Social Work: The Collected Writings *of* William Schwartz

Social Work: The Collected Writings *of* William Schwartz

Edited by
Toby Berman-Rossi

F. E. Peacock Publishers, Inc.
Itasca, Illinois

ISBN 0-87581-385-2
Printed in the United States of America
Printing: 10 9 8 7 6 5 4 3 2 1
Year: 98 97 96 95 94

Table of Contents

This volume is dedicated to
Ruth Efron Schwartz.
Bill's words of thanksgiving
in 1960,
upon completing his doctorate,
were
". . . and a final word of gratitude for my wife
Ruth Efron Schwartz,
whose casework training and experience served as
a continuous check on my ideas,
and whose professional contribution was
outdone only by
her inexhaustible faith and support
over a long stretch of time."

Foreword

This book is a celebration of William Schwartz's intellectual genius. The range and depth of his ideas are breathtaking. Published and unpublished materials present bold and exciting propositions about social work function and method. Twenty and thirty years later, his original ideas about the mediation function, professional method, contracting, mutual aid, and demand for work are well established in the profession's vocabulary, possibly without sufficient recognition of contributions. Toby Berman-Rossi's insightful discussion of his ideas deepens our understanding of the uniqueness and distinctiveness of what he offered us. His conceptualizations broke with traditional formulations, charted new directions, established a heuristic paradigm, and made important contributions to both professional practice and social work education.

As you read this book, you will be struck by the clarity and forcefulness of Bill's writing. He presents complex ideas with eloquent simplicity and uncommon clarity. Bill disdained academic and professional jargon. Each article is so comprehensively and beautifully polished, that it appears effortlessly written. However, those of us who were close to Bill knew how he labored over every word, making sure his ideas were presented clearly, succinctly, and actively. To fulfill his own expectations and standards, his writing required many drafts and much struggle. Bill worked on an article like a painter or sculptor creates a work of art: stroke by stroke, and redraft by redraft. No viewing of his art was allowed unless it met his standards for perfection. He had no interest in padding his curriculum vitae, in publishing for the sake of publishing. He had two "simple" criteria for publishing: his work had to offer a generative idea and it had to be expressed precisely. This book attests to how fully Bill lived by and met these compelling standards.

Neither of us were Bill's students at Columbia. Yet, he had a profound impact on our respective careers. Bill's clarity and forcefulness in assigning the profession a unique function—mediating—offered us a viable and heuristic functional statement. Bill's demand for clarity about one's professional function has been invaluable in our various roles as educators, practitioners, consultants, and workshop leaders. Moreover, Bill challenged us like he challenged all his students, colleagues, and professional associates to become fully invested in studying, conceptualizing, and illustrating professional method. To us, Bill's devotion to studying professional method seems analogous to studying the Talmud. To be truly learned and relevant, one has to commit his or her professional career to explicating the art and science of social work practice. To Bill, studying one's professional craft represented the highest order of scholarship. We are indebted to Bill for instilling us with this preoccupation and vision. Finally, Bill taught us and others to become emotionally as well as intellectually involved with the subject matter. By observing him in action, he taught us to create a learning environment that enables practitioners to discover and develop insights for themselves about the helping process. He agreed with Reynold's caution: "When education is oriented to the person who is to learn plus the situation to be mastered, there is something more to teaching than proving to the learner that one knows the subject."[1] So we are also indebted to Bill for many of our ideas about education.

We wish to express our gratitude to Ruth Schwartz. Her determination to have Bill's unpublished works published is the driving force behind this project. Her love and support fueled Bill's genius. Ruth's wisdom is evident in her selection of Professor Toby Berman-Rossi to edit this book. As a former student, a professional colleague, and devoted friend of Bill's, she offers us an inspiring understanding of the man and his ideas. To meet Bill's standards for excellence, editing this book had to be an intimidating challenge, both intellectually and emotionally. Toby, you have done Bill proud! Thank you for lending this project your personal commitment and professional competence.

Alex Gitterman
Lawrence Shulman

[1]Reynolds, Bertha Capen, (1942) *Learning and Teaching in the Practice of Social Work.* New York: Farrar and Rinehart, p. 83.

Preface

The idea for this volume was William Schwartz's. His notes reveal that he had been engaged in conversations with an eye to publishing a collection of his selected papers. "The Group Work Tradition and Social Work Practice" was the intended title. It was also the title of his final paper, delivered at the twenty-fifth anniversary of Rutgers University, School of Social Work. Also found among his papers was a tentative outline for the collection. The outline was organized thematically, rather than chronologically so that the reader might engage the fullness of his work by theme and particular areas. He wrote that the purpose of the work was "to convey both the progress of my own ideas and the intellectual and professional climate in which they grew." He divided his collection according to seven themes:

1. History and Tradition
2. Group Work Theory
3. The Field of Social Work
4. The Settings of Practice
5. The Art of Teaching
6. Research
7. Reviews and Short Pieces

He also specified his intent to include an introduction centered on the way in which his work has been addressed to:

> the various contradictions and dilemmas—what Thomas Kuhn would call "the anomalies"—besetting the practice of group work and social work in the past two or three decades. These ambiguities have taken several forms: the polarization of content and process; the preoccupation with abstract goals and philosophies, rather than the technical details of practice; the illusory "choices" as between the psychological and the social, the one "versus" the many; the inability to offer a limited and precise statement of our professional function; the meaning of gener-

> icism in the search for a unified profession; and the problems of putting our own principles into practice as we teach and translate ourselves to new generations of practitioners.

At the end,

> there would be an epilogue, a concluding piece on the state of the art, and some of the changes that have taken place in the past 20 years. The dualisms remain—content and process, intellect and feeling, the psychological and the social, private troubles and public issues—proliferating whenever our function is unclear, our understanding superficial, and we are afraid to look closely at what is bothering us. But the truth persists that social work is both a *structural* and a *personal* response to the problems of the system under which we live; and there is a growing realization that we are accountable not only for the efficiency of our organizations and the brave ring of our objective, but for the quality of our work with people. The struggle to call attention to the process will continue always, but there are signs (Shulman and others) that new professional energies are being directed to the technical tasks of defining and testing the skills of communicating, understanding, empathizing, tying feelings to knowledge, and translating human purposes into effective acts of helping people in trouble.

William Schwartz's outline has guided this presentation of his collected writings. Six of the intended seven sections are represented here. Only "Reviews and Short Pieces" has been omitted in favor of longer works. All major works are included, with the exception of "Social Group Work: The Interactionist Approach," which appears in the 1971 and 1977 editions of the *Encyclopedia of Social Work,* for which reprint permission was denied.

At first the decision regarding which works to include appeared uncomplicated. Once fully engrossed in the writings, the choice became somewhat difficult. *Social Work with Groups: The Search for a Method* was only partly completed at the time of Schwartz's death. Editorial efforts were focused on altering the work as little as possible. From time to time a word was deleted or inserted, references were hunted down, and care was taken to ensure that what appears in this volume was indeed the final copy on which he worked. The first three chapters of the book were completed by Schwartz. An initial decision was made to include only the first three completed chapters because of their virtually unique and powerful contribution to the literature on method. We also were concerned that Schwartz might not have wanted to present his work in progress. As more time was spent with the manuscript that decision gave way to the power and integrity of the remaining eight chapters. Even in their not quite finished state they make a distinctive contribution to our professional literature.

A similar thing happened with his dissertation. As it was initially reviewed and mulled, my thought was to include only Chapter 4, "The Learning Group and the Helping Function" in the collection. A later decision favored inclusion of the dissertation in its entirety. "Content and Process in the Educative Experience" remains in its wholeness as a statement of the author's initial effort to understand the nature of leadership in the group. It was his active and intense engagement with this question which ultimately generated the formulation, elaboration, and explication of his ideas in his writing. His later works, for example, "The Social Worker in the Group," of necessity, reflect only a small portion of his reasoning. To include his dissertation would have provided the fullest access to his ideas. The final decision not to include Schwartz's dissertation was made in the hope that the lowered cost of the volume would make it more accessible.

Editing this volume required and impelled a total immersion in Schwartz's writings and a reliving of a nineteen-year relationship, fundamental to the growth of my ideas and to the development of my practice as a social worker and teacher. Undoubtedly, the most difficult parts were reliving the loss and reconciling myself to Schwartz's absence in today's social work world, and wanting very much to do justice to the endeavor. Important learning came from the reengagement with the writings and the process of formulating this presentation of his ideas.

My introductory comments are designed to build upon previous commentary and to allow each theme or section to have its own integrity. In this way readers can work from beginning to end, or as many do, choose their own order. I have tried to avoid undue repetition and hope that my comments enhance, rather than detract from the power of the works included here.

The field of social work is indebted to Ruth Efron Schwartz for her sustained effort to have this manuscript published. Without her, this effort could not have gone forth. Support for this project also belongs with Alex Gitterman and Lawrence Shulman who, in recognizing the importance of this effort, brought the idea to Ted Peacock, of F. E. Peacock Publishers. We are all thankful to Ted Peacock who, in seeing the value of the book, agreed to publish it. It is with deep sadness that my appreciation to Derek Carter comes shortly after his untimely death. A friend of the Schwartz's, a student of Schwartz's and a colleague with whom Schwartz worked at the University of Ulster, at Coleraine, Northern Ireland, Professor Carter early on began to ready "Social Work with Groups: The Search For a Method" for publication by hunting down lost references. His support was always appreciated by them. For technical assistance I am grateful to Caryl Wenzel of Publishers Services, Inc. Irving Miller, Alex Gitterman, and Peter Rossi all generously contributed their ideas, their experiences with William Schwartz, and their experiences as group workers/educators within the profession. Their careful reading of the manuscript added greatly. Irving Miller's painstakingly detailed editorial comments added immeasurably to the quality of my endeavor.

Editing this volume was an honor for which I am deeply appreciative. I thank Ruth Efron Schwartz for the confidence she placed in me, for her patience, and for providing me with the opportunity to, once again so thoroughly, be a student of William Schwartz.

Toby Berman-Rossi

Overview

Schwartz's introduction to social work came in 1939, shortly after his graduation from Brooklyn College. He could not have realized that his first venture in camping would launch his career as a group worker. Years of work as a counselor, supervisor and director, and work with youth in "Y's," settlements, and community centers sparked and nurtured his belief in the value of the small group for the individual and for society at large.

His enrollment as a "social group work major" at the New York School of Social Work, Columbia University, from 1945 to 1947 came at a very interesting point in group work's history. The early history of group work was marked by a broad-based identification with other disciplines: psychology, sociology, education, recreation, and philosophy, and anthropology, religious and settlement work, all interested in small group phenomena. Issues of identity and affiliation were actively engaged in the 1940s and took precedence over matters of method.[1]

After several years of study, in 1948, the American Association of Group Workers, chaired by Grace Coyle, arrived at the "Definition of the Function of the Group Worker."[2] It was this definition that Schwartz labeled the "in such a way that" definition; that is, the worker behaves so that or in such a way that . . . but not defining the way. Progressive in its time in enabling group workers to come together around shared knowledge, values, and desired outcomes, this teleological emphasis and lack of specification of a professional technology remained problematic. While the merger in 1955 of the American Association of Group Workers with other social work professional membership groups, resulted in the formation of the National Association of Social Workers and put to rest the affiliation issues, the issue of method would remain barely attended to for a long time to come.

---

[1]See Schwartz's "Group Work and the Social Scene" and "The Group Work Tradition and Social Work Practice" for a discussion of the early history of group work.

[2]Kenneth E. Reid (1981) *From Character Building to Social Treatment,* Westport, Connecticut: Greenwood Press, pp. 146–47 discusses and presents this statement.

As a student, Schwartz was eager to study practice with groups. In class he learned about how group work's attention to articulating social goals and values helped forge a common identity and a common ground among those who practiced with groups in many different settings. He also was inspired by Grace Coyle who went beyond her vision of democratic ideals to an exploration of matters of process and relationship. At the same time, his appetite for discussion of method was unsatisfied. As an undergraduate, he was taken by the idea that "form follows function." In graduate school he brought with him a readiness "to think of function as part of a system, a job within a conglomeration of participating forces." What struck him immediately was how little the literature and his teachers actually addressed method. He felt that what was said about technique did not emerge from theory which would help social workers understand the relationship between what one was there to do and what one did. Technique separated from theory offered little more than "tricks."[3]

Schwartz found a ". . . big hiatus—[method] was mostly about philosophy, democratic goals, about self-awareness."[4] Like others, at the time, he was disturbed by the consequences of the unequal distribution of wealth within our capitalist society and was moved to try to contribute to a more just society. He shared group work's attention to articulating social goals and social values, but found his colleagues insufficiently attentive to the details of how to work toward their attainment. He believed it was not that philosophy, democratic goals, self-awareness, and knowledge about the problems of living in society were unimportant, but rather they were insufficient as guides for action. If we were to be of service to clients, and if we were to be a full-fledged profession, we would need to develop our methodology.

And so, early on, Schwartz's interest in method seemed to set him apart from many of his colleagues. For some, concern with technology represented movement away from social goals, for others it conveyed lack of sufficient interest in understanding clients and their problems. Only much later on would Schwartz find others similarly interested in the details of practice.

Two years after receiving his master's degree, Schwartz began to teach full-time, as an assistant professor at The Ohio State University School of Social Administration. He very quickly saw what he believed to be similarities between the social work group and the educational group. The classroom group was not an analogous situation, but rather a special case of the general situation of the relationship between a host institution, members with needs, and a person given the role of worker/teacher/leader charged with the assignment of being responsive to those needs. Both the classroom group and the social work group appeared to him to be ventures in collaborative learning

---

[3]Taped interview, April 14, 1982, between William Schwartz and Toby Berman-Rossi on the development of his ideas on method.

[4]Taped interview, April 14, 1982, between William Schwartz and Toby Berman-Rossi on the development of his ideas on method.

where the relationship among the members/students, and between the members and the worker/teacher influenced the learning itself.

It was at this point that he learned how little guidance there was for his work as educator and for his specific task of teaching practice with groups. In both social work and education, method was equated with the goals one wished to achieve or the knowledge of one's subject matter. It was as if the articulation of goals and the definition of what one believed to be true carried within them the means for their own implementation. The prevailing mode was "about philosophy, democratic goals, about self-awareness" and method was described in terms of desired outcomes rather than in terms of what the worker/teacher did.[5] Such beliefs felt untrue to Schwartz's experience as a worker with groups. He agreed that hoped for immediate outcomes should be clearly defined, and he agreed that he should be as knowledgeable about the troubles of his group members/clients. The more challenging problems, however, were technical ones, that is, what does one *do* with what one holds to be true about clients in their physical and social environment? What is the nature of leadership within the group? What are the skills one must develop to be of help? On behalf of what function were these skills to be applied? These were the questions the literature neglected.

Schwartz's reading of the literature suggested that educators, group workers, and others who worked with groups, had yet to solve the question of how to consider the contribution of the leader/worker/teacher, in her or his own right, separate from knowledge and separate from desired outcomes.

While Schwartz's interest in method was evident early in his career[6] his need to know more about the technology of teaching and helping became pronounced once in the classroom. His admiration for Grace Coyle[7] notwithstanding, he noted that even she believed that if group workers were "knowledgeable, self-aware and highly motivated" group work leadership would be exerted "by some delicate osmosis."

There were no questions more important than "what the social worker does for a living" and the manner in which that function is skillfully translated into helping activity. Unable to find what was needed, he carved out his

---

[5]While all of Schwartz's writings reverberate with the theme of the importance of method, he pays particular attention to the issue of the paucity of the study of method in: the early part of his dissertation; Part I. "The Problem of Method," the first three chapters of Social Work With Groups: The Search for a Method; and "Education in the Classroom."

[6]From October 1948 to September 1949, Schwartz was Research Director, Project on the Use of Volunteers in a Group Work Agency, Federation of Jewish Philanthropies Grant to the East Bronx Community YM-YMHA, New York City. In "A Comparison of Background Characteristics and Performance of Paid and Volunteer Group Leaders" (1951) *The Jewish Center Worker.* XII (1): 1–12, Schwartz points to ". . . the general need for a methodical spelling out of the concrete components of good leadership practice, as they manifest themselves in the observable performance of the group leader" (p. 4). He viewed his task of defining a set of measurement criteria ". . . as an attempt to translate the function of the group leader into a body of specific practices against which the performance of the leaders could be judged and compared" (p. 4).

[7]Schwartz's tribute to Grace Coyle, "Grace Coyle and Her Influence: A Personal Note," can be found later in this volume.

own questions for study. He approached his work recognizing the contributions of others. He believed that all ideas, no matter how diversified, had the potential to move the profession forward through stimulating exploration and stirring debate. Differences had the potential to point to areas of needed study. Schwartz was not a subscriber to the "great person" theory of history, but rather advanced the view that a society moves forward through the combined efforts of many and on the shoulders of those who labored before.

Schwartz's interest in function and method emanated from his need to understand and conceptualize his own experience. He wrote:

> I never set out to "create a model" of practice. My conclusions about what works with people are generalizations from my own practice and that of others; my efforts at all times, like everyone else who has put together a way of working, have been to generalize as effectively as possible from the needs of people, from what I have learned about people and processes, from my conclusions about what social work was invented for.[8]

Schwartz's doctoral studies at Teacher's College, Columbia University took place from 1953 to 1960. In his dissertation, "Content and Process in the Educative Experience," he posed what to him, at the time, was the most difficult and as yet unaddressed, question: what is the nature of leadership in the group situation? This interest in the worker's function and what the worker does to help, arose for him, years prior, with his first group meeting where he struggled with the issue of his influence. In the dissertation he asked: how do you reconcile the two aims of the classroom: *the what* (content) generated by the need to communicate the syllabus, and *the how* (process) generated by the learner's need to engage the educative experience? The challenge for him was to explore whether one could develop a way of looking at the teaching process which instead of polarizing or establishing dualisms between the set of prescribed expectations (the content) presented by society (in this case the host setting of the educational institution) and the set of personal goals (the process) presented by individuals (in this case students), actually brought them together. Viewing the classroom, "as a case in point" of the group situation with a "helping agent," allowed him to simultaneously arrive at a general definition of the assignment of the social worker in society and a particularization of the function within the classroom. By answering these questions for himself as educator, he was simultaneously answering them for himself as social work practitioner.

The study explored four main lines of inquiry:

1. the dualism between content and process and the dilemmas this polarization creates in the work;
2. the "system" within which workers take on their job and act to carry it out;

[8]In response to a letter from a student, January 24, 1980.

3. the formulation of a statement of function which reflects a conceivable social work job assignment; and
4. an elaboration of the functional statement into the operationalized tasks which would then represent "function in action."

Satisfactorily answering these questions would involve developing "a view of the *helping process* itself, of the nature of the helping skill and of the conditions under which guidance is given and received in the group situation" (p. 7). It was as a result of engaging these questions in the dissertation, that Schwartz's interactionist model was generated. By the end of the study Schwartz defined the function of the social worker within society, partialized this function into five operational tasks, and began to specify the nature of skills necessary to act upon these task assignments.

Schwartz's conceptualization of a generic theory of the helping process and the way that theory expresses the social worker's function in action, has been one of his most enduring contributions and influences upon the study of practice. These ideas, bold and challenging when "Group Work and the Social Scene" (1959a) and "The Social Worker in the Group" (1961) first appeared over thirty years ago, remain so today as the profession continues to struggle with the question of whether our helping method is generic or specific. While Schwartz's ideas were most frequently operationalized in the group situation, for him, the small group was always a case in point of the helping process in action rather than the medium for the expression of a separate method. His vision was always of social work with groups, not social group work.[9]

Central to Schwartz's generic vision was his belief that the problems of people do not lend themselves easily to the arbitrary divisions we have inflicted upon them through the division of labor between social agencies. To equate method with work with individuals, groups, and communities, was, he said, simply to mistake "the nature of the helping process itself for the relational system in which it is applied" (1961, p. 149).

While Schwartz's ideas of generic method set him apart from those who believed group work represented a distinct method, his model of the helping process also represented a bold departure from two more dominant and more familiar approaches to practice within the profession, that is, the "medical" model, and the "scientific" model (1964b; 1971e). Each of those approaches is based upon a set of beliefs and basic assumptions regarding the function of the social worker, the nature of the helping process, and the worker-client relationship, which are markedly different from those of William Schwartz. Each has associated with it a preferred knowledge base, preferred hoped for outcomes, and preferred instrumentalities for responding to client need which

---

[9]Schwartz's contribution to the generic vision of social work practice is discussed by Judith A. B. Lee in "Seeing it Whole: Social Work with Groups Within an Integrative Perspective," in Alex Gitterman and Lawrence Shulman (1985/86) (eds.), *The Legacy of William Schwartz: Group Practice as Shared Interaction, Social Work with Groups,* 8(4): 39–50.

further distinguish them from each other and from Schwartz's ideas.[10] Taken as a whole, both the "medical" and "scientific" models offer practitioners a strikingly different way of working with individuals, families, and groups.

Schwartz anchors his ideas in a third model, "a model of the organic system." He first distinguished between the "organic systems model" and the "medical" and "scientific" models in 1960 when asked to analyze various definitions of group work practice put forth by leading educators and practitioners as part of the Committee on Practice of the National Group Work Section of NASW. Schwartz characterized the differences among these three approaches in the following way:

> There was a kind of "medical" model in which "the steps in the helping process are described by assuming a sequence of movements through which the worker investigates, diagnoses, and treats the problem under consideration." There was a 'scientific' model "in which the steps in the helping process resemble closely the problem-solving sequence by which the scientific worker moves from the unknown to the known." And there was a "model of the organic system" in which "the total helping situation is viewed as a network of reciprocal activity," and in which it is impossible to describe accurately any part of the system without describing its active relationship to the other moving parts (1971e, p. 1255).

For Schwartz, differences among those three models were not reconcilable. He held that the scientific model so useful in advancing us into a period of enlightenment in which we learned how to understand and gain greater control over the world in which we lived went fundamentally awry when applied to the field of human relations.

It was in his doctoral study, "Content and Process in the Educative Experience" (1960a), that Schwartz fully developed his systems ideas and the implications of those ideas for a view of clients, the helping process, and professional function. His characterization of group workers as "action oriented, optimistic, and theoretically eclectic" (1971e, p. 1254) held for him as well. He studied the social interactionists and social philosophers and turned to John Dewey and William James to learn about the role of feeling, the importance of understanding the quality of experience, and the nature of reciprocal interaction. Martin Buber taught him about interdependence in relationships and the problems of dichotomizing intellect and feeling; while Soren Kierkegaard and the existentialists taught him how "truth exists only as the individual himself produces it in action" (1976, p. 177). The interactionism and systemic thinking of Kurt Lewin, Talcott Parsons, and Lawrence K. Frank

---

[10]Charles Levy discusses this schema of ". . . preferred conceptions of people, preferred outcomes for people, and preferred instrumentalities for dealing with people" in "The Value Base of Social Work," *Journal of Education for Social Work,* 9 (Winter) 1973, p. 34.

helped him understand the ways that "relations determine the properties of the parts" (1960, p. 99) and Mary Parker Follett taught him how "response is always to a relation" (1981b, p. 15).[11] These ideas remained with him throughout his life. They were expanded upon, applied to different settings, but not essentially changed.

To think systemically, Schwartz asserted, had necessary consequences for both a view of clients, the systems in which their lives were embedded, and a view of the helping relationship. "The interactionists emphasized experience and affect, step-by-step process, and situational rather than structural descriptions of people in difficulty" (1971e, pp. 1256–57). This was a substantively different conception than the notion of the client with characteristics stable enough to be diagnosed and analyzed by an external agent, who had the task of "fixing broken parts." Schwartz totally rejected the idea, so popular now, that it is possible to view the client as part of a system of interacting relationships and forces, while at the same time holding the worker-client relationship outside that system.[12] For him it was theoretically inconceivable to apply the concept of system to some relationships and to deny its validity in other instances. Necessarily then, practitioners could not stand outside a system of which they were a part for the purpose of studying, diagnosing/assessing, and treating clients. To intervene from within a system was simply not possible.

Using systems theory and interactionism as bases, Schwartz put forward four requirements for a definition of professional function: first, that this definition, as an action concept, must be expressed in the operational form of verbs rather than knowledge or values; second, that it must make explicitly clear how the worker moves in relation to all the other moving parts in the system of interaction; third, its influence is restricted to the field of interaction with which it directly interacts, and fourth, the idea that there is an "interplay of functions" prompts all parties in the system to answer the question, "What am I doing here?" (1961, pp. 152–53). Advancing a functional statement which met these requirements would represent a starting point in the profession's ability to define its realm of accountability. The ways that function was operationalized into professional tasks and then translated into the helping activity of the social worker would represent the next steps in the evaluation and measurement of our competence.

---

[11]For a fuller discussion of the diverse sources of influence on the development of Schwartz's thinking (including Freud's emphasis upon feeling and the irrational forces within), as well as his appreciation of B. F. Skinner's emphasis on operationalism, and his appreciation of the writings of the functionalists, see the first three chapters in his book, and his 1971e and 1976 writings.

[12]Christopher G. Petr distinguishes between what he calls "two systems perspectives," that is, a more traditional perspective which maintains ". . . a basic cause-effect relationship, reactive, mechanistic orientation, whereas the second perspective views cause-effect as secondary to the more primary, active, spontaneous, and autonomous nature of systems." In addition, the former view is characterized by "separateness and objectivity" whereas the second ". . . highlights the connectedness and reciprocity between observer and system," "The Worker-Client Relationship: A General Systems Perspective," *Social Casework,* (1988) 69(10): 620–26.

Schwartz's potent description of our professional function is one of his most distinctive contributions. Within our literature on professional method it is unrivaled in its clarity and percipience. Schwartz believed

> . . . that the general assignment for the social work profession is to mediate the process through which the individual and his society reach out for each other through a mutual need for self-fulfillment. This presupposes a relationship between the individual and his nurturing group which we would describe as 'symbiotic'—each needing the other for its own life and growth, and each reaching out to the other with all the strength it can command at a given moment. The social worker's field of intervention lies at the point where two forces meet: the individual's impetus toward health, growth, and belonging; and the organized efforts of society to integrate its parts into a productive and dynamic whole. (1961, pp. 154–55).

This conception arose out of his reading of history which convinced him that in our complex, class ordered society, innumerable obstacles arose which seemingly put individual need and social systems at odds with each other. The social worker would represent that centripetal force, intensely centered on individual-social ties.

The position of the social worker as mediator meant that Schwartz's social worker would also not choose between the vast numbers of dualisms besetting the professional: content v. process, directiveness v. nondirectiveness, activity v. passivity, intellect v. emotion, authoritarianism v. permissiveness, freedom v. control, leadership v. followship, the individual v. the group. For Schwartz choice was never possible, the identity of one was integrally related to the nature of the other.

By operationalizing his definition of function into five primary social work tasks, Schwartz demonstrated how "method is function in action" and how method was generic. Briefly stated, these tasks which would apply to all helping situations included: "searching out the common ground," "detecting and challenging the obstacles which obscure the common ground," "contributing data," "lending a vision," and "defining the requirements and the limits of the situation in which the client worker system is set" (1961, pp. 157–58). With professional tasks specified, Schwartz was then freed to define the skills which would carry out these tasks.

Perhaps no idea of Schwartz's has been more controversial and more misunderstood than the way his formulation of the social worker as mediator was operationalized, when people and systems seemed to pull apart from each other. "Private Troubles and Public Issues: One Social Work Job or Two" (1969a) was devoted to an elaboration of this idea, during a period in which society's pendulum moved sharply toward social protest. Though separated, by virtue of his ideas, from some within social work who actively supported social change, Schwartz never wavered in his belief that social progress could only occur by strengthening the connection between people and their social institutions. To destroy the very institutions designed to serve would leave clients bereft of the life-sustaining resources necessary for their survival. Some have attributed to him the idea that "man's impulse toward association 'is always productive of individual and/or social good'."[13] Actually, he said

> [t]hat there are quarrels over ownership and the terms of the contract is not surprising in a class society. And that, in a badly organized collective where the few rule the many, there will often be a nasty feeling between the service and its people is to be expected" (1969, p. 38). . . . "The mediating function is a skillful one, but it does not 'retreat into technique'; on the contrary, the engagements of people with their systems aim at real confrontations on real issues. This is not a call for peace, for there is no peace. The struggle is of a different order, designed to mobilize agencies rather than destroy them" (1969, pp. 42–43).

Schwartz is, sperhaps, most readily recognized for the ways in which his ideas were operationalized within the medium of the group, and in particular for his delineation of the social work group as a system of mutual aid. This designation of the social work group revolutionized the practice of work with groups and was a direct outgrowth of his belief that the individual-social relationship was symbiotic. The mutual aid group was comprised of people who needed each other to work on those tasks which brought them together, where this work proceeded in an agency receptive to those tasks. The group thus conceptualized brought with it ideas of "shared control, shared power, and the shared agenda" (1981b, p. 24). A multiplicity of helping relationships automatically decreased hierarchical power by increasing egalitarian relationships in which collective strength was emphasized. The view of the social worker as expert was automatically transformed into one among many; our activity designed not to lead members, but rather to help them to act in their own interests.

As the reader pursues Schwartz's application of his ideas to a wide range of settings, for example, residential treatment, the social work classroom, school settings, and child welfare, the breadth of his ideas becomes readily apparent. Their potency is realized by their ease of application in the varied settings in which social workers practice. Social workers equipped with a clear conception of function, a delineation of professional tasks, and an understanding of helping skills, are better prepared to conduct the business of the profession wherever it takes them. The writings that follow help us practice our craft. They stimulate, educate, challenge, and define a path through which art and science, head and heart can be joined. They take us a long way in the study of professional method and the helping process in social work.

Toby Berman-Rossi

---

[13]Written to a student on January 24, 1980, with reference to Catherine Pappell and Beulah Rothman's attribution to his "interactionist" model. See their article "Social Group Work Models: Possession and Heritage," *Journal of Education for Social Work,* (Fall 1966): 67–77.

Social Work with Groups:

The Search for a Method
1968–1972

William Schwartz

Social Work with Groups: The Search for a Method

Schwartz was a brilliant writer, who felt he had not published enough. One of his greatest regrets was not finishing *Social Work With Groups: The Search for a Method*. It is a great loss that the book was not completed. Much was finished, the rest was fleshed out, and only the final chapter "Transitions and Endings" had not progressed beyond notes.

It is difficult to pin down the period during which the book was written. Collective recall suggests between 1968 and 1972. References do not go beyond 1972. Considering the large number of reference materials used in his writings suggests that Schwartz did not stay with the work, in a sustained manner, after 1972. The period to 1972 was a very prolific one. Perhaps he needed a pause from the lonely endeavor of writing. Perhaps his energy shifted to his many agency consultations that were focused upon increasing the skills of practitioners, supervisors, and administrators. We know he gave generously to his former students who continued to work on problems of practice.

By the end of his dissertation in 1960, Schwartz had defined and elaborated upon the major components of his interactionist model. In his next three publications, he directed his attention to an exposition of the model, concentrating on the complexities of the subject of method. Subsequent writings showed the model at work in various settings of practice: child welfare, residential treatment, public schools, the social work classroom. In his work of 1969, he focused upon the implications of dichotomizing the social and psychological functions of the profession of social work.

By the late 1960s, having presented the model and having worked out the perplexities it engaged, Schwartz was ready to devote himself to the matter closest to his professional heart: the nature of professional practice in social work. *Social Work with Groups: The Search for a Method* represents that effort.

For Schwartz, attention to method reflected the highest calling of the profession. He believed that "[a] professional acts to help others to act"

(p. 22) and that "the work on technical problems, far from being precious or diversionary, is the only serious approach to the goals themselves." (p. 24). Thus, he said, *Social Work with Groups: The Search for a Method,* is "without apology, a book about technique" (p. 7).

This "how-to" book distinguishes itself from other social work practice texts by encasing its prescriptive emphasis in a "systematic approach to the art of helping people" (p. 1). The emphasis is not on knowledge, or philosophy, valued outcomes, and acts of helping alone, but instead actualizes Schwartz's belief that method theory represents the interdependence of its three component parts: knowledge, desired outcomes, and action as the implementing force.

Part 1 of the book, "The Problem of Method" is comprised of three chapters: "Introduction and Purpose"; "The Meaning of Method"; and "Toward a New Paradigm." These chapters occupy fully half of the uncompleted manuscript. These chapters on professional method are unrivaled in our professional literature for their clarity and power of elucidation.[1]

Part 1

As an introduction to a book on professional practice in small groups, "Part 1" serves to draw the reader into its subject matter by advancing the argument that for professionals to act as professionals, they must understand the theory of what they do. Without a consciously articulated theory of the helping process, professional activity is subject to randomness. "A talent divorced from its own theorizing cannot learn much from experience; it depends too heavily on inspiration from unknown sources" (p. 61).

Schwartz's theory of helping is guided by what was a new paradigm at the time, a paradigm dwarfed, even today, by older, more tenacious paradigms. He places the helping relationship within an "organic system model" and distinguishes it from the "medical model" and the "scientific model" which predominate in social work. This "organic system model" is one "in which the total helping situation is viewed as a network of reciprocal activity, and in which it is impossible to describe accurately any part of the system without describing its active relationship to the other moving parts."[2] The elements are action, interaction, relations, presentness, intimacy, and feeling.

Part 2

Part 2, "The Search for Function," including chapters four, five, and six, concerns itself with the search for an answer to the question Schwartz

---

[1]For an additional review, asserting the paucity of method theory, see: Toby Berman-Rossi (1985) "Theoretical Orientations of Social Work Practice Teachers: An Analysis." Unpublished Doctoral Dissertation. Yeshiva University, Wurzweiler School of Social Work, pp. 35–82.

[2]See also "Analysis of Papers Presented on Working Definitions of Group Work Practice" (1964) included in this volume, for Schwartz's concise definition of three distinct helping models: the medical model, the scientific model and the organic system model. Quoted material appears on page 60.

asked all his students: what does social work do for a living? Schwartz begins his analysis by taking us back into history and exploring the various definitions the profession has advanced. Most prominent are: (1) changing the individual (the casework tradition); and (2) changing the system (the group work tradition). These definitions compete with each other and ask social workers to align themselves with *either* the individual *or* society, the psychological or the social.

For Schwartz this "choice" represented an untenable dualism. He reasoned that the individual's relationship with society was symbiotic and that the individual could not be set against his or her own social/self interest no matter how diffused the tie between them and the system became. The worker would become a "third force," guarding the individual/social connection and identifying with neither the individual/client nor with the society/agency but rather with the common ground between them. Identifying with neither, the worker would become bound by neither. Thus freed, workers would not be neutral, but rather intensely partisan and focused upon mediating the engagement between individuals and their environments. All the skill they could bring to bear would be devoted to strengthening this symbiosis.

In Chapter six, "Systems: The Special Case," Schwartz brings us from function to a discussion of the "system part" of the mediating statement. He says that when the social worker mediates between clients and society, "society" becomes the term intended to convey the sum total of smaller systems; that is, the family, the peer group, the school, work, the club, the agency itself. The case for studying "the system" is clear. If, then, the helping process is essentially an effort to help people negotiate their systems, it becomes necessary that we devote at least as much time and effort to understand what it is they are trying to negotiate as we have in the past devoted to understanding (diagnosing/assessing) the personalities and characteristics with which they approach their life-tasks.

In turning his attention toward the agency as system, Schwartz defines two prevalent views, and differs with each. First, is the view of the functionalists that the "profession *is* the agency"; second, is the view that the agency is "mere housing" for independent practitioners responsible primarily to clients. In the first case, he argues, the concept of a profession weakens if social workers have no special identity (function) separate from their agency service. In the second case, the movement toward private practice separates social workers from their unique function and moves them toward the medical-therapeutic enterprise which is independent of agency service. For Schwartz, when social workers identify with the agency, as in the first instance, they lose their ties to clients; when identifying with clients in the second instance, they lose their ties to their agencies. The worker, pressured to make an illusory choice between client and agency, cannot establish a clear agreement for work, with agency or client, and therefore cannot practice honestly and well. Under these conditions "symbiotic diffusion" dominates and the worker becomes trapped by the dualism. A focus, however, upon the interaction between client and agency, strengthens the worker to work.

The final task of the chapter is to examine the system formed by the worker and his clients, wherein the peer group becomes another special instance of the individual-social encounter. Here Schwartz presents his now familiar "mutual aid definition" of the group as "*a collection of people who need each other to pursue certain common tasks, in an agency that is hospitable to those tasks.*" In this definition, both the individuals in the group and the group-as-a-whole become clients. He concludes by defining four group tasks to which the group-as-a-whole must attend: (1) formation; (2) internal structure; (3) negotiating its own environment; and (4) individual need satisfaction.

Part 3

Chapter seven moves us from function to method, as a prelude to the final chapters on the phases of the helping process, a process which involves the complex transition of moving from knowing to doing.[3] How does the social worker make use of the encyclopedic amount of knowledge that is continuously being generated? How do we reconcile our sense that everything seems relevant, yet the potential use of the material is unclear? How do we move from knowledge to action if "action is not directly deducible from knowledge"?

To engage these issues, Schwartz argues that we must answer three interdependent questions: *What is?* (social reality); *What should be?* (policy or valued outcomes); and *What should be done?* (action). Knowledge, action, and valued outcomes thus constitute the reciprocal components of method theory. In this way knowledge is particularized, action is specified, and only goals which are immediate in time are linked to worker activity.

To explore these questions Schwartz divides the work of the helping process into four time phases: tuning in, (beginnings), the work phase (middles), and transitions and endings. It is to these four phases of work that Part 3, "The Practice of Social Work with Groups," is devoted.

Schwartz intended that the major work of the book would "describe in a systematic way, the moves and skills through which the social worker carries out his function and carries it in the peer-group situation." No doubt, the last four chapters would have been highly developed, with his painstaking documentation and use of references and with the inclusion of rich practice examples to illustrate the work. What is striking, is that though unfinished, they offer a vital contribution to our practice literature.

In chapters eight through eleven, Schwartz follows his own definition of a theory of helping, organizing the content according to three method theory categories he had defined: reality assumptions, valued outcomes,

[3]The movement from knowing to doing is the subject of "Toward a Strategy of Group Work Practice," included in this volume.

and actions. The action category, or patterns of worker activity, includes a discussion of worker skills. For each phase of the helping process he spells out his core beliefs, the outcomes he hopes to achieve, and the actions he would have us take.

Schwartz asks what categories of worker tasks might express and emerge from the mediating sense of purpose? He suggests five interdependent rather than time ordered tasks, each of which is associated with a set of worker actions which would operationalize the tasks. His discussion provides guidance to social workers looking to attach their helping activity to an overall sense of professional purpose.

In *Social Work With Groups: The Search for a Method,* Schwartz does not ask that we agree with the ideas he has defined. He does ask that we risk ourselves and declare *our* own ideas, and hold them up for examination,

> . . . , when the purposes, values, aspirations, are unstated, the principles are unverifiable, except by those who (unconsciously) share the same assumptions and accept the same absolutes. When these creeds are made explicit, practice principles can be verified by all: given a fact, and given a valued outcome, the action will or will not provide the implementing force. This is how—and in no other way—practice can be said to be "testable."

Clearly, he believed that through comparison of our "testable" ideas the quality of our professional practice would advance.

Toby Berman-Rossi

Social Work with Groups:

The Search for a Method

Step by step the longest march
Can be won, can be won.
Many stones can form an arch;
Singly none, singly none.
And by union what we will
Can be accomplished still,
Drops of water turn a mill,
Singly none, singly none.

Folk Song

Contents

Part 1:

The Problem of Method

The first section leads us, via a kind of rationale, into the substance of the work that is to follow. I begin with the position that the subject of method has almost to be *created*—that is, that before one can begin to lay out the ways of working with people in groups, it is important that the reader become familiar with the meaning of "method" itself, how I *define* the problems of *defining* it, and the kind of need I mean for the book to fill. Thus, what is before us is not only a book on how to work, but a book that defends the thesis that there is such a subject. The first section is therefore a defense of the subject, an effort to create it, and stand it on its own two feet.

1

Introduction and Purpose

This book is written for those practitioners whose business it is to help people work together in small, face-to-face groups. It is a how-to-do-it book, in that I have tried to provide working strategies for the helping person. However, it is not meant to be merely prescriptive; it offers no mechanical or ready-made solutions to complex problems. What I have tried to do is to formulate a systematic approach to the art of helping people in groups—an approach that combines a concern for the science of human behavior, the dynamic of professional purpose, and the art of putting these together in action.

The basic ingredients are these: a number of people come together periodically to work on common tasks and problems; they meet in an agency that has formed and sponsored them, because that is how the agency carries out its function in the community; and there is a helping person—variously called the "leader," "teacher," "therapist," "enabler," "change agent," or simply the "worker"—who has been assigned to help these people do what they came together to do.

Many professions and their institutions have been interested in this arrangement. Social workers, teachers, psychiatrists, psychologists, nurses, clergymen, administrators—in schools, hospitals, social agencies, factories, churches, and other settings—have been attracted to the small group and its potential for intense human interaction, for the exchange of important ideas and feelings, and for sustained collaboration and planning. In fact, there is hardly an institution in American life that does not use the group in some way—to teach, treat, plan, mobilize, or organize people for work on specific tasks.

What follows here may thus be useful to practitioners in many fields. However, I will address myself most particularly to the practice problems of the social worker. The general understanding of how professional help should be offered, and how people use it, is still so meager that any single discipline can probably make its best contribution by examining its own work in detail, thus adding to what should eventually become a broader study of what all the helping professions have in common. I am convinced that the service professions are in fact moving in that direction—toward a general theory of the helping process that will belong to no single discipline alone, but to all who are directly involved in helping people manage some aspects of the world around them.

This convergence of method has, in fact, already begun to happen in the field of social work itself. Only a few years ago, a book like this would have taken "social group work" as its subject and addressed itself to the fellowship of "group workers" in the Ys and settlements, the leisure-time centers of recreation and informal education, and a number of selected institutions that played host (they were called the "host settings") to some specialized group services. In today's social work scene, this is no longer possible. A work on group practice must now speak to the entire profession, with practitioners operating in a broad range of social agencies that use the small group as a medium of service.

Social work's interest in groups is not new; it grew up alongside the concern with "cases." Samuel Barnett and Octavia Hill, Jane Addams and Mary Richmond, all played parts in the same social movement: indeed Barnett, the founder of the settlements, raised the slogan "One by One,"[1] even as Richmond, the theoretician of American charity organization, took early note of an interest in "small-group psychology."[2] But the peculiar tradition that developed, in which "case" and "group" expertise were segmented by agencies, by professional specialization, and by education, served for a long time to inhibit the development of group practice within the wide gamut of social welfare services.

Now, in our own social climate, this old tradition is giving way to a resurgent interest in the peer group and its potential for encouraging client action and mutual aid. The field has moved a long way toward meeting Eduard Lindeman's complaint of some thirty years ago: "I cannot see why . . . groups and group experiences do not stand at the very center of social work's concern."[3] The small group is now very much at the center of social work's concern—in the agencies, in the profession, and in the schools of social work.

Thus the change from "social group work" to "social work with groups" is more than a mere semantic turn. It is part of a growing trend in which social workers engage their clients in different relational systems—the one-to-one, the family, and groups of varied sizes and purposes—rather than continuing to specialize themselves, as their forbears did, by their claim to expertise in the "case," the "group," or the "community." Those who are still being educated in the old division of labor—and their number is decreasing—have had to adapt their "casework" skills to work with families and peer groups in the hospitals, clinics, public schools, welfare, and family agencies; while the "group work" specialists have for a long time been offering the individual services that grow inevitably out of any serious effort to help people in groups. In "community organization," the defining term is on another level of abstraction; but one does not, after all, work with "communities," except as one is involved with the individuals and groups of which they are composed.

As this tripartite system of specialization breaks down, each of the historic "methods"—casework, group work, and community organization—continues to lose visibility, both as a class of practitioners and a class of agencies.

The generic force pulls them all closer to the social work center and to the common skills by which they may be identified as members of a single profession. This momentum toward convergence has picked up considerable impetus—both in social work practice and in social work education—in the ten years that have passed since I noted that:

> . . . the single variable embodied in the number of people one works with at a time is simply not significant enough to be endowed with the designation of "method." Not significant enough, that is, if we reserve the term "method" to mean a systematic mode of helping which, while it is used differently in different situations, retains throughout certain recognizable and invariant properties through which one may identify the social worker in action. In this light, to describe casework, group work, and community organization as methods simply mistakes the nature of the helping process for the relational system in which it is applied. It seems more accurate to speak of a social work method, practiced in the various systems in which the social worker finds himself or which are established for the purpose of giving service: the family, the small friendship group, the representative body, the one-to-one interview, the hospital ward, the lounge-canteen, the committee, the street club, the special-interest group, and many others. Within this frame of reference, the task of safeguarding the uniqueness of the various so-called methods fades before the real problem of abstracting from all of these experiences the common methodological components of the helping process in social work.
>
> This is partly why any serious attempt to define a unique entity called "social group work" begins to turn, under one's very hand, into a description of something larger and more inclusive, of which the worker-group system is simply a special case. . . . the context has changed, and the moment has passed, for a definition of "group work method." Rather, we must now search for those common elements in social work practice . . . from which social workers in all settings can draw the specifics of their own practice. The job can no longer be done most usefully by first defining social group work (or casework or community organization) and then trying to fit the description into the general framework of helping theory. The process is now rather the reverse: by laying the ground work in a social work methodology, we may begin to analyze and clarify the activities of the social worker as he works with people in groups.[4]

This, then, is a book about social work skills and how they can be put to use in small group situations. Further, the point will be made repeatedly that the emphasis on skills is an emphasis on action. I will be concerned not with knowledge alone, or philosophy, or structure, or aspirations, but with how all of these can be put together in a way of *doing*—in a helping process drawn systematically from the work history of the total profession. It is thus, without apology, a book about technique.

The Trouble About Means and Ends

Why should it be necessary *not* to apologize for a book that is frankly technical? The answer is that in a time of social ferment such as ours, there is strong pressure on all professionals—in social work as in the other human relations disciplines—to view with suspicion the preoccupation with means. Many feel that the effort to refine one's methods is somehow diversionary, precious, a "retreat into technique" that encourages neutralism and blunts the commitment to social change. The fear is expressed in terms such as these:

> . . . the cult of the technician is spreading in our field. If agency memberships follow their professionals' lead, committed groups are going to be rare. By the cult of the technician, I refer to those professionals who really feel alienated from the broad purposes of social work—to help reconcile men to their society *and* their society to men—and who practice a technique like casework or even community organization for its own purposes alone.[5]
>
> The requirements for a social reform orientation are not easily reconcilable with the requirements of a professional service orientation. An emphasis upon the development of a scientific body of knowledge, disciplined and controlled use of relationships, and the need to have a precise and specialized competence is not normally the soil in which concern for social change can grow, unless it is consciously, deliberately, and insistently cultivated. The concern with and necessity for developing method and process disposes people to neutralism.[6]

In Buchler's general analysis of the concept of method, he states the problem as follows:

> Where interest in a method ceases to be merely primary and becomes militantly exclusive, where regard for a method begins to be related inversely to regard for its results, a peculiar type of problem arises, belonging to the sociology and ethics of query. For this kind of inverse relation has as eventual consequence an erasure of the sense of connection between activity and its aims. The uses and fruits of method become objects of disdain. Methodolatry enters the scene, and methodic activity becomes transformed into a continuing proliferation of conventions. . . . Men afflicted with methodolatry become self-righteous, and in their euphoria fancy themselves to have acquired unsuspected health.[7]

He might have pointed out that the reverse is also true: when the interest in *results* "becomes militantly exclusive," the opposite evil is brought into play. What Buchler might have called "*end*olatry" takes *method* as its "object of disdain," and creates its own forms of self-righteousness. The reverse image of the "continuing proliferation of conventions" is the frequent repetition of goals, values, and commitments, uttered with great feeling and conviction but unrelated to the study of means. Thus, just as Buchler warns against the worship of means without reference to purpose, so Dewey rejects the ritual formulation of ends without reference to process:

> An end established externally to the process of action is always rigid. Being inserted or imposed from without, it is not supposed to have a working relationship to the concrete conditions of the situation.[8]

Certainly the polarization of means and ends is inimical to meaningful action for social change; Schorr's fear of the "separation of technique from goals"[9] is soundly based. But the dualism is created by *method*olators and *end*olators alike, those who derive their "euphoria of unsuspected health" from the illusion that they can choose between the what and the how, and thus hope to avoid the more difficult task of finding the working relationship between the two. This approach to complex social problems runs through the professional literature in many forms, setting up a host of unworkable dichotomies: it pits content against process, the one against the many, the social against the psychological, freedom against discipline, stability against change, the past against the present, and others.

In social work, the struggle has revolved most often around the tension between what C. Wright Mills called "personal troubles" and "social issues."[10] In this version of the means-ends dilemma, the profession is asked to choose between its concern for people in trouble and the need to change the social system in which the trouble is brewed. The argument has been going on for a long time: Mary Richmond called for "retail," as against "wholesale," methods;[11] Kenneth Pray described the differing perspectives of "workmanship" and "statesmanship";[12] and Clarke Chambers wrote of the "misunderstanding and bad blood" that runs between the "priests" and the "prophets."[13] Chambers summed up the issue as follows:

> And so the two overlapping phases of social work continue to exist, not always harmoniously, but certainly in interdependence—the one focused on the individual and his welfare, strongly influenced by the psychological disciplines, introspective, dealing in personalized, retail services; the other concerned with reform, with reconstruction, informed primarily by the social sciences, extroverted, dealing with group or community or wholesale services.[14]

In the course of this historic "family quarrel,"[15] the swings of the pendulum have carried the profession back and forth between the social and the psychological conceptions of its function—from the early emphasis on individualism and soul-saving, to the reformism of the Progressive Era, to the strong formative influence of psychoanalytic thought after the first World War, to the renewed social consciousness of our time. These have been, as Chambers said, "overlapping phases"; one never excluded the other. And this is simply because one cannot choose between the two: both functions persist, precisely because we cannot conceive of a social work profession that does not continuously address itself to people in need, to the institutions that are supposed to serve them, and to the society in which all this takes place. The stubbornness of the "choice" illusion, and even the arguments about "emphasis," serve only to highlight the difficulties of the integrative task.

These difficulties are illustrated in Eveline Burns's statement that "the center of gravity has shifted away from an emphasis on what goes on inside the individual to an emphasis on improving the functioning of society,"[16] while she is unable to explain what this "shift" looks like in operation, and how the profession actually manages to choose between people's internal and external problems. And Roy Lubove urges social workers to "confront the hard questions of power and income redistribution which have been evaded historically by a stress upon social work's service role,"[17] without telling them which of the services he would cut off from the people who need them. All of which is a long way from C. Wright Mills's vision of the answer: "It is the task of the liberal institution, as of the liberally educated man, continually to translate troubles into issues and issues into the terms of their meaning for the individual."[18]

Meanwhile, the pendulum continues to swing; and as each side takes the ascendency, it fulminates bitterly against the other. In today's world, with its reigning spirit of militant social protest (not unlike the sense of outrage expressed by the human relations professions during the Progressive Era), much of the bitterness is directed against the profession's own service function and the technical interests that go with it. And since service is associated historically with individual "treatment," many seek to free themselves from the psychological yoke and to pursue their long-overdue commitment to social action and social change. Caught again in the means-ends dilemma, they proceed to make the "choice": the qualities of relevancy and statesmanship are attributed to those who stress the larger goals and programs; while the concern with method is seen as narrowly "psychological," overburdened with details, and excessively preoccupied with recording, supervision, and the rest—fiddling, in short, while Rome burns.

One can hardly argue with the sense of urgency out of which all this emerges. Rome is indeed burning: in fact, it is just that great gap between what society needs and the means available to achieve it that overwhelms those who are in the business of helping people take some control over the conditions in which they live. The contrast between what social workers know and what they can do about it is so enormous that many become hopeless about small steps, grow impatient with the subtleties of human communication, and choose instead to concentrate very hard on the goals, values, and structures they want so desperately to bring about. It is a form of *prayer*—just as, conversely, it is a kind of *ritual* to formalize the method and divorce it from social purpose. In both instances—prayer and ritual—the recourse is to magic, rather than art. As in pre-scientific societies, the search for means seems futile in the face of natural forces that are too large, too mysterious, and too difficult to master. The use of such magical thinking in social work is strikingly illustrated in Eisman's statement on the professional role in public welfare: "Social work, a profession dedicated to planned social progress, has the ability to develop skills and insights needed to bring about a successful welfare-class revolution."[19]

Nor is it surprising that a profession which has always been asked to pick up the pieces where the system fails should nourish a long-standing sense of guilt about its reputation, real or fancied, as "pallbearer for a dead society." Faced with the overwhelming discrepancies between ends and means in the society itself, more discouraging for social workers than for those with more limited and specific functions, it is no wonder that the profession yearns for a more central role within the system. Thus the problem is not in social work's impatience for new roles and programs, but in the failure to connect social action and social service, and in the assumption that the one subverts, rather than informs and strengthens, the other. A similar reasoning in the other professions would produce similar distortions: doctors would be urged to shift emphasis from the diagnosis and treatment of illness to the field of public health; architects would agree to build fewer houses, so they could have more time for city planning; lawyers would be pressed to lessen their preoccupation with cases and with courtroom work, so that more of them could become judges and politicians; and so on. In real life, all professions must move back and forth between the specific and the general, the particular and the universal. They must use cases to make policy, and policy to help them with cases; and they must draw from this exchange both the impetus and the evidence for social reform.

Unless these connections are understood, each "choice" defeats even its own purposes; the emphasis on goals produces not more action but less, while a sterile methodolatry fails to create an effective method. Most important, each side falls into the very errors of which it accuses the other. For example, each is guilty of its own charge of elitism. Those who are narrowly occupied with individualistic psychology are vulnerable to the charge of status-worship, lack of concern for social wrongs, and slavish imitation of the "independent" professionalism of, say, the psychiatrists. But the goals people, reacting against this syndrome, have produced their own version of the disease. It is expressed in their impatience with the slow pace at which people work on their own tasks, the eagerness to "plan" for them, and the intolerance for any discussion of the "feelings" of people as they work. The contempt for "process" often hides a contempt for the clients themselves, who will not understand their own problems as the expert understands them, and who refuse to move as fast as the professional thinks they should.

Social workers have always vacillated between these two images of their function; and in this version of the dualism, clinicians and activists are not ranged against each other, but internally divided. On the one hand, the profession has seen itself as a corps of experts, who understand (and "diagnose") individual, group and social ills, prescribe and plan for people, groups, and communities in trouble, and in general conduct the affairs of the needy in what they—the professionals—have defined as the best interests of clients and society. On the other hand, social workers have also taken considerable pride in their concern for democratic decision-making, for client autonomy and self-help, and for "helping people to help themselves."[20] Both these images are continuously reflected in the literature, often in the same articles, and practitioners are urged to do both, even as they are warned that they must choose between the two.[21] The ambivalence is in the desire to *change* people or to *help* them. The change-emphasis is on solutions growing out of the knowledge and wisdom of one who is trained to know about such things, to create good norms, and to move people toward them. The model is the practice of medicine, as such practice is commonly understood. The help-emphasis is on the energies of the client, who is perceived as one who is to regain direction of his own affairs, who is not to be "cured," but mobilized in his own behalf, and for whom the worker is instrumental to his, the client's, purposes rather than the other way around. The model is that of progressive education, existential psychiatry, and other schools of political and psychological thought that stress the processes of self-actualization and self-determination.

The Search for a Method

If we say that these models are not mutually exclusive—that is, that it should be possible to bring together both professional expertise and client initiative without doing violence to either—then we have simply stated the problem of method. How, for example, do we sustain a client-worker relationship that does away with elitism and the abuse of power, while at the same time dispensing with that unreal and patronizing "permissiveness" that distorts the meaning of freedom by denying the authority and the limitations that people have to deal with every day of their lives? The need to "choose" between client weakness and client strength is yet another instance of the professional inability to face the complexities of life, and the attendant compulsion to split the problems—and the people—in two. Having created his dilemma, the worker must then spend much of his time jumping back and forth from one horn to the other; for neither is ever a satisfactory solution to a complex problem. The resolution of these dualisms, so that we may move closer to how real people act in real situations, is a central task in the formulation of a methodical approach to the helping process.

Many of these realities are known to us; they have in fact been expressed so often that they have become clichés of the trade. We know, for example, that people have to do their own work, if what is achieved is to have lasting effects. This is not a moral imperative, but a pragmatic one; if they do not own the process, they will eventually disown the consequences. We know, too, that most people—and particularly the deprived, the punished, and the neglected—face serious obstacles as they try to cope with the confusing and ambiguous demands thrown at them by the society in which they live. How one identifies the source of these difficulties will depend on one's political and psychological orientation. But when the professionals are not attacking and defending their polarized positions, most will agree that the troubles are perpetuated by both internal and external conditions. Modern capitalist society is cruel to all but a few, and most of its institutions are designed to maintain a vastly unequal distribution of power and control, from which many suffer lifetimes of repression and injustice. But such punishment causes internal injuries. Cruelty injures the capacity for self-direction; and repressed people do not spring immediately into action on their own behalf simply because a professional has assured them that the doors have been opened.

We are convinced that a democratic society must create institutions that are responsive to its people, whether they are clients on welfare, families in their neighborhoods, patients in hospitals, children and parents in their schools, or participants in any of the other settings in which social workers find their clients. But the ways in which this responsiveness is kept alive are far more complicated than the oversimplified versions offered by both politicians and professionals. People who are unaccustomed to any measure of institutional control will not respond quickly and automatically, with active and enlightened self-interest, to a bloodless "war on poverty," or an abstraction called "maximum feasible participation," or any of the powerless "councils" and "therapeutic communities" offered by the professionals under the illusion that the concept itself, the vision of the outcome, and the invitation to freedom will somehow bring into being the processes they seek.

Nor can people use the leadership of a profession—however insightful knowledgeable, self-aware, and fired with liberal zeal it may be—that does not know what to do, and how to turn knowledge and purpose into a helping process that is consistent with human and social realities. This is as true for the social workers as it is, say, for the surgeons, who must turn their ethics, their beliefs, and their knowledge of human anatomy into a series of specific movements that can be identified and taught as surgical skill.

Unless the social work profession takes the responsibility for providing such skills, it can hardly hope to help turn the democratic ethic, everywhere so prevalent in words, into something resembling a democratic struggle. In a complex and disordered society, group action and mutual aid are among the most important devices through which some of the power can be redistributed and people can lay claim to their own institutions, small and large.[22] Where these processes fail, as they do most of the time, the power is preempted by elites. And these elites are composed not only of the forces we know and fear—the economic rulers, their politicians, and the whole constabulary of reaction—but of the ones to which we ourselves belong—the progressives, the human relations experts, and the professional helpers. People who are constantly being controlled and manipulated do not care much whether those who are doing the pushing are the "bad guys" or the "good guys." The feelings of impotence and humiliation are not mitigated by the assurance that the manipulation is being done for one's own good. In Dewey's words:

> There is a sense in which to set up social welfare as an end of action only promotes an offensive condescension, a harsh interference, or an oleaginous display of complacent kindliness. It always tends in this direction when it is aimed at giving happiness to others directly, that is, as we can hand a physical thing to another. To foster conditions that widen the

> horizon of others and give them command of their own powers, so that they can find their own happiness in their own fashion, is the way of "social" action. Otherwise the prayer of a freeman would be to be left alone, and to be delivered, above all, from "reformers" and "kind" people.[23]

Of course, the struggles of people to gain more control over their own conditions of life do not depend primarily on the social work profession, or any other profession, or indeed all of them put together. The idea that professional skill creates grass-roots power is an illusion dreamed up by those who are not happy in their work, and who need such magic to make it all seem worthwhile. But there is a connection, far less grandiose and more workable; and it grows from two related circumstances. First, people do need each other for this work; the Horatio Alger idyll of individual virtue triumphant is long gone, if it ever existed. And second, wherever such mutual aid is tried—by people in their neighborhoods, clients on welfare, children in clubs, patients on their wards, and others who combine to take strength from each other—there are powerful forces that operate to keep them alienated and apart. These forces are political and psychological, external and internal, social and personal; but whatever their roots, and whichever are "primary," they create an endless stream of difficulties for people who want and need to put their strengths together in work.

A profession can thus undertake to help strengthen the centripetal forces—those that drive people together, rather than keep them apart. And social work, strategically placed where people are trying desperately to negotiate difficult environments, is uniquely fitted for such a job. To do it, however, the profession must be able to describe and teach the specific skills by which its practitioners can help group members clarify their tasks, identify their strengths, face their own fears, break down old taboos, learn from each other's struggles, and use help to mobilize themselves in their own behalf. The social worker cannot stop with knowledge, intention, self-awareness, or any of the attributes that prepare him for action, but do not in themselves constitute action. The client, as we know, is in the same position: if he tries to substitute insight for action, we will, quite rightly, label him "resistive." A professional acts to help others act.

It is when the worker's acts lack skill—when they are vague, clumsy, obtuse, superficial, preachy, or unfeeling—that opportunities are lost and people suffer needlessly. It is then that the profession itself comes to be identified as part of the problem, rather than part of the solution. What was to be a collaborative, helping relationship turns into a battle of wills: clients become "unreachable" because the workers have not been able to reach them; and workers are perceived by the clients as hiding their humanity behind the vast institutions they represent.

In practice, these disappointments and failures abound: wherever the worker is so fixed on his preconceived "goals" that he cannot listen to what his people are trying to tell him; where he is vague about the nature of his service, and has to fall back on the long-winded jargon that social work clients hear so often; where he cannot help his people break a huge problem into smaller, more manageable parts; where he keeps missing the disguised messages through which people often send out their calls for help; where he is so frightened or angry about what is happening to his client that he hastens to "solve" the difficulty in his own terms, leaving the client far behind and unable to own or implement any of it; and in a host of other instances where the failure of skill turns the worker from a potential friend into another version of the enemy—a version more confusing, because he is so obviously well-intentioned.

Which is why I believe, and would like to show in this book, that the work on technical problems, far from being precious or diversionary, is the only serious approach to the goals themselves. The search for a method is not a "psychological" enterprise, nor is it a "social" one; and it serves neither means nor ends for their own sake. Instead, it is an effort to put together our knowledge of both the inner and outer determinants of action, and to focus in one view our aspirations for both individual well-being and social change. And it aims to create a scheme of action that can be broken down into the small, immediate steps through which social workers can use their knowledge and their purposes to help people act in their own self-interest, negotiate their environments, and make some more insistent claims on their own institutions.

It is precisely in these small steps that the professional identifies himself, and distinguishes himself from the layman in his field. General knowledge, personal sensitivity, and humanitarian goals are available to any liberal-minded citizen in the community. But the specific skills of the doctor, lawyer, engineer—and social worker—are the special responsibility of those who have been chosen and schooled to learn and perform them when they are called for by the people who need them. The problem of particularity is at the heart of the search for method. Bronowski, examining the similarities of both science and art in this respect, comments as follows:

> The test of truth is the known factual evidence, and no glib expediency nor reason of state can justify the smallest self-deception in that. Our work is of a piece, in the large and in detail; so that if we silence one scruple about our means, we infect ourselves and our ends together.
>
> The scientist derives this ethic from his method, and every creative worker reaches it for himself. This is how Blake reached it from his practice as a poet and a painter.
>
> > He who would do good to another must do it
> > in Minute Particulars:
> >
> > General Good is the plea of the scoundrel,
> > hypocrite & flatterer
> >
> > For Art and Science cannot exist but in
> > minutely organized Particulars.

> The Minute Particulars of art and the fine-structure of science alike make the grain of conscience.[24]

A Neglected Field

The "minute particulars" of the helping relationship have been virtually ignored by all of the service professions, and the literature reflects a good deal of uneasiness on this score. Freud himself, speaking for what is perhaps the most self-conscious and innerdirected of the disciplines, complained about the lack of curiousity about technique:

> It seems to me that among my colleagues there is a widespread and erroneous impression that this technique of searching for the origins of the symptoms and removing the manifestations by means of this investigation is an easy one which can be practised off-hand, as it were. I conclude this from the fact that not one of all those who show an interest in my therapy and pass definite judgements upon it has ever asked me how I actually go about it. There can be but one reason for this, namely, that they think there is nothing to enquire about, that the thing is perfectly obvious.[25]

This was in 1904. In 1940 Otto Fenichel commented that "it is amazing how small a proportion of the very extensive psychoanalytic literature is devoted to psychoanalytic technique and how much less to the theory of technique." And in 1958, Karl Menninger made the point again, quoting Fenichel in the introduction to his book on psychoanalytic technique.[26] Two years later, Strupp, in a pioneering investigation into the acts of the psychotherapist, noted that:

> Research on the therapist's contribution is not, of course, any more important than research on the personality processes which psychotherapy seeks to influence, but it is a necessary link in improving our understanding of what psychotherapy is about. Considering the obvious importance of the therapist variable, it is astonishing how little objective research has been conducted on the problem.[27]

Less surprising, perhaps, and certainly more widespread, is the failure of method-consciousness in the field of medicine as a whole. Engrossed in their technical problems, the physicians mystify their patients with private words and tend to identify any effort to move closer to the patient as something suspect called the "bedside manner." And yet Korsch and Negrete found, in a recent study of doctor-patient communication, that "the failure to establish empathy with patients can be a serious bar to communication and patient response."[28]

> The quality of medical care depends in the last analysis on the interaction of the patient and the doctor, and there is abundant evidence that in current practice this interaction all too often is disappointing to both

> parties. Systematic surveys confirm that there is widespread dissatisfaction among patients with doctors and among doctors with lack of cooperation by their patients.[29]

Korsch and Negrete observed and recorded 800 parent visits to an emergency clinic at the Children's Hospital of Los Angeles. They found considerable parent dissatisfaction with the doctor-parent interview; and they found that there was a high correlation between such dissatisfaction and noncompliance with the doctor's orders. Many physicians were unable to draw from the parent their version of the illness, or translate their terms into words the parent could understand, or show and elicit true feelings, or listen for hidden messages that were important to the clinical picture (as, for example, the fact that many mothers blamed themselves for the child's illness). Doctors and mothers often fell into irritated exchanges, with the latter soon lapsing into an anxious or resentful silence that the doctor construed as agreement. The physicians were frequently surprised by the feedback from these interviews, and particularly by the fact that they had done most of the talking. Interestingly, time was not a factor, even though it was an emergency clinic: "Indeed, on examining some of the longest sessions we noted that the time was consumed largely by failures in communication: the doctor and patient were spending the time trying to get on the same wavelength!"[30]

The researchers concluded that the patterns they uncovered are common in medical practice, and urged more attention to the skills of communication. And that even they tended to underestimate the complexity of such skills—finding that they "should not be difficult for any trained person to master"—simply goes further to demonstrate the strangeness of the methods terrain.

In the field of education, the methods question has been a center of controversy almost from its beginnings. It is focused most often on the issue of "process" versus "content," as fought between the "progressive," process-conscious perspective of John Dewey and his followers, and the "traditionalist" orientation of those who stress the transmission of knowledge and ideas. At its extremes, the arguments have been bitter. The traditionalist Bestor stormed that "the West was not settled by men and women who had taken courses in 'How to be a pioneer'. . . . I for one do not believe that the American people have lost all common sense and native wit so that now they have to be taught in school to blow their noses and button their pants."[31] Hutchins claimed that "all there is to teaching can be learned through a good education and being a teacher,"[32] and said that "personality is the qualification we look for in an antiintellectual teacher."[33] Mortimer Smith accused John Dewey of propagating

> . . . a doctrine that released the teacher from his responsibility for handing on the traditional knowledge of the race, a doctrine that firmly implied that one need not adhere to any standards of knowledge but simply cater to individual interests; and it was made the more attractive by the suggestion that this procedure was to be undertaken in behalf of

"self-realization," an ideal to which only a brutish sort of person indeed could oppose himself.[34]

On the other side, Dewey insisted that "the depreciation of action, of doing and making, has been cultivated by philosophers,"[35] and that these philosophers tried to escape their feelings of uncertainty by adopting "the method of changing the self in emotion and idea," rather than "the method of changing the world through action."[36] But some of Dewey's more enthusiastic followers did take some wild trips of their own:

> Through the years we've built a sort of halo around reading, writing and arithmetic. We've said they were for everybody—rich and poor, brilliant and not-so-mentally-endowed, ones who liked them and those who failed to go for them.
>
> We shall some day accept the thought that it is just as illogical to assume that every boy must be able to read as it is that each one must be able to perform on a violin.[37]

Strangely enough, however, the most significant aspect of this controversy is not that the progressives are interested in methods of teaching and the traditionalists are not. It is rather that the "process" people themselves have done so little to identify and teach the skills they so strongly espouse. Martin Mayer commented on this in his comprehensive examination of the schools in America. After observing in a school situation that seemed to go very well, he wrote:

> No one should be surprised that progressivism, or any other philosophy of education, works well when the teachers are people of the quality of the Bradts. The question is whether or not any philosophy is capable of fragmentation into specific techniques which can be acquired by teachers who are not remarkably gifted. Unfortunately, progressivism in America was always more interested in creating proper attitudes than in developing effective techniques.[38]

And from what some might regard as an unexpected quarter—the noted behaviorist, B. F. Skinner—comes a strong criticism of the failure of the field to interest itself in the process of teaching:

> The most widely publicized efforts to improve education show an extraordinary neglect of method. Learning and teaching are not analyzed, and almost no effort is made to improve teaching as such. The aid which education is to receive usually means money, and the proposals for spending it follow a few, familiar lines. We should build more and better schools. We should recruit more and better teachers. We should search for better students and make sure that all competent students can go to school or college. We should multiply teacher-student contacts with films and television. We should design new curricula. All this can be done without looking at teaching itself. We need not ask how those better

> teachers are to teach those better students in those better schools, what kinds of contact are to be multiplied through mass media, or how new curricula are to be made effective.[39]

It is in fact remarkable that two of the best-known books on the subject of teaching methods—one old and one recent—have almost nothing to say about methods of teaching. William Heard Kilpatrick's classic *Foundations of Method* contributed a great deal to our understanding of how children learn, but it did not address itself at all to how teachers teach. "The wider problem of method," he wrote, "has to do with all the responses children make as they work, and its concern is to help children build the total of these responses into the best possible whole."[40] But he failed to explain how such a concern is to be translated into a system of action. Instead, he said (and this is precisely what Martin Mayer was to comment on, many years later): "In particular the wider problem is much concerned to build attitudes and appreciations. In so doing, it builds the heart of the child; and out of the heart are the issues of life."[41]

More recently, Bruner's *Process of Education* summarized a conference held in 1959, in which "scientists, scholars, and educators [gathered] to discuss how education in science might be improved in our primary and secondary schools."[42] The conference was divided into five work groups, covering "Sequence of a Curriculum," "The Apparatus of Teaching," "The Motivation of Learning," "The Role of Intuition in Learning and Thinking," and "Cognitive Processes in Learning."[43] Except for the work on the teacher's use of mechanical apparatus, the implication is clear that the study of method is not a subject in itself, but is somehow supposed to emerge automatically from our knowledge of the material to be learned, the learner himself, and the order in which the material is presented. In Bruner's final chapter—on "Aids to Teaching"—he finally asks the question: "What can be said of the teacher's role in teaching?"[44] But it is then five pages from the end of the book; the discussion is brief, and it is closely tied to how the teacher uses mechanical devices in his work.

The problem is pervasive: in each of the helping professions, the literature reflects the mood of Blanton's comment as he discusses the training of clinical psychologists:

> The relationship between knowing and doing has as many puzzles for us today as it had for Socrates. Indeed, all of psychology is involved with it in one way or another.[45]

In social work, Pruyser's proposition that "to *be* a social worker is not the same as *doing* social work"[46] has been restated frequently, in one form or another, since the profession began. Mary Richmond complained in 1897 that "the most monstrous blunders are protected and perpetuated by being swathed in the cotton-wool of good intentions."[47] Two decades later, she was still concerned that "the investigation is stronger than the treatment"; a reader of case records had informed her that "after the investigation has been made and recorded, the treatment seems to drop to a lower level almost as suddenly as though it went over the edge of a cliff."[48] A similar impatience was later expressed by Eduard Lindeman, speaking from his perspective in group work and community organization: "But we have been surfeited with the sentimental appeals in all spheres of social work. . . . What we ask of the specialist is technique which rings true and organization which is unselfish."[49]

In our own time, Helen Harris Perlman reviewed developments in social work method over a ten-year period, and concluded: "We are surely and even rapidly adding to our store of knowledge: we have given tongue and ear to what we believe in and hold to be good; but the what and the how of carrying knowledge and belief into action—these are yet to be formulated."[50] And the report from the group work sector has the same ring:

> This specialized field is rich in democratic concepts; it has a wealth of examples; but in professionally unique concepts, "method theory," it has been curiously poor. . . . It is possible that no social or economic class in a community is beyond profiting from what goes under the name of a "group experience." But it is difficult for a social group worker to communicate how and why this near-miracle happens, except to another group worker.[51]

And so it goes: the nagging uneasiness about knowing, believing, and hoping for more than one can do anything about; and the equally stubborn inhibition against facing the problems of defining the doing, so that professionals may be taught to act with more skill and certainty. It is no accident, of course, that the helping disciplines suffer more than most from this condition. In science, industry, and the plastic arts, where the materials are inert and malleable, and their properties are fairly well understood, the worker can take more responsibility for the quality of his product; for the product is, in fact, of his making. Where the results are thus visible, and ascribable, he can, by referring to them, develop some notions of skill and make some distinctions between efficient movements and clumsy ones.

But in the human relations professions, the materials are people, with lives, energies, and initiatives of their own. The interaction between workers and their clients is so complex, and the contributing variables so numerous, that the product is often obscure and the responsibility for outcomes hard to place. Under these conditions, it is not only difficult to define skill; it is possible to deny that such a thing exists at all. Instead, the recourse is to something that might be called the "gimmickry of structures," where good ideas are roughly sketched out and put into operation as if the ideas were powerful enough to implement themselves, without having to define and teach the step-by-step skills through which a practitioner can make them work. Each helping profession has its own version of these slogans and structures—its "project method," "team teaching," "open classroom," "crisis intervention," "maximum feasible participation," "sensitivity training," and the rest. Porter Lee said it a long time ago, in the course of social work's persistent cause-function debate:

> To go from concept to program and from program to technique is to take the long dreary drop from ideals to routine, from the heroic to the humdrum, from enthusiasm to devotion. But technique is still the factor which rounds out our march toward social justice and every social program must in the end stand or fall upon the quality of its technique.
>
> . . . seen in its true relation to the other aspects of social work [techique] is as vivid and as appealing as the ideas which ought to guide it.[52]

The Task Ahead

But the professional conscience and the scientific tradition make it impossible to sustain such evasions indefinitely. As the work goes on, attention turns inevitably to the "minute particulars" of the worker-client engagement, and there is evidence that this is beginning to happen in several of the service professions.[53] In social work, a growing number of professionals, trained in the old traditions but impatient with the philosophizing and the global claims and ambitions, are turning to the task of studying the details of practice.[54] Our present stage of development may be close to that described by Rothman, as he discusses the movement from philosophy to experiment in the physical sciences:

> Scientists, being practical people in many ways, decided that there was no point in pursuing theories that did not lead anywhere in improving understanding. Toward the end of the nineteenth century, they came to the conclusion that the most they could accomplish was to give an accurate description of *how* the universe operates and let philosophers worry about the *why*. They concentrated on studying "what happens."
>
> With this approach, scientists found that their ability to find answers increased by leaps and bounds. By directing their efforts to questions that could be answered by observation, they were able to ignore questions which previously had used up much time and energy but had yielded no meaningful answers.[55]

Social workers—and particularly the group workers among them—have had more than their share of these questions that "use up much time and energy" without advancing their social usefulness in tangible ways. But the drive toward "meaningful answers" has never lost its impetus, and the profession remains in a favored position—between people and their environments—to integrate "cause" and "function" without sacrificing its devotion to either. Elsewhere, I have commented on social work's version of what Rothman describes as the transition from the "why" to the "how":

> When a profession is young, a considerable proportion of its thought and energy is devoted to the process of calling attention to the social

> need out of which it grew. From its special vantage point, the new group is intensely aware of this need, of the importance of doing something about it, and of the necessity for arousing a similar sense of urgency in the minds of the general public. This is another way of saying that a profession begins as a *movement;* its primary function at this stage is to agitate for a place on the social agenda, its workers are dedicated to the cause and its advocacy, and its major spokesmen are social philosophers, energetic social advocates, and commanding personalities who call attention to themselves and to the objects of their concern.
>
> . . . Having established the social need as a proper object of society's attention, it remains to be shown that the profession can do the job and do it well. Increasingly, then, a greater proportion of professional energy is diverted from what *should be* to what *is.* The concern with ends becomes a growing curiousity about the means for achieving them; the stress on intentions, motives, and enthusiasms gives way to a larger preoccupation with efficiency and productivity; and the working skills of practitioners take on a greater significance than their ability to formulate statements of philosophy and aspiration.

The reaction to this is a nostalgia for the old days and a sense of loss at the passing of the movement. The tone of the conversation has changed; the technicians have laid their cold hands on the work, and there is fear that there will be a general loss of feeling and vision. Nevertheless,

> The fact remains that the new social and professional climate makes it impossible to return to the days when the vision itself carried its own promise of fulfillment. That the emphasis on means can be used to evade social responsibility is, after all, no more surprising than the earlier discovery that the preoccupation with goals can be used in the same way. Both dangers simply point up the challenge to the modern profession: to draw upon a growing knowledge of social reality, to frame a sense of purpose consistent with that reality, to conceptualize its practice in forms that make it testable and teachable, and to retain in the process its initial vigor, its power of advocacy, and its driving vision of what society should be like.[56]

I believe that social work is better prepared for this challenge than most of the helping professions. For along with the means-ends confusions and the proneness to gimmickry, there has also grown a tradition that stressed the study of experience, the intimate engagement with human suffering, the accountability of workers to their agencies, and the responsibility of the agencies to their communities. Led by practitioners like Mary Richmond, Grace Coyle, Kenneth Pray, Bertha Reynolds, and others, there was an early emphasis on the details of practice. And it was from this emphasis that two of its most unique and characteristic procedures developed: the worker's detailed account of his conversations with the client—the so-called "process" record; and the strong supervisory discipline under which these records were used, in regular conferences between worker and supervisor, to exact accountability and improve performance through the study of the worker's practice skills in action.

But even as social work's interest in practice was early established, its efforts to theorize about it were never very successful. For reasons I will try to examine, it has been difficult to generalize from the experiences of a century. Now, at this stage of its history, the profession can no longer postpone the methodological inquiry; even as the concern with technique is under its severest attack, social workers must strengthen their efforts to turn their practice wisdom, of which there is a great deal, into practice theory, of which there is very little. "A few individuals," wrote John Stuart Mill, "by extraordinary genius, or by the accidental acquisition of a good set of intellectual habits, may work without principles in the same way, or nearly the same way, in which they would have worked if they had been in possession of principles. But the bulk of mankind require either to understand the theory of what they are doing, or to have rules laid down for them by those who have understood the theory."[57]

How does one construct a "theory" of the helping process? How do we build a "body of generalizations and principles developed in association with practice in a field of activity (as medicine, music) and forming its content as an intellectual discipline"?[58] Or even, ultimately, "a coordinated set of hypotheses which are found to be consistent with one another and with specially observed phenomena"?[59]

More specifically: How do we approach the search for a social work method, and then turn our formulation to effective use in guiding the work with people in groups? What does it mean to "operationalize" the language of practice, and why is it so difficult? Does the standardization of method preclude the variations of personal style? How do we develop a systematic plan of action that is neither rigid and prescriptive on the one hand, nor vague and global on the other?

These are some of the questions with which we begin. Needless to say, my approach to these questions will be drawn from my own experiences—as practitioner, supervisor, researcher, administrator, teacher, consultant—and my perspective will be but one among the many that will be needed by social work and the other helping professions. My aim is not to produce the Grand Theory, but simply to call attention to the importance of the subject, set out at least one way of approaching its study, and develop a working model of practice that should help to sharpen the group skills of those practitioners for whom this analysis may strike some echoes in their own work with people.

Notes and References

1. Canon Barnett, the founder of Toynbee Hall, wrote in his 1889 report: " 'One by one' is the phrase which best expresses our method, and the 'raising of the buried life' is that which best expresses our end'." This, incidentally, is one of the first recorded instances in which the relational

system ("one by one") is defined as the "method." In S. A. Barnett, *Canon Barnett, His Life, Work, and Friends* (Boston and New York: Houghton Mifflin Company, 1919), vol. 1, p. 320.

2. Mary Richmond commented "with great pleasure" on "the new tendency to view our clients from the angle of what might be termed *small-group psychology.*" From: "Some Next Steps in Social Treatment," *Proceedings of the National Conference of Social Work* (Chicago: University of Chicago Press, 1920), p. 256. (Emphasis in original).
3. Eduard C. Lindeman, "Group Work and Education for Democracy," *Proceedings of the National Conference of Social Work* (New York: Columbia University Press, 1939), p. 344.
4. William Schwartz, "The Social Worker in the Group," *The Social Welfare Forum, 1961* (New York and London: Columbia University Press, 1961), pp. 148–50.
5. Alvin L. Schorr, "The Retreat to the Technician," *Social Work,* vol. 4, no. 1 (January 1959), p. 29.
6. Mitchell I. Ginsberg and Irving Miller, "Problem of Conformity as Faced by the Professional Worker," *Group Work Papers 1957,* presented at the National Conference on Social Welfare (New York: National Association of Social Workers, 1958), p. 9.
7. Justus Buchler, *The Concept of Method* (New York and London: Columbia University Press, 1961), pp. 105–06.
8. John Dewey, *Democracy and Education: An Introduction to the Philosophy of Education* (New York: The Macmillan Company, 1916), p. 122.
9. Schorr, *op. cit.,* p. 32.
10. C. Wright Mills, *The Power Elite* (New York: Oxford University Press, 1957), pp. 318–19. For my discussion of the implications of this issue for social work, see also, William Schwartz, "Private Troubles and Public Issues: One Social Work Job or Two?" *The Social Welfare Forum, 1969* (New York and London: Columbia University Press, 1969), pp. 22–43.
11. Mary Richmond, "The Retail Method of Reform," in Joanna C. Colcord, ed., *The Long View: Papers and Addresses by Mary E. Richmond,* (New York: Russell Sage Foundation, 1930), pp. 215–16.
12. Kenneth L. M. Pray, *Social Work in a Revolutionary Age and Other Papers* (Philadelphia: University of Pennsylvania Press, 1949), p. 231.
13. Clarke A. Chambers, "An Historical Perspective on Political Action *v.* Individualized Treatment," in *Current Issues in Social Work Seen in Historical Perspective* (New York: Council on Social Work Education, 1962), p. 54.
14. *Ibid.,* p. 53.
15. For a discussion of the "family quarrel" aspect of the troubles-issues dilemma, see Schwartz, "Private Troubles and Public Issues." *op. cit.,* p. 23.
16. Eveline M. Burns, "Tomorrow's Social Needs and Social Work Education," *Journal of Education for Social Work,* vol. 2, no. 1 (Spring 1966), p. 16.

17. Roy Lubove, "Social Work and the Life of the Poor," *The Nation,* vol. 202, no. 21, May 23, 1966, p. 611.
18. Mills, *op. cit.,* p. 319.
19. Martin Eisman, "Social Work's New Role in the Welfare-Class Revolution," *Social Work,* vol. 14, no. 2 (April 1969), p. 86.
20. For two of the more cogent discussions of the self-determination principle and its implications in social work, see: Saul Bernstein, "Self-determination: King or Citizen in the Realm of Values?" *Social Work,* vol. 5, no. 1, (January 1960), pp. 3–8; and Alan Keith-Lucas, "A Critique of the Principle of Client Self-determination," *Social Work,* vol. 8, no. 3 (July 1963), pp. 66–71.
21. The poignancy of the prescriptive-permissive dilemma is illustrated in Harry Lawrence, "The Testing of Mr. Jennings," *The Group,* vol. 16, no. 4 (April 1954), pp. 11–14, 24–25. Here the author concludes that "democratic discussion" in his group of thirteen-year-old boys cannot take place unless the worker enforces a number of rules, by which only one boy may speak at a time, no interruptions may be tolerated, only one subject is permitted at a time, and other limitations inherently strange to the nature of his members. "The group work principle of 'taking the group from where it is'," he writes, "should not be interpreted to mean permissiveness on the question of order." He then points out that "the worker should encourage the group to formulate its own ground rules," following almost immediately with the warning: "It is essential that the above tenets of procedure are incorporated in whatever ground rules are developed." The conflict could hardly be more touching.
22. For a recent discussion of the use of collective power by small groups of citizens in ordinary walks of life, see Virginia Held, "Walking Out on the System," *The Nation,* vol. 213, no. 12, October 18, 1971, pp. 370–72.
23. John Dewey, *Human Nature and Conduct: An Introduction to Social Psychology* (New York: The Modern Library, 1930), p. 294.
24. J. Bronowski, *Science and Human Values* (New York: Harper & Row, Harper Torchbooks, Science Library, 1965), p. 66.
25. Sigmund Freud, "On Psychotherapy," *Collected Papers* (London: Hogarth Press and the Institute of Psycho-Analysis, 1950), vol. I, pp. 254–55.
26. Karl Menninger, *Theory of Psychoanalytic Technique* (New York: Harper & Row, Harper Torchbooks, Academy Library, 1958), p. v.
27. Hans H. Strupp, *Psychotherapists in Action: Explorations of the Therapist's Contribution to the Treatment Process* (New York: Grune and Stratton, 1960), p. 1.
28. Barbara M. Korsch and Vida Francis Negrete, "Doctor-Patient Communication," *Scientific American,* vol. 227, no. 2 (August 1972), p. 66.
29. *Ibid.,* p. 66.
30. *Ibid.,* p. 71.
31. Arthur E. Bestor, *Educational Wastelands* (Urbana, Ill.: U. of Illinois Press, 1953), p. 64.

32. Robert M. Hutchins, *The Higher Learning in America* (New Haven: Yale University Press, 1936), p. 56.
33. Robert M. Hutchins, *No Friendly Voice* (Chicago: University of Chicago Press, 1936), p. 29.
34. Mortimer Smith, *And Madly Teach* (Chicago: Henry Regnery, 1949), p. 23.
35. John Dewey, *The Quest for Certainty: A Study of the Relation of Knowledge and Action* (New York: G. P. Putnam's Sons, Capricorn Books, 1960), p. 4.
36. *Ibid.*, p. 3.
37. A. H. Lauchner, from a speech quoted in "Three R's Aren't for All," Champaign (Illinois) *News-Gazette,* February 14, 1951, p. 5.
38. Martin Mayer, *The Schools* (New York: Harper and Brothers, 1961), p. 53.
39. B. F. Skinner, "Why Teachers Fail," *Saturday Review,* Oct. 16, 1965.
40. William Heard Kilpatrick, *Foundations of Method: Informal Talks on Teaching* (New York: Macmillan, 1932), p. 134.
41. *Ibid.*, p. 135.
42. Jerome S. Bruner, *The Process of Education* (Cambridge, Mass.: Harvard University Press, 1960), p. vii.
43. *Ibid.*, p. xi.
44. *Ibid.*, p. 88.
45. R. Blanton, "Science and Art in the Training of Psychologists," *Journal of Clinical Psychology,* vol. 18, no. 1 (Jan. 1962), pp. 10–14.
46. Paul W. Pruyser, "Existential Notes on Professional Education," *Social Work,* vol. 8, no. 2 (April 1963), p. 85.
47. Mary Richmond, "The Training of Charity Workers," in *The Long View . . . , op. cit.*, p. 87.
48. Mary Richmond, "Some Next Steps in Social Treatment," *op. cit.*, p. 254.
49. E. C. Lindeman, "Organization and Technique for Rural Recreation," in *Proceedings of the National Conference of Social Work* (Chicago: University of Chicago Press, 1920), p. 324.
50. Helen Harris Perlman, "Social Work Method: A Review of the Past Decade," *Social Work,* vol. 10, no. 4 (October 1965), p. 175.
51. Frank J. Bruno (with chapters by Louis Towley), *Trends in Social Work, 1874–1956* (New York: Columbia U. Press, 1957), p. 422.
52. Porter R. Lee, "Technical Training for Social Work," in Lee, *Social Work as Cause and Function and Other Papers* (New York: Columbia University Press, 1937), pp. 30–31.
53. See, for example: N. L. Gage, ed., *Handbook of Research on Teaching* (Chicago: Rand McNally & Company, 1963), 1218 pages; Raymond J. Corsini and Daniel D. Howard, eds., *Critical Incidents in Teaching* (Englewood Cliffs, N.J.: Prentice-Hall, 1964), 222 pages; Arno A. Bellack, Herbert M. Kliebard, Ronald T. Hyman, and Frank L. Smith, Jr., *The Language of the Classroom* (New York: Teachers College Press, 1966), 274 pages; Hans H. Strupp, *op. cit.;* Karl Menninger, *op. cit.;*

Leonard Krasner, "Behavior Therapy," in Paul H. Mussen and Mark R. Rosenzweig, eds., *Annual Review of Psychology* (Palo Alto, California: Annual Reviews, Inc., 1971, vol. 22), pp. 483–532.

54. For example, in the area of group practice in social work, an increasing number of doctoral students have turned their attention to problems of method. See William Schwartz, "Neighborhood Centers and Group Work," in Henry S. Maas, ed., *Research in the Social Services: A Five-Year Review* (New York: National Association of Social Workers, 1971), pp. 171–75, for a review of this work.
55. Milton A. Rothman, *The Laws of Physics* (Greenwich, Conn.: Fawcett Publications, 1963), pp. 13–14.
56. William Schwartz, "Small Group Science and Group Work Practice," *Social Work,* vol. 8, no. 4 (October 1963), pp. 40–41.
57. John Stuart Mill, *A System of Logic* (New York: Harper, 1874), p. 22.
58. Under "theory," in *Webster's Third New International Dictionary of the English Language Unabridged* (Springfield, Mass.: G. and C. Merriam Company, 1964), p. 2371.
59. Under "theory," in C. F. Tweney and L. E. C. Hughes, *Chambers's Technical Dictionary* (New York: Macmillan, 3d ed. rev., with Supplement, 1961), p. 844.

2

The Meaning of Method

As we have seen, the helping professions have attached so many different meanings to the term "method"—the goals, the acts, the philosophy, the relational system itself—that it has been difficult to develop a common language in which practitioners can talk to each other about what they do and build on each other's work. Our search, therefore, is for a frame of reference out of which such a language may emerge. It will need a vocabulary that puts its faith in *verbs,* stressing the acts, the strategies, and the skills through which the worker tries to turn his knowledge, his values, and his purposes into the specific movements of a helping process.

If this were easy, the field would be further along. But what is it, exactly, that makes it so hard? What are the problems inherent in the helping process itself—in the very phenomena we are trying to understand? Let us begin by looking at a few recorded examples of the work itself, watching the "basic ingredients" in action—a group, in an agency, with a worker who has been assigned to help. The selections are excerpted from actual descriptions of agency practice.

The first is from the initial meeting of a group of foster parents, called together by a public agency to work on problems of rearing children who are not their own:

> Mr. T., a foster father, then spoke. He guessed he was the first man to speak this morning, and I gave him brief and good humored recognition for this. Mr. T.'s voice was calm and very earnest when he started; but as he finished his comment, his voice broke with emotion. He told the group that he was a stepchild, but that he was never told the truth. He regarded his stepmother as his real mother until he was 13 years of age, when a distant relative informed him of his true identity. His real mother was not only living, but residing in the community. He described the pain of this sudden discovery and said he would never want this to happen to his foster children.
>
> There was a hushed silence in the room.[1]

And, in the same agency, these are the foster children:

> F. said he always knew he was a foster child and knows the reason. M. said he knew why he was in foster care, too. F. wanted to know why M. was a foster child, and said that he didn't have to answer if it were too personal. M. said he didn't mind telling the group. He then asked me if I had ever been downtown near W's Department store. I said I had been in the area a couple of times. He asked F. the same question and F. said yes. M. continued: "Well, there is a man who sells pretzels in front of the store all year round." He hesitated, smiled and said, "He's my real father." Though M. smiled as he informed us of this, there were no smiles from the other boys.[2]

Here is a young worker meeting with her street club of preadolescent girls:

> When we were eating in the Center I said that I thought they had seemed kind of unhappy lately and asked if they wanted to talk about it. Kathy said they weren't unhappy about *anything*. I asked, "Even about my leaving in the summer?" Tata jumped up and shouted, "Nobody gives a shit about your leaving. Go ahead and leave now if you want to!" There were tears in her eyes as she spoke.[3]

And some tenants of a slum building move hesitantly to mobilize themselves in their own behalf. The worker writes:

> I received a phone call from the other worker about the heat being off in the building for a few days. The tenants were very angry and had called the Neighborhood Service Center for help. I went to visit them and we decided to have a meeting in the evening when the landlord could be reached.
>
> Everyone showed up on time and seemed eager to begin. . . . Three tenants described the situation and the ramifications of being without heat in the building for eight days. "The heat goes off when the superintendant leaves and comes on when he comes home at night." "It does no good to talk to the super. We have tried it for months and months. The time is to talk to the landlord."
>
> Mrs. N. suggested that I call the landlord, as I had once offered to do. I said that we had called the landlord and threatened him twice, and that Mr. N. had done the same, but it doesn't seem to do any good. H. said the problem was that he simply would not listen to the tenants. Everyone echoed this, and Mr. N. said that the landlord thought that "we are children." Mrs. N. thought I ought to call the landlord once again.[4]

These are the moments in which social workers are called upon to move, to speak, to act in some way that reflects their sense of what is going on and what they need to do to help. What is inside the "hushed silence" that follows Mr. T.'s poignant comment, and how much of it should the worker help preserve before she reaches in for what they are thinking? It has cost M., the foster child, a great deal to yield up his bit of heartache and share it with the others, and the temptation is strong to ease the tension with a light or reassuring remark. But this might flatten out an important moment and inhibit the others from responding to M.'s pain with some of their own. And how does the worker draw from Tata and the others their feelings about her leaving, and then, most probably, their bitterness about all the other separations and betrayals they have suffered at the hands of loved adults? Finally, what kind of immediate help do the tenants need in order to bell their cat and show the landlord that they are not "children," but people with dignity and the strength to act together when they have to? It is these "intermediate acts" that Dewey urged us to "take seriously," and pointed out that "of the intermediate acts, the most important is the *next* one."[5]

This is not to say that everything hangs on the worker's next step, or that there is a perfect move for every moment. Practitioners approach their opportunities with different styles and different perceptions. But every act, as well as every abstention, carries its own weight and meaning: it can stimulate or inhibit, clarify or confuse, clear the way or create new obstacles. And where the problems are the most difficult, and the clients most anxious or dependent, the influence of authority will be most strongly felt. An embarrassed worker can make Mr. T., or the child M., ashamed for having risked their private emotions in public, and can communicate subtly to the others that such talk is more than he bargained for. Tata and her friends can be stopped in their tracks by a worker who tries to convince them that they "shouldn't feel that way," because there are good and logical reasons why she must leave them. And an overzealous worker can take the tenants' problems away from them and show that he, too, thinks they are "children" who cannot act for themselves.

Further, this demand for the next step renews itself from moment to moment; no sooner has he made one move, than another is called for. The situation restructures itself continuously, new exchanges are created, and there is a steady flow of fresh cues and messages to which the worker must respond again and again in accordance with his perceptions of their needs and his purposes. As the worker reaches into the "hushed silence," or asks the boys to respond to M., or gives (or holds back) her immediate reaction to Tata's grief, or promises (or refuses) to call the landlord—each of these acts sets other acts in motion; the moment changes, relationships are altered, attention shifts, and a host of new cues call for the worker's attention.

He can, of course, register only a few of these cues, and respond to even fewer; inevitably, he will be attentive to certain messages and oblivious to others. In this fast-moving, ever-changing situation, the worker will always be selecting certain cues, ignoring others, and storing still others away for future reference. Certainly, not everything that happens is equally important; but every worker will, from moment to moment, make his own judgments about what is urgent, what to see and hear, what to stress and what to pass by, when to nod and when to speak and when to hold his tongue.

The matter is further complicated by the fact that these responses are not actually "chosen," in the usual sense. In the press of events, the worker has little time to weigh alternatives, deliberate on a course of action, and select his movements with care. He must act quickly, or the moment will pass him by. In the hectic give-and-take of the client-worker exchange—and particularly in its small-group version—there is little opportunity for the worker to choose his "interventions." Since his "waiting" moments are also experienced by the clients as acts—as judgments, thoughts, decisions, and other internal responses—he is actually "intervening" all the time, making his presence continuously felt, as does every other actor in the situation. In every spontaneous act and abstention, he shows how he has pulled together the mass of knowledge, attitudes, feelings, and purposes that have been built into his personal and professional preparation for this moment—and the next, and the next.

This process of ordering his ideas, beliefs, and intentions may be only dimly apparent to the worker himself; but order them he does, into some guiding scheme that tells him what to notice and what to do about it. Whether he is sophisticated or naive, experienced or raw, trained or unschooled, he has a frame of reference from which he draws his notions about what is "true," what is "right," and what should be made to happen. He has, in fact, a "theory" of his own—coherent or confused, conscious or unknown—about the nature of the helping process.

This brings us to the problem of method. Where this theory is vague, or internally inconsistent, or violates the realities of his subject, the worker's acts must reflect these confusions and fallacies to the same degree. If he hypothesizes (consciously or otherwise) that people tend to express their real intentions in their words—that they mean just what they say they mean—he will be unable to listen for the hidden voices of ambivalence. But if he also "knows" somehow that there is a life beneath the surface—that "still waters run deep"—he will at times hint darkly about hidden motives, perhaps even where the client's intentions are perfectly clear. Again, if he postulates (consciously or otherwise) that people act by choosing the most logical alternatives, he will spend considerable time in explaining, persuading, and convincing. But if he also "knows" that judgment is often shaped by emotion, he will move on this hypothesis too from time to time, intuitively searching out the client's feelings and bringing his own into play.

The problem is not, of course, in the fact that he shifts assumptions, changes tactics; human behavior is so complex that one may find many hypotheses plausible, and even be moved by several that seem to conflict. But where the worker does not know why he acts, or which moves go with which assumptions, his own beliefs will tend to dominate and surprise him, seeming to him alien and strange rather than the products of his own experience. Where he does not understand his own theory, or even know that it exists, he must treat his own behaviors as accidental and disconnected; he cannot *own* his own beliefs and use them deliberately in his work.

This does not bar occasional acts of sensitivity and skill performed by workers with perceptiveness and talent. But a talent divorced from its own theorizing cannot learn much from experience; it depends too heavily on inspiration from unknown sources. Where the worker does not seek to understand his own behaviors, or why some moves seem to work and others do not, or how to modify future attempts in similar situations, his accumulation of "practice wisdom" remains as amorphous and idiosyncratic as the talent itself. Further, if he has not, in Bentham's words, "arranged," or "methodized" his experience,[6] its fruits are as unavailable to others as they are, in any predictable way, to himself. His art is private: it cannot be studied, and it cannot be transmitted, except as others may watch him work and try to imitate his personal style. And a private art is too mysterious to become part of a continuous and cumulative professional tradition. The search of a profession is for consistency and repeatability—what Buchler, using the Greek word *methodos,* refers to as "the pursuit of a path."

> A road, a path, must continue to be that road, that path; it must be available and usable; it must be describable and recognizable, even when it ceases to be in fact available. . . . A "path" hacked through the forest in a semiconscious daze may be expedient, but it is not methodic.[7]

I have already touched on some of the problems that make it difficult to build such a road, but it would help to explore these somewhat more systematically here, as prelude to a new attempt. We need to know exactly why the task is so forbidding that so many expedients have been found to avoid it; and we need to learn how to recognize the expedients themselves, so that we may lessen their power to interfere with the search. The way to Buchler's *continuing, describable* path is obscured by certain illusions, the most serious of which is that the methodological problems have been resolved, when they have not even been tried. These devices have a kind of magical quality, reminding one of George Thomson's comment that "primitive magic is based on the idea that reality can be controlled by creating an illusion of controlling it."[8] We must see how this happens in social work before we can move to the subsequent task, which is to identify the analytical problems inherent in the worker-client encounter itself, and then pose the specific questions that need to be addressed in order to develop a theory and a language of action.

False Trails

The earliest efforts were those of a budding profession to list and then classify the intellectual and emotional equipment required of its practitioners. In their time, these attempts were necessary and progressive; it was important to bring some order out of the mass of professional attributes attached to a complex job, and to convert these into statements on the qualifications for practice and curricula for the schools of social work.[9] The first schemes were generally divided into three categories, calling for familiarity with the *objective* world around the social worker, the *subjective* states of mind that a worker should bring to bear, and the *actions* for which he should be held responsible. These became the familiar trilogy of "knowledge," "attitudes," and "skills." There was a satisfying ring to this scheme: it was as comprehensive as one could wish; and its organizing principle—the outer, inner, and performance demands on the worker—seemed to leave nothing to chance. Nonetheless, it contained the major error out of which most of the others then grew: these categories were presented as discrete, equal, and independent of each other. Although it was usually claimed that the separation was effected merely "for purposes of discussion," and although frequent mention was made that there must be interrelationships among the three, there was little effort to find out what these connections might be. The clusters remained separate and discrete, each encouraging independent speculation and elaboration.[10]

In the course of time, these classification schemes became more sophisticated and inclusive, culminating in the most carefully developed effort of its kind—the "Working Definition of Social Work Practice," prepared in 1956 by the Subcommittee on the Working Definition of Social Work Practice of the National Association of Social Workers.[11] This formulation offered five classes of attributes "basic to the practice of social work"—those of *value, purpose, sanction, knowledge,* and *method.* But here again, although the framers recognized that the categories should be in some way interconnected—the clusters were offered as a "constellation"—they made no effort to work out the actual relationships, and the five classes remained separate, equal, and independent. William Gordon identified this problem in his subsequent analysis, offered as a "Critique of the Working Definition":

> The components—value, knowledge, method, sanction, and purpose—appeared to stand separate and equal to each other, held together only by the assertion that all must be present in some degree for the practice to be considered social work practice. To take on any theoretical potence, the elements in a conceptual model must have propositions stating the relationships existing between them. . . . The present Working Definition . . . is silent with respect to any relationship between the components of practice except to assert their existence as a constellation.[12]

Why is it so important that the professional attributes—knowing, being, believing, intending, doing—be made explicitly interdependent? If it is generally true, as Gordon states, that "the elements in a conceptual model must have propositions stating the relationships existing between them," what, specifically, do we lose in the search for method for so long as the categories are kept discrete and studied independently?

The first problem is that, in such formulations, the classes of attributes do not limit or discipline each other in any practical way. Each category, free to run its separate course, makes no demands on the others and brooks none in return. This lack of accountability gives free play to all sorts of global claims and rhetorical excesses. For example, if "knowledge" is not carefully restricted by "value" and "purpose," it becomes *all* knowledge; since nothing human is indeed alien to the social work profession, it must proceed to claim the entire gamut of individual, social, and cultural expertise and range through virtually every field of human science. This creates some considerable difficulties for those entrusted with the education of professionals. In an article published in the *Social Work Education Reporter,* Catherine Chilman examines the "knowledge which underlies social work practice and permeates the curriculum." After pointing out that "the knowledge for social work is immediately related to its goals and tasks," she continues:

> In considering knowledge backgrounds for helping people in trouble, one must include the following disciplines: psychology, psychiatry, anthropology, sociology, consumer economics, and biology. In considering knowledge backgrounds for promoting social change, such fields as basic economics, sociology, and political science are clearly relevant. In order to understand the related professions, social workers also need considerable acquaintance with the fields of education, law, medicine, religion, and vocational and employment services. If social workers are also to develop knowledge for their own fields, expertise in research design and methodology become essential. If they are to communicate with other professions and the public, they need expertise in the communications professions. Thus, social work is called upon to be aware of and translate knowledge from many fields and to develop research-based knowledge specifically related to social work methodology and practice.[13]

At the end, the call for specificity is poignant, but futile; failing a framework for achieving it, the prospect of trying to encompass all of that "relevant" knowledge is overwhelming. To the question: how can we learn all that? the answer must be that of course we cannot, but we will "do the best we can." But this is a counsel of perfection, and it tends to immobilize rather than to empower. The practitioner must remain feeling guilty and incomplete, vaguely embarrassed about what he can never know, rather than sure and proud of what he can. The implications for method are, as Lasswell has pointed out, that "the idea of strategy does not depend upon omniscience";[14] and Millikan has suggested from his data that "an individual's capacity for making sound judgment about a complex situation may be seriously impaired by supplying him with a lot of information which he believes should be relevant but whose influence on the situation is not clear to him."[15]

Similar difficulties arise for each of the independent categories. When professional "purpose" is unlimited by agency and community "sanction," it becomes idiosyncratic and unreliable. An untamed "goals" category tends to make exorbitant statements about the responsibility of social workers to alter personality, create new value systems, and effect other profound changes in people and in their society. And when the "value" requirement is undisciplined by what we know about people and what we propose to do for them in certain specific circumstances, the words are absolutistic, vaguely poetic, and offer no real guide to practice. I have described this part of the problem elsewhere, as follows:

> A great deal has been said and written about the worker's obligation to acknowledge values and to profess them openly. But these injunctions are hard to obey, because they suffer from the same shortcomings as do the value formulations themselves—that is, they are too global, internally inconsistent, and unrelated to the specific conditions of group life. The professional commandments to stand for absolute and overgeneralized themes like "Jewish belongingness" or "social maturity," to "bear" values but not to "impose" them, to uphold both religious and secular-humanistic values at the same time, to extol modesty and thrift to children whose

> family modes are prevailingly those of conspicuous consumption—these are very complex materials from which to compose a rationale for the position of values in the strategy of practice. At this stage what is needed is more exact information about the value themes which merge or conflict within the lives of different groups and about the conditions under which these circumstances vary from group to group and from setting to setting—the religious and the secular, the sectarian and the nonsectarian, the therapeutic and the recreational.[16]

The second major problem of the unrelated categories is that such formulations obscure the primacy of action. By setting up "methods" simply as one class of attributes among others of equal importance, it becomes possible to spend large amounts of time and effort in exploring knowledge and value components without ever having to relate them to the study of professional skill. What is lost is the realization that states of knowing and being are professionally useless unless they are conceived as preparation for action, rather than as ends in themselves. A knowledge of anatomy does not make a surgeon; just as insight into human behavior and a desire for social progress do not in themselves distinguish the social worker from his liberal compatriots. Lawrence Durrell expresses this insight in his novel *Justine,* as he describes a frustrated painter: "He thought and suffered a good deal but he lacked the resolution to dare—the first requisite of a practitioner."[17]

This connection between professions and their skills has been stressed repeatedly by sociologists of the professions. Parsons notes that "the professional man is thus a 'technical expert' of some order by virtue of his mastery of the tradition and the skills of its use."[18] While Wilensky and Lebeaux, in their study of social welfare in modern society, state that "the profession represents a monopoly of skill, which is linked to standards of training and which justifies a monopoly of activity in an area."[19] The search for method is thus not merely another important area of concern, but the focus and payoff of the entire conceptual scheme.

> Professionals are paid for doing, for operationalizing, and not simply for speculating on the nature of life. . . . How-to-do-it is the bread and butter of the lawyer, the doctor, the engineer—and the social worker. Without it, they fail to differentiate themselves from the knowledgeable public, the informed layman, and the rest of those in society who are alive to its issues and have opinions about them. The professional distinguishes himself not by his general wisdom, his philosophy, or his goals, but by his ability to perform an operation, teach a class, build a bridge, plead a case, or use the resources of a community to help a person in trouble.[20]

What we need then is a scheme in which the demands for knowledge, value, and purpose will be defined and limited by their relevance to method. And, in fact, it is the failure to do this that brings us to the third, and perhaps the most troublesome, problem of the independent categories. It is that when the separate attributes are unrelated to means, *each then tries to become its own means.* We find ourselves, often against our better judgment, advancing the myth that each attribute will somehow, automatically, translate itself into useful action. Thus the literature offers us *knowledge* as means, *goals* as means, *values* as means, and the *worker himself,* in his charisma, self-awareness, and intuitiveness, as the means to his own ends. In fact, much of the professional discussion that purports to deal with problems of method finds itself trapped and isolated in one or another of these categories.

The error of *knowledge-as-method* appears in many forms, some of which have been mentioned in the preceding chapter: Hutchins's "all there is to teaching can be learned through a good education and being a teacher"; Kilpatrick's exclusive concern with the laws of learning, and none with teaching, in a book called *Foundations of Method;* and Bruner's similar tendency to equate cognitive with pedagogical tasks, in his *Process of Education.*[21] To these we could add, from a range of social work samples, Grace Coyle's statement that "among the essential skills of the group worker is the necessary knowledge about program activities likely to be of interest to a particular group."[22]

The importance of knowledge is, of course, not at issue here; no profession can maintain its grasp of the necessary realities without a rigorous orientation to scientific inquiry. Further, great works like the Kilpatrick book in education, and Mary Richmond's *Social Diagnosis*[23] in social work, made contributions of immeasurable value to the sophistication of practitioners. But insofar as these and similar works were as yet unable to differentiate sharply between knowledge and action, they helped create a tradition that we now call "scientism"—the belief that the ability to act flows directly from a knowledge of the subject.

> If we were suddenly and magically granted command of every shred of evidence ever produced on human behavior—if we were to learn it all by heart—we would as yet not have the slightest notion of what to do about it in practice. The idea that knowledge carries its own implications for action is what has come to be referred to as *scientism,* and it is no more useful than the old forms of *mysticism* by which it was assumed that appropriate professional activity followed directly from beliefs, values, and goals. Both expectations are unrealistic, in that they fail to take account of the fact that the road from knowing to doing is bridged by purpose.[24]

Mary Richmond understood this problem well, pointing out that social diagnosis was not the same as social treatment. "Although the level upon which the caseworker operates will also be raised, casework will still be needed; its adaptation of general principles to specific instances will not be automatic nor will good administration become so."[25] But she was not yet able to translate diagnostic knowledge and insight into casework method, and was still suspicious of "any narrow insistence upon technique."[26] Thus her call for diagnostic skills, even as it took the profession forward by a huge step, had also within it the seeds of what Millikan has called the "inductive fallacy—the assumption that the solution of any problem will be advanced by the simple collection of fact."[27]

Eventually there was a reaction, through all the helping professions, against what Gordon Allport criticized as the "faddism" involved in the "overemphasis on diagnosis." He said: "It is simply not true that successful treatment invariably presupposes accurate diagnosis."[28] But the illusion that knowledge does its own work dies hard—despite the "knowledge" of every practitioner that nothing could be further from the truth.

The other attributes proceed in much the same fashion, each in its own way begging the methodological question. *Goals-as-method* substitutes ends for means and covers the deficiency with transitional terms like "enables," "facilitates," and "in such a way that." The prototype of this device is in the "Definition of Group Work," produced by a committee of the American Association of Group Workers in 1948:

> Group Work is a method by which the group worker enables various types of groups to function in such a way that both group interaction and program activities contribute to the growth of the individual, and the achievement of socially desirable goals. . . . Through his participation the group worker aims to effect (*sic*) the group process so that decisions come about as a result of knowledge and a sharing and integration of ideas, experience and knowledge rather than as a result of domination from within or without the group.[29]

The teleological effect is tempting; there is a kind of easy magic in describing a complex process in terms of hoped-for outcomes, rather than what one has to do to achieve them. Thus the in-such-a-way-that syndrome is probably the most familiar in the literature. It appears in many forms:

> We want to be free to explore the philosophy of practice, leaving practice skills to follow once the aims of practice are thoroughly aired. . . . So as to keep our system of ideas as open as possible, we will hold out the hope that form will follow function, and that technique is not the largest of our worries.[30]
>
> The classic model during this early period was the view of the community organization practitioner as primarily an enabler who would help people to clarify their problems, identify their needs, and develop the capacity to deal with their own problems more effectively. The emphasis was clearly on skill in developing relationships.[31]
>
> To have any meaning, techniques must flow from the worker's identity and stance. Field practice should not attempt to teach techniques, but should allow or facilitate workers to acquire techniques in keeping with their identity and stance.[32]
>
> Competence in social work practice lies in developing skill in the use of the method and its techniques described above. This means the ability to help a particular client or group in such a way that they clearly understand the social worker's intention and role, and are able to participate in the process of solving their problems.[33]
>
> Social casework is a process used by certain human welfare agencies to help individuals to cope more effectively with their problems in social functioning.[34]

In the enabling method, the members are helped to learn new ideas, develop new skills, change attitudes, and deepen their personalities through participation in a social process wherein they make decisions and take the social action necessary to accomplish the purpose of the group. . . . We therefore see social group work as a process and a method through which group life is affected by a worker who consciously directs the interacting process toward the accomplishment of goals which in our country are conceived in a democratic frame of reference.[35]

And so it goes. *Value-as-method* usually begins with a deeply felt, often moving, effort to identify significant feelings and attitudes in the worker; then, failing the means to translate these sentiments into action, the writer must make them sufficient unto themselves. Thus Donald Yates, in an article entitled "A New Attitude for the New Instruction," states: "The teacher has to be concerned with learning as opposed to teaching. The child who is confident of his worth as an individual is eager to learn. In a classroom that makes individual growth possible, learning takes place." (Since he is interested in "learning as opposed to teaching," he cannot say how the teacher might help create such a classroom.) He concludes: "Moral leadership can only be offered by moral persons. Can we accept this basic responsibility of providing our students with models of courage and honesty? Accept the idea that the biggest change in our schools must be attitudinal."[36]

And Grace Coyle, in a beautiful passage so typical of her deep feeling for the work, begins with a moving insight, but ends on a mystical note that waives the need to translate the feelings into skill, since they are in themselves the "most significant contribution":

If a leader is himself achieving his own guiding values, his own delight in excellence, his own deep sense of validity and meaning of life, his own ability to function as part of the social whole, that achieving by a kind of delicate osmosis is likely to be his most significant contribution to the group.[37]

Closely related to the value category is that of *worker-as-method,* in which all of the practitioner's personal virtues—his compassion, sensitivity, self-knowledge, and eagerness to help—will, somewhat in the manner of Coyle's "delicate osmosis," make their effective impact on the client. Again, there can be no quarrel with the characteristics themselves; they are indispensable to good practice, and they are the raw materials out of which professional skills must be fashioned. But by themselves they accomplish little, to the classic frustration of those—laymen and professionals alike—who cannot rid themselves of the notion that kindness, especially when supplemented by "self-awareness," is all.

Furthermore, the position is not far removed from the one in which "artists are born and not made," behind which lurks the matching belief that any effort to teach method or theorize about it is futile, something invented by the "technicians" and the "educationists." In its extreme form, this argument is not worth any more attention than it has already received; it simply settles for a kind of lofty mysticism, and gives up the effort to find common elements in the practitioner's art because there are obviously so many variations.

Actually, however, the "artists are born" position appears more often in its milder, more troubled version, as part of a general anxiety about the problem of identifying the dimensions of an art without quenching its spark and rendering it stiff and unnatural. Even John Dewey, the greatest "educationist" of them all, fell prey to the fear that when "method is something separate," "it makes instruction and learning formal, mechanical, constrained." And so he concluded that "the traits of good method are straightforwardness, flexible intellectual interest or open-minded will to learn, integrity of purpose, and acceptance of responsibility for the consequences of one's activity including thought."[38] The traits are impeccable, indeed profound, and they show how close Dewey was to the most urgent demands of the teacher-student encounter. But as long as they were unrelated to method, to skill, they remained fixed as personal virtues, which one could claim—along with many others—without ever having to demonstrate them in actions that could be specified and taught. I believe that this was the rock on which "progressive education" foundered.

It is important to note that a rejection of the "artistic" approach is not a denial that there is such a thing as talent, or that some possess more of it than others, or that helping is indeed an art, practiced by every worker in his own unique fashion, or style. Social work practice is an art because it is, as in Herbert Read's definition of art, "emotion cultivating good form."[39] That is, the helping process is one in which the practitioner uses feelings to evoke feelings, and does it in a patterned, disciplined way that must be consistent with his sense of purpose and his reading of reality. An art, far from being inscrutable and inexplicable, is based on science; and the artist's need to master nature is as great as that of the scientist. In Bronowski's terms: "The exploration of the artist is no less truthful and strenuous than that of the scientist. . . . The great artist works as devotedly to uncover the implications of his vision as does the great scientist."[40] And John Stuart Mill comments on the art-science relationship as follows:

> Art necessarily presupposes knowledge; art, in any but its infant state, presupposes scientific knowledge: and if every art does not bear the name of science, it is only because several sciences are often necessary to form the groundwork of a single art. So complicated are the conditions which govern our practical agency, that to enable one thing to be *done,* it is often requisite to *know* the nature and properties of many things.[41]

When this relationship is not understood, art and science are torn apart and polarized, and some find it necessary "that there be less emphasis on feeling and more on thinking, less on hunching and more on disciplined study."[42] But the fact is that, as Bronowski has taught us, the thinking and the feeling "are as much parts one of another as are the Renaissance and the Scientific Revolution. The sense of wonder in nature, of freedom within her boundaries, and of unity with her in knowledge, is shared by the painter, the poet and the mountaineer."[43]

And the social worker. The helping art, like the other arts of life, is expressive, reciprocal, limited by knowledge and intention. It demands complex sensibilities that can be translated into a complex pattern of movements. And while every worker has his own "unique and private vision of the world,"[44] and there are certain stylistic aspects that cannot be standardized—lest the art become, as Dewey feared, "formal, mechanical, constrained"—there is a central core of disciplined, purposeful, reality-oriented activity that can be identified, criticized, evaluated, and passed on from generation to generation.

To conclude this section on the pseudomethods, I must mention two additional devices which, while they also produce only the illusion of method, do show a greater respect for the immediate necessities of the worker-client situation and an effort to develop something approaching a language of action. Both, however, fail for the same reason as the others, namely that they are not part of an action strategy that feeds knowledge, purpose, and belief into the situation in which they are needed. Again, the single dimension is important, but it remains isolated, independent, and left to do its own work.

The first of these is what I have referred to as the "gimmickry of structures";[45] here it can be called *structure-as-method.* In its worst forms, it appears as a kind of sloganizing, or word-magic, that gives few clues to the nature of real structures—as in "war on poverty," "progressive" or "traditional" education, "advocacy," and the like. Often, however, this approach does try to address the conditions under which the worker-client engagement takes place; its effort is to *set the scene* for effective action, by providing certain structures and activities designed to enhance individual treatment, or classroom learning, or institutional change, or group movement. The devices vary in complexity—from limiting group size, to putting the chairs in a circle, to the emphasis on "program," to the use of audiovisual aids and other machinery, to the democratization of structures and "maximum feasible participation," to the "open classroom" and the "team teaching," to the group and family work in the casework agencies, to "crisis intervention," group dynamics, and a host of others.

The difficulty is that, while all of these inventions deal with significant features of the *context* in which the helping process occurs, they ignore the details of the work itself. And in thus pinning their hopes on situation alone, they deny the fact that the effectiveness of structures depends on the powers of those who administer them.[46] A skilled doctor, teacher, or social worker will be strengthened by a clever situational device, a technical innovation, or a new freedom. But a clumsy doctor will practice clumsy medicine in the most modern of hospitals; an awkward teacher can make a prison of the "open classroom"; and an unskilled social worker is no more helpful in "crisis intervention" or "community mental health" than he was in ordinary casework. The frustration with structure-as-method is vividly expressed by Alan Cohen in an article in the British journal *New Society.* Cohen comments on writers who, in their emphasis on social reform, "raise real and serious issues," but persist in their "unwillingness to face up to the problems of technique which arise when making services available. They talk a lot about the organization, its product, the management, labour relations, consumer research and advertising, but very little about how the salesman finally gets the product into the hands of the consumer."[47] And he continues:

> For example, Adrian Sinfield [in his book *Which Way for Social Work?*] deplores the social worker's preoccupation with techniques and offers this as a job specification for social work: "A social worker imparts information about rights, makes services available, helps to communicate needs to those in authority and encourages action by the individual, family and group on their own behalf as well as on the behalf of the community." Fine. But how does a social worker do all this? Does Sinfield think it is just a question of explaining? As anyone who "imparts information" or "encourages action" knows, the problem of *how* to impart, *how* to encourage, *this* family, *this* individual—that is, the problem of technique—remains, and criticism of the role of the social worker in a capitalist society is not a substitute for dealing with this issue. It would remain a problem if all the deficiencies Sinfield pinpoints were remedied, and it would remain a problem in the kind of society which he, and I, would prefer.[48]

Here Cohen attacks not only structure-as-method but the second of the devices that tries for a language of action but produces only its illusion. In this latter approach, there is an effort to describe movement and to use verbs, as Sinfield does; but the problems of technique are too quickly abandoned. Thus, while we are brought closer to a concern for smaller steps and interactional details ("imparts information," "encourages action"), the same difficulties arise, because the "method" category itself is cut off from its context and made to operate independently. Unsupported by knowledge and purpose, as well as situation (even as "structure-as-method" puts its *entire* faith in situation), the search for method comes to ignore the very problems it had set out to solve—those of technique and of skill. What happens is that the worker's acts are defined either so broadly that they become another version of the "in-such-a-way-that," or so narrowly that they are oversimplified and trivial—what Fischer, in analyzing works of art, called "details drained of all meaning."[49]

Thus in the broader definitions, the practitioner is enjoined to "encourage," to "clarify," to "sustain," to "support," to "develop insight"—all of which mean simply that the worker acts *in such a way that* the client will have courage or will see things more clearly, or will feel sustained and supported. *How* this is done is concealed by the words of intention; it is as if we were to say that the surgeon acts "in such a way that" the appendix is removed. From such inventories of unrelated and unspecific items, it is difficult for the practitioner to understand the skills through which he acts to achieve the states of being he has in mind—of feeling encouraged, edified, insightful, supported, and the rest. Without a framework of interlocking and specific variables, there is little to guide him as he tries to invest *each movement* with what he knows, what he intends, and what he thinks his client may be asking for at any given moment.

Conversely, when the definitions are too narrow, the acts are rendered in such rudimentary form that one is left to wonder why professionals would be needed to perform them. So it is with items like "gives information," "listens sympathetically," "shows interest," and similar moves, all of which are real and important in the helping process but lack the context in which to determine when and how they are used by workers with scientific knowledge and professional purpose. It is probably this highly atomized language that irritates those who are contemptuous of "technique"; but the failure lies more with those who reject the whole effort out of hand than with those who are taking the first shaky steps toward a deeper understanding of a complex process.

Some of the difficulties in both the broad and narrow definitions are demonstrated by Hollis,[50] in one of the more sophisticated attempts to classify the movements of the casework practitioner. In a chapter entitled "The Sustaining Process, Direct Influence, and Ventilation" (all in the teleological mode), she moves from the intention-focused category she calls "sustaining procedures" to the "sustaining techniques" they require. These include "sympathetic listening," "bodily behavior," "attitude of interest," and others. The effort is made to include the element of situation, and the framework is admirably built to carry a wealth of practice, experience, and wisdom. But in its inability to integrate knowledge and purpose in each act of the worker, the scheme moves continuously back and forth between teleological and rudimentary items:

> In general it can be said that the greater the client's anxiety either initially or during the course of treatment, the more need there will be for the use of sustaining techniques. Chief among these is interested, sympathetic listening, which conveys to the client the worker's concern for his well-being. This skill comes naturally to most caseworkers, for it is an interest in people and their affairs that has brought them into social work in the first place. Nevertheless, workers do vary in their receptiveness and in their ways of showing it. It can be indicated by a subtle set of techniques, often not adequately recorded, for the necessary attitude is often expressed more in the worker's bodily behavior than in his words. Facial expression, tone of voice, choice of words, even his way of sitting as he listens, convey the worker's interest. The client is not seeking avid curiosity or over-solicitude on the worker's part, but neither does he want cold detachment. An attitude of interest is essential throughout treatment. Special pains must be taken to communicate it to the client whenever his anxiety is high unless, as we will see later, there is some special therapeutic reason for allowing tension to remain unrelieved.[51]

Similar problems emerge in the aforementioned "Working Definition of Social Work Practice."[52] Here an important advance is made, as the "Method" category is divided into sections on *method* ("an orderly systematic mode of procedure"), *techniques* ("instrument or tool used as a part of method"), and *skill* ("technical expertness; the ability to use knowledge effectively and readily in execution or performance"). Nonetheless, since the whole category is still separate, equal, and independent of the other classes (value, purpose, sanction, and knowledge), the difficulties persist. The *method* section defines itself as "the responsible, conscious, disciplined use of self in a relationship" that "facilitates interaction between the individual and his social environment," and that "facilitates change" in both. And the only acts named are those of "systematic observation and assessment," "formulation of an appropriate plan of action," and "continuing evaluation." The section on *skill* moves quickly to the in-such-a-way-that[53] and lists several items offered as "means of facilitating communication": "Setting the stage, the strict observance of confidentiality, encouragement, stimulation or participation, empathy, and objectivity."

In between *method* and *skill,* the section on *techniques* demonstrates clearly the heavy reliance on words of broad intention rather than action, interspersed with some rudimentary items, and all arranged on many different levels of abstraction:

> Incorporated in the use of the social work method may be one or more of the following techniques in different combinations: (1) support, (2) clarification, (3) information-giving, (4) interpretation, (5) development of insight, (6) differentiation of the social worker from the individual or group, (7) identification with agency function, (8) creation and use of structure, (9) use of activities and projects, (10) provision of positive experiences, (11) teaching, (12) stimulation of group interaction, (13) limit-setting, (14) utilization of available social resources, (15) effecting change in immediate environmental forces operating on the individual or groups, (16) synthesis.[54]

As I have noted, these efforts do reflect an effort to move closer to a view of the practitioner in action; as such, they represent an important first stage in the analysis. But the listings and classification schemes leave us short, because they have not yet moved close enough for a clear look. The professional attributes having remained independent and unintegrated—which is a way of saying that such schemes are atheoretical—the details of method emerge as an inventory of separate items, unrelated to each other and to the situation in which the work takes place. It is this situation—namely, the engagement of worker and clients—that creates the peculiar difficulties that confront any student of the helping process in action. In social work, and in the other human relations professions, these problems set certain special tasks for those who would develop a systematic way of describing the skills of the worker.

Theoretical Problems

The difficulties begin with the fact that we are trying to define an art whose achievements depend greatly on the efforts of someone other than the artist himself. For it is the client who retains the power to use help or reject it, to learn or not to learn, to change or to remain intact. These—the clients—are materials that offer a measure of resistance far beyond that which confronts the painter, the architect, or the musician. Like these other practitioners, the social worker also forges his skills through "the greatest degree of consideration for and utilization of the quality and capacity of the material."[55] But his materials are resilient and dynamic, with a will and energy of their own, rather than inert, malleable, and subject entirely to the skill of the artist. When the client learns, and finds new ways of dealing with problems, it is because he has invested quantities of motive and feeling in a task he has accepted as his own. Thus, when the practitioner says that he has "motivated" someone, he does not mean that he has implanted a motive where none existed, but that he has found a hidden interest and called upon a source of energy hitherto obscured. The impetus for change is controlled by the client, and it is his will, his energy, that empowers the worker. Even as the practitioner is striving to "enable," he is himself being "enabled" by his own materials.

Interestingly, this idea has been explored, in certain imaginative flights, even in the plastic arts. For example, the novelist Irving Stone describes the thoughts of the young sculptor Michelangelo about the marble under his hands:

> His first lesson had been that the power and the durability lay in the stone, not in the arms or tools. The stone was master; not the mason. If ever a mason came to think he was master, the stone would oppose and thwart him. And if a mason beat his stone as an ignorant *contadino* might beat his beasts, the rich warm glowing breathing material became dull, colorless, ugly; died under his hand. To kicks and curses, to hurry and dislike, it closed a hard stone veil around its soft inner nature. It could be smashed by violence but never forced to fulfill. To sympathy, it yielded; grew even more luminous and sparkling, achieved fluid forms and symmetry.[56]

If it is fanciful to imagine the "stone as master," it requires no such poetic flight to understand that the power of the social worker is only partly a function of his own imagination and skill. His art lies in the interplay with his clients; it feeds on their energies. And it is this interplay that must be revealed in the words we use to describe his actions.

The language of action that we seek is therefore a language of interaction. It must be able to express skill as a force that the worker exerts not *on* his clients but in his *engagement* with them. Those words are useless that tell us what workers do to people—"change," "teach," "move," "cure," "stimulate"; instead, the words must be *reciprocal,* showing the action-and-reaction of worker and clients in the same process. At the same time, these acts must also be recognizable and ascribable—movements for which the practitioner can take responsibility and be held accountable. We are thus put to the most difficult task of rendering *separately* a set of movements that are virtually *inseparable* from those of the clients around him. It is small wonder that we have gone to great lengths to avoid such a task. And yet it must be done, if there is to be any systematic development of method: the helping process can only be described in words that are interactive in structure, while they identify practitioner skills that are observable and teachable in their own right.

The next problem grows from the first: it is that the operations of *helping* and those of *using help,* while they are interdependent, are different and separate sets of tasks; the former belong to the worker, the latter to the client. Even as each energizes and reinforces the other, these are essentially *parallel processes,* each having its own problems and skills. At any given moment, there is a specific problem with which the client is engaged, and an immediate task to which the worker should be addressing his efforts. And both processes are subverted when one moves to take over the other. This happens, for example, when the members of a street club persuade their worker to identify with them so completely that he "joins" them as a peer, is trapped by the same anger and frustration as they, and loses sight of his function. And it happens also when a marriage counselor decides internally that a given marriage is good or bad, and sets his course to "help" his clients maintain or dissolve it in accordance with his own "diagnostic" prejudgments. In the first instance, the worker loses his identity and direction; in the second, the clients lose their dignity and control of their own affairs. The principle of "self-determination" can only mean that *both* workers and clients may risk entering into a helping relationship without either of them abandoning their right to do their own work, and to make the moves and decisions that belong to them, and to them alone.

This effort to distinguish between the tasks of helping and those of taking help is actually quite familiar to us in the literature of helping. Dewey, as we have seen, warned against attempts "aimed at giving happiness to others directly, as we can hand a physical thing to another";[57] Kenneth Pray, writing on the generic principles in casework practice, pointed out that "the helping dynamic, the source of healing power, is . . . in the client himself as he reaches out for help. It is not primarily in the worker."[58] And Freud, relating the case of Little Hans, described his psychoanalytic procedure in these terms:

> There will be a certain degree of similarity between that which he [the patient] hears from us and that which he is looking for; and which, in spite of all resistances, is trying to force its way through to consciousness; and it is this similarity that will enable him to discover the unconscious material. The physician is a step in front of him in knowledge; and the patient follows along his own road, until the two meet at the appointed goal.[59]

Freud also pointed out, in this account, that "therapeutic success is not our primary aim," by which he meant that he was concentrating on his work rather than its results as he moved from step to step in the psychoanalytic process.

This further implication of the "parallel processes" leads us to the next problem, which is that it becomes necessary to define the worker's skills *without reference to their effects.* This is not to say that there is no correlation of skills and results—my argument, of course, is quite to the contrary—but that the one cannot simply be assumed from the other. Thus, it cannot be reasoned that if the client appears to have done well, the worker must have performed skillfully, and if not, the worker must have failed in some way. This is a non-sequitur: for under certain conditions, people have done well with inept workers and with no workers at all; while others have, for their own reasons, failed to respond to the most skilled practitioners. All this means is that professional expertise is but one variable among many that enter into a person's complex existence; and it is grandiose (and demeaning to the client) for the professional to claim full responsibility for either good or bad outcomes. Further, such reasoning avoids the necessity of examining the worker's moves *in detail,* in favor of rendering gross judgments that stem from no other evidence than what are imagined to be the "results" of his work.

This demand, that we untie the work from its effects and describe it purely in its own terms, may remind us of the old jibe that "the operation was a success but the patient died." Indeed the implication is correct, and it must be accepted by any student of method, for we cannot in fact develop and teach an art of surgery until we can admit that it is possible for an operation to be well performed and for the patient to die. An operation may be based on all the realities available to the surgeon at a given time, only to have the patient's own processes exert forces outside the practitioner's control. A helping or a healing art can be shaped only when it strives for a collaboration with nature, rather than for full and independent control over it. Like Michelangelo's stone, the client can be "smashed by violence but never forced to fulfill." In surgery or social work, there is an engagement between a helping power and a person who brings his own strengths and limitations into play. Understanding this, the worker may be freed for the task of studying and describing the only force for which he alone is responsible—his own professional skills.

Nonetheless, having agreed to the task of describing skill in its own terms, we must still face the fact that every process carries within it a concern for its results. And this points up a further difficulty in the search for method. What is the practitioner's actual sphere of influence? What are the factors over which he can properly claim some degree of control? Once we have disavowed the illusion of transforming whole value systems, effecting huge social changes, "socializing" people, "adjusting" them, and rebuilding their personalities, we have yet to determine what a worker *can* achieve, given his limited role in the vast network of influences that shape a human life. Those concepts will be needed that will, as Millikan has put it, "place limits on the range of possible outcomes."[60] If a children's worker is empathic where other adults have been punitive, this will be a new experience for the youngsters in his group; but they will still be a long way from having "changed their perceptions of authority." And if one worker listens well, and supports where others have not, this will be gratifying to a client with a low opinion of himself; but it will fall considerably short of "changing his self-image." Perceptions of authority, and self-images, are made of stronger stuff than most social workers can alter singlehandedly.

On the other hand, the difficulty is not resolved by a false humility that denies the worker any significant impact on the client or the client group. The helping relationship can—indeed must—be a moving experience; and this is so even—perhaps especially—where it is focused in its work and limited in its effects. Thus the task here is not to eliminate statements of intention, but to scale them down to recognizable proportions and correlate them to the actual events of the client-worker exchange. One might say that the principle of "no action at a distance" applies as well to the helping process as it does in the physical sciences. The worker can affect only what he can touch, and a closer study of his actual influence-potential will carry us closer to an understanding of the helping process at work.

Another important problem in the study of method is that any effective description must be able to show how the worker brings together, in a single strategy, a number of role-expectations emerging from different sources of authority. Whom does the worker serve? On the one hand, the client claims him as his own—"my worker"—and expects him to identify with his problems, represent his interests, and be privy to ideas and feelings that he might reveal to few others in his life. On the other, the employing agency commands his loyalty, expects allegiance to its needs and interests, and perceives him as an operating arm of its function in the community.

The point here is not that these claims are inherently in conflict—although the elements of conflict, both real and imagined, will certainly be central to the study. The problem is rather that both sets of demands are clearly legitimate, but they are sharply different, that they represent different stakes in the client-worker relationship, and that any workable strategy must be able to integrate both into a single set of movements. The practitioner must bring these expectations together—not in his mind, abstractly, but in what he says and does—or he remains a wanderer between them, blundering back and forth and damaging both in the process. This is the condition I described in Chapter 1, with the worker torn between impossible choices—the one against the many, the individual versus the system, the client and the agency locked into a natural state of war, and the polarities stretching endlessly before him, splitting the psychological and the social, freedom and authority, consensus and conflict, process and substance, change and stability, treatment and advocacy,[61] and the rest. Each of these dualisms resists any unified conception of the social worker's function, or any coherent description of how he helps real people in real institutions—where worker and client are constantly and simultaneously besieged by the problems of client *and* agency, freedom *and* authority, consensus and conflict, change and stability, in the day-to-day exchanges between people and their systems.

Is there a relationship between clients and their agencies that will allow the social worker to find an honest job in the service of both? If not, the search for method is useless, for the worker is then trapped in a social system so unyielding that he can find no function; no function, that is, except to become part of the illusion that programs matter and social workers can help people. A community organizer put it this way:

> If we believe it is possible to move the community, we can continue to work for change through its institutions. If it is not possible, then God

> help us all, for then we must either continue to act in a drama that has lost its purpose or join in the destruction of society.[62]

The job, then, is to find and describe the actual working connections between people and their agencies in the same society. If we can understand what joins them together—issue by issue, in conflict and consensus, sickness and health—we may be able to conceive of a helping art that brings their aspirations into single focus instead of remaining torn between them. It is not a "consensus model" we are looking for, that recognizes no struggle, no dialectic, no quarrels between the individual and his collective at given points in time; but neither is it one of institutionalized warfare, a client-agency polarity that, paradoxically, gives up the struggle, awards the institutions to the enemies of the people, and calls for the clients to "overthrow" their services rather than to claim them—day by day, problem by problem, as their own. The kind of explanation we need does not call for either consensus or conflict as a permanent state, but should help us understand both, as workers help people and their agencies hammer out the terms of their relationship. The connections we seek are those that help put this relationship back to work, forcing client, worker, and agency to find their proper places in the process. These connections will thus be a crucial element in the whole design.

The problems cited so far—the client's autonomy, the parallel processes, the limits of influence, the diverse role-expectations—come together to create the most difficult conceptual task of all: How does one describe the uses of knowledge? What is the connection between what a worker knows about his client and what he does when they are together?

Almost from its beginnings, the profession has relied heavily on the model of study, diagnosis, and treatment—a conception taken partly from the physician's description of how he detects and treats disease, and partly from the traditional methods of research. Both are based on the image of a knowing practitioner, whose knowledge is the deciding factor in the solution of a problem. The problem itself is presumed to have certain fixed characteristics that can be identified and studied. And these traits are trusted to remain relatively stable while the decisions are being made as to what shall be done about them. Such an explanation of how we relate knowing and doing—by gathering data, then identifying the condition, and then acting to change it—is part of a strong intellectual and scientific tradition. We have been brought up to believe that we must *know* before we *move,* look before we leap, and the argument has a persuasive force. How else could intelligent action come about?

And yet there is something about the worker-client relationship—reciprocal, interactive, interdependent—that defies such descriptions, particularly when they are applied to the work with groups. Lawrence Frank, taking note of this problem of what he called "organized complexities," is among those who have called attention to the fact that, in such systems, the important knowledge is manufactured *in the event.* Frank suggested that "we need to think in terms of circular, reciprocal relations . . . through which the component members of the field participate in and thereby create the field of the whole, which field in turn regulates and patterns their individual activities."[63] And speaking to a meeting of psychologists, he called for a new model of research:

> Scientific research, until recently, has been guided by the analytic tradition; to study any situation or event we must analyze it into its various components and investigate the relation between pairs of variables in an adequate sample. I need not elaborate upon these procedures, which are familiar to you and which have been highly productive, except to say that they are not adequate for the study of total situations and organized wholes, and it does not seem that further and further analysis will help in such problems.[64]

Talcott Parsons also wrote about organic wholes, and pointed out that they are arrangements "within which the relations determine the properties of its parts."[65] And Hubert Bonner called attention to the fact that "research has shown that it is difficult to predict the behavior of persons in a group from premeasures of personality variables."[66] To the extent that this is true in the client-worker exchange—that it is the *relations* between the parts that determine their properties—to that degree it cannot be fruitful to see the client group, or even the casework interview, as an arrangement of fixed, stable, "diagnosable" entities. The diagnosing process becomes much more complicated if that-which-is-to-be-diagnosed is constantly shifting and changing before the worker's eyes, as new situations and new relations come into being from moment to moment. This does not mean that there are no constants at all—that the "personality" construct, for example, does not have useful elements. But these stable features may be more limited, in social work situations, than the diagnostic model leads us to believe. The idea that the social worker uses knowledge in practice by studying the data, then identifying and labelling, and then acting, may overestimate the reliability of structural descriptions and cross-sectional pictures taken at a moment in time.

The diagnostic model of explanation creates other problems as well. It tends to stress specific causes, disease entities, and individual malfunctioning, where the social worker is most often faced with complex interlacings of individual and social determinants. And if the worker is reluctant to oversimplify—that is, simply to "diagnose" the client before him—he finds it hard to locate a focus for his inquiry. What will he diagnose *about?* is a persistent problem, and Helen Perlman has commented as follows:

> Perhaps a major obstacle to the caseworker's pursuit of problem-solving in the systematic way that diagnostic thinking demands is that there has not always been clarity in the diagnostic literature or teaching as to the "what" of diagnosis. The essential content of the diagnostic design and the considerations that give it boundary and focus need more careful delineation. Faced in every case with a crowding array of facts and impressions, the caseworker must have some structured idea of how to find the center of his diagnostic concerns.[67]

More problematic still is the fact that, when the worker has decided what elements of a complex situation he wants to capture and label—when he has been able "to find the center of his diagnostic concerns"—he must still find a way to use this mental picture as he enters the engagement with his client. If, as Cameron has pointed out, "diagnosis is a design for action,"[68] we need to understand how the element of prior knowledge, prior insight, is brought into a field of "circular, reciprocal relations," where it is these relations that "determine the properties of its parts." Can the social worker really turn *diagnosis* into *prescription,* as when a physician tries to match a specific syndrome with an identifiable remedy? To what extent can a social worker appropriate the concepts of "treating" and "curing" without violating the parallel processes and taking over tasks that belong to the client? Certainly if the worker has found some stable elements in the picture, he will try to use this understanding as he interacts with the client. But how he does this is still a mystery. *To know* cannot but be helpful; the reservations about the diagnostic explanation are not arguments against trying to understand, or what Hollis calls the "critical scrutiny of a client-situation complex."[69] But *to prescribe* before the interaction occurs seems somehow incompatible with social work's conception of the helping relationship in action. And it is hard to understand a process in which a worker "thinks diagnostically" *during* an interview or group meeting, while at the same time trying to feel the client's pain, echo to his meanings, and leave his own spontaneity free and available in the exchange. The problem is illustrated in Hollis's description of how a worker gathers the facts necessary for making his assessment:

> *As the worker listens to the client,* he constantly asks himself questions such as, "What is the reality by which this person is confronted? Is this a realistic or exaggerated or distorted reaction? If it is not realistic, what might account for it? What does this tell me about the circumstances that provoke such a response? What does it tell me about the kind of person I am dealing with?" In other words, to what extent is this difficulty a matter of external deprivation, frustration, or provocation? To what extent is it a matter of unusual or excessive needs or demands? How much is it due to inadequacies or aberrations in the client's ego and superego functioning? The caseworker will be greatly helped in his assessment if he continuously orders his material according to a scheme which will help him locate the answers to these questions, some of which clearly refer to pressures or influences playing upon the client from his environment, and others to factors in the client's personality.[70]

No distinction is made here between cerebrations that occur *during* the interview and those that go on before and after it. Certainly there is a need to order one's material, think it through, and schematize it; but when does this process take place, and how will the results be brought back into the work with the client? The kind of "listening" the worker is asked to do here will plunge him deep in his own thoughts, attending with his brain instead of his "third ear," his affect cut off from the client and invested elsewhere. His process is parallel indeed; but it is detached and self-sufficient, rather than interactive and interdependent.

Aware of the difficulties attending the medical-diagnostic view of the uses of knowledge, many have tried to adapt it more specifically to social work practice. In fact, the problem is at the center of theoretical dispute in social casework: Bernece Simon, reviewing some of these theories, has pointed out that "diagnosis has been the height of the storm in this debate."[71] Some writers have stressed the flexibility and tentativeness of the worker's assessments (the word "assessment" itself is an effort to move away from the medical language toward a more indigenous formulation). Others have suggested that the steps of study, diagnosis, and treatment do not necessarily occur in that order, being not sequential but coexistent and continuous.

The importance of the knowledge problem is such that the attitude toward the diagnostic explanation is most often a key feature of the theory itself. From the functionalist view, Ruth Smalley has denied the usefulness of classification schemes, or of any effort to understand the client's "total situation"; instead, she focuses the worker's knowledge of the client on the "assessment of this person's capacity to use this service toward an end that is or can become his own, as it relates to the purpose of the particular service being given."[72] Edwin Thomas has worked out a behavioral approach to the job of assessment, defining the concept of "problem" more sharply, and calling for "behavioral specification" as a way of identifying the focus of change more precisely.[73] Florence Hollis emphasizes the importance of knowing the client in his situation, and cites three types of diagnostic inference—"dynamic," "etiological," and "classificatory."[74] And Helen Perlman has also tried to expand the concept of diagnosis, explaining the "dynamic" as "a kind of cross-sectional view of the forces interacting in the client's problem situation."[75] Perlman is among those who have made a strong case for defining diagnosis simply as an ongoing process of trying-to-understand:

> The fact is that whether we are "for" diagnosis or "against" it, whether we believe in its usefulness or not, whether we feel adept or inept at it, every one of us is diagnosing as he relates to another person in a purposeful, problem-solving activity. Every one of us in such a situation makes a mental note of what he is observing and experiencing, draws inferences from what his senses convey to him, and anticipates his next moves on the basis of the meaning that has been read into or drawn out of the signals. Consciously or not, we seek to clarify the nature and configurations of the material (person-problem-place-process) that we are attempting to influence. And, consciously or not, we try to organize our half-felt, half-thought impressions into some conclusions, temporary though they may be, that will give direction for what to expect and do next. This holds true in any kind of problem-solving work that is not blind hit-or-miss, whether it involves fixing a radio, painting a picture, arranging a party, or influencing the feelings and actions of another person.[76]

The logic is compelling: to organize our thinking, to categorize our experiences, to relate new events to old ones, to try to know before we act—this is the way of all intelligent beings, as they live and grow. Dewey called the process to our attention a long time ago: "If we inquire under what circumstances any object or event enters into our intellectual life as significant, we find that it is when it is connected in an orderly way with the rest of our experience."[77] This is as true of children as of adults; and, in fact, it describes the activity of the client himself, as well as that of the professional who serves him.

But this is what makes the argument disingenuous, equating as it does the ways of human thinking with those of a systematic process called diagnosis. Dewey pointed this out, too, stating that "scientific knowledge . . . differs from ordinary knowledge in being unified, systematic, connected knowledge." Science, he said, "finds one form, or a uniformity, in many facts apparently unconnected. The ultimate aim of science is to unify all facts and events whatever, so that it may not only *feel* that they are members of one system, but may actually realize their systematic unity."[78] Thus the simple equation of thinking and diagnosis begs the most important questions—of system, classification, prediction, treatment—that becloud the diagnostic explanation of how knowledge is used in the helping process. If it is just a way of thinking, it is unarguable; but it leaves the main problems untouched. If it is a more systematic and prescriptive procedure—as it is in the practice of medicine—it sets up new problems of its own, touching on how such cross-sectional, structural pictures are actually used in the circular, reciprocal, give-and-take of the helping relationship.

In fact, Perlman's analogies—fixing a radio, painting a picture—go far to reveal the nature of the problem. The radio and the canvas will remain constant while the practitioners examine them carefully and then move to change them. The "diagnosis" of the radio can be made by a skilled repairman with full confidence that if his assessment is correct his "prescription" will work. But insofar as no fully correct assessment of the "feelings and actions of another person" can be made outside of the situation in which they will occur, the "diagnosis" itself must be a shaky affair, and "prescription" is virtually out of the question. Only where *structure is all* can the expert use his prior knowledge without fear of interference from the materials themselves. To the extent that relations determine the properties of the parts, the assessment of structure without process simply produces a wrong answer, an unscientific result. Further, if the painter's canvas were suddenly to express an opinion about what ought to go on its surface, and if it were to refuse to accept certain combinations of line and color, the artist would then be faced with technical problems comparable with those of the social worker in the helping process.

Nevertheless, all such efforts to expand the diagnostic construct do reflect a growing professional awareness of the situational determinants and the complex relationships between individual and social factors. In fact, the experience of practice even leads one to suspect that the classic diagnostic model, however much it lends the profession a sense of status and order, may be more honored in the breach than the observance. Many workers, having carefully drawn up their assessments, put the pictures aside as they enter the helping situation and give themselves over to listening intently, empathizing closely, and feeling their way from moment to moment through the hectic exchange. Thus, even as they cling to the old ways of theorizing about the work, many find themselves moving intuitively to a practice model of a different sort. Again, this is not to be conceived as a move away from knowledge and intellectual activity; it would be self-defeating to deny the role of reason and simply swing to the other polarity. But it is a way of working in which knowing and feeling are to be combined in a manner that remains to be conceptualized.

Our problem, then, is to limit and locate the focus of knowledge; to distinguish among the kinds of reasoning that occur before, during, and after the helping encounter; and to show how the worker invests action with knowledge—as he works—without cutting himself off from the flow of affect and interaction between himself and his clients.

Having done all this, it will soon be clear that precisely the same operations must be performed on the element of *purpose.* Having cast aside preconceived goals as a way of describing practice, we are still left with the problem of including values and outcomes as a part of our theoretical scheme. Either that, or we fall into Millikan's "inductive fallacy"—the belief that the facts will tell us what to do. The gap between knowledge and action is still bridged by intention, and we cannot do without the dimension of purpose, *provided that* our goals and values are limited, specified, and monitored as they are brought into the helping process.

> The gap between what is known and what should be done is invariably bridged by value-goal orientations, often implicit and unformulated. When knowledge is converted into action on the basis of subtle and unstated values, the principle is unverifiable, except by those who unconsciously share the same assumptions. When creeds and valued outcomes are made explicit, practice principles are verifiable by all, on the basis of whether, given the first two variables—a fact and a valued outcome—the third will provide the implementing force. Practice cannot be "testable" in any other sense.[79]

It is at this point that the elements of a theory of helping should begin to fall into place: given the *knowledge* and the *intentions,* the *acts* must provide the force that implements and empowers them. Thus the appropriate facts and pictures, the immediate, valued outcomes, and the acts of skill should create a network of interlocking concepts, fitting together into a scheme that will integrate *science* (the way things are), *policy* (the way things should be), and *action* (what must be done). In such a scheme, facts and intentions will limit and specify each other, while it should be possible to see, in every act, the specific knowledge and purpose that brought it into being.

There is a final problem that needs to be mentioned—not theoretical in the same sense, but certainly of great interest, considering the array of difficulties discussed above. What are the qualifications that fit the worker to his tasks?

The traditional responses have been at two extremes: on the one hand, the worker is described as a kind of paragon, whose knowledge is encyclopedic, self-awareness profound, and motives entirely disinterested; on the other, no more is asked for than a pure, simple-hearted creature with no formal qualifications except the instinct to serve. This latter extreme is amusingly illustrated in a letter to *New Society,* where the writer responds to a case history published in the previous issue, and calls for volunteers who can help with such cases. The job analysis is sensitive and complex, and shows a real grasp of what needs to be done for the boy; but the denouement is fascinating:

> Sir: Denis could be a challenge—he's a bright lad, but when he comes out of Borstal he's going to need a friend—preferably someone who has made contact with him during the sentence. Volunteers in the probation and after-care service are put in touch with people like Denis (or sometimes with the family) by their local probation office. If they can possibly do so, they make contact with the client in Borstal or prison and try to help them on release and after. A volunteer for Denis could visit his mother and talk things over, put out feelers for a job for Denis, perhaps find him digs and help him to make a go of life.
>
> In general terms, a volunteer can help the inarticulate, who are often intimidated by the social services; he can raise objections to bureaucratic decisions; fight injustice, or simply be a shoulder to cry on. In short, he can make what he will of the job, in his own time and in as many ways as he thinks he is capable.
>
> *The only qualification required is to be human.* [!] Anyone interested in becoming a volunteer can get full details from the local probation office.
>
> Audrey Jones
> 42 Corringway, London w5[80]

Somewhere between the paragon and the person armed only with his humanity, there is a real practitioner with the skills—and the instrumental knowing, willing, and feeling—necessary to do the job. Here again, the task is to limit and to focus; in this case, it is to specify the qualifications that are most closely related to the work at hand, once that work is understood in detail.

In summary, then, any effort to theorize about the helping process must find a language of action, using words that describe the reciprocal, interdependent relations of the actors, the circular actions and reactions of the worker and his clients. It must show how the practitioner and the client can each do his own work, depending on, but not preempting, the work of the other. It must define skill in its own terms, rather than by implication from its effects. And in so doing, it must take into account, as must any art, both order and innovation, method and style, the standard and the unique aspects of the practitioner's skill.

It must emphasize immediacy, following step-by-step the details of the interaction between helper and client. And this concern with the moments of exchange will make it necessary to show how certain determinants of behavior, so often polarized, come together in action—the rational and the emotional, the past and the present, the structural and the situational. It must put boundaries to the worker's claims, limiting and specifying what he must be, know, feel, and believe, and what he can hope to achieve. It must show the worker moving in the context of the relationship between the clients and their agency. And it must describe the interplay of the worker's knowledge, purpose, and actions—his science, his policies, and his art—at every step of the helping process.

What kind of a scheme will it take to do all this?

Notes and References

1. William Schwartz, *Group Work in Public Welfare* (Chicago: American Public Welfare Association, 1969), p. 28. (Reprinted from *Public Welfare,* vol. 26, no. 4 (October 1968), pp. 322–70).
2. *Ibid.,* p. 22.
3. From a *Record of Service,* United Neighborhood Houses Pre-Teen Delinquency Project, 1964. Mimeographed. For a discussion of this recording instrument, *see* Goodwin P. Garfield and Carol R. Irizarry, "The 'Record of Service': Describing Social Work Practice," in William Schwartz and Serapio R. Zalba, *The Practice of Group Work* (New York: Columbia University Press, 1971), pp. 241–65.
4. From the records of a tenant group, University Settlement, New York City.
5. John Dewey, *Human Nature and Conduct: An Introduction to Social Psychology* (New York: The Modern Library, 1922), p. 35.
6. See Buchler's discussion of Jeremy Bentham's approach to the concept of method: Justus Buchler, *The Concept of Method* (New York: Columbia University Press, 1961), pp. 9–35.
7. *Ibid.,* p. 3.
8. Ernst Fischer, *The Necessity of Art: A Marxist Approach* (Baltimore, Md.: Penguin Books, 1963), p. 154.
9. See, for example, "Statement, Content of Group Work Practice with Implications for Professional Education," prepared by the Committee on Professional Education of the American Association of Group Workers, 1955. Mimeographed. This is an updated version of a similar statement, prepared in 1947, on the content of professional education in group work.
10. See, for example, *Building the Social Work Curriculum* (New York: Council on Social Work Education, 1961). Report of the National Curriculum Workshop, Allerton, Illinois, June 13–18, 1960. The report

revolves around the provision of objectives and experiences related to "knowing," "feeling," and "doing." See also, Werner W. Boehm, *Objectives of the Social Work Curriculum of the Future* (New York: Council on Social Work Education, 1959), pp. 71–197. This is Volume I of the Curriculum Study conducted by the Council on Social Work Education and directed by Mr. Boehm.

11. Harriet M. Bartlett, "Toward Clarification and Improvement of Social Work Practice," *Social Work,* vol. 3, no. 2 (April 1958), pp. 3–9.
12. William E. Gordon, "A Critique of the Working Definition," *Social Work,* vol. 7, no. 4 (October 1962), p. 5.
13. Catherine S. Chilman, "Production of New Knowledge of Relevance to Social Work and Social Welfare: An Examination of Knowledge Which Underlies Social Work Practice and Permeates the Curriculum," *Social Work Education Reporter,* vol. 17, no. 3 (September 1969), p. 49.
14. Harold D. Lasswell, "Strategies of Inquiry: The Rational Use of Observation," in Daniel Lerner, ed., *The Human Meaning of the Social Sciences* (New York: Meridian Books, 1959), p. 89.
15. Max F. Millikan, "Inquiry and Policy: The Relation of Knowledge to Action," *Ibid.,* p. 160.
16. William Schwartz, "Toward a Strategy of Group Work Practice," *The Social Service Review,* vol. 36, no. 3 (September 1962), p. 275.
17. Lawrence Durrell, *Justine* (New York: Pocket Books, 1965), p. 20.
18. Talcott Parsons, "A Sociologist Looks at the Legal Profession," in Parsons, *Essays in Sociological Theory* (rev. ed.; Glencoe, Ill.: Free Press, 1954), p. 372.
19. Harold L. Wilensky and Charles N. Lebeaux, *Industrial Society and Social Welfare* (New York: Russell Sage Foundation, 1958), p. 284.
20. William Schwartz, "Private Troubles and Public Issues: One Social Work Job or Two?" *The Social Welfare Forum, 1969* (New York: Columbia University Press, 1969), pp. 23–24.
21. Bruner, pp. 27–31.
22. Grace L. Coyle, "Some Basic Assumptions About Social Group Work," in Marjorie Murphy, *The Social Group Work Method in Social Work Education* (New York: Council on Social Work Education, 1959), p. 101. Volume XI of the Council on Social Work Education Curriculum Study.
23. Mary E. Richmond, *Social Diagnosis* (New York: The Free Press, 1965), 511 pages.
24. William Schwartz, "Small Group Science and Group Work Practice," *Social Work,* vol. 8, no. 4 (October 1963), p. 43.
25. Richmond, *op. cit.,* p. 370.
26. *Ibid.*
27. Millikan, *op. cit.,* p. 163.
28. Gordon W. Allport, *Personality and Social Encounter* (Boston: Beacon Press, 1960), p. 283.
29. "Definition of Group Work," in Dorothea F. Sullivan, ed., *Readings in Group Work* (New York: Association Press, 1952), p. 420.

30. Carol H. Meyer, *Social Work Practice: A Response to the Urban Crisis* (New York: The Free Press, 1970), p. 151.
31. Arnold Gurin, "Social Planning and Community Organization," in *Encyclopedia of Social Work* (New York: National Association of Social Workers, 1971), vol. II., p. 1332.
32. Alan F. Klein, *Social Work Through Group Process* (Albany, N.Y.: State University of New York at Albany, 1970), p. 148.
33. Bartlett, *op. cit.,* p. 7.
34. Helen Harris Perlman, *Social Casework: A Problem-Solving Process* (Chicago: University of Chicago Press, 1957), p. 4.
35. Gertrude Wilson and Gladys Ryland, *Social Group Work Practice: The Creative Use of the Social Process* (New York: Houghton Mifflin Company, 1949), p. 61.
36. Donald Yates, "A New Attitude for the New Instruction," *New York State Education,* vol. 58, no. 5 (March 1971), p. 30.
37. Grace Longwell Coyle, *Group Work with American Youth* (New York: Harper and Brothers, 1948), p. 216.
38. John Dewey, *Democracy and Education: An Introduction to the Philosophy of Education* (New York: Macmillan, 1916), p. 211.
39. Herbert Read, *The Meaning of Art* (Baltimore, Md.: Penguin Books, 1949), p. 31.
40. J. Bronowski, *Science and Human Values* (New York: Harper & Row, Harper Torchbooks, Science Library, 1965), pp. 71–72.
41. John Stuart Mill, *A System of Logic* (New York: Harper & Brothers, 1874), p. 18.
42. Joseph W. Eaton, "Science, 'Art,' and Uncertainty in Social Work," *Social Work,* vol. 3, no. 3 (July 1958), p. 10. Eaton refers here to Maurice J. Karpf, *The Scientific Basis of Social Work* (New York: Columbia University Press, 1931).
43. Bronowski, *op. cit.,* p. 71.
44. Read, *op. cit.,* p. 27.
45. See p. 33.
46. See Joseph Lelyveld, "City's New View of Welfare: A Job for Businessmen," *The New York Times,* February 1, 1972, pp. 1, 16. The story begins:

> Like managers everywhere, the new men at the Department of Social Services talk of productivity, time studies, utilization rates, and cost-benefit ratios. And they talk of the "bottom line," meaning the place on the balance sheet where you read the profit or loss.

And in the interview with Arthur H. Spiegel, the Department's executive director, Mr. Spiegel exults that "it's a good time to be in welfare."

> "Social workers are fine," Mr. Spiegel said, "but these are problems that need real resources, real teeth. It's the biggest data-processing show in town . . ."

See also, in the same issue of the *Times,* Jack Rosenthal, "Learning-Plan Test is Called a Failure," *The New York Times,* February 1, 1972, pp. 1, 30.

> The Office of Economic Opportunity pronounced a reluctant but blunt judgment of failure today on performance contracting—the use in public schools of private concerns, teaching machines, and incentive payments in an effort to conquer slow learning by poor children.

47. Alan Cohen, "Don't You Sweetheart Me . . . ," *New Society,* vol. 17, no. 435 (January 1971), p. 152.
48. *Ibid.*
49. Fischer, *op. cit.,* p. 200.
50. Florence Hollis, *Casework: A Psychosocial Therapy* (New York: Random House, 1969), xvi, 300 pages.
51. *Ibid.,* p. 84.
52. Bartlett, *op. cit.*
53. *Ibid.,* p. 7.
54. *Ibid.*
55. Virginia P. Robinson, "The Meaning of Skill," *Training for Skill in Social Casework* (Philadelphia: University of Pennsylvania Press, 1942), p. 12.
56. Irving Stone, *The Agony and the Ecstasy* (New York: Signet, New American Library, 1961), p. 48.
57. See p. 21.
58. Kenneth L. M. Pray, "A Restatement of the Generic Principles of Social Casework Practice," *Social Work in a Revolutionary Age* (Philadelphia: University of Pennsylvania Press, 1949), p. 249.
59. Sigmund Freud, "A Phobia in a Five-Year-Old Boy," *Collected Papers* (London: Hogarth Press and the Institute of Psycho-Analysis, 1950), vol. III, p. 262.
60. Millikan, *op. cit.,* p. 166.
61. For a fuller discussion of what I have called "the advocacy variation," see my "Private Troubles and Public Issues: One Social Work Job or Two?" *The Social Welfare Forum, 1969* (New York: Columbia University Press, 1969), pp. 30–34.
62. Harry Specht, "Disruptive Tactics," *Social Work,* vol. 14, no. 2 (April 1969), p. 15.
63. Lawrence K. Frank, "Research for What?" *The Journal of Social Issues,* Supplement Series, No. 10 (1957), p. 12. Frank's reference here is to Albert Einstein and Leopold Infeld, *The Evolution of Physics,* p. 259, where these authors point out that "it needed great scientific imagination to realize that it is not the charges nor the particles, but the *field in the space between* charges and the particles, which is essential for the description of physical events." (Emphasis in original.)
64. Frank, *Ibid.,* p. 8.
65. Talcott Parsons, *The Structure of Social Action* (Glencoe, Ill.: Free Press, 1949), p. 32.

66. Hubert Bonner, *Group Dynamics: Principles and Applications* (New York: Ronald Press, 1959), p. 20.
67. Perlman, *op. cit.,* p. 167.
68. D. Ewen Cameron, "A Theory of Diagnosis," in Paul Hoch and Joseph Zubin, eds., *Current Problems in Psychiatric Diagnosis* (New York: Grune and Stratton, 1953).
69. Florence Hollis, "The Psychosocial Approach to the Practice of Casework," in Robert W. Roberts and Robert H. Nee, eds., *Theories of Social Casework* (Chicago, Ill.: University of Chicago Press, 1970), p. 51.
70. Hollis, *Casework: A Psychosocial Therapy, op. cit.,* p. 179. (My italics.)
71. Bernece K. Simon, "Social Casework Theory: An Overview," in Roberts and Nee, eds., *op. cit.,* p. 374.
72. Ruth Elizabeth Smalley, *Theory for Social Work Practice* (New York: Columbia University Press, 1967), p. 137.
73. Edwin J. Thomas, "Behavioral Modification and Casework," in Roberts and Nee, eds., *op. cit.,* pp. 181–218. See particularly the section on "Assessment," pp. 199–204.
74. Hollis, "The Psychosocial Approach to the Practice of Casework," *op. cit.,* pp. 49–56, on the "Assessment of the Client in his Situation."
75. Perlman, *op. cit.,* p. 171.
76. *Ibid.,* p. 165.
77. John Dewey, *Psychology* 3d ed., rev. (New York: Harper & Brothers, 1892), p. 85.
78. *Ibid.,* p. 83.
79. Schwartz, "Toward a Strategy of Group Work Practice," *op. cit.,* p. 270.
80. Letter to the Editor, *New Society,* vol. 19, no. 486, January 20, 1972, p. 138. (My italics.)

3

Toward a New Paradigm

The methodological problems of the helping professions have their roots in the philosophical perspectives within which they were born and raised. Every age has its own ways of looking at the world; and as the professionals carry these habits of thought into action, they see and understand things in the terms provided for them by their time and place. Further, as these perspectives change with the times, so do the ways in which the professionals interpret their clients' behavior, view the world around them, and formulate their own objectives and their means for pursuing them. It is with such changes that we must deal now, and with ways of looking at the world that have produced new tasks for those who would understand the problems of method.

Thomas Kuhn, writing on the history of science, has shown that science develops not through a gradual evolution and accumulation of small bits of knowledge piled one upon the other, but in a series of dramatic leaps from old ways of looking at the world to radically new ones. Scientific history, he pointed out, is marked by revolutions, in which fields of inquiry move suddenly from old paradigms and "normal science" to startling new perspectives on the problems under study. In the new gestalt, "ducks become rabbits," and the field begins to ask new questions and formulate new problems for research.

A paradigm, as Kuhn describes it, is a set of "received beliefs," elaborated in the textbooks of its time and defining the legitimate problems of the field. These received beliefs are made up of "universally recognized scientific achievements that for a time provide modern problems and solutions to a community of practitioners."[1]

> The study of paradigms . . . is what mainly prepares the student for membership in the particular scientific community with which he will later practice. Because he there joins men who learned the bases of their field from the same concrete models, his subsequent practice will seldom evoke overt disagreement over fundamentals. Men whose research is

> based on shared paradigms are committed to the same rules and standards for scientific practice. That commitment and the apparent consensus it produces are prerequisites for normal science, i.e., for the genesis and continuation of a particular research tradition.[2]

The "normal science" of which Kuhn speaks is based on the notion that the professions in the field "know what the world is like"; and much of their activity is devoted to the unraveling of "puzzles"—that is questions and games in which the answers are already embedded and it is the job of the scientist to find them. This, says Kuhn, is an important stage in the history of science: "Acquisition of a paradigm and of the more esoteric type of research it permits is a sign of maturity in the development of any given scientific field."[3]

Nonetheless, in order to defend the paradigm's basic assumptions and to maintain its unity of vision, it becomes necessary to suppress novelty in the fear that diverse viewpoints are subversive of its basic commitments. "A paradigm can, for that matter, even insulate the community from those socially important problems that are not reducible to the puzzle form, because they cannot be stated in terms of the conceptual and instrumental tools the paradigm supplies."[4] (This effort is not conspiratorial or intentionally reactionary; it is simply part of the historical process by which a science moves from its preparadigm, preconsensual stage, to that of consensus and normal science, to a transcendent, revolutionary new gestalt.)

But novelty cannot be suppressed indefinitely, since it is in the nature of scientific inquiry eventually to expose the arbitrary. In time, the paradigm begins to spring certain leaks; certain "normal" problems stubbornly resist solution, even by the finest minds in the search; equipment designed to carry out normal research fails to perform in anticipated ways; and certain problems remain inaccessible and contradictory. Eventually, the field develops a number of "anomalies"—phenomena that cannot be squared with expectations engendered by the old paradigm.

> In these and other ways besides, normal science repeatedly goes astray. And when it does—when, that is, the profession can no longer evade anomalies that subvert the existing tradition of scientific practice—then begin the extraordinary investigations that lead the profession at last to a new set of commitments, a new basis for the practice of science. The extraordinary episodes in which the shift of professional commitments occurs are the ones known in this essay as scientific revolutions. They are the tradition-shattering complements to the tradition-bound activity of normal science.[5]

Kuhn shows how this "reconstruction of a field from new fundamentals" took place in the fields of light, motion, heat, electricity, astronomy, gases, and others. In each of these areas of inquiry, he demonstrates how scientists went through the "blurring" of the old paradigm, the build-up of anomalies, the crisis, and finally—the "desertion" of the old gestalt. Scientists then emerged into a world that was almost literally transformed.

> Led by a new paradigm, scientists adopt new instruments and look in new places. Even more important, during revolutions scientists see new and different things when looking with familiar instruments in places they have looked before. It is rather as if the professional community had been suddenly transported to another planet where familiar objects are seen in a different light and are joined by unfamiliar ones as well. Of course, nothing of quite that sort does occur; there is no geographical transplantation; outside the laboratory everyday affairs usually continue as before. Nevertheless, paradigm changes do cause scientists to see the world of their research-engagement differently. In so far as their only recourse to the world is through what they see and do, we may want to say that after a revolution scientists are responding to a different world.[6]

This new world is one in which the old answers—as well as the questions themselves—are not "wrong" but simply irrelevant. Where Aristotle saw a change of state, Galileo saw a process. Where early students of electricity saw a Leyden jar, Franklin saw a condenser. Aristotle's falling bodies in constraint became Galileo's pendulums. Kuhn provided a number of examples that show scientists undergoing the "shift of vision" find new phenomena with the same instruments; they then speak of "scales falling from the 'eyes,' " and the "lightning flash" that reveals the answer to a problem previously obscure.

> No ordinary sense of the term "interpretation" fits these flashes of intuition through which a new paradigm is born. Though such intuitions depend upon the experience, both anomalous and congruent, gained with the old paradigm, they are not logically or piecemeal linked to particular items of that experience as an interpretation would be. Instead, they gather up large portions of that experience and transform them to the rather different bundle of experience that will thereafter be linked piecemeal to the new paradigm but not to the old.[7]

Kuhn concludes that "at times of revolution, when the normal-scientific tradition changes, the scientists perception of his environment must be reeducated—in some familiar situation he must learn to see a new gestalt."[8]

What has all this to do with the search for method in the helping disciplines? Certainly we cannot take our comparisons directly from the developments in the physical sciences. The behavioral studies, despite considerable recent growth, are still largely in what Kuhn describes as a "preparadigm" condition; he points out that "it remains an open question what parts of social science have yet acquired such paradigms at all. History suggests that the road to a firm research consensus is extraordinarily arduous."[9] And if this is true of the social sciences in general, it is even more so of that segment dealing with the dynamics of the helping relationship—those processes through which someone offers assistance to people in need. We have no "normal science" in the same sense, and are in fact only just reaching the stage of organized and systematic investigation of problems.

And yet there is something in Kuhn's analysis that helps explain the polarities, contradictions, and problems explored in the first two chapters, and that may help us point some new directions in the search for method. We, too, have labored under a set of received beliefs, a kind of legitimized, consensualized outlook that frames certain questions and not others, that has a language of its own, and is elaborated in the textbooks of our time. And we too have, over the years, been aware of an increasing number of internal contradictions—very much like Kuhn's "anomalies"—leading to a sense of irrelevance and crisis that lurks under the certainties and reacts with outraged pride when new terms and formulations threaten to undermine the old gestalt. It is at these points that the arguments sound moral and religious rather than scientific, appealing more to faith and principles than to technical issues. Further, the warring paradigms cannot prove each other right or wrong, because they cannot find the concepts with which to talk to each other at all. There is no common language with which they can conduct the search for truth together. The "ducks have become rabbits," and one can see the picture only in a certain way.

Thus there is indeed a kind of revolution in progress, a sudden shift of perspective that changes the outlook, creates a new language, formulates new questions, and most important sees a new road along which to pursue the problems of method. It might even be said that, within this new gestalt, method itself—in the operational, instrumental way in which I have been using the term—can at last be invented.

In order to follow this new line of inquiry, we need to see how we have inherited a way of understanding people—and helping them—that though useful in its time, has now worn thin, allowing other possibilities to show through. These new possibilities involve few new discoveries of fact but call attention to knowledge that was there all the time but ran parallel to the accepted ways of thinking—both parallel and underground, so that it could be vaguely and uneasily sensed. These ideas have been around for a long time; appealing to an important part of human nature, they were always attractive and potentially powerful—so much so that they were widely "accepted" in the form of lip service. But they could not be acted upon or integrated into a theory of helping because they were foreign to the reigning gestalt. Eventually, however, they could no longer be suppressed, and as the old paradigm began to break down they were rediscovered in new forms. In a manner much as Kuhn described for the physical sciences, practitioners of the helping arts began to "see new and different things when looking with familiar instruments in places they have looked before."

The full story of this revolution is long and complex, involving all of the philosophical traditions within which the human relations professions grew up. We do not have to do it all; for our purposes, it will only be necessary to show briefly the main features of the old paradigm, how it was valuable in its time, and how it hangs on to create the anomalies and contradictions I wrote about in the first two chapters, even as the new way of looking at the world of human relations takes the center of the professional stage. It will then be possible to describe the major characteristics of the new gestalt and see how it helps us find a new direction in which to search for a theory of helping in social work, with particular attention to the practice of social work with groups.

The Old Paradigm

The world view used by our generation of practitioners is one in which social work was born and raised as a field of practice. The same is true of psychology, education, psychiatry, and the wide range of social studies that had their origins in America's Progressive Era, at the turn of the century.

The model has roots that are sunk deep into the history of man's struggle to understand himself. These roots are stuck in the study of science itself, where the main object of interest is the world around us, the objects which confront us. That is, man began to study the world before he turned his attention to himself, and when he got around to this, in the Progressive Era that marked the turn of the present century in America, he used the model of the physical sciences. In this model, the object of attention is the "objective" world around us, the world of objects that needed to be examined, understood, fixed when they go wrong. And to the extent that the human instrument lends itself to such a description, the results were good—the science of physiology led us to the practice of medicine. In this view, people are objects, independent entities, the objects of cause and effect, determined by their surroundings and by their history. When something went wrong with them, they could be examined, probed, then fixed.

The method was essentially positivist in philosophy and scientific in method, and it lent to the helping professions certain emphases that are easily recognizable today—the search for "objectivity," the rationalism, the stress on history and deterministic thinking, the prescriptiveness, the teleology, and the strong individualism. These emphases were not "wrong," in that they were misperceptions of reality—on the contrary, they were extremely useful in their day and remain formidable insights even to this day. They brought us forward, out of the dark ages of moralizing about people and hoping they could be exhorted to "do right," into the modern era, where man was seen as knowable and helpable. The problems of the old paradigm are not that it is no longer useful to us, but that it has hardened itself into such a form that its insights, taken alone, leave out too many dimensions of which we are learning more and more. They are no longer useful to us unless they can be integrated into a new world view, a new gestalt in which the old emphases, the old questions, can be changed into a form that includes dimensions that we have, incidentally, paid lip service to for a long time, but must now be taken into fuller account.

The fact is that each of the great ideas of the nineteenth century—the science, the rationalism, the structuralism—has within it the seeds of its own contradictions; each, over time began to spring its own leaks; and each began to produce the confusions and dualisms of which I wrote in the last chapter. The seeds of contradictions were there from the start, the ideas equally powerful, equally attractive, but apparently incompatible and ready to fight among themselves. Both modes were developed side by side, but one was suspect, romantic, of doubtful origins, even though the professionals knew it was there and were even compelled to pay lip service to its general importance. But the other, the scientific-positivist-rationalist mode, was the child of its time, and those who worshiped it were the ones who created the language, formulated the scientific questions, the questions for study, and set the problems and the "puzzles" to which the fullest attention was paid.

It is important to illustrate this thesis briefly before I go into the model we need to explore in the rest of this book. The history is long, of course, and I cannot dwell too deeply on the history of science, as fascinating as it would be for our purposes. But we need to do several things: first, to take a fleeting look at the scientific-positivist view and what it does for us; second, to examine the internal contradictions that led it to begin to "spring its leaks" and expose its anomalies; and finally, to show how our "ducks have become rabbits," and the new emphases we need in order to create a systematic view that will enable us to study the helping process in social work.

What we took from the pragmatic-positivist view of the world was, first, that human beings were products of their experience, and that they could hence be fathomed and understood just as any other part of nature could be understood. One could study man—he was, in fact, "the proper study of mankind"—as one studied other machines, namely, to make them work better. Man was *made* as well as *born,* and if we could contribute to the proper making of man, if we could make good things happen to him, he could be productive, useful, even happy: conversely, if bad things happened to him, his nature would reflect these distortions. Cause and effect and its laws would thus make it possible to prove, trace, verify—and predict. The sources of knowledge were observation and experience.

> As man finds regularities in the relationships between parts of the universe and between himself and these parts, he is able to foresee consequence of his actions and happenings among the parts, and to govern his actions, to a degree at least, in the light of these relationships.[10]

The positivist world view thus helped us gain certain useful attitudes towards people. It created *curiosities,* alongside of the *judgments* with which people, especially people in need, had been scrutinized for centuries. As "psychological science won its freedom from metaphysics"[11] in the late nineteenth century, we began to move away from the social Darwinism that marked the early stages of industrialization and capitalism.

> The pragmatist's most vital contribution to the general background of social thought was to encourage a belief in the effectiveness of ideas

> and the possibility of novelties—a position necessary to any philosophically consistent theory of social reform. As Spencer had stood for determinism and the control of man by the environment, the pragmatists stood for freedom and control of the environment by man.[12]

The idea that man was made by events, putting the emphasis on the need to understand what had happened to him, took the attention from his natural state of sin, and from the moral positions with which he could be redeemed. This created a more *hopeful* stance: man could control his destiny if he knew enough about the world; if we could thus conquer ignorance, we could rely on ourselves to further our own progress and development; and if man were perfectible, if people were not doomed by biology, class, status, and moral weakness, then there was a chance for something called Democracy. A better world could be envisaged, and it was tied to our ability to *know.* Science was the tool by which man could make all things possible.

There were several important offshoots of this basic position—scientific, materialist, pragmatic: Its *rationalism* was part of the mounting faith in intelligence and reason, along with its decreasing emphasis on inspiration and feeling and "mentalism." For the stress on intuition was regarded as untrustworthy, superstitious, interfering with objectivity and the scientific attitude. Knowledge was power; all things were knowable; what was not yet known were only things that had not yet been discovered.

This *objectivity* was, of course, a primary value, as it must be in any scientific-materialist view of the world. That is, it is important that the student of human nature maintain a detached attitude from that which he is studying. If he could separate himself sufficiently, his own feelings and emotions, his own "subjectivity" would be less likely to interfere with his ability to know the truth, which was outside himself. The student, the scientist, himself is a rather unreliable witness, for his predispositions, biases, "feelings" again, threatened always to cloud his view of objective reality. Therefore, he was to regard these feelings and intuitions as enemies of the truth; he must remain as detached, "disinterested" as possible in his pursuit of the laws by which the universe is run.

Historicity was another important feature of the scientific attitude. With the attention to causes and effects, hope was invested in the train of events by which one led to another and things were brought into being. This valuable way of explaining things, by reference to a chain of events, led quite naturally to the attitude that if one could find out what caused something bad to happen—maladjustment, disease (physical or mental)—one could then proceed to identify the malady and improve the organism. There was an easy transition from the medical wars against specific causes—biology, geneology, and microbes—to the psychological strivings to unearth the "reasons" for social and mental maladjustments. "Give us the child for the first six years, and you may have him for the rest of his life." This was the famous Jesuit maxim fortified by Freud's discoveries and by the heightened interest in the child and his fatherhood of the man.

Further: the *prescriptiveness* was part of the same picture. If the condition were known, if the causes could be found, the "cure" could be designed. Nothing could be more logical: to question the sequence of thought that led from cause and effect, to prediction, to prescription—so clear in the physical world of things—was to question the very basis of science itself and to poke holes in the structure of hopefulness that went with it.

Further: the study of man as a machine to be understood produced a strong kind of *individualism,* a strong psychological emphasis that accompanied the humanistic preoccupation. People were complex; they could be realized, studied, perfected, if one could understand their structures adequately. Although the deterministic approach understood that their development was caused, formed, shaped by events, they constituted studieable entities in their own skins; they were bounded by their physical structures. Thus, they could be typed, diagnosed, classified as entities, so they could be understood, treated, changed, perfected. If the structure could be improved, if the machine could be "fixed," it could then reenter its world and perform better. Psychoanalysis first, then casework, counseling, and the other individually oriented therapies, were essentially inventions designed to fix human machines that had, for good and sufficient reasons, been broken, distorted, and disrupted. Even in the group-oriented therapies, the emphasis remained for a long while on a new way—peer influenced—of repairing a recognizable individual structure that had been injured in its development. And again, to question this assumption would have been viewed as an attack on science itself.

Although many of the positivists themselves disputed the next offshoot, it remained a powerful source of inspiration for the scientific method itself, and for those interested in the helping process. It was the *teleological* mode that followed Aristotle himself, a way of envisioning the ending, and of using the inspiration of purpose. There was a kind of predestination in biology itself, Aristotle's "final cause," a kind of ideal state to which every organism, human and vegetable, aspired, if it was properly cared for. If this were true of man, then he could "realize" his true self, his own inherent force could burst into fruition. This idea formed the impetus to Bergson's *elan vital,* George Bernard Shaw's *life-force,* and the ego-psychologists, and the self-realization and growth-oriented therapists. It was an important vehicle for expressing one's aspirations about how the world and its people ought to look. It was, of course, deterministic, materialistic, and sought to remain "objective"; but it was also another part of the scientific optimism. If one could uncover the laws of things, one could know how they ought to look in their most realized state; things could be better if they lived up to their potentialities;[13] and these pictures of the future would emerge as the logical outgrowths of proper understanding, diagnosis, and prescription.

Finally, the scientific spirit brought professionalism into being. If knowledge, rather than metaphysical speculation was the hope of mankind; if observation and experience would discover the laws that would govern the changes in his condition; if people needed help rather than exhortation, then it would be necessary to develop a cadre of *knowers*—life and the new civilization were too complex to depend on home remedies, Sunday church, and sheer neighborliness. The complexity of the human and societal organism made it necessary to produce a group of trained people, a new ministry, those who could take the proper scientific, clinical attitude toward people and devote their lives to improving their structures, their psychological structures, in the same manner as the science of medicine had brought forth a corps of practitioners whose lives were devoted to curing their physical ills.

This was, in brief, the complex of attitudes and aspirations that took us a long step forward from the primitive, moralistic, absolutist approaches to people, to the modern, scientific, relativist, positivist, pragmatic attitudes of the nineteenth and early twentieth centuries. It performed wonders in its time, producing the modern array of social science practitioners and the helping professions, focusing their interest on the knowable, disciplining their observations and experiments, calling attention to the laws of nature, and in general creating an historic burst of optimism and hope for the future of man and the perfectibility of his state and his society. What could be wrong? And yet there was—not, certainly in many of their basic assumptions, which are valid to this day and will remain so. But things were left out, things, considerations, that were only vaguely felt, generally recognized, but had to wait until the scientific enthusiasms had done their trick and gone past their first victories. When these had begun to wear a little thin, they began to reveal certain contradictions, certain "anomalies"; for it was found that for every pragmatic certainty there was, lurking underneath it, another certainty of equal value that apparently ran counter to its opposite number. Each of these characteristics, described above, carried within it the seeds of its own trouble and self-contradiction. The old paradigm pledged its allegiance to a set of ideas that was not "wrong," but internally contradictory; and these contradictions, unresolved over the years, have in the past few decades begun to raise new questions, and ultimately created a new gestalt which attempts to "re-create the field from new fundamentals." As this process proceeds, our "ducks have become rabbits," and we are ready for a new vehicle with which to analyze the nature of the person in need, and the nature of the helping process. What are these anomalies, and what is the crisis?

Anomalies

The scientific world view put the professional in a position *outside* his subject, striving to maintain his "objectivity" and his detachment, so as not to contaminate his data with his own biases and preconceptions. The professional helping person was to act as a scientist does with his material under scrutiny—objectify it, watch it work, make comments about it, study it. The professional model was that of diagnosing the entity, as we have previously pointed out. This was a logical extension of the Cartesian dualism, the subject-object split of the seventeenth century, and its primary characteristic was the separation of what Buber was later to call the *I* and the *It.* Factors were to be *isolated* and studied: In the words of Rollo May,

> The result in our day is that science gets identified with methods of *isolating* factors and observing them from an allegedly *detached* base—a particular method which arose out of the split between subject and object made in the seventeenth century in Western culture and then developed into its special compartmentalized form in the late nineteenth and twentieth centuries.[14]

On the other hand, however, it is also understood that men, especially scientists and professionals, see things and events through the spectacles of their own experience and their summaries of their own experience. Further, and most especially in the human relations professions, they are deeply involved in the events they are trying to understand. In fact, as Freud himself showed us, what is happening between the helper and his client-patient is in essence the heart of the matter. The subjectivity of the helper is, in this light, not only something to be shunned and minimized, but something to be guarded, kept spontaneous, and understood as a helping event in itself. The relationship between helper and helpee should be helped to develop, to elaborate, and to exert its power. The humanity of the professional—his biases, of course, and his own agenda, and his ability to love and hate—while not to be used without discipline, was not part of that which must be understood.

The apparent contradiction between detachment and involvement produced considerable discomfort in its day, and created variables that precipitated much struggle that was essentially useless. As I have pointed out, such apparent irreconcilables produce dualisms, and this one created the formulations of "distant nearness," "involved-but-detached." These formulations and others like them, were attempts to get at a reconciliation of a difficult task—namely that thc professional had to develop the capacity to see events clearly, not by detaching himself in the "scientific" manner, but by risking himself in involvement while yet retaining his ability to do his job. Even as he was himself becoming part of the phenomena he was trying to understand. This was, in fact, Heisenberg's "Uncertainty Principle" seen on the ground of the helping process.

This was a difficult task, of course, and the recourse was to a series of movements that were designed to avoid the conflict rather than resolve the apparently opposite factors of which it was composed. Typically, the solution was to stick to the "scientific" (prestigious) mode, while simply paying lip service to the concept of "relationship" on which much of social work philosophy was built. It was necessary to say that relationship was the important ingredient, while at the same time objectifying and diagnosing the client as if he could bc properly understood without reference to the events of the helping relationship. For the social worker had allied himself with the positivist tradition, in which men could be isolated and studied, his history examined for "evidence," and the "social diagnosis" made.

> Positivist man is a curious creature who dwells in the tiny island of light composed of what he finds scientifically "meaningful," while the whole surrounding area in which ordinary men live from day to day and

> have their dealings with other men is consigned to the outer darkness of the "meaningless." Positivism has simply accepted the fractured being of modern man and erected a philosophy to intensify it.[15]

Again, it is important to point out that these insights—the analytic and the involved, the objective and the subjective—were conceived simultaneously; although one immediately took the ascendancy, the other remained alongside to comment, to correct, to play a minor role but always ready to move forward to center stage. As Barrett has put it, "Positivist man and Existentialist man are no doubt offsprings of the same parent epoch, but, somewhat as Cain and Abel were, the brothers are divided unalterably by temperament and the initial choice they make of their own being."[16] The problem through the recent centuries has been to keep the family together, rather than allow one to try to kill the other. Science cannot be killed by intuition, nor intellect by feeling. Neither would, in fact, stay dead, but would remain to haunt the feast, as in fact has always happened at each ostensible "victory" of a transcendent philosophy.

Each offshoot of the scientific model had its internal contradictions, and the conceptions of the helping relationship was forced with each one to fall into the dualisms that have plagued them to the present day. The *rationalist* mode, while emphasizing the importance of reason and intelligence and serving as an attractive model in the rise of professionalism, clashed with the realization that emotion, personal experience, and spontaneity were important and productive aspects of the human personality and the human relationship. Freud's use of the word *analysis* co-existed with his own stress on the irrational, the deep and subdued feelings one had to reach for in order to get at the real meaning of a patient's existence. Further, it was not only the patient's inner life that was important, as "illogical" as it sounded in any given exchange, but the doctor's as well. Thus, a dedication was established, very early in the game, to both the knowing and the feeling, and there was no real resolution of their relationship to each other in the therapeutic process. This has been a battle of the centuries, the tension between the rationalistic philosophies and the experiential ones, and it was a battle that the professions were called upon to resolve, not philosophically but in the development of their practice in relation to people in need.

Thus the scientific spirit, that flourished in the nineteenth century and flowered in the twentieth, made professionals aspire to the "analytic" model of progress, even as their patients and clients held them close to a recognition of the nonrational, the irrational, the idealist, and the mystical notions that neither understood, but intuitively realized that they were an important part of the total picture. It was seen that man's emotional, unfinished life was part of what had to be included in any realistic appraisal of what was going on, where the trouble was. Coue, Freud, and other psychological scientists taught us, even in the midst of their scientific inquiries, that we must include both the objective and the subjective, both the reason and the inchoate, vague associations of both the doctor and the patient.

Faced with this contradiction, the helping professions could either integrate the roles of knowing and feeling in one configuration or fall into the stance of "objectifying" their art and at the same time paying lip service to the role of feelings and emotions. Perhaps because the integration task was too difficult, the path of professionalism was along the latter route; while Dewey, James, Moreno, and others explored the life of the emotions, risked themselves in the inchoate world of experience, the major sectors of the field, and particularly in social work, clove to the rationalist tradition even as they spoke and taught of the importance of feelings.

The *historical* mode was, as we have seen, an important step forward in its teaching that events occurred in series, that prior events prefigured later ones, and that people were subject to influences other than simply moral and internal ones. But the deterministic view has other effects; it begins to lock us into a kind of hopeless state in which the past becomes so important that one begins to feel doubtful about present and future. As Dewey put it, trying to come to grips with the effects of determinism, if people had no choices to make, they must continue to act as if they did, or life would have no meaning. To find the laws of nature is one thing; but to envisage a set of laws so rigid that man has almost no choices to make leaves little room for the helping professions.

The job of the helping professions, after all, is to help people to widen, rather than narrow, their range of choices. A science that is enlisted to help free people from neurosis, ignorance, and confusion cannot find itself bound to a determinism that is felt as imprisoning people in circumstances beyond their control. How does one get free of such restrictions, while yet remaining true to reality, to the reality of circumstances, to the processes of history?

This tension between the past and the present also fell into a dualism, because the apparent contradiction was hard to resolve. How does one move from the question: How does *B* reflect the influence of *A*? to the question, equally vital: What alternatives remain to *B,* or in what specific senses does he remain free to choose? The present, in other words, needs to take on a new vitality, a new hope. The helper needs to become curious about it in a way that he has never been before, spending, as he has, most of his energies investigating the "depths" of the past. The present is in this new view no longer "superficial," "secondary," but the fighting ground on which the most difficult and crucial questions are worked out by the helper and the helpee.

Another aspect of the scientific, positivist paradigm is the professional's entry into the *prescriptive* mode, which puts the knowledge of the expert into play and extends the note of hopefulness so characteristic of this way of looking at the world. Knowledge leads to prediction and prediction to solution of problems. But here again, the prescriptive model ran into conflict with another important insight—namely, that people worked better, and the effects were more lasting, when they were permitted to work out their own solutions in the context of their own backgrounds and feelings. Prescriptiveness and self-determination could of course, with some considerable effort be reconciled in individual cases; but again the difficulty was great and the field fell into another dualism—taking prescriptiveness for granted and protesting its loyalty to self-determination all the while. What happens here, as in the other instances, is that the "scientific" form is followed *in action*—the diagnosis, the "objectifying"—while the other mode becomes a *cherished value.* Hence the difficulty of putting values into action—they cause too much trouble when they are mobilized, clashing into modes that need to be reconciled. It is best to keep them quiet, and so they are, in a sense, deified, mounted on a pedestal, and worshiped from afar. This is what happens to self-determination when prescriptiveness is the prevailing mode. On the one hand, the expert decides what is wrong and what should be done; on the other, the realization that people cannot carry out their solutions unless they own the problems and have a hand in the design to solve them.

And so here again the scientific model represents an important step forward for the professional community; but when it is applied by professionals engaged in work with people, it leaves out certain elements that the human subject insists on putting back in. And the tension between *changing* things, objects that one begins to know a great deal about, and *helping* people, dependent on their self-determining energies, ultimately creates the anomalies that mark the deterioration of the model itself. The question What *is* he? becomes much less relevant than the question How does he *act* in concert with others? What does he *do* in relations?

And this raises the corollary issues of structure and the *individualistic* mode, in which the *structure* of individual objects is the matter for study, and the professional helper applies this model of study to the work with people. Thus concentrating on the nature of things, the cross-sectional picture of the object that needs to be fixed, one begins to pay considerable attention to conditions that have not previously been sufficiently examined. And this is the great contribution of the positivists and empiricists. But the conflict arises when we begin to realize that man in motion is a different creature than man at rest. If man *is* what he *does,* any effective meaning of existence makes it necessary to understand that people do not carry their characteristics around inside them, but constitute instead a complex mass of *potentialities,* triggered and shaped by the circumstances in which they find themselves. The idea that man can be objectified, and studied, and fixed in his identity enough so that one can "understand" him and say what is generally to be done for him, becomes then a scientific myth. And it is a myth that one cleaves to, even as one is compelled to pay lip service to the importance of situation and the changeable, flexible nature of man. Again, one is compelled to *do* diagnostic things, to *act* as if the patient's psyche can be pinned down and described in cross-section, while at the same time holding flexibility and changeability up as an enshrined value. The doing is the paradigm in which we are enmeshed; the talking and valuing are the parts that have fallen out of the picture, which need to be put back in, and we don't know how, except by insisting on how important they are, so loudly that we will not notice that they have been left out in the doing.

And finally, the *teleological* emphasis, carrying the function of purpose and realization of potentiality, brought by the Aristotelian *telos* forward into the present era and birthed the self-realization emphasis so important to present-day psychology. The idea that every natural, living object had a destiny to fulfill was not only accurate in a very real sense, but it was inspiring as well, carrying the hopes of man, giving him something to reach for. Where it began to interfere with thinking was where it began to *substitute* the future for the present, where it began to view aspiration as an end in itself, as the job done, instead of merely seen in the mind's eye. Thus the *future* was misused, just as, in the deterministic, historical mode, the past was distorted. As Watts put it: "Awareness of time ceases to be an asset when concern for the future makes it impossible to live in the present."[17]

In its extreme form, the eye on the future took the position that one could not plan unless one could see the outcome beforehand. Further, the farther ahead one could see, the more "planful" one shows oneself to be. And here was the conflict: just as one restricted man's freedom by cleaving to the discipline and rigidities of the past, deterministically sovereign, so one could limit his freedom in the same way by betting everything on a number of previsaged outcomes. The prestructuring of outcomes became, in the hands of well-meaning professionals, self-fulfilling prophecies. The client, diagnosed and predicted and prescribed for, lost his freedom to move (a value that was strongly enshrined) and he could not retain his freedom to make decisions unless the way was left open for unforeseen consequences. In this way, teleology became problematic.

The Crisis

These are the internal contradictions, the anomalies, that have led us to the "crisis" of the old helping paradigm, and to the need for the emergence of a new one which sees the world, and the client, in a new, "absurd" way. The old gestalt shines the light in the wrong places and leaves whole areas in darkness. It was what Frank meant when he questioned the "analytic tradition" which was that "to study any situation or event we must analyze it into its various components and investigate the relation between pairs of variables in an adequate sample."[18] And he quotes Fritz Redl as follows:

> The practitioner—by whom I mean all those who deal directly with delinquents (including teachers and parents) has an old complaint. He is ready to pay tribute to the long-range usefulness of our fancy formulations, terminology and curves. He politely admits the research expert probably produces a lot that is important. His complaint is that the research expert does not answer the questions he asks.[19]

And the crisis is at the heart of Maurice Friedman's comment as he discusses Martin Buber's "philosophy of dialogue." He points out that "scientific method IS NOT qualified to discover the wholeness of man," and that this wholeness must be discovered

> not as a scientific observer, removed in so far as possible from the object that he observes, but as a participant who only afterward gains the distance from his subject matter which will enable him to formulate the insights he has attained.[20]

The contradictions inherent in the old positivist paradigm make it difficult for it to address the questions of the practitioner because the old way of looking at the client—individually, as an object to be understood, as structural entity, as restricted severely in his choices—cannot take into proper account several crucial dimensions that the practitioner has to cope with in every helping encounter. As I have indicated, these key factors have maintained their residence in the theory, so to speak, not as guides to action but as *values,* as things-not-to-be-forgotten despite the fact that they are not used, but worshiped from afar.

By the old light, it is difficult to see *the client in action,* although the latest perspectives stress "person-in-situation"[21] and social work has always stressed, verbally, the importance of action, in its debt to John Dewey, particularly in the group work segment of the profession. But, seeing the client as object, as individual structure to be analyzed, it is not possible to incorporate action into the theory of helping.

Questions of *process* are not asked, because the major curiosities are about structures and outcomes.

New ideas and insights are constantly being incorporated into the language of social work, with no ability to make them part of a technology, thus, "crisis," and "system," and "relation." The dualisms of doing one thing and valuing another makes it inevitable that we fall into certain distortions. For example, the inability to incorporate *feeling* and *experience* into the mechanistic, objective, positivist model makes us prey to quackery, as when the "feeling" components are isolated into "sensitivity training," and "encounter" as a way of life. Thus it is that it is possible to retain the old paradigm while giving ourselves the illusion that all the factors are taken into account. Action, relations, feeling, interaction are not emergent in a new and complete paradigm, but are installed by themselves, alone and inevitably spurious, producing monstrosities and parodies of the real thing.

The New Paradigm

Thus the new paradigm that is beginning to emerge is one that, in its best forms, does not reject the old, the experiential, and the scientific, but produces a new picture—"ducks become rabbits"—and the new gestalt stresses factors in man's situation that have lived for a long time underground. The factors are *action, interaction, relations, presentness,* and *feeling.* The model strives for a way of describing the helping process in which "the word of address and the word of response live in the same language."[22] These factors appear now not as values but as a technology, as guides to a way of helping people to live their lives more fully. They are, in this new framework, not *mottoes* but guides to professional skill.

If it is true, as Kuhn said, that "during revolutions scientists see new and different things when looking with familiar instruments in places they have looked before,"[23] then it would be useful to see how this works with social work's own "familiar instruments." Certainly, the notion of *action* is not new for social workers, or *relations,* or *present time,* and they have had the immediacy of crisis and emergency and pain to cope with since the beginnings of their work, so they are not strangers to feeling and *experience.* Doing and relationship and immediacy are as old as social work itself—in their practice that is, but somehow lost in the theorizing and the conceptualizing, where the thinking was trapped in the mainstream of scientism and detachment and objectifying. Now in the new light of the "revolution" that is brewing in ways of seeing the client and his world, and new ways of the helper seeing himself and his world, these familiar concepts take on a new and revitalized context. What is this new world of ideas that make this possible, and how does it get translated into new ways of viewing the helping process?

As Buber has pointed out, the world of objects is a safe world that offers the professional "all manner of incitements and excitements, activity and knowledge."[24] It has, in fact, sufficed us for a long time, and there is no reason to look for other perspectives, were it not that the old paradigm has become so adept at its abstract formulations that it has learned too well how to produce *truth* that is far from *reality.*[25] That is, its pursuit of the laws of nature have produced a greater curiosity about abstractions about "man" than it has about the day-to-day conditions in which particular men live. The old paradigm remains attractive and challenging, but it does not answer the practitioner's questions.

> In this chronicle of solid benefits the moments of the *thou* appear as strange lyric and dramatic episodes, seductive and magical, but tearing us away to dangerous extremes, loosening the well-tried context, leaving more questions than satisfaction behind them, shattering security—in short, uncanny moments we can well dispense with. For since we are bound to leave them and go back into the "world," why not remain in it? Why not call to order what is over against us, and send it packing into the realm of objects? Why, if we find ourselves on occasion with no choice but to say *Thou* to father, wife, or comrade, [or client] not say *Thou* and mean *It?* To utter the sound *Thou* with the vocal organs is by no means the same as saying the uncanny primary word; more, it is harmless to whisper with the soul an amorous *Thou,* so long as nothing else in a serious way is meant but *experience* and *make use of.*
>
> It is not possible to live in the bare present. . . .
>
> And in all the seriousness of truth, hear this: without *It* man cannot live. But he who lives with It alone is not a man.[26]

This is a demanding perspective, and one that brings in elements that have long been suspect in the language of science. It is in a sense, a kind of remarriage of the divorced couple Philosophy and Psychology. And it is not in truth a philosophy in itself that is represented in the new paradigm of the therapeutic and helping encounter. Not philosophy, but a technology that is based on a philosophy and a science that are brought together to explore and understand people as they are, and how they use help, and how it should, in the light of all these factors, be given.

The story of how these new factors have been emerging into the new gestalt is a long one and it is too complicated to tell here in detail. It is not, as I have said, a new development, but an old one that has been lying dormant, nodded to from time to time, but is only just emerging. Although I cannot review the whole development here, I need to point out a few highlights, in order to show the outlines of the picture and give us the framework we will use in the rest of this analysis. It is in effect the model of development that will be useful to me in the rest of this book.

Fundamental to the entire enterprise, and what produces the absurdity and excitement of the new paradigm, is the healing of the subject-object split. That is, the world of the helper-therapist-counselor-teacher changes when he accepts the fact that his involvement in the helping encounter can no longer be viewed as a peripheral aspect of the work, entered into only for the purpose of studying the client more thoroughly in his structure, but a pervasive phenomenon, in which the interaction itself is the stuff he studies; that is, his interest shifts from the subject under study to the processes, moving and changing, through which both he and his clients move together. This is what Buber calls the I-Thou, as against the *I-Him,* or *I-It,* that preserves, for the sake of a sense of safety, the detachment of subject and object, with one serving as an expert, the other as consumer, and each fearing to approach the other in fear of contamination. This does not mean that they are "equals" in function, for they are not; each has a different job to do. But the substance of the encounter is the encounter and what happens to both the helper and the helpee within it.[27]

This urge toward the healing of the classical subject-object split is part of a long tradition, as I have said; it is not a new idea, but one that has run underground, maintained as value, but developing technically all the while. Before, it was "interesting" but troublesome, fitting poorly with the positivist model and hence neglected in theorizing. But it had illustrious adherents: in the early existential philosophy of Kierkegaard, and his nineteenth century concept of relation-as-truth; in Nietzsche's later nineteenth century ideas which said that "every truth should be faced with the question, 'Can one live it?' "; to the pragmatism of James and the interactionism of Dewey; to the functionalists' conception of the part-whole relationship; to Reynolds's "conflict of opposite motives"; to George Herbert Mead, and Moreno's theory of spontaneity, Allport's psychology of participation; to the action emphasis of the behaviorists; to the client-centered therapy of Rogers; to transactionism, encounterism, sensitivity group dynamics; to Binswanger's existentialism, born even as the psychoanalytic movement was being born; to Buber's concept of the "dialogical," and "not group or individual, but the In-Between;" and to the dialectical notions of Hegel and Marx.

The tradition is rich and deep, and in social work itself, we can trace the opposite side of the positivist map of the world in many of the events of social work development: the emphasis of Richmond on the case, the specific, the experience of the client; Grace Coyle's emphasis on case examination; Konopka's deep feeling for practice, even as she cleaves to the classic diagnostic model that embodies the subject-object split; Florence Hollis, and Helen Perlman, in their emphasis on person-in-situation. But this only serves to illustrate and highlight what Buber called "the two ways of man," that is, the ability to cleave to the old I-It, even as one knew, from one's own experience, that the I-Thou could not be forgotten, at the risk of sterility and impotence.

More specifically, we can trace some of this out in four major headings, major implications of the subject-object split, that May commented on as follows:

> The result in our day is that science gets identified with methods of isolating factors and observing them from an allegedly *detached* base—a particular method which arose out of the split between subject and object made in the seventeenth century in Western culture and then developed into its special compartmentalized form in the late nineteenth and twentieth centuries.[28]

Kierkegaard's notion that there is no existential truth that can omit the relationship freed us from the old tradition that "the less we are involved in a given situation, the more clearly we can observe the truth."[29] Says May: "When we are dealing with human beings, no truth has reality by itself; it is always dependent upon the reality of the immediate relationship."[30]

Out of this relational, antistructural language there emerge four distinct and interrelated aspects that constitute the heart of the new gestalt, the new paradigm. They are the factors of *action, relation, immediacy* of time and place, and *inner experience.* These are, in truth, "familiar instruments," and "places we have looked before," but they are put together in a new way once we have disavowed the positivist paradigm; they are the same in that they are our old friends: the self, the world, and the interaction between them. But when we are no longer dependent on the separation between subject and object, on our own detachment from the one who is helped, the "ducks become rabbits," and the world is changed. It is just as when Heisenberg and Bohr, in the physical sciences, found that the measurer is part of what he must measure, we can no longer separate man from nature,[31] and the old clichés—that the scientist is involved with the world—cease to become values and bromides that satisfy the conscience while the body is doing something else; they come instead to be hard variables that have to be taken into account in the doing. Thus it becomes "possible to have a science . . . that . . . unites science and ontology."[32]

The emphasis on action, relations, presentness, and inner perceptions of experience makes it logical that the pressure to incorporate this new image of the world comes from those in the business of working with groups. In the group situation, the client stays in the world and brings it with him to the helping person, along with others in the same boat. In the small-group context, the factors of relations and immediacy come alive and take on a sense of urgency. This is not to say that the individual in treatment does not bring his world with him; certainly Freda Fromm-Reichman has correctly spoken of the "world in the consulting room." But the component of mutual aid, the fact that peer relationships are a part of the problem of group experience, lends a sense of urgency that gives the worker no choice but to regard the circumstances of the helping encounter as a living experience, in which "acting out" is not a forbidden variation but a natural part of the events of the encounter.

Let us, then, take each of these features briefly—action, relation, immediacy, and felt experience—and see how they contribute to a conception of the helping process. What we are after is not a general world view, but an approach that will guide a theory of helping. Although philosophy is important, since it colors our view of the world and orders what we see, it is not a reason for working in uncertain ways: we do not work in this or that way because we are carrying out a certain philosophy, but because we view the needs of people in a certain way and see their needs in certain terms; the philosophy adds up the events.

As we examine each variable, we need to look at two major aspects: one is the implication for how we view the client; the other is in how we view the role of the worker. In each case, the variable creates its impact in these two ways upon our conception of method and our plan for analyzing it into its components. *Action* is a way of moving, and our conception of method involves how we see the importance of action in both the client and the worker; *relations* is a way of interacting and being-with, and we need to incorporate a concept of client relating and worker relation; *immediacy* is a way of using time; and *felt experience* is a way of going through what Rollo May calls the *eigenwelt,* the owning of one's own world.

Beginning, then, with the construct of *action:* Why is it important in a scheme of helping? It involves the movement from what has been the mode of seeing truth as an abstract and absolute entity to the concept of *truth in action*—that is, as Kierkegaard put it "truth exists for the individual only as he himself produces it is action."[33] If, as Kierkegaard, and later, James and Dewey believed, the truth and meaning of people's lives emerged in the things they did and were or were not able to do, then it follows from that we will be less likely to put our faith in abstract conceptions of fixed personality, and more apt to put more belief in the power of situation to call forth the qualities that we need to be interested in.

For the professional, the same would apply. It is in the nature of his calling to seek the connections between "truth" and "reality"—that is, between what we think exists in nature and what people experience as their own reality, that which is real for them. The professional thus realizes himself in what he does; and one of the basic problems of theory then becomes: What is the basis for his actions? Is it possible to systematize and rationalize his strategies? For, although he is also beckoned into the deterministic, mechanized conception of events, he must maintain some conception of choice making; he has alternatives, and must make decisions, and must have some theoretical basis on which to make his plans for action. Somewhere in here, then, there must be a theory of action; in general, yes, for that would help him understand the movements of his clients; but also specifically, for his own role, as a special case for a theory of action. *A theory of helping is thus, in a way, a special case for a theory of action.* And for help, he must turn to the pragmatists, the functionalists, the existential philosophers, even the behaviorists. The latter, however much they eschewed the concept of mentalism, still held the line for a close examination of behavior, for their own reasons. In fact, those who study method need to provide the very integrative machinery necessary to heal the split between the idealism of *subject* and the hard-nosed positivism of *object.*[34]

On the question of *relations,* the central problem is to find a language that will express the engagement of people with each other, and the client with the worker. Buber's effort to find this language was in his construct of the I-Thou, in which he distinguished between the subject-object rigidity of the *I-Him* and the almost inexpressible (because of the traditional positivist view) condition of relations. Here is Buber describing the relationship between a psychotherapist and his patient, in *I-Thou* terms:

> If he is satisfied to "analyze" him, i.e., to bring to light unknown factors from his microcosm, and to set to some conscious work in life the energies which have been transformed by such an emergence, then he may be successful in some repair work. At best he may help a soul which is diffused and poor in structure to collect and order itself to some extent. But the real matter, the regeneration of an atrophied personal centre will not be achieved. This can only be done by one who grasps the buried latent unity of the suffering soul with the great glance of the doctor: and this can only be attained in the person-to-person attitude of a partner, not by the consideration and examination of an object.[35]

This striving for "the unity of the suffering soul with the great glance of the doctor" is an effort to find the language that will express what May and others have called the healing of the subject-object split. It is an effort to find the answer to what goes on in the relationship, not in the ministrations of an expert but in the things that go on between two people; each with his own function, in a series of exchanges that mark the ways in which they live together. It has within it, as does each of the variables, all of the others: *action,* in *relation, now,* and *as each partner experiences the events of their engagement.*

On the language of *immediacy:* what's involved here is the significance of time, and the way it is used. Whitehead's: "The present contains all that there is. It is holy ground; for it is the past and it is the future." It contains Dewey's work on the presentness of experience, the transition from moment to moment. It includes the concept of the "next step."

And the "absurd" proposition that it is possible to move without envisaging what the end should be, but simply what the beginning was. That is, to move *from* rather than *towards*—that the point of starting is a satisfying point of reference, risking the uncertainty of not "knowing" where one wants to end up.

It is possible, of course, to retain the old *ends* framework simply by making the ends, the future, very *immediate;* that is, what you see as happening in the next moment, and the next, and the next. Hence the concept of the next step.[36]

The language of *feeling:* May points out that Freud was an expert on the *what* of anxiety, that is, *knowing about* anxiety, what caused it, its symptomatology, its effects. But Kierkegaard was the one who *knew anxiety,* what it felt like to the person.

The therapist experiences the pain and anxiety of the client, not just observes and understands it. In social work, we have long paid lip service to this concept without emphasis on empathy, and our classical references to how the client feels. This is important, and gives us the tools with which to understand how this works when it is put into an action framework. Somehow, the irrational, the unrational, and the rational must be brought into a single framework.

Here is the effort to introduce *love* as a technical term; work as a way of loving. Here again, all flows from the healing of the subject-object split; and the effort to get into a kind of relationship in which relations are the important feature. There are familiar tools to work with. For example, the concept of empathy is the effort to feel with. But it has to be seen not as something the worker does to the client, but a way of risking himself in the *I-Thou* engagement. Feeling the pain, the tragedy of existence, not only in the unfortunate client, but in his own efforts to establish communication. The plight of man is the worker's and in a real sense the worker thus gets help from the client.[37]

The Systems System

What Bronowski spoke of as "the knot, the point at which several laws cross," is what is needed in order to pull together all of the necessities mentioned above—the functional, the existential, the interactional—and give us a frame of reference within which to pursue our investigation.

For this we must turn to a notion that has been gathering popularity in recent years, for precisely the reason that it promises to serve as an integrative model for the scientific and the existential. What attracts us all at this point in history is that it offers promise in the search for a more precise description of what actually happens in the human exchange, and to heal the subject-object split even as it remains amenable to close and methodical investigation. It is a model of relations, and thus offers us many advantages, as follows.

It gives us the opportunity to see moving parts within a system, people moving in relation to each other. It provides a model for action, and a justification for it, in its emphasis on function as a basis for action; it directs us to the problem of division of labor, as a justification for figuring out the basis of action.[38] For our purposes, we don't need it all—the complex mathematics, the technical inputs and outputs, the computer work. What we can use is the following:

the interrelationship of moving parts
the interdependence of functions
the division of labor
the workings and the process of action
the immediacy of movement
the inputs, both rational and non-rational
the limitation of power.

We are interested in the open, organismic system of learning, in which people act and react; in the division of labor; in the system within its own boundaries; in the relationship of systems. Chin puts it for us this way:

> In general, we find "system" and its modifications useful to practitioners since it emphasizes the functional interrelations between the parts of a client, be the client a person, group, organization, or culture. Its use thus requires thinking about behavior in terms of multiple determinants and factors—a model of thinking always required of intelligent practitioners in handling concrete situations.[39]
>
> The analytic model of system demands that we treat the phenomena and the concepts for organizing the phenomena as if there existed organization, interaction, interdependency, and integration of parts and elements.[40]

The systems idea has been attractive, as a way of reaching for the interdependence factor that is vaguely felt to be necessary in talking about man and his context. But the notion has not yet been brought into a theory of practice. Rather, in the manner of the old paradigm, the idea has been allowed to fall into the *object* mode, as another way of understanding the attributes of the client. The old paradigm still stands in the way, blocking off any real appreciation of how to apply the systems construct to the study of method. The new idea is again fitted into the procrustean bed of the old positivist world view.

Plan of Study

If then, a system comprises an interesting conglomerate of parts, each of which has its own function to perform, the parts together constitute an organism with boundaries, products. The system constitutes an interplay of functions, which means simply that each member has his own job to do, and needs the others, who in turn have their job to do. And this helps us to understand not only the functioning of the people we are trying to help, but the role of the worker as well. If the movements of the worker represent his way of carrying out his specially assigned function, then we have arrived by this route at a workable definition of method; namely, that it is a systematic process of ordering one's activity in the performance of a function. It is a strategy, then, by which the worker moves to carry out his assignment within the system's division of labor.

By this route, we come to understand that method is function in action. The acts required to carry out his job can then be differentiated from his objectives, his knowledge, his attitudes, and this without losing the importance of those attributes. It would then be necessary to describe the worker's moves in relation to the moves of the others within the system.

The transition from there to *skill* would be that the acts involved in the performance of the worker's function would be the most *direct* way of carrying out the job, considering the nature of the materials, the work of others, and the boundaried system in which they operate. Thus, the incorporation of action, relations, immediacy, and felt experience, all in the context of work—the worker's and the parallel efforts of the clients.

The systems that need to be considered are several, since both workers and clients operate within several: there is, first, the general society in which the profession is given its orders. What is social work assigned to do? Then, there are the special cases in which this assignment is carried out—the agency, the group, the interview, and any other system in which the client-worker encounter takes place.

Our job, then, is as follows, and will constitute the plan for the rest of the book:

First, it would be necessary to produce a statement of social work function, so formulated as to define the special assignment drawn by the profession of social work in the social system in which it was born and developed. This statement of function has certain requirements: it must be stated in verbs, in action, not in the end-states, as such statements are usually drawn. We cannot speak of "adjusting people to their society," or "democratic goals," and the usual litany to which we are accustomed.

Second, the statement must describe activity which affects and is affected by the activities of others within the system;

Third, it must explicitly demonstrate how the field of influence is limited;

And finally, it must reflect the interplay of functions, showing the uniqueness of social work function, while at the same time showing its interdependence with others.

Having found such a statement, it would have to be understood first in general terms, then in the specific subsystems in which the function is played out—the agency, the group, the interview.

The first job is historical, for if a statement of function is to be consistent with the history of the profession, rather than a statement of the writer's simple preference, it must be grounded in a rational perusal of a complex series of events that started a long time ago. No doubt such a statement will be controversial; with that kind of history, one would not expect, or need, consensus on its meaning. All that is necessary is that the statement can be said to square with at least some of the facts of history, and the subsequent methodological scheme be consistent with it, and can be evaluated in its own terms. It is not meant to be foolproof, or to achieve professional unanimity at a stroke; that would in itself mock the historical processes.

The second section, therefore, will constitute that kind of a search: what were the social circumstances under which social work was invented and found its work? How have these conditions changed over the years? What is constant through all of it? What does the function boil down to—in general terms, and in the specific settings in which the social worker finds himself?

Having completed that task, it then becomes possible to do the major work of the book: namely, to describe in a systematic way, the moves and skills through which the social worker carries out his function and carries it into the peer-group situation. We will be saying that a function can be described in action only as it can be broken down into the separate *tasks* required to carry it out.

Thus, the analysis will move from function, to tasks, to skill. This is the frame of reference for the search for method. It is a long way round, but given the nature of the problem, it is hard to see how one can arrive at a viable system of techniques in social work without committing either of the two great sins—to be superficial and mechanical, producing gimmicks and ready-made solutions; or, on the other extreme, to produce a philosophy and set of goals that say nothing about how it is to be achieved. Technology then, based on science and policy and the interworkings of knowing, believing, and doing, is inextricably linked in the helping process.

References

1. Thomas S. Kuhn, *The Structure of Scientific Revolutions,* (Chicago: University of Chicago Press, 1962), p. x.
2. *Ibid.,* pp. 10–11.
3. *Ibid.,* p. 11.
4. *Ibid.,* p. 37.
5. *Ibid.,* p. 6.
6. *Ibid.,* p. 110.
7. *Ibid.,* p. 122.
8. *Ibid.,* p. 111.
9. *Ibid.,* p. 15.
10. S. E. Frost, *Basic Teachings of the Great Philosophers* (Philadelphia: Blakiston, 1942), p. 81.
11. Rollo May, Ernest Angel, and Henri F. Ellenberger, eds. *Existence: A New Dimension in Psychiatry and Psychology* (New York: Basic Books, 1958), p. 8.
12. Richard Hofstadter, *Social Darwinism in American Thought* (New York: Brazillier, 1959), p. 201.
13. Gardner Murphy, *Human Potentialities* (New York: Basic Books, 1958).
14. May, et. al., *op. cit.,* p. 8.
15. William Barrett, *Irrational Man: A Study in Existentialist Philosophy* (Westport, Conn.: Greenwood Press, (1958), p. 21.
16. Barrett, *Ibid.,* p. 21.
17. Alan W. Watts, *Psychotherapy East and West* (New York: Pantheon Books, 1963), p. 28.

18. Lawrence K. Frank, "Research for What?" *Journal of Social Issues,* Kurt Lewin Memorial Award Issue, Supplement Series, no. 10, 1957, p. 8.
19. Frank, *Ibid.,* pp. 6–7, quoting Redl. See footnote, bottom p. 7.
20. Maurice Friedman, "Introduction Essay," in Martin Buber, *The Knowledge of Man: Selected Essays* (New York: Harper and Row, Harper Torchbooks, 1965), p. 20.
21. See, for example, the work of Florence Hollis, *Casework: A Psychosocial Therapy* (New York: Random House, 1969).
22. Martin Buber, *I-Thou,* 2d ed. (New York: Charles Scribner's Sons, Scribner Library, 1958), p. 103.
23. Thomas Kuhn, *op. cit.,* p. 111.
24. Buber, *op. cit.,* p. 34.
25. May, *op. cit.,* p. 13.
26. Buber, *op. cit.,* p. 34.
27. See the "Dialogue between Martin Buber and Carl R. Rogers," Appendix, pp. 166–84, in Martin Buber, *The Knowledge of Man* (New York: Harper and Row, 1965).
28. May, *op. cit.,* p. 8.
29. May, *Ibid.,* p. 27.
30. May, *Ibid.,* p. 27.
31. May, *Ibid.,* p. 26.
32. May, *Ibid.,* p. 36.
33. May, *Ibid.,* p. 12.
34. For a further discussion see: John Dewey, *The Quest for Certainty: A Study of the Relation of Knowledge and Action* (New York: G. P. Putnam's Sons, 1929); Capricorn Books, 1960; the transactionists; the functionalists; and Sartre's comment that the greatest freedom he ever achieved was under Fascism. The "freedom to say no."
35. Buber, *op. cit.,* pp. 132–33.
36. See Otto Rank and the functionalists for discussion on the use of time.
37. See the "Dialogue between Martin Buber and Carl R. Rogers," Appendix, pp. 166–84, in Martin Buber, *The Knowledge of Man* (New York: Harper and Row, 1965), for further discussion.
38. For a full discussion of the "systems system," see Ludwig von Bertalanffy, *General Systems Theory: Foundations, Development, Applications* (New York: Braziller, 1968).
39. Robert Chin, "The Utility of Systems Models and Developmental Models for Practitioners," in Warren G. Bennis, et. al., eds. *The Planning of Change* (New York: Holt, Rinehart and Winston, 1969), p. 299.
40. *Ibid.,* pp. 299–300. See also the efforts of Gordon Hearn, *Theory Building in Social Work* (Toronto: U. of Toronto Press, 1958), to bring the systems notion into social work. The model would include, first a general examination of the idea, then implications for social work, then the possibilities for the search for method.

Part 2

The Search for Function

4

The Search for Function

The problem in this chapter is to find a working function for the social worker, out of which he will fashion the techniques that will help him do most effectively what he is being paid to do. This function, first stated in general, social terms, must then be applied specifically within the two systems in which we are most interested—the agency in which he works, and the group in which he carries out his professional service.

In order to do this, we will have to go back a way into history and trace the changing conceptions of social work function in the developing American society. Although we will not be able to do this as thoroughly as a history book, we can at least highlight the major aspects of the search for a definitive function for social workers. Is it possible to carve out a coherent social assignment for a profession as complex and changing as social work? If our argument is correct, we must; for there is no way of conceptualizing a method without first providing a set of institutionalized purposes.

Our job is to find the unifying themes and to formulate a functional statement; to examine the way this function is carried out in the agency system; and to examine as well the client-worker system, with particular reference to the peer group as a client. We will then be ready in the succeeding chapters to undertake our analysis of the helping process itself.

The first important thing about the search for a social work function is that, after 200 years of work, it is still necessary to go through it at all. The fact is that it is still difficult to formulate a social work function that will encompass all of the activities that social workers perform—from rent collection, to treatment, to recreation, to education, to the administration of relief. Is there a common rubric, a common set of tasks that encompasses all of these and by which it may be known whether or not a given group of workers, or a given group of agencies shall consider themselves to be part of the social work field?

In order to get at this at all, one must do a bit of history by reviewing the ground a bit to see what all the different activities add up to. Without doing this too thoroughly—obviously for a book in itself—it should be possible to get a bird's-eye view that will begin to offer us some clues for a functional statement, clues that will include the welfare worker, the settlement worker, the recreationist, the camping people, the Ys, the community centers, public and private, the therapists—all holding the same membership card.

Before we move into this exercise, we need to do another. In any system of interdependent parts, from the cooking group, to the street club, to the agency, to society as a whole, in short, to any aggregation of people in meaningful relationship to each other, there are two major problems. One is composed of the tasks of *integration;* the other, the tasks of *differentiation.* The problems of integration are those that have to do with the business of organization, of running the ship, of establishing common rules and laws governing behavior, of pulling everyone's contribution to a common product and of transmitting these modalities from generation to generation.

On the other hand, the problems of differentiation are those involving the system's concern for its individual parts, its need to develop strong parts within the whole, well-differentiated, each of which does its own job well. The system, then, has two sets of tasks—those of building a strong and stable structure and those of developing strong parts that will, working together, make the system go. It is a part-whole problem, and it becomes necessary to understand the relationship of parts and wholes; how each affects the work of the other and how the organizational and individualizing functions affect each other.

Let us suppose, then, that our social system has developed among the professions a kind of division of labor as between those who are to take major responsibility for the integrating functions and those assigned primarily to the differentiating, or individualizing, ones. It would stand to reason that society, in order to get its work done, to be viable, will assign certain occupations and professions to the integrative jobs—coordinating, organizing, putting together, viewing the system as a whole—and assign others to worry about the individualizing—strengthening the individuals, curing the sick, helping the weak, making sure people don't get lost. Perhaps the prototype of the integrating professions might be the law, the ministry, perhaps education, in some of its aspects; and the model of the individualizers would be medicine, psychiatry, nursing, the clinicians. Education is, of course, a most interesting problem: the historic quarrel between the "progressives" and the "traditionalists" may have taken place precisely on the point of whether they have been designated to the integrative, system-maintenance tasks, or whether they are assigned to the tasks of differentiation, involving the concern with individual difference and individual expression.

If such a division of labor concept applies, and would be helpful in determining function, where does social work fit in? To which part of society's work are we assigned? Such a scheme crystallizes the issues of whose aspirations we represent, whether we are "therapists" "or" "social actionists." And, having been hung up on these either/ors for many generations, it has been difficult to discuss technique, except as one has chosen his role, which sometimes looks indistinguishable from that of a psychiatrist, and sometimes from that of a trade union organizer. Is it to be one *or* the other? Is it to be sometimes one and then the other? Are they reconcilable in the same package? Do they belong in the same club?

This is where history comes in. What can we learn from it? Over the history of this country, the specific job assignments of both the professionals and their agencies have changed and developed considerably, and the *practices* themselves, the concepts of skill have shifted with them. Let us try to trace these developments somewhat—the agency themes, the professional themes, and the practice themes—even if we have to do it sketchily.

Against the background of the period from colonial beginnings to the first stirrings of the Industrial Revolution—up to about 1850—we see old world patterns of class relations transferred to this country at a time when they are beginning to break up in their countries of origin. Industrialization began to find fertile ground in the north 100 years before it began to touch the south. We began as a nation half-feudal, half-mercantile. In the north, the process began with industrialization, urbanization, the rise of an independent middle class, the beginnings of a proletariat and the first movements toward trade union organization.

In this kind of social structure, you begin to have an increasingly visible group of "left-out" people, the ones that do not fit in, the indigents, the paupers, a group with which "something needs to be done." The idea of rugged independence, meant for the rising class of entrepreneurs, is poison when applied to the mass of wage-earners. At the same time, there is a rush of egalitarian ideas—Locke, Paine, the French revolutionaries—and this provides both a rationale for middle-class freedom and a rallying point for those who identify themselves with the depressed poor. Later, Herbert Spencer and William Graham Sumner will provide an answer in the philosophy of social Darwinism: those who are fit will survive, and that is how the race of man will progress. The ideas of social Darwinism will survive in the practices of these early years, emphasizing the worthy and unworthy poor, the administration of public assistance.

In the era of capitalist expansion, the years between 1850 and 1880, the Civil War joined the issue as to whether we should be half-feudal and half-industrial. Its close ushered in what Mark Twain called the Gilded Age—the age of pioneers, frontiers, and rugged individualism. Its prophets were Adam Smith, Spencer, and Sumner. As the country became richer, the people became poorer and as we reached the climax of middle-class power, in the 1870s, the problem was no longer that of a handful of paupers, but of large masses of economically marginal people; a class of poor. In the overcrowded, slum-ridden cities, their visibility rose sharply and the social effects proliferated: stereotyped and oppressive factory work, the complex maze of city life encountered by people from the villages and farms, and from the old country in successive waves of immigration. Over all, the amassing of large fortunes and the increasing concentration of economic and political power.

This concentration of economic power threatened the democratic idea and set the scene for the Progressive Era, or the humanitarian reaction. Here, from about 1880 to 1920, we begin to see the first organized protests and the disillusionment, from among the middle-class clergy, professionals, intellectuals, stimulated by the brute power of the middle class on its way up. In the clergy, the development of the "social gospel"; the rise of working-class movement; the burgeoning of the social sciences—Cooley's work on the peer group, Baldwin on the integrative relationship between the individual and the state. This problem is now important and very visible; the small group as building block of democracy—James, Dewey, Lindeman, and Follett restate the goals of a democratic state and show the connections between individual creativity, peer group organization, social action, and the democratic process. It is at this point that the whole idea of "process" comes into focus. In effect, it is a call for a distribution of power; the power lies in organization for self-interest; the democratic aspirations emerge from the clash of differences. In the field of psychology, the emphasis on environmental determinants constitutes an attack on the notion of inherent virtue and opens the way for a serious study of the effects and responsibilities of the social system on the lives of its people.

With the Depression and its aftermath, 1920 to 1940, there is a profound effect on the ideology of capitalism, the doctrine of individualism, and the concept of the "left-out" class. The growing responsibility of government in social welfare is a social index of the return to the concept of *mutual aid,* rather than that of the rich helping the poor. The instrumentality of government is the most stable and continuous way of providing the benefits of society to the mass of the people, in an institutionalized way, rather than a "residual" one.[1] The depression makes it clear, at least for a time, that a complex industrial society can no longer function effectively with the patched-up, residual notion as its only resource for integrating and organizing the system of social welfare services. At the same time, private philanthropy took new forms and the issue of public and private welfare (and the relationship between the two) becomes a major one. Is the public service a residual one, making up the gaps in private initiative, in approved capitalist, free enterprise style? Or, is it the other way around, with the private service serving a residual, experimental function?

In the current era, from 1940 to the present, *again occurs* the age of anxiety and again the threat of collective themes and the fear of social action. Before, it was the rising power of the middle class that was threatened; now it is the maintainance of power and influence. The trade unions purge themselves, as do all large associations. A big war, many little wars, and the threat of the last big bang. The automation issue; the prosperity of a war-preparation economy brings us back to a class of poor, the "left-out group", brilliantly explained by Harrington and Mills.[2] On the other hand, the counter-themes: the "affluent society" and the "substitution of sociology for socialism" on the one hand; and the powerful reaffirmation of mass action among the blacks and other minorities, the poor, the youth, and even spreading to the civil servants, the police, the firemen. Mutual aid is a rampant theme in the 1960s, and those who are for collective action are the ones with the people's causes; those who decry are the Establishment, by definition. In this era, the Establishment are the organized solidly, including the trade unions themselves, and even the Communist Party in a peculiar way. The issue of "action" v. "process" is a very urgent one and those professions that make their living serving in small ways are on the defensive. The cry now is to "change the system" and "change the people" is regarded as diversionary and reactionary.

Agency Themes

The agency themes begin with the transplantations of different national and cultural ideas and forms of organization for the care of the indigent—with the English Poor Law system as the primary form. At the beginnings, the rationale is *mercy,* not justice, and the social division of labor assigns the function to *religion,* the keeper of the social conscience. The implication that goes with that is that mercy must be deserved, one must not take advantage of the bounty of the well-to-do toward their less fortunate brethren. There is also a kind of Darwinism here: only the God-fearing are fit to survive. This is the beginning of the theme that identifies social service with salvation; and this theme will persist, in one form or another, until the present day: those who seek help will need to be saved, or their characters changed, or their psyches treated—the language of the day changes but the theme remains the same: the price of dependency is to submit oneself to some form of organized remodeling.

Another theme that develops here is the protection of society (those who have made it) from the left-outs—those who have fallen by the wayside. Those who have not "succeeded" are in some way dangerous to the rest; they must be identified, classified, and wherever possible, isolated. The social agency is established as the agent charged with the task of tabulating, identifying, classifying, isolating, and protecting society against the "exploiting" poor. In a strange sense, this identification with the poor is to join them and see that they are well-contained. All of them together—the poor, the agencies, the workers—are in the same bag—isolated from the society as a whole, invisible in the dark corners and the game is to keep them there.

The early "leisure-time" agencies—the Ys of the 1850s and 1860s—were protective associations with a strong religious and cultural admixture—protective associations against the various evils that sprung from rapid industrialization and urbanization. Against *alienation,* there was Barnett's "association in search of the best"; against the *removal from nature,* there arose the camping and playground movements; against *child labor,* the various youth movements; against the *powerlessness at the grass roots,* the neighborhood movements and the social action stance; against the *loss of group identity* (the Jews, the Italians, the Irish), the movement of the Ys toward protecting group identity—antiassimilationist efforts. Against the threats of alienation and intermingling were the strong ideological message of the Jewish Centers, the Ys, the settlements. And against the "Modern Times" routinization of work, the tendency to concentrate on skills-development ("program"), Americanization, culture, language, vocational. Thus, the group agencies were compounded of many traditions—recreation, education, mental health, social action, community organization, social welfare—in whatever area people could be urged to combine in their own interest. The social action theme is still largely undeveloped, despite the mythology on it, except as something influential people did for the less privileged.

Among the private welfare agencies, the function is to distribute small amounts of money and goods to the "deserving" poor; that is, those who conformed to the middle-class ethic and made strong efforts to return to the working force. Another function was to protect society against the

> ignorance, fanaticism, brutal ferocity, and animal appetites and lusts, unrestrained by self-knowledge or by mental discipline, (that) are always pursuing the orderly and educated classes like a pack of wolves. (R. M. Hartley, founder of the New York Association for Improvement of the Conditions of the Poor, writing in 1871.)

The NYAICP set itself against the strikes of the 1870s and idleness and profligacy often go hand in hand. At this stage, the trade union ferment finds no ally in the agencies of welfare; the identification of the agencies are basically with the ruling economic group. The conditions of the poor are to be improved by making them more worthy.

> It is a truism (again the NYAICP) to say that this charity is an outgrowth of Capital, and could not exist without it, or that the numerous benevolent institutions in this city and the world, with the gratuitous expenditures of untold millions for the help of the destitute and perishing have a like origin.

The growing concept of governmental responsibility nourishes the development of a network of public welfare agencies administered by larger units of government—state, federal. The theme of *mercy* now gives way somewhat to that of *justice,* and the private agencies take on the open function of *spokesmanship* for the poor, stressing the obligations of wealth rather than simply its prerogatives.

The private agencies begin to arrange themselves in an interesting pattern: the Charity Organization Society, with Mary Richmond as its guiding genius, tailors itself to the service of the individual and his family, stakes its hopes on the "friendship" between a "friendly visitor" from the middle class and a working-class recipient. The movement is impatient with "theorists" who question the system itself, and with any forms of government action for public welfare, as well as trade union organization itself.

The settlement movement is mainly concerned with *reestablishing the conditions for mutual aid,* in a complex urban environment that has almost destroyed such conditions. Here, too, in the settlements, the friendship theme is paramount, and the theme of *interclass friendship* is at the roots of the movement. But in the settlements the emphasis is more strongly on social reform and its sympathies are with worker organization—co-ops, trade unions—and its uplifting efforts are aimed at people together. "An association in search of the best"—the "best," of course, is in middle-class terms, but the emphasis on organization is important, and an important corrective. The social problems against which the neighborhood agencies set themselves are: alienation, loss of nature, the need for "culture," and the access to the finer things in life, the acquisition of skills for use in the new society.

Thus arose the first bifurcation of the agencies; the beginnings of what came to be called the "case work" and the "group work" agencies. The former are heavily favored by middle-class philanthropy. The COS is tailor-made to its needs—some minor redistribution of money and goods, a heavy emphasis on the one-at-a-time, a stress on treatment and control, the evaluation of the "deserving," and a disapproving attitude toward worker organization and government interference. The only price it asks in return is middle-class interest in good works and some money, as well as a curb on some of its most obvious excesses. The system is taken as given, and the concern is essentially with helping people live within it and find their proper subordinate places within it.

The settlements, on the other hand, seem slightly more dangerous, with their emphasis on association and their irritation with the injustices of the system itself. Actually, the tendency toward mass organization has been overrated; their concern was more with spokesmanship than with social pressure by the people themselves, the organization of working people in their own interest. There is little evidence that the settlements went much beyond the small interest group, designed to "adjust" people and make them more personally skilled. Certainly Addams and Barnett conceived of social action as action by the enlightened segment of the middle class, in favor of the less fortunate. The intervention of the well-to-do in the neighborhood was designed to make them more fit to rule, rather than share their power in any significant way. But the machinery was there, and more tolerated, to help the poor organize themselves; it simply was not—as to the present day—used very much in the agency's conception of its function. These were, very much as the casework agencies were, "charitable" organizations.

The sectarian agencies—the Ys, the Jewish Ys and centers, and the Catholic youth organizations—were basically ghettoized, developed problems of their own. Although they soon begin to identify with their social welfare counterparts (Jewish Family Service), they cut themselves off from the mainstream of social welfare activity. They are really *clubs* in themselves, associations banded together in self-contained homogeneity.

The third offshoot—to crop up somewhat later and complete the triad of "casework," "group work," and "community organization"—is already inherent in the charity organization aspects of the COS. Here the main social problem was to eliminate duplication of fundraising and distribution, to forestall "wasteful" philanthropy, and to stabilize philanthropy in a well-organized system of giving and distributing money. The function is one of husbandry, again with the framework of social stability rather than social service and certainly social reform. The fact that the CO people found it necessary to build in the concept of grass-roots organization is an interesting reflection of the persistent theme of change-versus-stability, and the tensions between these ideas that has characterized the social welfare field from the beginning.

Thus, case work as the individualizing force, designed to adjust people to the system; group work as the collectivizing force, potentially capable of addressing the problems of people in mobilizing themselves to point themselves and their mass strength to the social devices under which they live, but in the main not doing it; and the community organization people as another stabilizing force, designed to keep the system neat, serving an integrating function and bring order into the relations between the "giving" and the "taking" classes. The agencies develop around these three basic functions.

In the Depression period, the public sector sees the proliferation of insurance programs and the highly organized administration of public social services—inadequately staffed and only indirectly related to the emerging social work profession. At the same time, these agencies serve as a mass recruiting ground for the profession. The "professionalization of the client" brings into the field working-class people; it is a case of the working class beginning to serve their own, while middle-class workers are ensconced in the private agencies, most particularly the sectarian ones.

In the private sector, the growth of federated financing and their proliferating services, plus the development of further sectarianization of services. In the group work agencies, the emphasis begins to move from the "disadvantaged" to the higher classes, from social welfare with the poor to recreational, educational function, from the "uplifting" theme to the psychological, and the Freudian, treatment emphasis. While the casework agencies are differentiating themselves, generic and specific at Milford, the group work agencies grow more and more diffuse, uncertain of their function in the world. In the 1920s, they move into the Schools of Social Work.

In the current era, the stable establishment of the "host" agency as the place where social workers operate, and the preoccupation with the "team" idea. The generic and unifying themes; the Council on Social Work Education as a unifier of agencies and schools.

The further division of labor among the casework agencies: the private agencies will give "psychological" help, the public agencies will take on economic insecurity. In a sense, this is the final separation of "corrections" from "charity"; but in another sense, it drives social welfare to higher refinements and away from its base in the concerns of the mass of the people.

The group work agencies are slow to follow, and are left behind as the workers begin to leave them for the "psychiatric" settings. During the war, community organization agencies become firmly entrenched; their function now is essentially to supervise the collection of funds, administer the distribution, and hold the line against new demands for service or any other encroachments against the status quo of welfare.

Professional Themes

In the first stages, the practitioners of the day are those who are doing other jobs: low-status clerics, teachers, and rich volunteers; also local government employees who "oversee" the poor on behalf of local governmental units. Toward the end of the first period, there emerge the beginnings of an identifiable professional class—those who make their living in this kind of work.

Later, there appears the early beginning of a professional group and a division of labor between lay control and professional management. The professionals themselves are of middle-class origins—the lower segment of that class—but upwardly mobile and identified primarily with the promise of that system and its rewards. They have also, however, inherited from the clergy the job of keeper of the social conscience; the humanitarianism that led them into these jobs bends them toward some identification with the people to whom they minister.

This is where the great internal conflict of the social workers begins: the system or the client. Or, to put it another way, who *is* the client? The more complex the system gets, the more difficult the dualism—individual need *versus* social need is the way it gets read.

Another issue that begins here is whether the social worker is to devote his time to *amelioration* or *social change*. This is what, in politics, Julius Nyerere posed as the distinction between "the politics of complaint" or radical reform of the system itself. In social work, it is beginning to seem that one is a negation of the other. One must "choose" between the one-at-a-time, service, helping, "clinical" orientation, and the change-the-system movement, organizing, mobilizing approach. Is social work to be a "handmaiden" for class rule, or is it to be a profession of political protest, radicalism, striking wherever justice is deficient and changing the system wherever it can?

When the one-to-one v. one-to-group v. one-to-community division of labor arises within the agency field, the professionals go the same way, specializing by the number of people they are equipped to deal with at one time. The influence of the psychotherapeutic, Freudian approach to sick people is a part of this. The idea is that the one-to-one conversation is a treatment device and can work for social workers when they are trying to introduce some change into a person's life—get him to do something different from what he is doing now, so that he will be more acceptable to the system in which he lives.

Social work becomes early identified as *casework,* and professional training begins for caseworkers at about the turn of the century. The settlement group, at first individually identified with the "charity workers," come later to regard themselves as a kind of sub-profession of their own, splitting with the COS on several issues. In England, the relationship between Octavia Hill and Canon Barnett typified this encounter between the caseworkers and the group workers. In the COS, we begin to see the start of the clinical emphasis, the emphasis on case recording, the interaction between worker and client. In the settlements and Ys, the orientation is multifunctional; they are educators, recreationists, welfare workers, missionaries, nutritionists, social reformers, and a lot more. In a word, they are "good neighbors," reaching *down* from the heights of class to *do for* the poor what they need done for them. Their sense of democracy, guilt, "we-learn-from-them-too," may force them to fabricate the terminology of interactionism and self-help, but the fact seems pretty clear that they are, in Barnett's words, "in search of the best," as he and his young cohorts define "the best."

In the Depression era, the modern pattern of professional development comes clear—casework, group work and community organization. The professional associations begin to develop, by interest group or field of practice and by something that gets to be called "method." That is, they differentiate themselves by the social problems they serve (medical, psychiatric), and by the number of people they specialize in (group workers, co-workers and caseworkers). The National Conference of Social Work is a central forum that brings them all together once a year. The Schools of Social Work are really the only central point of reference for a single "profession"—in the separate organizations, they often act like *different* professions. The Milford Conferences are the first real unifying force among the caseworkers, but no effort is made here to handle the other organizational, identifying problems that will later go into the formation of a single profession.

In the Depression, a huge influx of new workers is brought into the public agencies. Many of these workers come from the client class itself—clients turned workers—and the class identification of the profession undergoes a marked change. As the social agencies of welfare become increasingly public, financed by tax funds, a huge body, about three quarters of the whole, is created—most "untrained" and unassimilated into the professional culture of the social work profession. This goes right into the present day, with a profession about three quarters of whose members are not eligible for membership in the professional association. The move is only just now being made to introduce them into the association on an "associate" level, and this is mostly a response to the pressure put on by the certifying bodies at the state level, where they will be certified as members of the profession by legal groups and professional recognition must follow hard by.

In the current era, the tripolarization begins to break down, as the agencies begin to understand their deficiencies and as the schools, a little belatedly, begin to drive toward the "generic" emphasis. Just as the "methods" identification is firmly established, it begins to break down. The National Association of Social Workers brings the subprofessional organizations in 1955; later, the "Sections" are eliminated and the unification of social workers moves ahead apace.

In the larger society, as the formal systems of power are increasingly detached from their grass roots, the repressive measures attack the philosophical roots of the profession itself. It is caught in the middle, between the "power," the establishment, on the one hand, and the "people," the poor, the blacks, the minorities on the other. It questions its function and its sources of strength. The soul-searching is both symbolized and intensified by the professional battles around standards, who to include, certification battles, private practice, the doctrine of "area of competence in matters of social policy, the role of the professional association (the "AMA model"), and other issues. If social demands are to hinge on areas of competence, what are these areas? *If competence derives from function,* as it surely must, what is this function? The question comes full circle, and the main issues are simply up-to-date versions of the age-old question: What are social workers supposed to do in society?

In the professional association itself, there are opposite pulls toward elitism and a broad base of membership toward status based on high-status clients, and that based on an exclusive concern with the poor and downtrodden.

In what are now called the "group-serving" (not "group work") agencies, the workers intensify their search for a reference group. The rapidity of development makes it difficult for them to find who they are as they move from stage to stage by the urgency of associational developments. Their visibility as a professional group declines as other social workers take on the group service function. As a fellowship, the same thing happens. As a "method" the term itself grows anomalous because it becomes obvious that they have not demonstrated their sole competence in this area. If the "method" inheres simply in the group being there, there is no "method"; there is, rather, a social-work method, applied in the various situations in which the worker finds himself.

Practice Themes

In the beginning, the idea that there may be something salutary in the interaction between the giver and the taker of help is not yet born, except in the notion that those who have made it—possess the world's benefits—should serve as behavioral models for those who have not. In this prescientific, preprofessional, prespecialized era, the basic measures for control of the indigent and alienated are example, exhortation, prayer and, where all else fails, confinement.

In the age of social Darwinism, social workers share the philosophy but it takes an interesting form: they share the premise, but not the conclusion. The "orderly and educated classes," they feel, were in truth fitter, more virtuous, thrifty, clean, but this is no reason to stand by and let the others perish. They could be saved, *taught* the finer things—culture, thrift, sobriety, and the "American way." The theme of education, in this context, means exhortation, example, and close supervision. In the Ys and centers and settlements, it meant all those things, plus skills, vocational and recreational—to make them useful to the system and to compete with the temptations of the city. Overall, the goal is to bring them into conformity with the society as it is, with perhaps some slight changes envisaged. The method is to urge them to equip themselves with characteristics that will make them more acceptable—sobriety and thrift. As in the religious mode, *guilt* is still a strong motivation for change. Reference is to authority—the Bible, the lives of the greats, particularly those who have risen from poverty, the Alger story. The theme of self-mobilization for social change is still a long way from being born; it is not permissible within a caste system.

Against the caste idea, however, is the Emersonian "self-reliance," the ideal of bootstrap democracy, but this is mostly for the well-to-do and the upwardly mobile, or at least the mobile poor.

Under the Humanitarian Reaction, there grows a new emphasis on the nature of the client-worker interaction; it begins with the familiar social model of *friendship*. It is, in fact, an extension and refinement of the ordinary ways in which people help each other. Mary Richmond and Jane Addams both saw—the former more clearly perhaps—that there is something in the feeling between the giver and the taker of help that is a healing and mobilizing force. (The friendship analogy is rounded out by Bertha Reynolds in the current scene.)

Mary Richmond, largely because of the way the agency function was organized, became interested in the process, wanted it recorded, studied; Addams was more concerned with larger movements, legislation, and so on, and with the salutary effects of peer association and comradeship.

The caseworkers' emphasis quickly moves to *professional* help, and it is a short step from there to the preoccupation with the medical model (the early rise of medical social work contributes heavily to this pull toward the medical model)—the helping person is one who "diagnoses," and then does something to the person to make him better. The group workers, at the same time, put their bets on mutual help, on peer group interaction and they turned, not to Freud and his cohorts but to the students of the small group—Lewin and Dewey. The group workers have no Richmond to guide them in focusing on the minutiae of practice; the "movement" phase persists for a long time, and the preoccupation with goals remains more important to them than the study of means to reach them.

In adopting the medical model, the social workers lent themselves to the traditional subject-object split that the medical profession inherited from Descartes; the phenomenological model and its emphasis are still a long way off—where the stress will be placed on the common experience between worker and client, the moment-to-moment, the here-and-now, the *becoming*[3], the interactionism of Dewey.[4] Even the research model of study, decide, and do will give way to the circularity of Frank.[5]

Later, the concept of "friendship" becomes that of "relationship," and a strong clinical emphasis is created under the influence of the psychoanalytic doctrine fathered by Freud and his followers in this country. The schools of social work are almost completely taken over by the medical-psychoanalytical model and the study-diagnosis-treatment paradigm. The social work discipline begins to take on what Mumford calls the "priestly monopoly of secret knowledge"—and this becomes identified as "professionalization"; the processes of status-gaining are, understandably, tied up with aping the fancier aspects of the historic professions—law, medicine, the ministry. When Flexner does his study of the social workers, in 1915,[6] he comes up with the conclusion that social work is not a "profession" because it orchestrates, rather than providing its own unique service; being a doctor, he forgets that, in a complex society, orchestrating can *be* the service—requiring its own skills and knowledge. The social workers, overwhelmed by his status and that of the doctors, buy his argument, hook, line, and sinker and proceed to take their direction from him.

At the same time, the Progressive Era has left its mark, and the transactional nature of the helping process is irrevocably launched—by the functionalists in social work, by the field theorists, the gestaltists, the progressive educational theory of John Dewey, the Rogerians, later the Existentialists, and transactionalists. The elimination of the "class of poor" idea, and the realization that those who have not "made it" have simply not been *allowed* to make it, rather than being cripples from birth (inherent defects), makes us begin to theorize around the potential *strength* of people, their ability to help each other, and the teaching-helping process turns to the notions of *volition and motivation* as part of the helping process. The rising ego-psychology, European existentialism create new themes—Horney, Adler, Sullivan, Fromm, and others are the harbingers.

As our society grows more complex, there is the developing professional concern with the issue of the *one versus the many,* the individual and the collective. The "versus" is an expression of the fact that people cannot find their way easily into the system and find their places in it. And the more difficult the fight to get in, the more specialized are our attempts to deal with the problems. Social workers begin to develop many specializations mostly by setting: the school, the hospital, the institution.

As the specializations proliferate, it becomes harder to conceptualize the function. There is fund-raising, fund-disbursing, ministering to the poor, recreation, informal education, therapy, social action, and child welfare. They deal in neighborhood politics, agency organization, individuals, families, basketball teams, and government programs.

Over the years, there is a visible relationship between themes of *practice* and those of *function.* As the arm of middle-class good works, they must learn to distinguish between the "worthy" and the "unworthy," and they develop the notion of "diagnosis" to meet this requirement.

As the uplifters of the poor, they must educate, exhort, and expose them to the better things of life.

As the organizers of peer groups for social control over their own destinies, they must learn to dig for strength—individual and mass—and to put action means within their reach.

As the catalysts of social change, they must interest themselves in the strengths of collective action—they must, in fact, make a study of action itself, what it means, how it happens. The latter-day interest in Parsons, Mills, the sociologists and psychologists of change. These are reflective of this need.

All of these tasks survive today, in mixed forms within the same workers and in clashes of conceptions about method and about the "true" function of the profession. All of the battles about the role of the profession, all of the issues about what is and what is not appropriate. Private practice and social action, process and organizing emphases are battles about function. What are social workers supposed to be doing in society? What do all of the tasks they've picked up over the years signify for their role in society? What does it add up to?

References

1. For a discussion of residual and institutional views of the institution of social welfare see: Alfred J. Kahn, "The Function of Social Work in the Modern World," in Alfred J. Kahn, *Issues in American Social Work* (New York: Columbia University Press, 1959), pp. 3–38; and particularly Chapter VI pp. 138–47 in Harold L. Wilensky and Charles N. Lebeaux, *Industrial Society and Social Welfare* (New York: Russell Sage Foundation 1958).
2. See Michael J. Harrington, *The Other America* (New York: Macmillan, 1963), and C. Wright Mills, *The Power Elite* (New York: Oxford University Press, 1957).
3. Gordon W. Allport, *Becoming: Basic Considerations for a Psychology of Personality* (New Haven: Yale University Press, 1955).
4. See for example, John Dewey, *Psychology* 3d ed., rev. (New York: Harper and Brothers, 1892); and Dewey, *The Quest for Certainty: A Study of the Relation of Knowledge and Action* (New York: G. P. Putnam's Sons, 1929; Capricorn Books, 1960).
5. Lawrence K. Frank, "Research for What?" *Journal of Social Issues,* Kurt Lewin Memorial Award Issue, Supplement Series, no. 10, 1957.
6. Abraham Flexner, "Is Social Work a Profession?" *Proceedings of the National Conference of Charities and Correction* (Chicago: The Hildmann Printing Co., 1915), pp. 576–90.

5

The Social Worker in Society

The search for a coherent professional function for social work in all this is a search for the unifying characteristics that cover the particular job assignment that has gathered up over the years. If we take the tasks one by one, the pattern is difficult to discern, involving such a diverse collection of jobs that they must be put together as one does the parts of a puzzle.

There is no trouble finding a general consensus that social workers are somehow concerned with the "social"—the term is used again and again in the literature and it comes through in notions like "social functioning," "social relationships," "social problems," "social goals." Furthermore, all are agreed that the social worker is somehow linked in his work to both the individual and his society. *But* the problem is that "social functioning" and the "enhancement" of it is not enough, because *all* functioning is *social* functioning. Pray saw this in 1947: "The word 'social' has none of the precision of such words as 'medical' or 'legal' . . . It is obviously not enough to say the social work treats 'social' problems. For virtually every life problem of every individual in this modern world is, in reality, a 'social' problem in one sense or another."[1] And he went on to say that not all of these "social" involvements could "lie within the province of a single profession."

The key question is asked by Gordon: "What does the social worker intervene *in*?"[2] And by Bartlett: "Where does the social worker *stand*?"[3] These questions are central because they try to go beyond what the worker is interested in—the individual *and* society—to the kinds of *processes* to which he is related. Bertha Reynolds's "We are ever and always a *go-between* profession" is a step closer, because it moves from *interest* to *action*. But a new element is still needed to complete the picture.

To understand that new element, one must see that the social worker is not only concerned with the individual *and* the social system, but he must understand something of the relationship between the two, and the energy that flows between the two. Can we understand the relationship between the individual and society so that one can take up a position that will make it unnecessary to "choose" between the two? Not, it should be emphasized, between the individual and the "establishment," but between the individual and his surrounding systems. What, exactly, is the relationship between the needs of the collective and those of the individuals who comprise it?

In pursuing this line of thought, it is necessary first to develop the individual-social relationship in a general sort of way; but then it is necessary to realize that every specific system of demand and relationship that a person has to negotiate between birth and death is a special case of that general relationship. Actually, there is no such thing as a relationship between man and "society"; there are only the relationships between a child and his mother, an adolescent and his peer group, the client and the agency, the patient in the hospital, the mother and her sewing group, the tenant and his council, the family and its neighborhood stores.

However, all of these social systems have certain things in common. The systems construct implies a patterning of relationships among a group of people, so that their activities are interdependent and that the well-being of all depends to some degree on each. A strong collective, therefore, will need to enlist its members in the tasks of preserving and developing its identity, to transmit the products—things, ideas, values—emerging from past experience, to inculcate the "social curriculum" it has developed over the years of its existence.

At the same time, however, it must also develop and maintain its capacity for change, for adaptation to changing conditions; a race of knowledgeable and cultured beatniks would lack the energy and opportunity and hope to reproduce itself and modify social institutions to adapt to the changing conditions of life. The *dialectic* must be served: society's task is to produce individuals who are well enough *integrated* to assume responsibility for perpetuating its culture, while they are also *differentiated* enough to question it, to take sides on issues, to fight for change, to invent new modes and to create new things from the remains of the old.

Society's need, therefore, is to create group members who can conform and rebel, who can love order and have a high tolerance for ambiguity, who can act both independently and interdependently. And it is important that these qualities be incorporated in the same people, so that social leadership will incorporate the dialectic—and the conflict—within themselves, rather than the "new men" v. "the old." The efforts of the collective are directed toward system maintenance and toward social change; and both processes require the type of individual indicated—free and controlled, conforming and inventive, with uses for both the old and the new. Social stability is not achieved by robots, nor lasting social change by those with utter contempt for the past.

So much for the requirements of the social system. What about the needs of the individual? On his part, he is faced with his own problems of identity formation and development. He, too, has a "curriculum" of his own, as he strives to affect the pattern of life around him so that the thoughts and acts of others will be responsive to his wants as he feels them. And, while he struggles to maintain his uniqueness, his difference from others, he also wants in; he needs a place to express his commonality with others; he wants to be assigned a purpose and set of roles with the collective that nurtures him. He asks, in his turn, to be both *integrated* and *differentiated.*

This is how it comes about that the individual's sense of personal need echoes the social requirement that the people be clearly integrated and differentiated—molded into a unit and strengthened in their individuality—*both.* In fact, one cannot actually take place without the other—strength is belonging, belonging (having a place and a job and entrée into the system) bespeaks strength. When Horney identifies psychosis as alienation, this is what she has in mind—there is no lonely splendor, and man takes much of his strength from his fellows. It is in the interest of both society and its people that the twin functions of organizing-integrating and individualizing-differentiating are interdependent and mutually fulfilling. Ballou's statement on this was that:

> The fullest possible development of the human personality is a necessary prerequisite to having that individual able and willing to make his maximum contribution to the community as a whole.[4]

What is being described here is a state of *symbiosis* between the individual and his surround, the culture that nurtures him—each needs the other to fulfill itself and each needs just about the same collection of qualities. The same dialectic nourishes the one as the many. Which is another way of saying that people *collect* and organize themselves into systems to make themselves stronger, to insure survival, to make life easier, and to draw support from each other in carrying on the jobs of which their lives are composed. And in each of the smaller systems—the family, the friendship, the peer group, the social agency—this relationship is played out again and again, every day of our lives. Each social encounter between an individual and some representative of social authority (the collective) is a *special case* of the symbiotic relationship between individuals and their society. Each is a specific form or structure in which the symbiosis works itself out.

What, then, goes wrong? What creates the sense of irreconcilable conflict between the individual and the society? What creates the need to make these "choices" between the needs of individuals and those of their systems, large and small? Somewhere along the line there is a *symbiotic diffusion,* a blurring of the one-many relationship into states of conflict, alienation, social rejection, and what appears to be a rigid dualism between people and their systems. When this happens, everybody—the individuals, the system representatives, the social analysts—is captured by the illusion of irreconcilable stakes, the symbiotic diffusion. It is not that these conflicts are not real; the rejection and bitterness and sense of overpowering force is real enough. That is exactly the point: the antagonisms are so real that they obscure the common stake between the collective and its people and that they are read as the normal state of tension, rather than something gone wrong. When this happens the individual and the society are set up as the great antagonists and one cannot but make his pledge of allegiance to one or the other.

How does the difficulty come about? How does the diffusion arise? At what point does the sense of conflict loom so large that it fills the picture, leaving no room for the more fundamental relationship between the two? My suggestion is that the problem of diffusion is essentially a function of *complexity*—that the simpler the system under consideration, the less likely it is that the symbiosis gets obscured. In a small, primitive society, where young people grow directly into the occupation chosen for them, where the rules are fairly clear, where the number of people is small, where roles and relationships are fairly well structured—in this kind of system, one finds little of the need to "choose" between individual and social demands. The same is true of the simple relationship between the infant and his mother, or mother substitute, where the need for each other is a similar prototype of the symbiotic relationship between the child and his surround. In both of these cases, the individual and his system have easy access to each other; each can reach out and make a connection without too much interference. Consequently, the "I v. they" problems play a minor role, are fairly quickly resolved as they arise, and do not, unless something else happens, get built in, either to the individual's self-image, or to the social institutions.

Unless what happens? Under what circumstances do the conflicts become rigidly fixed into both the individual's and the society's structure of responses? Again, the key is in the concept of "complexity"; the loss of the "symbiotic sense" is recapitulated in the life of each individual as he moves from the simple relational system of the family in which his role and function are clearly marked to the complex patterns of demand in the community at large. The symbiotic sense becomes more and more diffuse as the identification between the person and his surround becomes less and less clear.

More specifically, as the *access* of individual and society to each other becomes more and more difficult, the job of reaching is given up and war declared between the two. The "membership requirements" become more and more complicated; the child's efforts to "join the club" require more skill than he has available; power and control over his movements seem to reside more and more outside his own self. Power over the conditions that affect people's lives becomes more concentrated and slips out of their hands.

Under these circumstances, the individual asks for allies in his battle to regain some sense of dignity from the "they" who are controlling his life; and the "they" will pose the question as being "fixing" all the "I's" so that they will *adjust* to the system and carry on as the system thinks best. Each will call for sympathy and identification in the battle between them and the self-v.-society battle is joined. The situation is real, the feelings are real, the alternatives seem to make sense. But the game is lost, and all the "decisions" based on this analysis—the "Group think" school and the rest—are doomed to be tossed back and forth on the horns of the dilemma.

It is worth noting that the small peer group, and the adolescent peer group in particular, may be viewed as a device for reestablishing the conditions of a "simple" system in which one may, together with others similarly inclined, work out one's social relationships and find a mode of social functioning under conditions where it is still possible to retain some degree of control.

The developing diffusion thus creates a dualism between individual needs and those of the society, and this dualism becomes a major assumption on all fronts. The general anxiety about the loss of the symbiotic sense creates a major one-versus-many theme in philosophy, the arts, the social sciences. The teaching profession is an excellent example of the conflict in action between system-maintenance concerns and individual creativity (freedom) concerns. The great swings are familiar—between the traditionalists and the progressives—and we watch the battle as at a ping-pong game. The heads swing back and forth—now one side is up, now the other; the battle between the integrators and the differentiators, the system-people and the people-people. First we are warned to be very sensitive to the needs of the children, the psychological considerations. Then we are told we must move to the needs of society, Johnny can't read, enough of the psychological stuff.

The important thing to consider is that there is a pretty unanimous feeling that there *is* a choice to be made between individual need and social demand. In this, all the antagonists themselves agree; Freud with Hutchins, Rogers with Bestor. While they disagree with the choice itself, they agree that the allegiance has to be declared and one must plump for either the individual freedom or social demand. The complexity is overwhelming and its imperatives remain unchallenged. The dualism is accepted as a fact of modern life, rather than a lost symbiosis, waiting to be regained. What might be regarded as a temporary failure to implement the relationship between the system and its people is viewed as a "true" antithesis, irreconcilable; so that choices must be made between the individual and the collective, between psychology and sociology, between system-maintenance and individual freedom. In a word, the world is divided between the *integrators* and the *differentiators*.

The Function of Social Work

Into which of these categories does social work fit? From the historical review, it is clear that the role has been difficult to clarify—in contrast, let us say, with the roles of medicine, law, nursing, engineering, others—because it has taken so many different forms; because it has concerned itself with *both* system-maintenance and individual development; because it has found work to do in relation with a wide range of systems in society.

I will suggest now that the key to the unifying theme is that social workers seem, from the beginning, to have been placed precisely at the point where social opportunity and individual need reach out to each other. This assignment has always placed social work in the unique position of being equally concerned with *both* the integrative and differentiating tasks and explains why its internal development has produced the wide gamut of activities that runs from one end of the individual-social spectrum to the other—the fund-raiser, the social actionist, the recreationist, the educator, the psychotherapist. It also helps to explain why, in the course of this development, the social work profession has been sensitive to, and influenced by, the broad range of knowledge developed in the social and behavioral sciences, from medical information, to theories of society, to psychological and psychoanalytic ideas, and why the profession is caught up by every new idea as quickly as it makes its bid for public recognition.

The social work profession has seemed to develop as a kind of improvised social corrective for the growing schism between social and individual need in a highly complex and often disordered society. On the one hand, it has found itself plugging the loopholes in the system and repairing the effects of its malfunctioning; on the other, it has been asked to prepare the young, to retrain and rehabilitate the outcast and the disadvantaged, and to find places for all manner of individuals almost, but not quite, thrown out of the system. Thus it is that social workers have been occupied with the responsibility to "change the individual," "change the system," and have found themselves quarreling about "which is more important."

I am suggesting here that this particular argument is unresolvable because the social worker has historically been selected as the agent who must help individuals and their systems to make their proper impact on each other; in a word, to help the individuals change their systems and their systems to change the individuals. The professional assignment comes from the fact that the symbiotic necessities become obscured, diffuse, and someone must be assigned to the job of guarding the attachment between the two.

The professional work emerges from the growing obscurity of the symbiotic need, from the fact that people are weakened in their reach to the system and the system is too clumsy to incorporate the people it needs to serve. The specific situations range from the normal developmental problems of children, as in the group work settings, to the severe pathology of people whose symbiotic attachment to society is all but severed, as in the back ward of the mental hospital.

At every point where the complexities of the social system made it increasingly difficult for people to find their places and for the various subsystems to reach out to the people they were supposed to help, the social worker was called in to help both the individuals and the systems to reach out to each other—in the schools, in the distribution of relief, in the family, in the institution, in the hospital, in the neighborhood, and even in the industrial plant. At each of these places where the individual and his society come into meaningful exchange, someone had to help with the confrontation of individual and system.

The job here is to *mediate the transaction* through which individual and social need reach out to each other in each setting. The social worker was thus to be found in a broad range of agencies, each of which was designed to bring together certain specific individual needs and certain specific social resources. And, in each instance, the ground on which the profession walks is the agency's definition of the particular human problem to which the agency is enjoined by society to address itself. Placed thus, in Bertha Reynolds' old phrase, "between the client and the community,"[5] the social worker's job is *to represent and implement the symbiotic strivings,* even where these strivings are obscured from the individual, the society, or both.

It is important that it is not only "dysfunctioning"[6] that we are discussing here. While it is true that social workers operate in areas where the individual's ability to reach out is more or less seriously impaired, these situations are only part of the assigned field of action. The problems of symbiotic diffusion are as characteristic, in their own degree, of the developmental problems of youth as they are of the ordinary life tasks of ordering the individual-social encounters, as they are of areas in which the diffusion are so strong as to constitute "illness" of one sort or another. This is why the profession is so diverse, contains so many "subprofessions," and is so preoccupied with the problems of generic and specific.

The mediating function of social work is not a new idea. On the contrary, it has been stressed, though dimly viewed, by Richmond, Pray, and others. Our attempt here is bring it out more sharply, frame it schematically and, most importantly, relate the functional statement to the techniques involved in carrying it out. It is precisely the linkage between means and purposes that has escaped us over the years.

This mediating function, this special concern, is not with the individual alone, or with the system alone, but with the encounter between the two. This function is tacitly recognized by the other professions as they—law, medicine, education, the ministry—increasingly use social workers as allies in the pursuit of their own purposes; in the job of helping people use them and their institutions; in the hospitals, the prisons, the children's institutions, for the purpose of relating the integrating and differentiating functions. They use social workers more and more to provide a bridge between these two essential needs and to help people negotiate their services. The important point here is that social work is seen as a built-in *third force,* its function being to concern itself neither with the integration problems or the individualizing problems *per se,* but with the relationship between the two. To put it another way, the social worker is concerned with all the problems that arise in the relationship between people and their social systems; it works with the individual to use his systems; and it works with the systems to reach its people.

There is an implication here of "ombudsman"-ship, and the analogy is worth examining. The central notion behind the ombudsman function is that a society has grown too complicated to watch its people closely enough and that the system gets so difficult to negotiate that someone needs to be appointed to *guard the function* of serving people, to be sure that one does not fall between the cracks. Actually, it is a characteristic of dynamic systems that they must create a function like that. It is a hedge against their own complexity, wherein they, the people, together recognize that someone must be designated to see to it that the lines of communication do not become so snarled up that the whole thing gets too unwieldy to live with. Thus it is that the *equilibrating* force between the one and the many is built into the society as a whole. Note that it is *not* a "complaint department" wherein the ombudsman-social worker "represents" society and fixes its defects as they arise; nor is it an "advocate" that "represents" the individual and sees that his rights are not abrogated. It is the function of strengthening the interactive process between the two; so that the system *and* the individual can be strengthened in dealing with each other. When the social worker begins to act as an agent of of society whose job it is to identify completely with the message and transmit the values in toto, bringing the client into conformity with one or another pattern of predetermined behavior, *he loses his function* and with it his technical effectiveness as a practitioner. So it is, too, when he identifies completely with the individual and is seen by the client as an ally against the system. Both of these kinds of mistakes have been made and are being made all the time: in street club work, for example, we see practitioners fall into dysfunction both where they move to "prevent delinquency" and control antisocial behavior, and where they begin with the determination to "protect" the boys against the evil array of social pressures. Their job is to focus on the boys' efforts to find some role in society and the society's efforts to find a place for them. And where both parties have ostensibly "given up" the struggle to get together, the worker must remember that for each, they are the only game in town and remobilize the symbiotic strivings.

This functional position also has implications for the so-called "therapeutic" role, in which the social worker moves so completely into the individualizing process that he loses his connections with the tradition of the field with which he has been identified. In such instances, it has been properly said that the social worker may do quite effective work as a "therapist"; the question remains, however, whether he has not, in the process, entered another profession by the back door. The same may be said, of course, for the teacher, the nurse, who "qualify" themselves for therapeutic practice in a field where the criteria are vague, but leave their own particular fields of function as they move into a new and vaguely defined area of activity.

We have thus proposed a social work function that stimulates and protects the interaction between people and their systems, in a society where these channels are so fraught with dangers and so difficult to negotiate that someone must be designated to make them a primary focus of concern. The schematic representation for such a function places the social worker in this kind of position vis-a-vis both the client (individual or group) and the system (small or large):

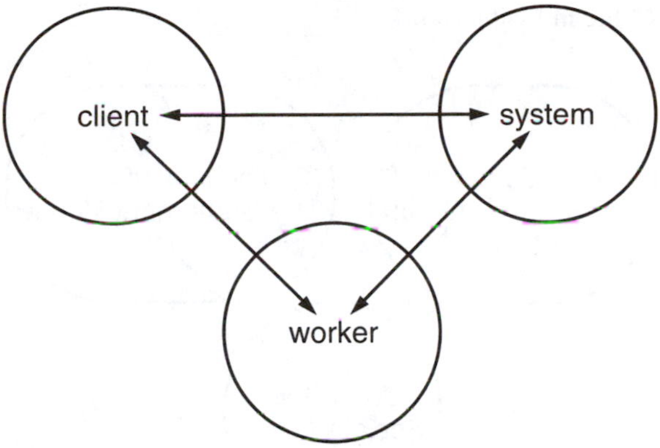

The arrows leading from client to system and back represent the core of the enterprise, the process that must be protected and facilitated; where it fails, the work fails, the system fails and the client fails, and the worker fails. Where it improves, all are closer to the spirit of the social work enterprise.

The arrows leading from the worker to the client and back represent all the work designed to help the client reach out to the system. The arrows leading from worker to system and back represent the work designed to help the system representatives reach out to the client. And *all* of the work that takes place, all of the acts that occur take place somewhere in this triangular relationship. If we would look for the technical skills of the social worker in society, we must find them somewhere along the worker-client and the worker-system axes. There is no place else to look. Another way of putting it is that if there is no work on one axis or the other, the function is lost. It should also be added that the same diagram is both universal and particular, depicting the role of the profession:

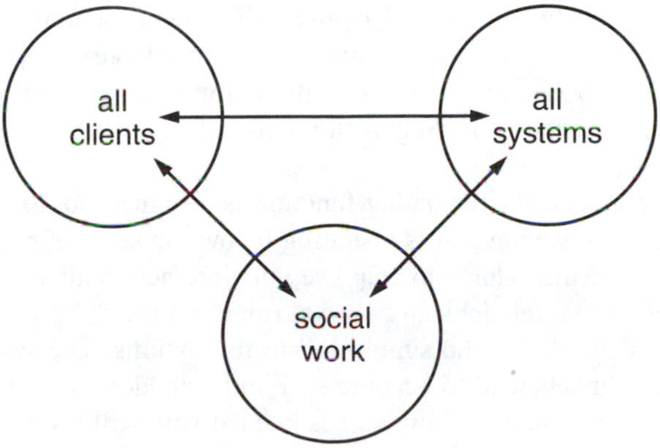

and the role of the individual worker:

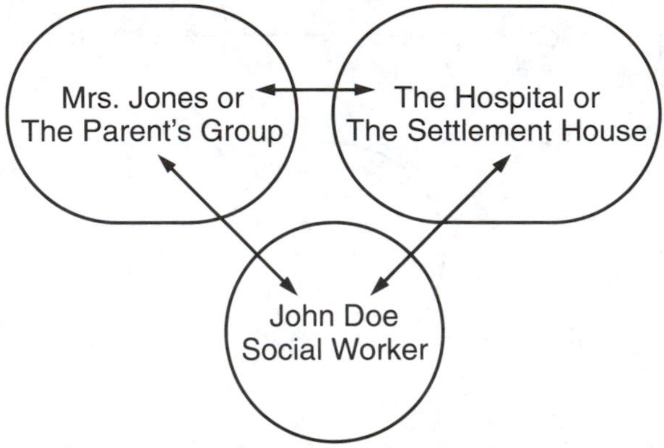

One may ask at this point: would it be possible to conceive of a division of labor within social work itself, allocating the left-hand arrow to one group and the right hand axis to another? One may, I suppose, make a case for that, but it would be difficult to carry it out technically, since the effort to help the client reach out to his systems is much more difficult where the worker cannot facilitate, through direct contact the simultaneous reaching out of the system itself, and vice-versa. The point is that the mediating function envisages two parties trying to get together, failing the means, and a third party trying to help them realize a difficult encounter.

There is another problem that needs to be addressed in order to understand this kind of function: it is the problem of conflict. The mediating role cannot be read as one which adopts a take-me-as-I-am, don't-try-to-change-me effort on the part of the worker. It is not, and cannot, be taken to mean that the effort is to get two parties to make peace and stop quarreling. Such an approach would call for soporifics, blandishments, reassurances—all of which would deny realities, rather than stress them and reach for them. Such an approach—often taken mistakenly by the "adjustment" school of human relations workers—moves almost inevitably into "missionary" type movements and, ultimately, becomes atechnical, calling for salesmanship and cover-up skills, rather than those of digging for real talk, allowing the chips to fall where they may.

On the contrary, the mediating function is designed not to avoid conflict but to bring it out wherever it is operating below the surface, because of fear. The object of the mediator is to help keep the interaction alive, not to allow it to deteriorate into a relationship between ruler and ruled, between those who steer the ship and those who simply roll to its rhythms. The system tends to rigidify, the channels tend to become stiff and orthodox, the arrows of influence tend to point one way. Someone is needed who will break up the rituals and reawaken the relationship as it was meant to function, so that the product of the whole is a composition that includes *all*—not just a few—of the aspirations of those who make up the system. When the interaction breaks down, it is not just the people who suffer; it is the collective itself, the organism that is established to serve the people. If one remembers that the profession is established not just to "save souls" (usually "left-out" souls), but to serve both people *and* systems to come into effective argument with each other, one begins to get a concept of the mediating job, one that will ultimately lead into a deeper understanding of the technical problems of developing social work skill.

Having now stated the general functional role of the social work profession, it remains to draw the action implications in specific terms. In order to do this, we will first have to look at the function in action, still in rather broad terms, laying out a broad strategy for work. Following this, we will be able to move, in subsequent chapters, into a detailed examination of the helping process.

References

1. Kenneth L. M. Pray, *Social Work in a Revolutionary Age and Other Papers* (Philadelphia: University of Pennsylvania Press, 1949), p. 275.
2. William E. Gordon, "A Critique of the Working Definition," *Social Work,* 7, 4 (October 1962).
3. Harriet M. Bartlett, "Toward Clarification and Improvement of Social Work Practice," *Social Work,* 3, 2 (April 1958), pp. 3–9.
4. Richard Boyd Ballou, *The Individual and the State* (Boston: Beacon Press, 1953), p. 9.
5. For a full discussion of Reynolds' thinking on the connection "between the client and community" see Bertha Capen Reynolds, *Between Client and Community,* New York: Oriole Editions, Inc., 1934, 1973.
6. Dysfunctioning as part of the purview of social work is discussed in Werner W. Boehm's curriculum study. See Werner E. Boehm, *Objectives of the Social Work Curriculum of the Future,* Volume I, Curriculum, New York: Council on Social Work Education, 1959.

6

Systems: The Special Case

I have said that the relationship between individuals and the specific systems that offer them demands and opportunities—the family, the peer group, the neighbor-clique, the agency, the welfare department and others—represents, in each instance, a *special case* of what we call, in general terms, the relationship between the individual and his "society." This means that the abstraction "society" is simply the sum total of all these very specific forms in which the collective—people together—presents itself in the life of all of us.

Thus, when we talk about "systems," we are talking about the society, except that we are showing in concrete terms how the society presents itself to people *at the point where they need help,* if indeed they need any. Indeed, the "minute particulars" of which I have spoken will, in each instance, deal with the specific efforts of people and their groups to negotiate one or another system in which it is necessary that they do something to make their lives more livable and more meaningful. If, then, the helping process is essentially an effort to help people negotiate their systems, it becomes necessary that we devote at least as much time and effort to understand what it is they are trying to negotiate as we have in the past devoted to understanding (diagnosing) the personalities and characteristics with which they approach their life-tasks.

This is not an effort to downgrade the inquiry and the preoccupation with *psychology*—that is precisely the error, positive and negative, of the "psychology v. sociology" arguers, and the one I am trying to warn against—but simply to point out that the concern with the *self*-work begs the question of what this is *for,* or the operations to which the self will be put to work. Or, more accurately, it separates the process into two parts. First, we will "get better" and then we will *do;* this again takes the "illness" approach of the medical model, leads us to think in terms of "therapy" and take us away from the problem which is central to the profession, namely that our job is to stimulate and protect the encounter between people and their systems.

Thus, they need a great deal about, not only the "psychology" of the client group, but the "sociology" of the institution they are trying to negotiate. The "right-hand arrow" is as important to us as the left. Most particularly, the two systems in which we will ourselves be present all the time and which will represent the everpresent point of negotiation—the *agency* in which the work takes place, and the *peer group* in which most of our helping movements will occur. The other systems will be important as they come into the foreground of concern, and it will be as important to us to understand how they operate, what moves them, what kinds of "resistance" and "ambivalence" they have institutionalized.

Let us begin, however, with the agency itself. What happens when the social purpose of a profession is brought into an agency with its own assigned social purpose? This relationship between institution and profession is, of course, germane not only to social agencies and their workers, but to schools and their teachers, hospitals and their doctors, and other institutions, like the settlements, that employ a variety of professions to carry out their tasks.

If we say (as have the "functionalists") that the professional *is* the agency[1] and that "his agency's purpose constitutes the whole of his effort"[2] then we deny the separate existence of a large, cohesive reference group, with its own subculture, its own tasks, its own social organization and, above all, its own charter and accountable function in society. It cannot be theoretically helpful to postulate a group of practitioners who have no special identity or social function until they deign to set themselves in the agency context, and who change their identity as they move from agency to agency. This seems to be contrary to the facts of history—the history of the development of professions in modern society.

It is, in fact, a kind of prehistory, reverting to a time when small groups of agendas banded together as *movements* to promote specific values and causes. In these settings, the workers carried the banner of *the movement,* with little awareness of that which they had in common with other workers doing similar work in other agencies. It was not until these connections became visible that a profession was born and began to work out its own contract with society. The new reference group then took its identity precisely from the fact that it was no longer bound to a particular agency and its function. The struggle is still operating in certain agencies, with staff wondering whether they are to be identified as "Jewish Center workers," or "Y" workers, or "settlement people," or as social workers capable of operating in any of these settings and others.

The issue was tackled considerably earlier in the Milford Conferences of the 1920s, where the attempt was made to find the core of professional practice that characterized the work going on in a variety of different settings. In group work, the struggle was delayed, the passage from "movement" to "service," from "cause" to "function" held up by the strong ideological origins of the group work agencies and the factors that brought them into being.

One may in fact say that the current concern with the "generic" and the effort to unify the practitioners of the various "methods" are continuations of the effort to develop and strengthen the identity and independence of the social work profession vis-a-vis the agency structures in which they operate.

Having said all this, it must now be made clear that it is equally unsound to view the social agency as a mere housing facility for a group of independent professionals, only vaguely and loosely connected to agency service and responsible only to their own professional codes of procedure. This is a current trend in casework practice—in the substitution of "consultation" by peers for traditional agency practice and supervisory accountability, in the de-emphasis on systematic recording, in the aspiration to private practice and, ultimately, in the "counseling centers" representing the private group practice of casework. This trend separates the nature of the skill from the nature of the service and moves social workers away from their function to a kind of misalliance with the medical-therapeutic enterprise.

Thus, while it is true that the profession and the social agency have two separate contracts with society, it is also true that the professional function is as closely tied to the institutionalized agencies of social welfare as the teachers to the schools and the mediating function of the social work profession begins in the effort to help the client negotiate the agency system through which it reaches out to the people it is supposed to serve. This is not a *healing* enterprise, essentially, but a *negotiating* one. Social workers heal neither agencies nor individuals; they help both these parties mobilize what they have by way of strength to reach out and do what they are supposed to do together. Hence the emphasis is on strength, not illness and the stress is on each one's ability to bring strengths to bear, with help, to play out their prerogatives within the agency context.

What is needed, then, is a conception of the agency-professional relationship that will preserve the identity of each and at the same time bind them together in a working interaction from which a definite and recognizable social service emerges—a product of two interdependent functions. The service produced expresses, simultaneously, a need of the collective, the society as a whole, and of the individuals who are served. The service must thus express the ways in which individuals call on their collective to do their work, which cannot be done by people alone; and the ways in which the people organize these institutions that will serve, organize them, and make them useful. The professional techniques have no other purpose but to facilitate the individual-social engagement and try to make them do what the exchange was intended to do.

We may thus define a social agency as a system of patterned relationships designed to address itself to the work that needs to be done on a designated social problem, clearly defined in the division of labor and held accountable by the public for that work. It is a relational system in which is played out the details of the symbiotic one-many relationship and it takes the form of a specific encounter between the needs of people and the demands and opportunities established by the collective. The agency thus represents, in concrete form, an effort of the collective to move out to its individuals with services which are of consequences both to the collective and to its people. It thus provides the meeting ground for the individual-social encounter—and, where necessary, the *battleground* on which will be fought out the individual's demand for attention and the collective's institutionalized, often rigid, demands for conformity and standardization.

The interplay, to be real, must be active, often quarrelsome, full of heat and excitement; if it is not, the terms of agreement are reached too easily and they must come under suspicion.

In each agency, the symbiotic strivings are seen in very specific form: the juxtaposition of a social need and an individual aspiration. In the Jewish Center, the drive toward cultural identification and unity on the one hand, and the needs of Jewish people to express their aspirations for group identification and belonging; in the family agency, the social need for family stability and the individual needs for fulfilment in the roles of mother, father, sibling; in the hospital, the social need for a healthy population and the need of individuals to be cured of disease.

Within each of these systems (agency), the function of the social worker is to mediate the transaction between the system and its clients—to represent and implement the symbiotic relationship between the agency service, representing society, and the individual who needs it. The worker thus offers the service of the agency to its people, and the experience of the people to the agency. He offers the service without becoming identified *as* the service; and he offers the troubles of the client to the agency without becoming identified *as* the client. His identification is *with the process itself* and it is this identification, and this function, that fashions and determines the nature of his skill.

The emphasis is thus placed, when we remove the "healing" stress that takes its power directly from the worker, with the building being largely incidental, on the terms of the engagement between the client and the agency. The precise nature of this engagement is expressed in a clear *contract* composed of a mutual understanding of both sets of need, both sets of stakes. Without such a clear understanding, the agency has few checks to exert on its power over the life of the client; it has no clear mandate for the extent of hegemony it will assert, beyond which it cannot go. And without such a contract, the client has no conception of the kinds of demands he may rightfully, and realistically place on the collective.

It follows, too, that where the contract between client and agency is not clear the social worker must fall into dysfunction: he cannot fail to feel that he must then make "choices," largely illusory, between the aspirations of the agency and those of the client—ending up by identifying first completely with one, and then with the other, bouncing back and forth on the horns of the individual-social dilemma. Under these conditions, the basis of the client-agency engagement is unclear (meaning that the symbiotic diffusion is ascendant and the worker is captured by it) and the worker, trapped by the dualism, orders his activity accordingly. In a settlement where the children are building model airplanes while the agency representatives are surreptitiously "building character," the opposite allegiances cry out for adherents; where there is not an open contract, the tensions draw the professionals into their orbit. Put another way, *there is no work to do* unless the terms of the individual-social engagement are open, honest, and explicit; where they are not, the professional is most often drawn into dysfunctional activity—"creating" the service himself, moralizing, "changing" people, therapeutics, teaching. His own aspirations, his own "social service," so to speak, rushes into fill the vacuum.

The Small Group System

The final step that remains, before moving into the details of the social work function in action—the nature of the helping process—is to examine the system formed by the worker and his clients.

We have, up to now, considered the relationship between individuals and their society, posing the social agency as a special case of this relationship. In this context, the social worker is designated to facilitate this interaction and help it do the work it is supposed to do. Similarly, we have suggested that the relationship between a social worker and a person in need of help is always an enterprise in systems-negotiation, whether that system be the agency, the welfare system, the schools.

Where, then, does the *group* fit? What kind of context is that? The situation here is complicated by the fact that two social processes are going on simultaneously: in one sense, the peer group is simply another special case of the individual-social engagement, in which each member needs help in negotiating the peer group system and enlisting it in his service, while the group itself needs assistance in integrating each of its individuals into the total scheme of activity.

On the other hand, and at the same time, the small group is an alliance of individuals, each using the group device as a way of assisting him to use the other systems of demand and opportunity with which they must come to grips. As such, the group may be defined as *a collection of people who need each other to pursue certain common tasks, in an agency that is hospitable to those tasks.* It is a mutual aid system and the efforts to make it strong are the efforts to provide a small society that will strengthen each individual in his efforts to cope with the demands of the larger.

This prospect offers the concept of the "two clients," in which the worker addresses himself to both the individuals in the group—helping them negotiate the peer group system—and to the group-as-a-whole, the collective itself—helping "it" address itself to the problems that collectives have to solve in order to survive and do the collective work. The idea here is that the social worker is always fixing his attention on two kinds of organisms in need of help: one is the individual, each individual, as he moves within the group; the other is the system itself.

When the worker faces his individuals, he is trying to help a member negotiate the others, find his place in the system, and address himself to the various tasks and demands that membership puts on him. Making his way in the world of the peer group is a difficult job—when to do and not to do, when to talk and not to talk, what kinds of roles to take and avoid, how to guide the perceptions that others have of him, how many risks to take, and so on. The tasks are complicated and demanding and it is not unreasonable to expect that the worker will consider part of his function to offer some help in coping with these. Further, as the group itself begins to set up a culture of its own, the demands on each member will increase. For now, the demands are composed of new elements that develop within the small society that is growing up around each member, the culture of the group. What emerges is a new set of values: what is right and what is wrong in *this* situation, what is allowed and not allowed, what is funny and not funny, appropriate and not appropriate. Negotiating this culture is no small job, and the worker addresses himself to the efforts of each individual to deal with the tasks of membership. In the process, he will be asked to help them negotiate other systems—the family, the school, welfare, employment, and others. How he responds to these requests will depend on the function of his agency, but the main point is that his work with them, the members, is most fruitfully seen as an enterprise in systems-negotiation, beginning with the present, small-group system itself.

Facing the group-as-a-whole—his "second client"—the worker's task is to help the members create a vehicle that will be useful to them. His aim here is to help them build a strong collective, one that will be responsive to their demands upon it, as each member makes his own unique set of demands. The collective, merging the aspirations of each member with the others, then faces its own set of tasks with which *it* needs help. What are these group tasks?

First, the group-client has tasks involving the processes of *formation,* in which it must make decisions about who is in and who is not, how to establish the procedures by which it will carry on its business. These are the *formation* tasks with which it may need help.

Second, there are the tasks of *internal structure* and organization, in which the collective must order its procedures to produce the processes it needs—the decision-making that it must produce in order to do its work.

Third, there are the tasks of *negotiating its own environment,* moving beyond its own borders and negotiating the systems with which it must come to grips.

And finally, there are the tasks of *individual need satisfaction* where the group must satisfy the demands of its members for meeting the needs for which it was formed.

In the foregoing, we have worked at establishing a sense of function out of which we could derive the tasks appropriate to the helping process and the skills needed to carry this process into fruition. First, we established a general sense of function in the general division of labor, in the society at large, and this sense of *assignment* had to do with mediating the efforts of individuals to use the systems through which society is supposed to serve them; and it had to do further with the mediation of the society's efforts to reach out to integrate its people. In more specific terms, this individual-social engagement, and the need for the mediating function was then envisaged in terms of the specific systems, the special cases, through which this individual-social relationship is carried out. And we saw how the social worker finds his place within each of these systems—the individual-worker, the family, the school, the group, the agency.

Having now established the sense of function—the mediating stance as a general concept—how does this translate itself into action? How do we now develop a scheme for showing the social worker in action, so that we can begin systematically to take inventory and describe in detail the movements by which he carries out the function, and further, how do we describe these movements so that we may get a sense of how these movements are carried out in the most direct way—that is, *skillfully?*

What we need now is a scheme that will carry out the ideas and concepts necessary to provide a theory of the helping process. In the next chapter, we will try to do this, preparing the way for the details of the helping process in action.

References

1. See Ruth E. Smalley's end comments on William Schwartz, "The Social Worker in the Group," *New Perspectives on Services to Groups: Theory, Organization and Practice, Social Work with Groups, 1961* (New York: National Association of Social Workers, 1961), pp. 7–34.
2. Smalley, *Ibid.*, p. 34.

Part 3:

The Practice of Social Work with Groups

7

From Function to Method: A Strategy

Our next job is to develop a general theoretical strategy around which to wind our examination of the helping process. What does it take to systematize the work on practice and produce a scheme that will carry the tactics and elaborate them in action?

We know that every profession has to stay close to the findings of science.

> Certainly the liaison of science and practice is a historic one; professions that do not keep pace with new knowledge soon cease to be professions. But it is also true that an orientation to scientific inquiry does not provide a simple method of converting facts into acts, scientific findings into appropriate professional behavior. The transition from knowing to doing is more complex.[1]

This complexity arises from two major problems: the first is that there is a growing, encyclopedic body of knowledge that needs to be taken into account—in the human relations fields, the knowing encompasses every conceivable aspect of human development and organization. Almost nothing is irrelevant to the one who would help people do their work in society and achieve some measure of peace with it. This overwhelming array of pertinent information produces what Millikan has commented on in the Bavelas-Perlmutter experiments at the Center for International Studies. He says that the data on these experiments suggest that "an individual's capacity for making sound judgment about a complex situation may be seriously impaired by supplying him with a lot of information which he believes should be relevant but whose influence on the situation is not clear to him."[2] And Harold Lasswell comments that "the idea of strategy does not depend upon omniscience."[3]

> The dilemma Millikan describes, a familiar one to group workers, seems to stem directly from the fact that the worker finds himself burdened with a great many answers for which he has no questions. He can

make little use of such information until he has ordered his experience into some coherent frame of reference from which he can develop his questions and focus his inquiry into the undifferentiated mass of scientific data. Thus the search for significant problems—for the questions that will draw forth the kinds of information most needed to throw light on the practical tasks of the group worker—calls for a theoretical effort designed to develop a system of interconnected concepts drawn from the experience of practice.[4]

The problem of finding the most relevant knowledge in an overwhelming mass of data is particularly poignant in a field like group work, where the productivity has jumped with startling suddenness in the last few years, turning out studies by the thousands, in addition to integrative efforts and theoretical ones in great number.[5]

> As the group work practitioner turns to face this overwhelming mass of material, how does he begin to make sense out of what is being offered, without abandoning his practice and devoting himself to the full-time study of social psychology? How does he establish connections not only with what has already been learned, but with the findings that keep purging from the laboratories from week to week? And, perhaps most important, how does he attain sufficient mastery of what has gone before so that he may tie in his own tentative and timid approaches to the systematic investigation of problems emerging from his own practice in working with groups? Obviously, if he is not to flounder in his own guilt and end with a sense of defeat at the whole prospect, he needs some approach by which he can limit and focus his search for knowledge.[6]

When we begin to make the effort to turn knowledge into action we run into the second problem, namely, that action is not directly deducible from knowledge.

> Those who assume that scientific evidence carries within it its own implications for behavior make the same mistake made by those in an earlier time who believed that action flowed inevitably and appropriately from one's convictions about values and goals. It is what Millikan refers to as the "inductive fallacy—the assumption that the solution of any problem will be advanced by the simple collection of fact."[7]
>
> . . . if we were suddenly and magically granted command of every shred of evidence ever produced on human behavior—if we were to learn it all by heart—we would as yet not have the slightest notion of what to do about it in practice. The idea that knowledge carries its own implications for action is what has come to be referred to as *scientism,* and it is no more useful than the old forms of *mysticism* by which it was assumed that appropriate professional activity followed directly from beliefs, values, and goals. Both expectations are unrealistic, in that they fail to take account of the fact the road from knowing to doing is bridged by purpose.[8]

Further, when the purposes, values, aspirations, are unstated, the principles are unverifiable, except by those who (unconsciously) share the same assumptions and accept the same absolutes. When these creeds are made explicit, practice principles can be verified by all: given a fact, and given a valued outcome, the action will or will not provide the implementing force. This is how—and in no other way—practice can be said to be testable.

> It is, therefore, suggested that practice theory, or method theory, can be defined as a system of concepts integrating three conceptual subsystems: one which organizes the appropriate aspects of social reality, as drawn from the findings of science; one which defines and conceptualizes specific values and goals, which we might call the problems of policy; and one which deals with the formulation of interrelated principles of action. Each of these constitutes a major area of investigation, each has its own conceptual problems and each is related to the others within a total scheme.[9]

The key word here is "integrated"—that is, it is not enough to make an inventory of the knowledge, goals, and skills, but it is necessary to show the relevant features of each area—relevant to one's function—and to show how one affects the other—the relationship between knowing and willing, willing and doing, and knowing and doing. To put it another way, what is the relationship between science and policy and between policy and action? For example:

> The relationship between science and policy is reciprocal. Science takes its cues from human problems and yields its best answers to those who are disciplined and urgent in their search for solutions. The contribution of science to policy is to define boundaries, limit expectations and clarify the range of alternatives.[10]

Similarly, the search for the most relevant areas of knowledge—to be culled out of the mass of data—is enhanced by the practitioner's experience with people. These experiences have, for example, singled out the problems of individual-social, structural-dynamic, internal and external determinants of change, the problems of stress, the relationship between authority dynamics and those of intimacy, and others.

The theory, then, will try to integrate the variables of *social reality, policy,* and *action.* Each sphere will have to identify its own problems and relate those problems to the other spheres of concern. Another way of putting this is that we will have to integrate problems related to what "is," what "should be" and what "should be done."

Thus, we will be asking, throughout, three main questions: What *assumptions* are we making about the nature of reality, and what science do we have at our command that may help us? Second, what do we want to make happen—what are the *valued outcomes?* And third, given these realities, and these purposes, what are the *acts* designed to implement these outcomes?

It remains to get somewhat more specific about the circumstances to which this scheme can be applied—knowledge about *what?* What specific *outcomes?* and action *where?* For this purpose, we will suggest that it would be helpful to divide the work itself into *four phases,* roughly corresponding to the chronological stages into which the worker's activity divides itself as he goes about his job with the client group. The stages are as follows:

First, there is a preparatory phase, in which the worker *tunes in* to the ensuing encounter with the client group; second is the phase in which the worker helps the group make its *beginnings;* third is the period of *work* on the matter for which they came together; and finally, there are the *transitions and endings,* concerned with the problems of leaving, ending, and separation. These phases, it should be realized, apply to the total group experience as well as the separate meetings—each encounter has its own tuning, beginning, middle, and ending phase. The same logic and the same necessities apply to the specific and the general aspects of the worker-group experience.

In each of these stages of work, one must then ask the three basic questions—what is, what should happen, and what do I do about it.

There are some general ideas that we must bear in mind as we move now into the work of describing the details of the helping process. First, as I have mentioned, the phases are being described as both those of a single encounter and a whole series of encounters; they are meant to apply to a single meeting and the entire life of a group. Second, I will be assuming that there is a kind of exchange between worker and client that I have called the *parallel processes*—that is, there is a process of helping, and there is a process of using help. These processes are interdependent but separate; each has its own characteristics and its own life and one must never be mistaken for the other. In the division of labor between worker and client, each has his own job to do and when either tries to step out of his own role there is dysfunctional behavior on both sides. Third, I will be trying throughout to avoid the dilemma of "feeling" v. "tasks." In order to do this, I will assume that in any given situation the members have work to do, certain tasks to pursue. I will assume, further, that they cannot do these tasks properly unless they can invest feeling in the job. Thus, my key to the problem is that people need to work on the problems for which they came together, that the work is mechanical and useless unless they are emotionally involved in what they are doing, and that the focus is therefore on *feelings in pursuit of a task.* It is therefore equally inappropriate to ask the client to "stop working and examine his feelings" as it is to ask them to "stop examining his feelings and start working." The game is *work,* that is the preoccupation with the task to be done, and the examination of feelings is important only as it is relevant to the work. And work, properly defined and understood, is activity invested with affect.

In the succeeding chapters, I will examine each of the stages of work in turn, relating knowledge, purpose, and action to the problems posed for the worker in each. Wherever possible, I will use records to illustrate the points about worker activity.

References

1. William Schwartz, "Toward a Strategy of Group Work Practice," *Social Service Review,* September 1962, p. 269.
2. Max Millikan, quoted in William Schwartz, "Toward a Strategy of Group Work Practice," *op. cit.,* p. 269.
3. Harold D. Lasswell, quoted in William Schwartz, "Toward a Strategy of Group Work Practice," *op. cit.,* p. 269.
4. Schwartz, *Ibid.,* p. 269.
5. For an extensive bibliography in this area, see William Schwartz, "Small Group Science and Group Work Practice," *Social Work,* 8, 4 (October, 1963), pp. 39–46.
6. *Ibid.,* p. 40.
7. Schwartz, "Toward a Strategy of Group Work Practice," *op. cit.,* p. 269–70.
8. Schwartz, "Small Group Science and Group Work Practice," *op. cit.,* p. 43.
9. Schwartz, "Toward a Strategy of Group Work Practice," *op. cit.,* p. 270.
10. *Ibid.,* p. 273. See also Max Millikan, *op. cit.,* and Harold D. Lasswell, *op. cit.,* for the science-policy relationship.

8

Preparation for Work: The "Tuning In"

What does it mean to prepare for entry into the life of a group? And how does this preparation phase repeat itself each time one gets ready to reenter group life from encounter to encounter?

The task of tuning in begins with the realization that you are about to enter a process that began a long time before you came and will continue for a long time after you leave. It is important for the worker to understand that he does not *create* a process, but simply enters one already in motion. The worker's problem is to prepare to become a meaningful factor in their lives—enter, make his impact, and leave. This perspective should serve to scale down his aspirations to manageable proportions, giving up at the outset any illusions about changing people's personalities in any fundamental ways, or revolutionizing lifestyles. The group experience may indeed have a very important impact on the consciousness of its members, but this can only happen when the experience itself is left to happen—and most often, the worker's aspirations about "changing" the members in radical ways will tend to inhibit rather than assist this process of group impact. Most of us know from our professional experiences that such aspirations are illusions—that people don't lend themselves to being readily invaded, that all professional impact is limited impact, even though some incidents have moved us profoundly for a time. People have a way of defending themselves against attempts to change them in ways that run counter to the ways in which they have organized their lives.

The tuning-in process thus addresses itself to the question: How can I prepare myself to enter (or reenter, if we are past the first meeting) the group's life-process, so that I may begin the work as soon as possible? With what *set* shall I make my entry? The worker will need to listen for the cues that will enable him to respond to the subtlest requests for help; thus this first problem will be to sensitize himself to the possible ways in which such requests will be made. The worker readies himself to receive cues that are minimal, subtle, devious, and hard to detect except by a very sensitive and discerning instrument. It is important to note that this notion is different from certain current conceptions about the preparation of workers, with the emphasis on the formulation of "goals" and the "diagnostic" emphasis that creates structural and cross-sectional versions of what the client *is* (and ought to be), rather than what he might *do* in a given situation.

If we say that a person tends to *do* what he *is,* and that he *is* what he *does,* the fact is that this is a proposition that needs more detailed examination. We have not been very successful in predicting behavior from our personality assessments; people tend to do different things in different situations, and they may very well be said to "be" different things in different situations.

In any event, the problem remains the same for the worker in the tuning-in phase: he must use his prior knowledge to anticipate clues that will be thrown up so quickly, and in such disguised ways, that the worker will miss them unless he is somehow "tuned" to their frequency. We may if we like call this a kind of "preliminary empathy," as the worker prepares to enter the process going on in the lives of his group members. For example, a young person properly tuned to a group of aged clients may instantly perceive the possibility that the comment "What a nice young man" may be a suspicious rather than an approving judgment: "What could you know about our troubles?"

In this phase, the worker tries to unearth the *themes* that may emerge in the group at the outset, and the ways (disguised) in which these themes may be expressed. For example, a group of adoptive parents in the period of agency supervision may be expected to express in various ways their fear of the "bad seed," the ordeal of "telling" the child that he is adopted, the perception of the agency as rigid and judgmental, the ambivalence toward the supervising social worker, and other specters. Thus, the tuning-in operation is designed to make oneself receptive to veiled communications, knowing as we do what may be of concern to this class of client—the aging, the adolescent, the adoptive parent—and from *these clients* in particular. It is an attempt to relate knowledge—general and specific—to action as the worker prepares himself for action. And the problem is to select those areas of knowledge that may be the most useful, rather than simply interesting and "potentially" valuable.

To illustrate, here is a worker preparing to move into a new group, and writing down her efforts to tune in to what may happen. It is a potential group of single parents, and it would be organized by a neighborhood center:

> I see this group as an opportunity for parents who are raising their children alone to get together and, with the help of a social worker, to work on the many problems they face in their situations. The emphasis would be on mutual aid—the sharing of their common concerns as single parents, with the purpose of obtaining support, advice and assistance with their problems. The parents would have a chance to share their feelings and experiences with others who are in similar positions and can

understand what is involved. The work would center around exploring and examining the problems they face, looking at them from various perspectives, dissecting and partializing them into handleable pieces and coming up with possible alternatives for dealing with them to lead to greater satisfaction for parents and children. The parents could use each other as well as the worker to sound out ideas, clarify their problems and feelings about them, obtain new perspectives and suggestions, and gain support and security in the knowledge that they are not alone.

The two main roles of the worker, that I see, would be (1) to facilitate work on problems by the group members by helping communication get started and flow and by helping members to deal with obstacles to their progress, and (2) to serve as a resource person and source of knowledge.

The group members might decide to bring in experts such as child psychologists, teachers, or others to increase their knowledge about development, child rearing practices, and other areas of concern. I would see these kinds of sessions as having the purpose of giving the parents more information which they could bring into their discussions and use in their own lives. However, I would not see this group as a lecture course, where answers were given by a teacher but as a chance for them to be actively involved in dealing with their own problems.

It is possible that prospective group members might want to use the group for a social purpose—either to make friends who "are in the same boat," or as a vehicle for meeting companions of the opposite sex. I feel that some decision should be made on an administrative level as to whether this agency wishes to offer this kind of service.

My suggestions for forming this group would be as follows:

1. Send a letter to all eligible parents describing the agency's ideas for this kind of group and inviting them to an open meeting. (I would be glad to help draft this letter.)
2. Follow up this letter with calls or home visits to obtain feedback and an estimate of potential interest.
3. Hold one or two open meetings to come up with a tentative contract of what the group will be for, incorporating agency service with members' desires and needs.
4. Close the group, formalize the contract, and begin the work.

I have purposefully not delineated specific problems or areas of focus for the group as I think this part of the work to be engaged in by all involved. However, I have some ideas about possible areas to be covered, including the following:

1. Difficulty of being both father and mother, and feelings of inadequacy and inability to do this. (Possible overcompensation, or rejection of child as a result)

2. Problems of explaining why one parent is absent. Bringing up a child with healthy attitudes toward absent parent and symbols of that parent.
3. Knowledge of (a) developmental needs of children, (b) consequences of loss of parent, and (c) child rearing techniques.
4. Loneliness and needs for adult companionship. Consequent guilt, resentment toward burden of children.
5. Realistic personal needs of single parent and how to deal with these without harming the children.
6. Specific problems with children—acting out, withdrawal, learning difficulties. Problems at various ages of children.

I feel there will also be internal group concerns, such as:

1. Finding ways of working together, selecting areas of mutual concern and relevance, while getting everyone's needs into the pot.
2. Developing bonds of intimacy and trust, which enable sharing of personal and emotional concerns.
3. Social concerns, establishing friendships.
4. Using the worker as a helping person.

In this excerpt, we see the worker tuning herself to the forthcoming engagement in several ways. We see her rehearsing the *contract,* so that she may be clear about the agency stake, the clients' stake, and the common ground between the two. Next, she tries to envisage what *her role* will be in the transaction, picking up cues for the kinds of action demands that may be made on her. She then considers some of the *action possibilities,* the "program" that may emerge from the work. She envisages the *procedures* by which the group may be formed and put on its way to work. And she tries to anticipate the *themes of concern*—including those of the members and those of the group-as-a-whole, external and internal pressures, personal concerns, and structural ones.

We note that she has the problem, in this exercise, of making herself as receptive as possible to future clues, but at the same time it is important that she not become so finely tuned that she will be oblivious to "static" as it were—so receptive to certain clues that she will ignore others that she had not anticipated. In the example above, we see the worker tuning herself *too grossly*—since she addresses herself to the problems of the class she is interested in—single parents—but neglects to interest herself in the specific people—the specific problems—that she will dealing with. Also, she remains too gross in her preliminary empathy by failing to speculate on how these "themes" may show themselves in action: for example, that the guilt about their own "personal" (sexual) needs may create a testing series in which they will try to find out from her what her moral codes are about extramarital intercourse—and from the others as well. If she anticipates not only the theme but the manifestation, she will be quicker to decode the messages and make it easier for them to move into this work more quickly.

Here is another example of a worker preparing herself to meet a new group. This is a group of girls in a residential treatment center, about to move into a public high school. The worker speculates as follows:

> I see as the purpose of this group to provide an opportunity for a number of youngsters who will be *entering a community school* to get together, and with the help of a social worker work on and help each other with the common concerns they have about this venture.
>
> My assumption, which I will present to the kids, is that they may have many concerns about entering the school next year. (Some of the kids have already talked with me individually about their concerns.) It is new and unfamiliar and very different from the small, protected, atmosphere of our public school. The rules are different, the requirements are different—and the people (teachers and other students) will be new. They may be worried or eager or scared or confused or want more information, or a million other things. My second assumption is that they can help each other around these concerns, so they'll be better prepared and more comfortable when they do go on to W. . . . The group can give the kids a chance to really talk about what it means to them to take this new step. It might help them to break down some of their larger questions into smaller, more manageable pieces. It might be an opportunity for them to express some of their fears and apprehensions and hopefully to gain some support and security in the knowledge that they are not alone. It might also help them pull out and recognize some of their strengths, and to focus on the positive aspects of moving to a community school. The group can be a chance to gain more information, so W . . . becomes more real and is not a big, frightening unknown. It might be a chance to test out new ideas about how to deal with the school situation—how to meet the demands, how to get along with the other kids, how to "make it" more successfully than they have in the past.
>
> I see as my primary task as the group worker to help the kids work. This would include helping them decide what issues and problems they want to work on, helping them set up and stick to the ground rules for the group, helping them get over obstacles to open communication. In the beginning, we'd have to carve out together a way of working—a way of talking freely and sharing with each other. We'd have to create an atmosphere of trust, where sharing of difficult feelings was sanctioned, where people could be honest even if it was painful. This will not be easy and as the obstacles come up I will help the kids deal with them. I also see my role to help the kids tackle their concerns in small pieces, by breaking down and partializing large problems and overwhelming feelings into their components so they can deal with them. I will try to help them pull out commonalities and differences among themselves so they can measure themselves, and examine their differences. In short, my role as the worker is to help the kids begin to work and then keep working on the task they've agreed to come together to work on.

Again, there is a question of making the tuning in *finer:* she leaves out her relationship to the system they will be trying to negotiate—her access to the W . . . school people; and her access to other resources and information about their problem.

Tuning-In Phase

I have tried to do some premeeting tuning in to the kids and their feelings and have come up with a number of themes which I feel may be operative as we try to begin to work as a group. By keeping them in mind and by being sensitive when they come up, however subtly, I think it will be easier to deal with them and help the kids tackle the problems they present. Through my awareness, I'll be conveying a number of messages which I think are important:

1. That I know what's going on and can help the kids recognize and sort out various, even conflicting moods, and feeling tones. That I try to understand how they feel.
2. That I can live with ambiguity and conflict and confusion and difficult times and can help the kids deal with these things.
3. That I try to be real and call things like I see them and that it's okay for the kids to do the same.

Below are some of the themes I have come up with:

1. Suspicion—of me as an authority and of the whole authority structure here at the institution as we offer this new service. The kids will probably be thinking, "What's the angle?" "What do they want from me?" "Why pick me for this?" "Where will it get me?" "What do I do to play ball?"
2. Unwritten code at the institution—don't talk real to adults when your friends (peers) are around. Don't let your friends know that you respect the authority figure enough to reveal pieces of yourself, especially emotional ones, to them, or that you'd go to them for real help.

Again, how would these come out in the group—in words and actions?

3. Another unwritten code of the institution—show plenty of bravado in front of peers. Don't acknowledge real fears or problems. Make them think you're cool, that no one and nothing can hurt you and that you have everything under your control. (Obviously this code will conflict with the group norm I'll be proposing of honest sharing and mutual aid—and this will cause problems.)

It is interesting that the worker presents only her perception of their negative affect—what is *their* stake in "honest sharing" and "mutual aid"? The grossness of the tuning in here will cause problems for all of them, when the worker is unprepared to reach for the *ambivalence* about the contract, rather than just the negatives.

4. Newness of legitimized mutual aid at the institution—this includes the above two "codes." Since this kind of group is new, the kids and I will

> have to hammer out together what it means and how to use it. This will include coming up with ground rules and deciding who sets what and who enforces what, working out discipline, use of language in front of me, appropriate topics. The kids will probably be especially interested in testing me to see if I will really allow them to help each other find solutions to their problems—solutions that I might not always agree with—or if I've gotten them together for a collective "brainwashing" on how to behave at the school. The group will give them a certain amount of strength and power which we will all have to recognize and deal with.

Note here the points at which the worker begins to get intellectualized and abstract—concentrating on her own need for order and to protect herself, rather than the *empathic* exercise that would stress their feelings and the cues they will give of what they see through their eyes.

Work Themes

I have also tried to tune in to possible problems and concerns around the general issue of the High School. My ideas are in no way meant to limit the kids, but to help me get closer to what they might be thinking about. I may offer some of these if it seems appropriate—if handles are needed to get to work, or if it seems they are thinking about them but are having difficulty verbalizing.

1. Reaction of other kids to the school . . . to our kids—"are we the crazy kids from the institution?"
2. The meaning of the label of being at the school—to teachers, other kids, themselves—"Are we emotionally disturbed?" "Do *they* think so?"
3. Fear of failure—"Can I make it with normal kids?" "Will I get along?" "Can I keep up with the work—is it harder?"
4. Consequences of difficulty or failure—"What'll happen if I can't make it?" "Who will be there to help me?" "Who will pick up the pieces?"
5. General information about the school: Objective—facts, rules, requirements, programs. Subjective—campus scuttlebutt—what the grapevine says.

Here we can note the absence of themes with regard to *this* group making it fun—will it be interesting, will she be strict. As the worker follows with a section on the "Involvement of Both Schools" and a "Proposal for Forming This Group," her thinking gets very "logical," and the tuning in is cased in broad strokes for *these* youngsters in *this* situation. For example, she does not use what she knows about *them,* speculating mostly about *class* phenomena, on which she does well. And she doesn't turn the speculation into anticipated behaviors.

As we move now into some of the *reality* assumptions pertinent to this stage of work, it is necessary to point out that the hypotheses in any phase of human endeavor are almost endless, depending on the level of abstraction one chooses, the particular phase of the subject one turns to, and so on. Therefore, as I have indicated before, the prospect is not one of finding *all* the relevant hypotheses, but just a few that seem to be the most immediately applicable to the situation in which we are interested.

One may wonder why I start with the objectivities, the facts, rather than the valued outcomes, or even the acts themselves. The truth is that there is no real reason, since wherever one begins one must relate the other two sets of variables anyhow. Thus, one may in fact begin with what you hope will happen, and go from there to what there is about human behavior that makes you think it might, and from there to the specific acts you think will bring about your purpose. Or one may begin with what you expect to do, showing how this is based on the following assessment of the way things are and the following things you hope to bring about in the immediate process. And so on. Our beginning with the reality variables is therefore arbitrary and not meant to signify anything but that this seems to me to be the best way to do the exercise.

Furthermore, it must be emphasized that what follows is indeed an exercise, not a definitive "proof" of anything at all. What I mean to do here is to choose from many possibilities; others may choose different facts, different purposes, and different acts. What matters is that my facts should be real, the purposes reasonable, and the acts based on the other two. In order to gain internal consistency, each set must be integrally related to the others; and it is internal consistency that we are after, in order to create a viable strategy, based on scientific findings and certain specific purposes consistent with the tasks at hand. What I am trying to create is a model of a helping theory; everyone is free to fill in his own details, if the model itself seems productive of useful strategies.

What, then, are some of the assumptions on which the worker will base his purposes and movements in the "tuning in" stage of work, the preparation for the client-group's encounter with the worker?

First, there is a *continuity* in human experience, meaning that people's expectations in new situations will be built on their memories of old ones.

Second, people will tend to respond, in these new situations, as they think others will expect them to respond, beginning with certain *roles* that have brought them rewards in similar previous situations.

Third, running throughout much of our speculation about human behavior, and particularly crucial to the opening stages of a relationship, is the idea that people's verbal communications generally convey only a small part of what they mean. There is a quality of *indirectness* in human interaction that serves to divert and obscure the messages that pass from one to the other.

Fourth, beginnings somehow call into question the matter of personal adequacy—that is, the fear of incompetence is heightened by finding oneself in a new situation.

Fifth, the fear of authority is stepped up by the expectation of new demands; these expectations and demands activate dependency and increases the fear of people who are able to do something to you, to take some of the control over your life.

Sixth, the new situation also tends to trigger expectations of *satisfaction,* the desire to achieve, as well as the hope that one will be recognized, drawn out, helped to achieve one's potential. There are a number of assumptions here on the relationship to authority, to the *new* authority, with the ambivalence including fears and hopes, demands and resistances, and so on.

Seventh, a new authority person entering one's life will tend to be cast in the role of *expert,* of one who knows, and this idealization will be in direct proportion to the degree of one's dependency on him for certain results. The worker will, in fact, judge the amount of dependency by the degree of idealization that occurs.

Eighth, the task for which the members are coming together will, in addition to its positive valences also generate patterns of avoidance; there is something about what they want to do together that will make them want *not* to work, as well as to work. There is something here that is akin to the familiar notion of resistance, but we need to get closer to the experience, the feeling involved in being repelled by the very task that attracts us.

We can continue to generate these assumptions almost indefinitely, trying to come in as closely as possible to the realities of what people will bring to the initial, or the next, encounter. What is important is not that we pin down each of the possible assumptions, or that we put these statements in one or another of the various theoretical languages (Freudian, or others) but that we try to isolate as many as will help us tune in and sensitize ourselves to the actual possibilities inherent in the forthcoming encounter. We can, of course, ritualize this process as other forms of professional preparation have been ritualized—but the emphasis on the *terms of the encounter,* rather than the *description of the clients* should go a long way to avoiding this kind of ritualization. We must prepare for a process, rather than steep ourselves in structural analysis. The emphasis is thus on what may happen, not what sort of creature, or creatures, we will be facing.

What, then, are my *valued outcomes?* That is, if I do it right, the tuning in, what will it look like? The important thing to remember about this concept of "goals," if you will, is that the accent is on *immediacy*—that is, if the aspirations are too big, too futured, too grand, they lose their value in guiding strategy and become mere "prayers," designed to give a sense of purpose without working for it. If I am to relate knowledge and action to what I hope to achieve, the achievement must happen soon, it must be small and measurable, and one must know whether it has happened or not. Thus, if my valued outcome is "adjustment" or "happiness" or avoidance of neurotic conflict, I can do little with it except, indeed, to pray for the best. If, on the other hand, it is to "bring out relevant feeling on the issue," or to "present the agency's reason for calling them together, in terms that will seem clear to them," I can begin to relate my knowledge of how people perceive and hear and listen, and fashion the words to do the job.

Another comment, which would be equally appropriate to make about the *knowledge* variables. I have said that all of them could not possibly be touched on, but that appropriate ones need to be selected. The same is true of outcomes, since here again the level of abstraction will determine the number of aspects that we can select for attention. We are actually a bit better off here in "outcomes" because the accent on *immediacy* and *recognizability* will tend to keep us to small movements and low levels of abstraction. However, it may still help to consider that one may *stratify* his sample of variables: that is, find the *areas* in which he will want to work, the *classes* of variables in which he is interested. In the tuning-in phase, for example, one would look for factors dealing with the *worker* and his perceptions, the *members* (individually), the *group,* the *setting* and situation.

Moving now to the valued outcomes of the tuning-in phase: I will be learning the language of hidden meanings, hidden agendas, so that I, the worker, will become a more sensitive instrument for decoding these messages and signals. I should become better prepared to understand the connections that will be implicit in the interaction, the connections between ideas and experience, ideas and their accompanying feelings.

I would like to understand better how they might perceive, rather than being totally preoccupied with how I might *wish* to be perceived. The worker, further, should be able to connect *his* feelings about beginnings to *theirs,* readying himself to move out to them as he wants them to move out to him. For example, if the worker is about to move in to work with a group of aged people—and if he has tuned in properly, he will be less apt to preen himself when they say, "What a nice young person!" and more apt to say "I know, but I'll do the best I can to understand."

The worker will try then to respond to the meaning of their words, their symbolic *communications,* rather than to the symbols themselves as if they constituted the only reality. In this stage, all of the valued outcomes are related to the *state of being* the worker wishes to achieve—and here is illustrated the *short-range* nature of the valued outcomes. One may get lost here by stating many aspirations about how the first meeting should turn out, what we hope to achieve there. But that would lose the emphasis of what the first stage is for—which is to produce certain states of readiness in the consciousness of the worker, in the hope that these "rehearsed" states will make him quicker to pick up cues that are difficult to discern and may very well be taken for something else.

The third task before us is to move now to the action components of this stage of work. What is it that the worker *does* as he prepares for his first, or next, encounter with the client group?

First, there is a whole category of acts that we might call the *empathic* movements. This involves a kind of *actor's exercise,* demanding the exercise of one's imagination to simulate the feeling and color of someone else's life and experience. The actor model seems significant here: this seems to be what Stanislavsky was trying to do—to get his actors to reproduce an experience with their whole selves, rather than just with their heads, or for that matter, just with their instincts. Stanislavsky had a strong sense of the connection between intellect and emotion, ideas and feelings. The empathic skills in the helping person demand a similar connecting between thoughts and emotions and demand, further, the ability to imagine himself into another person's existence—or as much of it as he can manage.

This is particularly difficult in those situations where the worker is about to project himself into experiences in which he has not stored up his own matching experiences, feelings, and ideas—a young worker with very old people, a male worker with an unmarried mother, a southern white with a black group, trying to help a young delinquent if we come from a protected middle-class culture. What does the world feel like to them? What will they see in me? What forms will their messages—to me and to each other—take, exactly? The attempt to develop this "preliminary empathy" is guesswork, it is speculative, it will misfire in part—but without it one can never develop any real and legitimate helping process, geared to the experience—the pain and the capacities—of the clients themselves.

It is important to remember that the inability to call up the exact life experience of the unmarried mother, the aged client, the young delinquent, is not necessarily a final deterrent to the worker trying to tune in. What he does is to call forth those elements of his own history that correspond most closely to what he is about to see before him. Thus, he has experienced rejection, as the unmarried mother is experiencing social punishment; he knows what it is like to disobey and be afraid and defiant, as is the young delinquent.

There is a category of skills that emerge from what one might call *acts of patterning,* involving the ability to put information together—from the record, from one's knowledge of the problems and their demands, from "diagnostic" attempts made by others—in order to create a mosaic of expectations. Here again the problem of making decisions about relevance creates certain complexities: we have for a long time deluded ourselves that the more knowledge we have about a particular case the more we will understand about it. This creates a search for "all there is to know" and the piling of datum on datum, a counsel of perfection and an unshakable thirst for the perfect diagnosis. The fact is that such an approach is just as apt to immobilize us, to prevent action, and distract us from the effort to *strategize* about the work. Bonner states that

> research has shown that it is difficult to predict the behavior of persons in a group from pre-measures of personality variables.[1]

And from Gordon Allport: It is simply not true that successful treatment invariably presupposes accurate diagnosis.[2]

The group work literature, on the contrary, tells us that what the group worker needs to know is human behavior, group dynamics, the community, the world. The prescription, of course, is what I have called a "counsel of perfection" and it leads to nothing but a vague conception of the pertinent knowledge that one uses in the preparation period. The real question for the worker is: what kinds of knowing will be most helpful in the forthcoming engagement—and it is in this respect that the patterning of useful information becomes crucial.

As it will be important to make larger ideas out of many small ones, it will also be necessary to make small ones out of large ones, or to *partialize* the information available, so that one may focus on that which is most specific in the upcoming situation. The demand to partialize requires that we make ourselves ready to read the cues not of *all* clients in this class (the old, the foster parent, the adolescent, the heart patient), but of *these* clients as well—not *all* of the poor people, but these in particular. The process of generalizing about classes in order to build our sophistication has gained us a great deal, of course—it is part of a scientific process; but it has on occasion also lost us a great deal—particularly when it becomes not a generalizing so much as a stereotyping. One may grow too comfortable with generalizations like "poor people don't talk" and "working-class men beat their wives"—until one has to work with real people and face the specific facts of their existence.

The stereotyping that comes from settling only for class characteristics usually comes from the worker's need to make some kind of theoretical point, a need that makes him tendentious in his thinking and loses the point of the tuning-in exercise. The point he wishes to make has generally to do with the effort to superimpose one set of variables *over* another—the "content" v. the "feeling," the "sociological" over the "psychological"—or vice-versa.

Another set of tuning-in skills has to do with the ability to plan a strategy, a focus for his work, carrying him into direct and unembarrassed involvement in areas that one may expect to be awkward, taboo, painful, or otherwise proscribed and difficult to enter. This again is our old friend the relationship between what one knows and what one is preparing to do—or, if we will, the connection between "diagnosis" and "treatment." Those who have worked in certain psychiatric settings are no strangers to the frustration of reading, or writing, a detailed statement that describes the patient very well but carries no implications for *strategy,* no focus for the ensuing encounter, no intimation as to what the worker should therefore do or say in the next interview or group meeting.

The payoff, therefore, for the kind of preparatory process designated as tuning in is in the planning of strategies, strategies designed to help the worker convert his heightened sensitivity into acts directed to the clients' responses. The worker is asked: In view of this preparation, in view of what you know and feel and expect, and in view of the decoding apparatus you have readied, how do you plan to move? It is this *impetus* that enables him to move more freely into ambiguity and conflict—so freely that he will, far from "cooling" difficult material, ask for it, reach for it, and make himself accessible to it where most people would treat it with apprehension and embarrassment.

An important footnote: the process of tuning in makes the worker highly attentive to important cues. However, it is important to achieve this state of attentiveness without becoming hypnotized. That is, one may be so finely tuned that he will be oblivious to cues he never anticipated, to which he is *not* attuned. Often workers will prepare so well that they cannot tolerate surprises and perseverate furiously for what they need to find, rather than for what is there in front of them. In the process of tuning in, one must be careful to keep one's peripheral vision intact.

References

1. Hubert Bonner, *Group Dynamics: Principles and Applications* (New York: Ronald Press, 1959), p. 20.
2. Gordon W. Allport, *Personality and Social Encounter* (Boston: Beacon Press, 1960), p. 280.

9

Beginnings: The Contractual Phase

This is the stage of work that describes the entrance of the helping person into the group process, both in the first contact and in all subsequent openings, meeting by meeting. The beginning phase is that in which the worker tries to help the group make its first moves under clear conditions for work. He asks them to understand the terms of the arrangement—the "contract"—under which they have established themselves within the agency context. In effect, he is asking the members to understand the connection between their needs as they feel them and the agency's reasons for offering help and hospitality: the contract embodies the stake of each party.

> By way of opening this first group meeting (of a series of four) I remarked that the couples had been parents for a matter of months now . . . many of them are still in the early stages of parenthood and are trying to make adjustments required of their new roles as parents. I said I was wondering what this new experience has meant to each of them; what adjustments have been necessary; what unexpected problems have been encountered; and what they anticipate in the future. We in the Adoption Agency have thought it would be helpful and supporting to them if they could get together and share their thinking and their experiences in their new roles. Could there be questions they would like to discuss? This would be a good place to share them.

Which is a fair description of the basis for a contract for work, although it implies that the agency has no stake in the proceedings except for how their work, the parents, can be made easier; when the fact is that they have a stake—the agency does—in raising the quality of parental behavior and making the parents happier with the adoption process itself and with the agency itself; that is, there are advantages to the agency in having its people think well of its efforts and see it in a helpful light, rather than as a watchdog and judgmentalist. All of which could have been said in a few words: "We're interested in what you do as parents, because we also want the best for the children." And, "We'd also like for you to know us better and see us as helpful."

Here's another, by way of illustration:

> My opening was brief—after a warm greeting, I mentioned that this was the first foster parents' group meeting we have held in this community. I explained the confidential nature of their comments, asking for their cooperation in keeping confidential anything that may be brought up during the meeting. I continued by stating that we are coming to them, as we recognize that travel can be difficult for them. Several mothers shook their heads vigorously in agreement. I added that being a foster mother is a tough job; but they have it even rougher because the area in which they live lacks so many essential services. We want to know their concerns; and what they think and feel will enable us to learn from and help each other.
>
> I then asked if someone would like to start us off. There was a brief silence, then Mrs. C. mentioned the therapy that her two foster children were receiving.

Here is a worker beginning with a group of paraplegic patients in a Veterans Administration hospital:

> I began the meeting by saying, "It might be helpful if I start out by explaining why I am here. I have done this with many of you individually—but in case there are questions, or if there are some people who I did not get a chance to talk to too much, I think it may help to go over it again. I am here because there are lots of problems on the Paraplegic Wards, which have been brought to the attention of the hospital by the PVA (Paralyzed Veterans Association) and by the patients themselves. My job is to try to help with some of these problems." Don S. interrupted and said, "The reason you are here is because of the pressure put on the Hospital by the PVA. The Hospital did not hire you out of the goodness of their heart." He continued, "So, you were really hired by the Hospital in response to the pressure from the PVA." "But I was hired by the Hospital," I said. Don did not answer. I said, "But I think behind that question, Don, is another one which may be bothering lots of patients—that is 'whose side will I be on—the patients' or the staff?'" There were some nods of the heads on this. I said, "And the answer is *neither.*" There were more curious looks. I said, "Well, I think that if I am going to be helpful around here I will need to be in good with the patients and also in good with the staff." Don said, "Yes, like a mediator." (I had talked with him about this during the week.) Nobody challenged this position.
>
> Somebody asked, "What are you going to help with?" I said, "That largely depends on what the patients want help with." Dick L. took it from there.

The above excerpt shows not only the worker's projection of his own perception of the terms of the agreement, but some of the feedback for which he reaches, with the understanding that contracts are not made on high, but are ultimately worked out by the parties to the agreement.

The beginning phase is particularly important, since it sets the terms of the engagement and does much to create the frame of reference from which the first responses will be chosen, by the group members, and by the worker himself. If the contractual tasks are not properly and directly addressed at the outset, they will plague both group and worker for a long time—in the prolonged testing, in the endless repetition of the what-are-we-doing-here theme and in the fits and starts with which the group approaches its business. Record analysis discloses many ways in which group members can raise and reraise the questions of who the worker is, what he is supposed to do, what the group is for, what the agency *really* expects, what are the hidden rewards and punishments, how much latitude they really have, and what the talk is supposed to be about.

Paul Abels, in an article on contract, subtitled "Playing it Straight," points out that:

> In essence, the client engages himself with a person having a particular area of expertise and agrees to follow certain procedures in order to obtain certain rewards. These may be concrete rewards such as funds, food stamps, jobs, or less concrete rewards such as insight, hope, ability to cope with problems, etc.
>
> The profession in turn has sought and at times received the sanction (contract) from society for the almost "exclusive rights" to be the mediators around the amelioration of social welfare problems. The profession in return for these exclusive territorial rights has agreed to carry out its mandate in an ethical, rational and effective manner, utilizing the most comprehensive knowledge and resources at its disposal.[1]

Daniel Lerner, applying the notion to medicine, says:

> Let me briefly review the elements making up the clinical core of medical work in general as two people. One is in need of help, the other is in possession of professional methods. Their contract is a therapeutic one.[2]

And thus Karl Menninger, in a book on psychoanalytic technique:

> Psychoanalysis, like other forms of psychotherapy, is a long continued two-party contract or compact. In all such two-party contracts, as we have seen, the interaction is a complicated one. Imagine how this might look to a man on Mars with a very powerful telescope: Out of a mass of milling, struggling individuals, two of them—here and there—are engaged in a regularly discontinuous series of vis-a-vis meetings. They come together, both remaining relatively motionless; they apparently engage each other in a communication; they exchange something. A balance of some invisible kind is established, and the two separate.[3]

And Menninger again:

> The trend of all that we have been saying . . . is to emphasize the following points: First of all, in any engagement between two individuals in

> which a transaction occurs there is an exchange, a giving and again of something by both parties with a consequent meeting of needs in a reciprocal, mutual way. When this balance is not achieved, either because one does not need what the other has to offer or because one does not give what the other needs or because there is the feeling on the part of one or the other that the exchange is not a fair one, the contract tends to break up prematurely.[4]

Abels again:

> Contracts are the dynamic agreements between the worker and the client system in which the problems to be worked, the goals, and the activities (means) by which the goals are to be accomplished are negotiated. The contract solicits and explores the mutual expectations, sets the boundaries of service and explicates the goals of the client, and worker and the means by which the problems may be solved.[5]

There is an important qualification to be made here. The Abels model in a sense accepts the medical model, as indicated by Menninger, namely that the contract is between the client and the *worker.* In a sense, there *is* a preliminary agreement between client and worker, as indicated in the efforts brought in the VA excerpt on the paraplegic patients. But, in essence, the fact is that the fundamental agreement, the contractual statement, is between the *agency and the client,* between the individual and the *system,* with the worker playing the mediating and facilitating role, directing himself to both, alternately. The contract thus partakes of the stakes of both the system and the individual, or group—reflecting the aspirations of the society on the other hand, and these of the client group on the other.

Reality Propositions

We may begin with the assumption that the way the worker and his client group begin together will affect the nature of their work in many ways. First, and most relevant, is the proposition that in general terms the encounter between the client and service is a small version—a special case of the symbiotic relationship between the individual and his society. The present client-agency relationship is a specific example—enacted before your eyes—of the ways in which individual and society reach out to each other. The terms on which this reaching is done will first become visible in the opening stages of the client-agency engagement.

Second, certain demands and expectations will flow from both sides of a new relationship, and these will be in effect whether or not they are put into words. These demands will constitute real forces at work; they will create certain behaviors, whether or not they are verbalized—or even recognized—by the parties involved. Certain consequences will flow from unverbalized—and unrecognized—stakes; others will emerge from stakes that are openly sought out and understood, insofar as they can be understood at that stage of the transaction.

Third, these demands and expectations are further complicated by the situation of the small group, where there is a complex amalgam of individual stakes and self-interest, where each individual's sense of need intersects and interacts with others, where there is a shifting consensus of how these demands should be expressed and where, in short, a new client—the group itself—is created and put into interaction with the service.

Fourth, for certain reasons not too well understood, any direct statement of what these demands and expectations are as experienced by both sides, and indeed the worker himself, as embarrassing and taboo. There is apparently something touchy and difficult about saying outright what it is they want from each other. The theoretical importance of the contract notion stems largely from this—that direct statements of mutual expectation are "not done" in polite society, that they are perceived as rude and impolitic and that, consequently the client-agency engagement is replete with hidden agendas. The examples are legion: the youngsters who are brought together to build model airplanes, while the staff is secretly plotting to "build their characters" and "socialize" them; the patients who are brought together "just to talk" about their troubles, while the decision has been secretly made that this will speed up the discharge rate; and similar situations.

Fifth, this indirectness creates a vague and ambiguous frame of reference, within which it is difficult for the clients to choose the appropriate responses. Further, the vagueness also creates an unnecessarily long period of testing, during which the members make many covert—we might call them "sly"—attempts to find out what they are supposed to do, what they are together for, the rules of the game, and the role of the worker. Where the group experience opens on this note, the record shows all of their signs of hesitation, testing, indirect attempts to establish a frame of reference and covert annoyance with the worker for putting the burden of purpose on their shoulders alone. Regard the following, in which the worker makes several attempts to set the framework; in the final one, at the third meeting, he makes himself clear—and it is only then that the work can begin:

> *First meeting:* . . . I then stated that they had common interests and concerns like most teenage boys, and said that their presence would give them an opportunity to discuss these concerns. I emphasized the fact that it was their group and it would, therefore, be their decision as to what they wanted to talk about . . . B. entered . . . sat down without taking his coat off . . . I asked if there were any questions that they wanted to ask. Each of them said no.
>
> After a long period of silence, I asked if they were in favor of attending the meeting when they first heard about it . . . Y. said that he wasn't . . F. said he didn't mind coming . . . I asked if they would like to talk about girls and there was a long period of silence . . .
>
> *Second meeting:* . . . the boys had engaged themselves in a discussion about camp. I joined them . . . Y. came into the room, very smartly dressed and wearing large sunglasses . . . they all started laughing . . . I

greeted Y. and introduced him to T. I then stated that I was sure T. would probably like to know the purpose of the group, since it was his first attendance. I wondered if someone would like to tell him about the purpose of the group. M. said he would give it a try . . . He began by stating that, as he saw it, this was their group; they talked about what they were interested in and added, pointing at me, that I was only there to supervise the meeting . . .

There was a brief period of silence which was broken by M., who reintroduced the subject of camp . . .

Third meeting: . . . T. asked me if I had ever gone on the Cyclone. M. responded to his question by saying that he had gone on the ride and enjoyed it . . . I interrupted him and asked if they could hold the discussion until we informed T. what the group was all about . . . (after they follow the pattern of "telling each other") I stated that I was a social worker with the Department of Welfare but I would not be visiting their homes or schools because they had their own (individual) social workers for that purpose. I also mentioned that all the boys in the group are foster children and that their concerns and problems are quite common. I paused and there was silence. I said, "How about it, are you concerned about your own parents, foster parents and about who you are and where you come from? M. started to speak, then stopped. I encouraged him to continue, telling him that I knew it wasn't easy to talk about such matters. M. said, "About our own parents, Mr. B. The only thing that bothers me is that they tell you about them." I asked M. what he meant. He said: "After you live in a foster home from a baby and think that you are living with your own parents, your social worker comes by one day and tells you that the people you are living with are not your real parents." To show him I understood how he felt, I replied that it is a rough deal and asked if the others felt the same way. F. said he always knew he was a foster child and knows the reason. M. said he knew why he was in foster care, too. F. wanted to know why M. was a foster child, and said that he didn't have to answer if it were too personal. M. said he didn't mind telling the group. He then asked me if I had ever been downtown near W.'s Department Store. I said I had been in the area a couple of times. He asked F. the same question and F. said yes. M. continued: "Well, there is a man who sells pretzels in front of the store all year round." He hesitated, smiled and said, "He's my real father." Though M. smiled as he informed us of this, there were no smiles from the other boys.[6]

Sixth, this kind of ambiguity about purpose creates a greater fear of the encroaching power of the agency and the invasion of their lives. Where purpose is vaguely defined, the client's perception will be that it could be about anything the agency says it is; the client must therefore be anxious about what the worker will do next, how the agency will use its power and the kinds of demands it may make at any time.

Seventh, contrary-wise, a clear consensus on group purpose limits the claims of each upon the other—client on service, service on client and, in the group, client on client. The opening agreement on the permissible demands tends to limit these demands rather than allow them to expand beyond control as the process continues.

There are a number of other propositions that deal with the more general problem of beginnings—propositions having to do with the effects of new situations, the tasks they imply, the perceptions they create, the movement from the familiar to the unfamiliar and the characteristics of first stages, in groups, in friendships, in school, and in other modes of human relationship. These first stages reveal fears of being tested under new conditions, the ambivalence of home and fear, with both negative and positive valences, and the effects of *time;* that is, the idea that the beginning is somehow attached to the ending, the limits and possibilities of time-limited groups, and so on.

Valued Outcomes

What immediate outcomes are we shooting for in the first stages of the group encounter? What is it that we want to happen, and not to happen?

First, we want to establish an opening consensus on what we are doing here together—what we have identified as the emergence of a "contract," embodying the stakes of both clients and agency, something of an understanding of the rules of the game and the limits of the enterprise. There is no intention to establish every aspect of the engagement in a rigid understanding that will brook no change; contracts are often "renegotiated" when the circumstances of the group's life reveal new facets of the arrangement and use up some variables, replacing them with others. But there is the hope in the mind of the worker that the opening moves will be made from a frame of reference that is fairly well shared at the outset, at least for the outset.

Second, the process of beginning with a viable contract calls for the partialization of tasks—that is, developing small operations out of the larger sense of purpose, seeing the prospect before them in terms of specific tasks to be approached more or less one at a time. That is to say, the worker hopes to move to a definition of work, rather than the ritualized repetition of broad goals and aspirations.

Third, we want to achieve some consensus on ground rules and procedures—a way of working. The impetus for work is provided by several common assumptions: self-interest is an important—it may be the only goal important—motive for work; the only group "patriotism" worth its salt is that which grows slowly and is a function of satisfied self-interests put together; an important ingredient in the group way of working will be their use of each other; and perhaps most important, the worker presents himself as one who will make a *demand for work;* that is, he will guard the focus of the work and ask only that they do what they came together to do. He makes no demand for progress, or achievement—only that they stay with the tasks they set out to tackle. This last ground rule is related to the problem of *relevance,* and the concern of all with being able to distinguish between what is relevant to the work and what is not. It is a distinction that is not easily made.

The key to relevance is the initial frame of reference, the first contract established between the clients and the service. A worker on a home visit who begins with something about wanting to "get to know you and you'll get to know us" courts irrelevance, because, in that context, *anything* is relevant. How does the client—or the worker, for that matter—choose his responses in that context? On the other hand, if the worker presents a specific reason for his visit, and a specific concern, the parent is much closer to what she might say, or not say, and the conversation can begin without the stylized ritual dance that often ensues in the testing and suspicion of the opening gambit.

Another aspect of the relevance theme is the professional practice—common in the neighborhood centers—of *making policy as one goes along,* inventing agency function everytime one comes up against a piece of client behavior he does not sanction. What happens here is that the worker falls into the trap of *creating* reality, rather than simply *explaining* it. A clear and unambiguous service makes it unnecessary for the worker to invent ground rules as he goes along, or in other terms, *inventing the service itself* from situation to situation. What we get here is a kind of private practice within the agency context: the service varies from worker to worker and varies in quality from worker to worker; some of which—the variations in quality particularly—may be inevitable, but when it characterizes the total effort of the worker, the mediating function is lost and even if some sensitive work emerges on a "personal" basis, the product is inconsistent, unstable, unpredictable, and essentially dysfunctional.

Finally, the worker wishes to avoid the necessity of making professional choices between the client's tasks and agency's aspirations. A clear opening contract puts the common ground between the two into the frame of reference and makes it unnecessary to bounce back and forth between such "choices." In the Radio Club record, for example, the face sheet declares that the agency purpose is "to develop interracial and intercultural understanding" while the members' purpose is appealed to as the interest in radio techniques of production and performance. The entire record then becomes a living testimonial to the confusion that is established, in both worker and members, when this contract, replete with hidden agenda, is established. The worker always happens to have a socially significant script in his pocket, picks them up on every chance social comment, and they begin to wonder why he responds to those cues all the time. He, on his part, is continuously frustrated by their "apathy" and their responses to his manipulation. The important element here is that their mutual frustrations are caused not by any bad will on either side, but by the fact that their expectations vary, that the variations are secret, and that they measure outcomes in different terms.

There are more of these valued outcomes—the move from the familiar to the unfamiliar, from their own sense of need to what will happen here, the first perception of the worker as a helping rather than a judging person, the perception of the worker as a knower and as one capable of controlling, using power benevolently. But let us leave the category now and turn to some of the *acts* implied for the worker in this opening stage of work.

Patterns of Activity

First, and for some reason extremely difficult to encompass are the acts necessary, the ability to make a simple statement about the service. The communication between professionals on this score is no indication of what these operations entail; their words are often so jargonistic that the shorthand is accented by both without the slightest idea of what either is talking about. As difficult as it might be, the act of making a simple statement is eminently possible; and the reason it is possible is that if one is talking about a real service—one that actually exists—all one has to do is to reach inside the reality for what is there, for what is actually being offered. This becomes clearer as we begin to make distinctions between those services that are easier, and those that are harder, to explain.

Second is the ability to offer the service without becoming identified *as* the service. This is connected to the point about explaining reality, rather than creating it. It involves presenting a service which is provided by the agency, rather than being embodied solely in the worker. The worker thus leaves himself free—by neither *becoming* nor *disowning* the agency—to help the client and the agency effect the engagement implied in the contract between them.

Third, an important skill involved in these opening processes is the ability to reveal one's faith in what is about to happen, the worker's belief in the relationship between the client and the agency. There is something about the worker's moves in the opening stages that reveals his investment in the engagement itself, and his stake in the possibilities; in this he is anything but neutral.

Fourth, there is the skill of reaching for feedback on the initial contractual statement. The contract idea is violated when one conceives it as a statement by the worker, uncorrected and unelaborated by the clients. The reach for feedback is the move that searches out "two signers" for the contract; it is an indispensable part of the beginning, and with the concomitant skills of reading and addressing the subtle ways in which people express their intentions and of engaging these motives in the work that follows.

In the aforementioned example of the opening attempts with the adolescent boys in foster care, the worker's first attempt leaves out the fact that they are foster children, that this is a child welfare agency and that he is a social worker—all of which they know and it is frightening for them to have him leave these facts out of the contract statement. He leaves it out because he is embarrassed and must pretend that this is an ordinary bunch of fellows who are going to have a club and can talk about anything they want to. The agency, he implies, has no special stake. It is only when he is encouraged to bring these factors—their stake, the agency's, and his function—into the proceedings that they are able to move into the work they were brought together to do.

Here is another example:

> The first patient came in at 10:50, and I began to feel anxious that nobody else would come. Then Mr. L. came in and he wanted to know the purpose of the meeting and I asked him to wait until I could tell all of them. Mr. C. came in and I introduced everybody. I went out to find out about some of the others and learned that Mrs. J. had gone to surgery, so the doctor said she could not come. I met Mr. O. as he was coming in. When I opened up, I was so anxious that my mind became a complete blank and I forgot everything I was going to say. I told them I got their names from the doctor and I was seeing them in a group instead of individually so that we could discuss common areas, and I said everything I should have said about common problems, helping one another, talking about how they feel. Mr. L. objected, as he felt each patient should solve his own problems, not through group therapy; Mr. O. agreed, and the others looked like they agreed, and this immobilized me further. I explained that I was new at leading discussions.

The last comment is at least a human touch, the worker beginning to recover as the process moves. But the problem is clear: the embarrassment one feels at confronting the condition that brought them together—they are foster children, or psychiatric patients, or very old, or welfare recipients—there is real struggle, and pain and the worker is afraid. Of what? What is it that keeps the professional doing the stylized ballet around the periphery of the problem? What is it that makes them pretend that there is really nothing serious—perhaps a little talk will help it get all cleared up?

The fact is that the next skill—*the demand for work*—takes its necessities from the fact that this is indeed "a group of people who need each other" and they will need to go hand in hand as they walk the paths of their common jungle. Thus the worker is not creating the trouble, or the work, or imposing the tasks—though he may feel as if he is. All he can do is safeguard the focus of the work—demand, prod, crystallize, and otherwise put the spotlight on the focus of the enterprise. They will have to put forward the energy for the work itself and, in the process, they will need help in using their differences as well as their common concerns.

Here the worker helps her group find a "handle" on which they grasp for a beginning; it is a continuation of a piece of work cited before:

> We in the adoption agency have thought it might be helpful if they could get together and share their experiences in their new roles. Could there be some questions they would like to discuss? This would be a good place to do it.
>
> Mrs. Harper said that she had hoped this was how the group meeting would be used. Mr. H. said he had some questions he would like the group to discuss and no doubt others had similar questions. He wondered where they should begin.
>
> I found they were thinking, and none seemed inclined to take the

first plunge. I then said since all of them had begun the new experience during the past year, I wondered if they did want to relate what being parents has meant to them. They began to speak of the joy that has come into their lives.[7]

On the business of the opening silence: it is an important part of the first efforts to establish contact. The key question, always, is "what's inside the silence?" The members are usually trying to decide what to share, what is appropriate, how much to give and who risks the first attempt at work. Though the worker's initial statement is helpful in establishing the frame of reference, it has not yet been conceptualized and the problem of beginning remains a real one for the members. Often, the first "problem" offered is what one might call a "near-problem," deciding to test the worker's seriousness and tolerance.

There was a brief silence, then Mrs. C. mentioned the therapy that her two foster children are receiving—the long trips to the city to see Dr. S., but she added hastily that everything is just working out fine. Her foster son, who never did his homework, now completes it regularly and responsibly. Another group member commented on the lack of success her child was having after two years of therapy.

It appeared to me that the group was disinterested in the topic, but felt they had to say something. Another mother stated that her daughter resisted therapy, because it made her feel even more different than her young friends. I picked up on why she thought the child felt different.[8]

It is only then, after this last "handle," that the work comes:

From this point, the discussion, which revolved around a foster child's search for identity, became more and more animated. For example, a member felt that it is too painful for a foster child to learn the truth as to why he is different. After a long discussion as to a child's uncomfortable feelings around using a name that was different from his foster parent, I asked if we could always protect a child from learning parts of the truth in the outside world.[9]

Later, in the same discussion:

I added that they seemed to be saying that, in many senses of the word, they are the real mothers . . . perhaps if they thought they were the true mothers, it might be hard for them to talk to their youngsters about their biological mothers. Several members said it is hard.[10]

Here is a brief excerpt from a long account in which a worker traces all the things she did with a group of ten- to- thirteen-year-old girls on the problem of developing a contract with them in a complex working situation:

A group of girls are friends. They join a center and a "worker" enters their lives. She says at the outset that she is there to help.

During the next eight months much passes between them, and there is a mutual revealing. The girls unveil themselves—their concerns, fears, questions and specific requests for help, while at the same time they discover in the worker a person who, through her affection and within her limitations, answers these requests by hearing what is being asked at a particular moment and responding with help.

The worker then describes some of the stages they go through in this business of trying to decide who she is, what she is there for and what her agency is offering them. This is from the second meeting:

As we were walking home, we discussed plans for next week. Carmen asked if they could have a party and Nilda added "with the boys." Margerita said that they could tell their mothers it was just a party—then later sneak the boys in. I asked what the reaction would be if I brought it up at the first parents' meeting, and Nilda replied that the parents would never allow it. She became quite angry and said she didn't know why they had to know everything. I said that I could see she and the others were upset about me wanting to talk to their parents about it. Nilda asked why the mothers had to meet at all anyhow. I said that this was part of my job—to work with families as well as with them. Martita exclaimed, "Well, if that's what she's supposed to do, Nilda, then that's what she's supposed to do." Nilda replied maybe, but she didn't think any parents would come to the meeting anyway.

A consultation with agency practitioners adds the following:

On the opening silence:

Yes, let's throw that open for some discussion; you've all had the experience of facing silences. My first question, for example, is always: "What's *inside* the silence?" The notion of what's inside gives a fuller, three-dimensional effect to the silence; if we don't develop some kind of constructive attitude toward it, it tends to become a diversion from the work, rather than part of the work itself. In the opening phases of work, the silences may have many different meanings in different groups, but in many instances I believe what is happening is that there is a question going through the members' minds—namely, what can I raise that would be appropriate to this setting, this group, this worker? I have something in mind, but is that what the worker wants?

On the business of *who establishes the service of the agency?* A member says:

There seems to be an underlying assumption in this whole framework that you gave today—it's bothering me—that the agency service has already been established for you. When I came to my agency, the primary reason they gave for hiring me was to get more girls to come to the settlement house. That's not a service, and I could not say "this is what

> the agency has to offer you." In the beginning, I was trying to establish what services they wanted—and I think this is even more general in the anti-poverty programs. They don't even know what the community wants, and the beginning is one in which you have to find out what they really want you to do. They don't like me, they don't know me, don't trust me—I can't say, now what do you want me to do for you . . . they don't "want" anything.

In the discussion: the idea of "work with" as an amorphous coverup for a lack of focus; it will be an "experience"—whatever that may mean; new programs and old ones;

> I would rather be in that situation (a new program) than to come into an established agency and begin working with 150 teenagers, trying to do good and be efficient and not have any idea of what the expectations are. The workers before me had set up completely different expectations; as a result the kids set up the new worker as an easy mark. And nobody knows: What's the program *this* year? You pay 25 cents down and $1.50 later, come in on Tuesday and Wednesday night, or Monday and Friday night, and nobody knows what to do. The worker has to develop his own identity in the agency; each worker does it on his own, without relationship to an agency service. He has to do it the best he can.

Question: How do you establish the nature of the service before you even come into contact with the client? My answer:

> Yes, V., this is the classical problem of the neighborhood agency, and it is why they get so embarrassed when no one asks them to define the nature of their service to the community. This has been inherited; it's part of their hundred-year history. What I'm suggesting is not that one concoct a concept of function out of whole cloth but that they dig in and find out what *this* agency is supposed to be doing in *this* neighborhood, with *these* people. The proposition is a fairly simple one: the agency is getting money from the community; what's it being paid to do? When I give my money to a hospital, I know pretty much what it's for; when it goes to a child placement agency, I have a pretty good idea of what they're getting paid for.

There was further discussion on the vested interest of Boards of Directors and their role, the "merely" of recreation; on the "renegotiation" of contracts; on the "interpretation" of arts-and-crafts pictures, without reference to group meetings and club talk, and sharing; and an interpretation of "agency"—the role of the Board and staff:

> Let me try an interpretation of "agency"; you check me on it, and address yourself to my comment. My interpretation would be that the Board of Directors has the primary responsibility for defining and redefining the service for which it is accountable to the community. It is financially responsible and it spends the money granted for its purposes.

> *But,* it cannot do this responsibly without the help of the professions it engages to help do its work. The same is true in a hospital . . .
>
> Now one of the major problems, I think, is that the laymen running the group-serving agencies have—with the collaboration of the professionals—abdicated their functions and allowed most of the power and responsibility to slip into the hands of the professional administrators . . . Any professional that accepts that assignment is wrong.

And then, a brief summary:

> Let me say where I think we are. Starting with the idea of developing clarity of purpose, we moved to the question of what happens if there is no clarity of purpose in the agency itself? How does the worker create a sense of clarity purely out of his own efforts? Then we went to the problem of whose fault is it that there is so little clarity in the definition of service—some people say well, if the professionals were sharper they would help the Board to make the service clearer and others say that if the Board were more responsible they would create the pressure for definition . . . and so on. Of course, both these things are true, and they move us to where we are now—which is, how do you establish a situation in which the Board staff relationship is such that their work constantly keeps what C. Wright Mills called *the interplay between public issues and private troubles.* His point, in *The Sociological Imagination,* was that there has to be a constant exchange between individual experience and the great human issues, and that a good sociologist can translate one in terms of the other. Where a Board derives its policies from what happens to the people in their agencies; and where the clients are directly touched by the public issues the Board calls attention to; this is the process that a good professional can stimulate and facilitate . . .

Finally, something on the use of beginnings to move from the familiar to the unfamiliar:

> Let me see if I can find an example . . . Well, in the foster parents group . . . the worker began with the feelings she knew they were familiar with—their isolation in a distant community, the lack of resources, their interest in their children—and they used her as a bridge to the unfamiliar—what are we going to do about that here, who are you, what will you do if I give you something? The worker is herself a bridge from the known to the not-known and they'll have to trust her in order to use her that way—trust her familiarity with what they're feeling and her ability to help them explore new ways of talking and doing.

A final note: How does one move from the initial requirement—function—to the last requirement (for a method)—*skill?* In the pressure to *operationalize,* we must be careful not to take a shortcut at the end and assume that *acts* and *skills* are the same thing. They are not: anybody can act; it takes more sophistication, and whatever, to act with skill. It's not *any* act, then, but a *kind* of act that we are looking for, a kind of act we define as skillful. What does it take then to define an act as skillful? It seems to me that that act is skillful to the extent that it exploits most directly the *nature of the materials* on which one is acting. A skillful act makes it easier for the *material to do its thing*—a piece of leather, a stone, paint and canvas—and the human being himself. An actor's material is the human emotion, the human experience—that is what he plays on and must make do its thing; a teacher's materials are the "subject" to be learned and the people who are trying to learn it; a social worker's skill depends on his ability to read the human being's impetus toward his systems and the systems' impetus toward its people. His *reality* is their impetus, and their ambivalence, and their past efforts, and their stake in the proceedings; his *policy* is the purpose with which he moves—to help them move—*he acts to help them act;* and his *acts* are chosen for their potential in applying his purpose to their realities. The degree to which he send his acts most *efficiently* (the least waste motion) through his purpose to their reality—that is what we recognize as skill.

To recap on the question: it starts with *function*—what am I doing in the systems in which I get involved—society, the neighborhood, the peer group. Then, from function it goes to *purpose*—in order to carry out this particular function, I propose to hand my efforts in this and that directions. Then, from purpose, it goes to *tasks*—in order to fulfill my purposes, I must take on these jobs. Then, from tasks, it goes to acts—in order to perform these tasks, this is what you have to do. Then, from acts, to *skills*—in order to do these acts *well*—anybody, or almost anybody, can do them badly—you have to do it *this way.* The limitation on skill definition has to be kept in mind: one must not get in the way of *personal style;* Cézanne and Picasso are highly skilled painters, but each one's style of expression is as different from the other's as can be (although one owes a great deal to the other).

Example? Function—to mediate
Purpose—facilitate the individual-system interaction
Task—find the common ground; and the other four major tasks
Act—reach for negatives; reach for opposites; recognize feelings, and so on
Skill—At the appropriate time—responsive to something that's happening; the skilled response takes its cue from an existential fact, and it can name it—in fact it does, in the acting

Notes and References

1. Paul Abels, "The Social Work Contract: Playing it Straight," presented at Cleveland Chapter National Association of Social Workers, p. 1.
2. From Abels, *Ibid.,* referring to p. 74 of Lerner, ed. *Evidence and Inference* (New York: The Free Press, 1959).
3. Karl Menninger, *Theory of Psychoanalytic Technique* (New York: Harper Torchbooks, 1958, p. 17.

4. *Ibid.,* p. 21.
5. Abels, *op. cit.,* p. 8.
6. Practice excerpt taken from William Schwartz, "Group Work in Public Welfare," *Public Welfare* (October 1968), pp. 21–22.
7. For a discussion of an effort to organize and offer group services to adoptive parents, see William Schwartz, "Group Work in Public Welfare," *Public Welfare* (October 1968), particularly pp. 31–35.
8. Practice excerpt taken from William Schwartz, "Group Work in Public Welfare," *Public Welfare* (October 1968), p. 27.
9. *Ibid.,* p. 27.
10. *Ibid.,* pp. 27–28.

10

Middles: The Work Phase

This is the substantive stage of the common work—the time in which the client group addresses itself to the matters at hand and the period in which the primary issues of process will have to do with the degree of productivity the members can command in elaborating the themes of which their subject is composed, sharing the ideas and experiences they need to share, investing the affect they need to invest in order to lend urgency to their efforts, making the decisions that are required, and using each other and the worker in the process.

It is at this point that we will begin to grapple in earnest with the symbiotic model—that is, the forces that lie along the client-system arrow on the three-cornered model. What are they indeed? What makes them operative? What assumptions are hidden in our definition of the term "work"? What facilitates work and what inhibits it? And what, operationally, are the expectations and tasks of the helping person within this effort?

Let us begin with our *reality* background for the problems of work and the middle phase. What assumptions are we making about this work as it proceeds?

Assumptions

First, the individual's major access to new ideas or attitudes or skills lies through his sense of their usefulness to him. The energy, or impetus, that provides *motive energy* for the reaching out process, for the effort to find new ways to conduct one's life, or a part of it, comes through—is generated by—the sense of self-interest, what's-in-it-for-me. Conversely, the sense of operating on *someone else's* stake is inhibitive; what feels like manipulation towards someone else's ends feels like imposition and contains a negative valence, a push away from learning and doing, whether the person is aware of it or not.

Second, learning will depend to a considerable extent on the degree to which the learner can invest affect, or feeling, or a sense of urgency, in the materials before him. Affect is the life's blood of investment and motive;

without it, one may think one is investing but the effort is mechanical and without energy. Energy then is feeling running through the meaning of the materials. Without feeling, all one can do is *simulate* ownership of the problem.

The more one gets into this business of finding the reality base, the scientific assumptions on which the helping process is based, the more one realizes that the job of laying them all out is impossible.

All I can do is select a few that will be closest to the helping work, identify them and explain them, indicate that there could be a whole set of others, and so on. The important thing is to relate the assumptions one has chosen to the *policy variables* and the *patterns of activity.*[1]

Third, the connections between the client's sense of his own stake and the requirements of social demand or expectation are always present in every specific issue. These connections are always there in one form or another, however obscure they may be to the participants.

Fourth, these connections manifest themselves in ways that are very specific and partial—not in generalized global terms like "maturity" "adjustment," "socialization," and the like. These words are substitutes for meaning, meant to disguise the fact that the connections are really unknown to us. The real connections are specific and existential—that is, they consist in small tasks that are being worked at *now.*

Fifth, the connections can never be permanently established—that is, one does not "do the job" once and for all. They are shifting, flexible, unstable, and change their terms from situation to situation; it is an illusion to think that things remain "established" for good. The child who is given the opportunity to "relate" to other children does not learn thereby to "relate" to all children. The Jewish child who participates in culture-related activities does not necessarily add anything lasting to his Jewish self-image. The assumption here is that the individual-social connections are always related to the particular situation, changing and shifting from meeting to meeting, from interview to interview. The implication is that these connections must continually be sought out anew in order to keep building the bridge between the individual's past and his future, between what has happened to him before and what he would like to have happen to him in the future.

Sixth, The client's access to social opportunity is continuously impeded by obstacles that are thrown up in the course of the engagement, or the "work" on specific tasks. An "obstacle" is an idea or a feeling that obscures the connections between individual need and social demand.

Seventh, the obstacle, or even its very existence, is often obscure to the client himself, his awareness limited by his incomplete vision of the common ground and by his own subjectivity; this makes it difficult for him to recognize his own defenses, to distinguish between internal and external deterrents, and to assess his own productivity at any given moment.

Eighth, these obstructions stem from many sources and appear in many forms: attitudes of the client; image projected by the worker, the nature of the problem to be worked on; the role and activity of the agency situation. In fact, the origins are so complex and interrelated that "causation" cannot in actual fact ever be satisfactorily determined. This means that workers are, most of the time, operating from motives and purposes that are existentially, rather than causationally determined. Or, to put it another way, short-term causes—moment to moment sequences govern the helping process to a considerable extent.

The eighth assumption gets into *interpenetrative assumptions,* that is, assumptions that arise not from the *intrapsychic* perspective, or the *sociological* perspective, but from an interaction between the two. Actually, it might be well to *categorize* the assumptions, beginning with *psychological* ones, intrapsychic, then moving to assumptions about the *group,* then the *agency,* then the *worker,* and then a host of *interpenetrating* ones, involving the interaction of factors and their origins. Or it may be that most of the emphasis ought to be put on the interactive ones, concentrating on the complexity and not trying to stay within the frame of reference of discrete psychological or sociological factors.

Ninth, the worker's offering represents only a fragment of available social experience. If he comes to be regarded as the fountainhead of social reality, he will begin to present himself as the object of learning, rather than as an accessory to it. Thus, there is an important distinction to be made between lending his knowledge to those who can use it in the performance of their own tasks, and projecting *himself* as a text, to be learned. In the first instance, the worker is used in accordance with his function as a mediator of the subject-object relationship; in the second the worker himself becomes the object.

Tenth, that data are most usable which are most closely related to the immediate tasks for which worker and client have been brought together. Often, the worker is tempted to "expose" the client to facts and ideas which "*may*" in some future context be found usable. Such efforts generally serve to confuse rather than enlighten, since there is no frame of reference within which the data can assume weight and significance. Where these workers' acts constitute a series of ideological "plugs," the effect is to breed a vague distrust of the worker's purpose and of his stated desire to assist the client with his problems.

Eleventh, that data are most useful when they are presented for what they are—opinion, or fact—rather than in disguised form.

Twelfth, there is a "charismatic" quality in the members' perception of the worker—that is, they invest him with ideas and feelings that emerge from their own attitudes towards authority, without too much relevance to his real qualities, particularly at the outset. When his actual behavior and his charismatic ascriptions come into some conflict, as they are bound to, there is a crisis in the life of the group.

Thirteenth, the "charisma" attached to the worker by the members is partly a function of their investment in the change process itself—that is, they will invest the worker with qualities related to their attitudes to the group task, clothing him with expertise and attitudes designed to do the job for them, or help them with it, or get in the way of the work.

Fourteenth, thus, the charisma is in part an *individual* and in part a *group* product; it is in effect a pooling of attitudes toward authority, as represented by the worker and there will be some conflict within the group as to what the "public image" of the worker should be.

Fifteenth, the charismatic effect can be used by the worker—and usually is—*both* to increase dependency and imitativeness and to foster creative, independent, solutions.

Sixteenth, the concept of "transference" and that of "counter-transference" can be used in this connection, but only in part. To some extent it is used superficially—when the abreaction of oedipal conflict ignores the fact that the perception of the worker is of one who represents access to social status and social opportunity, one who has "made it" and who has been designated to help others make it. Another way of looking at this is as the "friendship" theme, extended to that of a "professional relationship."

Seventeenth, the members will read the worker's behavior as a model for the prescription or proscription of certain kinds of behavior—his activity is seen as permitting or forbidding certain *similar* acts on their part—spontaneity, freedom of affect, tolerance of ambiguity, interest in new things, faith in the relationship, hope for change, and others.

Eighteenth, the worker's affect is thus a strong component in his relationship with the client. The professional relationship can be described as a flow of affect between worker and member, combining the expectations and perceptions of one with the other as they work together—each on his own tasks, within the helping system. Their interaction is based on the circumstances that brought them together, and it is in the work itself that their feeling for each other grows. In this light, the worker's efforts to "establish a relationship" go much deeper than a kind of wooing process in which he seeks to gain the members' acceptance and approval through the exercise of his personal warmth and attractiveness.

Nineteenth, the worker's feeling is related also to the material under discussion—that is, he cathects to the tasks ahead; his authority, too, lies in his interest in the tasks, in the work. These tasks, it should be clear, are not "solved" for him, but remain interesting and vital for him.

Twentieth, the agency, the worker, and the client system are related to each other by certain rules and requirements imposed upon them by the terms of agreement. These requirements emerge first in the conditions under which the relationship is established, its tasks identified, and its procedures initiated. Later, the rules are modified, amplified, reinterpreted, renegotiated, as their implications emerge more clearly in the transactions themselves.

Twenty-first, these expectations are not limited to those imposed by the agency upon the client; they are reciprocal, in that each actor imposes certain restrictions and is bound by others.

Twenty-second, to the extent that the terms of the agreement are specific and unambiguous, the participants are free to pursue their tasks within the system in their characteristic ways. Where the rules are, or become, obscure and vaguely defined, the major energies of both worker and client become diverted to exploring the boundaries repeatedly and testing the limits of each situation. Thus, freedom of movement is enhanced when the limits and boundaries of the situation are clearly perceived. And the less explicit the terms, the more time will be spent on covert explorations of the terms and the less on carrying them out. The limits of action and the areas of freedom are arrived at by a combination of factors, including the function of the agency, the purpose of the relationship and the ongoing conditions of work.

Twenty-third, moving to some *group* hypotheses, the work of a collective is the resultant of the extent to which it can develop a *shared impetus* in the pursuit of a common task. This involves the attempt to coordinate the perceived self-interests of several into a joint problem-solving process. This will involve some necessities around the *sharing of affect,* without which one may arrive at "consensus" that is false and inoperative.

Twenty-fourth, the problems of group problem-solving may be divided into two major categories—those under *authority* (their use of the worker), and those under *intimacy* (their use of each other).[2]

Twenty-fifth, the intimacy theme implies that one of the important features of the small-group situation is that it constitutes a *multiplicity of helping relationships*—that is, that the lines of assistance will arrange themselves not only from member to worker but from member to member. Thus, the affect that runs from one group member to the others will be as much a factor of group productivity as the feeling that runs between the members and the authority figure.

Twenty-sixth, further, the *interplay* of intimacy and authority themes create dynamics, behavior, that affect the nature of the helping relationship and the address to group tasks. For example, the ways in which members use each other will have considerable to do with how they use the worker's authority; misuse of authority can create disruption in the ranks—authoritative approaches can demoralize the members and make it more difficult for them to collaborate in problem solving.[3]

Valued Outcomes

One, that the members discern the connections between what they feel as important and what is going on in the situation around them. They may feel alone, and alienated and this feeling cannot be "taken away"; but they must also, it is hoped, feel that there is work to be done, that it is hopeful to work and that they will receive help in the process.

Two, that they will perceive their own self-interest, acting through "owning" their own motives, rather than through altruism narrowly defined—that is, that they are acting for someone else's good, in order to "prove" their goodness.

Three, that the members will combine feeling with ideas—that is, that they will invest affect in the work they are doing, and will express their thoughts with the emotion that accompanies them. The emphasis here is on "feeling in pursuit of a task," and reflects that emotion taken by itself, the pursuit of "feelings" devoid of substantive content, is a sterile, purely "self"-exploratory pursuit; while the idea of covering ideas without the spontaneity and feeling that attends them also produces sterility, but of a different kind—mechanical, unreal, and unproductive.

Four, that the clients perceive that which is relevant to their self-interest as they move from situation to situation—not relevant in general terms, but now, cathected to in this situation.

Five, the worker will want the members to have a sense of what it is they should be working on, giving their attention to, as the process unfolds. He will want to make his contribution to the clarification of tasks, bearing in mind both the client stakes and those of the agency.

Six, there is an outcome bearing on the worker's own perception, his own insight into the common ground, gained from moment to moment as he participates in the action; he is trying to refine his own ability to reach past the symbiotic diffusion and the battles of will to what it is that lies on the arrow leading from the client to the system and back.

Seven, he wants the group members to engage each other in finding these connections, using the group process to share their perceptions of their relationship to social demand and opportunity.

Eight, as obstacles arise to a clear view of the common ground, he hopes the members will achieve "insight"—the awareness of the relationship between previously disconnected events. As one begins to connect a series of small events in one's experience, the mosaic of connectedness gets richer, the different parts of one's experience get clearer and the "aha!" reaction signifies that new connections are visible. This somehow makes the obstacle less formidable, less frightening, and the valued outcome is that the members will resume the work as they rediscover their sense of direction.

Nine, that the mutual stereotypes—client of system and system of clients—will begin to break down as the obstacles are tackled. When the connections between the one and the many are more accessible, the oversimplifications will be harder to maintain intact: "all adolescents are rebellious," "give them a finger and they'll take a hand," "all teachers are culture-bound," "poor people don't talk," among others. All these oversimplifications connote a rigidity of approach; while the detection of obstacles *complicates* matters in the best sense of the term. That is, to stereotype is a way of *not working;* that is "they" are hopeless, what's the use. This is a way of "solving," or at least, "resolving" problems. The valued outcome of detecting obstacles is to *get on with the work,* retackle the tasks and pick up where we left off. By "complicating" the matter, we have taken *many* variables into account, thus unfreezing our capacity for action.

Ten, that the members should perceive the worker as a knowing, active, involved person, rather than someone who is passive, neutral, and past interest in the outcome or the subject under discussion. He wants them to perceive him as one who risks, takes chances, and is invested in the subject.

Eleven, the worker hopes, through his contribution of data and his own investment of feeling, to provide perspectives that are beyond what the members can produce at a given moment. This "expanding of horizons" is an old idea, here presented in more specific and tangible form—that is, not in the form of preachments but in the shape of data that the worker contributes from his own reconstructions of experience.

Twelve, there is an expectation that the worker's contribution of data will somehow provide a push for making choices, for commitments about what they think and feel about the problems under scrutiny. Allied to this is the idea of connecting feelings to thoughts, as previously mentioned; that is, that feelings alone add little unless they are part of important ideas, and that ideas in themselves mean little unless they are invested with the emotions and the sense of urgency that gives form and utility to the thoughts and concepts.

Thirteen, as the worker "lends his vision" to the process he hopes that they will view him as a real person, rather than a fabricated creature who has "solved" the problems into which they are moving. Here is a worker reflecting on the problem of professional honesty:

> For example, in the subway episode mentioned early in this record, when Tata had accused me of punishing her because I didn't like her, I experienced a sudden *pang of recognition.* What was it? Was it a part of what was going on in the group? Was it something that the girls were already aware of but I was still hiding beneath professional rationalizations? For only with great effort and loss of self-esteem could I admit to myself that not only didn't I like Tata, but I had a pretty good idea *before* I gave the command that she, and only she, would defy me.
>
> This brings me to my second point of concern, the conflict I felt initially between being honest or being professional. Somehow, I had the feeling that it wasn't "professional" to be too honest with the girls, because it might not be good for them. The most pragmatic of reasons made me look at the professional function in a different way. The girls seemed to know, in so many cases, and whether I wanted to tell them or not, what I was thinking and feeling. They were extremely sensitive and with great accuracy recognized my preferences, likes, dislikes and what things made me comfortable and uncomfortable.
>
> The real test they were putting me to was whether I would cover up these real feelings with a thousand rationalizations as did most adults they had known, or whether I could come closer to acknowledging something we both knew to exist. How in the world could I ask them to be honest with me—to examine what was really going on in the group—if I could not in some significant way acknowledge and deal with things we both knew I was feeling?[4]

Fourteen, thus the outcome has something to do with helping the members come to terms with the worker's real self, her humanity, her strengths and weaknesses, or face the fact that the relationship will be conducted *in words alone,* with everybody knowing that the emperor has no clothes, but nobody wishing to be the first to say so.

Fifteen, in helping the members face the requirements and limits of the working situation, the most important aspects of the boundaries are that they emerge from the nature of the client-worker system, and the necessities of work, rather than from the personal authority of the helping agent. As such, they are parts of a reality which is imposed by the nature of the setting and the purposes for which the engagement has been initiated. The worker is often frustrated by his inability to "set limits," when his real difficulty arises from his failure to recognize that his tasks are to explain realities, rather than create them. Club members, for example, find it a lot easier to accept situational realities and limitations—of dress, bans on smoking and other proscriptions—than those imposed by the worker in his name for reasons which are ambiguous, or moralistic, or designed to "build character." Since people do not join clubs to have their characters built, such taboos are not perceived as interpretations of reality, and in fact, they are not.

Sixteen, that the range of taboos will be narrowed, so that the members may approach their work with a minimum of proscribed pathways dictated by the culture in which they live—proscriptions of manners, mores, rituals, and other forms designed to create forms of behavior that are geared to the avoidance of truth rather than the confrontation of it.

Seventeen, to create a "culture of work," in which the members learn to guard the contractual focus in the same way that the worker does. That is, the outcome valued is that the members will reward work and frown on evasions of work, with a consensualized definition that "work" means attention to their concerns, participation in the problem-solving process, and investment of affect.

Eighteen, that they will see the worker as "unshockable," with a high tolerance for ambiguity, doubt, negative feelings, and conflict. This is the "strange adult" configuration, which produces its own kind of shock and jars the members into modes of communication they could not consummate without this kind of professional model.

Nineteen, that the worker's contributions are evaluated, as are other data, rather than perceived as mandates for action. Without this condition, the worker must be afraid to risk his own ideas for fear they will create immediate results and heighten the dependency on his authority. In this sense, he cannot work except in the *context of work;* that is, when they are evading he must wait, or deal with the obstacles, and it is only when they are working that he is free to make his own contributions to the work on the substance.

Twenty, a flow of affect between clients and worker, not always positive, but open and expressive.

Twenty-one, a clear understanding by the members of the claims, aspirations and expectations by which the group and the agency are bound to each other, and of the expectations attached to the behavior of the worker himself.

Twenty-two, a shortened period of boundary-anxiety and testing with regard to the limits of the situation.

Here again, the valued outcomes have to be categorized somewhat, for ease in the telling and general grasp—the "value" should emerge from the undercurrent of the mediating function, plus the assumptions of the previous sections—the "outcomes" should all be expressed in short-range terms, to be recognizable when they occur, and should be *located* in the *interpenetrating* variables of worker, member, group, agency, and other systems. Also, it should be clear that these variables are *chosen* for discussion, with no responsibility for handling them *all:* I am choosing the most relevant and interesting for me—others will have others; and I am providing a model for how this exercise goes.

Patterns of Activity

This is the phase in which the bulk of the work making up the helping process would be considered. The function of the social worker as we have conceived it is to mediate the individual-social transaction in the specific context of the agency service that sets the terms of the transaction in accordance with particular contractual agreement between the agency and its client. The job of translating this broad concept of function into the operations necessary to carry it out is essentially that of dividing a broad assignment into its component categories of activity, and, ultimately, into the more specific acts by which one recognizes the skilled use of the professional function to implement the function it is designed to carry out.

As an organizing notion, the term "task" may be helpful to gather up the various movements of the worker as he goes about the job of helping individuals and groups of individuals negotiate the various demands and opportunities facing them. The implication is that any function can be spelled out in the necessary tasks with which one moves to carry it out; further, that any specific act performed should then be identifiable under one or another of these task headings. These are, then, *categories* of activity, rather than an inventory of prescribed, highly specific acts. The latter would get us too close to mechanical, prescriptive, small movements and to matters of art and personal style. What we are trying to create is an art that is based closely enough on reality and purpose to apply to all practitioners and to create a teachable, universalized discipline—but not so operationalized that one has only to fill in the numbered spaces, so to speak. The methodological tasks are common and are based on a professional methodology held in common; the discrete acts in any given situation are heavily charged with the unique movements and lifestyles of the individual worker. A real understanding of any artistic enterprise is one that understands both the general and the specific—both the principles that bind all artists together and create a concept of "greatness" and "mediocrity," on the one hand, and the freedom of personal expression through which every artist is a different expression of these same principles.

If we were to take every single act a worker performs and enter it on a card; and if we were to shuffle these cards into categories, sorting like cards into piles, putting similar acts together—that is, moved by what seems to be the same intent, expressed in different ways—what directions would we find, what kinds of categories would we produce?

Of course, every card shuffler would come up with something slightly different, but each scheme would be a step forward in understanding the movements of the helping person. Several such studies have been done[5] in which categories of different kinds have emerged from the data. The problem with many of these attempts to *inventory acts* suffers from the fact that they begin with no attempt to link the acts to a functional frame of reference. The acts themselves cannot really be understood unless they are in some way hooked to an overall idea, an overall sense of purpose.

Beginning, as we have, with the mediating function—that is, the effort to relate the movements of the worker to the client and his systems and their efforts to negotiate each other—what categories of activity might express this sense of purpose? I will present five such categories, expressing what seem to be five major tasks of the worker, to which he must bend his acts and skills. Each of these tasks carries its own categories of activity and I will try to elaborate these, task by task.

The first major task is that of *searching out the common ground* between the clients' perceptions of their own need and those aspects of social reality and social demand with which they are faced, and with which they need to come to some kind of terms. This task calls for activity in which the worker tries to help the members clarify the focus of work and protect this focus against attempts to subvert it—either by the client, or the agency or the client group. This clarification of focus of work represents an active demand by the worker that the agency and the client begin their working relationship with a clear contract and a common understanding of the issue: What is this encounter about? What are we doing together? The search for common ground begins most auspiciously on a field where the members and their tasks have been, so far as possible, brought face to face. The effort to uncover and discover connections between individual goals and social realities is rendered infinitely more difficult when the terms of these realities are themselves shifting and unstable; as, for example, in the "character-building" activity disguised as teaching art or basketball. Furthermore, these attempts to guard the focus of work do not end when the initial statement has been made and the terms of the agreement reached. His activities in this regard persist as he continues to focus the work, helps change the focus where this is necessary, and asks the clients to consider such changes openly and realistically.

Another set of activities associated with this first task is the continuous effort by the worker to point up for the client those areas in which he feels, however faintly, an interest in the social objects which confront him. This is the effort to seek out the general lines of subject-object connection. This is a kind of internal process whereby he looks deeply into the characteristics of both subject and object—client and system—to find the elements of attraction and to make himself alert to the possibility of future engagement. What is the attraction between the gang member's hostility to social norms and society's demand for conformity to these norms? Between the "shock of diagnosis" experienced by patients in a mental hospital orientation group and the hospital's need for the patients to move smoothly into the necessary procedures, rules, and routines?

These are, in a sense, "diagnostic" attempts, but such preparatory insights cannot be effectively used to impose a series of prefabricated connections on a ready-made series of events. Such insights are used in three ways: to enable the worker to be more responsive to subtle and covert requests for help; to compel him to focus on the here-and-now, and to see through the client's evasions and denials of the strengths that lie hidden; and to structure the situation to favor strength rather than weakness.

By "guarding the focus of work" I mean those concerns which were initially established as the contract between members and service. By "pointing up the connections," I mean that when the gang member says "who needs them?" the worker reminds them that they do; and when the system says they are "hard to reach" and uses that as a reason for cutting off service, producing their own version of the "who needs them?" gambit, the worker can from his own function point up to the system-representatives that the diffusion is a mirage, and that they do need the kids as much as the kids need them.

The second major task is a corollary of the first, but has activities and characteristics of its own. This has to do with *detecting and challenging the obstacles* that obscure the common ground and frustrate the ability of both client and agency to identify their interest in the proceedings. The failure to search out these obstacles puts the worker in danger of being continuously entrapped by the symptoms of the symbiotic diffusion and falling into the deadly dualism of the one versus the many—man against his own society, and vice-versa.

The activity patterns associated with this task begin with those movements by which the worker reveals the existence of an impediment and accepts it as permissible. His acts here are not "interpretive" in the usual sense: he has no way of "diagnosing" the nature of the difficulty and no right to ask the client to deal with his causational explanations, even if he is very intuitive in this regard. He asks the client, simply, to recognize the fact that an obstacle exists, in the form of apathy, or evasion, or inconsistency, between the client and a desired objective. The "why"—the elaboration of causative factors—tends to tie clients up in knots, having to contend with complicated ideational notions while in the throes of some disturbance or other; while the simple fact of the struggle, the obstacle itself and recognizing the frustrations attached to the sense of immobilization tends to loosen them up, make them feel freer to work. The activity here is simply to ask the group members to face the fact that something has stopped the work, that it is understandable, and where do they want to go from there.

Second, the worker offers support and assistance as the client enters the area of taboo and seeks to determine the nature of the obstacle. That is to say that the worker helps them to examine the ways in which they are operating against their own interests in this situation. The attempt here is not to exorcise the taboo; that is, to eliminate its power for all time, but to help the members identify it and examine its effects. It is important only that the client recognize the source of his present frustration and free himself to determine the direction of his self-interest. In this aspect of the worker's activity, he is asking the members to recapture control of their own impetus, and to be discountenancing the illusion of work where there is no work. In effect, the worker is here helping the members respond to his invitation to enter a more difficult area of work, for he knows that the invitation itself is not enough. We see this often in the work of inexperienced people, as they become skilled enough to see the obstacle and offer the invitation to deal with it. The members respond, the worker is frightened and leaves the scene peremptorily. The invitation must be accompanied by moves that help the members move: "What you're doing now is not easy; let's take it a step at a time."

It is particularly important to remember that the worker is not trying to remove the obstacles once and for all. All he is trying to do is help the members identify and examine its effects on their work, thus lessening its frightening aspects and making it possible to bypass it for now. The attempt to achieve permanent "solution" of resistances simply leads to disillusionment on the part of the worker: he feels "we covered that already," "we went through that; what's wrong with them?" This activity is, of course, related to the assumption previously mentioned that the individual-social connections are constantly shifting, from problem to problem and from situation to situation.

The "illusion of work" is a common phenomenon in the worker-client encounter. In the field of education it takes a form with which we are familiar: the teacher talks, the learner listens, and the words are given back on prescribed occasions; everybody then agrees that all this represents some work on the part of the learner. This is a kind of ballet, or ritual dance, in which everybody learns his own steps and simulates the educative process. There is little learning in it, because the learner puts little energy into producing his own version of events and his own generalizations from experience. In social work, there are similar rituals in the conversations between worker and clients. Unless the worker shows an intolerance for such illusions the conversation often assumes this "game" aspect, in which all must work very hard to protect the illusion that something moving and meaningful is happening.

Another category of acts is that in which the worker moves to keep the purpose of the work alive, lest it be lost in the preoccupation with obstacles. The challenging of obstacles is based on the fact that they come between the client and the social product. When these impediments cease to be regarded as such and become objects of interest in their own right, the analytical process itself becomes an obstacle which needs to be dealt with. This calls for certain movements through which the helping process exercises a kind of "demand for work," an emphasis on focus and performance: the worker asks the client to continue with his tasks even as he examines the obstacles to their achievement. This is another way of saying that the examination of obstacles is part of the working relationship itself—that the contract is still in effect, so to speak, and that the examination of resistances can itself become an attractive prospect, so attractive that it forms a kind of resistance in itself. One can become so enamored of the resistances themselves, so interested in the "insights" that accompany this activity, that one can forget the main purpose of the enterprise. Once the attention to the obstacles has achieved its purpose—which is to move back to the work—the worker helps the group to act again, rather than have the members continue to gild the lily by understanding themselves better and better. It is not part of their contract to work on why they cannot work; they do it only because they are blocked and when they unblock, it is time to get back on the track. When "insights" produce action, they are productive; when they are objets d'art, to be admired for their own sake, they become obstacles themselves.

The third major task is that of *contributing data* which are not available to the client, but which may prove useful to him in the attempt to cope with that part of the social reality which is involved in the present problems on which the client is working. These "data" are meant to encompass not only "facts" but ideas and values as well—they are constructions of some reality and they represent social products of one sort or another. They are constructions, further, that are thrown out to them by the society in which they live, and, most particularly, by the system they are presently trying to negotiate. Whether the client's tasks are related to the specific problems of mastering facts and concepts in an established sequence, or to a less tangible complex of attitudes and feelings, the worker has a responsibility to offer what he feels the client can utilize from his store of experience. The worker's grasp of social reality is one of the important attributes that fit him to his function; while his life experiences cannot be transferred intact to other human beings, the products of these experiences can be immensely valuable to those who are moving their own struggles and their own stages of mastery.

Thus, nothing can be more destructive to the worker's function than the decision to withhold knowledge on the sole grounds that the client must make his own way. Such withholding is inevitably interpreted by the client as deprivation, hence rejection; and the result is usually opposite to what the worker intends. It is common, for example, to find the client straining to find answers that are hidden in the worker's questions; in this game of hide-and-seek, dependency increases as frustration mounts and as the client learns to search for the hidden answers, he ceases to explore the nature of the problem itself.

In providing access to data, the worker is in effect providing access to himself. His demand for a culture of work and for a free sharing of ideas can best be met if he makes himself available, as he would have the client make himself available to him. What he knows should be accessible, not after the client has tried to proceed "on his own," but in the course of their work together. The need to withhold is generally felt by workers whose helping relationship with the client is too fragile to be sustained in a culture of work. Where the dependence on authority is already great, the reluctance to offer more information to be swallowed whole is understandable. But the fear of creating dependency must be met in other ways. The worker who finds common ground, is sensitive to the climate in which the subject-object engagement proceeds, and is prepared to challenge the obstacles as they appear, will have no fear that the problem-solving process will be endangered by his assumption of full status as a knowing person in the helping relationship.

Thus, the worker provides data that can be used as instruments in the members' current work. The important point here is that the information is currently related, that it is a tool with which to work on a present concern, rather than an effort to "expose" people to data in the hope they will "catch" something that may be useful to them later. It is a foolish notion, unsupported by any evidence, that people will learn something from academic interest alone and will hoard the data as squirrels do nuts, for another season. People do not learn that way and they do not develop usable skills that way, nor do they form their values that way. The worker provides his data when it is needed—when it will provide an instrument with which to pry something open. It is also important that the data be presented for what it is: if it is a "fact," with some scientific support, it should be presented as such; if it is an opinion, a speculation, a tentative conclusion, it must not be improperly clothed, with the worker's professional authority used as a supporting datum; it is not. The familiar practice of "authorities" of presenting their own organization of experience as if it were a universal truth is a kind of "pulling rank" that inhibits inquiry and sets the model for dishonesty, rather than the search for truth.

In the matter of "program" development, the worker's interest in the formalization of activity must take the form of an orientation to the reality of their experience, rather than a prescription for their well-being. "Program" should be offered as a resource, rather than a moral responsibility; and the "character-building" organizations have always been hard pressed to allow their workers to use ideas for group activity as an *opportunity,* rather than a *demand.* The prescriptive aspects of group activity, masquerading as "diagnostic" and "treatment" devices, have made it difficult for group members to retain a sense of ownership of their own group life.

In this connection, the assertiveness of the worker in making his own contribution to the material of group discussion has long suffered from a peculiar fallacy. The accepted belief has been that the worker's initiative increases as the members' decreases and vice-versa; that is, when the members are working, there is no need for the worker to talk; and when the members are silent, the worker must move in to "prime the pump." Actually, effective work emerges from an opposite strategy. The fact is that when the group is active, the worker is freed to pursue his own function and to do his work, since his object is to help them work, and he cannot do so if they are immobilized. Conversely, when they are quiet and at odds, or resistive, he must be careful not to move in so strongly that he creates the illusion of work, obliterating the fact that something is wrong. Thus, the dance is more like a fox-trot than a tango: when the members work, the worker is freed to work and they move together; when the members block, he must be careful not to move forward as they move backward. *His work takes place in the context of work.*

The fourth overall task of the worker is one for which I have borrowed a term from Norman Kelman.[6] The term is "lending a vision," and these are the movements with which the worker reveals himself as one whose hopes and aspirations are strongly invested in the struggles of both the individual and his society to reach out to each other. He projects a deep feeling for that which represents for him both individual well-being and the social good, and this is largely because he sees the connection between the two. His investment, also, is not in any particular preconceived result, for that would interfere with the struggles of people to own their own solutions, but in the *process* through which they interact.

Based on the assumption, previously mentioned, that the worker's affect is a strong component in his relationship with the client, and that what he seems to represent represents for the client an important life-ingredient, the emphasis in these activities is on those movements through which the worker reveals his own hopes and aspirations concerning the importance of the individual-social encounter and the helping relationship itself. In these movements, the worker reveals himself as a person whose own aspirations are deeply invested in the interaction between people and society and who has developed a vision of what life can and should be like. In his enthusiasm, his sense of urgency, and his capacity for empathy, the worker demonstrates that his own life experience is involved here, that he has a stake in society, and that he is not here simply to dispense solutions to problems he has already "passed."

More specifically, the worker reveals his faith in the system itself—not as it is but what it could become—and in the conditions under which the growing experience takes place. By his activity, as he safeguards the function of the relationship, he expresses his respect for the dignity of the relationship itself and for the reasons which created it. *By his refusal to trade identities with either the client or the agency,* he demonstrates his faith in the constructive power inherent in the relationship between the two. And this is precisely what both the client and the agency need from him; it is his function as *guardian of the interaction* that they both look to for support. This is the only way they can both "own" him without losing him to the other.

His moves further reveal his attitude toward the relevant data under consideration. In this respect, the worker shows something of what the material means to him—its excitement, its depths, and its importance in the human scheme. As the worker shares his own intense involvement with the materials—the facts, attitudes, values, ideas—they have to come to grips with, he projects himself as a living example of their power to attract and intrigue the human mind. It is only in this sense that the helping agent is a "salesman," and without the slightest intent to be one. It is simply by virtue of his position as a "satisfied customer," so to speak. Without this sense of enthusiasm—and its reflection differs with the personal style and artistry of different workers—

this vision of immense possibilities, his contribution to the subject-object relationship resolves itself into mechanical question-and-answer, the "Socratic game," and the do-as-I-say, not-as-I-do. With it, there can be a driving curiosity, a challenge, and a strong motive for work.

The worker's affect is a strong device in his relationship with the client. Sensitized by his own need to cope with the complexities of living, growing, and learning, the worker has a fund of real feeling from which to draw his attempts to understand the members' struggles in detail. This understanding is reflected not in a generalized "wanting to help," or "giving love," or "accepting the client as he is"—although these purposes provide an important ideological base from which to operate. Rather, his understanding is communicated in his ability to empathize with the precise feelings engendered by the clients by the demands of a particular task in a specific situation. The worker's ability to call up parts of his own experience, to communicate his feelings, and to demonstrate an active faith in the productive capacities of the client are important parts of the image of *vitality* that he projects.

There is not the intent to imply that the worker must have available to him the exact components of every client experience with which he tries to empathize. This is impossible, and such a notion would tend to immobilize workers in many situations. Closer analysis of the empathic activity reveals that what is happening is that the worker tries to come as close as he can to the experience of the client with such materials, such feelings, as he can dredge up from his own life experiences. Thus, one does not have to be an unmarried mother to come close to the alienation and rejection she must be feeling, the ambivalence and confusion about whether or not she should keep the child, and other feelings for which we can provide analogues in our own lives. The familiar slogan about artists "needing to suffer" is a reflection of this requirement—all it means is that the artist needs to have available to him those deep feelings that will make it possible for him to move close to human experiences he has not gone through firsthand but can empathize and identify with in more than a superficial and mechanical way in order to meet the requirements of his job.

In all, the worker's affective involvement in the helping relationship demonstrates better than words his conviction that the process of growing and learning is complicated and difficult, but at the same time rewarding and challenging if one is left free to test one's reactions under conditions where one can err without fear of complete failure and humiliation. The worker lends his vision to the client not in order to exchange it for his, but because the helper's aliveness, his faith in work and his stake in it are inherent in his function as a helping person. Through this task, too, runs the current of "strangeness" in the makeup of the helping person: he is a "strange adult" because he concentrates so deeply on the importance of the work, rather than on the conventional responses the client has been taught, the fear of "bad thoughts" and "bad words" and other taboos and rituals by which the worker seems to be unbound—all he seems to worry about is the problem at hand and the work to be done. The lack of conventionality is a powerful, somewhat traumatic, force in the relationship; it calls for—creates a *demand* for—novelty, for a similar penchant for boat-rocking, a kind of *intolerance for illusion* without which it is hard to avoid the ritualistic, issue avoiding, symbolic, indirect, evasive ways in which people talk to each other and in which client and worker can talk to each other without the "strange" model provided by the worker himself as he conducts himself in the helping relationship. Conventionality is testimony to fear of the system, and one cannot urge the client not to be afraid while one is himself obviously afraid to be himself and to risk spontaneity in a repressive and critical world. The worker, by his model, "permits" expressions that the world represses and through which the client must move if he is to approach his tasks directly—spontaneity, freedom of affect, tolerance of ambiguity, interest in new things, risking new ways of approaching old problems, self-examination where it is necessary, faith in work and in the relationship.

The fifth and final task to be discussed is that of *defining the requirements* and the limits of the situation in which the client-worker system is set. These rules and boundaries establish the context for the working contract in which the helping relationship is set and establish the conditions under which both the client and the worker, as well as the system, assume their respective jobs.

The basic assumption here is that to the extent that the terms of the agreement between client and agency are specific and unambiguous, the participants are free to pursue their tasks within the system in their own characteristic ways. Where the rules are obscure and ill-defined, the major energies of both worker and client become diverted to exploring the boundaries and testing the limits of each situation.

The boundary-defining activities begin with the worker's first attempts to identify the specific responsibilities that have been undertaken by the agency, the client, and the worker. They proceed by *monitoring* these realities. And they call for clarification and redefinition where the rules, the limits, the freedoms and obligations become obscure in the working process.

As has been mentioned before, the important thing to remember here is that the worker must be careful to distinguish between *explaining* a reality and *creating* one—and he must never let one masquerade as the other, thus risking his reputation for honesty without which he cannot work for any length of time. It is indispensable for his third-force, mediating, "hedging" function (for the system) that he never be ordered, wheedled, or cajoled into treating the rules and regulations as either great friends or deadly enemies; these realities are simply there, and they are there to be used as the clients can use them—to live with them, or change them, or try to understand them better. When the worker begins to treat the rules either as if they were his own, or as if he would have no part of them—either owning or disowning them—he immobilizes himself. Both the client and the system need someone—there is no one else who can play this role—who can focus his entire attention on the engagement between client and system and not worry about protecting the conditions under which they must struggle together. If all are bound by the rules in the same way, there can be nothing but an endless battle of wills, shows of strength and, in the end, very little change. The worker's freedom from the role of rules protector is the system's effort to make itself available for internal change.

All of the tasks discussed above, it should be remembered, take place one within the other; they are not jobs to be done one at a time, in any given order. The search for common ground cannot be fruitful without a clear understanding of the limits of the situation; and the detection of obstacles is shot through with the vision-lending work, so much needed to establish a relationship that encourages the daring and risking necessary to find the taboos that frustrate and inhibit creative problem-solving.

Notes and References

1. For a fuller discussion of the relationship between knowledge and action, see William Schwartz, "Small Group Science and Group Work Practice," *Social Work,* 8, 4 (October 1963), pp. 39–46.
2. See Warren G. Bennis and Herbert A. Shepard, "A Theory of Group Development," *Human Relations,* IX, November, 1956, 415–38 and James Garland, Hubert Jones, and Ralph Kolodney, "A Model for Stages of Development in Social Work Groups," in Saul Bernstein, ed., *Explorations in Group Work: Essays in Theory and Practice* (Boston: Boston University School of Social Work, 1965), among others for a discussion of authority-intimacy relationships within groups.
3. A number of further hypotheses emerge here on the interplay between intimacy and authority in groups. See, for example, George Caspar Homan, *The Human Group* (New York: Harcourt, Brace and World, 1950); and Robert F. Bales, *Interaction Process Analysis: A Method for the Study of Small Groups* (Cambridge, MA: Addison-Wesley Press), 1950.
4. For a further elaboration of the worker's practice dilemmas see Goodwin P. Garfield and Carol R. Irizarry, "The 'Record of Service': Describing Social Work Practice," in William Schwartz and Serapio R. Zalba, *The Practice of Group Work* (New York: Columbia University Press, 1971), pp. 241–65.
5. See, for example, the categorizing efforts of Florence Hollis, *Casework: A Psychosocial Therapy,* New York: Random House, 1969, and Julie Aqueros *et. al.,* "The Nature of the Helping Process," submitted in partial fulfillment for the M.S. degree, Columbia University School of Social Work, 1965.
6. "Lending a vision" is a phrase borrowed from another context: Norman Kelman, "Goals of Analytic Therapy: A Personal Viewpoint," *American Journal of Psychoanalysis,* vol. 14, no. 1, January 1954.

11

Transitions and Endings[1]

There has been very little systematic work on the problem of endings—most of our time has been spent in close attention to the beginnings of work and the work itself. But the more we look, the more interesting it becomes and I would like now to suggest a few ideas on this business of endings. Let me begin by saying that there seem to be two parts to the problem: one has to do with what we might call "temporary" endings, or *transitions* from one client-worker engagement to the next, from conference to conference, from meeting to meeting; the other is the "permanent" ending, in which the experience itself comes to a close—the final interview, the last meeting. This is in line with what I've said before—that these phases of work I've been describing apply not only to the total experience but to each encounter, which has its preparation, its beginning, its middle, and its ending.

As with the other phases, I will now move briefly through some of the assumptions, valued outcomes, and patterns of activity that should help to light up this area of work.

My first assumption is that the client-worker experience is perceived by the client as an ongoing part of his life, part of a unity composed of all the other things that are happening to him at the same time. Further, that it—the interview, the group meeting—does not "end" when it is over, but is woven into the other parts of his life, into a continuity. This is another way of saying that the worker does not "create" an experience, but simply joins one that is already going on. He jumps on and jumps off, but the life experience goes on uninterrupted.

Second, this effect of the "continuous process" will vary in nature from group to group, depending on how much continuity there is between contacts—varying from institutional groups, to friendship groups, to aggregations that collect only when they formally meet. But the continuity effect, the flow of life, continues in all of them, in different ways. Thus, the effort of the worker to "pick up where we left off" almost never works; it falls on its face for the simple reason that they are no longer where they were last time.

A third assumption I find interesting in its ramifications is that the period of ending lends itself to an intensification of work; it seems, somehow, to carry less *risk* for the client. There is a kind of "doorknob therapy" phenomenon, in which the client says the most significant thing on his way out the door, and the last few minutes of group meetings seem to gather up some of the most important concerns of the members. What one does with this material presents interesting problems; the attempt to tack it on to the beginning of the subsequent meeting rarely works, again, because it has a different function. I am thinking of an instance where a foster mother said something critical about the agency at the end of a meeting and asked for discussion on the point; when, at the beginning of the next meeting, the worker raised the matter, this mother went out to get a drink and never came back to the meeting. So the doorknob issues have a kind of life of their own. In any event, the point I am interested in here is that the ending is often used as a way of asking for help but not hanging around long enough to get involved in using it.

Let's look at some valued outcomes. First, that the group members understand that the interim work is important and legitimate, so that they do not feel they are bootlegging it—that their problem-solving is a process in their lives, and that the worker does not own it. Two, that the members add this in-between work, the transitional processes, to their agenda-making, seeing the work as a continuous process and bringing their developing concerns into each encounter as they go along. Three, that the members feel free to use each other between the formal meetings—that they accept the validity of the informal system. And finally, that this informal system be narrowed; that is, that the gap be narrowed between what happens in the official encounters and the informal contacts that transpire between these encounters. This is another way of saying that the worker would rather have the informal elaborations, including the negatives, the afterthoughts, happen before him, rather than outside his notice. While he does not try to eliminate the informal communications system—that would be neither possible nor desirable—he wants as much freedom as he can get in incorporating their productions into the "official" working system. The wider the gap between the formal work and the interim developments, the more mechanical and ritualistic grows the matter for which the group has gathered.

Staying now with the transitions, or "temporary" endings, let us move to some of the action implications. First, the worker credits, or approves, the interim contacts and the informal system, accepting this existence as a fact of life and legitimizing it with his own interest and curiosity. He reaches for this material and encourages the expression of transitional developments, leaving room for it at the beginning of meetings, urging its significance, and stressing its relevance. In the classroom, for example, I make it a point to begin with the question: "Any questions?" and my students understand that the reason I do this is that they have thought and talked about the work during the week and I am being careful not to crowd out their material and assume that one can pick up exactly where one left off. Many will wonder whether I am "risking" the curriculum itself with this device—taking a chance that I will not be able to "cover" the subject matter, and so on. And that raised all the right questions about how one integrates the needs of the curriculum with those of the learners—questions not too different from those of the social worker and her desire to bring together the aspirations of the service with those of the client.

The main point I am raising here is that the worker's activity is designed to make the process accessible to the client—that people will know that they do not have to fight for a place on the agenda, as the work proceeds from engagement to engagement. I suppose what I am really saying here is that these transitions constitute an extension of the *demand for work* to the entire time period of the helping experience and the assumption is that both the formal and informal systems are relevant to this experience. We cannot isolate the "official" contacts between worker and clients; people don't live that way, or work that way.

Let me now move into the problem of *permanent* endings—where strategies cannot be redone, or undone, because the work is over and the separation process is therefore felt more deeply by both worker and clients. First, some assumptions, beginning with what seems to be a fairly general tendency to resist the idea of ending itself. Why should this be so? There seems to be a reluctance on the part of the members to tear down a social structure that was built with such struggle and to give up the hard-won intimacy they have gained in the course of the group experience. There is often a kind of guilt, a feeling that if only they had more time they could work better, do more, play their own roles more adequately—"give us another chance." There are transference and countertransference problems, involving the sense of "unfinished business" in the relationship between the members and the worker. In our records of long-term experiences, we see the need to work off intense feelings of love between the helper and the members; and in shorter contacts, the quality is less intense perhaps, but unmistakably connected to the affect that has grown between and among the people as they worked together on problem after problem. Throughout, the intimacy, the guilt, the ambivalence, marks the process of terminating with an authority person around whom have been heaped a number of complex feelings.

Moving from the tendency to resist the ending, there is also a kind of "graduation" quality—where do we go from here, a sense of having "made it" and an urge to use and stretch one's new-found skills in life situations. This sense of a new stage, a new phase, is probably directly related to the image of group success and the quality of morale with which the group has moved into its own final phase of work.

My next assumption is that the more sudden, the more precipitous the ending, the more difficult it is for the members to encompass and deal with openly and honestly. There seem to be a number of stages to this business of ending, and a need to go through them in fairly systematic order. The first reaction by the members seems to be evasive, they don't admit that it's true, that there will be an ending. They move from that, then, to some expressions of anger, both open and covert. The third stage, if enough time is left, has something to do with their attempts to face the separation directly and to go through a kind of mourning period while the experience is still going on. And finally, we begin to see some ability to try on the idea for size, rejecting the worker in subtle ways, directing conversations to each other; partly this is anger, but it is also a kind of effort to see "how it will be without her."

> Walking back from the bus, I noticed again what had frequently been happening lately: the girls were "busy" talking to themselves and teasing each other and although it looked as if we were together, I was quite obviously apart. At one point, they actually walked in front of me, laughing over some joke, while I walked behind alone.
>
> This had essentially not happened since last summer and I felt much as I had then—isolated from them. It made me very sad, a feeling that must have been reflected in my face, for suddenly Judy "noticed" I was walking alone and came and took my arm condescendingly. Tata's response was "shit on her," at which she, Judy, Carmen, and Kathy laughed hysterically.
>
> When we were eating in the center, I said that I thought they had seemed kind of unhappy with me lately and asked if they wanted to talk about it. Kathy said they weren't unhappy about *anything*. I asked, "Even about my leaving in the summer?" Tata jumped up and shouted, "Nobody gives a shit about your leaving. Go ahead and leave now if you want to!" There were tears in her eyes as she spoke.
>
> I replied I would be very unhappy if I thought she meant this. Kathy interrupted, jumping up and raising her hand and shouting with authority, "We are not talking about this anymore."

The anticlimax usually consists of a kind of release period, the good-byes, and so on; but even here one detects the ambivalence, the reluctance to mark finis on an experience. In a recent student record, one saw the kids saying not good-bye but, "We'll be seeing you," when they knew they wouldn't. Some years ago, a student responded to this by saying, "No you won't; you must understand that I'm leaving this job and won't be back." It was a rough way to handle it, but he was trying, however clumsily, to stay close to this reality of ending.

This final phase often develops into what I sometimes call the "Farewell party syndrome," the object of which is to "celebrate" the occasion—lauding the worker, saying how grand everything was, patting the whole experience over—rather than using the occasion to *work* on the things they feel as they end. This delaying action makes it impossible to work together as they live it together; and so most of the work happens individually, after it's all over, and the mourning and easing off, and so on, is put beyond the reach of worker help and mutual aid. By the way, the camping experience is an example par excellence, where, because of the lack of counselor experience in handling endings, the weeping and wailing at the last moments of parting are loud and shrill, and are mostly carried off by staff and camper alike, to lick their wounds in private. This farewell party syndrome is a condition that has to be examined carefully; it is generally a collaboration between worker and members, for the feeling is shared and the evasions of the opportunity to *finish with work*—to use the last moments as part of the contract, rather than something different, anticlimactic. For the worker, the inability to *resolve* his function—"the client is dead, long live the client"—makes it difficult for him to end with feeling, even as he looks forward to the next beginning, with new people. We're beginning to develop some beautiful material on the stages of endings, and I hope we'll have some time to look at some of it.

The patterns of activity begin with the worker's efforts to call attention early to the imminence of ending, so that the process will have time to establish itself and take the various forms it needs to take. He reaches for the clues that emerge from the various stages of ending—the evasions, the expectations, the mourning—and holds them up for the members to see, so that they may understand a little of what is happening to them. Here again, the demand for work is made in specific terms, not in global, overgeneralized ones: not "this is our last session, let's evaluate"; not "how did it go?" asking for a kind of report-card judgment, passed or failed, good or bad, but a specific request for thought about what happened, what they got their kicks from, what they learned from, what held them up, what they feel remains to be done. This includes the search for negatives; and this search will often disturb those who want the experience to "end happily," in the "farewell party"—emphasizing the high rapport with the worker and each other and the great quality of the whole performance. It is hard here for the worker to reach behind this and ask for times when they were angry with him, when he stepped on what they were trying to do—all this in the face of their need to tell him how wonderful he was.

There is activity here that is directed to the difficulty of helping the members share *diverse* reactions to the ending, as they have tried to share such diversity in the body of the work itself. There are many differences in the ways they react to the experience of ending, and they can learn from these differences. One member will say that he had a great time, what are they all carrying on about? Another will be glad it's over and looking forward to the "graduation." And yet another will be angry with the worker, feel unfinished. It is good that they should contend with these differences, learn about their own diversity, compare reactions to this experience.

Finally, the worker remembers to put himself into the evaluation, the recollections, the feelings about separation—because he is an important part of what they are separating from and the failure to deal with the authority piece leaves a significant gap in the final work.

These are just a few ideas about endings; as I said, there's a lot more to be done in this area, both theoretically and in the examination of the records of practice.

Notes and References

1. At the time of his death, Schwartz had not begun Chapter Eleven. The following material on transitions and endings has been taken from the

final tape-recorded session of a Spring Institute, Group Work Area, Schwartz conducted on "Theory and Practice in Social Work with Groups." This institute was conducted at Columbia University School of Social Work from April 14 to June 9, 1966. The inclusion of this material was at the suggestion of Professor Alex Gitterman. Additional material on phases of work can be found in the following writings by Schwartz: "On the Use of Groups in Social Work Practice," in William Schwartz and Serapio Zalba, eds., *The Practice of Group Work* (New York: Columbia University Press, 1971), pp. 3–24; "Between Client and System: The Mediating Function," in Robert W. Roberts and Helen Northen, eds., *Theories of Social Work with Groups* (New York: Columbia U. Press, 1976), pp. 171–97; and "Social Group Work: The Interactionist Approach," *The Encyclopedia of Social Work,* vols. 16 and 17, 1971 and 1977.

Bibliography

Abels, Paul. "The Social Work Contract: Playing it Straight." Presented at Cleveland Chapter National Association of Social Workers.

Allport, Gordon W. *Becoming: Basic Considerations for a Psychology of Personality.* New Haven: Yale University Press, 1955.

Aqueros, Julie *et. al.* "The Nature of the Helping Process." submitted in partial fulfillment for the M.S. Degree. Columbia University School of Social Work, 1965.

———. *Personality and Social Encounter.* Boston: Beacon Press, 1960.

Bales, Robert F. *Interaction Process Analysis: A Method for the Study of Small Groups.* Cambridge, MA: Addison-Wesley Press, 1950.

Ballou, Richard Boyd. *The Individual and the State.* Boston: Beacon Press, 1953.

Barnett, S. A. *Canon Barnett, His Life, Work, and Friends.* Boston and New York: Houghton Mifflin Company, 1919, Vol. 1.

Barrett, William. *Irrational Man: A Study in Existentialist Philosophy.* Westport, CT: Greenwood Press, 1958.

Bartlett, Harriet M. "Toward Clarification and Improvement of Social Work Practice." *Social Work,* vol. 3, no. 2 (April 1958): 3–9.

Bellack, Arno A., Herbert M. Kliebard, Ronald T. Hyman, and Frank L. Smith, Jr. *The Language of the Classroom.* New York: Teachers College Press, 1966.

Bennis, Warren G. and Herbert A. Shepard. "A Theory of Group Development." *Human Relations.* IX, (November 1956): 415–38.

Bernstein, Saul. "Self-Determination: King or Citizen in the Realm of Values?" *Social Work,* vol. 5, no. 1 (January 1960): 3–8.

Bertalanffy, Ludwig Von. *General Systems Theory: Foundations, Development, Applications.* New York: Brazillier, 1968.

Bestor, Arthur E. *Educational Wastelands.* Urbana, IL: University of Illinois Press, 1953.

Blanton, R. "Science and Art in the Training of Psychologists." *Journal of Clinical Psychology,* vol. 18, no. 1 (Jan. 1962).

Boehm, Werner E. *Objectives of the Social Work Curriculum of the Future.* Volume I. Curriculum. New York: Council on Social Work Education, 1959.

Bonner, Hubert. *Group Dynamics: Principles and Applications.* New York: Ronald Press, 1959.

Bronowski, J. *Science and Human Values.* New York: Harper and Row, Harper Torchbooks, Science Library, 1965.

Bruner, Jerome S. *The Process of Education.* Cambridge, MA: Harvard University Press, 1960.

Bruno, Frank J. (with chapters by Louis Towley). *Trends in Social Work, 1874–1956.* New York: Columbia University Press, 1957.

Buber, Martin. *I-Thou.* Second Edition. New York: Charles Scribner's Sons, Scribner Library, 1958.

———. *The Knowledge of Man: Selected Essays.* New York: Harper and Row, Harper Torchbooks, 1965.

Buchler, Justus. *The Concept of Method.* New York and London: Columbia University Press, 1961.

Burns, Eveline M. "Tomorrow's Social Needs and Social Work Education." *Journal of Education for Social Work,* vol. 2, no. 1 (Spring 1966).

Cameron, D. Ewen. "A Theory of Diagnosis," in Paul Hoch and Joseph Zubin, eds., *Current Problems in Psychiatric Diagnosis.* New York: Grune and Stratton, 1953.

Chambers, Clarke A. "An Historical Perspective on Political Action *v.* Individualized Treatment," in *Current Issues in Social Work Seen in Historical Perspective.* New York: Council on Social Work Education, 1962.

Chilman, Catherine S. "Production of New Knowledge of Relevance to Social Work and Social Welfare: An Examination of Knowledge Which Underlies Social Work Practice and Permeates the Curriculum." *Social Work Education Reporter,* vol. 17, no. 3 (September 1969).

Chin, Robert. "The Utility of Systems Models and Developmental Models for Practitioners," in Warren G. Bennis, et. al., eds. *The Planning of Change.* New York: Holt, Rinehart and Winston, 1969.

Cohen, Alan. "Don't You Sweetheart Me. . . ." *New Society,* vol. 17, no. 435 (January 1971).

Committee on Professional Education of the American Association of Group Workers. "Statement, Content of Group Work Practice with Implications for Professional Education." 1955. Mimeographed.

Corsini, Raymond J. and Daniel D. Howard, eds., *Critical Incidents in Teaching.* Englewood Cliffs, NJ: Prentice-Hall, 1964.

Council on Social Work Education. *Building the Social Work Curriculum.* New York: Council on Social Work Education, 1961.

Coyle, Grace. *Group Work with American Youth.* New York: Harper and Brothers, 1948.

———. "Some Basic Assumptions About Group Work," in Marjorie Murphy. *The Social Group Work Method in Social Work Education.* New York: Council on Social Work Education, 1959.

Dewey, John. *Psychology.* 3d ed., rev. New York: Harper and Brothers, 1892.

———. *Democracy and Education: An Introduction to the Philosophy of Education.* New York: Macmillan, 1916.

———. *The Quest for Certainty: A Study of the Relation of Knowledge and Action.* New York: G. P. Putnam's Sons, 1929; Capricorn Books, 1960.

———. *Human Nature and Conduct: An Introduction to Social Psychology.* New York: The Modern Library, 1922, p. 30.

Durrell, Lawrence. *Justine.* New York: Pocket Books, 1965.

Eaton, Joseph W. "Science, 'Art,' and Uncertainty in Social Work." *Social Work,* vol. 3, no. 3 (July 1958): 3–10.

Einstein, Albert and Leopold Infeld. *The Evolution of Physics.*

Eisman, Martin. "Social Work's New Role in the Welfare-Class Revolution." *Social Work,* vol. 14, no. 2 (April 1969).

Fischer, Ernst. *The Necessity of Art: A Marxist Approach.* Baltimore, Md.: Penguin Books, 1963.

Flexner, Abraham. "Is Social Work a Profession?" *Proceedings of the National Conference of Charities and Correction.* Chicago: The Hildmann Printing Co., 1915, pp. 576–90.

Frank, Lawrence K. "Research for What?" *Journal of Social Issues.* Kurt Lewin Memorial Award Issue. Supplement Series, No. 10, 1957, pp. 5–22.

Freud, Sigmund. "On Psychotherapy." *Collected Papers.* London: Hogarth Press and the Institute of Psycho-Analysis, 1950, Volume I.

———. "A Phobia in a Five-Year-Old Boy." *Collected Papers.* London: Hogarth Press and the Institute of Psycho-Analysis, 1950, Volume III, pp. 149–295.

Friedman, Maurice. "Introduction Essay." in Martin Buber. *The Knowledge of Man: Selected Essays.* New York: Harper and Row, Harper Torchbooks, 1965.

Frost, S. E. *Basic Teachings of the Great Philosophers.* Philadelphia: The Blakiston Co., 1942.

Gage, N. L. ed. *Handbook of Research on Teaching.* Chicago: Rand McNally & Company, 1963.

Garfield, Goodwin P. and Carol R. Irizarry. "The 'Record of Service': Describing Social Work Practice." in William Schwartz and Serapio R. Zalba, eds., *The Practice of Group Work.* New York: Columbia University Press, 1971, pp. 241–65.

Garland, James, Hubert Jones, and Ralph Kolodney. "A Model for Stages of Development in Social Work Groups." in Saul Bernstein, ed., *Explorations in Group Work: Essays in Theory and Practice.* Boston: Boston University School of Social Work, 1965, pp. 12–53.

Ginsberg, Mitchell I. and Irving Miller. "Problem of Conformity as Faced by the Professional Worker." *Group Work Papers 1957.* Presented at the National Conference on Social Welfare. New York: National Association of Social Workers, pp. 7–19.

Gordon, William E. "A Critique of the Working Definition." *Social Work,* vol. 7, no. 4 (October 1962).

Gurin, Arnold. "Social Planning and Community Organization." in *Encyclopedia of Social Work.* New York: National Association of Social Workers, 1971.

Harrington, Michael J. *The Other America.* New York: Macmillan, 1963.

Hearn, Gordon. *Theory Building in Social Work.* Toronto, Ontario, Canada: University of Toronto Press, 1958.

Held, Virginia. "Walking Out on the System." *The Nation,* vol. 213, no. 12 (October 18, 1971): 370–72.

Hofstadter, Richard. *Social Darwinism in American Thought.* New York: Brazillier, 1959.

Hollis, Florence. *Casework: A Psychosocial Therapy.* New York: Random House, 1969.

———. "The Psychosocial Approach to the Practice of Casework," in Robert W. Roberts and Robert H. Nee, eds., *Theories of Social Casework.* Chicago, IL: University of Chicago Press, 1970.

Homans, George Caspar. *The Human Group.* New York: Harcourt, Brace and World, 1950.

Hutchins, Robert M. *The Higher Learning in America.* New Haven: Yale University Press, 1936.

———. *No Friendly Voice.* Chicago: University of Chicago Press, 1936.

Jones, Audrey. "Letter to the Editor." *New Society,* vol. 19, no. 486 (January 20, 1972).

Kahn, Alfred J. "The Function of Social Work in the Modern World," in Alfred J. Kahn, ed., *Issues in American Social Work.* New York: Columbia University Press, 1959, pp. 3–38.

Karpf, Maurice J. *The Scientific Base of Social Work.* New York: Columbia University Press, 1931.

Keith-Lucas, Alan. "A Critique of the Principle of Client Self-Determination." *Social Work,* vol. 8, no. 3 (July 1963): 66–71.

Kelman, Norman. "Goals of Analytic Therapy: A Personal Viewpoint." *American Journal of Psychoanalysis,* vol. 14, no. 19 (January 1954): 105–114.

Kilpatrick, William Heard. *Foundations of Method: Informal Talks on Teaching.* New York: The Macmillan Company, 1932.

Klein, Alan F. *Social Work Through Group Process.* Albany, NY: State University of New York at Albany, 1970.

Korsch, Barbara M. and Vida Francis Negret. "Doctor-Patient Communication." *Scientific American,* vol. 227, no. 2 (August 1972).

Krasner, Leonard. "Behavior Therapy," in Paul H. Mussen and Mark R. Rosenzweig, eds., *Annual Review of Psychology.* Palo Alto, CA: Annual Reviews, Inc., 1971, Vol. 22, pp. 483–532.

Kuhn, Thomas S. *The Structure of Scientific Revolutions.* Chicago: University of Chicago Press, 1962.

Lauchner, A. H. in "Three R's Aren't for All." *News-Gazette,* Champaign, Illinois, February 14, 1951.

Lasswell, Harold D. "Strategies of Inquiry: The Rational Use of Observation," in Daniel Lerner, ed., *The Human Meaning of the Social Science.* New York: Meridian Books, 1959.

Lawrence, Harry. "The Testing of Mr. Jennings." *The Group,* vol. 16, no. 4 (April 1954): 11–14, 24–25.

Lee, Porter R. "Technical Training for Social Work," in Porter R. Lee *Social Work as Cause and Function and Other Papers.* New York: Columbia University Press, 1937.

Lerner, Daniel, ed. *Evidence and Inference.* New York: Free Press, 1959.

Lelyveld, Joseph. "City's New View of Welfare: A Job for Businessmen." *The New York Times.* February 1, 1972, pp. 1, 16.

Lindeman, E. C. "Organization and Technique for Rural Recreation," in *Proceedings of the National Conference of Social Work.* Chicago: University of Chicago Press, 1920.

———. "Group Work and Education for Democracy." *Proceedings of the National Conference of Social Work.* New York: Columbia University Press, 1939.

Lubove, Roy. "Social Work and the Life of the Poor." *The Nation,* vol. 202, no. 21 (May 1966).

May, Roll, Ernest Angel, and Henri F. Ellengerger, eds., *Existence A New Dimension in Psychiatry and Psychology.* New York: Basic Books, 1958.

Mayer, Martin. *The Schools.* New York: Harper and Brothers, 1961.

Menninger, Karl. *Theory of Psychoanalytic Technique.* New York: Harper and Row, Harper Torchbooks, Academy Library, 1958.

Meyer, Carol H. *Social Work Practice: A Response to the Urban Crisis.* New York: The Free Press, 1970.

Mill, John Stuart. *A System of Logic.* New York: Harper and Brothers, 1874.

Millikan, Max F. "Inquiry and Policy: The Relation of Knowledge to Action." in Daniel Lerner, ed., *The Human Meaning of the Social Sciences.* New York: Meridian Books, 1959.

Mills, C. Wright. *The Power Elite.* New York: Oxford University Press, 1957.

Murphy, Gardner. *Human Potentialities.* New York: Basic Books, 1958.

Parsons, Talcott. *The Structure of Social Action.* Glencoe, IL: Free Press, 1949.

———. "A Sociologist Looks at the Legal Profession," in Talcott Parsons, Rev. ed. *Essays in Sociological Theory.* Glencoe, IL: Free Press, 1954.

Perlman, Helen Harris. *Social Casework: A Problem-solving Process.* Chicago: University of Chicago Press, 1957.

———. "Social Work Method: A Review of the Past Decade." *Social Work,* vol. 1, no. 4 (October 1965).

Pray, Kenneth L. "A Restatement of the Generic Principles of Social Casework Practice." *Social Work in a Revolutionary Age and Other Papers.* Philadelphia: University of Pennsylvania Press, 1949, pp. 224–61.

———. *Social Work in a Revolutionary Age and Other Papers.* Philadelphia: University of Pennsylvania Press, 1949.

Pruyser, Paul W. "Existential Notes on Professional Education." *Social Work,* vol. 8, no. 2 (April 1963): 82–87.

Read, Herbert. *The Meaning of Art.* Baltimore, Md: Penguin Books, 1949.

Reynolds, Bertha Capen. *Between Client and Community.* New York: Oriole Editions, Inc., 1934, 1973.

Richmond, Mary E. "Some Next Steps in Social Treatment." *Proceedings of the National Conference of Social Work.* Chicago: University of Chicago Press, 1920.

———. "The Retail Method of Reform," in Joanna C. Colcord, ed., *The Long View: Papers and Addresses by Mary E. Richmond.* New York: Russell Sage Foundation, 1930.

———. "Some Next Steps in Social Treatment," in Joanna C. Colcord, ed., *The Long View: Papers and Addresses by Mary E. Richmond.* New York: Russell Sage Foundation, 1930.

———. "The Training of Charity Workers," in Joanna C. Colcord, ed., *The Long View: Papers and Addresses by Mary E. Richmond.* New York: Russell Sage Foundation, 1930.

———. *Social Diagnosis.* New York: The Free Press, 1965.

Robinson, Virginia P. "The Meaning of Skill." *Training for Skill in Social Casework.* Philadelphia, PA: University of Pennsylvania Press, 1942.

Rosenthal, Jack. "Learning-Plan Test is Called a Failure." *The New York Times.* February 1, 1972, pp. 1, 30.

Rothman, Milton A. *The Laws of Physics.* Greenwich, CT: Fawcett Publications, 1963.

Schorr, Alvin L. "The Retreat to the Technician." *Social Work,* vol. 4, no. 1, January 1959.

Schwartz, William. "The Social Worker in the Group." *The Social Welfare Forum, 1961.* New York and London: Columbia University Press, 1961, pp. 146–171.

———. "Toward a Strategy of Group Work Practice." *Social Service Review,* vol. 36, no. 2 (September 1962): pp. 268–79.

———. "Small Group Science and Group Work Practice." *Social Work,* vol. 8, no. 4 (October 1963): 39–46.

———. "Group Work in Public Welfare," *Public Welfare,* vol. 26, no. 4 (October 1968): pp. 322–70.

———. "Private Troubles and Public Issues: One Social Work Job or Two?" *The Social Welfare Forum, 1969.* New York and London: Columbia University Press, 1969, pp. 22–43.

———. "Neighborhood Centers and Group Work," in Henry S. Maas, ed., *Research in the Social Services: A Five-Year Review.* New York: National Association of Social Workers, 1971, pp. 130–91.

———. "On the Use of Groups in Social Work Practice," in William Schwartz and Serapio Zalba, eds., *The Practice of Group Work.* New York: Columbia University Press, 1971, pp. 3–24.

———. "Social Group Work: The Interactionist Approach," in *The Encyclo-*

pedia of Social Work. New York: National Association of Social Workers, 1971.

———. "Between Client and System: The Mediating Function," in Robert W. Roberts and Helen Northen, eds., *Theories of Social Work with Groups.* New York: Columbia University Press, 1976, pp. 171–97.

———. "Social Group Work: The Interactionist Approach," in *The Encyclopedia of Social Work.* New York: National Association of Social Workers, 1977, pp. 1328–38.

Simon, Bernece K. "Social Casework Theory: An Overview," in Robert W. Roberts and Robert H. Nee, eds., *Theories of Social Casework.* Chicago: University of Chicago Press, 1970.

Skinner, B. F. "Why Teachers Fail." *Saturday Review.* October 16, 1965.

Smalley, Ruth Elizabeth. *New Perspectives on Services to Groups: Theory, Organization and Practice, Social Work with Groups, 1961,* New York: National Association of Social Workers, 1961, pp. 32–34.

———. *Theory for Social Work Practice.* New York: Columbia University Press, 1967.

Smith, Mortimer. *And Madly Teach.* Chicago: Henry Regnery, 1949.

Specht, Harry. "Disruptive Tactics." *Social Work,* vol. 14, no. 2 (April 1969).

Stone, Irving. *The Agony and the Ecstasy.* New York: Signet, New American Library, 1961.

Strupp, Hans H. *Psychotherapists in Action: Explorations of the Therapist's Contribution to the Treatment Process.* New York: Grune and Stratton, 1960.

Sullivan, Dorothea F. *Readings in Group Work.* New York: Association Press, 1952.

Thomas, Edwin J. "Behavioral Modification and Casework," in Robert W. Roberts and Robert H. Nee, eds., *Theories of Social Casework.* Chicago: University of Chicago Press, 1970, pp. 181–218.

Tweney, C. F. and L. E. C. Hughes, 3d ed., rev. *Chamber's Technical Dictionary.* New York: Macmillan, with Supplement, 1961.

United Neighborhood House, Pre-Teen Delinquency Project. *Record of Service.* 1964. Mimeographed.

Watts, Alan W. *Psychotherapy East and West.* New York: Pantheon Books, 1963.

Webster's Third New International Dictionary of the English Language Unabridged. Springfield, MA: G. and C. Merriam Company, 1964.

Wilensky, Harold L. and Charles N. Lebeaux. *Industrial Society and Social Welfare.* New York: Russell Sage Foundation, 1958.

Wilson, Gertrude and Gladys Ryland. *Social Group Work Practice: The Creative Use of the Social Process.* New York: Houghton Mifflin Company, 1949.

Yates, Donald. "A New Attitude for the New Instruction." *New York State Education,* vol. 58, no. 5 (March 1971).

Collected Works

History and Tradition

Introduction

As time passes, we move further and further away from our professional beginnings. Social work reconfigures itself continuously, new forms of service develop, and new patterns of practice emerge. The proliferation of experience makes it more difficult for us to hold on to our past. The belief that "all past is prologue"[1] loses sway as students and educators are required to expend increased energy to mine the past for the wisdom derived from earlier times. The significance of history becomes more difficult to discern. The press of serving vulnerable populations understandably rivets students' attention on the present. In the wish to reduce student anxiety, discussion of the historical roots of professional practice is a neglected afterthought, if at all. Distance from our origins becomes prominent in present-day practice. As dependence upon current technologies increases, we find ourselves increasingly alienated from the teachings of our forebears. Repeatedly we are left to "reinvent the wheel."

It seems fitting that Schwartz's first major work, in 1959, and his last, in 1981, presented and mined group work's history for its lessons for the present. He believed that one cannot understand the present well without delving into how issues were defined and thought about in the past. New ideas, he posited, do not emerge in isolation, but rather in the context of their times, what has preceded them, and through the efforts of those who have gone before.

His thinking about group work theory and social work practice was deeply rooted in his reading of history and his belief that social work function is embedded in the social function of the profession. For him it was the social conditions themselves which gave rise to the need for a centripetal force expressly designed to mitigate some of the negative effects of capitalism and the growing separation between people and their social institutions. By attending to the processes between the individual and society, the symbiotic tie between them would be strengthened. Because function arose in response to environmental conditions it would become imperative to understand these conditions and their consequences for people's lives.

"Group Work and the Social Scene" represents Schwartz's first major effort to advance his definition of social work function as one of mediating between individuals and the social systems of importance to them. In this chapter, he traces the growth of industrialization during the latter part of the nineteenth century. This was a period in which developing capitalism created the rise of a small monied class which profited at the expense of

[1]William Shakespeare, *The Tempest.*

the masses of people whose labor produced wealth for them. Alienation, abuses of power, and the inability of people to redress grievances through their own individual efforts would become important themes to which group work paid attention.

As with all change, this oppressive economic order created the conditions which prompted the need for a countervailing force. Group workers became part of that effort. They shared a more equitable vision and with other democratic forces pressed for social change. The pragmatism of William James and the instrumentalism of John Dewey added strong voices to a growing progressivism.

Early group work history celebrated union among people. In contrast to those who believed that natural law was one of competition, Schwartz emphasized that the movement towards mutual aid and cooperation was equally a part of what occurred naturally. The theme of mutual aid became integral to Schwartz's view of the social work group as a prototype of the democratic system itself. Concern *with* the small group was a concern *for* ". . . the salutary social and personal effects of group association" (1959, p. 115). Concern *with* the development of leadership within the group was a concern *for* "the mobilization of group life in a democracy" (1959, p. 115).

To Schwartz, 1959 was an interesting point in group work's development. While group work's search for a reference group had concluded in 1955 with the formation of the National Association of Social Workers, its heritage had been forever enriched by its long-term association with a wide group of disciplines interested in small group phenomena. Themes of interactionism, social determinants of attitudes and values, motivation as a basis for learning, the small group as an instance of democracy in action, and the creative force in all people which when sufficiently liberated would allow the individual to act together and in the interests of all, would remain integral to the character of group work. His fond remembrance of Grace Coyle (1979) points clearly to her contribution to these ideas: the small group "as the prototype of the democratic process in action"; the union between social reform and social service; and self-help and self-determination as bedrock of the client-worker relationship.

By 1959 group work had progressed to view leadership as a process rather than a trait. It also began to distinguish professional influence from peer influence, and started to design a "teachable methodology." For some, the movement toward method represented a retreat from, and thus a betrayal of, social goals. For Schwartz, "[t]he ensuing efforts to build a scientific base and a unique methodology were undertaken not to replace the sense of mission, but to implement it" (1959, p. 122). He believed that "[a]t this moment in history, the concern with method far from representing an abandonment of larger aims constitutes a high form of dedication to their achievement" (1959, p. 129). Knowledge was sufficiently defined for the time being, desired outcomes sufficiently specified; it was now necessary to move toward method as the link between the two.

In the ensuing twenty-two years, Schwartz devoted himself to the development of a "teachable methodology" for the practice of social work, focusing on practice with groups. While much had been accomplished, he remained concerned that though NASW was formed in 1955 to further the goal of a unified profession, the profession was "more like a coalition of the old 'methods' than it [was] an integrated discipline combining the richest and most effective elements of each" (1981, p. 9).[2]

"The Group Work Tradition and Social Work Practice" represented Schwartz's final effort to further a common technology irrespective of the number of persons with whom the social worker was working at any point in time. His vision of social work practice remained a generic one throughout his career. This universal view prompted him to look beyond practice with groups, to the practice of social work. There he developed a broad appreciation of the contribution of others, for example, Bertha Capen Reynolds (1981) who put forward the vision of a unified profession based in the link between "private troubles and public issues."

In "The Group Work Tradition and Social Work Practice" Schwartz pursued the view he advanced in 1959 that the search for a common technology would best be furthered if each of the old "methods" explored its own traditions. Then, through comparison and testing, the "richest and most effective elements of each" could be woven together.

Schwartz's examination of group work's history and tradition for those elements which could guide practice will be familiar to those who have ventured into "Content and Process in the Educative Experience" and *Social Work With Groups: The Search for a Method.* At the outset, what was striking to him was that these themes and elements were more readily visible in the group situation than in the one-to-one situation where "the work is private, . . . and under the worker's almost total control" (1981, p. 23). Group work provided a different milieu in which "the traditional worker-member relationship in group work was that of coactive, reciprocal, functional, first-among-equals, mentoring collaboration in the pursuit of group tasks" (1981 p. 20).

Schwartz's study of group work history revealed four key elements which had importance for understanding the helping process. First was the idea that the worker practiced from inside the helping system, thus making the concept of intervention a contradiction in terms because one cannot intervene in a system from inside. Second was the value of action and activity and the use of program to engage members through other than cognitive processes. Third was an appreciation of the place of feeling and impulse in the helping experience where process does not necessarily (or

---

[2]Method is written in quotes to reflect Schwartz's belief that casework, group work, and community organization did not represent separate methods, but rather arrangements for working with different numbers of people at different times. See "The Social Worker in the Group" (1961), in this volume, for elaboration of these ideas.

at all) proceed through a tight, orderly, and logical progression of ideas. And fourth the worker was called upon to match members' emphasis upon strengths, and the connection between feeling and action. These themes highlighted that the deeper truth of the settlement "lay in its vision of a relationship in which the qualities of leadership were expressed in the joys of human collaboration, rather than in the action of the knower on the naive, the strong on the weak, the expert on the uninitiated" (1981, p. 23). "[S]hared control, shared power, and the shared agenda" (1981, p. 24) were at the heart of the helping process rather than the tenets of the coveted medical model built upon "a unilateral power exercised over an objectified, inert, malleable client" (1981, p. 24). The image of the "broken client" needing to be "fixed" would not do as a guide for an expanded theory of the helping process.

Toby Berman-Rossi

Group Work and the Social Scene

William Schwartz

In the decades immediately following the Civil War, a reunited America gave itself over to the development of its vast economic and industrial potential. As the country set out to fill its territories and exploit its unlimited physical and human resources, there was a surging sense of power, emerging from the promise of man's ingenuity and technical genius.

Mark Twain called that period the Gilded Age. It was an era of frontiers, and the frontier spirit was individualistic, bold, adventurous, and competitive. And since the open frontiers were everywhere—geographic, social, industrial—the heroes of the time were the pioneers, the empire-builders, and the self-made men.

The philosophical mood was expansive, materialistic, and dynamic; "utility" and "change" were the bywords, and Herbert Spencer's doctrine of the inevitability of progress caught the imagination of Americans. Freedom and the machine were to go hand in hand as a prosperous people took increasing control over its political power. The ability of the machine to do the work of society would soon create a new element in life, which was leisure. Already, all things seemed possible for those with talent, resourcefulness, and the middle-class virtues.

For the mass of the people, converging on the new centers of industrial development, the prospect was somewhat grimmer:

> . . . this picturesque America with its heritage of crude energy—greedy, lawless, capable—was to be transformed into a vast uniform middle-class land, dedicated to capitalism and creating the greatest machine-order known to history. A scattered agricultural people, steeped in particularistic jealousies and suspicious of centralization, was to be transformed into an urbanized factory people, rootless, migratory, drawn to the job as by a magnet.[1]

[1]Vernon Louis Parrington, *Main Currents in American Thought* (New York: Harcourt, Brace, 1927), III, 26.

With the growth of large, sprawling cities and the concentration of the labor force, grinding poverty was out in the open for all to see. The scale of expansive creation and construction was soon matched by a similar scale of deterioration in conditions of urban life. As the nation grew richer, a large proportion of its people grew poorer, with families broken by want, children working in mines and factories, and gathered together in slums that perpetuated their own evils.

Moreover, the industrial system brought with it difficulties that transcended the purely economic. Factory work was stereotyped and oppressive, as Chaplin later illustrated so vividly in his film "Modern Times." Urban life was a complicated network of human relationships, and those who failed to meet its demands experienced the new phenomenon of loneliness in the midst of crowded cities. As the organization of society grew more complex, it became increasingly difficult to retain a sense of control over one's own destiny.

Since it was this element of control that constituted for many the central concept of a democracy, there was a growing concern—barely heard at the outset but swelling into an insistent clamor toward the turn of the century—that we were moving further from the democratic vision rather than closer to it. This fear was accentuated by rapidly increasing concentration of power and wealth in the hands of the few.

The social Darwinism of Spencer and William Graham Sumner provided the intellectual undergirding for the new competitive and individualistic order. The philosophy of the "survival of the fittest," applied to the facts of social and economic existence, offered a strong rationale for those who might have moral problems to solve as they surveyed the American scene:

> In the Spencerian intellectual atmosphere of the 1870's and 1880's it was natural for conservatives to see the economic contest in competitive society as a reflection of the struggle in the animal world. It was easy to argue by analogy from natural selection to social selection of fitter men, from organic forms with superior adaptability to citizens with a greater store of economic virtues. The competitive order was now supplied with a cosmic rationale. Competition was glorious. Just as survival was the result of strength, success was the reward of virtue.[2]

But, in the words of Tawney, "there is no touchstone . . . which reveals the true character of a social philosophy more clearly than the spirit in which it regards the misfortunes of those of its members who fall by the way." Further, it was not possible "to consign to collective perdition almost the whole of the wage-earning population."[3] The disillusionment rode on the heels of two

---

[2]Richard Hofstadter, *Social Darwinism in American Thought* (rev. ed.; Boston: Beacon Press, 1955), p. 57.

[3]R. H. Tawney, *Religion and the Rise of Capitalism* (New York: Penguin Books, 1947; originally published in 1926, Harcourt, Brace), p. 222.

depressions, the agitations of labor, and the political unrest of the 1890s. The voices of protest insisted that a true democratic freedom could not be built on the hopes of a propertied elite and the promise of a static evolutionism. And they proceeded to reinterpret the evolutionary theme in a manner that was perhaps less strange to Darwin himself than it was to some of his prophets.[4]

If man was an animal, he was at least a new kind of animal, one who could by his wits and collective power control the forces of nature rather than submit himself docilely to its inexorable laws of survival and selection. Society was not a jungle, in which life for one meant death for another, but a system of cooperative and interdependent relationships designed to raise the level of existence for all men. Cooperation, it was shown, was at least as much a law of nature as competition; people were responsible to each other and government was their instrument of action. Social reform, far from being an unwarranted intrusion upon nature's laws, was man's way of adapting those laws to his own needs and conditions.

The philosophical voice of the new progressivism made itself heard through an organized labor movement, an aroused clergy, and the new relativistic thinking of economists, sociologists, and social philosophers. The pragmatism of William James and the instrumentalism of John Dewey were potent tools in the hands of those who saw democratic freedom as a social development rather than as a prerequisite of rugged and powerful individuals:

> The pragmatists' most vital contribution to the general background of social thought was to encourage a belief in the effectiveness of ideas and the possibility of novelties—a position necessary to any philosophically consistent theory of social reform. As Spencer had stood for determinism and the control of man by the environment, the pragmatists stood for freedom and control of the environment by man.[5]

Agency Beginnings

These developments fashioned the social context in which the first leisure-time community agencies assumed their form and took on their function in American society. In their inception, they were native adaptations of services brought about by earlier and similar developments in the industrialization and urbanization of the English economy. The sectarian "Y" 's appeared first, just after the turn of the mid-century; the settlements followed, in the 1880s and 1890s; and the first two decades of the twentieth century saw the beginnings of the national youth-serving organizations and the recreation movement.

In many respects, the agencies were protective associations against the problems created by city life in a rising industrial society. They ranged themselves against the mobility and rootlessness, the stultifying, noncreative work,

---

[4]Hofstadter, *op. cit.*, p. 201.

[5]*Ibid.*, p. 125.

the rising rates of delinquency and crime, the patterns of neighborhood segregation, and, pervading all, the inability of transient and disorganized populations to pool their interests and take action in their own behalf.

To counter these forces, the agencies projected themselves as the protagonists of social responsibility in a competitive order and of individual and cultural identity in a faceless crowd. They stressed the need for individualizing, for a kind of collective security, and for the equalization of political and economic power. They stressed, too, the rehabilitating force of play and recreation and they made a key issue of the relationship between responsible citizenship and the creative use of leisure time. "In the play group (i.e., the free-time group)," wrote Mary Simkhovitch in her later account of the values of group living, "may be seen the happy exercise of power unrelated to oppression, the use of energy that brings no reward but the satisfaction of capabilities, and a sense of comity that enriches the spirit and is symbolic of a kind of society the world has not yet known."[6]

Above all, there were two common emphases which, taken together, constituted perhaps the community agencies' outstanding contribution to the American scene. One was their shared belief in the salutary social and personal effects of group association; the other was a tested conviction that the development of sound leadership was a central problem and a special task in the mobilization of group life in a democracy.

In their preoccupation with human association, they created a great laboratory of group experience, in which attention was called to some of the major hypotheses later to be elaborated and tested by the social scientists: people in groups were more teachable, more reachable, and more susceptible to change; small groups in particular were crucibles of attitude and value formation; people together tended to solve problems more efficiently, since "group work" is more lasting and more accurate than individual work. Further, in acting together people could exert greater impact on their environment, and the group thus became the symbol and the instrument of the democratic ideal. A democratic society is one that acts through a multiplicity of active groups, trained in their own broadly conceived self-interest. As a further development of this idea, the group itself must be democratically evolved, structured, and oriented—a prototype, or special instance, of the democratic system in action.

In a similar way, the early work of the agencies served to dramatize the nature of influence within the structure of group experience. The fact that people seemed more amenable to the ideas of others directly involved in their activity than to ideas in the abstract brought with it a searching concern with the attributes of leadership and with its importance as an instrument of agency purpose. Although the first conceptions differed among agencies, they held certain important notions in common: "leadership" was seen as a fixed personality characteristic, distinguishing those who "lead" from those who

[6]Mary K. Simkhovitch, *Group Life* (New York: Association Press, 1940), p. 34.

"follow"; the term itself was used to describe the personal influence of group members and agency workers alike, without differentiating their separate functions within the group experience; and the exercise of influence, since it was a natural concomitant of personal strength and character, was essentially an intuitive process rather than a planned and conscious method of intervention in group life. The later efforts to identify leadership as a process rather than a trait, to distinguish peer influence from professional guidance, and to design a planned and teachable methodology of intervention were to constitute the first significant steps toward the development of modern group work practice.

Taken together, the agencies projected a strange and varied assortment of aspirations and functions: they were established to educate and to reform, to serve youth, to mobilize neighborhoods, to perpetuate religious and cultural identities, to preserve ethical (largely middle-class) values, and to exert a benevolent moral pressure on those whose low position in society rendered them especially susceptible to the confusions and temptations of the time. Some were specifically concerned with the vast throngs of immigrants from abroad and with the streams of young people moving from their homes on the farm in search of city opportunities. Thus, when Margaretta Williamson studied the job definitions of workers in leisure-time agencies in the late 1920s, she reported that:

> The objectives of these various agencies would at first thought seem so divergent as to make it impossible to treat the duties and responsibilities of their workers in the same analysis. The evangelical motive, so strong a feature in certain of the agencies, is entirely lacking in others; some are concerned with group experience and leisure-time activities for the average everyday person of any walk of life, others for the so-called "underprivileged" person; neighborhood relationships, community organization, education, concern for the young man or woman away from home, or appreciation of out-of-door life, may loom large in the program of a particular agency. Upon closer scrutiny, however, and after acquaintance with methods and procedure, it becomes apparent that along with other motives and interests peculiar to the particular agency, they all have a common desire so to guide the leisure-time activities of the individual, through group experience and education, that he may develop an integrated personality with the capacity for living a full life, and accustom himself to the give and take of group life as an introduction to social responsibility. Quite apart, moreover, from the purposes of these organizations, it is certain that group activity has commended itself as a medium of work to a variety of agencies pursuing a variety of aims.[7]

---

[7]Margaretta Williamson, *The Social Worker in Group Work* (New York and London: Harper, 1929), p. 17.

In function and philosophy, the agencies combined the scientific, pragmatic, and materialist outlook of the new society with its equally characteristic heritage of puritanism and moral absolutism. Drawing their inspiration and sponsorship from middle-class philanthropy and from radical social protest, from religious idealism and from the scientific spirit of the progressive era, they both reflected and rejected the social Darwinism against which, collectively, they had set their faces. Emerging from both the revolutionary and the conservative spirit of the age, group work was born as a true child of its time.

The Search for a Reference Group

Those who began to gather around the discussion tables in the 1920s and 1930s to explore the problems of working with people in groups represented a wide variety of identifications and interests. They were educators and psychologists, settlement workers, church workers and social workers, recreationists, anthropologists, sociologists and social philosophers.[8] It was an unprecedented working collaboration of practitioners, philosophers, and social scientists; it was also short-lived, lasting only until academic and professional loyalties began to harden and the separate fields and disciplines began to move off along their own lines of emphasis.

The substance of their communication was centered in three major areas of concern. They shared the results yielded up by the newly developing social sciences, finding both verification and inspiration in the emerging emphasis on the laws of change, the dynamics of interaction, the social determinants of attitude and value, and the motivational basis of learning. Said a psychologist:

> If you believed in the constancy of temperament, personality, intelligence, etc., your groups could promise to be of little or no therapeutic value in these directions. Basic tenets of group work such as education and re-education would remain Utopian ideas. But there is already implicit in group work a dynamic approach. There is already present at least the hope of effecting change. It is on this ground that the new psychology and the new group work must meet.[9]

Second, they sought to develop a guiding ethical system and to specify the objectives of group education—both formal and informal—in a democratic society. They translated the philosophy of James and Dewey into the specific meanings of democracy in action;[10] inspired by the optimism of Mary Follett and Eduard Lindeman, their statements reflected a strong conviction about the perfectibility of human nature and the connection between self-interest and

---

[8]See, for example, list of contributors to Joshua Lieberman, ed., *New Trends in Group Work* (New York: Association Press, 1939).

[9]Dan L. Adler, "Contributions of Psychology to Social Group Work," in *Group Work 1939* (New York: American Association for the Study of Group Work, 1939), p. 8.

[10]Cf. Eduard C. Lindeman, "The Roots of Democratic Culture," in *ibid.*, p. 1.

the social good. They stressed the existence of benevolent and creative forces in people, forces which needed only to be liberated by circumstances to enable individuals to act together in the interests of all. The connection between the *one* and the *many* was, in fact, so clear and obvious that it was not yet considered necessary to describe the precise nature of the enabling process; the goals and values themselves, could they be clearly enough formulated, seemed powerful enough, in the hands of a mature, self-aware "leader," to produce alert, responsible citizens in socially active groups.

Finally, they attempted to define the "group work" entity itself, and to understand its scope and function, in a way that would provide an identification and a sense of direction for its practitioners and teachers. Group work, seeking a reference group, found itself bound by heritage and loyalty to a wide assortment of fields, agencies, social interests, and academic disciplines.

Our society has established certain institutions, beyond the family, which are designed to carry out its functions. Needing to transmit its accumulated heritage of knowledge, values, and skills to succeeding generations, it has institutionalized a system of education; seeking to provide means through which people can play, exercise, relax, and develop their cultural tastes, we have developed a field of recreation; to bring the sick back to health, a complex of therapeutic activity is organized; the field of social welfare functions to ensure its citizens against emotional and physical deprivation and to bring needs and resources into balance; and, to provide a climate and a machinery through which people may act to effect change and express protest, we have institutionalized structures through which people may exercise their right to influence social policy through social action.

To which of these systems did the developing entity of group work—or, as it was sometimes called, "social" group work—belong? In a real sense, it was all of these things, having brought together agencies, practitioners, and students of group phenomena in each of these areas of function. It was certainly, in its various aspects, a reform movement, a therapeutic tool, an educational method, a field of service, a small part of the recreational movement, and a moving spirit in the affairs of many social welfare agencies.[11]

There was another sense, however, in which group work was none of these, but something quite new, with an identity all its own. In this respect, it seemed to be developing as a unique and highly refined skill, limited primarily to functioning in small groups of people in intimate psychological interaction, and directed toward helping the group members to work together on their common goals and concerns, whatever these might be. A distinctive profession built around such an area of expertness could conceivably be utilized anywhere that people needed or wanted to be together, play together, work together, or even learn together. It could be used in industry, in social agencies, in education, in hospitals, and in other organizations and institutions.

---

[11]Cf. Grace L. Coyle, "Social Group Work," in *Social Work Year Book 1937* (New York: Russell Sage Foundation, 1937), pp. 461–64.

There were, in fact, many who felt that this development was exactly what should happen and who pointed to the dangers of a premature or exclusive identification with one or another field of service. As late as 1939, Hugh Hartshorne, reporting as chairman of the Commission on the Objectives of Group Work of the American Association for the Study of Group Work (AASGW), said, "It is probably fortunate that the notion of group work has not yet settled down into a new educational stereotype."[12] And, after delineating the various kinds of tasks amenable to group work assistance, he continued:

> Viewed in this way, group work has no objectives of its own, but represents, instead, the increasing sensitiveness of agencies to the conditions under which the social skills and attitudes needed in a democracy may be expected to develop. . . . the immense variety of objectives that have been proposed for group work is the consequence of this confusion between group work as an agency device and group work as an educational principle.[13]

In 1938, in a chapter entitled, "To What Profession Does Informal Education Belong?" Charles E. Hendry wrote:

> It seems quite clear that we are not yet in a position to decide definitely on this question of the professional classification of informal and group education and recreation. Whether we have here an independent profession or a substantial segment of an existing profession remains to be determined. Just as a scientist would not want to restrict his participation to a single scientific society, so group educators, presumably, will not want to identify themselves solely with one professional organization or to isolate themselves from any professional organization that operates within the area of their social function.[14]

Thus, too, William Heard Kilpatrick, in his *Group Education for a Democracy,* published in 1940 under the auspices of the AASGW:

> The author takes responsibility here for stating his personal opinion, assisted at points by publications of the Association, that group work is a highly worthy new interest, whether this go on in school classes or in recreation and other informal education. This group work is, however, not to be thought of as a separate field of work, but rather as a method to be used in all kinds of educational effort. "Group work" in this sense is just now more or less of a movement, and as such deserves support and success. But its success will be achieved when, and to the degree that,

---

[12]Hugh Hartshorne, "Objectives of Group Work" in *Group Work 1939,* p. 39.

[13]*Ibid.*

[14]Hedley S. Dimock, Charles E. Hendry, and Karl P. Zerfoss, *A Professional Outlook on Group Education* (New York: Association Press, 1938), p. 47.

effective working in groups has established itself as an essential part of any adequate education of youth, however and wherever conducted.[15]

The reluctance to harden into a "field" persisted through the years, even as many of the agencies offering group work services were being gradually but steadily drawn into the social work fold. The AASGW, started in 1936, did not become a professional association of group workers until 1946; until its amalgamation into the National Association of Social Workers ten years later, its membership was open to those with training and experience in public recreation, physical education, education, or social work. Even today, though the search for identity has slackened, it has not ceased. It has its present-day repercussions in the controversies on the psychiatric emphasis, the call for a revitalized program of social action, the attempt to distinguish the practice of "social group work" from that of "work with groups"[16] and, most recently, the proposals that group work withdraw completely from an educational to a therapeutic function.[17]

Group Work and Social Welfare

Despite the ebb and flow of other influences, the historical impetus of group workers and group-serving agencies was toward the identification with social work as a profession and with social welfare as a field of service. The roots of group work were in the activities of agencies reflecting concern with social conditions and their effects on people. Its origins lay in the general movement for social amelioration and social protest. Even as its workers drew inspiration from educational theory, psychiatric learnings, and small-group research, these developments were seen by many as instruments to be used in achieving social objectives. The ensuing efforts to build a scientific base and a unique methodology were undertaken not to replace the sense of mission, but to implement it.

This tendency was expressed, on another level, in the fact that a substantial number of the group-serving agencies were sponsored and financed under the same auspices as the social casework programs and those devoted to social welfare organization and planning. The relationship among these various efforts took on new strength and meaning during the great depression of the 1930s; thrown together around common problems and a common clientele, caseworkers, group workers, and community organization workers came increasingly to regard themselves as partners in the same enterprise.

---

[15]William Heard Kilpatrick, *Group Education for a Democracy* (New York: Association Press, 1940), p. vii.

[16]Gertrude Wilson, "Social Group Work Theory and Practice," in *The Social Welfare Forum, 1956* (New York: Columbia University Press, 1956), pp. 143–59.

[17]See, for example, letter to the editor by Max Doverman, *Social Work,* III, No. 2 (1958), 127, 128; see also reply by Mary Dot Monte and Rita Comarda, *Social Work,* III, No. 3 (1958), 126–27.

Social work, with its early emphasis on the individual in his environment, was a congenial host for those whose work lay at the very point of interaction between the two. Social work's concern with the total individual, the importance of community life, and the role of government in human affairs offered a comfortable resting place for group work's unique blend of scientific, humanitarian, and missionary zeal—more so than either education or recreation, each of which had for some time seemed to present a logical professional identification. The former was being increasingly torn by internecine conflict with regard to the most fundamental assumptions on the holistic nature of human psychology and human learning—many of which assumptions had been taught to group workers by the educators themselves. Recreation, slow to recognize the small-group potential, to individualize its clients, and to embrace the mental hygiene movement, became "merely" recreation and was relegated by many to a minor role in the field of human relations practice. It was a role, incidentally, somewhat similar to that assigned by caseworkers to the group workers themselves.

The identification had significant implications for both parties. It served to expand the scope of social work itself, bringing it back to earlier and broader conceptions of its function and responsibility at a time when these were being interpreted in ever narrowing terms. It brought fresh sociological thinking into a profession that was coming more and more to explain human behavior and social phenomena in biological and individualistic terms; it carried a renewed interest in social treatment, where the emphasis had been shifting almost entirely to individual therapy; the interest of the leisure-time agencies in prevention, in education, and in the broad range of human problems encountered in everyday living, made it necessary to extend concern to millions of new clients. The prospect of the "normal" client was completely antipathetic to the development of social work as a therapeutic profession, auxiliary to that of medicine in general and psychiatry in particular.

For group workers, the move lent strength and discipline where the need was greatly felt: it created a clearly marked professional identification, broader than that of a single agency or movement and hence more socially significant and status-giving; it gave promise of yielding a clearer and more distinct sense of function and focus, for which qualities many group workers hungered, and looked to casework for its skill and sophistication in these areas; it strengthened the movement toward developing a conscious method of working, supervising, and recording; and it stimulated awareness and understanding of some much-needed concepts regarding the psychodynamics of human behavior.

In its more negative aspects, the identification tended to bring about a gradual disengagement of group workers from some of their most fruitful professional and theoretical connections. The spirit of inquiry that had marked their early association with many sources of knowledge and insight gave way, in many quarters, to the prevailing uncritical acceptance of a single explanation of human behavior. Following casework, they embraced the

Freudian system—part science, part doctrine—with characteristic missionary enthusiasm, weakening its essential contribution by holding it up as a theory that excluded all other theories and constituted a kind of loyalty test for any new ideas that might bear upon our understanding of people and society.

Over all, the alliance between group work and social work has been a dynamic one, strengthening both entities while posing significant problems of integration with which the field is still struggling.[18] These problems have been rendered more difficult, rather than less so, to the extent that group work has tended to follow the path of casework development rather than to identify and elaborate its own unique contribution to social work theory and practice. Wrote Clara Kaiser in 1957:

> For better or for worse, social group work as it has been developed conceptually and as a field of practice is an aspect and method of the profession of social work. . . . Group workers often feel like "poor relations" in the family of social work practitioners, but instead of feeling resentment toward our sibling, casework, let us emulate her where this will deepen our insights and skills and let us develop the special methods which pertain to the helping process through the medium of group interaction and participation.[19]

And Louis Towley, summarizing the group work contribution, states:

> Social group work has found a comfortable professional family in social work during the past thirty years—though who adopted whom is occasionally a question. The way has not been smooth. The younger member of the profession relied on social casework for many of its concepts. But the psychoanalytic view of the individual adapts poorly to the group, and its explanations by no means always consort with observed group facts. Then came a dynamic kind of sociology-anthropology: the concept of status, role, caste, and pattern, and the influence of the situation on conduct.
>
> Social group work responded to these sympathetic, explanatory, group-rooted ideas. Many workers shared [Nathan E.] Cohen's belief that the social group work field is closer to these developments than is casework and therefore should bring the ideas to social work as a whole.[20]

In the Current Scene

Any attempt to evaluate the present problems of social group work must begin with the effects upon its thought and work of our "age of anxiety"—to

---

[18]See Harleigh B. Trecker, ed., *Group Work—Foundations and Frontiers* (New York: Whiteside and William Morrow, 1955), pp. 383–88, for examples of comments by social group workers on the group work-social work relationship.

[19]Clara Kaiser, "Characteristics of Social Group Work," in *The Social Welfare Forum, 1957* (New York: Columbia University Press, 1957), pp. 168–69.

[20]Frank J. Bruno (with chapters by Louis Towley), *Trends in Social Work, 1874–1956* (New York: Columbia University Press, 1957), pp. 426–27.

use Auden's phrase—fraught with doubts, pessimism, and the fear of imminent catastrophe. In a paper delivered at the National Conference of Social Work in 1955, Nathan E. Cohen traced the relationship between group work practice and the American scene and described the social climate in these terms:

> Uncertainty, doubt, confusion and fear are the order of the day, intensified by an ever threatening international situation. The insecurities resulting from a structureless, and ofttimes contradictory climate add to the mental health problems of the nation. The reactionary political climate which is accompanying this period of change has brought an attack on our humanistic philosophy which has been the base of our more modern approach in family life, education and social welfare.[21]

In such a time, the group itself, regarded in a more optimistic era as a bulwark of democratic society, begins to take on sinister connotations. Against the faith in social action is counterposed the feeling that concerted movement is somehow dangerous, that all collectives are somehow tinged with subversion, and that those who seek to assert their interests in this fashion are likely to be antidemocratic and revolutionary. The suspicion also takes a converse form, charging the group with creating inaction and conformity: against the vision of group relationships as a force which liberates creativity and individual power, there grows the fear of "group-think" and the "organization man"; and against the conviction that the group is an instrument for learning and change, there appears the fear that the changes are for the worst, toward the least common denominator, trampling on talent and individual creativity in the exalted name of the group product.[22]

Thus, as any anxiety creates both immobilization and the fear of it, so in the present climate the group experience stands accused of creating both conformity and rebellion. The call for a new individualism is an attempt to find a solution to the loss of human dignity; but in its plea for a new assertion of self, it proposes the one against the many and seeks the sources of freedom in man's liberation from his fellows rather than in the combined efforts of men to control their environment.

The theory and practice of social group work have been trapped, to an extent, by the pessimism of the time. Having developed their outlook on life in an age which had clearly identified the common interest of man and men, group workers built their practice on this insight and were certain, even in bad times, that worth-while ends could be achieved if men trusted the process by which, together, they could find the means. Today, many of their discussions reflect a pervasive anxiety lest social values be lost in the search for means by

---

[21]Nathan E. Cohen, "Implications of the Present Scene for Social Group Work Practice," in *The Social Welfare Forum, 1955* (New York: Columbia University Press, 1955), p. 49.

[22]Cf. William H. Whyte, Jr., *The Organization Man* (Garden City, N.Y.: Doubleday and Co., Inc., 1956), pp. 57–59.

which to gain them. As one writer has put it, they "cannot be left to chance";[23] the value system that is abstracted by the social group worker and designated as socially desirable, cannot be subjected to the trials and errors of the life process and the ways in which people use help to find their way toward what they need. A "positive methodology"[24] is one which produces the predetermined end.

Back in 1939, Eduard Lindeman had said:

> The distinction between education and propaganda is simple: in the former there is visible a constant aim to formulate ends and then to invent means which are consonant with those ends; in the latter there is a constant tendency to utilize whatever means are available to achieve ends, already determined.[25]

And before that, in the 1920s, John Dewey's profound effect upon group work thought came through statements like the following:

> To say that the welfare of others, like our own, consists in a widening and deepening of the perceptions that give activity its meaning, in an educative growth, is to set forth a proposition of political import. To "make others happy" except through liberating their powers and engaging them in activities that enlarge the meaning of life is to harm them and to indulge ourselves under cover of exercising a special virtue. . . . There is a sense in which to set up social welfare as an end of actions only promotes an offensive condescension, a harsh interference, or an oleaginous display of complacent kindliness. . . . To foster conditions that widen the horizon of others and give them command of their own powers, so that they can find their own happiness in their own fashion, is the way of "social" action. Otherwise the prayer of a freeman would be to be left alone, and to be delivered, above all, from "reformers" and "kind" people.[26]

Shaken from their own philosophical foundations and captured by the false dualisms of an anxious era, many have urged impossible choices between the "psychiatric" and the "social," means and ends, "process" and "content." The true measure of an anxious conflict is in its grandiose visions of outcomes and its accompanying distrust and fear of concentrating on hard, step-by-step methods of achieving them. So, in social group work, the rejection of process goes hand-in-hand with an obsessive formulation and reformulation of objectives. Ends without means must, in fact, have recourse to magic, and there is a mystical, prayerful quality about these exhortations to

---

[23]Harold Arian, "Developing Positive Jewish Attitudes through Jewish Center Activities," *Jewish Social Service Quarterly,* XXX (1953), 160.

[24]*Ibid.,* p. 165.

[25]Lindeman, *op. cit.,* p. 5.

[26]John Dewey, *Human Nature and Conduct* (New York: Random House, 1922), pp. 293–94.

achieve something important without skill and without method, but merely through the sheer power of intent.

Thus, while the preoccupation with social outcomes remains a vital part of the group work inheritance, the conviction is growing that the field of service must send its "humanitarianism in search of a method"[27]—or court disillusionment with the goals themselves, with the group work process, or with both. At this moment of history, the concern with method, far from representing an abandonment of larger aims, constitutes a high form of dedication to their achievement. Writing on the development of social work as a whole, Cohen draws this connection between individual and social aspirations, and thence to the requirements of a professional method:

> Better family life, improved schools, better housing, more understanding courts, more protected economic conditions, better relations between the various racial and religious groups, and more adequate medical care will all help the individual in his adjustment and development. On the other hand, the achievement of these desirable conditions depends on the use the individual can make of existing institutions and the resources he can mobilize both personally and in cooperation with other people . . .
>
> . . . Integral to these objectives, however, is the method through which we arrive at them. An approach which seems to accomplish the goal but which, in the process, destroys the very values from which it stems is a false accomplishment. On the other hand, without the security of an adequate standard of living, our "ideal" values can be reduced to hollow and empty slogans. For social work, therefore, both objectives must be pursued together through methods that reflect the "ideal" values from which they arise and grow.[28]

The problem of defining the nature of the helping process as it is carried out by social group workers has been rendered more difficult by the fact that it has been a "profession without professionals," depending on volunteers and unskilled personnel to document what actually happens in practice. Although this situation has changed somewhat with the advent of professionally educated practitioners into clinical and institutional settings, the picture remains much as Towley described it in 1957:

> This specialized field is rich in democratic concepts; it has a wealth of examples; but in professionally unique concepts, "method theory," it has been curiously poor. . . . It is possible that no social or economic

---

[27]Nathan E. Cohen, *Social Work in the American Tradition* (New York: Dryden Press, 1958), chap. i.

[28]*Ibid.*, pp. 8–9.

class in a community is beyond profiting from what goes under the name of a "group experience." But it is difficult for a social group worker to communicate how and why this near-miracle happens, except to another group worker.[29]

On Method

The historical tendency, culminating in the 1948 "Definition of the Function of the Group Worker," has been to define the function of the worker not by the nature of his acts, but by what he *knows,* what he *believes,* what he *is,* and what he *hopes to achieve.* Thus, it is stated that the group worker has knowledge of individual and group behavior, that he holds certain attitudes and beliefs about human dignity and the social good, that he is mature, aware of his own psychological needs and sensitive to others, and that he works in such a way that the group experience will produce individual growth and socially desirable goals.[30]

The qualities of knowing, believing, and aspiring, indispensable as they are to the practitioner, describe neither his function nor the nature of his skill but simply the equipment he needs in order to carry these out successfully. In a dynamic, interactional system,[31] the function of any of its actors can only be stated in dynamic terms, describing a moving part within a system of moving parts, and emphasizing the way it moves rather than what it looks like or what it may help—in a small way, for it is only a part of a relational system—to achieve. It would be as futile to say that the function of a carburetor is "to make the car go," or to act "in such a way that" the car does not stall, as it is to describe the function of the worker as enabling the group members "to use their capacities to the full and to create socially constructive group activities."[32] It is not that these things may not be true, but simply that such a description enlightens us only on ethics and intent rather than on the nature of the helping process.

In theorizing about the helping process, the initial emphasis on function emerges from the basic principle that what one does in any situation should express his purpose in being there. Thus, the establishment of a consistent and workable function for the group worker in the group situation should yield valuable clues as to the roles he must play in order to carry it out. In this

---

[29]Bruno, *op. cit.,* p. 422.

[30]Dorothea F. Sullivan, ed., *Readings in Group Work* (New York: Association Press, 1952), p. 422.

[31]See Talcott Parsons, *The Structure of Social Action* (Glencoe, Ill.: Free Press, 1949), pp. 30–38, for a discussion of the properties of organic systems. See also Lawrence K. Frank, "Research for What?" *Journal of Social Issues,* Supplement Series, No. 10 (1957), for discussion of systems of "organized complexity."

[32]Sullivan, *op. cit.,* p. 422.

context, the term "role" is used to designate the dynamic aspects of a function, or the active, implementing ways in which the worker proceeds to carry out his own unique *raison d'être* within the group system.

To return to our analogy, we may say that the function of the carburetor, within its own dynamic system, is to regulate the mixture of air and gasoline, and then proceed to describe the various kinds of acts it performs in order to fulfill this function. The acts thus described would have several characteristics: they would be appropriate to the ascribed function; they would be directed at tasks for which only this part is uniquely fitted, and which would remain undone if there were no carburetor, or substitute mechanism, in the system; they would express relatedness with other parts of the system, deriving much of their utility from them and being, in fact, inconceivable without them. What is perhaps most important is the fact that the results of its action are limited, and the sphere of its influence defined, by the number of factors over which it has some control.

The mechanical analogy is not meant to be carried to its extreme, but simply to provide a model for considering the relationship between function and movement in a system of reciprocal interaction. In describing the nature of the helping process it implies that: the description should begin with an assignment of function within the group process, and the assignment must be made in terms of concrete and immediate action rather than ultimate, hoped-for outcomes; the functional statement should then point the way toward the elaboration of certain roles, also expressed in the terminology of action, which are appropriate to the worker's function, unique and specialized within the system, and interrelated with the movements of the group members; and the roles themselves—which actually constitute categories or classifications of acts—should be amenable to further breakdown into discrete acts, which serve to illustrate the movements of the worker and the events of the helping process.

To see the process in these terms would make it difficult to project objectives and outcomes that go beyond the worker's actual sphere of influence. In this perspective, goals like "preventing juvenile delinquency," "enabling people to become mature," and "creating a healthy social climate" would be revealed as obviously unrealistic for a given worker or agency, or even for a single profession.

It should be mentioned at this point that such an effort would not represent an attempt to reduce the helping process itself to an automatic, "scientific" procedure, or to deny that professional ways of helping contain artistic components unique to the specific movements of each worker. The art of helping cannot be standardized without defeating its own purpose. But an art cannot become individualized and creative until it establishes its roots in science and in a discipline of knowledge and purpose. While techniques will, inevitably, vary with each worker, a theory of method must be formalized, transmissible, and amenable to interpretation to those in whose service it is pledged. Without a theoretical foundation for method, we have knowledge and cannot use it, or we have goals without a sense of how they can be reached. Both these conditions lead to systems of exhortation rather than of helping. Method, properly understood, is neither mystical nor mechanical.

Within this general frame of reference it is suggested that the history of social group work lends itself strongly to a conception of function in which the group worker assumes, as his area of responsibility, the task of searching out and clarifying the vital connection between the driving motives of the group member and the external requirements of his social situation. This connection becomes increasingly obscure as a society grows more complex; the function of the group worker emerges from his conviction that the normal biological and social development of individuals carries them toward and into the nurturing group. "It is only through social survival that the individual survives, but it is only through the survival of the individual and of some measure of his self-centered concerns and ambitions that society survives."[33] In Baldwin's words, written early in the history of modern sociology:

> It is, to my mind, the most remarkable outcome of modern social theory—the recognition of the fact that the individual's normal growth lands him in essential solidarity with his fellows, while on the other hand the exercise of his social duties and privileges advances his highest and purest individuality.[34]

What Jessie Taft called the "living relationship"[35] between the individual and his significant milieu is essentially a compelling mutual attraction, a symbiosis which, however diffuse or obscure it may become in complex social situations, persists in the life process and offers the only ground on which help is given and received. It is only on this common ground that the worker can offer his skill and the group member can utilize it to help himself to learn and grow.

Representing as he does the mutual attraction between two dynamic, changing entities—the individual and his culture—the group worker finds it thus unnecessary to choose between them. He has no need to create impossible alternatives between goals and methods, process and content, but can assume full status as a helping person. He is, in fact, a third force, focusing his activity on the task of uncovering—where it is obscure—and clarifying—where it is confused and conflicted—the member's sense of identification with his own past and present. In the helping situation, he knows he cannot

---

[33]Arthur T. Jersild, *Child Psychology* (3d ed.; New York: Prentice-Hall, 1942), p. 158.

[34]James Mark Baldwin, *The Individual and Society* (Boston: Richard G. Badger, the Gorham Press, 1911), p. 16.

[35]Jessie Taft, "The Relation of Function to Process in Social Case Work," in Virginia P. Robinson, ed., *Training for Skill in Social Work* (Philadelphia: University of Pennsylvania Press, 1942), p. 100.

"meet the member's needs," but he attempts to help the member relate these needs to the tasks before him.

The worker is thus enabled to distinguish between presenting a value—as a fact of the member's life—and sponsoring it. His lack of anxiety lest the value perish if he does not "sell" it is born of the knowledge that if it has no utility it cannot be sold, and if it has, it need not be sold, but only revealed and made accessible.

Such a statement of function, further elaborated and clarified, presents the group worker with working problems requiring the utmost in personal maturity, knowledge, and skill. In the roles which emerge, he must find ways of searching out the common ground where it is often hidden by overlays of bitterness and antagonism on both sides; he must help to clarify the nature of the obstacles between people and their immediate tasks; he must provide access to information and ideas they need as they pursue these tasks; he must reveal his own identity and his sense of function so that people may come to know him and be encouraged to use his help; and he must offer the function of the agency as an additional fact of life with which they must come to grips.

Closer analysis will reveal other roles which stem from the function designated above. The illustrative acts which dramatize these roles cannot be specified here for lack of space, but the records of group workers are rich with examples; often intuitive and unfocused, these instances nevertheless reflect Towley's judgment that:

> Social work's secret tool is the infinite untapped, unused, unsuspected capacity for growth in the sovereign individual personality. . . . Of all types and breeds of social worker, the social group worker most consciously accepts this democratic premise in his work.[36]

The above is obviously only a brief attempt and a crude beginning in the process of building a functional theory of method which may serve ultimately to remove some of the mystery from the helping process in general, and from the group work process in particular. The studies of practice undertaken by the Council on Social Work Education, the National Association of Social Workers, and the Group Work Section of the NASW, indicate that important discoveries will soon be made in this area of concern.

Toward the Future

A transitional phase provides a difficult vantage point from which to see the future, and social group work is, in many ways, in transition to a new identity. It is, on the one hand, still preoccupied with many of the normal problems of a self-sufficient profession, with its own structure, its distinctive agencies, and its own clientele. In the pursuit of these problems, its practitioners are concerned with the interpretation of its function, with its public relations,

---

[36]Bruno, *op. cit.,* pp. 421–22.

with the economic status of its workers, with the effort to recruit personnel for the enormous number of job vacancies, and with the educational program for those who will carry on its service and tradition.[37]

Simultaneously, social group workers are working on the common social work task of welding the total profession into a unified entity, and contributing their share in the general effort to uncover its generic foundations. The repercussions of the generic hypothesis are being felt in many ways in the professional association, in the schools of social work, and in the functions of agencies. As professionals work together, as the schools learn how to teach social work rather than a particular method, and as the agencies become increasingly multifunctional, the common base for the profession may extend even further than has been envisioned in some quarters. Beyond a common ethic, common knowledge, and common aspirations for mankind, there are those who are convinced that the helping process itself is essentially generic and that the time is not far off when a social work method can be developed and taught. Such a method would be abstracted from the accumulated skill and experience of caseworkers, group workers, and community organization workers over more than a century of practice.

Social group work's history of close association with people where they live, its continuing concern for collective action in the social interest, and its experience with the strength of people in action predispose it to make a significant contribution to a mature, full-bodied social work profession. The group will always be the most potent instrument of social change, and to work closely with people in groups is to become oneself an instrument through which people gain a more civilized condition of life.

---

[37]See Trecker, *op. cit.*, pp. 373–418, for comments by social group workers on an "agenda for the future."

Grace Coyle and Her Influence: A Personal Note

William Schwartz

This assignment had been a kind of sentimental journey for me, going back over the years in which Grace Coyle was writing her books, and I was growing up into my own career, I remember with strong feeling the inspiration she provided, the ideas she stood for, and the tasks she set for all of us in the field of social group work. I am grateful for this opportunity to take a look back, aided by Betty Hartford's excellent paper, and recall some of the ways in which Miss Coyle stirred my imagination and affected the course of my work.

First, there was her profound dedication to democratic values as a guiding force in professional work. No one before her had spelled out in such detail the importance of self-help and self-determination as fundamental aspects of the client-worker relationship. Carried into the small-group setting, these ideas took on a special excitement: the notion of viewing the peer group as a prototype of the democratic process in action was particularly powerful for those of us who sought in the field of social welfare an outlet for the progressive impulses and political activism forged in the Great Depression of the 1930s. This committment to both social reform and social service was exhilarating, even as it created certain problems that each of us had to think through for ourselves. How, for example, did one reconcile the needs of individuals with the problems of society as a whole? Did social workers have to choose between helping people and working to reform society? How could we help people—particularly those in small groups—to reach their own decisions, rather than turning them into catspaws to achieve our own "higher" intentions? The marriage of professionalism and self-determination was easier to celebrate in theory than to carry out in practice.

Her second major contribution to our thinking lay in the fact that she was a political creature, and not simply a democratic philosopher. That is, she

Schwartz, William. Grace Coyle and Her Influence: A Personal Note. *In Sonia Leib Abels and Paul Abels (Eds.), Proceedings of the 1979 Symposium, Committee for the Advancement of Social Work with Groups.*

thought always of social *action* as an end of social *process,* and she offered us keen insights into the connections between the two. Like her great contemporary, Bertha Reynolds, she called for no false choices between ends and means, the social and the psychological, the one and the many, but sought to bring these concepts together in a deeper understanding of social activity. Coyle's vision was of a democratic, nonmanipulative professional who is at the same time guided by "socially desirable goals." This was, as I have said, a difficult ideal to translate into practice, for it contained many contradictions and left important questions unanswered. But it was a challenge to us to develop the practice implications in detail, without either abandoning the values of self-determination and turning utterly prescriptive, or assuming a kind of neutrality that would reduce us to a band of echoers and headnodders. In my own work, the direction lay in finding the common ground between the client's self-interest and the social good, and then describing the professional function as it sought to help bring these closer together in specific tasks. Others went in different directions, but we were all mobilized by Coyle's uncompromising conviction that human need, group action, and the professional stimulus were indispensible to each other in the scheme of social change.

Third, she was a *profession-builder,* whose concern for intellectual discipline, ordered knowledge, and the details of the small-group experience legitimized and set standards for the practice of social group work, as Mary Richmond had done for social casework. She wrote about instances and examples, teaching us to use process and the group record as tools with which to develop our craft. In 1930 she gave us *Social Process in Organized Groups;* in 1937, she produced her *Studies in Group Behavior;* and in 1948, her major work, *Group Work with American Youth,* was subtitled "A Guide to the Practice of Leadership," and was written "primarily for the professional worker." In a field which, at the time, boasted few such trained practitioners (as against supervisors and administrators), it was a bold effort to write for a level of practice which scarcely existed, and from which it was difficult to draw satisfying examples. But what emerged from all her work was a fascinating description of how groups of people—and particularly young people—played and worked together, and a new clarity about what professional leaders needed to know, to believe in, and to aspire to, in their efforts to help. It was an organized vision of faith and purpose, and it opened up a new world of work for those of us who were looking for a profession that could, through its own art and discipline, help people build their individual and collective powers.

At the same time, I also remember my growing uneasiness with certain aspects of her formulation. There was still the strong hint of prescriptiveness, the missionary flavor, that was part of the tradition in which her work was couched. Could we, in practice, reconcile our eagerness to teach "desirable social goals," and "socially constructive group activities," with the image of a self-realizing, self-directing client, so well drawn up by Coyle herself? And who was to define what was socially constructive and desirable? Was the professional worker to be cast as the arbiter of moral values and proper behavior?

Surely this must be an odious role for social workers who were to be trained to "accept the clients where they are." Or was it that the worker was meant to offer such acceptance only *on condition* that the client would, after a decent interval, go where he was being led? Professional prescriptions and client self-assertion continued to bump into each other at every turn.

As we struggled with this problem in practice, it became increasingly clear that the effort to resolve it philosophically, rather than technically, was doomed to failure. It would be necessary to *operationalize* the attitudes and intentions that Coyle had formulated so well. By what means, exactly, were these professional aspirations to be achieved? What *worked* with people, and what didn't? "The Group Worker," wrote the Coyle Committee on the Function of the Professional Group Worker, "enables various types of groups to function *in such a way that* both group interaction and program activities contribute to the growth of the individual, and the achievement of desirable social goals" (my italics). The statement went on to cite the knowledge, awareness, and responsibilities of the professional group worker; but the means remained mysterious, hidden behind the "in such a way that," and leaving unspecified the special skills and behaviors that mark the trained worker and distinguish him or her from the highly motivated and equally well-intentioned amateurs traditionally associated with group work in general and youth work in particular. We were now brought to questions that went beyond what do we know, and what do we believe in, and what do we hope to achieve, to *how* such attributes are translated into professional behaviors. And it was to these questions that some of us turned our hand.

In summary, then, this is what Grace Coyle's work meant to us, in the professional generation that followed:

> She expressed our aspirations in clear and inspired terms, at a time in history when there was a great need for social workers to find the living connections between social work and social reform in a democracy.
>
> She described the work with small groups in dramatic, detailed, exciting ways, stirring our imaginations and opening up new possibilities for working with people in a real-life atmosphere of action and mutual aid.
>
> She held out the image of a disciplined professionalism, with its own ordered knowledge, an ethical base, a sense of purpose, and a systematic effort to record its experience, its processes, and its practice.
>
> In this emphasis on recorded experience, and in her scholarly formulation of knowledge, value, and purpose, she paved the way for future generations to take on the task of further refining and identifying the particular skills of the social worker in the group.

In these ways and others, she is the godmother of us all. We are all working the ground she prepared so well.

Bertha Reynolds as Educator[1]

William Schwartz

Bertha Reynolds was a complicated human being who lived through two world wars, the Great Depression, revolutionary ferment at home and abroad, the birth of the trade unions, the Cold War, the civil rights movement, and other profound changes in the political and social climate of twentieth century America. Her career spanned a period stretching from the virtual beginnings of social work—she was thirty-two when Mary Richmond published *Social Diagnosis*—to the issues and concerns of modern-day social work. Through it all, she worked, taught, agitated, formed and re-formed ideas and opinions about the major political and professional events of her time. She was a willing speaker and a prolific writer, leaving behind a large body of work reflecting an active life.

Such a life cannot be summarized easily, even in parts, especially when that part—her work as an educator—was a central theme of her career. For her, "education spilled over into life at every point.[2] Her teaching was strongly connected to her enormous sense of social responsibility; it presented her with some of the most challenging and vexing problems of her professional life and it helped her mold her lifelong conceptions of what helping people was about—not only in the classroom, but in supervision, consultation, group work, community work, and casework itself. Although she "did not want to be a teacher like Mother,"[3] teaching was actually her first job. Having been graduated from Smith College "with a B.A. degree, a Phi Beta Kappa key and a determination to serve the world,"[4] she worked for a year in the high school department of Atlanta University. Then, following an intense period of soul-searching, she found her vocation in the new field of psychiatric social work, and pursued it for the next fifteen years. In 1925, at the age of forty, she began her career as an educator when she accepted the position of Associate Director and teacher of social casework at the Smith College School for Social Work. After ten years, she switched her responsibilities at Smith to the

William Schwartz is Emeritus Professor of Columbia University School of Social Work.

Schwartz, William. (1981). Bertha Reynolds as educator. Catalyst, *3(3) 5–14.*

famous "Plan D," out of which grew her pioneering work in the education of field supervisors and, ultimately, her major contribution to the professional literature, *Learning and Teaching in the Practice of Social Work.*[5]

After thirteen years at Smith, she left in 1938 and established herself as a private "Consultant in Staff Development for Social Agencies," conducting seminars and small-group workshops for practitioners and supervisors in agencies, school, and other settings. She pursued this work for the next twenty years, excepting her five-year wartime experience with the United Seamen's Service. She also taught for brief periods at various universities and maintained a huge correspondence with social work practitioners and supervisors all over the country.

What She Brought to Her Teaching

Bertha Reynolds was no systematic philosopher or theory-builder; rather, she brought to bear a "brilliant common sense"[6] that lit up her study of the professional experience. Like social work itself, she was a child of the Progressive Era, and the themes of experiential learning, action and interaction, the study of man in nature, and the values of social responsibility ran through her work from its beginnings. It is strange that she did not mention John Dewey in her *Learning and Teaching* but the term "progressive education"[7] occurred often, there and in her other writings, and she used it as a kind of general reference from which she drew many of her ideas about teaching, casework, supervision, group work, and other situations that called for "drawing out and leading forth."[8] In many ways, she did for social work education what Dewey had done for the larger field of formal and informal education, weaving these dominant themes—the faith in science, the devotion to experience, the social vision—into patterns of professional method. When she came to review her life's work, she identified some of these life-long convictions: she remembered her feeling that "systematic study was futile as long as it could not be used in action."[9] Her "guiding light," she said, "was to live in harmony with nature, but nature expressed for man in terms of social living."[10] Finally, "if one word is needed . . . to begin to sum up what fifty years of living have taught me, that word is *relatedness.*"[11]

Professionally, she conceived of the social work function in the broadest terms. Social work was a part of social living[12] and her students needed to "see the living material of social work in relation to the price of fish, the latest popular song, a new theory of treatment of disease, recent legislation, or whatever concerns human beings."[13] Her experience as an educator, she said, "shaped my philosophy of casework to an important degree. I came to see casework itself as helping clients to do a job . . . ."[14] She made the point at different times, in different ways, that "social work is itself a form of educational work."[15]

She was strongly influenced by the functional school, greeting Virginia Robinson's *Changing Psychology in Social Case Work,*[16] published in 1931, with "wonder and deep delight."[17] She was attracted by its emphasis on client self-determination, clarity of agency function, and the importance of relationship in the casework process. Later, although she retained much of the functional emphasis in her way of practicing, she rejected what she perceived as its rigidity and philosophical mysticism.[18]

She believed in agencies as a setting for social work practice. Although she warned against their power to subvert the professional function, she nonetheless saw professional work as a world of specific services, facilities, community contacts, and social institutions. "It's not possible," she wrote, "to do good social work without equipment."[19] Speaking as a psychiatric social worker, she was often coolly received by her colleagues when she said that "there was a field for casework permeated with psychiatric understanding which would be neglected if everyone were diverted to practicing psychotherapy."[20] She clung to her conviction, despite the trend of the times, that this was a "*social* profession . . . not to become confused with other services which have mental hygiene as their main professional function."[21]

Politically, she was a Marxist, coming to it in the latter years of the Great Depression. "After an earthquake," she wrote, "it is well to look to the foundations."[22] She was at an age when most people are giving up their youthful radicalism; she was past fifty when a student gave her Marx and Engels to read, exacting from her the promise to write one of the "reading reports" she was wont to assign. Then, as she had studied Freud because she needed a science of man, she studied Marx to find a science of society, and as her researches in psychiatry had deepened her grasp of human behavior, her newfound socialism brought insights that helped her understand and take part in the struggles of the 1930's and their aftermath.

Her leftism never led her into the egregious errors attendant on having to "choose" between Freud and Marx. She wanted both, and as she was suspicious of Freud's bourgeois origins and his ethnocentric view of human nature, so she was also aware of the tendency of great movements to forget individual freedom in its pursuit of social justice.

> Social case workers find those who think that individuals are not worth bothering about opposing case work for very different reasons. Those who would use men and women as cogs in an industrial machine prefer that personal development be kept to a minimum lest it interfere with contented acceptance of monotonous labor. Those who want to free humanity from exploitation by a mass movement sometimes count on able leadership and a following that will act in unison without the loss of momentum involved in making room for individual differences . . . the habit of being herded, whether by a beneficent or by an evil force, is as fatal for stability and progress as for individual growth.[23]

Thus it was that *method,* for Reynolds, was a *political* issue: bad practice robbed people of their rights. And the false issue of "working with feelings" vs. "working for social progress" was subversive of both individual freedom and social reform. Democracy was not only a political word, but a technical and professional one as well. In the classroom, the casework interview, the group meeting, and the supervisory conference, one could create prototypes of the democratic process in action. Where John Dewey had said:

> To foster conditions that widen the horizon of others and give them command of their own powers, so that they can find their own happiness in their own fashion, is the way of "social" action. Otherwise the prayer of a freeman would be to be left alone, and to be delivered, above all, from "reformers" and "kind people."[24]

Bertha Reynolds wrote:

> Can anyone, except as he is actually a part of a situation, make these delicate adaptations to the other persons involved that must be the basis for action? Without these adaptations to personal feeling, how can case work "action" be anything but interference with life processes?"[25]

Through all this complexity, there ran a single, unifying theme. She was the great synthesizer of social work, the integrator of factions that have since torn the field apart. Because she worked directly from experience, she spent her life drawing together the lines that threatened to come apart long before she left the scene. She was a Freudian and a Marxist, a practitioner and an activist, a psychiatric social worker who was our leading advocate for social change. She was dedicated to the union of content and process, a professional who made her reputation both as a technician and a political radical. Where others polarized the social and the psychological and exhorted us to choose between them, she saw them as different aspects of the same human struggle. Her firsthand, working knowledge of the connections between the individual and the social—what I have elsewhere called "private troubles" and "public issues"[26]—made it possible for her to say that "oppression produces the resistance which will in the end overthrow it,"[27] and know that this was, at one and the same time, both a political and psychological statement.

Her Way of Teaching

Teaching was not easy for her. She approached the job at Smith with great misgivings, worried about her lack of formal education (she had no master's degree), her identification of academia with upper-class superiority, her unorthodox views about social work, and the interruption of her casework practice—"my art and my predominant satisfaction in life."[28] Also, she was concerned that she "did not know how to teach and had no time to learn."[29]

Some of her fears were well-grounded: "I proved to be more a maverick in education than I had supposed I was in social work."[30] A year after she began, she talked seriously with her Director about resigning: "I could not get a grip on teaching and felt I ought either to leave it or to take time out for adequate preparation leading to a master's degree."[31] In any event, she did neither, but went into a personal analysis, which freed her in many ways. Her teaching "took hold," and she began to find a type of her own, less Socratic and more in tune with her casework talent for listening and gentle probing. "Instead of being 'Socrates, the gadfly' . . . I loved to see people grow."[32] Later in her life she said of those early years with her students: "That they and I survived is a tribute to the toughness of the human animal."[33] And she regretted the fact that "there was no organized preparation for becoming a supervisor, nor, for that matter, a class teacher of casework. Here was the bottleneck in the development of our profession."[34]

Mainly, her difficulties lay—as they do for all serious teachers—in finding the working connections between structure and freedom in the educational process. It was constitutionally impossible for her to work in the tradition of spooning out her ideas and getting them back in their original, undigested form. She was too much imbued with the spirit of "progressive education" for that. But these theories, rich in democratic concepts and liberal philosophy, had little to say about method. Like most teachers of the progressive persuasion, Reynolds had to forge out of her own inclinations some effective ways of working in the classroom. She had been instinctively attracted to the discussion method, but she discovered that she was continually "overestimating" her students' ability to rise to it without a great deal of help from the teacher. How did one "put in" enough material to feed their raw curiosity, so that there would be enough to "draw out" when the time came? It was the classical question that Bertha Reynolds faced, in her own time and her own way: how did one integrate the *what* and the *how,* the substance and the method in the give and take of the classroom?

To this effort, she brought everything she had. Her fifteen years of casework experience helped her create the "type-situations" she used in case discussion. Her growing understanding of the dialectic brought her closer to the dynamics of resistance and the realization that "the learning one eventually does results from conflict of opposite motives."[35] Her faith in experience sent her students into the streets, stores, and public places, to observe people and write about them. Her determination to integrate theory and practice created the writing exercises in which her students brought together what they read, thought, felt, and practiced. And years, there were the occasional brief lectures that she had taught herself to use as part of her overall educational strategy.

Through all of her work ran her deep conviction about social interaction and mutual aid. She saw the classroom and the workshop as prototypes of the small group in action, and stores to develop group work skills in her role as teacher. She reveled in "the joy of thinking with a group in a comfortable situation."[36] To a large extent, *Learning and Teaching* is a book about the use of groups in the educational process.

By the time the supervisors' course known as "Plan D" came into being ten years later, her educational methods were considerably more surefooted. The year was 1935, and the curriculum reflected clearly her view of the social work function the offerings were divided into four sections—casework supervision, group process, economics, and psychiatry. In her teaching, she continued to struggle with the problem of "putting in and drawing out," but she had developed a rich store of experience in the classroom, more confidence in her group skills, a deeper conception of the common elements in all social work helping, and a clearer view of the relationship between classroom and field work teaching.

"Plan D" gave her the opportunity to bring all this learning into focus on a close study of the supervision of social work students in the field and it was out of this experience that she formulated what was to be her major contribution to social work education—her "Five Stages of the Use of Conscious Intelligence."[37] The conception was based on her insight into the frightening aspects of new learning—"what will it do to me?—and the realization that the student's progress depends on his or her growing ability to release the energy being used in his or her protection of self. Reynold's stages of learning lit up large areas of the educational experience, and the scheme remains a powerful tool in the analysis of social work still, both during and after professional training.

When a loved one dies, everyone feels guilty. We feel we did not do enough to honor her, to show support when she needed it, to let her know we understood what she was doing. We should have talked with her, engaged her, warmed ourselves more before the light went out.

One longs to continue the conversation with her on the issues she raised during her lifetime. What was it that soured her so completely on functionalism—after having been so excited by it—that she lost her sense of the dialectic and declared the functional and diagnostic schools to be "irreconcilable"? Why was it so difficult, as she tells it, for her students to go beyond Stage 3—"the stage of understanding the situation without power to control one's own activity in it"?[38] Could she have progressed faster if she had examined the students' practice earlier, instead of deferring close scrutiny until they had worked for a long time on understanding the client? Surprisingly, *Learning and Teaching* has no process records of her own work, and many of her technical distinctions would have been clearer if it had. And her courageous support of agency supervision—she said an agency "is something much more than . . . a housing project for a number of independent practitioners"[39]—would have generated more power if she could have shown how the record can be used to examine the movements of a skilled worker in step-by-step detail.

Further, what *is* the role of the social agencies today, weakened as they are by slow starvation and suffering from the attacks of the advocates on one side and the private practitioners on the other? How can progressive social workers, isolated as they are even within their own profession, find their real allies in the struggle for human welfare? Do they have to go on choosing between their radicalism and their professionalism, or can they somehow find the synthesis of which Bertha Reynolds' career was a living example?

We have these questions, and many more. And since we can no longer hear her voice, we must go back and study her writings. She has left us with a lot to do.

Notes

1. Paper read at National Conference on Social Welfare, Philadelphia, Pennsylvania, May 16, 1979. Grateful acknowledgement is given for the help of Yvonne Cullen, who generously shared her unpublished paper on the subject, as well as other materials gathered in her researches.
2. Bertha C. Reynolds, *An Uncharted Journey: Fifty Years of Growth in Social Work* (New York: The Citadel Press, 1963), p. 94.
3. *Ibid.,* p. 20.
4. *Ibid.,* p. 16.
5. Bertha Capen Reynolds, *Learning and Teaching in the Practice of Social Work* (New York: Rhinehart & Company, 1942).
6. This was a phrase that Reynolds herself enjoyed, and quoted from an article by Zona Gale on the life of Charlotte Perkins Gilman. *See* Bertha Reynolds, "Social Case Work: What Is It? What Is Its Place in the World Today?" *The Family,* December, 1935, p. 235.
7. See her acknowledgement of her debt to the principles of progressive education, in her Ruth Kotinsky Memorial Lecture at the Bank Street College of Education, on April 21, 1961. Bertha C. Reynolds, "Mental Health Concepts in the Practice and Teaching of Social Work," mimeographed, 10 pages.
8. This is the title of Chapter 6 in her *An Uncharted Journey.*
9. *Ibid.,* p. 310.
10. *Ibid.,* p. 308.
11. *Ibid.,* p. 314. Emphasis in original.
12. This is a thought she used as the title of her book on her wartime work with the United Seamen's Service. *See* Bertha Capen Reynolds, *Social Work and Social Living: Explorations in Philosophy and Practice* (New York: Citadel Press, 1951).
13. Reynolds, *Learning and Teaching,* p. 157.
14. Reynolds, *An Uncharted Journey,* p. 94.
15. Reynolds, *Learning and Teaching,* p. 139.
16. Virginia P. Robinson, *A Changing Psychology in Social Case Work* (Chapel Hill: The University of North Carolina Press, 1931).
17. Reynolds, *An Uncharted Journey,* p. 120.
18. *See* Bertha C. Reynolds, "A Changing Psychology in Social Case Work—After One Year." *The Family,* 13 (June 1932), pp. 107–111; Bertha C. Reynolds, "Digging Deep: A Critique of Diagnostic-Functional Casework Concepts," *Trends in Social Work,* (February 1951), pp. 2–3; and the reply by Grace Marcus, "A Leap to Conclusions: Another View of the Diagnostic-Functional Controversy," *Trends in Social Work,* (June 1951), pp. 4–5, 8.

19. Reynolds, *Social Work and Social Living,* p. 2.
20. Reynolds, *An Uncharted Journey,* p. 233.
21. Reynolds, "Mental Health Concepts," p. 6.
22. Reynolds, *An Uncharted Journey,* p. 170.
23. Reynolds, "Social Case Work: What Is It? What Is Its Place in the World Today?" p. 240.
24. John Dewey, *Human Nature and Conduct: An Introduction to Social Psychology* (New York: Henry Holt and Company, 1922), p. 294.
25. Bertha C. Reynolds, "The Art of Supervision," *The Family,* 17 (June 1936), p. 104.
26. William Schwartz, "Private Troubles and Public Issues: One Social Work Job or Two?" in *The Social Welfare Forum, 1969,* Official Proceedings, 96th Annual Forum, National Conference on Social Welfare (New York: Columbia University Press, 1969), pp. 22–43.
27. Reynolds, *An Uncharted Journey,* p. 187.
28. *Ibid.,* p. 83.
29. *Ibid.,* p. 84.
30. *Ibid.,* p. 85.
31. *Ibid.,* p. 125.
32. *Ibid.,* p. 129.
33. Reynolds, "Mental Health Concepts, p. 8.
34. *Ibid.*
35. Reynolds, *Learning and Teaching,* p. 58.
36. *Ibid.,* p. 119.
37. *Ibid.,* Chapter 7.
38. *Ibid.,* p. 79.
39. Reynolds, *An Uncharted Journey,* p. 307.

The Group Work Tradition and Social Work Practice

William Schwartz

The social work profession is one of the primary institutions designed to help people negotiate the complicated systems in which they live. Its efforts have followed three major impulses. The most prominent of these has been to deal with people individually, "case by case," seeking to remedy the psychological and social conditions that have brought their problems about. Theories of responsibility vary with the times—individual and social, moral, economic, and psychological—but in most instances those who seek help are seen as somehow personally inadequate, and the effort is made to render them more self-sufficient, psychologically stronger, less dependent on help from the outside. The worker-client relationship is intimate, confidential, and takes place on the professional's own ground. The client is carefully examined, and the condition "diagnosed"—in the adopted medical language—as a prelude to "treatment." The rationale for this thorough personal inquiry is today largely scientific, following the medical approach to illness. But the tradition goes back a long way. Thomas Chalmers, an early precursor of the Charity Organization movement, said of those who came to seek economic assistance: "He who seeks another's bounty shall also submit to another's scrutiny."[1] This one-on-one approach to human problems is the discipline we have called social casework, and it has been the dominant feature of the social work profession since its inception.

This paper was presented at the 25th Anniversary Symposia. Graduate School of Social Work, Rutgers, the State University of New Jersey, and is republished with permission from *Social Work Futures: Essays Commemorating Twenty-Five Years of the Graduate School of Social Work,* Edited by Miriam Dinerman, published by the Graduate School of Social Work, Rutgers, The State University of New Jersey in cooperation with the Council on Social Work Education, 1983, New Brunswick, NJ.

Schwartz, William. (1985). The group work tradition and social work practice. Social Work with Groups, *8(4), 7–27. Published by The Haworth Press, 12 West 32nd Street, New York, NY 10001.*

A second direction has been to help needy people in their own milieux, surrounded by their peers and working in an atmosphere of mutual aid. Here the effort is to find, in the people's own conditions of life, the energy and the resources with which they can help each other act together on common problems. People are brought together for many reasons: to organize themselves for action on special interests and common concerns; to help each other face difficult personal problems; to learn new skills with which to enrich the quality of their lives. The setting is the small, face-to-face group, placed in some shared community context; experiences are communicated among the members, rather than held confidential between member and worker; and the worker is surrounded by a host of surrogate helpers, each claiming a share of the supportive function. The lines of communication are intricate, and the worker's authority is diffused in the network of relationships that goes to make up the pattern of mutual aid. This is the direction we came to know as social group work, and it has grown over the years to occupy an increasingly significant place in the work of the profession.

The third approach has been to deal with the social problems themselves, rather than the people who suffer under their effects. The lines between direct service and social planning have not always been distinct, nor has it been necessary that they be so. In fact, both the early settlements and the Charity Organization movement were prime examples of the integration of direct practice and what we now call community organization and social reform. But the deepening troubles of industrial capitalism, and the accompanying complexities administering social welfare, created this specialized field, with its own knowledge and skills, that addressed itself to the tasks of social and legislative action, the development and distribution of resources, intergroup cooperation, and—maintaining its ties to direct service—the organization of grass-roots action on community problems.

The history of social work is the story of how these different ways of helping people in need came together to find a single professional identity. In 1873, the National Conference of Charities and Correction first offered the humanitarians a chance to share their common aspirations and working problems.[2] In the 1920's, the Milford Conference found some theoretical unity for social casework, at a time when that was considered tantamount to integrating the entire profession.[3] And in the 1950's, the National Association of Social Workers was born of a long organizational process that merged seven independent social work organizations into a single association that represented social workers of America who had formal educational preparation.[4,5]

The search for a common identity for social work did not end when this union was effected. Today, a generation later, it still remains to find the common technology that could render its practitioners recognizable as part of a single professional entity. It has been relatively easy to describe the common objectives, the shared values, even the relevant areas of knowledge; but it has been much more difficult to define the basic skills that bind them together and constitute a special claim to conpetence in serving the community. Parsons, in his study of the legal profession, defined the professional as a "technical expert . . . by virtue of his mastery of the tradition and skills of its use."[6] How would such a principle be applied to social work? What is its common tradition, and to what special skills does it lay its claim? What abilities do the family worker, the camp director, the organizer, the club leader, the clinician-therapist have in common? Are they in any measure interchangeable, considering that they all hold the same graduate degree?

It is, of course, the old search for the generic, in a jungle of specifics. The merger of professional associations, however desirable it may have been, left yet to be done the task of merging the separate experiences and histories of social work into a commonly understood way of working with people. Although structurally unified, the profession is still more like a coalition of the old "methods" than it is an integrated discipline combining the richest and most effective elements of each.

It is true that such development does not happen overnight; the Milford Conference, for example, took close to a decade to sort out the generic and the specific in social casework. In our own generation, we have had some thoughtful work on the subject,[7,8] and there will be more. But I believe that such an effort would be considerably advanced if each of the so-called "methods" were to explore its own traditions of practice to find those unique elements that might help to put its own special stamp on a unified conception of the function and practice of social work. My effort here is to examine something of the group work heritage, looking back on some of its early history, its theoretical underpinnings, its conception of the client, the worker-member relationship, and its conduct of the helping process. In a short paper, one can only touch on the main themes; but I would hope to give some of the flavor of such an enterprise, and stimulate others to work along similar lines.[9]

The Early Years

There is a common misconception that group work is considerably younger than its casework sibling. In fact, the ancestors of both movements began their work at about the same time in history, with the group work agencies following the casework establishments by only a few years. Canon Barnett, the founder of the first settlement—Toynbee Hall in London—was a close associate of Octavia Hill, who played a similar role in the beginnings of the London Charity Organization Society; Barnett was in fact influential in both movements.[10] In this country, Jane Addams and Mary Richmond were colleagues and very much aware that they were part of a common enterprise. Both in England and in the United States, the settlements and the Societies were not far apart: the London COS in 1868, Toynbee Hall in 1884, the Buffalo COS in 1877, Jane Addams's Hull-House in 1889. As to the seminal works in both fields, Mary Richmond's *Social Diagnosis* was issued in 1917,[11] while Grace Coyle's *Social Process in Organized Groups* came in 1930.[12] In general, the early workers were all part of the same group of social reformers that came out of the Progressive Era. Their motives were much the same, and they knew and worked with each other long before the casework-group work distinctions were drawn. Canon Barnett's favored motto—embroidered and hung in his drawing room in Whitechapel—was "One By One."[13]

The historical difference between the two movements was that casework, or individual work, became almost immediately synonymous with social work as its practitioners sprang into action, defined themselves as a body, formed a national conference, began to systematize their thinking,[14] and produced a steady stream of writing about their experiences in the field. The group workers, on the other hand, were much more diverse in their outlook, identifying themselves with many fields of endeavor, among them education, recreation, camping, and mental hygiene—each with a tradition of its own going back to 1861[15]—as well as social work. The American Association for the Study of Group Work, founded in 1936, numbered among its members people from all these professions, as well as those with purely academic and scientific interest in the small group, without any particular reference to its professional uses.

This wide range of interests and allegiances was reflected in a study of the leisure-time agencies in the 1920's, which concluded that "the objectives of these various agencies would at first thought seem so divergent as to make it impossible to treat the duties and responsibilities of their workers in the same analysis."[16]

Group work's ambivalence about where it belonged continued even after its place was established, both in social work education and as part of the National Conference of Social Work, in the mid-'30s. In 1940, the noted educator William Heard Kilpatrick asserted that "this group work is . . . not to be thought of as a separate field of work, but rather as a method to be used in all kinds of educational effort."[17] And as late as 1946, we find Grace Coyle herself still concerned about the "alignment" of group workers: "One baffling problem has plagued the development of professional consciousness among group workers over this decade. It is usually phrased in terms of alignment, and a dilemma is presented. We must, it seems, be either educators or social workers."[18]

Ultimately, the choice was made, and group work practitioners found their place within the social work profession. It was, after all, group work's natural habitat, having had its origins in the humanitarian movement and its major development within the agencies of social welfare.

> Social work, with its early emphasis on the individual in his environment, was a congenial host for those whose work lay at the very point of interaction between the two. Social work's concern with the total individual, the importance of community life, and the role of government in human affairs offered a comfortable resting place for group work's unique blend of scientific, humanitarian, and missionary zeal. . . .[19]

It was at that point that the question changed from whether group workers would identify themselves as social workers to what they would bring with them into a unified field of practice. Undoubtedly, there was much in their world view that was the same as that of the other approaches within the profession. But there must also be, from the settings and circumstances of their encounters with human beings in need, a great deal that was different, through which group work could make a valuable contribution to a generic conception of the work of the profession. To find these, one would have to look closely at several key areas in their collective early experience.

Group Work Purposes

If the caseworkers were the "priests" of social welfare, and the social planners were its "prophets," the group workers were a kind of cross between the two.[20] On the one hand, they were deeply involved in direct service to the poor, ministering to their needs in day-to-day contact; on the other, because they worked where the people lived, they were first-hand witnesses to the cramped quality of the people's lives and the limitations of a political and economic system in which huge sections of the population were neglected, uninvolved, and relegated to the fringes of power. Catherine Cooke Gilman suggested that the motto of the settlements might be: "Keep your fingers on the near things and eyes on the far things."[21]

These were the twin emphases that pervaded the work of the first agencies—the "near things" of individual need and the "far things" of social reform. On the one hand, the early settlement papers were replete with references to "self": self-development, self-sufficiency, self-respect, and the like.[22] At the same time, there was a strong preoccupation with the need for education for political power. "If power is to be dispersed, then everybody is to be trained to exercise it. . . . Democracy becomes a farce, not because it has lost its ideal force but because its devotees are, democratically speaking, illiterate; they do not know how to operate in and through groups."[23]

In order to provide a new version of society, a community in which people could regain some control over their immediate environment, the early workers turned to the small group as a context for action. This connection between individual and social strength may seem naive to us today, but it appeared to the settlement pioneers to be compelling; they had an enormous faith in human association, and the small group was to be an instrument of personal growth as well as what they called a "building block of democracy." Jane Addams spoke of exchanging "the music of isolated voices [for] the volume and strength of the chorus."[24] And Canon Barnett said: ". . . if it be a great matter to be an individual, it is a greater matter to be part of a whole . . ."[25]

Underlying all of these purposes, there lay the urge to restore to the people those aspects of life that had been denied to them by the ravages of industrialization. The crowded city streets, the dearth of recreational opportunities, the absence of trees and country spaces, the lack of time for play—all of these produced a great yearning for space, country, and leisure. It was the need that spawned Barnett's Children's Country Holiday Fund in England,

and vitalized the camping and playground movements in this country. The group work pioneers waxed particularly eloquent on the subject of play. "A people's play," said Mrs. Henrietta Barnett, "is a fair test of a people's character. Their recreation more than their business or their conquests settle the nations' place in history."[26] And consider this paean to its virtues:

> Play has physical, psychological, social, ethical, and spiritual significance. . . . Play is joy-producing and hence develops mental optimism. Play naturally and unconsciously places the individual in right relations with his social group. Play is the testing-laboratory of the individual and the social virtues. Play rounds out our fragmentary lives and makes us spiritually whole.[27]

This concern with enhancing the quality of life was at the heart of the preoccupation with cultural activities—music, art, literature, drama, trips, discussion—as well as occasions, entertainments, and general atmosphere of intimate and informal exchange. Barnett claimed that his ultimate resource was his wife's tea-table.[28] The themes of informality, social intercourse, shared experience, and, above all, friendship, were at the very roots of the settlement movement. Friendship was the bond that would unite them all—the residents and the neighbors, workers and members. Indeed, friendship was to be a political instrument. The young, well-favored, well-to-do students who came to the first university settlements—of which Toynbee Hall was one—were being trained to rule more wisely by making real friendships with the poor and learning at first hand their way of life. The class struggle was in their eyes a product of misunderstanding between the rich and the poor, and it could be mitigated by working out these failures of communication on the people's home ground. "The classes are out of joint," wrote Barnett "and do not work together to one end. The call is still for a way of peace, and for a means of promoting good fellowship between man and man."[29]

And so group work came to the people with an active agenda and a sackful of hopes and prayers for individual salvation and social change. Although Barnett himself went to some pains to point out that settlements are not missions, and should not be used for "doing good," or for preaching a message,[30] the total effect over the years has been to invest the worker-client engagement with urgent conviction and well-marked educational purposes. Later, when "cause" began to edge its way toward "function," there would be considerable difficulty in distinguishing means from ends. But there was rarely any danger that the group workers would go passive, or neutral, about what the world should be like. They would carry their strong sense of the individual-social connections with them into the social work arena. It was a heavy load, and they often carried it clumsily; but always the worker was an active and intimate participant in the client's experience.

It was a new kind of relationship, this collaboration between a worker and the members of a group, and it raised questions that went beyond the Freudian explanations that were being studied so intently by the rest of the profession. Unbound as they were to any one field of exploration, they had a whole world to turn to; and they did—to the educators, the sociologists, the psychologists, and the host of disciplines that were exploding with new insights at the turn of the 20th century.

Theoretical Foundations

The intellectual renaissance that took place in America as part of the Progressive Era was in many ways responsive to the needs and curiosities of the group work movement. New knowledge came from many directions—religious, philosophical, social, psychological, political—and the group workers, not yet tied to any hard-and-fast identifications, were free to look where they chose for enlightenment and inspiration. The Freudian answers found some ready group work adherents, as they did in casework, but the fit was uncomfortable, the explanations skirting many of the situational questions raised by the group experience. It was not that the group workers had no interest in personality development; obviously they must have. But their point of vantage led them to observe human behavior in its social, relational context. Their curiousities were essentially what we would now call *systemic,* having to do with interrelational networks; and their questions were oriented to issues of action and interaction, the nature of shared experience, and the processes of communication—verbal and nonverbal—within the small group.

Their field of inquiry was broad, and it would take a much longer work than this to trace the precise connections between the growing body of early 20th century knowledge and the development of group work thinking. But certain influences are fairly clear, and important to our present purpose. The great progenitor of small-group analysis was, of course, Charles Horton Cooley, whose researches into the nature of the primary group provided a profound rationale for the social uses of human togetherness. It was Cooley who took his stand against the opposition of self and society, uniting these into a single, unified concept. He said: "By primary groups I mean those characterized by intimate face-to-face association and cooperation. They are primary in several senses, but chiefly in that they are fundamental in forming the social nature and ideas of the individual."[31] It was a radical idea, and it explained much of the group workers' experience with people. " . . . human nature is not something existing separately in the individual, but a *group-nature . . .*"[32] And he echoed another part of their experience as he described the feeling of "we": "one lives in the feeling of the whole and finds the chief aims of his will in that feeling."[33]

The concept of the social nature of human personality was a landmark in our intellectual history, and it was highly congenial to those who worked in the context of community. The group workers turned to others with the same idea—Baldwin,[34] Kropotkin,[35] and Dewey[36] in the early years, and later Mead,[37] Sherif,[38] Lewin,[39] and the host of others that followed. The implications of this insight moved directly to the heart of one of the great issues of group work practice, namely the persistent tendency to dichotomize the needs of individuals and those of the collective. Baldwin put it this way:

> It is, to my mind, the most remarkable outcome of modern social theory—the recognition of the fact that the individual's normal growth lands him in essential solidarity with his fellows, while on the other hand the exercise of his social duties and privileges advances his highest and purest individuality.[40]

Like all great insights, this one raised new questions to replace those it answered. How, for example, did one understand the processes of interaction between people who were not fixed entities but social creations, the ever-changing products of those same interactions? For this they turned to Mary Follett, an ex-settlement worker in working-class Boston, who wrote books analyzing the group experience, the uses of authority, the nature of freedom, and similar, eagerly debated, issues affecting group work practice. Her concept of "circular behavior" emphasized the *reverberating* character of human exchanges, in which each actor responds to a situation he helped create a moment ago. She pointed out that "response is always to a relation. I respond, not only to you, but to the relation between you and me."[41] This idea took on considerable meaning as workers tried to describe a helping process in which they did not attempt to change the fixed and immutable "personality" of their members, but viewed both client and worker as in a continuing process of shifting and changing under the moment-by-moment impact of each upon the other. In the spontaneous, ever-active ambience of the group experience, this latter version, however difficult to describe, was felt to be closer to experience than the subject-object, "change-agent," what Buber was later to call the "I-It" rather than the "I-Thou"[42] version of the helping process.

It was a day-by-day discovery of the group workers that communication was only partly a formal, verbal affair, and that much of the human exchange could be read in the language of action—in games, body language, and expressive play. In this area, their teacher was Neva Leona Boyd. Using her long experience as a pioneer of the recreation movement, and taking her cues from the literature of spontaneity and progressive education, she asserted that "the only morality there is is bound up with action."[43] She urged the group workers to free themselves "from the limitations imposed by an overemphasis on verbalized aspects of expression."[44] And she said: "Only in the spontaneous, uncalculated response of human beings to each other can sensitivity to undefined subtleties function."[45]

There was a great deal more, and as the field moved into the '30s and '40s, it was Grace Coyle and her colleagues who pulled it all together and made it into a syllabus. The time for building their own theoretical base was getting short; there would be less than ten years between the formation of the American Association of Group Workers in 1946 and its merger into the National Association of Social Workers in 1955, and there were many important questions left to be resolved.

The Group Work Client

There are those who claim that all of social work is a kind of "battlefield medicine," in which the object is to patch up the victims as best one can and put them back in the field as soon as possible. If this is so, then the triage was arranged so that the group workers took those who were the less incapacitated and somewhat more capable of conducting their affairs as part of a small community. This is not to say, as it is so often, that their people were "normal"—there are so few of those around—but simply that they had enough energy to engage themselves with others in common tasks. The emphasis was on working with strengths, rather than curing illness. At the 1935 National Conference of Social Work, LeRoy Bowman said: "Group work . . . is not a service to those who ask for help—it is the social mechanism perfectly competent people utilize to achieve their own ends."[46] And just as Virginia Robinson had written that "one does not go to a [casework] agency joyfully,"[47] Grace Coyle stresses the "true enjoyment [that] comes when the self is . . . actively and vitally engaged, its powers expanding in fulfillment."[48]

Thus it was that the very concept of "client" was somewhat strange, even distasteful, for many group workers, preferring as they did the designation of "member." Bowman was careful to make a point of this at the same conference in 1935, asserting that group workers "must help to relate the members of their groups (I did not say 'clients') to the national or mass concerns of the day."[49] The argument about terms was, of course, part of the aforementioned ambivalence about social work itself; but it had a deeper significance in that the "member" orientation helped bring millions of new middle-class consumers into group work's field of action, as the group work skills were sought out by the youth movements, community centers, "Y"s, and Jewish Centers that were coming into being all over the country.

The distinction between "client" and "member" was not always easy to maintain: group workers were constantly dealing with group members who were struggling under a heavy load of personal problems as they tried to meet the demand for responsible group participation. Thus workers faced what came increasingly to feel like a choice between their concern for individuals in trouble and their aspirations for the group as a whole. Here again was the self-society dilemma in its practice manifestation: whether to get on with the collective tasks or to stop for those who needed help in catching up with the others. The "choice," though it was much discussed, always turned out to be an illusion, in the small group as in the larger community: when one "chose" the individual and abandoned the others, the group foundered and all suffered; and when the worker addressed himself exclusively to the collective, ignoring those who needed special help, there was a mounting residue of anger and guilt, felt by both members and worker.

Out of this dilemma there emerged what has been called the "two clients" conception, in which the worker's function is to help both the individual and the group, the one to meet his needs within the system, the other to pursue its collective tasks. The value of this idea was that it called for considerable skill and forced the worker to try to unify his responsibility for both the individual and the group, instead of hovering indecisively between the two, always worrying about whether he should be sacrificing one for the other.

But the trouble with the "two clients" idea was that it was still dualistic in nature. While "both" was superior to "either-or," it was really only a different version of it, and it tended to produce a kind of pseudo-solution that obscured a deeper insight into the problem. What was needed was a closer look at the working relationship between a person and his group, to find the common need, the common ground, the common impetus that carried them toward each other.[50] In this view, the worker's function was to act as a bridge across which the individual could reach out to negotiate the system of demands and opportunities offered by his group, while at the same time helping the collective reach out to incorporate each of its members in the group life.[51] The worker would thus define his "client"—or his major responsibility—as neither the individual nor the group, but the *processes* that passed between them. The group workers had learned about process from Dewey, Follett, Lindeman, and others; it was a natural outgrowth of their interest in social action and social experience. It was no accident that Coyle's first landmark publication was called *Social Process in Organized Groups,* while Mary Richmond's was entitled *Social Diagnosis.*

The group workers could not always muster the skills necessary to help carry people and their significant groups toward each other; the burden of process is not easy to carry in a product-oriented society. Nevertheless, operating where these problems were always right before their eyes, they could not but form the habit of viewing people in their social context. When they looked at an individual—be he "client" or "member"—they could not fail to see him as surrounded by his culture, his family, and his friends.

The Worker-Client Relationship

The earliest conception of the helping relationship in group work was of one that took place within a community of equals. As I have indicated, the theme of friendship was paramount in the minds of the founders: "Charity is friendship," said Canon Barnett, "and . . . institutions which don't give friends are not charity."[52] The Charity Organization Society also used the slogan "not alms but a friend,"[53] but the settlements used the term literally, and carried it into action with its daily opportunities for physical contact, joint action, group entertainments, and the like.

The theme of camaraderie—of comradeship as an instrument of helping—had a lasting effect on the development of the group work tradition. It became a subject of humor in the sophisticated fellowship into which it subsequently entered, but when the idea of friendship was later transformed into that of leadership, the group workers found themselves formulating an important problem in the uses of professional authority. How did one maintain an active, intimate, spontaneous relationship with a person in need, while yet retaining the distance and discipline necessary to carry out a professional function? How did a worker act freely without acting out?

Freud's discovery of the "transference" in the doctor-patient relationship[54] was a revelation to workers in the helping disciplines, and it was eagerly taken up by the newly emerging social work profession. He had written that "eventually all the conflicts must be fought out on the field of transference,"[55] and, in advising physicians on the use of the psychoanalytic method, he had laid great stress on the absolute "impenetrability" of the doctor in the face of this phenomenon:

> The loosening of the transference, too—one of the main tasks of the cure—is made more difficult by too intimate an attitude on the part of the doctor, so that a doubtful gain in the beginning is more than cancelled in the end. Therefore I do not hesitate to condemn this kind of technique as incorrect. The physician should be impenetrable to the patient, and, like a mirror, reflect nothing but what is shown to him.[56]

Obviously, such a doctrine, however useful in helping workers understand more deeply the meaning of professional authority, was difficult to apply directly in the hustle-bustle of the group experience. And, as we might expect, there was some horror at the prospect. Again it was Bowman who stated the problem:

> Any good group worker knows, as does any good progressive teacher, that such a relationship is the opposite of that desired by the group leader. It is not transference to the leader at all, but cross transference between the members, that should form the dynamic influence in group activities.[57]

In this area as in others, the group workers found the new, system-oriented ideas more congenial to their experience. While always troubled by their tendency towards counter-transference, and their vulnerability to its effects, it was difficult to remain "impenetrable" in a game of steal-the-bacon, or a trip to a strange place, or a discussion of serious group problems. But they could echo to Follett's description of the helping relationship as circular and reciprocal—"a reaction to a relating." And they could respond to her brilliant insight, realized as early as the '20s, that leadership was not essentially a factor of personality—what she called "ascendency traits"—but a functional, situational manifestation. "Don't exploit your personality," she said to them. "*Learn your job.*"[58]

Later in their development, the group workers would be heavily influenced by Grace Coyle's distillation of the educational process and her conception of the *mentoring* and *modelling* aspects of the professional relationship.

> In this interacting mesh of life, whatever the content of program, teaching and learning are a mutual process. If the leader is himself achieving his own guiding values, his own delight in excellence, his own deep sense of the validity and meaning of life, his own ability to function as part of the social whole, that achieving by a kind of delicate osmosis is likely to be his most significant contribution to his group.[59]

Thus the traditional worker-member relationship in group work was that of a co-active, reciprocal, functional, first-among-equals, mentoring collaboration in the pursuit of group tasks. What kind of helping process was it that emerged from all this?

On the Nature of Helping

The legacy of group work, like that of many of the helping professions, lies more in its accumulated experience and its sense of social purpose than in its understanding of its own technical skills. Towley commented on this at about the time when group work was merging its identity with that of the social work profession:

> This specialized field is rich in democratic concepts; it has a wealth of examples; but in professionally unique concepts, "method theory," it has been curiously poor. . . . It is possible that no social or economic class in a community is beyond profiting from what goes on under the name of a "group experience." But it is difficult for a social group worker to communicate how and why this near-miracle happens, except to another group worker.[60]

It was true; but from their "wealth of examples"—that is, the social history of their experiences with people—it is possible to bring into clearer focus some of the action implications of what the group workers thought about their purpose, knowledge, professional relationships, and the rest. Given these conceptions, and given the demands of the settings in which they worked, they were compelled to fashion certain kinds of working skills. Whether or not they were always equal to these demands—early records leave some doubts on that score—the group workers nevertheless developed certain perspectives on the helping process that were unique to their calling.

First, since the worker found himself located inside the group members' sphere of activity—a part of their play, their talk, and their transactions—his comments had to be made not as a detached observer and interpreter but as an active participant with his own functional stake in the proceedings. The concept of "intervention," although it would later become fashionable, was essentially inappropriate since one does not "intervene" in a system from the inside; it is a contradiction in terms. Within the system, the worker's function was to provide the skills with which to mediate the transactions between each individual and the group, reinforcing the energies with which they reached out to each other. In this position, two major, concurrent tasks are faced: on the one hand, to help each member come to grips with the worker's authority and use it to the member's own advantage; while at the same time, to help members use each other in the collective effort. Later, Bennis and Shepard and others would teach them more about these processes of *authority* and *intimacy,* how they operated, and the connections between the two.[61] But whether or not they understood exactly what was happening, group workers' skills were fashioned by such demands, as were their conceptions of the helping process in action.

Second, since the workings of groups made them often restless and mobile, group work skills were at the outset less tuned to introspection and the pursuit of insight than to the advancement of action. Their early interest in non-verbal, extra-logical forms of communication had helped them develop proficiency in many of the expressive phenomena—phantasy, play, drama, music, travelling, and the rest; it is only recently that formal courses in these "program" subjects have been dropped from the graduate school curricula. What remains, however, is the sensitivity to the language of action, and the awareness that talk and action are not antithetical, the former serious and the latter trivial and distracting, but different, often simultaneous, aspects of the communication between worker and clients.

Third, it was not possible for the worker to maintain an orderly and logical progression of ideas when constantly being called upon to react quickly in the press of events. The agenda was often controlled by impulse and feeling, and the worker had to develop the ability to make quick connections and find underlying themes, protecting professional purposes even while moving spontaneously into the action. The sight of a worker sitting wrapped in thought while those around him were feeling and acting was not calculated to inspire confidence in the interest and empathy of professional help. It was not possible for a worker successfully to urge freedom and openness on one's members while serving as a model of caution and circumspection. It called for considerable risking on the worker's part; but risking, after all, was a major ingredient in the client's prescription, and it was a poor sort of authority that gave the message to the client to "do as I say, not as I do."

Finally, since the members' main source of enjoyment and profit came from their ability to show their strengths with others, the group workers had to develop the skills with which to help the members find those strengths and use them in the group. The workers' efforts were primitive at first, relying heavily on urging and exhortation. Later, taught by Alfred Adler, Carl Rogers, and the ego psychologists, they fashioned more sophisticated techniques to mobilize client strength: partializing difficult issues; reaching for real feelings; using role-playing to help translate feelings into action; turning members toward each other for support and reality-testing; reaching for ideas that were hard to express publicly; and connecting private troubles with group concerns.

One could explore many more aspects of the group work gestalt that emerged from the need to do a helping job within a setting that, because it was social, public, and on the clients' home ground, made unusual demands upon the worker. This is not to say that the helping process in group work was *sui generis,* or totally different from other approaches; indeed the point of this paper is that it was only a special manifestation of social work in action. But, over and above the similarities, group work's special character lay in the fact that its experience brought into focus certain phenomena that are less easily seen when the work is private, one-on-one, and under the worker's almost total control.

Toward an Expanded Paradigm

The old settlement idea of the helping relationship as a shared experience meant that residents and neighbors, workers and group members, were on a voyage of discovery, affecting each other's lives, tied together with a common bond, fulfilling each one's own special purposes in the process. The idea was drawn from the very air of Victorian society; it was class-dominated, idealistic, and amateurish in many ways. But its deeper truth lay in its vision of a relationship in which the qualities of leadership were expressed in the joys of human collaboration, rather than in the action of the knower on the naive, the strong on the weak, the expert on the uninitiated. As I have indicated, the intimacy of worker and members created the need to guard one's function carefully, lest it be lost in the close exchange. But the opposite view—detached, "objective," and often identified as more *truly* professional—raises a more serious problem; the distance between worker and client is then so large, and the worker's position on the periphery of the system so secure, that there is no longer any risk at all, and the worker is too safe to worry about it. The group worker's emotional involvement, and tenuous control of the situation, felt dangerous but it was often salutary. Caseworkers who have moved into service with groups have experienced this sense of danger as the feeling, "there are so many of them and only one of me!"[62] They have found that

> . . . the group leadership role demands that the worker give up much of the interview control to which she has, often unconsciously, become accustomed. Caseworkers have often told me that they had never realized how rigidly they controlled the client-worker interaction until they began to function as group workers, where changes of subject could be effected by anyone in the group, where people often turned to each other rather than to the worker for reinforcement and support, where clients could verify each other's "wrong" ideas, where mutually reinforced feelings could not be turned off when they became "dangerous," and where, in short, one's faith in the client's autonomy and basic strength were put to its severest test.[63]

These are the themes of shared control, shared power, and the shared agenda, which are among those I have tried to identify in this paper. That their appearance is so disconcerting to those who first move into group service speaks well for their potential uses in helping to evolve a richer model of the helping process in social work. Each theme needs to be explored in some detail: the social self, the faith in action, the helping relationship as a reciprocal system, the shared power, the sense of immediacy, the eclecticism, the collective sources of individual strength, and even, in some respects, the didacticism that pervaded the group workers' outlook.

The ideas themselves are not new; many have in certain ways been accepted over the years. But they are easy to lose sight of, in a model of practice—perhaps it is the coveted medical model—of a unilateral power exercised over an objectified, inert, malleable client. For example, the definition of the self as a social creation, culturally formed and culturally modifiable, is well ensconced in today's scientific atmosphere; but it is hard to keep before us in the paradigm of the client as a broken object who comes to be repaired by an agent of change who operates single-handedly on self-contained, privately-owned personalities.

As to what it is that does help people change in their own chosen direction,[64] that question will be with us for a long time. The group workers' experience told them that there was something in the nature of *doing,* and particularly collective doing, that helped people find new ways of looking at themselves and the world around them. Many, like Neva Boyd, suspected verbal and logical explanations that went under the name of "insight," but seemed to produce more "aha"s than lasting changes in problem-solving behavior. And it was Kierkegaard, a generation before Freud, who said that "truth exists for the individual only as he himself produces it in action."[65] Ultimately, of course, the answer will lie not in pitting action against insight, but in finding the connections between the two, and the techniques with which to distinguish real understanding from verbal games, and meaningful action from a mechanical behaviorism.

And so it would go: there is obviously a great deal more to be done with these issues than can be attempted here. The major threads are reciprocal, systemic, existential, and would lead us back into studies that might rescue these constructs from their stereotypes and translate them back into their implications for practice, both one-to-one and one-to-group. For the present, this brief analysis may help bring their roots in the group work experience back into view and lead the profession forward in the process of locating the traditions that indeed make up the profession.

Footnotes and References

1. Kathleen Woodroofe, *From Charity to Social Work* (Toronto: University of Toronto Press, 1962), p. 46.
2. Robert H. Bremner, *American Philanthropy* (Chicago: The University of Chicago Press, 1960), pp. 95 ff.
3. American Association of Social Workers, *Social Case Work, Generic and Specific: An Outline: A Report of the Milford Conference,* 1929, 92 pages.

4. "The TIAC Report: Principles, Proposals and Issues in Inter-Association Cooperation," *Social Work Journal,* Vol. 32, No. 3 (July 1951), pp. 112–57. Entire issue on the subject.
5. Melvin A. Glasser, "The Story of the Movement for a Single Professional Association," *Social Work Journal,* Vol. 36, No. 3 (July 1955), pp. 115–22.
6. Talcott Parsons, "A Sociologist Looks at the Legal Profession," in *Essays in Sociological Theory* (Glencoe, Ill.: The Free Press, 1954, Rev. Ed.), p. 372.
7. *See,* for example: Harriet M. Bartlett, "Toward Clarification and Improvement of Social Work Practice," *Social Work,* Vol. 3, No. 2 (April 1958), pp. 3–9. *See* also her "The Generic-Specific Concept in Social Work Education and Practice," in Alfred J. Kahn (ed.), *Issues in American Social Work* (New York: Columbia University Press, 1959), pp. 159–90.
8. William E. Gordon, "A Critique of the Working Definition," *Social Work,* Vol. 7, No. 4 (October 1962), pp. 3–13.
9. For an earlier historical effort of my own, *see:* William Schwartz, "Group Work and the Social Scene," in Alfred E. Kahn (ed.), *Issues in American Social Work* (New York: Columbia University Press, 1959), pp. 110–37.
10. Henrietta Barnett, *Canon Barnett, His Life, Work, and Friends, By His Wife* (Boston and New York: Houghton Mifflin Company, 1919, 2 Volumes), Vol. 1, pp. 27 ff.
11. Mary E. Richmond, *Social Diagnosis* (New York: Russell Sage Foundation, 1917).
12. Grace L. Coyle, *Social Process in Organized Groups* (New York: Richard R. Smith, 1930).
13. Henrietta Barnett, op. cit., p. 184.
14. *See:* Mrs. Glendower Evans, "Scientific Charity," *Proceedings of the National Conference of Charities and Correction, 1889* (Boston: Geo. H. Ellis, 1889), pp. 24–35.
15. *See:* William Schwartz, "Camping," *Social Work Year Book, 1960* (New York: National Association of Social Workers, 1960), pp. 112–17.
16. Margaretta Williamson, *The Social Worker in Group Work* (New York and London: Harper, 1929), p. 17.
17. William Heard Kilpatrick, *Group Education for a Democracy* (New York: Association Press, 1940), p. vii.
18. Grace Coyle, "On Becoming Professional," in *Toward Professional Standards* (New York: American Association of Group Workers, 1947), pp. 17–18.
19. Schwartz, "Group Work and the Social Scene," op. cit., p. 123.
20. For the distinction between the "priests," who minister to the needy without judging them, and the "prophets," who thunder and hold up standards to follow, *see:* Clarke A. Chambers, "An Historical Perspective on Politi-

cal Action *vs.* Individualized Treatment," in *Current Issues in Social Work Seen in Historical Perspective* (New York: Council on Social Work Education, 1962), p. 54.

21. Quoted in Clarke A. Chambers, *Seedtime of Reform: American Social Service and Social Action, 1918–1933* (Minneapolis: University of Minnesota Press, 1963), p. 150.
22. Ibid., p. 149.
23. Eduard C. Lindeman, "Group Work and Democracy—A Philosophical Note," reprinted in Albert S. Alissi (ed.), *Perspectives on Social Group Work Practice* (New York: The Free Press, 1980), p. 81. Originally published in 1939.
24. Jane Addams, *Twenty Years at Hull House* (New York: The New American Library, A Signet Classic, 1960), p. 97. First published in 1910.
25. Henrietta Barnett, *Canon Barnett, His Life, Work, and Friends*. . . . , op. cit., p. 110.
26. Henrietta Barnett, "Principles of Recreation," in Canon and Mrs. S. A. Barnett, *Towards Social Reform* (New York: The Macmillan Company, 1909), p. 289.
27. Eduard C. Lindeman, "Organization and Technique for Rural Recreation," *Proceedings of the National Conference of Social Work* (Chicago: University of Chicago Press, 1920), p. 321.
28. Henrietta Barnett, *Canon Barnett, His Life, Work, and Friends*. . . . , op. cit., p. 115.
29. Canon Barnett, " 'Settlements' or 'Missions'," in Canon and Mrs. S. A. Barnett, op. cit., p. 273.
30. Ibid., pp. 271–88.
31. Charles Horton Cooley, *Social Organization: A Study of the Larger Mind* (New York: Schocken Books, 1962), p. 23. First published in 1909, by Charles Scribner's Sons.
32. Ibid., p. 29. Emphasis in original.
33. Ibid., p. 23.
34. James Mark Baldwin, *The Individual and Society* (Boston: Richard G. Badger, The Gorham Press, 1911), p. 16.
35. P. Kropotkin, *Mutual Aid, A Factor of Evolution* (New York: Alfred A. Knopf, 1925).
36. John Dewey, *Human Nature and Conduct* (New York: Random House, 1922).
37. George Herbert Mead, *Mind, Self and Society* (Chicago: University of Chicago Press, 1934).
38. Muzafer Sherif, *The Psychology of Social Norms* (New York: Harper, 1936).
39. Kurt Lewin, "Conduct, Knowledge, and Acceptance of New Values," in *Resolving Social Conflicts: Selected Papers on Group Dynamics* (New York: Harper, 1948), pp. 56–68.
40. Baldwin, op. cit., p. 16.

41. Mary Parker Follett, "Constructive Conflict," in Henry C. Metcalf and L. Urwick (eds.), *Dynamic Administration: The Collected Papers of Mary Parker Follett* (New York and London: Harper, 1940), p. 45. Paper first published in 1926.
42. Martin Buber, *I and Thou* (New York: Charles Scribner's Sons, 1958).
43. Neva L. Boyd, "The Social Education of Youth Through Recreation: The Value of Play in Education," in Paul Simon (ed.), *Play and Game Theory in Group Work: A Collection of Papers by Neva Leona Boyd* (Chicago: The Jane Addams Graduate School of Social Work at the University of Illinois at Chicago Circle, 1971), p. 43. Paper written in 1924.
44. Neva L. Boyd, "Social Group Work: A Definition With a Methodological Note," in Paul Simon (ed.), op. cit., p. 149. Paper written in 1937.
45. Ibid.
46. LeRoy E. Bowman, "Dictatorship, Democracy, and Group Work in America," *Proceedings of the National Conference of Social Work* (Chicago: University of Chicago Press, 1935), p. 385.
47. Virginia P. Robinson, "The Dynamics of Supervision under Functional Controls," in *The Development of a Professional Self: Teaching and Learning in Professional Helping Processes, Selected Writings, 1930–1968* (New York: AMS Press, 1978), p. 254. Article first published in 1948.
48. Grace Longwell Coyle, *Group Work With American Youth: A Guide to the Practice of Leadership* (New York: Harper, 1948), p. 32.
49. LeRoy Bowman, op. cit., p. 383.
50. For a discussion of this "symbiotic" relationship between the individual and his group, *see:* William Schwartz, "The Social Worker in the Group," *The Social Welfare Forum, 1961* (New York and London: Columbia University Press, 1961), pp. 156 ff.
51. For a discussion of the social work function in regard to the needs of the one and the many, *see:* William Schwartz, "Private Troubles and Public Issues: One Social Work Job or Two?" *The Social Welfare Forum, 1969* (New York and London: Columbia University Press, 1969), pp. 22–43.
52. Henrietta Barnett, *Canon Barnett, His Life, Work, and Friends*. . . . op. cit., p. 169.
53. Mrs. Glendower Evans, op. cit., p. 25.
54. Sigmund Freud, "The Dynamics of the Transference," (1912), *Collected Papers* (London: The Hogarth Press and The Institute of Psycho-Analysis, 1950, 5 Volumes), Vol. II, pp. 312–22.
55. Ibid., p. 318.
56. Sigmund Freud, "Recommendations for Physicians on the Psycho-Analytic Method of Treatment," (1912) *Collected Papers* (London: The Hogarth Press and The Institute of Psycho-Analysis, 1950, 5 Volumes), Vol. II, p. 331.
57. LeRoy Bowman, op. cit., pp. 385–6.

58. Mary Parker Follett, "Some Discrepancies in Leadership Theory and Practice," in Metcalf and Urwick (eds.), op. cit., p. 272. Emphasis in original. Article first published in 1928.
59. Grace Longwell Coyle, *Group Work With American Youth. . . .*, op. cit., p. 216.
60. Frank J. Bruno (with chapters by Louis Towley), *Trends in Social Work, 1874–1956* (New York: Columbia University Press, 1957), p. 422.
61. Warren G. Bennis & H. A. Shepard, "A Theory of Group Development," *Human Relations,* Vol. 9 (1956), pp. 415–37.
62. William Schwartz, "Discussion of Three Papers on the Group Method with Clients, Foster Families, and Adoptive Families," *Child Welfare,* Vol. 45, No. 10 (December 1966), p. 572.
63. Ibid., p. 575.
64. *See,* for example: Allen Wheelis, "How People Change," *Commentary* (May 1969), pp. 56–66.
65. Quoted in Rollo May, "The Emergence of Existential Psychology," in Rollo May, (ed.), *Existential Psychology* (New York: Random House, 1961), p. 12.

Group Work Theory

Introduction

The writings in this section reveal the systematic manner in which Schwartz worked at developing his ideas on method theory in general, and practice with groups in particular. As a student of history, he studied the profession's development and planfully labored to engage the difficult questions which he believed would take the profession forward in developing its methodology. The examination of history, he maintained, pointed to the profession's omissions, as well as to its achievements.

Schwartz (1963) wrote that as a profession begins, it concerns itself with problems of social need. Matters of social vision predominate as the profession must draw support for its cause. Gradually, as some success is achieved there is a shift from social advocacy to social effectiveness wherein the profession is required to demonstrate that it can do the job and can do it well. Energy shifts from what should be to what is. The concern about ends prompts inquiry toward means. The skills of the practitioner take on greater importance in comparison to motives, intentions, philosophy, and aspiration. The movement toward science, "the systematic appraisal of reality" (1963, p. 4), becomes stronger.

As the profession pressed on into the 1960s it had clearly and eloquently described its social cause and had yet to specify the methodology which would help it achieve its desired ends. Movement toward a unified profession in the 1950s seemed based more on matters of shared values and philosophy than on a shared definition of helping activity. In "The Social Worker in the Group" (1961), "Toward a Strategy of Group Work Practice" (1962), and "Small Group Science and Group Work Practice" (1963) Schwartz attends to the subject of methodology and the complexities of method theory as a subject unto itself. In each of these works, he poses a series of questions inherent in the subject of method. He hoped that as the profession engaged the questions, arrived at and compared its answers, it would move forward in understanding and defining the nature of the helping process in social work.

In "The Social Worker in the Group" (1961) Schwartz engages us immediately, by asking us to consider the historic ways in which method has been characterized by the profession. Traditionally, he says, method has been defined by the number of persons with whom one worked at any one point in time, that is, casework, group work, or community organization. Schwartz's ideas of method represent a complete departure from such a notion. A generic theory of the helping process and the application of this theory to the small group system were what Schwartz advanced. His theory was about social work with groups, not group work as a separate method in social work. He believed that to consider casework, group work, and community organization as separate methods "simply mistakes the nature of the helping process itself for the relational system in which it is applied" (1961, p. 149). Rather, method was "a systematic process of ordering one's activity in the performance of a function" (p. 151). Having specified that "[m]ethod is function in action" (p. 151) Schwartz devotes the remainder of the article to three critical theoretical questions: First, what is the professional assignment of social work (function)? Second, how can we specify the tasks, or activities of the social worker which will carry function into professional activity? And, third, how are these ideas elaborated in the small face to face group?

As with most of his writings, Schwartz begins "Toward a Strategy of Group Work Practice" (1962) by locating his subject matter within an historical context. Not long after the 1955 forming of NASW, the early 1960s was a period in which the process of the practitioner was slowly becoming an acceptable subject for study. At this point, discussion of method used words like *enables, provides for, aims to, functions in such a way that,* to characterize our helping activity. Schwartz contended that these words reflected our strong teleological emphasis which did little to advance defining a strategy of professional practice.

"Toward a Strategy of Group Work Practice" is devoted to an exploration of how a profession proceeds "to develop and systematize its concepts of practice" (p. 269). This question concerns itself with the movement from knowledge to action and the complexity of this transition. Two issues for the human services predominate: (1) how to make use of the encyclopedic body of potentially useful knowledge and (2) how to move from knowledge to action since "action cannot be deduced directly from knowledge no matter how vast that knowledge may be" (p. 269).

His answer to these two questions is the thesis that method theory consists in three interdependent/integrated conceptual subsystems: (1) knowledge, (2) action, and (3) hoped for immediate outcomes. He advanced the idea that the gap between what is known and what is done is immutably bridged by what one hopes to achieve. *If* one can define what one believes to be true, and *if* one can define the immediate outcomes one hopes to achieve, *then,* and only then, can one specify the action required as the implementing force.

The paper goes on to explore some of the major conceptual problems in each of these areas and demonstrates how the interdependence among knowledge, action, and hoped for immediate outcomes, determines the clarity and coherence of method theory. While each area has its own integrity, their value as components of method theory is realized when each is viewed in relation to each other.

"Small Group Science and Group Work Practice" (1963) continues the discussion of method by examining a profession's need to turn toward science as it progresses from a movement to a profession. How does social work link scientific inquiry to professional activity? By what strategy can group workers make use of burgeoning material about groups without becoming so enamored with the social psychology of groups that interest in practice is secondary?

These were important questions to group workers whose growing identification with the profession, rather than with their employing organizations, prompted the need to become articulate to colleagues about their knowledge base and its relationship to practice. Despite the fears of others, that the turn toward science might move group workers from their humanity, Schwartz was absolutely convinced that to be a professional meant establishing the ways in which knowledge informs practice while simultaneously holding on "to retain in the process its initial vigor, its power of advocacy and its driving vision of what society should be like" (1963, p. 5).

Central to his ideas was his belief that the purpose of science is *not* to puzzle out the problems of the practitioner. Science, is not a "design for action" but rather a way of organizing ideas which represent "bits of verified human experience." Having stated that something is "true" does not yet offer what should be done about it. Science is not the generator of ideas, with practice the receiver of them. Rather, the relationship between science and practice is an interactive one in which each informs the other. If, then, the practitioner cannot look to science for practice instructions and if the amount and range of potentially useful information is limitless, how does the practitioner proceed?

All inquiry, according to Schwartz begins with a felt need. By articulating questions, uncertainties, ambiguities, the social worker is provided with the impetus for inquiry. This "need to know" becomes the driving force prompting group workers to spell out their basic assumptions, hoped for outcomes, and methodological preferences. Spelling out this frame of reference prompts lines of inquiry which then become the working grounds for research about practice.

This then, in 1963, was the major task before group workers—that of lessening the gap between practice and science by looking to their own experiences for the systematizing and studying of practice, all of which was well within their grasp.

The systematic studying of group work practice theory was at the heart of the Project of the Committee on Practice, of the National Group Work Section of NASW—1959 to 1963. Under the editorship of Margaret E. Hartford, this report was published in 1964[1] and reflected the efforts of the committee to produce a new "Working Definition" of social group work practice. Schwartz's "Analysis of Papers Presented on Working Definitions of Group Work Practice" (1964) is a discussion of the efforts of

---

[1]*Working Papers Toward a Frame of Reference for Social Group Work,* ed., Margaret E. Hartford. New York: National Association of Social Workers, 1964. Prepared as a Project of the Committee on Practice of the National Group Work Section of NASW—1959 to 1963, Bernard Shiffman, Chair.

group work educators and practitioners to arrive at a shared definition of group work practice, one which would attend to components of values, purpose, sanction, knowledge, and method. Schwartz's distinguishing of three different models: the medical model, the scientific model, and the organic systems model, "each with its own implications for how one defines and teaches the nature of the helping process" (1964, p. 60) provides a clear conceptual framework for a comparative analysis of models of working with groups.

By 1971 the use of groups was becoming more widespread within the settings in which social workers practiced. Under the press of clients' troubles, the barriers between caseworkers and group workers had begun to soften somewhat and work with groups was making its way into what was traditionally considered "casework" settings. *The Practice of Group Work,* edited by William Schwartz and Serapio Zalba, emerged from the planning process of the Annual Forum of the National Conference on Social Welfare under the then chair of the Group Work Section, William Schwartz. The intent of the conference was to study social workers' efforts to assist with practice problems within a wide range of settings. Process records became the basis for identifying and discussing the skills used in the work. As always, Schwartz's emphasis was on the technical problems of helping people and he developed a volume in which the visible actions of the social worker were integral to the discussion of practice. Process recording brings to life what the social worker does to help. In fact, it is the degree to which the writers reveal their practice that provides this volume with its unique quality.

Published as an introduction to *The Practice of Group Work,* "On the Use of Groups in Social Work Practice" (1971) was first presented to the field instructors and faculty of the Columbia University School of Social Work. It was written to serve as a general frame of reference for the practice papers within the volume, most of which were prepared for the conference. As Schwartz introduced his subject matter he appealed to us not to think of group workers as educating caseworkers, but rather to view the profession as moving forward toward defining the social worker's function in a way which explains what all social workers do. His plea was for us to move together, as a profession, toward our study of the ways in which social workers help clients negotiate difficult environments. His introductory chapter serves as a concise reference for practitioners with groups and very quickly acquaints the reader with the interactionist model, Schwartz's phases of the helping process, and the importance of beginning under clear conditions of work.

"Between Client and System: The Mediating Function" (1976) represents a full presentation of the mediating model, as it applies to work with small groups. For those already acquainted with *Social Work with Groups: The Search for a Method* and "Content and Process in the Educative Experience," this chapter constitutes a more highly summarized presentation of familiar ideas. The unfamiliar can begin to become familiar with the ways by which Schwartz developed his interactionist model. His beginning discussion of the scientific paradigm from which the profession of social work emerged, enables the reader to understand the history of social work method within the context of the times in which it developed. Though he differed greatly with the scientific model, he believed that these ideas were progressive in their time and helped us move away from and beyond the notion that people had innate attributes which could not be altered. The problem arose, Schwartz believed, when these ideas were applied to the helping profession. If people were influenced by events, then, a whole world of study and thinking could open up in which we would need to pay attention to the relationships between people and events rather than imposing moralistic standards on those believed to be "fundamentally incapable of change."

Schwartz writes that for generations there has been a long line of scholars who have worked toward a paradigmatic shift and have offered an alternate view. The positivist separates self and environment, dichotomizes feeling and intellect, and holds a view of science partial to the external and visible. The antiobjectivist view emphasizes the power of experience, and the idea that "truth" for the individual can only be created by the individual in action. Schwartz builds these ideas into his theory of practice. Thus, he offers us a model of the helping process which is irreconcilable with either the medical or scientific models.

Toby Berman-Rossi

The Social Worker in the Group

William Schwartz

Professions have a way of moving periodically through eras of rediscovery in which an old truth comes alive with the vigor and freshness of a new idea. Such an occurrence seems to be taking shape in social work practice as we face the realization that the problems of people do not lend themselves easily to arbitrary divisions of labor among the various agencies of social welfare. In fact, this particular truth has been rediscovered several times, cutting deeply, in each instance, into established forms and calling for new institutional and professional alignments.

This stubborn fact has precipitated a reexamination of social work's historic system of designating the functions of agencies by reference to the number of people involved in the client-worker system at one time. Thus the casework agency, as we have known it, was one which derived its distinguishing characteristics from the fact that its workers talked to people one at a time; the group work agency (later called the "group service agency") worked with people in small, cohesive groups; and the community organization agency assumed the function of leadership with representative bodies and similar associations.

This typology emerged at an early stage of specialization and has remained relatively stable over the major course of social work history—not, however, without a certain marked degree of uneasiness throughout. Group workers have struggled for years with the need to "individualize," wondering whether they were "doing casework" when they dealt with individual problems, and continually raising the issue of whether individual or group problems should take priority. The agencies of social casework have been concerned about the reluctance of workers trained in the one-to-one relationship to carry these skills into committee work, multiple interviewing, group consultation, and other group constellations. And the community organization workers have been faced continuously with the vital connection between

Schwartz, William. (1961). The social worker in the group. In The Social Welfare Forum, *Proceedings of the National Conference on Social Welfare. Copyright © 1961, Columbia University Press, NY. Used by permission.*

the tasks that people undertake and the uniquely personal ways in which they approach them.

These vague but pervasive concerns have now begun to crystallize into new conceptions about the appropriate client-worker systems through which agencies carry out their functions. The rapid development of social work services in the institutional therapeutic settings has created a community model which lends itself poorly to a type of specialization based solely on the number of people with whom the social worker interacts at a given time. In these settings, the caseworkers have been pressed into group service, just as the psychiatrists and the psychologists had before them;[1] and the group workers have found themselves involved in a degree of intensive individualization beyond anything they had ever experienced.

In general practice, the developing emphasis on the family as a unit of service has forced both caseworkers and group workers into new modes of activity. The former have been constrained to understand and work with the dynamics of family interaction; the latter, to replace the comfortable aura of friendly visiting with a more sophisticated and focused approach. In both agency types, the traditional forms have been changing, with caseworkers turning more and more to the group as a unit of service and group workers rekindling their old concern with ways of offering skilled individual guidance for those who need it.[2]

In the area of community organization, the picture is less clear. There seems to be little doubt, however, that its conceptualizers are recognizing another old truth, namely, that the only way to work with communities is to work with people, singly and together, and that skill in the helping process needs to be abstracted and formulated into teachable concepts. The newer theoretical attempts lean heavily toward organizing the experience of community workers into concepts that reflect the language and central concerns of social work method. Genevieve Carter, for example, has addressed herself directly to an analysis of the helping process in community organization, and her concept of "cumulative sequence" is an interesting attempt to relate the order of community change to that of individual growth and development.[3]

Concurrently, the unification of social workers within a single professional association and the efforts of the social work schools to conceptualize the common elements in practice have dramatized the need to combine the

---

[1]See, for example, "The Psychiatric Social Worker as Leader of a Group," Report of Committee on Practice, Psychiatric Social Work Section, National Association of Social Workers (New York: the Association, n.d.; mimeographed).

[2]See, for example, *The Use of Group Techniques in the Family Agency: Three Papers from the FSAA Biennial Meeting, Washington, D.C., April, 1959* (New York: Family Service Association of America, 1959); "Committee Statement on the Role of the Caseworker in a Group Work Agency" (Chicago: Chicago Area Chapter, National Association of Social Workers, 1958; mimeographed).

[3]Genevieve W. Carter, "Social Work Community Organization Methods and Processes," in Walter A. Friedlander, ed., *Concepts and Methods of Social Work* (Englewood Cliffs, N.J.: Prentice-Hall, 1958), p. 248.

learnings of workers from the various fields and settings into a functional scheme that can be taught and practiced under the name of "social work." Such a scheme would not eliminate specialization but would certainly redefine it; most important, it could create a new integration within which the component parts could be differentiated on a basis more consistent with the facts of life as they actually exist in the community.

The new conceptual framework would be built on the recognition that the function of a social agency is determined more realistically by the social problem to which it has been assigned than by the specific relational systems through which the social worker translates this function into concrete services. It would accept the fact that there is no known correspondence between a function such as child placement, or family welfare, or recreation, or social planning, and the exclusive use of the one-to-one or the one-to-group structure to carry it out. And it would become increasingly clear that any agency should be capable of creating, in each specific instance, that system of client-worker relationships which is most appropriate to its clients' requirements.

A significant corollary would then emerge quite naturally, namely, that the single variable embodied in the number of people one works with at a time is simply not significant enough to be endowed with the designation of "method." Not significant enough, that is, if we reserve the term "method" to mean a systematic mode of helping which, while it is used differently in different situations, retains throughout certain recognizable and invariant properties through which one may identify the social worker in action. In this light, to describe casework, group work, and community organization as methods simply mistakes the nature of the helping process for the relational system in which it is applied. It seems more accurate to speak of a social work method, practiced in the various systems in which the social worker finds himself or which are established for the purpose of giving service: the family, the small friendship group, the representative body, the one-to-one interview, the hospital ward, the lounge-canteen, the committee, the street club, the special-interest group, and many others. Within this frame of reference, the task of safeguarding the uniqueness of the various so-called methods fades before the real problem of abstracting from all these experiences the common methodological components of the helping process in social work.

This is partly why any serious attempt to define a unique entity called "social group work" begins to turn, under one's very hand, into a description of something larger and more inclusive, of which the worker-group system is simply a special case. Having now, after many years of shifting identification, found a resting place in social work function and the social agency network,[4] group workers can indeed make a significant conceptual contribution to the theoretical problems involved in working with groups. But the context has changed, and the moment has passed, for a definition of "group work

[4]For a more detailed account of the developing integration of group work and social work see the writer's "Group Work and the Social Scene" in Alfred J. Kahn, ed., *Issues in American Social Work* (New York: Columbia University Press, 1959), pp. 110–37.

method." Rather, we must now search for those common elements in social work practice—the very elements which attracted group workers into the social work fold—from which social workers in all settings can draw the specifics of their own practice. The job can no longer be done most usefully by first defining social group work (or casework or community organization) and then trying to fit the description into the general framework of helping theory. The process is now rather the reverse: by laying the groundwork in a social work methodology, we may begin to analyze and clarify the activities of the social worker as he works with people in groups.

To both of these endeavors—building the common model and describing the special case of the group system—those who have been schooled in the traditions of social group work have a rich store of experience from which to contribute. The task is, of course, rendered doubly difficult by the fact that any worker who attempts it must break the bonds of his own training, since he himself has been reared in the ancient fallacies. But, clumsy though these first efforts must be, it seems inevitable that they will be made, and in increasing number;[5] for they represent an indispensable part of the still larger task of conceptualizing the generic framework of the social work profession as a whole. These larger issues are embodied in the Curriculum Study of the Council on Social Work Education[6] and in the work of the Commission on Social Work Practice of the National Association of Social Workers.[7] The present segment of this over-all task deals only with those activities through which the social worker functions in direct relationship with people of established or potential client status; the focus is on the helping process itself and on the factors which determine its nature and its variations. In what follows, we shall not presume to create a comprehensive theoretical statement but simply to highlight a few of the essential components around which such a statement will need to turn.

Let us begin, then, with three fairly simple propositions:

1. Every profession has a particular function to perform in society: it has received a certain job assignment for which it is held accountable.
2. This assignment is then elaborated in certain characteristic modes of activity—certain action patterns designed to implement the professional function.
3. These action patterns are further fashioned and developed within the specific systems in which they operate.

---

[5]Although not dealing specifically with the method component, an outstanding effort to develop a foundation for a unifying theory in social work has been made by Gordon Hearn, *Theory Building in Social Work* (Toronto: University of Toronto Press, 1958). See also Joseph W. Eaton, "A Scientific Basis for Helping," in Kahn *op. cit.*, pp. 270–92, and Harriet M. Bartlett, "The Generic-specific Concept in Social Work Education and Practice," *ibid.*, pp. 159–90.

[6]Werner W. Boehm, *Objectives of the Social Work Curriculum of the Future,* The Comprehensive Report of the Curriculum Study, Vol. I (New York: Council on Social Work Education, 1959).

[7]Described by Harriet M. Bartlett, "Toward Clarification and Improvement of Social Work Practice," *Social Work,* III, No. 2 (1958), 3–9.

These propositions lead to a working definition of method as a systematic process of ordering one's activity in the performance of a function. Method is function in action.

This line of reasoning thus calls for three major lines of inquiry, each of which carries its own theoretical problems. The first line of inquiry is designed to produce an accurate functional statement which formulates as precisely as possible the particular assignment drawn by the social work profession in the society which creates and sustains it. The second inquiry is designed to convert the functional statement into those patterns of activity through which the social work function is implemented. The third line of investigation is directed to seeking out the specific adaptations of the general methodological pattern in the various concrete situations in which the social worker performs his job.

Requirements for a functional statement. The central requirement is to recognize at the outset that the very idea of function implies the existence of an organic whole, a dynamic system, in which the worker performs certain movements in relation to the movements of others. In Parsons's words:

> The very definition of an organic whole is as one within which *the relations determine the properties of its parts*. . . . And in so far as this is true, the concept "part" takes on an abstract, indeed a "fictional" character. For the part of an organic whole is no longer the same, once it is separated factually or conceptually from the whole.[8]

And Lawrence Frank, in describing what he calls "organized complexities," speaks of the need for a field concept describing

> circular, reciprocal relations . . . through which the component members of the field participate in and thereby create the field of the whole, which field in turn regulates and patterns their individual activities. This is a circular, reciprocal relation, not a serial cause and effect, stimulus and response relation.[9]

This model of a dynamic system which surrounds and incorporates the movements of the worker provides specific clues for our statement of social work function. First, it helps us realize that function is itself *an action concept* and that it cannot be understood as a description of what social workers know, or feel, or hope to achieve. To say, as we often do, that the social work function is to "understand behavior," or "be sensitive to need," or "effect changes," is to beg the functional question entirely. Such statements remain

---

[8]Talcott Parsons, *The Structure of Social Action* (New York: McGraw-Hill Book Co., 1937), p. 32; italics added.

[9]Lawrence K. Frank, "Research for What?" *Journal of Social Issues,* Kurt Lewin Memorial Award Issue, Supplement Series, No. 10 (1957), p. 12.

fixed at the level of what the worker may need in order to carry out his function, or what he may envision as a result of having performed it well—they say nothing about the function itself. The social worker's philosophy, social aspirations, attitudes toward people, and even his knowledge about them, are not unique to the profession and do not, in themselves, represent its assignment in society. Properly viewed, these qualities are simply prerequisite to the forms of action through which the profession justifies its social position.

Second, the model illustrates the need for the statement to reflect the activity of the social worker *as it affects, and is affected by, the activity of others* within the system. The failure to understand this feature of the helping system has created great difficulties in both the practice and the theory of social work. The inability to see the system as one "within which the relations determine the properties of its parts" has made it possible to imagine that one may deal with human beings by reference to certain discrete characteristics rather than to their movements within the relational system through which they seek help. To "diagnose" the client, to inventory his "needs," and to recapitulate his life history leave undone the task of understanding how these facts, if such they be, may be moving the client as he acts and reacts within the present field. Where the properties of parts are determined by their relations, the search for discrete characteristics is at best "interesting" and at worst produces a situation in which, in Merton's words, "understanding is diminished by an excess of facts." It should be stated that the uneasy attempt to take over the language and the sequence-of-treatment concept of the medical profession has confused and retarded our own attempts to find terms and concepts which would truly describe the helping process in social work. For the helping relationship as we know it is one in which the client possesses the only real and lasting means to his own ends. The worker is but one resource in a life situation which encompasses many significant relationships. And movement, at any given moment, is based on the movement of the preceding moment, as each new event calls for a reorientation of the worker to a new complex of demands for his skill. Such a process is patently different from one in which the function of the person in difficulty is to supply information and the function of the worker is to create action based upon this information, by which division of labor a "treatment" or a "cure" is effected.

The third clue offered by the organic model is the need to represent the *limited field of influence* in which any part of a dynamic system operates. This involves acceptance of the fact that, within such a system, any single part affects only those with which it interacts; and, further, that it affects even these in a limited way, in accordance with its specific function. This recognition can help to scale down the grandiose, cure-all aspirations of any single profession, and to avoid couching its objectives in the language of absolutes—"achieving individual maturity," "fulfilling human needs," and the like.

Fourth, the model points to the fact that, within a dynamic relational system, the interplay of movements of the various actors is in effect an *interplay of functions.* Thus, as the worker is moved by the question "What am I doing here?" so are the others in the situation moved, consciously and unconsciously, by the same question. The worker-client interaction is one in which each needs and uses the other in order to carry out his own sense of purpose within the relational system.

Our next question must then be: What are the systems within which the social work profession in general, and the social worker in particular, derives and carries out the social work assignment?

First, there is the general system of society itself, within which the profession has been set in motion and assigned to a given sphere of influence consistent with its ability to perform certain necessary tasks.

Second, there is the social agency system, within which the social worker translates agency function into concrete services. The agency situation represents a kind of partialization of the larger social system, from which it draws its own special assignment; and the agency creates, in addition, a unique subculture of its own, out of its own mode of living and working.

Third, there is the specific client-worker relationship—one-to-one or one-to-group—in which the social worker expresses both his general function as a professional and his specific function within the agency complex. The client-worker relationship, viewed from a distance, may thus be seen to be a system within a system within a system.

This is, of course, a simplified version of the relationship of parts to a dynamic whole. It is simplified precisely because we need to choose, from the immensely complex network of relationships in which the social worker finds himself, those which exercise the most significant determining effects upon his movements.[10] We may say that the social worker's movements, within any specific helping relationship, reveal certain constant elements, which he derives from his professional identification, and certain variant elements, which he derives from his agency identification and from the situations in which he operates. The common components of social work function emerge from the social work position within the social scheme; its adaptive components are those which express the specific ways in which the professional function is put to work.

Function: the professional assignment. Let us now venture a proposal for the functional statement itself. We would suggest that the general assignment for the social work profession is to mediate the process through which the individual and his society reach out for each other through a mutual need for self-fulfillment. This presupposes a relationship between the individual and his nurturing group which we would describe as "symbiotic"—each needing the other for its own life and growth, and each reaching out to the other with all the strength it can command at a given moment. The social

[10]The interdependence of dynamic systems and the problems of abstracting one or another for analysis are discussed in Ronald Lippitt, Jeanne Watson, and Bruce Westley, *The Dynamics of Planned Change* (New York: Harcourt, Brace and Co., 1958), pp. 5–11.

worker's field of intervention lies at the point where two forces meet: the individual's impetus toward health, growth, and belonging; and the organized efforts of society to integrate its parts into a productive and dynamic whole.

More specifically, the social work assignment emerges from the fact that, in a complex and often disordered society, the individual-social symbiosis grows diffuse and obscure in varying degrees, ranging from the normal developmental problems of children growing into their culture to the severe pathology involved in situations where the symbiotic attachment appears to be all but severed. At all the points along this range, the social work function is to mediate the individual-social transaction as it is worked out in the specific context of those agencies which are designed to bring together individual needs and social resources—the person's urge to belong to society as a full and productive member and society's ability to provide certain specific means for integrating *its* people and enriching their social contribution. Placed thus, in Bertha Reynolds's old phrase, "between the client and the community," the social worker's job is to represent and to implement the symbiotic strivings, even where their essential features are obscured from the individual, from society, or from both.

It should be emphasized that this conception is different from that which places the social worker in a sphere of concern known as "dysfunctioning." While it is true that the profession operates in areas where the individual-social interaction is impaired, these areas are only part of the social work field of action. The problems of symbiotic diffusion are inevitable in any complex society and apply not only to social pathology but to the normal, developmental processes and to the ongoing social effort to order the relationship between needs and resources. The concern with developmental tasks has provided part of the traditional preoccupation of the leisure-time agencies, while the ordering of needs and resources has engaged those agencies concerned with social planning and action.

This is obviously only a brief outline of the symbiotic model; its rationale has been elaborated by Kropotkin,[11] Mead,[12] Sherif,[13] Murphy,[14] Bergson,[15] and many others. For our present purposes, the important points are: the fundamental impetus of people and their groups carries them toward each other; this impetus is often blocked and diverted by a diffusion of the relationship between self- and social-interest; where the impetus can be freed to operate, it constitutes the basic motivation, for both individual and social change, with which the social worker engages himself.

---

[11]P. Kropotkin, *Mutual Aid, a Factor of Evolution* (New York: Alfred A. Knopf, 1925).

[12]George Herbert Mead, *Mind, Self and Society* (Chicago: University of Chicago Press, 1934).

[13]Muzafer Sherif, *The Psychology of Social Norms* (New York: Harper, 1936).

[14]Gardner Murphy, *Human Potentialities* (New York: Basic Books, Inc., 1958).

[15]Henri Bergson, *The Two Sources of Morality and Religion;* tr. R. Ashley Audra and Cloudesley Brereton, with the assistance of W. Horsfall Carter (Garden City, New York: Doubleday, 1954).

This strategic location of social work as a kind of third force implementing the basic identity of interest between the individual and his group creates its own problems when the social worker falls prey to the very diffusion against which his function is set. It is at these times that we hear the controversies about whether he should be more concerned with social or with individual problems, with "content" or "process," "ends" or "means," and so on. This debate disregards the most essential characteristics of social work: that it stands on the meeting ground between the two; that it is inextricably involved with both; and that it sees no contradictions, even where the dualism looms large in the popular mind. The social work function is based on "the recognition of the fact that the individual's normal growth lands him in essential solidarity with his fellows, while on the other hand the exercise of his social duties and privileges advances his highest and purest individuality."[16]

Method: the professional tasks. The transition from function to method is essentially a problem in dividing a broad assignment into its component activities. For this purpose, we have chosen the term "task" as an organizing concept around which to gather up the various movements of the worker in any given client-worker system. The implication is that any function can be broken down into a number of tasks necessary to carry it out, and that any specific act performed should come under one or another of these headings. Our emphasis here is on categories of activity rather than on small discrete movements; for the latter may involve us in problems that lie outside the scope of method as we conceive it. While the concern with specific acts is important, the units of activity cannot be so small as to take us either into mechanical prescriptions for worker responses or into problems of personalized style and technique. The tasks are common and are based on a professional method held in common; but many of the helping acts in a given situation are heavily charged with the unique movements and personal artistry of the individual worker.

We envisage the following tasks as those required of the worker as he carries out his social work function within the helping relationship:

1. The task of searching out the common ground between the client's perception of his own need and the aspects of social demand with which he is faced
2. The task of detecting and challenging the obstacles which obscure the common ground and frustrate the efforts of people to identify their own self-interest with that of their "significant others"
3. The task of contributing data—ideas, facts, value-concepts—which are not available to the client and which may prove useful to him in the attempting to cope with that part of social reality which is involved in the problems on which he is working

[16]James Mark Baldwin, *The Individual and Society; or, Psychology and Sociology* (Boston: Richard G. Badger, the Gorham Press, 1911), p. 16.

4. The task of "lending a vision"[17] to the client, in which the worker both reveals himself as one whose own hopes and aspirations are strongly invested in the interaction between people and society and projects a deep feeling for that which represents individual well-being and the social good
5. The task of defining the requirements and the limits of the situation in which the client-worker system is set. These rules and boundaries establish the context for the "working contract" which binds the client and the agency to each other and which creates the conditions under which both client and worker assume their respective functions.

The social worker in the group. As we move this methodological pattern into the worker-group situation, the first problem is to specify some of the salient characteristics of the small-group system which help create the social climate within which the worker functions.

First, the group is an enterprise in mutual aid, an alliance of individuals who need each other, in varying degrees, to work on certain common problems. The important fact is that this is a helping system in which the clients need each other as well as the worker. This need to use each other, to create not one but many helping relationships, is a vital ingredient of the group process and constitutes a common need over and above the specific tasks for which the group was formed.

Second, the group is a system of relationships which, in its own unique way, represents a special case of the general relationship between individuals and their society. The present group is, in other words, but one of the many associational forms through which its members interact with social values, social objectives, and social resources. More specifically, the cultural climate of the group is drawn from three major sources: Generalized social attitudes about what is good and bad, right and wrong, worthy and unworthy, permeate the group and form a part of its culture. The agency in which the group is embedded has drawn from the general culture its own characteristic and unique constellation of approved attitudes and behaviors. The group itself, by the nature of its central problem, by the activities in which it engages, and by the particular personalities it brings together, creates its own conditions for success and failure.

Finally, the group is, as we have indicated, an organic whole: its nature cannot be discerned by analyzing the separate characteristics of each component but by viewing the group organism as a complex of moving, interdependent human beings, each acting out his changing relationship to society in his present interaction with others engaged in a similar enterprise. In this framework the worker is more concerned with what the member does and feels in

---

[17]A phrase borrowed from another context. See Norman Kelman, "Goals of Analytic Therapy: a Personal Viewpoint," *American Journal of Psychoanalysis,* XIV (1954), 113.

the present situation than with what the member *is*. Further, the demands of society can be understood more clearly as they present themselves to the group member in the immediate situation than in abstract, holistic terms like "democratic responsibility" or "social maturity." It is, in fact, this very partialized and focused character of the present enterprise that makes helping and being helped possible and manageable. The implications for the worker himself are that his ability to help is expressed in action and that this action is limited, as in any functional system, to certain areas in which he has some control. He acts to help others act, and the emphasis on new ways of moving, of interacting, is more realistic and productive than the concern with total being, with discrete characteristics, and with totalistic conceptions of change.

With these observations in mind, let us examine the activities of the social worker in the group, following the pattern of the five major tasks outlined above:

1. As he pursues his search for common ground, the worker's movements are fashioned by four major assumptions about the connections for which he is seeking. The first is that the group member's main access to new ideas, new attitudes, and new skills lies through his ability to discern their usefulness to him and to invest affect in the tasks required to make them his own. The second assumption is that such connections—between individual aspirations and social objects—are always present, no matter how obscure they may seem to the members themselves. To conceive of a situation in which the connections do not exist would be to postulate a group in which the members are completely beyond the call of social demands—a situation in which the group itself would be a futile device since its members could exercise no effect upon each other. The third assumption is that these connections are both specific and partial. A gang of adolescents does not rush eagerly toward the ideal of "democratic values"; youngsters in a Jewish Center do not respond quickly to the generalized notion of "Jewish identification"; hospital patients do not invest themselves equally and evenly in the tasks of rehabilitation. In each of these instances, the attraction between the individual's sense of need and the aspirations of society is present and inherent; but it is partial, elusive, and comes into the open only at certain significant points.

The final assumption is that these connections cannot be established in any permanent sense. From meeting to meeting, almost from moment to moment, the group members meet reality on new ground, with new connections constantly to be discovered as each member works at the job of building a bridge between past and present experience.

The worker's search for common ground is expressed in two major forms of activity. One is his efforts to clarify the function of the group and to protect this focus of work against attempts to evade or subvert it—whether by the agency, the group, or its individual members. The other is represented by consistent efforts to point up for the members those areas in which they feel, however faintly, an interest in the social objects which confront them. The clarification of group function represents an active demand by the helping agent that the agency, the group, and its members begin their working relationship with a clear "contract" and a common understanding of the issue: What are we doing here together? All of this is based on the worker's conviction that the search for common ground begins most auspiciously on a field where the members and their tasks have been, so far as possible, brought face to face. The endeavor to uncover and discover connections between individual goals and social realities is rendered infinitely more difficult when the terms of these realities are themselves shifting and unstable; as, for instance, when the worker "builds character" while pretending to teach basketball, or "improves social relations" when the group has enlisted his skill in clay modeling. Further, these attempts to guard the focus of work do not end when the initial statement has been made and the terms of the agreement reached. His activities in this regard persist as he continues to guard the focus of work or, where change in focus is feasible and permissible, he helps the group to consider such changes openly and realistically.

The second complex of activities through which the worker searches for common ground begins with the worker's efforts to seek out the general lines of subject-object connection. This is a kind of internal process whereby he looks deeply into the characteristics of both subject and object to find the elements of attraction and to alert himself to the possibilities of future engagement. What is the attraction between the gang member's hostility toward social norms and society's demand for conformity to these norms? Between the Jewish youngster's desire to be like others and the agency's emphasis on Jewish belongingness? Between the shock of diagnosis experienced by patients in an orientation group and the hospital's need for the patients to move smoothly into the necessary procedures, rules, and routines?

These are, in a sense, "diagnostic" attempts, but such preparatory insights cannot effectively be used to impose a series of prefabricated connections on a ready-made series of events. For the most part, this awareness of the general lines of connection is used in three ways: it enables the worker to be more responsive to subtle and covert requests for help; it compels him to focus on the here-and-now, and to see through the members' evasions and denials to the strengths that lie hidden; and it helps him to structure the situation to favor strength rather than weakness.

2. As the search for common ground continues, the helping agent is constantly confronted with another task which, though it is a corollary of the first, is important enough to be considered on its own terms. This task evolves from the fact that the member's access to social reality is constantly impeded by obstacles which are thrown up in the course of the engagement. The existence of these obstacles is usually obscure to the group member himself. His awareness is limited by his incomplete vision of the common ground and by his own subjectivity, which makes it difficult for him to recognize his own defenses, to distinguish between internal and external deterrents, and to

assess his own productivity at any given moment. Thus, a force is needed within the learning group system that will challenge the obstacles as they appear, by calling attention to their existence and asking the group to come to grips with them. This is the second major task of the helping person.

These obstructions stem from many sources and appear in many forms. They originate in past experience and crystallize in the moment-to-moment events of the group situation. They are created by the attitudes of the members, the human image projected by the worker, the nature of the things to be learned, and the function of the agency. The origins of the obstacles are, in fact, so complex and interrelated that it is impossible for the worker to define causation as he approaches them in the context of the group experience.

Fortunately, it is unnecessary for him to do so. What is necessary is that he recognize these phenomena, that he accept them as relevant to his professional responsibilities, and that he offer help with the concrete learning problems they indicate. Whatever its underlying source, each obstacle always takes the form of a very specific struggle between the members and their present tasks: the group has a decision to make, has stressed its importance again and again, but falls into aimless chatting whenever the subject comes up; a member accepts a task with enthusiasm, and repeatedly fails to perform it; a group proceeds, halfheartedly and unsuccessfully, on a course unanimously approved by the members but, in fact, subtly imposed by the worker; another group moves independently, but guiltily, along its "chosen" lines of action.

In these instances, there is an obstruction that lies between the group members and a valued objective, distorting their perception of what is valued and frustrating their efforts to act openly in their own self-interest. There is a path they need to take, and cannot—because its entrance is blocked by taboo. The taboo may be present in the conditions that surround them; often, its complexity is such that it combines several factors. A discussion group may become dull and unproductive because it has built up a fund of resentment against a respected but authoritarian leader. Unable to deal with their need to conform, with the leader's unassailable correctness, or with the general subcultural proscription against self-assertion, the members have no recourse but to express their resistance in listlessness and apathy.

The area of taboo may be painful enough to ward off recognition and remain buried in consciousness as it invisibly directs the actions of the members; or, the group may be aware of its existence but does not dare to enter an unsafe and risky region. Thus, in our example, the members' respect for the leader and their need to be liked by him can be so great that they cannot accept any flaw in him, but can feel only guilt for their own unexplainable lapse of ambition; or they may, on the other hand, feel their resentment against the beloved autocrat but shrink from hurting him or from exposing themselves as rebels.

In either event, the effect is evasion of the obstacle that impedes their path to productivity. Consciously or unconsciously, the members withhold their energies from the task before them. Instead, they devote themselves to movements which reflect no real investment in content, but only their efforts to create the best imitation they can muster.

In the activities designed to carry out the worker's task of dealing with obstacles, he directs himself toward three major forms of endeavor. The first includes those actions in which he reveals the fact that an impediment exists and that this is permissible. His actions here are not "interpretive" in the usual sense; he has no way of "diagnosing" the nature of the difficulty, and no right to ask the members to deal with his causative explanations, even if he were extremely intuitive in this regard. He asks them, simply, to recognize the fact that an obstacle exists, in the form of apathy, evasion, or inconsistency, between them and a desired objective.

The second category includes those movements by which the worker offers support and assistance as the members enter the area of taboo and seek to determine the nature of the impediment. This is to say that the worker helps them to examine the ways in which they are operating against their own interests in this situation. The attempt here is not to exorcise the taboo—that is, eliminate its power for all time—but to help the members identify it and examine its effects. It is important only that they recognize the source of their present frustration and free themselves to determine the direction of their self-interest. In this aspect of the worker's activity, he is asking them to recapture control of their own impetus, and to begin by discountenancing the illusion of work where none exists.

In the third category of activities, the worker moves to keep the function of the group alive lest it be lost in the preoccupation with obstacles. The challenging of obstacles is based on the fact that they come between the member and the social product. When these impediments cease to be regarded as such and become objects of interest in their own right, the analytical process itself becomes an obstacle which needs to be dealt with. This calls for certain movements through which the helping person exercises a kind of "demand for work," an emphasis on performance; he asks the group members to continue with their functional tasks even as they examine the obstacles to their achievement. This is still another way of saying that the examination of obstacles is part of the group function itself and that one does not cease as the other begins.

3. The third task encompasses those movements in which the helping agent makes a contribution of data in the group situation. The term "data" is used here to denote any ideas, facts, or value concepts which the members may find useful as they involve themselves within the system. Whether the members' tasks are related to the specific problems of mastering facts and concepts in an established sequence, or to a less tangible complex of attitudes and feelings, the worker has a responsibility to offer what he feels they can utilize from his own store of experience. The worker's grasp of social reality is one of the important attributes that fit him to his function; while his life experiences cannot be transferred intact to other human beings, the products

of these experiences can be immensely valuable to those who are moving through their own struggles and stages of mastery.

Thus, nothing can be more destructive to the worker's function than his decision to withhold knowledge on the sole grounds that the member must make his own way. Such withholding is inevitably interpreted by the individual as deprivation, hence rejection; and the result is generally the very opposite of what the worker intends. It is common, for example, to find situations where the group members spend a major part of their energies in straining to find answers which lie hidden in the worker's questions; in this game of educational hide-and-seek, dependency increases as frustration mounts and as the members learn to search for hidden answers rather than to explore the nature of the problem itself.

In providing access to data, the worker is, in effect, providing access to himself. His demand for a culture of work, and for a free sharing of ideas, can best be met if he makes himself available, as he would have them become available to him and to each other. What he knows should be accessible to the members of the group, not after they have tried to proceed "on their own," but in the course of their deliberations so that they may use him in their work. The need to withhold is generally felt by workers whose relationship to the group is too fragile to be sustained in a culture of work. Where the dependence on authority is already great—and not necessarily created by the worker—the reluctance to offer more information to be swallowed whole is a natural one. But the fear of creating dependency must be met in other ways. The worker who finds common ground, is sensitive to the climate in which the subject-object engagement proceeds, and is prepared to challenge the obstacles as they appear, will have no fear that the problem-solving process will be endangered by his assumption of full status as a knowing person in the group system.

As the worker makes his contribution of data, several major considerations guide his movements. The first is his awareness that his offering represents only a fragment of available social experience. If he comes to be regarded as the fountainhead of social reality, he will then have fallen into the error of presenting himself as the object of learning rather than as an accessory to it. Thus, there is an important distinction to be made between lending his knowledge to those who can use it in the performance of their own tasks and projecting himself as a text to be learned. In the first instance, the worker is used in accordance with his function as a mediator of the subject-object relationship; in the second, the worker himself becomes the object.

The second consideration lies in the relationship between the information he shares and the function of the group as this function is understood by the members and by the agency. Often, the worker is tempted to "expose" the group to certain facts and ideas which may, in some future context, be found useful. Such efforts generally serve to confuse rather than enlighten, since there is no frame of reference within which the data assume weight and significance. Where these acts of the worker constitute a series of ideological "plugs," the effect is to breed a vague distrust of the worker's purpose and of his stated desire to assist the group to carry out its own function.

The function of the group may be considered a general frame of reference to be considered by the worker as he selects the data he will share with the members. Even more important as a factor is the specific working context within which he makes his contributions. Again, this assumes the existence of a culture of work, within which the worker's offering is but a single, important ingredient and the worker is but one of many sources of social reality; with his data, as with everything else, the test of utility will inevitably lie in its appropriateness to the demands of the current task. This is the sense in which the old group work injunction that "program is a tool" is important. It is a tool, not of the worker, but of the group and its members; and, like all tools, each fact, idea, or concept must be fashioned to the specific job for which it is to be used.

The final consideration is that, while the worker's own opinions represent important data, they are such only when presented honestly as opinion rather than as fact. There are many occasions where the member is at the mercy of the worker's power to disguise the distinction between the two. The temptation to becloud this distinction is strong, and often unconscious; culture-bound and ego-bound, the worker is himself unclear in many important areas about the difference between reality and his own constructions of it. But the struggle to distinguish between subjective perceptions and external reality is at the heart of all human learning and growing, and the worker who is not engaged in this struggle himself will find it impossible to help others in the same endeavor. As he helps them to evaluate the evidence they derive from other sources—their own experiences, the experience of others, and their collaboration in ideas—so must he submit his own evidence to the process of critical examination. When the worker understands that he is but a single element in the totality of the member's experience, and when he is able to use this truth rather than attempt to conquer it, he has taken the first step toward helping the member to free himself from authority without rejecting it.

4. The responsibility for contributing data is related to the fourth task that expresses the function of the helping agent. This involves those activities through which the worker reveals, frankly and directly, his own hopes and aspirations concerning the outcome of the group experience. Borrowing a phrase used by Norman Kelman in another context, we would designate this task as that of lending a vision to the members of the group.[18]

In these activities, the worker reveals himself as a person whose own aspirations are deeply invested in the interaction between people and society, and who has, through his own struggles, developed a vision of what life can

---

[18]*Ibid.* Dr. Kelman speaks of the necessity to "lend our vision to the patient" as the psychoanalytic process proceeds. Although his meaning here is slightly different from ours, his general intent is similar to the one we mean to convey.

and should be like. In his enthusiasm, his sense of urgency, and his capacity for empathy, the worker demonstrates that his own life experience is involved here, that he has a stake in society, and that he is not here simply to dispense solutions to problems that are beneath him and irrelevant to his own concerns.

More specifically, the worker reveals his emotional involvement in three important ways. The first is his faith in the system itself and in the conditions under which the growing experience takes place. By his movements to safeguard the function of the group, he expresses his respect for the dignity of the group itself and for the reasons which created it. By his refusal to trade identities with either the members or their materials, he demonstrates his faith in the constructive power inherent in the relationship of one to the other.

The second aspect of the worker's personal investment is revealed in his attitude toward the relevant data of the group system. In this respect, the worker's activity reflects something of what the material means to him—its excitement, its depths, and its importance in the human scheme. As the worker shares his own intense involvement with the materials, he projects himself as a living example of their power to attract and intrigue the human mind. It is only in this sense that the helping agent is a salesman; and without the slightest intent to be one but simply by virtue of his position as, so to speak, a pleased consumer. Without this sense of enthusiasm, this vision of immense possibilities, and his status as a model of mastery, the worker's contribution to the subject-object relationship resolves itself into a mechanical questioning and answering; with it, there can be a challenge, a driving curiosity, and a strong motive for work.

Finally, the worker's affect is a strong component in his relationships with the members of the group. The professional relationship can be described as a flow of affect between worker and member, combining the expectations and perceptions of one with the other, as they work together—each on his own tasks—within the group system. Their interaction is based on the circumstances which brought them together; and it is in the work itself that their feeling for each other grows. In this light, the worker's efforts to establish relationship go much deeper than the kind of wooing activity in which he seeks to gain the member's acceptance and approval through the exercise of his personal warmth and attractiveness. The human qualities of the worker, however engaging they may be, should not be used to divert, to charm, or to build personal dependency.

The worker, sensitized by his own need to cope with the complexities of living and growing, has a fund of feeling from which to draw his attempts to understand the member's struggles in detail. This understanding is reflected, not in a generalized "wanting to help," or "giving love," or "accepting them as they are," although these purposes provide an important ideological base from which to operate. Rather, his understanding is communicated in his ability to empathize with the precise feelings engendered in the learner by the demands of a particular task in a specific situation. The worker's ability to call up parts of his own experience, to communicate his feeling, and to demonstrate an active faith in the productive capacities of the member are important parts of the image of vitality that he projects.

In all, the worker's feeling involvement in the group system demonstrates better than words his conviction that the process of growing is complicated and difficult, but also challenging and rewarding if one is left free to conjure with it and to test one's experience under conditions where one can err without failing completely. The worker lends his vision to the members, not in order to exchange it for theirs, but because his aliveness, his faith in productivity, and his stake in work are inherent in his function as a helping person.

5. The agency, the worker, the group, and its members are related to each other by certain rules and requirements imposed upon them by the terms of their agreement. These requirements emerge first in the conditions under which the group is established, its function identified, and its procedures initiated. Later, the rules are modified, amplified, and reinterpreted as their concrete implications become clearer in the events of group life. These expectations are not limited to those imposed upon the members by the agency, or by the worker; they are reciprocal in that each actor imposes certain restrictions and is bound by others. Thus, while the group and its members are held to certain policies and procedures, the agency and the worker are also limited by standards such as equal treatment, consistency in approach, the members' concept of fair play, and so forth.

To the extent that the terms of the agreement are specific and unambiguous, the participants are free to pursue their tasks within the system in their own characteristic ways. Where the rules are, or become, obscure and vaguely defined, the major energies of both worker and members become diverted to exploring the boundaries and testing the limits of the group situation. This leads us to the final task of the helping agent, in which he calls upon the participants of the learning group to face the necessities inherent in the conditions of their association. This definition of the requirements begins with the worker's first attempts to identify the specific responsibilities that have been undertaken by the agency, the group, and the worker himself; it continues as he monitors these realities and calls for clarification at those points where they become obscure.

The most important aspect of these requirements is that they emerge from the function of the group and the necessities of work rather than from the personal authority of the helping agent. As such, they are parts of a reality which is imposed by the nature of the setting, the conditions of group life, and the purposes for which the group has been assembled. The worker is often frustrated by his "inability to set limits," when his real difficulty arises from his failure to recognize that his task is to explain a situation rather than to create one. Club members find it a great deal easier to accept situational realities and limitations—dress requirements, bans on smoking, and so on—than those imposed by the worker in his own name for reasons which are ambiguous, or moralistic, or designed to build character. Since people do not join clubs to have their characters built, such taboos are not perceived as interpretations of reality, and in fact are not.

Science and art in the helping process. Because of our emphasis on viewing the social worker in action, we have concentrated our analysis on his movements within the group system rather than on the personal and professional equipment which he brings to the job. Most attempts to identify the foundations of professional skill have resulted in an encyclopedic and somewhat frightening inventory of virtues. There is, after all, no sphere of knowledge, no personal strength, and no field of competence which is irrelevant to the responsibilities of the human relations worker. And yet we know that the tasks of helping are not performed best by paragons but by those who want to help, know what they are trying to do, and have sufficient mastery of themselves and of social realities to offer their strengths in the struggles of others. Thus, the central problem for the helping agent does not lie in his nearness to perfection but in the extent to which he can mobilize the powers he does possess in the service of others. In order to find the common ground, he must use certain specific knowledge about human beings; in order to contribute data, to reveal his own stake in society, to define the rules, and to challenge the obstacles in the learner's path, he must be free to share what he has of sensitivity, science, and personal maturity. Where the worker proceeds from a clear sense of focus and function, his own strengths are tools that he uses in the specific tasks that he is called upon to face. As such, his powers are not pitifully inadequate replicas of a formidable ideal but full-blown strengths which he is free to own and to share.

There is nothing in the conception of a professional methodology which denies or subordinates the uniquely personal and artistic component which each worker brings to his administration of the helping function. On the contrary, the concept of a disciplined uniqueness is inherent in the definition of art itself. In a broad sense, we may view artistic activity as an attempt, by someone innately endowed with extreme sensitivity to the world about him, to express strong personal feelings and aspirations through a disciplined use of his materials. The analogy between the helping agent and the creative artist can be struck at several points. In both, there is an emphasis on feeling, on an empathic quality which is cherished as a tool of the craft; both feel a constant need for fresh insights into the nature of things and for new ways to express their view of the world; in both, there is a strong preoccupation with essences and basic principles; there is a high degree of subjectivity, of self-consciousness, which constitutes a major element in their ability to create new vistas and new perspectives; in both, the creativity is nourished by the continuous search for truth and is, in fact, an expression of this search; and both require an atmosphere in which one is free to explore, to err, to test reality, and to change.

If we add to these the powerful urge of both the artist and the social worker to communicate their view of life and to affect the experience of others through their artistry, then the sense in which the helping art is distinguishable from that of the painter, the musician, or the writer lies only in that which they are impelled to express, the nature of their materials, and the processes through which they move in order to carry out their functions.

Toward a Strategy of Group Work Practice

William Schwartz

In the long history of the helping professions, it has been only recently that the working processes of the practitioner have been accepted as an appropriate field for scientific study. Once it has defined its body of knowledge, its social aspirations, and its goal-commitments, a profession must say something equally precise about the ways in which these entities are put to use in the working relationship between the practitioner and his clients.

In the group work segment of the social work profession the methodological problem had not yet become apparent when, in 1948, a committee of the American Association of Group Workers issued the now classical "Definition of the Function of the Group Worker."[1] This statement, used as a basis for teaching and interpreting group work practice during the past decade, has until recently served as an excellent model of the state of professional thinking. In its time, it served to formulate social goals, define the field of operations, stake a claim to certain kinds of expertness, and reveal some basic assumptions about people and groups in a democratic society.

What it did not do was to make the necessary distinctions between means and ends which could have helped to dissipate the strong teleological emphasis and to challenge the intrenched assumption that professional skill was somehow inherent in the worker's goals, his knowledge, his feeling for the client, his value-commitments, and certain of his personal attributes. The gap between the worker's intent and his effect was bridged with terms like "enables," "provides for," "functions in such a way that," "aims to," and other phrases that produced closure without coming to grips with the theoretical

---

The author is a member of the faculty of the New York School of Social Work of Columbia University. This article is based on a paper read at the Problem-finding Conference, Research Institute for Group Work in Jewish Agencies, Arden House, New York, April 28, 1961.

---

[1]Dorothea F. Sullivan (ed.), *Readings in Group Work* (New York: Association Press, 1952), pp. 421–22.

Schwartz, William. (1962). Toward a strategy of group work practice. Social Service Review, *XXXVI(3), 268–279.*

problems involved in designing a strategy of professional practice.[2] The difficulty was aptly summed up by Louis Towley, who pointed out in 1957 that "this specialized field is rich in democratic concepts; it has a wealth of examples; but in professionally unique concepts, 'method theory,' it has been curiously poor."[3]

The newer interest in the systematic study of professional practice is part of a similar impetus in social work as a whole. Although there are those who see this development as a "retreat into technique" and as a distraction from the "real" purposes of the profession, practitioners and teachers are gradually becoming excited by the possibility of finding out, after many years, what the exact nature of group work skill is, what it looks like in action, and how it can be conceptualized and taught.

How does a profession proceed to develop and systematize its concepts of practice? To say that it needs to build a more intimate working relationship with science is only the beginning of an answer. Certainly the liaison of science and practice is a historic one; professions that do not keep pace with new knowledge soon cease to be professions. But it is also true that an orientation to scientific inquiry does not provide a simple method of converting facts into acts, scientific findings into appropriate professional behavior. The transition from knowing to doing is more complex.

The complexity arises from two major problems faced by all the human-relations professions as they survey their appropriate fields of knowledge. One is that the body of potentially useful information is encyclopedic, encompassing every conceivable aspect of human development and organization; the other is that action cannot be deduced directly from knowledge, no matter how vast that knowledge may be.

In relation to the first problem—the overwhelming array of pertinent information—Max Millikan has pointed out that the Bavelas-Perlmutter experiments at the Center for International Studies suggest that "an individual's capacity for making sound judgment about a complex situation may be seriously impaired by supplying him with a lot of information which he believes should be relevant but whose influence on the situation is not clear to him."[4] Harold Lasswell comments that "the idea of strategy does not depend upon omniscience."[5] The dilemma Millikan describes, a familiar one to group workers, seems to stem directly from the fact that the worker finds himself

---

[2]For a more extended historical treatment of the means-ends relationship in group work, see William Schwartz, "Group Work and the Social Scene," *Issues in American Social Work,* ed. Alfred J. Kahn (New York: Columbia University Press, 1959), pp. 110–37.

[3]Frank J. Bruno (with chapters by Louis Towley), *Trends in Social Work, 1874–1956* (New York: Columbia University Press, 1957), p. 422.

[4]Max F. Millikan, "Inquiry and Policy: The Relation of Knowledge to Action," *The Human Meaning of the Social Sciences,* ed. Daniel Lerner (New York: Meridian Books, 1959), p. 160.

[5]Harold D. Lasswell, "Strategies of Inquiry: The Rational Use of Observation," *The Human Meaning of the Social Sciences,* p. 89.

burdened with a great many answers for which he has no questions. He can make little use of such information until he has ordered his experience into some coherent frame of reference from which he can develop his questions and focus his inquiry into the undifferentiated mass of scientific data. Thus the search for significant problems—for the questions that will draw forth the kinds of information most needed to throw light on the practical tasks of the group worker—calls for a theoretical effort designed to develop a system of interconnected concepts drawn from the experience of practice.[6]

It is when we question what these concepts shall be about that we come to the second difficulty mentioned above—that action is not deducible from knowledge. Those who assume that scientific evidence carries within its own implications for behavior make the same mistake made by those in an earlier time who believed that action flowed inevitably and appropriately from one's convictions about values and goals. It is what Millikan refers to as the "inductive fallacy—the assumption that the solution of any problem will be advanced by the simple collection of fact."[7] The fact is that the gap between what is known and what should be done is invariably bridged by value-goal orientations, often implicit and unformulated. When knowledge is converted into action on the basis of subtle and unstated values, the principle is unverifiable, except by those who unconsciously share the same assumptions. When creeds and valued outcomes are made explicit, practice principles are verifiable by all, on the basis of whether, given the first two variables—a fact and a valued outcome—the third will provide the implementing force. Practice cannot be "testable" in any other sense.

It is, therefore, suggested that practice theory, or method theory, can be defined as a system of concepts integrating three conceptual subsystems: one which organizes the appropriate aspects of social reality, as drawn from the findings of science; one which defines and conceptualizes specific values and goals, which we might call the problems of policy; and one which deals with the formulation of interrelated principles of action. Each of these constitutes a major area of investigation, each has its own conceptual problems, and each is related to the others within a total scheme. The purpose of this paper is to point up some of the major conceptual problems in each of these areas and to show how each area depends upon the others for its own clarity and coherence.

Problems of Social Reality

As we turn to the social sciences for information about human behavior and social organization, our task is to establish those lines of inquiry which emerge most directly from our experiences with people. Gordon Hearn has

---

[6]For a discussion of theory-building and empiricism, see James B. Conant, *Modern Science and Modern Man* (New York: Doubleday Anchor Books, 1953).

[7]*Op. cit.,* p. 163.

suggested some proposals to focus the study of social work practice in general[8] and Robert Vinter has discussed some lines of work within the context of his frame of reference for group work.[9] From my own orientation to the tasks of the group work practitioner,[10] the following are suggested as some of the central themes around which the struggles of practice have taken place.

The individual and the social. Probably the most enduring and pervasive methodological problems have stemmed from an inability to develop an integrative conception of the relationship between individual need and social demand. This is the difficulty that gives birth to the issue of "content versus process"—the dilemma wherein the practitioner is forced to make impossible choices between the functional necessities of individual growth and the social requirements of the culture in which he operates. The early efforts of Sherif,[11] Mead,[12] Kropotkin,[13] and others to effect a workable synthesis were significant, but group workers were not yet in a position to formulate their problems so that these concepts could be used. In recent years, social scientists have come alive to the issue. Alex Inkeles' attempt to analyze this work without regard to internal professional boundaries has been helpful.[14] For practitioners, the present problem is that much scientific work is pegged either at a very high level of abstraction or at empirical laboratory efforts with artificial groupings that are difficult to translate into terms relevant to group work experience. As in so many other problem areas, the need is to break down the general question into some middle-range propositions that can be tested in our own situational field. Lippitt, Watson, and Westley have suggested work on the "forces toward innovation" through which people attempt to use, control, and change the people and things around them.[15] Another more specific line of inquiry might consist in the effort to develop

---

[8]Gordon Hearn, *Theory Building in Social Work* (Toronto: University of Toronto Press, 1958), p. 25.

[9]Robert D. Vinter, "Group Work with Children and Youth: Research Problems and Possibilities," *Social Service Review,* XXX (September, 1956), 310–21. See also his "Small-Group Theory and Research: Implications for Group Work Practice Theory and Research," *Social Science Theory and Social Work Research,* ed. Leonard S. Kogan (New York: National Association of Social Workers, 1960), pp. 123–34.

[10]William Schwartz, "The Social Worker in the Group," *Social Welfare Forum, 1961* (New York: Columbia University Press, 1961), pp. 146–71.

[11]Muzafer Sherif, *The Psychology of Social Norms* (New York: Harper, 1936).

[12]George Herbert Mead, *Mind, Self, and Society* (Chicago: University of Chicago Press, 1934).

[13]Peter Alekseevich Kropotkin, *Mutual Aid: A Factor of Evolution* (New York: Alfred A. Knopf, 1917).

[14]Alex Inkeles, "Personality and Social Structure," *Sociology Today: Problems and Prospects,* ed. Robert K. Merton, Leonard Broom, and Leonard S. Cottrell, Jr. (New York: Basic Books, 1959), pp. 249–75.

[15]Ronald Lippitt, Jeanne Watson, and Bruce Westley, *The Dynamics of Planned Change* (New York: Harcourt, Brace, 1958), pp. 4–5.

motivational typologies with which to ascertain elements of consensus among group members and agency personnel. From my own frame of reference, which assumes a symbiotic interdependence between the individual and his culture and which conceives the agency as a special case of the individual-social engagement, my prediction would be that mutually perceived "success" would take place primarily in these areas of motivational consensus.

The group work setting—as a living laboratory of the individual-social encounter—has failed conspicuously to produce its own research and add to the systematic study of this relationship in action. The field was so completely captured, early in its development, by the character-building, social-conformity pressures of the group work "movement" that the need to change people far outweighed the need to understand them and to examine carefully the ways in which their natural tendencies carry them into the society in which they develop. Thus, the move was made from socialization as a process—which needed to be analyzed and understood—to socialization as a demand. From that point, the road was a short one to the dilemma of "content versus process" and, ultimately, to the individual versus the group.

The structural and the dynamic. Our historic tendency has been to rely heavily on structural descriptions—"diagnostic" typologies—to describe the people with whom we work. The study-diagnosis-treatment model—based partly on the physician's detection and cure of disease and partly on the methods of research—is built from the assumption that these structural characteristics are stable enough for workers to base predictions, referrals, and "treatment" decisions upon them. However, it has been difficult to show that this model bears any practical relation to the moment-to-moment, situationally fluid realities of the helping process in action. Hubert Bonner reports that "research has shown that it is difficult to predict the behavior of persons in a group from pre-measures of personality variables,"[16] and Gordon Allport has scored the "faddism" involved in the "overemphasis on diagnosis." "It is simply not true," he states, "that successful treatment invariably presupposes accurate diagnosis."[17]

Interest is mounting in elaborations of a newer approach, which has particular implications for the situational field in which the group worker operates. This approach points up the "circular, reciprocal relations . . . through which the component members of the field participate in and thereby create the field of the whole, which field in turn regulates and patterns their individual activities."[18] This model calls attention to the interdependent transactions within a functional system—an organic whole "within which the relations

---

[16]Hubert Bonner, *Group Dynamics: Principles and Applications* (New York: Ronald Press Co., 1959), p. 20.

[17]Gordon W. Allport, *Personality and Social Encounter* (Boston: Beacon Press, 1960), p. 283. Discussed in chapter entitled "Social Service in Perspective."

[18]Lawrence K. Frank, "Research for What?" *Journal of Social Issues,* Supplement Series, X (1957), 12.

determine the properties of its parts."[19] The emphasis on relational determinants of behavior, while at the same time subjecting structural determinants to more critical scrutiny, has a strong potential impact on all group work practice conceptions. It may provide the stimulus for closer analysis of the differential forms of stress, social demand, and social opportunity offered by the various settings of group work practice.[20] It may also stimulate the development of terminology—and perhaps new typologies—that will help us to express relations as well as structure and to distinguish more clearly between the two.

The group as "it" and as "they." We have not yet developed a working conception of the group as a whole which might help the group worker to implement his traditional claim that group work skills are directed to the group as well as to the individuals within it. If the small group is a system which—like society itself—both integrates and differentiates its parts,[21] group workers remain far more perceptive about the attributes of individuals than they are about the activity of the group as a whole. Familiar evidence is found in recorded anthropomorphisms like "the group laughed," in references to the group as "they," and in models of confusion, like "the group looked at each other." This failure to distinguish between the attributes of members and those of the collective has made it difficult to isolate and describe those professional skills which are designed to affect the system itself rather than any of its component parts.[22] Efforts have been made to use the wealth of empirical research on group dimensions, but again the lack of theoretical models has been a barrier. Much energy has been devoted to building longer inventories of group traits, but there is little knowledge of how these traits may be related to each other in the life of the group.

The recent work of the organizational theorists,[23] the developing insight into the interdisciplinary implications of the system construct,[24] and other integrative attempts now offer group workers the opportunity to analyze the group work experience in a new way. In the process they may begin to make their own unique contribution to this field of inquiry. The growing diversity of small-group systems in which they operate gives group workers the chance to observe both similarities and differences in the ways in which different kinds

---

[19]Talcott Parsons, *The Structure of Social Action* (Glencoe, Ill.: Free Press, 1949), p. 32.

[20]For a limited attempt of this type, see William Schwartz, "Characteristics of the Group Experience in Resident Camping," *Social Work,* V (April, 1960), 91–96.

[21]See A. Paul Hare, Edgar F. Borgatta, and Robert F. Bales, *Small Groups: Studies in Social Interaction* (New York: Alfred A. Knopf, 1955), pp. 345–47.

[22]Robert D. Vinter's conception of "indirect means of influence" is an effort in this direction. See his "Small-Group Theory and Research . . .," *op. cit.,* p. 128.

[23]See, for example, Mason Haire (ed.), *Modern Organization Theory* (New York: John Wiley & Sons, 1959).

[24]See Roy R. Grinker, M.D., *Toward a Unified Theory of Human Behavior* (New York: Basic Books, 1956).

of groups integrate and differentiate their human components and relate themselves to the larger systems in which they operate.

Internal and external determinants of change. Much of the discussion on "self-determination versus manipulation" has been carried on in a high moral tone, while a great deal of work needs to be done in studying the specific conditions under which people enlist the aid of others in their attempts to solve problems. The group worker is in a unique position to study the uses of help and the nature of influence, since he works within a system the essence of which is that people create many helping relationships in addition to, and concurrent with, the one formed with the worker. The problems of the group members in using each other are coexistent with their problems in using the worker. The group worker has an opportunity to examine in microcosm a very old idea, long since forgotten in a highly specialized civilization. This is the idea that the client-worker relationship is simply a special case of what Kropotkin described as the evolutionary theme of mutual aid[25]—that is, the social devices through which human beings establish conditions of mutual support in the struggle for survival. More specifically, the group work situation offers the conditions for studying peer help and professional help within the same dynamic system, guided by the strong possibility that these two sets of movements have much in common and that, in fact, the latter may be a stylized, intensified version of the former.[26]

Problems of Policy

The relationship between science and policy is reciprocal. Science takes its cues from human problems and yields its best answers to those who are disciplined and urgent in their search for solutions. The contribution of science to policy is to define boundaries, limit expectations, and clarify the range of alternatives.[27] This idea of knowledge as a disciplining, limiting force is important in each of the problems to be discussed briefly below. It should be remembered that we are still in the context of the study of practice, and these problems are viewed from that perspective.

Functional definition. Much of the difficulty in understanding the nature of group work skill stems from the lack of a clear and limited statement about the unique, operative function of the worker in his group. Such a statement, made in terms of action rather than intent, of function rather than purpose,[28] would provide a focal point for a general strategy of practice. The

---

[25]Kropotkin, *op. cit.*

[26]Bertha Capen Reynolds' *Social Work and Social Living* (New York: Citadel Press, 1951) explores this basic proposition in detail.

[27]For a detailed discussion of the science-policy relationship, see Millikan, *loc. cit.*, and Lasswell, *loc. cit.*

[28]The distinction between purpose and function is helpfully discussed in Robert K. Merton, *Social Theory and Social Structure* (Glencoe, Ill.: Free Press, 1957), chap. i.

strategic lines of action would be appropriate to the worker's ascribed function, would be directed to certain tasks and not to others, would be related to the functional performance of the members, and would be directed to the specific and limited factors over which the worker exercises some influence.[29]

The components of the functional statement would be drawn from three main areas of investigation: the specific problems faced by group members as they move to relate their own sense of need to the social demands implicit in the collective tasks of the group; the functional assignment of the agency within its own dynamic system of neighborhood and community; and the social function of the profession itself as it lends itself to the agencies in which it works.[30] This general orientation to the operational problem offers many questions for study: In what precise ways does the practice of group workers reflect the degree of conflict—and consensus—about the proper function of the worker within the group, as viewed by group members, agency administrators, and the worker himself? What are the conditions under which certain kinds of group behavior may be functional to the members and dysfunctional to the requirements of the agency, or vice versa? Under what conditions is it desirable to convert latent functions into manifest ones?

Structural ordering. The task here is to study the circumstances under which the group establishes and maintains its position within the agency, for these circumstances create the framework within which the worker interprets and performs his tasks. If the structure is unclear and ambiguous—as in situations in which the agency secretly aspires to build character while it teaches clay-modeling—the worker's function becomes diffuse and unmanageable.

Several aspects of the relationship between the client group and its host system seem profitable for study. One is the process through which the stage of group formation or group intake establishes conditions of consensus or conflict about the nature of the "contract" between the group and its agency—what each may expect from the other, the normative requirements to which each may be held, and other factors which bind them together. Another important structural aspect lies in the complex of prepared events, activities, and ethical commitments which agency administrations perceive as integral to their function and as substantial elements in their contributions to group life. Under what conditions do these prepared events and prestructured experiences become functional or dysfunctional for the groups for which they are intended?

---

[29]These criteria are elaborated in Schwartz, "Group Work and the Social Scene," *op. cit.*, pp. 130–32.

[30]Cf. Everett Cherrington Hughes, "The Study of Occupations," *Sociology Today: Problems and Prospects,* pp. 442–58: "The composition of an occupation can be understood only in the frame of the pertinent social and institutional complex (which must in turn be discovered, not merely assumed). The allocating and grouping of activities is itself a fundamental social process" (p. 455).

Much of this problem of structural ordering lies in the relationship between what George C. Homans calls the "external" and the "internal" systems of the group—between "group behavior that enables the group to survive in its environment" and "group behavior that is an expression of the sentiments towards one another developed by the members of the group in the course of their life together."[31] The tension between these two systems of group behavior sets up some of the central methodological problems of the group worker.

Value orientation. A great deal has been said and written about the worker's obligation to acknowledge values and to profess them openly. But these injunctions are hard to obey, because they suffer from the same shortcomings as do the value formulations themselves—that is, they are too global, internally inconsistent, and unrelated to the specific conditions of group life. The professional commandments to stand for absolute and overgeneralized themes like "Jewish belongingness" or "social maturity," to "bear" values but not to "impose" them, to uphold both religious and secular-humanistic values at the same time,[32] to extol modesty and thrift to children whose family modes are prevailingly those of conspicuous consumption—these are very complex materials from which to compose a rationale for the position of values in the strategy of practice. At this stage what is needed is more exact information about the value themes which merge or conflict within the lives of different groups and about the conditions under which these circumstances vary from group to group and from setting to setting—the religious and the secular, the sectarian and the non-sectarian, the therapeutic and the recreational. Content analyses of group work recording may help uncover some of the conflicts and inconsistencies which have made it difficult to break up the problem of value orientation without seeming to attack value systems themselves. Most important would be an attempt to isolate and formulate value items of limited scope which apply directly to the life of the group itself, which are drawn from its own history, and which represent normative guides without which the worker actually could not function.

Goal setting. What kinds of knowledge would be best designed to help "place limits on the range of possible outcomes"?[33] Here, as in the value question, the first requirement is that we begin with a willingness to drop exorbitant claims.[34] Caught up early in the social promise of the small-group experience, it has been hard for group workers to give up the claim that the

---

[31]George C. Homans, *The Human Group* (New York: Harcourt, Brace, 1950), p. 110.

[32]For a thorough discussion of this point, see Alfred J. Kutzik, *Social Work and Jewish Values* (Washington, D.C.: Public Affairs Press, 1959). Also see Herbert Bisno, *The Philosophy of Social Work* (Washington, D.C.: Public Affairs Press, 1952).

[33]Millikan, *op. cit.*, p. 166.

[34]Barbara Wooton, *Social Science and Social Pathology* (London: George Allen & Unwin, 1959). Chapter ix, entitled "Contemporary Attitudes in Social Work," makes particular reference to the American scene. Here the author characterizes some claims of American group workers as "arrogant" and "self-deceptive."

club group in the leisure-time agency alters personality, creates new value systems, and effects other profound changes in people's lives. This abstract and totalistic way of framing its objectives has prevented the field from examining the real, if limited, influence that skilful group work practice probably has, and the kinds of specific help that people in groups are actually able to use.

There are several lines of study that may help to bring practice goals closer to reality. There is, for example, the problem of separating worker goals from member goals, so that one can distinguish between the process of teaching and the process of learning—or, in social work terms, the dynamics of giving help and those of taking help. Study of the moment-to-moment interaction of these two processes should help clarify the means-ends structures of each and relate the desired outcomes more closely to possible ones.

A second line of inquiry may be directed toward the definition of outcomes that may reasonably be expected. If, for example, a worker aspires to help a group develop a wider variety of problem-solving devices, he may then create instruments to measure his degree of success. This is what Martin Wolins calls "a single, readily ascertainable development."[35] By contrast, a change-objective like "achieving socially desirable goals" is both unmeasurable and unachievable since the behavioral indexes are undefined and, even if they were defined, they would still remain far beyond any conceivable range of influence to be expected of a single worker operating in a small sector of people's lives.

Problems of Action

Given a body of knowledge about the social realities of group experience, and given a use of this knowledge to work out a realistic function and achievable value-goal objectives, one must next lay out a plan of action. Such a plan is essentially a way of breaking down a broad functional assignment into its component classes of activity.

At this point an organizing construct is needed from which to create the categories in which to gather up the various acts that the worker performs as he goes about his job. This is the point at which there might be advantages in using the "role" construct, an action-oriented idea designed to relate the worker's movements to those of others in a dynamic system. However, the term is so overladen with ambiguities and special uses that one experiences difficulty in using it without developing a specialized rationale for its meaning in this context. For the present, the term "task" may serve. Any function can be divided into a number of tasks necessary to perform it, and any specific act may be understood as related to one or another of these task headings.

---

[35]Martin Wolins, "Measuring the Effect of Social Work Intervention," *Social Work Research,* ed. Norman A. Polansky (Chicago: University of Chicago Press, 1960), p. 263.

Once having determined what these implementing tasks are, one must define and describe the skills necessary to carry them out. In this framework, then, the problems of action which climax the methodological study are those of task definition and skill definition.

Task definition. The problems of task analysis revolve around three main points. Each task (*a*) must emerge from the theoretical scheme to which it is related, (*b*) must be directed to the tasks of the group members themselves, and (*c*) must be broad enough to encompass a number of helping activities, which should be specifiable in concrete terms.

For example, if "the general functional assignment of the social work profession is to mediate the process through which the individual and his society reach out for each other through a mutual need for self-fulfilment,"[36] we may then conceive of five implementing tasks: (1) to search out the common ground between the client's need-perception and the social demands with which he is faced; (2) to detect and challenge the obstacles that obscure this common ground; (3) to contribute otherwise unavailable and potentially useful data; (4) to reveal and project the worker's own feeling for the client and his problem; and (5) to define the limits and requirements of the situation in which the client-worker relationship is set.[37] The analytic process in examining the second of these tasks, for example, would proceed as follows. It would begin by describing the ways in which this task is designed to implement the functional statement. It would then proceed to describe and document some of the specific social realities involved—the origin of obstacles, what they look like in action, and the forms in which they are perceived by the members. Finally, it would describe the worker's activities—revealing impediments to action, supporting the members as they enter the area of taboo, and protecting the focus of work, lest it be lost in the preoccupation with obstacles. This is of course a highly condensed account but it may serve to give some inkling of the possibilities offered in carving out limited areas for intensive study.

Skill definition. The difficulty in defining skill in human relations is the problem of describing an act in its own terms, rather than in terms of its results. One may jibe at the notion that "the operation was a success, but the patient died," but the fact remains that it is impossible to develop a communicable art of surgery until we are willing to admit that it is possible for an operation to be well performed and for the patient to die. All this means is that the human material has a dynamic of its own and that the process of helping consists of two interdependent processes—the offer of help (the worker's act) and the use of it (the client's response). To say that the skill of an act is to be measured by its effect is to equate skill with predictive certainty and to leave out the client entirely. Social work cannot use a model borrowed from

[36]Schwartz, "The Social Worker in the Group," *op. cit.*, pp. 154–55.

[37]*Ibid.*, pp. 157–58.

those who work with completely controllable materials—that is, inanimate objects.

It is true, of course, that the concern with skill is designed to help us narrow the range of uncertainty—that is, to find those acts which go most directly toward their purpose. Such acts must reflect "the greatest degree of consideration for and utilization of the quality and capacity of the material,"[38] but unless we can develop some descriptions of skilful activity, independent of effect, we cannot judge skill or order its "levels," or teach it; we certainly cannot, as we have often complained, interpret it to the general public.

This is a difficult job, but there are some indications that it is not an impossible one. We know, for example, that skill is an action concept. Skill is observable behavior of an actor-with-a-purpose toward others in a relational system. There are, of course, a number of mental acts—expressed mainly in the concept of "diagnosis"—but these have no value until they are translated into overt behavior guided by purpose. We know, too, that the factor of immediacy is important—that is, the further we move from the idea of present purpose, the "next step," the more difficult it is to define an act in its own terms. Thus, the ability to read a hidden message and to show the client his problem in a new form is a response to an immediate problem in helping. As such, it is definable, teachable, perhaps even measurable. By contrast, the attempt to formulate skills designed to "make the client more self-sufficient" is an impossible task.

A major contribution can be made in this area by those whose responsibility it is to educate for professional skill—social work teachers, agency supervisors, administrators of in-training programs. In this connection, an interesting attempt has been made by a group of field instructors to develop some models of group work skill, to make some determinations about levels of practice, and to describe the specific teaching and learning problems associated with the various models.

A Note on Research

Despite the impatience of those who would like to move as quickly as possible into studies of outcome and effectiveness, our main progress for a time will probably be in studies of process and of limited effects.[39] In the course of what Bartlett has called "learning to ask better questions,"[40] our important devices are still descriptive, exploratory, and theory-developing; our major tools are still the group record, the life-history, the critical incident, and other

---

[38]Virginia P. Robinson, "The Meaning of Skill," *Training for Skill in Social Casework* (Philadelphia: University of Pennsylvania Press, 1942), p. 12.

[39]See Wolins, *op. cit.*, for his distinction between "effectiveness" and "effect."

[40]Harriet M. Bartlett, "Ways of Analyzing Social Work Practice," *Social Welfare Forum, 1960* (New York: Columbia University Press, 1960), p. 205.

techniques for codifying and conceptualizing the experience of practice. Perhaps our most critical problem is that so much of this experience is unavailable to us, since so little systematic and analytic work has been emerging from our potentially richest sources of information—the leisure-time agencies and their practitioners.

This is a period in which the social scientists are increasingly aware that the study of social systems—small and large—presents new challenges to the partnership of science and practice. Lawrence Frank put it this way to an assemblage of psychologists:

> Perhaps we can devise new and appropriate methods if we will focus on the situation or difficulty, as in operations research, instead of relying so much on the assumptions and formulations of our discipline, especially since these offer little help in approaching organized complexities.
>
> What the practitioner seeks is not merely a presentation of what exists or is occurring, or what trends may be revealed, no matter how precisely these are measured or correlated. Rather, he needs a plan of action, a strategy for dealing with situations so that desired ends may be attained through a kind of action research which will help people to change their ideas, expectations, and behavior.[41]

It is this development of a "plan of action"—a strategy of helping people in groups—that represents the next major task of the group worker in social work.

New York School of Social Work
Columbia University
Received November 25, 1961

---

[41]Frank, "Research for What?" *op. cit.*, p. 19.

Small Group Science and Group Work Practice

William Schwartz

The growing interest of group workers in small group research and theory raises some important questions about the working relationship between professional practice and scientific inquiry. This operating connection between knowledge and practice must be understood in different terms from those implied by the usual question, "What is new in small group research, and how can we use the findings in our work?" The fact that such a question can yield no productive answer makes it necessary to clear some ground before we can profit from some of the substantive contributions of small group science to group work practice. Such an effort will in the long run justify itself far beyond the customary attempt to get that fine scientific feeling by citing, and trying to remember, long inventories of studies and their results.

This attention by group workers to scientific investigation in general and to small group research and theory in particular has been stimulated by several factors. Their developing identification with the social work profession provides them with a reference group that goes beyond single-agency loyalties and creates a professional self-image more in keeping with what Gouldner calls the "cosmopolitans" than with the "locals."[1] The extension of group services to the specialized host settings has challenged the group workers to give some evidence of their small group expertise and to present themselves to their co-workers in the more advanced professions as respectable members of the clinical team. Like-wise, the expanding use of

[1]Alvin W. Gouldner, "Organizational Analysis," in Leonard S. Kogan, ed., *Social Science Theory and Social Work Research,* (New York: National Association of Social Workers, 1960), p. 55. The distinction drawn is "between those who are primarily oriented to their professional specialization and those who are primarily committed to their employing organization."

group services in other sectors of the field—the private family agency, public welfare agencies, and others—has spurred on the efforts of group workers to organize and systematize the group experience accrued to them over a century of practice.

Concurrently, over the past decade there has been flourishing interest in small group phenomena within the social sciences themselves. Stimulated not by the needs and demands of social group work but by those of other institutions that have discovered the group and come alive to its possibilities, the scientific enterprise has turned to small group study with increasing energy; as a consequence, the bibliographies of small group research are no longer the simple affairs they were in the thirties and forties. Even before the profusion of work accomplished over the past few years, Strodtbeck and Hare's review of the literature from 1900 to 1953 listed over fourteen hundred items.[2] Most recently, an attempt to integrate small group research and cross-tabulate the variables under study yielded an inventory of 2,155 items, culled from thirty-one periodicals that produce such materials regularly.[3] Each year the *Annual Review of Psychology* selects for comment over one hundred small group studies conducted during the preceding year,[4] and a recent book on the leadership factor lists 1,155 items associated with this single area of study.[5]

In addition to the empirical work being poured out, a new emphasis has been urged on the integration of concepts and the formulation of theory,[6] and results have not been long in coming. During the past five years, integrative works of considerable importance have been produced by Bonner,

---

[2]F. L. Strodtbeck and Paul Hare, "Bibliography of Small Group Research (from 1900 through 1953)," SOCIOMETRY, Vol. 11 (1954)

[3]See I. Altman and A. Terauds, MAJOR VARIABLES OF THE SMALL GROUP FIELD, A. Terauds, I. Altman, and J. E. McGrath, A BIBLIOGRAPHY OF SMALL GROUP RESEARCH, and I. Altman, G. Pendleton, and A. Terauds, ANNOTATIONS OF SMALL GROUP RESEARCH STUDIES (Arlington, Va.: Human Sciences Research, November, April, and October 1960, respectively).

[4]See, for example, R. W. Heyns, "Social Psychology and Group Processes," in P. R. Farnsworth and Q. McNemar, eds., ANNUAL REVIEW OF PSYCHOLOGY (Palo Alto, Calif.: Annual Reviews, Inc., 1958), pp. 419–442; and H. W. Riecken, "Social Psychology," in Farnsworth and McNemar, eds., ANNUAL REVIEW OF PSYCHOLOGY (Palo Alto, Calif.: Annual Reviews, Inc., 1960), pp. 479–510.

[5]B. M. Bass, LEADERSHIP, PSYCHOLOGY, AND ORGANIZATIONAL BEHAVIOR (New York: Harper and Brothers, 1960)

[6]See, for example, Robert F. Bales, "Small-Group Theory and Research," in Robert K. Merton, L. Broom and Leonard S. Cottrell, jr., ed., SOCIOLOGY TODAY: PROBLEMS AND PROSPECTS (New York: Basic Books, 1959), pp. 293–305; Dorwin Cartwright, "A Decade of Social Psychology," in CURRENT TRENDS IN PSYCHOLOGICAL THEORY (Pittsburgh: University of Pittsburgh Press, 1961), pp. 9–30; Robert K. Merton, "Notes on Problem-Finding in Sociology," in Merton, Broom, and Cottrell, eds., op. cit., pp. ix–xxxiv; and Mildred B. Smith, "Recent Developments in the Field of Social Psychology," in J. Bernard, ed., TEEN-AGE CULTURE (Philadelphia: Annals of the American Academy of Political and Social Science, 1961), pp. 137–143.

Hare, Heider, Homans, Schachter, Sprott, Stogdill, Thibaut and Kelley, and others.[7]

As the group work practitioner turns to face this overwhelming mass of material, how does he begin to make sense out of what is being offered, without abandoning his practice and devoting himself to the full-time study of social psychology? How does he establish connections not only with what has already been learned, but with the findings that keep pouring from the laboratories from week to week? And, perhaps most important, how does he attain sufficient mastery of what has gone before so that he may tie in his own tentative and timid approaches to the systematic investigation of problems emerging from his own practice in working with groups? Obviously, if he is not to flounder in his own guilt and end with a sense of defeat at the whole prospect, he needs some approach by which he can limit and focus his search for knowledge.

The purpose of this paper is thus to explore the general orientation of the professions to the sciences, to examine some of the problems involved in converting the results of the scientific effort into patterns of professional activity, and to design a practical strategy by which the group worker can relate himself to small group data.

From Movement to Profession: Turn Toward Science

When a profession is young, a considerable proportion of its thought and energy is devoted to the process of calling attention to the social need out of which it grew. From its special vantage point, the new group is intensely aware of this need, of the importance of doing something about it, and of the necessity for arousing a similar sense of urgency in the minds of the general public. This is another way of saying that a profession begins as a movement; its primary function at this stage is to agitate for a place on the social agenda, its workers are dedicated to the cause and its advocacy, and its major spokesmen are social philosophers, energetic social advocates, and commanding personalities who call attention to themselves and to the objects of their concern.

---

[7]Hubert Bonner, GROUP DYNAMICS: PRINCIPLES AND APPLICATIONS (New York: Ronald Press, 1959); A. P. Hare, HANDBOOK OF SMALL GROUP RESEARCH (New York: Free Press of Glencoe, 1962); F. Heider, THE PSYCHOLOGY OF INTERPERSONAL RELATIONS (New York: John Wiley and Sons, 1958); George C. Homans, SOCIAL BEHAVIOR: ITS ELEMENTARY FORMS (New York: Harcourt, Brace and World, 1961); Stanley Schachter, THE PSYCHOLOGY OF AFFILIATION: EXPERIMENTAL STUDIES OF THE SOURCES OF GREGARIOUSNESS (Stanford, Calif: Stanford University Press, 1959); W. J. H. Sprott, HUMAN GROUPS (London: Penguin Books, 1958); R. M. Stogdill, INDIVIDUAL BEHAVIOR AND GROUP ACHIEVEMENT (New York: Oxford University Press, 1959) J. W. Thibaut and H. H. Kelley, THE SOCIAL PSYCHOLOGY OF GROUPS (New York: John Wiley and Sons, 1959).

As this effort begins to achieve some success, and as the group and its cause begin to take on some stability and permanence within the social division of labor, the concerns of the profession undergo a gradual shift from the problems of social advocacy to those of social effectiveness. Having established the social need as a proper object of society's attention, it remains to be shown that the profession can do the job and do it well. Increasingly then a greater proportion of professional energy is diverted from what should be to what is. The concern with ends becomes a growing curiosity about the means for achieving them; the stress on intentions, motives, and enthusiasms gives way to a larger preoccupation with efficiency and productivity; and the working skills of practitioners take on a greater significance than their ability to formulate statements of philosophy and aspiration. The profession then turns toward more systematic appraisals of reality and toward science as an institution designed to make such appraisals.

Inevitably, there are those who decry the tendency and who are nostalgic about the rough excitement of the old days, the old call to action; they mourn, in short, the loss of the sense of "the movement." It disturbs them that the tone of the conversation has changed, that the vision is less clear and that the values are less often dwelt upon, and they take this to mean that professional hopes and aspirations are fading, that there has been a "retreat into technique," and that the group has become "overprofessionalized." As Frankel stated this attitude:

> He is tinkering with the broken products that are brought to the repair shop, but he is not asking himself why so many of these broken products are being brought in.[8]

The turn toward science brings such problems in its wake as the fear that systematic approaches imply immunization against social vision, the notion that a professional concern with understanding human behavior somehow leads to a cold-hearted approach to those human beings, and the ensuing confusion of science and art that leads some, at the other extreme, to hope that the profession itself is on its way to becoming a science.[9]

But, whether or not the turn toward science actually causes a general loss of feeling and vision, the fact remains that the new social and professional climate makes it impossible to return to the days when the vision itself carried its own promise of fulfillment. That the emphasis on means can be used to evade social responsibility is, after all, no more surprising than the earlier discovery that the preoccupation with goals can be used in the same way. Both dangers simply point up the challenge to the modern profession: to draw

---

[8]C. Frankel, "Obstacles to Action for Human Welfare," THE SOCIAL WELFARE FORUM, 1961 (New York: Columbia University Press, 1961), p. 281.

[9]Joseph W. Eaton, "Science, 'Art,' and Uncertainty in Social Work," SOCIAL WORK, Vol. 3, No. 3 (July 1958), pp. 3–10.

upon a growing knowledge of social reality, to frame a sense of purpose consistent with that reality, to conceptualize its practice in forms that make it testable and teachable, and to retain in the process its initial vigor, its power of advocacy and its driving vision of what society should be like.

This is essentially where the social work profession is today, with different segments more or less advanced on the movement-to-profession continuum. The trend is clear even in those corners of the profession that—like group work—are the most newly disciplined, agency centered, and movement oriented: the growing practitioner irritation with vague and global goal formulations, the awakening curiosity about the specific manifestations of professional skill, and the felt desire to establish a stable and ongoing orientation to the systematic organization of knowledge about human beings in action.

Problems of Scientific Orientation

But the orientation to scientific inquiry brings with it certain problems of its own, and there are found in the literature of every profession comments similar to that of Blanton in a recent discussion of the relationship of art and science in the training of psychologists:

> The relationship between knowing and doing has as many puzzles for us today as it had for Socrates. Indeed, all of psychology is involved with it in one way or another.[10]

What are these "puzzles" and what do we need to understand about the knowledge-practice relationship in order to develop a viable practitioner's approach to the data of science?

First, it must be understood that it is not the direct purpose of the scientific effort to resolve the immediate problems of the working practitioner. The search for knowledge about human behavior must be kept independent of day-to-day problems or it loses its value as science. This is not to say that the scientific process cannot be useful to the practitioner as it moves from stage to stage, but that its utility is of a different order from that assumed by those who look to the social sciences for specific answers to specific questions. A research finding is not a fact, but a piece of experience systematically confirmed and evaluated; a theory is not a design for action, or even a direct attempt to reflect reality, but a way of organizing a system of ideas that will be productive of further experiment.[11]

The significant point here is that the findings of research are not sanctified by some magical touchstone of truth, but are simply bits of verified

---

[10]R. Blanton, "Science and Art in the Training of Psychologists," JOURNAL OF CLINICAL PSYCHOLOGY, Vol. 18 (1962), p. 10.

[11]James Bryant Conant, MODERN SCIENCE AND MODERN MAN (Garden City, N.Y. Doubleday and Co., 1953).

human experience out of which may be formed hunches and insights somewhat comparable to those formed out of the events of practice. What makes the research process valuable is that its experiences are consciously designed, observed, and evaluated so that one may with greater assurance believe that what he thinks happened actually did happen. The Lippitt-White experiments on autocratic, democratic, and laissez-faire modes of leadership were valuable to the group worker not because they "proved" anything, or because the findings were constituted as absolute knowledge, but because they represented a systematic and well designed affirmation of the practitioner's experiences with children in groups.[12] (One might speculate, for example, on whether practice would be different today if the experimenters had found that the more constructive group patterns emerged from the techniques of the autocratic leader.)

The relationship between science and practice is not, therefore, that one provides knowledge and the other uses it; it is a more dynamic process of interaction, in which each plays its hunches into the other, each feeds on the other's experiences—and this goes on for a long, long time before a multitude of "findings" becomes a tiny piece of predictable human behavior. Both science and practice are creative attempts to fathom the human experience; in Bronowski's words, "the symbol and the metaphor are as necessary to science as to poetry."[13]

The second fact that must be faced is that the range of potentially useful information for the human relations worker is virtually unlimited, and it is a fantasy—a counsel of perfection—for the practitioner to hope that it can ever be "learned," in the sense of achieving fingertip control over the information he needs as he needs it. And if the scientific process has taught us nothing else, it has surely helped us to understand that the pursuit of knowledge is essentially a problem-finding venture, a process of formulating the most appropriate questions with which to focus our inquiry into the inchoate mass of available data. This puts the burden of initiative on the profession, for it means hard work in defining its problems rather than waiting with mouth open to be fed the "facts." But it is work without which a profession cannot hope to maintain a productive relationship with the scientific process.[14]

The third aspect of the problem is that if we were suddenly and magically granted command of every shred of evidence ever produced on human behavior—if we were to learn it all by heart—we would as yet not have the

---

[12]Ronald Lippitt and R. K. White, "An Experimental Study of Leadership and Group Life," in Eleanor E. Maccoby, Theodore M. Newcomb, and E. L. Hartley, eds., READINGS IN SOCIAL PSYCHOLOGY (New York: Henry Holt and Company, 1958), pp. 496–511.

[13]J. Bronowski, SCIENCE AND HUMAN VALUES (New York: Harper and Brothers, 1956), pp. 48–49.

[14]For a more detailed discussion of this point, and the one that follows, see William Schwartz, "Toward a Strategy of Group Work Practice," SOCIAL SERVICE REVIEW, Vol. 36, No. 3 (September 1962), pp. 269–270.

slightest notion of what to do about it in practice. The idea that knowledge carries its own implications for action is what has come to be referred to as scientism, and it is no more useful than the old forms of mysticism by which it was assumed that appropriate professional activity followed directly from beliefs, values, and goals. Both expectations are unrealistic, in that they fail to take account of the fact that the road from knowing to doing is bridged by purpose.[15]

All of which brings us to the point where we may begin to see the scientific process in something like its proper perspective from the vantage point of the practical arts: its findings are not "truth," but tentative insights—like the practitioner's, but more systematically fashioned—into the nature of human experience; it produces too much material to be "learned" and it does not tell us what to do. We must create our own filing system, our own receptacles in which to carry away the information we need.

This is another way of saying that the practitioner needs theories—organized perceptions of experience—as much as does the scientist. Indeed, it is because of the lack of theoretical approaches to the problems of practice that there has been so much difficulty in integrating the work of the behavioral sciences into the graduate school curriculum in social work. Without theory, the crucial questions cannot be formulated and the student is overwhelmed by the demand that he somehow learn all there is to know about human behavior—intrapsychically, in the group, in the community, in the world.

In the group work specialization, for example, the typical exercise of "group analysis," devoid of any theoretical work on the nature of the small group, produces long inventories of group characteristics, internally unrelated and throwing little light on the life of the group. The result is not analysis at all, but a crude typology that adds little to the student's understanding of a complex group situation. Until it is able to produce more integrative approaches, the group work segment will remain about where it is: intrigued by the scientific ferment of the day, vaguely attracted to its glamour, slightly disappointed in its results, and unable to do very much about it.

An Approach to the Data

With these considerations in mind, let us now examine what might be a practical approach for the group worker to the body of information available to him in the small group literature; in the process, we will in effect be designing a model for similar approaches to other specific areas of scientific investigation.

1. The group worker needs to become familiar with the history of the inquiry. As with all facets of the human experience, the study of the past is essentially a device for formulating the most searching questions about the present. One cannot, for example, see deeply into the current work on group

[15] *Ibid.*, p. 270.

cohesiveness without some knowledge about the early controversies between those who sought for a quality of "group mind"[16] and those who asserted that the study of groups was simply the attempt to understand individuals in group situations.[17] It is easier to understand Gertrude Wilson's attempt to distinguish between "social group work" and "work with groups"[18] when one becomes aware of the group worker's historic preoccupation with the socialization process and the forces that made Cooley's formulations so attractive in the early years of practice.[19] The story of the awakening interest in the small group as a social instrument, the social significance of the first speculations it aroused, the ensuing movement from sociological speculations to the empiricism of the psychologists—these are some of the events that illuminate the area and make it familiar ground on which to find one's way.

The task is not so difficult as it may appear. Several brief surveys exist that provide the broad outlines of the story: Shils's "The Study of the Primary Group," published in 1951, is an excellent early review.[20] Riecken and Homans, Smith, Allport, Trow, Bernard, and Olmsted have also produced brief accounts which, taken together, fill out the historical development of issues and problems in this field of study.[21]

2. The group worker needs to develop search techniques with which he can go to the evidence he needs when he needs it, in much the same way that a doctor or a lawyer goes to the literature to get help with a problem posed to him in his practice. The ability to use the reference literature in this way is in fact a professional hallmark and involves a knowledge of where the evidence is stored and how it is labeled. The social work profession will some day reach the point of ordering and arranging its own reference data, case materials, and professional terminology; for the present, the practitioner must develop his own devices and depend largely on his knowledge of the history of the

---

[16]W. McDougall, THE GROUP MIND (New York: G. P. Putnam's Sons, 1920). See also G. Le Bon, THE CROWD: A STUDY OF THE POPULAR MIND (London: Earnest Bean, Ltd., 1952).

[17]F. A. Allport, SOCIAL PSYCHOLOGY (Boston: Houghton Mifflin Company, 1924)

[18]Gertrude Wilson, "Social Group Work Theory and Practice," SOCIAL WELFARE FORUM, 1956 (New York: Columbia University Press, 1956) pp. 143–159.

[19]Charles Horton Cooley, SOCIAL ORGANIZATION (New York: Charles Scribner's Sons, 1909.)

[20]Edward A. Shils, "The Study of the Primary Group," in D. Lerner and Harold D. Lasswell, eds., THE POLICY SCIENCES (Stanford, Calif. Stanford University Press, 1951), pp. 44–69.

[21]Henry W. Riecken and George C. Homans, "Psychological Aspects of Social Structure," in Gardner Lindzey, ed., HANDBOOK OF SOCIAL PSYCHOLOGY (Cambridge, Mass. Addison-Wesley Press, 1954) pp. 787–832; Mildred B. Smith, "Recent Developments in the Field of Social Psychology," op. cit., pp. 137–143; Gordon W. Allport, "The Historical Background of Modern Social Psychology," in Lindzey op. cit., pp. 3–56; W. C. Trow, "Group Processes," in C. W. Harris, ed. THE ENCYCLOPEDIA OF EDUCATIONAL RESEARCH (3d ed. New York: The Macmillan Company, 1960), pp. 602–613; L. K. Bernard, "Social Psychology," in THE ENCYCLOPEDIA OF THE SOCIAL SCIENCES, Vol. 14 (New York: The Macmillan Co., 1942), pp. 151–157; M. S. Olmsted, THE SMALL GROUP, (New York: Random House, 1959).

inquiry and on his familiarity with the periodicals, reviews, and existing anthologies of related disciplines.[22]

3. The worker needs his own working theory of the phenomena in which he is interested. This does not mean that every practitioner should be a systematic theoretician. What is meant is that every worker already has a number of unstated theories about what he is doing, that he would be immobilized without some such structure of related assumptions, and that he is better able to add to his knowledge if he makes these assumptions explicit rather than allowing them to operate outside his own awareness.

Every group worker, for example, perceives his groups in some particular way—as a network of competitive strivings, as a mutual assistance pact, as a horde led by its strongest members, as a family of siblings with himself in the parent role, and so on—and his conception will determine the way he evaluates events, the kinds of information about which he is curious, and the types of predictions he makes about future events. When his assumptions are covert and hidden from his own awareness, there will be a tendency to assign many of them to the sphere of absolute truth and to regard them as settled rather than open questions, which is as far from the scientific orientation as one can get. Martin Loeb, in a recent and valuable article on theory-making and model-building, makes a strong point of the need for practitioners to generalize openly from their experience:

> The belief that it is possible to make generalizations above the level of experiencing is the first major step in developing a climate in which social work theories can be made and exciting models can be built.[23]

4. With his own frame of reference made fairly explicit, the worker is then in a position to mark out those issues and questions with which he is most concerned and on which he most needs clarification. These problems are not then merely "interesting," but become central to his understanding of his own work. They constitute the lines of inquiry that have more meaning for him than for others, they focus his investigations into the literature, and they become his particular areas of specialization, serving to guide both his study of the data and his appraisals of evidence emerging from his own practice. If,

---

[22]See, for example, Altman and Terauds, op. cit., Dorwin Cartwright and Alvin Zander, eds. GROUP DYNAMICS: RESEARCH AND THEORY (Evanston, Ill. Row, Peterson and Co., 1953); Paul Hare, Edgar F. Borgatta, and Robert F. Bales, SMALL GROUPS: STUDIES IN SOCIAL INTERACTION (New York: Alfred A. Knopf, 1955); H. H. Kelley and J. M. Thibaut, "Experimental Studies of Group Problem Solving and Process," in Lindzey, op. cit., pp. 735–785; Maccoby, Newcomb, and Hartley, ed., op. cit., E. Sapir, "Group," in THE ENCYCLOPEDIA OF THE SOCIAL SCIENCES, Vol. 7, op. cit., pp. 178–182; and Luigi Petrullo, "Small Group Research," in A. J. Backrach, ed., EXPERIMENTAL FOUNDATIONS OF CLINICAL PSYCHOLOGY (New York: Basic Books, 1962), pp. 211–253.

[23]Martin B. Loeb, "The Backdrop for Social Research: Theory-Making and Model-Building," in Leonard S. Kogan, ed., SOCIAL SCIENCE THEORY AND SOCIAL WORK RESEARCH, op. cit., p. 12.

for example, he views the small group as a type of family arrangement and a reenactment of childhood relations, he will be interested in the ways in which he fortifies or weakens the members' perception of him as a parent, he will be curious about the relationship between the sex of the worker and member behavior, the issues of competition and cooperation will take on certain special meanings, and so on. The development of such specialized lines of work makes it possible to envision the day when the group work practitioner will be able to use the scientific work of the academic disciplines as an adjunct to his own conceptualized body of experience based on the events of group work practice itself.

Thus, to summarize the points made above: the study of history tells what the study variables have been and how they came to bc regarded as important; the development of search techniques provides the instrument for finding the evidence on these variables when it is needed; a theory of one's own helps one to select those that are most crucial and to invent new ones as new models and paradigms emerge from the events of practice; and one's own lines of inquiry help one to formulate the central questions around which to organize one's ongoing search for useful insights, both in the scientific literature and in one's own working experiences.

Conclusion

Space limitations make it impossible here to demonstrate in detail the steps outlined above and the ways in which particular frames of reference open up specific lines of inquiry into the scientific data. In a limited way, the author has tried to do this in an article previously mentioned,[24] where certain directions are extrapolated from his own theoretical orientation to the problems of practice.[25] The major task for group workers, at this stage of their professional development, is to eliminate the sharp dichotomy drawn between science and practice, for, the wider the gap between them, the less creative will be the work of each.

The tasks of generalizing and systematizing are as necessary to professional practice as are the practical problems of the field to the over-all scientific effort. In this sense, the professional is a scientist within the limits of his practice, and the scientist grows sterile and academic without first-hand knowledge of the human phenomena he is trying to study. Group workers and their agencies have been unduly awed by the scientific label and frightened at the prospect of doing research with a capital "R". As a consequence, they have failed to realize that systematic observation of their experiences and generalizing from those experiences are quite within their competence—and

---

[24]William Schwartz, "Toward a Strategy of Group Work Practice," op. cit.

[25]Schwartz, "The Social Worker in the Group," THE SOCIAL WELFARE FORUM, 1961 (New York: Columbia University Press, 1961), pp. 146–171.

that these processes are, in fact, indispensable to maintaining and improving the quality of their practice. When this becomes clear, and when the agencies begin to structure action along these lines, group workers will take a major step toward establishing a stable relationship with man's organized effort to find out more about himself.

Analysis of Papers Presented on Working Definitions of Group Work Practice

William Schwartz

Background

At a meeting in June, 1959, the Practice Committee of the Group Work Section, NASW, took on the task of producing a new "Working Definition" of social group work practice. There were two reasons given for this decision: one was the Section's own expressed need to create greater technical and conceptual clarity to guide the work of its members and their agencies; the other was the need of the National Association to test out, in the various sections, the recently formulated "Working Definition of Social Work Practice," written by the Subcommittee on the Working Definition of the NASW Commission on Social Work Practice.

At that time, the following steps were projected: 1) the Practice Committee would invite a selected number of group work practitioners and teachers to submit their own present formulations of a working definition of group work practice; 2) they would be asked to structure their statements in accordance with the categories employed in the Subcommittee definition of social work practice—namely, *Value, Purpose, Sanction, Knowledge, and Method;* 3) simultaneously, a member of the Committee would undertake to write an historical paper on group work's search for self-definition over the past 30 years; 4) all of these documents would then be brought together and reviewed by the total Committee; and, 5) a small group would then be asked to create a synthesis in the form of a single statement which could then be proposed to the NASW Subcommittee and to the membership of the Group Work Section.

Excerpt from minutes of Practice Committee and Group Work Section, March, 1960

What follows here is a part of the fourth step in the process described above; it is an attempt to summarize and relate the various statements prepared for the Committee in order to facilitate its review of the material at its meetings in March, 1960. The documents under consideration were as follows:

1. The "Working Definition of Social Work Practice" prepared by the NASW Subcommittee, reported in the article in SOCIAL WORK, by Harriett Bartlett.
2. Six working definitions of social group work practice, which follow the five categories in the general statement closely, and can thus be related directly to it. (Helen Northen, Helen Phillips, Marjorie Murphy, Paul Deutschberger, Merrill Conover, Irving Canter).
3. Four group work definitions which employ not the given categories but other more or less related frames of reference. (Mary Lee Nicholson, Norman Polansky, David Austin, Gisela Konopka).
4. Two full-length articles, not prepared expressly for the Committee, but definitive in nature and contributed to the pool of documents on request. (Robert Vinter, William Schwartz).
5. The historical article, "The Search for a Definition," by Margaret Hartford, a member of the Practice Committee.

The procedure in this analysis is based on the two purposes indicated at the outset: to reach for some internal clarity and consistency within the group work "field" and to relate our definitions to the overall NASW task of creating a working definition of social work itself. It begins with a brief summary of the Bartlett definition, according to its major categories—value, purpose, sanction, knowledge, and method. The group work definitions are then examined to determine the ways in which they might tend to add to, modify, agree with, or disagree with the social work statement. The attempt is then made to compare the group work statements with each other, seeking internal agreements and disagreements on problems of definition. And finally, some general observations will be made on the nature of the materials and some of the overall problems involved.

It should be stated that this review was done quickly and cursorily, and was intended to serve as a discussion device rather than a thorough analysis of the material under scrutiny. The possibilities for analysis and comparison of the various documents are still largely unexploited, and it may be important to undertake such a project at some future time.

Highlights of the NASW "Working Definition"

This statement is an attempt to identify social work as a unique and recognizable institution in our society. Its use of the term "practice" is meant to convey something more than a *method* of working, or the way social workers act in the process of helping. This is only one of its concerns. The statement also encompasses, in its concept of "practice," the *values* shared by its practitioners, the *purpose* for which social work was organized by its society, the social *sanction* from which it draws its authority, and the range of *knowledge* its practitioners must acquire in order to carry out its social function.

Taking each of these areas in turn, these seem to be the essential features against which any definition of group work (or casework, or community organization) would have to be measured.

Value—the concept of individual worth; the interdependence of human beings; the importance of active participation of people in social affairs; and the notion that society—the collective—carries responsibility for each of its parts.

Purpose—to "assist" people; to "identify" problems; to "strengthen maximum potential." To cure, to prevent, to maximize strength.

Sanction—social work as an expression of society's recognition of need and assumption of responsibility. Permission, support, and authority given to social work through three channels: machinery of law and the agencies of government; voluntary, privately-supported agencies; and the establishment of a profession to provide the practitioners of the social welfare services.

Knowledge—derived from sources outside itself and from its own practice; list nine areas of knowledge which, taken together, represent every department of social science known to man.

Method—the "responsible, conscious, disciplined use of self in a relationship." Social workers "facilitate" the achievement of certain desirable results as, for example, interaction, awareness, change. The "systematic mode of procedure" which has this facilitating effect is not described. Definitions are given of "techniques" (tools or instruments) and "skills" (expertness in using techniques).

The Social Work Definition and the Group Work Statements

Area by area, the group work definitions showed broad agreement with the essential features of the NASW document. There were also some interesting additions and modifications, emerging from the special interests and sensitivities of those working in group settings. By category, the comparison went somewhat as follows:

1. In the area of *value,* there was a common emphasis on the Subcommittee concepts of individual worth, interdependence, responsible activity, and social responsibility. Paul Deutschberger called for recognition of the values inherent in the group itself as a medium through which social work goals are attained. Marjorie Murphy and Helen Northen devote considerable attention to an elaboration of the value scheme contained in the social work document. Merrill Conover offers several "values or assumptions more specific to group work," such as the importance of group life, its social carryover, and others.

   In general terms, one may say here that the working definitions of social group work are easily assimilable into the framework of the social work definition, insofar as the identification of the value system is concerned. The effect of the group work statements is to add some values to which the group work tradition is especially alive, and to elaborate others in terms which apply to groups and communities.

Also, the group work statements reflected a conceptual problem which was evident in the Subcommittee statement as well. With the exception of the Irving Canter statement, all of the definitions failed to make proper distinctions between "conditions" and "norms"—that is, between something judged to be a scientific hypothesis (e.g., that people are interdependent) and something regarded as socially desirable (e.g., that society should function as a protective agent for its individuals). The failure to separate the "is" from the "should" tends to weaken both the philosophical and the scientific structures on which social work is built and from which it draws its identifying features.

2. In the category of *purpose,* the group work statements, while not disagreeing with the social work definition in its essentials, seem to be reaching for greater precision and a more satisfying conceptualization. The Subcommittee's term, "equilibrium," seems unsatisfactory to most; Deutschberger and Murphy prefer a concept like "the integration of social roles." Murphy, in speaking of "goals," refers to the concept which guided the Curriculum Study, namely, the "enhancement of social functioning." The stress, in these and other of the group work statements, is strongly on the necessity to conceive of social work purpose in general developmental terms, rather than solely as a therapeutic agent—as a righter of wrongs, curer of illness, strengthener of weakness, etc.

   Another major modification is introduced by Helen Phillips who emphasizes the notion that the articulation of social work purpose is not a function of the profession alone but of the agency in which it functions and the clients (here, the group) which it serves. This approach would have the effect of designating any general statement of social work purpose as incomplete and partial until it is fixed in its agency framework.

   Somewhat peripheral, but important, is Robert Vinter's representation of the group as a "means and context for treatment" rather than as a client entity in itself, upon which one may focus social work purposes. Vinter's denial of the historic group work emphasis on "the group as a client" highlights one of the major issues involved in making a definitive statement about the practice of social work today. The "context of treatment" theme is one of the ways in which the therapy "versus" social action issue has been stated in its clearest form.

   Generally, the *purpose* area is another in which both a semantic and conceptual confusion is reflected—again—in both the Subcommittee statement and the group work definitions. Here, it is the failure to distinguish between *ends* and *means, goals* and *functions,* between what Boehm has called the "vision-of-the-outcome" and the unique *way-of-acting* assigned to the social worker in the social scheme. "To identify" a problem, to say what one thinks is wrong, is clearly a *function* one may take on in a given situation. If this is a social work function, it is easy to see it in operation, to make judgments as to whether it is being done or not, whether badly or well, etc. "To assist" somebody, "to change" his thinking or his way of living, simply means that your aspirations for him include this or that vision-of-the-outcome. That social work is committed to democracy, mental health, social action, etc., is implicit in its values; and unless *purpose* is conceived as an action-category, it simply becomes a restatement of the value scheme. "To identify problems" is a step forward—but it is a small step, and in the face of the difficulties involved in identifying other patterns of action, the statement of purpose falters and lapses into a restatement of the previous category.

3. Under *sanction,* the most significant consensus arrived at lies in the common agreement that the professional support on which social group work builds its activities and services is that of social work. The "sub-professional" aspects of the group work tradition have, in the statements before us, all but disappeared and the primary effort is to define an entity which is an integral part of the social welfare field and the social work profession.

   Deutschberger proposes a different framework for understanding sanction, suggesting that there are three forms of authority—*legal, professional and leadership,* the latter being "conferred on the worker by the client or the client-group" and thus "irrespective of both agency employment and professional authority." (In direct disagreement here, Phillips' emphasis is on the sanction provided by agency and community). Deutschberger makes an interesting suggestion in his statement that social work skill is an expression of the worker's ability to use all three kinds of authority appropriately, rather than depending primarily on any one of them.

   Finally, Northen and Murphy make the point that the multifunction agencies need to be included in any realistic discussion of social work sanction.

4. On the knowledge component: the group work definitions include much the same basic ingredients as the Bartlett statement, though several undertake different categorical systems. The Phillips statement is useful in that it is almost unique in its stress in the importance of knowledge about *processes* (the meaning of "experience" the "nature of process," etc.), rather than an exclusive concern with entities (the individual, the group, the community, etc.). Marjorie Murphy's discussion of the knowledge item attains a high degree of specificity, a quality lacking in many of the statements, and in the Bartlett statement itself.

   For the most part, however, the group work definitions tend to compound rather than correct the basic error of the Subcommittee statement in this area of concern. This error lies in staking out a field of knowledge so extensive and unlimited that it cannot be taught and learned in all of the professions put together—much less one single profession with a limited function. To say that social workers need to "know" all about the dynamics of human behavior, the dynamics of group living, the cultural heritage, the history and development of communities, and so on and on, is simply to indicate that it would be nice if we could know all there is to know about Man in Society. But this adds nothing to the solution of the real problem—which is to work out, with some attempt at precision, those special areas of knowledge which lend themselves most immediately to the performance of the social work function, and by the possession of which the social work practitioner may be identified.

5. Finally, on the subject of *Method:* just as the key element in the social work definition is the *conscious use of self in relationship,* so this combination of *purposive movement* and *interactional process* is part of the general conceptual framework of the group work statements. The differences in point of view begin to emerge only as one examines the ways in which a particular definition explains the *focus* or *intent* of the helper's movements. In this respect, one may distinguish two different types of methodological explication: one is *teleological,* stating the method of helping as *being defined by its results*—the worker acts "in such a way" that change is effected, or facilitated, self-awareness is achieved by the client, etc.; the other approach may be termed *process-oriented,* in which the attempt is made to describe the method of helping in its own action terms, rather than in terms of what it hopes to achieve.

The Bartlett statement is a concise model of the teleological approach to the definition of social work method, and all but a view of the group work definitions deeply influenced by the classical group work statement of 1948, follow the "in-such-a-way," teleological tradition. In the statements under consideration here, only Austin, Phillips, Vinter and Schwartz attempt to focus on the helping process itself as part of a practice definition, even though each, in his own way, finds it difficult to avoid completely the trap of defining a means by describing its intended end. Austin's concept of "reality" focus is a promising notion; Phillips' consistent emphasis on process is partly diluted by the failure to see "function" itself as an action concept that cannot itself be defined by its results; and the formulations of Vinter and Schwartz, unrestricted by the demand for brief definition, are the only elaborated attempts to define the helping process itself.

One point that stands out clearly is that the semantic problem is an imposing one, where the attempt is made to compare the assumptions and concepts of different writers working at the tasks of definition. The terminology itself, generally speaking, is the same; but the meanings ascribed to the various terms—"method," "technique," "skill," "purpose," "goal," etc.,—vary considerably from statement to statement and, often, within the same statement.

Internal Comparisons

In comparing the various group work definitions with each other, the areas of general agreement stand out clearly. I would list them somewhat as follows:

1. It seems to be unanimously accepted, among these respondents, that social group work is a social work function. The general feeling is that group workers, their traditions, and their agencies now find themselves squarely within the field of social welfare and appropriately related to the social work profession.
2. There are no major difficulties encountered in attempting to write a group work definition on the model of the Bartlett statement. Although a better, perhaps less mechanical, categorical scheme may ultimately be arrived at, the present one is useful for pointing up the basic similarities, differences, modifications, etc., among the casework, group work, and probably community organization frames of reference.
3. There is general agreement among all the group work statements in matters relating to the value system of its workers, the social aspirations to which they are committed, and the general image evoked by concepts like "maturity," "democracy," "citizen participation," "social change," and the like. There is also a generally shared curiosity about the same things; the knowledge aspirations, while too broadly and vaguely stated, tend to focus on the same areas of human concern. Thus in matters of philosophy, value and knowledge, these statements reflect a kind of common origin, a shared tradition, a kind of family tie.
4. There is a striking sense of urgency, in almost every statement about the need for fresh theoretical formulations in the area of practice. Each effort reflects not only the need to move away from the old shibboleths, but also the willingness of the writers to risk themselves in attempting some new ways of thinking about the problems. The result is a group of statements that are stimulating and exciting beyond anything our literature has produced for some time.

Moving now to what seems to me to be the general area in which disagreements occur and issues are posed, as one contrasts and compares the various group work definitions, I would list these as follows:

1. As previously mentioned, there is great disagreement about the meanings which should be assigned to various terms: *purpose,* for example, is made to mean *goals* ("the purpose is to help the client attain health relationships"), or *means* ("the purpose is to identify problems"), or *activities* (where the "purpose" of a group is to play basketball); *function* is used to signify goals, means activities, the intent of the agency, the intent of the member, or that of the worker, etc.; *method* is another difficult word which is applied to the knowledge of the worker, his aspirations, the general frame of reference, or the total situation in which both the group and its worker find themselves.
2. There are significant variations in the type of working models used by the various writers to study the helping situation and the client-worker relationship. I can distinguish three different models, each with its own implications for how one defines and teaches the nature of the helping process:

a. The *medical* model, in which the steps in the helping process are described by assuming a sequence of movements through which the worker investigates, diagnoses, and treats the problem under consideration. Although the Bartlett statement does not use the medical terminology, its conception is essentially the same. Among the group work statements, Konopka and Vinter represent this point of view most strongly, the latter in a highly developed form.
b. The *scientific* model, in which the steps in the helping process resemble closely the problem-solving sequence by which the scientific worker moves from the unknown to the known. This is a strong tradition in group work, coming out of the progressive education movement and its inspiration from Dewey's *How We Think* and similar works of that period. In the group work statements, Canter and Northen developed this line most effectively.
c. The model of the *organic system,* in which the total helping situation is viewed as a network of reciprocal activity, and in which it is impossible to describe accurately any part of the system without describing its active relationship to the other moving parts. This model, elaborated in most detail by the Schwartz statement, is basically alien to either the medical or the scientific model and produces a mode of explanation which is different from both.

3. There is wide variation in the levels of abstraction on which the different writers tackle the problem of defining the group work method. The attempts range all the way from eliminating altogether the attempt to deal with how to help ("in such a way that"), to the most highly simplified, limited, and concrete acts performed by the worker.
4. Finally, the issue is raised—most sharply by Bob Vinter—as to whether it is still valid to regard the group itself as an entity, a *client,* to be served by the worker. Vinter's claim is that the group should be viewed *solely* as a "context of treatment," a place in which individuals are helped to get well, or solve certain developmental problems, etc. The entity itself, the group, has no purpose other than this and cannot be "helped" to develop, mature, etc.

Final Comments

It will, of course, be recognized that this brief analysis must suffer throughout from my own biases which seek expression on all of the points and issues mentioned above. Also, I must reiterate the fact that none of the writers are done justice by it, and some are badly neglected. However, its sole objective is to facilitate discussion, and perhaps it is enough to do that.

He who would do good to another must do it in
Minute Particulars:
General Good is the plea of the scoundrel,
hypocrite & flatterer,
For Art & Science cannot exist but in minutely
organized Particulars.

William Blake

On the Use of Groups in Social Work Practice

William Schwartz

IN THE INTRODUCTION to his book on social behavior, George Homans describes his subject as a "familiar chaos." By this he means that we "have been at home with the evidence since childhood," but our knowledge remains unsystematic and poorly organized, and generalizations consist mainly of proverbs, maxims, and other half-truths (2, p. 1).*

Many social workers think of their small group experiences in just this way; they have been in groups all their lives and they have developed maxims to express their understanding of those experiences. But they feel vaguely inexpert when asked to consider this area of work from a professional's point of view. Nevertheless, it is important to remember that the familiarity is as vital as the chaos. Any theorizing about the group experience should have a familiar ring as one measures the ideas against his own sensations and recollections. This requirement has important implications for both professionals and their clients.

*The parenthesized numbers refer to the bibliographical references listed alphabetically at the end of each paper.

Some Background Issues

It is helpful to recall some of the institutional and professional events that have led up to the present situation in which workers trained in the traditional settings of "social group work" talk to audiences composed largely of "social caseworkers" for whom the subject of groups is fast becoming highly relevant to their professional tasks and to the service of their agencies.

We should understand, for example, that this is not a new tradition but a tradition reclaimed. Group work historians are now fond of quoting Mary Richmond on the importance of groups; and she did, in fact, comment "with great pleasure" in 1920 on "the new tendency to view our clients from the angle of what might be termed *small group psychology*" (emphasis in original) (4, p. 256). But the paths of individual and small group preoccupation soon diverged and went their separate ways—to the point where Eduard Lindeman complained, in 1939, that "I cannot see why . . . groups and group experiences do not stand at the very center of social work's concern" (3, p. 344). Now, more than 40 years after Mary Richmond's observation, the group experience has indeed begun to move closer to the center of social work's concern, and caseworkers are again coming to view their clients from the vantage point of small group psychology. What is it about today's world that has compelled social workers to look again to the forces of mutual aid and peer group association—not only in the group work and community organization settings where you might expect it, but in the family agency, the hospital, the school, the child welfare setting, and others that have from the outset identified themselves as the "casework agencies"?

The rebirth of interest seems due more to the necessity in clinical settings for professionals to utilize techniques that help meet the needs of their clients than to any particular influence exerted by the traditional group workers; the latter have indeed complained of the paucity of classical group work references—the Coyles, Treckers, Wilsons, *et al.*—in the developing literature of group services in the casework and clinical settings. One might, in fact, say that the lines of influence have been reversed; as the small group has become a more general instrument of social work practice, group workers in the traditional leisure-time agencies have had to re-examine some of their historic confusions and ambiguities. The portion of their work that is related to creating people in their own image—good Americans, good Christians, group-identified Jews, middle-class prototypes—seems less and less useful, and the part that is connected with the traditional social work function of helping people negotiate difficult environments assumes new significance. So, as we move into this new era of group work, we must think not of an old service teaching a new but of both services striving together to redefine and clarify the function of the social work profession. And this presents another theoretical problem undergirding the problems of group service—namely, how to define social work function in a way that will explain the operations of all social workers.

When professionals grow tired of a difficult problem it is a familiar gambit to sneer at the problem itself. So it is with the current fashion to belittle efforts at defining social work function in generic terms. But no amount of indifference or disdain will change the fact that the various parts of social work have been drawn together from the most diverse sources of experience, and that there is a strong need to examine their relationships to each other to find out what they have in common. It is no accident that we are developing into a single, unified profession, integrating the widest differences in practice, philosophy, and social origins—no accident, but something of a mystery. Over the years we have made many efforts to probe the mystery, but from rather safe ground. We have said, for example, that we are held together by a common body of knowledge, common values, common aspirations; but we have hesitated to explore what it is we *do* that identifies us as social workers, and by what professional *skills* we want to be recognized. It is this formulation of a common methodology—a commonly characterized way of working—that provides the context in which any contemporary definition of group practice must be embedded.

In actual fact, the requirements of practice are forcing most workers into the role of expert in the generic enterprise. The work itself is beginning to persuade us that the idea of a common method is neither utopian nor premature. On the contrary, practitioners will inevitably fashion their group skills out of those they learned in their work with individuals; and they will learn, in the process, the integral connections between the two. Casework students comment repeatedly that the group work courses help them understand their casework more deeply; and I have no doubt that a good casework course is similarly significant for group work students. And so it is that as we build our understanding of social work in groups, we are both drawing from and adding to a general theory of social work practice.

It would be possible, in a longer exposition, to describe in detail how the face-to-face group is a special case of the encounter between the one and the many—between the individual and his social surroundings. What are the ways in which people try to negotiate the various systems of demands and relationships with which they must come to terms in their daily lives? And what are the ways in which collectives—people working together—integrate their individuals into a working whole, producing things, dividing the work, and making decisions? How we view this encounter between a human being and his society will fashion our view of work, our conception of function, and our theories about how to have an impact on this children's club, that patients' group, this group of mothers on welfare, and others.

Finally, there are issues related to the problem of coming to terms with the tremendous upsurge of knowledge and hypotheses emerging from the small group research of recent years. How does one develop work strategies incorporating this overwhelming accumulation of new knowledge about group behavior?

Having thus outlined all the themes that *could* be developed, let me now try to move into the middle of my subject by citing a few connected propositions about the nature of group experience, the settings in which groups are embedded, and the operational skills of group work practice. I would also like to make a few points about the problems faced by agencies moving anew into the area of group services.

The "Client" Described

In considering the nature of the client group, what we have before us is *a collection of people who need each other in order to work on certain common tasks, in an agency that is hospitable to those tasks.* This simple definition carries within it all of the necessary ingredients for a strategy of practice. The following are some of the propositions it yields.

Need. The group members' need for each other constitutes the basic rationale for their being together. If people do not need to use each other, there is no reason for them to be together—which may seem like a truism until we recall all the experiences in which the mutual need was not apparent and the members struggled to understand what brought them together and why someone thought they had to interact with each other.

Tasks. This need for each other is specifically embodied in certain common tasks to be pursued. Defining "tasks" as *a set of needs converted into work,* we may say that these common tasks will constitute the purpose of the group and the frame of reference from which the members will choose their responses. It follows, then, that unless there is some fair degree of consensus about what these underlying tasks are, the members will find it difficult to find responses, judge the appropriateness of their responses, and plan their impact on the culture of their group. The number and complexity of these common tasks will, of course, vary with the nature of the group—ranging, in a broad spectrum, from the multipurpose adolescent gang, to the six-session group of foster parents discussing child-rearing problems, to the single-meeting group of prospective adoptive parents, and others.

Agency. The group purpose is further clarified and bounded by the agency service in which it is embedded. In society's division of labor the agency has been designated to apply itself to some human problems and not to others. Thus, the agency has a stake in the proceedings; it is not simply a meeting place, or a place of refuge. Its own social tasks are involved and become an integral part of the group experience.

Contract. The convergence of these two sets of tasks—those of the clients and those of the agency—creates the terms of the *contract* that is made between the client group and the agency. This contract, openly reflecting both stakes, provides the frame of reference for the work that follows, and for understanding when the work is in process, when it is being evaded, and when it is finished.

Work. The moving dynamic in the group experience is *work.* Let me define the term "work" as I am using it: (a) each member is trying to harness the others to his own sense of need; (b) the interaction between members thus reflects both the centripetal force of the common tasks and the centrifugal force of those tasks that are unique to each member; and (c) there is a flow of affect among the members—negative and positive in varying degrees—

generated by their investment in each other, their sense of common cause, and the demands of the *quid pro quo.* This emphasis on the importance of work, on an output of energy directed to certain specific tasks, is also a comment on the common fallacy that the group process, in itself and in some mysterious way, solves problems. This naive belief that the sheer interaction of people with problems is somehow productive is often reflected in the records of workers who describe the group process in great detail yet all but obliterate their own movements. Indeed, the function of the worker emerges from the fact that the group process is not a panacea: the members must work for everything they get; they must invest heart and mind in the process; and they need all the help they can get in doing so.

Self-Consciousness. At any given moment the group members may be working on their *contract,* or they may be occupied with their *ways of working.* As in any problem-centered enterprise—casework, research, education, psychotherapy—obstacles to the pursuit of the group's basic work will require diverting energy to the task of finding ways through and around them. When a group is frustrated by such obstacles it will need to work collaboratively on them; and when the obstacles are, for the moment, cleared away, the members are then free to put their strengths together to work on what they came together for. The important point here is that group self-consciousness—attention to its own processes—is not an end in itself, however, attractive this might be to the worker; it is a way of wrestling with the obstacles that impede the group's work.

Authority and Intimacy.* In the culture of the group two main themes come to characterize the members' ways of working together: one, quite familiar to the caseworker, is the theme of *authority,* in which the members are occupied with their relationship to the helping person and the ways in which this relationship is instrumental to their purpose; the other, more strange and threatening to the caseworker, is the theme of *intimacy,* in which the members are concerned with their internal relationships and the problems of mutual aid. It is the interplay of these factors—external authority and mutual interdependence—that provides much of the driving force of the group experience.

The Tasks of the Worker

Having described some of the essential features of the client group system, let us turn now to the job of placing the worker inside it. What is his part in the internal division of labor? What is his function within the system? I have written elsewhere about the movements of the worker in the group[5] and will not repeat the details of the scheme here. For present purposes, let me simply present some general propositions about the worker's major tasks.

*For further inquiry into the group themes of *authority* and *intimacy,* see Bennis and Shepard's discussion of the T-group experience (1).

Parallel Processes. Most important is the fact that the tasks of the worker and those of the clients are different and must be clearly distinguished from each other. Where one takes over the tasks of the other—as workers are often asked to do by supervisors who demand that they state their "goals for the client"—the result is a typical confusion. The worker, trying hard to understand the nature of his helping acts and their impact on the client's process of taking help, is, in effect, asked to obliterate the differences between the two sets of movements rather than to sharpen and clarify them. I have tried to clarify the differences by positing the principle of the *parallel processes,* by which I mean that the worker has his tasks and the client has his, that these processes are interdependent but different, and that any violation of this division of labor renders the work dysfunctional and the encounter itself manipulative, sentimental, and generally frustrating for both parties.

Mediation. The worker's central function is to mediate the engagement of client need and agency service. For a long time we have been ruled by two major fallacies about how needs are met in social welfare: one is that we meet a need when we have learned to identify it; the other is that needs are met when we have established the appropriate structure of service. Granted that both of these achievements are necessary, the sad fact is that the landscape is littered with identified but unmet needs within elaborate but impotent agency structures. The encounter between client and agency is not in itself productive; it can, and too often does, misfire. What is needed is a catalytic agent to activate both client and service. That catalyst is the skill of the worker, which helps the client reach out actively for what he needs and helps the agency reach out for the clients whom it seeks to serve.

Demand for Work. In general terms, the worker carries out the mediating function by clarifying and calling for adherence to the terms of the contract that keeps client and agency together. This means that the worker, of all the participants in the system, must see most clearly into the symbiotic relationship between the client and the agency—must see the specific ways in which they need each other to carry out their own purpose. Furthermore, the worker also represents what might be called the *demand for work,* in which role he tries to enforce not only the substantive aspects of the contract—what we are here for—but the conditions of work as well. This demand is, in fact, the only one the worker makes—not for certain preconceived results, or approved attitudes, or learned behaviors, but for the work itself. That is, he is continually challenging the client to address himself resolutely and with energy to what he came to do; and he is also, at the same time, trying to mobilize his agency to clarify what it has to offer and to offer it wholeheartedly.

Authority. In the group, as in the interview, the authority theme remains; there is the familiar struggle to resolve the relationship with a nurturing and demanding figure who is both a personal symbol and a representative of a powerful institution. But the theme is modified by the addition of numerical reinforcements to the dependent member of the relationship. The caseworker first experiences this as "there are so many of them and only one of me." From both sides of the relationship interesting things begin to happen:

the worker moves—a little reluctantly at first—to share his authority and to learn to live with a "diluted" control over the events of the helping process; and the client's battle with authority is markedly affected as he learns that his feelings about dependency and strength are part of the human condition and not necessarily a unique and personal flaw. The "all-in-the-same-boat" dynamic has a strong impact on the nature of the transference phenomena.

Intimacy. Complementing the work with the authority theme, the social worker in the group helps his clients exploit the theme of intimacy, mobilizing the healing powers of human association and mutual aid. The group members' investment in each other constitutes the new dimension to which professional skill must be addressed. Not only must the worker be able to help people talk but he must help them talk to each other; the talk must be purposeful, related to the contract that holds them together; it must have feeling in it, for without affect there is no investment; and it must be about real things, not a charade, or a false consensus, or a game designed to produce the illusion of work without risking anything in the process. We might say that much of the client's "internal dialogue" should be out in the open, with the internalized parts represented by real people, and the worker's movements directed more clearly and openly to the actions and reactions among them.

The Power of Specific Purpose. Finally, it should be pointed out that just as the member's role is limited by time and purpose, so is the worker's. This is a limitation that adds to the power of the worker because it directs his energies to what he and his clients are working on *together,* what they are doing together, rather than what the clients *are,* how he can make them different, or how he can change their characters, their personalities, their morals, their manners, or their habits. As a practitioner I am strengthened by the idea that I do not have to change anybody's basic state of being; but there is work to be done and my skills can help the work. And, in order for the professional to accept this idea, he must accept another—namely, that the life processes into which he enters and makes his limited impact have been going on for a long time before he arrived and will continue for a long time after he is gone. The process by which the client reconstructs his experience is not one that the worker creates; he simply enters, and leaves. Another way of saying this is that he is an incident in the lives of his clients. Thus the worker should ask himself: What kind of an incident will I represent? What kind of impact will I make? More specifically, how do I enter the process, do what I have to do, and then leave?

The Phases of Work

The above questions serve to introduce another dimension that may be helpful in describing this way of analyzing work with groups—the dimension of time. I believe the tasks of the worker can be understood more precisely if we watch him move through four separate phases of work in sequence. The first is a preparatory *"tuning-in"* phase, in which the worker readies himself to enter the process, to move into the group experience as a professional helping person. The second phase is that in which the worker helps the group make its *beginnings* together. The next is the period of *work,* encompassing the essential business of the enterprise. And the final period of *transitions and endings* concerns itself with the problems of leaving, of separation and termination.

As I discuss each of these phases, I am suggesting that they apply not only to the total group experience but to each of the separate meetings that comprise it. Each encounter has its own tuning-in, beginning, middle, and end-transitions; the same logic and the same necessities of work make the terms of the analysis equally applicable, although considerable work remains to be done in testing out the details of this conception in action.

The process of preparation, described here as the "tuning-in" period, is one in which the worker readies himself to receive cues that are minimal, subtle, devious, and hard to detect except by a very sensitive and discerning instrument. It is important to note that the tuning-in idea is different from certain current conceptions about the preparation of workers, where the main emphasis is on the formulation of "goals" and the construction of "diagnostic" pictures—that is, on developing a structural and cross-sectional version of what the client *is* (and what he ought to be) rather than of what he might *do* in a given situation. If you say that a person tends to do what he is, and is what he does, that proposition needs more detailed examination. The fact is that we have not been very successful in predicting behavior from personality assessment; people tend to do different things in different situations, and they may thus be said to "be" different under different conditions. In any event, the tuning-in process tries to use prior knowledge to anticipate clues that will be thrown away so quickly, and in such disguised forms, that the worker will miss them unless he is somehow "tuned" to the client's frequency. We may, if we like, call this a kind of "preliminary empathy," as the worker prepares to enter the life-process of his clients. A young person properly attuned to a group of aged clients may instantly perceive and address himself to the possibility that the comment "What a nice young man!" may be a suspicious rather than an approving judgment—that is, "What could you know about our troubles?" In this phase the worker tries to unearth both the themes that may emerge in the worker-group engagement and the ways in which these themes may be expressed. For example, a group of adoptive parents in the supervision period may be expected to express in various ways the themes of the "bad seed," the problem of whether, how, and when to tell the child that he is adopted, the tyranny of the agency, and the ambivalence toward the supervising social worker. Thus, the tuning-in phase is devoted to making oneself receptive to veiled communications, making use of our knowledge about the issues that tend to be of concern to any particular type of client—to the aging, the adoptive parents, adolescents under stress, and others—and our knowledge about these clients in particular. It is an attempt to relate knowledge to action as the worker prepares himself for this action.

The second phase is that in which the worker tries to help the group make its beginnings under clear conditions of work. He asks them to understand the terms of the "contract" under which they have established themselves within the agency context. In effect, he is asking the members to understand the connection between their needs as they feel them and the agency's reasons for offering help and hospitality; the contract embodies the stake of each party. This beginning phase is particularly important; if its tasks are not properly and directly addressed at the outset, they will plague both group and worker for a long time—in the prolonged testing, in the endless repetition of the what-are-we-doing-here theme, and in the fits and starts with which the group approaches its business. Record analysis discloses many ways in which group members can raise and re-raise the questions of who the worker is, what he is supposed to do, what the group is for, what the agency *really* expects, what the hidden rewards and punishments are, how much latitude they *really* have, and what the talking is supposed to be about.

Simply put, the worker's tasks in this phase are: (a) to make a clear and uncomplicated (unjargonized) statement of why he thinks they are there, of their stake in coming together and the agency's stake in serving them; (b) to describe his own part in the proceedings as clearly and simply as he can; (c) to reach for feedback, for their reactions to his formulation and how his formulation squares with theirs; and (d) to help them do whatever work is needed to develop together a working consensus on the terms of the contract and their frame of reference for being together.

It is not assumed that this settles everything; nor is it true that contract work is limited to the opening stage of the group experience. Negotiation and renegotiation take place periodically, as they do in any relationship. But this does not negate the need to develop an initial working agreement, a frame of reference from which to choose one's first responses. The only alternative is ambiguity of purpose, which results in a prolonged period of subtle dickering about the terms of the engagement.

The third phase is related to the main body of the work together and is directed to the primary tasks of the helping process. Assuming that the worker has sensitized himself, that he has helped establish a fairly clear sense of purpose, and that the members have begun to address themselves to the job ahead, the worker's skills can now be employed freely in carrying out his part in the process. His central questions now become: Are we working? What are we working on? At this point there is a high premium on the worker's ability to make accurate judgments in identifying when work is going on, what it is about, when it is being avoided, where it runs into obstacles, and when the group is remobilizing itself.

I have written elsewhere about what I believe to be the five major tasks to which the worker addresses himself in the group situation[5]. I have suggested that these consist of: (a) finding, through negotiation, the common ground between the requirements of the group members and those of the systems they need to negotiate; (b) detecting and challenging the obstacles to work as these obstacles arise; (c) contributing ideas, facts, and values from his own perspective when he thinks that such data may be useful to the members in dealing with the problems under consideration; (d) lending his own vision and projecting his own feelings about the struggles in which they are engaged; and (e) defining the requirements and limits of the situation in which the client-worker system is set. For present purposes let me simply identify some of the skills required to carry out these tasks. I have mentioned the ability to perceive when work is going on and when it is being avoided; further, there is the ability to reach for opposites, for ambiguities, for what is happening under the good feelings or the bad; there is the skill of reinforcing the different ways in which people help each other; of partializing large problems into smaller, more manageable pieces; of generalizing and finding connections between small segments of experience; of calling not only for talk but talk that is purposeful and invested with feeling; of being able to handle not only the first offerings but the second and third stages of elaboration; and, throughout, of being able constantly to make the demand for work inherent in the worker's helping function.

Most of these skills are familiar to those working with individual clients; what is less familiar is the set of adaptations required in the small-group situation where, as I have said, "there are so many of them and only one of me." What is crucial here is that there is a *multiplicity of helping relationships* rather than just one, and this is disconcerting to many who have not realized how much professional control they are accustomed to using in the one-to-one interview. The role of the authority factor comes home with renewed force to the caseworker who begins to work in the spontaneous, interactive, mutually-reinforcing, rather unpredictable climate of the small group. Workers begin to question how much control they have really been using and how comfortable it has been to be able to regulate the flow of the interview, to turn themes off and on, and to take a new tack when the present one is too confusing to them.

However, the disease is not incurable; when such an evaluation takes place it often has significant effects on the worker's practice—not only in the learning of group skills but in deepening the casework skills as well. The group process has the power to move the worker as well as the members.

In the final phase of work—that which I have called "transitions and endings"—the worker's skills are needed to help the members use him and each other to deal with the problem of moving from one experience to another. For the worker it means moving *off* the track of the members' experience and life-process, as he has, in the beginning, moved *onto* it. There is a great deal to be said about how people join and separate, what beginnings and endings mean to them, and the kinds of help they need in the process. For example, one of the most interesting of the separation phenomena is what has come to be called "doorknob therapy." Within the life of any particular group we have found that the last few minutes of every meeting yields us the most significant material; that is, people will raise their most deeply-felt concerns as a "by-the-way," almost with a hand on the doorknob. We find, further, that these themes do not lend themselves to easy reintroduction at the beginning of the next meeting. The intention to "start with that at our next meeting" is more often subverted, and the theme re-enters only at the next doorknob period. The point is that beginnings and endings are hard for people to manage;

they often call out deep feeling in both worker and members; and much skill is needed to help people help each other through these times.

The Move to Group Services

What happens when the "casework" agency begins to serve some of its clients in groups? The first point that needs to be made is that those involved should not be trapped into making invidious comparisons between the one-to-one situation and the small group as contexts of treatment. There is a kind of tempting chauvinism in this "battle of methods," but it is a useless enterprise that blocks the development of agency service. The fact is that the authority theme creates certain kinds of demands for professional skill, and the intimacy theme calls for others, with different possibilities and limitations. There are things clients can do in a group that they will find more difficult to do in an interview; and there are things they feel free to share with a worker alone that they will not part with in the peer group. We need to learn more about what these differences are, and we are learning all the time. But we are learning from the work itself, not from the arguments of those who, by a strange historic arrangement, first learned to specialize by numbers.

The workers in one agency, evaluating their first group experiences to determine which phenomena seemed to offer the most interesting new dimensions for service, described the following factors[6]. A worker reported on the "amazing rapidity" with which her group members moved into intensive consideration of their problems. She felt there was something about the small group climate that stimulated an early sharing of important ideas and feelings. Another worker talked about the ways in which her members found "echoes" in each other of wishes and feelings that were hard to express; this seemed to create an atmosphere in which there was "less emphasis on denial." One commented on the release of anxiety that seemed to accrue from "the knowledge that such feelings are shared by all."

There was emerging awareness among the workers that the group created a considerable degree of peer pressure to face reality and work on it. A dramatic example was given of a father who produced heart symptoms while the group was on a difficult subject; he was reminded forcefully by the members that this was his familiar reaction to tough problems, and he promptly returned to what he was struggling with. This was offered as an illustration of how the members regulated and supported each other in their reactions to pain and shock. In several connections the point was made that the group seemed to make more demands for tolerating negatives than the professionals themselves dared to make, and that it supplied, in addition, both the support and the incentives for the members to reach for difficult themes, explore self-doubts, endure painful feelings, and search into tabooed areas.

The group process seemed to lend itself particularly well to the way problems need to be broken down and elaborated in order to work on them. The members called for more information, swapped examples, asked for details on this or that aspect, contributed ideas, and shared their interpretations from different perspectives.

These points are all related, of course. The thread that ties them together is the theme of *mutual aid,* and the helping process is tangibly affected by the ways in which people challenge and support each other in the common work. I have already mentioned some of the effects upon the worker—the problem of giving up some controls, the need to adjust to a situation in which there are not one but a multiplicity of helping relationships, the feeling of "so many of them and only one of me." In addition, there is at the outset a considerable uneasiness about what is experienced by caseworkers as a "lack of privacy" in the group situation. Reared in the rigorous and respected tradition of confidentiality, many workers have begun by promising their group members that material emerging in the group would not be shared with other workers and stipulating that they should observe the same rules of confidentiality. To their surprise, they have subsequently found that their clients wanted more communication between their different professionals rather than less. A worker with a group of adolescent boys in foster care found himself repeatedly charged with messages to take back to the caseworkers, to be sure they understood what had happened in the group. Another found it impossible to prevent communication between her girls and their parents about what was happening in both the daughter and the parent groups. Furthermore, the sharing of information, far from creating the problems she expected, actually seemed to contribute greatly to the process in both groups. She concluded that in this context "confidentiality is a myth." It takes time for the caseworker to learn that the group has its own regulatory powers, and that people will make their own decisions as to what they will and will not share with workers, with peers, and with those outside the system.

However, the practice similarities far outweigh the differences; it has become a familiar event to hear caseworkers exclaim, as they discover a group work principle, that this is just what they have always done in the one-to-one relationship. It is true. The group work problems of developing a clearcut contract, helping the members talk to each other with feeling, breaking big problems into smaller, more manageable parts, putting small clues together into generalized learnings, setting the tone of tolerance for ambiguity and struggle, helping the group deal with the various parts of its environment, and helping the members use the resources of this and other agencies are familiar to the caseworker and are part of his stock-in-trade.

What is most important is that, in moving into work with groups, the object of the enterprise should not be to develop a new esoteric terminology to take its place alongside the old; the language of group dynamics can be as seductive and as mystical as that of psychoanalysis. Workers should be prepared not to write articles about the group process but to learn how to *move* in the group situation, how to develop the skills and perform the operations needed to help people in groups. And I do not believe it is possible to teach these skills to social workers by placing them in groups as observers, or even by making them co-leaders with members of other disciplines. I am not saying that these may not be interesting experiences, or that workers cannot learn from them. What I do question is whether they can learn what needs to be taught—namely, the skills of practice. I believe that what we know of pedagogy will bear out the idea that the student can learn how to do something only by taking the responsibility for doing what he is trying to learn to do.

There is a related problem here about which I would like to state another bias; it concerns the question of who should supervise the work with groups—whether this function should go to specialized personnel in group work "departments" or to existing casework staff making itself expert in the new form of service. I believe the latter is the only feasible alternative if the new service is to be securely incorporated as a basic requirement, and if the conditions created are to be the most effective for education of social workers. The unnecessary specializing and the dual supervision that often accompanies it (the group practice supervised by group workers and the casework by caseworkers) create both administrative and technical confusion without any sound professional reasons to justify the arrangement. My position implies that casework supervisors will need to work with groups of their own, at least in the first stages of the enterprise. They can then begin to teach from their own practice, from first-hand experience with the problems their workers are being called upon to face.

It is most important—returning to the note on which I began—that the subject of groups be kept close to the professional experience, uncluttered by any new mystique. To the professional, good practice in any context should have the same moving quality and the same ring of simplicity. Here is a caseworker in one of her first group assignments:

> My opening was brief—after a warm greeting I mentioned that this was the first foster parents group meeting we have held in the community. . . . I continued by stating that we are coming to them, as we recognize that travel can be difficult for them. Several mothers shook their heads vigorously in agreement. I added that being a foster mother is a tough job; but they have it even rougher because the area in which they live lacks so many essential services. We want to know their concerns; and what they think and feel will enable us to learn from and help each other.
>
> I then asked if someone would like to start off. . . .

Later in the meeting:

> From this point, the discussion, which revolved around a foster child's search for identity, became more and more animated. For example, a member felt that it is too painful for a foster child to learn the truth as to why he is different. After a long discussion as to a child's uncomfortable feelings around using a name that is different from that of his foster parent, I asked if we could always protect a child from learning parts of the truth in the outside world. Mrs. W. felt that even though she had told her youngster about his natural mother, the child thinks of her as his "real" mother. This statement brought forth many contributions by the group that were in a similar vein. I added that they seemed to be

> saying that in many senses of the word they are the real mothers. A group member said this was really so; but she thought that a child should be helped to understand that he also had a different biological mother. I said that perhaps if they thought they were the true mothers it might be hard for them to talk to their youngsters about their biological mothers. . . .
>
> Mr. F., a foster father, then spoke. He announced that he guessed he was the first man to speak this morning, and I gave him brief and good humored recognition for this. Mr. F.'s voice was calm and very earnest when he started; but as he finished his comment, his voice broke with emotion. He told the group that he was a stepchild, but that he was never told the truth. He regarded his stepmother as his real mother until he was thirteen years of age, when a distant relative informed him of his true identity. His real mother was not only living, but residing in the community. He described the pain of this sudden discovery, and said he would never want this to happen to his foster children.
>
> There was a hushed silence in the room; but the expressions on the faces of the foster mothers showed that Mr. F. had their sympathetic understanding. I supported Mr. F. by telling him that his sharing of his childhood experience with us certainly helped us understand a great deal.

And here is a group worker talking to an individual member of her group:

> At Coney Island Judy and I were standing alone while the others were on a ride. Judy asked if we were going to the beach, and I said I thought so if they all wanted to go. Judy said she couldn't understand why some people wanted to get tans. She looked up at me pointing to her skin. "You know, most colored people would like to take their color away," and she laughed as if it were the funniest joke. I didn't laugh or say anything, and she added, "It really isn't so pretty." I replied, "On you it looks good, Judy." "No," she answered, "black don't look good on nobody." She didn't move away as I had expected but just stood beside me, now with a perfectly serious face. She seemed to have expressed so directly and with such feeling the essence of this whole issue and struggle. I felt very moved by her words and said, "I guess it is easy for me to say that, just standing here looking at you. But the hard part is to know what you are really feeling like inside your skin." We were interrupted by everyone rushing back, screaming from the ride, and with them I began gathering up things to move to another place. As we started walking along, Judy slipped her arm through mine.

References

1. Warren G. Bennis and Herbert A. Shepard, "A Theory of Group Development," in Warren G. Bennis, Kenneth D. Benne, and Robert Chin (eds.), *The Planning of Change* (New York: Holt, Rinehart & Winston, 1962), pp. 321–40.

2. George Caspar Homans, *Social Behavior: Its Elementary Forms* (New York: Harcourt, Brace & World, 1961).
3. Eduard C. Lindeman, "Group Work and Education for Democracy," *Proceedings of the National Conference of Social Work* (New York: Columbia University Press, 1939), pp. 342–47.
4. Mary Richmond, "Some Next Steps in Social Treatment," *Proceedings of the National Conference of Social Work* (Chicago: University of Chicago Press, 1920), pp. 254–58.
5. William Schwartz, "The Social Worker in the Group," *The Social Welfare Forum, 1961* (New York: Columbia University Press, 1961), pp. 146–77.
6. William Schwartz, "Discussion" (of three papers on the use of the group in providing child welfare services), *Child Welfare,* Vol. 45, No. 10 (December 1966), pp. 571–75.

Between Client and System: The Mediating Function

William Schwartz

The Scientific Paradigm

The profession of social work was born and raised under the influence of a scientific model which showed an objective investigator at work, exploring his materials, learning their properties, and developing skill in manipulating them for the good of society. The scientists and the engineers studied their objects, found the laws that regulated their behavior, and used the knowledge to make nature operate to man's advantage. So, too, in the helping professions: the physician, faced with a person whose machinery had gone wrong, examined it, diagnosed the difficulty, and proceeded to put it back in working order. Following closely, the psychiatrist, the psychologist, the educator, and the social worker took over this view of the helping relationship. They posed the same problems, set themselves the same tasks, and laid their claims to science in the terms laid down by this positivist view of the world. In this conception, an independent worker-*subject* acts upon a client-*object* from a distance, to understand him, to change him, to fix him, using standards drawn from his own special area of expertise.

In its time, this image of science worked very well. It brought man into his age of enlightenment and helped him gain greater control over the world in which he lived. It taught people that they were products of their experience and could, like nature itself, be studied and understood, tested and improved. And it helped create new attitudes toward people in need: if men were made by events, we needed to understand both men and events and not simply judge people in abstract moral terms; further, we had to do something about the conditions of the poor, rather than rely entirely on exhortations to be "worthy" of society's help. To the budding human-relations professions of the

Progressive Era, the spirit of science and experiment lent a view of the client-worker relationship that reflected the modern spirit. It was historical, rational, determinist, prescriptive, individualist, objective.

But something went wrong in the adaptation of this model to the art of human relations. In fact, the very qualities that helped bring these professions into being soon began to tear them apart. The historicism that brought them to the study of causes and effects created a determinism so rigid as to magnify the importance of the past until it blocked out the worker's vision of the present. The rationalism that valued knowledge and logic (Freud's term for his therapy was psycho-*analysis*) turned into what John Dewey later described as the "quest for certainty," where knowledge was considered more elegant than action, and the nonlogical and the intuitive became elements in a lower, "unscientific" order.[1] The prescriptiveness that we borrowed from the doctors helped us to think more specifically about human problems, but it soon came into conflict with our growing emphasis on the importance of self-determination. Further, the stress on individual differences served to focus our attention on the study of human behavior, but the increased preoccupation with early character formation made it too easy to underplay the social and interpersonal forces that continue to change people throughout their lives, as they move from situation to situation. And the objectivity that brought us closer to science and research also created a detachment so formidable that the client suffered from the distance put between him and his helper. In fact, professionalism itself came to be defined as the ability to maintain one's distance from the client; we thus found ourselves bound to what Rollo May called "the traditional doctrine, so limiting, self-contradictory, and indeed often so destructive in psychology, that *the less we are involved in a given situation, the more clearly we can observe the truth.*"[2]

A new vision was needed to illuminate the nature of the helping process. Fixing broken things was not the same sort of work as helping people to mobilize their own energies in their own behalf. The worker-client relationship was one in which the client was not an object at all, but a dynamic force with a will and energy of his own. The client did not hold still to be examined, labeled, and treated, and the engagement was not between a detached expert and malleable entity—between fixer and fixed, teacher and taught, changer and changed. The person in need retained the ultimate power—using it both consciously and unconsciously—to accept help or reject it, and much of the impetus for change came from the client. Thus, even as the worker strove to "enable" his client, he was himself being enabled by the latter's own motives and energies.

---

[1]John Dewey, *The Quest for Certainty: A Study of the Relation of Knowledge and Action* (New York: Putnam, 1929; Capricorn Books, 1960).

[2]Rollo May, "The Origins and Significance of the Existential Movement in Psychology," in Rollo May, Ernest Angel, and Henri F. Ellenberger (eds.), *Existence,* p. 27. Emphasis in original.

A Shifting of Paradigms

In response to these persistent realities, some professionals began to move to a new model of the helping process. This move represented a revolution in thinking similar to that described by Kuhn in his work on the history of science. In his *Structure of Scientific Revolutions,*[3] Kuhn showed that science advances not through a gradual accumulation of bits of knowledge but in a series of dramatic leaps from old ways of looking at the world to radically new ones. As the gestalt changes, the "ducks become rabbits"; the field of inquiry shakes itself loose from the "normal science" of its day and shifts to a new paradigm from which there emerge new kinds of questions and brand new problems for research.

The old paradigm, as Kuhn defined it, is a set of "received beliefs," written into the textbooks of its time and defining the legitimate areas of inquiry. Normal science, productive in its time, sets the tasks for the paradigm, creating a climate in which the professionals all "know what the world is like." They talk the same language, ask the same questions, and work on the same "games and puzzles"—that is, on problems in which the answers are already embedded.

It is the very solidity of this world, however, that makes it necessary ultimately to suppress novelty, motivated by fear that diverse viewpoints might be subversive of the paradigm's basic commitments. "A paradigm can, for that matter, even insulate the community from those socially important problems that are not reducible to the puzzle form, because they cannot be stated in terms of the conceptual and instrumental tools the paradigm supplies."[4] This effort is not conspiratorial; it is simply part of a historical process through which a field of inquiry moves as it passes from the preconsensual stage, to that of normal science, to the transcendant revolutionary leap. In any event, the jump from normal science is precipitated by the fact that science cannot suppress its novelties indefinitely, since it is not in its nature to tolerate the arbitrary for too long. In time, the paradigm begins to spring leaks; and it develops a number of anomalies—phenomena that are contradictory and do not square with expectations.

It is at this point, said Kuhn, that there "begin the extraordinary investigations that lead the profession at last to a new set of commitments, a new basis for the practice of science."[5] He showed how such revolutions took place in the fields of light, heat, electricity, astronomy, and others, describing how scientists emerged, after the crisis, into a world that was almost literally transformed:

> Led by a new paradigm, scientists adopt new instruments and look in new places. Even more important, during revolutions scientists see new and different things when looking with familiar instruments in

---

[3]Thomas S. Kuhn, *The Structure of Scientific Revolutions.*

[4]*Ibid.,* p. 37.

[5]*Ibid.,* p. 6.

places they have looked before. It is rather as if the professional community has been suddenly transported to another planet where familiar objects are seen in a different light and joined by unfamiliar ones as well. . . . In so far as their only recourse to the world is through what they see and do, we may want to say that after a revolution scientists are responding to a different world.[6]

In all this, the analogy to social work development can be overdrawn; the social sciences in general are still in what Kuhn called the preparadigm state. But the similarities are striking, nonetheless. We too have our received beliefs, embodied in the paradigm of study-diagnosis-treatment as it was taken over from medicine, research, and positivist science. We have our consensualized language, and the games and puzzles that frame only certain kinds of questions and can imagine no others.[7] We have our stubborn contradictions, the anomalies that face us at every turn: the need to hedge on the sequential character of study, diagnosis, and treatment, maintaining that each step occurs simultaneously, since the imagined process is so obviously at odds with what actually happens between worker and client; the vexing inability to reconcile the demands for both prescriptiveness and self-determination; the call for both professional detachment and deep empathy in the same relationship; the problem of integrating concepts of changing people with those of helping them; and many others. And the crisis is unmistakable as professionals try to live with the traditional subject-object view of the helping relationship.

The problem that faces the social work profession, and the other helping disciplines as well, is to describe an art whose achievements depend only partly on the skill of the artist. Since his power is a function of the power of his materials—his clients—a model is needed that will show the acts of the professional as a force exerted not only on people but in interdependent relations with them. The worker-client engagement is one in which, in Parson's terms, "the *relations* determine the properties of its parts."[8] Or we may view it as Frank's "organized complexity," where "we need to think in terms of circular, reciprocal relations and feed backs . . . through which the component members of the field participate in and thereby create the field of the whole, which field in turn regulates and patterns their individual activities."[9] The

---

[6]*Ibid.*, p. 110.

[7]A colleague asked, incredulously: "If you don't teach diagnosis and treatment goals, what can you teach at all?"

[8]Talcott Parsons, *The Structure of Social Action* (Glencoe, Ill.: Free Press, 1949), p. 32. Emphasis added.

[9]Lawrence K. Frank, "Research for What?" *Journal of Social Issues,* Suppl. Ser. No. 10 (1957), p. 12. Frank also refers to Albert Einstein and Leopold Infeld, *The Evolution of Physics* (Cambridge, England: Cambridge University Press: New York: Simon and Schuster, 1938), p. 259, where these authors point out that "it needed great scientific imagination to realize that it is not the charges nor the particles, but the *field in the space between* charges and the particles, which is essential for the description of physical events. . . ." (emphasis in original).

language of description will have to be a language of action, showing how the worker *moves,* and not only what he knows, what he values, and what he hopes to achieve. In effect, such a model undertakes to describe *separately* a number of professional acts that are virtually *inseparable* from those of clients around him. It is indeed a different world for the professional who changes his image from that of a fixer of broken objects to that of a participant in a network of active, reciprocal relationships, where he finds his own special piece of the action and then fashions the skills necessary to carry it out.

Theoretical Foundations

The new gestalt that springs from all this does not abandon what was useful in the old. Kuhn himself noted that "the new paradigm must promise to preserve a relatively large part of the concrete problem-solving ability that has accrued to science through its predecessors."[10] In fact, many of the necessary themes are there in our history, running underground for part of the way but surfacing in certain features of the old paradigm itself. When they do, they are frequently honored more in the breach than the observance—as when we devise a "treatment plan" for a client without reference to his work on the problem, even as we stress his right to self-determination. For when two sets of desirable but opposing aspirations cannot be reconciled, we tend to act on one and pay homage to the other.

It was, in fact, a version of the reciprocal construct on which John Dewey based his interactionist view of the teaching-learning process, although he found few, even among those in progressive education, who understood what he meant and could translate his vision into a theory of pedagogy.[11] Martin Buber tried to find a reciprocal language, distinguishing between the interdependent relationship of "I-Thou" and the detached, subject-object encounter that he called "I-It."[12] As Buber explored the "dialogical" character of human relations, he showed us two men observing each other:

> The essential thing is not that the one makes the other his object, but the fact that he is not fully able to do so, and the reason for his failure. We have in common with all existing beings that we can be made objects of observation. But it is my privilege as man that by the hidden activity of my being I can establish an impassable barrier to objectification. Only in partnership can my being be perceived as an existing whole.[13]

---

[10]Kuhn, *Structure of Scientific Revolutions,* p. 168.

[11]The most systematic presentation of Dewey's ideas on education can be found in John Dewey, *Democracy and Education.*

[12]Martin Buber, *I and Thou* (2d ed.; New York: Scribner, 1958).

[13]Martin Buber, "The William Alanson White Memorial Lectures, Fourth Series," *Psychiatry,* 20:106 (May 1957).

Buber's "barrier to objectification" is the central theme of any reciprocal, transactional approach to the helping process.[14] The tradition from which it draws is part of the historic revolt against Descartes' early 17th century polarization of the self and the environment, his dichotomy of feeling and intellect, and his rigid definition of science as the study of that which is external and visible.[15] The opposition to this individualist and objectivist thesis has surfaced in every generation since, taking one form or another as part of the history of philosophy, the physical sciences, and the social sciences. Wherever it appears, its ideas are expressed through a curiosity about processes, the nature of experience, the influence of feelings on human behavior, and the conduct of people in interaction.[16] Gordon Allport has traced the development of two antithetical traditions: the one, engendered by John Locke, an admirer of Descartes, stresses the "scientific," environmental, behavioristic factors in human psychology; the other, begun by G. W. Leibnitz soon after the death of Descartes, emphasized the purposive, internal forces of man, and led toward the work of Kant, Herbart, Wundt, and the gestalt psychologists.[17]

Soren Kierkegaard, a contemporary of Freud's who went unnoticed by the new human relations professions, pointed out that "truth exists only as the individual himself produces it in action."[18] Rousseau's intuitionism, Jame's phenomenology, and Dewey's analysis of the emotional aspects of human experience, all helped to translate the tradition into a new view of the educational enterprise. Mary Follett, a social philosopher of the Progressive Era, helped lay the foundations of social work thinking with her observation that "experience is the power-house where purpose and will, thought and ideals, are being generated."[19] And in the present day, social workers with an existential perspective have stressed the antiindividualist theme:

> To understand existentialism it is essential to have a feel for its conception of man's most fundamental need that distinguishes him as a human being. This may be described as the hunger for unity, belonging, eternalization of personality by somehow overcoming the separateness he

---

[14]For further elaboration of Buber's ideas on "objectification" in human relations, see Maurice Friedman's introductory essay in Martin Buber, *The Knowledge of Man: Selected Essays,* edited by Friedman (New York: Harper & Row, Torchbooks, 1965), pp. 11–58.

[15]Rene Descartes, *Discourse on Method and Other Writings,* translated with an introduction by F. E. Sutcliffe (Baltimore: Penguin, 1968).

[16]See Rollo May, "Origins and Significance of the Existential Movement in Psychology," in May, Angel, and Ellenberger (eds.), *Existence,* pp. 3–36. See also Fritz Heider, "On Lewin's Methods and Theory," *Journal of Social Issues,* Suppl. Ser. No. 13 (1959), pp. 3–13. See also William Schwartz, "Social Group Work: The Interactionist Approach," *Encyclopedia of Social Work* (2 vols., 16th ed.; New York: NASW, 1971), 2:1252–63.

[17]Gordon W. Allport, *Becoming: Basic Considerations for a Psychology of Personality* (New Haven: Yale University Press, 1955).

[18]Cited by May, "Origins and Significance of the Existential Movement," p. 12.

[19]Mary P. Follett, *Creative Experience* (New York: Longmans, Green, 1930), p. 133.

feels between parts of himself, as well as between himself, others, and the universe as a whole.[20]

In fact, the ideas that helped fashion our concepts of social interaction and social influence, as well as the empirical work that elaborated these ideas, have flowed from so many sources that it would take an essay as long as this one merely to trace its barest outlines. For those interested in the most recent philosophical implications of the existential view as it is joined to latterday phenomenology, Luijpen's book on the subject has interesting implications for a professional's view of human behavior.[21]

In psychiatry, Freud himself, representing as he did the prototype of positivist science, also provided entry for the dark forces of subjectivity and irrationalism in his therapeutic emphasis on feeling, instinct, and the unconscious. And his successors—Adler, Horney, Rank, and others—developed and enriched his concept of the ego and its efforts to gain control of its immediate environment. In psychology, the theoretical and experimental work of Carl Rogers directed attention to the details of the helping process, stressing the powers of the patient and the efforts of the therapist to enter into a genuine collaboration with him; Gordon and others carried the Rogerian implications into work with groups.[22]

In sociology, the stream of thought flows from Cooley and McDougall, who gave us our first real glimpses into the entity of group, over and above the properties of its individual members,[23] to the contemporary work of Parsons, Frank, and Grinker, whose emphasis on the organic whole brought the interactional insight to its most dramatic development and helped us begin to grasp the idea of group-as-client.[24] In social psychology, we learned about the uses of spontaneity from Jennings and Moreno,[25] the effects of group pressure on individual judgments from the experiments of Asch[26] and

---

[20]Donald F. Krill, "Existentialism: A Philosophy for Our Current Revolutions," *Social Service Review,* 40:292 (September 1966).

[21]William A. Luijpen, *Existential Phenomenology* (rev. ed.; Pittsburgh: Duquesne University Press, 1969).

[22]Carl R. Rogers, *Client-Centered Therapy* (Boston: Houghton Mifflin, 1951.) See also Carl R. Rogers, "The Process Equation of Psychotherapy," *American Journal of Psychotherapy,* 15:124–46 (1961); Thomas Gordon, *Group-Centered Leadership* (New York: Houghton Mifflin; Cambridge, Mass.: Riverside Press, 1955).

[23]Charles Horton Cooley, *Social Organization* (New York: Scribner, 1909); and W. McDougall, *The Group Mind* (New York: Putnam, 1920).

[24]Talcott Parsons, *The Social System* (Glencoe, Ill.: Free Press, 1951); Frank, "Research for What?"; and Roy R. Grinker et al., *Psychiatric Social Work: A Transactional Case Book* (New York: Basic Books, 1961).

[25]Helen Jennings, Leadership and Isolation (New York: Longmans, Green, 1943); Jacob L. Moreno, *Who Shall Survive* (Washington, D.C.: Nervous and Mental Diseases Publishing, 1934) Jacob L. Moreno, "Foundations of Sociometry," *Sociometry,* 4:15–35 (February 1941).

[26]Solomon E. Asch, "Effects of Group Pressure Upon the Modification and Distortion of Judgments," in Eleanor E. Maccoby, Theodore M. Newcomb, and Eugene L. Hartley (eds.), *Readings in Social Psychology* (3d ed.; New York: Holt, 1958), pp. 174–83.

Lewin,[27] the analysis of interaction from Bales,[28] the effects of different leadership styles from the work of Lewin and his colleagues,[29] and, most recently, the history of the nonverbal, "beyond science" tradition embodied in the sensitivity and encounter movements from Kurt Back.[30]

In an interesting way, we may also be said to have learned from the behaviorists and their concern with action; their interest in external behavior is akin to our preoccupation with the observable skills of the worker in interaction with his client. In fact, whether or not we agree with his methods, B. F. Skinner has shown a greater concern with the process of teaching than have the proponents of progressive education themselves.[31]

Again, a thorough review of all the appropriate theory and research that has led us to our present understanding of a way in which "the word of address and the word of response live in the same language,"[32] would take a long effort of its own; this writer has essayed three such reviews, from the perspective of the history of small-group study.[33]

Thus, it can be seen that the basic elements for a radical shift in our view of the helping process have been developing for generations, contributing steadily to social work—and group work—theory, but always somehow in contradiction to the accepted positivist gestalt and never put together in a coherent and consistent pattern of ideas that would help us build a reciprocal model of the worker and his clients in action. What was actually called for was a kind of "relativity theory" of human relations, along the lines of the uncertainty physics of Bohr and Heisenberg, and in the sense that Polanyi meant it as he discussed the discovery of relativity. "When Einstein discovered rationality in nature," he wrote, "unaided by any observation that had not been available for at least fifty years before, our positivistic textbooks promptly covered up the scandal by an appropriately embellished account of his discovery." Polanyi then continued:

---

[27]Kurt Lewin, "Conduct, Knowledge, and Acceptance of New Values," in Lewin, *Resolving Social Conflicts: Selected Papers on Group Dynamics* (New York: Harper, 1948), pp. 56–68.

[28]Robert F. Bales, *Interaction Process Analysis: A Method for the Study of Small Groups* (Cambridge, Mass.: Addison-Wesley, 1950).

[29]Ronald Lippitt and Ralph K. White, "An Experimental Study of Leadership and Group Life," in Maccoby, Newcomb, and Hartley (eds.), *Social Psychology,* pp. 496–511.

[30]Kurt W. Back, *Beyond Words: The Story of Sensitivity Training and the Encounter Movement* (New York: Russell Sage Foundation, 1972).

[31]See, for example, B. F. Skinner, "Why Teachers Fail," *Saturday Review,* October 16, 1965, pp. 80–81, 98–102. See also, for an excellent summary of the behaviorist contribution to the tasks of practice, Robert D. Carter and Richard B. Stuart, "Behavior Modification Theory and Practice: A Reply," *Social Work,* 15:37–50 (January 1970).

[32]Buber, *I and Thou,* p. 103.

[33]William Schwartz, "Small Group Science and Group Work Practice," *Social Work,* 8:39–46 (October 1963), "Neighborhood Centers," in Henry S. Mass (ed.), *Five Fields of Social Service: Reviews of Research* (New York: NASW, 1966), pp. 144–84; "Neighborhood Centers and Group Work," in Henry S. Mass (ed.), *Research in the Social Services: A Five-Year Review* (New York: NASW, 1971), pp. 130–91.

There is an aspect of this story that is even more curious. For the programme which Einstein carried out was largely prefigured by the very positivist conception of science which his own achievement so flagrantly refuted. It was formulated explicitly by Ernst Mach, who . . . had extensively criticized Newton's definition of space and absolute rest on the grounds that it said nothing that could be tested by experience. He condemned this as dogmatic, since it went beyond experience, and as *meaningless,* since it pointed to nothing that could conceivably be tested by experience. Mach urged that Newtonian dynamics should be reformulated so as to avoid referring to any movement of bodies except as the relative motion of bodies with respect to each other, and Einstein acknowledged the 'profound influence' which Mach's book exercised on him as a boy and subsequently on his discovery of relativity.[34]

Toward a Theory of Practice

Polanyi's admonition "to avoid referring to any movement of bodies except as the relative motion of bodies with respect to each other," is apt for social work as well. The model of the open, organismic system offers us the opportunity to put together all the dimensions we need into an image of the helping relationship in action. The systems idea is far-reaching, ranging across the whole scientific spectrum; Bertalanffy called it "a new world view of considerable impact."[35] But we do not need the whole technology for our purposes. What we do need are certain basic features to which the model calls attention: bodies in motion within a limited space, the interdependence of parts, the division of labor and the interplay of functions, the specificity of purpose, and the permeability of boundaries between the organism and its environment.[36]

The systems terminology is growing in popularity, precisely because it promises to meet the need for an active and reciprocal view so sorely missed in our traditional descriptions of the helping process. But too often it is only the words that are used, rather than the total gestalt; the latter would require a surrender of the old paradigm, rather than simply garnishing it with up-to-

---

[34]Michael Polanyi, *Personal Knowledge: Towards a Post-Critical Philosophy* (New York: Harper & Row, Torchbooks, 1964), p. 11. (Emphasis in original.)

[35]Ludwig von Bertalanffy, *General System Theory: Foundations, Development, Applications* (New York: Braziller, 1968), p. vii.

[36]Definitions vary in complexity, but these are the most concise: "A system is a set of objects together with relationships between the objects and between their attributes." "The analytic model of system demands that we treat the phenomena and the concepts for organizing the phenomena as if there existed organization, interaction, interdependency, and integration of parts and elements." And "system is typically understood as a whole made up of interdependent and interacting parts." A. D. Hall and R. E. Fagen, "Definition of System," in Walter Buckley (ed.), *Modern Systems Research for the Behavioral Scientist. A Sourcebook* (Chicago: Aldine, 1968) p. 81; Robert Chin, "The Utility of System Models and Developmental Models for Practitioners," in Warren G. Bennis, Kenneth D. Beene, and Robert Chin (eds.), *The Planning of Change: Readings in the Applied Behavioral Sciences* (New York: Holt, Rinehart, and Winston, 1962), p. 203; Irma Stein, *Systems Theory, Science, and Social Work* (Metuchen, N. J.: Scarecrow Press, 1974), p. 3.

date terms. The models are in fact irreconcilable: either the ducks become rabbits or they remain ducks. The effort to have it both ways produces strange effects, as when the worker is said to intervene in the client-worker system. The idea of intervening in a system of which one is an integral part violates the whole model and obscures the tasks it sets before us.

In social work these tasks are as relevant to the worker-individual relationship as they are to the worker-in-the-group. The tasks begin with the search for a function for which the professional should be held accountable, whatever the relational system in which he operates. The statement of function must be phrased in active terms, describing what social workers *do,* showing how these acts affect, and are affected by, the acts of others within the system in which they meet. Further, the description must make it clear that the worker operates within an immediate sphere of influence, touching directly only those with whom he interacts, within the limits of his specific function within the system.

By the function of the profession is meant not its hopes and visions of the outcome, but its specific part in the division of labor, both in the larger social system from which it takes its assignment and in the smaller subsystems in which its practitioners work—the one-to-one, the family, the committee, the peer group, and others. In each of these, the worker's acts are adaptations of his general function, showing his part in the division of labor: how he translates his knowledge and purpose into skill.

Practice theory—what Loeb called a "professional science"[37]—leans heavily on both knowledge and philosophy, but it cannot end there. For a theory of practice is a theory of action, and action is not deducible from either knowledge or intention working alone. If we knew everything there is to know, we would still have to decide what to do; and if our purposes were impeccable, the action based on them would still not be self-evident. Each of these areas influence and limit each other in every specific situation: given the appropriate evidence, and given a set of valued outcomes, the principles of action provide the implementing force. Throughout any practice theory we might build, every step must show how we bring together science, policy, and action within a total scheme.[38]

A Concept of Function

The effort to find a general function for social work in our society is complicated by the very wide range of jobs and settings in which it has worked over the past hundred years—from rent-collecting to psychotherapy, recreation

---

[37]Martin B. Loeb, "The Backdrop for Social Research: Theory-Making and Model-Building," in Leonard S. Kogan (ed.), *Social Science Theory and Social Work Research* (New York: NASW, 1960), p. 11.

[38]For further discussion, see William Schwartz, "Toward a Strategy of Group Work Practice," *Social Service Review,* vol. 36 (September 1962).

leadership to social action, family counseling, neighborhood organization, athletic coaching, child placement, and other functions, performed in settlement houses, family agencies, sectarian community centers, camps, playgrounds, hospitals, children's institutions, industry, and many other auspices. The common themes have not been easy to uncover. But there is one that has asserted itself continuously over the years: the preoccupation with the "social" begins with the name of the occupation itself and repeats itself in its attention to the psychosocial, social relationships, social functioning, social action, and the like. Still, as they stand, such terms are inchoate, expressing more a concern and an aspiration than an active function for the profession. To do that, there must be some description of the forces into which social workers wish to move, and how they plan to affect such forces. To say that we are concerned with the social is almost tautological, since it is hardly possible for any profession to exist without some sense of urgency about the conditions in which it works. As Pray noted:

> The word "social" has none of the precision of such words as "medical" or "legal". . . . It is obviously not enough to say that social work treats "social" problems. For virtually every life problem of every individual in this modern world is, in reality, a "social" problem in one sense or another.[39]

The tendency to see the social merely as the situation, and to demand simply that "it" be taken into account, fails to find the specific processes we want to address. Historically, it has set the scene for the ancient quarrel between those who would—as if they could—choose one or the other, the individual or society, therapy or social planning.[40] And those who have urged that we do both, or assign primary and secondary emphases to one or the other, have helped to maintain the dualism and failed equally to find what Jessie Taft called the "living relationship" between individual needs and their collective, institutionalized forms.

The author's reading of history suggests that social work's function in the society we know has been most powerfully expressed when it directs itself not to the individual *or* the social but to the relationship between the two. Social workers seem clearest about what they are doing when they are addressing themselves to the energies that flow in both directions between people and their institutions—to the reaching and pressuring and straining that goes on between them as both strive to carry out their sense of need and purpose. The relationship between people and their environment begins as a symbiotic one,

---

[39]Kenneth L. M. Pray, "When is Community Organization Social Work Practice?" in Pray, *Social Work in a Revolutionary Age and Other Papers* (Philadelphia: University of Pennsylvania Press, 1949), p. 275).

[40]For further discussion of this issue, see William Schwartz, "Private Troubles and Public Issues: One Social Work Job or Two?" *Social Welfare Forum, 1969* (New York: Columbia University Press, 1969).

with each needing the other for its own life and growth, and each reaching out to the other with all the strength it can command at a given moment.[41] In any complex system, however, and particularly one in which great power exists and is unequally distributed, a force is needed to guard the symbiotic strivings and keep the interaction alive when each party is tempted to dismiss the other as unreachable. But whether the relationship is harmonious or conflicted, the function of social work is to mediate the transactions between people and the various systems through which they carry on their relationships with society—the family, the peer group, the social agency, the neighborhood, the school, the job, and others. The mediating skills are designed to create not harmony but interaction, based on a sense of strength, feeling, and purpose, drawing on the often all-but-forgotten stake of people in their own institutions, and of the institutions in the people they are meant to serve. The worker's job analysis, in any specific system in which he and client find themselves, can thus be expressed as follows:

> If each service system is . . . regarded as a special case, or small version, of the individual-social relationship, the social worker's skills are fashioned by two interrelated responsibilities: he must help each individual client negotiate the system immediately crucial to his problems; and he must help the system reach out to incorporate the client, deliver its service, and thus carry out its function in the community.[42]

The relationship of forces is presented diagrammatically below. This model may be used at two different levels of abstraction: on the one hand, it shows the general function of social work in society; on the other, it depicts the specific relationships at work in any given situation.

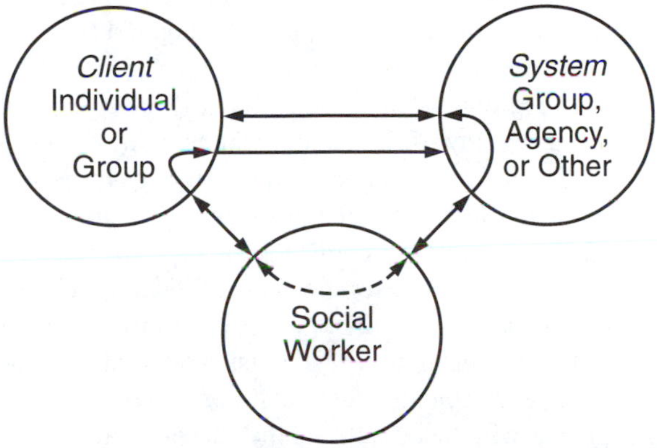

This arrangement shows the impetus of the client (individual or group) toward its system, and the system (group, or agency, or family, or school, or

[41]For further discussion, see William Schwartz, "The Social Worker in the Group," *Social Welfare Forum, 1961* (New York: Columbia University Press, 1961).

[42]Schwartz, "Social Group Work," p. 1258.

other) toward its member or client. It also shows the lines along which the social worker uses his skills to encourage the approaches of each toward each. These approaches may involve conflict, cooperation, confrontation, negotiation, or any other form of exchange emerging from the realities of the situation. Again, the demand is not for conciliation, but for a realistic exchange, based on the actual business between them.

The Worker and the Group

When we consider this arrangement as a picture of the social worker in the client group, we have the characteristic two-client responsibility well known to group workers. In part of his work, he addresses himself to each member—in the member's part-whole relationship to the group which he needs to negotiate. In the other aspect, his client is the collective itself, the group-as-a-whole, as it moves to negotiate the larger systems of which it is a part—the agency, the neighborhood, the peer-group culture, and others. As the worker moves into this small-group system, he finds himself in *a collection of people who need each other to work on certain common tasks, in an agency that is hospitable to those tasks.* The group is a project in mutual aid, focussed on certain specific problems, and set within a larger system—the agency—whose function it is to provide help with just such problems. It is an alliance of moving, interdependent beings, each pursuing his own purposes together with others similarly engaged.

The worker is one of those moving parts, and his professional function is conceived in action terms, which are then elaborated in the specific acts and skills designed to carry it out. The worker's movements must reflect the movements of the others, as he acts to help others act. His moves are directed toward specific purposes, limited in scope and time, and touching only those within his immediate reach.

The definition of group as presented above is specific enough, and yet broad enough, to include any of the client groupings in which social workers are apt to function. It has four major features: the group is a *collective,* in which people face and interact with each other; the people *need each other* for certain specific purposes; they come together to *work on common tasks;* and the work is embedded in a relevant *agency function.* The designation is *specific* in that it demands an identifiable group purpose, and is stated not in vague, aspirational form but in active, understandable tasks. And it is *broad* in that it makes few requirements other than that the people need each other and can work together, with help, on tasks they accept and understand.

In this sense, the formulation is not limited by whether the group is natural or formed, therapeutic or task-oriented, open or closed, voluntary or captive, time-limited or extended, age-or-sex homogeneous or heterogeneous, or other quite legitimate small-group distinctions that will of course affect the nature of the group processes, but will leave intact the model diagrammed above and the professional function illustrated there. The requirements are simply that people can give and take from each other however slight their capabilities, that the agency and the worker have some stake, however slight, in allowing the freedom to work, and that there is some real reason for the people to be together.

The professional acts that are fashioned by this arrangement of separate and interdependent forces, each pursuing its own function and purpose, can be described most clearly with reference to the time in which they occur. The sequence of acts divides itself naturally into four phases, extending from the worker's preparation for entry, to his beginnings in the group, to the actual work on the tasks that brought them together, to the processes of ending and separation. These phases can be viewed both as they cover the entire life of the group and the events of a single meeting: from either perspective there is a preparation, a beginning, a period of work, and an ending that is either permanent or transitional to the next encounter.

The Phases of Work

There is space here only to develop a general strategy for each phase of work, with just enough specificity to demonstrate the mode of analysis. In response to the aforementioned need to bring together the elements of science, policy, and action, each phase must address three major questions. First, what *assumptions* can we make about the laws of nature appropriate to the tasks of the worker in this phase? Some of these assumptions may have been tested, some not, but in either event the judgments are operative and need to be brought into the open in a form that is clear and arguable. Second, what are the immediate *valued outcomes* that need to be brought about? The key here is immediacy: the worker's expectations are focussed on next steps rather than long-range goals that are only abstractly related to the work at hand. And third, given these assumptions and these immediate expectations, what are the *implementing acts* which the worker may bring to bear?

The "Tuning-In"

As the worker prepares himself to enter (or reenter) the group, he must understand that the life-processes with which he is about to join forces began long before he came, will continue after he leaves, and will, even during his tenure, be subject to many influences other than his own. The worker is about to move toward processes already in motion, establish his function quickly, do his job, and leave. These preparations, which he will go through each time he readies himself for a new beginning, are based on a number of assumptions about human behavior. He knows, for example, that there is a continuity in human experience, which means that people's expectations in new situations will be built on their memories of old ones. Thus he knows, too, that people will tend to respond, in these new situations, as they think others expect them to respond. Further, he suspects that beginnings tend to stir up feelings of self-doubt and hesitancy about one's competence to play the new game. With regard to the worker's own reception, he may assume that a new authority will engender both a fear of new demands and a heightened initial dependency, with expectations of reward and love. And he expects that these cues and others will be communicated in a kind of code; that his clients will convey directly, to him and to each other, only a small part of how they feel.

There are, of course, many other assumptions relevant to this phase of work, governing the members' ambivalence about work itself, the group climate in the opening stages, the members' demands on each other, and more. What is important is not that the worker build a ready-made inventory of all the possible hypotheses, but that he identify as many as will help him sensitize himself to the possibilities inherent in the forthcoming encounter.

The valued outcomes of this opening phase consist in the worker's ability to "tune" himself to the coded messages and disguised meanings through which the members will be communicating their messages as they begin the work together. His is a kind of preliminary empathy, as illustrated by the young worker who had tuned herself so keenly to the feelings of old people in a home that when they commented on how young and pretty she was, she smiled and replied: "I know, but I'll do the best I can." In such an exercise, the worker is less interested in drawing pictures of the outcomes (goals) and analyzing the structures of each client (diagnoses) than in visualizing the terms of the future encounter—the actions and reactions through which he and the members will deal with each other in the opening stages of the experience. He does not ignore prior knowledge of the class of clients or the specific personalities, but operationalizes this knowledge by anticipating the possibilities and rehearsing his expectations. He wants to bring himself to understand how they may perceive him, how his own sensations will connect with theirs, and how he may decode their meanings from the symbols they use.

The skills of the tuning-in phase are largely empathic, invoking demands similar to those made on the actor, who must generate from his own imagination the feeling and color of another's experience, particularly when the one is as yet unknown to him. It is something like the Stanislavskian effort to help actors create a new experience by using both their knowledge and their feelings, their observations and their instincts. The worker's exercise in preliminary empathy demands a similar ability to connect his thoughts and his emotions as he readies himself for his opening moves with the clients. In addition, he needs skill in both generalizing and partializing the data at his command—both organizing the bits of information into a pattern of expectations and breaking down his general knowledge into smaller propositions that are relevant both to the class of clients he is to meet (the aged, or foster children, or parents of the handicapped) and to the particular members (*these* aged, *these* children) whose folders he has before him. The process of generalizing must make the worker *more* receptive, rather than, by stereotyping ("poor people don't verbalize," "deaf children can't conceptualize"), less so. Thus, it is important that the worker's heightened attention to certain expected cues not serve to cut out his peripheral vision for those he does not anticipate. And finally, the tuning-in skills are strategic in nature, involving his plans for bringing clients and agency together in the work that lies before them. Using his knowledge of both the client stake and the agency interest, he prepares to ask both members and agency representatives to enter into open, unjargonized recognition of what the work will be about.

The Beginnings

The second phase is that in which the worker moves into the group and asks both members and agency to make their beginnings under clear conditions of work. In the group he asks for an explicit understanding of what they are there for; and in the agency he verifies the nature of the service and the contract that exists between the agency and the group. To the worker, this relationship between these clients and this agency is a special case of the processes through which people and their society reach out to each other, and the terms of this particular engagement will first show themselves in the opening stages of their relationship.

The heart of these beginnings is the contracting process, and several assumptions underlie the work. First, the new relationship will engender certain demands and expectations of each upon the other, and these demands will create certain behaviors and forces at work, whether or not they are verbalized, or even recognized, by clients and agency. Second, these demands and expectations are further complicated by the small group itself, where there is a complex interaction of individual stakes, where there is a shifting consensus of how these should be expressed, and where the new client—the group itself—is put into interaction with the agency. Third, and for reasons not well understood, any direct statement of what these demands and expectations are is experienced by both sides as embarrassing and taboo. In fact, the theoretical importance of the contracting process lies precisely in the fact that direct statements of mutual expectation are perceived as rude and impolite, that consequently the client-agency engagement is often replete with hidden agendas, and that a force is needed that is uninhibited by such taboos. Fourth, the taboo about explicit purposes creates an ambiguous framework within which it is difficult for the clients to choose their responses. Fifth, the vagueness also tends to create a prolonged period of testing during which the members make covert attempts to discover the nature of the enterprise, the rules of the game, and what the worker represents. Building from one consequence to the next, a sixth assumption would be that the ambiguity and the testing creates a greater fear of the power of the agency and the worker's power, under cover of clarity, to invade their lives without restriction. Contrariwise, a further assumption is that a clear consensus on group purpose limits the claims of each upon the other—client on service, service on client, and even client on client. There are a number of other propositions dealing with the more general problem of beginnings—on the effects of new situations, on the interactions they foster, on the fear of being tested in unfamiliar situations, on the hopes engendered, and more. In addition, further hypotheses are needed to explicate the ways in which each meeting of the group constitutes an entity with its own beginning, middle, and end.

Moving to the valued outcomes, what the worker wants to help bring about in this phase is an opening consensus: from the members, on what they need, and from the agency representatives, on what they offer. The worker also wants a partialization of tasks, beginning to break down the work before them into some of the specific jobs of which it is composed. And he seeks to help establish some of the ground rules and procedures designed to move them as quickly as possible to a collaborative and independent style of problem-solving.

The skills of the beginning phase begin with the worker's ability to feel his way so deeply into both the client need and the agency service that he can make a simple statement of their connections. If there is a viable relationship—not necessarily harmonious—between the agency and its clients, and a real service and an urgent need, then an agent is needed who will understand both the service and the need and accept both stakes without reservation or embarrassment. If there is not such a relationship, the contracting process is defeated from the outset, and the defeat lies hidden behind jargon and obscure agendas that none is brave enough to pierce. The worker's skills also extend to his ability to reach for feedback and encourage specifics, refusing to allow comfortable but fuzzy formulations to rest undisturbed. He must also learn to make the "demand for work" with which he challenges the members to move through their timidity to the words and feelings they need to express in order to own their problems and aspirations without coloring them in euphemisms. In this stage, the worker prepares himself to monitor the terms of the contract; later, he may have occasion to ask both group and agency to renegotiate as they pass through the various stages of the work.

The Tasks

The tasks of the middle phase have been elaborated elsewhere in some detail.[43] Briefly, there is the search for common ground between the needs of clients and those of the systems they have to negotiate. There is the process of detecting and challenging the obstacles that come between the members and their systems. There is the worker's responsibility for contributing ideas, facts, and values, as he feels these data may be useful to the members in the course of the work. Further, the worker needs to share his own vision of the work, his feelings about the process, and his faith in the clients' strengths. Finally, he must help to define the limits and requirements of the situation in which the work takes place. Each of these tasks requires its own framework of professional assumptions, valued outcomes, and strategies for action. For example, the worker's search for common ground proceeds partly from the assumption that an individual's major access to new ideas lies in his sense of their usefulness to him, and in his consequent ability to invest feeling in the job of making them his. Similarly, with respect to the common-ground task,

[43]Schwartz, "Social Worker in the Group," pp. 156–70.

the worker will have in mind the valued outcome of having the client examine his self-interest, situation by situation, in very specific terms. And, with regard to his strategy, he will be reaching repeatedly for feelings of self-interest that are buried under considerations of politeness, self-denial, and the desire to cooperate with one's oppressor.

In this fashion, each of the major tasks of the worker in this phase is powered by specific assumptions, valued outcomes, and actions:

> . . . all call for explicit variations on the symbiotic theme; each demands specific hypotheses on the nature of self-interest, the relationship between people and their systems, the group processes through which pooled self-interest yields a social product, how both individuals and systems strive simultaneously for equilibrium and change, the role of the mediating authority, and others. The immediate outcomes, throughout, are envisaged by the worker as the investment of affect, the engagement of energies, the expression of conflict, and the translation of feelings and ideas into work. And the professional skills involve the ability to decode messages, to reach for ambiguities, to probe for negatives, to show love and energy in the work, to partialize tasks, to point up the connections between fragments of experience, to find and mobilize resources, and, throughout, to make the "demand for work" inherent in the contract and in his helping function.[44]

Transitions and Endings

In the final phase of work, the essential task is to make a transition from one stage of experience to the next. In both the temporary endings that mark the passage from one meeting to the next and the final separation that brings the entire experience to a close, there are a number of problems concerning the uses of time, the way energy is distributed in beginnings, middles, and endings, and the relationship between the opening and closing phases of group experience. There has been little experimental work on the subject of time and the group experience; the most valuable studies have been philosophical and poetic. However, we might hazard a few assumptions based on experience with groups.[45] For example, group records indicate that, as part of an ebb and flow of productive work, there tends to be a rush of energy toward the closing moments of the group meeting. This phenomenon can be called "doorknob therapy," in which the members seem to save their most important disclosures for the time when they are on their way out of the door. Subse-

[44]Schwartz, "Social Group Work," pp. 1260–61.

[45]For an excellent description of developmental stages in groups, based on analysis of agency records, see James A. Garland, Hubert E. Jones, and Ralph L. Kolodny, "A Model of Stages of Development in Social Work Groups," in Saul Bernstein (ed.), *Explorations in Group Work* (Boston: Boston University School of Social Work, 1968), pp. 12–53.

quent attempts by the worker to tack these subjects onto the following meeting fail almost invariably, revealing another interesting fact about group experience—namely, that the meeting does not end when it is over, but moves, via the informal system, into an interim phase of communication in which the difference is that the worker is not present. This is another way of saying that the life of a group does not proceed in quantum jumps, but in a continuous and unbroken process, with the meetings constituting a special—but not an isolated—event in that process. Thus, in a group that meets weekly for ten weeks, there is a considerable difference in whether the life of the group is regarded as ten meetings or ten weeks.

The permanent ending that brings the group life to a close seems to go through a number of stages, protracted or brief depending on the variables of *authority* (their use of the worker) and *intimacy* (their use of each other). There is an evasive period, in which the prospect of ending is ignored and denied. There is a sullen, angry stage, in which the worker finds himself back in the beginning aspects of the relationship, resisted and suspected. There is a period of mourning, in which the members are close to their complex feelings about the worker and the others in the group, and are capable of intensive work on the meaning to them of the experience. Finally, if there is time and skill in dealing with the mourning period, there is a kind of graduation effect—the future is regarded with optimism, there is a tendency to reject the worker, and there is considerable rehearsing for new stages of experience. The resistance to endings seems to be marked by a general reluctance to tear down a social structure built with such difficulty, and to give up intimacies so hard to achieve. Members may also experience a sense of guilt that is based on feelings that they could have played their roles more adequately. There are strong feelings, often, that members could be better members if they had the chance to do it again. There may, in fact, be a kind of inverse logic in the relationship between group members' satisfaction with the experience and the emotional intensity of the closing phase: successful groups seem to end more easily and go through their ending stages more quickly than those whose experience has been more frustrating, with the latter generating more dependency and pain in the separation process.

The valued outcomes in this final phase include the following: that the members make the ending a serious part of their work together, attentive to what is happening to them and learning from it as they have from the events of the work phase; and that the endings-work be regarded as part of the contract, rather than a kind of farewell party in which the worker is eulogized, the negatives obliterated, and the experience suffused in a rosy glow. Another way of putting this is that the ending should have substance as well as feeling: where the content is stressed and the feeling repressed, there is apt to be a kind of mechanical recital of what the members "learned in school", and where the reverse is true, there is an orgy of expressiveness, equally evasive of the total reality. The valued outcome is that the ending be not a moratorium of the work but a significant episode in it. In considering the transitional endings, the worker wants the members to respect the interim events in the life of the group, valuing the informal system and accepting its workings as legitimate. He wants them to weave these between-meeting themes into the continuity of the group meetings themselves, bringing in as many of the negatives, the afterthoughts, and the rethinking as they can muster for his notice. While he does not try to eliminate the private, informal system of the members—for that would be neither possible nor desirable—he wants to include their productions in the official working system. The wider the gap between the meeting-work and the interim developments, the more mechanical and ritualistic grows the work for which they have gathered as a group.

Moving to the action implications—but staying with the temporary endings—the worker credits the informal system, accepting its existence and legitimizing it with his own interest and curiosity. He reaches for this material, leaving room for it at the beginning of meetings and urging its relevance. In effect, the worker's activity in this regard constitutes an extension of the *demand for work* to the entire time period of the group's existence rather than merely to the meetings themselves. The worker also monitors time, developing a sense of the rhythm of the meeting and the transitions from the opening stage, to the body of the work, to the closing moments which carry with them a sense of achievement or self-doubt, vagueness or clarity, hope, frustration, and other feelings affecting the outlook for the next meeting.

In the permanent endings, the monitoring of time safeguards the amount needed to allow the group to pass without haste through the various stages in which they come to grips with one aspect of the problem at a time. The worker calls attention to the imminence of the ending, and watches for and reaches for the cues that emerge in devious forms from stage to stage. Here again the demand for work is made in specific terms: the worker asks the members to recollect their time together, to review both positive and negative experiences, to deal with their present feelings about him and about each other, and to think about next steps. And again, the confrontation of feelings is not undertaken simply because the feelings are there, but because their work at this phase is as much a part of their contracted tasks as all the rest. Also, and for the same reason, the demand upon the worker is that he involve himself closely in the separation experience, sharing his own feelings even as he retains his function as the authority within the system.

Generic Linkages

Given what has gone before, it is hardly necessary to dwell on the helping process as a pattern of activity that retains most of its salient characteristics regardless of the number of people within the system. The worker's sensitivity to cues, his ability to read human behavior, the generalization and partialization of tasks, the reaching for feelings that lurk beneath those which are expressed, the integration of feeling and substance in the work, the uses of authority, the demand for work, the contracting and the separating—all of these acts are as relevant to the worker in the one-to-one interview as they are to the worker in the group.[46] Certainly differences do occur when the group element, the dimension of mutual aid, is introduced. As the intimacy theme appears alongside the theme of authority around which the casework process is built, the worker finds himself in a situation where there is not just one helping relationship but a multiplicity of them; and this calls for some new knowledge and some new skills. The worker is now put to the additional task of helping people not only to help themselves but to help each other as well. There are also certain strains attached to the distribution of authority, the de-monopolizing of professional control, and the new skills needed in fostering group interaction and decision-making. But the knowledge of human behavior, the aspirations for client autonomy, and the communications arts indicated above all remain the same and are familiar to the caseworker in another context. The historic reasons for the original tripartite arrangement of casework, group work, and community organization are interesting to pursue,[47] but it has certainly lost whatever functional validity it may once have had.

As to any criteria which may exist for a differential assignment of clients to either group or individual help, there is little evidence that such criteria actually have been formulated. Further, it is questionable whether they are needed. It is this author's impression that all people—"sick" or "well," with severe problems or ordinary ones—need and use both the personal help of authority figures and the peer help of people in the same "boat," often at the same time. To suggest that social workers can decide which form is more appropriate is to defy the social processes through which people use others, and to try to mold their lives to the profession's ways of working, rather than the other way around. Group demands may be difficult for some clients, as those of the one-to-one relationship may be for others; but such difficulties are often productive, and not reason enough to substitute a professional prescription for an actual experience skillfully conducted.

Some Problems

The symbiotic view of the client-agency relationship is a difficult one to grasp, in the face of considerable experience with the antagonisms between the two. That the tensions exist is beyond question; but the problem remains as to how to deal with them in the helping process. If the adversary relationship is accepted as normal, and seen only as a continuous running battle between the two, the social workers can only see themselves as collaborators in further separating the institutions from the people to whom they belong.

---

[46]For further discussion of the use of groups by caseworkers, see William Schwartz, "Discussion of 'The Group Method with Clients, Foster, Families, and Adoptive Families' ", *Child Welfare,* 45:571–75 (December 1966).

[47]For some historical background on this development, see William Schwartz, "Group Work and the Social Scene," in Alfred J. Kahn (ed.), *Issues in American Social Work* (New York: Columbia University Press, 1959), pp. 110–37.

The professional strategy that emerges from this view is a war strategy, and as in most wars, the intellectuals do the planning and the people do the suffering. If, on the other hand, the troubles between client and agency are seen as a relationship under stress, then a professional strategy can be developed to help both parties re-address the work they are meant to do together. In keeping both client and agency in the field, the client is helped to establish his claim, service by service, through the worker's knowledge and skill, the strength of the group, and, when necessary, confrontations with the agency. In all this, the theoretical problem is to develop a more dynamic view of agencies. This involves eschewing the devil theories, always a feature of war strategies, and finding the forces within agencies that need novelty and change as much as they do equilibrium and the status quo. Social workers have learned to do this with individuals, balancing the analysis of pathology with the search for ego strengths, and thus deepening their understanding of the forces that drive clients toward society as well as away from it. In the same manner, more work needs to be done on the symbiotic-mediating model so that it more clearly depicts the forces that drive agencies both toward and away from the people they are designed to serve. Here, systems theory and organizational theory can be most specifically useful in helping to identify the agency structures and processes to which the worker might best address himself as he carries out his mediating function.

The need for a more detailed exposition of the elements that keep client and agency together in a working relationship is but one of the problems of the triangular model showing the forces that keep client, agency, and worker operating in the same orbit. The others are located on the lines of energy running between worker and client and worker and agency. Here the model makes its case on its ability to call attention to the moves by which a professional is judged, translating the worker's states of knowing, being, believing, and aspiring into acts of skill. The difficulty lies in achieving more refined degrees of specificity without becoming trivial, prescriptive, or vague. By focusing on the worker's *function* within a system, a new realm of specificity is entered. When this function is partialized into its component *acts,* yet another step is taken. But a step remains: the move from *acts* to *skills* has yet to be made with confidence—from *what* the worker does to *how* he does it in its most economical and effective form. There is still a tendency to equate the what and the how, thus settling for an insufficient measure of operationalism.

Finally, more study is needed of the problems involved in analyzing the phases of work in the double perspective of both the single meeting and the life of the group. Using the time sequence is undoubtedly a productive way of identifying and ordering the worker's moves, for they are in fact located somewhere along a time continuum, and each measure of time reflects a different task. But the array of knowledge, outcomes, and skills in each phase has not yet been worked out in detail. In each phase, the skills must be seen in interaction with both client and agency people, and reflecting on both lines the same degree of sensitivity, awareness, and clarity of purpose.

The problems and questions that emerge from this model call for a research program, just beginning to emerge, that stresses analysis of processes rather than the study of outcomes and long-term effects. For until more is known about what goes on in the helping process, social workers will be unable to decide what "it" was that worked or did not. It is believed that the main progress for a time will be in studies of process and limited effects. In the course of learning to ask the right questions, the major devices will for a time remain descriptive, exploratory, and theory-developing, and the primary tools will be the group record, the life-history, the critical incident, and other techniques for codifying and conceptualizing the experience of practice.

Bibliography

Bertanlanffy, Ludwig von. *General System Theory: Foundations, Development, Applications.* New York: Braziller, 1968.

Bronowski, J. *Science and Human Values.* New York: Harper & Row, Torchbooks, 1965.

Buber, Martin. *I and Thou,* 2d ed. New York: Scribner, 1958.

Buchler, Justus. *The Concept of Method.* New York: Columbia University Press, 1961.

Coyle, Grace L. *Group Experience and Democratic Values.* New York: Woman's Press, 1947.

Dewey, John. *Democracy and Education: An Introduction to the Philosophy of Education.* New York: Macmillan, 1916.

Kropotkin, P. *Mutual Aid, a Factor of Evolution.* New York: Knopf, 1925.

Kuhn, Thomas S. *The Structure of Scientific Revolutions.* Chicago: University of Chicago Press, 1962.

May, Rollo, Ernest Angel, and Henri F. Ellenberger (eds.). *Existence: A New Dimension in Psychiatry and Psychology.* New York: Basic Books, 1958.

McGrath, Joseph E. and Irwin Altman. *Small Group Research: A Synthesis and Critique of the Field.* New York: Holt, Rinehart, and Winston, 1966.

Reynolds, Bertha. *Learning and Teaching in the Practice of Social Work.* New York: Rinehart, 1942.

Robinson, Virginia. *Training for Skill in Social Work.* Philadelphia: University of Pennsylvania Press, 1942.

Schwartz, William and Serapio R. Zalba (eds.). *The Practice of Group Work.* New York: Columbia University Press, 1971.

The Field of Social Work

Introduction

The field of social work is always beset by conflicts and contradictions centered on its nature and social function. Beginning with our roots in the nineteenth century, we have felt the tension between a host of dualisms. Should we align ourselves with the individual or society? Are psychological or social matters more important? Are we agents of social control or social liberation? We have wondered whether our profession and clients are best served by practitioners or planners, and whether adequate planning would eliminate the need for practitioners.

Perhaps most poignant are the ways in which we have set ourselves against each other, accused each other of caring less about social issues and individual pain, and worked toward establishing complex structures which accord status and privilege to some while casting others aside. We have acted as if we believe that choice between a wide range of dualisms is both possible and productive in the practice of our professional function.

Schwartz believed that these "function-splitting," dialectical pulls were not surprising, given our professional function as a "built-in hedge against the imperfect distribution of opportunity and power—[which] creates a profession into which is built most of the ambivalence our society entertains for problems emerging from the nature of its own imperfections" (1973, p. 7). Our profession would naturally be pulled by opposing forces which, over a hundred years ago, generated the need for our centripetal function. Understandably, both the individual and our society would intuitively make claim upon our allegiance as each struggled with complex problems spawned in our society.

Schwartz held that to define professional function in this way brought with it certain difficulties stemming from our closeness to those without power. In addition, the sense of familiarity with what we do, could make it seem as if little expertise and specialized knowledge was required. On both counts, he suggested, our status and prestige within society became compromised, marginalizing us and those whom we served.

Schwartz's writings in this section concern the many "part-whole" tensions within the field. His approach to these tensions came from his belief that social work's mediating function applied to all within the profession, whether practitioner, programmer, planner, administrator, or educator. Thus guided by an integrative view, Schwartz devoted himself to understanding "part-whole" pulls and offered that the tenaciousness of these pulls reflected concerns with status and the profession's resistance to tackling the more difficult question of integration. Schwartz was not surprised that we were so challenged by the task of finding the common ground among us. He noted that the development of social work differed from that of other professions. For us specialization developed prior to the concept of a unified profession. Social work, drawn together from partialized visions of over a half century, would take a different path toward becoming an integrated profession.

Part-whole tensions have also been tenacious within our own professional associations. "On Certifying Each Other" (1962) and "Professional Association in Social Work: Some Structural Problems" (1962) were written not too long after the formation of NASW, and once again show Schwartz's unifying eye being applied to our professional associations. "On Certifying Each Other" bravely took a stand against the prevailing currents and was consequently controversial, i.e., it was applauded by many but resented by most. He believed that creation of the Academy of Certified Social Workers fragmented the profession, that the certification requirements for membership had no relation to standards of competence and offered an illusion of protection to the public. Ultimately, he said, an elite status-bestowing group, which bore a circumscribed relation to the profession as a whole, would be created.

"Professional Association in Social Work: Some Structural Problems" was presented at a meeting sponsored by the Group Work Section, National Association of Social Workers, at the National Conference on Social Welfare in New York City, May 31, 1962. The occasion was a review of the newly formed NASW and a consideration of how group work had fared in the merger. Schwartz directed his remarks to two themes "the sense of the importance of professional unity and the fear that such unity may become a blanket that covers and conceals the identity of its parts" (p. 1). Schwartz believed that group work was particularly vulnerable to the dissolution of its special identity. Group workers, from many different settings, who had worked hard at defining the common ground among them, shared concern about what would happen to Group Work when it joined with Casework to form NASW. Would the loyalty of group workers to their special interests be viewed as disloyalty to the "larger goals of professional unity"? Could the larger organization be attentive to the part-whole relationship without viewing it as a matter of a part versus whole relationship? Schwartz's remarks have a prophetic ring as we have witnessed the formation of the Association for the Advancement of Social Work with Groups, in the late 1970s, exactly because those who work with groups increasingly found their interests unrepresented within their membership organizations.

Schwartz's position was consistent with his response to other dichotomizing strains. The part-whole relationship was a symbiotic one and the task was to work at understanding how organizational structure might reflect connections between the whole of social work and its parts within; that is, group work. To pay little attention to the part, allowing it to wither away, would inevitably change the nature of the whole.

Perhaps no issues has been more stubborn, for us, than has been the part-whole tension implicit in whether we are "a profession of private troubles *or* public issues," or "a profession of private troubles *and* public issues." No question was more important to Schwartz than was this question of our professional function. "Private Troubles and Public Issues: One Social Work Job Or Two?" (1969) and "Thoughts From Abroad: Some Recent Perspectives on the Practice of Social Work" (1973)[1] are concerned with "function-splitting" within the profession, the psychological and social "tracks" established within our schools, the generic perspective, and the search for an integrative definition of social work function.

Schwartz posited that even though we proliferated "clinical" social work societies and journals identifying with psychotherapy as the roots of our traditions, the characterization of planners as "progressive" and "clinicians" as "reactionary" propelled us on a path which could only set us against ourselves and against the totality of client need. He believed that each generation of social workers produces its own version of the tension between the social with its concern for social reform and the psychological with its concern for individual change. As a part of our larger society, we continuously reinvent our hierarchy of valued positions counterposing psychological explanations against sociological ones, and posing action against insight. Schwartz's letter to *The Nation* (1966) presents what he believed occurs when we ask ourselves to choose between direct service and social action roles.

As an educator, Schwartz was particularly anguished by the ways in which our educational programs perpetuated these untenable choices. He wrote that a two track system in which professionals are distinguished by their objectives, i.e., a practice track and a social welfare policy track, created "a living symbol of the schizophrenia induced by the failure to understand the connections between private troubles and public issues" (1969, p. 35). The separation of the "clinicians" from the "social planners" denies each a basis for understanding what the other does. The reinforcing power of each is lost when they are separated.

Schwartz never failed to recognize "[t]hat there are quarrels over ownership and the terms of the contract . . . in a class society. And that, in a badly organized collective where the few rule the many, there will often be a nasty feeling between the service and its people" (1969, p. 38). But for him, the answer was always an integrative one centering on the ways in

---

[1]"Private Troubles and Public Issues: One Social Work Job or Two?" was first presented as the Eduard C. Lindeman Memorial Lecture of the National Conference on Social Welfare, New York City, 1969. "Thoughts From Abroad: Some Present Perspectives on the Practice of Social Work," an unpublished paper, was first read at a social work conference in Northern Ireland, at the New University of Ulster, Institute of Continuing Education, Magee University College, Londonderry, on June 25, 1973. Schwartz presented this paper at the invitation of Derek Carter.

which a mediating definition of function and skill can be "designed to mobilize agencies rather than destroy them" (1969, p. 42–43). For him, the agencies, created to provide service, could never be set against those in need of service.

Toby Berman-Rossi

On Certifying Each Other

William Schwartz

WHEN AN ORGANIZED group makes a major decision, there is no intention that debate and discussion on the subject should end. It is, in fact, inherent in the democratic process that those members who oppose the move should take up a responsible critical role—clarifying their position to the others, urging reconsideration of the action, and carefully watchdogging its consequences.

Such a course is particularly important in the matter of the newly organized Academy of Certified Social Workers, formed by decision of the Delegate Assembly of the National Association of Social Workers in October 1960. It is important because the issues involved have at no time—either before or after the move was made—received their share of public attention and concern. There was some attempt to precipitate such activity in the preparations for the 1960 Assembly, but these efforts were not productive, and there is no evidence that they produced the kind of widespread membership analysis and discussion that was intended. Further, if we examine the total output of the professional journal, SOCIAL WORK, from its beginnings, we will not find the elaboration of the problem, the historical comparisons with other professions, and the responsible debate of pros and cons that one might expect from a profession preparing to make a significant move of this nature. In its six years of publication from January 1956 through December 1961, the journal has in fact produced exactly two articles on the subject of regulation,[1]

WILLIAM SCHWARTZ, Ed.D., *is associate professor of social work, New York School of Social Work of Columbia University, New York City. This paper was first presented at a meeting of the NASW Group Work Section, Chicago Area Chapter, January 1962.*

[1]Virginia Laurence and Anne Baeck, "Voluntary Certification vs. the California Title-Licensing Bill," *Social Work,* Vol. 5, No. 1 (January 1960), pp. 9–13; Eileen S. Cassidy and Margaret M. Bullard, "The California Story," *Social Work,* Vol. 6, No. 1 (January 1961), pp. 56–65.

four letters to the editor,[2] and one peripheral comment in the "Notes and Comments" section of an early issue.[3]

The effect of all this silence has been to create the belief, in a large segment of our membership, that there are no real issues involved in the recent action, that there is no significant division of opinion within the association, that their own doubts are unworthy and unshared, and that an accomplished fact exists about which nothing can or should be done. As social workers, we should be particularly sensitive to the ways in which such *faits accomplis* can come about without in any way representing the wishes of the members had they all the facts in hand. In this instance, the repeated insistence that the certification plan is voluntary in its intent makes it doubly urgent that it not become compulsory through the lack of available alternatives.

The purpose of these comments, then, is to stimulate some open discussion on the subject by setting down some of the basic issues, clarifying the points of opposition, and suggesting some ways by which we may yet—even at this late date—save ourselves from the consequences of an action which is against the best interests of both the profession and the general public.

Professional Regulation

This is not the place for a detailed analysis of the issues involved in the social regulation of professional practice; but it will help to take note of a few basic propositions. By far the most essential of these is that such regulation is a device by which society protects itself against incompetent and unauthorized practice in those areas where the public stands to suffer harm or injury by such practice. To this end, society creates what Greenwood has called a "professional monopoly," and develops certain instruments by which this monopoly is protected against invasion.[4] The processes of standardization, exclusion, and imposition of sanctions are designed to insure that the qualifications, training, and modes of practice in a given profession shall be made highly visible to the public and thus more subject to its control. The granting of professional status is a means to the end of social control.

The regulatory devices by which social control is exerted fall into two major categories: there are those embodied in forms of *legal* regulation, where the public will is expressed in legislation designed to define requirements and certify those who meet them; and there are those constituted by forms of *self*-regulation, where the profession itself undertakes to provide, in the public interest, the machinery designed to protect society against unautho-

---

[2]*Social Work,* Vol. 5, No. 2 (April 1960), pp. 125–127.

[3]"Legal Opinion in Michigan," *Social Work,* Vol. 1, No. 2 (April 1956), p. 114. Signed by B.M.B.

[4]Ernest Greenwood, "Attributes of a Profession," *Social Work,* Vol. 2, No. 3 (July 1957), p. 49.

rized practice. It is not the purpose here to argue the merits of one or the other of these forms of control. Rather, the point should be made that there is nothing inherent in one or the other which is inimical to the goal of public protection. Used wisely, both can achieve the desired end; used badly, either can defeat its purpose. The medical profession has in fact used both forms to good advantage. And the best case can undoubtedly be made for a regulatory structure that incorporates both professional and legislative activity.

This is an important point: the central objection to the NASW plan for voluntary certification is not that it is a self-controlling mechanism. Both legal and professional approaches are valid to the end of rendering the profession more accountable to the public which finances it and uses its services. What is significant is that neither of these approaches eliminates the basic problem of establishing certification standards which bear some clear relation to the issue of competence. That is, the standards of eligibility should be so defined that they make sense to the public and that they distinguish clearly between the relative likelihood of competence in those who are eligible and those who are not. This does not mean that only maximum standards are permissible; *but it does mean that trivial ones are not.* For in the latter case, the only distinction made is between those who take the trouble to apply and those who do not.

Admittedly, this problem creates some difficult tasks: defining standards of competence, translating such definitions into terms the public can understand, demonstrating the need for the "professional monopoly," and convincing the public that only certain people should be allowed to perform certain services.[5] It must be remembered that all professions grow out of familiar forms of self-help and that, invariably, the professionals themselves will be the first to perceive the need for a special expertise and a new social specialization.[6] Convincing the uninitiated that it is in their interest to recognize this is another matter. But there are no short-cuts to this end, and every advanced profession has learned this in its own process of development.

In social work, such efforts have met with a singular apathy among the professionals themselves. For reasons which none seem able to understand, NASW chapter leaders interested in control legislation in the various states have met with indifference and negativism from their own people. Invariably, such campaigns have been poorly fought, the members themselves badly prepared, and the profession itself revealed to the legislators as one which is uninterested in a measure it has itself called to their attention. When the effort has failed, the leaders correctly ascribe the failure to poor membership educa-

---

[5]Harold L. Wilensky and Charles N. Lebeaux, *Industrial Society and Social Welfare* (New York: Russell Sage Foundation, 1958), Chapter 11.

[6]The process is well described, in both general and specific terms, in Henry J. Meyer, "Professionalization and Social Work," in Alfred J. Kahn, ed., *Issues in American Social Work* (New York: Columbia University Press, 1959), pp. 319–40.

tion, call for a continuous educational campaign within the association—and proceed to forget about the whole thing until just before the next bill is introduced. This unfortunate cycle of events takes place periodically in many states throughout the country.

It is hard to resist the conclusion that we have now, as a profession, come around to the position that if nobody wishes to certify us we will have to certify ourselves. Which brings us to the 1960 Delegate Assembly and the Academy of Certified Social Workers.

At the Delegate Assembly

The certification proposals of the NASW Commission on Personnel Standards and Practices, published in *NASW News* (February 1959) and again in the Delegate Assembly issue (February 1960), were based on preliminary discussions at the 1958 Assembly and a subsequent report prepared by the Southern Minnesota Chapter. In essence, these proposals called for a basic title of Certified Social Worker, restricted eligibility to members of the association, and set up an additional requirement of two years of paid employment under the supervision of a certified worker. All present members of the association were to be blanketed in if they applied; in addition, special consideration was to be given in situations where certified supervisors were in short supply.[7]

Again it should be emphasized that, beyond these presentations and the two articles published, as previously mentioned, in SOCIAL WORK, the literature shows almost nothing in the way of public analysis, debate, and discussion of a move that had been impending since before the Delegate Assembly of 1958. We believe it would be accurate to say that the same general apathy manifested in the matter of legal regulation was apparent on the issue of certification by the profession itself, and to say also that no intensive efforts were made by the national Commission on Personnel Standards and Practices to educate the members on the issues in all of the intervening time. We believe, too, that it would not be too farfetched to assume that the 264 delegates to the 1960 Assembly were, in the main, not properly prepared or instructed for deliberation and action on the proposal—if we believe that such preparation should represent a distillation of widespread local activity and consideration of the issues involved. It may be significant to note that some of the larger chapters, which are generally more successful in generating local engagement with national issues, offered the most serious reservations to the plan.

At the Assembly itself, the delegates were informed that legal advice had made it necessary to propose an alteration in the plan. By restricting eligibility to members of the association, NASW had laid itself open to charges of illegal monopoly. Therefore, a legal fiction had been devised, namely another

[7] *NASW News,* February 1959, p. 28; February 1960, p. 17.

"organization," to be called the Academy of Certified Social Workers. The Academy would be run by the same Board of Directors as that of NASW and be administered by the same staff. That this fiction was specifically designed to circumvent certain legal and ethical requirements drawn up to protect the public evidently held no terrors for the sponsors; in any event, it was not discussed by them.

The floor debate was long and heated. Its most striking feature, to this participant, was that *no arguments were advanced to show that this was a measure designed to protect the public.* When challenged to do so, the proponents argued that the plan was "a step forward," that an enhanced professional status would ultimately bring such protection, and that it was "better to have some plan than no plan at all."[8]

The primary opposition was raised by the two largest chapters, New York and Chicago, with important amendments also offered by Philadelphia, Los Angeles, Lehigh Valley, and others. The opposition focused on the monopolistic aspects of the plan, its attempt to create the illusion of public protection in the face of eligibility requirements barely above NASW membership itself, and the deceptive aura around the Academy device. The reservations held by delegates from some of the smaller chapters that they would be disadvantaged by the difficulty of acquiring certified supervisors were dispelled by assurances from the commission chairman that consideration would be given to difficult cases. The measure was passed, intact, by a vote of 178–64.

The Morning After

In the year or more since its passage, the paper Academy has been established and many thousands have paid their registration fees and received their certificates. It is noteworthy that, up to this point, the shower of materials merchandising Academy membership far outweighs any information regarding the "next steps" indicated as being in the offing—despite the fact that the 1962 Assembly is not far off. In the literature advertising the Academy, a small note of guilt was struck by the symbol of the small "a" preceding the CSW, but one would assume that this was too much for some to digest, and the small "a" has since been capitalized.

But small "a" or large, the problems remain the same. We now face the task of implementing and interpreting a plan which is inherently defective in both intent and application. Its defects may be summed up as follows:

1. As presently constituted, the plan provides certification requirements which bear almost no relation to standards of competence. None will seriously argue—and none did at the Delegate Assembly—that two years of supervision after the master's degree discriminates competence with sufficient clarity

---

[8]This last argument was the most interesting, in view of the oft-heard comment by opponents of specific legislation that "it is better to have no bill at all than a bad one," since it is more difficult to change a measure than to get it adopted in the first place.

to justify the elaborate Academy machinery and the $200,000 that will be spent on it. If there are any such arguments, the "special consideration" provisions should remove even these.

2. We are deliberately offering the public the illusion of protection where there is none. The label "certified," so heavily emphasized in the Academy materials, means something important in American life and while we may understand our own *sotto voce* qualifications, the general public does not. When we show an elaborately wrought document prominently proclaiming a state of "certification" it is plainly our intent that people should assume it to mean more than it does—which they will. This is misleading and—the only suitable word is a harsh one—unethical. It is a terrible price to pay for professional prestige, even if one is foolish enough to believe that any lasting prestige can be built on so shaky a base.

3. The measure serves to cheapen our really hard-won symbols of competence—the MSW degree and the NASW affiliation itself. We have created confusion in the public mind, at a time when board members in many parts of the country have just begun to accept the master's degree in social work as a mark of proper preparation for practice. When we are ready to replace this symbol with one more advanced, let it be one that is unambiguously so and one which we can respect and explain. Can anyone truthfully say that he can interpret this new requirement to an intelligent lay leader, or to a member of another profession?

4. The public deception is matched by an equally unfortunate deception of our own members. An illusion of *voluntarism* has been created where none is intended; if the Academy is to succeed at all, it must eliminate the voluntary features as far as possible by creating a bandwagon so large that agencies and supervisors will be forced to adopt the device in order to attract young workers. The way to do this—and this is what the Academy does—is to tie the eligibility requirements not to any inherent standard of competence (an examination, long years of practice, and so on) but to a term of service under another member of the Academy. The plan is thus built to eliminate alternatives as soon as possible, and the so-called "voluntary" feature is illusory.

5. The plan must necessarily create the effect of further concentrating the location of new MSW's in the larger cities—a result that is precisely opposed to the present social need for a wider distribution of professionally educated social workers. It is doubtful whether the assurances given in the smaller chapters can be implemented and the "special considerations" ground out fast enough to offset the inclination of young workers to find a locale in which there are enough Academic workers around to offer the needed supervisory conditions.

6. The same consequences will accrue to the public agencies, which are having even now a difficult time recruiting and holding trained workers. This move will tend to freeze them in their present status, insofar as their ability to recruit young workers is concerned. The argument that these agencies—as well as those, public and private, in the smaller communities—have but to

"raise their standards" to compete is more than slightly arrogant on on part, and unworthy of our vaunted understanding of how such changes come about. A more likely consequence is that board members in these agencies, having just begun to take an interest in the MSW degree, will be puzzled by this new requirement, more than a little bewildered as to its intent, and ultimately discouraged by the twists and turns of this strange profession.

7. If it is our desire to raise the standards of practice and to create classes of advanced professional competence, we have a strange way of showing it. As far as the public is concerned, we have twice during the past six years "blanketed in" many thousands of workers with little or no professional training at all, offering them first the NASW designation and now the ACSW symbol of advanced competence. The first such procedure can be honestly justified on the grounds that it was a necessary step in unifying the profession. The second, however, is more serious in its consequences; it creates a huge pool of unqualified but "certified" supervisors who will, for many years to come, be providing the supervision under which young workers will themselves become certified, and so on. This can only be explained by our unseemly haste to certify at any cost; or, as it was put at the Assembly, "better some plan than no plan at all."

8. Finally, and despite the assurances of the Commission on Personnel Standards and Practices, the measure diverts our professional machinery from the important struggle for legal regulation of social work practice. Many of the people who have worked hard in this area will regard somewhat wistfully the projected Academy budget of more than $200,000, and wonder how much they could accomplish with this kind of money. It will, of course, be argued that no such fund could be raised for a legislative campaign; but this is a peculiar argument, for it presents us as a group that will pay almost a quarter of a million dollars for the machinery needed to print self-certifying certificates of little intrinsic value, but which can raise no such funds for a fight to win public recognition and a secure place in the social scheme. There are many who will not believe this, and the proposition has never been tested: no such campaign, elaborated on a scale equal to the Academy effort, has ever been undertaken by our association.

What Can We Do?

Although we hear that Academy membership is booming, the most optimistic estimates reveal that there is still a high and significant percentage of NASW members that has not responded to the call. Further, of those who have purchased their certificates there are many who have done so mechanically, as an act of routine loyalty and without the full implications before them. It would certainly be a mistake to assume that every $7.00 paid in represents a vote of confidence in the certification plan.

For those who feel, and may come to feel, that our association has made a bad move, there are two important courses of action left open. The first is to safeguard the voluntary character of the plan by retaining one's own independence of it—in short, to stay out of it—or, if one is already in, to fail to renew. As indicated, the program is such that it requires near-unanimity in order to succeed at all. Having within it no inherent mark of achievement, its band-wagon attraction is its only force for compliance. If the young worker has a genuine alternative—that is, if there are a visible number of non-Academy members around—he will go to the job he wants and to the supervisor he wants, regardless of whether or not the latter is "certified." This is the real concern in the retention of voluntarism. Insofar as board members are involved, it is doubtful that they will accept Academy membership in itself as a badge of competence; they will defer to it only if it is needed in the race for workers. If, then, the young workers retain their alternatives, so will a considerable number of supervisors who have no stomach for the Academy program. The ACSW symbol will then be reserved for those who need it for special reasons of their own—as, for example, the private practitioners, those who may feel it necessary to impress psychiatrists and doctors in the special settings, and some others. This is in itself unfortunate, but for the present it is the lesser of the evils.

The other major course of action is to urge, and give leadership to, serious preparation at the local level for discussion of the issue at the 1962 Delegate Assembly. Both chapter and Section meetings should be used for intensive discussion and education on the problems and for formulating proposals for the national meeting. In constructing such proposals, consideration should be given to three primary objectives:

1. In view of the probability that we have already gone too far to rescind the present plan, we should at least make every effort to convert its machinery into a respectable certification device designed to cover the profession as a whole, rather than merely our own in-group. One way to do this is to change the status of the Academy of Certified Social Workers from a legal fiction to a working reality—by opening it to non-NASW members who meet the same objective requirements and by establishing a separate Board of Control that would include non-members of the association, as well as some distinguished members of other professions.

2. Establish qualifying criteria of a more rigorous nature than those presently constituted. As a guiding principle, it should be accepted that the certification tag should carry its own clear mark of advanced competence, rather than be dependent on the indirect "passing on" of competence from one worker to another.

3. Press for an active and dynamic program for legal regulation of social work practice and demand leadership from the national association on this score.

Professional status is a precious charge, handed over by society for its own protection. It is meted out slowly and carefully, in return for recognized service, conspicuous achievement, and consistent concern for the common good. Pinning medals on ourselves will not hasten the process, and what may sometimes look like a "step forward" may, if it is a false and hurried step, turn out to be more than one step backward.

This particular misstep is still retrievable if those of us who can see its dangers will delay no longer in making our voices heard. There is not a great deal of time left, but there is enough, if our members exercise their right to re-examine these problems and if our association meets its responsibility for creating the necessary conditions. In the long run, we will then have done much more for our "public image" than we can hope to achieve with yet another diploma on the wall.

Professional Association in Social Work: Some Structural Problems*

William Schwartz

This is a significant period in the associational history of group workers, and it may indeed mark the closing of an era in social group work as we have known it. As we examine the structural proposals contained in the report of the Committee on Review of Structure of the National Association of Social Workers,[1] the spirit of the event is somehow familiar to those of us who have sat in so often on those sober discussions at which a group of youngsters has been trying to decide whether or not it was time to "break up the club."

This would explain some of the difficulties I sensed in the efforts of the Group Work Section planning committee to develop an approach to the meetings held in May at the National Conference. On the one hand, its communications stressed the importance of the whole association and the need for overall professional strength and unity. On the other, there was a strong concern about the relationship between the parts and the whole and the feeling came through that the pervasive question was: what will happen to us? What will become of our identity if we break up the club? Thus two themes emerged that will undoubtedly dominate our discussions for the months to come: the sense of the importance of professional unity and the fear that such unity may become a blanket that covers and conceals the identity of its parts.

Once before, in the early 1950s, we addressed ourselves to such problems as we examined the unification proposals of the Temporary Inter-

*Based on a paper presented at meeting sponsored by Group Work Section, National Association of Social Workers, at National Conference on Social Welfare, New York City, May 31, 1962.

[1]*Report on the Review of NASW Structure* (New York: National Association of Social Workers, May, 1962). See also: "Interim Report on the Review of NASW Structure," *NASW News, 6,* 3 (May 1961), 6–30.

Schwartz, William. (1962, May). Professional association in social work: Some structural problems. *Paper presented at the National Conference on Social Welfare in New York City.*

Association Council of Social Work Membership Organizations.[2] But that demand was of a somewhat different order: the pull toward unity was then new and strong; it was only a first step in a long, indeterminate process; the threat to subgroup identity was hedged about with many assurances as to the preservation of specialized autonomies; and the structure of the new association was carefully designed to both allow and assist the separate groups to pursue their historical processes and problems while they combined to take up the new processes and problems of a unified professional association.[3]

Nevertheless, it still took seven years of intensive effort—from the first joint meetings in 1948 to the NASW consummation in 1955—to iron out the doubts and uncertainties that arose in the process of determining the relationship of the whole and its parts in an association of professional social workers.[4] The formula then devised has been seven more years in the testing, and we are now being asked to decide whether this initial approach is in fact outdated and whether the time has come to develop a new structure within which to conduct our internal divisions of labor.

As we approach our discussions, there are several ways in which we could go wrong at the outset. One way would be to deny that a problem exists and to exercise our feelings with the rationale that they are unworthy, that there is no conflict of concerns, and to imply that there may be is simply to be disloyal to the larger goals of professional unity. Another would be to insist that Structure Review changes nothing, but simply rearranges the old relationships under new labels—which is a neat way of both accepting and depreciating the work of the Review Committee.

Nor would it help us to make a quick choice of either horn of the part-whole dilemma and evaluate the proposals in that light: to say, for example, that the "important" goal is unification and all other considerations are minor; or that the "basic" problem is subgroup autonomy and let the unity come in where it may.

It seems clear that the only reasonable course is to admit that a problem exists, to hold to our feeling for a while rather than to deny it, and to bring

---

[2]Temporary Inter-Association Council of Social Work Membership Organizations, *Plan for a Single New Organization of Social Workers,* December, 1962. See also: *National Association of Social Workers: Proposed By laws and Memorandum of Understandings,* as approved by TIAC, November 15, 1954.

[3]See Melvin A. Glasser, "The Story of the Movement for a Single Professional Association," *Social Work Journal, 36,* 3 (July 1955), 115–22.

[4]For additional material dealing with the discussions around the TIAC proposals and the processes that led up to them, see: "Inter-Association Organization," *Social Work Journal, 30,* 3 (July 1949), entire issue; "The TIAC Report: Principles, Proposals and Issues in Inter-Association Cooperation," *Social Work Journal, 32,* 3 (July 1951), entire issue; Helen Rowe and Sanford Solender, "A Challenging Decision for AAGW," *The Group, 14,* 1 (October 1951), 9–28; Benjamin E. Youngdahl, "Plan for a Single Professional Organization: Comments on the TIAC Report," *Social Work Journal, 34,* 2 (April 1953), 55–8, 88–9; and Nathan E. Cohen, "Professional Social Work Faces the Future," *Social Work Journal, 36,* 3 (July 1955), 79–86.

our analysis to bear on the job of understanding how organizational structure might reflect a viable connection between our subgroup aspirations and those we hold for the profession as a whole. And since an examination of structure must necessarily call up fundamental questions about professional goals and functions, we may in the process gain some deeper insight into the nature of our own specialized identity, the problems of unity and diversity in the social work profession, and some of the larger issues involving professionalization and specialization in our society.

Professionalism and Association

When a vocation makes a bid for professional status, it projects certain claims for which it asks social recognition.[5] It asserts, first, that it carries a significant and definable part of the cultural tradition in which it is embedded;[6] second, that its tasks in the social division of labor are important enough to warrant a reservation of function and a set of social devices designed to insure control of practice and of practitioners;[7] third, that its job requires not only manual but intellectual skills, involving the exercise of knowledge, science, and the theoretical organization of its own experience;[8] and finally, that the vocation has achieved enough collective identity and strength to be entrusted with a professional monopoly in matters of training, self-definition, self-discipline, and social accountability.[9]

This last claim of a definable identity and the collective strength to nourish and enforce it led Carr-Saunders and Wilson, in their classic work on the professions, to propose an integral connection between the social conditions that led to the rise of professional group consciousness and the emergence of

---

[5]For some of the many attempts to define and describe professions and their characteristics, see: A.M. Carr-Saunders and P. A. Wilson, "Professions," *Encyclopedia of the Social Sciences,* Vol. XII, 476–80; Morris L. Cogan, "The Problem of Defining a Profession," *The Annals,* 297 (January 1955), 105–11; Grace L. Coyle, "On Becoming Professional," *In Toward Professional Standards* (New York: AAGW, 1947), 11–21; Ernest Greenwood, "Attributes of a Profession," *Social Work, 2,* 3 (July 1957) 45–55; Everett C. Hughes, "The Study of Occupations," in Robert K. Merton, Leonard Broom, and Leonard S. Cottrell, Jr. (eds.) *Sociology Today: Problems and Prospects* (New York: Basic Books, 1959), 442–58; Robert K. Merton, *Some Thoughts on the Professions in American Society,* address, Brown University Papers, No. 37, 1960; Henry J. Meyer, "Professionalization and Social Work," in Alfred J. Kahn, ed. *Issues in American Social Work* (New York: Columbia U. Press, 1959), 319–40; "Profession," *Oxford English Dictionary,* Vol. VIII, 1427–8; Talcott Parsons, "A Sociologist Looks at the Legal Profession," *Essays in Sociological Theory* (Glencoe, Ill.: The Free Press, 1954, rev.ed.), 370–85; Roscoe Pound, "The Professions in the Society of Today," *New England Journal of Medicine, 241,* 10 (September 8, 1949), 351–7.

[6]For discussion of the profession and the cultural tradition, see: Parsons, *op.cit.,* pp. 372ff.

[7]On the reservation of function, see elaboration by Coyle, *op. cit.,* p. 15.

[8]See Greenwood, op. cit., p. 47. See also discussion by Carr-Saunders and Wilson, *op. cit.,* p. 476.

[9]William J. Goode, "Community Within a Community: The Professions," *American Sociological Review,* 22, 2 (April 1957), 194–200.

the full-fledged professions in society.[10] The interdependence of professional status and professional association becomes clearer as we realize that the association serves important functions both for the growth and maturation of the profession itself and for the social control that every society must demand of the functional groups designated to do its work. Externally the association is a public symbol of the specific social concern that it serves to define and implement; it is a visible piece of social machinery designed to do the job and do it well; and it is a body of policies and programs that the public can recognize, evaluate, and hold accountable. Internally, it is a welding together of the diverse forms and specializations through which the profession effects its own division of labor; it is a device through which these specializations are refined and strengthened; and it is a vehicle for the development of individual status and self-betterment—both for those who have achieved membership and, in the newly emerging professions, for those excluded practitioners who depend for their own developing aspirations on the extent to which the profession grows more identifiable, status-connected and socially accepted.

Thus, just as the profession, working to develop the strength and cohesion necessary to play its proper role in the social structure, stands in relation to society as a part to the whole, so it stands in relation to its own sub-specializations as a whole to its parts, requiring its own well-defined subgroups in order to develop as an effective instrument for doing its job. Any complex social organization needs unity to carry on its work, but effective unity requires the maintenance of well-defined, specialized parts operating in functional interdependence.

The major structural problem is not then one of the whole *versus* its parts, or of unity versus diversity, since neither can be properly conceived without the other. Rather, the problem is to determine the nature of the organizational tasks and the best way in which these tasks can be divided. Unity is not an end in itself; nor is it a problem in the simple elimination of inefficiency and waste motion. The fundamental question is Unity for what? For what purposes? What is the organized and unified "image" to represent? When this is determined, the problems of specialization fall into place: what units are needed in the division of labor, and how can they best be placed in functional interdependence?

I am not suggesting that such questions are decided in the rational way in which they are presented here. On the contrary, there is a factor of institutional inertia which is inevitable in the process of change and which, further, contains a dynamic that needs to be guarded and respected, insofar as such resistances represent a valuable safeguard for the protection of certain real-life modes of growth and development against conceptions of progress that may exist only in the minds of a small but powerful elite. What I am saying is that where the rational process is employed, these are the questions to which

---

[10] A. M. Carr-Saunders and P. A. Wilson, *The Professions* (Oxford: Clarendon Press, 1933), pp. 298–304.

it should be addressed; and further, that even where it is not employed, much of the internal part-whole tension stems from subgroup differences as to what the answers to these questions should be.

Professionalism and Social Work

How then should we conceive the model of a unified social work profession? Talcott Parsons, in his analysis of the legal profession, has stated that "The professional is distinguished largely by the independent trusteeship . . . of an important part of the major cultural tradition of the society."[11] To what part of the American tradition does the social work profession claim trusteeship—a trusteeship which will be held in the name of its professional association?

It was only a few years after the term "social work" was itself created that Dr. Abraham Flexner delivered his historic paper[12] in which he asked whether social work was a profession, and concluded that it was not, because the social worker did not carry "primary responsibility"[13] for his decisions about the client. Social work appeared to him to be "not so much a definite field as an aspect of work in many fields."[14] He asked:

> To the extent that the social worker mediated the intervention of the particular agent or agency best fitted to deal with the specific emergency which he has encountered, is the social worker himself a professional or is he the intelligence that brings this or that profession into action? The responsibility for specific action thus rests upon the power he has invoked. The very variety of the situations he encounters compels him to be not a professional agent so much as the mediator invoking this or that professional agency.[15]

That Dr. Flexner was confused by the diversity of social work practice and by its integral connection with agency functioning, and that he was unable, from his medical frame of reference, to conceive a model of professionalism different from that of the private and "independent" practitioner, is no longer important today, almost fifty years later. What is important is that his analysis has served to set the tone and direction for all subsequent discussions of professionalism by social workers themselves, down to the present day. The point that was missed by Flexner was missed also by his social work audience—namely, that it may be possible to conceive of a profession that is formed for the precise reasons that led Flexner to exclude social work from the charmed circle: that, in a complex and often disordered society it may be necessary to

---

[11]Talcott. *Parsons, op. cit.,* p. 372.

[12]Abraham Flexner, "Is Social Work a Profession?" *Proceedings of the National Conference of Charities and Correction* (Chicago: The Hildmann Printing Co., 1915), pp. 576–90.

[13]*Ibid.,* p. 585.

[14]*Ibid.*

[15]*Ibid.*

organize a group of specialists whose function it is to mediate the encounter between the individual and the agencies of social betterment and to monitor the efforts of society to provide for the common good, and, further, that such tasks might be of a complexity that would require advanced learning and skill. Such a profession would then, far from trying to emulate the existing order of professionalism, establish its very basis for recognition in those qualities which, for others, might signify a lower ranking in the professional hierarchy. Professional independence, as Dr. Flexner himself admitted, was a kind of social myth even in 1915; and certainly the function of reducing complexity, of arranging the maze of social services into something like a comprehensible pattern, of restoring in people and their groups a sense of control over the events that shaped their lives, and of educating and agitating for a more equal distribution of power, might reasonably be included as a significant part of the social division of labor. However, this peculiar function—this built-in hedge against the imperfect distribution of opportunity and power—creates a profession into which is built much of the ambivalence our society entertains for problems emerging from the nature of its own imperfections. The job, necessary as it is, does not draw the quick gratitude, the recognition, and the symbols of status accorded to the "cleaner," more respectable professions. Most of its clients are those at the lower end of the social scale—the excluded, the dependent, the deviant, those who have failed to achieve the middle-class ideal; its practitioners are closely tied to the agencies of philanthropy and function mainly in the context of agency supervision and the mechanics of agency accountability; and the problems with which it deals are so close to the very fabric of society, so familiar to the life experience of its citizens, that everyone regards himself as a kind of expert in those areas where the social worker feels himself most in need of special knowledge and training.

And so it happens that our studies of social work status and prestige[16] show that these are indeed the factors which form the general basis for social work's "marginality" as a profession; and they also show that social workers have to a considerable extent introjected these criteria and accepted the guilt, rather than attempting to hold to an identity based on difference and on the nature of its work.[17] From Flexner's time to the present day—when it was recently suggested that the term "social work" is in itself a status-reducing factor, because it contains the word "work"[18]—it has been difficult for the

---

[16]See for example: Norman Polansky, William Bowen, Lucille Gordon, and Conrad Nathan, "Social Workers in Society: Results of a Sampling Study," *Social Work Journal, 34,* 2 (April 1953), 74–80; R. Clyde White, "Social Workers in Society": Some Further Evidence," *Social Work Journal, 34,* 4 (October 1953), 161–64; Alfred Kadushin, "Prestige of Social Work—Facts and Factors," *Social Work, 3,* 2 (April 1958), 37–43 Lydia Rapoport, "In Defense of Social Work: An Examination of Stress in the Profession," *The Social Service Review, 34,* 1 (March 1960), 62–74.

[17]See discussion by Norman A. Polansky of the phenomenon of "distraction into the status struggle" (pp. 311ff) in his "The Professional Identity in Social Work," in Alfred J. Kahn, ed. *Issues in American Social Work* (New York: Columbia U. Press, (1959), pp. 293–318.

[18]Otto Pollak, "Image of the Social Worker in the Community and in the Profession," *Social Work, 6,* 2 (April 1961), 106–11. See pp. 110–11.

profession to seek its status not in eliminating its off-beat and unusual characteristics, but in showing that they are necessary, that they were created for a purpose, that they call for learning and skill, and that social work represents in these very attributes an important, if submerged, part of the cultural tradition of the society in which it works.

Thus, in developing what Cogan calls the "persuasive definition"[19] of the profession—the unified image we wish to present—the structure of the professional association may reflect either the real and ongoing effort to build a true working model of its place in society, or what Wilensky and Lebeaux have termed the "enthusiastic pushing of a tenuous package."[20] In this latter endeavor, the profession and the association take on the psychology of a beleaguered state—defensive, compulsively homogeneous, superficially unified, and dedicated to the Madison Avenue version of the "public image," where what is sold is not the product but the image of the product. In a beleaguered state there can be little tolerance for difference, little patience with developmental processes, little room for grass-roots groupings and discussions, and little chance for leadership to take its cues from those being led.

In discussing the form and substance of professional unity, I have so far been concerned largely with social work's external relationship to the society in which it lives. Let us now turn our attention to some aspects of the internal process through which many of these questions will ultimately be decided. Which brings us to the problem of specialization, within the profession itself.

In an article which discusses the effects of professional differentiation on the processes of professional change, Harvey L. Smith observes:

> The modern professions are complex social institutions which select people of varied skills, often from different social strata, and organize them into different levels of operation and diverse interest groups. Each level and group may be sensitive to contingencies not shared by the profession as a whole. Thus different parts of the profession may "metabolize" at different rates, and any single action may have many, diverse, and often conflicting effects within the professional institution. In addition, our complex modern professions have multiple relations, directly and, through their professional associations, with other occupational groups and with the public. Here, too, there are important problems of differential sensitivity. Such problems are highlighted during periods of professional change.[21]

As we can see, the problem of coordinating specialized identities is not unique to the profession of social work. It does, however, make its appearance

---

[19]Morris L. Cogan, *op.cit.,* p. 107.

[20]Harold L. Wilensky and Charles N. Lebeaux, *Industrial Society and Social Welfare* (New York: Russell Sage Foundation, 1958), p. 334.

[21]Harvey L. Smith, "Contingencies of Professional Differentiation," in Sigmund Nosow and William H. Form, eds. *Man, Work, and Society: A Reader in the Sociology of Occupations* (New York: Basic Books, Inc., 1962), p. 219.

in certain unique ways. "It is important to note," observed Nathan E. Cohen, commenting on the imminent formation of NASW, "that the pattern of professional associations in social work was different than that of other professions. Specializations preceded the general organization and were being built up before social work had found a common base."[22] This process of growth by accretion meant, in effect, that the social work tradition had been pieced together from a number of different, partialized versions that had taken organized form over a period of more than half a century. That it was possible to draw these pieces together into a single association in 1955 indicated that three important developments had already taken place: first, that the commonalities had been sufficiently crystallized to provide a common base for organized professional activity; second, that each of the specializations was ready to give up some part of its visibility and its autonomy to the larger collective; and finally, that each specialization could see this giving-up process not as a total threat to its identity but, conversely, as a move toward strengthening its own performance and its own assigned area of social work practice.[23]

The move toward unification was thus not intended as a surrender of the separate professional identities, or even as a paving of the way for such a surrender. Instead, it was a new process set in motion—a process directed to the search for common skills, common learnings, and a common identity; to learn which aspects of specialized practice could best be developed by the total association and which might best be left to the various subgroups themselves; and to refine and strengthen specialized practice in both its institutional and methodological aspects.

During the past seven years, much of the Association's work has in fact been devoted to these problems of exploring commonalities and learning to distinguish between the tasks of the specializations and those of the Association as a whole. In this sense, the process has been one of cooperation rather than integration as the separate groups have learned to recognize the problems of living and working together.

But the "problems of differential sensitivity" to which Smith referred[24] are still very much in the picture; as the concept of total integration is projected, to replace that of subgroup cooperation, it would be well to review some of these problems. In Smith's analysis, the following are among the internal resistances to which he make reference as he surveys the processes of professional change:

(a) The divergence of aims between rank-and-file members and "future-oriented" leaders who are insensitive to those "whose security systems are rooted in the *status quo*";[25]

---

[22]Nathan E. Cohen, "Professional Social Work Faces the Future," *op. cit.*, p. 82.

[23]See Grace White, "Multiple Associations or a Single Association—Values in Each," *Social Work Journal*, 30, 3 (July 1949), 116–22.

[24]See page 7.

[25]Harvey L. Smith, *op. cit.*, p. 219.

(b) the fact that the professional association tends to represent one interest group within the profession: "in such a case important components of a profession may remain effectively disenfranchised at the level of professional politics."[26] (In this connection, it is interesting to take note of a comment made by Wilensky and Lebeaux on the newly-formed National Association of Social Workers: "It may be predicted," they wrote in 1958, "that the new membership standard in the professional association, if sustained, will have the effect of strengthening the place of casework in professional social work at the expense of other types of practice."[27] Pointing out that 86 percent of social work students were enrolled in casework specializations, they went on to state: "Administration, community organization, development of social policy, social insurance, research—these are in danger of becoming even more peripheral to the professional image of social work than they were under the more loosely defined professional associations which existed prior to the establishment of the National Association of Social Workers."[28]);

(c) the loss of the sense of colleagueship: "In every established occupation shared values and expectations are developed around the bonds of colleagueship, the meaning of the occupation, and its place in the world. This occupational culture may be threatened or torn apart during periods of drastic professional change."[29]

(d) the problems of structural complexity and communication difficulties: "Authority systems and formal structures may become more firmly established and grow apart from the informal working patterns of members of the profession."[30]

Smith concludes his analysis by restressing the need to reconcile the search for formal solutions with a respect for the normal growing processes of the profession: "technical solutions achieved by professions with regard to functions, standards, and qualifications must satisfy, at the same time, the demands of professional integration and adaptation."[31]

The Group Work Specialization: A Case in Point

As the social work profession was building up its bid for a collective identity, a similar process was going on in a budding profession called Group Work with a complex root-structure set in the settlement tradition, the field of sectarian neighborhood organization, the playground movement, the camping movement, and the fields of recreation, and progressive education. Beginning as a number of diverse and disconnected social movements, the new social

---

[26] *Ibid.*

[27] Wilensky and Lebeaux, *op. cit.*, p. 313.

[28] *Ibid.*, p. 314.

[29] Harvey L. Smith, *op. cit.*, p. 221.

[30] *Ibid.*, p. 222.

[31] *Ibid.*, p. 225.

specialization moved to establish a sense of professional community based on a common interest in peer interaction for the solution of social and individual problems.

But the shift from a collection of movements to a sense of common function—from what Gouldner has called the "locals" to the "cosmopolitans"[32]—started late and took longer to gather momentum.

When the American Association of Social Workers was formed, in 1921, the group workers were still holding informal conversations and tentatively exploring their common interests.[33] Even when, in 1936, these conversations were given structure and form through the founding of the American Association for the Study of Group Work, the question of professionalism was still wide open. There were many who felt, deep into the 1940s, that it was not profession-building in which they were engaged but a common exploration of a way of working with people[34]—a way that could be used in a variety of fields and professions, in much the same spirit that Flexner had described social work back in 1915.

But the forces that drive occupations toward the professional ideal were too strong, and in 1946 the American Association of Group Workers bent itself to the task of building a unified profession. It should be remembered that this new association of group workers was born just two years before it accepted the invitation of the American Association of Social Workers and the American Association of Schools of Social Work to join with other social work membership organizations to consider a merger. It should also be noted that even at this time the group workers had not yet made the full social work committment; the AAGW membership requirements still reflected its orientation not only to social work but to the field of recreation and education as well.

What was perhaps most important was that these multiple professional identifications reflected the diversity of the employing agencies themselves, which were struggling to develop definitions of function consistent with the various services offered within their walls. Group work was never a disembodied "method," and could never really become one; it was too closely tied

---

[32]Alvin W. Gouldner, "Organizational Analysis," in Leonard S. Hogan (ed.) *Social Science Theory and Social Work Research* (New York: National Association of Social Workers, 1960), p. 55.

[33]For additional material on the early history of group work, see: William Schwartz, "Group Work and the Social Scene," in Alfred J. Kahn (ed.) *Issues in American Social Work* (New York: Columbia U. Press, 1959), pp. 110–37; Charles S. Levy, *Education for Social Group Work Practice* (New York: Yeshiva University School of Social Work, 1959) 124 pages (mimeo); Murray Schneier, "A History of the American Association of Group Workers 1936–1953," unpublished master's thesis, University of Connecticut School of Social Work, 1954. 130 pages.

[34]See for example: Hedley S. Dimock, Charles E. Hendry, and Karl F. Zerfoss, *A Professional Outlook on Group Education* (New York: Association Press, 1938); William Heard Kilpatrick, *Group Education for a Democracy* (New York: Association Press, 1940) p. vii; Charles E. Hendry, "A Review of Group Work's Affirmations," *Proceedings, National Conference of Social Work,* 1940, pp. 539–51; Charles E. Hendry, "Group-work Imperatives in Wartime," in *Group Work in Wartime* (New York: American Association for the Study of Group Work, 1943), pp. 9–17.

to the fortunes and aspirations of certain well-marked social agencies and traditions. The developing interplay of professional and agency history is a thread that runs through the part-whole struggles of the group work community, the attempts to find a reference group, and its own generic-specific concerns. Group workers are no strangers to the professional problems of unity and diversity.

The final solution was precipitated in the events of 1948 to 1955, when the separate associations hammered out the terms under which they agreed to merge. However pressing was the need for social work unity, the demand presented a serious problem for the group work association—namely, that of turning its attention from the tasks of finding its own identity, defining its own technical contributions to the field, and determining its relationship to other fields of practice, to those of the social work profession, its needs and indeterminancies, and its collective identity. In effect, it changed its perspective from that of a whole defining its parts to that of a part trying to find its place within the whole. The problem persists to the present day, with the group workers "on the one hand, still preoccupied with many of the normal problems of a self-sufficient profession, with its own structure, its distinctive agencies, and its own clientele . . . and . . . simultaneously . . . working on the common social work task of welding the total profession into a unified entity. . . . "[35] Group workers are alternately referred to as a "profession" and as a "field of practice" within social work[36]; they may even, on occasion, produce material which looks longingly toward their old community of interest with the fields of recreation, informal education and physical education.[37]

Thus the rapid pace of events—in which a loosely formed union based on common interest became a disciplined segment of a single profession in one generation, and the entire vocational-professional gamut was run in the space of a single lifetime—created a situation in which the natural process of developing an identity out of the events of practice and experience underwent a kind of forced growth. In the course of this forcing process, progress was rapid but the price was high—individual practitioners held in a state of insecurity because of the need to cope with constantly changing frames of reference, and an unstable group identity put to the task of working out its relationship to a larger identity. The old question, "What is group work?" now became: "If we knew what group work is, what would be its relationship to social work?" As late as 1957, Clara Kaiser commented on the group work-social work liaison with the uneasy phrase "for better or for worse."[38]

---

[35]Schwartz, *op. cit.*, p. 136.

[36]NASW Commission on Social Work Practice, "Identifying Fields of Practice in Social Work," *Social Work, 7,* 2 (April 1962,), 7–14.

[37]Kenneth W. Hindelsperger, "Common Objectives of Group Work, Physical Education and Recreation," *The Group, 16,* 3 (February 1954), 13–18; 25–27. This article was published a year before the official absorption of AAGW into the National Association of Social Workers.

[38]Clara Kaiser, "Characteristics of Social Group Work," in *The Social Welfare Forum, 1957* (New York: Columbia University Press, 1957), p. 168.

The situation has been further complicated by the fact that the "we" element in the group work segment has become progressively more fuzzy as the integrative process continues; the identifications have begun to slip away even before they are defined. Where we could previously identify each other by the agencies for which we worked, this becomes more difficult as group services proliferate in every field of social work practice; where we could recognize ourselves as a colleagueship bound by tradition, philosophical ancestry, and a common language, this too grows diffuse as the subgroup ties give way to those of the larger Social work culture; and where we could with some confidence cooperate in a common search for a unique and identifiable "method," the evidence grows that the major technical task of the profession is not to define "case-work," "group work," and "community organization," but to develop a theory of social work practice that can undergird the work with individuals and groups in whatever situations we may find them. Thus the visibility of the group work segment declines in its three basic areas of ingroup identification—the institutional, the professional, and the methodological.

But to say that an ingroup is waning is one thing; to create a self-fulfilling prophecy is another. The dangers in trend-spotting lie in the temptation to accept their inevitability, thus creating the conditions under which they run their full course. That the old conditions of association have passed is without question; but it is similarly unquestionable that this or any other interest group within the Association still has the power and the responsibility to make some intelligent and planful impact on the way the processes of change will go from here. The fact is that in any large and complex organization members with common interests and common working loyalties will always be drawn together by their sense of colleagueship, and will find ways of working on their problems together. The question is whether such alliances—both local and national—will be built into the formal structure of the Association, or whether they will be forced to take recourse to the informal system, thus weakening both the parts and the whole.

We cannot predict what structural changes the normal processes of intergroup cooperation would have brought about if no present demand were being made for structural reevaluation and decisions as to whether subgroup identities, as we know them, shall be dispersed. We do know that most, if not all, of the problems reported to Harleigh Trecker[39] by the group workers in 1955 are still current and perplexing to workers and their agencies: defining the nature of social work practice in the leisure-time agencies; problems of job classification; need for recruitment on a larger scale; problems of interpretation of group services; group work contributions to the fields of recreation and education; the integration of research from the social sciences; the practice of group work in the rehabilitative settings; the development of personnel standards and practices; group work and social change; the increased

---

[39]Harleigh B. Trecker, ed. *Group Work–-Foundations and Frontiers* (New York: Whiteside and William Morrow, 1955).

production of case materials and publications; professional education for agency practice; problems of group work research; and many other areas pointed up by group workers as those of sharp and immediate concern to the field.

We know, too, that just as these constellations of problems—those concerned with practice and technique, those dealing with the processes and goals of social action, and those pointed at the improvement of agency service and structure—emerged and developed together, so they can only be worked on together; it will be difficult, perhaps impossible, to disengage them for convenience into separate working groups without weakening and diluting the efforts in each area.

Out of their history, group workers have brought three major assets to the work of the combined Association—a strong and identifiable tradition, a body of technical experience, and a set of unfinished tasks. Their tradition of collective action, social reform, the meaning of grass-roots democracy, and the working connection between individual and social problems fits them for the job of providing a driving force within the Association, turning its efforts toward a strong social policy and vigilant social action on the issues of the day. This is the job, as C. Wright Mills put it so brilliantly, of working "continually to translate troubles into issues and issues into the terms of their human meaning for the individual."[40] The group work tradition also fits this segment of the profession to the task of monitoring our own organizational democracy, to the end that it preserve both the sense and the reality of grass-roots control; we are as prone as any large organization to the manipulations of "future-oriented" leaders, the "secret exercise of power,"[41] and the failure to differentiate between the mere symbols of democracy—elections, representation, and so on—and the process of democracy itself. I do not think it is presumptuous to impute to group workers a special sensitivity in this area, or to suggest that a special responsibility exists, for which a certain degree of organized strength may remain necessary.

As to their body of technical experience, group workers have only just begun to analyze its content, to untangle its threads, and to develop some theoretical conceptions based on the teachings of science. The job is enormous, the more so because so much of the work is dependent on the degree of clarity achieved by the lay leaders of the leisure-time agencies themselves, as they struggle to find their function in the community, to stop building their hopes on what Iago Galdston has called the "Champagne pretension and the Root Beer performance,"[42] and to work out a realistic relationship to the field of social welfare and the profession of social work. This interdependence of

---

[40]C. Wright Mills, *The Power Elite* (New York: Oxford U. Press, 1957), p. 319.

[41]*Ibid.*, p. 316. See pp. 316–20, for Mills's discussion of power, authority, and the manipulation of masses.

[42]Iago Galdston, "How Social is Social Work?" Address presented at Alumni Conference, New York School of Social Work of Columbia University, March 26, 1955. Eight pages, mimeo. p. 1.

technical and institutional themes—of professional and agency attempts at self-definition—makes it unlikely that the group workers can with profit be segmented into separate subgroups, with some working on something called "method" and others working on the "field of practice." Divorced from each other, or even separated, these elements may lose so much of their strength and meaning as to throw some doubt on the elaborate organizational process by which they were parted.

The unfinished tasks, as conceived by group workers in the field, were partly indicated in the list gathered by Trecker and referred to previously.[43] The fundamental question here is: Which of these tasks can safely be entrusted to the general processes of the total Association, and which must continue to be invested in an identifiable and visible body of group workers operating freely in the areas of professional practice, agency improvement, and social action?

There is not a great deal of time between now and the time of decision; too much time has already gone by, if there is to be thorough and intelligent work by the total membership on these complex issues. But perhaps our history has accustomed us to making important decisions at breakneck speed, and there is enough time if it is used well at every level of organizational activity.

---

[43]See page 13.

The Nation

Nation Associates, Inc.
333 Sixth Avenue
New York, New York 10014

May 23, 1966

Dear Sirs:

It has become fashionable for certain sociologists to demonstrate their radicalism and their passion for the poor by saddling the social workers with all the responsibility for the evils of the system and publicly beating up on them for their insensitivity, their cowardice, their "welfare colonialism," and other sins. This display would be considerably more impressive if these critics were themselves to rock the boat a bit in the process and produce some sharp and radical analyses of the economic system that creates the conditions they rightfully deplore. But Mr. Cloward has no criticisms of capitalism, only of welfare; and he would solve the problems of public assistance by sabotaging the whole program. Further, he will "end poverty" through the guaranteed annual income, which he naively assumes will be pegged at rates far above the bare subsistence levels of public assistance.

What Mr. Lubove comes up with is that social workers should transform themselves into "hawks," eschew their "service role," and "confront the hard questions of power and income redistribution." One needs to ask which of the "service roles" he wants deleted and what such a "confrontation" would look like. If he is advocating more radical forms of income distribution and wants the social workers to join him in such a program, let him say what he has in mind; let him suggest specifically what social services he would have us eliminate and what economic solutions he would have us advocate. Anything less is mere brave talk.

This kind of cheap and easy scapegoating simply diverts attention from the real problems of the people and the work that needs to be done. And it is a serious matter that the establishment of the social workers as a group of convenient villains serves to discredit the necessary work in which they are

---

engaged. For all of the fulminations against the so-called "service role," I have heard none of these critics—with the exception of the savagely irresponsible plan of Cloward and Piven—suggest that certain specific services be cut off from people who need them.

It takes considerable naivete not to realize that the social work profession—like any profession—is only very partially responsible for defining its own tasks and setting the institutional framework in which it functions. We should not have to remind sociologists that professions do not lead revolutions, nor do they make the major economic decisions in our society. Further, they are hardly ever in a position to "decide" whether they will do the jobs for which they were trained or lead broad social movements for the redistribution of income—however desirable that might be.

There is no real choice between serving human beings in trouble and changing the system in which they live, and one does not prove one's commitment to one by openly despising the other. It was C. Wright Mills who pointed out to his sociologist colleagues that they must understand deeply the connections between public issues and private troubles, and that they must take responsibility for showing the interplay between the two. To this idea most social workers and sociologists are committed and neither their interests or those of the people are served when they turn their guns on each other. The enemy is in another direction.

Sincerely,

William Schwartz
Associate Professor of Social Work

Private Troubles and Public Issues: One Social Work Job or Two?

William Schwartz

There are certain human issues that are never laid to rest. They are "solved" by the best minds of every generation, yet they remain troublesome, suspended, permanent centers of uneasiness. These issues tend to persist in the same form in which they began—as polarized absolutes between which we are asked to choose. We are urged to decide whether we are for the individual or the state, for freedom or discipline, nature or nurture, means or ends, structure or process, the past or the future. The specific controversies change, but the demand is always the same: you must be for the one or the many; you are a process man or a goals man; permissive or restrictive; for stability or for change; and so on into dualism after dualism.

These "choices" never satisfy. We feel trapped in the array of absolutes, wanting some of each and feeling that the problems have somehow been misstated. Those who have only to speculate about life can abstract the problems from the people and be satisfied with the clean ring of deductive logic. But those who must put the issues to work must look for solutions that not only include both polarities—the how and the what; the means and the ends; and the rest—but integrate them so completely that they cannot be pulled apart into false alternatives and inoperable choices.

The dualisms make it necessary to create *religious* solutions rather than technical ones, those where faith is more important than fact and strong belief is its own justification. Having sworn allegiance to one of the alternatives, there is no need for evidence, for records, for research, or any other effort to translate objectives into ways of achieving them. There is a kind of magical quality about it, a form of prayer, where solutions are invoked by forming the proper words and saying them with a certain emphasis and conviction. Hutchins, for example, urges the "pursuit of knowledge for its own sake"[1] (the content *vs.* process dualism) in the following tones: "Education implies teaching. Teaching implies knowledge. Knowledge is truth. The truth is everywhere the same. Hence education should be everywhere the same."[2] He tells us further that "the aim of education is to connect man with man, to connect the present with the past, and to advance the thinking of the race. If this is the aim of education, it cannot be left to the sporadic, spontaneous interests of children or even of undergraduates."[3] His conclusion is irresistible, a haunting strain from the old days: "One objection may be that the students will not like it, which is, as we have seen, irrelevant."[4]

A frequent consequence of the polarization of complex problems is that the adversaries forget who their real enemies are and fall on those closest to them. What ensues is a kind of "family quarrel" which takes on a ferocity not ordinarily wasted on strangers. The following was written by social workers about other social workers in public welfare:

> . . . recipients who have now learned to organize and fight the welfare system may not submit any longer to the preachments of case workers. Indeed, the movement may soon demand that welfare workers stay out of the ghettos and barrios, thus putting a halt to routine invasions of recipients' homes which take place under the guise of establishing rapport and conducting rehabilitation (in probable violation of the Fourth Amendment).[5]

Each profession creates its own versions of these dilemmas, with their trumped-up "choices," the verbal magic, and the family quarrels. But since they are professions, the frustrations are particularly acute. Professionals are paid for doing, for operationalizing, and not simply for speculating on the nature of life. The need for technical rather than dogmatic solutions is inherent in their social role. Although they may sometimes be a little apologetic about it, the fact is that their stock in trade is technique, and society holds them responsible for their ability to perform their work with skills not available to the ordinary citizen. How-to-do-it is the bread and butter of the lawyer, the doctor, the engineer—and the social worker. Without it they fail to differentiate themselves from the knowledgeable public, the informed layman, and the rest of those in society who are alive to its issues and have opinions about them. The professional distinguishes himself not by his general

---

[1]Robert M. Hutchins, *The Higher Learning in America* (New Haven: Yale University Press, 1936), p. 36.

[2]*Ibid.*, p. 66.

[3]*Ibid.*, p. 71.

[4]*Ibid.*, p. 86.

[5]Richard A. Cloward and Frances Fox Piven, "Finessing the Poor," *The Nation*, October 7, 1968, p. 332.

wisdom, his philosophy, or his goals, but by his ability to perform an operation, teach a class, build a bridge, plead a case, or use the resources of a community to help a person in trouble. Those who have studied the sociology of the professions have made a special point of their relationship to action and to skill. Parsons notes that "the professional man is thus a 'technical expert' of some order by virtue of his mastery of the tradition and the skills of its use."[6] And Wilensky and Lebeaux state that "the profession represents a monopoly of skill, which is linked to standards of training and which justifies a monopoly of activity in an area."[7]

Thus, when these polarizations appear in the professional arena, they are disruptive of technical advancement. They may serve for a while to dramatize important issues,[8] but the banner-waving, the quarrels over abstractions, and the ritualistic emphasis on goals without means, all impede the work on the central professional tasks. The dualisms inhibit action, and the term "technique" itself becomes invidious rather than the symbol of highest achievement.[9] As long ago as 1920, it was Eduard Lindeman, always sensitive to this problem, who complained:

> But we have been surfeited with the sentimental appeals in all spheres of social work. And sentiment, unsupported by scientific fact and principle, saps the dynamic forces of community life, making of our attempts at social progress a series of trial-and-error, hope-and-delusion spasms. . . . What we ask of the specialist is technique which rings true and organization which is unselfish.[10]

It is not that sentiment is unimportant to professionals. On the contrary, their hopes and convictions are indispensable to them as they work. It is simply that these are preludes to action, not accomplishments in themselves or debaters' points that carry their own ring of finality. Such have been the issues of "child *vs.* curriculum" in education, "justice *vs.* mercy" in law, "innate *vs.* cultural" determinants in psychiatry.

Social work has created its share of these dilemmas. It has had its "diagnostic *vs.* functional"; it is currently enjoying its "generic *vs.* specific"; and there will be others. But the granddaddy of them all, the oldest and still most vigorous, is the issue of the "social" *vs.* the "psychological"—its responsibility for social reform on the one hand, and individual help to people in trouble

---

[6]Talcott Parsons, "A Sociologist Looks at the Legal Profession," in *Essays in Sociological Theory* (rev. ed.; Glencoe, Ill.: Free Press, 1954), p. 372.

[7]Harold L. Wilensky and Charles N. Lebeaux, *Industrial Society and Social Welfare* (New York: Russell Sage Foundation, 1958), p. 284.

[8]This point was made to me in a conversation with Dr. Hyman Weiner.

[9]See, for example, Alvin L. Schorr, "The Retreat to the Technician," *Social Work*, IV, No. 1 (1959), 29–33.

[10]E. C. Lindeman, "Organization and Technique for Rural Recreation," in *Proceedings of the National Conference of Social Work* (Chicago: University of Chicago Press, 1920), p. 324.

on the other. The issue has all the elements of the classical dualism, with the polarized abstractions, the family quarrel, the self-realizing objectives, and the persistent, unsolved feeling despite the attention of the best professional minds of every generation since social work began. In today's unstable and uproarious American scene it has taken on new forms, a new language, and a fresh sense of urgency.

As always, the problem has been identified by each generation in its own terms. In 1913 Porter Lee was already engrossed in his search for the connections between the spirit of reform and the technical problems of service to people. He called it "the crystallizing of enthusiasm into programs,"[11] and he said:

> To go from concept to program and from program to technique is to take the long dreary drop from ideals to routine, from the heroic to the humdrum, from enthusiasm to devotion. But technique is still the factor which rounds out our march towards social justice and every social program must in the end stand or fall upon the quality of its technique.
>
> . . . seen in its true relation to the other aspects of social work [technique] is as vivid and as appealing as the ideas which ought to guide it.[12]

Then, in 1929, Lee summarized the issue as that of "cause *vs.* function" and tried to reconcile the two. Beginning with Bryce's notion that the struggle for democracy comes not out of positive ideas but from the need to remove certain tangible grievances,[13] Lee pointed out that "a cause is usually a movement directed toward the elimination of an intrenched evil."[14] When the evil is disposed of, the interest lessens. He went on to say:

> The momentum of the cause will never carry over adequately to the subsequent task of making its fruits permanent. The slow methodical organized effort needed to make enduring the achievement of the cause calls for different motives, different skill, different machinery.
>
> . . . an outstanding problem of social work at the present time is that of developing its service as a function of well-organized community life without sacrificing its capacity to inspire in men enthusiasm for a cause.[15]

---

[11]Porter R. Lee, "Technical Training for Social Work," in Lee, *Social Work as Cause and Function and Other Papers* (New York: Columbia University Press, 1937), p. 29.

[12]*Ibid.*, pp. 30–31.

[13]James Bryce, *The American Commonwealth* (London and New York: Macmillan, 1888).

[14]Porter R. Lee, "Social Work as Cause and Function," in Lee, *op. cit.*, Presidential Address, National Conference of Social Work, 1929, in *Social Work as Cause and Function and Other Papers* (New York: Columbia University Press, 1937), p. 3.

[15]*Ibid.*, pp. 4, 5.

Much earlier, Mary Richmond had written of the "wholesale" and "retail" methods of social reform, avowing her strong belief that "the order of march for most minds is from the particular to the general,"[16] asking her followers to "stick to the individual case," and concluding that "the whole of social reform is in the retail method, when we follow faithfully wherever its careful working out may lead."[17] Even earlier, in 1896, she had warned against the diversionary effects of the settlement movement.[18]

Clarke Chambers, reviewing the "wholesale-retail" dimensions of social work, states that "over the past 40 or 50 years, it was inspired more by St. Sigmund than St. Karl,"[19] and continues:

> And so the two overlapping phases of social work continue to exist, not always harmoniously, but certainly in interdependence—the one focused on the individual and his welfare, strongly influenced by the psychological disciplines, introspective, dealing in personalized, retail services; the other concerned with reform, with reconstruction, informed primarily by the social sciences, extroverted, dealing in group or community or wholesale services.[20]

Chambers's analysis of the tensions between the "prophets"—those who thunder and hold up absolute standards—and the "priests"—those who minister, listen, and judge not—illustrates what I have called the "family quarrel": "Between the 'movers and the shakers' on the one hand, and the 'seekers and the sojourners' on the other there has often been misunderstanding and bad blood."[21]

Kenneth Pray wrote of "workmanship" and "statesmanship."[22] Others have stressed the polarities of clinician and activist, technician and reformer, Freud and your favorite sociologist, the "service" and the "movement." A few years ago, I tried my hand at the service-movement theme:

> When a profession is young, a considerable proportion of its thought and energy is devoted to the process of calling attention to the social need out of which it grew. From its special vantage point, the new group

---

[16]Mary Richmond, "The Retail Method of Reform," in Joanna C. Colcord, ed., *The Long View* (New York: Russell Sage Foundation, 1930), pp. 215–16.

[17]*Ibid.*, p. 221.

[18]Mary Richmond, "Criticism and Reform in Charity," in Colcord, *op. cit.*, pp. 50, 51.

[19]Clarke A. Chambers, "An Historical Perspective on Political Action *vs.* Individualized Treatment," in *Current Issues in Social Work Seen in Historical Perspective* (New York: Council on Social Work Education, 1962), p. 52.

[20]*Ibid.*, p. 53.

[21]*Ibid.*, p. 54.

[22]Kenneth L. M. Pray, *Social Work in a Revolutionary Age and Other Papers* (Philadelphia: University of Pennsylvania Press, 1949), p. 231.

> is intensely aware of this need, of the importance of doing something about it, and of the necessity for arousing a similar sense of urgency in the minds of the general public. This is another way of saying that a profession begins as a *movement;* its primary function at this stage is to agitate for a place on the social agenda, its workers are dedicated to the cause and its advocacy, and its major spokesmen are social philosophers, energetic social advocates, and commanding personalities who call attention to themselves and to the objects of their concern.
>
> As this effort begins to achieve some success, and as the group and its cause begin to take on some stability and permanence within the social division of labor, the concerns of the profession undergo a gradual shift from the problems of social *advocacy* to those of social *effectiveness.* Having established the social need as a proper object of society's attention, it remains to be shown that the profession can do the job and do it well. Increasingly, then, a greater proportion of professional energy is diverted from what *should be* to what *is.* The concern with ends becomes a growing curiosity about the means for achieving them; the stress on intentions, motives, and enthusiasms gives way to a larger preoccupation with efficiency and productivity; and the working skills of practitioners take on a greater significance than their ability to formulate statements of philosophy and aspiration.
>
> . . . That the emphasis on means can be used to evade social responsibility is, after all, no more surprising than the earlier discovery that the preoccupation with goals can be used in the same way. Both dangers simply point up the challenge to the modern profession: to draw upon a growing knowledge of social reality, to frame a sense of purpose consistent with that reality, to conceptualize its practice in forms that make it testable and teachable, and to retain in the process its initial vigor, its power of advocacy, and its driving vision of what society should be like.[23]

This would seem to have tucked the issue away rather nicely—except that in the six years since that was written, the world changed again, and the cause-function dilemma became sharper and more demanding than ever before.

In today's world, the initiatives have changed, and the actionists within the profession are no longer in the minority. It is the "psychological" emphasis now that is on the defensive, and, at least in the literature and the open forums, the militants rule the roost. This does not resolve the historic dilemma, or even ease it; it simply drives it underground. The battle for supremacy continues, the impossible choices, and the family quarrel.

Thus Eveline Burns tells us that "the center of gravity has shifted away from an emphasis on what goes on inside the individual to an emphasis on

---

[23]William Schwartz, "Small Group Science and Group Work Practice," *Social Work,* VIII, No. 4 (1963), 40–41.

improving the functioning of society"[24]—without explaining how such a shift takes place and how, specifically, one manages to choose between the two. The fact is that no such choices are made within the professional arena; the practitioners on whom troubled people depend could easily explain to us that their clients would take small comfort from knowing that the social workers are out somewhere "improving society."

As the rhetoric mounts, the polarities widen. Against Vinter's sideswipe at "group workers in search of a cause"[25] there is Frankel's accusation that the social worker "is tinkering with the broken products that are brought to the repair shop, but he is not asking himself why so many of these broken products have been brought in."[26] Roy Lubove urges us to eschew the "service role," become "hawks" instead of "doves," and "confront the hard questions of power and income redistribution."[27] Typically, he does not tell us which of the social services he would eliminate and what specific forms his "confrontation" might take.[28]

In effect, what began as a necessary and overdue attack on the idea that if the *people* are changed the system will take care of itself, has turned into its opposite: if the *system* is changed, the people will take care of themselves. The reaction against purely psychological explanations has been so fierce that it has produced purely sociological ones, spawning analyses that romanticize "action" as the previous ideas romanticized "insight" and glorify structural solutions as we previously glorified individual ones.

In the process, a new utopianism has emerged, with much talk about "destroying systems" and "power and income redistribution"—all naïvely set within the existing economic structure. Cloward and Piven actually propose to end poverty by forcing public welfare out of existence and creating a guaranteed annual income, which, whatever its merits, is not likely to escape the limits of least eligibility and soar too far above the present rates of public assistance.[29] Eisman's vision is dramatic: "Social work, a profession dedicated to planned social progress, has the ability to develop skills and insights needed to bring about a successful welfare-class revolution."[30] Others would

---

[24]Eveline M. Burns, "Tomorrow's Social Needs and Social Work Education," *Journal of Education for Social Work,* II, No. 1 (1966), 16.

[25]Robert D. Vinter, "Group Work: Perspectives and Prospects," in *Social Work with Groups,* 1959 (New York: National Association of Social Workers, 1959), p. 147.

[26]Charles Frankel, "Obstacles to Action for Human Welfare," in *The Social Welfare Forum, 1961* (New York: Columbia University Press, 1961), p. 281.

[27]Roy Lubove, "Social Work and the Life of the Poor," *The Nation,* May 23, 1966, pp. 609–11.

[28]See William Schwartz, "Bucking the System," letter to the Editor, *The Nation,* June 27, 1966, pp. 762, 780.

[29]Richard A. Cloward and Frances Fox Piven, "A Strategy to End Poverty," *The Nation,* May 2, 1966, pp. 510–17.

[30]Martin Eisman, "Social Work's New Role in the Welfare-Class Revolution," *Social Work,* XIV, No. 2 (1969), 86.

dispense with the profession itself, the prime scapegoat for the plight of the poor. Here the attack is no longer directed to the bad practices of social workers, but to the social work institution itself: "It may even be unfair," concludes Lubove, "to ask a dove to become a hawk."[31]

The "Advocacy" Variation

The most recent effects of the cause-function dilemma are evident in the present preoccupation with the "advocacy" role now being pressed by a committee of the professional association[32] and discussed at some length in a recent issue of the professional journal devoted to the subject.[33] As explained by one of its major proponents:

> . . . the role of advocate has been co-opted from the field of law. Often the institutions with which local residents must deal are not even neutral, much less positively motivated, toward handling the issues brought to them by community groups. In fact, they are frequently overtly negative and hostile, often concealing or distorting information about rules, procedures, and office hours. By their own partisanship on behalf of instrumental organizational goals, they create an atmosphere that demands advocacy on behalf of the poor man. . . .
>
> In short, the worker's posture, both to the community residents and to the institutional representatives with whom he is engaged, is that of advocate for the client group's point of view. While employing these techniques, the worker is not enabler, broker, expert, consultant, guide, or social therapist. He is, in fact, a partisan in the social conflict, and his expertise is available *exclusively* to serve client interests.[34]

Beginning with a real social problem—the breakdown of service to people in need—the advocates, with the best will in the world, find no way but to create a permanent "social conflict" between an unchangeably evil system and a hopelessly alienated client. The worker must then "choose" the client and devote himself "exclusively" to his interests. "To whom, then, is the worker's primary responsibility: the agency or the client? If the former, the issue is simply met. If the latter—as in the case of the advocate—the agency may well become a target for change."[35] If, indeed, the worker feels that it must be the one or the other, he can do no less than choose the client and be prepared to cast his lot with the enemies of those who pay his salary. But this,

---

[31]Lubove, *op. cit.*, p. 611.

[32]National Association of Social Workers (NASW) *Ad Hoc* Committee on Advocacy, "The Social Worker as Advocate: Champion of Social Victims," *Social Work,* XIV, No. 2 (1969), 16–22.

[33]See *Social Work,* Vol. XIV, No. 2 (1969).

[34]Charles F. Grosser, "Community Development Serving the Urban Poor," *Social Work,* X, No. 3 (1965), 18; italics added.

[35]George A. Brager, "Advocacy and Political Behavior," *Social Work,* XIII, No. 2 (68), 7.

of course, is the ultimate dualism, the polarization of the people and their own institutions. The advocate must now, presumably, agree with the very establishment he despises that the agencies are the natural enemies of the people who need them. "Change the people" has become "change the system," since they can no longer hope to change each other through the skilled use of the client-agency encounter.

The results are predictable. Again, much of the talk is revolutionary, but it is essentially romantic rather than programmatic, because social workers do not lead revolutions. Within the professional context it turns into a kind of "let's-you-and-him-fight" position that confuses both clients and workers.

From the first false choice, others emerge. The NASW *Ad Hoc* committee tells us not only that "the obligation to the client takes primacy over the obligation to the employer,"[36] but also that NASW has an obligation to the worker that takes priority over the obligation to the agency."[37] Wineman and James extend the approach to the social work schools, setting them against their training agencies and demanding that the student be given an opportunity to see his school "put its action where its mouth is"[38] And so it goes: school against agency; agency against professional association; social work practitioner against social work administrator; "social worker" against "welfare worker";[39] some clients against other clients.[40] All is absolute, all is split into halves, and all is stereotyped.

Indeed, the split is so sharp that in the advocacy programs put forward by both the *Ad Hoc* Committee for the professional association and Wineman and James for the social work schools not one of the many steps proposed calls for an offer of assistance to the agency itself. It is as if any contact with the agency system would contaminate them, or throw their identification with the poor into serious question.

But, as always, the problem of method is the most serious. The disdain for means is evident in the definition of "process" as a straw man: ". . . the process orientation is distinct from the others in that process is valued for its own sake"[41]—an accusation frequently made but impossible to document. Brager points out that "although the concept [of the social worker as advocate] is both important and in current use, its methodological implications have not yet been seriously considered."[42] Nevertheless, some discussion of tactics must be held sooner or later, and here we find ourselves developing a

[36]NASW *Ad Hoc* Committee on Advocacy, p. 18.

[37]*Ibid.*, p. 21.

[38]David Wineman and Adrienne James, "The Advocacy Challenge to Schools of Social Work," *Social Work*, XIV, No. 2 (1969), 32.

[39]See Eisman, *op. cit.*, p. 82.

[40]See NASW *Ad Hoc* Committee on Advocacy, *op. cit.*, p. 19.

[41]Brager, *op. cit.*, p. 9.

[42]*Ibid.*, p. 6.

literature of guile, with Machiavelli as the new culture hero. Brager cites studies to show that people in influencing roles, as well as bright college students, are in significant agreement with Machiavelli's ideas.[43] He points out that "in the context in which social workers function, advocacy requires political behavior, and political behavior includes manipulation."[44] In action, the method looks like this:

> He [the social worker] must then walk the tightrope between conflicting demands. If client identification is uppermost to him, he will present the case to his agency in a way most likely to garner support for a client-oriented course of action. This may require that he minimize the risk to his agency while underscoring the importance of his client's interests. He may even argue the case with more passion than he feels, if he believes that his emotional tone will positively affect his gaining administrative support. He will, in short, engage in political behavior.[45]

It is important to note that guile is not reserved for the employer alone; it is elevated to a general methodological principle. It is recognized, however, that the approach has some dangers, and Brager's discussion of professional technique concludes:

> The potential costs of political strategies must always be assessed against their potential gains, so that one's morality is supported by expedience. Social workers may use up their currency as, for example, when a person develops a reputation for guile. With his motives suspect, his hidden agendas revealed to view, and his word in doubt, he can hardly be an effective advocate. Since people resent being treated as means to an end rather than ends in themselves, those who appear to use them instrumentally are likely to be ineffective.[46]

Precisely so; and the advocates present clear evidence of how manipulativeness emerges from an unresolved means-ends problem. The fact is that manipulation, which C. Wright Mills defines as the "secret exercise of power,"[47] diminishes both those who use it and those on whom it is used. To people in need, it makes little difference whether they are being pushed around by the "good guys" or the "bad guys." The loss of freedom and dignity is the same.

The methodological issue is deeply troublesome for many within the advocacy camp itself. Specht states:

> The question for the professional is whether his objective is to enable people to make choices or to assert *his* choice and cast his lot with those

---

[43] *Ibid.*, pp. 9, 14.

[44] *Ibid.*, p. 9.

[45] *Ibid.*, p. 8.

[46] *Ibid.*, p. 14.

[47] C. Wright Mills, *The Power Elite* (New York: Oxford University Press, 1957), p. 316.

who have arrived at *the* solution. Social work operates in a framework of democratic decision-making, and if one decides that the framework is no longer viable, then there is no profession of social work to be practiced.[48]

Finally, the family quarrel is pushed to its furthest point when the *Ad Hoc* Committee recommends to NASW a program that would go beyond "mere urging" in holding members to the "obligation under the Code of Ethics to be an advocate," and states that "under certain circumstances . . . the obligation is enforceable under the Code of Ethics."[49] It is further noted that the NASW Commission on Ethics "reviewed these findings . . . and . . . interprets the Code of Ethics as giving full support to advocacy as a professional obligation."[50] Unfortunately, the Committee itself deplores the general lack of understanding of advocate behavior and admits that "most social workers seem wholly deficient in this area."[51] Thus the members of the professional association seem about to be punished for not doing something that has not yet been defined.

The motives of the advocates are not in question here; it is the analysis that is weak. They subvert their own real identification with the poor and the oppressed by their neglect of the dialectics of the client-agency relationship. An agency is not a static organism with no play of internal forces; and those who insist that it is must cut themselves off from the most progressive elements within it, and take their clients with them. It was Brager himself who said that the agency is "a coalition of diverse interests"[52] and that "the task is to foster that influence within the agency coalition, so that goals congenial to the value system of social work may be specified and attained."[53]

One Job or Two?

The psychological-social dilemma has cut so deep as to suggest to some social work educators that society would be served best by a "two-track" system of social work education. Such an arrangement would create two broad specializations in the profession: the "technicians," who would devote themselves to the tasks of practice, treatment, and psychological theory; and the "planners," who would be taught the theories and strategies of social policy and action. Miller and Rein suggest, in one of their "models for change," the

---

[48]Harry Specht, "Disruptive Tactics," *Social Work,* XIV, No. 2 (1969), 13–14. See also, for a discussion of the "troubles and issues" theme. Ronald A. Feldman and Harry Specht, "The World of Social Group Work," in *Social Work Practice, 1968* (New York: Columbia University Press, 1968), pp. 77–93.

[49]NASW *Ad Hoc* Committee on Advocacy, *op. cit.,* p. 21.

[50]*Ibid.,* p. 21 n.

[51]*Ibid.,* p. 20.

[52]George Brager, "Goal Formation: an Organizational Perspective," in *Social Work with Groups 1960* (New York: National Association of Social Workers, 1960). p. 35.

[53]*Ibid.,* p. 36.

separation of casework from the other social work fields and discontinuance of the search for the "generic."[54] Kahn remarks on the variety of new social roles required of the profession, and issues a call for "some other kinds of people" who would have to be appraised by new criteria and . . . perhaps even trained in new ways."[55] Burns draws her implications for professional education as follows:

> In place of the "methods" ideology, it should be recognized that there are two types of professional workers who are differentiated by their *professional objectives*. The first, the social caseworker, is concerned with bringing about change in the individual and is essentially clinically and therapeutically oriented. The second, the social welfare specialist, is concerned with change in social institutions and is non-clinical. One could also differentiate them by saying that the professional activity of the first justifies—indeed, requires—certification or licensing because an unqualified person can do so much harm to the individual client) whereas the second does not. Freed from the necessity to pattern itself on the clinical model, the curriculum of the social welfare practitioner could then be developed in accordance with the nature of its subject matter, the presenting problems, and the professional orientation of its students, whether they are aiming toward community organization, leadership in a variety of roles, administration, or research.[56]

A half-licensed profession would indeed be a living symbol of the schizophrenia induced by the failure to understand the connections between private troubles and public issues. To create a "department" for each would in fact institutionalize the very evils they mean to solve. The "clinicians" would be shielded from any further pressure to bring the weight of their experience with people in trouble to bear on the formation of public policy; and the "social planners" would be set free from the realities of practice and left alone to fashion their expertise not from the struggles and sufferings of people but from their own clever and speculating minds. It would be as if the legal profession were to decide to train its lawyers in one curriculum and its judges in another. Practice and statesmanship are functions of each other, and each is informed by the demands of the other. The planner who has not practiced will be as shallow in his policy-making as the practitioner who has not made his impact on policy will be in his work with people.

Thus, the question for the profession is whether it now gives itself over to the polarization of the individual and the social, building it into its very structure, or tries to see more deeply into the connections between the two so that it may create a single vision of the professional function. To remain split in

---

[54]Miller and Rein, *op. cit.*

[55]Alfred J. Kahn, "The Function of Social Work in the Modern World," in Alfred J. Kahn, ed., *Issues in American Social Work* (New York: Columbia University Press 1959), p. 38.

[56]Burns, *op. cit.*, p. 18.

this way is to remain uncertain of our identity, accusing each other of not being the "real" social workers, and providing the forces of reaction with the ammunition they need to keep watering down programs and diluting services to people in need. If, on the other hand, we can find a function that will integrate insight and action, service and policy, psychology and sociology, the individual and the group, the people and their institutions, we may develop a profession that spends much less energy on the family quarrel and more on building a unified conception of professional knowledge and skill. The problem is deeply felt in many corners of the profession. "It is not fitting," says Konopka, "for this profession to indulge in the destructive practice of arguing an 'either-or' position—either direct help to individuals or a change of society."[57] And a graduating social work student said to me, in a last-semester seminar: This school has taught me to be a good caseworker; and it has also taught me to be ashamed of it."

Toward a Single Focus

How can we merge the twin images of individual and social need into one? In a complex and disordered world, there are forces constantly working to pull them apart, and the search for unity is an old one. Back in the social ferment of the Progressive Era, James Mark Baldwin studied the relationship between psychology and sociology and commented, in 1911:

> It is, to my mind, the most remarkable outcome of modern social theory—the recognition of the fact that the individual's normal growth lands him in essential solidarity with his fellows, while on the other hand the exercise of his social duties and privileges advances his highest and purest individuality.[58]

Mary Follett searched for "a method by which the full integrity of the individual shall be one with social progress."[59] She preferred to think of "individual" and "social" rather as the "short view" and the "long view."[60] And she said: "The problem of democracy is how to develop power from experience, from the interplay of our daily, concrete activities."[61] Eduard Lindeman saw "adjustment" as a "dual process," noting that "the forms of social organization need to be adjusted in such a manner as to produce cohesion among the constituent units, and the individuals need to be adjusted to the social forms without sacrificing their essential freedom."[62] The literature is

---

[57]Gisela Konopka, "Social Values and Social Action: the Place of History in the Social Work Curriculum," Annual Program, Council on Social Work Education, 1967.

[58]James Mark Baldwin, *The Individual and Society; or, Psychology and Sociology* (Boston: Richard G. Badger, the Gorham Press, 1911), p. 16.

[59]Mary P. Follett, *Creative Experience* (New York: Longmans, Green, 1930), p. xiv.

[60]*Ibid.,* pp. 37, 38.

[61]*Ibid.,* p. 197.

[62]Eduard C. Lindeman, "From Social Work to Social Science," *New Republic,* (June 2, 1926), p. 48.

huge, and we have established again and again the general thesis that "it is only through social survival that the individual survives, but it is only through the survival of the individual and of some measure of his self-centered concerns and ambitions that society survives."[63]

In our own time, C. Wright Mills has seen most clearly into the individual-social connections and their implications for professionals identified with social struggle. He points up the distinction between what he calls the "personal troubles of milieu" and the "public issues of social structure,"[64] and notes that *trouble* is a private matter, while *issue* is a public one. Most important, he stresses that each must be stated in terms of the other, and of the interaction between the two. Taken in time, this way of posing the problems of an era brings us closest to its central characteristics. The task of the social scientist, he continues, is to clarify both the private troubles and the public issues of his time; it is here that the sociological imagination is most needed.

Earlier, Mills had said: "It is the task of the liberal institution, as of the liberally educated man, continually to translate troubles into issues and issues into the terms of their human meaning for the individual."[65] In this light, the polarization of private troubles and public issues cuts off each from the reinforcing power of the other. There can be no "choice"—or even a division of labor—between serving individual needs and dealing with social problems, if we understand that a private trouble is simply a specific example of a public issue, and that a public issue is made up of many private troubles. To speak of confrontation as an alternative to service is to betray one's misunderstanding of both.

Every agency is an arena for the conversion of private troubles into public issues. The agency begins, in fact, as an effort to provide a service that is of specific consequence both to society and to its individuals; each system is a special case of the individual-social encounter. That there are quarrels over ownership and the terms of the contract is not surprising in a class society. And that, in a badly organized collective where the few rule the many, there will often be a nasty feeling between the service and its people is to be expected. But the fact remains that the basic relationship between an institution and its people is symbiotic; each needs the other for his own survival. Each individual needs to negotiate the systems with which he must come to terms—school, welfare, occupation, neighborhood, and others. Each agency, on its part, needs to justify its existence by serving the people for whom it was designed. It is a form of social contract; and when the arrangement goes wrong, as it frequently does, those who claim that the contract is broken do no service to the people or to the agency. The arena of need remains the

---

[63]Arthur T. Jersild, *Child Psychology* (3d ed.; New York: Prentice Hall, Inc., 1942), p. 158.

[64]C. Wright Mills, *The Sociological Imagination* (New York: Oxford University Press, 1959), p. 8.

[65]C. Wright Mills, *The Power Elite* (New York: Oxford University Press, 1957), p. 319.

same, and the symbiosis remains intact—merely obscure to the unpracticed eye.

In the individual's struggle to negotiate the various systems of demand and opportunity that his society offers him, he will, wherever it is made possible, enlist the aid of people who have similar tasks and similar systems to manage. The peer group or mutual aid system then becomes a way of helping him negotiate the larger system and getting what it was designed to offer him. It cannot, however, substitute for the institutional structure and provide the volume of resources available to the larger society. What it can do is strengthen its members and heighten their sense of poise and security in the processes through which they reach out to fulfill the terms of the symbiotic relationship. The institutions are theirs; they do not belong to anyone else, for there is no one else. And the move is toward the agency, not against it—to make the system-representatives listen if they are not listening, to take responsibility for their part in the process, and to institutionalize their own roles in the service encounter. The client and the clients together need their institutions; they have no stake in destroying them.

The agencies, as do the clients, reach out with all the strength at their command at a given moment, and all the ambivalence. They have devices dedicated to both stability and change, and their managers are torn between the need to make people fit into preconceived structures and the desire to create and to innovate. They are not devils, they simply represent both the worst and the best motives of the communities that pay them. In Bertha Reynolds's words:

> Our agencies are social institutions, molded by the same contending interests in our communities that produce both the relationships which bring people together and those that drive them apart. Whatever we find in our communities, we find also in social agencies.
>
> Social work and social living, then, instead of being in contrast, or being artificially brought together, are inextricably mixed, and inseparable.[66]

On the ambivalence of systems, Lippitt, Watson, and Westley offer the following in their analysis of systems, individual and social:

> We need always to remember that when examined closely all dynamic systems reveal a continuous process of change—adaptation, adjustment, reorganization. That is what we mean by dynamic, by being alive. . . .
>
> But it is equally true, as we can learn both from experience and from the results of scientific studies, that all these systems exhibit a high

---

[66]Bertha Capen Reynolds, *Social Work and Social Living* (New York: Citadel Press, 1951), p. viii.

> degree of stability, constancy, or rigidity, in many aspects of their operation and organization.[67]

Thus the problem, throughout modern society, is one of complex, ambivalent systems that are hard to negotiate by all but the most skillful and best organized. How can such systems be kept functional? What they need, and what each tries feebly to provide in some form or other, is a force within the system itself that will act as a hedge against the system's own complexity. Its charge is to see that people do not get lost, that the system does not overpower its consumers, and that the processes through which client and system reach out to each other remain viable. Although this is a system role, necessary to its proper functioning, it places the role-occupant in a unique position in which he is not exclusively identified with either the client or the agency, but with the processes through which they reach out to each other. The practitioner is required neither to "change the people" nor to "change the system," but to change the ways in which they deal with each other.

I believe that it is this "mediating" or "third-force" function for which social work was invented and that historically it is the function in which it has done its best work.[68]

A Professional Function

Rein and Riessman discuss a "third-force" role for the community action programs (CAPs), in these terms:

> These new programs constitute a form of third party intervention between the poor who represent the demand side of the social service market system and the established community institutions who represent the suppliers of service. As a third party they fully represent neither, but rather they are an attempt to produce a better juncture between both. They can be seen as a strategy for bringing together the citizen and the bureaucracy; its techniques of "linkage" are an attempt to provide greater coherence into a highly fragmented system.[69]

What I have called the "hedging" role in complex social systems has been institutionalized in many forms throughout the world. Rein and Riessman discuss a number of these phenomena in this country and Europe, citing the political clubs, the various information and referral services, the trade union counselors, the veterans' representatives, the British Citizens' Advice

---

[67]Ronald Lippitt, Jeanne Watson, and Bruce Westley, *The Dynamics of Planned Change* (New York: Harcourt, Brace & World, 1958), p. 10.

[68]For a fuller development of the mediating construct, see William Schwartz, "The Social Worker in the Group," in *The Social Welfare Forum, 1961* (New York: Columbia University Press, 1961), pp. 146–71.

[69]Martin Rein and Frank Riessman, "A Strategy for Antipoverty Community Action Programs," *Social Work,* XI, No. 2 (1966), 3.

Bureaux, the Swedish Ombudsman,[70] and others.[71] These, however, and the third-party role that Rein and Riessman describe for the CAPs, are positions taken up outside the system to be negotiated; many, like the Ombudsman, direct themselves largely to abuses of government authority.

Where, on the other hand, such a function originates within the agency itself, the image is that of a built-in monitor of the agency's effectiveness and a protection against its own rigidities. From such a position, the social worker moves to strengthen and reinforce both parties in the client-agency relationship. With the client, and with mutual aid systems of clients, the worker offers the agency service in ways designed to help him reach out to the system in stronger and more assertive ways, generalizing from his private experiences to agency policy wherever possible and avoiding the traps of conformity and inertia. In many instances, the activity thus produced is similar to that desired by the advocates except that the movement is toward the service and the workers are interested in the process rather than having lost faith in it.

With the system—colleagues, superiors, and other disciplines—the worker feeds in his direct experience with the struggles of his clients, searches out the staff stake in reaching and innovating, and brings administration wherever possible into direct contact with clients who are seeking new ways of being served. The role is difficult, but it is not new. It is what we have meant all along by the "social" in social work and have implied by our interest in "social functioning," "social relationships," the terms "psychosocial" and "social problems." We have long been agreed that the social worker is somehow related both to the individual and to the society in which he lives. Some have even understood that it is the individual *in* society. But the term "social functioning" has not explained enough, because *all* human functioning is social functioning.

When we begin to ask, as Gordon does, "What does the social worker intervene *in?*"[72] we go beyond the social worker's "interest" in the individual *and* society to the kinds of *processes* to which he is related. Bertha Reynolds's "We are ever and always a *go-between* profession"[73] is closer because it moves to *action.* But a new element is needed, and that is the energy that flows between the individual and his systems. That is what the social worker intervenes *in,* and it is for that function that he needs all his specialized knowledge and skill.

---

[70]For a discussion of the Ombudsman role in various countries see Donald C. Rowat, ed., *The Ombudsman: Citizen's Defender* (London: George Allen & Unwin, Ltd., 1965). See also Richard A. Cloward and Richard M. Elman, "Poverty, Injustice and the Welfare State. Part I: An Ombudsman for the Poor?" *The Nation,* February 28, 1966, pp. 230–35.

[71]Rein and Riessman, *op. cit.,* pp. 4–8.

[72]William E. Gordon, "A Critique of the Working Definition," *Social Work,* VII, No. 4 (1962), 12.

[73]Bertha C. Reynolds, "The Social Casework of an Uncharted Journey," *Social Work,* IX, No. 4 (1964), 17.

The skills, it should be emphasized, are directed not only to clients, but to system-representatives as well; both require the same sensitivities, the same listening, the same partializing, generalizing, reaching for negatives, decoding messages, and the rest. We are collecting records of such "systems work," and Weiner has made valuable contributions from his work in hospital settings and the trade unions.[74]

The mediating function is a skillful one, but it does not "retreat into technique"; on the contrary, the engagements of people with their systems aim at real confrontations on real issues. This is not a call for peace, for there is no peace. The struggle is of a different order, designed to mobilize agencies rather than destroy them. There are other forms of social action—disruptive, revolutionary—and we have a right to join them. But we have no right to confuse this with the professional function, for we must then find ourselves exploiting people in need in order to satisfy our own need for social protest. As long as our living is made in the professional arena, our responsibility is to make *those* processes as dramatic and as vital as we can. If we can help to revolutionize the nature of service and the relationship of people to their agencies, we will have performed an important, and difficult, social function. The *cri de coeur* is from our young advocate:

> If we believe it is possible to move the community, we can continue to work for change through its institutions. If it is not possible, then God help us all, for then we must either continue to act in a drama that has lost its purpose or join in the destruction of society.[75]

---

[74]See Hyman J. Weiner, "Toward Techniques for Social Change," *Social Work,* VI, No. 2 (1961), 26–35. See also Hyman J. Weiner, "A Group Approach to Link Community Mental Health with Labor," in *Social Work Practice, 1967* (New York: Columbia University Press, 1967), pp. 178–88.

[75]Specht, *op. cit.,* p. 15.

Thoughts from Abroad: Some Recent Perspectives on the Practice of Social Work

William Schwartz

The visiting professional is always on unfamiliar ground: he knows that his concerns are somehow relevant to those around him, but he cannot be quite certain about what they mean here, how these ideas grew in the present climate, and how they are put into words. As an "expert" he feels bound to provide answers; but he does not yet know the questions. Actually, all he can do is lay the groundwork for more talk, and for what may turn out to be an interesting and useful new friendship. This is my first offering toward that end.

Despite the strangeness, I have a strong feeling that the most pressing issues now troubling American social workers are also worrying practitioners on this side of the ocean. Happily for you, these do not include—at least not in the same way—Watergate, Cambodia, and other humiliations we share with others in the American community and feel perhaps more strongly than most. But you have your own troubles: every country has its own absurdities, and suffers under the arrogance of its power figures and the failures of leadership that create the issues that we professionals then formulate in our own terms. These formulations may sound highly technical, or esoteric, or removed from the real worries of the world; but they are not, for they must inevitably reflect the same popular anxieties and the same aspirations. When a government loses touch with its people, when innocents are bombed, and

Paper read at Conference on "New Interventions in Social Work," at New University of Ulster, Institute of Continuing Education, Magee University College, Londonderry, Northern Ireland, June 25, 1973.

Schwartz, William. (1973, June). Thoughts from abroad: Some recent perspectives on the practice of social work. *Paper presented at the social work conference at the New University of Ulster, Institute of Continuing Education, Magee University College, Londonderry, Northern Ireland.*

when $60 million are spent to re-elect a president, even as he is slashing benefits for the old, the sick, and the poor, these events will be reflected in the professional conversations of the doctors, the teachers, the nurses, and the social workers—each in their own technical terms and their own ways of surveying the work to be done. And when a top presidential aide suggests that social workers will now have to go out and find honest work, there are strong repercussions within the profession itself. These feelings are directed inward as well as out, and are translated into theoretical and conceptual forms, issues, and strategies that mirror the anxieties of the time. I want to describe three of these major issues to you now, and discuss them with you in the days to come. If they sound familiar, as I hope they will, it is because the American struggles are not ours alone, but part of a common historical and social context.

The most compelling urge at work right now seems to be to define more precisely the function of social work in society—to write a clear description of who we social workers are, why we were invented, and what we are paid to do. Such a task requires that we find unity, perhaps for the first time, in a complex set of origins and a motley crew of workers with traditions reaching back into the hospitals, the community centers, the schools, the adoption agencies, the settlements, the personnel departments, the youth camps and recreation services, the psychiatric centers, the sectarians and the nonsectarians, the public sector and the private, the character-builders, the educators, the psychotherapists, and more.

This job is difficult at best; but we have complicated it even further by *polarizing* the answers to our identity problems. Aggravated by the attacks and anxieties of the time, the condition takes on the typical characteristic of a neurotic state, where the solutions range themselves in opposites. In social work, the battle lines are pitched between those who identify us with the individual or the state, means or ends, process or goals, stability or change, the client or the system. The either-or reigns supreme and there is created a great illusion that we can solve our problems by choosing between one or another of a wide range of extremes. Of course—and here the neurotic analogy is still striking—the dilemmas thus created become part of the problem rather than part of the solution: for when one horn of the dilemma is "chosen," the other begins to appear very attractive, and the chooser finds himself jumping continually back and forth between the two pseudosolutions.

One of the oldest of these dichotomies has recently, under modern stresses, been reborn in all its power and is now having considerable impact on social work education and concepts of practice in the United States. It is the polarization of what C. Wright Mills called "personal troubles" and "public issues," and there is a great family quarrel as to whether social work should represent one or the other as it carries out its job in society. It sounds something like this: shall we be a "psychological" profession, attending the mental ills of troubled people, developing therapeutic relationships with our clients, and defining ourselves to the community as a part of the healing tradition? Or shall we be a "social" profession, addressing ourselves primarily to the conditions under which people live, and allowing the clinical tasks to fall to those who put their faith in mental states and individual solutions? The need for such choices may seem strange to the outsider, unversed in our mysteries. But they are deadly serious for the social work profession, having come down to us in one form or another over a hundred years of social work history. Each generation has cast the issue in its own terms: Mary Richmond spoke of the choice between "wholesale" and "retail" methods, opting for the latter and urging her followers to "stick to the individual case," since "the whole of social reform is in the retail method, when we follow faithfully wherever its working out may lead";[1] Porter Lee tried to reconcile "cause" and "function";[2] Kenneth Pray wrote of "workmanship" and "statesmanship";[3] Clarke Chambers contrasted the influences of "St. Sigmund" and "St. Karl," described the tensions between the "priests" and the "prophets," and cited the antipathies that have existed between the "movers and the shakers" on the one hand, and the "seekers and sojourners" on the other. Chambers summed the matter up in this way:

> And so the two overlapping phases of social work continue to exist, not always harmoniously, but certainly in interdependence—the one focussed on the individual and his welfare, strongly influenced by the psychological disciplines, introspective, dealing in personalized, retail services; the other concerned with reform, with reconstruction, informed primarily by the social sciences, extroverted, dealing in group or community or wholesale services.[4]

In its most recent form, the struggle has evolved into the so-called "advocacy" variation, in which the social worker is called upon to choose between the client and his agency. This is perhaps the most painful form of the individual-social dilemma. Here is a professor of social work on the subject:

> In short, the worker's posture, both to the community residents and to the institutional representatives with whom he is engaged, is that of advocate for the client group's point of view. While employing these techniques, the worker is not enabler, broker, expert, consultant, guide, or social therapist. He is, in fact, a partisan in the social conflict, and his expertise is available *exclusively* to serve client interests.[5]

In this spirit, a committee of the National Association of Social Workers has urged that the obligation to the client takes primacy over the professional's obligation to his employer,[6] and that such a responsibility is enforceable under the Association's Code of Ethics.[7] Others have urged the schools of social work to set their students against their own training agencies, exhorting the school to "put its action where its mouth is."[8] The excitement runs high, and the rhetoric is broad and brave. But the analysis is weak, as I have noted:

> Beginning with a real social problem—the breakdown of service to people in need—the advocates, with the best will in the world, find no

> way but to create a permanent "social conflict" between an unchangeably evil system and a hopelessly alienated client. The worker must then "choose" the client and devote himself "exclusively" to his interests. . . . If, indeed, the worker feels that it must be the one or the other, he can do no less than choose the client and be prepared to cast his lot with the enemies of those who pay his salary. But this, of course, is the ultimate dualism, the polarization of the people and their own institutions. The advocate must now, presumably, agree with the very establishment he despises that the agencies are the natural enemies of the people who need them. "Change the people" has become "change the system," since they can no longer hope to change each other through the skilled use of the client-agency encounter.[9]

The polarity of change-the-system produces practice as poor as that of change-the-people. The advocacy variation ultimately degenerates into a rigidity as severe as the over-psychological emphasis it deplores. This time not Freud but Machiavelli is the culture hero. Here is another social work professor discussing some problems of professional technique: after describing the social worker's "political behavior," he becomes aware of the accompanying means-ends dilemma and provides some cautions to go with the general approach.

> The potential costs of political strategies must always be assessed against their potential gains, so that one's morality is supported by expedience. Social workers may use up their currency as, for example, when a person develops a reputation for guile. With his motives suspect, his hidden agendas revealed to view, and his word in doubt, he can hardly be an effective advocate. Since people resent being treated as means to an end rather than ends in themselves, those who appear to use them instrumentally are likely to be ineffective.[10]

No doubt. As we can see, this struggle is part of a long history, in which each generation resolves the problem in its own terms; however, when it fails to integrate its view of the psychological and the social, the individual and his surroundings, the one and the many, it leaves the basic dilemma untouched. Those who say that the solution lies in doing "both" are in no better position than the "choosers," since the concept of "both" simply resigns itself to the dualism, accepts the polarization of psyche and social, and enjoins us only to take a more temperate stance. This may, for a while, abate the ferocity of the family quarrel; but only for a while. Since the dichotomy remains unresolved, no deeper understanding of social work function is achieved, and the pendulum effect, the jumping-back-and-forth, continues.

In fact, the notion of "both" is now being institutionalized in social work education, appearing in the form of a "two-track" system now gaining popularity in American schools of social work. In this arrangement, the entering student is asked to choose between a "clinical" and a "social policy" specialization, although the degree itself makes no such distinction for the benefit of the consumer of social service. In this connection, Eveline Burns has suggested that the schools educate two kinds of social worker—the people-changers, who would be licensed to practice the psychological arts, and the institution-changers, who would require no such license.[11] My own opinion of such a structure has been expressed elsewhere:

> A half-licensed profession would indeed be a living symbol of the schizophrenia induced by the failure to understand the connections between private troubles and public issues. To create a "department" for each would in fact *institutionalize* the very evils they mean to solve. The "clinicians" would be shielded from any further pressure to bring the weight of their experiences with people in trouble to bear on the formation of public policy; and the "social planners" would be set free from the realities of practice and left alone to fashion their expertise not from the struggles and sufferings of people but from their own clever and speculating minds. It would be as if the legal profession were to decide to train their lawyers in one curriculum and their judges in another. Practice and statesmanship are functions of each other and each is informed by the demands of the other. The planner who has not practiced will be as shallow in his policy-making as the practitioner who has not made his impact on policy will be in his work with people.[12]

Why is the dilemma so persistent? Certainly not because the answer itself is so hard to figure out. Our social philosophers, as far back as those of the Progressive Era, had a vision that merged man and his society into a single image. In 1911, James Mark Baldwin commented that "the individual's normal growth lands him in essential solidarity with his fellows, while on the other hand the exercise of his social duties and privileges advances his highest and purest individuality."[13] Mary Follett, Eduard Lindeman, John Dewey, and others perceived a society in which there was certainly a continuous struggle among people and groups for what was rightfully theirs; but the individual and the state, the one and the many, the psychological and the social, freedom and structure, were but different expressions of the same human condition.

In our time, it was C. Wright Mills who took this insight a step further, reaching for the obligation of the professionals to find the connections between the problems of individuals and those of the state. It is, he said, the task of the liberal institution "continually to translate troubles into issues and issues into the terms of their human meaning for the individual."[14] In this view, social problems are the generalized forms of individual pain, just as personal troubles are the individual manifestations of social malfunctioning. Thus there can be no choices between the two; each reinforces and explains the other, and each is a function of the other. And there can be no meaningful division of labor that has one set of professionals attending to the individual problems, while another specializes in the social ones.

And yet, we continue to discuss social work function in those terms. Sometimes it seems as if we must need the problem; but more likely our dilemma simply reflects the fact that we work in a society where the relationship between people and their supporting environments is so confusing and torn with strife that we shy away from the difficult job of holding the integrated vision against attack, moving instead to the more facile one of representing one side or the other, and getting our satisfactions from the call to arms. But as we fall victim to the dualism, we lose our function instead of defining and clarifying it. For some force is needed in our society that will guard the connections between people and their systems; there are plenty around who shout the familiar dualisms. It is my belief that social work was invented—both in your countries and mine—for precisely that purpose: to find the person in his situation and the situation in the person, the psyche in the social and the social in the psyche, and to base our practice on the knowledge that they are mutually interdependent, symbiotic forces. The "choosing" between these forces is an academic exercise; and it is in fact done mostly by those academics whose theories are derived from their logical minds rather than from the tasks of working directly with real people who need help in the real world.

The repercussions of the function-splitting process are pervasive: the "two-track" concept will change the social work schools in many important ways; further, there is a sharpening schism between the "progressive" planners and the "reactionary" clinicians, where each reserve their finest epithets not for the rich supply of real reactionaries on the American scene but for each other; and there is a growing industry of private practice, with a proliferation of societies of "clinical social workers" and new journals that identify the profession with the history and traditions of psychotherapy. No doubt there is a need to expand the supply of competent therapists in America; but it is not yet clear as to whether the private practitioners of social work are simply substituting the "therapeutic" for the "social planning" definition, or whether they are leaving the social work profession entirely and joining a new one.

In any event, and by an interesting dialectic, these events occur at the very time in our history that an opposite tendency is receiving considerable attention in American social work. It is the problem of "genericism" in professional practice, and this is the second major issue that I would like to call to your attention. Unlike the two-track solutions, genericism seeks to be a unifying force, a study of the roles and tasks that can draw together practitioners from a wide range of settings and a huge array of human problems—as, for example, those represented here at this Conference. Historically, this trend is a continuation of the integrating moves of the 1950s, that brought together a number of social work organizations into a single professional group known as the National Association of Social Workers. For a long time, the unification processes were largely formal and structural; but more recently, the Bartlett Commission undertook the technical work of finding the common base in the practice of social work itself, and this effort aroused considerable interest both in the field of practice and in the schools of social work.[15]

In order for such a search to proceed, we need what amounts to a new idea, a new dimension, to add to the already powerful incentives for unification—the political, the economic, the philosophical. We need, quite plainly, to invent the concept of skill; and it must be a "generic" concept, that will undergird the practice of social work wherever it takes place.

This may seem strange: to "invent" the idea of skill in a profession that has been at work for a hundred years. But the fact is that when we try to describe the actual operations that should be taught and learned in social work, our literature has little to say. Much has been written about what social workers should *know,* and *be,* and *believe in,* and hope to *achieve*—but the work itself, the technical moves by which we distinguish ourselves from the other professions, are undefined. The underlying assumption is that the proper knowledge, attitudes, and aspirations are somehow automatically converted into skillful acts. At the same time, of course, "everybody knows" that this is not so—that you may have great knowledge, be a paragon of insight and virtue, and believe in all the right things, and yet not be able to do the things that can help a person in trouble. A knowledge of anatomy does not make a surgeon. Helen Perlman, in a review of developments in social work method over a ten-year period, concluded that "we are surely and even rapidly adding to our store of knowledge; we have given tongue and ear to what we believe in and hold good; but the what and the how of carrying knowledge and belief into action—these are yet to be formulated."[16] And from the group work sector, the complaint has the same ring:

> This specialized field is rich in democratic concepts; it has a wealth of examples; but in professionally unique concepts, "method theory," it has been curiously poor. . . . It is possible that no social or economic class in a community is beyond profiting from what goes under the name of a "group experience." But it is difficult for a social group worker to communicate how and why this near-miracle happens, except to another group worker.[17]

Our responses to the job of defining method have tended toward the extremes: on the one hand, the social worker is described in sweeping absolutes, with no limits to his knowledge, self-awareness, and commitment; on the other, no more is asked for than a pure, simple-hearted creature with no qualifications except the desire to serve. The first approach is well-illustrated in the professional literature, in discussions that pass for method-analysis. The following is a not untypical example, published in a journal of social work education, and purporting to examine the "knowledge which underlies social work practice and permeates the curriculum":

> In considering knowledge backgrounds for helping people in trouble, one must include the following disciplines: psychology, psychiatry, anthropology, sociology, consumer economics, and biology. In considering knowledge backgrounds for promoting social change, such fields as basic economics, sociology, and political science are clearly relevant. In

> order to understand the related professions, social workers also need considerable acquaintance with the fields of education, law, medicine, religion, and vocational and employment services. If social workers are also to develop knowledge for their own fields, expertise in research design and methodology become essential. If they are to communicate with other professions and the public, they need expertise in the communications professions. Thus, social work is called upon to be aware of and translate knowledge from many fields and to develop research-based knowledge specifically related to social work methodology and practice.[18]

The other extreme is amusingly shown in a letter to *New Society,* where the writer responds to a case history published in the previous issue, and calls for volunteers who can help with such cases. The job analysis laid down by the letter-writer is sensitive and complex, showing a real grasp of what needs to be done for the boy in the case; but the denouement is fascinating:

> SIR: Denis could be a challenge—he's a bright lad, but when he comes out of Borstal he's going to need a friend—preferably someone who has made contact with him during the sentence. Volunteers in the probation and after-care service are put in touch with people like Denis (or sometimes with the family) by their local probation office. If they can possibly do so, they make contact with the client in Borstal or prison and try to help them on release and after. A volunteer for Denis could visit his mother and talk things over, put out feelers for a job for Denis, perhaps find him digs and help him make a go of life.
>
> In general terms, a volunteer can help the inarticulate, who are often intimidated by the social services; he can raise objections to bureaucratic decisions; fight injustice, or simply be a shoulder to cry on. In short, he can make what he will of the job, in his own time and in as many ways as he thinks he is capable.
>
> *The only qualification required is to be human.* (!) Anyone interested in becoming a volunteer can get full details from the local probation office.
>
> Signed, etc.[19]

The problem is not ours alone; it affects all of the helping professions. Kilpatrick's great educational classic, *Foundations of Method,*[20] has not a word in it about method; it taught us a great deal about how children learn, but said nothing about how teachers teach. More recently, Jerome Bruner's *Process of Education,* a summary of a conference on the teaching of science, discusses curriculum, machines, learning motivation, intuition and cognition in learning—and devotes only the last five pages to the question "What can be said of the teacher's role in teaching?"[21] Freud himself complained that "not one of all those who show an interest in my therapy and pass definite judgements upon it has ever asked me how I actually go about it. There can be but one reason for this, namely, that they think there is nothing to inquire about, that the thing is perfectly obvious."[22] Thirty-five years later, Fenichel still commented that "it is amazing how small a proportion of the very extensive psychoanalytic literature is devoted to psychoanalytic technique and how much less to the theory of technique."[23] And in the field of clinical psychology, Blanton has pointed out that "the relationship between knowing and doing has as many puzzles for us today as it had for Socrates."[24]

In any event, the problem is pervasive. And it must be addressed directly in every profession, for without clearly defined skills, there is not a profession at all but a kind of fraternity with a set of shared beliefs, knowledge, attitudes, and aspirations that are accessible to all educated and right-thinking people, and not the unique function and expertise that qualifies a certain group of people to offer a special, complex service in a certain kind of way. Thus, Merton has written of the "systematic knowledge, technical skill, and the mobilization of knowledge and skill in the service of others" that make up "the concept of a profession."[25] Parsons noted that "the professional man is thus a 'technical expert' of some order by virtue of his mastery of the tradition and the skills of its use."[26] And Wilensky and Lebeaux speak of a "monopoly of skill" that justifies a "monopoly of activity" in a given area.[27] If I may quote myself again, I have summarized this point elsewhere as follows:

> Professionals are paid for doing, for operationalizing, and not simply speculating on the nature of life. The need for technical rather than dogmatic solutions is inherent in their social role. Although they may sometimes be a little apologetic about it, the fact is that their stock in trade is technique and society holds them responsible for their ability to perform their work with skills not available to the ordinary citizen. How-to-do-it is the bread and butter of the lawyer, the doctor, the engineer—and the social worker. Without it they fail to differentiate themselves from the knowledgeable public, the informed layman and the rest of those in society who are alive to its issues and have opinions about them. The professional distinguishes himself not by his general wisdom, his philosophy or his goals, but by his ability to perform an operation, teach a class, build a bridge, plead a case, or use the resources of a community to help a person in trouble.[28]

In social work, the search is, in fact, beginning to go forward, in the very social climate that has made "technique" a bad and precious word. The two-track concept, wrong-headed as it is, nevertheless offers those who work closest to the clients the chance to develop their common interest in the details of practice. As the caseworkers, group workers, and grass-roots community organizers come together on the "clinical" track, they can begin to share their experiences in practice, their records of work, and their curiousities about the technical skills by which all social workers should be known. This represents a historic opportunity to identify our common purposes, to unify our function, and to describe our practice with people wherever it takes place.

Thus the "genericizing" will emerge from our direct work with people—not, this time, by the numbers, as with "case," "group," and "community" work, but as a single discipline using certain distinctive ways of working and helping. There will be specialization, of course, as in any large and complex institution; but the dimensions will be different, perhaps by field of service, by types of human difficulty, by agency setting, or others. But psychology and sociology will come together again, as they were at the dawn of social work. Casework was not, in its beginnings, so heavily individualistic; nor was group work so inextricably committed to service by multiples. Mary Richmond stressed the "social" diagnosis, and expressed her "great pleasure" in the "new tendency to view our clients from the angle of what might be termed *small group psychology.*"[29] And Canon Barnett's favorite slogan, even as he founded the first settlement house and laid the groundwork for the group work movement on both sides of the ocean, was "one by one."[30]

And so it has happened that no sooner did the dualism take over than it began to offer itself for resolution in the search for method. The need to operationalize, to identify our skills in action, forces us now to dig deeply into the connections between what goes on *inside* people and *outside* them, and to build such understandings into a useful theory of the helping process. The inquiry is barely begun, and still unfocussed; but the necessary curiousities are in play.[31] At the same time, the interest in method is being taken up by many of the other helping professions—psychiatry, education, psychology, and more—and we in social work are becoming part of a general effort to probe the details of the encounter between a worker and the people who use his help. In the process, new perceptions are emerging, new models being fashioned, that will seem strange to eyes trained in the old ways of seeing and ears tuned to the old semantics. This is my third and final theme for your consideration.

I believe that the growing interest in the meaning of method is moving us toward a radical reorientation to the nature of the helping process—a "revolution" roughly akin to those described by Thomas Kuhn in his work on the history of science. In his *Structure of Scientific Revolutions,*[32] Kuhn points out that science has developed not through the gradual accumulation of knowledge, bits piled one upon the other, but in dramatic leaps from old ways of looking at the world to radically new ones. He shows how the history of science is marked by such revolutions in gestalt, where fields of inquiry move suddenly from old "paradigms" to startling new perspectives on the problems under study. Then, as the field jumps from what he calls "normal science" to the new gestalt, "ducks become rabbits"; the investigators begin to ask brand new questions, and new problems are formulated for research. A "paradigm," in Kuhn's view, is a set of "received beliefs," written out in the textbooks of its time, and defining the "legitimate problems" in language that all practitioners understand in much the same way. In the normal science of the day, the professionals "know what the world is like." Furthermore, the paradigm is productive: it asks the questions everybody understands; it produces research; everybody talks the same language and shares the same assumptions; and they are all working on the same "games and puzzles"—that is, on problems in which the answers are already embedded. In the process, many useful answers are brought to light.

But then something begins to happen to the old view of life. In order to continue to defend its basic assumptions and maintain its unity of vision, it becomes necessary to suppress the exceptions, the doubts, and the novelties, for fear that diverse viewpoints may subvert the paradigm's basic commitments. Kuhn says: "A paradigm can, for that matter, even insulate the community from those socially important problems that are not reducible to the puzzle form, because they cannot be stated in terms of the conceptual and instrumental tools the paradigm supplies."[33]

However, novelty cannot be suppressed indefinitely, since it is in the nature of scientific inquiry eventually to expose the arbitrary. In time, the leaks in the structure become obvious: certain "normal" problems stubbornly resist solution; equipment fails to perform in expected ways; certain questions remain contradictory and unapproachable. Eventually, "anomalies" develop—phenomena that do not square with expectations engendered by the old paradigm. Here is Kuhn again:

> In these and other ways besides, normal science repeatedly goes astray. And when it does—when, that is, the profession can no longer evade anomalies that subvert the existing tradition of scientific practice—then begin the extraordinary investigations that lead the profession at last to a new set of commitments, a new basis for the practice of science. The extraordinary episodes in which the shift of professional commitments occurs are the ones known in this essay as scientific revolutions. They are the tradition shattering complements to the tradition-bound activity of normal science.[34]

He then shows how the revolutions took place in the fields of light, heat, electricity, astronomy, and others, demonstrating how, after the crisis and the desertion of the old gestalt, scientists emerged into a world that was almost literally transformed.

> Led by a new paradigm, scientists adopt new instruments and look in new places. Even more important, during revolutions scientists see new and different things when looking with familiar instruments in places they have looked before. It is rather as if the professional community had been suddenly transported to another planet where familiar objects are seen in a different light and joined by familiar ones as well. . . . In so far as their only recourse to the world is through what they see and do, we may want to say that after a revolution scientists are responding to a different world.[35]

What has all this to do with us? Without presuming to take our example directly from Kuhn's analysis of the history of science—social work is actually in what he calls a "pre-paradigm" state—there is nevertheless a striking analogy to our condition. We too have our set of "received beliefs" about the nature of the helping process, and we have a self-contained model that is written into our textbooks, establishes certain kinds of questions as relevant and disallows others, and sets up the "games and puzzles" on which we work. Furthermore, this ruling view seems now to be wearing thin, producing a growing number of anomalies and leading us toward a crisis in our study of the helping function.

The gestalt in which our profession was born and raised emerged from the Cartesian paradigm, the time-honored scientific model, in which an expert versed in the study of causes and effects examined certain objects, explored their nature, learned their "regularities," and gained increasing skill in manipulating them for the good of society. Thus the physicist, the chemist, the biologist, the engineer, all studied their materials, found the internal relationships, and used their knowledge to make their objects operate to better advantage, as such advantage was defined by the expert. And so, too, in the helping professions: the physician, faced with a person whose machinery had gone wrong in some way, examined his object, "diagnosed" his difficulty, and "treated" him in ways designed to put him back in working order. Following closely, the psychiatrist, then the psychologist, the social worker, the educator, and the other human relations workers took on this view of the relationship between the helper and his client. They used the same words, asked the same questions, and defined their claims to the status of "science" in the terms laid down by the pragmatic-positivist world view. In time, they institutionalized what Buber was to call the "I-It" relationship,[36] wherein an independent worker-subject acted upon a client-object from a distance—to understand him, fix him, change him, in accordance with criteria drawn from the professional's wisdom and knowledge of his materials.

In its ascendancy, it was an excellent model; as Kuhn pointed out, the old paradigm serves us well in its time. The positivist revolution brought man into an age of enlightenment and helped him gain enormous control over the world in which he lived. Applied to the study of human relations, the mechanical view of nature taught us that men were products of their experience; they could be studied and understood just as all of nature would surely and eventually be understood. Man was, in fact, "the proper study of mankind"; and his machinery could be made to work better and last longer. The search for regularities was as appropriate in the field of human nature as it was in the physical sciences, and the laws of cause and effect would guide us in the effort to test, to verify, and to predict the factors associated with the course of human development.

Such a view also helped create new attitudes toward people in need. If men were made by events, we were challenged to understand people rather than merely to judge them; and we had to do something about the conditions in which they lived, rather than rely solely on moral admonitions and exhortations to be "worthy" of society's care and attention. As "psychological science won its freedom from metaphysics,"[37] the scientific spirit lent to the budding human relations professions a view of the client-worker relationship that was historical, rationalistic, deterministic, prescriptive, individualistic, objective. These characteristics were, in fact, the original building blocks of professionalism itself.

Nevertheless, the adaptation of the positivist model to the art of human relations lost something in the translation. The problems appeared very soon and have remained persistently troublesome, both in practice and theory, over the generations. For the very qualities that helped bring the helping professions into being soon began to tear them apart. The historicism that helped us understand causes and processes also created a rigid determinism that magnified the importance of the past to the point where it blocked out the worker's view of the present. The rationalism that, quite properly, put a high value on knowledge and reason (psycho-"analysis" was Freud's term for his therapy) turned into what Dewey was to call "the quest for certainty,"[38] wherein knowledge was considered more elegant than action, and the irrational, the illogical, and the intuitive were elements of a lower, "unscientific" order. (A contemporary of Freud's named Soren Kierkegaard was hardly noticed by the new professions). The prescriptiveness that we borrowed from the doctors helped us to put our knowledge at the client's disposal, but it came into conflict with a growing emphasis on self-determination, as we learned to help people use their own energies to work out their own solutions. And again, our individualism served to focus attention on the study of personality, but the concepts that emerged counted so heavily on early character determination and cross-sectional "diagnosis" that it was too easy to underplay the social and interpersonal connections that continue to change people as they move from situation to situation. It was indeed Kierkegaard who said that "truth exists only as the individual himself produces it in action."[39] Rollo May put it that "when we are dealing with human beings, no truth has reality by itself; it is always dependent upon the reality of the immediate relationship."[40] And Maurice Friedman, discussing the thought of Martin Buber, pointed out that when the forces of the unconscious are placed within the individual alone, "the basis of human reality itself comes to be seen as psychical rather than interhuman, and the relations between man and man are psychologized."[41] Finally, and perhaps most important, the objectivity that had brought us closer to the scientific method and helped us to study people in their own terms brought us, ultimately, to a detachment so complete that the client had to shout to make himself heard, much less touched. In fact, professionalism itself came to be defined as the ability to maintain one's distance from the client; we found ourselves chained to "the traditional doctrine, so limiting, self-contradictory, and indeed often so destructive in psychology, *that the less we are involved in a given situation, the more clearly we can observe the truth.*"[42]

The fact is that the more we study the process of helping, the more we realize that a new set of ideas is needed to illuminate its details. Fixing broken things is not the same sort of work as trying to help people mobilize their own energies in their own behalf. In the exchanges between worker and client, the "object" is no object at all, but a moving, dynamic force with a will and impetus of its own. The client does not hold still to be examined, labelled, and "treated," and the encounter is not between a detached expert and a malleable entity—the fixer and the fixed, the teacher and the taught, the changer and the changed. The person in need retains the ultimate power—whether or not he uses it consciously—to use help or reject it, to change or not to change, to learn or not to learn. When a person finds new ways of dealing with his environment, it is because he has invested something of his own energy and motive in a task he has accepted as his own. And thus the impetus for change resides in the *taker* of help; it is his power that empowers the giver. Even as the professional strives to "enable," he is himself enabled by the strengths of his client.

All of which creates an interesting theoretical problem: how do you define an art whose achievement depends only partly on the skill of the artist, and ultimately on the power of the materials themselves? This is the issue that Dewey sought to emphasize in his early interactionism, and found few, even in the "progressive" movement, who understood what he meant. More recently, it is the dimension Buber reached for as he sought to distinguish the intertwined relationship of "I-Thou" from the detached, subject-object perspective of "I-It." In his William Alanson White Memorial Lectures, Buber explores the elements of "distance and relation," the "dialogical" nature of human relationships, and the concept of the "interhuman." At one point in his search, he asks us to examine the situation of two men observing each other:

> The essential thing is not that the one makes the other his object, but the fact that he is not fully able to do so, and the reason for his failure. We have in common with all existing beings that we can be made objects of observation. But it is my privilege as man that by the hidden activity of my being I can establish an impassable barrier to objectification. Only in partnership can my being be perceived as an existing whole.[43]

If the reality of human relations does in fact lie in what Buber calls the "between," and the "dialogical," we are indeed carried very close to Kuhn's "revolution" in gestalt. We need new ways of talking about the helping relationship, new kinds of questions, and new concepts to help us describe professional skill—concepts that will identify both the worker's acts and those of his clients *as aspects of each other.*

This is not to say that the new gestalt abandons totally what was useful in the old model; Kuhn himself does not claim that for his revolutions in science. He notes in fact that "the new paradigm must promise to preserve a relatively large part of the concrete problem-solving ability that has accrued to science through its predecessors."[44] In our case, the status of student, knower, professional helper, cannot be covered over without producing yet another kind of illusion. Buber himself pointed this out in a conversation with Carl Rogers:

> Martin Buber: . . . First of all, I would say, this is the action of a therapist. This is a very good example for a certain moment of dialogic existence. I mean, two persons have a certain situation in common. This situation is . . . it is a sick man coming to you and asking a particular kind of help. Now—
>
> Carl R. Rogers: May I interrupt there?
>
> Martin Buber: Please do.
>
> Carl R. Rogers: I feel that if from my point of view this is a *sick* person, then probably I'm not going to be of as much help as I might be. I feel this is a *person.* Yes, somebody else may call him sick, or if I look at him from an objective point of view, then I might agree, too, "Yes, he's sick." But in entering a relationship, it seems to me if I am looking upon it as "I am a relatively well person and this is a sick person"—
>
> Martin Buber: Which I don't mean.
>
> Carl R. Rogers:—it's no good.
>
> Martin Buber: I don't mean it. Let me leave out this word sick. A man coming to you for help. The essential difference between your role in this situation and his is obvious. He comes for help to you. You don't come for help to him. And not only this, but you are *able,* more or less, to help him. He can do different things to you, but not help you.[45]

Buber and Rogers then continued to explore the differences in function between the professional helper and his client, with Buber trying to bring together in a single vision both the professional power and the power of the person in need. This in fact is one of the primary tasks of the new gestalt, for if we cannot merge these processes in a single account we are doomed to continue to act on one and make a high value of the other. The more we "diagnose" and "treat" people, the more we will have to carry on in praise of self-determination and client autonomy. This is the kind of pseudoresolution that we call "lip service": where we cannot reconcile two equally desirable and apparently opposing values, we are forced into the position of practicing one and worshipping the other.

The new paradigm will also have to find a language that expresses the *presentness* of the worker-client experience, along with our curiousity about the past and our aspirations for the future. The words will have to be those of *action,* describing what we do, rather than simply what we know, and are, and profess to believe. Professional skill must then be defined as a force that we exert, not *on* people but in our interdependent relations with them in an undertaking we both understand. The terms must be reciprocal, not unilateral, showing not what we do to people—change them, cure them, teach them—but how workers and clients *resonate* to each other in an ongoing process. In effect, we are put to the task of describing separately a set of professional acts that are virtually inseparable from those of the clients around him. And describe them we must: for we cannot take refuge in the complexities of interactionism to avoid the job of explaining exactly what we do in the helping process. The social worker's acts must be definable and recognizable, and it must be possible to distinguish between skillful moves and clumsy ones. Unless we can make such distinctions, we cannot be held accountable to the people we serve; nor can we lay claim to the technical, operational skills by which professions are known.

No wonder we have shied away from such a task. It does indeed require a kind of revolution in thought to change from a model of an expert fixer of broken objects to that of a participant in a network of relations, where the worker finds his own special part in the process and develops the skills he needs to carry it out. To find himself thus in the middle of things, with his own work to do, is a far cry from the view of himself as an outside "intervener,"[46] detached from the objects of his concern and acting on them for their own good.

It is in this context that the "systems" construct takes on special meaning for the helping professions; and it is no accident that this idea is growing in importance on the American scene. It is a complex notion, with dimensions ranging across the whole scientific spectrum; Bertalanffy calls it "a new world view of considerable impact."[47] But we do not need the whole technology for our purposes. What we do need are certain basic features to which the model calls attention—the interdependence of functions, the division of labor, the specificity of tasks, and the "circular, reciprocal relations . . . through which the component members of the field participate in and thereby create the field of the whole, which field in turn regulates and patterns their individual activities."[48] When we can view the worker-client relationship as a system in which "the *relations* determine the properties of its parts,"[49] we can see the person in need not as an object of help but as an active system-within-a-system, with his own energies, strengths, and purposes, and the need to know what those purposes are, so that he can move more decisively and responsibly to carry them out. In this view, the professional is not an outside expert but a moving actor among moving actors, driven by his special function and bringing to bear the skills he needs to carry it out. And we can see more clearly that what happens between them—client and worker—is a complex collaborative process that goes forward a step at a time, concerned at each step with limited and specific tasks rather than the global and abstract goals—"maturity," "adjustment," "socialization"—that neither will ever see in any tangible, recognizable form.

With these thoughts in mind, it is not hard to see why the use of groups has become such an important theme in American social work. Not, it should be noted as a system superior to individual work; the one-to-one will always be important as a way of helping. But the work with client groups offers us a special opportunity to be in the center of the action, in the heart of those mutual aid systems through which people use and support each other as they take on problems they have in common. The peer group is a network of relationships in which the worker uses his knowledge and skills from the inside: caught up in the action, sharing a common experience, he has little time for the detachment and "objectivity" of the old paradigm. He and his clients "stay in the world" together as they tackle the problems before them. It is no accident that much of the impetus toward new ways of looking at the helping process has come from those in the group work corner of the profession.[50]

As you have no doubt noticed, the three major issues I have brought to your attention are closely interconnected—the polarization of functions, the search for generic, unifying skills, and the move toward a new paradigm of the worker-client engagement. Each of these issues is a part of the others, and as we begin to see more clearly into one, the others too come into focus. If the search for method begins with function within a system, then we must start by finding out why we were invented in the first place, what part we were meant to play in society's division of labor. From that point, the question "what am I doing there?" will help us understand the tasks that are necessary to carry out our piece of the action within the various systems in which we work—the one-to-one, the peer group, the family, the committee, the agency itself, and the rest. Each of these systems is indeed a tiny version of the society that created us; and the skills we use represent the most direct and efficient way of performing the tasks through which we translate our function into action. This interest in *how* we do the job will bring us together in action, as we are for the most part together in philosophy and objectives. It means that we are ready to be held accountable not only for our general program, but for the details of its execution.

From there, the work gets harder but its outlines become clearer. This is an interesting time for us all, social workers on both sides of the ocean. I am looking forward to our time here together, as we work to understand what we are about and how we are to strengthen ourselves in the service of people.

References

1. Mary Richmond, "The Retail Method of Reform," address to the Ethical Culture Society of Philadelphia, April 17, 1905, in *The Long View* (New York: Russell Sage Foundation, 1930), p. 221.
2. Porter R. Lee, "Technical Training for Social Work," address delivered at the opening of the New York School of Philanthropy, 1913, in *Social Work as Cause and Function and Other Papers* (New York: Columbia University Press, 1937), p. 29.
3. Kenneth L. M. Pray, *Social Work in a Revolutionary Age and Other Papers* (Philadelphia: University of Pennsylvania Press, 1949), p. 231.
4. Clarke A. Chambers, "An Historical Perspective on Political Action *vs.* Individualized Treatment," *Current Issues in Social Work Seen in Historical Perspective* (New York: Council on Social Work Education, 1962), p. 53.
5. Charles F. Grosser, "Community Development Serving the Urban Poor," *Social Work,* vol. 10, no. 3 (July 1965), p. 18. (My italics.)
6. National Association of Social Workers, Ad Hoc Committee on Advocacy, "The Social Worker as Advocate: Champion of Social Victims," *Social Work,* vol. 14, no. 2 (April 1969), p. 18.

7. *Ibid.,* p. 21.
8. David Wineman and Adrienne James, "The Advocacy Challenge to Schools of Social Work," *Social Work,* vol. 14, no. 2 (April 1969), p. 32.
9. William Schwartz, "Private Troubles and Public Issues: One Social Work Job or Two?" *The Social Welfare Forum, 1969* (New York: Columbia University Press, 1969), p. 31.
10. George A. Brager, "Advocacy and Political Behavior," *Social Work,* vol. 13, no. 2 (April 1968), p. 14.
11. Eveline Burns, "Tomorrow's Social Needs and Social Work Education," *Journal of Education for Social Work,* vol. 2, no. 1 (Spring 1966), p. 16.
12. William Schwartz, *Op. Cit.,* pp. 35, 36. Italics added.
13. James Mark Baldwin, *The Individual and Society, or Psychology and Sociology* (Boston: Richard G. Badger, The Gorham Press, 1911), p. 16.
14. C. Wright Mills, *The Power Elite* (New York: Oxford University Press, 1957), p. 319.
15. Harriet M. Bartlett, "Toward Clarification and Improvement of Social Work Practice," *Social Work,* Vol. 3, No. 2 (April 1958), pp. 3–10. See also: William E. Gordon, "A Critique of the Working Definition," *Social Work,* vol. 7, no. 4 (October 1962), pp. 3–13.
16. Helen Harris Perlman, "Social Work Method: A Review of the Past Decade," *Social Work,* vol. 10, no. 4 (October 1965), p. 175.
17. Frank J. Bruno (with chapters by Louis Towley), *Trends in Social Work, 1874–1956* (New York: Columbia University Press, 1957), p. 422.
18. Catherine S. Chilman, "Production of New Knowledge of Relevance to Social Work and Social Welfare: An Examination of Knowledge Which Underlies Social Work Practice and Permeates the Curriculum," *Social Work Education Reporter,* vol. 17, no. 3 (September 1969), p. 49.
19. Letter to the Editor, *New Society,* Vol. 19, No. 486, January 20, 1972, p. 138. (My italics; and the exclamation, too.)
20. William Heard Kilpatrick, *Foundations of Method: Informal Talks on Teaching* (New York: Macmillan, 1932).
21. Jerome S. Bruner, *The Process of Education* (Cambridge, Mass.: Harvard University Press, 1960), p. 88.
22. Sigmund Freud, "On Psychotherapy," *Collected Papers* (London: Hogarth Press and the Institute of Psycho-Analysis, 1950), Vol. I, pp. 254, 255.
23. Quoted by Karl Menninger in the introduction to his *Theory of Psychoanalytic Technique* (New York: Harper Torchbooks, Academy Library, 1958), p. v.
24. R. Blanton, "Science and Art in the Training of Psychologists," *Journal of Clinical Psychology,* vol. 18, no. 1 (1962), p. 10.
25. Robert K. Merton, "Some Thoughts on the Professions in American Society," Address to the Graduate Convocation, Brown University, June 6, 1960, Brown University Papers, no. 37, p. 9.
26. Talcott Parsons, "A Sociologist Looks at the Legal Profession," *Essays in Sociological Theory,* rev. ed. (Glencoe, Ill.: Free Press, 1954), p. 372.

27. Harold L. Wilensky and Charles N. Lebeaux, *Industrial Society and Social Welfare* (New York: Russell Sage Foundation, 1958), p. 284.
28. William Schwartz, *op. cit.,* pp. 23, 24.
29. Mary Richmond, "Some Next Steps in Social Treatment," *Proceedings of the National Conference of Social Work* (Chicago: U. of Chicago Press, 1920), p. 256. Emphasis in original.
30. S. A. Barnett, *Canon Barnett, His Life, Work, and Friends* (Boston and New York: Houghton Mifflin Company, 1919), Vol. 1, p. 320.
31. See, for example, Catherine P. Papell and Beulah Rothman, "Social Group Work Models: Possession and Heritage," *Education for Social Work,* vol. 2, no. 2 (Fall 1966), pp. 66–77. And, for my own effort to explore some of the theoretical problems involved in building a theory of practice, see William Schwartz, "Toward a Strategy of Group Work Practice," *Social Service Review,* vol. 36, no. 3 (September 1962), pp. 268–79.
32. Thomas S. Kuhn, *The Structure of Scientific Revolutions* (Chicago: University of Chicago Press, 1962).
33. *Ibid.,* p. 37.
34. *Ibid.,* p. 6.
35. *Ibid.,* p. 110.
36. Martin Buber, *I and Thou* (Second Edition, New York: Charles Scribner's Sons, 1958).
37. Rollo May, "The Origins and Significance of the Existential Movement in Psychology," in Rollo May, Ernest Angel, and Henri F. Ellenberger, eds., *Existence: A New Dimension in Psychiatry and Psychology* (New York: Basic Books, 1958), p. 8.
38. John Dewey, *The Quest for Certainty: A Study of the Relation of Knowledge and Action* (New York: G. P. Putnam's Sons, Capricorn Books, 1960).
39. Rollo May, *op. cit.,* p. 12.
40. *Ibid.,* p. 27. (May, *op. cit.*)
41. Maurice Friedman, "Introductory Essay," in Martin Buber, *The Knowledge of Man* (New York: Harper & Row, 1965), p. 35.
42. Rollo May, *op. cit.,* p. 27. Italics in original.
43. Martin Buber, "The William Alanson White Memorial Lectures, Fourth Series," *Psychiatry,* vol. 20, no. 2 (May 1957), p. 106.
44. Thomas S. Kuhn, *op. cit.,* p. 168.
45. Martin Buber, *The Knowledge of Man, op. cit.,* pp. 170, 171.
46. In this period of transition from an old paradigm to a new one, many find themselves straddling both, in an effort to keep up with the times while yet not relinquishing the old way of looking. The use of the word "intervene" is a sign of this dilemma, when in conjunction with an apparent acceptance of systems theory. It is simply not possible to "intervene" from the inside—only from the outside, looking in.
47. Ludwig von Bertalanffy, *General System Theory: Foundations, Development, Applications* (New York: George Braziller, 1968), p. vii.

48. Lawrence K. Frank, "Research for What?" *Journal of Social Issues,* Kurt Lewin Memorial Award Issue, Supplement Series, no. 10 (1957), p. 12.
49. Talcott Parsons, *The Structure of Social Action* (New York: McGraw-Hill Book Co., 1937), p. 32. Italics added.
50. For a fairly recent review of group work practice research, see William Schwartz, "Neighborhood Centers and Group Work," in Henry S. Maas, ed. *Research in the Social Services: A Five-Year Review* (New York: National Association of Social Workers, 1970).

The Settings of Practice

Introduction

Once having presented his ideas and his mediating model, in the early 1960s, Schwartz moved toward the exploration of how his generic vision was operationalized within various settings of practice. His interest lay in showing how function was translated into action through an examination of what the social worker actually did to help. He believed that showing the details of practice would make the subject come alive and would provide a clearer basis for practitioners to explore their own helping activity.

Schwartz approached consultation work both as student and expert, intent upon learning "how his subject takes on its special shape and form within a particular setting" (1971, p. 38). Each setting provided a welcomed opportunity to learn more. In each setting he sought to understand what was unique, distinctive, and universal, and to use this knowledge to inform his ideas about practice. His files are filled with the process records written after each consultation session. These recordings provided him with the basis for his careful documentation in "Group Work in Public Welfare" (1968) and "The Practice of Child Care in Residential Treatment" (1971). They also provided the basis for his analysis of his practice.

His little known early writings about camping, return us to the roots of group work (1960b; 1960c). Camping, through the auspices of "Ys," settlements, and later on through social agencies, was a traditional setting of group work practice. Like the early settlement worker, the group worker learned about the meaning of the child's camping experience by living within the child's milieu. It was Schwartz's fifteen summers in the field of camping which positioned him to understand the relationship between the individual group member (the camper) and the experience of the group as a whole (the bunk). It was this understanding which early on, strengthened his ideas about the symbiotic tie between the individual and the group as a whole, and prompted the development of his thinking about the action implications of this knowledge.

With a set of ideas and principles to guide him, Schwartz became a consultant to the Bureau of Child Welfare, New York City, from October 1962 to June 1966. His agreed-upon task was to work with the Bureau toward the "development of staff skills in the use of groups [where] from the beginning it was assumed that staff's work with clients in groups and administrators' work with staff in groups bore significant similarities" (1968, p. 4). The monograph "Group Work in Public Welfare" (1968) is Schwartz's documentation of that effort.

Schwartz's way of proceeding in this and other consultations reflected a set of working assumptions: skill in groups could be described and defined; discussion of skills could best be explored through the recording of practice; workers and administrators learning to work with groups would learn an adaptation of skills they were already practicing, rather than learning a new discipline or "method"; it was more beneficial for group skills to be learned as widely as possible than to create a group work department; institutionalization of a new way of working is dependent upon personnel at every level of the hierarchy using the new ideas, and consultants teach as much by what they do as by what they say should be done.

"The Use of Groups and School Social Work Function" (1969b) was originally presented at the New York State School Social Workers Association, May 10, 1969, Saratoga Springs, New York. What intrigued Schwartz so much about school social work was that it "dramatizes most effectively several problems with which social workers struggle no matter what the setting in which they work" (1969b, p. 1). The stories Ruth Efron Schwartz (a school social worker) told daily were filled with the complexities of social workers trying to establish a position between the children and the school which did not jeopardize a relationship with either. This paper is devoted to defining the function of the school social worker between child and school, to discussing the skills of the social worker which put the function to work, and to showing how groups fall within that function. The use of student recording makes the dilemmas and skills come alive.

A newly graduated group work student's interest in the residential cottage and the application of group work skills to the tasks of child care practice led to Schwartz's consultation in residential treatment. This graduate's employment as a professional child care worker reflected his and the agency's interest in exploring the potentiality of the child care role. A three-year consultation ensued in which Schwartz was invited to "help [the agency] identify the child care tasks and define the skills necessary to carry them out" (1971a, p. 38).[1] Once again Schwartz saw how considerable tension was generated for the child care worker placed within the child's milieu. The pulls by the agency to side with it, and the pulls by the children to side with them, generated "flip-flop" behavior which often obscured a clear service role. The demand to choose from a host of dualisms made for impossible choices. Who could pick from instrumental *v.* expressive; custodial *v.* treatment; doing *v.* feeling; limiting *v.* loving; superego *v.* ego; structure *v.* freedom, aspects of our practice. The dilemmas of ambiguous expectations and status dissonance and the dilemma of group living where the group itself was both suspect and a source of help only served to intensify the distress within the child care position.

"The Practice of Child Care in Residential Treatment" (1971a) is a careful, detailed, presentation of Schwartz's consultation, directed at identifying the function and skills of the child care staff, clarifying the tasks

---

[1]David Birnbach tells his story of his experience as child care worker in "Residential Treatment: The Skills of Child Care," in W. Schwartz and S. Zalba, eds., *The Practice of Group Work*, New York: Columbia U. Press, 1971, pp. 177–98.

and skills of the supervisors of child care workers, and exploring the interdisciplinary arrangements which affected the entire child care enterprise. Inclusion of process recording, once again, literally breathes life into Schwartz's discussion of the practice of child care.

It seems fitting to end this section with "Rosalie" (1978), an article made up entirely of a worker's practice strategies, reflections, and process recording. In publishing this article, Catherine Pappell and Beulah Rothman, editors of *Social Work with Groups* wrote that "[t]his article is a departure from the traditional form of professional literature. We are pleased to present it to our readers in an effort to stimulate writing about group work practice" (p. 265). Based on a Record of Service, submitted by Judith A. B. Lee,[2] and using some of her actual language, Schwartz tells the moving story of Lee's efforts to help a twenty-year-old, isolated, mentally retarded young woman to negotiate her peer group. "Rosalie" is a striking example of the way in which many of Schwartz's students carried on his tradition of revealing the details of practice through recording. It is also a stunning example of the ease with which Schwartz could present his theory of helping in groups through the particulars of a worker, an individual, and her peer group.

Toby Berman-Rossi

---

[2]Dr. Judith A. B. Lee is now Professor of Social Work, University of Connecticut School of Social Work.

Camping

William Schwartz

CAMPING, in its broad meaning, signifies the establishment of temporary living quarters in an undeveloped area. The term has been popularly applied to a form of activity in which individuals and families spend periods of vacation from school or work living in the outdoors and utilizing the natural environment for recreational purposes. With the increased scope and significance of leisure in American life, the camping movement has expanded considerably in recent years and has created a vast vacation industry designed to provide facilities, equipment, and supplies for the growing number of American campers. The federal government has, through its Department of the Interior, taken a leading role in the conservation of the natural areas in which informal camping activity is conducted.[1] State and local park agencies have also attempted to protect and conserve the wooded areas and natural resources necessary to meet the growing recreational needs of an expanding population.

In addition to these individual ventures into outdoor living, the camping tradition in America has assumed a unique institutional form, in which the attempt is made to develop the values of an organized group experience in a natural environment. This movement, generally referred to as "organized" camping, establishes small, temporary communities in which the participants live in close proximity and engage in planned activities under the leadership of trained personnel. The organized camp is distinguished by its emphasis on outdoor skills and activities, its concern with the effects of group experience on individual personality, its stress on improving the quality of its leadership, and its formulation of specific objectives. Through its administrative processes, the organized camp seeks to create a unified structure of purpose and program designed to control the design and quality of the camping experience.

Scope and Sponsorship

The first attempt at organized camping is believed to have been undertaken by Frederick William Gunn and the students of the Gunnery School in 1861.

[1]*See* Secretary of the Interior, *infra.*

This program was continued until 1879, when the School deferred to the innovation of the long summer vacation. Notwithstanding this effect on Camp Gunnery, the institution of the summer vacation was an important factor among the circumstances that ushered in the era of organized camping. In 1876 "The North Mountain School of Physical Culture" was established by physician Joseph Trimble Rothrock in Luzerne County, Pennsylvania, for the purpose of "mingling exercise and study" for "weakly boys" during the summer months. In 1880, the first church camp was founded by the Rev. George W. Hinckley in Rhode Island, with a program based on the inspiration of "Adirondack" (Rev. W. H. H.) Murray, considered by many to have been "the father of the modern outdoor movement." In 1881, Ernest Berkeley Balch established Camp Chocorua in New Hampshire, expressing his primary purpose as that of taking the children of the well-to-do out of the summer hotels and offering them an experience in responsibility and creative labor. Because of Balch's emphasis on the educative, character-building effects of the camping experience, the present organized camping movement has been referred to as the "lengthened shadow" of Camp Chocorua.

The movement of the social agencies into the camping field followed swiftly, led by the Young Men's Christian Association of Newburgh, New York, in 1885, the Salem, Massachusetts, Boys' Club in 1900, and the Boy Scouts, Girl Scouts, Camp Fire Girls, YWCA's, YM and YWHA's, settlement houses and other leisure time agencies, in the early decades of the twentieth century.

In the hundred years of camping practice since the advent of the Gunnery Camp upon the American scene, the field has expanded into a complex network of services, with a wide variety of sponsorships, settings, and objectives. The growth of the movement has been phenomenal: from an estimated 106 camps in 1910,[2] the number grew to an estimated 1,248 in 1924,[3] 6,200 in 1939,[4] and 12,600 camps in 1951.[5] A new survey is currently being undertaken by the National Park Service, in cooperation with the American Camping Association, and is expected to produce the most accurate count as yet achieved. It is anticipated that this survey will be completed in 1960.

The sponsorship of organized camping falls into three major categories. The largest segment is administered by the nonprofit agencies and organizations deriving their financial support from voluntary contributions and community fund-raising efforts conducted by community chests and other local groups. The second largest group of sponsors consists of private individuals and groups who undertake to establish camps as private, commercial enterprises designed to provide a means of livelihood for their entrepreneurs. The third sponsoring group—a relative newcomer to the field, but rapidly expanding its scope—consists of the tax-supported agencies, such as the public

---

[2]*See* Gibson, "The History of Organized Camping," *infra.*

[3]*Ibid.*

[4]*See* Dimock and Hendry, *infra.*

[5]*See* McBride, *infra.*

schools, local park districts, and state and local departments of recreation and conservation.

The structure of organized camping has been extended, in recent years, to encompass the field of day camping, in which school-age children participate in a daytime program of outdoor activity during the summer months. The prevailing philosophy of the organized day camp partakes of the basic ingredients of the camping rationale: the use of the outdoors, the values inherent in group association, the importance of creative play, and the adherence to a specified set of objectives of an educational-developmental-character building nature.

Both in its resident and day camp manifestations, the field of camping is structured to address itself to a broad variety of specialized needs. In addition to its provision of educational and recreational experience for normal children, adults, and families, the camp setting is being increasingly used to serve the physically handicapped, the emotionally disturbed, and other groups requiring specialized care and unique adaptations of the traditional camp program. In addition, there are camps which attract clientele around particular interests, such as music, dance, art, canoeing, and even some forms of rugged outdoor living which have become subordinated, in many camps, to other aspects of the organized camping program. To these should be added those camps conducted by labor unions, industry, fraternal societies, service clubs, churches, and other associations.

By age, the largest group served in organized camping is that of the nine to fourteen year-olds, although the proportion of adults and family groups has increased as social agencies, fraternal groups, and others have moved to develop new camping opportunities to meet this need.

By length of stay, it is generally characteristic of agency, as against private, resident camps to offer shorter camping periods ranging from five days to four weeks. In the privately owned camp, the period generally extends through eight weeks of the summer season. It should also be mentioned that, while organized camping activity is still largely concentrated in the summer months, there is a developing trend toward the use of camping facilities throughout the year, by the public schools, the leisure-time agencies and national youth-serving organizations.

The Evolution of the Camping Tradition

Organized camping has been described as "a folkway of an urban civilization."[6] Striking root in the latter decades of the nineteenth century, it had its beginnings in the social revolt against the disorganizing effects of the Industrial Revolution in America. It expressed a strong reaction against the softness and stultification of city life, the competitive ideology of a rising industrialism, and the depreciation of individual, creative labor in a mass production system. In its social agency development—particularly the phase of the "fresh air" movement—the interest in organized camping represented

[6] *See* Busch, *infra.*

an attempt to remove people, at least briefly, from the unhealthy, crowded conditions of the newly created city slums.

The early camping leaders stressed the restoration of the simple, age-old values which they regarded as inherent in a life close to nature. They emphasized the dignity of work, the healing effect of life in the outdoors, and the importance of communal responsibility. The basic philosophy was essentially Spartan and their early heroes were the Indians, the pioneers, and the builders of the American frontier. The romanticism and the back-to-nature aspects of the early tradition in organized camping have remained essential ingredients in our present conceptions of camp programming.

Soon after the turn of the century, the flourishing camping movement began to replace its initial reactive emphasis with a more positive exploitation of its own special ability to make a significant contribution to American life. This tendency emerged largely from a growing realization by many other professions and fields of practice that the camp setting possessed certain unique characteristics which made it flexible to many uses. The total control of the individual's environment, the high morale factor induced by close and intensive living together in work and play, the separation from home and city ties, the development of interpersonal relationships of an intense nature, the moving psychological effect of the natural environment—all of these features combined to offer the camp setting as a ready instrument for those interested in the conditions of individual and social change.

As a result, the history of the camping movement is one of attracting and absorbing the traditions and objectives of many other fields and interests in American life. Soon after the turn of the century, the rugged, Spartan tradition in camping underwent its first modification under the impact of the newly developing recreation movement. In this phase, camping incorporated the concern of recreationists with the development of the creative faculties through participation in games, music, dance, dramatic play, and other such activities. This added a new dimension to the camping program, introducing activities which have become as identified with the events of the camp day as the tent, the axe, and the blazing campfire.

Thus too, the movement was profoundly influenced by the "progressive" revolution of the 1920's and 1930's in the field of education. This development was reflected in the "progressive camping" era represented in Dimock and Hendry's *Camping and Character,* Joshua Lieberman's *Creative Camping,* and other works which characterized camping's prolific literary output of the 1930's. Here again, as with the recreational impact, the identification of American camping with American education has become so complete as to make it difficult to find a camping definition which does not incorporate certain precise educational objectives.

In approximately the same historical period, "the wedding of education and recreation in the great out of doors" found an answering echo in the leisure-time group-serving agencies—settlements, Y's, Jewish Centers, and national youth-serving organizations—then developing into a prominent feature of American urban life. The group workers' concern with both learning and play, coupled with the intense preoccupation with the benefits of the small-group experience, found in camping both a stimulating outlet for service and a ready-made laboratory for demonstrating the social importance of group interaction under professional leadership. The primary contribution of the group workers to the developing camping tradition lay in their emphasis on leadership training, the psychological significance of the small-group experience, and the central importance of the relationship between the cabin counselor and the small group of children with whom he lived. *See* SOCIAL GROUP WORK.

In a similar manner—and hastened by its early connections with the field of social group work—the philosophy and program of camping have been deeply influenced by the mental hygiene movement and by the traditions and practices of social work and social welfare. This has been reflected in its increasing preoccupation with psychological problems, its emphasis on individual differences, its developing role as part of the year-round pattern of social welfare services, and its growing importance as a residential treatment facility for the emotionally disturbed. Having, earlier, drawn heavily on the new social science of the early twentieth century, organized camping has itself developed into a significant resource for those who regard the circumstances of camp life as providing an ideal laboratory for observing and changing human behavior.

Toward Professional Development

Throughout the years, camping leaders have faced a major problem in their efforts to combine the various public and private interests into a common and recognizable pattern of practice, with enforceable standards of health, safety, leadership, and program. The efforts to increase public accountability and to formulate professional standards have come from legislating bodies, welfare councils, local health departments, national youth-serving organizations, and, most prominently, from the American Camping Association.

The American Camping Association, beginning in 1910 as a small group of camp directors, now numbers 8,000 lay and professional members and 3,600 camps, both public and private, throughout the nation. Its activities include the administration of an accreditation program, implemented by the issuance of a Camp Member Seal and the publication of a national directory of approved member camps. In addition, the Association works to refine and extend standards, to improve the quality of camping personnel, to stimulate the development of the camping literature, to affect public policy on matters affecting camping, and to interpret the field to the general public.

In the Current Scene

Organized camping began as an institution designed to serve the very rich; subsequently, under the impetus of the fresh-air movement, it expanded its scope to include the very poor. In the intervening decades, it has evolved as a movement that seeks to establish the camp experience as "the right of every child." This development has altered the perspective of organized camping from that of a special facility for particular segments of the population to one which seeks to permeate the educational and social welfare fabric of the community.

The prognosis for such an expansion of camping opportunities is seriously affected by certain problems of modern America. In the face of our rapidly shrinking areas of open space, the "exploding metropolis" continues to exert an overwhelming pressure for further subdivision and industrial use. Civic leaders throughout the country are calling attention to the need for legislation and group action designed to prevent a further melting away of open areas. The National Park Service's Mission 66,[7] and the Camping Survey mentioned above, represent action of this nature. Many feel, however, that the public has not yet been sufficiently alerted to the full scope of the problem. With an estimated increase in the national population to 240 millions in the next 20 years, a considerable increase in available land and buildings will be necessary merely to maintain the present relative volume of camping service.

These factors, added to the soaring land and building costs of the past few years, have produced considerable local interest in plans by which existing facilities may be more extensively used—in winter camping under agency auspices, the use of public recreation areas for year-round camping, and the use of privately owned camp facilities by public schools during the fall, winter, and spring months.

There are many who feel that any substantial expansion of organized camping beyond its present stage must await the further development of public school camping in America. Although less than 100 schools throughout the country have incorporated camping programs, these experiences have created a good deal of interest, and the outdoor education movement has stirred up considerable ferment in recreational and educational circles.

Bibliography[†]

American Camping Association, *Bibliography of Studies and Research in Camping.* Bradford Woods, Martinsville, Indiana, Undated. 13 pp.

———. *Day Camp Standards.* Martinsville, Indiana. Undated. 7 pp.

———. *1959 Directory of Camps Affiliated with the American Camping Association.* Martinsville, Indiana. 276 pp.

———. *Family Camp Standards.* Martinsville, Indiana. Undated. (As Adopted July, 1958).

———. *The Place of the Organized Camp in the Field of Education.* Rev. ed. 1956. 7 pp. First published in 1929. First revision in 1945.

---

[7] *See* Secretary of the Interior, *op. cit.*

[†] For addresses of periodicals listed see Appendix. All U.S. Government publications may be obtained from the Superintendent of Documents, Government Printing Office, Washington 25, D.C.

———. *Resident Camp Standards.* (As revised in 1956). Martinsville, Indiana. 1956. 11 pp.

Blumenthal, Louis H. *Group Work in Camping.* Association Press, New York. 1937. 100 pp.

———. "Group Work in Camping, Yesterday, Today, and Tomorrow," in *A Decade of Group Work,* ed. Charles E. Hendry. Association Press, New York. 1948.

Bogardus, LaDonna. *Planning the Church Camp for Juniors.* National Council of Churches, Chicago. 1955. 96 pp.

Brimm, R. P. "What Are the Values in Camping and Outdoor Education?," *Camping Magazine,* January 1959.

Busch, Henry M. "Camping," *Encyclopedia of the Social Sciences.* Vol. III.

Camping Magazine. Monthly. November–June.

Carr, Lowell Juilliard and others. *Integrating the Camp, The Community and Social Work.* Association Press, New York. 1939. 230 pp.

Clawson, Marion. "Recreation Land Resources. . . . For the Year 2000," *Recreation.* January 1959.

Crocker, Olive. "Integration of Social Work Concepts Into Camping Practice," in *Selected Papers in Group Work and Community Organization.* National Conference of Social Work, Columbus, Ohio. 1952.

Dimock, Hedley S., ed. *Administration of the Modern Camp.* Association Press, New York, 1948, 283 pp.

——— and Charles E. Hendry. *Camping and Character.* Association Press, New York. 2nd ed. 364 pp. With a foreword by William H. Kilpatrick.

——— and others, eds. *Character Education in the Summer Camp.* Reports of institutes held at Y.M.C.A. College, Chicago, and George Williams College, Chicago. Association Press, New York. 1930–1948. 9 parts. (Monographs no. 1–9).

Gibson, H. W. *Camp Management: A Manual on Organized Camping.* Greenberg, Publisher, Inc. Rev. ed. 1939. 304 pp.

———. "The History of Organized Camping," *The Camping Magazine.* January through December 1936.

Gilliland, John W. *School Camping, a Frontier of Curriculum Improvement.* Association for Supervision and Curriculum Development, National Education Association, Washington, D.C. 1954. 58 pp.

Howett, Harry H., ed. *Camping for Crippled Children.* The National Society for Crippled Children and Adults, Inc., Elyria, Ohio. 1945. 120 pp.

Ingram, Helene. "The Value of the Fresh Air Movement," *Proceedings of the National Conference on Charities and Correction,* 34th Annual Session, Minneapolis, Minnesota, 1907. William B. Burford, Indianapolis. 1907.

Irwin, Frank L. *The Theory of Camping, An Introduction to Camping in Education.* A. S. Barnes and Company, New York. 1950. 178 pp.

Jobe, Mabel Lyon. *The Handbook of Day Camping.* Association Press, New York. 1949. 189 pp.

Joy, Barbara Ellen. *Annotated Bibliography on Camping.* American Camping Association, Martinsville, Indiana. 1955. 34 pp.

Kolodny, Ralph L., and Virginia M. Burns. "Group Work with Physically and Emotionally Handicapped Children in a Summer Camp," in *Social Work with Groups, 1958,* Selected Papers from the National Conference on Social Welfare. National Association of Social Workers, New York. 1958.

Lieberman, Joshua. *Creative Camping.* Association Press, New York. 1931. 251 pp.

McBride, Robert E. *Camping at the Mid-Century, a Census of Organized Camping in America.* American Camping Association, Chicago. 1953. 41 pp.

McNeil, Elton B., issue ed. "Therapeutic Camping for Disturbed Youth," *The Journal of Social Issues,* Vol. XIII, No. I, 1957. 62 pp. Entire issue.

"Psychopathology and Psychotherapy of Camping," *Nervous Child,* April 1947. Entire issue.

Secretary of the Interior. *Sound Use of Our Natural Resources.* 1958 Report. Washington, D.C. 36 pp.

Characteristics of the Group Experience in Resident Camping

William Schwartz

When Louis H. Blumenthal, writing in the middle thirties, stated that "the essence of camping is its group life"[1] he was calling attention to one of the significant discoveries that changed the face of organized camping during the intense self-examination of that decade. The prolific literary output of the period—ushered in by the publication of *Camping and Character* (1929)[2] and *Creative Camping* (1931)[3]—was created by a kind of interlocking intellectual leadership, demonstrating the close identification of three budding movements: organized camping, progressive education, and social group work. In this "wedding of education and recreation in the great out-of-doors," an essential unifying theme was the significance of peer group experience in child development, and the realization that the resident camp setting was an ideal model for studying and demonstrating the effects of this experience.

In time, other members of the human relations professions—social psychologists, social caseworkers, psychiatrists, and more—came to find camping a fertile field for study and service, and their advent heightened the interest and attention focused on the ways in which children live, work, and play together in the resident camp situation. In the process, considerable information was gathered about the effects of group interaction on children's

---

WILLIAM SCHWARTZ, M.S., *is associate professor of social work at the University of Illinois School of Social Work. This article was chosen for publication by the Group Work Section.*

[1] *Group Work in Camping* (New York: Association Press, 1937), p. 14.

[2] Hedley S. Dimock and Charles E. Hendry, *Camping and Character,* 2nd ed. (contains a foreword by William H. Kilpatrick) (New York: Association Press, 1939). First printing, Young Men's Christian Association, May 1929.

[3] Joshua Lieberman, *Creative Camping* (New York: Association Press, 1931).

---

attitudes and behavior and these learnings served further to modify the camping tradition and to add new dimensions to its original conceptions of purpose, structure, and program.

Over the years, these insights have been built into the structure of resident camping in various ways: in the increased emphasis on cabin-group planning and activity, in the decline of highly organized competitiveness, in the decentralization of unit activity, in the efforts to group campers in accordance with certain grouping criteria, and so on.

As these implementing attempts continue, however, they are hampered by the fact that much of what has been learned about the nature of group experience is still taught and applied in general terms. A great deal remains to be done in relating abstract conceptions of group life to the unique problems and circumstances of the camp setting. What are the special factors inherent in the resident camp situation which fashion the child's reactions and relationships and create a very particular kind of group experience? The ability to understand this uniqueness in specific terms will determine the extent to which camp personnel can translate a general awareness into concrete measures through which to help children live up to their experiences at camp.

The camping literature—sparse at best since the thirties—reflects the fact that little systematic work has been done on this problem.[4] Beyond Fritz Redl's notable contribution[5] only a few limited attempts have been made to explore in detail the special characteristics of the resident camp setting.[6]

The present effort is brief and rudimentary, offered in the hope that some renewed interest can be stimulated in the questions involved. Of the salient operable factors in the camp situation, several seem most readily observable and seem to have the most immediate implications for the structuring of the

---

[4]In addition to other citations throughout the article readers may be interested in the following list of references: American Camping Association, *Bibliography of Studies and Research in Camping,* undated, and *The Place of the Organized Camp in the Field of Education* (3d ed. rev.; Indiana, Bradford Woods, Martinsville, 1956); Louis H. Blumenthal, "Group Work in Camping, Yesterday, Today, and Tomorrow," in Charles E. Hendry, ed., *A Decade of Group Work* (New York: Association Press, 1948), pp. 9–16; R. P. Brimm, "The Issues in Camping and Outdoor Education," *Camping Magazine,* Vol. 31, No. 1 (January 1959), pp. 14–15; Olive Crocker, "Integration of Social Work Concepts into Camping Practice," in *Selected Papers in Group Work and Community Organization* (Columbus, Ohio: National Conference of Social Work, 1952), pp. 33–44; Howard G. Gibbs, "Camping as a Tool in Social Welfare," in *Group Work and Community Organization, 1955* (New York: Columbia University Press, 1955), pp. 87–96; Barbara Ellen Joy, *Annotated Bibliography on Camping* (Bradford Woods, Martinsville, Ind.: American Camping Association, 1955); Elton B. McNeil, ed., "Therapeutic Camping for Disturbed Youth," *Journal of Social Issues,* Vol. 13, No. 1 (1957), entire issue; "Psychopathology and Psychotherapy of Camping," *Nervous Child,* Vol. 6, No. 2 (April 1947), entire issue; Paul Simon, "Social Group Work in Camping," in *The Social Welfare Forum* (New York: Columbia University Press, 1952), pp. 194–204.

[5]Fritz Redl, "Psychopathologic Risks of Camp Life," *The Nervous Child,* ("Psychopathology and Psychotherapy of Camping"), Vol. 6, No. 2 (April 1947), pp. 139–147.

[6]*See,* for example, Paul Gump, Phil Schoggen, and Fritz Redl, "The Camp Milieu and Its Immediate Effects," *The Journal of Social Issues* ("Therapeutic Camping for Disturbed Youth"), Vol. 13, No. 1 (1957), pp. 40–46.

camp experience. Within the space allowed, I shall try to point up some of their implications for practice. The task here is not to develop a comprehensive formulation, but to suggest some ways of thinking which may be profitably developed.

Characteristics of the Setting

The child's group experience at camp seems to be fashioned by four major situational characteristics.[7] *First,* this is a situation in which the child places unusually high demands and expectations on an experience which is relatively brief in time. This combination of great expectation with a limited time perspective produces, in the cabin group, a kind of "pool of excitement," in which each camper, in his own manner, demands immediate priority for his needs as he sees them. Group life thus begins in a hectic, competitive, and highly charged atmosphere. It is in this climate that each child begins to establish his relationships with both peers and adults.

Begun in this fashion, the cabin group experience appears as a kind of *telescoped version* of small-group life as we have come to know it in the year-round settings. The normal processes of testing for status, establishing role, pairing and subgrouping, sizing up the worker, finding the limits, and so on, are all distinctly observable, but in accelerated and often exaggerated form. The processes are accelerated because they represent certain problems and tasks inherent in small-group membership; they cannot be omitted or by-passed simply because the relationships involved are short-lived. The forms in which they appear are exaggerated, because the situation calls for quick resolutions, with much less time available for the customary caution and the elongated maneuvers of hanging-back and feeling-out engaged in by children in groups of indefinite tenure.

For similar reasons, the cabin group as a whole goes through what seems to be a *reverse order* of group development. In the typical long-term group, what we generally see is a gradual gathering of group momentum; the development of activity and organization reflects the extent to which the members have established their footing and learned to create group products out of the push and pull of individual demand. The camp group, on the other hand, plunges immediately into highly organized action and forms itself, as it were, in the breathing spells, as it goes along. The camp environment is such that the cabin group is immediately called upon to produce certain types of group behavior—like program-planning, limit-setting, role-differentiating—that we have come to regard as symptoms of high group cohesion emerging from an extended period of group life. In response to this necessity, the cabin group goes through a period where it must *simulate cohesion* until such time as it

---

[7]The implications of any such analysis will, of course, vary with the length of time that the camp groups stay together. These considerations are directed primarily to the 2- to 3-week camping period traditional to most social agency camps.

can organize and mobilize itself as an actual group through its own processes of group interaction.

Second, camp is a setting in which each child must adjust himself to an existence marked by constant and highly intimate contact with youngsters he scarcely knows, in a group not of his own choosing. This demand for *intimacy with strangers* carries within it three basic problems for the camp child. One is that it takes place in the context of what is essentially a peer society, in which the demands upon each other are severe and the general tolerance for weakness is low. At the same time, visibility is extremely high; the intimacy of camp life is such that close involvement with others is practically a condition of life, and the ordinary defenses are difficult to maintain. And finally, the child must deal with these demands in a group which is formed and accidental—meaning that he must develop his friends and allies *within the situation itself,* beginning more or less from scratch rather than having access to a given amount of group support at the outset.

Third, it is an experience away from home. Because of its intimacy and intensity, the child will invest it with the qualities of home and carry into it the unfinished business, the problems, and the attitudes involved in his home relationships with both siblings and adults. What he has grown to expect in the way of protection—and rejection—he will expect from those who surround him here. At the same time, the camp experience also represents something which is different from home, an opportunity for developing new ways of dealing with people and being dealt with by them. This is a chance to get out from under certain home patterns that seem dull, or repressive, or otherwise unsatisfactory. This striving for new and independent expression often produces the familiar changes in behavior—eating patterns, self-care, and the like—which surprise parents and gratify camp personnel.

Further, this striving often finds its best expression in group behavior, where the combined efforts of the cabin members provide the support and strength needed to try out new and unstereotyped relationships with adult authority. This is one of the factors that make it possible for a cabin group of tough, undisciplined youngsters to rise to new heights of co-operation and conformity, and for a cabin composed of conforming, middle-class children to take on all the earmarks of an antisocial gang.

And *fourth,* the resident camp constitutes an environment in which life is, to a large extent, both isolated from and insulated against outside influence. In this respect, camp is considerably more than simply a home away from home, since it concentrates the sources of both satisfaction and frustration within a tiny living space, offering none of the collateral outlets and compensations made possible by the school, the club, the street, and the larger family. This greatly reduced opportunity to *hedge his relationships* is the basic challenge of the camp experience for the camper. If he wants to be liked and respected, he has little alternative but to reach inside himself for qualities that are—in this camp community—socially valued; for these are the qualities that will help him to establish himself as a worth-while member of the community.

This is a difficult task, both for those children whose sense of self is not strong and for those to whom the present value system is strange. And it is in this search for personal strength that the child is most in need of help.

Aside from the ever crucial factor of staff skill, the fact is that much of this kind of help will be sought by the campers from each other. In order to find a place in the community, the camper must secure a fairly firm footing in his cabin group, and his feeling of *camp*-belonging will depend largely on the extent to which he has achieved the status of *cabin*-belonging. Thus, in studying the dynamics of the cabin group, we are examining a living unit that carries the major burden of success or failure for each of its members. With this kind of stake in the outcome, the child takes on participation as a matter of vital necessity, rather than choice; his efforts to effect successful relationships with the group carry an unusually high potential for general social success or failure.

Some Implications for Structure and Program

The cabin-group image that emerges from the above is that of a highly charged, dynamic organism that makes many demands and meets many in return. Its special features seem to stem primarily from the conditions of group formation, the nature of its community, the scope of its influence, and the nature and quality of member involvement. In each of these areas, the resident camp setting presents certain special problems and conditions that mold the forms of group interaction.

To the extent that these observations are valid, they should be translatable into techniques and devices that could sharpen the focus of camp work. Here again, the present effort will be to outline briefly some of the general directions in which such implementing efforts might move.

First, I would suggest that the resident camp setting should be understood and accepted as an *artificial community,* in the sense that it derives its basic stability and structure not from the strengths and weaknesses of its constituent groupings but from the efforts and activities of professional personnel. This should not mean that the individuals and groups within it have no control over the events of camp life, but that the *degree* of control will vary within an established framework. This idea may run counter to an ancient notion, namely, that camp is a model of "democracy" in action. But in actuality the analogy is poor, for—as in a school or an institution—the reins and responsibility of government must be tightly held by those accountable to the general community. The failure to recognize this produces an illusory system of "government," which is far from the real meaning of democracy. On the other hand, an acceptance of the realities of power in the camp setting makes it possible to create genuine opportunities for group policy-making and environmental control in areas where such decisions are really binding and effective.

If it is true, for example, that the cabin group begins its life with more problems that it is equipped to handle, a premature preoccupation with the signs of group strength and cohesiveness may result in practices which are essentially manipulative rather than democratic. Even if we do not trouble ourselves with the semantic problem of whether the cabin actually constitutes a "group" at the outset, it seems clear that its initial capacity for joint problem-solving is severely limited by its internal pressures and by its group immaturity; hence nothing can be gained by fostering an illusion of group strength where it does not exist. Rather would it be wiser to accept, without guilt, the proposition that the over-all context and structure of camp program is provided by staff, with a view toward creating a stable and well-defined system. Within this system, groups and units of groups may be helped gradually, and according to their growing strengths, to make those decisions of which they are capable at a given time. Inevitably, the ability to create a significant impact on this prefabricated culture will vary from group to group; it should, in fact, be a foregone conclusion that some of the cabin groups will never achieve this degree of strength.

A second set of implications arising from this analysis may move us further in the direction of offsetting the intense concentration of energy invested by the camper in his interaction with members of his cabin group. In this connection, it may be important for us to examine the camp regimen for the opportunities it provides for (1) widening the child's range of significant groups and (2) finding, through acts of individual choice, periods of time in which he can set his own tempo and regulate his own involvement in the affairs of others. Camps have developed a number of devices aimed in this general direction—mass activities, unit activities, hobby groups, free-play periods, free-choice programs, and so on. But, again, these are often accompanied by some sense of violating cabin "groupness"; further, these opportunities themselves have often been so severely routinized as to lose their original purpose. What is needed here is a conceptual framework for evaluating these various levels of camper involvement and a machinery for implementing them on an individualized basis—a difficult task but a necessary one, if the problem is correctly stated here.

Olive L. Crocker has suggested, for example, that the "early use of staff activity and use of milieu (rather than the group)" can "give a camper the feeling of being expected as an individual, being prepared for, and being given to immediately." She makes the further point that it is only after the child has had some "tasting experiences," in which he has felt the various forms of excitement offered by the camp environment, that he is ready to participate in a creative program-planning process with his fellows.[8]

A third area of interest lies in the development of means by which the camper may be helped to expand his circle of significant adults within the camp community. In orienting counselors, camp leaders have tended to interpret their responsibilities as combining the roles of mother, father, uncle,

---

[8]These comments were developed by Miss Crocker in a statement prepared as a reaction to the present paper, in the form in which it was read to the Chicago Group Work Section of the National Association of Social Workers in April 1958. See *Group Work Papers, 1958* (Chicago: Group Work Section, NASW Chicago Area Chapter). (Mimeographed.)

aunt, and grandparent. The unreality of such a conception—for both counselor and camper—is patent, even where staff skill and maturity are considerably greater than is usually the case. The insularity of camp life and the reduced opportunity for the "emotional shopping" children do among adults cannot be compensated for in a more intense relationship with the cabin counselor. Without underestimating the importance of this central relationship, the need remains to provide opportunities for the campers to create a wider range of "significant others" within the adult population. This need has been recognized, to an extent, in the growing use of caseworkers, "roving" counselors, and in certain individualizing functions of the unit leader. But these relationships—important as they are when the need arises—are essentially trouble-oriented and curative, rather than built into the normal pattern of camp activity. In this connection, the specialty counselor may once more come into his own, having been overshadowed for some time by an old group work notion that a skilled cabin counselor could render the role of the specialist relatively unnecessary in the camp setting.

Finally, if it is true that the rewards of the camp experience are available only to those with certain marked strengths and capacities, it should be possible to specify these characteristics in fairly precise terms, in order to guard against the premature exposure of those who may be hurt by it. Although camp personnel have learned to be wary of the undifferentiated referral of children who "need a group experience," they have not been helpful to those who need to understand the personality factors involved in a child's ability to use such an experience in the camp milieu. Simply by way of example, I would suggest that there may be considerable evidence to indicate that there is a close connection between a child's perception of his own attractiveness to others and his chance of success in the camp situation. Whether or not such a hypothesis holds up, the fact remains that such formulations are needed, and that they are available from the store of experience built up by camping people over the years.

The field of camping has moved a long way from the early days in which the emphasis on individual strength and achievement created a culture in which only the fittest survived. However, the newer stress on group strength and group achievement carries its own potential for danger when it remains stereotyped and abstract in the minds of those who work with it. Understood in its own concrete terms, the camp group can be helped to provide a richer source of significant experience for its members.

Group Work in Public Welfare

William Schwartz

It is now fairly well established that social work with small groups is no longer a monopoly of the "group workers," but a common feature of social work practice in a wide range of settings. The interest in groups has spread rapidly in a short time; it was only a few years ago that we were beginning to note the impending breakdown of the old, three-cornered, "methods" arrangement under which social work had grown up. In 1961 I called attention to the forthcoming

> . . . reexamination of social work's historic system of designating the functions of agencies by reference to the number of people involved in the client-worker system at one time. Thus the casework agency, as we have known it, was one which derived its distinguishing characteristics from the fact that its workers talked to people one at a time; the group work agency . . . worked with people in small, cohesive groups; and the

WILLIAM SCHWARTZ, D.Ed., Professor of Social Work, *Columbia University School of Social Work, New York, New York.*

The program described in this monograph was financed by the Children's Bureau, Department of Health, Education, and Welfare, from Child Welfare Services funds disbursed through the cooperation of the New York State Department of Social Services, with 100 percent reimbursement.

Dr. Schwartz, who is widely known and admired as social work educator, philosopher, and practitioner, has made a distinctive contribution to the field through the writing of this report for the journal. In transmitting it to the Editor, he expressed his heartfelt appreciation and respect for public welfare personnel whom he has met at Institutes and Conferences in different parts of the country and in his classroom at Columbia. He further stated, "The program described here was conducted through the office of Evangeline James, then Director of Training, Bureau of Child Welfare, New York City Department of Welfare, and owed a great deal to her intelligent leadership, professional discipline and warm cooperation. Thanks are also due to James Dumpson, then Commissioner of Welfare; Elizabeth Beine, Director of the Bureau of Child Welfare; Murray Ortof, who as Training Director of the Department of Welfare first set the program in motion; Rose Thomas, who succeeded him in that position; Patricia Garland, Emanuel Fox, Winifred Lally, and a host of superb administrators, supervisors and practitioners too numerous to mention here."

Schwartz, William. (1968). Group work in public welfare. Public Welfare, *XXVI (4), 322–370.*

community organization agency assumed the function of leadership with representative bodies and similar associations.[1]

It was clear even then that the time had come for a more reasonable perspective on the division of labor within the social welfare field:

> The new conceptual framework would be built on the recognition that the function of a social agency is determined more realistically by the social problem to which it has been assigned than by the specific relational systems through which the social worker translates this function into concrete services. It would accept the fact that there is no known correspondence between a function such as child placement, or family welfare, or recreation, or social planning, and the exclusive use of the one-to-one or the one-to-group structure to carry it out. And it would become increasingly clear that any agency should be capable of creating, in each specific instance, that system of client-worker relationships which is most appropriate to its clients' requirements.[2]

I noted further that it was a *social work method* that should now be emerging, practiced in the various situations in which social workers find themselves—the family, the friendship group, the representative body, the interview, the client group, the hospital ward, the lounge-canteen, the interest group, the street club and many others.[3] The idea of a social work method has since become increasingly attractive and both agencies and schools of social work have been exploring its meanings.[4] While it may not yet be safe to say that the generic rationale is commonly understood and accepted, the fact is that the expanding service to groups is being developed, for the most part, as a form of social work rather than as a group work specialization. There seems to be little question that the interest in groups has weathered its "fashionable" phase and is now firmly fixed in the social work conception of service. Further, it seems clear that the skills of group practice will increasingly be expected of social workers, whatever "method" they have been taught in schools of social work still operating under the old conceptions of practice.

Whatever it is that triggers the adventure into group service, the effect of the move is to place a powerful new instrument in the hands of social workers and their institutions. While clients are formed into groups, the combined strength of their feelings, troubles and aspirations provides a new dynamic in the helping process itself. There is a demand for new skills on the part of workers still struggling to master the old ones, but convinced that there are important connections between the two. And the developing interest in mutual aid, interpersonal sharing and group spontaneity begins to spread to the staff processes themselves—the meeting, the committee and the supervisory conference. If peer group support and shared work helps clients, why should these processes not be effective for staff as well? Altogether, the new work carries with it a fresh sense of aliveness, a search for new forms of communication, a kind of existential faith in the ability of people to help each other, and a calculated break from the formalism of some of the traditional patterns of client-worker relationship.

It may be this very need for new ways of grappling with immensely complicated problems that has put the field of public welfare so much in the forefront of the growing preoccupation with group services. In the large and complex bureaucracies that administer the public welfare services, the sheer enormity of their technical and administrative tasks may dispose them to the search for larger devices and group solutions. In any event, the achievements of the public agencies in this area are impressive and a significant portion of the new literature and case material have been contributed from this field. In a pioneering work, Fenton and Wiltse[5] have described 25 group service experiences in 13 county welfare departments in California. The history of their County Project in the Social Welfare Program recapitulates the development of group services, and the training for group skills, from its earliest beginnings in the areas of corrections and public assistance.[6] The group work described is with a wide variety of clients—foster parents, applicants for Aid to Needy Children, prospective adoptive parents, unemployed older workers, alcoholics, adolescent girls and other groups from the caseloads of public welfare. And the problems discussed anticipate those that would subsequently characterize each similar effort—the search for the connections with casework skill, the struggle with dubious distinctions between "educational" and "counseling" groups, the problem of developing a clear sense of group purpose, and others.[7] In a young literature, writing on the subject has been given considerable impetus by the Federal coordinating and program agencies such as the Bureau of Family Services[8] and the Bureau of Public Assistance,[9] both of the United States Department of Health, Education, and Welfare. In addition, public-private collaborations have produced some interesting accounts[10]; and there is a fast-growing bibliography of individual articles, reports and technical papers dealing with the practice of social work with groups in public welfare settings.[11]

When an agency becomes interested in the use of groups it takes on a number of problems, bearing on where the new expertise will come from, how to incorporate a new form of work into an existing pattern of service and how to create a climate in which staff members will see the work as important to them, rather than a new set of demands dreamed up by the powers above. If the agency must go outside for help—and the need to do so has created an imposing new consultation industry—it will bring a stranger into its midst. Much will then depend on the degree to which the "expert" can become a part of the working force, engaging himself with staff in a genuine collaborative relationship. Staff members—like learners everywhere—will not take lessons from a bore, or a pedant, or one so far removed from the perplexities of practice that every problem is an exercise in reason and his words do not echo the workers' pressing sense of urgency and immediacy.

The consultant, on his part, is faced with the fact that he is far from expert in the working problems of the agency that has called him in. He cannot possibly know as much about child welfare, or public assistance, as those who have struggled with those tasks for many years. What the consultant knows is a new (for them) way of working, and he must adapt this knowledge to a new (for him) agency setting. He must thus be prepared to learn from them as fast as they learn from him, and at exactly the same time.

A further consideration affecting the consultative relationship is that it is in constant danger of sinking into *triviality*—where the work will become merely "interesting" and "educational," rather than a carefully constructed and lasting addition to the agency's structure of service. Many circumstances may conspire to rob the consultation work of its meaning and produce little but a brief flurry in the life of the agency—remembered at its worst as a tedious burden and at its best as an "interesting experience." The work may be confined to a small corner of the agency, rather than demanding time and attention from a cross-section of the hierarchy; the expert may try to "hand over" his knowledge and skills, *talking* them across, rather than helping the staff members work hard to own them; the premium may be put on developing a fancy, "in" lexicon rather than a precise definition of the acts of skill that must be learned. These and similar approaches create an illusion that something important is happening, while no demands are made of the agency, no commitments are established and no one is asked to undergo the pain and struggle of learning to do something new and difficult.

In fact, the consultative enterprise, taken seriously, draws heavily on the energy, commitment and skill of all who are involved. The agency administrators must face the impact of the training on the service and be prepared to implement the changes called for as the work proceeds. The staff workers must risk themselves, enter areas in which they feel inadequate and shaky, and reveal their working weaknesses in records and staff presentations. And the consultant is called upon to show not only an exact knowledge of his subject but an ability to carry out—in the consultation process itself—the kinds of helping skills he is trying to teach.

More specifically, the group work consultant must be able to do three things: he must identify the *group work skills* and help the workers put them into action on their jobs; he must engage the staff in a *learning process,* where the consultation work provides its own model of how people use each other in groups and what it takes to help them; and he must help the agency develop a way of using consultation for the purpose of *institutionalizing* the new service—that is, of building it in so securely and integrally that it will continue to operate after he has left.

These are the areas that will require the most careful study by those interested in the expanded use of groups in the public settings, and our working experiences should be examined closely for the generalizations we can draw about them. The following account is one such attempt, drawing on the efforts of a large public child welfare setting to intensify its use of groups and to use consultation as a way of working at the tasks involved. As the consultant, I made a conscious effort from the outset to direct our work and our recording to these three major problems—identifying the group work skills in detail, learning and teaching them in a new setting, and building them into the agency's pattern of work with both clients and staff. It is not an easy story to tell, for it deals with a number of processes moving at the same time and one is tempted to draw attention to the chronology, the working themes, the theoretical perspectives and the practice itself, all at the same time. What this illustrates, of course, is the inseparability of all these factors and the account must indeed manage to convey each perspective as it operates in relation to the others.

The presentation will begin with an overview of the total experience, describing its objectives, basic assumptions and the design of the work of the four-year consultation period. The second section deals with the involvement of the agency administrators in the processes of establishing the consultative purpose, beginning the work and maintaining a close and proprietary interest in the developing problems of training staff members for group practice. The third is a section on the formation of client groups, the client problems that we addressed and the group work skills on which we worked. Fourth is the section on the use of groups in staff work, with particular reference to the skills required to turn the staff meeting into a more effective instrument for staff education and coordination. And finally, there is an attempt to summarize and draw some conclusions from the entire experience.

Overview: Scope and Design

The experience began in the autumn of 1962, when I was called in to work with the Bureau of Child Welfare of the New York City Department of Welfare (now the Department of Social Services) on the development of staff skills in the use of groups. The Bureau of Child Welfare (BCW) is a large and complex operation, providing a wide range of services to over 22,000 children both in their own facilities and in those of voluntary agencies in New York City. Working through eleven separate Divisions, it offers foster care, adoption, homemaking, protective services, filiation services, day care, prenatal and postnatal care and child welfare consultation to local public assistance centers. The Bureau has over 1200 social service workers, in various stages of training and experience, and conducts an extensive program of inservice education at the various levels of the staff hierarchy.

The Bureau's interest in groups was based on the conviction that they could be usefully employed both to enrich its program of services to clients and to increase the skill and effectiveness of its staff in carrying out the work of the agency. Thus, in my early meetings with top training personnel, these two major areas of consultation were established. One was to teach group work skills to those who were working—and those preparing to work—with groups of clients; such groups had already been used to some extent and these efforts had pointed up the need for additional training. The other was to help BCW administrators and supervisors use their staff meetings more effectively, employing group skills to help their staff members work together on common problems. It was assumed at the outset that these two processes—client work and staff work—had much in common and called for skills very similar in nature; in both instances, one brought together people with common tasks and concerns and tried to help them pool their strengths to work together on these common problems. The account will show that these similarities became increasingly clear as the work progressed.

Some Working Assumptions

In consultation, as in any helping relationship, both parties operate on certain assumptions—some shared, some divergent—as to what the work is for and how to go about it. These assumptions will—consciously or otherwise—fashion the procedures, determine the ground rules and establish the criteria for success. Thus, the more clearly these propositions are understood at the outset, the more likely it is that the experience will be focused and controlled by the aspirations of those involved. At the BCW, we reached early agreement on several important points and these shaped the pattern of consultations through which we worked.

First, it was clear that our emphasis was to be on the development of group *skills,* on learning the specific *acts* of helping people in groups. This was not to be a "seminar" in "group dynamics." Although it would certainly help to become more sophisticated about how people behave in groups, we would be more concerned with how such knowledge could be converted into skilled performance with people. So it was with qualities like "self-awareness," "sensitivity," "social aspiration" and other desirable professional attributes; all of the *knowing, being* and *hoping* would be important only as they were put to use in *doing.* This stress on the importance of the deed—the only quality that is after all visible and useful to the client—grew from the assumption that one can indeed define and describe the explicit acts of helping[12] and this was a dominant and persistent theme in the course of our work together.

Second, we agreed that the best way to work on skills was to base our discussions almost entirely on their own records of practice. Our emphasis on recording and case presentation cannot be overestimated: the decision to learn from watching people work, rather than from abstract discussion, speeded up the formation of groups and immediately involved a large number of workers in actual group practice; an atmosphere was created in which top administrators and supervisors, applying the same rule to themselves, moved into work with groups so that they could acquire first-hand experience and develop materials they could present at their own consultation meetings; and the need to look closely at the records before us made it difficult for us to lose ourselves in abstractions, semantics and theoretical wanderings.

Third, we took the position that we were bringing not a new discipline but an adaptation of skills they were already practicing in their work with individuals. This was of course the "generic" theme, appearing now in a form that could be useful to them in their development as social workers. We assumed—and events were to bear us out—that group work problems would be recognized by the BCW workers as resembling the casework problems they had been struggling to master, involving the same communications and human relations skills set in a wider context. And we believed that the preoccupation with group skills would reinforce the concern with method itself—that is, that the discussion would eventually turn from "casework" and "group work" to the more basic problems of helping people in trouble, reading their problems and helping them use their strengths, in whatever context the worker-client relationship developed.

Fourth was a corollary, namely that we would try to develop the group skills as widely as possible, rather than establish a "group work department" within the Bureau. We agreed that a group work specialization would defeat the purpose of the program, restricting the responsibility to a few, emphasizing the uniqueness of the work and inhibiting its integration into the basic service of the agency. This approach carried several implications for the use of consultation: it meant that we would not be using trained group workers to lead the way into group practice, but would try to develop these skills with as many of the BCW people as we could, whatever their training or lack of it; further, the agency was serving notice that it would ultimately expect its workers to include group skills as part of their professional equipment; and finally, the coordination of individual and group services could be conducted as a continuous feedback between social workers doing different jobs at different times, rather than between two bodies of specialized personnel.

Fifth, the consultation plan was geared to the conviction that the institutionalization of group services would depend on the degree of interest, knowledge and urgency developed at *every level* of the staff hierarchy. A program in which the workers alone were interested might be accepted by the administrators in a general kind of way, but such acquiescence would soon give way to the overwhelming pressures of the "regular" workload. Conversely, a strong sense of administrative urgency might well leave the practitioners with the feeling that this was simply another burden imposed by people who did not have to do the work. Thus, the consultation process was to be directed to the different levels of responsibility and as close together in time as we could manage. We also believed that one does not really *own* a form of work until one has grappled with its problems and tried to carry out its tasks; therefore, we were not merely to "expose" the top level staff to the new ideas, or to "interest" them in general terms, but to strive for as much technical sophistication as we could get, at each staff level. It was hoped that the group work discussions would be taken over by each supervisor along the line, as a regular supervisory item, however inadequate they might feel in this area at the beginning. For it was only when the work on groups found its way from the consultation sessions to the supervisory agendas that it would be safe to assume that any real degree of group work integration had been achieved.

Sixth, we assumed that the consultation process itself would model all of the phenomena we would be studying—how people work on common tasks, how they help and frustrate each other, how they learn and how they resist, how they use help from a worker and how the worker uses his skills to help them. Whether we planned it that way or not—and it would be best *not* to work up artificial situations to illustrate this point—we would reproduce all of the group processes that they would experience with their clients and their staff, simply because we would in fact be a group of people trying to master some problems with the help of a worker. And the worker (the consultant) would inevitably illustrate his points quite as much in what he *did* as in what he *said.* This did not mean that we should be spending all or most of our time examining our own processes; but neither should we hesitate to do so if we had the opportunity to look closely at a skill in action, or a mistake, or a crucial event in our own work together as a group.

This working model would show the consultant in the act of practicing—or not practicing—his own teachings about the role of the helping person. He must not, for example, dedicate himself so rigidly to the necessities of "group process" that he pretends to know nothing at all and forces everything to "come from the group." On the other hand, he must not swing to the opposite extreme and show his expertise at great length, solving all the problems himself and restricting the group discussion to a period of "any questions?" He must, in short, demonstrate a worker's ability to be active without interfering, to give and to take, and to use himself fully, openly and honestly in the hectic interaction of a group. This approach created the strategy for beginning the work in each new consultation group: I would open with a very brief theoretical framework, simply phrased and offering an opening perspective on the problem of working with groups; I would then ask for some "problem-swapping" about their previous attempts to do this kind of work in this and other settings; there would be some "contractual" talk, sharing our ideas about the purpose of our work together; and we would do some planning on the use of future sessions, the kinds of material we wanted to examine, the nature of the recording and any other necessary mechanics. The effort throughout would be on keeping the opening communications as real as possible, reaching past the dull and lifeless forms of acquiescence, calling for actual problems rather than slogans ("finding out where the client *is,*" "help them *work through* their problems," etc.) and openly identifying some of their own conflicts and doubts about the work ahead.

Finally, we understood that my work was to be limited to the tasks of developing group skills; I was not to direct myself to the various problems of administrative policy that might arise as the work proceeded. I would of course be interested in these problems, as I was interested in the agency and its success. But I would be careful to avoid undue involvement in questions of value growing out of their responsibility to the agency. It would be presumptuous to advise them on matters for which I had no accountability and on decisions with which I would not have to live. Although I would certainly not disavow the connections between program and policy—there would undoubtedly be many—I would be careful not to claim the authority or function in the latter that I could stand for in the former.

There were of course a number of other assumptions built into the first planning sessions with the training personnel of BCW; but the above will illustrate our basic approach to the purposes and processes of the consultation program. Some of these propositions were clear enough at the outset to be stated in so many words. Others were identified as we moved along in the first stages of the work itself. The important point is that there was a firm consensus, not only on the need to understand these foundations but on the substance of the assumptions themselves. I was thus able to represent their own training aspirations, rather than an alien "educational" force preparing to do things to them for their own good.

Chronology

Guided by these considerations, we established a consultation program that ultimately involved about 500 participants[13] in 20 working groups of varying duration, in about 125 meetings and conferences held between October 1962 and June 1966. The following is a brief account of the succession of events, showing how the time was used, the range of work and the tasks undertaken over the four-year period. Having done that, I will then be free to concern myself less with the story in sequence and more with the substantive problems that occupied our time.

First Year: Our first major problem was to establish a framework of ideas about working with groups—ideas not to be "learned" at the outset, but to be used as a common reference point for the problems that would emerge as we began to look at the work. From that point, the consultation program could begin fairly simply, designed only to begin on the two major tasks—the work with staff groups and with client groups—and to involve as many strategic personnel as possible in the lessons to be drawn from our first attempts. Accordingly, two consultation groups were established, each numbering about 30 members and each meeting monthly between November and June.

Group I, consisting of the BCW Director and her associates, the Director of Training and her assistant, the eleven Division Directors and a number of Senior Supervisors and Case Supervisors from each division, devoted itself to the problem of using the small group as a device for "training and orientation of workers to carry on the functions of the division."[14] The nature of their concerns may be illustrated by the kinds of presentations they offered for group deliberation and consultation: a Senior Supervisor in the Division of Under Care offered his record of a meeting in which he had led five unit supervisors and 30 social investigators in a discussion of a new form to be used as a control of prospective cases of permanent neglect; a Case Supervisor in the Division of Auxiliary Services presented her record of a meeting in which she had tried to help six trainees discuss the results of their first field visits; a Case Supervisor in the Division of Maternity Shelter and Allocation presented a meeting with three unit supervisors and 17 social investigators, on an inquiry from a private agency regarding their decrease in referrals to that agency; the Assistant Director of Training brought a record in which he had discussed with 17 recently appointed social investigator trainees their reactions to a popular article in the current press attacking the Department of Welfare; and other presentations covering work with staff groups on problems such as incomplete dictation, the need for some staff consensus on certain aspects of agency philosophy and practice, case reviews for the purpose of standardizing the decision-making within the divisions, and other issues crucial to the work of the agency. In each of these presentations, our work was focused not primarily on the issues themselves but on the efforts and the skills necessary to help staff members hold live and meaningful discussions about them, reach decisions they could implement and achieve a genuine involvement in division affairs.

Group II consisted of personnel from the three placement divisions of the Bureau—Homefinding, Adoptions and Foster Home Care. Its membership ranged from the BCW Director, the Training Director and the three Division Directors to selected Case Supervisors and—a step lower on the hierarchy—Assistant Supervisors from each of the three divisions. Their work was directed to the organization of client groups and the skills required for group services:

> In my opening presentation, I described the growing interest, in both public and private family and children's agencies throughout the country, in the small group as a medium of service to clients. I also pointed out that, although this interest carries a great potential for service, there is also the danger that it may become a kind of fad that will wear out its welcome after a flurry of activity. One way to prevent this outcome is to guard against the notion that group service is a kind of cure-all, a panacea for all the problems that workers find difficult to resolve through the one-to-one relationship. Group work creates its own helping problems and its own demands for professional skill; used where it is most appropriate to the needs of clients, it can play an important part in the agency if it is carefully built into the total program of services. Thus my job would be not to sell them the benefits of group work, but to help them understand the nature of this activity, the skills it calls for, and how it might be helpful to them in carrying out their respective functions. In so doing, I hoped that we could focus as closely as possible on problems and concerns that emerged directly from their own work.[15]

Again, the work of Group II may be illustrated by the kinds of case presentations they offered for discussion: the Director of Training herself presented a record in which she had led 25 foster parents, in the temporary care program of the Division of Homefinding, in a discussion of the problems of the foster mother in the neighborhood; an Assistant Supervisor in the Division of Foster Home Care made three presentations in the course of her work with a six-session group of foster mothers, meeting to work together on the problems of raising adolescent children in foster care; a Case Supervisor in the same division also presented an entire six-session sequence of work with a group of foster mothers, offering us another opportunity to see the progress of a short-term group with which we helped the worker to begin, watched and helped him carry out his purpose and then helped him to end; the Director of the Division of Adoption Services offered her record of a first meeting with a group of seven adoptive parents in the supervision period (laying the groundwork for the subsequent development of this kind of service in her Division); and an Assistant Supervisor for Group Homes in the Division of Foster Home Care presented her meeting with four adolescent girls discussing certain group living problems they were experiencing.

In both consultation groups, I and II, we followed the same work format: we began with a small planning session with a few key personnel, outlining their main concerns and day-to-day problems in the area under discussion, planning the use of consultation time and deciding who should participate in the consultation groups; then, in the first meeting with the entire group, I presented a brief, theoretical frame of reference, following which we spent some time in "problem-swapping" and concluded with some plans for future group organization and case presentation; the bulk of the remaining sessions were then spent on these presentations—one or two, sometimes three per meeting—in analyzing the work line by line, drawing principles from it and helping the worker plan for future work; and there was a final session devoted to a summary of the learning and implications for future planning.

Second Year: In the second phase, the agency moved into more intensive group programming with both clients and staff. The consultation process, while maintaining close engagement with upper-echelon staff, made its way downward on the hierarchy, working with a large number of Assistant Supervisors on problems of staff management, and with a substantial group of casework practitioners on group services to clients in their care.

The work with staff groups was concentrated in the population of Assistant Supervisors, otherwise known as the *unit supervisors* since each is responsible for a small operational unit of six caseworkers in direct contact with clients. The focus of consultation was on their use of the unit meeting as an instrument of administration and education. The unit supervisors were arranged in three large consultation groups, about 35 in each and each meeting monthly between November and June. The work format was now fairly well standardized: each group devoted its first session to developing some consensus on purpose, establishing the frame of reference and working up a kind of agenda of their working, day-to-day problems; subsequent meetings were then given over to discussion based on submitted records of unit meetings and other administrative meetings in which they had assumed leadership; and the final session in each group was evaluative, sharing reactions to the substance and process of our work together and drawing implications for the future. In the course of these sessions, we worked together on 23 different record presentations, representing activity in every division and describing a wide range of problem situations for the unit supervisor: trying to help a unit of trainees—some new and some experienced—work together on how to get closer to clients; a new supervisor meets with her unit for the first time; an inter-agency meeting, in which the supervisor tries to relieve the tensions between the various professionals in a day care center; other inter-agency conferences in which the supervisor leads the discussion of cases held in common; a supervisor presents her work in a unit meeting held to discuss the role of unit meetings; another takes on the difficult task of chairing a group of seven supervisors sitting as a Program Committee for the administrative meetings of the division; yet another works with his unit on their real reactions to the new group services for adolescents in foster care; and many other recorded presentations showing the units at work on new procedures, practice skills, relating to other agencies, expressing anger at the agency, discussing the fear of home visiting in troubled neighborhoods, evaluating their progress and morale and a host of other issues on which unit teamwork was crucial to agency success.

The consultation on client groups was directed to the establishment of three such groups in the Division of Foster Home Care, trying to develop the organizational processes, the involvement of all appropriate staff in the planning, the measurement of time and facilities required and the implications of all these factors for the further expansion of group services to other divisions in BCW. Two of these groups were formed of adolescent boys in foster care, meeting to help each other with the common problems of children growing into maturity in foster families. I met with the worker (an Assistant Supervisor) once a month, received his process recording regularly and met monthly as well with the entire staff of caseworkers carrying the boys and their families. As always, our format consisted of a first meeting that focused the work, a series of sessions based on record presentations by the worker and a final meeting for evaluation and planning.

The third group was composed of foster parents—mostly mothers—living in an outlying community; the staff felt that the distance created a sense of isolation and rendered the parents less accessible to service. A Case Supervisor was assigned to the group. It was her second such undertaking; she had led one of the six-session foster parents' groups in the first year of consultation. The consultation pattern involved four sessions with the worker and five associates, one of whom served as an observer in the parents' group and all of whom were being prepared to take on group service responsibilities.

The consultations with the administrators continued, with 40 to 50 top echelon BCW staff attending each of three meetings. These were spaced to plan the work, to discuss it while it was in progress and to evaluate its effects from their respective points of vantage.

By the end of the second year, certain factors were fairly well established: there was a general theoretical base, with some shared assumptions about the themes of mutual aid, open contracts, directness and spontaneity and other constructs; staff motivation was high and many were prepared to risk themselves in the new work; and there was agreement on a general strategy of building the service gradually—out of conviction and real need—rather than as a crash program designed to produce impressive participation figures. We were also developing some specific ideas about the adaptability of casework skills and the level of practice we could achieve at given stages of work.

Third Year: There were several points from which we could now move to the next stage: some specific group services had been incorporated into the Bureau's pattern of work; a small cadre of agency personnel was actually engaged in group work and developing practice skills; a larger group of caseworkers and supervisors was now familiar with the work and growing more knowledgeable about its concepts and problems; a close involvement had been maintained by the administrative staff and there was no question of their support of the program and their increasing sophistication about its demands; and the consultation pattern was now clearly worked out, allowing us to move quickly and with a clear sense of what we were to do together.

Based on this assessment, the consultation tasks for the third year were to expand group services in those divisions where they had taken hold, increase the number of workers willing and able to move into group practice, continue to work with administrators and supervisors on the skilled use of staff meetings and encourage top staff to put the group item on their regular supervisory agendas.

Specifically, the work with adolescent boys was continued and the same worker put in his second year of group service; his supervisor now took over the meetings with the caseworkers carrying the families, thus institutionalizing this segment of the work. The consultation group consisted of the worker, his supervisor, other personnel preparing to lead groups, the Senior Supervisor and the Division Director. Also, a number of individual conferences were added to the consultation program: there was an interview with the Division Director in Foster Home Care, on strengthening the supervision of group practice; there was a conference with the boys' group worker, helping him review his work; and there was a series of meetings with the leader of last year's foster parents' group, to develop a teaching record of this experience.

Consultation was also extended to new client groups in the Divisions of Adoptions and Homefinding. These two divisions, having continued their group services while consultation had been concentrated in Foster Home Care, were now combined into a single consultation group, with which I met monthly during the third year. This was a group of about 25 caseworkers, supervisors, training personnel and Division Directors, working on materials emerging from practice in the two divisions. Four group experiences were recorded and presented: a one-meeting group of prospective foster parents; two separate four-meeting groups of adoptive parents in their year of supervision; and a one-meeting group of new applicants for adoptive parenthood.

In the area of staff work, a program was established in which all the Case Supervisors met regularly with their Assistant (unit) Supervisors in small groups designed to carry forward last year's work on handling unit meetings and other supervisory problems. This was an answer to the call of the unit supervisors, sounded in last year's sessions, for more support and supervision; it also gave the Case Supervisors a chance to try out their own group skills, in the very processes they were trying to teach. They used a syllabus, prepared over the summer by the Training Division in collaboration with the

Case Supervisors. I now worked with the Case Supervisors, about 35 in number, meeting monthly with them in discussions based on their recorded accounts of their meetings with the unit supervisors. These records were presented by the group leader, or by a colleague observer, or, in some instances, by both leader and observer giving their versions of the same group session. The device of the individual consultation was used once, with a Case Supervisor who requested special help in preparing her materials for presentation to the consultation group.

The sessions with the administrators called attention to specific problems arising in the work and helping them share their reactions to developments in their own separate spheres of authority.

At the end of the third year, group methods were firmly established in some sectors of the Bureau and variously understood and attempted in others. In services to clients, the group skills had advanced demonstrably and no apologies needed to be made for the quality of practice. In staff work, there was progress but it was not yet clear how these gains would be stabilized and intrenched in ongoing supervisory and administrative practice. The next major emphasis would have to be on strengthening the hand of those who would be supervising the work with groups; only if supervisory skills could keep pace with practitioner skills could the agency ensure that group work would remain a permanent feature of their program.

Fourth Year: In the final stage, a high priority was placed on the practice and supervision of client group services. Much of the staff work was now moved into the regular program, with the Case Supervisors' meetings and the Assistant Supervisors' sessions continuing under their own impetus. The administrators, now closely related to the program were worked with less intensively during the fourth year.

In the Division of Foster Home Care, program decisions were complicated by several factors. The high staff turnover characteristic of the large public agency made it difficult for the division to commit itself permanently to a service in which much-needed trained personnel would be required to perform new kinds of tasks. Further, the turnover had the effect of vitiating the careful work that went into explaining the group service to the rest of the staff, dealing openly with the feelings involved and building a systematic feedback between individual and group help. Where large numbers of new workers came into the division every year, the process would have to be repeated again and again, and this too would require large investments in time.

At the same time, the pressure to expand the work with groups came from the results of the work itself. Once a service was begun, it was hard to look away from the needs it uncovered and the opportunities it offered. It had become increasingly evident that good work creates pressure for more work; every new move opened vistas for new ways of improving the program. Thus, the foster parents' groups had dramatized the parents' problems, as well as their ability to involve themselves deeply in work with a skilled helper. The group work with the adolescent boys had impressed the staff with the boys' open and energetic approach to their own problems, and had created an eagerness to offer the same service to the girls. In addition, the group records had thrown new light on some important problems—the relationship between the parents and the agency, the mutual ambivalence that hung between the boys and their mostly young and female caseworkers, the use of outside agencies as sites for group service, and other issues.

It had also become increasingly clear that the individual work and the group work were inextricable parts of the same service, that they must be kept closely related in spirit and philosophy and that they could not support any traces of rivalry between them. This would require a continuous effort to avoid the intrenchment of discrete casework and group work roles; it would call for flexible assignments, record-sharing, case discussion and other forms of interaction. Most important, it would require the steady development of confidence and skill in those who were to supervise the group practice; the agency would have to generate these skills from its own resources and become increasingly independent of the consultative function.

These needs produced three main bodies of consultative work. The first was on the problems of direct practice: a new group of adolescent boys was formed and led by a young untrained worker, from among youngsters referred from different caseloads; and a girls' group was similarly organized by a young woman professionally trained as a caseworker. The consultation group consisted of these two practitioners (the girls' worker left the agency and was replaced during the season), their immediate supervisors and several top echelon personnel in the division, including the Director. They worked not only from the records of practice but from the supervisors' activity with both the staff group and the foster parents' groups, as these were involved in the opening stages of group formation.

The second body of work in Foster Home Care was with the larger group of supervisors, meeting monthly to examine and discuss the conference records of those who were supervising the group practice with the adolescents. In the typical mode of work in this group, the supervisor would offer her worker's record of a group meeting, then her own record of the supervisory conference that followed. The assembled supervisors—about 20 in the group—would first make their own notes on the worker's record, as if they were themselves about to go into the conference as the supervisor. They then moved into the actual supervisory conference material, to discuss what had happened between the supervisor and her worker.

The third area of consultation focused on the special conferences that were increasingly serving to catch up specific aspects that could be handled more profitably with individuals and subgroups. This device took a new and interesting turn in the fourth year, as we developed a conference form involving both a supervisor and her worker *together* in discussion of the practice problems, the supervisory problems and the interplay between the two. I had tried this before, in the first stages of client service; however, the supervisor did not yet "own" the work, there was no common experience for them to discuss and they were not yet ready to build the group work into the supervisory agenda. In these present conferences, the atmosphere was markedly different; worker and supervisor interacted with candor and perception on each other's problems and the process of giving and taking helps with these problems.

This emphasis on joint work with practitioners and their supervisors had begun early but was brought to a special emphasis in the fourth year. It prevailed throughout the work on client groups—in individual consultations, in the larger sessions, in Foster Home Care and in Adoptions:

> It should be understood that this mode of work represented a kind of transitional phase in the process of institutionalizing group services. On the one hand, the supervisors had now taken the step of putting group practice problems on their supervisory conference agendas, rather than leaving these discussions entirely to the consultant. On the other, they were reluctant to declare themselves ready to assume full professional responsibility for this service. This caution was in itself perfectly responsible and understandable and resulted in a mode of consultation that would allow them to watch and work at the same time—to watch the consultant as he tried to help the practitioners develop their practice, and to work out their own supervisory approaches with familiar ideas and materials. Our relationship was such that possible duplications and contradictions were not problematic; in fact, such contradictions did occur from time to time (between the supervisor's judgment and mine), but there was little embarrassment as we faced each issue as openly as we could.[16]

The Division of Adoptions was the other locale for the activity on client groups, and here the consultations were focused on service to four groups of adoptive parents, each meeting four times at two-week intervals, during their year of supervision following legal adoption. As a result of the third year work, these parents had been prepared at Intake and were expecting to be called together for this group experience. The purpose of the groups was to offer the new parents a chance to share and discuss problems in child rearing and other issues emerging from their status as adoptive parents.

In the consultations, I spent a bloc of time with the workers and their supervisors together, helping them study the practice and bring their work to the larger staff of the Division. In each monthly consultation, I met with the worker-supervisor teams first, following which we moved into the staff meeting to discuss the records, develop strategies of practice and supervision and exchange client information as drawn from both individual and group practice. Individual conferences were also held as needed.

In this division, the intensive work on short-term groups provided an opportunity for the agency to develop a sense of how much client work they could expect over a given span of time. Having looked at two four-session groups in the winter and two more in the spring, there was agreement that more experience with groups of varying duration would help them develop some sophistication about the variables that determine the pace and depth of social work help when it is carried on in groups.

Finally, the work with the administrators was confined to a single meeting, held early in the season and devoted to a review of progress and problems and plans for the forthcoming consultation year.

Other Activity

It will be noted that we made a consistent demand for written recording; there was in fact a clear assumption throughout that written work is an indispensable element in any serious approach to the problems of practice. Thus, the consultation process carried with it a demand that the work be recorded in some detail, that it be open to the scrutiny—and help—of peers and, ultimately, that it be offered to a wider professional audience through the publication of journal articles and teaching materials.

However, the demand by itself was useless unless it was accompanied by the help needed to carry it out. Our efforts to provide a practical approach to the recording problem will be described later, in the context of the work itself. In addition, consultation time was allocated to the task of helping workers prepare presentations, reports and articles for publication. The first published accounts—on the work with foster parents[17] and adolescent boys[18]—soon appeared in the agency's own outlet, to which I also contributed a piece on the work with staff groups.[19] Later, four staff members read papers at the 1967 Annual Forum of the National Conference on Social Welfare[20]; two of these accounts subsequently found their way into a professional journal[21] and the four are now collaborating on a paper to be included in a forthcoming book on group work practice.[22] The Director of Training and her associates have from time to time described the work at state conferences and other professional meetings.

Out of the rich yield of group records, materials were drawn for use in a number of institutes I have conducted for other workers in the field of public welfare, and at a workshop for field instructors of the Columbia University School of Social Work.[23] And there was an effort, not yet concluded, to develop a comprehensive teaching record on the work with foster parents. The volume of practice materials is in fact so huge that such efforts can conceivably continue for some time to come.

Time was also made available for my own recording efforts. My Log, or diary, was a vehicle for carrying the detailed quantitative and qualitative descriptions on which I based my annual Report on Consultations. The Reports were distributed widely within the Bureau and created considerable discussion, both agreeing and disagreeing with my interpretation of events and always producing a high degree of honest and animated evaluative activity. Outside interest was also shown in these Reports and, with agency permission, they have been shared with public and private agency professionals throughout the country.

Finally, my relationships within the agency were enhanced by participation in appropriate agency events wherever possible; such were the Arden House Conference on the Role of the Supervisor in Child Welfare, and an all-day training institute for Case Supervisors in the Bureau of Public Assistance.[24]

With this overview in mind, we may now move to a more detailed discussion of the major work themes, showing the interplay of theory and practice as it emerged in the integrative work of the administrators, in the consultations on client services and in the activity focusing on the work with staff groups.

The Administrators

It must be clear by now that we envisaged the administrative group—from the Director of the Bureau through the Division Directors, their associates, the Senior Supervisors and the Case Supervisors—as a principal power in determining whether the new work would go through a temporary vogue or be built securely into the future of the agency. Many decisions would be called for in the course of the work and it would be in the best interests of both the program and the agency if these decisions were made *expertly,* rather than from naive enthusiasm or an equally vague prejudice against "extra work." To do this, they would have to go much beyond merely being "kept informed" of developments; they would need sophisticated judgments about the nature of the service, its real demands on staff and its practical uses in carrying out the work of the agency. In short, they should develop the same authority and expertise on the work with groups as they were expected to have on any other aspect of the agency's operation.

How then do busy administrators involve themselves seriously in a new effort, using relatively small amounts of available time and energy to study the work, practice it themselves and make it a permanent part of their professional equipment? It was a difficult requirement, but we felt that much could be achieved if our aspirations were specific, if we used the time well and if we were honest about appraising our efforts as we went along.

From this perspective, the administrators followed four main lines of work. They *theorized* about the work with groups, starting from a general frame of reference and moving from there to their own generalizations, based on their experiences and others', about the nature of groups, the service of their agency and the practice skills that emerged in the interaction between the two. They *practiced* working with groups wherever they could, struggling with its problems, recording the meetings and presenting their work to their peers. They *watched* the work in progress very carefully, helping to plan the consultant's approach to their staff members, reading the records and learning from the efforts of their own workers. And they *evaluated* its effects, particularly in their own spheres of influence, trying to discriminate between what worked for them and what did not and to carry the best parts forward from year to year.

Obviously, these lines were intertwined at many points; nonetheless, each had its own tasks and each may be described, however briefly, in its own terms.

The Frame of Reference

Early in the work with the administrators, in the context of their first efforts to share problems and present and discuss their own materials, I offered several aspects of my own theoretical stance on the meaning of work with groups. These ideas, presented briefly and in general terms, were offered as a beginning, as a handle for grasping the first problems of practice, not as a dogma to be "learned." Care had to be taken that these notions be treated as tentative and biased, that they be tested against the administrators' sense of reality and that they be questioned seriously when they did not "feel right." Hopefully, they would soon take their proper place among the many generalizations that the staff people would be developing from their own experiences.

In this spirit, I suggested that a group could be defined as a *collection of people who need each other to work on certain common tasks, in a setting that is hospitable to those tasks.* Concise as it is, this definition poses all the problems with which the worker must come to grips if he is to understand the helping process in groups. It calls for insight into the phenomenon of *collectivity* and the character of small-group, face-to-face behavior; it points up the process of *mutual aid* and the ways in which people use each other in giving and taking help; it demands definition of the *specific tasks* for which the people have come—or been brought—together; and it necessitates an equally specific understanding of the *agency function* from which the group takes its purpose and its sanction.

Thus the emphasis was immediately placed on the work that people needed to do together, their common stake in this work, the connections between individual (each member) and social (the agency, the group) purposes, and the members' ability to help each other. The productivity of any given group would depend on its ability to reach some consensus on what the members were supposed to be doing together, the extent to which members could identify their own self-interest with the group purpose, and the nature of the collaboration itself—their ability to talk to and listen to each other as they create the ideas and activities they need. And as one began to define the specific helping skills, it would be seen that each of them was fashioned by one or more of these necessities.

In the staff group, all of the work stems from the task of carrying forward the service of the agency most effectively, and this generates the problems to which joint thinking and action must be addressed. The staff meeting is neither a social occasion or a therapeutic enterprise, but a collaboration on the business of the agency. Further, it is a collaboration in which the administration and staff have certain (not all) interests in common, however obscured these may sometimes be: administration is charged with maintaining and improving the service of the agency, which depends in turn on high staff morale and the steady improvement of practitioner skill; staff members, on their part, want to feel competent, that they are working for a "good agency," that they have a contribution to make and that they can get help in making it.

Nevertheless, real staff involvement is difficult to achieve, hinging as it does on certain realities about how people learn, how they work together, how they give and take help and how they use authority. As the leader faces his group, he is looking at many of these social and psychological realities: people remember things selectively, unconsciously choosing what they want and need to forget; open communication is a risky business—punishments abound and people will not reveal their half-formed ideas to those they do not trust; ideas that do not conform to group or agency consensus will often be treated by member, group or agency as taboo; the taboos themselves continue to operate in hidden ways, often inhibiting action even when there is apparently a considerable "agreement" on what ought to be done; and many more of these forces exert a powerful and mysterious impact on the life of the group. Every administrator is familiar with the fact that many ideas and feelings too risky for workers to share in the "formal system"—the staff meetings, the supervisory conferences and other official devices—will run quietly through the "informal system" of the coffee break, the private chat and the office conversation. When no effort is made to reduce the risk and bring these feelings into the open, the informal system may begin to determine agency events more consistently than its formal machinery. The staff meeting then takes on a kind of mechanical quality, an "illusion of work," where instructions are given, procedures explained, agreements reached—and very little is implemented. Most often it will be the skill of the leader that will determine whether the staff group has clarified its work, found the common ground between the interests of the agency and those of its workers, found ways of "talking real" and reached for difficult material before it has turned destructive.

In the client group, the common tasks are those to which the agency service is committed, but the basic definition remains essentially the same—a collection of people brought together to help each other work on common tasks, in an agency hospitable to those tasks. Here too the working elements that fashion the helping skills are the character of the collective, the process of mutual aid, the clear definition of specific tasks and the social responsibility of the setting in which the transaction takes place. And here again the "illusion of work" fills the vacuum created by distrust of others, a failure of hope, a repressive social situation, a fear of authority and other forces that alienate people from the open search for reality and rob the group of its potential for creating new strengths and capabilities. The helping skills are directed to the same basic questions: What are the tasks for which these people have been brought together? How are these related both to the service of the agency and the felt needs of the clients? How can I help them focus on these tasks and work on them? And how can I help them use each other in the process? The last question carries important implications for the major difference between individual and group help: the group is an enterprise in mutual aid, where people establish a whole network of helping relationships, rather than just the one with the worker; and this means that the worker is asked to support a process that he cannot entirely control since it involves the feelings, wisdom and experience of many others beside himself.

As the presentations unfolded, we became increasingly specific about the helping role of the worker, first creating a kind of general backdrop against which to pick out his movements and then, as their experience grew, beginning to identify the actual skills in detail. The backdrop was a scheme for separating the worker's movements into four *phases of work:*

> As often as possible, the records were used to describe the phases of work a leader goes through in carrying out his role: *the preparation phase,* in which his effort is to "tune in" to the attitudes and ideas with which his members may approach the meeting, so that he may be more alive to the subtlest cues they may express in the course of the meeting; *the beginning phase,* in which he opens his meeting with the attempt to make as clear as possible the purpose of the meeting, the problems under consideration, so that the focus of attention and discussion is as clear and unambiguous as it can be; *the work phase,* in which the leader concentrates his attention on whether the group is working, what it is working on, and how he may help them use each other in their attack on the problem; and *the ending phase,* in which the group leader helps the group to summarize and make some transition to the next steps and implications for future action.[25]

This frame of reference helped us operationalize our approach to the record presentations offered by the administrators in the consultation sessions. That is, it kept us close to the identification of practice skills, rather than general discussions of human behavior, group process, social work philosophy and other interesting subjects that so often obscure the specific movements of the helping person. In examining a piece of work—a meeting of supervisors, or a first meeting of a client group, or a session with a group of trainees—we would put ourselves into the presenter's shoes and search for the skills required in each of the four phases. As we repeated the work in situation after situation—going through the "tuning in," making a purposeful beginning, addressing the work themes and effecting a meaningful ending or transition—ideas that had been "learned" were rediscovered again and again in new forms. And each time an act presented itself in a new light, through another concrete example, they moved deeper into its meaning and became more "expert" at identifying it in action.

It was in this framework that they defined, discussed and tried out a wide range of group skills, including the "preliminary empathy" of the preparation period, the ability to make a clear and simple statement of purpose, helping members talk to each other with feeling, breaking big ideas into smaller, more manageable ones, reaching for ambiguities and taboos, demanding work, risking one's own feelings, reading silences, connecting small events into larger patterns of meaning, and others that I will discuss in detail in the subsequent sections on the work with clients and the work with staff.

The Reports carried many examples of the kinds of generalizing the administrators did in the course of their work. Their theorizing ranged over many themes—technical, structural and administrative. These examples will give some of the flavor of this activity:

> When a worker poses a question to his group, it ought to be a real question—that is, one to which he does not have a concealed answer. He

asks the question because he wants to stimulate work in some area. The "false question" is a dubious—and unfortunately familiar—technique that creates a kind of guessing game in which the clients try to find out what the worker has in mind, rather than devote their energies to the problem at hand. Inevitably, it is experienced by the group members as a process in which they are led by the nose to the "proper" solution that the worker, in his wisdom, has already figured out. As such, it is not only undignified but tends to distract the people from their own tasks in order to pursue the answers hidden in the worker's mind. If the worker has a suggestion to offer, he should offer it for what it is worth, and ask the members to consider it along with their own ideas and any other evidence they have at hand.[26]

Several records pointed up the problem of the worker in dealing with the overassertive member, the one who expresses himself freely and frequently, often negatively; workers discussed their fear that such members tended to overwhelm and inhibit other members of the group. Close examination of the material revealed that such clients often play an important role in the group—expressing ideas that others may feel but be afraid to express, catalyzing issues more quickly, bringing out negatives that need to be examined, etc. This helped us to see that such members should not immediately be thought of as "enemies" of the group, diverting it from its purposes, but as clients with needs of their own, and that these needs are often dramatic and exaggerated versions of those of the other group members. We discussed ways in which the worker might help the others relate to these ideas, counter the pressures offered by the "deviant" and respond to him as one of the group rather than as an outcast.[27]

And in another vein:

There was also discussion . . . of the relationship between the tasks of training and those of administration; it was becoming clearer that the training division was setting certain processes in motion that administration was then hard put to implement and sustain.[28]

. . . the point was made that the underlying concept of family service calls for a staff of older, experienced professionals; and, since so few of these are available, the conduct of skilled group services supports the efforts of the younger workers and provides much additional help to clients. At the same time, there were advantages to using some of the trainees themselves in the program of group services: they tend to have fewer prejudices about specializing in a single "method"; they have less to unlearn about the fearsomeness of groups, not having been taught that they are "harder" than individuals one at a time; and this flexibility makes it easier to assign mixed work loads—individuals and groups—and to train workers in both kinds of work from the beginning.[29]

And another:

How do people learn new ways of thinking and acting? Our records and discussions showed how many of us, despite our formal knowledge to the contrary, hold on to a deep-dyed conviction that learning is essentially a rational process—that, somehow, if we put something into words it is automatically learned by those who are listening. There is a kind of magical faith in the power of the verbal explanation and when we have "covered" a point in the training process we get a sense of satisfaction that this part of the job is done. We are then surprised to find later that the point has been ignored, or read in different ways, and become impatient with the "stupidity" or "indifference" that makes it necessary for us to "go over it" again.[30]

Practicing and Recording

As previously indicated, many of the administrators tried their hand at recording and presenting their own work with both staff and client groups. Most of these presentations were offered in the first year—in consultation groups I and II—and during this period they made 18 such presentations of meetings with 14 different groups of varying purpose and duration.[31]

In putting themselves into the work this way, it was natural that they should immediately come to grips with the problem of recording. On the one hand, it would be foolish for them to expect themselves—or their staff workers—to produce elaborately "processed" accounts of each meeting; such a system might hold up for a while, but would certainly deteriorate as it went along, simply because the time demand would be unrealistic. On the other hand, no constructive work could be done—either in consultation or in regular supervision—without *some* systematic recording of the "process" through which the group members had worked and the leader had tried to help. While too much detail is impractical and unnecessary, too little is an invitation to irresponsibility and aimless talk.

The emphasis on writing down what one has done was also tied to the fear of faddism and of the all-too-common agency practice of using group work as a kind of "hobby," where groups were formed by any worker who "wanted one," where every aspect was "voluntary," where there was "no time" for recording and where there was virtually no accountability to one's superiors. The position on which the administrators and I reached immediate agreement may be illustrated by a comment I later made to the staff of a private child welfare agency:

> And, inevitably, we come to the problem of recording the work. What can one say about recording except that there is no way out of it? The "hobby" aspects of group work in the casework agency are in no respect more clearly revealed than in the reluctance to follow the same rigorous demand for recording in group work that resulted in the raising of casework to its present state of system and discipline. Admittedly, the task is imposing; it is a frightening prospect to consider describing the events of group interaction over a 60- or 90-minute period.

> But the solution is not to ignore the job, or to make it voluntary, or even to use the tape recorder—although tapes and movies may have real value for certain purposes—but to devise practical forms of recording the work so that we may supervise from it, learn from it, and transmit our experiences to the field.[32]

The "practical form" I then suggested was the one we used extensively at BCW:

> I have had some success with a format that calls for a fairly detailed account of the opening of the meeting, a similarly exact description of its closing, and a brief summary of what when on in between—the entire record not to exceed one page, or a page and a half at most. This simple procedure stresses brevity, provides a kind of structure by calling for the details of the beginning and ending, and uses what I call an "accordion principle" for recording the main body of events—expanding and contracting the amount of detail according to the worker's judgment of what is significant. I have found that the records produced according to this formula are sufficiently faithful to experience to provide material for service, for supervision, and for consultation.[33]

This is not to say that workers did not on occasion produce longer accounts, or that such would not be useful for purposes of teaching and publication. However, we were careful not to hold such records up as norms—even discouraging such efforts at the outset—lest they begin to set standards that would make each succeeding record harder to write.

The practice itself provided the administrators with several opportunities. To begin with, they could experience at first hand how it felt to move into group leadership and try to find a way of working in a strange medium. The following is from my Log in the Spring in the first year:

> *March 20, 1963:* M. (a Division Director) expressed interest in how the workers' perceptions about working with groups have changed in the course of our work, and with the opportunity to practice group work. S. (a Case Supervisor) explained that he is much less anxious now, and also much more confident that he is capable of keeping his group together. Another interesting comment by S.: the history of each group member is so much less important now—what is important is the kind of experience they have together in the group. He gave an expressive account of trying to "catch the train as it goes rushing by"—meaning all the things that happen at the same time. Also, on the problem of control, he had felt that he was losing control, as the group members began to interact so rapidly.
>
> A., another supervisor, talked about her "stage fright," and the anxiety about "is there going to be a group?" However, she said, after you get started, you're too busy listening to worry about those things.

The practice also gave them the opportunity to experience some of the striking effects that sometimes occur in the group situation. A., the supervisor in the above excerpt, concluded her comment with the statement that

> . . . at her third meeting, she had accomplished something—on the problem of foster parent identity—that she feels she could not have accomplished in five months of individual interviewing.

In this connection, it should be mentioned that we tried hard not to fall into a pattern of making invidious comparisons between individual work and work with groups. We repeatedly pointed up the fact that these were different structures for service and each had its own unique strengths and problems. In the practice, we were able to see many problems on which people could work more productively with one helping person, and many others on which the stimulation of peers created effects that were surprising to the staff. In this context, it was possible for A. to make her comment without setting up competitive or defensive tensions between the "old" and the "new."

There were other effects from the work on practice: the administrators made most of the mistakes, happily, that their workers would make and need help with; they saw themselves beginning to produce some of the skills they would be asking for; they began to read group records with some of the acuity and confidence they felt in reading case materials; and they watched themselves taking the specific, line-by-line help from the consultant that they would ultimately be trying to give to their own subordinates.

Observing and Supporting

The administrators' attention to all the segments of the group development program both deepened their understanding of the service and helped them make a substantial contribution to the consultation process itself. For example, as I prepared to move into the program with the Assistant Supervisors,[34] the administrators discussed some of the problems inherent in this position, some ways in which they might facilitate the training process and some specific areas of work on which the Assistant Supervisors could be helped to present case materials at the consultation sessions:

> In their discussion of (the unit supervisors') training needs, several themes emerged that later proved to be valid items of concern: the struggle of new appointees to give up the caseworker role and move wholeheartedly into a position of authority; the fearfulness of most Assistant Supervisors at the prospect of meeting with their workers as a group; unit problems arising from the working combination of older and younger caseworkers in the same units; the reluctance to take on the supervisory conference as a working device and the lack of basic supervisory skills that lay behind this; and a number of technical issues involving difficulties in caseload management, interpretation of agency procedures, methods of evaluating their workers, and some others.
>
> Moving then to ways in which they could support the training process, the administrators agreed that it would be most important for the Case Supervisors—no matter how "inexpert" they might themselves feel—to add these group methods to their own supervisory agendas. They would

> need to offer direct and ongoing help to the Assistant Supervisors in discussing their unit meetings, in preparing materials for presentation, in focusing their questions and in evaluating how the presentations had been received. Substantively, the administrators felt that presentations should be encouraged on such problems as: (their) efforts to interpret agency forms and procedures; situations involving group morale; the use of the staff group in certain kinds of decision-making; (etc.) It was understood, of course, that such themes were advanced only tentatively and that the major determinant of the case presentations would be the concerns expressed by the Assistant Supervisors themselves.[35]

And later, in evaluating the progress of the program, their discussion was searching:

> I reported on the work I was doing with the unit supervisors, the content and the major themes that were coming through the patterns of both cooperation and resistance that were showing in our sessions together . . . The administrators, from their perspective, reported some of their impressions: many saw their people as trying to work in new ways, several with some success; several reported that their Assistants had real question as to whether the agency really intended for them to work with the degree of freedom and creativity that was stressed at the training sessions; some of the Assistants had expressed fears about presenting their work in the training sessions, feeling they should be more expert than they were and fearful about exposing themselves; and it emerged that many of the Assistants regarded the training sessions as a demand of the agency rather than as an opportunity for themselves.
>
> In the discussion, many administrators indicated that there was a general feeling among the Assistant Supervisors that they needed a great deal more help from the agency on many fronts other than their skill as group leaders at unit meetings; many, in fact, had serious questions as to whether this was their primary need. When I asked to what extent the unit supervisor had an ongoing opportunity to put his concerns on the supervisory agenda—that is, with his own Case Supervisor—the answer was, not a great deal; "95 percent" of their supervisory agenda is occupied with emergencies requiring immediate attention.[36]

And, at the final evaluative session:

> . . . there was a careful identification and thorough discussion of the working problems of the Assistant Supervisor in the Bureau of Child Welfare. Of equal importance was the recognition that the agency needed to find new ways of offering more supervision and support to the unit supervisors in carrying out their very difficult tasks. Thus, the effort to strengthen the hand of the Assistant Supervisor was seen as inextricably tied to similar moves to strengthen the role and skills of his immediate supervisor, the Case Supervisor. This was subsequently implemented by

the Training Division in its development of a training syllabus for use by the Case Supervisors in a special group training program for the unit supervisors.[37]

The above has been presented at some length to show something of the seriousness with which the administrators monitored and supported the various aspects of the program. They went through a similar process in examining the subsequent staff work of the Case Supervisors and the client group services offered in the different divisions of the Bureau. In the third year:

> We discussed the anxieties of the Case Supervisors as they prepared to take on regular group leadership responsibility (with the unit supervisors) and the ways in which the administrators could help them develop and evaluate their work as it went along. We also examined the training syllabus prepared by the Case Supervisors for their own use, the level of aspiration it represented and its use as a teaching device. And we discussed the focus of consultative help in this effort . . .
>
> The March meeting was devoted to a full review of the work in progress—the client groups in Foster Home Care, Adoptions and Homefinding, and the staff training work with the Case Supervisors. We also prepared for the evaluation discussions that I would be conducting in each sector, in the final meetings of the season. In this connection, the administrators did some close work on their own perceptions of progress and problems . . . (client group) services, they said, could no longer be regarded as "auxiliary," but were needed as an integral part of the work of the Bureau. They saw the staff management work as harder to incorporate, but pointed to specific signs of progress in this area as well . . . There was agreement that the Case Supervisors had learned a great deal from working together across divisional lines; they had taught one another, watched each other work and, "for the first time," they had developed a feeling of group support with people from outside their own immediate service. A division director stated that the handling of the strike and its aftermath could not have been as effective as it was without the work the Case Supervisors had done together in the consultation sessions.[38]

One of the most interesting aspects of this "watching" process was their observation of themselves at work in the consultation process itself—drawing lessons from their own feelings, their own ways of working together and how I behaved, as their "worker." Although we were careful not to let self-examination become an end in itself, or a mechanical gimmick, there were several occasions where their own feelings and activities were of considerable interest to them. The following brief example is excerpted from a Log entry on the administrators' discussion of the problems of the unit supervisors:

> *May 27, 1964:* There was a comment about my own leadership: someone said I "grew"—that I was not "ready for *them* at the beginning"; I encouraged this tack—some felt I had been "too elementary,"

others that I had been at "too high a level." Could be I had been both—alternating between the two.

(After some talk about the survival value, for the unit supervisors, of "playing the system" and keeping their mouths shut) M. asks: "Can we handle (all this) group feeling among the unit supervisors? Do we really want it?" This hits like a bombshell . . . it took some courage to say it at all. What they do then is to leave it, go back to the fears of the unit supervisors, their fear being exposed . . . etc. . . .

But the comment is repeated by M.: "How much initiative and independence by the unit supervisors can we really handle?" This time I hold them to it, don't let them get away. They get into this deeply . . . their own feelings of being pushed, what they really want in good performance, how much conformity they really need and don't need, etc.

Evaluation and Planning

As will be noted from the excerpts given above, the evaluative process ran through all of our work together; we sought to draw implications wherever we could and we moved constantly back and forth between specifics and generalizations. However, we also built in a periodic evaluation procedure that demanded specific judgments about what was happening, how useful it was and what should be done next. As always, this was used both for our own work and as a model for their approach to staff and client groups. It was introduced in every consultation group, but it took on particular importance with the administrators, because of their special modeling and supporting role.

The procedure itself was fairly simple, requiring that each member prepare for the final session each year by culling his recollections of our work together for one idea that had struck him with particular force and one area that still seemed fuzzy and incomplete. When these private choices—these "*one* ideas"—were pooled in the ensuing discussion, they produced a comprehensive review of the major concepts and problems that had emerged in our work sessions. Further, the "remembering-back" enhanced the element of feeling and frank subjectivity ("I don't know about the rest of you, but the notion that hit me hardest was . . . "; and "I still remember how startled I was when you said that . . . "). The specificity and the affect, combined with the focus on substance and ideas, kept them close to reality and helped them move naturally into implications and next steps.

Aside from its importance for learning and planning, the evaluation process was also an exercise in the significance of endings. It dramatized the fact that the last stage of a meaningful group experience can be an occasion for important work, rather than the bland exchange of awards and pleasantries ("it was a very good experience . . .") that we came to call the "farewell party." Properly handled, the ending is an opportunity to catalyze all of the intimacy, the mutual help and the preparation for action that the group has been building in the course of its career.

From the Log again, the following brief excerpts show something of the tenor of these evaluation discussions, both early and late in the consultation process:

> *June 12, 1963:* Purpose: general summary and evaluation. Focus: particular ideas which seem to have been useful. In the first part of the discussion, the following points were made: so much of what we talked about seemed to deal with plain common sense; I agreed—disciplined common sense . . . the idea of "tuning in" as a concept in preparation . . . the group as a device in which "people use each other" . . . the "step by step," rather than the preoccupation with results. Discussion of our own group as a model: all the things that had happened in our work together. Miss K.: There is a difference in our staff groups . . . somehow it seems easier to listen to clients than to our staff members—there is so much to "get done." How do you create a sense of trust . . . as an authority person? The very freedom we try to create threatens us. (Group worked hard at this) . . . meeting ended on a high note; feeling of having worked well . . .
>
> *June 23, 1965:* I began: Three (main) bodies of work this year—the Case Supervisors, the adolescent boys' groups in Foster Home Care and the meetings with Adoptions and Homefinding. This meeting to look at this work, assess where we are now in use of groups, and draw some implications for future planning.
>
> (On the Case Supervisors' work) Mrs. K. cited need to have had more involvement of the unit supervisors in planning their own training sessions with the Case Supervisors . . . S. reinforced this . . . also felt that once in two weeks was too much . . . also felt that the multiple leadership thing was a problem—"we're all in different stages."
> . . . I said: "We have spent three seasons now on the staff management problem—where are we now? Are we any further along?" Miss G. responded: "I'm very conscious now of staff management techniques." Miss R.: "The Case Supervisors are doing things now they never thought they could do." Mrs. N.: "The unit supervisors are much more reflective, introspective—there is much less projection of their problems, more taking of responsibility." S.: "But only *some* of the teaching process was really good . . . the whole thing was newer than we thought it would be." B.: "The carryover in *interagency* conferencing—"easy to see the beneficial effects here." Mrs. A.: "Some of the unit supervisors are now wanting to try their hand at working with groups of clients." S. and B.: "We're not making a polite chit-chat any more . . ." and they cite some specifics in the work.
> Miss D. then picked up on an earlier comment of mine about the fact that I might have shaken up the unit supervisors a bit too much . . . they had (then) passed my comment by. Now she said that they (had been) angry with me when the Report came out. Miss T. elaborated, described . . . their annoyance about my comment that they felt inferior to the private agencies. (Now we were into it).

I read the exact words from the Report, on their feelings about public-private. Wasn't it true, and wasn't it just as true of the Case Supervisors (themselves)? Yes, and they speculated on the degree of insecurity that makes it so difficult to face these kinds of realities in the open. I asked: "Is it also true that the lower you get on the status scale, the more difficult, the more rigid, the harder to loosen up?" Yes, and they worked on *implications for supervision* . . .

(After review of client groups) . . . M. felt that they have made more dramatic progress in their service groups than they have in their staff groups. B. disagreed . . . "We have observed real change in our staff processes." Miss D. commented that they have had more consistent feedback from staff than they have had from clients . . . Miss G. said they'd had considerable feedback from their adolescent boys when they'd made a move to close down the groups. Mrs. N.: "The work with clients is more exciting, more dramatic, part of the service . . ."

Re *implications for future work:* I pointed out that in the beginning they had "all started even," supervisors and workers; now, the top people would be called upon to assume expertness, supervisory responsibility for group services; they needed to be "learning with the left hand and teaching with the right." Discussion, some support from Miss G., some reluctance from Miss D.: "I'm not ready to teach it yet." S. said that they have a strong tradition of the "supervisor as expert," which makes it hard for the supervisor to take chances unless he's sure of his expertise . . . Mrs. J. suggested that the consultation pattern might now be related to the nature of the work, the level of practice—rather than the particular division or job title; sounded like a good idea . . . to begin to work more around the nature of the group problem, pulling these practitioners together.

The Service to Clients

During the four year period, we worked on a wide assortment of client groups; however, the major effort was spent on four types—the adolescents in foster care, the foster parents, the adoptive parents in supervision and the one-session groups of prospective parents conducted by the Homefinding Division. These were intensive, well-documented experiences and only a brief glimpse can be given into each; but I will try to show something of the *group formation* process, the *client problems* that were addressed, the *practice skills* we discussed and the *agency impact* that the work created.

All these efforts were built on the exploratory work of the first year, in which the Bureau staff formulated their problems, organized some new groups and began their discussions of group practice. These introductory themes established the framework around which the agency subsequently developed its service to client groups.

First Themes

When the first planning group of training personnel, Division Directors and supervisors from the placement divisions named the problems on which they would like consultation, they expressed their concerns in these terms:

> *Problems of group formation:* optimum group size, and the relationship between size and purpose; criteria for determining group membership; the issue of open groups vs. closed ones, with particular reference to the problem of continuous and sporadic intake; and the varied purposes for which group formation might be appropriate. Interest was expressed in the orientation of prospective adoptive and foster parents, work with groups of parents during the mid-study and supervision periods, and educational groups of active foster parents.
>
> *Problems of practice:* the tendency of workers to fall into the practice of lecturing, thereby losing the interest of their group members; workers' difficulty in handling questions and concerns emerging at the meetings; problems of stimulating free expression of real problems, in the face of agency authority and the fear that they would reveal themselves as poor parents; and the confusions inherent in differentiating between what was social work practice with groups and what was "group therapy."
>
> *Problems of recording:* records showed a tendency to produce the "minutes" of a meeting, rather than a social work record, written by the worker himself and designed to reveal his manner and focus of help with client problems; there was discussion of ways in which such a recording process might be structured so that it would not be too time-consuming, yet would provide a continuous record of service.[39]

Out of the first forays into the work with foster parents, adolescents and adoptive parents,[40] these themes and others began to take shape in experience and certain of them were to repeat themselves again and again in the work to come. These central problems emerged from the practice itself and they emerged so often that they began to take on *theoretical* importance—that is, staff members began to identify them quickly, predict them, build explanations around them and teach from them. Most important, these themes became part of the permanent agenda, as they must in any group service setting; they could not be "solved"—mastered and disposed of. One could only try to understand their central role in the scheme of things and become increasingly skillful in handling the action difficulties they presented.

Many of these problems could be generally classified as inherent in one or another of the four "phases of work" previously described: the "tuning in" process that prepares the worker to enter the group experience armed with the special sensitivities to the subtle ways in which people express their needs and ask for help; the beginning process, in which the worker helps to clarify the "contract" and focus the work they are to do together; the middle, or work, phase that calls on the worker's skill in helping the members use each other as they address themselves to the problems that brought them together; and the end, or transition, process in which the worker helps to create the continuity that carries the group from meeting to meeting.

More specifically, one of the themes that ran most frequently through our work was the relationship between clarity of group purpose and the clarity of the worker's focus in helping. Vague and fancily-expressed notions of purpose confused the members and made it difficult for the worker to know where to take hold. Conversely, where the group's reason-for-being was worked out beforehand in specific and achievable terms, and was stated briefly and simply at the outset, the members could begin to work more quickly and the worker could more easily plan and focus his helping activity.

Another recurring theme was that of finding the common ground between the stake of the clients in coming to the group and that of the agency in forming the group. Where this common ground was not understood, the worker frequently found himself in the position of "choosing sides" between the two—a position that led to struggles of will, lecturing, exhorting and other futile attempts to "change" the client against his own judgment. In each instance, closer examination revealed the client's underlying need for help—and his subtle calls for it—on the very problems with which the agency was concerned: ways of rearing children, being better parents, using the agency well, and others.

There were many questions about the worker's role with the "group-as-a-whole"—involving the skills required to help strengthen the group as an instrument of mutual aid. This subject—sometimes expressed in the phrase "the group as a client"—can become highly academic and mechanical; there is considerable vagueness about it in the literature. We stayed as close as we could to some simple constructs: helping a group own its own problems, by giving the members a chance to work together on difficult issues, rather than rushing in with premature closure; helping members listen and react to each other's ideas and feelings; and providing opportunity for the group to develop its own structure, its leaders and its deviants without controlling all these outcomes at every step.

Interestingly, the "is it group work or is it group therapy" issue never developed into a major theme, despite its troublesome potential. We took the position early that we ought to describe and understand the helping process, rather than worry about fixing the labels; thus, the question of what-do-we-call-it came up once, during the first meeting, and did not recur. It lost its importance as the members became involved in the real problems of clients and in trying to understand the movements through which one helps. There was no special effort required for them to stay clearly within the social work—rather than the "therapeutic"—frame of reference; in this they were aided by their clear understanding of the function of their agency, our consistent emphasis on clear and limited group purposes, our definition of specific group tasks and the concept of mutual aid within the groups to be served.

There were other specific and repetitive practice themes. There was the tendency to be afraid of silences and to rush in to fill them with words. There was the false "democracy" that makes only those ideas valid that "come from the group." There was the passivity that comes from the fear of manipulating the client and the over-activity that comes from the fear that the client is reaching a "wrong" solution. In all of this, the working similarities between the approach to groups and what they knew as good casework were a constant center of curiosity. At the same time, there was considerable interest in why it *felt* so different, when so many of the working principles were obviously the same. Primarily, it emerged that when the caseworkers moved into group leadership there was apprehension about the loss of control: with so many people affecting the turn of events, and with so much emphasis on spontaneity and free expression, how does one retain "control of the interview?" Also, the wariness was attached to the fear of being "ganged up on;" it was expressed by a caseworker as "there are so many of them and only one of me!"

Perhaps the most important by-product of these casework-group work discussions was the continuous re-examination of their casework practice as they struggled with the problems of adapting these skills to the group of clients. For example, when they discovered their fear of loss of control in the group, they began to wonder about how much control they tended to exert in the interview, where their power is undiluted by the presence of others and where the client finds it so much more difficult to make his own impact on the course of events.

In addition to these practice themes, there were a number of recurring *structural* concerns, bearing on the institutionalization of the service. There was discussion of the relative merits of open and closed groups—those with shifting, come-and-go membership as against those with fixed rosters of people kept together for the life of the group. I encouraged experimentation with these forms, as a way of arriving at group formation procedures through the agency's own experience, rather than through concepts that sounded "scientific" but have not been sufficiently tested. And there was discussion about the use of observers, the uses and abuses of "confidentiality" between the individual and group service, the recording, sharing and storing of materials and others.

There were other significant themes, many of which will come through as we proceed to examine the work with each type of client group. The above was offered to show something of the quality of the early concerns that dominated the first efforts to adapt their skills to the demands of the new service.

The Adolescents

After a preliminary, short-term experience with adolescent girls in a group home,[41] two groups of adolescent boys in foster care were formed in the second consultation year. Trying to encourage a transition to the use of local services, the agency arranged to use leisure-time community centers in two boroughs as sites for the group meetings, providing center memberships as part of the process. These groups were continued in the third year, with the same worker and some turnover in membership. In the fourth year, a new worker was assigned to a new boys' group and a girls' group was also organized.

In the first preparation process, a staff committee was established that aided in the selection of boys and set up the entry processes with staff, foster parents and adolescents: caseworkers carrying the families assisted in selection and were oriented to the new service; they visited the homes and explained to boys and parents what the agency had in mind; and separate letters of invitation and explanation were sent to the foster parents and adolescents. These procedures were subsequently experimented with and altered in several ways—for example, the group leader later played a more prominent role in the first explanations and discussions with parents. But the basic elements of preparation remained the same—keeping the caseworkers close to the process, seeking the understanding and support of the foster parents from the outset and involving the adolescents in individual discussion as part of the group formation process.

The groups were formed of adolescents who had given evidence not of severe emotional problems (these were being treated by a psychiatrist in group therapy) but of a range of developmental difficulties involving their foster status, relationships with people in authority, adjustments to school, vocational preparation, use of the agency and related problems. Many of their interests and concerns were common to all adolescents—the school problems, family tensions, sexual guilt and curiosity and the urge to learn the patterns of dating, dancing and courting behavior; others arose from their role as black adolescents, with all the emerging feelings of outrage and hope common to their time; and they were foster children, together in the search for a stable identity—preoccupied with differences in last names, yearning to be like other youngsters in as many ways as possible, torn with fear and guilt about their natural parents and deeply ambivalent about "welfare," about social workers in general and about young, female, white social workers in particular.

As we began with each group, the first task was to help the worker move from a general awareness of these problems to a specific sensitivity to the language and feeling with which they would be expressed at the meetings. This was the "tuning in" process previously mentioned, and it constituted an important part of our preliminary work with each leader. It was not simply a "diagnostic" exercise, but an effort to merge psychological insight with the dimension of *purpose*. That is, there were reasons for this engagement: the youngsters had reasons, the agency had reasons, and there was concrete ground on which these reasons met. Our effort to begin with a fair consensus about what the group was *for* involved several operations—finding the simple and honest words to say it with, rehearsing the opening scene, anticipating reactions, reaching for real, unembarrassed responses and other movements designed to help establish a clear "contract" for the work ahead.

It was a difficult discipline—specificity comes hard for social workers—but when it began to come under the workers' control it produced a culture of work and a depth of involvement that often surprised workers grown used to reticence and monosyllables when they talked to adolescents. In the following excerpts from the first three meetings of an adolescent boys' group, the worker makes three separate attempts—interspersed with consultative and supervisory work—to make a statement that will help the boys begin doing what they came to do. In the first, he confuses (and probably alarms) them by leaving out the fact that they are foster children—which, as they know, is why the agency is interested in them. In the second, he passes the chore to a group member in an awkward attempt to develop some interaction on the subject. Both efforts produce silences, some chatting and a kind of restless movement from subject to subject. In the third attempt, he makes a clear and simple invitation, reaches for a response and the work begins, dramatically.

> *First meeting:* . . . I then stated that they had common interests and concerns like most teenage boys, and said that their presence would give them an opportunity to discuss these concerns. I emphasized the fact that it was their group and it would, therefore, be their decision as to what they wanted to talk about . . . B. entered . . . sat down without taking his coat off . . . I asked if there were any questions that they wanted to ask. Each of them said no.
> After a long period of silence, I asked if they were in favor of attending the meeting when they first heard about it . . . Y. said that he wasn't . . . F. said he didn't mind coming . . . I asked if they would like to talk about girls and there was a long period of silence . . .
>
> *Second meeting:* . . . the boys had engaged themselves in a discussion about camp. I joined them . . . Y. came into the room, very smartly dressed and wearing large sunglasses . . . they all started laughing . . . I greeted Y. and introduced him to T. I then stated that I was sure T. would probably like to know the purpose of the group, since it was his first attendance. I wondered if someone would like to tell him about the purpose of the group. M. said he would give it a try . . . He began by stating that, as he saw it, this was their group; they talked about what they were interested in and added, pointing at me, that I was only there to supervise the meeting . . .
> There was a brief period of silence which was broken by M., who reintroduced the subject of camp . . .
>
> *Third meeting:* . . . T. asked me if I had ever gone on the Cyclone. M. responded to his question by saying that he had gone on the ride and enjoyed it . . . I interrupted him and asked if they could hold the discussion until we informed L. what the group was all about . . . (after they follow the pattern of "telling each other") I stated that I was a social worker with the Department of Welfare but I would not be visiting their homes or schools because they had their own social workers for that purpose. I also mentioned that all the boys in the group are foster children and that their concerns and problems are quite common. I paused and

there was silence. I said "How about it, are you concerned about your own parents, foster parents and about who you are and where you come from?" M. started to speak, then stopped. I encouraged him to continue, telling him that I knew it wasn't easy to talk about such matters. M. said "About our own parents, Mr. B. The only thing that bothers me is that they tell you about them." I asked M. what he meant. He said: "After you live in a foster home from a baby and think that you are living with your own parents, your social worker comes by one day and tells you that the people you are living with are not your real parents." To show him I understood how he felt, I replied that it is a rough deal and asked if the others felt the same way. F. said he always knew he was a foster child and knows the reason. M. said he knew why he was in foster care, too. F. wanted to know why M. was a foster child, and said that he didn't have to answer if it were too personal. M. said he didn't mind telling the group. He then asked me if I had ever been downtown near W's Department store. I said I had been in the area a couple of times. He asked F. the same question and F. said yes. M. continued: "Well, there is a man who sells pretzels in front of the store all year round." He hesitated, smiled and said, "He's my real father." Though M. smiled as he informed us of this, there were no smiles from the other boys . . . (M. continues to tell his story, the others listen, exchange observations, then move into a discussion of fathers drinking, what drinking means to them, etc.).

It was true in each group: when the worker dug behind the professional jargon to exact a clear and limited conception of the group purpose, when he could face this purpose honestly and say it to his clients, they accepted the invitation gratefully and the work themes poured forth:

One girl said that she was ashamed to walk down the street with her (white) worker as the people would think that the worker was her cousin (brief laughter) . . . I asked her if she had white friends and white classmates who walked down the street with her. She felt that this was different. Their friends didn't ask them personal questions about their mothers and how do you feel about your (own) mother. The girls made faces, poking fun at the workers . . .

A discussion of venereal disease developed when J. said a fellow is afraid to smoke, you can get cancer, and afraid to have sex because you can have a venereal disease. B. thought if J. was so afraid maybe he should tie his penis up. This drew quite a few laughs. I said it was quite real that some people could develop an unusual amount of fear around contracting a venereal disease . . . the boys were eager for information . . .

M. continued by saying: "No matter what, when I get married I'm going to treat my wife good." He had learned all about what happened to his mother from his older brother . . . his father drove his mother crazy because he was no good; his actions led to her confinement at Y. State

> Hospital. M. said his mother was now dead. He stopped and said: "You know, Mr. B., I was born in Y. State Hospital, but I didn't know my mother."
>
> G. opened a discussion around the foster mothers' use of the agency's money in their care, complaining about his foster mother not buying the foster children clothing. He accused his foster mother of using the agency's money to buy clothing for her grandchildren and getting nothing for the foster children. I recognized this had been bothering him for a long time and I was glad he had decided to talk about it. (After some details) he was so mad he almost exploded. S. said foster parents only got a little amount of money and it wasn't enough. R. said that's one thing the agency was cheap about . . . G. said his social worker was always discussing things with his foster mother—"just talk, talk but nothing gets better for us." He feels it is just about time that his social worker had a "man to man" talk with him. He received an open applause from the group after this statement.
>
> . . . A. mentioned that one of the things that bugs him most is to be tagged at school as a foster child . . . at the beginning of school, the teacher calls your name and asks for your parents' names and addresses and when your name was different from the foster parents, some children ask if you are foster . . . B. said he tells them his parents are dead . . . H. said people believe that the parents of foster children are bad and didn't want them . . .

When the adolescents began thus to respond to the sharper invitation to talk seriously about their real ideas and feelings, the practitioners' next problem was to turn these productions into sustained work. And as they moved to this next task, it became possible to make some distinctions between the group skills that could be drawn most readily from their casework experience and those that were more difficult to master. For example, they achieved their first skills in making a clear statement of purpose, listening for hidden cues, openly identifying with the youngsters' sense of urgency, reaching for ambiguities and negatives and responding to "bad" feelings without shock. However, as the children began to move into these areas of taboo, as they accepted the invitation to share anxieties, the workers were often nonplussed as to where to go from there; the need to handle and elaborate this material made more complicated demands on the workers' professional skills.

In the consultations, we were able to specify—working line-by-line from their recorded experiences—what some of these demands were: to break down large problems into smaller, more manageable pieces of work; to reach for the details of a problem and help others in the group add to the inventory from their own experiences; to ask for *more* of the feeling, both negative and positive, and help the members support each other in its expression; to help them try out new ideas in public and rehearse new ways of handling old problems; to help them generalize from their experiences and others'; to ask them to define their realities, without underplaying or overplaying the difficulties;

to hold them to their work; to help them talk to and listen to each other; to invest their own (the workers') compassion and spontaneity without losing their special helping role; and other moves designed to help the youngsters examine their world in detail and teach each other some new ways of handling it.

These were the tasks of the middle, or "work," phase. Many of these problems were not new ones for caseworkers; but they were rendered more complex in the group setting—by the potential explosiveness of group-reinforced feelings, by the need to balance many different individual themes at the same time, by the sheer rapidity of the interaction, by the reluctance to "interfere with the group process" and similar factors. The reasons varied from worker to worker, but the symptoms were the same: there would now be a clear and specific invitation to honest talk; the adolescents would respond to the kindness and skill by sharing some of their most intimate anxieties and curiosities; and the worker would cut them off before the themes could be developed.

It should be made clear that this was not a fallow period; indeed it was far more exciting and productive than the tentative and uncertain fumblings of the first phase. But it was still, at this stage, somewhat short of reaching the real potential of group service. In the following, the members begin to express some important concerns, but the action deteriorates as the worker cuts off their productions—through passivity and vagueness, as in the first example, or a fear of the outcome, as in the second, or a premature call for action, as in the third excerpt, or from a need to "explain" away the tension, as in the last:

> The discussion was then focused on school when M. said he made 35 on his midterm in math; F. laughed and said he made 15 on his. M. said it wasn't funny . . . math is his weakest subject . . . he cannot even do his multiplication tables and he is in the ninth grade . . . I wondered if he had asked his parents for help in math and he said no, he hadn't, because his parents don't know math themselves. Y. agreed . . . B. nodded his agreement but did not speak . . . I wondered whether they had brought this problem to the attention of their workers . . . if his social worker was aware of the problem, he may be able to work something out. A period of silence followed . . .

> With biting sarcasm and biting criticism, one group member related that her social worker would religiously arrive for her appointment at meal time . . . the worker would graciously comment on how delicious the food smelled, forcing the foster mother to offer the worker lunch . . . at one point, when the girls were going at the social workers strongly, I asked if anyone felt that her social worker had done anything good for her . . . none of the girls could or would pick up on this.

> I observed that everything that had been mentioned seemed quite real in their lives. I wondered if we shouldn't talk about why they didn't seem to care about them. In spite of his declaration not to talk,

> A. plunged in. He verbalized strongly that you couldn't count on anyone. He related his situation around trying to get transferred to another high school . . . he couldn't cound on his foster parents to give him much help with anything. He needed his social worker to go to the school to handle the transfer. When I asked what the group thought should be done about this, R. suggested that someone from the agency should take care of it . . .
>
> S. asked, "Why do social workers always want to know about your business?" I inquired what she meant and she stated that they were always asking how you felt about someone or something. Both C. and D. nodded their heads vigorously. I commented that as social workers we are interested in people and how they feel about things. It is important that we know how you feel so that we will be able to help you. D. stated in a low tone that her previous social workers always asked how did she feel about her natural mother . . .

Despite these fits and starts, the material continued to flow because of the group stimulation and the workers' ability to listen, empathize and keep trying. The themes appeared again and again, and each time they did the workers showed more skill in helping the youngsters elaborate them and dig more deeply into their meanings. Increasingly, their ability to focus on specifics, to be direct, to help the group members move slowly and to reach for the accompanying affect made it possible for the youngsters to do some intensive collaborative work on matters of considerable importance in their lives. As the work deepened, it began to look more like this:

> . . . I returned to the issue of their feelings about being cared for and given to by the agency. W., who was about to devour her last cookie, asserted that she didn't mind getting things from the agency because no one else cared enough about them to give to them. T. added that she agreed with W. that they didn't care. I got at whom they were referring to and W. blurted out "our foster parents." She went on, "You know, Mrs. W., they make you feel different by treating you different." W. was emotional as she continued. I asked how they were treated differently. W. told about having to do special chores . . . own children have special privileges . . . no one who was not a foster child could understand how it feels. I commented to W. and the group that from what they say, it must be a tough pill to swallow and that I wanted them to help me understand what it was like to be a foster child.
>
> . . . B. contributed that it hurt her for her friends to know that she was a foster child and that she hated to explain the different names. I asked what did she tell them. She said she told them that her name was B_______ D_______ and left it at that. E. interrupted to say that she would be ready to fight if anyone pushed her to tell them why her name was different. S. added that she used to fight all the time about the names, but fighting didn't help. B. agreed with S. that even if you fight it still hurt you to be treated like a step-child.

> I encouraged T. to share some of her feelings by asking her to tell us about some of the ways she felt hurt and left out. T. shared a revealing incident about another foster child who was a friend of hers. Apparently, T. had gone to visit this child on a rainy day, and . . . the foster mother referred her around to the backyard . . . her little friend was tearfully sitting on a box out in the rain being punished. So the two of them just sat there in the rain. I asked T. if she had cried with her friend . . .
> . . . I commented to the group as a whole that I got the feeling that they didn't always speak up for their rights. T. picked up on this to say "if you are foster, you don't have no rights." W. contributed that although she felt she had some rights, since you weren't with your own, you feel silly trying to say something about the way you are treated . . .
> . . . as I looked at each girl, she apparently sensed that I was asking her to open up a little more . . .

Some of the problems of the fourth phase—the transitions and endings—have been touched on in the previous discussion of the significance of endings and the dangers of the "farewell party" cult problems remains itself a difficult problem syndrome.[42] In addition, the fact that sharing diffi was evidenced by the frequent introduction of touchy material at the end of a meeting, when there was little time left to deal with it; this was a phenomenon we came to know as "doorknob therapy." In this connection, we worked on the skills necessary to help the groups make transitions between meetings and pick up more quickly the tempo and momentum of the sharing process. Carrying a "doorknob" theme mechanically into the next meeting ("John, you were saying that . . .") almost always drew a blank, since it failed to recognize the delicacy of the theme and the ambivalence about bringing it up. Similarly, all the routine transition devices—"let's review what we talked about last time," "at the end of the last meeting, we were discussing . . ."—tended to dampen the work rather than stimulate it. At the other extreme, the "silent treatment"—refusing to open the meeting because the transition should "come from the group"—and the lazy "what shall we talk about today?" most often created resentment and precipitated a battle of wills that dominated the rest of the meeting.

The workers' examination of the transition processes threw more light on the meaning of group experience and added to their store of skills. When they came to realize, for example, that the life of a group is continuous—a part of the members' lives—and not restricted to the meeting times, alone, they began to incorporate this "interim" dimension into their search for carryover from meeting to meeting. They could then eliminate the artificial "think about that for next time" gimmick—so popularly used, so easily tossed off and so unreal, for hardly anyone ever actually thinks about it for next time. They could also understand that meetings often begin before they are "called to order;" that the time of "waiting" is often used for important work, even when the worker himself fails to realize that the "chatting" is closely connected to their purpose in being together.

> While we were waiting the boys continued their discussion about school. B. was expressing his concerns about white teachers and how they were prejudiced toward Negro students. He cited several examples of incidents to support his feelings. F. felt that white people in general were very prejudiced and dramatically told the group about his physical battle with white students in school. The discussion touched on many phases of the social conflicts within our society. There was strong agreement with the concept of "black power," and the boys talked of their displeasure over having to join the service, fight in wars, and return home to be discriminated against. . . . B. was concerned about "Negroes not sticking together." He felt that, in many instances, they were responsible for their troubles. F. related how funny he felt in school when they discussed subjects like race riots and other crimes by Negroes.
> I interrupted the boys at this point to officially call the meeting to order.

There were other practice themes that emerged from their growing understanding of transitions: they learned to expect and to reach for the regression and "apathy" that almost always followed a highly productive session; they learned to open meetings gingerly, reaching for possibilities but open to messages about what might be uppermost in their minds; and they learned to use endings to *credit* their productions, thus reinforcing the emphasis on work and empathizing with the demands it imposed.

> I terminated the meeting and told the boys that they really had worked hard and talked about things that were difficult. I added that I knew it wasn't easy to do, and that they showed great strength.

The group work with adolescents drew the staff of the Division of Foster Home Care into discussion of a wide range of issues affecting its service to clients. Perhaps the most important was the realization that the adolescents had been somewhat bypassed in the natural pattern of service. Following is a Log excerpt from the first end-year staff evaluation of the group work with adolescents:

> *June 17, 1964:* . . . Mr. B.: I find I'm now paying more attention to the child in the family; I think we have been neglecting them. I asked why: *are* you all more comfortable with the parents than with the children? A big *yes* from the group, and animated discussion: how hard it is for them to get the kids to talk to them; the tendency to let the kids go and deal mostly with the parents. Someone raised the question as to whether they can actually work effectively with the mothers and the children at the same time—the problem of having close rapport with both. Another said: These children have had so many workers—can *they* feel comfortable with *us?* . . .

In this connection, it was a source of continuing interest and surprise to the staff that the adolescents were so verbal in the group situation. At an early point, a caseworker stated that he was "jealous" of the "spectacular" things that were happening in the group and felt it was important for him to be kept informed of these developments. Under this impetus, they examined the differences between the demands of the interview and those of the group experience, and explored the ways in which the peer group lends itself, on certain problems, to a measure of free expression sometimes harder to achieve in the interview.

The staff's desire to be kept informed of the work with their clients ran into some initial conflict with the group service worker's feeling that he must promise "confidentiality" to his members, in order to encourage freedom of expression. Having agreed at the outset that we would, wherever possible, begin with the workers' own hunches and test our procedures from there, the staff experimented with various forms of anonymous and semianonymous recording and modes of sharing the written materials. The problem of sharing went both ways—from family work to group service, as well as from the group to the caseworker:

> *June 17, 1964:* . . . Y.: What about the reverse angle? How much does the group worker want to know about what is happening in the caseworker contact? How much does he want to know about the boys beforehand? W. (the worker) gives an example of how this information might have helped him in a particular case—the "smooth" boy and his special kind of defense . . .

Later, the attitudes about confidentiality began to change as it became evident that the boys themselves seemed to want *more* communication between the group leader and their caseworkers, rather than less. When I later asked the first boys' worker whether the members were talking about things they would not be talking about if confidentiality had not been promised, he said he did not think so. In this—as with the staff's first fears that the youngsters would share *with each other* material that was not suitable—it was found that the professionals' fear of excessive sharing was greater than that of the clients themselves. Actually, the adolescents developed their own modes of revealing and concealing in accordance with their sense of self-protection; for the most part, they seemed to derive a greater sense of security from the feeling that their various workers were together in their knowledge, rather than removed from each other. The growing frequency with which the youngsters asked their workers to "take messages" to each other was a sign of their need to integrate the services, rather than compartmentalize them.

From time to time, the staff also re-examined agency policies that had come under attack in the adolescents' group discussions:

> Strong feelings against the agency's policy of requiring older adolescent children to secure receipts for haircuts and hairdressings came out in group sessions. As a result, this policy has been changed; money for such needs is now included in payments for board made to foster parents. The groups have also influenced the division to take a more practical look at

the ways it meets many general needs, especially in regard to allowances for clothing and personal needs.[43]

There was much discussion on the interpretive and preparatory work with the foster parents in the process of forming the children's groups. The work with the parents revealed more resistance and fearfulness than had been expected; attendance at orientation meetings was often low, there was a range of ambivalent attitudes and the parents often used the occasion primarily to air grievances about the staff turnover and other problems. On the other hand, several of the parents were eager to learn more about the children's groups and about the problems they were designed to address. As they worked, several points became clear: there was considerable variation in the kinds of explanations offered to the foster parents by the referring caseworkers—variations in clarity, enthusiasm and opportunity for feedback—and there was much work to be done to achieve a common language with which to describe the new service; it became evident that parent fears were most readily allayed when they met the group worker face-to-face and received their explanations and impressions at first hand; and there was growing evidence of the specific connections between the work with the children and the service to their foster parents.

For example, it was soon clear that a single meeting of foster parents at the outset would not be enough to help the parents understand the group service, perceive it as a support to their own efforts and express their own need for help from the agency. Unless the division could bring the work with the adolescent groups into close harness with the efforts of the caseworkers and the foster parents, there would be some danger of splitting, rather than helping, the foster home. With children already torn between natural and foster parents, care would have to be taken not to create additional tensions between home and agency, between caseworkers and group leaders.

There were many more such issues, growing out of the work with the adolescents and stimulating staff work of some importance to the division. The discussion of acting-out children in the group raised the possibility of more rigorous screening but this was rejected on the grounds that they would rather take their chances with the more difficult ones than exclude children who needed the help. The experience with the local recreational centers was examined, to find criteria determining when such settings could be hospitable to this kind of work, and relevant differences were found in social atmosphere, flexibility, informality and tolerance for deviance. Ways were discussed of incorporating the group records into the main body of service data constantly being fed into the agency files. The experience with a young and talented trainee gave them an opportunity to examine the possible strengths and limitations of untrained personnel in group service tasks. The loss of the girls' worker in midseason made it necessary to study the factors involved in helping clients make transitions of this nature, from a trusted worker to a newcomer who makes a fresh bid for their confidence. There was discussion of using the training period to induct new workers into group skills as well as individual and family work. And there was all of the technical work, involving the examination of group skills, relating them to social work practice as they knew it and rehearsing the supervisory skills necessary to intrench and enrich the service to groups.

The Foster Parents

The first consultations on group work with foster parents began in the first year, as part of the initial practice explorations in the placement divisions.[44] At that time, both Homefinding and Foster Home Care presented early experiences in this area of work: Homefinding brought in the fourth of a series of "in-service training meetings . . . focused on infant and child physical and psychological development;" while Foster Home Care organized and presented two complete six-session groups, designed to stimulate discussion on common concerns and to "improve the functioning" of the foster parents. These groups ranged in active membership from about six to ten, met once a month and consisted mostly of foster mothers, with a few fathers and couples attending from time to time.

In the second year, the focus of consultative attention was on a group of foster parents who lived in an outlying community,[45] the group met six times, at two-week intervals, and was led by one of the workers active in the previous year's experience. Her report later offered the following rationale for the group's formation:

> For many years the casework staff in the Division of Foster Home Care had been particularly concerned about the large number of foster parents in ______ County and the outlying areas of ______ County. We were aware that because of the distance involved the social workers carrying out the supervision of these homes could not offer the same intensive services as foster homes within the five boroughs of New York City receive. In addition, many of these communities lacked essential community services such as special classes in school, medical and psychiatric facilities, etc. We were also aware that many of the foster families located there might feel somewhat alienated from the agency.[46]

Later, the group work with foster parents was geared to the process of enlisting their self-interest and collaboration in the group program for adolescents. These meetings were handled by the supervisors, and consultations were addressed to helping them prepare, examining their records and drawing implications for further programming.[47]

In the work with the foster parent groups, the consultation activity wound itself around the same basic themes—the phases of work, the staff feedback and the impact on the agency service. What was different were the specific ways in which these were put to use with the special problems of the foster parents. The problems, as they emerged, ranged widely: their concern about the natural parents and the uneasiness about the "bad blood;" the problem of whether, how and how soon you tell the child about his background; the realization that it might be that they, rather than the children, were not "ready" for the "telling;" the child's anxieties about his own identity; the pain of separation when they lose the foster child; similar feelings of the natural sibling on separating from the foster child; the problems of raising adolescents, with their sexual problems, school difficulties and home behavior; their need to develop child-rearing and disciplinary strategies; their concern about inadequate board rate allowances from the agency; their relationships with caseworkers; their resentment at community attitudes toward foster families; their efforts to use the group and the worker productively; and many others.

We soon learned that there was a kind of typical pace at which these problems unfolded. The parents' first reaction was to agree that foster parents certainly had problems but that they, individually, were among the fortunate ones. They might, in a variation of this response, admit that there had been some problems in the past, but these were solved now. They might even go a step further and offer a few items that had the ring of "problems" but were not urgently felt as such:

> (After the introduction) the foster mothers presented a positive attitude toward the children. They were verbal and spontaneous . . . the words seemed to rush out and sometimes they jumped from one point to another that did not seem to be logically related.
> They expressed deep religious feelings, with much emphasis on its daily importance in their homes. They were proud about their foster children's religious activities . . . they had no problems now. Some had them in the past (but) with God's help, with their efforts and those of the children, and in a very few instances with the help of foster fathers, therapists and workers, they overcame them. Mrs. H. said her children were "too young" (not yet adolescents) to have problems.
>
> Each foster mother and the foster father introduced themselves, relating one or two incidents that they felt were particularly meaningful that had occurred while caring for their foster children. The inference seemed to be that although the related incidents represented past problems, they had all been relatively successfully handled.
>
> I then asked if someone would like to start us off. There was a brief silence, when Mrs. C. mentioned the therapy that her two foster children are receiving—the long trips to the city to see the doctor; but she added hastily that everything is just working out fine—her foster son, who never did his homework, now completes it regularly and responsibly. Another group member commented on the lack of success her child was having after two years of therapy. It appeared to me that the group was disinterested in the topic but felt they had to say something. Another mother stated that her daughter resisted therapy because it made her feel even more different than her young friends. I picked up on why she thought the child felt different.

In this last example, the worker's last comment turns a vague beginning into work, and the record continues as follows:

> From this point, the discussion . . . became more and more animated . . . a member felt that it is too painful for a foster child to learn the truth as to why he is different. . . . Mrs. W. felt that even though she had told her youngster about his natural mother, the child thinks of her as his "real" mother. This statement brought forth many contributions by the group that were in a similar vein. I added that they seemed to be saying that, in many senses of the word, they are the real mothers. A member said that this was really so; but she thought that a child should be helped to understand that he also had a different biological mother. I said that perhaps if they thought they were the true mothers it might be hard for them to talk to their youngsters about their biological mothers. Several members said it is hard . . .
>
> Mr. T., a foster father, then spoke. He . . . guessed he was the first man to speak this morning, and I gave him brief and good humored recognition for this. Mr. T.'s voice was calm and very earnest when he started; but as he finished his comment, his voice broke with emotion. He told the group that he was a stepchild, but that he was never told the truth. He regarded his stepmother as his real mother until he was 13 years of age, when a distant relative informed him of his true identity. His real mother was not only living, but residing in the community. He described the pain of this sudden discovery and said he would never want this to happen to his foster children.
>
> There was a hushed silence in the room; the expressions on the faces of the foster mothers showed that Mr. T. had their sympathetic understanding. I supported Mr. T. by telling him that his sharing of his childhood experience with us certainly helped us understand a great deal.

So it was that when the foster parents began to realize that the worker was serious, was not testing their fitness as parents and would not punish them for being less than perfect, the real feelings began to emerge and the work began.

The contract was fairly clear; in the tuning-in work, we had mapped out a broad common ground on which the workers could help bring parent and agency stakes together, with hardly a trace of hidden agenda. For example, in what came to be known as the "Center Village Group," some of this work on finding the common ground is shown in the following Log excerpt:

> *March 6, 1964:* . . . a) what do these parents want from us? The isolation, the lack of agency attention, the paucity of local services, the school problems, etc.; b) what is the agency's stake? We want to reach out . . . "They're part of us" . . . helping them negotiate new services, deal with the schools, share their problems, get a sense of help from others, etc. (The worker) is quite clear, serious, direct—I encouraged her to be as specific as she could be, offer a tangible service, connect up directly with their sense of problems. She understands this, has learned this lesson well and has the guts to apply it.

This, and further work on specifics,[48] later produced this opening statement in the group:

> My opening was brief—after a warm greeting I mentioned that this was the first foster parents' group meeting we have held in this community. I explained the confidential nature of their comments, asking for their cooperation in keeping confidential anything that may be brought up during the meeting. I continued by stating that we are coming to them, as we recognize that travel can be difficult for them. Several mothers shook their heads vigorously in agreement. I added that being a foster mother is a tough job; but they have it even rougher because the area in which they live lacks so many essential services. We want to know their concerns; and what they think and feel will enable us to learn from and help each other.

The opening remark on confidentiality reflected an experience similar to that in the work with adolescents; the practitioner began by favoring the offer of confidentiality and then changed her perspective in the course of the work. At the third consultation, she asserted that we needed to rethink the issue: "We are trained to use information professionally," she said, and pointed to evidence that the parents seemed less concerned about it than the professionals. As with the adolescents, the parents wanted more staff communication, not less.

In the main body of work, each theme made its appearance—sometimes faint and hesitant—sometimes in "doorknob" fashion, sometimes strong and vigorous and often repeated in a different way when the worker missed it the first time. Through it all, it was the validity and strength of the contract—the real need and the constant effort to keep the purposes clear and straightforward—that kept the work moving despite false starts, ambiguities and mistakes along the way. With increasing frequency, the interaction of parent concerns, self-help processes and worker skills produced intensive work on matters of real concern.

> Mrs. S. said that the former director had assured her that the children she received were for long term care and barring unforeseen circumstances would remain with her until age 18. She said that two had been taken from her not because they went home to relatives, but because they were placed in another foster home. She asked "Was this right?" Another mother said that "barring unforeseen circumstances" means that there is always a "maybe" in foster care. It is different than having natural children or in adoption, for it is always there. Mrs. A. mentioned that it is something you want to forget, and perhaps you conveniently do. Then, when the child has to be moved, you almost don't remember you were ever told about this "maybe."
>
> I asked if there was any way that . . . foster parents could be more comfortable with that "maybe" which is always there in the background. A great many comments were made which included that perhaps you can't; but a foster mother always seems to try over again with the next child and that every separation is painful. But the first one is surely the worst. Mrs. B. said quietly and thoughtfully, "I guess everyone cannot be a foster par-

ent." At this point, there were so many undercurrents of cross-conversation that I had to ask Mrs. B. to repeat her remark. She did, emphasizing what she had said. There was some realization within the group that there was something "special" in them that made them continue to want to help children in spite of the pain of separation . . .

Three meetings later, an important connection is made as they discuss the children:

> . . . I said I guessed they were sick and tired of having everything attributed to "a child's insecurity." There was a general titter and nodding of heads. Mrs. S. said, boy they sure were. Mrs. L. said "But what else can you call it?" . . . Mrs. B. added that when one of her foster children had to leave, the others fall down in their school work. She attributed this to their fear that they might have to leave, too . . .
>
> I said as they were talking and discussing this point, it seemed to me they were saying that like the foster parents had to always live with a "maybe" . . . our foster children too had to live with a "maybe." I recapped quickly the earlier meeting, but it was almost unnecessary. They remembered, and they gave many gestures and looks which indicated their understanding.

In another group, there is a long discussion about the "bad blood" anxiety and the worry about rearing children who "do wrong because it is in them." The worker thought "it hurt to put in so much and see a child doing well turn bad," and they move to thoughts about the children:

> Mrs. J. spoke about foster children feeling different from others. They wonder about their natural parents, their identity and why they are in care. I and the others claimed in . . . there was also the agency involvement: visits by social workers, these group meetings, checks, forms, etc. . . . Maybe foster children do not do well at times because they see their status in a negative way. They generally tell their children about their identity only when they have to . . . (Mrs. J.) asked, "How can you tell a child his mother is a prostitute?"

In the Center Village Group, there was an important piece of work on the agency's financial allowances—an effort that became productive as the worker learned to keep the channels open for work, rather than "cool out" the members with premature "solutions" and reassurances. The theme appeared at the third meeting, and began as follows.

> Mrs. C. then said she did not want to hog the meeting, but she had something else on her mind. After encouraging her to say whatever she wished, Mrs. C. said she felt the allowances we give the children, especially teenagers, are woefully inadequate. She continued by stating that her 15-year-old foster son receives $3.60 a month from the agency, and since bowling costs $1.25 and movies are $.90, one can see that this allowance is just not sufficient.

> I asked how the other group members felt about the allowances, and there was unanimous agreement that the amount was completely insufficient. Almost the entire group participated in this discussion.
> I said that the agency is also questioning the entire area of allowances, and it will be reevaluated. However, I cautioned that this takes time and it is not only up to the agency administration. This seemed to be accepted and understood—there was a great deal of nodding of heads . . .

When the record was brought to consultation, we looked closely at how and why the work had been cut off:

> *April 16, 1964:* We went to the discussion about the allowances . . . the worker's handling: luckily, the agency is "considering" and will give them their answer, but it will take time, etc. They propose and the agency disposes—is that the name of the game? She questions my implication seriously . . . "it would stir up a hornet's nest!" But as we work, she begins to wonder . . . thought must be allowed to lead where it will, does she have the right to cut it off, how can she help them handle this problem realistically, etc.

Then, with characteristic courage, the worker moved into the next meeting determined to make it happen again, so that she could get another chance to help. Fortunately, the group had its own impetus and the theme came through again, in a new form:

> . . . As I reconstructed the last meeting, many of the foster parents were nodding and reminiscing about the incidents that had occurred previously. Mrs. B. then interjected that she feels there is a very severe problem about clothing. She added that she has a ten-and-a-half-year-old girl who wears very large sizes . . . in addition, the child has had her period and requires personal hygiene items such as sanitary napkins, yet the money we give for clothing goes according to age rather than to the child's maturation. It was unnecessary for me to stimulate the discussion about clothing. The members of the group felt that this was a real problem for them. Mrs. R. pointed out that if you buy cheap clothing it does not wear. Mrs. C. indicated that older children have to have a "say so" in the selection of their clothes, or they won't wear them. The discussion drifted briefly to comments about the different high styled clothing that children demand . . .
> I brought them back to the problem at hand by saying that they "seem to feel that they have a tough time managing on the clothing allowances." Mrs. S. said, "Tough, it's impossible—those allowances must have been figured out 15 years ago." Mrs. O. said, "No, I don't think so, but they expect you to buy in John's Bargain Store . . . and those cheap things just will not last—it's throwing your money out . . ."

> I said quietly that since almost all of you seem to be having the same problems, what have you done about it? Mrs. A. said bitterly, "We tell our caseworkers." There was a great deal of group interaction, with many of the foster mothers talking at once. I interrupted by saying, "Let's hear what Mrs. S. has to say." Mrs. S. said that her caseworker just says if she spends more clothing money than she should, she can take it out of the next clothing check. . . . She added helplessly, "It just doesn't work out. I just have to use my own money."
>
> There was general agreement with Mrs. S.'s comments . . . many of them had also discussed it with their caseworkers, only to receive similar comments.
>
> I added to their frustration by stating, "What do you think you might do about it?" Mrs. C. answered helplessly, "What can we do?" Mrs. B. said hesitantly, "Could we send a petition to Miss G.?" (the Division Director). There was a brief silence and then many remarks were made agreeing with the suggestion . . .

Out of this came an exchange of letters between the group and the Division Director, where the foster mothers made a strong and detailed case for increased allowances and the Director expressed her thanks for their work on this problem. Shortly afterwards, the personal and clothing allowances were raised; and while the parents had certainly not effected this outcome singlehanded, they had provided some of the pressure that went into making the change. And, with some further expenditure of time and skill, they could learn to do more.

In the matter of endings, the consultation work was again focused on the skills required to help the members avoid the "farewell party syndrome"; it was important that they not complete their experience in a euphoric bout of mutual admiration, but that they be helped to work seriously at figuring out what they had accomplished and what they had left unexplored. This was always a difficult demand on the workers themselves; their tendency was to express their separation feelings too soon, thus cutting off some of the negatives they hoped to elicit in the evaluation process. Although an ending could have warmth and gratitude and feel good, a "happy ending" was artificial and unreal. Serious endings were complex and should be allowed to remain that way, for in a real sense they were not endings at all, but transitions to new experience.

> I asked that we now consider the group meetings as a whole. As I had said when we first met, these were new for us all . . . what did they get out of them? . . . Mrs. L. and Mrs. T. found them supportive. It was good to hear what other mothers have to say and that they have similar problems. Mrs. T. is encouraged. They are not alone and implied interest in attending other meetings.
>
> Mrs. H. and Mrs. J. disagreed. Mrs. H. felt it was a lot of repetitive talk and she is back where she started at the first meeting—still without an answer to her problem of why her foster children turn bad. . . . Mrs. J. felt

> that . . . the meetings made no difference. They could talk to each other like this on the telephone or in the park . . . she expected something to take home . . . maybe a lecture or a movie . . .
> We were running over time and some mothers were ready to leave when Mrs. T. spoke with deep feelings. These meetings meant a lot. So many times she felt like calling us to take the children out. She spoke of an incident last year when she bore the cross alone. The others nodded and yessed as she spoke.

The group services to foster parents, like the work with adolescents, involved the division staff in regular sessions designed to examine the experience and its impact on them and the agency. These meetings became part of agency routine, conducted by one of the workers without the presence of the consultant. Again the discussions ranged over many technical and structural issues, including the parents' concerns, the group skills, the sharing of information, the impact on casework service, the problems of supervision and others.

The experience with the Center Village Group produced, in addition to the process record of the six meetings, a running account of other events, including the preparation process, the use of consultation, the correspondence and the meetings with casework staff. Because of the confidentiality principle earlier described, the worker also produced a brief, summary version of each group meeting, for use at the staffing sessions.

Some learning accrued from our use of an observer, introduced into a foster parents' group for the purpose of training another worker for group leadership. We found, for example, that the group members were more threatened by her silence than by her participation, construing passivity as judgmental and alien. Thus, the observer was increasingly drawn into the discussion and she had to work out a way of responding that was easy and natural, while being careful not to interfere with the work focus of the group leader. We found, too, that the perceptions of the observer greatly enriched the insights of the worker as to what had happened at the group meetings and added to the substance of the consultation sessions.

In the final stages of the Center Village Group, the question was raised as to whether the members should be invited to continue after the stipulated number of sessions had expired. It was decided that it would be better to hold to the time space visualized in the original contract and to arrange for new groups as they were needed. It was reported that the experience had produced a number of continuing associations and neighbor-finding, some of which had emerged from the ironing out of transportation arrangements. Among the staff, there was considerable discussion of how much "like casework" the group skills were and, on the other hand, how different was the group situation, with its "public" character, its "scariness" when the negatives appear and its threat to the worker's control. Several caseworkers made the point that their group work courses at school had been too formalistic and unreal to prepare them for this kind of work.

The Adoptive Parents

In the Division of Adoptions, the interest in groups was directed primarily to their use with both approved and post-adoptive parents under agency supervision. There were a few presentations of one-session groups of new applicants; and there was some preliminary exploration of the possibilities of group work with families under study. But most of the consultation work was focused on the short-term (four-session) groups of adoptive parents in supervision. One such group was presented by the Division Director in the first consultation year[49] and six more were subsequently organized, presented and followed in consultation. These groups generally met at two-week intervals, thus covering a two-month period; they were homogeneous with respect to age of children, with parents of older children clustering in the groups formed from inter-country, own-kin adoptions; and active group membership ranged from about six to twelve couples.

After some preliminary work, they began to prepare parents at Intake for the group experience, and by the fourth year the groups were formed of parents who had been expecting to be called together as part of agency procedure. The groups were interpreted as offering the parents the opportunity to share and discuss, with each other and the agency, problems in child-rearing, agency relationships and other questions emerging from their status as adoptive parents.

As with the other populations, the opening work on group services to adoptive parents focused on tapping the staff's rich knowledge of their clients and on "tuning in" to the major themes that could be expected to make their appearance.

> *May 1, 1963:* Took them through systematically, a step at a time: first, the tuning in—they anticipated questions about how to share information about adoption, with the child and with the neighborhood—the stigma of infertility—the loss of control over the child when he finds out—the notion of the bad seed (even more scary in adoption than in foster care)—the fear that the child won't love them when he finds out they are not his "real" parents; also, their own attitudes toward "pseudo" parenthood. Then, my focus: Given this tuning in, how can they prepare to help?

In preparing for later groups, they continued to work at sharpening their receptivity to parent concerns. They discussed the child-rearing ideas and practices they might expect to find among group members of different class, culture and occupation, the tensions in the relationships between biological and adopted children, the guilt and concern about the natural parents, the ambivalence toward the agency and its staff, the problem of husband and wife working together in the same group meetings, and similar themes. And, as in the other services, the workers rehearsed their beginnings in the groups—explaining purpose, reaching for feedback, making a contract, helping the members start talking to each other, reading silences and keeping the conversation open and real.

The work in Adoptions followed much the same course as it did in the other services, with staff trying to develop the same basic skills, in the context of their own special tasks and the special problems of their clients. However, there were some issues that came through with particular clarity and emphasis in this setting.

For example, the work with new adoptive parents seemed to create a tendency for the practitioner to be particularly distressed by the "wrong theories" of the members, especially on questions of child-rearing. In response to this anxiety, the workers did a great deal of "teaching," hoping to offset the effect of the "wrong" ideas on the others in the group. Then, when they realized that the teaching had sounded to the clients like preaching, they were left with the feeling that they had accomplished little but to make the parents more cautious about expressing their real feelings and ideas. Often, the teaching took the form of the all-too-familiar "Socratic game," in which the "questions" were designed to elicit answers already in the worker's mind:

> I wondered how many parents were "sticklers" when it came to following schedules. A couple of hands went up . . . others said they'd tried schedule feeding, but they often fed their infants on demand . . .
> I wondered if anybody had an idea of how feeding problems develop. Mr. M. said . . .
> I asked what would lead a mother to fear that her child was not getting enough nourishment? Mrs. H. said . . . I asked how is it determined that a child is supposed to drink a certain amount of milk or eat a certain amount of solid food? Mrs. R. replied . . .
> I said I was wondering when the child would be brought into the discussion. There were a few amused smiles . . .

Their struggle with this "pedagogical pull" precipitated some intensive work by the practitioners on the importance of trusting their own theories of child care enough so that these ideas would not have to be *sold*—"subtly" or otherwise—but would emerge from people's experience, from their love for the children and from their ability to learn from each other. The skill of helping people explore their own experience and come up with something they could own was, in the end, far more exciting to the practitioners than the crude polemicizing with which they sometimes began. Here is the same worker in a later group:

> (In a discussion of discipline) The group agreed that the child would show anger. I wondered how did they handle this anger. This was a new approach to discipline for them. . . . I asked them to slip back in memory to their childhood once more and recall an incident. . . . What happened to the anger and resentment? Mr. B. said he had never thought of it. What does happen to it? . . . Mr. L. said . . . it piles up and finally it comes out by a person's striking out at something or somebody. He cited a recent

> instance in which a young man was refused the use of his girl friend's car and, in anger, he ran his fist through the window shield. He said this was like so many adults who strike out in anger. He never learned to control his anger. "I was never disciplined properly as a child."
> I said it isn't easy for adults to acknowledge that they haven't disciplined their children properly, but if we could look at what precedes the discipline we might recognize the weaknesses. . . . Someone said the parent's patience reaches the end of the rope. They said that at this point the parent becomes angry and he may strike the child. The discussion was rapid at this point . . . the parent punishes in anger. The child too is angry because he can't get what he wants. In anger, the parent orders the child to obey and sometimes the child strikes out too . . .
> I asked if there were others who could recall their feelings or their child's actions before an outburst . . .

There was also something in this work that made it difficult for the practitioners to be direct and assertive, lest they be perceived by the parents as "threatening." This sometimes led to fuzziness and ambiguity about group purpose. There was a tendency for the workers to express purpose as if it were solely dedicated to the needs of the parents, with no agency stake or demands and the worker's role left vague and unexplained, or worse.

> I again introduced myself (Mrs. F. and I had greeted each member at the elevator) and spoke briefly about the purpose of our group meetings, emphasizing that there will be a series of four meetings to be held every other Tuesday evening. I said that this was their meeting to discuss the things that they felt were most pertinent to them as adoptive parents. I would serve as their chairman.
> I suggested that they might start by introducing themselves . . .

When this record—which the worker signed as "Chairman"—came to consultation, we examined some of the problems of beginning:

> *January 27, 1966:* Long record of first meeting signed by "L ________ B________, Chairman"). These are recent placements, good experience with the agency, have known about the group and looked forward to it. Worker had "expected more pauses," was surprised that the talk had moved so fast . . .
> To the record: The (worker's) opening statement—I point out how the agency's stake is left out: include this in the contract . . .
> (Later, in discussing the work) she sees the relationship between the two themes—the "telling" problem and the natural mother problem. On both these themes, the group "patches it up" again (smooths it over). I suggest: "This is a worrisome thing for them" and perhaps it will come up again. Mrs. B.: "But that would be threatening!" Exactly! I said. At this point, we have a good discussion, they begin to see what's involved in the "demand for work"—it's a new idea for them—runs counter to old ideas

about being "supporting," etc. Mrs. B.: "That's probably why I wanted to be the 'chairman'." Beautiful insight.

The beginnings in Adoptions also taught us a few things about group formation. It became very clear, for example, that there was much to be gained (as we were also learning in Foster Home Care) from having the group leaders participate prominently in the first invitations and explanations to the parents. Although the other workers' interpretations were conscientiously done, they tended to lack the specificity, authority and sense of conviction imparted by those who were actually slated to do the group work themselves. Further, we found that it was important to reach more deliberately for resistance to the group experience in these first interviews; in several instances, the parents would agree amiably, promise to come and then simply not show up.

This initial parent resistance was most marked in the intercountry adoptions group and reflected several factors: there was hostility to the whole process of legal adoption of their own kin; the group experience had not yet begun to be interpreted at Intake and was felt by the parents as something tacked on, rather than integral to the entire proceeding; the children had already been with the parents for some time; and the parents were generally older and less connected to the need for help with child-rearing problems. By contrast, the parents of infants and toddlers, who responded with alacrity to the group service, were younger, more recently involved in child-rearing tasks, more eagerly related to the agency and the adoption process, had been informed about the group experience in the early stages of home study and had been looking forward to what it could do for them. In the next round of groups, better results were achieved with the intercountry group as the group worker made her own contacts and spent more time with each prospective member discussing whether they really thought the group was a good idea, what they thought they might get out of it, what the agency had in mind and whether the time and place were in fact feasible for them. The connection between this preparatory activity and the early work of the groups themselves was clearly visible.

As in the work with foster parents, the problems of the adoptive parents emerged slowly and in a certain order: at first, the parents expressed great satisfaction with the way things were going—no problems existed and they were very happy with the children; then, tentatively, they began to offer some mild and permissible concerns—the children's attitude toward school work and some mild and occasional acting-out; and finally, as trust developed in the group and the worker, the real and troubling anxieties began to make their way into the discussion. Underlying this caution were several factors: there was the feeling that the agency expected them to be perfect parents, without any "neurotic" tendencies; there was the fear that their modes of child-rearing were not in accord with the best social work thinking; and, underneath, there was a pervasive feeling that adoptive parents do not have the same privilege of making mistakes, getting angry at the children and feeling anxious about them, as do their "natural" parents.

When the real concerns came through, the problem of "telling" the child—whether to tell, how to tell and when to tell—led all the rest; it appeared in every record and revealed a complex pattern of attitudes and feelings reaching into every aspect of the adoption process.

> Mrs. R. emotionally stated that she found it very hard to say "adoption"; she knows that she will have to tell the child, but she is still very uncomfortable about the word adoption . . . she felt so strongly that this was her child and cannot say the word. . . . Mrs. M. told her that maybe if she keeps saying it, it will come easier . . .
>
> Mr. S. felt that part of this fear that adoptive parents have was due to the image of adoption agencies in the community. He said he felt that most adoption agencies give the parents the feeling that they are constantly being judged and never really accepted. He said he believed the voluntary agencies had created this impression. Mrs. S. added that "social workers do not bite and the ones in this agency are especially easy to talk to." Mr. and Mrs. F. expressed their definite feelings that a child needs to be told about adoption and should be told by the parents. Mr. L. said, "A lot of you are saying that because she is here, (pointing to the leader) but you know you are not going to really tell."
>
> Mrs. T., with much feeling, told how she felt that adoption meant love. She said that people adopt other people, animals, etc., because they want to give and receive love and to care and be cared for. She had explained adoption in this way to her three-year-old when they secured a puppy. The group was silent and thoughtful for a moment. Mrs. W. shook her head in the negative: she said that she understood, but still did not feel that she could do it. The group was sympathetic and several people said it was not easy.
>
> Mrs. M. said, "I realize I am the one who has the problem, not the child, but no matter how I talk to myself, I can't do it." She understands why some parents say "they died," or "they were too sick to care for you." The group laughed understandingly and agreed that this was easier, but Mrs. R. said, "You can't kill off everybody," father, mother, total family. Mrs. W. said, if you can just bring yourself to use the word once, it will get easier. I wondered if a child could understand the word "death" any more easily than "chosen." The mothers of the three older children felt their problems are more difficult than Mrs. M.'s . . . Mrs. R. said Michael brought his "memories" of previous parents and this hurts.

Obviously, these struggles were of considerable interest to the caseworkers carrying the families and they used the staff sessions to follow the relationship between the two helping processes:

> *April 28, 1965:* I picked up on: How *are* the clients using these meetings? Are they (the caseworkers) getting new stuff coming through? Are the parents talking about the meetings in their interviews? V., D. and

> M. gave examples of clients bringing group experiences into the interview; they talked about the group as a stimulant, as a preparer, causing deeper work in the interview. . . . Mrs. K. pointed out that Mrs. W. (the group worker) had "telescoped" the process with Mr. S. and precipitated a great deal of important material into the open when the interview came later, after the meeting. She said, "I want to thank Mrs. W."; everybody laughed and Mrs. W. looked pleased.

Another caseworker told of how a parent had been "resisting" her pressure to talk to the child about the adoption; after a group meeting on the subject, the worker had read the record and it had "opened her eyes" to the depth of the problem from the client's perspective. Later, she was able to raise it with the parent again, tempering her approach. In this connection, it should be noted that the group leaders in Adoptions were not promising confidentiality; earlier work in the division had convinced them that the adoptive parents themselves did not want to separate the two experiences. This conviction was borne out as the parents increasingly confided group events and reactions to their caseworkers. And these perceptions were fed into the ongoing exchange between the caseworkers and their counterparts in group service.

Another theme that emerged in the feedback process was the question of how much specific family information the group worker should have before beginning with her group. The issue of how much information would be helpful was raised by the group leaders themselves, precipitating discussion of how the case record should be used, the positive and negative effects of anticipating certain problems and, ultimately, the relationship between *knowing* and *doing* in group practice. There was no attempt to formulate an answer here, for the alternatives would have to be crystallized in the process of work. But there was a tentative synthesis of a construct called the "central problem"—suggesting that any given case record could be distilled into a very few key family issues, and that these central themes would be useful to the group leader as she prepared to move into a new group experience.

On the corollary question of whether the group leaders should work with groups of their own clients or those referred from other caseloads, our approach was to try both of these modes—and a combination of the two—and develop our generalizations from experience. The initial staff predisposition was strongly in favor of "other" rather than "own" clients in the groups; but the worker whose groups contained both reported that it seemed to make little difference. Her working problems remained essentially the same and as the group interaction developed she could detect no tendencies to exploit special positions or to use her in any way other than that of the helper in the group. However, here again more experience will be needed before any firm positions can be taken.

There was a distinct advantage, in the fourth year, in having a format in which they could staff two groups at a time and then repeat the whole experience with two new groups and a change of workers. Working concurrently with two groups took some of the pressure off each worker and gave the staff a chance to make some distinctions between problems of personal style and those inherent in the work itself. Staffing two complete series in turn offered them the opportunity to reexperience the several stages of work—the preparation, the beginnings, the mutual aid and the endings—and to test their growing knowledge as they went through each set of problems a second time. And it was clear that the learnings from the first round were put to use in the second.

As we worked, I was able to feed in references to similar problems and experiences that were coming through in my consultations with the Division of Foster Home Care—on the confidentiality issue, the tasks of group formation, casework-group feedback and the stages of work. These references were supportive, as they pointed up similar tasks in both divisions, tied both efforts to a larger program and offered specific suggestions based on related work in another corner of the agency.

A final comment should be made on the brief but important experience with the one-meeting groups of new applicants for adoption. Here the stake of the agency was to create a break in the long wait after application and a transition between the first inquiry and the interview; to save some time by taking this step in a group; to provide the kind of preliminary work that would quicken and deepen the work of the first interview; to bring the "mythology of adoption" into the open and handle common concerns; and to explain the service in simple, non-jargonized terms. In this work, the beginnings highlighted the worker's effort to move from the members' expectations to those of the agency and combine both in a brief working contract. In the main body of the meeting, the focus was on the skill of "telling" and "listening" almost at the same time, combining facts with feelings so that misconceptions could be freely aired, real expectations simply interpreted and the first real client-agency encounter brought off with a minimum of defensiveness by either party. The termination process was then seen as a transition to the ensuing casework that would take the client through application, study, and on. The one-session group gave us the opportunity to study the working construct of beginning, middle and end as it applied in the space of a single meeting.

The Homefinding Groups

The problems of the one-session group were most sharply focused in the work of the Division of Homefinding, where group efforts had been going on for some time and the one-meeting model received its greatest impetus. This vehicle—used mostly with prospectives and applicants—presented skill problems somewhat similar to those of short contact casework, where many feelings, ideas and expectations have to be dealt with in a very short time. In these brief sessions, the worker was beset by a host of apparently conflicting demands: she had many "facts" to dispense, but knew they would not be heard or remembered if she lapsed into a long and boring account; she wanted to "get at their feelings," but time was pressing and she found it hard to listen as well as she knew how; she must impress the applicants with the seriousness of the enterprise, but not scare them off; she wanted a dialogue, and group interaction, but there were many things to "cover" and she could not trust them to raise all the proper questions.

The work on these concerns came through in consultation somewhat as follows:

> *February 17, 1965:* Presentation by Miss L., Homefinding: A single group meeting with prospective foster parents. On a question from another supervisor, she explained that the invitation to the meeting followed a telephone inquiry, SSE clearance based on the inquiry form, a postcard return from the prospective to the meeting invitation, and the mailing of the application form to the prospective parent; they may bring the application with them, or they may mail it in.
>
> In answer to my question about how she felt about the meeting, Miss L. said that she'd been a bit disturbed that some of the questions she'd expected didn't come out. Like what? The amount of time they'd be allowed to keep the child, the problem of giving it up, etc. I asked: Did she raise this herself, as something they might be concerned about? Miss L.: (embarrassed) No.
>
> After some more questions and answers on procedure, Miss L.: "Mostly, I felt like I was lecturing too much." And, "I wanted them to identify with the children" . . . the fact that they're not so different from other children, etc. She didn't feel she'd accomplished that.
>
> I had them all start from the beginning—tune in before the meeting—a member said this would be experienced by the prospectives as a pleasant experience, anticipation, etc. Mrs. S.: They'll be thinking, will the agency accept me? How much red tape will I have to go through? Mrs. A.: They'll feel good about being invited. Also, they'll feel like they're on inspection, they'll be on guard, best foot forward. And, most important, they'll be feeling partly, do they really want a child, now that it might be close. I picked up on this last: Do you want this ambivalence to come out? Yes, immediately. I: Then you'll have to reach for it. More tuning in: Do I want to be with these others? Am I the same as them? The class distinctions.
>
> Among the implications of these thoughts: How realistic is it to shoot right at the outset for Miss L.'s objective of having them identify with the children? Not very, and Miss L. saw it immediately.
>
> Based on this tuning in, we moved to the record of the meeting . . . what were Miss L.'s aspirations? She listed: Convince them to stop shopping; that our kids are not easy; that this is an important job, has status. Then she said: "I should have left out all the agency history—it took forever—about 20 minutes too long." Mrs. A. suggested they could do some of this in a brochure and Miss L. agreed. I pointed up: The usual mode is first to talk and then to listen—how about turning it around—*first listen and then talk.* This would give you a chance to say what you want to say, but to do it *in the context of work* and feedback. I asked Miss L. how that sounded—was it feasible? Yes, very definitely.

> Having discussed Miss L.'s aspirations for the meeting, we moved to what the parents wanted . . . then, Mr. C. (with his ideas) on discipline, etc. What does he represent? The other side of the coin—my caution to the worker not to flatten it out, but to use Mr. C. as a kind of "Mr. Id." saying things others might feel but not be able to say. There was also some work on a mother and father not agreeing on a point (helping them accept the idea that they need not present a united front, either to the children or to the agency).
> On the *home study* theme: Miss L. answers some excellent questions and there is a good flow of talk and feeling. Her role? She says: "to keep the questions coming—the time is passing." . . . the worker can work *harder* when the discussion goes well—not a "discussion leader" who has no work to do when the (talk) is moving well.
> They made an important point about the parents' perfectionistic model of what the agency will be looking for in the home study; at least say that it is not perfection the agency seeks.
> Some work on the *board rate:* the worker's embarrassment on the money theme is shared by the members; they want more work on this—workers, parents, youngsters, all have feelings about the money angle; need work on how to handle this . . .

The consultation effort was only briefly related to the work in Homefinding, but it was quickly obvious that they had a significant contribution to make to group practice in social work. It seemed clear that their successes—better use of Intake, greater cooperation in the home study, quicker action for the prospective parents and readier identification with the agency—warranted continued use of the group device and study of the skills required to use it well.

> *June 16, 1965:* . . . the hardest thing is to give up the "educational focus" . . . a "teaching point" comes up and they feel: "Do I have to let this go by?" . . . the one-shot meeting is particularly difficult in this respect. . . . Mrs. S. said that . . . "there *is* another shot." More opportunity will arise in the home study to say what you have to say.
> More on skills: L.: How do you get them to talk, and do it fast? (We worked on) the brief and direct statement of purpose; the waiting of silences; handling their productions as they come out. Miss A. talked about their need to *trust* the group process as they have come to have faith in the interview as potentially productive . . .

The Use of Groups in Staff Work

In an article written for the agency's training publication at the end of the first year, I stated the central problem of staff work in these terms:

> The effectiveness of a social agency is finally determined by the skill with which each practitioner carries out its service to people. Behind this work lies an agency structure designed to enrich these skills, increase the

efficiency with which each worker manages his job, and coordinate many workers and their functions into a smoothly articulated whole.

The administrator's concern with these factors—skill, efficiency, and coordination—sets him certain ongoing tasks. His need to sharpen professional techniques makes it necessary to create a process of staff education, through which workers can study their ways of giving service and learn from their successes and failures. His desire to increase efficiency and productivity is a problem in building staff morale and developing positive attitudes toward the job and the agency. And the task of coordinating many different functions calls for a high order of organization, through which each worker understands his own job, respects those of others, and lends himself to the implementation of the necessary regulations and procedures.

The interesting thing about these administrative tasks is that they cannot be accomplished by administrators, that is, they cannot be "legislated" or "administered" from on high, but depend almost entirely on the interest and energy that the staff members themselves are able and willing to throw into them. Thus, the quality of staff education is determined by the extent to which workers feel free to reveal their problems, share their mistakes, and use the wisdom and experience of both their supervisors and their peers. So too, morale is a group product, involving a sense of group support, a feeling of being "in the same boat," and an atmosphere in which workers can draw strength from each other as they face common problems. And the business of organizing human beings into a harmonious unit of work hangs on their ability to lend themselves wholeheartedly—which means privately as well as publicly—to the job of making policies and procedures come alive in action. The old folk saying about leading a horse to water is nowhere so amply demonstrated as in the complexities of an agency culture, where the subtle operation of hostilities, confusions, and simple ignorance can so effectively undercut policies on which everybody is in apparent agreement.

It is this interdependence of administrators, supervisors, and practitioners that makes the regular, problem-solving, face-to-face staff meeting so important in the life of the agency.[50] (Emphasis added.)

This part of the consultation program was thus addressed to the skills with which supervisors could help staff members work together more effectively to improve the service of the agency. It was a hard, pragmatic exercise with real, day-to-day problems, and not an attempt to introduce exotic new group techniques to enliven staff meetings. Nor was it for the purpose of doing "group therapy" on agency time:

March 25, 1964: (A group of unit supervisors, discussing a "resistive" worker at a unit meeting, and whether they would want his attitudes to be brought into the open) . . . I sharpen it further: When you have a resistive client, what do you do? Mr. C.: Get at the underlying feeling. I role-played the resistance, and they pitched in, alive, talking to each other, talking without raising their hands, a high degree of affect. J.: Is this close to the role of therapist? In answer, I took them through some of their feelings about presenting material in our group—they talked about the embarrassment, the fear of exposure, etc. I asked: Is *this* "therapy?" J.: No. Why not? Well, it's close to what we're supposed to be doing together; it's about our work. Precisely.

The work on staff group leadership was begun by the administrators in the first year of consultation. Subsequent staff populations that used consultation in this area were the Assistant Supervisors in the second year, and the Case Supervisors in the third.

First Steps

The first-year activity of the administrators[51] laid the basis for much of the work that was to come. First, they put to use a frame of reference that helped them seek out the common elements in *all* their group attempts. The definition of a group—any face-to-face group—as a "collection of people who need each other to work on certain common tasks, in a setting that is hospitable to those tasks" pointed up the need for workers in all groups to understand collective behavior, to help the members help each other, to make the "demand for work," to focus the limited and specific tasks for which they had come together and to help clarify the group's relationship to its setting.

Second, they examined these connections in action, using their own practice—in both staff and client groups—to define the skills they used to prepare for a meeting, to establish purpose, to help the members talk to each other in real terms and to make the transitions from encounter to encounter.

Finally, having established the common core of work in all their groups, the administrators were in a position to make some of the genuine distinctions that emerged from differences in group composition and purpose. In this connection, the members of consultation Group I uncovered many of the major problems of staff group leadership that were to appear again and again in the later work with the Assistant and Case Supervisors. For example, many of their presentations illustrated the problem of the "false consensus," in which staff workers "agree" on a course of action, only to fail repeatedly to implement it. Here the supervisor's frustration is born of the fact that he can raise neither disagreement nor compliance, but only acceptance of the logic of the official position and an implacable inability to do anything about it. In most of the meetings reported—on instituting new forms, keeping dictation up to date, carrying out new service decisions and others—it was not open, or even conscious, defiance that held up the action. Rather, it was a kind of bland passivity that muffled the feelings and immobilized the energy either for or against the move. What had happened was that the "rightness" of the decision had been so incontrovertibly established—by both supervisor *and* workers—that one would require great courage to mention any of the lurking negatives, even though they were there, and would thereafter proceed to work underground. In this climate, the staff had made what we came to call a "New

Year's resolution," in which the will is registered, but the work necessary to make it function has been left out. In the following, a Case Supervisor in Group I records a meeting with four unit supervisors, on the problem of incomplete dictation:

> I began by saying that one of the purposes of the meeting was to discuss the workers' failure to dictate their contacts regularly and to examine together how this relates to the effectiveness of their supervision. I said that I was shocked, as they knew, with what I had found and I was sure this bothered them too . . . Admission that this was true was general . . .
> I emphasized that training from case material was one of the biggest tools of supervision. Workers are helped to identify problems and attitudes and to plan treatment. While the group accepted this in principle (how can one train without the case record?) one who had the most difficulty in this area said, "They (meaning the administration) are living in a dream world." I asked, "They?" She got the point. They protested that our area had more pendings than other areas and I said that I was aware of it and would be discussing this on a higher level with a view towards relief, but am concerned about the relaxation of adherence to conference schedules by the supervisors, as well as the dictation schedules of the workers. Didn't they think that regularity in this area would save time in the end? . . .
> There was discussion around how the "ideal" could be implemented. Active discussion regarding what was needed followed . . .
> I ended the meeting with a reminder that keeping recording current is an agency requirement. We agreed we will be discussing in individual conferences our progress in the areas that were reviewed in this meeting.

With all the work there was to be done, it was easy to understand this relentless march toward the "New Year's resolution." But the fact remained that the "rightness" of a decision rarely generated the energy necessary to carry it out, and the administrators were forced by their own experience to look closely at what they knew about the mechanisms of resistance, how they operated with staff-people as well as client-people, and the skills required to reach deeply for doubts and ambiguities, bring them into the open and help workers make decisions they could own and live with.

Out of this problem came another, closely related. It was no accident that the "we versus they" question was raised—and stifled—in the excerpt above; the we-they issue was almost always involved in the problem of the false consensus. For, in order to derive some hope from an open and direct confrontation of issues, one had to believe that staff and administration could find some common ground on which to develop strategies of service that both could own and act upon. Was there a real relationship between the stake of the agency and that of its workers? Was it always a "versus" or could the administrator find the common interest between them—not in broad, philosophical terms, but on a given problem of service? Much of the we-they feeling is certainly inevitable in any worker-employer relationship, and particularly in a large bureaucracy. But in every meeting record we examined, on every specific practice question, the motives of staff and administration could be harnessed so that the job that brought them together could be done more effectively. Both had a stake in solving the problem—because it would make their jobs easier and more enjoyable, because they wanted a better service to people and because their own performance would look better in the process. And the administrator's skill lay in finding the way—often tangled and obscure—to this common ground. Where he could not find it, all the exhorting, persuading and cajoling he could muster would not produce the action he needed on any important problem. But where he could, he was able to precipitate an open and dignified problem-solving process that had at least the ring of reality, however difficult the issue.

There were other staff-group problems that were first explored by the administrators in Group I. The phenomenon of the "informal system" was examined when a Case Supervisor from the Division of Allocation and Maternity Shelter Care offered a record describing her work in opening up a situation in which her staff, faced with a private agency with which they had a problem, had "solved" the problem, tacitly and without discussion, by simply ceasing to make referrals. Another issue was that of the relationship between "forms and philosophy," which was discussed when records showed how supervisors often created artificial distinctions between "cut-and-dried" procedures—that could presumably be "disposed of" quickly, at the beginning of a meeting—and the "deeper" problems of professional practice. They found instead that these were two sides of the same coin: what started as the introduction of yet another printed form often called up serious questions about agency philosophy; and discussions of "professional" issues would precipitate a close interest in the paperwork necessary to carry them forward in a new direction.

By the end of this first period, certain ideas had been rather thoroughly investigated and were fairly well established as guidelines for future work. The use of group processes as an aid in agency work was accepted and the administrators felt somewhat more confident in their ability to give leadership to small group discussion. The "group work" expertise was not as mysterious as it had appeared to them at the outset. They saw connections between some familiar social work skills and the group skills they wished to acquire. And they had become acutely aware of the need to provide a clear focus of work in the staff meeting; their case presentations showed a growing ability to eschew the vague and abstract statements of purpose and to move their people directly into what they were supposed to be talking about.

Other problems were more tenacious. The practice of facilitating free discussion and creative group thinking was easier in the conceptualizing than in the doing, and they were frustrated by the frequency with which they had been so intent on delivering their message that they could not listen for underlying cues, even where they "knew" that this would help in reaching a solution. The faith in explanations and exhortations was also hard to overcome, though again they "understood" that simply being right about a problem did not always get them the action they needed. And the specific skills involved in partializing problems, making connections with prior events and helping staff members use each other's strengths would require continuous testing and improving. Much of this work was elaborated and deepened in the work that followed.

The Assistant Supervisors

As I described earlier,[52] the unit supervisors were organized into three consultation groups, numbering about 35 in each. Each group met once a month and our purpose was to work on the skills required to use their unit meetings as a more effective educational and administrative instrument.

The planning for these meetings began with the administrators and extended into the first sessions of each consultation group. The administrators discussed group formation and decided to organize the three groups heterogeneously, across divisional lines and combining older and younger workers. They speculated about what they thought the Assistant Supervisors needed and identified several themes: many had recently been promoted from the ranks and were shaky about role-switch from social investigator to supervisor, teacher and—most frightening—"boss"; there was some fear of the unit meeting itself as a working device; the younger supervisors were apprehensive about working with both older and younger caseworkers in their units—some of their veteran workers had been there much longer than they; and all of them had the normally overwhelming problems of caseload management, staff morale and the supervision of workers in need of considerable help. And finally, we discussed the interaction of my work and theirs, touching on how they, the administrators, could help the unit supervisors prepare their presentations and the importance of keeping the staff leadership problems on their own supervisory agendas.

This tuning-in provided some valuable clues to the problems ahead. But the full dimensions of the job and the real poignancy of the Assistant Supervisor's position in the agency came through only as the first sessions began. It was soon apparent that the motives for the work were far from clear: several were not holding unit meetings at all and many others were using the device sporadically; some pointed to worker resistance, others blamed administration for ordering unit meetings but giving them no place to get together except restrooms, hallways and interview cubbies, and a good many confessed that they were at a loss as to what to do with such meetings; and there was a strong feeling throughout the groups that there were so many urgent and pressing problems in "the job itself" that supervision and training were luxuries they could not afford.

As I encouraged them to move into more detailed discussion of their jobs, their difficulties and their aspirations, they described the "box" of the Assistant Supervisor, as they felt it: he is caught between the workers of the front line and the administrators at the rear; he has no real power and it is not his job to "rock the boat"; he is, in effect, a *messenger* between the workers and those who have real authority. When they looked at their own supervisors, they wondered how interested they were in the problems of the unit supervisor; and when they looked at their workers, they saw people so bogged down with work that all these supervisory devices seemed like so many interruptions and academic exercises.

> *November 13, 1963:* (Unit supervisors discussing supervisory processes and unit meetings) . . . A supervisor saw it through a worker's eyes: "We carry the heaviest load that any human being was ever asked to carry—(so) who needs all that leadership?"

Nevertheless, along with these expressions of irritation and self-doubt, there was a strong current of curiosity, pride of work and a stubborn desire to master their job. The "social criticism" was sharp, astute and real enough; but the day-to-day work of administering a unit was also real, and they wanted to be good at it. And these questions, too, began to emerge: How do you induce workers to speak up at a meeting? How do you "make it interesting" for them, so that the meetings would be "something to look forward to?" So many of the meetings, they said, were simply procedural and hence pretty boring. We can teach them procedures, but we don't seem to be able to get them to share their real feelings with us; and this has something to do with the general problem of raising group morale within the unit.

These first meetings also included some didactic work on my part, offering a few ideas on the meaning of group experience, the concept of mutual aid and the importance of watching our own group as a kind of laboratory of group processes and leadership.

Finally, the initial sessions were used to work out a plan for recording and presenting accounts of their unit meetings. These materials were duplicated and distributed before the sessions in which they were presented for discussion. In most instances, two presentations were made at a single consultation session, and these generally illustrated work in two different divisions. One of the peripheral benefits of the program was that many of the unit supervisors learned, for the first time, something of the workings and problems of other divisions within the Bureau.

From that point—working as always, line-by-line from their recorded accounts—we proceeded to develop their themes of concern. Again as always, the first major problem was that of learning to make a clear beginning, with a direct statement of what a meeting was to be about, rather than a vague or global opening designed to hide the supervisor's real intent. The "hidden agenda" was a frustrating device for both workers and supervisor:

> The supervisor was recently transferred from an operating unit in the Division of Intake to the Application Unit. With a recognition of the fact that the Application Unit is a focal point of the agency, I observed the activity of the workers and I had a growing awareness of the tendency of staff to see themselves functioning only in the peripheral areas of the total agency's services.

> This was (my) first meeting with the unit. The agenda was prepared by the unit supervisor (me) following a conference with the Case Supervisor. Workers were informed of the date of the meeting and the general content of the agenda. It was held in one of the small interviewing booths . . .
>
> The Unit Supervisor opened the meeting by asking whether the workers had any pressing problems which they might want to discuss. There was no response. The leader asked the group what their feelings were in relation to the number of changes in supervisors over a short period of time. It was generally accepted that the unit's routine was proceeding as established by the previous supervisors . . .
>
> The meeting was planned because of the apparent apathy, differences in attitudes and approaches by the different workers. Individual conferences and review of case records indicated a general lack of involvement by the workers prior to the trial discharge period . . .
>
> The leader opened the meeting by introducing the topic and reviewing basic concepts pertaining to the procedures and policies of BCW as they applied to the workers' involvement in the pre-discharge plan . . .

The work on beginnings began with the tuning-in exercise previously described,[53] extended to the involvement of staff in the agenda-making process and took them, ultimately, into the heart of the problem of direct and honest communication with their workers. In this context, they began to work on the task of dealing with feelings openly rather than allowing them to go underground and take their course at the coffee sessions of the informal system. When the unit supervisors decided that they would rather have unit decisions made before their eyes—*at* the meetings rather than *outside* them—they began to examine the techniques that tended to encourage evasion and false consensus and discourage public discussion of troublesome issues. They were then able to examine the fact that they "generally do all the talking," that they somehow perceive directness and assertiveness as "rude" or "impolite," and that their timidity in reaching for what they wanted made it hard for their workers to deal openly with difficult subjects. And it was exactly these difficult areas—problems of morale, attitudes toward the agency, feelings about work, confusions about the service—that the supervisors needed most to bring into the open.

In the course of the work, they kept returning to the problem of identification, expressing a deep concern about the role of the Assistant Supervisor in the agency hierarchy. On the one hand, they defined themselves as practitioners, working close to the line of service. On the other, there was considerable pressure, both internal and external, to identify themselves as "bosses," as figures of administrative authority. As this conflict became clearer to them, they discussed the dilemma and how it intruded itself into the different areas of their work.

> *March 11, 1964:* Miss S. said: We need an "our group" feeling, vis-a-vis administration, and workers need to trust us in what we transmit to

> administration—they need to know that we are discreet. I asked: *Are* your workers afraid to talk, lest they will be discussed with superiors? No, they said, they didn't think so. Miss A.: Who *is* administration? Isn't it us? I said: You seem to feel like both, workers and administration, alternately. L. affirms this strongly; he objects to the notion of "I'll pass it on to *them*" and says "we *are* them!" M. responded to my comments: "We *are* both—rank-and-file *and* supervisors—this is our strength—we should understand the problems of both." D. likes this point; so do I, and drive it home.

There was considerable work on how people behave in the small group climate and how the interactive process can be helped along by the group leader. This took them to the problem of silences, passivity and resistance and they became interested in the various forms taken by this resistance as it appeared in their unit meetings. They illustrated many of these in their presentations: as when workers "accepted" orders too readily, without expressing any reservations at all; where they listened selectively, remembering and forgetting according to their needs; where they used discussion as a way of avoiding action, rather than precipitating it; when the talk became elaborate, abstract and devoid of affect; and other ways of producing what we came to know as the "illusion of work."

Most difficult for them was their attempt to come to terms with the fact that effective supervision and unit leadership called for an ability to encourage freedom and initiative, as well as discipline. They could see, and had experienced it many times, that repression and over-conformity served only to harden resistance to learning, that these worked against group morale and that they needed ways to stimulate continuous communication about feelings, attitudes and work frustrations, as they arose. But they were afraid that free discussion would "get out of hand," that "our supervisors really don't want this kind of thing," and that conditions in the Department were so difficult to change that it would be both futile and dangerous to encourage open discussion on most issues.

> *December 18, 1963:* (Unit supervisors, discussing a record of a unit meeting, called to handle the "confusion, irritations and uncertainties on the part of staff as to what was expected of them, both with respect to their own job functions and their relationships with two new supervisory persons") . . . Discussion lively. They want to know: Were workers taken into account in making the administrative change? Apparently not. I asked: What kinds of things would you like to have happen as you move into this meeting? What would you like to see come out? Mrs. W., with others pitching in, make several points, all of them having to do with some complaint they want to see voiced. Then she said many of these did come out and she feels there is stuff for many meetings to come. "We learned a great deal." I pushed: "What did you learn?" As she talked, an important thread became visible: (her workers were saying) "There's too much supervision going on around here." That's what her workers are

> thinking. I asked: "Why isn't this on the agenda? Do you want it out?" They asked a question: "What do you do when you have a hunch like that, and it may be wrong?" I turned it back: "What do you do with your hunches in casework?" You usually play it, is the answer. I: Then what about here?
>
> Then it comes out: What about the attitudes of administration; such gripe sessions can "get out of hand." I point it up: Their conflict between the need to encourage freedom and the need to sweep stuff under the carpet, for fear it may look too messy. I also stressed that this kind of conflict is no reflection on them, but is always part of the work, especially in a big bureaucracy. They were thoughtful, this was it, but not, I think, too hopeful about working on it: it's too big, to pervasive. Go fight City Hall."

The bind around "letting sleeping dogs lie" had several ramifications for them. First, it was very hard for the unit supervisors, feeling as powerless as they did, to encourage others to work more independently, more assertively and more hopefully to make some impact on their surroundings. Second, they had the feeling that they were asking their workers to "do as I say, not as I do," since they were as cautious and conforming with their own Case Supervisors as their workers were with them.

> *February 26, 1964:* I talked about their problem of "waking people up," while they themselves often preferred to let sleeping dogs lie. If meetings are so important to them in their work, why do they let them sink to such a low level of priority? Their work as supervisors makes them an enemy of passivity: yet they have so much of it themselves, right? This hits home—and they get into their own resistance to being "the boss"; many of them have only recently come out of the ranks. Intensive discussion here, alive and meaningful.

Finally, and most important for our purposes, they correctly interpreted the consultation process itself as an attack on hidden agendas, and they resisted it in many of the same ways they were experiencing resistance from their own workers. The effect was to produce a sporadic way of working, alternating periods of apathy and inertia with flashes of feeling and creative work. But it also produced before our eyes many of the very conditions that troubled them, and about which they were trying to learn. About midway in the consultation period, I confronted each group with its way of working and asked them to come to grips with how they were using consultation. They made a thoughtful and serious response and it was at this point that they were able to crystallize many of their deepest feelings and ideas about their work.

In each group, this confrontation session marked a turning point in our work together, and it was thus in the context of their own groups that they could see how fuzziness and fear could hinder creative work among people and how a direct and honest attempt to deal with the feelings could trigger deeper work and some hope for future possibilities.

> *March 25, 1964:* (Mr. C. presents his record of a unit meeting in which he set out "to obtain more cooperation, freer expression, function more as a unit . . . to confront the group . . . with some of their shortcomings, as a means of galvanizing the meeting.") . . . Mr. C. says he took his cue from *my* confrontation of this group at our last session; at this time, he realized that what I had done had started *him* to talking at our meetings; he had decided he would try this with his unit. He feels it worked out; he got what he was after.

> And in the record that Mr. C. presented:
> Supervisor said that he felt unit meetings were degenerating into his telling them what procedures to follow, etc., and this was ineffective. Several workers felt this was not the case. They felt that they profited by this method. I brought up the fact that the group was never chosen a topic for discussion . . .
> (After some discussion) Supervisor cited an example of several cases that had come up recently . . . in which one of the workers had much experience . . . it was felt she could help the supervisor and the other workers by sharing her knowledge. The worker said that she would gladly help any workers who came to her individually . . .
> (After more work, the supervisor notes) . . . there is now a certain readiness to go on to more imaginative uses (of the unit meeting) after working through the negative feelings . . . the worker who was initially opposed to the idea of sharing experience and knowledge at the meeting manifested (later) an astounding change of attitude in actually sharing her knowledge at this meeting.

Having taken hold of the possibility that they might, through their own skills, take some real control of the unit of service that belonged to them, they moved with great strength into the specific skills they needed—the listening, the partializing, the connecting of events, the reaching for negatives, the demand for work, the focusing of affect, the transitions, the agenda-making, and others.

Several of the presentations focused on problems in interagency work, where an Assistant Supervisor met with personnel from other social agencies and institutions in the community. It became clear from their records that these meetings often take place without any real notion of auspice, that neither agency takes any responsibility for agenda preparation or leadership in the work of the meeting and that, again, the "let's just talk" syndrome militates against the implementation of agreements; somehow, if everyone "gets things off his chest," things will be put right. We worked on the task of focusing the problem on which the agencies were meeting, putting aside the myth that they have met "just to get to know each other" and moving directly to the business at hand.

In addition, there was even more serious work involved in their discussions of interagency relationships. There was a strong tendency for the BCW supervisors to enter their meetings with the "professionals" from the private agencies burdened with strong feelings of inferiority. Later, a unit supervisor pointed out with some warmth that it was time public agency people stopped approaching their work with the private agencies as if they were second-class citizens. "We are a responsible agency!" she protested, and they worked well on how such attitudes made their impact in the unit meetings. Interestingly, they could also see from these records that there were lower positions in the agency pecking order; there were agencies—for example, the public schools—that they rated lower in the status hierarchy and to which they felt superior. Here the roles were reversed and the unit supervisors talked about "what we want them to know," "how they will misuse our information," and so on. The meetings between agencies often took on the character of councils of war, rather than efforts to seek meaningful collaboration between institutions with clients in common. In this connection, we worked on how, with attitudes clearer, purposes acknowledged, discussion focused and leadership skills applied, these encounters could be more productive for both agencies.

In the final evaluations, much of the work drew its lessons from what had happened in the consultation groups themselves. They reviewed the fuzziness of the initial contract, their inability to take hold until they had worked out their own stake and their fears about being forced into something they did not want to do. They analyzed my leadership role, showing where I had helped, where I had not and how I had "learned from them" as I worked. One said: "I didn't think any change was possible here, but it happened." All agreed that much of the progress dated from the confrontation—my "demand for work"—and several told of how they had subsequently tried this process in their own groups and stimulated more dynamic unit discussions.

It is difficult to assess the actual improvement of group skills; much of the work was clearly a kind of reorientation of approach, a serious examination of their role and expectations and a general preparation for moving more deeply into their work with the units. They gave evidence of trying new techniques, brought back some successes and some frustrations and developed some new perspectives on "rocking the boat" and the possibilities for change. There seemed to be little question that the program stepped up the sheer frequency of unit meetings.

Probably the most significant effect of the program was the considerable attention and recognition given by upper-echelon personnel to the problems of the unit supervisors.[54] Certainly this is a group whose strategic position in the agency calls for the strongest measures of assistance and support.

The Case Supervisors

The Case Supervisors' consultation group, formed in the third year,[55] consisted of 35 experienced professionals, most of whom had already been involved in some aspect of the consultation program—either in the administrative groups or in those of the placement divisions. Thus, the conceptual language and framework for working with groups were somewhat familiar to them and we could move quickly into the details of their work with the unit supervisors.

After the second-year consultations with the Assistant Supervisors, a follow-up program had been organized under the leadership of the BCW Training Director: teams of two and three Case Supervisors worked with stable groups of Assistant Supervisors, meeting bi-weekly over a six-month period; the Case Supervisors changed roles, serving alternately as leader, recorder and observer, and collaborated in planning and evaluating their group sessions; a syllabus was written by them and put to use as a guiding device; and various forms of recording were employed—by the leader, by the recorder, and in some instances a kind of postmortem worker account of the leadership problems that had arisen at the meeting. The groups were formed in two ways: some were organized within their own divisions, with their own Case Supervisors acting as group leaders; others were formed of unit supervisors from different divisions, representing a wider range of experience. The consultation program was, of course, only a small part of this total effort; I joined the Case Supervisors and the Training Director once a month for a two-hour session.

In the beginning, there was considerable interest in how they could use their training syllabus as an educational tool. The problem was basic, since it contained within it the crucial "content-process" issue, in which they must learn to integrate their "teaching points" with the inductive, step-by-step way in which people actually build ideas that will be useful to them. Later, there was pressure from the unit supervisors to share the syllabus with them, against the feeling of some Case Supervisors that the instrument was not designed for that purpose.

> *December 2, 1964:* When I arrived, discussion was under way . . . they were talking about whether they should or should not respond to the demand of the unit supervisors . . . for the syllabus to be shared with them. They see it as a "secret weapon" that the Case Supervisors have prepared for—or against—them. The Case Supervisors are now concerned both about the syllabus decision and the "original illness" that makes the unit supervisors so distrustful. There is good sharing and discussion going on at this point. Miss Y.: "The agenda items we drew up together were pitiful—we're just now, after three sessions, beginning to be ready to work together." Another: "We have to reread the fine print in our 'contract'."
>
> . . . somewhere along here, I wondered whether the best way to get the syllabus problem off their backs was to give it to the unit supervisors if they wanted it . . . nods at this point, but Mrs. O. . . . would like more work on this . . .
>
> I moved to: the "knowledge fallacy" . . . everybody has a piece of this feeling—that somehow to *know* is to ward off the evil. A.: But their having the syllabus doesn't have to stifle the discussion. I asked: Does anybody have the feeling that "it would give the show away"? Reaching for what is really bothering them about all this. No, they said, but I noticed that the discussion was now turning from *whether* to distribute the outline, to *how* to issue it and use it.

The decision was soon made to make the syllabus available, if only to eliminate the battle of wills so that the real work could proceed. The apprehension about "secret weapons" was part of an interesting ambivalence about the whole problem of open communication within the agency. There was, for example, considerable attention given—by both Assistant and Case Supervisors—to the wording of minutes, the role of recording and the sharing of documents: on the one hand, they were cautious about making certain realities part of a written account—and were upset with me when I mentioned, in my Second Report, their sense of inferiority vis-à-vis the private agencies; on the other, however, they were eager to put it all down, so that their superiors would receive the full impact of what was going on.

The reconciliation of "process" and "content"—how to address themselves *simultaneously* to the "*how* to work" and "*what* to work on"—was the most persistent technical theme in the work with the Case Supervisors. Their small group leadership brought them closer to this problem than ever before; with considerable discipline and courage, they dug again and again into the complexities of their own material. In record after record, it was clear that the "what" and the "how" were contained in each other: when they "analyzed their feelings" in the group, it was unproductive and irritating unless it was somehow related to their work together and what they were supposed to be learning; and when the leader began to "worry about the content," it became mechanical, abstract and without emotional investment. But when there was "feeling in pursuit of a task," the "content" was alive with feeling and the "process" was about the work of the agency:

> One young supervisor raised specific questions throughout the sessions; he seemed to be struggling to demonstrate that he could participate, at the same time that he showed real concern about understanding the conceptual material. Thus, when I offered a verbal transition from a report of an individual conference to . . . how a worker's . . . agenda affects the content of the . . . conference, (he) saw no correlations. When he further asked if "we should always handle a worker's personal problems," I realized that the group was not ready to move on, and encouraged clarification of the problem presented in the conference material . . .
> . . . as the meeting continued . . . I was impressed by the participation of several members who were quite involved in the material. The member who had raised the initial questions about the material then asked what he should do when his workers disagree with agency policy. Should he always agree with them? This led to a consideration of what is policy, is it fixed, etc.
>
> The next half hour was characterized by group interaction as we related to a worker's written agenda (raising) questions as to interpreting policy to foster parents. The group was initially hesitant about relating to this material . . . but what then began to come through was a hesitant attempt to speculate whether we could learn anything about this worker and her relationships with families from the questions she raises in her . . . agenda for the conference. The most difficulty was experienced by the member

> who had raised the most questions . . . the most hostile was the member who seemed to be consistently challenging the leader . . . Because of her hostility . . . she was quite verbal . . . in the course of (which) she offered many helpful and concrete suggestions to the beginning supervisor . . .

The records showed a great deal of collaborative work on many of the central problems of the Assistant Supervisor—caseload controls, priority management, unit programming, supervisory techniques, use of the unit meeting, conference planning, the evaluation process, interagency work, routines and procedures, and others. There was also considerable preoccupation with their own group events, in which they paid close attention to their own model of group learning and the Case Supervisor's model of leadership. In this connection, the Case Supervisors began to build some generalizations about the twin themes of group help: the *intimacy* theme, in which the leader helps the members to use each other in the work; and the *authority* theme, involving their equally complex efforts to use the helping person.

Our most intensive discussions, and the most dramatic demands on their skills, emerged from the professional problems created for them by the aftermath of the Department of Welfare strike in mid-year. Our meeting in February, soon after the strike ended, began with a routine presentation but soon developed into a serious exploration of their feelings about the strike, the bitterness among friends of long standing, the deep estrangement of strikers and non-strikers at every level of authority, the fear of feelings run rampant ("It's like a war!") and the hopelessness about ever being able to work together again in carrying out the agency's service to its people.

Then gradually, as it became clear that the common ground for all was the desire to take up the work again, the focus of the meeting shifted to the planning of their first post-strike meetings with their groups. In planning their strategies, they drew from their own group process in the consultation session: they agreed that it would be a mistake to impose an "artificial order" by conspiring in a general pretense that nothing had happened; they saw how it was possible to work on common tasks without giving up their differences on the strike issues themselves; they saw that their ability to face the unpleasant issues head-on would help their workers do the same, and then help them do the same for their own staff; and they defined the technical skills that would be required to bring the problems out, handle the recriminations honestly as they came up, focus on what was to be done and use the power of mutual aid to help their people talk to each other about the service of the agency.

> *February 3, 1965:* We began with Mrs. M.'s material. She introduced, describing how she was trying to understand what her group was saying. (I asked her to) tell us how it felt while it was happening. She responded, openly and expressively, and moved to describe her blackboard device, apparently inhibiting to her group; the silence that ensued, and I asked, "What's inside the silence?" (Discussion continues for a few more minutes.) Suddenly, it happened . . . Mrs. D. asked: "How do we face our groups at the next meeting? The strike has been so terrible for

all of us . . . some stayed in (did not strike), some went out, long-standing friendships have broken up . . . how do we pick up the threads now?" More specifically, she wanted to know: Shall we just begin to work, as you just did? Or should we ask them to talk about the strike more self-consciously?

I invited the work, and they plunged in with much feeling. They talked about the prevailing "which side are you on?" running through the agency, the bitterness about who had stayed in and who had gone out; there was much need to justify their own positions on the strike . . . they rehashed, and I didn't try to stop it. Somebody (mentioned) the "selective communication" now going on: people are afraid to talk frankly about the strike—the coming back, the bitterness, etc. Many feel the bad part will go away somehow, they don't know how, if they don't talk about it.

Miss Y., very shrewdly: The strike crisis was a huge symbol of the whole authority thing—we can't be so "comfortable" any more in our own authority; we can't avoid the authority thing and hope that people will cooperate "voluntarily." As the *horizontal* lines get stronger—the strength between peers—the *vertical* ones get weaker, unless they are formally strengthened and paid attention to. Mrs. M., in another way: "The workers have shown that they *can* fight City Hall!"

I tried to clarify this feeling: "If they don't work for *us* personally, because they like us, what's left?" W.: "The work is left." I agreed heartily—perhaps they could now see and accept . . . the idea of being "boss" and being able to work "aside from friendship." The feeling poured out: Somebody said, "it's like a war!" as they tried to face the implications. Gradually, then, some opposite reactions began to become possible: "There can be respect and liking *and* being boss" . . .

I warned against trying to achieve "artificial order" . . . by reasoning the feeling away: "If they had the facts, they'd have done as I did" . . . the differences remain—between jobs, between levels of work, between political feelings, between orientations toward authority . . . all right, if we don't try to create "artificial commonality," what's *really* common among them all at this point? Answer: Everybody has a stake in getting back to work; everybody wants to reestablish relationships . . . very few really want the bitterness to go on much longer. Can they work on these common tasks without giving up their differences? (The answer is obvious, because that's exactly what they're doing right now between Case Supervisors who went out, those who stayed in, both still feeling betrayed by the others, guilty about what they did, on whatever side . . . D. and F. sit near each other but can hardly look at each other . . . old friends who wound up on opposite sides in this struggle, now estranged but working here very intensely on how to help their workers and themselves get back to work.)

D. (I think it was) asked about my own strategy: Why had I started with Mrs. M.'s record, rather than with the strike issue I knew must be on everybody's mind? I tried to explain: The *work* is the focus for us all, our

> reason for being together; the feeling underneath either facilitates or blocks the work; where it is the latter, the feeling would have to be looked at, and it would be brought out either by them (as happened today) or by me (if they hadn't been able to work and hadn't raised it themselves). To do otherwise, I thought, would be to make a demand on their privacy, a demand not undergirded by the requirements of the work. If it's real, and they need to get to it, it will come . . . if they could work without needing to tackle the problem head-on, then fine, that's what we'd . . . do. I said I didn't know if it would happen that way in their groups, but that's how I had felt it before coming in to work with them today. Perhaps they would like to try it differently, and I'd be interested to have them do so and see what happens. From there to: Strategies for their next meeting with their unit supervisors. What, specifically, are they most afraid of, at these meetings? W.: What to do when the recriminations come up, between strikers and non-strikers . . . they discuss this, what they will try . . . they realize, and I verbalize, that their political feelings . . . will have to be suspended—"a moratorium"—for the two hours of group leadership . . . they will need every ounce of energy for listening, helping, focussing, working . . . (This does not mean that they cannot) make themselves (and their sympathies) clear; (but their workers expect) reassurance that they won't abuse their power by enforcing their own opinions.
>
> I reminded them: This is happening all over town, all over the country, everywhere they've heard about the strike—the tension is echoed, the sides are chosen, the bitterness played over, the needing to get back to work; it hasn't just happened here, even though this was the locale. I reviewed what they have going for them, as they move into their next meetings: aside from their common need to pick up, to give service . . . our work today may help them feel less fear of the ambiguity, the conflict, and have less need to "play nice" and shove the thing under the rug. Their ability to face the uneasiness openly should make it easier for others to do the same, have it out, accept the differences and get back to work. They seemed to feel better about their next move.

In the consultation sessions that followed, several of the presentations were about these post-strike group meetings and there was evidence that this preparation had helped the Case Supervisors work their way through a difficult time. The records were dramatic as they revealed the process through which they tried together to restore an honorable balance: as the unit supervisors picked up the argument and tried to convince each other that they had been right in their respective positions; as they told how terrible the whole experience had been for them and the suffering that ran through it; as they expressed their rage at an administration that had "let it happen"; as they talked about their feelings of hopelessness and helplessness; and, finally, as they began to experience some small sense of mastery in picking up the threads of work and painfully putting staff relationships together again. Following are some brief excerpts from the Recorder's notes of a long meeting of one of the groups:

> . . . The leader encouraged the group by briefly commenting that this was one of the reasons why we should discuss this here and clear the air, for otherwise we are in a state of limbo which will undoubtedly result in impairment of service to clients . . .
>
> Another group member spoke, with tears in her eyes, stating that if those who were *in* gain additional benefits because of those who were *out,* how can she manage her guilt feelings? Other members said that they would have no guilt about achieving benefits and if they had to do it all over again, they would make the same decision. They would not leave their jobs . . . Another group member said emotionally, "What is the purpose of these meetings? Let's lay our cards on the table—what do we as social workers believe in? Has an individual a right to make a decision—it was a nightmare—how I wish it would go away!"
>
> . . . One person felt that even though she had conviction about her decision to come in, she wondered whether her evaluation of the issues meant that she did not feel enough for her fellow workers. She said that she had spoken to enough people in Public Assistance to recognize that their situation may have been intolerable . . . Another, with tears welling, said she did not feel guilty for coming in, but felt keenly for those who were out . . .
>
> Many questions were raised by group members as to why nothing was done to prevent the tremendous amount of dissatisfaction and unrest which was so clearly evidenced by the staff before the demonstration. They wondered if it was possible that the administration really did not know about these basic dissatisfactions . . . how important it is for a person not to be dehumanized . . . to have to resort to a strike to get these needs and feelings made known is a terrible thing . . .
>
> . . . The group recognized that criticism in itself is insufficient and that we have to give concrete suggestions to help the situation . . . some of those who were in, will also do their best to fight for the amendment of the Condon-Wadlin Act . . .
>
> It was mentioned that one of the conditions for returning to work was that there would be no reprisals against those who were in or those who were out, but it is not always possible to legislate feelings. At the end of the meeting, we realized that the discussion had been so earnest and involved that no one even thought of taking our usual break at the end of the first hour.

In the year-end evaluation, the Case Supervisors worked both on summarizing their work together and the skills necessary to help their groups to do the same. In identifying the areas they wished to emphasize in the future, they named the skills of supervision, the use of case materials in individual and group conferences, the specifics of preparation as a working process, the feedback between the staff meeting and the supervisory conference, the importance of maintaining formal supervision at higher levels of authority, the need to enrich the orientation program for new workers, and the importance of addressing themselves to the pervasive sense of powerlessness that seemed to characterize so many of the staff, particularly at the level of practice.

* * * * * * * * *

One can only speculate about what was accomplished here, and what the possibilities are for other programs like it. There is no question about the excitement it created, the attention to practice, the heightened communication among staff—both horizontally and vertically—and the new services to clients.

The institutionalization we strove for came harder; the service caught fast in a few parts of the agency and was probably lost among more pressing priorities in others. But the work throughout was intense and moving, and some difficult but powerful ideas did, I think, find a permanent place, particularly with those who struggled with them again and again—the importance of a clear working "contract," the integration of feeling and action, the power of mutual aid, the need to reach for negatives and tolerate ambiguities, the ability to work step-by-step rather than rushing in with premature "solutions," and others. Above all, there is a new commitment to the concept of *skill*—that is, that "knowledge" and "sensitivity" and "insight" must all pay off in action, in a way of *doing* things that separates the professional from the layman.

On the development of group skills, much remains to be done; but as the work progressed there was little question, in my mind or theirs, that the level of skill was increasing steadily. Some skillful acts were more easily transferable from their casework experience, and after the first shock of "so many of them and only one of me" they began to appear—developing clarity of purpose, focusing the talk, demanding the work and even, after a while, reaching into areas of taboo. Others were harder, like moving directly into areas of high group feeling, helping members elaborate each other's ideas and experiences, helping them turn feelings into action and handling openly their concerted resentments against the worker, fellow professionals and the agency itself. But even these difficulties were beginning to give way, and the later stages produced some moving examples of leadership skill and mutual aid, in both staff and client groups.

There are many counts on which one can, and should, attack the welfare system; but the quality of the people who are trying to make it work is not one of them. This was an amazing group of professionals, in their great capacity for work, their driving intellectual curiosity, their ability to risk themselves in action and their unsentimental but profound commitment to people in need. They and their clients deserve all the help they can get, both from people in authority and—through the small group medium—from each other.

References

1. William Schwartz, "The Social Worker in the Group," *The Social Welfare Forum, 1961* (New York: Columbia University Press, 1961), p. 146.

2. *Ibid.*, p. 148.
3. *Ibid.*, p. 149.
4. The growing literature on the generic characteristics of social work practice is now making its way from the comprehensive attempts of Harriet M. Bartlett ("Toward Clarification and Improvement of Social Work Practice," *Social Work, 3,* 2, (April 1958)) and William E. Gordon ("Toward a Social Work Frame of Reference," *Journal of Education for Social Work, 1,* 2, (Fall 1965)) to some specific efforts to work out the practice and teaching implications of a social work helping process in action. *See,* for example, Beulah Rothman, "Contributions of Probation to Social Work Education Emerging from a Joint Project on Multi-Methods," *Social Work Education Reporter, 14,* 2, (June 1966); Alice Overton, "The Issue of Integration of Casework and Group Work," paper presented at the Annual Program Meeting, Council on Social Work Education, January 1968, mimeo; and Gary A. Lloyd, "Integrated Methods and the Field Practice Course," paper read at the Annual Program Meeting, Council on Social Work Education, January 1968, mimeo.
5. Norman Fenton and Kermit T. Wiltse, *Group Methods in the Public Welfare Program* (Palo Alto, Calif.: Pacific Books, 1963).
6. *See:* Kermit T. Wiltse and Justine Fixel, *The Use of Groups in Public Welfare* (California State Department of Social Welfare, 1962); and *Guide for Use of Group Methods in County Welfare Departments* (California State Department of Social Welfare, 1962).
7. For a further discussion of the Fenton and Wiltse book, *see* my review in *Social Casework, 45,* 4, April 1964, p. 232.
8. *See* Harleigh B. Trecker, *Group Services in Public Welfare,* Bureau of Family Services (Washington, D.C.: Department of Health, Education, and Welfare, 1964); Marjorie Montelius, *Working with Groups: A Guide for Administration of Group Services in Public Welfare,* Bureau of Family Services (Washington: Department of Health, Education, and Welfare, 1966); and *Helping People in Groups: Six Background Papers from the Workshop on Group Services,* Bureau of Family Services (Washington: Department of Health, Education, and Welfare, 1965).
9. *See Training for Service in Public Assistance,* Bureau of Public Assistance (Washington: Department of Health, Education, and Welfare, 1961).
10. *See,* for example, Janice Bowen, *A Study to Determine the Feasibility of Developing a Demonstration Project in Group Care for Young Children within the New York City Department of Welfare* (New York: New York Fund for Children, Inc., 1966); and *Reducing Dependency in AFDC Families Through the Use of Group Treatment* (Palo Alto, California: Santa Clara County Welfare Department and Family Service Association of Palo Alto and Los Altos, 1964).
11. *See,* for example, *Potentials for Service Through Group Work in Public Welfare* (Chicago: American Public Welfare Association, 1962); Louise P.

Shoemaker, "The Use of Group Work Skills with Short Term Groups," in *Social Work With Groups, 1960* (New York: National Association of Social Workers, 1960); Louise C. Youngman, "Social Group Work in the AFDC Program," *Public Welfare, 23,* (January 1965); and Hans S. Falck, "Helping Caseworkers Use the Social Group Method," *Public Welfare, 22* (April 1965); Murray Ortof, "Group Services to Families Receiving ADC," in *Group Method and Services in Child Welfare* (New York: Child Welfare League of America, Inc., 1963).

12. For a detailed discussion of this problem, *see* William Schwartz, "Toward a Strategy of Group Work Practice," *The Social Service Review, 36,* 3 (September 1962).
13. The unduplicated count would include about 300 staff members, since many participated in more than one consultation group.
14. From my Log, November 21, 1962.
15. From my first "Report on Consultations," dated November 1962 to June 1963, mimeo., pp. 11, 12. The four Reports on Consultations and the aforementioned Log, or diary, reproduced the consultation process in some detail as we went along. I will draw on these materials freely in the course of this account, making specific page references only where it serves some particular purpose.
16. "Fourth Report on Consultations—October 1965 to June 1966," p. 6.
17. Adolin Dall and Seymour Fass, "Use of the Group Method with Foster Parents," *Staff Development News, 1,* 2 (Sept.-Nov. 1963), pp. 1, 5.
18. Woodrow W. Carter, "A Group Counseling Program in BCW," *Staff Development News, 2,* 3 (Fall Issue, December 1964), p. 4.
19. William Schwartz, "Some Comments on the Function of the Staff Meeting," *Staff Developments News, 1,* 2 (Sept.–Nov. 1963), pp. 3, 4.
20. Florence E. Boyd, "Work with Adoptive Parents and Recruitment"; Woodrow W. Carter, "The Group Counseling Process as a Helping Tool for Adolescent Foster Children"; Adolin G. Dall, "Instituting Group Work Services for Foster Parents"; and Seymour K. Fass, "The Institutionalization of Group Services through Supervision and Administrative Practice."
21. Adolin G. Dall, "Group Learning for Foster Parents: In a Public Agency," *Children, 14,* 5 (September–October 1967), pp. 185–187; and Woodrow W. Carter, "Group Counseling for Adolescent Foster Children," *Children, 15,* 1 (January–February 1968), pp. 22–27.
22. William Schwartz, ed., *The Practice of Group Work,* soon to be published by the Columbia University Press.
23. Two selections: "At a first meeting of adoptive parents in the supervision period," and "A group of foster parents in a public agency, discussing the child's identity—and theirs," in *The Practice of Social Work with Groups: Some Examples from a Variety of Settings,* casebook of the Annual All-Day Workshop for Field Instructors and Faculty, Columbia University School of Social Work, March 21, 1966.

24. For a description of this latter event, *see:* Esta Bloomfield and Sylvia Goldberger, "Case Supervisors in Public Welfare: Challenge and Reassessment," *Staff Development News, 1,* 2 (Sept.–Nov. 1963), pp. 1, 6.
25. First "Report on Consultations . . .", pp. 6, 7.
26. From the summary of the discussion, first "Report . . .", p. 17.
27. *Ibid.*
28. "Third Report . . .", p. 4.
29. "Fourth Report . . .", pp. 3, 4.
30. "First Report . . .", p. 8.
31. To review the range of recorded experiences presented in these consultation groups, *see* pp. 6, 7.
32. William Schwartz, "Discussion of Three Papers on the Group Method with Clients, Foster Families and Adoptive Families," *Child Welfare, 45,* 10 (December 1966), pp. 573, 574.
33. *Ibid.,* p. 574.
34. *See* pp. 7, 8.
35. "Second Report . . .", p. 3.
36. *Ibid.,* pp. 3, 4.
37. *Ibid.,* p. 4.
38. "Third Report . . .", pp. 3, 4.
39. "First Report . . .", p. 11.
40. *See* p. 7.
41. *See* p. 7.
42. *See* pp. 17, 18.
43. Woodrow W. Carter, "Group Counseling for Adolescent Foster Children," *Children, 15,* 1 (January–February 1968), p. 26.
44. *See* p. 7.
45. *See* p. 8.
46. From the worker's report, March 8, 1964 through May 20, 1964, Division of Foster Home Care, Bureau of Child Welfare, New York City Department of Welfare. Mimeo., p. 1.
47. *See* p. 26.
48. *See* Adolin G. Dall, "Group Learning for Foster Parents: In a Public Agency," *Children, 14,* 5 (September–October 1967), p. 186.
49. *See* p. 7.
50. William Schwartz, "Some Comments on the Function of the Staff Meeting," *1,* 2 (Sept.–Nov. 1963), pp. 3, 4.
51. *See* pp. 6-7 and 11-19.
52. *See* pp. 7, 8.
53. *See* pp. 13 and 21.
54. *See* p. 16-17.
55. *See* p. 9.

The Use of Groups and School Social Work Function

William Schwartz

I have the distinct feeling that the important part of the meeting is really over—so many wonderful and interesting things happened that I got all caught up in them, and I'm ready to join. You know—show me where to go! The fact of the matter is, that as your chairman indicated, I'm no stranger to the affairs of the Association. A part of every dinner hour is devoted to them at home, so "me and the kids" are quite the experts on the affairs of your group. The fact of the matter is, from my point of vantage as a social work teacher, and more particularly as a group work teacher, I have been interested for a long time in the role of the social worker in schools—even, I might say, before my wife took the job.

My wife, if I may take a moment, is one of our symbols at the school of a generic social worker, the reason being that she works wherever I happen to be, so that the closest job might be that of psychiatric or school social worker or medical social worker, but whatever it is she does it and she is a kind of living proof of the fact that it really is a generic craft.

The reason I'm particularly interested in the school setting and have been for a long time is that it has seemed to me that in all the settings in which social workers find themselves, the school dramatizes most effectively several problems with which social workers struggle no matter what the setting in which they work. One of these problems is the complex of tasks and problems that large and complicated systems take on, in reaching out to incorporate and to integrate the people they serve. The second major area of problems are those of the people who try to make use of these complicated bureaucracies and systems that are supposed to serve them, and finally, the problems of social work as it tries to take up some kind of a stance, a position vis-a-vis with both of these major sets of problems; that is, those of the system with respect to its people and those of the people with respect to the system. In

Schwartz, William. (1969, May). The use of groups and school social work function. *Paper presented at the New York State School Social Workers Association, Saratoga Springs, NY.*

other words, the major problem of social workers, that is, of finding a function in the various settings in which they work, seems to me to be most poignant and most interesting in the school situation. The problem is, What are we doing there?

I happen to believe that most of the mistakes that social workers make in any setting, and most particularly in the schools because they are so close to the action there, come out of an incomplete or distorted or a fuzzy sense of function, an inability to explain to themselves or to others just *what* it is they are doing there and are *not* doing there. Now if this is true, if I am right about this, it becomes important, setting by setting, to try to understand why this is so difficult; that is, why it is so hard to make a clear and brief and definitive statement of what we are doing in that particular setting.

Let me say by way of preface, what I think some of these functional problems are. The first is that most of us have not been taught and are not used to thinking and talking about function in precise terms. The literature of social work is replete with vague, global statements of what social workers do. We talk about bringing about adjustment; we talk about maturity; we talk about democracy and there are several things wrong with these attempts at explanation. One is that they are too global, that is in most cases we claim to do things that we cannot possibly do or that any single institution cannot possibly do. No agent can claim a corner on democratic values or an adjustment to society. These are such complicated and usually unrealized processes that for any profession to come along and claim responsibilities for those processes, is palpably untrue and palpably becomes part of the jargon of the profession.

The second thing that is wrong with these kinds of statements is that essentially they emphasize the goals of a profession or to put it more simply, the prayers or the hopes or the aspirations of a profession. The problem is not what we hope will happen, the problem is not how grandly we can state our objectives; the problem essentially is what do you do. Any kind of a system is made up of parts each of which has its own thing. The principal administers; the teacher teaches; the psychologist does whatever it is he does—psychologizes; the barber cuts hair, the lawyer defends clients, the engineer builds bridges; what does the social worker do? It is at that point, you see, that the problem of globalness, the problem of vagueness take on a rather important role in the efforts of people to understand us and the efforts of social workers to make their work clear. The question then becomes how do we describe the function in action?

The second major problem, aside from the globalness and the vagueness with which we state our operations, is to translate the notion of function into method. That is, simply speaking, what a person is doing in a given situation should determine how he moves. So the problem is one of translating function into method; that is, the problem of translating the notion of what are you doing there? What do you do and how do you do it? Therefore, the discussion soon has to turn to problems of skill, and I may say that this problem has been dogging the social work profession for a long time and particularly in the area in which I am most interested, that of working with groups. The problem is that until a profession communicates its skills; that is, the things it can do that other's cannot do, it will not be accepted as an important enterprise, either in the schools or in the society at large. It does not take special expertise to talk about objectives, to talk about philosophy, to talk about democracy and social maturity. But it does take a special expertise to be able to teach a class, to help a client to do an operation and so on.

We now move into the third problem I want to say something about, which is essentially substantive. Again it is common to all social work but has a particular relevance in the school situation. It is the problem Who is my client? Whom do I represent? To whom do I belong? Is it the system, in this case the school, or is it the client, in this case the child and his family. Is it the system that hires me (and pays me, by the way), or the member who is having trouble? There are a hundred ways to ask the child to the system or the system to the child? Do we advocate for the child or do we represent the system? Do we change the child or change the system and so on? The question has an urgency today that it has not had in many years. In all the areas of social work to which we turn, we find the same pressing sense of upset, sense of nervousness about the problem. For those of you who work in the schools, the problem is almost a day-to-day sensation, a day-to-day feeling. The most interesting thing about this problem, that is whom do I represent, the system or the child, is, that no matter how you ask the question, it is impossible to answer.

Why is it so impossible to answer? Because no matter how you ask, the question always assumes that there is a need to make a choice between system and person and such choices are impossible to live with. The typical machinery through which we have all moved can be described as that of a neurotic dilemma, that is when you move in one direction, you wish you had moved in the other, and then when you have moved in that direction, you wish you had moved in the first. This is in fact what is meant by a dilemma. It has two horns. When you are on horn A, you wish desperately that you were on horn B and vice versa. Specifically, the worker who identifies closely with the child against those lousy cops, lousy teachers, lousy administrators, and so on, soon finds himself feeling vaguely guilty about that fact he has somehow lost his function, his sense of a society into which the person has to move. Then when he moves around and tries to get the kid to shape up, he begins to feel vaguely guilty about imposing standards that do not come from the client. So the dualism is unresolvable as long as it is kept in terms of Whom do I represent? Make yourself a choice. This choice thing assumes a basic conflict of interest between the two, or else you would not find it necessary to think in those terms. There is a basic conflict of interest between the society and the people who live in it. Social workers somehow desperately have to find out which is right and which is wrong. Most of us, perhaps because of the very reasons we came into the profession, assume we know the answer, almost by definition. Obviously the systems are wrong and people are right.

This presents us with some very, very difficult problems when we begin the most important enterprise, which is basically to ask ourselves What is the real relationship between people and their systems, or more specifically, between a child and his school?

Now I want to spend a moment on presenting to you a few ideas which have helped me in trying to resolve the dilemma both for myself and for pedagogical purposes; that is, to help students, each of whom comes into the school of social work carrying this particular dilemma on his back. The necessity to make these choices become unnecessary as soon as one realizes that the relationship between people and their institutions is what I call symbiotic. That is, they live off each other. People are constantly striving to move into or to negotiate the various systems that make up their lives—school, welfare, jobs, housing, family, friends, etc. While each system in order to stay alive and in order to do its thing, the thing society is paying it to do, must reach out to integrate and to incorporate the people it is supposed to serve. Now, that this relationship, this symbiotic affair between the two, gets obscure and hard to read, that it often looks like its very opposite; that the stupidity, the fear, the ineptness with which the parties reach out to each other is a part of your everyday lives and somewhat overwhelming. All this is undeniable. The more complicated the system, that is the larger the school, the larger the welfare bureaucracy and so on, the more complex the system, the more diffuse and unrecognizable this symbiosis becomes. But, it is always there. It is there almost by definition. The system and its members, the school and its kids need each other in order to do their thing; the kids to get educated and the educator to teach his kids. How then does a complicated system see to it that its people do not fall between the cracks? When it fails, the people do fall between the cracks and the cracks in many of the systems that you know are so wide that it's almost impossible not to fall between the cracks. But how is it arranged that any system tries to set up some machinery to see to it that its own complexity can be negotiated? How does the system rescue these symbiotic strivings from obscurity as both system representatives and members all but lose track of their needs for each other? This is the condition with which we are most familiar—the unreachable client and the impossible bureaucracy. To all intents and purposes, both have ruled each other out and the slogan is "the hell with them, who needs them anyhow." Underneath that slogan is a profound need on the part of all people to use their own institutions or part of institutions to make it with the people they are supposed to serve. Thus you have a situation in which only what is underneath (and this should be familiar to social workers) represents the driving force which we need in order to bring them together; what on the surface is a tremendous obscurity and a tremendous kind of looking the other way.

So back to our question, the question of how the system can offer some rescue operation for this symbiosis that gets lost. The answer is that every system creates a hedge against its own complexity. It designates a special group that is still *of* the system but in a very special kind of way. The job of this special group is to remember and protect the symbiotic relationship when everybody else has forgotten it, and its special task is to mediate the symbiotic strivings between the school and its families, helping them to reach out to each other on their common tasks. I believe that this is the job for which social workers are hired. This is the special function of the social worker in the schools.

When you designate a function, it is important to go back a little bit and ask yourself what then is dysfunctional? Now by this concept of function it becomes dysfunctional, as I said before, to fix one's sights on only one or the other member of this relationship. That is when, I believe, the social worker fixes his sights only on the child and his family, only on their psychological attributes without regard to the special system for which they have some responsibility. The social worker becomes dysfunctional and feels it.

When, on the other hand, the social worker fixes his sights on the demands of the system, on the behavioral demands, on the job requirements, and so on, without regard to the individual psyches with which they have to come to terms in order to do their job, he becomes again dysfunctional, which presents us with a kind of interesting idea. Essentially what I am saying to the social worker, is that you are *not* primarily responsible for the child nor are you primarily responsible for the system. Basically you are responsible for the ways in which they handle each other; for the ways in which they interact. This creates a function which has not to do with particular parties, but with processes through which these parties reach out to each other. You might put that another way; in fact you might put it the opposite way, and say the social worker has responsibility for both the individual and the social; for both the child and the school. It then becomes unnecessary; in fact, dysfunctional for him to try and make choices and declare allegiances for one or the other. His job, as I said, is not to range himself with one against the other, but to help them recognize their common ground and work on it together.

In this context, the social worker is then called upon to deliver certain skills which I believe most of them have not yet been called upon to deliver. For example, within the context of this kind of reasoning, the contact between the social worker and the system, or more exactly the representative of the system, must reflect all the skills and sensitivities usually reserved for the client alone. The listening, the reaching for real talk rather than the ritual words, the close connection to underlying feelings are as relevant in talking with the teacher as they are in the conversation with the child. Most generally, in the overidentification with the child, the conversations with the system representative, have largely been a huge, conning type of operation, where essentially we are swinging these people (because they are obviously not as smart as we are) with subtle arrangements whereby we are trying to get them to do something for *our* child. The quarrel for the client, of course, is hectic, and conversely, very often it happens that the conversation with the family, let us say, has none of the skills that the social worker is able to exert when talking to a child in trouble. That is on the one hand there is skill and listening and sensitivity and on the other hand there is swinging, there is manipulation and there is conning.

I'm not going to have time today to do something which I generally enjoy doing most, and that is to begin to develop the specific operations, the specific skills that this kind of a concept of function actually leads to, but let me mention just a couple and perhaps when I read some of the examples that I have with me, they may be highlighted a little bit and then perhaps when we have our question period, which I'm hoping to leave time for, we'll be able to develop a few more. But as the social worker begins to face both his student and his system, he begins to develop certain skills which have to do with pointing them in each other's directions; with helping them to find the common ground between them; with pointing up the obstacles over which they trip as they try to reach each other with a coordination of community resources and with a certain reliance on the processes through which people work. Anyhow, when it works well, it looks something like this. This material comes out of our work with one of our second year group work students in a group with preadolescent youngsters, all of whom have records of deviance and disturbance, in the schools.

The worker says:

> In another meeting, Charles describes a fight he has had in class. He is furious at the teacher for not taking his side in the argument. Later in the day the teacher reprimands him and several other youngsters for clowning. Charles becomes furious, accuses the teacher of picking on him and storms out of the classroom. He gets into a great deal of difficulty and requests help from his group on what he should do and this is how it reads. Eddie says "shouldn't have hit him, you wouldn't have gotten into trouble." I said (the worker) "Well, Charles was so mad that he had to say how mad he was some way." Charles told how mad he really was. Then there was a silence which I let go for awhile because it was obvious that they were all thinking and looking for solutions. All of a sudden, Ronald, a big husky kid who just looks like he gets into lots of fights, said to Charles, "You shouldn't have hit him. You'll just get into trouble. Instead you go up and tell the teacher and she'll get him into trouble. Then, beat him up after school." The response was that this made a lot of sense. Greg said, "No, not after school, you could still get into trouble, beat him up on Saturday." Charles said he liked that solution for the time being. Charles encouraged, then brought out his real concern. What do you do about the teacher not liking him and picking on him. The worker picks this up and suggests: "Charles, do you want to know what to do to make the teacher not pick on you and like you?" He said yeah, he did. Somebody said he shouldn't have run out of the class, that didn't help. They still had a rough time. I then (the worker said) had to take a more active role after they showed some signs of frustration. I said, "You know, this is similar to what happened here with Bill's gripe earlier. Bill thought

that I was playing favorites and I was picking on him and then he did something that solved his problem. Do you remember what it was?" Angel said "yeah, he came in and said he quit; he got mad." I said "that's right; that's true, but he didn't get any good results until he told me what was bothering him, what he was mad about and what I did that made him mad." Bill's face lit up and he said in a long, drawn out way "yeah." The others then caught on because they could see that Bill really believed that that is what had helped him. Then they started telling Charles what he could do. The group recommendation turned out to be to go to the teacher after class and tell her that he's mad because she always picks on him. Then Charles said to me, "But she's not like you." Other said "yeah, you understand." I said, "I'm different, but lots of times I understand because you tell me what's bothering you. She doesn't know what's bothering you; she can't understand. She probably doesn't know that you even think she's picking on you." The others said to Charles "Well, you can give it a try." They were through with this when I said, "You can give it a try, and if it doesn't work, you can bring it back here and we'll try to see what else we can do." So much for the client.

Now the worker turns to the system and this is what it looks like. He goes to talk to a teacher not in relation to Charles here, but in respect to his relation to Bill, the person whose experience was used by the group to help Charles. And this is the worker now talking to the teacher.

I said that I could tell by the way Mr. Smith was talking that Bill causes him a lot of trouble. He went on to tell me a little about how the class gives him a bad time and so on, and then he gets mad at them. I said I'm sure he has his hands full. Then I asked him why Bill had failed art. He said that Bill just seems to prefer fooling around to doing his work. Or else he would sulk in his seat and do nothing. I said "right, that's the way Bill acts when he takes something as criticism or he's disappointed in himself." Mr. Smith then began talking about how I was right. He was surprised, although his statement showed respect for a social worker and one who might know what's going on in these kids minds. He said "that's exactly when Bill starts sulking." I told him that Bill takes anything that's critical that way, usually because he thinks you don't like him. Mr. Smith showed interest, talked a little bit and then asked how it would be if he gave Bill a monitor's job (the classic pedagogical panacea) and moved him up to the front of the class where he could give him more attention. Then he said he had already moved Bill up to the front. I said I could see where he thought giving Bill a monitor's job would make things easier all around. But, I continued, "if you're willing to try something, I think that you could help Bill with his problem. That would involve not necessarily giving him a monitor's job but helping him work at his moods and his anger and his overreaction to criticism." He said he'd like to help. I said, "Well, what I've done to help Bill when he reacts with anger at criticism is to say, "hey, you're acting like I don't like you. I did that because you did something wrong, not because I don't like you'." Bill seems not to be able to see the difference between criticism and rejection. Of course, I talked to him about why he reacts the way he does and so on but you have your hands full and that would be hard for you." Mr. Smith said excitedly that that sounds like a good idea, he'd like to give it a try. I said we could get together and compare notes later if he wished.

Later in the discussion, it goes like this:

The worker says: "You know, I'm not sure what you say to them." (He is now beginning to generalize from Bill's experience to the experience of the other youngsters in the group). He says, "You know, I'm not sure what you say to them but they hear it wrong. You know, lots of times kids get different things out of what you say to them, they get a different meaning. But something you've said to these kids over and over again is giving them the idea that you think they are the stupidest class and that they are all stupid and dumb." Mr. Smith thought for a moment and then he said, "Well, they're right, I have said that. I've gotten so mad at them that I have said that and I can see how they would have taken it." I said I could see that they made his job almost impossible for him. He said that initially he said these things because they didn't finish their work. Then he said that he definitely thought that he shouldn't have said those kinds of things. I said "because you are telling them they're stupid, they get mad and they're gonna get back at you probably by acting bad and giving you a lot of trouble." He said he thought that made a lot of sense.

At the end we discussed other types of actions. He thanked me for the help I had given him and I thanked him for the information. We set up a future meeting time.

You understand that it doesn't always happen that way. But sometimes it's nice to have it happen that way and the important thing about it is not so much that the teacher responded well because the teacher could just as well have responded defensively and angrily to an angry approach. It was not so much that the teacher responded well but that you see the worker trying to do this thing I have been talking about; that is, taking responsibility for steering the kids toward the teacher which is ultimately where they have to make their peace and steering the teacher toward the kid which is ultimately what is going to give him his sense of being a good teacher or a lousy one. I have never yet met a teacher that wants to be known as a lousy one, no matter how lousy he is.

The second part of my assignment is to ask the question where do groups fit in? You know that I have taken a route, which is by the way, the typical route that I tried to take, in understanding the work with groups. We are no longer, you see, historically in a frame of reference where group work is by itself a profession or a sub profession or, in any event, a reference group of its own. This is how we grew historically but we have passed the period.

In teaching social work with groups now it becomes necessary first to understand social work and then to understand how it is carried into the group. The implications of this kind of approach are many. For example, one of the most important implications is that group work departments are now an anomaly or, where they still exist, should be phased out as gracefully as possible. The problem is not who is the expert on groups and who is the expert on "one-at-a-time"; the problem is how do you apply your sense of social work function to whatever situation you find yourself in—the individual, the family, the group, the teachers meeting—wherever you are, you are a social worker and you should lay claim to certain skills which are relevant. Now you may say that that is very easy for a group worker to say, but the fact is that wherever I have worked as a consultant to caseworkers on opening up group services, it always happens that they tell me "but this is just social work" and I say "exactly." The fact of the matter is that those things which they are good at, they do well in the interview and they do well in the group, and those things which they are bad at, they do equally badly in either situation. So you see, we must move in understanding group services from the sense of What you do and what you are as a social worker to How you use this stuff when you meet with a family or when you meet with a group of kids or a group of parents. It is interesting, I might say briefly, that this dysfunctional choosing between systems and people can be extremely obvious in a group situation—as workers that move into using a group as a way of changing deviant children into conforming ones; of parent educating; or of lecturing parents upon their responsibilities; or of identifying with the children against the tyrannical school; or of offering "group therapy" to acting out children who may, in fact, be less ill than the children who play it cool. We know intellectually that the kids who call attention to themselves are often in a less serious way than those who are afraid to call attention to themselves and yet, the loudmouths find their way into group therapy which is why they were hollering in the first place.

Let me say a word about the group itself as an organism. Let me in a sense define it for you. I am not really defining it as much as I am saying that when I use the term "group" this is what I mean. A group, essentially, (I am talking about the peer group at the moment) is a mutual aid system of its own. You might say a system within a system. It is a collection of people, an alliance of people, if you will, who need each other in order to work on certain common tasks within a setting that is hospitable to those tasks. Let me repeat that. A collection of people who need each other in order to work on certain common tasks within a setting that is hospitable to those tasks. The interesting thing about this definition is that it is an agenda for the study of group work. You might say that we take two years in a school of social work to examine that definition phrase by phrase. Let me show you what I mean by that, by trying to break down the definition to see what it contains. When I said the group is a collection of people, I am therein setting an agenda for the study of collection behavior. That is, you will find, as every teacher knows, and as you inside of you know from your own participation in groups, that people act in the small group very often in peculiar ways, to peculiar meanings that you didn't expect them to react to. There are certain things that happen when people sit around looking at each other and talking to each other and reacting to each other that call up certain parts of themselves which may not so quickly be called up when they are talking to people one at a time, or, when they are in a different kind of situation. The parent doesn't understand why the kid acts that way in the home; the teacher doesn't understand why the kids act that way at camp. So much for the collection of people; the agenda for the study of interaction of collective behavior.

Now the second part of that definition was that these are people who need each other, not just the worker. I'll say more about that in a moment. The implication, of course, is that if people have no palpable use for each other, there's no point in calling them together in a group. There is something about the panacea quality, especially in today's world, about group experience which somehow assumes that if you pull six, eight, ten people together, something good will happen. That isn't true. They must have something to do and they must see each other as potential carriers of good, that they are useful to each other. This is one of the problems on which many groups fall. People look around saying What am I doing here? What do I need them for? The worker unconsciously feels pretty much the same—that is, not understanding what their need for each other is, only what their need for him is.

The third part of the definition has to do with working on *certain* common tasks and when I underline certain, what I mean is that a group, unless it has something specific to do, flounders. The efforts of people to describe that floundering in terms of something good really goes against all human experience. "Let's just talk," they say; "let's just express our feelings," they say, "and good things will happen." Well, most often embarrassing things happen, bad things happen, humiliating things happen and so it seems to me in trying to understand the helping in groups, that all present have to have at least some beginning concensus about what their tasks are, what they are working on. If you say to them, "you are working on yourselves," that is no more satisfactory to them than it would be to you. I might say parenthetically with a big parenthesis around it and then go on tantalizingly to something else, that this is what's wrong with the current rage, for the encounter and for the sensitivity and for the T groups. They have no work to do, except to express their feelings. Anybody who just needs to express his feelings without reference to any particular task, either has a terrible need to express his feelings in general because they are overwhelming to him, in which case you get into some kind of therapeutic enterprise, or he is an exhibitionist who enjoys that kind of game or is lending himself to something which he feels is fashionable. The fact of the matter is that the helping process, the function of a specific profession in a specific situation, is best carried out through the medium of people applying their emotional energy and applying their feeling to a job that they understand, The kid who is having trouble in school, and I say to the kids "you're all having trouble," look at each other, talk to each other, find out what the hell the trouble is about and what you can do about it. They know where to pick it up, they know what's relevant and not relevant and they can begin to work. What I'm saying here is, that unless there is some kind of a clear contract about what the group is about, (and a clear contract means limited tasks and stuff that you don't get into, as well as stuff that you do) unless there is some kind of a clear contract, it is hard to help people in a group situation.

The fourth part of the definition says that this group that we're talking about, these people with a common task and this worker who is trying to help, are in a setting which is hospitable to just those tasks. Now that means that a group that operates in a welfare setting, that a group that operates in a community center setting, that a group that operates in a school setting, are to some extent governed by the function of the agency in which they operate. That is that that agency has certain jobs to do and *not* others. That is what helps to keep the group straight and sane and together. This definition is most interesting to me because, as you might have noticed, it is not limited to deviant or to sick children or to any people who need some sort of remodeling. It may include groups of teachers or parents or children with special interests. Indeed it includes the classroom itself where group skills and the respect for the power of mutual aid, have helped many teachers since teaching began and could help a great many more.

The group, therefore, is an alliance of people who are in the same boat with respect to certain tasks with which they can help each other. The group is designed to help make people stronger in the performance of their roles. In a mutual reaching out that takes place between people and their systems, each side benefits from the strength of the other. This is an important point, because those who fear the strength of the other, are always trying to break up, as they put it, kid's groups or gangs or what have you, and are still operating from the mistaken notion of where their own self interest lies. This might include the school administrator who would rather talk to the parents one at a time than put his trust in building a strong and attentive group of knowledgeable and responsible parents, those who distrust children's peer groups, based on the old notions that groups are threatening, that they can unseat you, (which in fact they can, if your perch is so tenuous) that any expression of strength can unseat you. In the history of a labor movement, for example, it took us many years, perhaps generations, for employers to find out that a strong negotiating union was much easier to deal with than a weak one divided among themselves.

Now the exact group skills themselves, as I said before, would take too long to elaborate here. I have written about them elsewhere, but it is important to note in this audience that they are not mysterious, that they stem from a common social work function and that the skills that have been learned in casework are as sharply relevant in groups as they are in the individual interviews. They have to do with studying a clear contract, with helping people to say what they really mean, with helping people integrate the task and the feeling, with reaching for negatives, with breaking large problems into smaller pieces, with guarding the focus of work, with using community resources and all of the other technical skills with which you are all familiar. Where the group situation differs (and we must say just a word about differences because obviously looking at one pair of eyes presents a different psychological situation than looking at eight or ten); where the group situation differs is the area in which people who have had almost all of their experience in the individual interview, need the most help in the earliest stages of working with groups. For example, the worker who moves from the primary situation of helping a client to use him in the classic transference and countertransference kind of relationship now moves into a situation in which the use of him is only a part of the scene and in which the use of each other becomes an important dynamic. The worker is now in the group situation helping people not only to use his authority constructively, but to use the intimacy of their relationships with each other and draw on each other's strengths. This means that in a group situation there are two major themes; the theme of *authority* which is What are you doing there? Who are you? How can I use you? and the theme of *intimacy* which is How can we help each other? How can you help each other?

Another important difference comes out. Again everytime I work with caseworkers around these problems, they point out that they never realized before they moved into a group service situation, how much control they needed over the interview. That is, the forms in which they take control of the interview had become so refined and so subtle that they don't even know they're happening. If you analyzed the interview, they're the ones who change the subject, they're the ones who decide what's relevant, they're the ones who pick up the negatives, they're the ones who end the interview, and so on. And doing it for so long without realizing that they are taking as much initiative as they are, now when they move into a group situation the spontaneity factor begins to take control. There are many forces and the worker begins to realize that he is being asked to relinquish a certain amount of control which produces a certain amount of anxiety at the outset, but a sense of excitement that goes along with it. That is, the ability to really participate in a process in which people are trying to develop some control over their own immediate situation in an exciting prospect.

In general, and in conclusion, there is this growing excitement about social work with groups in schools, and many of my own students are now beginning to turn their attention to job possibilities in this area. Unfortunately, there aren't enough of such jobs. We are now beginning to gather the records, to elaborate the themes that worked, to define the skills more sharply. As the workers begin to write about their work with teachers, their meetings with groups of parents and children, and their—what we have begun to call "systems work" with school administrators. The power of the group continues to impress us: the force and insight that people can pick up from each other, and the things that presumably nonverbal and inarticulate children can begin to say to each other.

> Let's go back to our group. "The talk hit a number of things," said the worker, "none too deeply." Bill said to Charles, "Hey, what are you mad about?" Bill was very proud of himself. He looked at the rest of them and said, "See, I can be a leader. I knew what he was feeling." Then, feeling that maybe he had hurt me, he said to me, "Sorry" with a smile on his face. I said immediately, "You didn't hurt me. In fact, I would be delighted if you could do more of that. You all can if you try." They said, "We can all be leaders?" I said, "I'd love it if you could all be leaders." Bill said jokingly, "Good, I'm first." Then he began taking a pad of paper and a roll sheet. I said, "No, you lead by helping, not by taking the roll or having a pad of paper." He said with a smile, "I know."

Discussion

Question 1: Dr. Hirning. I was very much interested in all you have to say about the dilemma between the system and the individual which is presented to the school social worker, which leads me to ask a question relative to the pertinency of an integration of a school of social work and a school of education at a University level. I note you have an Ed.D. from Teachers College. I've spent almost twenty-two years at Teachers College, mostly helping train guidance counselors. Especially when we had an NEA institute geared to training guidance counselors for working with the socially disadvantaged, I was very eager for an interrelation between the Columbia School of Social Work and Columbia Teachers College. I always wondered where the stumbling blocks were that we couldn't get together; that there weren't at least some common courses or some courses in pupil personnel services which would bring people from the School of Social Work and from Teachers College together.

Now I stopped there in 1964; maybe things are much different now. Perhaps you can tell us what the stumbling blocks are?

Answer: The question is really a very important one. I really don't know what the specific stumbling blocks are in the New York situation, but I know—I think I have a sense of what socially these stumbling blocks are. I think that socially what has happened in a sense is that the professions have grown up alongside each other rather than together, so that you find people in one profession having all kinds of insights, for example, that the people in the other had—like a generation or two ago—they just weren't listening to each other. The college campus is a beautiful symbol of all this distractiveness, and this convergent business that goes on. I have worked in three schools of social work in each of which I never had occasion to meet the faculty from the other schools of social work in the same community; so that actually what is happening is that the psychologists, for example, are developing their own line of thought and their own history of what it means to be helpful; the teachers are developing their own, the social workers their own, the psychiatrists their own, and so on. Some day, and I don't think any of us will be around at the time, somebody will begin to conceptualize a helping art, a helping profession, out of which it will build its own generalizations from the experiences of all the others. Our present attitudes toward each other are that somehow we have made it, and the others haven't, which means that there is a kind of status system that has to go. For example, if I raise it at a faculty meeting tomorrow, the general feeling will be that teachers aren't smart enough to understand what we're saying. If I were to raise it at a meeting of educators in my capacity as an educator, they would say, "Oh, those social workers, they are only talking about Freud, what do they know?" I have been lucky in my own education in that I have constantly been extremely nosey about what's going on in the other professions, and I have wound up and been accused of being a little eclectic—that's a curse word, by the way, in the profession!

Question 2: I am concerned when you talk about the dilemma of choice between the system and the client. It would seem to me that you can't decide for yourself where you stand on this dilemma in a constant sense. Doesn't that have to be a moving decision on a case by case basis as it would be if you were working with a family agency in a parent-child situation, perhaps where the parent is the system and the child the client? You have to constantly set yourself different in each situation. Wouldn't you have to in schools too?

Answer: Let me attempt to clarify this. What I'm really saying here is that wherever you make the choice, it doesn't work—whether you make it in general or whether you make it in specific. You are perfectly right that the business of systems negotiation takes place whenever somebody is trying to negotiate some kind of complex of demands and relationships. So it could be a kid in this group; it could be a child in his family, etc. Now if you had got to the situation where you have to opt for the child against his family the situation has already gotten so bad that you can't get too much satisfaction out of it anyhow. And I'm not saying that such situations do not occur. Or where you've gotten to a situation where a certain family has to be chosen as against the school that it is trying to make it with, you've already gotten into an impossible situation. What I would say further is that you have gotten into such a bad situation that you really are in many ways already dysfunctional. So what I'm saying is that in any situation that you would present me with as a social worker, my eyes would immediately move in both directions. That is what can I do with this child vis-a-vis the family and with this family vis-a-vis the child. I am interested in that arrow that goes between the person and the system and I am interested always in trying to smooth or facilitate or get them together. Now, it is important to remember that this is not a Pollyanna notion that all things are good in the best of all possible worlds, but it is a notion which precipitates conflict rather than avoids it. But it is based on the notion that the people and their systems in order to make it, had to look at each other; they had to holler at each other, if necessary; they had to come into conflict if that's what happening. The moment they start talking "play nice," the game is lost.

Question 3: Alex Mindes. That's very relevant to the question I want to raise which is how the common purpose can be used or what special adaptations it might need with the alienated client, the very resistive client.

Answer: Alex is asking what happens with the very alienated, the very resistive client. This has to be studied, and studied in the record. We're gathering more and more records, and again we have to apply the concept, *resistive,* and its sibling concept *ambivalent,* not only to clients but to systems, because essentially what you have in every situation where there is resistance, it takes two to set up a decent conflict, decent resistance. With a resistive child, you are looking at a resistive school, or a resistive principal. In other words, resistance to what? Resistance to facing squarely the work they have to do together in order to get on with it. The moment we begin to accept this kind of mediated conception, we're freed not to psychologize the client too much, to sociologize the social situation, but to bring them together. So the question then becomes, "What happens when the diffusion of the symbiosis, that is, it's obscurity is so bad, the situation is so black, that neither the client nor the system understands at all its common ground. That is the thing we need to look at more and more. My impression would be, for those who would say, "This kid is hopeless" or for those who say, "This system is so rigid it's just impossible," my impression would be, "That may be. But let's see if we've done all the work that leads us to those conclusions." But if you've left out any of the work that leads to those conclusions I don't trust your conclusions. Let me give you an analogy. In a mental hospital not too long ago they went into the back wards with patients who had been there for thirty and forty years. If the diffusion, if the lack of connection between people and their society is any more obvious than that, which is "these people are almost dead." They pulled some of them out of the wards and they put them with their chairs looking, facing each other, and several of them turned their chairs around to face the wall. And they sat there meeting after meeting after meeting with their chairs next to the wall. And then, after I don't know how many meetings, one turned his chair around, you see, and the symbiosis was alive—that is, he was looking for a connection. My answer really is, and call me an optimist if you will but a realist if you won't, you have to be dead for the connection to be missing. Now I may not be good enough to put the vibrancy back in the connection or it may in truth be so bad, so obscure, so confused, that it needs more ammunition than I have to give, but my check on that is I do not allow anyone to make the statement, "They are impossible"—anyone that I have anything to do with, that is, students, consultees, and so on to make the statement, "They are impossible," until I have seen all the work that leads up to it. Then I may believe, but they've not been able to do that yet.

Question 4: A brief question that the reference to sensitivity training brought home. Social workers are no more immune to fashion trends than any other group. Some of us find ourselves in a situation where the only way to change the system is to get people together in groups for discussion of issues. Will you make further comment on how we can be helpful?

Answer: Yes, I was hoping I'd get a rise out of that. I'm either very courageous or very foolish. I did this at Meninger's a few months ago—made a crack at sensitivity—and they may have a whole department on sensitivity training, so I had a real session with the guy in charge of it afterwards! Let me tell you what my thinking is on that. The fact that this is a society that tends to cut people off deadens them, that is tends to offer few rewards for spontaneity and affect is undeniable. In other words, the whole move toward sensitivity is an important one. My objection to it is that in striving to reach for the lost feelings it is again dichotomizing feeling from the task; that it is committing the same error that society has committed in reverse. Whereas, if society is saying, "Get the job done, get the job done, the hell with this feelings crap, let's get on with it, get on with it. If you are angry, swallow it, if you are hurt, eat it—get on with it." In reaction, this very often happens in our society, we tend to react to the opposite extreme, in reaction to that dichotomizing of task from feeling, we have said in the same way that I have described the dualing between individual and system, we have said, "You have opted for task; we will now opt for feeling." And I say that that mistake is in a way as bad, although it may be experienced as not quite as bad because at least it breaks some people loose. "I have a better alternative," is what I am saying. And my alternative is not to be trapped by dualism, not to be trapped by either task or feeling because that's not how people live. My slogan is "Feeling in pursuit of a task." That is, if you are doing something and you are feeling something it's got to be *about* something. Not just the feeling itself. John Dewey said a long time ago that in order to describe the practice of eating, you have to describe the jaw moving up and down with food in it. If there's no food in it, it's just a jaw moving up and down. What happens very often in a sensitivity arrangement is that the people who lend themselves in good will to the process begin to experience some kind of resurgence within them. The fact that it can't eat, you know, bite on something, makes it distressing. Very often in the literature on sensitivity there is no provision for handling the feelings that get left over. And I have seen situations in which people who are not as strong, when I say as strong I say who cannot handle it as the game it is, and it can be a productive game, these people get left out, get terribly upset, and get set back even further. So what I'm saying is, the effort to relieve feeling is a good one. But it's separation from task that is a bad phenomenon.

In working with principals, with teachers, as I have for example, I want to sit down and say, "Teachers, running a class is a rough job. What are some of the problems of running a class? What are some of the problems of getting kids to work with each other in the classroom?" And then they start to work on that. If they say, "We get very angry when they . . ." I say, "You don't sound angry; if you're angry, be angry!" Now—But angry about what? And then the feeling begins to come out and they say, "Those goddam parents, if it wasn't for the parents, we'd have . . ." and so on. And now, what we have got is feeling which is attached to work. We can stop it at any point without losing anything, because nobody has given his whole self, but only a piece of himself.

Mary O'Hagan: Dear MSW's. For a long time many school districts have wanted us to change our name from school social worker, and today we've found our new name, and the translation is, in a sense of MSW, it is MSR, Mediators of Symbiotic Relationships.

The Practice of Child Care in Residential Treatment

William Schwartz

A good consultation process is a training course for the expert; what he learns is how his subject takes on its special shape and form within a particular setting. In the experience from which this paper is drawn, I learned a great deal about the relevance of social group work to the specific problems of child care practice in a residential treatment center. Having been called in from another branch of the service, as it was, I was not in any sense an expert in child care; those who had been struggling with these problems for some time were closer to them in sense and feeling than any outsider could be. My job was to help them identify the child care tasks and define the skills necessary to carry them out. In the course of this effort, several ideas emerged that may have some value for those interested in the development of institutional child care as a field of practice.

Background

The Hawthorne Cedar Knolls School serves approximately 200 disturbed and delinquent boys and girls from 9 to 16 years of age, referred to them by courts, social agencies, hospitals, and schools in the Greater New York metropolitan area. My association with Hawthorne began when one of our group work students from the Columbia University School of Social Work was placed there in a field assignment. It was a fairly traditional assignment; he worked with leisure-time activities, interest groups, and clubs. In the process, however, he became interested in the cottage situation itself and in the application of his developing group work skills to the day-to-day tasks of child care practice. The director of the institution also became absorbed in this problem and when the student was graduated he was employed as a child care

Schwartz, William. The practice of child care in residential treatment. From M. F. Mayer & A. Blum (Eds.), Healing through living: A symposium on residential treatment, *1971. Courtesy of Charles C. Thomas, Publisher, Springfield, Illinois.*

worker, at a professional salary and with special supervision to be given by the executive himself.[1]

Under this arrangement, the young worker[2] became an operational model of what group work skills, albeit freshly acquired, would look like as they were applied to the problems of child care in a residential treatment center. Given a receptive climate, professional supervision and systematic recording, how would the work appear in action? Of course, even under the best of conditions such an effort would be encapsulated and set off—a kind of island, around which the usual practice would continue and the usual concepts prevail. But the capsule would have translucent walls; each would see and be affected by what the other was doing, an experimental atmosphere would be created and the child care job itself would take on a new importance in the agency.

My consultative role began a short time after, with a visit directed to the problems of recording child care practice. In the process, we moved rather quickly to the need for a clearer description of the child care function; what the worker writes down must obviously be related to the tasks for which he is accountable. We also took notice of the growing importance of bringing the young professional out of his isolation and making him less *exceptional* in the scheme of things. This was a way of saying that the new approaches to child care must eventually be institutionalized—built into the regular pattern of agency service. The new work had been calling attention to the helping process in the cottages and the task of defining the skills in fairly precise terms. Such an effort was in fact needed not only in this agency but in the field itself; while the literature of residential treatment is voluminous and rich in both theory and experience, there is little in it about the practice of child care—few records, not much theory, little analysis of technique, and almost no operational descriptions of skilled workers in action.[3]

---

[1]Some of the Director's early attempts to rethink the child care job are reflected in Jerome M. Goldsmith: A New Concept of the Child Care Function. Presented at the American Orthopsychiatric Conference, Los Angeles, 1962 (mimeo, 19 pages).

[2]Whose name is David Birnbach, and to whom we were all indebted for the quality of his work, his detailed recording and his willingness to expose his professional movements to continuous staff examination and discussion.

[3]For some recent work along these lines, see Maier, Henry W. (Ed.): *Group Work as Part of Residential Treatment.* New York, National Association of Social Workers, 1965, which includes a brief annotated bibliography; Hromadka, Van G.: Child Care Worker on the Road to Professionalization. A task-analysis research presented at the Annual Meeting of the American Association for Children's Residential Centers, October 1966; Bettelheim, Bruno: Training the child care worker in a residential center. *American Journal of Orthopsychiatry, 36*(4):692–705, 1966; Goldsmith, Jerome M. and Birnbach, David M.: Professionalizing the Child Care Task in Residential Treatment. Presented at the American Orthopsychiatric Conference, Washington D.C., March, 1967; and Burmeister, Eva: *Tough Times and Tender Moments in Child Care Work.* New York, Columbia, 1967. *See also:* Berman, Netta: The group worker in a children's institution. In Schulze Susanne: (Ed.) *Creative Group Living in Children's Institution.* New York, Association Press, 1951; Konopka, Gisela: The role of the group in residential treatment. *American Journal of Orthopsychiatry, 28*(4):679–684, 1955; Mayer, Morris Fritz: *A Guide for Child-care Workers.* New York, The Child Welfare League of America, 1958); and Grossbard, Hyman: *Cottage Parents: What They Have to Be, Know and Do.* New York, The Child Welfare League of America, 1960.

A few months later, I was called in to begin work as a regular consultant on the problems of cottage life and the dynamics of child care. In the ensuing three-year period, I met regularly with the unit supervisors, conducted workshops for child care personnel, observed and talked with children and held individual and group conferences with social workers, teachers, psychiatrists, psychologists, and others. All of my work was recorded in a professional diary, which I used later to summarize and conceptualize the learnings that emerged from the experience.

My work was directed to three main areas: The first was to identify the function of child care and the specific skills required to do the job. The second was to clarify the tasks of the supervisors—in this case, the unit administrators—as they strove to integrate the services required for treatment, supervise the practice of child care, develop programs for the entire unit, and learn the very group skills they were trying to teach. The third area developed somewhat unexpectedly but became a central focus of concern, namely, the division of labor within the institution and the complex of professional relationships within which the child care worker must find his function; these interdisciplinary arrangements affected the child care enterprise in many ways as they addressed themselves to the problems of power, status hierarchies, who owns the child, who has the best theory, and other lines of internecine struggle.

During this three-year period, the practice model provided by the professional child care worker began to reproduce itself: two group work students from Columbia were placed under his field work tutelage; these, as they were graduated, took child care jobs in their turn; and three additional students were subsequently placed in child care field assignments.

I should make it clear that these ideas emerged from one agency setting and are not meant to be stretched any further than they can go to cover others. I should also add that this was a dynamic situation, with staff people who were highly motivated for self-examination and change. This made each problem more interesting, since most of the frustrations and failures must then be ascribed not to idiosyncratic attributes but to the complexities of the system itself. These complexities were in fact such that one was constantly amazed and impressed by the vigor with which the director and his staff lent themselves to the persistent probing and challenging in which we were engaged.

My presentation will begin with what appeared to me to be the major dilemmas of the child care practitioner. From there, I will try to identify a special function for child care work within the residential treatment institution. That will lead us to the attempt to define some of the specific skills that seemed to be required in order to carry out this function. I would like then to discuss some of the special problems that seem to be involved in the professionalization of the child care service. Finally, although it would take another paper to do the subject justice, I would like to try out just a few ideas on the division of labor among the various disciplines represented on the treatment team.

The Dilemmas of Child Care

My work with cottage personnel offered many examples of the internal contradictions hidden in the child care role. The first of these might be termed *the dilemma of ambiguous expectations,* in which the child care worker is called upon to act on what seem to him to be conflicting models of what he is supposed to do in the agency. On the one hand, he is told that he must establish and maintain order, enforce the rules, run a tight ship and, above all, never risk the reputation of the institution. These are the system-maintenance expectations, embracing all of the demands for stability, equilibrium, and the rule of law. And the fact is that these demands are necessary, for no bureaucracy, particularly a large and complex one, can do its job effectively without them. In the residential treatment center, no real work is possible without stability of structure and some orderly arrangement of rules and procedures. The call for staff responsibility in this area is eminently reasonable, not as a "necessary evil" but as an integral factor in the treatment process itself.

On the other hand, however, the worker is also told that he must "individualize," that each child has different needs, that "behavior is symptomatic," and that he should be adjusting his expectations from moment to moment as he reads the feelings and problems of each child in his group. And this too is real, for without such a child care norm the institution cannot fulfill its function. The child care workers themselves, after the first twinges of annoyance with unrealistic administrators and ivory-tower professionals, will understand this demand: What is the point of working in a treatment institution if one is to feel like a policeman most of the time?

This is the dualism in which every staff member, from top to bottom in the hierarchy, is trapped. It is called many things, depending on whose terminology is being used, and it always poses one set of variables "versus" another—the instrumental vs. the expressive, custodial vs. treatment functions, doing vs. feeling, limiting vs. loving, superego vs. ego, structure vs. freedom, and a host of other polarities. The "versus" always implies that one must choose and, as in every true dilemma, the choice is always wrong, that is, when one has climbed out on one of the horns, he wishes he had chosen the other. The professional literature itself reflects this pendulum effect, as a rash of articles on the importance of structure and stability is followed by another on the need for individualization and symptom tolerance.

Of course the plain fact is that both sides are right and the opposing articles ought to be read at the same sitting. Life in the cottage, as in life outside the institution, calls for an integration of freedom and discipline and one cannot solve one problem without tackling the other. The theoretical preoccupation with one side or the other does the child care worker no good at all; for he must, in his work from day to day, integrate the two sets of demands *in precisely the same movements.* He cannot "choose," or even alternate between the two; in his interaction with the children, he must learn to merge the so-called "instrumental" and "expressive" tasks in a single concept of function and skill in the helping process.

In the meantime, however, the effect of the dilemma is to create a pervasive sense of frustration and incompleteness. When he is trying to make things run smoothly, he feels vaguely like a tyrant. "The more needy the child," a cottage worker said to me, "the more he gets me mad; there's something wrong with that!" Another said, "I find myself saying to my kids, Don't act sick around here!" On the other hand, when the worker is trying to listen and to individualize, he lives in fear that the lid will blow off. "If you give them a finger," he worries, "they'll take the whole hand." A trained caseworker, acknowledging the child care dilemma, observed ruefully, "When I spend some time in the cottage, I find myself acting and sounding like a layman."

Is there a way out of this dilemma? Can the child care job be explained so that the movements of the worker can be seen as *simultaneously* social and psychological, integrating the ordering and the listening, the proscriptive and the permissive? The point is that it must, and that many of the skills of child care work will flow from such a description.

The next set of contradictions is found in what might be called *the dilemma of status dissonance,* in which the worker is offered opposing versions of his position in the treatment hierarchy. The fact that the cottage worker is low man on the institutional totem pole is not the most damaging blow to his self-image; what is far more serious is that there is a pronounced dissonance between what he hears about his status and how he is actually treated in the professional family. It is demoralizing to be told that you are an indispensable part of the treatment team because you are so close to the child and his problems, while at the same time it is being conveyed to you in more subtle ways that you are incapable of understanding difficult children, you should avoid complex material, and you should make no attempt to talk to children about their troubles. The sociogram of the unit meeting was revealing: the professionals around the table, engaged in a rapid crossfire of scientific talk; the child care workers on the fringe of the circle, waiting for someone to ask them a question, feeling slightly stupid about the discussion, yet knowing they had specific and relevant experiences to contribute. I remember one such meeting, called to discuss a rash of runaways, in which an hour of intense professional discussion went by before someone thought to ask the child care workers whether something had happened in the cottages that might have set off the elopements.

As with any oppressed minority, the child care people vacillate between feelings of self-hate and those of anger at the oppressor. On the one hand, the worker accepts the image of incompetence projected on him by his superiors; on the other, there is anger at the psychiatrists, social workers, and psychologists, and the conviction that these top level professionals could not do the child care job themselves. Added to this is the fear that their lowly status will be observed by the children: "How can the kids respect us if the professionals don't?" The following is abstracted from my log:

> Jack, an old-timer in the institution, brought to the child care workshop a taped interview he had conducted with one of his kids. The interview showed how, under the workshop impetus, he had ventured to talk to the child—at the latter's request—about a problem. The boy had complained to Jack that the place had no walls, and this worried him, because if he ran away the judge would throw the book at him. Jack had asked some good questions and the child had begun to answer in detail and to elaborate a little on some of his anxieties. Suddenly, Jack said to the boy, "Hey, wait a minute, you think I'm your therapist or something?" And the interview ended.
>
> In our discussion, Jack explained how he had panicked as he found himself entering the area everyone had told him was forbidden; you're not supposed to talk to the kids about their problems. This precipitated an earnest discussion about how child care workers were viewed by the professionals in the institution.

Through all of this there is a strong feeling, particularly in the younger workers, that child care is an exciting job, that they really do own the child, that they *can* tell the difference between one child and another, that they can do a sensitive job and that they can learn more if they are helped. The conviction came through clearly and frequently in the workshops: "Our work is in fact the most important in the institution, even if we can't use big words to describe it."

Finally, there are the contradictions inherent in *the dilemma of group living,* where the peer group itself, purportedly the major treatment vehicle in a residential center, is the primary object of the institution's fear and distrust. The anxiety has several elements: there is fear of the "gang," and the feeling that mutual aid among the residents is an alliance against authority (which in certain respects it is, and needs to be); there is ambivalence about the desirability of group discussion ("too much talk weakens authority"); and there is a pervasive sense of apprehension about group spontaneity ("once they start expressing themselves, who knows how it will end?"). It is easier to face one or two children at a time than to risk oneself against a multitude ("there are so many of them and only one of me"). The themes of risking, trusting, and the possible abuses of group power were anxiously repetitive ones at the child care workshops—and, it should be added, at the meetings of the supervisors themselves.

Under these conditions, the "Cottage Six" psychology must prevail, that is, the informal group processes are left entirely to the children, with few attempts by the adults to affect the real conditions under which they live. This rigid division of power, the formal system for the staff and the informal system for the residents, makes it impossible for the child care workers to make their proper impact on the culture of the cottage and influence the norms and values by which the children order their lives within the cottage system. Polsky's comment is important:

> Institutionalized adolescents are probably socialized more by their peers than any other young people in American society. Living together twenty-four hours a day, they have little respite from one another. When one boy is "acting out" against another, he is fulfilling needs traceable to his unique pathological history. But his outburst is publicly enacted and, together with peer spectators, he is institutionalizing a subculture—a world-within-a-world . . .
>
> The fundamental task of the residential treatment center is not only to rehabilitate individual youngsters but to create a therapeutic youth culture; the latter mediates institutional values and exerts a profound influence upon each boy.[4]

At the times when these rigidities broke down and child care workers found themselves entering the cottage culture and engaging the children in heart-to-heart, informal group talk, they reported their pleasure in the newly found intimacy, their fresh respect for the youngsters, and how impressed they were with the children's desire to talk to staff and to each other. And invariably, the youngsters would wonder why they did not do this kind of thing more often. These adventures into group intimacy were both tempting and threatening to the child care workers, requiring skills they did not have and with which they received little help.

With these dualisms before us, how do we proceed to conceptualize the child care job so that we may understand its tasks more clearly and help integrate some of these dilemmas? The first problem would seem to be that of describing the function of child care in terms sharp enough to lead us to the skills necessary to carry it out.

The Child Care Function

Certain criteria must be applied if we are to design a functional statement that works as a guide to action, rather than the customary inventory of broad goals and aspirations. We might begin, for example, with the stipulation that the child care job must claim only a specific part of the agency's function, not all of it. The statement should identify a well-marked set of tasks that can then be seen alongside those of the teacher, caseworker, psychiatrist, psychologist, nurse and others. This may appear to be a truism until one has seen the all-encompassing characterizations with which each discipline identifies itself—as if it were not part of a system in which the labor is divided, but working single-handedly to produce "adjustment," "maturity," "altered self-images" and the like.

---

[4]Polsky, Howard W.: *Cottage Six—The Social System of Delinquent Boys in Residential Treatment.* New York, Russell Sage Foundation, 1962, pp. 181–182.

Second, the statement of function must emphasize what the child care worker is supposed to *do,* not what he should know, or be, or feel. The focus should be on the movements he performs and on the acts that are in demand. If it is important that the child care worker understand human behavior, be sensitive to feelings, and model certain traits of character, it is only because these attributes may add up to some specific acts and skills that will benefit the children in his care. To describe one's function within a dynamic system is to define how one *moves,* not simply to identify one's characteristics; as "love is not enough," neither is knowledge, or sensitivity, or self-awareness. The preoccupation with knowing can, in fact, impede the helping process itself. Often I found the child care workers following the professionals into what I came to call the "talmudic trap"—where the need to pile insight on insight, datum on datum, made it extremely difficult for them to turn their attention to the development of *strategies* for dealing with the problems under discussion. In several instances, after a cottage worker had presented a child for discussion and then listened patiently to a brilliant diagnostic exposition by a psychiatrist, I asked the worker whether he felt he could now use what had been said to him. The answer was always a sheepish negative, and I would urge him to put his question again. It is not true that if one understands a client's problem in detail, he is somehow programmed to do something effective about it. The bridge between knowing and doing is harder to build than that. Knowing and feeling and modeling are all important, but they are preparation for action, not substitutes for it.

Third, this action requirement—this demand to describe the doing—is not satisfied by the usual role designations that pass for operational description. To call a child care worker a "parent," or a "nurturer," or an "ego-ideal," or an "enabler" is to beg the question of *skill* and settle for *intent.* It is *how* one nurtures, or enables, or administers, or offers love, that is the crucial factor in describing his work; there was a time, for example, when one "enabled" a child to learn to swim by throwing him into deep water. This, I think, is what child care people mean when they say to their experts, again and again, that they would like to be told less about what to do and more about how to do it. The role inventories are legion, but all of them put together do not explain a single skill or clarify any detail of the helping process in action.

Fourth, the worker's movements must be clearly related to those of his children; his work takes its meaning from theirs and his tasks can be understood only in interaction with theirs. He acts to help them act. When we describe the worker's moves in unilateral terms, as when we see him "diagnosing," speculating, making decisions for the child and otherwise operating independently of what the child himself is working on, the effect is essentially unreal. Any helping process, child care no less than supervision, administration, teaching or therapy, must reflect the efforts of the helper to articulate his energies with those of the ones being helped. In our child care workshops, the first case presentations were geared to the assumption that to describe a child was to describe his illness, and they gave long and detailed accounts of his inadequacies. The first time I asked "What is the kid working on?" the discussion came to a puzzled halt. But it was only when they could begin to discuss the child's intentions, the function of his behavior, what he was spending his energies on, how he was using his peers and the worker—it was only then that they were able to talk about the children as real people rather than as a collection of illnesses. From this point, they began to include in their presentations comments about the child's strengths, his ambivalence and anxiety and his efforts to master his environment. Most important, they were then able to focus more directly on their efforts to help the child use these strengths in his own behalf.

Fifth, the statement must put its emphasis on process, rather than goals. The concern with small steps, with the here-and-now, calls for close attention to the moment-to-moment exchanges between the worker and his group; while the preoccupation with goals creates global formulations, promising achievements that are impossible for one worker, or one institution, to attain. The statement should stress working on problems, not solving them: the work-in-process theme sounds real and manageable; the goal-achievement theme creates the kind of "professional lying" that sounds high notes and fanfares but soon becomes quite discouraging.

Sixth, we must avoid the temptation to distinguish between "instrumental" and "expressive" tasks—between work designed to "get things done" and that addressed to the problem of "feelings." To split life in two this way can only be attempted by people who do not have to do the work in the cottages. Such a concept divides the worker from himself and must inevitably lead to the effort to divide the child as well. Where it governs, the institution tends to create what we came to call a "feelings department" which, set off against a "strictly business department," constitutes a fairly accurate model of schizophrenia itself. The fact is that everything the child care worker does is invested with all the qualities of life: what is "to be done" cannot properly be done without feeling and investment; and where there is feeling, it is always *about* something. What the worker seeks, always, is "feeling in pursuit of a task."

Finally, the functional statement should make it clear that the child care worker is responsible for "two clients," with each demanding its own appropriate skills and strategies. On the one hand, there is each individual child within the cottage group, establishing a concurrent series of one-to-one relationships in which the worker carries out his institutional assignment. On the other, there is the group itself, the mutual aid system on whose strength so much of the therapeutic enterprise will depend.

With these criteria in mind, it seems to me that the special function of child care in the residential treatment center is to help the children negotiate the various complex systems that they must mobilize for their own use in order to get better and get out. Each of these systems—the cottage, the school, the clinic and others—presents the child with certain demands and opportunities designed to add its special function to the total pattern of treatment; and the child care worker is strategically placed to assist both the child and the system to do what they are supposed to do together. Oriented thus to the *encounter* between the children and their systems, the worker moves to facilitate the work between the two and finds it unnecessary to choose between them or to declare his loyalty to one or the other. Instead, he acts from the assumption that the child and the institution have a common stake in the treatment process, that the network of treatment systems is complicated and difficult to negotiate and that his assigned function is to mediate these transactions. Thus, in any given encounter between a worker and a child, the central question is, What system are you trying to help him use? And in every contact with a system-representative, the central question is, How are you helping this system reach out and incorporate which children into its part of the treatment pattern? The following is from a child care report:

> Sam had a history of changing his school program whenever he began to have trouble with a teacher, other students or the demands of the subject. This semester, Sam and the school guidance counselor had agreed that he could choose his own school program but that he was expected to remain with that program for the rest of the school term unless the three of us agreed beforehand that there were valid reasons to change it.
>
> One day, the guidance counselor telephoned me to say that Sam had been ejected by one of his teachers for disrupting the class. The boy had then demanded a program change and the counselor had refused to give it to him. It seemed to me that Sam and the counselor were caught in a dilemma and didn't know what next step to take. They had committed themselves to a specific school program and now one of Sam's teachers was complaining that he was too unruly for her class. I suggested that the counselor, Sam and I sit down together to discuss the problem.[5]

When they did, the worker's skills were fashioned by his efforts to carry out the function of mediating the interaction between the two, as he talked alone with the child, alone with the counselor, and with the two of them together. Here is another instance:

> Most of the boys in the cottage were becoming more and more resistant to the idea of attending religious services. In addition, they were becoming more restless and unruly while the services were in progress, and the rabbi was finding it more difficult to hold their attention. They constantly complained to me about the services and searched for ways of being excused from attending . . . I approached (the rabbi) and informed him that the boys in the cottage wanted to meet with him in order to express some of their concerns and to offer suggestions that might make the services more appealing to all the students in general. The rabbi thanked me for my interest and declined the offer.
>
> The services continued to be a painful experience for all concerned. About three weeks later, the rabbi telephoned me to say that he had reconsidered and would accept the boys' offer to meet with him. Before

[5]For this and the subsequent examples from practice, we are indebted to the professional child care worker, David Birnbach. They are taken mostly from his own work; a few are from the practice of workers he later supervised.

> the meeting took place, I met separately with the rabbi and the boys in the cottage, in order to clarify the purpose of the meeting. As I saw it, both the boys and the rabbi wanted to find ways of improving the religious services . . . my task with the rabbi was to help him listen . . . to the feelings of the boys. The rabbi said that he would be willing to listen to constructive suggestions, but that he would not allow the boys to make statements that would demean him or undermine the dignity of his position . . . My task with the boys was to help them express themselves in ways that would serve their interests.

Again, this time with the whole cottage group as his focus, the worker's skills would be judged by his attempts to implement the aspirations of both the clients and the particular system they were trying to negotiate.

When the mediating function is thus applied to the cottage itself—the group as a whole—it proceeds from the fact that the peer group plays two roles in the life of the institution. First, it is one of the various systems of demand and opportunity with which each child must come to terms, and which each child is continually trying to negotiate as he seeks to use this difficult instrument in his treatment. Second, it is a mutual aid society in which each member is trying to do much the same thing and for which they need each other's strengths. The process of child-system negotiation is much the same as with the other systems and the helping skills will emerge from similar necessities. Helping the collective, the alliance itself, will produce some additional movements and requirements. The group, as a whole, has much of its own work to do, and this work will be done either *sub rosa*—Cottage Six style—or openly and "officially," in line with the members' formal responsibilities to each other for mutual help in their shared goal of getting better and getting out.

This problem, helping to strengthen the peer group itself, calls for the development of skill in several areas: in the *contractual* work, which sets the climate of mutual aid and elevates the treatment values to a position of prominence on the cottage agenda; in the *structural* work, where he helps the group to order its internal affairs, develop work machinery for planning and decision-making, regulate the system and assign roles and statuses; in the *environmental* work, involving the group's relations with neighbors and other systems and its "public image" within the institution; and in the *individual* work, in which the group inducts its newcomers, finds places for its deviants, exerts its discipline, resolves its power struggles and develops its subgroupings. It would take too much time to elaborate each of these areas, but some of the elements of work come through in the following. We call it our "brother's keeper" record:

> Three boys had been involved in getting beer and drinking it in the cottage on Friday evening after lights out. When I arrived on Sunday, I saw each of the boys involved individually and called for a cottage meeting after dinner.

I began the meeting by saying that I guessed everyone knew about the incident on Friday and I thought we should get together to discuss how the guys felt about what had happened, what could have been done and what should now be done.

SAL: I feel that we can't always be there to stop situations. JOE: Is it our job as friends to stop them? I felt guilty because I could have prevented it; instead, I went along with it. No one would do anything. PETER: The guys thought it was only a cigarette run . . .

I said that the feeling I had picked up was that nobody really cared what Hal did or whether he messed up, but that feelings were more complicated where the other two boys were concerned.

SAL: The next day the guys wanted to hit Hal. Why not the others? Hal was masochistic, but the others didn't have to go along with him. HARRY: You should have gotten the beer away from them. JOE: I feel as guilty as they. I enjoyed it as much as they did. I wondered what to do and I began to worry. Anyone could have stopped it and nobody did. They wanted to be stopped.

ARTHUR: Yes. JACKIE: Yes and no. . . . ARTHUR: I expected Sal to stop it. JACKIE: I expected Sal and Joe to stop it. HAL: I expected Joe to stop it. . . .

(Later in the discussion, the worker reaches for contrary feelings, and succeeds.) STEVE: I hate to say it, but I don't really care. I've taken enough deprivations for other guys. I don't care about the cottage anymore, or anything. . . . BOB (to me): Is not caring a problem?

I answered: I don't know. I guess you either feel it or you don't. You can't force people to care for others.

And so it goes—the struggle to understand what they have in common, what the peer group means to them at this point in their lives and how to use the worker without succumbing entirely to his values and expectations. Out of these problems and others grow the worker's efforts to turn his special function into the specific skills he needs to make it work.

Let us now make the attempt to describe these skills specifically and show what they might look like in action.

The Child Care Skills

This attempt to translate function into skill is not meant to be comprehensive, but simply to offer some examples and develop a model of the exercise itself. Time will not allow me to give enough examples; ideally, I would like to show each of the defined skills as it operates in the encounter with individual residents, with cottage groups, with subgroups and with representatives of the various treatment systems—teachers, nurses, therapists and others. However, the few I will offer do come directly from the Hawthorne experience. In the course of our work together, these were the special skills that seemed most crucial to the work of the child care staff.

We may begin with the ability "to talk with a purpose"—to state openly one's reason for being there, and to focus without embarrassment on what needs to be talked about.

> Pete's volunteer Big Brother had agreed to allow Pete and three other boys to spend four days with him during the Christmas vacation, and the agency gave its approval. A week before they were to go, Pete, who had been pushing very hard for the visit, came to see me and admitted that he didn't think it was a very good idea, because it placed too much responsibility on his Big Brother, whom he sincerely liked; he felt he was taking advantage of him.
>
> I told Pete it must have been hard for him to tell me this and he agreed, saying that he usually could not admit that he was making a mistake and he would end up digging holes for himself. I asked what did he want from me on this? He said he had made the decision, but he didn't know how to tell the others. We then proceeded to work on how he could tell the others.

And here is a record entry by a student of ours, in his second year of study, as he struggles with the problem of mastering the purposive approach and tries to learn the stance.

> On the first day: What I decided to do was to begin interviews with each boy. . . . I made several specific demands that I felt were clear to the kids: "As I begin working in the cottage I want to get to know you, how you feel things are going in the cottage, some of your ideas about the way things are done, what's been done so far. It's a lot, but let's try. Before I know how I want to move and how I can help, I have to know what's happening from you. So start wherever you want." Where the kid seemed unclear, I got more specific: "What are some of your feelings about cottage routines, the way guys get along, relationships with staff . . . what kind of help do you think you need?"
>
> . . . I was saying that this is the way I work—and I want to hear from you because I want you to work, too. . . .

Second, there was the ability "to feel the child's struggle," the ambivalence and pain, and to show that you know what he is going through. The professional word for this is *empathy,* but the movements in it are as old as human relationship itself. The difficulty is in really feeling what the other is feeling, rather than simply saying you do. What the child seeks is not the mechanical I-know-how-you-feel-about-it-routine, but a deep and serious reaching into what it is that he feels but cannot describe.

> Morrie came to tell me that he wasn't going home for the weekend, because he didn't think he'd be able to resist his mother's food. He also complained about the lack of cigarettes, but as we were talking I got the feeling that Morrie wasn't really concerned with what we were talking

about. I said to him: "What really is the matter, Morrie?" He answered abruptly: "Nothing . . . it's this place." He got up angrily, saying: "Well, never mind," and walked out.

Five minutes later, I saw him pacing the halls in front of the kitchen. When I went up to him, he was still standing in the hall near the kitchen, his head turned in toward the hall, crying. I said to him softly: "Come on, let's go for a walk," and we left the cottage. For a while, we walked in silence. He said: "I don't even know why I'm crying." I answered: "It's OK to cry sometimes." Then he started to unburden himself, talking about the tremendous strain he was feeling in school, how hard it was to concentrate on his homework because he could think only of food, that he was struggling not to eat but was losing control, etc. I listened, and would comment from time to time: "it's rough," "you're trying to accomplish an almost impossible task," "the strain is getting to you," "you feel so alone in it," and so on.

After about a half hour of this, Morrie again expressed his sense of hopelessness. I said: "I see how you can feel that, but I also remember that six months ago you couldn't sit in a classroom to do an hour's homework because *that* was an impossible job. You said the same thing then. Now you're carrying a heavy academic program." He smiled and said: "Yeah, I remember."

. . . I asked him for no commitment that he would "go out there and try," but rather reiterated that the struggle was rough . . . and that I hoped he felt a little better. . . .

About ten minutes later, he quietly started to do his homework and worked steadily for the next seven hours. Midway through the evening he came to me with a broad grin: "I made it, Dave. I'm over another hurdle. I have the desire to learn again. It feels great!" I smiled, was glad for him and reminded him that "there will be other hurdles, but we'll work those through also."

At the end of the evening, when I sent him to bed, he said: "I wish I could tell you how much you helped me . . . I wish I could tell you how I feel. But I guess you know. Thanks."

A third major skill that came through the work was the ability "to avoid the battle of wills." This involved the recognition by the worker of the earliest signs that he and the child were mobilizing each other's resistance around a given issue and the ability to change the course of the encounter before matters got any worse. In the following engagement, the battle of wills is avoided and a rather important point is made:

LOU: Dave, do I need a shave for tonight? (Friday)
DAVE: (Looks) Yeah, I think you can use one.
LOU: I don't feel like taking a shave. Why do I have to take one? I shaved day before yesterday.
DAVE: Wait a second. Let's start all over.
LOU: OK. Dave, do I need a shave for tonight?

DAVE: I think you need one, but you'll have to make your own decision.

LOU: In that case I guess I'll take one. But I still don't feel like shaving.

DAVE: That's OK. You don't have to feel like shaving in order to shave.

And another example:

> Pete, on a deprivation that I had suggested, was protesting loudly to the recreation counselors as I drove up. "I'm not going to take this crap." "OK." "If you think I'm going back to the cottage you're crazy." "OK." "What are you going to do if I don't go back?" "I don't know. I haven't thought about it. I guess I can always come up with something if it's necessary." "Yeah, I'll bet you can." "So long. I'll see you later."
>
> I drove off. Shortly thereafter, Pete apologized to the recreation counselor and took his punishment. Back at the cottage, he said to me: "Man, trying to get through you is like trying to walk through a brick wall."

Fourth, I would call attention to the ability "to reach past consensus" to the lurking negatives that cannot easily be expressed, but which return inevitably to plague the child or the group if they are not faced in the course of the decision-making process. This is a primary demand in the work—that the worker "reach for trouble" when things are apparently going "his way."

> I had called a cottage meeting in order to find out how the boys felt about admitting another boy into the cottage who was having trouble in his own cottage, and whom the unit administrator wished to transfer for his own welfare. The impression I got as I listened to the boys talk was that, although the boy in question might be disrespectful towards staff and create certain problems for our cottage, they did not feel threatened by his entry. They were pretty well agreed that he should be given a chance in the cottage. . . . As one boy said: "I feel he should come in and let our counselors struggle with him." Nobody seemed upset at the prospect.
>
> However, I continued to ask whether they could think of any reasons why he should *not* come in. Finally, Art said: "Well, I think a little inconvenience on our part is worth it if we can help the guy, but I don't like to see the cottage used as a dumping ground for guys who can't make it anywhere else." Immediately, several boys responded with comments like "Yeah, how come we get all the trash?" Suddenly, we were talking about something else—the fact that the boys had strong feelings about how they were viewed by the rest of the campus as the cottage that had all the "sickies" who couldn't make it anywhere else.

The point here is that the worker would never have gotten their real feelings on this issue—only to have to face them later on—if he had not reached for these realities, despite the fact that things were going "his way" on the transfer of the troubled youngster.

The fifth skill involves the persistence with which the child care worker holds his youngsters, individually and in their cottage group, to the work at hand. This *demand for work* puts a sharp focus on the contract between the child and the institution and holds the children to their share in the treatment enterprise. In the "brother's keeper" record, the worker makes a firm demand that they use the beer-drinking incident as an episode in their treatment and weave it into their ongoing attempts to develop more control over their own lives.

> I ended the meeting by saying that guys had raised some rough problems that they were obviously struggling with. I said that I didn't think there was any right answer that would work for everybody and that, if they were unhappy with a solution they had chosen, they would have to think about it and try to find another one that worked better.

And here is the worker with an individual member of the cottage:

> I had told Art that he wasn't working . . . that he had loads of insight and understanding into the causes of his problems, but that he was now using these as excuses for not trying to do anything differently—as if to say: "Let me tell you my sad story and then you'll know why I'm the way I am." Art agreed that this was so, and said: "I'm using it as a rationalization." I said: "What's that?" He said: "I don't know, but it sounds good." I asked him what he was doing. He said: "I'm talking about my problems and trying to get more knowledge about them as a way of avoiding actually doing anything about them." I told him that if all he's gotten out of his treatment is a lot of words and "knowledge," he can consider it a failure, unless he can somehow do something different that's hard for him. "I want you to bleed a little, sweat a little," I said. He said: "You're right. I've been too comfortable. I haven't been struggling."
>
> Two days later, I asked him: "Been bleeding lately?" He told me of an incident in which he had tried something new (talking to a girl) when he didn't have to. He explained that it was hard, he didn't really want to, but he'd forced himself to try. The incident had turned out well and we talked about it. Art and I agreed that he would try and report back at least one new step or experience each day, no matter how small it was.

As the worker carries out his mediating function, this demand to do what one is there to do is found not only in his approach to the children but also in his work with the representatives of the systems in which they need to become involved. It shows up in the previously cited encounters with Sam and his school counselor and between the cottage and the rabbi. Here is the child care worker involved in a similar problem between Harold and his therapist:

> Harold, after working one year with an individual therapist with whom he had had a warm relationship, was assigned to another therapist. The problem that he brought to my attention was that virtually no work was taking place with the present therapist . . . he explained that he felt extremely uncomfortable with the new man, who sat in silence and stared at Harold, whereas his former therapist had been extremely personable and outgoing. He referred to the therapist as sitting in stony silence and

staring at him "with his beady eyes," increasing his anxiety and making it more difficult for him to talk . . . the silences had become unendurable . . . I shared my own concern that if his sessions were less productive than they could be, it was a loss not only for him but for all of us, since it meant that we were not helping him as effectively as we should be.

After we had talked a while, Harold said that the sessions were not serving his own interests and that they would not get any better unless he did something about them. He felt it would be very hard, but that it was now imperative for him to assert himself with his therapist. I helped him rehearse how he might present his feelings and I offered to speak with the therapist and introduce the idea that Harold was concerned about how they were working together and wanted to share some of his feelings with him. Harold agreed to the suggestion . . . he especially wanted me to convey the idea that he was not doing it to be mean. . . .

When I spoke with the therapist, I explained the situation and told him that Harold wanted to raise it with him in their next session. I added that my stake was in seeing to it that Harold used all the resources of the institution as effectively as possible and that whatever problems existed in their relationship had to be worked out between the two of them. The therapist acknowledged the problem and said that it was difficult for him to compete with the ghost of Harold's former therapist . . . he shared his awareness and concern . . . I offered my own impression that Harold seemed to be asking for the therapist to share a piece of his humanity in order to then be able to express his own honest feelings and concerns. I added that Harold wanted to talk about their working relationship but was fearful of hurting the therapist's feelings; he would need some help from the therapist in order to express his feelings openly. The therapist said it might be easier to talk if they took a walk together . . . I told him it was an idea, and I was sure the two of them could come up with others, since they both had an investment in working more effectively together.

Finally, there is the ability *to integrate both feeling and task in a single movement.* Such integration occurs when the worker begins to reach for the feeling in every task and the task that is the target of every feeling. No work is useful if it is done mechanically, without investment; and no feeling is real if it is sought in the abstract, unattached to a piece of work. It is only by focusing directly on this relationship between feeling and task that the child care worker can avoid the trap that lies at either polarity: either "never mind all this feeling stuff—get the work done;" or, "we can't work on this job until we've first explored the feelings." Here is an entry in which the worker speculates about the feeling-task connections:

Staff members are trying to do what they feel is asked of them; they give lip service to the idea of therapeutic management, but they will find

> their direction from what they feel the administrator wants. If the premium is on stability and orderliness, they will perform tasks to accomplish that end. For example, two youngsters are doing a cottage house job and the stronger kid bullies the other into doing all the work. The staff response was "I don't care, as long as the job gets done." If the attempt were made to deal with the relationship between the kids, the set of tasks would be entirely different. The latter choice is the more difficult and requires greater skill. As it was the kids had to feel "you care more about having a clean floor than you do about me."

As I have said, this brief inventory of skills is not meant to be comprehensive, but simply to show some of the connections between function and skill and to elaborate the point about the need to operationalize our conceptions of the child care job. It remains now to say a few words about the process of *ordering* these skills so that we may better understand the contexts in which they appear and the circumstances under which they may best be taught. Again, this aspect of the theoretical task requires more time than I can give it here; but I would suggest that a time perspective may be useful to us, that there is a progression of events in the worker-child, worker-group encounter which highlights the various stages of work that fashion the tasks and skills of the child care worker. Specifically and briefly, the demands on the worker seem to arrange themselves somewhat as follows:

There is a preliminary, *preparatory* period, in which the skills of the worker are wound around the ability to "tune in" to the specific perceptions with which each child will enter the institution and with which each cottage enters into its relationship with the worker. This "preliminary empathy" into how the children will approach each of their systems and the specific feeling-states that will affect their ability to work, will determine to a considerable extent the child care worker's ability to decode the children's messages and shorten the agonized, early periods of testing to find out what is real and what is illusory in this strange new world.

There is then a *beginning* period, in which the child care skills are directed primarily to the "contract-making" enterprise between the children and the institution. It was clear to me, in this as in other settings, that those children who had been helped at the outset to understand their relationship with the agency, their purpose for being there and some of the ground rules were considerably better focused in their work than those who were left to draw their own conclusions. The latter usually decided they had been sent to some peculiar sort of prison and waited defensively to see what would be done to them.

A *work* period then ensues, in which each partner in the therapeutic regime elaborates his role in detail. In this phase, the skills of child care are divided—if not equally in time, certainly in care and concern—between the cottage members and their systems. With the children, the effort is to help them, individually and collectively, to reach out to school, clinic, hospital and the other systems of demand and opportunity while supporting their attempts to establish terms that do not destroy their dignity in the process. Unless the child can maintain some sense of control over the conditions under which he lives and works, his ego will suffer under the "treatment" rather than benefit from it. With the various systems, the worker's effort is to help their representatives—doctors, teachers, nurses, psychologists, social workers and others—to understand the specific conditions of the child's life in the cottage, the work the child is trying to do and the strategies that might be required to involve him with, rather than simply deliver him to, the various treatment functions in the institution.

Finally, there is an *ending* period, in which the worker's skills are fashioned by the need to help both the child and the institution work out the steps by which the child can make the transition from one mode of life to another—from the period of reassessment and change to the delicate time in which the child prepares to re-enter the world in which he had once failed.

In an interesting way, these phases of work, the tuning-in, the contracting, the work and the transitional ending, are as applicable to the *single* encounter—the interview or the group meeting—as they are to the whole course of the relationship. There is nothing mysterious about this; it is simply because the theoretical importance of beginnings, middles and endings in human experience persists whether one is looking at large or small segments of time.

It is also true that as we apply these phases and skills to the work with both individuals and groups, we get a deeper sense of the *generic* character of the helping process in residential treatment. By force of circumstance, the child care worker cannot afford the luxury of specializing by the number of people he addresses at one time. He is generic by definition, as he moves from ones to twos to tens, from child to group to system-representative, using the same basic skills in each situation: focusing, talking with purpose, empathizing, avoiding the battle of wills, partializing, generalizing, reaching past consensus and moving to integrate task and feeling from moment to moment.

The Professionalization of Child Care

If we assume from the above, as I think we must, that the child care job is complex enough to be subjected to the rigors of training and discipline, how does this process of "professionalization" take place? And what are some of the problems that arise as the institution begins to take steps in this direction? Drawing from the Hawthorne experience, I would like to address a few questions that were particularly interesting to me in this connection. First, what are some of the supervisory dilemmas involved in the present work with child care personnel? Second, what, specifically, can you teach child care workers to do and at what point do your expectations become unrealistic? And finally, what implications can we draw for the task of converting the service of child care into a professional discipline?

The dilemma of the child care supervisor begins with the fact that his ability to fulfill his own function depends on the least equipped and least educated members of the agency staff. It is literally true that the supervisor's own professional aspirations and sense of adequacy ride on the efforts of people who have been judged least competent and placed lowest on the institutional totem pole. Thus, while the supervisor is constantly trying to build efficiency and autonomy in his child care staff, he is at the same time poised to snatch back responsibility at the instant that something goes wrong. When this happens, the child care worker feels cut down and demeaned before the children, while the supervisor, feeling slightly guilty, is nevertheless convinced (often correctly) that the situation calls for a level of skill beyond the cottage worker's powers. In this institution, certain issues tended to provoke considerable amounts of supervisory anxiety: the inmate behaviors most frightening to top staff were unorthodox patterns of dress, rebelliousness directed at staff members and the use of narcotics. I would imagine that each institution has its own particular areas of administrative sensitivity, and these are precisely the areas in which the alternatives available to child care workers are the most severely limited.

A second dilemma arises from the fact that the supervisor creates new complexities for himself as soon as he raises his level of aspirations for the child care service. When he begins to encourage his cottage workers to talk seriously with the youngsters and to individualize their needs, he changes the workers' lives and raises the stakes appreciably. Specifically, the "professionalized" child care worker dilutes the supervisor's power: the worker is himself "individualized;" he begins to expect more autonomy and one must take more risks with his performance. A supervisor said "You know, it's easier to blame them than to teach them." Most important, the worker begins to create a demand for supervisory skill on a higher level. The supervisors found themselves in fact trying to teach the very skills they were themselves trying to master. It was a humbling experience for them to realize that the problems of order-and-freedom, tolerance of ambiguity, empathizing, reaching for negatives, integrating task and feeling, and so on, were difficulties that they were experiencing in their own work. This meant that they had to examine quite seriously the tempting and all-too-common fallacy that a teacher has mastered the tasks he is trying to teach. This was an excellent lesson, but a difficult one; and the embarrassment began to dissipate only when they moved to the more productive thesis that a supervisor and his staff were human beings struggling for the same answers to the same perplexing problems on different levels of professional accountability. Having thus accepted their own vulnerability, the supervisors then needed help in examining the specific movements of the helping process and the devices that all authorities, workers and supervisors alike, use to subvert it. They explored the phenomena of word magic, the false consensus, the ambiguous message, the distrust of small steps and the "Socratic game"—an exercise in which the helper, with the "answer" in his head, leads his charge by the nose to his "solution."

Through it all, we were constantly digging at the supervisors' basic sense of hopelessness about how much one could actually teach an untrained person about the sensitive care of sick children. There was a persistent feeling that they were being asked to build bricks without straw. Thus, the question that needed to be probed more deeply was the one into which I would now like to move. What is a realistic aspiration for the orientation and supervision of untrained child care personnel? In very specific terms, what can they learn?

At this point, it becomes necessary to begin work on a kind of "hierarchy" of skills, or, to change the image, a "continuum" ranging from the simplest skills to the most complex and difficult. Much work is needed in this area; our typical model of orientation and training is to throw the book at the untrained worker and hope that he will "get as much of it as he can." This counsel of perfection creates more guilt than education, mainly guilt about all the things the worker cannot do, rather than some realistic sense of what he can. The orientation sessions that purport to "expose" the untrained worker within a few days to massive doses of psychology, social psychology, psychoanalysis, social anthropology, community relations and more are gruesome examples of what I mean.

As I enter into this skill-ordering exercise, I am aware of the dangers of stereotyping the untrained workers; they are not all the same and in fact represent wide differences in background, age, sensitivity, and personal experience. What they do have in common, however, is the lack of formal preparation and discipline geared to their child care tasks; and, despite the limitations, it is worth trying to make some beginning generalizations about what we can reasonably expect from the unsophisticated workers and where we begin to approach the limits of what they can generally do. From my experience, it looks something like this:

1. You can get the untrained worker to enter the culture of talk, that is, to engage the children in serious conversation and draw them out on problems that disturb them. *However,* it is hard for the worker to sustain the conversation, because directness is embarrassing to him. Having not yet learned to distinguish between assertiveness and hostility, he mistakes the one for the other and is afraid that the child will perceive his openness as anger and attack. On a deeper level, of course, the worker is afraid that some of his real anger will in fact betray itself if he risks any of his real feelings in open and direct talk.

2. It seems to be possible for the untrained worker to learn to suspend his temptation to moralize for a while. *However,* it is only for a while. What seems to happen in the course of agency training is that the workers will learn first to listen to the child and try to decipher what he is trying to say; they will then learn to invite the child to open up and talk, promising attention and concern; under this impetus, many of the children will actually begin to respond and share something of themselves; and it is at this point that the workers will swoop in for the lesson, the moral and the sermon—they cannot resist the opportunity to "teach" the children "something about life." In the child care

workshop, they would say, "But if I'm not teaching, I don't feel like I'm doing anything." This strong need to have everything add up to a moral lesson emerges as what Kurt Lewin called the "intolerance for ambiguity;" to the child, it comes through as the worker's own need for closure, in every meeting and in every interview; each must end "right"—with an answer, a solution, and a reassurance.

3. They can be brought to sympathize with the children's struggles and can even, in training sessions, engage themselves in certain empathic exercises. I have seen them work together intensively on what it might feel like to be a compulsive child, an ambivalent, or anxious one, relating these feelings to their own life experiences in, say, trying to stop smoking, feeling rejected by their parents, deferring certain gratifications, experiencing anger, and reproducing other intense emotions. However, in actual practice it is very difficult for them actually to enter into a child's experience and feel his feelings at the moment. The worker is afraid, and with some justification, that if he closes the distance between himself and the child, he will lose his own sense of self. He feels that if he gets too close, he will be unable to retain the sense of difference between the child's interests and his own. Thus, the struggle to maintain the social distance is the effort not to betray one's role. This is of course one of the more poignant variations on the theme of "if you give them a finger, they will take the whole hand."

4. You can widen their range of symptom-tolerance, making it possible for them to be hospitable to some deviant behaviors, having learned to accept these behaviors as signals of distress. *However,* they cannot stretch these tolerances much beyond the behaviors they can tolerate in themselves; they cannot allow the child to enter their own circle of taboos. This is of course a familiar problem for professionals and nonprofessionals alike; but the trained worker, conditioned to self-appraisal with a deeper insight into his own defense mechanisms, is less apt to apply absolute criteria to human behavior and thus has a better chance to extend his hospitality to a wider range of symptoms. It should be noted that one of the most crucial symptoms of the disturbed child, defiance of authority, seems to be among the most difficult for the untrained worker to accept without retaliation. The personal taboo against rebelliousness seemed to me to be the most pervasive and the most difficult to unseat in the untrained child care workers. No matter how prepared the worker felt himself to be, as, for example, after a satisfying case conference, the actual defiant behavior of the child in action would turn the worker bitter and vengeful.

5. You can add to their knowledge of human behavior and deepen their understanding of why children do what they do, the function of defensive behavior and the meaning of certain psychological mechanisms. *However,* it is a towering problem for them to relate what they "know" to what they do. The demand to respond differently to the children is more than just a call for "applying new knowledge" to their work; it means asking them to change the reactions and response-patterns of a lifetime and reordering the judgments

and biases on which they have based their lives. Thus, the demand to do different things will feel to them like a personal attack, which, to some extent, it really is. To give up a deep-set norm for treatment purposes feels to them as if you are asking them to betray the norm itself. "After all," they said, "one has to stand for something." To be asked to give up this "something," even temporarily and for a specific therapeutic reason, is to invoke feelings of sinfulness and guilt. It is a full-fledged superego violation.

6. The educational progress that is made with the untrained worker is largely confined to his performance in the one-to-one relationship. The problems of developing group skills are more complicated: the group is a frightening device, often perceived as a multiplied version of individual anger and defiance; the worker feels outnumbered—"there are so many of them and only one of me;" and they tend to adopt a stereotyped or conventional stance in the group meeting—they "chair" the session, or socialize, or use the platform to make speeches. Thus, while it is often possible to improve the quality of individual conversations between worker and child, it is much harder to develop skills that will empower the worker to function more helpfully in the group arena—to strengthen the mutual aid processes, to help children negotiate their peers, to deal with problems of cottage morale, to promote more effective group planning and to facilitate the processes of programming and decision-making.

7. There are some special problems related to the unsophisticated use of written records of practice, the analysis of work and the use of supervision. Nevertheless, it is certainly true that much more can be done with these devices than is commonly imagined or attempted. I saw some very positive examples of how older, untrained workers could be stimulated to use recording, to tape their work, to make formal presentations of their practice and to use supervision with eagerness and a desire to learn.

What then are some of the implications for the professionalization of the child care function? I think it means that, although much more can be done with proper training and supervision of present personnel, it seems clear that such work must still be regarded as making the best of a poor bargain. It cannot, I believe, ever bring the level of child care to where we say it is, or to the point where it can live up to the real and pressing needs of residential treatment. While we certainly should be doing more intelligent things about the in-service training of the untrained worker, we should not delude ourselves that such efforts can go too far beyond the constant, nagging work that feels like building bricks without straw. To turn the job of residential child care into an accountable discipline, with a professional self-image and a teachable expertise, will require some formal preparation, some scholarship, some practice in separating the self from the client, some induction into the modes of empathy and self-evaluation and some of the other devices designed to carve out a distinctive function within the helping professions.

As to how much education will be required and what its specific content should be, we will learn more about that as we become more intelligent about the tasks and skills of child care. I am not now making the case for social group work, although I have found that what I teach social workers seems very close to what the child care worker needs to do his job. What is most important is that the residential treatment center recognize that the child care function is at the heart of its service, that it is complex and difficult work and that those who perform it must become full-fledged, unpatronized, disciplined members of the treatment team.

Conclusion: Some Thoughts on the Division of Labor

The professionalization of child care seems to depend to a considerable degree on the resolution of a number of other problems in the institution. These begin with the task of defining who does what for the child and whether the institution will develop a culture of treatment, rather than a continual battle about who owns the client. In the above, I have discussed the child care dilemmas and then the supervisory dilemmas; it now becomes necessary to examine some of the dilemmas of administration.

The administrator needs to make clear job distinctions among the various professions he employs to carry out the agency function. This meets both his need and that of the professions themselves, for no discipline, including child care, can assume its proper function and stature until it is fairly clearly marked off from the others. On the other hand, such distinctions cannot be drawn so as to "wall off" the separate functions so completely that the institution begins to look like the world outside in which each service is kept in its own compartment—something you "go to." In such a climate, the child does not enter a "therapeutic community;" he simply "lives" in the cottage, "goes to the doctor," "goes to school," and so on. The basic error that emerges, and robs the cottage and the child care workers of their function, is that the gap between the cottage and the treatment program distorts the essential character of residential treatment. The cottage is "instrumental," the clinic is "expressive," and the cottage life is conceived as a kind of baby-sitting operation that takes care of the child between visits to the therapist. The artificiality of this concept reached its height when the professional suggested that the clinic could actually be conceptualized as the aforementioned "feelings department," to which all matters involving the emotional life of the child should be referred.

Another administrative problem arises from the general ambivalence about the need for more sophisticated work in the cottages. On the one hand, the administration and the professional core of therapeutic personnel are eager for more effective child care work, realizing that peer group life carries an important dynamic for advancing or impeding the therapeutic enterprise.

However, there are also strong fears, representing a composite of administrative and professional interests: "all this new talking" in the cottages will make the cottage workers "soft" on matters of discipline; child care staff will make treatment judgments that may conflict with those whose function it is to make such judgments, cottage people will get too close to the children, close enough to alienate their affections and rob the therapists of their influence. A psychiatrist bitterly accused a child care worker of this "softness:" "With all this talk, you're suspending your disciplinary function!" At one meeting, my log reflected the varied perspectives of the psychologist, case-worker, unit supervisor, child care worker and executive director, as they sat around a seminar table and discussed the problems of institutional child care. I noted, "There is a major disagreement here on the kind of world they are living in," which brings me to my final point.

The administrator, surrounded by many professions, each with its own professional jargon, technical language, and frame of reference, is in the center of a kind of "Tower of Babel." It is necessary not only for him to understand something of each language, all talking at the same time, but also to help make these talkers intelligible to each other, so that they can integrate their efforts in the interest of the children. What often happens around the conference table is that each discipline makes its speech, contributes its piece of knowledge, makes its contribution to the pile of diagnostic perceptions, and leaves without being much affected by the work of the others. The task of orchestrating all this becomes increasingly crucial as the administrator realizes that the basic need is not to pile knowledge on knowledge but to create a common treatment *strategy* from the integrated contributions of each discipline. The emphasis on strategy rather than knowledge revolutionizes the staff conference and the processes of teamwork, as each profession tries to tell what it *does,* not what it *knows,* and shows how its analytic tools can be used as levers for action rather than as finished pictures to be admired for their own beauty.

In the institutional system then, as in any complex arrangement of interdependent parts, the separate functions must be clearly *differentiated,* while at the same time *integrated* so that the child experiences not a struggle for who owns him but an articulated network of acts designed to help him negotiate the institution, work with his peers, use his therapy in his own self-interest, learn what he has to learn, keep his lines open to his family and the outside world, and reconstruct his sense of self and his relationship to the demands and opportunities around him. The child care movements are a significant part of this network of professional activity.

Rosalie*

William Schwartz

Dear Professor:

If I were back in Group Work II at the dear old School of Social Work, I'd be giving you the story of Rosalie and me in the form of a "Record of Service," as:

> ROSALIE B.: *Age:* 20. *Member of:* Group of mentally retarded young adults in a neighborhood center. *Period of Work:* About six months, from November to May. *System to be Negotiated:* Her own peer group. *Problem and Focus of Work:* Client unable to participate actively in the life of her group; she was withdrawn, isolated, alone. I tried to help her open up and share some of her feelings and experiences with them. *How the Problem Came to My Attention:* From the very first meeting, I noticed that . . .

And the rest. Then I'd wait eagerly for the exercise to come back to me, covered all over with those big fat scrawls of yours, made with the famous black felt pen. And now I'm a thousand miles away, without a supervisor to my name and workload that leaves me little time for any writing at all. But when I do something I like, a bit of practice with class and skill, I think of the old days and our work together, and I grow nostalgic for the dialogue.

So let me tell you about Rosalie—my big, fat, beautiful Rosalie, who belongs to this group of retardate young adults that I've been working with at the Tom Paine Neighborhood House here in the Midwest. TPNH is a little box of a house, about 100 years old, underfinanced, understaffed, underpainted, with gloomy corridors, rickety floors, creaky doors, and suspicious smells

*[This article is a departure from the traditional form of professional literature. We are pleased to present it to our readers in an effort to stimulate writing about group work practice. Your comments are welcome.—The Editors]

William Schwartz is Distinguished Visiting Professor, Fordham University Graduate School of Social Service, New York, New York. This article is based on a record of practice submitted by Judith Lee, currently Assistant Professor, New York University School of Social Work.

Schwartz, William, (1978). Rosalie. Social Work with Groups, *1(3), 265–278. Published by The Haworth Press, 12 West 32nd Street, New York, NY 10001.*

coming from the corners. But somehow, when the place is full of people, it takes on a kind of warmth and excitement, and it feels good to be there.

What I'm doing with these young people only God, and maybe Tom Paine, knows, but I do enjoy them immensely and am developing more and more respect for them as people. They're exasperatingly slow sometimes (as I am often, to them, frustratingly quick), but they crack me up with their cheerfulness, their eagerness to have a good time, and their plain, goddamn love. I think we have a contract of sorts, even if they can't put it into words. Let me see if I can.

In the fast, jerky world outside, they're out of step; people are always shoving them impatiently out of the way or nagging them to get on with it. But here, in our little enclave, the place is theirs, the rules are theirs, and everybody *else* is out of sync. They talk, compare notes about how they live in the world, and figure together how to handle the slings and arrows. They eat, they dance, they laugh and cry together, and in general use each other to develop their own sense of community. My job is to point them toward each other and help them listen as well as talk, take as well as give. I reach for thoughts and feelings they've been taught to fear, including the deep sense of shame and guilt that has been built into them. I break up their large, inchoate notions into ideas small enough for them to handle. I demand honesty and candor, rather than the sham compliance that they've learned to use with the powerful ones in their lives. And I try to show as much honesty as I ask for, sharing my joys and sorrows in the things we do together. I try to legitimize their pace instead of making them use mine. And I show a stubborn and persistent confidence in their ability to think serious and worthwhile thoughts.

There, that didn't come out too bad, did it Professor? So now back to Rosalie.

When I first laid eyes on her, I saw a very depressed young lady, with a spark so faint she hardly seemed alive at all. Her responses were almost nil. She never shared an experience or expressed a feeling. Meeting after meeting, while the others were talking, Rosalie would sit there like a stone, a large dead weight, her eyes clouded over and revealing nothing. She would cling, the whole obese lot of her, to her boyfriend of the moment; it was not an active, or affectionate, or "making out" sort of clinging, but a kind of inert hanging on. For whole meetings she would remain with her head on Harold's shoulder, her hand in his, hardly stirring. Then, at meeting's end, she would rouse herself to eat with the others. Once in a while, she would joke a bit with her friend Sylvia—a silly, heavy kind of joking, with a tiny trace of spontaneity hidden somewhere deep beneath.

So . . . a hard case, my Rosalie. Nevertheless, I had some hopes: the clinging, the eating, the joking—these were Rosalie's *Imitation of Life,* the closest she would come to what you and I would feel as love, humor, enjoyment. But there was life in the old girl yet, and I wasn't going to give up without a struggle. What to do? I'll tell you what I did.

To begin with, I started right off by treating her as a member of the group, rather than as an isolate. Through my eyes, she was to see herself reflected as part of what the others were doing, even when it didn't look that way to anyone else. A smashing success I wasn't; it usually went something like this:

> "Rosalie, everybody's talking about Kevin's problem with his mother and their problems at home, but you haven't said a word. What's wrong?"
> Rosalie closed her eyes and turned toward Harold's shoulder. I tried again.
> "Something's hurting you and you feel better holding on to Harold?"
> At this it was Harold who smiled. Rosalie looked down.
> "Rosalie, something must be going on inside you while everybody's talking."
> Her head moved from side to side, slowly.
> Nothing. I turned back to the others.

The joking thing would get me some results from time to time. At one meeting, Rosalie suddenly said something to Sam in Yiddish (which they knew that I, being a *shikse,* don't dig). It was something about not pestering her, and Rosalie obviously meant it to be very funny. Which, apparently, it was, since they all began to laugh hysterically and then make up English equivalents. Sam said it meant that their parents want to hock them to China. I said ruefully that I'd like to do that myself since we'd now lost whatever it was we were talking about. This produced gales of laughter, in which Rosalie the instigator joined. I said it was good to see Rosalie laugh once in a while, and I pulled down the corners of my mouth, imitating her expression as she sits with us in the group. This drew more laughter, this time at her expense, but she joined in. I turned them toward some work, saying that maybe Rosalie and Sam were really making a point that wasn't so funny. Maybe their parents do sometimes consider them to be pests, and maybe tell them that. Rosalie said it's all she ever hears from them, and we went into some important talk about it. She stayed with us for a little while before lapsing back into her coma.

I found myself using humor a lot, trying to ease some of the tensions brought on by my demand for work, while at the same time reaching for a deeper level of feeling. Sometimes it got primitive. Once Rosalie suddenly announced—again in Yiddish, the language of humor and her favorite way of keeping me in my place—that she had to go to the bathroom. She and Sam and Sylvia went into hysterics. I said she'd better go before it was too late, and they squealed with delight, surprised that I had understood the remark. She and Sylvia ran to the toilet and returned after a few minutes, still laughing. We all joined in, and again I turned the incident into talk, allowing as how they'd all probably had some funny and not-so-funny experiences about having to run to the bathroom. We got several stories about not quite making it, the embarrassment, and the rest, and Rosalie was with us part of the way. The Yiddish quip remained Rosalie's favorite way of coming to life, and I continued to play the benighted *shikse,* sometimes verging on the *goyishe kop.* It became one of our main ways of communicating, of being together. But it didn't always get me the mileage I wanted. The real stuff was to come later.

You know, it was strange how the group itself was in some ways my worst enemy as I fought to get Rosalie to take full citizenship in her little community. The others really liked her—and that would eventually help a lot—but at the outset they would fall all over themselves to protect her from me, especially when I was about to hit paydirt. Like when there was an important discussion going and they were talking up a storm; no sooner would I reach for Rosalie to join us than they would find all kinds of excuses for her to stay out. Like headaches, for example. Headaches were very large. There was the time when Sylvia—small, dark, slow of speech—was angry about a fight she'd had with her mother, because her mother had been "babying" her again. The others waited patiently as she laid it out, and I said: "You've all felt that? Your folks baby you and you get mad?" You bet they did, and they moved in with feeling, each giving their own version, supported by the others with much nodding of heads. Their parents wouldn't let them grow up, didn't trust them, treated them like children, were always saying no, and the rest.

All except Rosalie. So I reached for her—timidly, gently, but directly. I asked whether she too felt babies sometimes, and got angry. Yes, she said, and looked away. "Rosalie, how does it feel to be so angry and not be able to say anything?" Silence, and the others watching nervously, looking first at me, then at her, then back to me. I was about to try again—I felt her almost within reach—when Sylvia said that Rosalie wasn't feeling so good; she had a headache. The others nodded gravely, and so did Rosalie. I looked around at their anxious faces; then I put my hand on Rosalie's arm and said I was sorry and hoped she would feel better soon. We went back to our discussion.

So I really had *two* jobs: one was to help Rosalie into her group, by making the demand for work and giving her every loving opportunity I could to meet it; the other was to get her friends to reach out for her, too—to stop holding her off with the protective bit, and to show their caring by respecting her ability to give as much as they did to the common work.

On job no. 1, with Rosalie herself, I forced my way past the aches-and-pains barrier and made my first real breakthrough. The next time she reached for her pillbox, I said:

> "Rosalie, you keep saying you have a headache, and I know it's painful to suffer with a headache. But if you'd only try to talk about the things you're thinking and feeling, the headaches might just ease up." At this point, Ralph, bless him, moved in to say that his dad had told him

that if you keep your feelings in, you can explode. "You got to let it out," he assured her eagerly. The others—Kevin, Harold, Sylvia, Sam—all made appropriate remarks, agreeing with Ralph, and for once so interested in the point itself that they forgot to haul out the first-aid kit.

And Rosalie responded. Quivering with feeling, she said: "I try to talk to my mother, but she always tells me to shut up, because she's always watching television or something. I try to talk to her in the street, but she says (imitating, shrilly) 'You're talking nonsense!' Just today, on the train, she said I was talking shit and I should shut up!"

Harold, flushing to his hair, stammered: "Your *m-m-mother* is full of shit!"

"Rosalie," I asked softly, "how did that make you feel, when your mother said that?"

"Like a lump of shit!"

"Wow, like you're not a person—worth nothing."

And Rosalie, quietly now: "I am nothing. One big nothing. A lump of dirt, that's all. No matter how nice they treat you, you feel like dirt, ..." Her voice trailed off, and she was silent again.

Poor Rosalie. But for those few moments she was with us, in the open. She was not old Deadweight Rosie, but a throbbing, suffering young woman, with a life and a mind of her own. She was . . . how shall I put it? . . . *interesting* . . . to me, to the others, even to herself.

This was only the beginning of course, and the job of tackling the group itself remained. But I was encouraged, and as I turned to this piece of work it was Kevin who gave me my chance. He had just gone through a list of ten—count 'em—complaints against his parents, and the others were picking up on his theme, elaborating it, and telling their own stories. They were getting very good at telling each other their troubles, what Mom or Dad did, how they responded or didn't, what they'd do if it happened again—all recounted with great feeling and excitement. They're used to each other's pace and style, and they don't get impatient, as I sometimes do, with the slowness of speech and the time it takes them to put together an idea. They wait each other out: little Sylvia looks intently at the speaker's mouth, her body tense and concentrated; skinny Harold looks up at the ceiling and around at the walls, apparently detached but listening carefully all the while; Kevin jiggles up and down and smiles a lot, his thick glasses bobbing on his nose; red-headed Sam spends much of the time watching my eyes and reflecting every expression on my face; and round Ralph, tubby and serious, stares at his hands, frowns weightily, and looks as if he's thinking deep thoughts.

Anyhow, there we were, each in our customary stance, everybody picking up somewhere, hot on the trail of injustice. (I should mention that the poor defendants, the long-suffering parents, have been invited by the agency to form a group of their own.) Sylvia had just completed her litany of woes when I turned to Rosalie and said I knew she had lots of complaints too, and was just as angry as the others, but she wasn't saying anything. Remember what we had found about keeping it all inside? Rosalie shook her head, that slow, ponderous, wagging movement of hers from side to side. Right away, Sylvia said that Rosalie's ear must be bothering her. Harold and Sam jumped in to corroborate, telling about her ear problem as the others set up the chorus of nodding. (This was the third earache meeting.)

I asked Rosalie if that was why she was so quiet? She looked off to one side and whispered that her ear did hurt, and she had her drops with her, but if she put them in she wouldn't hear anything. I asked if she wanted to hear. "Yes," she said, a little surprised. "Good," I said, "then you want to work!" She looked straight at me then, and I asked if her ear hurt very badly? At this, she softened somewhat, her voice got a little louder, and she said "no, not really." I turned to the others, looked slowly around our little circle, and said "You know it doesn't help Rosalie to let her off the hook by saying that her head or her ear aches. We have to find out what's hurting her *inside.* I think she wants to be with us, and share things the way you all do, but it's hard and she needs your help." Sam nodded sagely, turned to Rosalie, and asked her if her mother lets her have friends? "That's it," I said, "that's what I think will help Rosalie." She sat up straight in her chair and answered that the only time friends come in is when her mother goes out, and anyhow, she has no friends except boyfriends. I said it must be lonely for her, and Sam and Kevin told her they had the same problem about finding friends. Sylvia and Ralph came in, too, and Harold, with enthusiasm. Rosalie joined the work and sustained her energy for the rest of the meeting.

I was real proud of her, and the others, and not too displeased with myself, either. But when I was through congratulating myself, I knew—as you must be thinking right now—that the work was far from over. In fact, it was just about to begin.

Now I have to tell you—reluctantly, but dutifully—about one of my most formidable obstacles, and it was a lot harder to face than Rosalie's inertia or the group's overprotectiveness. It was *me,* no less, in my most regressive moments. Those were the times when I got it into my head that something Rosalie was doing was wrong, and I was going to change it. At these points, I was no longer trying to help her do something *she* wanted to do and couldn't, like when I was pulling her into a group activity and using her own energy to help her find a way in. No, these were the times when I in my wisdom decided she was doing something wrong, or bad for her, and she should stop. Rosalie is retarded, right? And I am a college grad-u-ate, and Master of Social Work, too, right? So wouldn't I naturally know better than she how to conduct her own affairs? In other words, poor Rosalie was sometimes saddled with yet another Jewish Mother; and a JM with an MSW is a formidable opponent. When I would decide—"diagnostically," as we say in the trade—that something that felt good to Rosalie was, in fact, bad for her, I would begin to push her around, with all the "social work skills" at my command. It was terrible. I only did it a little bit, because it felt so lousy that I stopped. But it was awful while it lasted. I'll give you a for-instance:

One of my problems was that Rosalie was spending large amounts of money on her fellow members—buying them food with it, lending it, even giving it away sometimes. And they, I felt, were exploiting this need of hers to use money as a way of being in the group. So I asked my girl to come and talk to me after one of the meetings.

While the others hung around, waiting to go home together, Rosalie dragged after me into my little office and sat down across from me. Her face was a mask, expressionless, her eyes fixed on the wall over my shoulder. I smiled—my reassuring smile—and got to the business.

> "You know, Rosalie, maybe it's not my affair, but I'm worried about the way you carry around so much money, and spend so much on your friends in the group. I'm not blaming you or anything, but I'm curious about it. Why do you do that?"
>
> Rosalie lowered her eyes to mine. "Are you going to tell my mother?"
>
> "Rosalie! I'm not bawling you out! I'm just wondering why you want to do it. Can't we just talk about it a little?"
>
> The downward gaze . . . and the silence . . .
>
> "Is it that you feel they won't like you if you don't give them things?"
>
> She shrugged, a bit flushed now, some beads of perspiration showing on her nose and upper lip. I was trying to be casual and "nonjudgmental," but it sure as hell didn't seem to feel that way to her. Retarded and all, she was reading my mind, not my words. A note of desperation entered my voice as I persisted, trying to get it right.
>
> "Rosalie, you're nice enough to like without having to give away your money."
>
> She looked up, straight into my eyes: "I'm sorry," she said, "I won't do it any more." God! "But Rosalie, you must be doing it for a reason. Have you thought about why?" She answered in a small voice: "Because I like them." A start? "Do you feel they like you?" She shrugged, was silent, then: "I'm sorry. I won't do it any more."
>
> Wiped out. I let her escape, back to her friends. God knows what she told them.

Instead of letting bad enough alone, I pushed my point with the others, figuring I could get my message across in the group and pick up some allies there. After the next meeting, Kevin said he felt like having a pizza. As usual, Rosalie went for her money, but this time she said she couldn't have any, because her doctor had put her on a diet. Using this as a pretext, I asked the others what they thought about Rosalie treating again, especially since she couldn't have any. They agreed, cheerfully enough, that it wouldn't be fair, and Sam volunteered to treat, with Sylvia chipping in. Mission accomplished

. . . big deal. At the pizza parlor, I saw Rosalie slip Kevin a slice of pizza when she thought I wasn't looking. So much for me and my message. Rosalie had her way of being in the group; and whether it was "right" or not, "mature" or not, it was her way. Thank God she was dumb enough, or strong enough, or stubborn enough, to resist my invasion.

But enough of that; let's go back to my real career as a social worker. (This *is* a long letter!) I want to tell you about the dancing, and then about the Big Finish, which had some of the most thrilling action in my long and varied experience. Are you ready for this?

First, the dancing. It was their favorite activity, and from time to time they'd have some of their school friends in to join them after the meeting. They'd clear away the chairs, roll up the raggedy rugs, and put on the records. Then they'd sail toward each other, couple up, and move off dreamy-eyed, box-stepping vigorously around the dimly lighted room. The couples were either boy-girl or girl-girl, depending on who was there, and I would move around pretty good myself, especially when there were more boys than girls. Usually, everybody would dance every number.

Except Rosalie, of course. She would sit and watch, a kind of half-smile on her face, waving her body the tiniest bit in time with the music, and shaking off any of the boys who came toward her. From time to time, I would sit down with her and wave silently along, sometimes letting my hand rest lightly on her shoulder.

Once I picked up a spark of real interest as she watched Sylvia and her boyfriend move across the floor, and I tried to break it down a little for her. How come she wasn't dancing? She didn't know how? She didn't enjoy it? She couldn't dance as well as Sylvia? This last guess brought me a nod and a small sentence: She didn't feel like it. I smiled and said her eyes said she did. She returned my smile, and went back to her silent vigil.

The next time we had the dancing, I went a little further. As the first record began, I danced over to Rosalie, took her hand, and pulled ever so gently. The weight gave, and she came to her feet. But she kept me close to her chair, dancing a kind of standing-in-place step, her arms extended outward, her eyes closed, her lips half-smiling. I stood there watching her, waving my body slightly to make like a partner, but mostly just watching this great hulk of a girl as she moved with a strange, elephantine grace, a great sweetness shining from her face; the effect was somehow elegant, feminine, almost sexy. It only lasted a few moments: suddenly she stopped, turned back to her chair, and sat down. I said that was beautiful. She really liked to dance! She gave me the old Mona Lisa, turned her attention to the dancers, and that was all for then.

After that, Rosalie started to bring her own records and contributed them to the common pool. But she wouldn't leave her seat at all during the dancing, and I didn't push. I would look over at her often, smile, and let her know with my eyes that I was available to dance with her whenever she liked. Again, I would sit with her from time to time, the two of us watching . . . and waving . . .

Then, one night, I took another step. It was a risky shot, but I counted on what we had going together. I was dancing with Kevin, with Rosalie watching, when suddenly I moved away from him, faced her, stretched my arms outward, closed my eyes, and danced a slow, standing-in-place step. After a few moments, I half-opened my eyes and saw that Kevin was watching me with interest, while some of the others had stopped, too, and were observing the little scene. I told them I was doing Rosalie's dance, and sneaked a look at her . . . she was grinning!

It was time for the circle dance with which we always end our sessions, so as we formed for it I fell into Rosalie's step again and reached for her hand to join us. She rose, protesting that her step (her step!) didn't fit into this kind of dance, and she couldn't do it right. I made a little adaptation, coming out of place a little, and she started to do it with me, all the while objecting that she didn't know how. Holding her hand tightly, I went through it with her again and again, until she seemed more comfortable. Then we joined the circle. She smiled at me, and I laughed out loud, saying "you're doing it fine!"

At the next meeting, Rosalie got up by herself and danced with Ralph. Between them, believe me, they took up a lot of floor. I took care to comment out loud, publicly noting the change: "Remember when you used to sit and watch, while everybody was dancing?" She laughed—no half-smile this, but a real laugh!—and straightened up a little, pleased with herself. Later, she reached for me: "If you do my step with me, I'll dance too." "You mean 'The Rosalie'?" I asked. And as we sailed majestically onto the floor, I looked into her baby-blues and said, "It looks like you've decided to join the world." She laughed again, nodded, then turned her attention to the demands of the dance.

We taught "The Rosalie" to the others. I leave it to your imagination what that scene was like: the gang of us, me included, dancing grandly in place, eyes half-closed, arms outstretched, while the star of the show modelled our movements from the center of the floor, watching me carefully to be sure she had it right.

All of which was great fun; but it was also a preparation for a time when Rosalie could join her friends more openly, more expressively, in the common effort to which their little group was dedicated. It was now near the end of our time together, and I decided to build more boldly on what Rosalie and I, and the others, had going for us. I reached directly for the depths of her sadness and engaged a part of her that none of us, including Rosalie, had but barely seen. It started with the medicine thing; then I took a long chance, laid on a big demand, opened a wide space for her to get in, and got a startling effect. I wrote up this part of the work in some detail, so I'll give you the record itself. Here's how it went, Professor, so grab your black felt pen and head for the margins.

The group had been working on a problem of Sam's—one of many he had brought in that night—when:

> . . . there was a pause in the discussion, and something made me look at Rosalie. She was looking up, over our heads, and her eyes were

> very sad. I asked the others to notice how Rosalie looked. Sylvia said she was quiet, Harold said sad, and others used the words upset, lonely, sick. Rosalie said she thought she should take a tranquilizer. I looked sympathetic, and wondered why she thought so. She said she's supposed to take them when she's nervous or sad or something. I said she did seem sad tonight; but if she couldn't talk, we couldn't help her. Last week, I said, she had opened up a little—and now there are only four meetings left, and there isn't much time for us to help her with the things that are making her sad. The others were leaning forward, watching intently, pulling for her. Ralph sat quietly, hands in his lap, his eyes fixed on her face. Sam was watching mine. Harold smiled encouragingly, if a bit uncertainly, at Rosalie, then at me, then back at her. Kevin's expression was impenetrable behind his heavy glasses. Sylvia was all tender concern, anxiously waiting. And Wendy, a newcomer, smiled nervously, troubled by the encounter but eager to do what everybody else was doing.
>
> Rosalie's eyes were dull as they met mine, and then travelled slowly around the circle. As if in answer, the others began to talk. Sam said he's learned that if you keep it in you explode, like he did last week. Sylvia stated: the last time she talked in the group, she was embarrassed, but she felt much better afterwards, and she got real help with her problem. Kevin, Harold, and Ralph each took a stab at guessing what Rosalie might be worried about (each of them projecting his own particular struggle).

You see, they were all working hard to help her, and to help me help her, but at the same time I could feel that the guessing and the filling-in were their way of smoothing it over for Rosalie, not letting her deal with the silence and her own thing. I wanted to let her have it back; it felt to me like she was ready to take over her own part of the affair.

> I asked Rosalie what was she feeling right then, as we were talking? The silence again—but this time the others held it, sensing that I wanted it, and that Rosalie needed it in order to make her move. About half a minute went by (I think!) and then Rosalie spoke. She said she looks sad because she is angry. "Good!" I answered. "Angry at what?" Her voice rose: at the people in school. Nobody likes her there; she has no friends there; they all walk away from her. Her eyes deepened as she talked, and I noted it to the others, saying that Rosalie feels so badly that she wants to cry. She nodded and the tears welled up.
>
> I said, "Go ahead and cry, Rosalie, it will make you feel better, not worse." Sylvia said, "Yeah, sister" (a pet name), "it sort of clear out your system, the whole inside of you." Rosalie looked down and fell silent again. I said gently, "no words, no help"—and then (balancing the demand with the invitation) I said she must be feeling very hurt and alone. She nodded vigorously, sniffing deeply, the tears beginning to come.

> I tried to give her a handle she could use to start talking. "What's wrong?" I asked, "Why don't you have friends at school?" She shrugged, but I persisted. "What do they say when they walk away? Do they talk about you? Do they talk about how you look?"

Now the others, deeply moved, began to react as if the complaints were theirs, not just Rosalie's. It was about them too now, and they pitched in, guessing about what the enemy was saying, each offering the comment that hurt them most. The Big One was on its way, of course, and now it came.

> Suddenly, Sylvia said she knows what it is—they must have called her *retarded!* Rosalie's head came up sharply. "That's right," she choked, and really began to cry . . . a deep, sobbing, breaking-up kind of crying. Kevin stood up next to her and put his hand on her shoulder, his head moving from side to side in embarrassment and agony. I nodded and smiled at him. Sylvia looked at me, and I said of course she could comfort Rosalie if she wanted to. Sylvia put her arm around Rosalie's big shoulders from the other side, and kissed her on the cheek. Sam was red-faced, furious: "I don't know what to do," he fumed, "they got some nerve . . . they're all retarded . . . we're all the same . . . they should talk like that and hurt you!" Wendy was in tears, her pretty face contorted. She said that the kids on her block always laugh and call her retarded, and she knows how Rosalie feels . . . she gets so mad she doesn't know what to do.
>
> I said that it hurts them very much to be retarded, and to have people use that word like a curse word. They all picked up on that, agreeing that the word shouldn't be used at all by people who don't understand what it means. Each gave examples of times when they'd been called names, and how it hurt, and they didn't know what to do. Rosalie had stopped crying and was nodding eagerly at what the others were saying.
>
> Our time was almost up, so when there was a lull in the conversation I said that Rosalie had worked very hard tonight, and shared a big hurt with us, and it had turned out to be everybody's hurt. Sam said she sure did, and she sure hit the nail on the head! I said I'd like for us to talk more about this next week: about the times people make fun of them, or are impatient with them; what it feels like when they do; what they do about it; and what they might be able to do that would make them feel more proud of themselves, and not so ashamed. They nodded gravely, Rosalie too, everybody looser, eyes more alert, than I had ever seen. Rosalie had sure done as much for them as they had for her.
>
> Kevin ran over and put on the record for the goodnight dance, and they moved to the center of the floor. Rosalie hung behind, sitting down alone. I went over and asked her if she was still feeling sad. She said no, and I pushed to keep up our winning streak: "But you want to sit there behind your stone wall while everybody dances?" She smiled that angelic smile, grabbed my hand, held it tight, and went into "The Rosalie" as she fell in with the others.

So . . . that's how it all happened. And now I find myself trying to put it all together in my head. What has happened, exactly, and what does it add up to? You taught me that social workers don't trade new lives for old, and that they shouldn't say they do. Well, it's true: Rosalie is still Rosalie, and the major burdens of her life remain. She is a lonely, depressed character, too fat, terribly shy and uncertain, and with a self-image so tiny it could get lost in her voluminous handbag. But she has finally applied for membership in this little gang of hers, these fellow-sufferers, all in the same boat. She talks to them now, and she has seen herself put some of her own deep and painful feelings into the common fund. She has been able to give—and give not only food and money, but something of her own secret self. She has known, if only fleetingly, what it's like to choose action over the passive, stony, silent suffering, broken only by an occasional joke to show that she was still breathing. And perhaps most important of all, she has laughed out loud, allowing herself to be seen enjoying, admitting publicly that she can feel some happiness and have a good time with her friends. For a chronic depressive, that's not bad.

Mind you I'm not claiming, as we often do in this business, that Rosalie has "learned" all these things—to share, give, feel, enjoy. Just because she's done something once or twice, or even a few times, it doesn't mean that these behaviors now belong to her, or that her character has been transformed. As I said you said, no new lives for old. I don't know how these experiences transfer over to other places, other times, or how long the effects last; I suspect that will depend on more than me, or the group, or even Rosalie herself. All I know for sure is that she has done things that are new for her, that she has been able to enjoy them, that she is more involved with the others, and that she seems closer to her own feelings, at least when she's with us, than I've ever known her to be.

As to her use of grown-up authority—that's me—she's also taken a few steps. She turns to me more often now, to help her negotiate the risky business of group participation. She reacts more to what I do with her, rather than just sitting back and watching cooly as I lay another egg. What I'm trying to say is that Rosalie has taken me on: she makes demands, however subtle; she acts like she wants to please me a little; and she seems to have decided that it's my job to help her. You might say that Rosalie has become a client.

I think some of Rosalie's recent progress comes from the fact that we're coming to the end of our time together. It's a sort of last-ditch stand: "Hey, all of you, pay attention . . . don't leave me, just as I'm beginning to get into it . . . and you, social worker, don't give up on me yet. . . ." The others, too, are beginning to show some of the same uneasiness as we get closer to my impending desertion. I hate this endings business worse than they do; it kills me that we have to work in "seasons" this way, and I have to deal as much with my guilt as I do with their anger. I know, I know, it comes with the territory; and I'll handle the separation feelings like a good pro should. But the end is not yet. Maybe we'll be together again next year and maybe we won't, but right now we're still in business. And far from turning our last few meetings into one big farewell party, I'm planning to step up the work. Like so:

I want to help Rosalie *own* the progress she's made in the group—that is, admit it to herself and take credit for it. So I have to call attention to what she's doing while she's doing it. It mustn't get mechanical, of course; it's just a way of showing her, and them, that I understand what she's trying for, that I'm enjoying it, and that I want her and her friends to face it and get pleasure from it, too. I know that such attention-calling can be experienced as more pressure, more demand, so I'll be getting even more nudgy than I have been. But that's all right: I'm a Nudge by function, and I think they understand that. It's what you taught me as the "demand for work"; they know that about me, they expect it, and further, they welcome it. It means that I dignify them with expectations that nobody else thinks enough of them to make.

However, the strategy with Rosalie has to go further than just demand and expectation. Even as I'm urging and nudging, I'll have to leave space for her to retreat to when the going gets rough. When she's too afraid, and harassed, and depressed, I'll have to make it possible for her to duck back into her shell with my full understanding and approval. In fact, there will be times when I have to get her off the hook even when she herself hardly knows she wants out. So there I'll be—encouraging her to move in opposite directions, forward and backward. It's tricky; but so is Rosalie. If I get so enthusiastic about her "progress" that I lose her in the process, there I am again, a JM with an MSW; and again Rosalie will find herself being pushed around for her own good. She's had enough of that—and so have I.

As for the group itself, there's a lot I want to do about a number of things we've been working on together; but this letter is about Rosalie, so I'll stick with that. In a few words, her peers also need to own the strengths they used to band together to help one of their members—Rosalie—find her place within their fellowship. They've been wonderful with her—showing their feelings, putting a bit of pressure, protecting her when they felt she needed it, and showing their love and respect for her in lots of ways. The greatest thing is their lack of jealousy at all the attention she gets; somehow they feel what I've been trying to get across, namely that my attention to Rosalie doesn't mean that I "prefer" her, but that my love and concern are for each of them as they need it. The fact is that they've each gotten their own special piece of me as we went along. I could write you letters called "Sylvia," and "Kevin," and "Sam," and the rest. (Don't get scared; I won't, just yet).

The important thing for the group as a whole is that when one of them gives us some hard work on an important problem, it pushes each of the others deeper into the group experience. So, as I keep Rosalie close to her feelings of sadness and anger, I'll pick up the same yearnings in the others and try to help them come alive to the same feelings. I expect this to get pretty heavy as I begin to call attention to our growing sense of loneliness and mourning as we get closer to the moment of parting. I want Rosalie in the middle of all that, and I'll make the full demand on her, together with all the affection I feel for her.

One more thing. I mention it timidly, because it seems the hardest expectation of all, and maybe the most presumptuous. But let me say it anyhow. I would like to help Rosalie take *me* on a little, as she will have to take on all the grownups in her life, in order to free herself a little. That interview with her, about giving money to her friends, still haunts me. Wouldn't it have been great if she could have fought me off more openly? Like, "Look, madame social worker, you're supposed to help people, not run their lives. If I want to buy things for my friends, don't—what's the word?—di-ag-nose it, OK? And I'll do the same for you, every time you want to do something just because you want to do it. No hard feelings, OK?" That's my fantasy. Of course, that's way beyond the likes of Rosalie and her buddies; but I'd like to try for something close to a reasonable facsimile. Or am I drunk with the power?

With love,
Judy

The Art of Teaching

Introduction

For thirty-one of his thirty-three years of professional experience, Schwartz worked formally as an educator. He began this career, in 1950, at the Ohio State University School of Social Administration, leaving as Associate Professor, after six years of service. For the next six years he taught at the University of Illinois School of Social Work. In 1977 he retired, as Professor Emeritus, after fifteen years of service to Columbia University School of Social Work, New York City. His final teaching role as Distinguished Visiting Professor, Fordham University Graduate School of Social Service, New York City, began in 1977 and continued until his death.

It was Schwartz's experience that our profession, for the most part, acted as if attention to the details of the classroom and to the strategies, tasks, and skills of the teacher was unnecessary.[1] In this way, he suggested, we were similar to other professions which believed that subject matter competence was sufficient for the classroom. Rarely, he said, had he participated in discussions with other educators where their method of teaching was the subject of conversation.

The ideas contained in "The Classroom Teaching of Social Work with Groups: Some Central Problems" (1964c) and "Education in the Classroom" (1980) run directly counter to the belief that attention to method is unimportant. Schwartz believed that the challenges before social work educators were similar to those before social work practitioners. He reasoned that each group needed to develop a strategy which would reveal its definition of professional function; each group needed to identify the tasks which would carry that function into action, and each group needed to specify the skills to actualize the work the professional was there to do.

"The Classroom Teaching of Social Work with Groups: Some Central Problems," was published not long after the formation of NASW. This was an interesting time for group workers who were involved in the process of defining their difference from and common ground with others in the profession. Intended as a starting point for discussion, this article concerns: (1) the nature of group work process; (2) its connection with other social work processes; (3) the problem of teaching an art rooted in science; (4) the organization of classroom experience; (5) the function of the teacher in the classroom system; and (6) the interaction of the class and field.

---

[1]A review of the *Journal of Education for Social Work* from 1964–1981 reveals little attention to *how* social work teachers teach or to the theoretical orientations of classroom teachers. See Toby Berman-Rossi (1985), Theoretical Orientations of Social Work Practice Teachers: An Analysis. Unpublished Doctoral Dissertation. Yeshiva University, Wurzweiler School of Social Work, p. 26.

As readers engage these areas of thought they will quickly see the reverberations between Schwartz's ideas about social work practice and his ideas about social work teaching. Once again we see his emphasis on defining objectives in operational terms and a belief in the primacy of skill as central to the achieving of desired outcomes. It was not that he believed we taught skill in the classroom; that could only be learned in the field where students practiced what they were to learn. Rather, he saw the classroom as "teach[ing] behaviors associated with the analysis of skill and with modes of theorizing about the nature of the helping process" (1964c, p. 8).

By 1980, when "Education in the Classroom" was published, little of our professional literature was directed toward the nature of the teaching process and the analysis of teacher skill. First submitted to a leading social work journal, Schwartz was advised that though well written, "Education in the Classroom" would not be published because the journal believed it probably would not have a wide enough audience of interest.

"Education in the Classroom" is distinctive in our professional writing. It is not concerned with such important areas as curriculum content and design, or training priorities, but rather with Schwartz's own theory and perspective on teaching. He does so through a discussion of teaching strategies, operationalized objectives, and teaching skill. Like "The Classroom Teaching of Social Work with Groups: Some Central Problems," Schwartz hoped that "Education in the Classroom" would stimulate discussion about teaching, its relationship to how students learn, and the events of the classroom. He hoped that inclusion of process recording, from his own classes, would encourage others to do the same.

Toby Berman-Rossi

The Classroom Teaching of Social Work with Groups: Some Central Problems

William Schwartz

The job of developing a "conceptual framework for the teaching of the group work method in the classroom" presents a formidable array of problems. The term "conceptual framework" carries some kind of theoretical challenge; "teaching" means that we want to conceptualize the pedagogical processes along with those of the "group work method" itself; and the reference to the "classroom" indicates that we are focusing here not on the total educational enterprise—which would be difficult enough—but on precisely that part of the experience that emerges from the interaction between the group work teacher and his class. The task requires that a number of questions be tackled in turn, and each of us will undoubtedly come up with a somewhat different display and arrangement of such questions. This in itself will be our first step toward revealing and comparing the various theoretical orientations from which we work.

Concepts and Frameworks

My own order of questions begins with a need for some clarity about what we mean when we use the term "conceptual framework." I have read articles in our literature that purport to offer conceptual frameworks of one sort or another, yet seem to formulate no concepts and reveal no frameworks. Aside from the scientific allure attached to the use of such language, what kind of an instrument is this, why is it important that we have one, and how accessible is it to us at this stage of our professional development?

This article was first published in A conceptual framework for the teaching of the social group work method in the classroom, *and is reprinted here with the permission of the Council on Social Work Education.*

The term "concept" has been variously used to mean both simple ideas and complex abstractions, single words and the ideas behind the words, cognitive propositions, and normative "shoulds."[1] There seems to be general agreement, however, that concept formation is a process of generalizing from immediate experience. It is a *categorizing* activity, designed to group events into classes of like things, so that the categories thus formed will be useful for thinking.[2] Thus, if we were to agree that our first task is that of concept formation, it would mean that we should begin to define the categories in which we have arranged our preceptions of the teaching-learning experience in group work. More simply put, we would be identifying the generalizations on which we base our work.

Necessary Interrelationship of Concepts

But concept formation alone does not satisfy our need for understanding. Unless the generalizations are related to each other in some significant way, the major theoretical tasks remain unsolved. Merton's comment on this point is that "an array of concepts—status, role, *Gemeinschaft,* social interaction, social distance, *anomie*—does not constitute theory, though it may enter into a theoretic system. . . . It is only when such concepts are interrelated in the form of a scheme that "a theory begins to emerge."[3] And Carl Hempel notes that "concept formation and theory formation are so closely interrelated as to constitute virtually two different aspects of the same procedure."[4]

What is required of us, then, is not only that we risk some inferences and classify the significant elements of our experience, but that we arrange these concepts in a network that reveals the relationships between them. It is at this point that the going becomes particularly rough, for this is a diverse family of notions that needs putting together. The problem cannot be solved by a clear and forceful definition of group work—even if we had one to offer—followed by a bow in the direction of "good teaching." This is a kind of salesmanship mode, in which the emphasis is on "knowing your product," and then "putting it across." It cannot even be handled by an exposition on the problems of pedagogy, without reference to the group work model with which the teacher is identified. This latter is closer to the experiential truth—namely, that the "subject" is not a thing intact, but is fashioned for the learner in the course of the search itself—but it fails to conceptualize that which the search is about. We might say, for our purposes, that two conceptual frameworks—one for the

---

[1]On the subject of concepts and concept formation, see: Jerome S. Bruner, Jacqueline J. Goodnow, and George A. Austin, *A Study of Thinking* (New York: John Wiley and Sons, Inc., 1956), Chapters 1–3; Lillian Ripple, "Problem Identification and Formulation," *Social Work Research,* ed. Norman A. Polansky (Chicago: University of Chicago Press, 1960), pp. 41–44; and Robert K. Merton, *Social Theory and Social Structure* (Glencoe, Ill.: The Free Press, 1957), pp. 89–93.

[2]Bruner, Goodnow, and Austin, *op. cit.,* pp. 8–10.

[3]Merton, *op. cit.,* p. 89.

[4]Quoted in Ripple, *op. cit.,* p. 43.

"subject" and one for the "teaching"—are almost as bad as none at all. What we need, ultimately, is a single framework that will define and interrelate concepts dealing with the nature of the group work process; its connections with other social work processes, the problems of teaching an art rooted in science, the organization of classroom experience, the function of the teacher in the classroom system, the interaction of the class and field, and other facets of the teaching-learning problem in the group work classroom.[5]

Such schemes can be important to us in many ways. They can help us reduce a mass of experimental data to its essential elements. They can lay open the assumption on which we work. They give deeper meaning to the concepts which are forced to stand up under the pressure of other ideas within the same framework. By putting ideas into working juxtaposition, they tend to show up inconsistencies that might otherwise operate undisturbed. They serve to focus the collection of data. And they may help us to communicate with each other in a common conceptual language that has hitherto been unavailable to us.

Nonetheless, one has only to state the problem clearly to realize that we are not yet in a position to produce theoretical models of this order of complexity. Group workers have only recently settled into a profession that is itself struggling to find its rationale and its own conceptual language. Furthermore, we have only recently emerged from the missionary-movement stage, where the major problems were essentially philosophical rather than scientific and professional. There is still a good deal of work to be done in simply clearing away the debris of slogans and stock phrases which have for so long hampered our efforts to talk to each other about our work and build on each other's professional experiences.

But whether or not we are ready to provide complete and internally consistent frameworks, we can certainly continue to move forward in the process of generalizing from our experiences as teachers of group work in the social work context. And the most immediate question seems to be: Where do we most productively direct our search for relevant concepts?

---

[5]For some of our professional attempts to generalize about the problems of teaching group work, see: Charles S. Levy, *Education for Social Group Work Practice* (New York: Yeshiva University School of Social Work, 1959); Marjorie Murphy, *The Social Group Work Method in Social Work Education* (New York: Council on Social Work Education, 1959); Walter L. Kindelsperger and Gladys Ryland, "Assessment of Progress Made by Group Work in Identifying Basic Concepts and Methods for Utilization in Social Work Education," *New Developments in the Theory and Practice of Social Group Work* (New York: Council on Social Work Education, 1956); see also: articles by Vinter and Sarri, Pernell, and Saloshin, in *Educational Developments in Social Group Work* (New York: Council on Social Work Education, 1962); articles by Hartford, Lodge, and Middleman, in "Methods of Teaching Social Group Work" (New York: Council on Social Work Education, 1959), mimeographed; see also: articles by Cockerill and Kaiser, in "Methods for Formulating and Teaching the Common Elements of Social Work" (New York: Council on Social Work Education, 1953), mimeographed.

Problem-finding

I suggest that the best place for us to begin is with the enterprise of *problem-finding;* reaching for those concepts that are most immediately relevant to the problems we are trying to solve. My intention here is to raise three such problems, to describe briefly some of their working ramifications, and to suggest some possibilities inherent in each. The problems are these:

1. What specific professional tasks are we preparing our students to undertake? The question is asked without regard to who does what in the educative experience, but in terms of general educational objectives.
2. When we have developed some conceptions about general educational objectives, what part of this assignment is best performed in the classroom? In other words, what is the division of labor between class and field?
3. Having thus established the work of the classroom, what experiences are most relevant to this work?

Preparation for What?

One of our most serious conceptualizing problems is created by our inability to state our educational objectives in operational terms. "The most useful form for stating objectives," says Tyler, "is to express them in terms which identify both the kind of behavior to be developed in the student and the content area of life in which this behavior is to operate."[6] For us, this principle points to two basic concerns: the specific social problems we are preparing our students to tackle; and the specific professional skills with which we are equipping them to do the job. We suffer from a marked lack of clarity in both these areas—partly because the field of service is itself shifting and changing from year to year, and partly because of our uncertain part-whole relationship to the larger social work profession. But these questions must be answered by every profession, if it is to gear its training to its social function, and if it is to refine the skills it must propagate from generation to generation.

This emphasis on the *primacy of skill* as an educational focus carries several implications. First, it throws doubt on the efficacy of our tripolarization of educational objectives—knowledge, attitudes, and skills—presented as if they were of the same order and of equal importance. From our experience, we can testify that there are "knowers" who cannot help anybody and there are "feelers" who cannot put their feelings to use in the service of people. Ultimately, both cognition and affect must be transmuted into ways of listening and responding, and it is these operations, consistently reproduced, that

---

[6]Ralph W. Tyler, *Basic Principles of Curriculum and Instruction: Syllabus for Education 360* (Chicago: University of Chicago Press, 1950), p. 30.

represent the educational payoff in any profession. The client is not interested in the worker's store of knowledge, in his aspirations for humanity, or even in his degree of self-awareness. His questions must be: Does he seem to know what to do for me, and has he been able to help me? It is unfortunate that many professionals are known for the glibness of their talk and the sophistication of their language, rather than for the helping movements by which the community could characterize them as professionals. It should be made clear here that there is no intention to negate the importance of knowing, believing, and aspiring, but that these characteristics should be conceived as instruments to be employed in the development of skillful behavior. With this emphasis, the problems of knowledge and attitudes would become more specific than we have so far been able to make them. What, specifically, does the student need to know in order to develop these specified behaviors? What purposes can best lend themselves to the movements of the helping process? We may, perhaps, thus be able to work ourselves out of the unreal perfectionism of our current educational claims—that our students are being trained to know all about human behavior, group behavior, community life, social forces, and all the ways of the world.

Skill Identification

Second, the emphasis on education for skill would make it necessary for us to turn our attention to the problems of skill identification. If we can formulate some conceptions about what these professional behaviors look like—create some professional models, as it were—it would then be possible for us to develop some tools for measuring student progress, beyond the vague criteria of "insight," "growing knowledge," and "self-awareness" with which we are presently struggling. I envisage the conceptual tasks in this area to be somewhat as follows: (a) to identify the areas of performance in which professional skills are to be taught, in both class and field; (b) to describe the skills to be taught in each of these areas of performance by projecting a professional model of what these skills look like in action; (c) to delineate the specific areas of fact and purpose that the student will need to feed into the task of skill development; and (d) to develop an inventory of the kinds of opportunities and demands, in both class and field, through which the student will pursue his search for skill. What kinds of problems will we ask him to tackle along the way?

Categories of Performance

Space will not permit me to explore these themes in detail, but let me illustrate them briefly by giving some suggestions as to how they may be carried forward. I have found it helpful to conceive of four categories of professional performance, and to develop a professional skill-model for each category: *professional practice,* in which the skills taught are those involved in helping people, individually and in groups, to work on the tasks and problems that have brought them into the agency's sphere of service; *professional impact,* in which the skills are those required to implement a course of action designed to make one's professional contribution to the processes of social change—in the agency, in the neighborhood, and in the profession itself; *job management,* involving the skills required to organize one's professional tasks and to conceptualize the learnings one derives from one's practice—including the recording of experience, the collection of data, the publication of results, etc.; and *professional learning,* in which the skills taught are those required to work on professional problems and to use the help available—supervision, the literature, colleagues, specialists—while incorporating these resources into an ongoing approach to professional problem-solving.

The model-building process may be illustrated in one of the areas outlined above—that of *professional practice.* The professional model here is one of a worker who, because he understands both the service of his agency and the needs of his clients, can establish a working relationship between the two and help his clients mobilize their strengths in getting the assistance they need. This calls for the following skills in his work with people, both individually and in groups: the ability to establish purpose, to read subtle communications and respond to them directly, to find the focus of the client's concern, to show the client his problem in a new and more manageable way, to partialize concerns that are vague and global, to point up connections between apparently disconnected events, and to provide information relevant to the client's tasks. The general emphasis is thus on the identification of problems, the establishment of focus, helping the client to work, and helping him to separate himself from the service when it is completed.

In addressing itself more specifically to the skills required in service to groups, the model would emphasize the fact that these behaviors are rendered more complex by the multiplicity of simultaneous relationships. The group situation is one in which the student's primary task is to help the members use each other, exploit each other's strengths, direct themselves to each other's perceptions of experience, and enlist each other in the performance of the common tasks that brought them together. In addition, the worker must address himself to certain additional tasks which belong to the collective itself, and each of which presents its own attendant problems: group formation, with its problems of contract, task-consensus, etc.; group structure and maintenance, with its problems of the division of labor, status assignments, productivity, etc.; the group's relationship to its environment; and its efforts to provide satisfactions for its members. Each of these major group tasks calls for certain professional skills which can be explicated and taught.

The above is rather hastily presented, but it is hoped that some of it may provide perspectives that will be helpful to our discussion.

Division of Labor: Class and Field

In exploring the division of responsibility between the class and field experiences, there is no intention to create rigid, nonoverlapping distinctions, but simply to develop some understanding of the different demands that can most productively be made on each situation. It is difficult to imagine how one might conceptualize the classroom problems and processes without some prior insight into their function within the total educational scheme.

We have had some fallacies obscuring our view on this problem for years: the false allocation of "feeling" processes to the field and "intellectual" processes to the class; the assignment of "knowledge" to the sphere of the classroom, and the concern with "practice" to the work of the field; etc. One may note sympathetically what those who created these distinctions were reaching for, but the fact remains that the problem here is to divide the labor without flying in the face of known facts about how people learn and how they invest themselves in the educational process.

As a place to begin, let me suggest a principle enunciated by Ralph Tyler as part of a discussion of "general principles in selecting learning experiences." It is, in fact, the one with which he begins: "The first of these is that for a given objective to be attained, a student must have experiences that give him an opportunity to practice the kind of behavior implied by the objective."[7]

In other words, *the student should work at what he is supposed to learn.* If this principle is valid for our experience, it would mean that the division of labor between class and field must be closely tied to the operational opportunities and limitations inherent in each of these situations. The field situation, for example, is designed to provide the student with a series of professional tasks to be carried out as part of an ongoing social welfare service in the community. As the student performs these tasks under professional supervision, he is expected to bring his organization of knowledge and purpose to bear on the practice of social work in a particular setting. Field learning is thus geared to the demands of practice, and its dynamic for teaching and learning is created by the problems of the client, the pressure to produce a service, the responsibility to the agency, and the immediacy of the helping experience. This places certain functional limitations on the need to err and to experiment, but it does not categorize the field experience as one in which the student does not generalize, think, evaluate, read, or even write papers. It simply means that the work emerges from the necessities of service, and that it is from this dynamic of service that both the teacher and the learner derive their impetus for work.

What then is the function of the classroom? By Tyler's principle, it becomes obvious that we have erred in the notion that the class is a setting in which we *teach* the skills of group work—for the student cannot "practice the kind of behavior implied by the objective." If we then ask what kinds of use behaviors *can* he practice, several clues emerge as to the uses of the classroom experience. We see, for example, that, while we cannot teach the skills of practice in the classroom, we can teach behaviors associated with the analysis of skill and with modes of theorizing about the nature of the helping

[7]*Ibid.*, p. 42.

process. We see, too, that the classroom calls for certain other behaviors important to the making of a professional: he must learn to pursue and research a line of inquiry; he must learn to reach into the historical context within which he will perform his function; he must learn to generalize comfortably enough so that he can risk his theories in the give-and-take of peer interaction; and he can test his analytic skills in the context of a living group—the classroom itself—of which he is a part, that makes demands on him as a member, and that replicates many of the problems about which he is studying. The class is thus a rehearsal stage where one can speculate and try things out without fear of hurting anyone; a place to risk negatives and "wrong" ideas, that is, ideas that do not fall easily into the professional consensus. It constitutes a model of group activity and the demands of individual participation; a model, in the teacher himself, of the helping process; and a place in which to assemble the experts, and to come to grips with the formulations and theories of the most immediate and imposing "expert" of them all—the teacher.

It should be clear that whether one does or does not like this modeling aspect of the classroom experience—whether or not one is given to pronouncements like "the class is not a group," "the teacher is not a group worker," and so on—the fact is that these things happen. The students need each other; they use each other, openly or otherwise; they watch the teacher at work and are acutely aware of the extent to which he is at home with his own principles; and they will draw lessons from the mode and the feeling, as well as the cognitive demands, of the classroom experience. As one who once attended a series of fifteen lectures on the evils of lecturing, I speak from experience on both sides of the desk.

We may say in summary that the educational power of the field experience comes largely from the fact that we must take it whole, intact, and respond to what it wants done. The power of the classroom, on the other hand, lies precisely in its artifice, its organization, and its consciously designed succession of educational problems. What kinds of experiences would be most relevant to this work?

Work of the Classroom

Central to the organization of classroom experience is the problem of the relationship between structure and freedom in the educative process. In a class in professional methodology, the problem is even more pressing than usual: How does a teacher explicate a theory of practice without tying his students to it and thus smothering the very creativity and spontaneity that is indispensible to the helping art? As personally skillful as the teacher may be in his own professional practice, he cannot deliver these skills to the student. As clearly as he may have thought through and simplified the elements of his subject, he cannot transplant his insights into a student's vaguely formed and unprepared frame of reference. Yet the teacher's effectiveness will depend on both these abilities: to present a workable theory in which he has some investment; and, simultaneously, to set them free to their own analytical tasks. It is not our job to stamp out copies of ourselves and our personal solutions to professional problems, but to lead students in a search for the components that will ultimately go into their own uniquely-formed theories about what they are doing.

It is important to recognize that the teacher's responsibility for a clear formulation of his own model of practice emerges not from the need to have "something to teach," but from his need to integrate the demands of structure and freedom. Such model-building helps him to *simplify* his subject, *partialize* it, and *set the tasks* of investigation. By the word "simplifying," I mean his ability to see so deeply into his subject that he can abstract its essentials, distinguish between central and peripheral problems, and show his students an open path into the possibilities of the inquiry. By the "partializing function," I refer to the teacher's ability to order the stages of complexity—that is, to so understand the problems along the way that he can visualize the learning continuum from simple to complex. And both these processes—simplifying and partializing—make it possible for him to set the tasks that guide the students' search without legislating its outcome.

I have found it useful to embody these ideas in a format that seems to address itself to the requirements of both structure and freedom, by establishing certain Areas of Investigation, within each of which certain Lines of Inquiry are laid down in order to help the student begin his search of the Area. This "mapping" of the terrain, together with the use of certain instruments—the Log, the case presentation, the theoretical group analysis, the critical incident analysis, the critical review of the literature, and others—seem to help maintain the delicate balance of initiative and demand, discipline and freedom, about which we need to know so much more in our work.

Conclusion

This is an interesting time in which to be a group work teacher, despite the mourning and lamentations of those who think we are dead because they can only recognize us in the old costume. The process of weaving some new clothing can be an exciting one both for us and for our students.

In conclusion, I would caution against trying to reach premature agreement by the unfortunate method of "voting" on ideas, as in the past, we have been wont to do. We have had too much agreement; what we need now is independent work and creative reconstruction of our experiences as practitioners, teachers, and consultants in the field of practice. "The basis of every discord," says Whitehead, "is some common experience, discordantly realized."[8] As we work together, we should share our discordances with pleasure, and accept only those agreements where we are certain that what we have earned is true conceptual, rather than merely semantic, accord.

---

[8]Alfred North Whitehead, *The Function of Reason* (Boston: Beacon Press, 1929), p. 86.

Education in the Classroom

William Schwartz

Learning and teaching are separate processes; they can go on without each other, and often do. People learn from books, experiences, relationships, even their own thoughts. And others teach, explain, propound, while nobody learns or even listens. Ivan Illich would have it that these processes are not only independent but antithetical, that we have seriously confused one with the other, and that in fact "most learning happens casually" [29, p. 12].

But for the professional teacher there is nothing casual about the problems of teaching and learning. How students learn and teachers teach are complicated processes, difficult to understand and even harder to master. It is not surprising that professors of many years experience feel they have never quite got it right, and are amazed and gratified when the will to learn and the desire to teach come together in a few moments of excitement, pleasure, and joyful discovery.

Our situation is complicated by the fact that we were never trained for this job. Under the general assumption that scholarly competence alone, or successful experience in the field, qualifies one to teach a subject to others, most university teachers are turned loose upon their students without any formal recognition that teaching is an art that requires its own knowledge and skill. "The American college teacher," Blegen and Cooper have pointed out, "is the only high level professional man in the American scene who enters upon a career with neither the prerequisite trial of competence nor experience in the use of the tools of his profession" [6, p. 123]. And B. F. Skinner commented that "the most widely publicized efforts to improve education show

This article is based on a paper read at the Annual Program Meeting of the Council on Social Work Education, Boston, March 5, 1979.

William Schwartz is Distinguished Visiting Professor, Graduate School of Social Service, Fordham University.

an extraordinary neglect of method. Learning and teaching are not analyzed, and almost no effort is made to improve teaching as such" [44, p. 80]. The problem gathers force as we go higher in the field of education: at the university level, and particularly in the graduate professional schools, the lack of attention to the quality of teaching is striking.

The failure to create a climate congenial to the study and improvement of teaching is not essentially a condition imposed on us from the outside. The fear and suspicion of method, that have made it a kind of non-subject on the American campus, have come largely from within the profession itself, and, oddly, from both the conservative and progressive ends of the educational spectrum. Classicists like Hutchins and Barzun repeatedly stressed the irrelevance of method in education. From Hutchins came the axiom: "All there is to teaching can be learned through a good education and being a teacher" [28, p. 56]. "Education implies teaching. Teaching implies knowledge. Knowledge is truth. The truth is everywhere the same. Hence education should be everywhere the same" [28, p. 66]. Barzun's observation was that "all 'methods' in the 'educator's' sense of the word are wholly beside the point" [2, p. 44]. "Given a mastered subject and a person committed heart and soul to teaching it, a class accustomed to think, attend, and be led; the result will be, under God, as near to the discourse of men and angels as it is fit to go" [2, p. 45]. As a teacher, one would pray to be given all those givens, but would probably have to go on learning how to manage with a good deal less.

Even from those more alive to the importance of teaching, the message is ambivalent. Nisbet, in an article emphasizing the need for the teaching function to hold its own against the demand for research, suddenly finds it necessary to remind us that "for either administration or faculty to take method or organization of teaching too seriously is, of course, fatal" [37, p. 31]. Mandel, in a sensitive account of a creative teaching-learning experience, conjures up an image of students who are "too literate and imaginative to need a teacher at all" [34, p. 16]. And Bruffee, who has done new work on the processes of "collaborative learning" in the field of creative writing [8], would solve many of the problems of traditional teaching by having the teacher relinquish authority and assume a position "at the edge of the action" [9, p. 466], rather than at the center of it, with a clear and active function aimed at developing the desired kind of collaboration.

As for the literature of teaching, it goes back a long way [38, 48], but the bulk of it is essentially philosophical and inspirational, illustrating how rich we are in our aspirations for the educative process and how difficult it is to turn these ideas into work [17, 33]. Of those who have tried to bring us closer to an interest in method, most have stopped short at the study of learning, rather than teaching: Kilpatrick's classic *Foundations of Method* [32] is a book about how children learn, rather than how teachers teach; Bruner's emphasis, and his excellence, is in his ability to find the logic of the subject matter [10, 11]; William James's *Talks to Teachers* [31] is another classic entry in the literature of learning, with little attention to the acts of teaching.

The most important modern source of inspiration for the study of method is in the work of John Dewey, whose *Democracy and Education* [17] called attention to technical problems and helped create an atmosphere in which they could be studied. In this tradition, our own generation has produced many demonstrations of how modern attitudes and values have been transformed into dynamic teaching, by sophisticated practitioners like Cantor [13, 14], Moustakis [36], Dennison [16], and others, and in a number of absorbing classroom experiences described by teachers in England [26, 30, 46]. Such accounts lean heavily on personal experience, progressive and humane approaches, and strong, charismatic leadership. At their best, they show a deep interest in the work of the classroom and a vision of what teaching can be like when it is done well. What they do not do is identify the skills the teachers use, or offer us some systematic way of studying them further.

Most recently, there has developed a small but promising body of work on what Flanders [20, 21] has called the "small events" of the classroom. Bellack [3, 4] has used interactional analysis to examine the nature of the "pedagogical move." Gage [24, 25] has surveyed and analyzed various approaches to the study of teaching. In the field of higher education, the work is thin on the ground: Shulman [42, 43] has studied the "hidden group" in the college classroom: I have written on graduate school teaching in the field of social work [41]; Lee's [33] collection of articles makes a strong case for the improvement of college teaching, and includes important data on the subject, while contributing little specific technical work on the art and science of teaching itself.

In any event, the subject of classroom teaching is much neglected, perhaps even slightly disreputable, on the American campus. In my own experience of almost thirty years of teaching in four different large universities, I have not until very recently attended a single formal faculty meeting devoted to discussion of teaching methods, comparison of classroom events, or examination of teaching theory and research. For the educators themselves, ways of teaching do indeed seem to be "beside the point."

Nevertheless, in Atherton's words, "something called teaching happens" [1, p. 90]. There is a great deal of it going on—some of it exciting, much of it dull, and all of it alive with possibilities. It has been in process for a long time, but we still know too little about it, and are only just beginning to take a real interest in what works, what doesn't, and what creates the sterile game-playing that so often takes place in its name. My effort here will be to draw from my years of work in the classroom some observations that may stimulate other teachers to take a fresh look at their own experiences.

Teaching and Telling: The Transmitting Function

A class is a group of students that meets face to face to explore a given area of human knowledge. It usually includes a person in authority, assigned from the outside and invested with the responsibility for establishing the mode of communication—what Bellack calls the "pattern of discourse"—designed to teach and learn certain facts, ideas, concepts, or skills for which both teacher and students will be held accountable. Conventionally, the test of learning will be the students' ability to remember and reproduce the data at stated intervals. The teacher determines what the relevant data will be, tries to instill them in one way or another, and stands guard to be sure that no student who has not learned them will be allowed to go on to the next stage in the educational process. Thus, at the heart of the teacher's authority lie these three functions: to represent the data and their major sources; to qualify those who have passed the tests of learning and are free to move on; and to set up the rules of the game by which they will carry on their work together.

The last is probably the most important, affecting as it does the quality of the whole experience—the pleasure and the boredom, the motivation for work, the attitude toward the subject, the classroom relationships, and ultimately the way it will all be remembered. And this interactional structure is almost entirely within the teacher's power to establish. Especially in higher education, the academic freedom of professors is augmented by a professional freedom to order the classroom operation in any way they see fit, using lectures, discussions, assignments, formal demands, informal exchanges, and the rest.

Thus free to establish the conditions of work, where does the professor go from there? Having spent one's working life mastering a subject, one feels its importance deeply; it is in fact closely connected to the very meaning of one's life. And with all there is to be learned, it seems most logical to assume that the best and fastest way to transmit all these data is for someone who knows the material to tell it to those who do not. The teacher's job, then, is to say what he or she knows, and to make other experts available as well. The students' tasks are to listen, read, ask questions if they do not understand, remember what they have heard and read, and later to give evidence that they have registered the material in their minds.

The logic seems unassailable; there is great power in the idea that if you want people to know something you tell it to them. And the teacher's responsibilities follow clearly; to present the data in terms that are interesting and alive; to organize them in logical sequence; to mention all of the relevant aspects; to motivate and sustain curiosity. The salient skills are organization, flair, and the wit and force to inform, command attention, excite interest, and model one's own enthusiasm and mastery.

This form does not require that teachers talk all the time. In fact, they may often use short question-and-answer exchanges—the prevailing "teaching cycle" discovered by Bellack and his associates [4]—or play a kind of "Socratic game" in which questions are designed to elicit from the students the "correct" answer, as represented by the one the teacher has in mind. These moves are designed to produce the appearance of student participation, while maintaining the basic rule that the teacher is the one who knows, and will in time share, all the information the students need in order to show that they have learned the course.[1]

This is the model as we have known it, often learned in it, and in varying degrees practiced it. Most of the literature of teaching is about it; and although the teachers' colleges continue to enjoin the young teacher that "teaching isn't telling," the fact is that most teaching is exactly that. The art of teaching is generally practiced as an art of telling—of exposition, explanation, dissemination.

But this conception, as common as it is, has always carried dissatisfaction in its train. Dr. Samuel Johnson thought much of the talking was unnecessary, since there were now so many books around for students to read. McKeachie found research showing that "students learned as thoroughly from reading material as from listening to it," with the better students actually learning more from the reading [35, p. 220]. Paolo Freire wrote that "education is suffering from narration sickness" [22, p. 57]. And John Dewey wondered: "Why is it, in spite of the fact that teaching by pouring in, learning by a passive absorption, are universally condemned, that they are still so intrenched in practice?" [17, p. 46].

From the student's viewpoint, there is a pervasive resentment at the expectation that one learns complicated things simply by being told and asked to repeat, at the lack of intimacy and feedback, at the dearth of activity and participation in the classroom. Drosnin complained about "the limited interest the professor displays in his classroom performance" [18, p. 253]. Whether the pattern of discourse is the lecture form or any of the other ways of giving answers where there are no questions, the system feels imposed, one-sided, too often dull. In education for the helping professions, it is often seen as poor training for students who are at the same time being taught that one does not help people that way.

Why then does the practice persist? In Gage's words, "lecturing embarasses but prevails" [23, p. 245]. At least part of the answer to Dewey's question must be that the tendency to teach by telling is a natural one, and cannot simply be ruled out of the teaching process. If one has something important to tell, and takes one's teaching seriously, there is no power that can interfere—unless the teacher chooses to become artificial, "Socratic," devi-

---

[1]Bruffee calls this the "Socratic Convention," where "the teacher asks questions and approves or disapproves the answers students offer. In this way, the teacher leads students to say what he might as well have said himself. The line of reasoning is his own, and it leads to a point he has, more or less, decided upon beforehand" [9, p. 459]. B. F. Skinner has also discussed this device: "The archetype is the famous episode in the *Meno* in which Socrates takes an uneducated slave boy through Pythagoras's theorem for doubling the square. In spite of the fact that this scene is still widely regarded as an educational triumph, there is no evidence that the child learned anything. He timidly agrees with various suggestions, and he answers leading questions, but it is inconceivable that he could have reconstructed the theorem by himself when Socrates had finished" [44, p. 100].

ously "permissive," ultimately withholding. Indeed in its most creative form, the telling function has inspired, informed, and set processes in motion that have lasted a lifetime. I have such an experience in my own student career, with an English professor whose love of learning, profound knowledge of his subject, and attitudes toward life and people turned me to ways of thinking and studying that are with me to this day. His pattern of discourse was always the lecture—he was too shy for anything else—interrupting himself from time to time only to be sure he was not too far ahead, which he often was, with some of us running hard to catch up. His influence was enormous—not with everyone in the class, but with those few of us who knew what he was looking for and wanted to be with him in the search. Such experiences are not common, but they happen, and every teacher has had those moments in which his or her contribution of data and grasp of the subject have been an important part of the classroom process.

Both those who attack and those who defend the transmission function are prone to dichotomize "content" and "process," "teacher-centered" and "student-centered" education, "knowledge" and "feelings," and the rest. These were the polarities that confused the arguments about "progressive education" from its beginnings, and they have never been very useful in helping us to understand the function of the teacher and the skills that go with it. I would like to suggest that the analysis hangs on other questions, and turn my attention to what these are and how they arise.

Beyond Discovery

Bronowski has described three modes by which science achieves its changes; they are *discovery, invention,* and *creation.* "A fact is discovered, a theory is invented" [7, p. 7]. And an act of creation is a profoundly personal distillation of experience into a new and original vision. I think this idea may be useful to us in our understanding of teaching and learning.

In giving information, in transmitting new facts, ideas, and constructions of the data, the teacher's work is designed to facilitate the act of discovery. When the telling is well done, with clarity and conviction, many students will make new and exciting finds, and perhaps even gain access to worlds they never knew existed. But what happens next? At what point do we begin to identify the experience as learning? From many fields—education, science, philosophy, social work, others—we are urged not to stop there, but to define useful learning in terms that go beyond the stage of discovery, to those of invention and creation. Whitehead spoke of ideas that are "merely received into the mind without being utilized, or tested, or thrown into fresh combination" [49, p. 13]. Buber cited the power that may "grow up in each man in the special form of that man" [12, p. 111]. Pruyser said that "knowing is agreement and disagreement" [39, p. 86]. And Bronowski warned against the idea that "the existence of a thing leaps of itself into the mind, immediate and whole. We know the thing only by mapping and joining our experiences of its aspects" [7, p. 42].

Back in the year 1710, the historian and philosopher Giambattista Vico put it this way, in his theory of *verum ipsum factum:* "The rule and criterion of truth is to have made it. . . . We can know nothing that we have not made" [19, p. 490]. I believe this is true of the process by which students learn: they cannot *own* their knowledge until they have "made" it, worked it over, imposed their own order on the data, and altered it to fit with what they already have. What Bronowski called the "mapping and joining" have not yet happened at the moment when the ideas of the teacher have been taken down and entered into the student's notebook.

But they will happen, more often than not. There are, of course, those students who, left alone, will be content to let the teacher's facts lie there quietly, study them, and then return them in their original state. But many, perhaps especially in the professional school, will try to make the material work for them. They will elaborate the data, apply them to their practice, agree and disagree, hone their insights on each other, and try to go beyond discovery to generalization and invention, fitting their findings to what they already know and believe.

The question is, where will they do all this? If they cannot get help with these tasks in the formal system of the classroom, they will be limited to the informal system of the hallway, the cafeteria, classmates, friends, and private study. All of which are, of course, legitimate resources, and create an excitement that is an integral part of the learning process. But the teacher's problem is one of function: where does the job end? One possibility is to pass knowledge on and leave it to the students to work it over in their own way. That is the path that many teachers have chosen.

But there is an alternative, and that is to extend the teaching function to include the *aftermath* of discovery: the elaboration, the testing of the data, the struggle with authority, the agreeing and disagreeing, the students' use of one another, and the other individual and group events that make up the hard and painful process of learning. In this view, the problem of the transmitting function is not that it is "unprogressive," or even unproductive, but simply that it does not go far enough into the educational process. When the facts are told, the notes taken down, the "truth" laid out, the work is only just begun. The hardest part remains.

When teachers so enlarge their vision of the job, and move into the center of the action, the climate of the classroom changes; new strategies and skills are demanded, and the work grows more difficult. They will not abandon their command of the subjects they teach, or withhold their knowledge and experience; but in this new context, their roles will change from chief purveyors of the truth to that of expert guide in a common search for useful meanings. The class is no longer an audience but a search party, with the teacher at its head. The professor's presence remains central, because leadership is badly needed on this dangerous, unfamiliar terrain; but the authority stems more from knowing the questions than the answers. The force of his or her leadership will lie in understanding how students work and learn, and in the ability to help them use one another, the teacher, and all the other resources they can muster, to find out what they need to know.

In this kind of teaching-learning enterprise, the rules of the game change in certain dramatic ways: the preoccupation with certainty gives way to an open recognition of ambiguity and ambivalence—what Bertha Reynolds called the "conflict of opposite motives" [40, p. 58]; learning difficulties are exposed, rather than concealed; it is accepted that learning is not a gradual accretion of knowledge that fills in the empty spaces of ignorance, but a process that moves shakily, in fits and starts; the teacher, closely engaged in the action, lays his status and authority open to attack; feeling and knowing can no longer be polarized, but become part of the same search for meanings; and the mutual aid factor—the working relationships between students—takes its place somewhere near the teacher as a source of strength and power.

In such a climate, the students also take on tasks that are new, difficult, often frustrating. And the strategies and skills with which the professor moves to help them work are what constitute the nature of the teaching art.

The Search for Meanings: Learning Tasks and Teaching Skills

The effort to relate teaching strategies to student tasks is my way of trying to understand the classroom events of which I have been a part for many years. My own strategies are, of course, formed and limited by my beliefs and experiences, as well as by the nature of my subject, which is social work practice. I believe, however, that when students are freed to search for their own usable answers, their problems are very much the same, regardless of subject.[2] They must all begin, for example, by finding a structure that provides both the freedom to work on their own and the discipline to meet the demands of the course. They must deal with an authority figure who somehow stands in the way of their freedom even as they are urged to think independently. They must develop ways of using one another, harnessing diverse personalities and backgrounds into a collective effort. They must learn something about how to learn: to call things by their right names instead of the euphemisms and evasions with which they have been taught to address difficult problems; to work back and forth between the general and the specific; to tolerate ambiguity instead of rushing to premature solutions. And they must use the events of the classroom itself, the process before their eyes, to find out about their own resistance to learning, to face their pleasure and their anger in the work, and

[2]At the Faculty Workshop on Teaching of the Fordham University Graduate School of Social Service, some professors from different subject areas are indeed finding such common ground, as they record and discuss their work in the classroom in an effort to identify and define the skills of teaching.

to make the experience a part of their lives, rather than a game played between students and teachers.

In the following, I will describe some of my own efforts to help students learn in such a framework. Using examples from my classroom records, I will touch briefly on each of the tasks mentioned above: the integration of structure and freedom; the struggle with authority; the problems of mutual aid; the effort to learn how to learn; and the use of the events of the classroom itself. Each needs more elaboration than the present space allows; but the following may serve as introduction and groundwork for further description and analysis.

To begin, the need for more freedom in the classroom is not solved by the elimination of structure. In fact, and especially in the early stages of work, teacher passivity, or indecisiveness, or "permissiveness," will engender weakness rather than strength, dependency rather than freedom. As the students sit there—uncertain, docile, unconnected to one another—they begin by needing someone who can provide an energy, force, and direction that they cannot yet muster for themselves. They are, and feel themselves to be, within the teacher's power; and they look to the teacher to offer them meaningful work, an interesting time, and a reasonable chance to learn. The teacher who is to be a guide had better look as if he knows where he is going.

I believe the teacher should meet this need for structure at the outset, and offer the class a clear contract, a way of working, and a quick beginning into the work itself. To withhold one's energy and sense of purpose because one insists that the class exert a unity and initiative it has not yet developed, is to precipitate a battle of wills that can set the tone for the whole experience. The real issue is not whether structure is to be offered, but what form it will take; for the initial framework within which the work begins will demonstrate how the teacher's function and the pattern of discourse preferred are defined. If certainty and "truth" are in the teacher's view predetermined, they will be set up as objectives and arrangements made to "cover" each of their aspects in turn. But if the learning process is seen as a quest, and the class as a party of searchers, the teacher will lay out devices and strategems for putting this idea into action. The emphasis will be on where and how to dig, what questions to pursue, and how to use both their private work and their classroom processes to pursue them.

My own procedure is to devise a syllabus that defines the course's "Areas of Investigation," lays out some of the beginning questions—called "Lines of Inquiry"—in each area, defines some of the students' responsibilities briefly and clearly, and offers a large bibliography in which the students are free to range, without any specifically required readings. The primary communication device is a study diary, called the "Log," in which students are required to enter their comments and observations on all their readings, their work in the field, the events of the classroom, and other thoughts that seem to them pertinent to the work of the course.

This opening structure calls for both discipline and initiative, order and freedom. It is what Torbert has called a "liberating structure" [47], and it is important not only for the opening needs it meets, but for the fact that it provides the walls against which the students will begin to hammer when they later develop a heightened sense of their own self-interest and begin to enlist one another's aid in expanding their areas of freedom. At that time, the teacher will be accused of four egregious errors—too much structure, too little structure, too much freedom, and too little freedom. The ambivalence of the students toward both structure and freedom will be a major theme in the life of the classroom, as it is in life's other aspects.

But at this point the problem is to get under way. The following is excerpted from my record of a first session of a class on social work with groups in the second year of study; it shows something of my effort to define the course and its expectations, the opening interactions, and my moves to take them into the work itself.

> We did some contract work: the course emphasis is on the skills of the worker; I cited the requirement that they have small groups or families to work with, if they were to be eligible for the course. Some anxious discussion of this: possibilities in field work, other opportunities, and I offered to help them find groups in the community. Further: there will be no exams; explained the Log and its uses, my demand for extensive reading, their comments to reflect their own thinking, rather than "little compositions" for the teacher. We looked at the syllabus, two students offered to make more copies of the bibliography for each other.
>
> . . . we talked about some of their group experiences of last year. We got into discussion of two of the groups, the students' understanding of what the groups were about, and members' perceptions of the group purpose . . . this took us into some discussion of contracting, and the relationship between *need* and *service*. . . .
>
> The class worked well: we slipped in and out of role-play as we explored their group experiences, without any big deal about it, and they responded well to the demand in the work. At the end, I asked how did they feel? Anxious, they said, but excited by the possibilities. Good, I said, just the right frame of mind.

This quality of being "anxious but excited" about the prospects ahead comes out clearly in the following Log entry, written after the first session of a class in the second semester:

> Well, things certainly got off to a roaring start—had an incredible class today. I'm about as shook as I expected to be but the shakiness is founded in reality and not just wondering what the class will be like. It's going to be super challenging—he never lets up for a second—push, push, dig, dig, why? why? which is scary but good. Going to have to learn to have enough guts to put myself out and get stomped on.

Thus rescued from anomie, the students begin the work, grateful for the promising start and intrigued by the possibilities that lie ahead. They are in the stage that Bennis and Shepard [5] call "dependence-flight"—obedient, superficial, their attention riveted on the teacher, still trying to figure out what kind of power he represents, if he really means what he says, and how to win his approval.

But such a situation is not tolerable for long. Under the impetus of the work itself, their ambivalence begins to emerge and find expression. Bennis and Shepard, coming from a frame of reference quite different from mine, have aptly described the processes by which the students bring under attack the very strengths they were so thankful for at the outset. In their analysis, this struggle with *authority* is one of the two great problems students bring with them, the second being their struggle for *intimacy,* or their relations with one another. Thus the problem is common; but the immediate provocations for the struggle with authority lie clearly before them. The business is more serious than they had bargained for: not simply because of the amount of reading and studying—many enjoy that and are good at it—but the "push, push, dig, dig," the demand that they tie their feelings to their ideas, the intensive search for real meanings, the classroom interaction with others who question and disagree, and the active participation of the teacher, who also has strongly held views. In a second-year group work class, a student suddenly wailed: "I didn't want to get into all this. I just want to do a *little bit* of social work!" All of these factors conspire to heighten the feelings of involvement and risk, highlight the anger and frustration, and ultimately produce the daring that it takes to challenge this strange figure of authority who invites the challenge and helps create the conditions that make it possible.

That the teacher knows it is coming—it happens every time, and one can read a thorough description of the process in Bennis and Shepard—does not make it any easier. It is a hectic and difficult time, calling on all the energy, love, self-confidence, and skill the teacher can command, to hold on to one's function, to stick to what one believes in, and to offer the students the help they need in their dilemma. If I hide my feelings and keep my "cool," in the "I understand how you feel" tradition, they will mark me off as a phony and I will be lost to them in the next stages of work. On the other hand, if I act out and strike back in revenge, I will lose my function, perhaps irretrievably. Somewhere between the unreal blandness and the acting-out, there is a line of work in which I show how I feel, the hurt and the resentment, but also that I can—as I have been trying to teach them to do—use my feelings as I continue to work: I can name their feelings and my own, help them get things out in the open, point them toward one another, and call on them to translate their emotions into ideas and action. Following is an example from my record of such an event in the life of an integrative seminar, which included graduating students from the various specializations within the field of social work practice:

> Ken and Nat persisted in trying to turn the work into a sole concern with the black power issue. [In view of the recent arguments, and trying to stay out of trouble] I did not engage them on the substance but worked on keeping the other issues in the picture, as people tried to introduce them.
>
> Then the shit hit the fan. Audrey accused me of cutting off the discussion, not allowing them to get into the black power issue with Ken,

> and we were off to the races. I said that Audrey was very angry, and that we ought to get it all out in the open; perhaps others felt that I was cutting them off, too; there is this duel that comes up again and again. So they let me have it, most of them, with the group work students remaining silent—I guess they also felt attacked, as they actually were at one point. Audrey let me have it, angry and with both barrels. I stood up to it as well as I could, not returning the anger but trying to help keep the discussion going.
>
> In moving them toward some kind of resolution, I said, glum and depressed, that I would play whatever role they wanted me to. I had tried different tacks and nothing I did seemed to work with them; what did they want me to do? We agreed that the presenters would chair their own discussions; they wanted me to participate, and so on, but they would take over leadership of the discussions themselves. I agreed. It was mean and murderous; the "revolutionaries" had staged their rebellion, won over the masses, and prevailed. It remains to be seen what they will do with it.

Fortunately, not all the rebellions are as threatening as that; but the point is that the students must, in one way or another, deal directly with the authority in the classroom before they can with full energy turn to one another for help in the search for what they need. It is only when they have put the teacher in his place that they can achieve genuine mutual aid—talking directly to each other, criticizing each other's productions seriously, sharing resources, and using the teacher as a part of their work rather than as the sole focus of attention. It is not that the work begins here; it has been going on all along. But it is the time when the search intensifies and becomes a serious collaboration of forces.

This is the stage at which the class, gathering force and self-confidence, needs all the help it can get in learning to avoid some of the pitfalls in the path of people trying to learn. Where, for example, the students begin to wax vague and abstract, the teacher reaches for the specifics that will bring them back to the problems at hand. Where they lose themselves in philosophical meanderings, he seeks out the feelings attached to their ideas, to heighten their responsibility for the work they need. Where they settle into a kind of "false consensus," self-congratulatory and superficial, he reaches to find the negatives hidden somewhere among them. He shows them how to live with ambiguity for a while, instead of rushing toward quick pseudo-solutions. He helps them break up huge ideas into smaller ones that they can manage more easily, and to gather up bits of knowledge and experience and form them into conclusions and generalizations.

I have recorded examples of each of these efforts, but there is not the space to deal with all of them here. The following excerpt illustrates a few of these moves, as I tried to help a second-year class with a difficult problem in mutual aid. A student had presented a record of work with an old couple in a housing situation. After some discussion, she was attacked by a fellow student for the manner of her presentation It was soon clear that the presenter, the attacker, and the rest of the class all needed help in retaining their focus of work and helping one another learn from the work before them.

> Before long, it was clear that the class members were getting as tied up as Carol was, and it was hard for them to stay with the work. Mac got furious with the housing authority people, who were trying to kick this poor old couple out of their home; and he and I got into a thing about his anger and my trying to stay with Carol's moment-by-moment work. Carol's response to each of the criticisms of her failure to listen to her clients and make connections was to say yes, she had learned that, and it was included in her final summary. After several repetitions of this, Ike burst out at Carol, saying he didn't understand what she was doing, and what was the use of presenting if she kept saying that she knew all her own mistakes? This shut everybody up for a few moments, the usual discomfort at an angry comment by a class member, and then there was a rallying and everybody started to get on Ike. I stayed out for a while, as several attacked Ike for his intolerance. Carol's response was to defend herself by talking to me and laughing a lot; I suggested that she turn around and address herself to Ike, which she did, mostly admitting her sins and trying to hold her own. It was a painful time for them all, but I tried to hold them to it, pointing out to the class members that they were not listening to Ike, but simply dumping on him. At the same time, I wondered out loud what Ike was getting so sore about, since we had all seen Carol's defensiveness, but she was working at the same time, doing her best to keep the discussion going.
>
> My efforts to make them listen to one another began to turn the course of events a little, and Lenore took a new tack when she said to Ike that maybe he was upset about something in the work itself, something about the situation Carol was describing. Ike pooh-poohed the suggestion, still very angry. At that point, May (a friend, and in the same field work placement as Ike) turned to him and explained that different people present their work for different reasons; some people do it to learn for themselves; some present work so that general questions can be opened up; some are more defensive than others; etc. This was Carol's presentation, she continued, and she was doing it in her own way. Ike started to pooh-pooh again, still fighting everybody off, and I suggested to him now that he "try to shift his weight a little." He asked what I meant, and I explained that he was sitting flat and dead center, set in his position and unmoved by anything that was going on. For instance, May had just said something important and he hadn't listened. Half grudging, half interested, Ike turned to May and asked her to repeat what she had said. She did, and Ike nodded, trying to let it in. I asked whether he understood what she was saying, and he seemed more relaxed as he said yes, he did.
>
> This done, Lena then picked up the action, saying that she simply didn't understand anything that was going on; whereupon I asked her

> please not to be a spectator, but to try to get in with us and try to figure out what was happening. There was some more interaction for a few minutes, and suddenly Lena exclaimed that she knew what was going on; it was, she said, that everybody was simply avoiding the pain in Carol's situation. This old couple was in an impossible bind, and they, as workers, kept getting into these very painful situations about which they could do nothing.
>
> This was really it, finally, and I pointed it up for us all: the dozens of ways in which they try to avoid the pain of the work, as well as the pain of the struggle right here in class to learn from the work. I reviewed Carol's situation: an ambivalent agency, wanting to get rid of this couple, while at the same time wanting to maintain a legitimate service; an ambivalent couple, with a relationship that was complex and a problem of finding their own best way; and in the middle (they finished it for me in chorus), an ambivalent worker, not knowing which way to turn and how to offer the most direct and honest kind of help. And, here in class, Mac's anger at the system, Ike's anger at the presenter, and everybody showing so many different ways of avoiding the step-by-step, moment-by-moment moves of the worker.
>
> This was the note on which we ended, with everyone more relaxed, yet still intense, the general feeling that we had broken through to something very important. At the end, I thanked Carol for her work; and I also thanked Ike for the cantankerousness without which we would not have gotten to where we did.
>
> After the class, considerable excitement, etc.

The teaching strategy by which attention is called to the events of the classroom involves an examination of the uses and abuses of self-consciousness in the process of learning. The fundamental task of the class is to pursue the learning for which teacher and students are contracted; as far as possible, all energies should be bent to that task. When, however, something gets in the way of learning—an authority problem, an obstacle to mutual aid, a bit of suppressed anger, a perceived slight, a disagreement too soon cut off, an explanation too readily accepted, a false consensus, or any of a host of other underground noises—it is sometimes necessary to ask "what just happened here?" If the question remains unaddressed, it rankles and distracts from the work: the action slows, there is a deadness, a loss of energy, a sudden attack of "laziness" that the teacher is at a loss to explain. Where the pattern of discourse is such as to allow the existential question to be asked—either by the student or the teacher—without guilt but as part of a way of working, the class can be helped to proceed to the immediate task, which is to find out what is holding them up and robbing them of their energy. Then, because the classroom is a life experience and not something stylized and unreal, they may discover other things as well—something about resistance, about how they learn, about the uses of authority, and about the relationship between knowledge, feeling, and action.

The point is that when a class is working well, "content" and "process" are a seamless whole; it is neither necessary nor possible to distinguish one from the other. *How* we work and *what* we are working on are of the same focus and impetus, owing so much to each other that there is no interest in regarding them as separate entities, even if it were possible. But when the pursuit of learning is interrupted from within, a kind of classroom neurosis takes form, in which conflict and frustration act insidiously to inhibit action. The self-examination that ensues is a way of identifying the obstacle, robbing it of its secret power, and regaining the unity of content and process. If they can do this—and fairly quickly—they can go back to what they were working on. If they cannot, there are deeper problems to search for that are interfering with the progress of the work.

Thus, classroom self-consciousness should go no further than what is needed to help students and teacher go back to their work. When the process is prolonged, it becomes narcissistic and self-indulgent—in a sense too "enjoyable"—changing the contract of the course and luring the members from their purpose. The students are not there to heighten their general self-awareness, or to become more sensitive people, or to build their characters in any way whatever. They have a job to do; something blocked their energies and interrupted the search; they stopped to see what went wrong, found it, made it public, and gave it as much attention as it needed. They then went back to their work with renewed energy, having learned from the experience some new things about how people learn.

The teaching strategies in this area are several: to model tolerance for a variety of different and opposing assessments of what is wrong; to enter with one's own views without cutting off theirs; to invite students to move through their hesitation and embarrassment to make their necessary disclosures: to decode the euphemisms and evasions with which they will tend to approach the difficult material; to call for specifics, examples, and real feelings that go with the ideas; and then, to ask the class to risk a less-than-perfect solution of the problem as it makes its first effort to return to the work of the course.

In concluding, it is customary to call for more research on the subject; and I would certainly agree that research is needed. But the lack of formal study is only part of the deeper problem I mentioned earlier—namely, that the subject itself, that of skill in the classroom, hardly exists in the profession's awareness. What is most needed at this stage is for interested teachers and professors to find one another, share their records of classroom experience, and compare their conclusions about the art of teaching, its science, and its purpose. In little corners of the academic world, the process has begun: timidly, fearfully, a few brave souls have been taping their work, showing themselves in action, and opening themselves to the criticism that they do not know everything there is to know about the art of helping people learn.

As for the students themselves, who from their vantage point know a great deal about the state of the art, there is great respect for those teachers who put their own work on the line. At the end of a three-hour interview with eleven graduating students [45, Appendix 7], I asked them to sum up what it was they really wanted in a teacher. A student said: "A human being who's not afraid. I think it boils down to not being afraid. I really do."

References

1. Atherton, J. W. "Expectations and Responsibilities of the Employing Colleges." In *Improving College Teaching,* edited by C. B. T. Lee. Washington, D.C.: American Council on Education, 1967.
2. Barzun, J. *Teacher in America.* Garden City, N.Y.: Doubleday, Doubleday Anchor Books, 1954.
3. Bellack, A. A. (ed.). *Theory and Research in Teaching.* New York: Teachers College Press, 1963.
4. Bellack, A. A., H. M. Kliebard, R. T. Hyman, and F. L. Smith, Jr. *The Language of the Classroom.* New York: Teachers College Press, 1966.
5. Bennis, W. G., and H. A. Shepard, "A Theory of Group Development." *Human Relations,* 9 (1956), 415–57.
6. Blegen, T. C., and R. M. Cooper (eds.). *The Preparation of Teachers.* Washington, D.C.: American Council on Education, 1950.
7. Bronowski, J. *A Sense of the Future: Essays in Natural Philosophy.* Cambridge, Mass.: MIT Press, 1977.
8. Bruffee, K. A. *A Short Course in Writing.* Cambridge, Mass.: Winthrop, 1972.
9. ———. "The Way Out." *College English,* 33 (January 1972), 457–70.
10. Bruner, J. S. *The Process of Education.* Cambridge, Mass.: Harvard University Press, 1960.
11. ———. *Toward a Theory of Instruction.* Cambridge, Mass.: Belknap Press of Harvard University Press, 1966.
12. Buber, M. "Elements of the Interhuman." William Alanson White Memorial Lectures, Fourth Series, *Psychiatry,* 20 (May 1957), 105–13.
13. Cantor, N. *Dynamics of Learning.* New York: Agathon Press, 1972. First published Buffalo, N.Y.: Foster and Stewart, 1946.
14. ———. *The Teaching ↔ Learning Process.* New York: Dryden Press, 1953.
15. Conant, J. B. *The Education of American Teachers.* New York: McGraw-Hill, 1963.
16. Dennison, G. *The Lives of Children: The Story of the First Street School.* New York: Vintage Books, 1969.
17. Dewey, J. *Democracy and Education.* New York: Macmillan, 1916.
18. Drosnin, M. "College Teachers and Teaching: A Student's View." In *Improving College Teaching,* edited by C. B. T. Lee. Washington, D.C.: American Council on Education, 1967.

19. Edie, J. M. "Vico and Existential Philosophy." In *Giambattista Vico: An International Symposium,* edited by G. Tagliacozzo and H. V. White. Baltimore: Johns Hopkins Press, 1969.
20. Flanders, N. A. *Analyzing Teacher Behavior.* Reading, Mass.: Addison-Wesley, 1970.
21. ———. "Teacher Influence in the Classroom." In *Theory and Research in Teaching,* edited by A. A. Bellack. New York: Teachers College Press, 1963.
22. Freire, P. *Pedagogy of the Oppressed.* New York: Herder and Herder, 1972.
23. Gage, N. L. "The Need for Process-Oriented Research." In *Improving College Teaching,* edited by C. B. T. Lee. Washington, D.C.: American Council on Education, 1967.
24. ———. "Paradigms for Research on Teaching." In *Handbook of Research on Teaching,* edited by N. L. Gage. Chicago: Rand McNally, 1963.
25. Gage, N. L. (ed.). *Handbook of Research on Teaching.* Chicago: Rand McNally, 1963.
26. Grainger, A. J. *The Bullring: A Classroom Experiment in Moral Education.* London: Pergamon Press, 1970.
27. Highet, G. *The Art of Teaching.* New York: Vintage Books, 1950.
28. Hutchins, R. M. *The Higher Learning in America.* New Haven: Yale University Press, 1936.
29. Illich, I. *Deschooling Society.* New York: Harper & Row, 1971.
30. James, C. *Young Lives at Stake: The Education of Adolescents.* New York: Agathon Press, 1972.
31. James, W. *Talks to Teachers.* New York: W. W. Norton. The Norton Library, 1958.
32. Kilpatrick, W. H. *Foundations of Method: Informal Talks on Teaching.* New York: Macmillan, 1932.
33. Lee, C. B. T. (ed.). *Improving College Teaching.* Washington, D.C.: American Council on Education, 1967.
34. Mandel, B. J. *Literature and the English Department.* Champaign, Ill.: National Council of Teachers of English, 1970.
35. McKeachie, W. J. "Research in Teaching: The Gap Between Theory and Practice." In *Improving College Teaching,* edited by C. B. T. Lee. Washington, D.C.: American Council on Education, 1967.
36. Moustakis, C. *The Authentic Teacher: Sensitivity and Awareness in the Classroom.* Cambridge, Mass.: Howard A. Doyle, 1966.
37. Nisbet, R. A. "Conflicting Academic Loyalties." In *Improving College Teaching,* edited by C. B. T. Lee. Washington, D.C.: American Council on Education, 1967.
38. Payne, J. *Lectures on the Science and Art of Education.* New York: E. L. Kellogg, Second Edition, 1884.
39. Pruyser, P. W. "Existential Notes on Professional Education." *Social Work,* 8 (April 1963), 82–87.

40. Reynolds, B. C. *Learning and Teaching in the Practice of Social Work.* New York: Rinehart, 1942.
41. Schwartz, W. "The Classroom Teaching of Social Work With Groups: Some Central Problems." In *A Conceptual Framework for the Teaching of the Social Group Work Method in the Classroom.* New York: Council on Social Work Education, 1964.
42. Shulman, L. "Group Work and Effective College Instruction." Ed. D. dissertation, Temple University, 1972.
43. ———. "The Hidden Group in the Classroom." *Learning and Development.* 2 (November 1970), 1, 6.
44. Skinner, B. F. "Why Teachers Fail." *Saturday Review.* October 16, 1965, 80–81, 98–102.
45. Soffen, J. *Faculty Development in Professional Education.* New York: Council on Social Work Education, 1967.
46. Stuart, S. *Say: An Experiment in Learning.* London: Thomas Nelson & Sons, 1969.
47. Torbert, W. R. "Educating Toward Shared Purpose. Self-Direction and Quality Work: The Theory and Practice of Liberating Structure." *Journal of Higher Education,* 49 (March/April 1978), 109–35.
48. Trumbull, H. C. *Teaching and Teachers.* Philadelphia: John D. Wattles, 1885.
49. Whitehead, A. N. *The Aims of Education, and Other Essays.* New York: Macmillan, 1949.

Research

Introduction

1951

A Comparison of Background Characteristics and Performance of Paid and Volunteer Group Leaders

1966b

Neighborhood Centers

1971d

Neighborhood Centers and Group Work

Introduction

Throughout his career, Schwartz maintained his conviction that the goals of the profession could not be advanced without serious and substantial attention to matters of method. All his writings were intended to contribute to the profession's social mission by focusing attention on the technical problems of practice.

Schwartz chose three works to be included in the "Research" section of this volume. At first glance one might infer little attention to research. Such a view would be mistaken. Using Zimbalist's framework, Schwartz considered research, "as any effort to collect and analyze data in a planned attempt to answer questions or test hypotheses arising out of the planning and practice of relevant agencies" (1966, p. 145). Employing this definition, one can readily see that Schwartz emphasized that generating and organizing data about practice were, in fact, an effort to support research about practice. His interest in fashioning tools for the analysis of practice was part of his research agenda.[1]

Not unlike Glaser and Strauss (1967)[2] Schwartz's approach was an inductive one. He began with no a priori hypotheses to be tested, no carefully controlled experiments. His efforts were exploratory and formulative in nature. He believed that the state of our knowledge about the nature of the helping process and skill in work with groups was so limited that our study priorities could best be realized through an approach which began with generating data for analysis. The data to be created were the details of what the worker did to help and the contexts in which those helping activities were conducted. Schwartz (1962b) believed that

> [d]espite the impatience of those who would like to move as quickly as possible into studies of outcome and effectiveness, our main progress for a time will probably be in studies of process and of limited effects . . . our major tools are still the group record, the life-history,

---

[1]Several of these tools can be found in the literature. See, for example: J. Agueros et al. "A Study of Social Work Practice: An Exploratory Investigation into the Nature of the Helping Process," Unpublished master's thesis, Columbia University School of Social Work, 1965; "Identification of Worker's Responses in Group Situations," Memorandum to Gertrude Wilson and others, NASW, February 20, 1958; George S. Getzel (1988) Teaching Group Work Skill Through Reflection-in-Action, in Marcos Leiderman, Martin L. Birnbaum, and Barbara Dazzo (Eds.) *Roots and New Frontiers in Social Group Work,* New York: Haworth Press, pp: 115–129. Selected Proceedings Seventh Annual Symposium on the Advancement of Social Work with Groups. See Appendix B for how Schwartz used the "Identification of Worker's Responses in Group Situations" (the "Critical Incident") in his classroom.

[2]B. Glaser and A. Strauss approach the task of generating theory by grounding themselves in the phenomena under investigation. Their approach is an inductive one which begins with experience. See for example their 1967 work: *Grounded Theory,* Chicago: Aldine Publishing Co.

the critical incident, and other techniques for coding and conceptualizing the experience of practice (p. 278).

A reading of Schwartz's first published article demonstrates how early his ideas formed on the importance of the particulars of practice. "A Comparison of Background Characteristics and Performance of Paid and Volunteer Group Leaders" (1951) is a study Schwartz conducted shortly after earning his Master's. It focused on the role of the volunteer in group service agencies and examined "[a]t what specific points does he make his most—and least—productive contribution?" (p. 1).

The research methodology chosen reflected Schwartz's belief that helping and being helped were two distinct though interrelated processes. The study examined actual practitioner behavior rather than effectiveness and set as its first task the establishment of a set of performance criteria. This was not a small assignment, for as Schwartz later suggested, "[t]he difficulty in defining skill in human relations is the problem of describing an act in its own terms, rather than in terms of its results" (1962b).

This investigation was unusual in its time, for its emphasis upon an operational definition of worker skill cut into the prevailing mode of discussing worker activity in terms of its intentions, values, and philosophy. The task of defining a set of measurement criteria was "an attempt to translate the function of the group leader into a body of specific practices against which the performance of the leaders could be judged and compared" (p. 4). Process records provided the data and became the basis for defining, measuring, and studying worker action. This emphasis upon examining function in action, through process recording, remained with Schwartz throughout his career. Even at this early date, it was clear that he believed that interest in a high quality of practice was synonymous with interest in the study of practice.

"Neighborhood Centers" (1966) and "Neighborhood Centers and Group Work" (1971) were written as part of a response to a call from the Council on Social Work Research of the National Association of Social Workers, to examine critically what has been learned through systematic study in five fields of practice. In these exhaustive reviews including hundreds of entries, Schwartz presented the state of knowledge about the systematic study of neighborhood centers and group work. His first review (1966) was organized according to five areas: the client, the agency, the community, the professionals, and evaluations and outcomes. In his final observations Schwartz cited three obstacles to research in this field: (1) the hesitancy of centers to institutionalize inquiry into practice issues, (2) the absence of any systematic recording of agency practice, and (3) the reality that workers "are badly trained in the skills of research" (p. 183). He suggested that on balance, the picture was not all bleak. There were some beginning signs of theorizing about practice with groups. In his second review in 1971 (1971d), using the same categories for analysis, Schwartz was slightly encouraged. He felt that while "the gaps are still large, the continuity weak, and the commitment spotty"

(p. 180) there were signs of a more developed picture in which "official curiosity" was growing. He remained hopeful that as the relationship between neighborhood centers and the social work profession was strengthened, so too would be research into the activity of group work in neighborhood centers.

Toby Berman-Rossi

A Comparison of Background Characteristics and Performance of Paid and Volunteer Group Leaders*

William Schwartz

As a growing number of group work agencies take steps to define their function and improve their service to the community, the role of the volunteer, once central and undisputed, becomes a deepening source of confusion to both lay and professional workers alike. Much of this confusion stems from the failure to think through and spell out the function of the unpaid worker in the new and growing context of agency practice. What is the role of the volunteer in the total picture of agency service? At what specific points does he make his most—and least—productive contribution?

The general process of growth also brings with it a growing realization that the ability of the agency to live up to its aspirations for service lies directly in the hands of those workers who maintain a close, ongoing relationship with the members themselves. Where, as in most settings, these relationships are carried mainly by those who lead clubs, there has developed a greater concern with the problems of leadership selection, orientation and supervision. This preoccupation with the quality and efficiency of group leaders has, to a large extent, stimulated the movement toward re-examination of the use of volunteers in the agency setting. It has also, particularly among

*Summary of a study undertaken at The East Bronx Community Y.M.-Y.W.H.A., New York City, October, 1948 to June, 1949.

Presented at the Conference of the National Association of Jewish Center Workers, June, 1950, Atlantic City, N.J.

Reprinted from The Jewish Center Worker, *Vol. xii, No. 1, Jan. 1951.*

agencies with a history and tradition of volunteer club leadership, posed a practical problem both for those who direct and those who finance agency policy.

Assuming for the moment—as would many professional workers and lay leaders—that group leadership positions should be assigned to trained, full-time personnel, it is clear that such a course is presently unrealizable in the vast majority of communities. Agency settings are most generally such that leaders are engaged—whether paid or volunteer—on a session basis. It is also largely true that, where session workers are paid, agency budgets provide only for fairly nominal payments to leaders working with small friendship groups.

Within this context, will there be any real and tangible difference between the performance of volunteers, carefully selected and professionally supervised, and that of paid session workers? If no such difference actually exists, the wisdom of a system of payment can certainly be called into question. Strong support would then be given to the hypothesis that the central issue is not payment but better orientation and supervision of volunteers. If, however, a clear distinction would be found, it would be important to locate and define it more carefully. Is it a function of the payment, per se, or do leaders hired under circumstances of payment offer a different set of qualities and characteristics from those who volunteer their services? If the latter is true, the issue of payment would be linked to a larger configuration of factors than the single dimension of financial incentive alone.

The study to be briefly described in this paper was an attempt to explore these and related questions within the experience of a single agency during the course of one season of activity.

Background

In the summer of 1948, the East Bronx Community YM-YWHA of New York submitted to the Federation of Jewish Philanthropies a request for funds with which, for the first time in its history, the agency could hire and pay personnel for the direct leadership of groups. The Federation, aware of the agency's outstanding history of volunteer participation, felt that a study of this type of experience would be important to the field in general, and that this would be an ideal setting for such an effort. Accordingly, it was decided that a sum, similar to the one requested, would be allotted for the purpose of conducting a research project designed to study "the validity of the wide use of volunteers in their program."

The East Bronx Y, in fourteen years of service to its community, had developed and grown mainly through the efforts of volunteers and their contributions to the agency; its contact with the community was a close one and neighborhood people had been represented on the Board of Directors for some time. During the previous season, it had made use of more than 75 volunteers, throughout the program and in direct contact with the membership. Over many seasons, the agency had developed a host of techniques designed to stimulate volunteer involvement, conscientiousness and morale. These techniques had been refined to a point where they constituted somewhat of a model for agencies faced with a similar situation.

In recent years, the Y had expanded its key professional staff and developed its consciousness of goals and function. At this point it felt that it could offer a better service to the community were it put in a position to offer financial payment to club leaders. The budget request was an expression of the belief that volunteer leaders, regardless of orientation and supervision, carried a severely limited potential, as compared with workers hired under a system of payment.

The Federation grant represented an opportunity to examine this hypothesis and several of its implications in some detail. The study was initiated in October, 1948, under the supervision of the Functional Committee on Community Centers. From the general mandate regarding the examination of "the wide use of volunteers," the Study Committee focussed the research effort on a comparison of the background characteristics and performance of paid as against volunteer group leaders in the teen-age division of the Y during the season October, 1948 to June, 1949.

Setting and Focus

The unit of study consisted of twenty-two club leaders, concentrated in a single division of the agency program, namely, the 13 to 17 year age grouping. The leaders were under the supervision of a single full-time professional worker, and comprised his total supervisory load. This division supervisor was an older worker, partially trained, who was in turn supervised by the Assistant Director—the latter a social work graduate with some years of experience.

The total group of twenty-two consisted of three leader categories: the *paid* grouping was composed of 6 leaders, hired on a session basis, for fees ranging from \$3 to \$5 per session; the *volunteer* grouping, with 9 leaders, was recruited from the community at large in accordance with past agency practice; and a *student* grouping consisted of 7 undergraduate students, unpaid, but receiving project credit for at least the first three months of work with the agency. These students, sent by the Social Research laboratories of local colleges, had been used by the agency for the past several seasons. The last two categories named represented an attempt to explore the possibility of a distinction between two different types of volunteer recruitment with which the agency was realistically concerned.

The fact that no attempt was made to control the hiring process by some effort to effect an equation of qualifications, such as training, motivation, experience, etc., was, of course, in direct line with the central focus of the study. Actually, the study was an effort geared to the single experience of a fairly typical urban group work agency, within a single large division of the program. It was hoped that a close and systematic examination of this experience would yield some answers to a practical question being asked by the agency, namely: What kind of leadership can we offer to our groups when we are able to pay session workers, as against when we use people who have volunteered their services? Will there be a difference in the kind of people we get?

In pursuing the comparison between the paid and unpaid workers—or, more specifically, among the three categories of *paid, student* and *volunteer*—our objectives were as follows:

First, to determine whether significant differences existed in the quality of group leadership performance demonstrated by the group leaders in the categories under study. It should be noted that the word "performance" was used, rather than the concept of "effectiveness." This was purposefully done, with the realization that the measurement of "effectiveness" involved the necessity to scrutinize not only the techniques of the leader but also their actual effect upon the group and its members. While it was recognized that these would be difficult to separate, it was decided that the measurement instruments should be designed mainly for what they could tell us about the actual behavior of the leaders. Any attempt to study group growth, except in a related and subjective manner, would lead us into an effort of mammoth proportions, far beyond the present limitations of time and staff. The assumption was thus made that a set of Criteria for the Performance of Group Leaders could be drawn up that would cut so closely to the heart of good group leadership, as presently defined, that it would serve as an evaluative instrument without close reference to the actual responses of the group and its members.

The second objective was to determine whether significant differences existed in the composition of the separate leader categories in relation to certain background characteristics chosen for their potential relationship to the quality of leadership performance. The chosen areas of identification by no means exhausted the possibilities; they were selected from among many, the choice being dictated by considerations of accessibility of information, possible motivational clues, and general significance to the task of group leadership. They included the following: age, educational status, educational emphasis, experience as a group leader, experience as a group participant, circumstances surrounding the leader's affiliation with this particular agency, career goal, interests and skills, conceptions of the agency's function, and some very limited aspects of personality orientation and attitudes.

Finally, it was hoped that it might be possible to relate these characteristics and attributes to the behavior of the leaders under study and to isolate those that seemed to bear most directly on the quality of group leadership performance within the current setting. This objective, though a subsidiary one, was regarded with great interest by both the agency and the Study Committee for its potential usefulness in the area of screening and hiring.

Scope and Limitations

An obvious limitation of the entire plan was the small size of the sample, which left room for any number of accidental variables to throw doubt on the results. However, it was felt that, while the sample was certainly not statistically unassailable, it was large enough to offer significant data for some preliminary conclusions. We hoped, too, that the comparisons would yield additional material that was important to the whole question of group leadership and point some directions for future research in this vital area of practice.

As to methodology, our efforts brought home to us very clearly the complicated nature of any attempt to evaluate scientifically the performance of a group leader in all of its subtlety and complexity. No one who has attempted to pin down and observe the factors inherent in human relationships, all the more elusive in their group manifestations, can fail to come away with less than a huge respect for the job of the leader of clubs, nor underestimate his role in the agency picture. The material that emerged was so vast, and its implications so broad, that it soon became apparent that our efforts at delimitation had been largely unsuccessful. Of necessity, the originally conceived emphasis on quantitative documentation was restricted to fewer areas, with the remainder being subjected to a more qualitative analysis of the material emerging from the records.

The full report of the completed study* carries a detailed account of the methodological considerations and the process through which these were analyzed and dealt with along the way. It also describes fully each of the techniques designed for data collection and data analysis. For the purposes of this limited presentation, we will merely describe the instruments briefly and attempt to deal somewhat more fully with the main points embodied in the findings themselves.

The Criteria

Our first task was the formulation of a set of Criteria against which the performance of the leaders could be measured. Investigation into the literature of group work and of progressive education offered only a partial solution to this problem and gave early indication that a new formulation would be required. While the literature revealed many attempts to define the contribution of the group leader, each effort represented a commingling of related and unrelated, measurable and unmeasurable, factors. The focus would shift from the leader's equipment, to his function, to his behavior in the group situation, to his actual effect upon the group itself. This mixture of cause and effect, role, background and function, pointed up the general need for a methodical spelling out of the concrete components of good leadership practice, as they manifest themselves in the observable performance of the group leader.

Our formulation represented an effort in this direction. It was an attempt to translate the *function* of the group leader into a body of specific *practices* against which the performance of the leaders could be judged and compared.

Three major considerations had to be met in the final document. One was that the assumption of translatability could not be followed to a reduction ad absurdum which would deny the complex nature of the group leader's job and reduce his contribution to a series of mechanical acts. This would give us a

*Copies of the full report can be obtained from the East Bronx Community YM-YWHA. 1288 Southern Boulevard, Bronx, New York.

number of trees without anything resembling a forest. The attempt to isolate and particularize must be done with a constant eye for the "feel" of the total subject and a concurrent concern with both the subjective and the objective.

Further, the formulation would have to be theoretically correct and comprehensive enough to insure a balanced picture.

And finally, it would have to be so formulated as to achieve general acceptability by layman and professional alike. The new and untested nature of the instrument made it extremely important that it represent the widest possible distillation of knowledge, experience and feeling that could be achieved.

The process out of which the Criteria emerged was geared to the above considerations and was an attempt to draw together as many different levels of thought and opinion as could be focussed on the problem. In addition to a survey of the theoretical literature, the formulation was arrived at through a series of discussions by the agency staff, agency lay leadership, and other professional and lay people in the field. The final form was established by the Study Committee.

Lack of space makes it necessary to refer to the full report for a complete listing of the Criteria themselves. It should be mentioned, however, that they were divided into five areas of leadership responsibility, as follows: 1. Criteria relating to the club leader's responsibility toward the job itself. (Conscientiousness, dependability, etc.) 2. Criteria relating to the leader's role and performance with the group as a whole. 3. Criteria relating to the leader's role and performance with individuals within the group. 4. Criteria relating to the leader's responsibility for his own growth and learning. 5. Criteria relating to the leader's responsibility to the total agency structure of which he is a part.

Data Collection

The instruments that were designed to probe the experience of the division under study bore an important relationship to the ongoing agency program. Since these tools constituted an attempt to draw specific information from every point of vantage, they were designed to establish contact with every individual in any way connected with the leader's experience in the agency. This included the supervisor, the specialty-area workers, our group observers, and the leaders themselves. Thus, many demands were, of necessity, made upon the workings of the teen-age division. Failing a constant sensitivity on the part of the research worker, these demands would place an undue load upon everybody's time and provoke serious psychological obstacles to cooperation.

On the positive side, the informational requirements of the research plan coincided closely with the functional needs of the program itself; the challenge to the research worker was to create, with the cooperation of the division supervisor, recording instruments that would be equally useful to the agency and to the research project.

This process gained some impetus from the fact that the data-gathering tools had to be fashioned from scratch for our needs. Owing mostly to the scarcity of similar research efforts in the field, and partly to the peculiar demands of this project, it was impossible to find ready-made instruments that could be put to use for our purposes.

The following forms were used:

1. An Interview Schedule, designed to draw from the leaders themselves, in an early-season interview with the research worker, information necessary to identify them in relation to the factors previously mentioned.

2. A Leader's Group Record form, designed to standardize, in some measure, the information submitted by the group leaders in their regular recording of the club meetings. The Record was, at different points, both structured and unstructured, representing an effort to combine objective reporting with free narrative recording and subjective interpretation.

3. An Observers Record, incorporating a system of both horizontal and vertical recording, and designed to yield similar information from different observers.

4. A Record of Supervisory Conferences, which was kept by the research worker with information taken from the division supervisor in a weekly interview. These interviews were based on a prepared schedule and grew out of the necessity to devise a plan whereby the supervisor would be free of the time-consuming responsibility for keeping detailed supervisory conference records.

5. An Anecdotal Record, which was used by agency workers in semi-mass and activity areas, such as the gymnasium, lounge, game-room, etc. This form was designed to yield information emerging from the informal contacts of these specialty workers with members, sub-groups and leaders in a setting other than the club meeting.

Findings: Summary and Discussion

Moving now into a consideration of the material that emerged, it should be remembered that the study represented a broad attack on a complex problem with the aid of a very limited sample. Viewed, however, as a pilot study, designed to explore some meaningful hypotheses, the broad nature of the attempt offered the advantage of eliciting a mass of evidence touching upon, and partially illuminating, many facets of the total problem.

Of these, we will attempt to highlight those which seemed closest to the central questions. The following will, of necessity, represent a brief summary and discussion, making it necessary to refer to the full report for most of the accompanying documentation and statistical material.

1. *The student and volunteer categories were essentially similar in every aspect under analysis.*

Though it was true that, if the comparison were restricted to these two groups, a case could be made for a slight superiority of the student group, these differences were so insignificant as to create a general pattern of similarity that far outweighed that of difference. By contrast, as will be shown, the distinctions between the paid category on the one hand, and the students and volunteers taken together, on the other, were clear and sharp. This discovery tended to strengthen the hypothesis that the essential choice lay between *paid* and *volunteer* workers, with the latter category being more broadly defined. The fact that the students voluntarily undertook this type of school obligation (much more time-consuming and exacting than the alternative of writing a term paper) lent added support to this development.

Thus, in our future references to the categories *paid* and *unpaid,* the latter term should be taken to embody the broader concept of "volunteer", and will include all of the 16 unpaid workers.

2. *Examination of the characteristics and attributes of the leaders under study revealed clear differences between the paid and unpaid categories in certain well-defined respects.*

The total group, we found, was fairly homogeneous in age, averaging 21 years, with the great majority of leaders falling between the ages of 18 and 22. It was a group made up almost entirely of college students, fairly evenly distributed in the second, third and fourth year. In their subject orientation, the predominant emphasis was upon education and the social sciences. With regard to group work training and experience, the total picture was that of an untrained group which, while presenting marked differences in the amount of previous leadership experience of a disciplined nature, was still as a group fairly limited in this area. Thus, there was no question here of trained vs. non-trained, or professional vs. non-professional workers. Differences did exist in the extent to which this factor was present in the separate categories, but in the main, there were only leaders with more or less experience, more or less schooling, and more or less group work background.

The differences that emerged between the paid and unpaid workers followed a consistent pattern and, under further examination, seemed to fall into three major areas.

The first of these dealt with the leaders' own life experiences as participant group members, their apparent success or failure in effecting such identifications, and some of the indicated results of such experiences. In this connection we found that the paid workers presented a personal history of group activity and participation that far outweighed that of the unpaid leaders. In each of the four fields of activity examined—school, natural-group, camp, and agency—the pattern of difference was consistent. The evidence strongly indicated that the paid workers, as a group, were people who had moved out to group experiences, had participated and involved themselves to a considerable degree, and were currently carrying on the same pattern of group-involvement. There was also evidence to indicate that these experiences were part of a configuration—whether cause or effect—of wider and more diversified areas of personal interests and curiosities, as well as a disposition to pursue these preoccupations and exploit them. The unpaid leaders, on the other hand, seemed in the main to present a picture of general past insecurity in the area of group relationships and around the problem of belonging. Some seemed to be coming to this experience belatedly, having recently joined groups, for the first time, of a small, intimate nature. Many of them, some consciously and explicitly, seemed to have come to a realization of their problem and were looking to their current assignment as a group experience for themselves. A typical example was the volunteer who stated that he took this job so that he "could be before a group."

The second area of difference covered those points in our analysis that bore upon the relationship of the worker toward the practice of group work as a career goal. Here we found that, beginning with the circumstances under which they became members of the staff and ranging through their leadership experience, career goals, and conceptions of the function of the agency, the paid leaders gave many indications of regarding their present position as a stepping stone to a career slanted in the direction of social work in general and group work in particular. In each of these aspects, the findings revealed a marked difference between paid and unpaid workers: the "professional-referral" nature of the paid group's introduction to the agency, as against the predominant "self-referral" of the unpaid category; the greater amount of previous experience, both supervised and unsupervised, of the paid group; the greater incidence of "career goals related to social work"; and the somewhat more precise understanding of the function of the agency, based in part on their own experiences as members and in part on their previous leadership experiences in such settings.

The third area was included primarily for the purpose of recording some impressions in an area that seems to constitute a fertile field for future study. While we were obviously not geared to derive findings in the complex field of personality configuration, the interviews yielded certain very striking impressions which seemed, in many ways, to be related to the points discussed above.

In examining our "Interviewer's Comments" section—an attempt to form a total diagnostic impression of the leader, based on the interview—we found a marked emergence, with variations, of two distinct "types."

One of these seemed to lend itself to the term "*mission*-centered." These leaders were, in the main, a poised, articulate group, with a definite feeling that they were in possession of a value-system that could and should be transmitted to teenage youngsters. The outstanding characteristics of this group were reflected by our repeated use of the words "controlling," "driving," "aggressive," and particularly, "strong helping need." They were active, outgoing, and seemed willing—and able—to involve themselves in a host of new experiences. Primarily, they demonstrated a strong need to influence, to help—actually, to teach.

The other grouping seemed somewhat at the other extreme. Here the key diagnostic references seemed to be "self-effacing," "guarded," "reveals little feeling," "lack of self-involvement", and in some instances "shy and fearful." These were workers who seemed quite hesitant about their ability to contribute anything of value to the group situation. Their responses in the interview tended to be under-elaborated, sometimes vague and tentative. There was a strong impression that the experience of group leadership was immensely challenging and fear-provoking for them. To distinguish this group—and for want of a better name—we applied the term "*self*-centered."

Moving a step further, we found that the "*mission*-centered" group included 5 *of the 6 paid leaders, and 3 of the 15 unpaid workers*—8 in all. The connection between membership in this "type" category and their own group-orientation was particularly striking. In all 8 instances, the leaders presented a picture of active participant experience, either at school or in adolescent groups, or both. 5 of the 8 had had significant adolescent group experiences; 6 had been campers; 4 had had experience as agency members. In relation to Career Goals, 7 of the 8 had chosen *Goals related to Social Work,* the single exception having named the vocation of "courtroom lawyer."

Of the 13 remaining, 10 leaders seemed to fit very definitely into the second "type" category. Of these 1 was a paid worker and 9 were unpaid. Here again the participation figures were striking. Of the 10, 9 leaders reported extremely limited participant experience, while the other had had some, of a mass organizational nature. Only 1 of this group had had experience as a camper; only 1 had had a childhood experience as an agency member (2 had recently joined). With regard to Career Goals, only 4 of the 10 had named *Goals Related to Social Work.*

What these considerations lead to is a matter for present conjecture and future research. It seems indicated that the above touches, at some decisive points, on the whole area of group leadership motivation, a field in which further systematic work is sorely needed.

It seems quite probable that the similarity of pattern in regard to career-orientation and to group-orientation was more than accidental. The evidence appeared to point to the fact that the former was an extension of the latter; that the career direction contemplated by the paid workers had been considerably influenced by both the group experiences themselves and the very psychological drives and motivations that led them to their original disposition to active group involvement and participation. In any event, it seemed likely to us that, out of their group experiences, these leaders had derived much of their impetus toward the practice of group leadership, as well as some of the tools—both attitudinal and practical—with which they felt they could proceed. The previously described *"mission*-centeredness" seemed to represent in part a transfer of their enthusiasm for the group experience to a setting in which they now functioned as leaders rather than members. Again, without going into questions of cause and effect, the teacher-missionary configuration so markedly noted in these workers appeared directly related to their desire to produce, in the members of their clubs, a repetition of their own past experiences and learnings in the group experience. In this sense, our speculation would lead us to the conclusion that—in an antithetically different manner from the unpaid leaders—the paid group was also using the current experience as a projection of its own needs and relationships to the problem of group involvement and participation.

It might be stated, in essence, that the paid workers were attempting to *duplicate* a successful experience, while the unpaid leaders were trying to *achieve* one.

The emergence of certain perceivable experiential, motivational and, to the extent that we were able to judge, personality differences between the paid and unpaid leaders opens up an important area of conjecture bearing upon the role and significance of the *payment factor* in the hiring of part-time leadership personnel. Discussions on the issue of payment often tend to focus upon the relationship between payment and financial *incentive,* the assumption being that the crucial variable is the introduction of a payment tie, which binds the worker to his responsibility with the agency. While we have no way, at this time, of assessing the degree of decisiveness of the financial-incentive factor, both the nominal nature of the payment and the generally high level of reliability reached by many of the leaders, paid and unpaid, tends to weaken the thesis that it constitutes, in itself, a crucial consideration.

3. *With the exception of certain changes that occurred within the paid category near the close of the season, both the paid and unpaid workers had been largely unsuccessful in understanding their groups, discovering their potential and helping them to realize it, even on the simplest levels.*

This inability to successfully perform a helping role in their relationships with the groups they were leading was both general and unmistakable. The indications were that it stemmed from a strong and fixed preoccupation with rapid and concrete evidences of group movement and growth; that this in turn reflected a conception of themselves as bearers of values and, unconsciously, the embodiment of their definition of the good teacher and the benevolent parent; and that their investment in the group situation represented, to a large (and visible) extent a projection of their own needs. The general emphasis on group accomplishment, seen only as reflected by immediately tangible evidence such as "program," organization" and "order", served to create situations in which the leaders were seen by their groups as demanding, authority figures—however benevolent; groups responded with guilt and tension, and competitive relationships emerged between workers and indigenous leaders. This pattern of leadership dominated the total picture so completely as to tend to obscure many of the more subtle evaluative considerations contained in the Criteria.

The effect of this discovery was to dramatize a point related to the type of contribution the agency could properly expect from its group leaders. It served to shift the focus of expectation—and, simultaneously, the focus of comparison—to areas whose importance was now radically heightened. If none of the hiring systems under study produced competent leaders, and if these systems represented the only real and practical alternatives available to the agency, it now became necessary to move the emphasis into areas in which the agency could realistically demand a high quality of performance. These demands would necessarily center upon those aspects of the group leader's job which dealt with his responsibility for cooperation with, and amenability to, the agency's processes for orientation and training. Specifically, the important questions would be: Does he attend club meetings regularly? Can he participate in the supervisory process and involve himself in discussions of his own role and performance? And, finally, can he learn from supervision and show some modifications in approach as a result of this learning?

These were areas involving both *intent* and *ability:* they were concerned, on the one hand, with questions of conscientiousness, largely requiring only a sense of responsibility to the job at hand; on the other, they were related to considerations that went deeper and called other attributes and characteristics into play. Taken together, they represented expectations that, while limited, were both valid and crucial in this setting.

4. *In each of the areas mentioned above—Reliability, Participation in Supervision, and Flexibility—the paid workers showed a marked and consistent superiority.*

In the area of *Reliability,* the first fact of major importance was that, of the 8 leaders who failed to finish the season (all representing more than one-third of the total group under study) *all* were in the *unpaid* category. Of the 7 performance indications that went to make up the total *Reliability* aspect, we found that the paid workers showed higher than the unpaid in all but one, in which latter no difference appeared. In 4 of the 7 areas, the differential was particularly striking and the superiority of the paid workers unquestionable. The *Total Reliability Score,* compounded of all 7 areas, revealed a group score for the paid leaders which was almost double that of the unpaid.

Examining the nature and degree of the leaders' *Participation in Supervision,* we found that the records of the supervisory conferences revealed little difference between the leader categories in the amount of verbal participation, elaboration and responsiveness. However, when we studied the nature and content of this participation, we discovered a sharp difference, with the paid workers demonstrating a markedly superior ability to involve themselves at a level of *feeling*—expressing their doubts, discussing and attempting to understand their own roles, and using help in thinking their way through the problems that arose in their work.

Thus, it seemed clear from the evidence that while both groups found it possible to participate actively on the verbal level, the unpaid workers were unable to involve themselves freely in a more personal, and what we would take to be a more meaningful, relationship to the supervisory process.

Turning to the question of *Flexibility,* our attempt to discover the extent to which the leaders were able to make use of their supervisory help was necessarily tentative and was centered on a single phenomenon. A close study of both the group records, submitted by the leaders, and the supervisory conference records, submitted by the supervisor, revealed that the majority of the leaders were unable, in spite of repeated conferences on the problem, to relax their pressures upon the groups to live up to the leaders' demands for achievement. In four instances, however, there seemed a great deal of evidence to show that group situations improved considerably as a result of a change in approach on the part of the leaders. In each case, a group which was close to disbanding was helped by the leader to find new and important strengths with which to continue together. These four groups, all of them led by paid workers, were among the six clubs that finished either strongly and together or, in one instance, with new indications of group strength. Five of these six groups were led by paid workers.

In a very real sense, the touchstone of difference between the paid and unpaid workers seemed to lie in their respective reactions to the frustrations and disappointments of the first half-season. Faced with a job whose difficulty and complexity became clearer week by week, and with groups whose reactions they could not understand and whose failure to "move" they regarded as a personal rejection, the responses of the paid leaders as a whole differed considerably from those of the unpaid. A careful examination of the records of the unpaid leaders who dropped out convinces us that many of these took this way out of a situation that was too difficult to pursue. Their records show a marked increase in disillusionment and hopelessness preceding their failure to continue. Those who remained turned more directly and intensively to the supervisor for help. It was at this point that the leaders' ability to accept responsibility for what was happening and to subject their own values to critical examination was vitally important. In the main, the unpaid workers found this too difficult; they externalized, found fault with their groups, fantasied the removal of troublesome individuals within the group, or passively and uncomprehendingly listened to the supervisor's interpretations. These manifestations, it goes without saying, were far from absent in the supervisory conferences of the paid workers; nevertheless, it seemed clear that they were able to take a much larger degree of responsibility, tended more toward self-examination, and participated more actively in the actual diagnostic and interpretive process. In an interesting manner, the "*mission*-centeredness" played a salutary role in this regard. While this quality tended strongly to increase their manipulativeness, it also seemed to make them extremely sensitive to this very tendency, which was sharply out of line with their own intellectual conception of the leader's role.

5. *Analysis of the background and equipment of the top-ranking leaders revealed certain significant attributes and characteristics held in common.*

Restricting the present discussion to the actual results of our work, their inherent significance lies in the possible interconnection of the following revealed facts: a) the paid group presented, almost unanimously, certain characteristics which were diametrically opposed to those of the unpaid group; b) in the performance areas under examination, the paid group was consistently superior to the unpaid, with the individual performance-ranking showing all six paid leaders at the top of the list; c) the paid workers who ranked *lowest* in relation to their own category were those who offered *fewest* of these differentiating characteristics; d) the unpaid workers who ranked *highest* in their own category were those who presented *the greatest number* of these characteristics; and e) the workers at the very bottom of the performance ranking were furthest away from the attributes in question.

To some extent, these results tended to represent verification of the hypotheses which dictated the focus of the original interviews in which the identifying material was gathered. In addition, the interviews also produced other factors which were not anticipated and which added to the total pattern of differences and the number of possibly significant variables.

We have seen that these variables—the attributes and characteristics alluded to above—seemed to group themselves into three major configurations: *group-orientation,* including those factors relating to that portion of the leader's life-history which dealt with his own relationship to group experience and the extent to which he had successfully involved himself in such experience; *career-orientation,* including factors reflecting the leader's estimate of the present job as a step in the direction of a career goal closely related to group work; and "*mission*-centeredness," involving factors reflecting an approach to the role of leadership which focussed primarily in an outward direction—upon the values to be "taught"—rather than inwardly, toward his own status in the group situation and toward the opportunity to indirectly work out a positive group relationship where there had been failure in the role of group member.

We have also presented the strong possibility that these three configurations were closely interrelated and that, taken together, they represent parts of something which, when broken down more acutely and at a level of deeper perception, would provide important clues in the relationship between personality and successful group leadership.

For present purposes, there seemed to us to be many indications that these attributes contributed to the performance results. From the point of view of *group-orientation,* the record material illustrated dramatically many of the differences between leaders who regarded the group experience as exciting and challenging, as remembered from their own histories of involvement, and those to whom group participation had always constituted a threatening and rejection-fraught experience. While the leaders whose own group participation was enthusiastically brought to bear tended to move in like a hurricane and carry out his mission with perhaps destructive fervor, this very quality seemed also to have militated in favor of a keener sensitivity to the supervisory process and a willingness to try out new perceptions and insights derived there from. Certain it was that these leaders had collected certain tools which were helpful to them in this situation: their diversity of interests, repertoire of skills, and greater amount of experience, in other jobs, with the process of supervision, its demands, and its usefulness as a helping device.

Conversely, those workers who—as the leader who wanted "to be before a group"—were moving into the leadership experience at least partially motivated by a desire to win their own battles, found themselves in a position where they were attempting to guide others in an experience in which they were themselves badly in need of guidance. Not only were they facing psychological blocks which made them ineffective as leaders; they were also, because of their own background, lacking in the social skills, interests and experiences which would have enhanced their ability to contribute to the situation of which they were now a part.

It would of course be possible to speculate at much greater length as to the possibilities inherent in this aspect of our investigation. We have attempted only a limited presentation in the hope that it may open the way for further exploration and study.

Other Areas

In conclusion, we would wish to call attention to the wealth of record material left behind by the present study, and to the fact that a major portion of this material remains to be developed and exploited for the tremendous amount of learning contained within it.

As an example of the latter, we believe the material has within it important lessons for the orientation and supervision of untrained workers. The evidence in this area came through so clearly that we presented it to the professional staff in a discussion which served as part of the post-season Evaluation Conference held by the agency. At this meeting, we offered the thesis that methods of orientation and supervision of workers without professional training and experience would have to be radically altered if we hoped to utilize their potential in a healthy and constructive manner. This change would provide that the supervisory emphasis be shifted from those attributes which the leader *does not* bring to the job, to those he *does;* from efforts to teach group work, psychodynamics, psychology and sociology in the space of a single season, to a healthier and more helpful stress on the positive qualities which the leader actually brings with him: his own memories, not far behind, of the problems and aspirations of adolescents; his own strengths and weaknesses as a functioning human being; his desire to involve himself with people in a shared experience; his eagerness to help; his willingness to learn; and his own special interests and skills, whatever they may be. When orientation and supervision are based on these attributes—which are the leader's own and of which he may be proud—the emphasis shifts from the *intellectual* to the *feeling,* and tends to replace guilt and confusion at *not knowing* with the kind of learning which is based on intimate contact with the nature of each problem as it arises.

A study of the supervisory conference records would show evidences of such guilt and would, we believe, show quite clearly that real understanding and participation took place only at those points where both leader and supervisor were talking about material that stemmed directly from the leader's own experience and with which the leader was able to deal on a feeling level. The records would also show many instances where such discussions were abruptly cut short by an "interpretation" by the supervisor or an attempt by him to generalize feeling into an intellectual concept.

This has been intended simply to highlight the possibilities in this area of research; even without actually focussing on this aspect, enough evidence was derived to develop this thesis to a considerable degree. It is hoped that steps will be taken to utilize the records for the investigation of this and other aspects not approached in this project.

Neighborhood Centers

William Schwartz

From Williamson's 1929 personnel study of the agencies that "have a common function of dealing with individuals in groups" to Vinter's analysis of group work and recreation services in Detroit thirty years later, it has been pointed out many times that group work is practiced not in a unified field of service but in a loose assortment of agencies with diverse traditions and purposes.[1] Even as this inquiry is limited to the "neighborhood center" segment—excluding the psychiatric and medical hospitals and clinics, institutions, camps, family agencies, public recreation facilities, and other settings in which group work is practiced—there still remains an array of different objectives and client groups, as well as a wide gamut of commitments ranging over the fields of education, recreation, social service, psychotherapy, and social reform.

Yet whether or not one can define the field precisely, these agencies—*building centered* like the settlements, "Y's," Jewish Centers, and Boys' Clubs; and *program centered* like the Boy Scouts, Camp Fire Girls, and the B'nai B'rith Youth Organization—operate in the heart of the American urban neighborhood and are historically connected, in varying degrees, with the field of social welfare and the profession of social work. As such, they have a potential as yet only barely realized for affecting deeply the scope and quality of the social welfare performance where it is most needed. Much will depend on the extent to which these agencies can follow both the field and the profession into a closer working relationship with science and research.

To this end, it becomes useful periodically to review past research, to reveal some of the work currently in progress, and to draw some implications

[1]Margaretta Williamson, *The Social Worker in Group Work* (New York: Harper & Brothers, 1929); Robert D. Vinter, "New Evidence for Restructuring Group Services," in *New Perspectives on Services to Groups: Theory, Organization, Practice,* selected group work papers from the 1961 National Conference on Social Welfare (New York: National Association of Social Workers, 1961). *See also* William Schwartz, "Group Work and the Social Scene," in Alfred J. Kahn, ed., *Issues in American Social Work* (New York: Columbia University Press, 1959), pp. 110–137.

for further study. An attempt should also be made to assess related research from allied fields, but here the problem of relevance is a difficult one. When agency purposes are so all embracing and ill defined, when the client group is almost unlimited, and when the "client" concept itself includes not only the people but the vehicles in which they move together (the family, the group, the neighborhood), the relevant scientific data are encyclopedic. Nevertheless, additional references will be pointed out in this review for those interested in particular lines of inquiry.

In choosing agency studies for inclusion, an attempt has been made to be as comprehensive as possible, while neither overstating nor underplaying the achievements to date. Following Zimbalist, "research" has been defined here as any effort to collect and analyze data in a planned attempt to answer questions or test hypotheses arising out of the planning and practice of relevant agencies.[2] Published accounts have been favored, but many mimeographed documents describing some important work and a number of studies in progress are also included. Student research has been drawn in where possible, but any systematic review of this work would require a special effort similar to those of Van der Smissen in the field of recreation and Gordon in his analysis of thesis titles in social work.[3]

Although there have been a few research reviews relevant to some aspects of group work practice, this seems to be the first attempt to draw together a fairly inclusive summary of neighborhood center research as such; it may thus be expected to suffer from the crudeness of a first try. Some background material was particularly helpful: historical and technical discussions by Zimbalist, Kahn, Tyler, and Greenwood; group work research reviews by Vinter, Konopka, Northern, Klein, and Zander; summaries of unpublished work by two research committees of the professional association; and some more specific agency materials from Hillman, Brown, Sanua, Eaton and Harrison, and the Boy Scouts of America.[4]

The studies will be discussed in five sections: (1) clients and their problems; (2) the agency as a vehicle of service; (3) neighborhood and community problems related to the function of the centers; (4) the worker and the practice

---

[2]Sidney Eli Zimbalist, "Major Trends in Social Work Research: An Analysis of the Nature and Development of Research in Social Work, as Seen in the Periodical Literature, 1900–1950," p. 12. Unpublished doctoral dissertation, George Warren Brown School of Social Work, Washington University, 1955.

[3]Betty Van der Smissen, "A Bibliography of Research (Theses and Dissertations Only) Related to Recreation" (Iowa City: State University of Iowa, 1962) (mimeographed); and William E. Gordon, *The Focus and Nature of Research Completed by Graduate Students in Approved Schools of Social Work, 1940–1949, as Indicated by Thesis and Project Titles* (New York: American Association of Schools of Social Work, 1951).

[4]Zimbalist, *op. cit.;* Alfred J. Kahn, "The Design of Research," in Norman A. Polansky, ed., *Social Work Research* (Chicago: University of Chicago Press, 1960), pp. 48–73; Ralph W. Tyler, "Implications of Research in the Behavioral Sciences for Group Life and Group Services," in *Social Welfare Forum, 1960,* proceedings of the National Conference on Social Welfare (New York: Columbia University Press, 1960), pp. 113–126; Ernest Greenwood, "Social Science and Social Work: A Theory of Their Relationship," *Social Service Review,* Vol. 29, No. 1 (March

of group work; and (5) the measurement of outcome. Some final comments will be directed to implications for future research.

The Client

The traditional approach of the neighborhood centers to those they serve has been that of an organization to its "members," rather than a social agency to its "clients." The complex historical issues involved in the use of these terms have been discussed by Reynolds and more recently by Vinik, and they are not within the scope of this review.[5] It should be noted, however, that the membership concept creates interest in certain kinds of problems—notably those of recruitment, dropout, and factors involving the interests of current and potential members. These are, of course, important to social agencies as well as membership groups, but the latter emphasis sometimes invests the research effort with a kind of "market research" quality, when the investigation is designed to uncover the "buying habits" of a target population so that the product—or program—can be fashioned to meet consumer demand.

In addition to these studies of member participation, needs, and interests there is a body of work directed to certain special problems and populations and to the group itself as an instrument of service—a concept sometimes expressed in the term "the group as a client."

1955), pp. 20–33; Robert D. Vinter, "Group Work with Children and Youth: Research Problems and Possibilities," *Social Service Review,* Vol. 30, No. 3 (September 1956), pp. 310–318; Gisela Konopka, "Group Work with Children and Youth: Unanswered Questions," *Social Service Review,* Vol. 30, No. 3 (September 1956), pp. 300–309; Helen Northen, "What is Researchable in Social Group Work?" in *Social Work With Groups, 1959,* selected papers from the National Conference on Social Welfare (New York: National Association of Social Workers, 1959), pp. 149–160; Alan F. Klein, "Role and Reference Group Theory: Implications for Social Group Work Research," in Leonard S. Kogan, ed., *Social Science Theory and Social Work Research* (New York: National Association of Social Workers, 1960), pp. 32–45; Alvin F. Zander, "Current Research in Group Work," in *Toward Professional Standards* (New York: American Association of Group Workers, 1947), pp. 37–50; American Association of Group Workers, Research and Study Committee, "Selected Studies and Research Projects in Group Work, 1948–1953" (New York, 1954) (mimeographed); National Association of Social Workers, "Inventory of Research of Group Work Practice, 1955–1960" (New York, undated) (mimeographed); Arthur Hillman, *Neighborhood Centers Today: Action Programs for a Rapidly Changing World* (New York: National Federation of Settlements and Neighborhood Centers, 1960), chap. 7; Susan Jenkins Brown, *The Helen Hall Settlement Papers: A Descriptive Bibliography of Community Studies and Other Reports, 1928–1958* (New York: Henry Street Settlement, 1959); Victor D. Sanua, "Social Science Research Relevant to American Jewish Education: Fifth Bibliographic Review," *Jewish Education,* Vol. 33, No. 3 (Spring 1963), pp. 162–175; Allen Eaton and Shelby M. Harrison, *A Bibliography of Social Surveys: Reports of Fact-Finding Studies Made as a Basis for Social Action* (New York: Russell Sage Foundation, 1930); and Boy Scouts of America, "Bibliography of Studies on Scouting" (New York, 1962) (mimeographed).

[5]Bertha Capen Reynolds, *Social Work and Social Living* (New York: Citadel Press, 1951); and Abe Vinik, "Role of the Group Service Agency," *Social Work,* Vol. 9, No. 3 (July 1964), pp. 98–105.

Participation Factors

The studies on hand reveal a number of factors that seem to affect the process of client selection in the neighborhood centers. The clearest case seems to have been made for the fact that agency membership, in both the building-centered and the program-centered organizations, tends to be drawn from the higher, rather than the lower, socioeconomic groups in the community. These findings are similar to those reported by Cloward on the clientele of the private family agencies.[6] The Survey Research Center of the University of Michigan, in studies of the general population of boys 11 to 13 and 14 to 16 years of age, undertaken for the Boy Scouts of America, found that those who were most involved in organizations tended to live in the smaller central cities, had more possessions, better educated parents, more autonomy within the home, and were punished less by their parents.[7] In a study of Boy Scout membership, the Survey Research Center verified the greater participation of boys from higher-status families, and also found that Negro membership was about proportional to its percentage in the general community—a significant finding in view of the greater need and lower social status of this segment of the population.[8] In yet another SRC study, this time for the Girl Scouts, Douvan and Kaye found that the unaffiliated segment of a large general sample of adolescent girls—about 25 percent—was predominantly from the lower socioeconomic group.[9] Again, a study of the Girl Scout membership by the SRC produced verification and an additional finding that lower-income children tended to drop out sooner, with reasons less often related to loss of interest.[10] Many years before, in 1937, Young's *Report of the Girl Scout Program Study* had pointed out that

> the proportion of Girl Scouts to all girls in all communities is much larger in the middle and upper income groups, although admittedly large numbers of girls from low income groups are to be found in Girl Scout-

---

[6]Richard A. Cloward and Irwin Epstein, "Private Social Welfare's Disengagement from the Poor: The Case of Family Adjustment Agencies" (New York: Research Center, Columbia University School of Social Work, 1964). (Mimeographed.) To be published in Arthur Pearl and Frank Riessman, eds., "Poverty and Low Income Culture: Ten Views," by the National Institute of Mental Health.

[7]Survey Research Center, Institute for Social Research, University of Michigan, *A Study of Boys Becoming Adolescents* (Ann Arbor: Survey Research Center for the National Council, Boy Scouts of America, 1960); and S. B. Withey and E. Douvan, *A Study of Adolescent Boys* (Ann Arbor: Survey Research Center, Institute for Social Research, University of Michigan, 1955).

[8]Survey Research Center, Institute for Social Research, University of Michigan, *A Study of Boy Scouts and Their Scoutmasters* (Ann Arbor: 1960).

[9]E. Douvan and C. Kaye, *Adolescent Girls* (Ann Arbor: Survey Research Center. Institute for Social Research, University of Michigan, 1957).

[10]Survey Research Center, Institute for Social Research, University of Michigan, *The Program of the Girl Scouts of America* (Ann Arbor: Survey Research Center for the Girl Scouts of America, 1958).

ing . . . Where Girl Scouts are found in lowest proportions, there the percentage of foreign born is greatest and the delinquency and dependency rates are the highest.[11]

In other settings, studies of youth memberships show some agreement. Lippitt's "game-board" interviews of 1,117 Camp Fire Girls in a nationwide sample disclosed that the agency served a high economic group—92 percent native born, 98 percent white, and 79 percent Protestant.[12] Sanua, in a demographic study of four Jewish community centers, found a broad distribution on the Hollingshead-Redlich class scale, but generally high-status educational, religious, and professional characteristics.[13] Jacobs, in a study of the membership of eleven recreational agencies in the Germantown section of Philadelphia, found that the membership was again roughly equal to the racial composition of the area but that the nonwhite members were a distinctly younger group.[14] Even the Boys' Clubs of America, serving primarily a working-class group, found that a high proportion of its members were from the more stable segment of the population—native born, predominantly white, from a high proportion of intact families, and almost 100 percent of Catholic or Protestant religious affiliations.[15]

Other studies cite findings that might reasonably be considered class related. Some small studies of dropouts in three New York City settlements revealed a preponderance of member comments directed to factors of association ("the crowd is too rough," "too many non-Jews," and so on); agency demands and procedures ("the rules are too strict," and so on); and other possible indicators of a drift toward class homogeneity and agency-client norm discrepancies.[16] The New York City Youth Board, investigating the high agency dropout rate of 15- to 19-year-olds, received responses from sixty agencies, in which high importance was ascribed to rigid agency requirements and to "workers who act like policemen or preachers."[17] Ellsworth, in a

---

[11]Charles H. Young *et al., Report of the Girl Scout Program Study* (New York: Girl Scouts of America, 1937), p. 16.

[12]Rosemary Lippitt, *They Told Us What They Wanted—Report of the Camp Fire Girls Program Study* (New York: Camp Fire Girls, 1946).

[13]Victor D. Sanua, "Preliminary Research Findings in Jewish Community Centers." *Journal of Jewish Communal Service,* Vol. 40, No. 2 (Winter 1963), pp. 143–152.

[14]Jerome H. Jacobs, "Who and Where? A Survey on Recreation in Germantown," Special Report No. 10 (Philadelphia: Health and Welfare Council, 1961). (Mimeographed.)

[15]Boys' Clubs of America, *Needs and Interests of Adolescent Boys' Club Members* (New York, 1960).

[16]Canio J. DeVito, "A Study of Drop-outs," unpublished master's thesis, New York School of Social Work, Columbia University, 1955; Melvin M. Kuwamoto, "A Study of Seventeen Dropouts," unpublished master's thesis, New York School of Social Work, Columbia University, 1955; and Sheila Pekowsky, "Where Have They Gone?" unpublished master's thesis, New York School of Social Work, Columbia University, 1954.

[17]New York City Youth Board, *Reaching Teenagers Through Group Work and Recreation Programs,* Monograph No. 1 (New York, 1954).

study of young adults, found that the YMCA members in his population had little concept of the "deeper meaning of Y membership" and were "least in accord with staff in relation to program."[18]

There are some scattered data suggesting other factors that affect participation. On *area of residence,* an early study of New York City settlements, a recent self-study of thirteen Los Angeles settlements, and some other studies have found that the great majority of neighborhood center members live within a few blocks' radius of the agency.[19] On *age,* it has been suggested that the ages 11 to 13 are optimal for membership in organized club groups, that organized group participation decreases progressively as age increases, and that there is a "slow evolution" of attitudes and concerns in boys 11 to 13 years of age, when "the pace of change is more often set by school grade rather than by age."[20] On *membership motivation,* it has been found that both children and adults tend to join an agency because of specific activity interests rather than a general commitment to agency philosophy and objectives.[21]

Needs and Interests

Field-generated knowledge about client needs is scanty and substantively diffuse, emerging largely from broad population surveys and opinion studies. Many of the researches mentioned in the previous section have yielded information, more or less penetrating, in this area. The Survey Research Center found that four out of every twenty boys in the 11- to 13-year-old group chose a glamour figure as their hero, but "by the time these boys are 14–16, that figure is more than cut in half."[22] They found, too, that the younger boys seemed more likely to refer openly to their anxieties about war, accidents, and disasters.

The Metropolitan Chicago YMCA, in an opinion survey of 30,000 adolescents in the Chicago area, reported that two out of every five boys expressed an active fear of failure, and three out of five expressed doubt that

---

[18]Allen S. Ellsworth, *Young Men and Young Women: New Insights on Becoming Adult* (New York: Young Men's Christian Association, 1963), pp. 3–4.

[19]Albert J. Kennedy, Kathryn Farra, and associates, *Social Settlements in New York City: Their Activities, Policies, and Administration* (New York: Columbia University Press, 1935); and Margaret Hirschfeld, "Neighborhood Centers" (Los Angeles: Welfare Federation of Los Angeles Area, 1961) (mimeographed).

[20]Lippitt, *op. cit.;* Boys' Clubs of America, *op. cit.;* Alvin Zander *et al.,* "Straight from the Boy on Why Scouts Drop—And What to Do About It." in *Scouting for Facts with a Local Council* (New York: Boy Scouts of America, 1945); Douvan and Kaye, *op. cit.;* and Survey Research Center, *A Study of Boys Becoming Adolescents,* p. 206.

[21]Boys' Clubs of America, *op. cit.;* Kennedy, Farra, and associates, *op. cit.;* Stanley W. Harris, "The Expressed Interests of Two Hundred Jewish Teen-Agers," *Journal of Jewish Communal Service,* Vol. 32, No. 4 (Summer 1956), pp. 406–415; Ellsworth, *op. cit.;* and Harry Specht, "Jewish Young Adults and the Jewish Community Center," unpublished doctoral dissertation, Florence Heller School for Advanced Studies in Social Welfare, Brandeis University, 1963.

[22]Survey Research Center, *A Study of Boys Becoming Adolescents,* p. 207.

their minds work normally.[23] Lippitt, in her previously cited study of grouping preferences among the Camp Fire Girls, found that respondents wanted to be in the middle of their age range, preferring companions either one year older or younger.

Some data point to a kind of continuing struggle between clients and agency staff to define the germane needs and interests of the clients. Thus, almost all of the program and interest studies noted above found desires on the part of the children for more active programs, fewer "social" themes and conversations, more autonomy, less dependency, and more member-direction. Such desires, increasing with age, might account for a great part of the organizational dropout rate in adolescence.

Zander and Hogrefe's research on five hundred dropped Boy Scouts from ten communities traced differential dropout patterns relating to age, scout rank, tenure, economic group, and other factors.[24] Similarly, Harris found that his B'nai B'rith adolescents had less interest in community service activities as they grew older; that their greatest interest lay in concrete, informal, active programs; that "Jewish content activities rated last for the boys and second to last for the girls"; and that interest declined as program emphasis moved from local to national concerns.[25] Sanua's Jewish Center mothers "did not perceive the center as an agency which fosters Jewish identification for their children," and had little objection to non-Jewish members and leaders in the program; in his study of adolescents, he found the term "Jewish" identified as a religious rather than a cultural concept.[26]

The divergence between client and staff perceptions of need is dramatically illustrated in some studies of the relationship between young adults and the neighborhood agencies. Ellsworth, Olds and Josephson, Rosenthal and Schatz, and Specht have all noted that young adults are a most difficult age group to involve in organized agency activity, and they have commented that staff workers tend to ascribe this reluctance to such young adult characteristics as superficiality, restlessness, and narrow horizons rather than to inadequate provision for their developmental needs.[27] Ellsworth found his YMCA

---

[23]Sears, Roebuck and Company, National Personnel Department, Psychological Services Section, "The Youth of Chicagoland: A Study of Its Attitudes, Beliefs, Ideas, and Problems," a study conducted for, and in conjunction with, the Young Men's Christian Association of Metropolitan Chicago (Chicago, undated). (Mimeographed.)

[24]Alvin Zander *et al., op. cit.*

[25]Harris, *op. cit.,* p. 408.

[26]Sanua, *op. cit.*

[27]Ellsworth, *op. cit.;* Edward B. Olds and Eric Josephson, *Young Adults and Citizenship* (New York: National Social Welfare Assembly, 1953); William Rosenthal and Harry A. Schatz, *Young Adults and the Jewish Community Center* (New York: National Jewish Welfare Board, 1956); and Specht, *op. cit.*

members "least in accord with staff in relation to program."[28] Olds and Josephson called particular attention to the discrepancy between organizational aims and what staff workers perceive as the "merely social" interests of young adults, and Specht pointed out that Jewish Center personnel "appear to frown on the types of programs which are geared to meet the courtship needs of young adults."[29]

Special Problems and Populations

A number of studies have been generated by the agencies' concern for particular clients with special problems. The bulk of this work seems to be concentrated in three categories: (1) the research on cultural identification and "belongingness," with which the Jewish Centers have been particularly concerned; (2) the studies emerging from the various "reaching-out" programs aimed at street-club adolescents who do not lend themselves easily to service within agency walls; and (3) the newer work with handicapped people whom agencies have undertaken to integrate into their ongoing programs.

Identification and belongingness. Space does not permit an adequate summary of studies on the identification problems associated with minority group membership. While the research is still sporadic, the group survival emphasis of the Jewish Centers has stimulated some interesting work, much of it generated by Kurt Lewin's field theory on belongingness.[30] Aside from references already made to studies by Sanua, Harris, and Specht, fruitful lines of research have been opened by Hurwitz, Chein, Canter and Rothman.

Hurwitz studied the self-perceptions of Jewish Center children in twenty-four groups and found differences among children designated as "orthodox oriented," "center oriented," or "community oriented."[31] His orthodox-oriented children, closely related to their religion, seemed more secure when younger, but developed more intense antagonisms toward nonobservant elements in their own culture as they grew older; the center-oriented children, defined as those who tried to live in two cultures, generated more rebellion against the culture of the parents as the difference in cultures became more marked; and his community-oriented children, fairly well adjusted to the American culture, tended to accept anti-Semitic positions along with other majority group values, thus demonstrating most clearly Lewin's concept of "self-hate."

---

[28]Ellsworth, *op. cit.*, p. 4

[29]Specht, *op. cit.*, p. 444.

[30]Kurt Lewin, *Resolving Social Conflicts* (New York: Harper & Brothers, 1948), Part 3.

[31]Jacob I. Hurwitz, "On Being a Jew: Perceptions, Attitudes, and Needs of Jewish Children," *Jewish Center Worker,* Vol. 9, No. 2 (May 1948), pp. 6–12.

Chein, commenting on the Hurwitz study in what he calls an "action research perspective," points out that what these three groups have in common is the fact that their Jewishness is for them "a source of confusion, ambivalence and divergent goals." He concludes that, for the Jewish child:

> the help he most needs in finding himself is not *teaching,* but assistance in unravelling his own problems in the order and within the psychological settings in which they present themselves.[32]

In a later collaboration, Chein and Hurwitz studied 166 boys in fourteen different Jewish Centers in metropolitan New York, comparing attitudes of group members by age, socioeconomic grouping, and the extent to which they were exposed to Jewish observances in their homes.[33] They found significant differences, which they summarized as follows:

> If we were to reduce these patterns to a single statement, it would be the following: with increasing acculturation (a process that probably goes on—though perhaps in different ways—with aging, with improved socioeconomic status and, as a rule, with a perceptible decrease in Jewish environment) there is an increasing desire for social and cultural integration with the general community. In the case of the age and socioeconomic breakdowns, this desire for social integration is clearly associated with increased defensiveness and feelings of insecurity.[34]

Canter surveyed the sociopsychological research relevant to the problems of training workers in the Jewish settings, and he abstracted a number of "developmental tasks" of the Jewish adolescent.[35] He studied the effects of the Christmas holiday in the life of adolescents in the B'nai B'rith Youth Organization, and examined over one thousand records kept by workers on twenty-five groups that met at the Irene Kaufman Center in Pittsburgh between 1944 and 1946, defining and analyzing "situations of a Jewish nature" and the problems they create for both the member and the worker.[36] Rothman challenged some of Lewin's assumptions about the relationship

---

[32]Isidor Chein. "The Problem of Belongingness: An Action Research Perspective," *Jewish Center Worker,* Vol. 9, No. 2 (May 1948), p. 16.

[33]Isidor Chein and Jacob I. Hurwitz, "The Reactions of Jewish Boys to Various Aspects of Being Jewish" (New York: National Jewish Welfare Board, 1949, reissued 1959). (Mimeographed.)

[34]*Ibid.,* p. 6.

[35]Irving Canter, "What Research Tells Us About Training for the Jewish Component in the Practice of Group Work in Jewish Settings," *Journal of Jewish Communal Service,* Vol. 39, No. 3 (Spring 1963), pp. 266–285.

[36]Irving Canter, *Christmas in the Life of a Jewish Teenager* (Washington, D.C.: B'nai B'rith Youth Organization, 1960); and Irving Canter, "How the Jewish Center Members are Relating to Their Jewishness: A Study of Group Process Records," *Jewish Center Worker,* Vol. 11, No. 1 (February 1950), pp. 10–16.

between ingroup identification and outgroup association, and has developed an instrument designed to identify and measure the "belongingness" variable itself.[37]

Interest in the problems of minority group members vis-à-vis the larger culture is, of course, not restricted to the Jewish agencies; settlement and other neighborhood workers are continually concerned with these problems in the lives of Negroes, Catholics, and the various ethnic groups they serve. However, no evidence of any systematic study of these issues in these settings could be found.

The "hard-to-reach." Despite the traditional claim that the work of the neighborhood centers is related to the prevention of delinquency, it was not until the relatively recent movement of staff out of the buildings and into the streets that the agencies undertook their first serious engagement with nonconforming youth. It was at this point that they began to tap the street-work tradition of Aichhorn, Thrasher, Shaw, and Whyte; and to focus with some purpose on the body of delinquency research and the theoretical work of Cohen, Cloward and Ohlin, Kobrin, Miller, and others.[38] Typically, however, the centers have over the years produced some excellent service and very little research of their own. As Hogrefe and Harding put it: "Doing something with gangs has been easier than measuring the effectiveness of what was done."[39] It was not until the emergence of the more recent, well-financed, multifunction community-based projects that most of the continuous empirical work began.[40]

One of the earliest studies was produced by the Central Harlem Street Clubs Project, an action-research venture that leaned heavily on the analysis

---

[37]Jack Rothman, "Construction of an Instrument for Measuring Minority Group Identification Among Jewish Adolescents: An Exploratory Attempt," *Journal of Jewish Communal Service,* Vol. 34, No. 1 (Fall 1957), pp. 84–94; and Jack Rothman, "In-Group Identification and Out-Group Association: A Theoretical and Experimental Study," *Journal of Jewish Communal Service,* Vol. 37, No. 1 (Fall 1960), pp. 81–93.

[38]August Aichhorn, *Wayward Youth* (New York: Viking Press, 1935); Frederick M. Thrasher, *The Gang* (2d rev. ed.; Chicago: University of Chicago Press, 1936); Clifford R. Shaw, *The Jackroller* (Chicago: University of Chicago Press, 1930); William Foote Whyte, *Street Corner Society* (Chicago: University of Chicago Press, 1955); Oliver Moles, Ronald Lippitt, and Stephen Withey, *A Selective Review of Research and Theory on Delinquency* (2d ed.; Ann Arbor: Survey Research Center, Institute for Social Research, University of Michigan, 1959); Albert K. Cohen, *Delinquent Boys: The Culture of the Gang* (Glencoe, Ill.: Free Press, 1955); Richard A. Cloward and Lloyd E. Ohlin, *Delinquency and Opportunity: A Theory of Delinquent Gangs* (Glencoe, Ill.: Free Press, 1960); Solomon Kobrin, "The Chicago Area Project—A 25 Year Assessment," *Annals of the American Academy of Political and Social Science,* Vol. 322 (1959), pp. 19–29; and Walter B. Miller, "Lower Class Culture as a Generating Milieu of Gang Delinquency," *Journal of Social Issues,* Vol. 14, No. 3 (1958), pp. 5–19.

[39]Russell Hogrefe and John Harding, "Research Considerations in the Study of Street Gangs" (New York: Commission on Community Inter-relations of the American Jewish Congress, 1947), p. 1. (Mimeographed.)

[40]*See* Martin Gold and J. Alan Winter, *A Selective Review of Community-Based Programs for Preventing Delinquency* (Ann Arbor: Institute for Social Research, University of Michigan, 1961).

of case materials.[41] It developed some important insights into worker techniques, street club structure, the dependency needs of "hardened" youth, and the problems of working with those who withdraw into the use of drugs. The pioneer work of the New York City Youth Board has also been of great interest to the practitioner, although a good deal of its published material leans heavily on program description and interpretation rather than research.[42]

Some of the more theoretically oriented studies on the "hard-to-reach" have been published by Miller of the Boston Delinquency Project and by Short and his associates, working with the Program of Detached Workers of the YMCA of Metropolitan Chicago, and later followed up in the Youth Studies Program of the University of Chicago.[43] Miller has summarized his findings on the relationship between gang delinquency and lower-class culture:

> 1. Following cultural practices which comprise essential elements of the total life pattern of lower class culture automatically violates certain legal norms. 2. In instances where alternate avenues to similar objectives are available, the non-law-abiding avenue frequently provides a relatively greater and more immediate return for a relatively smaller investment of energy. 3. The demanded response to certain situations recurrently engendered within lower class culture involves the commission of illegal acts.[44]

Short and his associates have tested hypotheses derived from the theoretical positions of Cohen, Miller, and Cloward and Ohlin—"hypotheses concerning the values of gang, non-gang lower-class, and non-gang middle-class boys." They found that:

> . . . contrary to expectation, the data indicated no differences between gang, lower-class, and middle-class boys, both Negro and white,

---

[41]Paul L. Crawford, Daniel I. Malamud, and James R. Dumpson, *Working with Teen-Age Gangs,* a report on the Central Harlem Street Clubs Project (New York: Welfare Council of New York City, 1950).

[42]New York City Youth Board, *Reaching the Fighting Gang* (New York, 1960).

[43]Walter B. Miller, "The Impact of a Community Program on Delinquent Corner Groups," *Social Service Review,* Vol. 31, No. 4 (December 1957), pp. 390–406; Miller, "Lower Class Culture as a Generating Milieu of Gang Delinquency"; Miller, "Preventive Work with Street-Corner Groups: Boston Delinquency Project," *Annals of the American Academy of Political and Social Science,* Vol. 322 (1959), pp. 97–106; Robert A. Gordon *et al.,* "Values and Gang Delinquency," *American Journal of Sociology,* Vol. 49, No. 2 (September 1963), pp. 109–128; James F. Short, Jr., "Street Corner Gangs and Patterns of Delinquency: A Progress Report," *American Catholic Sociological Review,* Vol. 28, No. 2 (Spring 1963), pp. 13–32; James F. Short, Jr., and Fred L. Strodtbeck, "The Response of Gang Leaders to Status Threats: An Observation on Group Process and Delinquent Behavior," *American Journal of Sociology,* Vol. 48, No. 5 (March 1963), pp. 571–579; James F. Short, Jr., Fred L. Strodtbeck, and Desmond S. Cartwright, "A Strategy for Utilizing Research Dilemmas: A Case from the Study of Parenthood in a Street Corner Gang," *Sociological Inquiry,* Vol. 32, No. 2 (Spring 1962), pp. 185–202; and James F. Short, Jr., Ray A. Tennyson, and Kenneth I. Howard, "Behavior Dimensions of Gang Delinquency," *American Sociological Review,* Vol. 28, No. 3 (June 1963), pp. 412–428.

[44]Miller, "Lower Class Culture as a Generating Milieu of Gang Delinquency," p. 18.

> in their evaluation and legitimation of behaviors representing middle-class prescriptive norms . . . The samples differed most in their attitude toward the deviant behaviors, tending to form a gradient, with gang boys most tolerant, middle-class boys least tolerant.[45]

Short's project has also yielded data on the use of outgroup aggression by gang leaders as a means of reducing threats to their status; the sociological, cultural, and personal concomitants of illegitimate fatherhood; and the behavioral dimensions of group delinquency based on data collected from 598 members of sixteen delinquent street clubs with assigned workers.

There have also been reports on the Hyde Park Youth Project, which studied case-finding, street club work, and community self-help in co-operation with the Hyde Park Neighborhood Center in Chicago; the Hunting-ton-Gifford project in Syracuse, New York, which developed instrumentation to measure individual movement and "group tone"; the ongoing five-year project of the Seattle Atlantic Street Center, designed to demonstrate and evaluate social work effectiveness in serving boys of junior high school age in the central area of Seattle; the Neighborhood Youth Association in Los Angeles, working with school referrals of acting-out adolescents; and the work of the Wesley Community Centers in San Antonio with Mexican-American conflict gangs.[46] Promising research projections have been published for New York's Mobilization for Youth, Harlem Youth Opportunities Unlimited, Cleveland's Community Action for Youth, and other such projects that are under way in Boston, New Haven, and elsewhere throughout the country.[47] There is hope that the pattern of building research designs into project proposals, encouraged by the federal grant system, will soon begin to produce a substantial body of research emerging directly from the practice of social work with working-class children not amenable to the routine ministrations of the neighborhood centers.

The handicapped. Contrary to the tradition that the neighborhood agencies were somehow assigned to the "normal" client, leaving the handicapped and afflicted to the "special settings," the centers have recently begun

---

[45]Gordon *et al., op. cit.*, p. 109.

[46]Charles H. Shireman. *The Hyde Park Youth Project* (Chicago: Welfare Council of Metropolitan Chicago, 1955–1958); Norman R. Roth, *Reaching the Hard-to-Reach* (Syracuse, N.Y.: Huntington Family Centers, 1961); Seattle Atlantic Street Center, "Effectiveness of Social Work on Acting-Out Youth: Second Year Progress Report," September 1963 to August 1964 (Seattle, 1964) (mimeographed); Helen Northen, "Social Group Work: A Tool for Changing Behavior of Disturbed Acting-Out Adolescents," in *Social Work with Groups, 1958,* selected papers from the National Conference on Social Welfare (New York: National Association of Social Workers, 1958); and Buford E. Farris and William M. Hale, *Mexican-American Conflict Gangs: Observations and Theoretical Implications* (San Antonio, Tex.: Wesley Community Centers, undated).

[47]Mobilization for Youth, *A Proposal for the Prevention and Control of Delinquency by Expanding Opportunities* (New York, 1961); Harlem Youth Opportunities Unlimited, *Youth in the Ghetto: A Study of the Consequences of Powerlessness and a Blue-Print for Change* (New York, 1964); and Greater Cleveland Youth Services Planning Commission, *Community Action for Youth* (Cleveland, 1963). For other projects in progress, *see* Gold and Winter, *op. cit.*

to undertake projects designed to help those with special physical and emotional illnesses to use the agency as a bridge to the general community. Again, there is not yet any significant production of research data, but there are signs that some important investigations are in progress.

The integration project for orthopedically handicapped children of the Mosholu-Montefiore Community Center of the Associated YM-YWHA's of Greater New York has already produced some first documents, including a study of the social and recreational patterns of these children by Schwartz and Holmes's "scale of deviance, in which individual and group factors are taken into consideration . . . to predict 'how deviant' a deviant individual will be, when cast into a particular social milieu, here represented by the various children's groups."[48] Cole and Podell surveyed agency staff attitudes toward working with physically handicapped children and discovered reactions likened to minority group stereotyping.[49] At New York's Greenwich House, Quartaro and Pierson studied the experience of settlements with narcotics addicts and found that most of the agencies simply excluded them for fear of alienating the community, and because of repeated failures in practice and lack of adequately trained personnel.[50]

The Henry Street Settlement has reported a project in "preventive psychiatry," and in Chicago, Bunda has issued promising preliminary reports on the Girl Scouts of Chicago project for integrating 7- to 18-year-old girls with mental and physical handicaps into the ongoing program of troops and camps.[51] Parnicky and Brown, at the Bordentown, New Jersey, YMCA, have reported a study designed to probe the reactions of institutionalized retardates in their first experiences in the community, suggesting that it may soon be possible to develop an "index of readiness for community placement."[52]

---

[48]Associated YM-YWHA's of Greater New York, "Progress Report on 'A Study of the Problems of Integrating Physically Handicapped Children with Non-Handicapped Children in Recreational Groups' " (New York, 1963) (mimeographed); Arthur Schwartz, *Social and Recreational Patterns of Orthopedically Handicapped Children* (New York: Associated YM-YWHA's of Greater New York, 1962); and Douglas Holmes, "A Consideration of Deviance in Conducting Programs for Clinical Populations in a Community Center Setting," paper presented at the National Conference on Social Welfare, Los Angeles, May 29, 1964 (mimeographed), p. 14.

[49]Minerva G. Cole and Lawrence Podell, "Serving Handicapped Children in Group Programs," *Social Work,* Vol. 6, No. 1 (January 1961), pp. 97–104.

[50]Peter Quartaro and Arthur Pierson, "A Survey of Settlement House Experience with Narcotics Addicts" (New York: Greenwich House, updated). (Mimeographed.)

[51]Harry Joseph, Annelise Thieman, and Evelyn Hamilton, "Preventive Psychiatry at the Henry Street Settlement: A Five-Year Experimental Project," *American Journal of Orthopsychiatry,* Vol. 22, No. 3 (April 1952), pp. 557–569; and Bertha Bunda, "Project for Working with Exceptional Girl Scouts." Progress Reports Nos. 1–5 (Chicago: Girl Scouts of Chicago, 1961–64) (mimeographed).

[52]Joseph J. Parnicky and Leonard N. Brown, "Introducing Institutionalized Retardates to the Community," *Social Work,* Vol. 9, No. 1 (January 1964), p. 83.

The Group As Client

There is a large and fast-growing literature of research on the small group, and all of it is in some way relevant to those agencies whose primary interest lies in the group as a medium of service. Interestingly enough, the body of research on the small group has been built up in many settings—the army, the factory, the school, the laboratory—with the virtual exception of the neighborhood centers, where thousands of groups meet every day in the year. Several researchers have expressed concern about this and tried to relate the center practitioner to this body of work, both as consumer and producer.[53] It is impossible to review here even a representative segment of this research. Some helpful introductions, surveys, and bibliographies have been provided by Terauds, Altman and McGrath, Berelson and Steiner, Hare, Schwartz, and many others.[54]

There are several lines of research from related fields of practice that should be mentioned, however briefly, for their importance to the work of the centers. The social influence and "behavioral contagion" studies, conducted in the camp setting by Lippitt, Polansky, Redl, and others, pointed strongly to the social origin of children's behavior.[55] They have noted:

> The fact that it has proved possible in this study to make a number of generalizations about the behavior of individuals in groups almost independently of any real knowledge of the internal working of the individuals concerned, but solely in terms of functioning group positions, is seen as indicative of the necessity for an interest in *groups* as having dynamic reality in the same sense as do personalities.[56]

---

[53]*See,* for example, Edgar F. Borgatta, "What Social Science Says about Groups," *Social Welfare Forum, 1957,* proceedings of the National Conference on Social Welfare (New York: Columbia University Press, 1957), pp. 212–237; Klein, *op. cit.;* Edwin J. Thomas, "Theory and Research on the Small Group: Selected Themes and Problems," and Robert D. Vinter, "Small-Group Theory and Research: Implications for Group Work Practice Theory and Research" in Leonard S. Kogan, ed., *Social Science Theory and Social Work Research* (New York: National Association of Social Workers, 1960), pp. 91–108 and 123–134.

[54]Anita Terauds, Irwin Altman, and Joseph E. McGrath, *A Bibliography of Small Group Research* (Arlington, Va.: Human Sciences Research, 1960); Bernard Berelson and Gary A. Steiner, *Human Behavior: An Inventory of Scientific Findings* (New York: Harcourt, Brace, and World, 1964), chap. 8; Paul A. Hare, *Handbook of Small Group Research* (New York: Free Press of Glencoe, 1962); and William Schwartz, "Small Group Science and Group Work Practice," *Social Work,* Vol. 8, No. 4 (October 1963), pp. 39–46.

[55]Ronald Lippitt *et al.,* "The Dynamics of Power: A Field Study of Social Influence in Groups of Children," *Human Relations,* Vol. 5, No. 1 (February 1952), pp. 37–64; Norman A. Polansky, "On the Dynamics of Behavioral Contagion," *The Group,* Vol. 14, No. 3 (April 1952), pp. 3–8, 21, and 25; and Norman A. Polansky, Ronald Lippitt, and Fritz Redl, "An Investigation of Behavioral Contagion in Groups," *Human Relations,* Vol. 3, No. 4 (November 1950), pp. 319–348.

[56]Polansky, Lippitt, and Redl, *op. cit.,* p. 348. Emphasis in original.

The games and activities studies of Gump, Sutton-Smith, Redl, and others, also in the camp context, have explored the effects of games on the group experience of children and have produced some clear results enabling the authors, as Gump has observed, to "look forward to the day when workers will . . . have more accurate expectations regarding the impulses a given activity is likely to provoke and gratify, the defenses or control measures it will likely call forth, and the interaction it will stimulate."[57] Attention is also called to the prolific work of the Sherifs in the areas of intergroup relations and adolescent group behavior—particularly the well-known "Robbers Cave Experiment," in which intergroup friction among camp groups was experimentally induced by heightening ingroup feeling and dissipated by creating "superordinate goals," leading to the conclusion that "the limiting condition determining friendly or hostile attitudes between groups is the nature of functional relations between them, as defined by analysis of their goals."[58] Aside from their substantive contributions, these studies did much to establish the camp setting as a research laboratory; McNeil has reviewed some aspects of this relationship between social research and the field of camping.[59]

Also in the category of related research, Lippitt has summarized the conclusions about group morale drawn from the Lewin, Lippitt and White studies of leadership and group behavior in which the effects of complete freedom, authoritarianism and disciplined freedom, authoritarianism and disciplined freedom are seen to produce varying effects upon the "climate" of the group.[60] Kolodny and Waldfogel have summarized the research carried on by the Department of Neighborhood Clubs of the Boston Children's Service Association, a unique structure of group services in a casework setting and one that has been extremely sensitive to the need for

---

[57]Paul Gump, "Observational Study of Activities for Disturbed Children," in *Group Work and Community Organization, 1953–54,* papers presented at the National Conference of Social Work (New York: Columbia University Press, 1954), p. 22; Paul Gump *et al.,* "Activity Setting and Social Interaction: A Field Study," *American Journal of Orthopsychiatry,* Vol. 25, No. 4 (July 1955), pp. 755–760; Paul Gump and Brian Sutton-Smith, "The 'It' Role in Children's Games," *The Group,* Vol. 17, No. 3 (February 1955), pp. 3–8; and Fritz Redl, "The Impact of Game Ingredients on Children's Play Behavior," in Bertram Schaffner, ed., *Group Processes* (New York: Josiah Macy, Jr. Foundation, 1959), pp. 33–81.

[58]Muzafer Sherif and Carolyn Wood Sherif, *Groups in Harmony and Tension: An Integration of Studies on Intergroup Relations* (New York: Harper & Brothers, 1953); Muzafer Sherif and Carolyn Wood Sherif, *Reference Groups: Exploration into Conformity and Deviation of Adolescents* (New York: Harper & Row, 1964); and Muzafer Sherif *et al., Intergroup Conflict and Cooperation: The Robbers Cave Experiment* (Norman, Okla.: University of Oklahoma Press, 1961), p. 208.

[59]Elton B. McNeil, "The Background of Therapeutic Camping," *Journal of Social Issues,* Vol. 13, No. 1 (January 1957), pp. 3–14.

[60]Ronald Lippitt, "The Morale of Youth Groups," in Goodwin Watson, ed., *Civilian Morale,* Second Yearbook of the Society for the Psychological Study of Social Issues (Boston: Houghton Mifflin Company, 1942), pp. 119–142.

research.[61] Luck has studied the intensity of children's peer relationships within groups in a child guidance clinic, isolating differences in learning problems, psychological remedial work, size of groups, and types of program activity.[62]

In the same area of related research, Somers compared four small-group theories with respect to their ideas on the individual in the group, relationships among members, the relationship between group activities and group process, the group's relations with its environment, and longitudinal growth and decay in group life.[63] A particularly provocative study by Mann and Mann indicated that group interaction produced more personality and behavior changes among members in "task-oriented" groups than in self-directed "role-playing" groups.[64] This study suggests a line of investigation that may ultimately challenge the vague "personality" emphasis in agency work and replace it with one more clearly focused on the common and concrete tasks that bind group members to each other.

Moving closer to work emerging from the practice problems of the centers themselves, one finds a few problems that have attracted the interest of students of group process, but no continuous body of work on any single theme, with the possible exception of the work with street clubs. Spergel has developed a "typology of gangs within a sociocultural framework," with special reference to the "anomie tradition" as it has been developed by Cloward and Ohlin.[65] Spergel found that he could identify the "racket," "conflict" and "theft" subcultures in the neighborhoods he studied, and relate the emergence of these subcultures to certain distinguishable neighborhood conditions under which they tended to flourish.

Short's work at the YMCA of Metropolitan Chicago, previously mentioned, has yielded data on the structure of the gang, with the study by Short and Strodtbeck revealing several dimensions of gang behavior.[66] They found, for example, that although intragroup aggression was high, gang norms were

---

[61]Ralph Kolodny and Samuel Waldfogel, "Summary of Research Carried on by the Department of Neighborhood Clubs, Boston Children's Service Association, 1955–1958." Unpublished paper, Boston, Mass., undated.

[62]Juanita M. Luck, "A Study of Peer Relationships," *The Group,* Vol. 17, No. 3 (February 1955), pp. 13–20.

[63]Mary Louise Somers, "Four Small Group Theories: A Comparative Analysis and Evaluation of Selected Social Science Theory for Use as Teaching Content in Social Group Work." Unpublished doctoral dissertation, School of Applied Social Sciences, Western Reserve University, 1957.

[64]John H. Mann and Carola Honroth Mann, "The Relative Effectiveness of Role Playing and Task Oriented Group Experiences in Producing Personality and Behavior Change," *Journal of Social Psychology,* Vol. 51, Second Half (1960), pp. 313–317.

[65]Irving Spergel, "An Exploratory Research in Delinquent Subcultures," *Social Service Review,* Vol. 35, No. 1 (March 1961), pp. 33–47.

[66]"The Response of Gang Leaders to Status Threats: An Observation of Group Process and Delinquent Behavior."

not generally supportive of internal aggression aimed at the establishment of individual dominance, even by the leaders themselves. They found, too, as had Whyte before them, that gang leaders were cautious not to use their leadership arbitrarily but were sensitive to the needs and tolerances of group members. There was evidence that the relationship between leaders and staff workers was often such as to stabilize the leadership structure and reduce the need for status-asserting forms of intragroup aggression. Yablonsky obtained data on thirty New York City street clubs over a four-year period and developed a typology that yielded the concept of the "near-group," located on a continuum from group to mob and distinguished by characteristics such as diffuse definitions of membership, limited membership responsibility, self-appointed leadership, limited goal consensus, shifting stratification systems, norms in conflict with the larger society, and indeterminate size varying with circumstances.[67]

Studies of organized groups in, and related to, neighborhood center programs have focused on various dimensions of group life. On the *role of the member* in youth clubs, Maas contrasted the ways in which this role is filled by lower-class and middle-class urban adolescents.[68] He studied ten paired groups in action, noting "collaborative," "aggressive," and "digressive" interactions and their direction—toward adult leader, peer president, or other members. He found that the role relationships between members and adult leaders in the lower-class clubs were similar to those between the members and their own peer leaders in the middle-class clubs, where the adult seemed less important to the members.

On *indigenous leadership,* Lowy examined leadership patterns in adolescent groups and secured some verification for the idea that leadership is not identical with office-holding, that it varies with group size and group events, and that it cannot be regarded as a personality characteristic in the old tradition of youth work.[69] On *group size,* Hare arranged 150 Boy Scouts in discussion groups of different size and found that, as the size of the group increased from five to twelve, consensus resulting from discussion decreased when time was limited, leaders had less influence, skill was a more important factor, there was an increase in factionalism, and amount of expression decreased, as did degree of member satisfaction.[70]

On *group-influenced attitudes,* Kelley and Volkart, also working with a Boy Scout population, found that a speech criticizing the scout emphasis on

---

[67]Lewis Yablonsky, "The Delinquent Gang as a Near-Group," *Social Problems,* Vol. 7, No. 2 (Fall 1959), pp. 108–117.

[68]Henry S. Maas, "The Role of Member in Clubs of Lower-Class and Middle-Class Adolescents," *Child Development,* Vol. 25, No. 4 (December 1954), pp. 341–351.

[69]Louis Lowy, "Indigenous Leadership in Teen-Age Groups," *Jewish Center Worker,* Vol. 13, No. 1 (January 1952), pp. 10–15.

[70]Paul A. Hare, "A Study of Interaction and Consensus in Different Sized Groups," *American Sociological Review,* Vol. 17, No. 3 (June 1952), pp. 261–267.

camping had more impact on those who placed less value on their membership, and that this feeling was expressed more readily under private rather than public conditions.[71] Avigdor, working with groups of children in a New York City settlement, found a relationship between the traits chosen by children for group stereotyping and the functional relations between groups.[72]

On *group cohesion,* French compared the reactions of organized social and athletic clubs with those of unorganized undergraduates to frustrating situations, represented by the need to solve insoluble problems.[73] He discovered that the organized groups manifested more frustration and aggression, but because the cohesive forces were also stronger, this did not in turn create more group disruption. The unorganized groups showed lower motivation, hence less frustration and aggression but more tendencies toward disruption.

On *group development,* little has been done until very recently to elaborate or document Bernstein's *Charting Group Progress,* published in 1949.[74] A significant contribution has now been made by Garland, Jones, and Kolodny, whose "Model for Stages of Development in Social Work Groups," emerging from the work of the Department of Neighborhood Clubs of the Boston Children's Service Association, is a long step forward in analytic sophistication.[75] Distilled from the experience of practice, the model deals with a client population close enough to that of the neighborhood centers to offer valuable assistance in their work.

The Agency

As the centers have responded to changing times, new functions have tended not to displace the old but to move in alongside them. As a result, the agencies present a kind of agglomeration of services and objectives; one may almost read their histories in a cross section of their current issues, their interpretations to the public, and their internal problems. Such a situation poses questions for historical and empirical research on which little has yet been done, although there are signs that some of the newer work on the study of organizations is being noted with interest by agency personnel.[76] Studies on

---

[71]Harold H. Kelley and Edmund H. Volkart, "The Resistance of Change to Group-Anchored Attitudes," *American Sociological Review,* Vol. 17, No. 4 (August 1952), pp. 453–465.

[72]Rosette Avigdor, "The Development of Stereotypes as a Result of Group Interaction." Unpublished doctoral dissertation, New York University, 1952.

[73]John R. P. French, Jr., "The Disruption and Cohesion of Groups," *Journal of Abnormal and Social Psychology,* Vol. 36, No. 3 (July 1941), pp. 361–377.

[74]Saul Bernstein, *Charting Group Progress* (New York: Association Press, 1949).

[75]James A. Garland, Hubert E. Jones, and Ralph L. Kolodny, "A Model for Stages of Development in Social Work Groups." Unpublished paper, Boston, Mass., undated.

[76]*See* Peter M. Blau and W. Richard Scott, *Formal Organizations* (San Francisco: Chandler Publishing Co., 1962); Alvin W. Gouldner, "Organizational Analysis," in Kogan, ed., *op. cit.,* pp. 46–63; and Mason Haire, ed., *Modern Organization Theory* (New York: John Wiley & Sons, 1959).

hand are best presented in three categories: those dealing with the clarification of *agency function* or purpose, work on the problems of *agency structure,* and research on *agency program* that defines the nature of the service itself.

Functions

Several studies bear on the question of whether a given agency will be perceived by board, staff, client, and community as a social service or part of a social movement, an issue with which the ideologically oriented agencies in particular have been increasingly concerned.[77] In 1948, Janowsky set out to clarify the "fundamental purpose of the Jewish Center" in an extensive study of agency history, records, reports, opinions, and programs in Jewish Centers throughout the country.[78] He emerged with the conclusion that "the Jewish Center is one of the agencies Jews join in order to satisfy their distinctive Jewish needs."[79] Perhaps because the Janowsky study failed to distinguish clearly between philosophical questions and empirical ones, it has precipitated a good deal more heated debate than scientific research and follow-up.

In 1960, Dodson undertook a study of the Young Women's Christian Association as "part of an effort by the YWCA to redefine its relationships to the YMCA in light of changes that are taking place in both organizations and stemming at least in part from changes in American life."[80] Dodson reaffirmed the need for an independent women's organization, pointed up the balance between local service programs and national purposes, and tried to bridge the gap between movement and service: "The art of lacing together involvement in service and intelligent action is perhaps the greatest social frontier of all."[81]

The most sophisticated of these organizational analyses is undoubtedly that of Zald and Denton in their recent study of "the transformation of the YMCA from an evangelistic social movement to a general service organization."[82] Their structural analysis points up the agency's dependence on a paying clientele, its federated structure, factors of professional ideology and lack of it, and the range of programs and services legitimized by concepts of character development. In addition, Zald and Denton develop some general propositions about organizational change, which they feel can be helpful in the analysis of other agencies. They suggest, for example, that

---

[77]*See* William Schwartz, "Small Group Science and Group Work Practice."

[78]Oscar I. Janowsky, *The Jewish Welfare Board Survey* (New York: Dial Press, 1948).

[79]*Ibid.,* p. 7.

[80]Dan W. Dodson, *The Role of the YWCA in a Changing Era: The YWCA Study of YMCA-YWCA Cooperative Experiences* (New York: National Board of the Young Women's Christian Association of the U.S.A., 1960), p. 76.

[81]*Ibid.,* p. 106.

[82]Mayer N. Zald and Patricia Denton, "From Evangelism to General Service: The Transformation of the YMCA," *Administrative Science Quarterly,* Vol. 8, No. 2 (September 1963), p. 216.

> organizations that are dependent on some form of enrollment economy (a form of competitive market place) are forced to recognize quickly the environment changes affecting the demand for services. On the other hand, organizations protected from the market place, such as religious organizations, welfare organizations, or social movements, may soon find themselves poorly adapted to the changing order.[83]

Meeting community needs. Another body of research on function is comprised of the numerous self-studies and surveys designed to determine the extent to which a given agency, or group of agencies, is "meeting the needs" of its community. In these studies, the primary emphasis is generally on the service, rather than on the ideological, components of agency work; attempts are made to elicit neighborhood problems, measure the agency's facilities against them, or evaluate the agency's role in the community. One of the earlier and more comprehensive of these was the Kennedy and Farra study of 1935, designed to appraise the "activities, policies and administration" of eighty New York City settlements, the major concentrations of which they found in areas of declining population.[84] More recently, the National Federation of Settlements and Neighborhood Centers published its *Review and Revision,* a self-study that drew information by questionnaire from 288 member agencies in all parts of the country concerning the attitudes and opinions of board, staff, and members on common agency and neighborhood problems.[85]

In Los Angeles, a self-study by thirteen community chest-supported settlements was designed to "define the modern role of the neighborhood center in Los Angeles" and included "an attempt to formulate practice theory by relating agency objectives and goals to program activities."[86] The study produced a carefully worded statement on the settlement function, but "encountered great difficulties" in fulfilling its task of relating the nature of the service to specific community problems. This, of course, is the heart of the functional problem, and the one on which the least progress has been made—the development of a statement of agency purpose directed at the social and individual problems they are meant to address, as hospitals address the cure of illness, schools the propagation of learning, and the courts the administration of the law.

It is impossible to review here even a small part of the single-agency studies in this self-study category; most of them have been helpful to their sponsors in some measure but have not lent themselves to generalization or been built one upon the other into a body of work useful to the field as a

---

[83] *Ibid.*, p. 234.

[84] Kennedy, Farra, and associates, *op. cit.*

[85] National Federation of Settlements and Neighborhood Centers, *Review and Revision: A Report of the Self-Study Committee of the National Federation of Settlements and Neighborhood Centers* (New York, 1960).

[86] Hirschfeld, *op. cit.*, p. 7.

whole. Several have aspects that could be so used if the attempt were made. New York's University Settlement and the Educational Alliance re-evaluated their functions in a changing neighborhood; the Alliance found some interesting differences about agency function among board, staff, and members.[87] For example, board and staff ranked "developing the total personality" first in their priority of functions, while the members ranked this item seventh; on "promoting Jewish loyalty," staff put the item second, members fourth, and board seventh; and on the item "combat delinquency," members thought it should be first, board fourth, and staff fifth.

In Chicago, the Erie Neighborhood House studied various aspects of life in its neighborhood, each having some bearing on the agency's service to adolescents. They found certain neighborhood attitudes toward youth that had implications for their use of local volunteers as group leaders.

> The new awareness of the hostile attitude of the more conforming group toward the less conforming teen-agers provided knowledge which clarified our administrative problem. Among the changes now in process we are trying to select leadership which can freely move toward the teen-agers without loss to their own sense of self-esteem.[88]

Scheidlinger compared the various forms taken by the Boy Scout movement in different cultural groups and concluded that "the institution of Scouting has become a tool for inculcating into the young a total system of integrated behavior patterns considered desirable by the particular national or social group which is making use of the Scout program."[89] Lewin's comparison of the Boy Scout organization with the Hitler Youth movement examined the goals and practices of two highly organized youth groups in a democratic and totalitarian state.[90] Proceeding by content analysis of literature aimed at both members and leaders, he found significant differences in what he called the "experience context" of his "ends" items: for ends recommended as a member of the national community, the Hitler Youth literature had 66 percent to the Boy Scouts' 25 percent; for those ends recommended for the sake of personal growth and satisfaction, the Boy Scouts had 47 percent, the Hitler

---

[87]New York University Center for Human Relations, *Building Neighborliness,* Human Relations Monograph No. 8 (New York: National Council of Christians and Jews and University Settlement, 1957); and Nathan E. Cohen, *A Summary of the Survey of the Educational Alliance,* summary prepared by Emanuel Fisher (New York: Educational Alliance, 1950).

[88]Robert Armstrong and Edna Raphael, "Relating a Neighborhood Study to Programming," *The Group,* Vol. 17, No. 3 (February 1955), p. 21.

[89]Saul Scheidlinger, "A Comparative Study of the Boy Scout Movement in Different National and Social Groups," *American Sociological Review,* Vol. 13, No. 6 (December 1948), p. 750.

[90]Herbert S. Lewin, "A Comparison of the Aims of the Hitler Youth and the Boy Scouts of America," *Human Relations,* Vol. 1, No. 2 (November 1947), pp. 206–227.

Youth 15 percent. There was marked agreement between the two organizations on the emphasis on learning by doing and on the strong emotional appeal, particularly to the sense of patriotism.

Structure

Studies about the relationship between agency structure and its impact on clients are generally beyond the present level of research sophistication. The work of Cloward and his students, however, provides a foretaste as to where such a line of research may lead.[91] Cloward's research proposal represents the convergence of three different viewpoints:

> . . . the leisure-time agency as an organization, direct social relations between individuals, and the community setting. Seen in this way, an agency is, first of all, a formal structure with definite goals, program, and organizational machinery; it is also a social framework within which people are in constant interaction. The interplay between "structure," "interaction" and "community characteristics" has implications for agency policies and for what happens to them as they are translated into action.[92]

He projects a number of specific questions for research meant to "identify and understand the ways in which unintended consequences arise." Further, these consequences "are not haphazard, but can be systematically located."[93] Among the major sources of such consequences, he suggests the "formal structure of the agency," and it was this formalization variable that was taken up in a student project aimed at comparing two sets of agencies differentiated by defined differences in degree of formalization "in order to ascertain what consequences or functions the operation of these agency structures have [sic] for the client group that they are serving."[94] Cloward's students found that the agencies they had defined as more highly formalized served fewer members, had larger budgets, employed more paid staff workers, and allocated larger proportions of service to group and club structures. In these more formalized agencies, members perceived themselves as having more voice in decision-making, tended to carry personal problems to workers lower in the administrative hierarchy, and were more likely to share such

---

[91]Richard A. Cloward, "Leisure-Time Agencies and Adolescents: A Proposal for Research" (New York: New York School of Social Work and Bureau of Applied Social Research, 1955) (mimeographed); Richard A. Cloward, "Agency Structure as a Variable in Service to Groups," in *Group Work and Community Organization, 1956,* papers presented at the National Conference of Social Work (New York: Columbia University Press, 1956); and Greta Anhisiger *et al.*, "Some Consequences of Agency Structure for Teen-Age Perceptions and Participation," unpublished master's thesis, New York School of Social Work, Columbia University, 1956.

[92]Cloward, "Leisure-Time Agencies and Adolescents: A Proposal for Research," p. 10.

[93]*Ibid.*

[94]Anhisiger *et al., op. cit.,* p. 1.

problems with staff. This important inverse relationship between degree of formalization and the social distance between client and practitioner staff has been discussed by Cloward in a general summary of the findings of this study and its implications for future research.[95]

Material pertinent to the structure of boards of directors and the government of agencies can be found in the Glaser and Sills reader on leadership in voluntary associations.[96] Among the studies sampled here is one by Arsinian and Blumberg exploring sources, status, and expectations of volunteers in the YMCA.[97] Their group of ninety-three volunteers, about evenly divided between board members and club leaders, was examined on factors of age, sex, marital status, religion, education, occupation, community activities, community residence, previous "Y" experience, church activity, and parental family activity in community affairs. Both board and volunteer staff members tended to be active in other organizations, to have had satisfactory "Y" experiences in their own backgrounds, and to have come from families with a tradition of community activism. Board members were older, more educated, more likely to be married, higher on the status ladder in occupation, and had lived for a longer period in the same community. Group leaders were more likely to be female, non-Protestant, and with more previous participant experience in the YMCA.

In another study, Reece collected data from a representative 25 percent of all YMCA board members throughout the country in 1960; he found the typical "Y" board member to be male, white, in a high-status professional or managerial occupation, and generally inactive as a program participant or client.[98] One of the factors that generally has operated to obscure the study of boards is the common confusion engendered by combining, in a single category called "volunteer," those who govern the agency with those who may lead a group without compensation, offer a single lecture, or help out from time to time with clerical chores.

Fierman's survey of intake practices in 1952 is one of the very few evidences of agency interest in the intake process.[99] One might speculate that this general lack of interest in how persons are introduced to neighborhood center programs is related to other issues affecting the practice of social work in the neighborhood centers—for example, uncertainties about the "member"

---

[95]"Agency Structure as a Variable in Service to Groups."

[96]William A. Glaser and David L. Sills, eds., "The Government of Private Organizations: A Social Science Reader for Leaders of Voluntary Associations" (2 vols.; New York: Bureau of Applied Social Research, Columbia University, 1963). (Mimeographed.)

[97]Seth Arsinian and Arthur Blumberg, "Volunteers in the Y.M.C.A.," in *ibid.*, Vol. 2, pp. XI:2–15.

[98]Sanford M. Reece, *YMCA Boards and Committees of Management: A Study of the Membership, Structure and Practice of YMCA Boards* (New York: National Council of the Young Men's Christian Association, 1963).

[99]Frank Fierman, "Intake Policy and Procedure for the Jewish Community Center," *Jewish Center Worker,* Vol. 13, No. 2 (May 1952), pp. 27–30.

as "client," ambiguities surrounding agency function, and a historic reluctance to impose conditions on the offering of service. Finally, a nostalgic reference is in order to a 1941 study reminiscent of another era—Stoney's "Rooms of Their Own," in which he examined the origins and structure of twenty-eight "cellar clubs" in the Henry Street Settlement neighborhood in New York City.[100]

Programs

Most of the national agencies and federations have produced periodic program studies, more or less objective and varying considerably in their interest in generalized knowledge. Reference has already been made to several of these general surveys and inquiries.

In this category is Hillman's survey conducted for the National Federation of Settlements and Neighborhood Centers, presenting thirty-three case studies of programs under way in various parts of the country.[101] In addition, his final chapter on "Research as a Function of Settlements" reviews some settlement research in progress and suggests some lines of inquiry on family life, neighborhood organization, and other subjects related to the work of the settlements.

Weisman has studied the reactions of 231 adolescents in eleven groups meeting in four centers, developing data on member attitudes, activity preferences, member perceptions about agency power distribution, and reciprocity of feelings between members and group leaders.[102] She also studied groups ranked as "effective" and "ineffective," comparing them on variables of participation, member-leader communication, group climate, involvement in decision-making, and program achievement. In contrasting her Type I ("high-effective") groups with those of Type II ("low-effective"), she found that (1) there was more reciprocity of feeling between members and group leaders in the Type I groups; (2) Type I leaders underestimated the degree to which they were liked by their members, while Type II leaders overestimated this factor; (3) Type I leaders underestimated the positive feelings members had about each other, while Type II leaders overestimated them; and (4) Type I leaders perceived more power concentrations than the members did, while the reverse was true in the Type II groups. In examining the rankings of program activities, she found that "a great discrepancy emerges when it is found that there is a very low correlation between the supervisors' and executive directors' actual rankings and the members' perceptions of the agency ranking."[103]

---

[100]George Stoney, "Rooms of Their Own" (New York: Henry Street Settlement, 1941). (Mimeographed.)

[101]Hillman, *op. cit.*

[102]Celia B. Weisman, *A Study of Jewish Community Center Teen-Age Programming* (New York: National Jewish Welfare Board, 1960).

[103]*Ibid.*, p. 47.

Among the studies produced by the Research and Statistical Service of the Boy Scouts of America was the well-known "Boys in Wartime," which examined the attitudes of scouts and their leaders toward the war and their part in it.[104] Of particular interest was the extent to which the scouting program seems to have created, along with the high morale and active participation in the national war effort, many highly stereotyped reactions to the nature of the enemy, the differences between the Germans and the Japanese, and the aims of the war. Also significant was the fact that, while scouts and nonscouts were generally similar in the frequency of their intolerant responses, this was not true in the poor environments of the metropolitan areas; in these populations, the scouts were twice as intolerant as the nonscouts.

An "experience survey" conducted by Chein *et al.* at the Commission on Community Interrelations of the American Jewish Congress was designed to crystallize the major issues and develop hypotheses regarding the content of Jewish school curricula and Jewish Center programs.[105] In interviews with sixty-four leading Jewish educators and group workers, they addressed themselves to the general question: "Taking into account the fact that the Jewish child has a dual role to play, and all that this implies, what should the major emphases of Jewish schools and group work agencies be in their dealings with Jewish children?"[106] Respondents were differentiated on their central viewpoints, specific goals, over-all emphasis, and the extent to which non-Jewish experiences should be provided. This technique, aimed at crystallizing the experience of working practitioners, seems ideally suited to the task of clarifying and dramatizing the research issues in an area where little systematic work has yet been done.

There is a sizable segment of the group work literature devoted to what was once called "casework-group work"—an enterprise devoted to improving the service to individuals both by interagency referral and by instituting improved modes of personal service within the agencies.[107] Linderman, for example, reported a project in which eight Pasadena neighborhood centers experimented with the use of the Social Service Exchange for children under 18 and found that about half of the cases they registered were previously known to other social agencies in the community.[108] However, the material

---

[104]Boy Scouts of America, "Boys in Wartime: Special Research Supplement," in *Scouting for Facts* (New York, 1942).

[105]Isidor Chein *et al.*, "Basic Issues in Jewish Education and Group Work" (New York: American Jewish Congress, 1950). (Mimeographed.)

[106]*Ibid.*, p. 3.

[107]*See*, for example, Saul Scheidlinger, "Patterns of Case Work Services in Group Work Agencies," *The Group*, Vol. 8, No. 1 (November 1945), pp. 1–7; and Gertrude Wilson, *Group Work and Case Work—Their Relationship and Practice* (New York: Family Welfare Association of America, 1941).

[108]Wanda Taylor Linderman; "An Experiment in Casework-Group Work Cooperation," *The Group*, Vol. 8, No. 1 (November 1945), pp. 11–13.

that generally emerged from this type of research effort was largely descriptive and hortatory, and interest seems to have dried up in recent years.

The Community

The interest of the centers in their neighborhoods and in the social problems of the larger community has been reflected in three main lines of research: the community survey, which had its moments of glory in the first two decades of the twentieth century; the study of specific social problems of immediate concern to the big city settlements in particular; and the development of indices for measuring the community's need for group work and recreation services.

The Community Survey

> The early social survey was a process for effecting social improvement by means of a large-scale, one-time investigation of a community's social welfare needs. . . . Major emphasis was placed throughout upon publicizing the survey and its findings and conclusions as widely and effectively as possible, so as to arouse the community to action and implementation of its recommendations.[109]

Zimbalist and Eaton and Harrison have described and documented the centers' historic interest in the social survey; in its day, it commanded considerable community attention and produced some action on social problems of great urgency.[110] Over the years, the traditional survey approach, primarily designed to make a strong case for action on social issues, fell into decline. "Because of the many changes and extensions of use which the term 'survey' has undergone over the years, it no longer appears to provide a meaningful referent in social work research."[111]

The community study nevertheless remains an important part of the catalogue of techniques used by social welfare councils and other planning bodies, both public and private, to study conditions bearing on the need for social services. Every community has its own local landmark survey, which it uses as a continuous point of reference.[112] Some recent efforts may be noted: the "self-portrait" of the Greater Mission District in San Francisco, developed by the Mission Neighborhood Centers; the New York City Youth Board's studies of delinquency trends in New York City between 1953 and 1962; Jacobs'

---

[109]Zimbalist, *op. cit.,* p. 179.

[110]*Ibid.,* chap. 7; and Eaton and Harrison, *op. cit.*

[111]Zimbalist, *op. cit.,* p. 200.

[112]Helen Hall, "Community Studies," in *Group Work and Community Organization 1953–1954,* papers presented at the National Conference of Social Work (New York: Columbia University Press, 1954); and Jean M. Maxwell, "Group Work and Community Surveys," *The Group,* Vol. 11, No. 4 (Summer 1949), pp. 9–17.

recreation survey of the Germantown area in Philadelphia; the Bergen County, New Jersey, study of Jewish population trends and community needs; and two larger surveys by Wolins in Berkeley and Jenkins in New York City.[113]

The Jenkins study, sponsored by the research department of the Community Council of Greater New York, is one of the most comprehensive efforts undertaken in recent years to develop the relationship between recreational needs and services in a large and enormously complex metropolis. Also in New York City, Cloward and the staff of the Institute of Public Administration studied and made recommendations to the city government on "the organizational and administrative relationships involved in services rendered by the various agencies, departments, commissions, officers and boards of the City of New York dealing with child and youth problems."[114]

Selected Social Problems

In her "descriptive bibliography" of the Helen Hall Settlement Papers, Brown notes:

> . . . over the years, settlements have done sampling or surveying repeatedly—to obtain information about the most pressing social and economic problems of their neighbors at the moment when the facts might serve best, whether it was unemployment, medical care, public relief policies, or milk consumption, to name just a few of the fields in which we have investigated the needs or attitudes of neighborhood families.[115]

Among the best of the early examples were Lenroot's "Children of the Depression," published in 1935, and *Case Studies of Unemployment,* compiled by the Unemployment Committee of the National Federation of Settlements under the chairmanship of Helen Hall and edited by Marion Elderton in 1931.[116] Elderton's 150 case studies were selected in a survey conducted between June 1928 and March 1929, with the co-operation of 104 neighborhood houses in thirty-two cities and the District of Columbia. Coming as it

---

[113]Mission Neighborhood Centers, "A Self-Portrait of the Greater Mission District in Southeastern San Francisco" (2 vols.; San Francisco, 1960) (mimeographed); New York City Youth Board, *Ten-Year Trends in Juvenile Delinquency in New York City: Offenses for Ages 7 Through 20 Years, 1953–1962* (New York, 1964); Jacobs, *op. cit.;* YMHA of Bergen County, *A Survey of the Jewish Population of Bergen County* (New York: National Jewish Welfare Board, 1963); Martin Wolins, *Welfare Problems and Services in Berkeley, California* (Berkeley: Berkeley Council of Social Welfare and School of Social Welfare, University of California, 1954); and Shirley Jenkins, *Comparative Recreation Needs and Services in New York Neighborhoods* (New York: Community Council of Greater New York, 1963).

[114]Richard A. Cloward, *The Administration of Services to Children and Youth in New York City* (New York: Institute of Public Administration, 1963). The quotation above is from the letter of transmittal sent with the recommendations.

[115]Brown, *op. cit.,* p. 4.

[116]Katherine Lenroot, "Children of the Depression: A Study of 259 Families in Selected Areas of Five Cities," *Social Service Review,* Vol. 9, No. 2 (June 1935), pp. 212–242; and Marion Elderton, ed., *Case Studies of Unemployment* (Philadelphia: University of Pennsylvania Press, 1931).

did before the actual onset of the Great Depression, the study was a striking demonstration of the potential ability of the neighborhood agencies to serve as a barometer of impending problems and to dramatize them in terms drawn from their own firsthand experiences with people where they live.

More recently, agencies have produced other studies of current social problems. Caplovitz, under the sponsorship of three New York City settlements, has researched the consumer practices of the poor, examining buying habits, modes of installment purchase and other aspects of the "peddler economy."[117] The Union Settlement Association, studying the impact of a new low-cost housing project in New York's East Harlem, found that the new community showed little evidence of neighborhood feeling; it was not an integrated community, with only the barest representations of white, single, middle-income, and aged populations.[118] The most stable families resented the impersonal treatment and invasions of privacy in project living more than they appreciated the improved physical facilities. Also studied were friendship selection, participation in organized activity, management problems, and the characteristics of the "problem tenant."

In another East Harlem study, the East Harlem Project of the James Weldon Johnson Community Center, in co-operation with the New York City Commission on Human Rights, examined the effects on parents and children of a busing program designed to take minority group children, mostly Negro, from an overused, segregated school facility to underused schools in white neighborhoods.[119] Parents who had given permission to have their children transported had relatively high educational achievement of their own and higher educational aspirations for their children, although of fifty-two fathers in the home, forty-one were in the manual labor class. Parents' motivation for giving consent was expressed primarily as wanting improved educational opportunities and relief from overcrowding, with a "chance to integrate" as a low-order choice. They also reported changes in their children as a result of the new experience, noting improvements in "work habits" and "interest in school."

Urban sociologists and others unaffiliated with settlements have shown a continuing interest in social problems of immediate relevance to the tasks of the neighborhood centers. For example, Handlin, Deutschberger, and Fellin and Litwak have studied changing neighborhoods and newcomer

---

[117]David Caplovitz, *The Poor Pay More: Consumer Practices of Low-Income Families* (New York: Free Press of Glencoe, 1963).

[118]Ellen Lurie, *A Study of George Washington Houses, A Federally Aided, Low Cost Housing Project in East Harlem: The Effect of the Project on its Tenants and the Surrounding Community* (New York: Union Settlement Association, 1955–1956).

[119]East Harlem Project and the New York City Commission on Human Rights, "Releasing Human Potential: A Study of East Harlem-Yorkville School Bus Transfer" (New York, 1962). (Mimeographed.)

integration.[120] Komarovsky, Mann, and Dotson have worked on patterns of voluntary association and "neighborliness."[121] White and others have examined social class differences in the use of leisure time.[122] The list is long and cannot appropriately be reviewed here, but examples are cited to suggest some of the areas of knowledge to which the centers can make a contribution from their experience, and upon which they can draw for a firmer knowledge base for their practice.

Measuring Need

Carter has called attention to the problems involved in studying the need for welfare services in the community, stressing the importance of relating such research to a theoretical context:

> Research on need for services is guided by content theory, but we do not always clarify this in our written reports. . . . The point is that we are not conducting research unaffected by theory, although in most instances the theory is speculative rather than verified, implicit rather than explicitly stated, and fragmentary rather than systematized.[123]

Among the index-building studies she cites as having been both based on and productive of theory is the Youth Project Yardstick.[124] The Yardstick research was developed by the research department of the Welfare Council of Metropolitan Los Angeles, on a request from the Los Angeles Youth Project for an index that would serve as an administrative tool in identifying areas needing service. Here the research problems are identified as extracting criteria from the practitioners, obtaining agreement among experts, and translating the criteria into quantitative symbols that could be expressed in an index. Seven years earlier, Sorenson had developed, in the same project, an Index of Relative Social Need, substantiating the fact that the Los Angeles Youth Proj-

---

[120]Oscar Handlin, *The Newcomers: Negroes and Puerto Ricans in a Changing Metropolis* (Cambridge: Harvard University Press, 1959); Paul Deutschberger, "Interaction Patterns in Changing Neighborhoods: New York and Pittsburgh," *Sociometry,* Vol. 9, No. 4 (November 1946), pp. 303–315; and Phillip Fellin and Eugene Litwak, "Neighborhood Cohesion Under Conditions of Mobility," *American Sociological Review,* Vol. 28, No. 3 (June 1963), pp. 364–376.

[121]Mirra Komarovsky, "The Voluntary Associations of Urban Dwellers," *American Sociological Review,* Vol. 11, No. 6 (June 1946), pp. 686–698; Peter H. Mann, "The Concept of Neighborliness," *American Journal of Sociology,* Vol. 60, No. 2 (September 1954), pp. 163–168; and Floyd Dotson, "Patterns of Voluntary Association Among Urban Working-Class Families," *American Sociological Review,* Vol. 16, No. 5 (October 1951), pp. 687–693.

[122]R. Clyde White, "Social Class Differences in Uses of Leisure," *American Journal of Sociology,* Vol. 61, No. 2 (September 1955), pp. 145–150.

[123]Genevieve Carter, "The Concept of Measurability of Need for Social Work Services," in *Group Work and Community Organization, 1953–1954,* papers presented at the National Conference of Social Work (New York: Columbia University Press, 1954), pp. 64–65.

[124]Genevieve Carter and Elisabeth R. Frank, *The Youth Project Yardstick: Measuring Youth Services Needs,* Special Report Series No. 36 (Los Angeles: Welfare Council of Metropolitan Los Angeles, 1953).

ect boundaries were identical with the "areas of greatest need" and using five major factors—the presence of minority groups, the absence of professional and managerial occupations, unemployment in 1940, contract rents, and delinquency rates.[125]

The later Yardstick researchers cited the Sorenson study as having represented considerable progress at the time, but tried in their own work to overcome some of the shortcomings, perceived by them as overly gross area units, overweighting of economic factors, the overgeneralized nature of the "social need" concept, and the crudeness of the ranking method used to distinguish areas.[126] The weighting procedures used by Carter and Frank were designed with the aim of producing a composite index, comparable, for example, to the consumer price index of the Bureau of Labor Statistics.

> The "yardstick" can then be applied by a new worker or by a lay leader in Youth Project territory with the same results as those a practitioner could deduce from his years of experience in directing special services to needy areas.[127]

Several other attempts at index construction have been made, generally under the auspices of community-wide groups and councils. Jenkins' study of recreation needs and services in New York City proposed

> . . . to provide information on selected neighborhood characteristics and on existing recreation and group work programs, and to analyze these data to determine comparative neighborhood needs for group work and recreation services.[128]

In the process, she utilized two main concepts: "one is the index, as the tool which relates all data to the city-wide average; and the other is the concept of comparative need, based on the relationship of the various indexes to each other."[129]

Similarly, White, for the Welfare Federation of Cleveland, set out to develop "criteria for determining what constitutes need for community-subsidized leisure-time services," and to evolve a method "for measuring relative need among various geographic areas of the community."[130] The White study emphasized four points: (1) the relativity of the "need" concept; (2) the distinction between "growth" needs and "social" needs; (3) the partialization

---

[125]Roy Sorenson *et al., Recreation for Everybody* (Los Angeles: Welfare Council of Metropolitan Los Angeles, 1946).

[126]Carter and Frank, *op. cit.*, p. 12.

[127]Carter, *op. cit.*, p. 69.

[128]*Op. cit.*, p. 1.

[129]*Ibid.*, p. 3.

[130]Virginia Kann White, "Measuring Leisure-Time Needs: A Report of the Group Work Council Research Project" (2 vols. and appendix; Cleveland: Welfare Federation of Cleveland, 1955), p. 6. (Mimeographed.)

of objectives needed in the field of recreation; and (4) the self-study aspects, involving the importance of the community processes set in motion by the study itself.

Reference should also be made here to the "guideposts" effort of the Group Work and Recreation Division of the Hennepin County Community Welfare Council, and to the New York City Youth Board's *Indices of Social Problems.*[131]

Future efforts to quantify and measure the need for group work and recreation services will owe much to those who can begin to specify what is meant by both the "needs" and the "services." It is in this sense that there is a critical interplay between the agencies' ability to clarify what they do and the community's efforts to plan for its people.

Vinter, from his research for the Policy Committee on Services to Groups of the Metropolitan Detroit United Community Services, has challenged the ambiguities surrounding current references to both needs and services:

> The indeterminacy of needs contributes to vagueness in formulating service objectives and confusion in designing service programs. Given such unclear purposes as "character-building" or "personality development," it becomes extremely difficult to plan for their implementation through the strategic allocation of services within metropolitan areas, and impossible to determine how effectively particular services accomplish these general aims.[132]

Vinter concluded that "the view that all these services constitute a unitary field—such as 'group work and recreation'—was mainly due to the absence of criteria for differentiating among the diverse services being offered."[133] His attempt to identify "the outcomes deliberately intended in the provision of services" produced a classification of group services into three major fields—"socialization," "rehabilitation," and "facilities provision"—roughly equivalent to the leisure-time, clinical, and public recreation settings.[134]

The Worker

The major factor affecting the study of professional practice in the neighborhood centers is that the professionally educated group workers, of whom the centers garner about three-fourths of the available pool, do not serve the

---

[131]Community Welfare Council, "Guideposts for the Location of Group Work and Recreation Services In and Near Minneapolis, Hennepin County, Minnesota (Minneapolis, 1955) (mimeographed); and New York City Youth Board, *Indices of Social Problems: Selected Socio-Economic Characteristics of New York City by Borough and Health Area* (New York, 1962).

[132]Vinter, "New Evidence for Restructuring Group Services," p. 58.

[133]*Ibid.*, p. 54.

[134]*Ibid.*, p. 51.

clients directly but manage the agencies as administrators and supervisors.[135] Pernell, summarizing the data from Wilson's study of members of the Group Work Section of the National Association of Social Workers in 1956, noted:

> . . . the social group worker who wants to use his knowledge and skill in direct services aimed toward effecting the social adjustment of individual members of agency groups, has a much better chance of finding the opportunity to do so in the "special setting" than in the traditional.[136]

The fact that the agency's service to clients is carried out by people not formally educated in the work has left the method of work largely undocumented and unstudied; what research exists has, for the most part, been inspired by administrative curiosities rather than technical ones.

For present purposes, studies will be reported in three different sections: (1) factors defining the population of paid and full-time professionals; (2) data on the body of volunteer practitioners; and (3) findings related to the study of group work practice—the worker-group encounter and the nature of the helping process.

The Professionals

General characteristics. The Wilson study mentioned above is still the most comprehensive analysis on record of professional group work personnel in all settings. Acting for the Committee on Practice of the Group Work Section of the National Association of Social Workers, she analyzed responses from 665 section members—about 25 percent of the total—to questions dealing with their backgrounds, selected characteristics, conditions of work, their agency policies and programs, the use of their time, and their observations on certain issues of practice. Her data are not rendered in strict accord with the "neighborhood center" definition used here, since she includes the field service personnel of the national agencies in a separate classification. Her "traditional settings" category, however, consisting of personnel from the local group-serving agencies and representing two-thirds of her sample, is close enough to give some of the salient characteristics of the professional group in the neighborhood centers.

According to Wilson's data this professional group is about evenly divided between men and women, with a slight shading toward the latter; 38 percent were under 35 years of age, 57 percent under 40; 6 percent were in

---

[135] Gladys Ryland, "Employment Responsibilities of Social Group Work Graduates" (New York: Council on Social Work Education, 1958) (mimeographed); Robert D. Vinter, "Group Work: Perspectives and Prospects," in *Social Work With Groups 1959,* selected papers from the National Conference on Social Welfare (New York: National Association of Social Workers, 1959), pp. 128–148; and Gertrude Wilson, "The Practice of Social Group Work" (New York: National Association of Social Workers, 1956) (mimeographed).

[136] Ruby Pernell, "Members and Their Positions," in Gertrude Wilson, ed., "The Practice of Social Group Work: Summary of the Report" (New York: National Association of Social Workers, 1957), pp. 18–19. (Mimeographed.)

"direct service" jobs, 33 percent were listed as supervisors, 61 percent as administrators; 43 percent reported that they spent no time in direct service to clients, or "social group work" activity, while 13 percent said that they spent 25 percent to 54 percent of their time in direct service. Pernell's summary of the characteristics of the average professional worker in the traditional settings points out that "in taking this job, she found she was presenting both experience and educational qualifications beyond the level required by the agency. . . ."[137]

In contrast to the neighborhood centers group, Wilson found that her "special settings" respondents were more apt to be women (55 percent); they were younger, with 57 percent under 35 and 69 percent under 40; they were closer to practice, with 45 percent in direct service positions, 32 percent supervisors and 23 percent administrators; and they spent more of their time in direct service—only 20 percent reporting no time thus spent, and 36 percent indicating that they used 25 percent to 54 percent of their time working directly with clients.

The Wilson study produced a great deal of additional data, too voluminous to report here; further aspects of the work will be discussed below. Main and Macdonald, in a more limited attempt to develop similar information, studied the responses of 151 members of the Chicago Area Group Work Section of NASW in 1962, seeking information about "the functions that social group workers are performing, their perceptions of these functions, and something of their professional aspirations for themselves and for social group work practice."[138] It may be significant, or it may simply be a regional characteristic, that in this more recent study a much smaller proportion of the total sample—54 percent, as against Wilson's 67 percent—were employed by what Wilson called the "traditional" agencies.

Like Wilson, Main and Macdonald found a slightly higher proportion of women—54 percent—and a large percentage of members with ten or more years of experience, raising some question about the absence of younger workers from the professional association. Also like Wilson, they found a great diversity of named functions and few clear distinctions among responsibilities designated as administrative, supervisory and practitioner: "nearly everybody seemed to be giving attention to practically everything."[139] Of those employed in direct service agencies, thirteen respondents classified themselves as practitioners, thirty-one as supervisors and fifty-two as administrators.

The Main and Macdonald study also reveals some confusion within the profession itself as to the importance of direct practice. Asked where they would place new workers if there were personnel shortages, 101 out of

---

[137]*Ibid.*, p. 18.

[138]Marjorie W. Main and Mary E. Macdonald, "Professional Functions and Opinions of Social Group Workers," *Social Service Review,* Vol. 36, No. 4 (December 1962), p. 421.

[139]*Ibid.*, p. 427.

143 responded that they would put them into direct service positions. On the other hand, when those in the direct service agencies were asked to select the job to which they aspired, without reference to salary or preparation, over two-thirds selected supervisory and administrative positions. Further, when the respondents were asked in which of eight aspects of practice they considered the recent graduate to need the *most* further preparation and the *least,* there was a bipolar response, with fifty-two calling for direct work with groups as a top-priority area of further training and fifty-five stating that this was the area of least need. The authors concluded:

> [Although] efforts are being made to distinguish the goals of social group work practice from the more inclusive goals of the multi-purpose agencies with which they are identified, the present findings indicate the existence of widely divergent expectations of the social group work practitioner.[140]

Further data on allocation of time appear in two other studies. Adler and Kleinstein found that, of the 43 percent of agency time spent on program activity at the Jewish Community Center of Los Angeles, 17 percent was devoted to direct work with clubs. In the Los Angeles self-study mentioned earlier, Hirschfeld reported that 9 percent of the workers' total time was spent in direct leadership, 11 percent in free play and mass activity, 14 percent in routine office work, and 26 percent in preparation and planning.[141]

The National Jewish Welfare Board, in a preliminary study of full-time professional workers in the Jewish community centers, found a dramatic increase of professional staff during the past decade, serving to create a worker population that is young, mobile, and relatively inexperienced.[142] In the only psychological study of worker characteristics in group work that could be found, Koepp tested a sample of graduate and undergraduate social work students at the University of Wisconsin with Form D of Rokeach's Dogmatism Scale and found that social group work candidates were more authoritarian than those in corrections, child welfare, and psychiatric social work.[143] Such studies must be replicated in other regions, of course, for their findings to have any more than very limited significance.

Mobility. There are several studies of professional mobility in the neighborhood centers. In her 1929 examination of 11,877 full-time positions

---

[140]*Ibid.,* p. 432.

[141]George M. Adler and David Kleinstein, "Our Professional Time—How Do We Use It?" *The Group,* Vol. 13, No. 1 (October 1950), pp. 11–15; Margret Hirschfeld, "Neighborhood Centers" (Los Angeles: Program Division, Welfare Federation of the Los Angeles Area, 1961) (mimeographed).

[142]National Jewish Welfare Board, "Educational and Experience Background of Full-Time Professional Workers in Jewish Community Centers—1962: A Preliminary Report" (New York, 1964). (Mimeographed.)

[143]Edwin F. Koepp, "Authoritarianism and Social Workers: A Psychological Study," *Social Work,* Vol. 8, No. 1 (January 1963), pp. 37–43.

in the leisure-time agencies, Williamson had no access to precise figures on turnover, but she was able to determine that mobility was higher among workers than executives, and higher among men than women.[144] She also disclosed the major reasons for leaving advanced by the executive group—long hours, inadequate salaries, better offers in other fields, return to school for further study, the feeling that their professional status was not accepted, and the difficulties they encountered in working with volunteers. In 1954, the Girl Scouts' "Exit Study" explored factors causing resignations of professional workers in Girl Scout Councils from November 1951 through July 1953 and came up with many of the same reasons, adding factors related to problems with supervisors and difficulties in staff relationships.[145]

Vinter studied a group of 125 full-time workers who had left their positions in member agencies of the National Federation of Settlements and Neighborhood Centers between January 1955 and January 1956, and he elicited identifying information, previous work history, plans on taking and leaving the position, and reasons for leaving.[146] He found that they were educationally superior to the remaining workers, with 62 percent having undertaken or completed graduate study, as against 45 percent of all settlement workers. Over 40 percent had left their positions within the first two years, while another group of almost 25 percent had been in their jobs for more than four years. Vinter concluded that, to the extent that his group is a representative sample, it appears that the greatest turnover occurs in the first few years after taking a position.

He also reported that the greatest salary differences were those between executives and assistant executives; that workers tended to express their commitment to settlements as a whole, rather than to a particular agency; that salary inadequacies were given as a relatively minor reason for leaving; and that "work content"—degree of satisfaction inherent in the work to be done—was given as the major reason for leaving by the highest percentage of respondents.

Herman sought the "personal" and "institutional" determinants of job mobility among Jewish Center workers. Studying agency reports, work histories, and questionnaire responses from over three hundred workers in seven professional group work categories, he developed his findings along several dimensions.[147] His description of the field disclosed that less than one-tenth

---

[144]*Op. cit.*

[145]Girl Scouts of the U.S.A., "An Exit Study of Local Professional Workers in Girl Scouting" (New York, 1954). (Mimeographed.)

[146]Robert D. Vinter, "Report of the Personnel Turnover Study," *The Round Table* (Journal of the National Federation of Settlements and Neighborhood Centers), Vol. 21, Nos. 5–6 (May–June 1957), pp. 1–5.

[147]Melvin Herman, *Occupational Mobility in Social Work: The Jewish Community Center Worker* (New York: National Jewish Welfare Board and the Research Institute for Group Work in Jewish Agencies of the National Association of Jewish Center Workers, 1959).

of the Jewish Centers employ one-third of all Jewish Center professional personnel, with the jobs of executive director, program director, and program assistant accounting for almost 85 percent of all positions. The center worker is young—the median age being just under 35. The analysis of "amount of job movement" disclosed that the mobility of center workers declines with age, but remains high among those 30 to 50 years old. The study of "movement propensity" yielded the conclusion that the center worker is "poised for flight," with almost 40 percent reporting that they expected to leave their jobs within two years and more than 25 percent actively seeking new employment at the time of the study. The "significant determinants" of this condition are described as "level of aspiration," "perception of the road to advancement," "salary increase," and "status anxiety," wherein the worker perceives "movement as being associated with advancement."[148]

Herman makes an important contribution to future work in this area with his analysis of three "patterns of job movement": (1) horizontal change, involving movement from one agency to another without change in job title; (2) vertical change, describing movement upward in the job hierarchy in the same agency; and (3) diagonal change, with a difference in both agency and job title. He found that horizontal movement was the most common form of job change, encouraged by differences in salary for the same job title in the larger agencies, by the prestige attached to these agencies, and by the condition of status anxiety.

The Volunteers

Whatever reservations one might have about the use of volunteer and other untrained personnel in the neighborhood centers, it seems clear from a study by Pins that the practice has helped cast the centers as a major recruiting agent for the social work profession.[149] Studying factors affecting the choice of social work as a career, Pins found that 76 percent of the students entering schools of social work in the fall of 1960 had first learned about social work from a prior work experience in the field; that 74 percent of this first-year class ascribed their career choice to these work experiences; and that the group service agencies had provided this volunteer and part-time work for the largest number of these students—36 percent of the total, with public assistance next at 31 percent. This recruitment role yields only a small return of workers to the centers themselves: of the 2,771 entering students in the United States and Canada at this time, only about 10 percent, or 272, had elected the specialization in social group work. The centers, then, are apparently well suited to introduce young people into the social work arena but may not promise the kind of professional experience that would attract them into the field of service in which they began.

---

[148] *Ibid.*, p. 72.

[149] Arnulf M. Pins, *Who Chooses Social Work, When and Why?* (New York: Council on Social Work Education, 1963).

The centers' historic stake in voluntarism has produced a rich descriptive and philosophical literature, but there has been little systematic study of the volunteer's role in the administration of a social service. However, the few reportable studies offer some interesting data and some promising clues for future work. Findings have been developed on the group characteristics of those who volunteer, some motivational factors, and the analysis of volunteer performance.

General characteristics. Thursz, for the B'nai B'rith Youth Organization, and Arsinian and Blumberg, for the Young Men's Christian Association, have studied the characteristics of volunteer group leaders.[150] Although Thursz's sample was a very large one, and Arsinian and Blumberg's group leader sample very small, the similarities are worth mentioning. Both found an older population than they had expected—one-half of the BBYO sample was between 26 and 40 and 93 percent were over 21. One-half of the "Y" group was between 30 and 47. Both had a high married population—80 percent for the BBYO and 61 percent of the "Y" leaders. Both had a high proportion of leaders—about one-third—who had been educated at the college level and above. Both had a high proportion of leaders in the middle- and upper-status occupations. Both found a very high percentage of "satisfied customers"—that is, group leaders who had themselves come through a satisfying agency experience as a participant or "client."

Thursz also found that volunteer qualifications were higher in the small cities than in the large metropolitan agencies, while Arsinian and Blumberg developed additional data identifying the volunteer leader as one who is more active in other community activities, has lived in his community a relatively long time, and comes from a family with a tradition of community service. The figure on length of residence, it may be added, replicates a finding of Sills in his study of the March of Dimes volunteers.[151]

Motivation. Both the BBYO and YMCA studies found evidence that might support a theory that the motive for volunteering is more closely related to what Arsinian and Blumberg called a "trait of volunteerism" than to a desire to implement the purposes of a particular agency. Almost half of Thursz's respondents "gave as their motive for volunteering a self-oriented or self-fulfilling reason," while only 25 percent gave "motives which can be classified as organization-centered."[152] Arsinian and Blumberg's leaders indicated that they derived their satisfactions from certain social and psychological factors, rather than from factors closely related to a "high regard for the purposes of the Y.M.C.A.," such as "wholesome Christian activities," "religious reasons," and the like. The researchers were led, in conclusion, to ask: "Would these people just as readily volunteer in some other agency?"

---

[150]Daniel Thursz, *Volunteer Group Advisors in a National Social Group Work Agency* (Washington, D.C.: Catholic University of America Press, 1960); and Arsinian and Blumberg, *op. cit.*

[151]David L. Sills, *The Volunteers: Means and Ends in a National Organization* (Glencoe, Ill.: Free Press, 1957).

[152]Thursz, *op. cit.*, p. 330.

The problem of motivation is sharply raised in Schwartz's small comparative study of paid and volunteer club leaders at the East Bronx Community YM-YWHA in New York City.[153] He found the two groups to be similar in age, education, and work experience, but strikingly different in three major respects, exclusive of performance. In each of four fields of prior experience—school, natural group, camp, and agency—he found that "the paid workers presented a personal history of group activity and participation that far outweighed that of the unpaid leaders."[154] Second, the paid workers were more oriented to social work and group work as a future career. Finally, the paid workers tended to fall into what was designated as a "*mission*-centered" category, denoting strong value systems and the desire to transmit them, while the volunteers fell mainly into the "*self*-centered" group, marked by under-elaborated responses, difficulties in self-involvement, and fearfulness of, though eager to try, the group experience. On this aspect of the study Schwartz concluded that "it might be stated, in essence, that the paid workers were attempting to *duplicate* a successful experience, while the unpaid leaders were trying to achieve one."[155]

Richards and Polansky investigated the question of why the participation of women in voluntary organizations tends to vary with their class position.[156] Working from the perspective of girl scouting and its concern about the paucity of volunteer leadership in working class neighborhoods, the authors state that they realized early that it would be a mistake to assume that the agency program was appropriate, and that only adaptation and intelligent public relations were needed.

They compared samples of working-class and middle-class women in two different neighborhoods, found markedly greater participation by the latter, and proceeded to search for determining factors. They found few differences in what they called "reality factors"—family size, outside employment, spatial mobility, and chronological age; greater differences emerged in family participation and activity patterns—significantly lower in the working class families, even among the adolescents. Their most impressive results came in the area of "general morale and personality," with the working class women more often describing their health as poor and producing responses characterized as "depressive." They concluded:

> . . . larger numbers of working-class women . . . appear to feel defeated, alienated, powerless to help themselves and others. Moreover, if

[153]William Schwartz, "Group Leaders—Paid and Volunteer: A Comparison of Background Characteristics and Performance" (New York: East Bronx Community Y.M.-Y.W.H.A., 1949) (mimeographed); and William Schwartz, "A Comparison of Background Characteristics and Performance of Paid and Volunteer Group Leaders," *Jewish Center Worker,* Vol. 12, No. 1 (January 1951), pp. 32–44.

[154]Schwartz, "A Comparison of Background Characteristics and Performance of Paid and Volunteer Group Leaders," p. 38.

[155]*Ibid.,* p. 40. Emphasis in original.

[156]Katherine Richards and Norman A. Polansky, "Reaching Working Class Youth Leaders," *Social Work,* Vol. 4, No. 4 (October 1959), pp. 31–39.

> you look at their backgrounds, they come to adult life with less ingrained self-expectation of participating, and less experience in their own adolescent years.[157]

Performance. The Baden Street Settlement in Rochester, New York, has used volunteers as case aides in a family-visiting program designed to make more agency and community services available to "hard-to-reach" families who "would respond to a less formal and less demanding relationship."[158] First reports showed that the aides perceived their roles as satisfying, that concrete modes of practice were being worked out, and that marked success had been demonstrated in 38 percent of the cases, with the "health problems" group being the most productive of movement. Later reports pointed to reduced figures on neglect petitions, arrests, truancies, and evictions, with "only slight changes" in welfare status and growth in financial independence.[159]

In St. Louis, McAllister evaluated the work of 102 "program volunteers" in fourteen group-serving agencies, using supervisory ratings on "enrichment of experience," "creative learning," "emotional adjustment," and "social adjustment."[160] His highest-rated volunteers were women over 30 from the metropolitan area, with superiority in education and experience.

Schwartz's previously cited comparison of parttime paid and volunteer club leaders revealed no differences in the quality of their actual work with clients "even on the simplest levels."[161] The paid workers, however, showed marked superiority on those performance criteria that required not professional skill but motivation and ability to learn, scoring higher on the criteria related to reliability, flexibility, and participation in supervision.

> Faced with a job whose difficulty and complexity became clearer week by week, and with groups whose reactions they could not understand and whose failure to "move" they regarded as a personal rejection, the responses of the paid leaders as a whole differed considerably from those of the unpaid. . . . It was at this point that the leaders' ability to accept responsibility for what was happening and to subject their own values to critical examination was vitally important. In the main, the unpaid workers found this too difficult. . . . In an interesting manner, the "*mission*-centeredness" [of the paid workers] played a salutory role in this regard.

---

[157]*Ibid.,* p. 38.

[158]Baden Street Settlement Staff, *Final Evaluation of the Volunteer Case Aide Demonstration Project* (Rochester, N.Y.: Baden Street Settlement and Junior League of Rochester, 1959), p. 4.

[159]Baden Street Settlement Staff, *Patterns of Change in Families Assigned to the Volunteer Case Aide Program* (Rochester, N.Y.: Baden Street Settlement, 1960).

[160]William A. McAllister, "Program Volunteers and Their Job Performance," *Smith College Studies in Social Work,* Vol. 23, No. 1 (January 1952), pp. 93–119.

[161]"A Comparison of Background Characteristics and Performance of Paid and Volunteer Group Leaders," p. 40.

> While this quality tended strongly to increase their manipulativeness, it also seemed to make them extremely sensitive to this very tendency, which was sharply out of line with their own intellectual conception of the leader's role.[162]

The Method

The state of practice research in group work can be judged by the fact that discussions on the subject are still apt to begin and end with a study conducted outside the field more than twenty-five years ago. The Lewin, Lippitt, and White research, dealing with the effects of "authoritarian" and "democratic" leadership behaviors on the social climate of children's groups, impressed both group workers and teachers with its unique interest in the details of practice, its experimental daring, and its direct confrontation of the worrisome issue of permissiveness and laissez-faire as factors in group leadership.[163]

Lippitt and White summarized these experiments, showing "the interdependencies of leadership role, group composition, group history, and membership personality structure in this study of four experimental clubs of preadolescent boys."[164] Aside from reassuring group workers on several of their working articles of belief, this research also developed data—in terms more specific than had yet been made available—on group patterns of aggressiveness and passivity engendered by the behavior of the worker and the group's history of previous relations with adult control. Of equal importance were the research implications: " . . . it was found in this exploratory study that the process of small-group life could be experimentally manipulated in a satisfactory way for scientific study and could be recorded adequately for meaningful quantitative analysis."[165]

Unfortunately, the study remained a conversation piece instead of becoming a stimulant to research in the neighborhood center field. Moreover, the social sciences have not since yielded any comparable bonanza of data on professional leadership in the small-group context. Steiner's recent review of group dynamics research states:

> . . . the term "group dynamics" refers to the interpersonal transactions which occur in groups, and to the antecedents and consequences of

---

[162]*Ibid.,* p. 42. Emphasis in original.

[163]Kurt Lewin, Ronald Lippitt, and Ralph K. White, "Patterns of Aggressive Behavior in Experimentally Created 'Social Climates,' " *Journal of Social Psychology,* Vol. 10, No. 2 (March 1939), pp. 271–299; Ronald Lippitt, "An Experimental Study of Authoritarian and Democratic Group Atmosphere," in Kurt Lewin, Ronald Lippitt, and Sybylle Escalona, eds., *Studies of Topological and Vector Psychology I* (Iowa City: University of Iowa Press, 1940), pp. 45–198; and Ronald Lippitt and Ralph K. White, "An Experimental Study of Leadership and Group Life," in Eleanor E. Maccoby, Theodore M. Newcomb, and Eugene L. Hartley, eds., *Readings in Social Psychology* (New York: Henry Holt and Company, 1958), pp. 496–511.

[164]*Op. cit.,* p. 510.

[165]*Ibid.,* p. 511.

> those behaviors. Unfortunately, many studies of group phenomena have examined the presumed antecedents and consequences without giving careful attention to the mediating interpersonal transactions.[166]

It is these "mediating interpersonal transactions," involving the professional worker in his client group, that have remained largely undocumented and unstudied. Some work, nevertheless, has been done, and some lines of inquiry are beginning to take shape. There is interest, for example, in clients' and workers' perceptions of each other as they interact. Maas, pointing out that "group life . . . depends partly on the nature of the leader's perception of members' behavior in the group," undertook "an exploratory study of factors related to the modification of such perception."[167]

He examined the work of twenty-two college juniors leading youth groups in neighborhood agencies over an eight-month period: ten groups were designated as "open," with informal, unstructured membership and activities, and twelve were "closed" groups, with elected members and more formal programs and procedures. Leaders were characterized as "x-type"—those who tended to project blame—and "y-type"—those who tended to introject responsibility. "Desirable" changes in leader perceptions were defined as a decrease in "j-reactions"—perceptions distorted by moral judgments—or an increase in "c-reactions"—perceptions with causal inferences. Using diary content analysis, group observation, and the California Test of Personality, Maas found the personal and group factors related to the workers' perceptual changes: x-type leaders (the projectors) showed more desirable changes when they led open groups; y-type leaders (the introjectors) showed more desirable changes when they led closed groups; reverse placements produced more undesirable changes; and the members' demands on leaders were greater in the open groups. Maas concluded that x-types were probably less frustrated in the open groups, while the y-types probably functioned with less anxiety in closed, well-structured groups.

In 1958, the Group Work Section of the Southern Pennsylvania Chapter of the National Association of Social Workers published a research proposal focusing on intragroup perception variables and their relationship to measures of "social functioning" and "relationship competence" in groups led by social group workers.[168] In casework practice research, Polansky, Thomas, and Kounin have studied the expectations of the client vis-à-vis the "potentially helpful person," with special emphasis on the client's experienced "freedom

---

[166]Ivan D. Steiner, "Group Dynamics," in Paul R. Farnsworth, Olga McNemar, and Quinn McNemar, eds., *Annual Review of Psychology,* Vol. 15 (Palo Alto, Calif.: Annual Reviews, 1964), p. 440.

[167]Henry S. Maas, "Personal and Group Factors in Leaders' Social Perception," *Journal of Abnormal and Social Psychology,* Vol. 45, No. 1 (January 1950), p. 54.

[168]"Group Workers Design Practice Research," *NASW News,* Vol. 4, No. 1 (February 1958), pp. 9–10.

to communicate" and "freedom to reveal one's feelings."[169] "This particular index [freedom to reveal feelings] correlated significantly with every other dimension having to do with satisfaction with the interview, and it was about the only one that did."[170] Along similar lines, Wormby has studied adolescent perceptions of the "potentially helpful person."[171]

Other lines of interest have been developing. Vinter has suggested, in an approach similar to the "planned change" emphasis of Lippitt, Watson, and Westley, that study be directed to the worker's means of influence, defining "direct" means as "those interventions utilized to effect change through immediate interaction with one or another group member," and "indirect" means as "those interventions utilized to effect modifications in group conditions which subsequently affect one or more members."[172] Schwartz has called attention to the need for an operational definition of practitioner skill: "The difficulty in defining skill in human relations is the problem of describing an act in its own terms, rather than in terms of its results."[173] Along these lines, there had been, in Schwartz's leader-comparison study mentioned earlier, a formulation of a set of criteria for measuring performance of group leaders. Later, in work with a professional committee, an instrument was designed for the identification of worker responses in group situations; and there have been recent indications that the interest in operational analysis is being carried forward in graduate classrooms, student research, and, most important, in the agencies themselves.[174]

There have been studies stemming from an interest in what might be called self-definition. This line of research raises questions about what group work is and what it is not, where it should be practiced, and what activities are consistent with its historic goals and functions. In this category is Wilson's attempt to draw reactions and discussion from her respondents to a distinction

---

[169]Norman A. Polansky, "Small-Group Theory: Implications for Casework Research," in Kogan, ed., *op. cit.,* pp. 109–162; Norman A. Polansky and Jacob Kounin, "Clients' Reactions to Initial Interviews," *Human Relations,* Vol. 9, No. 3 (August 1956), pp. 237–264; and Edwin J. Thomas, Norman A. Polansky, and Jacob Kounin, "The Expected Behavior of a Potentially Helpful Person," *Human Relations,* Vol. 8, No. 2 (May 1955), pp. 165–174.

[170]Polansky, "Small-Group Theory: Implications for Casework Research," p. 113.

[171]Marsh Wormby, "The Adolescent's Expectations of How the Potentially Helpful Person Will Act," *Smith College Studies in Social Work,* Vol. 26, No. 1 (January 1955), pp. 10–59.

[172]Ronald Lippitt, Jeanne Watson, and Bruce Westley, *The Dynamics of Planned Change: A Comparative Study of Principles and Techniques* (New York: Harcourt, Brace and Company, 1958); and Vinter, "Small-Group Theory and Research: Implications for Group Work Practice Theory and Research," p. 128.

[173]William Schwartz, "Toward a Strategy of Group Work Practice," *Social Service Review,* Vol. 36, No. 3 (September 1962), p. 277.

[174]William Schwartz, "Identification of Worker Responses in Group Situations," memorandum to Gertrude Wilson *et al.,* Chicago, 1958, (mimeographed); and United Neighborhood Houses, Pre-Teen Delinquency Prevention Project, "Recording Devices: Guiding and Documenting Work" (New York, 1963) (mimeographed).

she had made between "social group work" and "work with groups"—producing 69 percent agreement that such a distinction was valid and a fascinating symposium revealing many of the confusions in the profession's own thinking about its practice.[175]

The quest for definition is also reflected in Wilson's earlier practice study at the Educational Alliance in New York City.[176] A good deal of the value of this account lies in its close examination of research problems in the agency context and in the internal effects of the study process. And also to be included in this category is Hartford's "Search for a Definition," undertaken for the Committee on Practice of the former Group Work Section of NASW as part of a project designed to compile a number of "working definitions of social group work" drawn up by leading professionals.[177]

Finally, there are a few studies related to the tasks of leadership training, when such tasks demand a synthesis of knowledge about the practice of group work. Kolodny and Johnson have reviewed the contributions of social research to leadership training in group work and concluded that social scientists have dealt more with the method and structure of the training process than with the content of practice.[178] For those interested in the body of research related to leadership, Bass has provided the most recent comprehensive account.[179]

At the Treasure Island Camp of the Philadelphia Boy Scout Council, Lippitt and Hogrefe worked as part of the camp staff and produced one of the first close explorations of the leadership training process in action.[180] Bavelas, in a co-operative project of the Child Welfare Station of the State University of Iowa, the Iowa WPA and the Home Camp of the Des Moines Jewish Community Center, conducted an experiment designed "to test under controlled conditions the efficiency of certain methods for rapid retraining of leaders in a particular field."[181] Bavelas reported highly successful training effects on

---

[175]"The Practice of Social Group Work."

[176]Gertrude Wilson, "Measurement and Evaluation of Social Group Work Practice," *Social Welfare Forum, 1952,* proceedings of the National Conference of Social Work (New York: Columbia University Press, 1952), pp. 205–219.

[177]Margaret E. Hartford, "Social Group Work 1930 to 1960: The Search for a Definition," Cleveland, 1960. (Mimeographed.)

[178]Ralph L. Kolodny and Edwin Johnson, "The Contributions of Research and Experimentation in the Social Sciences to Leadership Training in Group Work," *The Group,* Vol. 14, No. 4 (June 1952), pp. 13–16 and 26.

[179]Bernard M. Bass, *Leadership, Psychology, and Organizational Behavior* (New York: Harper & Brothers, 1960).

[180]Ronald Lippitt and Russell Hogrefe, "Camp as a Laboratory for Scoutmaster Training," in *Scouting for Facts* (New York: Boy Scouts of America, 1944).

[181]Alex Bavelas, "Morale and the Training of Leaders," in Goodwin Watson, ed., *Civilian Morale* (Boston: Houghton Mifflin Company, 1942), p. 146.

the morale, involvement, and productivity of both the leaders and the children's groups they led, ascribing these effects to a "democratic" training experience in which the trainer had stressed "attitudes versus techniques," " 'sensitizing' the leaders," "broadening and restructuring the goal region," "development of techniques," "integration of work with broader social objectives," and "sensitivity of morale to leadership."

Many have tried to explain the paucity of practice research in the neighborhood centers and many have discussed remedies. Vinter has tied the problem closely to the need for practice theory; by contrast, Polansky has suggested that a concrete "how to" approach should not be shunned because it seems superficial at the outset.[182] "Theory," he stated, "does not always come from posing 'theoretical questions.' " These approaches are not, of course, mutually exclusive; on the contrary, any point of departure for a systematic search is valid, and future study will depend a great deal on the growing ability of professionals to think their way from the specific to the general and the general to the specific.

Evaluations and Outcomes

Since the study of outcomes is so closely tied to the clarity of expectations, one might foresee that evaluation research would present particular difficulties for the neighborhood centers. It is hard to measure "character changes," even if agency personnel were to believe their own claims that this is the business they are in; so, too, with "socialization," "maturity," and similar abstractions. Thus, along with the need to limit and operationalize their goals, there is the added problem of clarifying the essential service of the agency, so that an open contract can be established with each client. It would, for example, seem a more practical enterprise to measure success in imparting a new skill, if that was what the client had come for, than to try to determine whether he had, without his knowledge or co-operation, become more social, more independent, or more mature. This is not to say that experiences do not have complex effects and side-effects, or that these cannot be measured; but the demands of rigorous inquiry would seem to call for some ability at the outset to "distinguish between one's vision of the product and the by-product.

There is evidence that the processes of concretizing and clarifying are under way, and the problems of evaluation may soon seem less formidable to neighborhood center professionals. The studies on hand fall into three categories: the "movement" studies of individuals and groups, the evaluations of program effectiveness, and the work dealing with the impact of agencies in their neighborhoods.

---

[182]*See* Vinter, "Small-Group Theory and Research: Implications for Group Work Practice Theory and Research"; and Norman A. Polansky, "Comments on Papers by Vinter and Konopka," *Social Service Review,* Vol. 30, No. 3 (September 1956), pp. 318–321.

Movement Studies

Northen has reported a project in which a professional research committee evaluated fourteen summaries of individuals in group experience.[183] Using Hunt's family agency movement scale, an instrument that will probably be a point of departure for movement research for some time to come, the committee concluded that it had found ten cases of progress, two of regression, and two of no change.[184] The study throws light on the problems of studying individual growth in the group work context and serves also to illustrate the major problem of overstated and global objectives: "The general goal of all social group work is to effect changes or adaptations in an individual's attitudes, relationships, and behavior to the end that he may develop greater personal adequacy and improved social adjustment."[185] Such statements are generally based on the historic "Definition of the Function of the Group Worker," a document prepared by a professional committee in 1948 under the leadership of Grace Coyle.[186] The definition was indeed a landmark, but its major achievement was in its summary expression of philosophy and purpose, rather than its precision of language for use in research.

There is some work in progress on the more precise identification of client problems, clearly marking the areas in which an agency might reasonably expect to measure the effects of its service over time. From the casework perspective, Purcell has developed "a preliminary classification system for the identification and evaluation of problems encountered in the course of social work and counseling."[187] He addressed himself to the task of categorizing the "systems" with which clients need to cope—such as educational, employment, welfare, family, and housing—thus not only sharpening the client's problems and the worker's focus but also synthesizing the social and psychological aspects of the difficulties at hand. In a similar approach, a rare instance of convergence in social work, the United Neighborhood Houses' Pre-Teen Delinquency Prevention Project has emphasized the client's specific tasks as he tries to negotiate the various systems of demand and relationship with which he needs professional assistance.[188]

In a laboratory study, Maas studied the effects of group work services on the behavior of 7-year-old boys in two clubs under the supervision of a social

---

[183]Helen Northen, "Evaluating Movement of Individuals in Social Group Work," in *Group Work Papers 1957* (New York: National Association of Social Workers, 1958), p. 28–37.

[184]J. McV. Hunt and Leonard S. Kogan, *Measuring Results in Social Casework: A Manual on Judging Movement* (New York: Family Service Association of America, 1950).

[185]Northen, "Evaluating Movement of Individuals in Social Group Work," p. 29.

[186]American Association of Group Workers, "Definition of the Function of the Group Workers," in Dorothea F. Sullivan, ed., *Readings in Group Work* (New York: Association Press, 1952).

[187]Francis P. Purcell, "A Suggested Classification for Problems in Social Functioning" (New York: Mobilization for Youth, 1964). (Mimeographed.)

[188]*Op. cit.*

group worker.[189] In a forty-five-minute experimental situation calling for intragroup planning and co-operation, he found that the members of Group A, composed of boys "with no social group work experience," displayed more ego-centered behavior, intragroup hostility, dependence on the worker, and inability to collaborate in planning than did those in Group B, consisting of boys who were "members of an organized club in a YMCA (Indian Guide) social group work program" for six months prior to the study.

"If these ten boys," Maas stated, "were well matched on all relevant factors except their prior participation in a social group work program, some of the effects of one social work program seem to have been dramatically demonstrated."[190] Maas then asked: "How were they matched?" and proceeded to discuss the "five concepts and fifteen factors" used in the studies, building on a biological concept ("organism"), two psychological concepts (the "self" and "personality"), and two social concepts ("membership and reference group" and "social role"). What is important about these concepts and their constituent factors is that they are shown to be interdependent within a conceptual framework. Earlier formulations, such as Bernstein's "Individual Evaluation Chart" in *Charting Group Progress,* as well as similar devices, had suggested important factors for observation but had not yet gone beyond the simple listings or inventories of discrete and unrelated items.[191]

The study of group movement is still virtually untouched within the field. Group workers were enthusiastic about Cattell's early offering of the "syntality" construct, which "defines for the group precisely what personality does for the individual," but they have not yet been able to produce the body of narrative and descriptive data against which this and subsequent work might be applied.[192]

The previously cited Garland, Jones, and Kolodny "Model for Stages of Development in Social Work Groups" is an encouraging example of what can be done through a disciplined examination of case materials. The United Neighborhood Houses' Pre-Teen Delinquency Prevention Project has completed preliminary work on a design for a "Group Problems Inventory," designed to abstract from group records and staff discussion the tasks and problems that a *collective* may be said to have had—and with which "it" has been given certain specific kinds of professional help. Finally, it should be added that whatever inadequacies a sophisticated observer might properly

[189]Henry S. Maas, "Evaluating the Individual Member in the Group," in *Group Work and Community Organization, 1953–1954,* papers presented at the National Conference of Social Work (New York: Columbia University Press, 1954), pp. 36–44.

[190]*Ibid.,* p. 38.

[191]*Op. cit.,* p. 15.

[192]Raymond B. Cattell, "New Concepts for Measuring Leadership in Terms of Group Syntality," in Sullivan, ed., *op. cit.,* pp. 387–417. *See also* the section in this review on "The Group As Client," pp. 154–158.

find in Bernstein's early inventory of group characteristics, it still contains a number of ideas that have never been adequately explored.

Program Evaluation

Several of the street club projects have addressed themselves to studies of their own effectiveness. The most thorough going of such attempts seems to have been that of the Boston Delinquency Project, reported by Miller to have taken "as its principal target of change the value system of the group itself."[193] He described a "definite and measurable impact" on patterns of group behavior, incidence of recorded acts of law violation, commitment rates, and the dynamics of community relational systems. He also pointed to certain factors that militated against effects that would represent "the true potential of this method and its developed operating rationale."

In Chicago, Gandy reported on the efforts of the Hyde Park Youth Project to provide intensive staff services to youths with high delinquency potential. He reported:

> . . . comparison of the frequency of individual antisocial behavior at the outset of the staff service and termination indicated that the youths who were participating in little or no antisocial behavior when staff service was first provided continued to avoid delinquency. The staff was least successful with youths who, at time of first contact, already had a history of antisocial behavior.[194]

In Minneapolis, Wright and Magoffin studied the effects of the "Floating Worker Service" on the social adjustment of adolescent delinquents in six groups, using controls.[195] They found that school records on ten items of adjustment favored the six groups served, but official delinquency records favored the control groups. Generally speaking, one must still agree with Miller's judgment in 1959: "The corner-group method of attempting to prevent 'gang' delinquency is in fairly wide use, but little substantial evidence as to its effectiveness is available."[196]

Studies have illustrated the kind of work that can be done by local centers in collaboration with skilled researchers. The Horace Mann-Lincoln Neighborhood Center and the Commission on Community Interrelations of the American Jewish Congress conducted an experiment designed to test the

---

[193]Miller, "The Impact of a Community Program on Delinquent Corner Groups"; and Miller, "Preventive Work with Street-Corner Groups: Boston Delinquency Project," p. 98.

[194]John M. Gandy, "Preventive Work with Street-Corner Groups: Hyde Park Youth Project, Chicago," *Annals of the American Academy of Political and Social Science,* Vol. 327 (1959), p. 107.

[195]Charles F. Wright and John Magoffin, "Floating Worker Service Study" (Minneapolis: Community Welfare Council of Hennepin County, 1959). (Mimeographed.)

[196]"Preventive Work with Street-Corner Groups: Boston Delinquency Project," p. 97.

effects of interracial club experience and certain prescribed leadership behaviors on the reduction of intergroup prejudice among children.[197] Although they produced no significant findings on the experimental leadership variables, they did find marked differences on subsequent projective test responses between the neighborhood center children and the control non-neighborhood center group, with the former showing more avoidance of segregation patterns.

At the Friends Neighborhood Guild in Philadelphia, Lewis evaluated the effects of a training program for housekeepers rated poor by housing personnel and social service staff. Lewis found no evidence for the "hard-core" or "life-pattern" explanations currently in vogue. The poorly rated housekeepers were of average intelligence, optimistic, capable of warm interpersonal relationships, and their housekeeping patterns were susceptible to changing circumstances. He found clear improvement in the group that received training, as against a control group whose only stimulus for change was the threat of eviction.[198]

Other outcome studies in progress have been reported at the Goodrich-Bell Neighborhood Center in Cleveland and the Lighthouse Settlement in Philadelphia, both studying the effects of "intensive" group work on given populations; at the Child-Parent School of the University Settlements in Philadelphia, in an early-detection project; and at the Oakland (California) YWCA, studying the formation of community-based groups for on-leave mental patients.

Agency Impact

By far the most popular instrument of agency evaluation is and has been the "self-study," in which the major emphasis is frequently on the study process itself as an educational device for clients, board, and staff. Often, too, the search for information is broad and comprehensive, rather than focused on any particular problem, hypothesis, or outcome. Serotkin has described this process in some detail.[199]

In the 1940's, Reed directed himself to the question of the effectiveness of the neighborhood centers in preventing delinquency, beginning with the hypothesis that "the group-work agencies worked more largely with youths

---

[197]Russell Hogrefe, Mary Catherine Evans, and Isidor Chein, "The Effects on Intergroup Attitudes of Participation in an Inter-Racial Play Center," paper presented at the 55th annual meeting of the American Psychological Association, Detroit, 1947.

[198]Harold Lewis, "Implication of Evaluation," in "Housekeeping—A Community Problem: Summary of Workshop" (Philadelphia: Friends Neighborhood Guild, 1961). (Mimeographed.)

[199]Harry Serotkin, "The Evaluation of Recreation and Informal Education Agencies," in *Social Welfare Forum, 1953,* proceedings of the National Conference of Social Work (New York: Columbia University Press, 1953), pp. 250–265.

from families which by reasons of better fortune and character were less productive of delinquency and that this might be the reason that fewer group-work youths got into court."[200] He studied randomly selected samples of 1,679 children served by the Cincinnati group-serving agencies in April 1942, and 246 cases from the juvenile court files of 1941. The samples were proportionate for sex and race. He found that the group work agency youth were younger and had a smaller proportion of Negroes, a significantly smaller percentage of them lived in the highly depressed areas, and they tended to come from more stable and socially adequate families than the court sample, rated by Social Service Exchange registration and other criteria. He also found that the highest proportion of the group work youth lived in both the highest and lowest economic areas and that they represented a more secure group in all economic areas.

Two years later, the group work names were checked against court files, showing a lower delinquency rate, fewer repeated offenders among those with court records, and higher delinquency rates as they grew older. Reed concluded that the study raised serious questions about the agencies' screening-out processes, with age and socio-economic factors rendering them favorable to lower delinquency rates.

Several years later, Reed repeated his study, this time restricting his attention to a single, highly deteriorated section of Cincinnati.[201] He compared the social and economic status of families served by the leisure-time agencies with the general population of the area. Gathering data on 5,675 client youth, he found again that the agencies were serving an above-average group for that area of the city. He also found that, under these conditions, the Social Service Exchange registration rates, being pervasive, were poor indicators of social status and stability; more suitable were figures on delinquency, public assistance, and other factors.

More recently, Brown and Dodson studied the impact of the Louisville, Kentucky, Red Shield Boys' Club on the delinquency rates of its neighborhood.[202] Because the Boys' Club had been established in 1946, they did an ex post facto statistical study of the period 1944 to 1954 and found that the area's delinquency figures had decreased markedly—from one in nineteen in 1946, to one in thirty-nine in 1954. At the same time there was an increase in the city as a whole—from one in twenty-nine to one in eighteen. Comparable neighborhoods used as controls had also increased. In their discussion of

---

[200]Ellery F. Reed, "How Effective are Group Work Agencies in Preventing Delinquency?" *Social Service Review,* Vol. 22, No. 3 (September 1948), p. 340.

[201]Ellery F. Reed, "Families Served by Group Work Agencies in Deteriorated Area Compared with the General Population of That Area," *Social Service Review,* Vol. 28, No. 4 (December 1954), pp. 412–423.

[202]Roscoe C. Brown and Dan W. Dodson, "The Effectiveness of a Boys' Club in Reducing Delinquency," *Annals of the American Academy of Political and Social Science,* Vol. 312 (1959), pp. 47–52.

results, the authors pointed up other neighborhood factors that may have affected the outcome: commercial expansion, leadership structure, intergroup relations, organizational activity, and others. They suggested that the same social stabilizers that had led to the establishment of the agency may also have contributed to the improved delinquency situation.

In general, it is probably safe to predict that a number of other difficulties will have to give way before the neighborhood centers can make any real progress in evaluation research. To repeat an earlier injunction:

> Despite the impatience of those who would like to move as quickly as possible into studies of outcome and effectiveness, our main progress for a time will probably be in studies of process and of limited effects . . . our major tools are still the group record, the life-history, the critical incident, and other techniques for codifying and conceptualizing the experience of practice.[203]

Some Final Observations

One is tempted to conclude by offering one's own list of research priorities, urging study of certain crucial questions and exploration of certain neglected areas of knowledge. The fact is, however, that the list of possible questions is endless. Further, few of these questions are, in any absolute sense, more important than others. While such lists, reflecting one person's theoretical stance and sense of urgency, are for him a logical way to proceed, they rarely stimulate research by others. The field has produced many such agendas for research, each marking out problems of unquestioned importance and then taking its place in the realm of unfinished business.

Heuck's "A Challenge to Group Work" in 1946 showed awareness of the need for scientific study, and the responses to her challenge were written by personages no less important than Lewin, Slavson, and Trecker, each of whom specified particular problems of knowledge and methodology to be pursued.[204] A year later, Zander published a comprehensive review and prospectus for future research.[205] In 1955, Coyle projected a number of "proposed areas for concentration and study," and subsequent research agendas have been put forward by Hurwitz, Konopka, Vinter, Northen, Hillman, Schwartz, and others.[206] Thus, there is no lack of research problems—only of

---

[203]Schwartz, "Toward a Strategy of Group Work Practice," p. 278.

[204]Julia F. Heuck, "A Challenge to Group Work," *The Group,* Vol. 8, No. 3 (March 1946), pp. 1–4; Kurt Lewin, "The 'Challenge' Should Be Met," *The Group,* Vol. 8, No. 3 (March 1946), pp. 4–5; S. R. Slavson, "Problems of Research," *The Group,* Vol. 8, No. 3 (March 1946), pp. 8–10; and Harleigh B. Trecker, "A Methodology for Research in Group Work," *The Group,* Vol. 8, No. 3 (March 1946), pp. 6–8.

[205]*Op. cit.*

[206]Grace Coyle, "Proposed Areas for Concentration and Study," *The Group,* Vol. 17, No. 5 (June 1955), pp. 7–10; Jacob I. Hurwitz, "Systematizing Social Group Work Practice," *Social Work,*

research. Rather than proliferate questions for study, it may be more profitable to attempt some brief assessment of the factors that impede the scientific effort, as well as some positive indicators for the future.

A major obstacle to research in this field is the failure of most of the centers to institutionalize the process of raising and formulating the questions that emerge from agency practice. This lack of "official curiosity" creates an atmosphere in which research becomes a kind of hobby, pursued independently and sporadically by an occasional staff member if he has the time, rather than a formal responsibility stemming from the job analysis of the agency itself. A second problem, stemming partly from the first, is the absence of any systematic logging or recording of agency practice. Despite, or perhaps because of, the heavy recording emphasis in the formal training of group workers, the agencies have never given more than lip service to the discipline of documenting their work with people. The problem goes beyond the narration of events or the recording of "process"; even the development of uniform statistical procedures, such as common definitions of units of service, remains about as it was twenty-five years ago, when the U.S. Children's Bureau made a valiant but short-lived effort in this direction.[207]

Finally, mention should be made of the fact that the profession upon which the centers depend is itself badly trained in the skills of research. Social workers still tend to view systematic inquiry as an alien task, rather than as part of their professional equipment. This alienation increases the dependence of the agencies on outside experts. Also, the research interest, when it appears, is often expressed in a kind of perfectionism—wherein a study design is either very intricate and ambitious or it is not "research" at all. Such a perspective discourages the use of limited but consistent modes of study through which the agencies can, within their resources, systematically scrutinize their practice and build up their findings over the years.

On the credit side, the achievement to date, though not as rich as one might expect from a century of practice, is not as poor as many have supposed. There are small bodies of work and growing signs of activity in key areas of concern: class factors in client selection; the relationship between agency structure and service; the "need" perceptions of worker and client; conflicting concepts of agency function among board, staff and clientele; modes of leadership and professional impact on group life; the cultural iden-

---

Vol. 1, No. 3 (October 1956), pp. 63–69; Konopka, *op. cit.;* Vinter, "Group Work with Children and Youth: Research Problems and Possibilities"; Northen, "What is Researchable in Social Group Work?"; Hillman, *op. cit.,* chap. 7; and Schwartz, "Toward a Strategy of Group Work Practice."

[207]*See* Frances Adkins Hall, *Statistical Measurement in Group Work: A Manual on Statistical Records for Use by Staff Members* (Washington, D.C.: U.S. Department of Labor, Children's Bureau, 1939); and Louis J. Owen, "The Group-Work-Reporting Project of the United States Children's Bureau," in *Proceedings of the National Conference of Social Work, 1938* (Chicago: University of Chicago Press, 1939).

tification and "belongingness" work of the Jewish Centers; the developing attention to the details of the helping process in the group context; and the many other lines of inquiry discernible in the work reviewed above. There is a developing literature on the experience of center research and the nature of the ongoing relationship between agency service and the discipline of study.[208]

Similarly, there is a growing body of experience in action-research collaboration between the professional practitioners and the social scientists.[209] From the profession, there is a growing technical literature projecting new and more sophisticated attempts to theorize about the practice of social work with groups and to take on some of the research problems inherent in the study of group service in action.[210]

Ultimately, much will depend on the developing relationship between the neighborhood centers and the social work profession. When the agencies continue to clarify their conceptions of service, they will be increasingly less occupied with questions of faith and doctrine and more with the problems of science. Within these settings, a maturing profession can then be asked to turn its attention to the systematic pursuit of the knowledge it needs in order to practice.

---

[208]*See* Irving Canter, "Pittsburgh's Adventure in Research," *Jewish Center Worker,* Vol. 9, No. 2 (May 1948), pp. 19–22; Ralph L. Kolodny, "The Research Process—An Aid in Daily Practice," *The Group,* Vol. 16 No. 1 (October 1953), pp. 17–20 and 24; Eli Picheny, "Research Comes to the Center," *Jewish Center Worker,* Vol. 9, No. 2 (May 1948), pp. 17–19; and Wilson, "Measurement and Evaluation of Social Group Work Practice."

[209]*See* Isidor Chein, Stuart W. Cook, and John Harding, "The Field of Action Research," *American Psychologist,* Vol. 3, No. 2 (February 1948), pp. 43–50; William Schwartz, "Action Research in a Group Work Setting: A Record of a Cooperative Experience," unpublished master's thesis, New York School of Social Work, Columbia University, 1948; and James F. Short, Jr., "Notes on Action-Research Collaboration: Research Design and Some Not-So-Technical but Vital Problems" (Seattle: University of Washington, undated) (mimeographed).

[210]*See* Gordon Hearn, *Theory Building in Social Work* (Toronto: University of Toronto Press, 1958); William Schwartz, "The Social Worker in the Group," in *Social Welfare Forum, 1961,* proceedings of the National Conference on Social Welfare (New York: Columbia University Press, 1961), pp. 146–171; David F. De Marche and Michael G. Iskander, "On-Lookers," *The Group,* Vol. 12, No. 3 (June 1956), pp. 7–12 and 17–18; Hans L. Epstein and Arthur Schwartz, "Psychodiagnostic Testing in Group Work," *Rorschach Research Exchange,* Vol. 11 (1947), pp. 23–41; Norman A. Polansky *et al.,* "Problems of Interpersonal Relations in Research on Groups," *Human Relations,* Vol. 2, No. 3 (July 1949), pp. 281–291; Vinter, "Small-Group Theory and Research: Implications for Group Work Practice Theory and Research"; and Vinter, "Group Work with Children and Youth: Research Problems and Possibilities."

Neighborhood Centers and Group Work

William Schwartz

In the writer's previous review of research in the neighborhood center field, written for the first volume of this series (199), some problems in defining the field were identified and note was made that

> group work is practiced not in a unified field of service but in a loose assortment of agencies with diverse traditions and purposes . . . an array of different objectives and client groups, as well as a wide gamut of commitments ranging over the fields of education, recreation, social service, psychotherapy, and social reform. [199, p. 144]

The writer noted further that the global character of agency objectives, the agencies' view of themselves as both social movement and social service, their emphasis on ends without a corresponding curiosity about means, all served to inhibit both the pursuit of research and the use of research from other fields. The effort to assess the relevance of scientific work from other disciplines was in itself a formidable task:

> When agency purposes are so all embracing and ill defined, when the client group is almost unlimited, and when the "client" concept itself includes not only the people but the vehicles in which they move together (the family, the group, the neighborhood), the relevant scientific data are encyclopedic. [199, p. 145].

At the same time it was pointed out that these agencies—the *building-centered* "Y"s, settlements, Jewish centers, and boys' clubs and the *program-centered* Scouts, Campfire Girls, B'nai B'rith Youth Organization, and others—are built into the American urban scene and emerged historically from the same impulses that created the social welfare field and the social work profession (196).

> As such, they have a potential as yet only barely realized for affecting deeply the scope and quality of the social welfare performance where it is most needed. Much will depend on the extent to which these agencies can follow both the field and the profession into a closer working relationship with science and research. [199, pp. 144–145]

At this time, some six years later, both the pattern and the promise remain essentially the same, although there are some signs of movement in certain quarters. The field of service is still vaguely defined and the agencies have characteristically taken on even more functions without first clarifying those they already had. The volume of research is still thin, the production sporadic, and the study themes unconnected and atheoretical. On the other hand there is evidence of a growing "official curiosity" about questions emerging from agency practice; some sectors report what seem to be serious attempts to institutionalize research rather than leaving it to occasional bursts of individual effort. In addition several of the young practitioners now moving into doctoral work have taken with them their interest in direct practice and have begun to produce published accounts of their dissertation research in this area. Finally, some long-standing work in which the neighborhood centers have been much involved—notably the street club projects of the past two decades—have recently matured and produced some significant scientific findings. These trends should become clear as the specific studies are reviewed in the pages that follow.

The decision to extend this review's scope from neighborhood centers (the sole subject of the earlier chapter) to group work—from the traditional agencies to other settings for social work practice with groups—stems partly from the fact that six years is a short follow-up period and this provided an opportunity to use a broader compass that would help to enlarge and enrich the material under review. Actually, the writer had laid the basis for this approach in the earlier chapter, in which much of the classical small group research that has affected group work thought and practice both in the neighborhood centers and elsewhere was included. In this spirit, the writer has again tried to catch up some of the more relevant studies made by other fields and disciplines interested in the dynamics of small group behavior.

An Overview

Our search for studies—helped by students and other friends—took us through the 1964–69 issues of 125 periodicals in the fields of social work, education, recreation, psychology, psychiatry, rehabilitation, public welfare, and crime and delinquency, among others. In addition, we examined national agency house organs, recent research anthologies, and mimeographed accounts of work as yet unpublished. The yield, as indicated, was not large and yet there was no intent to report it all. Rather, we have tried to develop a sense of what has been happening since the earlier review and to highlight the major trends and research directions of the past few years. In making the choice of work to report we may have missed some studies that should in fairness have been included, and to these researchers we apologize. Certainly, in the use of mimeographed accounts of work in progress we will inevitably reflect a bias in favor of work being done close to home and miss a great deal of what is going on elsewhere. Selected student research has been used without any systematic review of this work throughout the country being attempted. Throughout, the choice of studies has been guided as before by Zimbalist's definition of social work research as any effort to collect and analyze data in a planned attempt to answer questions and test hypotheses arising out of the planning and practice of relevant agencies (255, p. 12).

While research reviews are still scarce, reviews of the literature have been appearing in greater number. The "state-of-our-knowledge" articles have been especially helpful in assessing the quality of scholarship in the field and calling attention to the areas that need more light. Silverman (208), for example, examined all the group work articles published between 1956 and 1964 in *Social Work, Social Service Review,* and *Social Welfare Forum;* his attempt was "to identify some of the strengths and weaknesses in the literature and consequently suggest fruitful areas of inquiry for the future" (208, p. 56). To do this he sorted his material into two major categories—the kinds of knowledge with which the authors were concerned and the professional sources from which they drew their references. He found a high proportion of the content to be descriptive of specific programs and service settings, rather than technical and practice oriented. And he found too that his authors drew little from the scientific journals in sociology, social psychology, and other social science disciplines.

In a similar analysis of the broader field of social work knowledge, Taber and Shapiro (223) used a one-issue-a-year sample from *Social Work, Social Casework,* and *Social Service Review* and examined 124 articles covering about fifty years of the periodical literature. Their conclusions for the field as a whole were both similar to and somewhat more encouraging than those reached by Silverman for the group work sector. Their findings are as follows:

> The increasing interest of the field in reliable knowledge is indicated by the findings. While reports of practice experience accounted for over half the empirical material, the reports became more generalized and less personal in recent years. Evidence of borrowing knowledge from other fields was found in the use of recognized authorities, concepts, and theories for exposition or interpretation. . . . On the other hand, the findings could not be interpreted as showing progression toward "relatively well-confirmed theory." The theory and concepts found were used for exposition and there were no attempts to revise concepts or to develop and add to theory in a systematic way. Research reports were few and were not related to each other or to a common frame of reference. [223, p. 106]

Arkava's (5) examination of the relationship between social work knowledge and practice traced the history of the effort to organize social work knowledge. He described "the three faces of social work" as its "art form face," "empirical technology face," and "scientific face," pointing out that the field must move toward closer connections among practice, values, and knowledge, rather than trying simply to extrapolate knowledge directly from its practice experience.

Other works provided useful references and research collections. Rostov's review of the literature on group work in the psychiatric hospital (185) classified articles by their emphasis on background information, goals, functions, relationship to other services, relationship to social service, and implications for practice. She noted, as Silverman did later, that she found little cross-referencing among authorities:

> Although much has been written on the subject of group work in the psychiatric hospital, there is a notable scarcity of references by one writer to others. Each writer describing a program tends to write as if his is the first and only one of its kind that has been tried. [185, p. 29]

And she pointed out, also as would Silverman, that the work was essentially descriptive rather than theoretical, and that little attention was paid to the technical problems of practice.

Walton's (244) review of research on the community power structure was an interesting attempt to find generalizations about the methodological and substantive correlates of different power arrangements. There were other useful reviews that will be mentioned as their area of investigation comes under consideration in the pages that follow.

Several research collections have gathered studies together around themes of importance to social workers in general and group workers in particular. The memorial volume published by the National Association of Jewish Center Workers after the untimely death of Irving Canter (25, 26) was both a fine tribute to the moving spirit in the development of research on the Jewish community centers and an important addition to the literature on that subject. Thomas's *Behavioral Science for Social Workers* (226) and Zald's reader in social welfare institutions (254) were also valuable resources. The January 1965 issue of *Journal of Social Issues* combined a number of articles in pursuit of

> three interrelated purposes: to encourage comparative studies of the new emerging poverty intervention bureaucracies; to contribute to the elaboration of the strategic variables in the system of poverty; and to make our organizational efforts in the "war on poverty" increasingly congruent with our enlarging understanding of such organizations and their focus of effort, improving the lot of the poor. [113, pp. 1, 2]

The United States government continues to publish bibliographies and reviews on current social themes important to social workers in the neighborhood setting. Several recent publications were especially thorough and informative. From the U.S. Public Health Service came four annotated bibliographies on training methodology (234, 235, 236, 237), two on in-service training for key professionals in community mental health (230, 231), a publications catalog on community health services (232), and a comprehensive bibliography on human deprivation (233), embedded in an exhaustive summary of the issues, review of research, and account of the literature from biological, psychological, and sociological perspectives. From the U.S. Children's Bureau, the annual *Research Relating to Children* is an inventory of work in progress (229). The Department of Agriculture has provided a well-selected bibliography on the literature on the poor (142). And, in another sphere of interest, the Department of the Interior issues an annual "reference catalog" of research in progress in the field of outdoor recreation (159).

Other reports of research in progress were obtained from agency associations such as the Community Council of Greater New York (41), the National Federation of Settlements and Neighborhood Centers (178), the Center for Community Research of the Associated YM-YWHAs of Greater New York (34), the National Council of the YMCAs (9), Boy Scouts of America (14), and others. Attention should also be called to a new quarterly journal first issued in the winter of 1969: the *Journal of Leisure Research,* published by the National Recreation and Park Association, 1700 Pennsylvania Avenue, N.W., Washington, D.C.

Finally, researchers will be grateful for Casper's ingenious new *KWIC (Key-Word-In-Context) Index* (32, 33) of journal articles relevant to group work practice. Two volumes have now appeared, encompassing the years 1965 through 1968, and those who take the trouble to master the device itself will find it a valuable tool for digging out specific issues and themes from the group work literature.

Studies will be presented here in much the same order as in the last review and under the same rubrics whenever possible, so that the reader may follow more easily the unfolding of the various research themes over the years and make comparisons between old and new trends. The major headings will be as before: (1) the client and his problems, (2) the agency as an institution of service, (3) neighborhood and community problems affecting service, (4) the worker and social work practice with groups, and (5) evaluations and outcomes.

The Client

Like most institutions in these times, the neighborhood centers have been drawn into deeper involvement with the social problems that surround them. In the process the centers have continued to grow more and more related to the social welfare enterprise, and as they do the client concept takes increasing primacy over that of the member (199, p. 146). This may explain why the flood of "market research"—stressing dropout rates, membership analyses, activity "buying habits," and other "consumer" approaches—has diminished to a trickle. Correspondingly there is a larger output of research on special problems and populations that need attention. No doubt the spur of antipoverty financing over the past decade has jogged this development, and it remains to be seen whether the more recent drying up of many of these federal sources will result in a retreat to the more traditional preoccupations.

Participation

The question of "Who participates?" seems to have been relegated to a subordinate role; it appears as part of other studies, but it drew relatively little attention compared to the intense interest shown earlier. Something has been lost in this, since study of participation has often reflected the connections between agency service and the social scene.

The Yankelovich survey commissioned by the National Executive Board of the Boy Scouts of America asked, "Is Scouting in Tune with the Times?" and found that "while Scouting is highly regarded as part of the American scene, it has some serious problems in attracting and holding today's youth" (109, p. 2). The problems cited are interesting, for they apply to the wide range of youth-serving agencies. In discussing their discovery that the program "fit" becomes less close as the boys grow older, the researchers note: "As boys mature Scouting does not point the way toward contemporary American adulthood: it points the other way toward childhood" (109, p. 2). Nearly a quarter of all boys between the ages of 8 and 18 are now members of the Boy Scouts of America, but an additional 25 percent have expressed a liking for the program while either dropping out or failing to join at all. The inhibiting factors are given by respondents as over-organization, irrelevant programming, inaccessibility in poor and nonwhite neighborhoods, leadership insensitivity, and interest in coeducational activities. The responses reflected the difficulties of most of the group- and youth-serving agencies and in particular their failure to offer services perceived as exciting by older adolescents and young adults.

Simon's analysis of the girl-boy imbalance in the B'nai B'rith Youth Organization (209) begins with a concern about the constant membership figure of Aleph Zadek Aleph boys as against the rising entry rate of B'nai B'rith girls; he proceeds to examine the BBYO and adult B'nai B'rith statistics and concludes:

> The higher the concentration of Jews in a given area, the lower the percentage of affiliated Jewish males in the area as compared to Jewish females and this is true of adults as well as adolescents but more true of adolescents. [209, p. 6]

Simon notes also that "males tend to be users of facilities while females become users of services" (209, p. 8) and speculates further about inhibiting factors that may keep adolescents from using service and may be especially deterrent to males: overorganization, the stress on "Jewish" programming, the agency's apparent disinterest in open approaches to the problems of dating and sex, and the boys' interest in smaller groups, among others. As with the Scouts and the "Y"s, there is the recurring idea that the age of single-sex agencies may be over:

> Perhaps we ought to conclude that the time has come for the B'nai B'rith Youth Organization to merge its programs on the adolescent as we did on the Young Adult level and not to be concerned with separate or different programs for boys and girls. [209, p. 15]

Essentially these are recruitment studies out of which the field often derives valuable insights about client needs and patterns of agency use. In another tradition are the sociological researches that come from outside the field of practice and serve the agencies by illuminating social participation phenomena at work in the general community. In this category are Pope's study of the relationship between social participation and economic deprivation (168) and Kraus's research on black participation in public recreation and the administrative practices that affect such participation (119). Pope studied high-seniority white workers in a single factory, obtaining work histories that provided data about the number and duration of unemployment and layoff periods and relating these to participation in voluntary associations and attendance at union meetings and church services. Middle-aged (45–54) and blue-collar workers were overrepresented in the high-deprivation group, and Pope found that participation in formal associations was indeed negatively related to cumulative economic deprivation. Interestingly, the better educated, younger, and higher income workers showed the strongest inverse relationship between economic deprivation and participation in voluntary associations.

Kraus, working under the sponsorship of New York's Center for Urban Education, gathered data from supervisors and directors of recreation in the park and recreation departments of the five boroughs of New York City, as well as from park and recreation administrators in twenty-four suburban communities in New York, New Jersey, and Connecticut. Using structured interviews, analysis of printed brochures and reports, ethnic maps, meetings with specialists, and direct observation of programs and facilities, Kraus developed information on black participation patterns, administrative problems and practices, the relationship between public recreation programs and other community activities in the areas of antipoverty, civil rights, and school desegregation, and the extent of employment of blacks as leaders, supervisors, and administrators in public recreation. The region under study includes some 13.5 million people, of whom 2.5 million are between the ages of 5 and 19. Kraus chose for his study suburban communities with a population of more than 10,000, with public recreation departments operating under full-time year-round leadership, and with nonwhite populations of at least 7 percent.

In his background chapter Kraus traced the growth of public recreation in the United States, citing the expansion of public funds devoted to such programs (from $262 million in 1948 to $894 million in 1960) and the proliferation of public agencies concerned with providing recreational facilities and services (over 3,000 throughout the country by 1966). He also reviewed the history of discrimination in both private and public recreation, giving instances of segregated patterns of service in "Y"s, settlements, Scouts, and neighborhood centers: "Thus we find, in the North as well as in the South, a conscious pattern of separation between the races, both in public and private recreation programs" (119, p. 13). He then proceeded to describe the progress of civil rights in the field of recreation and the efforts to desegregate facilities in northern cities, pointing out that "the relationship between racial disturbance and inadequate recreation facilities is only one aspect of the broad problem of recreational opportunity for Negroes" (119, p. 19).

Kraus's findings covered a wide range of concerns. On *patterns of participation* in activities he found "a striking contrast between the reported recreational involvements of Negro and white participants" (119, p. 31), with blacks tending to dominate in track and field, swimming, basketball, and boxing and to participate less in tennis, golf, archery, and bocce, "which are of an individual or dual nature and which have certain social-class connotations" (119, p. 31). Blacks were lightly represented in programs designed for physically handicapped, blind, and retarded children, with involvement well below their estimated proportion of the population. In the case of outdoor activity, blacks made widespread use of inexpensive and unstructured programs and participated little in the more costly pursuits. Kraus concluded:

> Both in terms of the kinds of choices they make and the overall percentages of their participation, it therefore may be said of Negroes as a group that their pattern of recreational involvement differs widely from the white-community population. [119, p. 32]

On *participation by age groups* he found "a striking shift of interest and involvement according to age levels" (119, p. 32), with extremely high participation by those under 12, especially in the neighborhood playgrounds, high teen-age activity in most programs (except for the suburbs), and declining participation by black adults and older people. On *integration within programs,* although

> recreation is regarded within the professional literature, and in programs of professional training, as a means of achieving racial or ethnic integration in community life [the] findings of this study indicate . . . that these claims are generally not realized. [119, p. 32]

Team segregation follows neighborhood patterns, especially among teenagers and adults, and "the entire field of athletic competition, as reported by many directors, is characterized by increasing racial antagonism and examples of conflict . . ." (119, p. 33).

Regarding *administrative problems related to race,* Kraus's respondents perceived the situation in different ways: the directors in suburban communities tended to blame black youths for their "aggressive behavior" and "racial antagonism"; city administrators, on the other hand, tended to ascribe their problems to the fact that white residents often withdrew from programs in which blacks became involved. In both settings the administrators, invariably white, found themselves working with heavily segregated programs, predominantly black, especially in the evening centers.

On *equality of opportunity* all the directors emphasized de jure accessibility of all facilities and resources, while offering many instances of de facto exclusion, tension, and white resistance. Facilities in and near black neighborhoods were asserted to be equal in quality, but closer examination disclosed that these were usually of the most basic type, while the more attractive and diversified facilities were located at a distance from the older town center where the black population resided. Recreation directors reported that black residents tended to be less persistent in making demands for improved resources, but offered instances in which antipoverty groups had in fact mobilized such pressure in black neighborhoods.

Serious criticism of these antipoverty agencies emerged in Kraus's examination of the *relationship with other community agencies;* directors often scored them as "troublemakers" and charged that they represented unnecessary competition for both staff members and the children to be served. Contacts between the public recreation agencies and neighborhood groups representing blacks were found to be "superficial" except for the widespread hiring of Neighborhood Youth Corps trainees financed by the Office of Economic Opportunity. Kraus also found, interestingly for these times, that recreation directors often felt it "improper" to make special efforts to attract specific ethnic and racial groups in the community. "Most indicated that they publicized their programs with all groups, and anyone who attended was welcome" (119, p. 35).

On the *employment of Negroes* Kraus reported, not unexpectedly, that blacks are substantially represented, that they are employed at the lower levels of pay and responsibility, and that most directors said they would like to change this but that "it was difficult to locate qualified personnel with the proper academic background" (119, p. 35).

And finally, on *recreation and school desegregation,* recreation directors reported:

> The present practice is to bus Negro children back to their home neighborhoods almost immediately at the close of the school day . . . rather than permit them to remain for extracurricular or other organized recreation activities. This procedure suggests that desegregation efforts have been seen narrowly in terms of academic involvement, rather than in terms of achieving the broader benefits of social integration as well. [119, p. 35]

Kraus concludes with a quotation from a director:

> It seems to me that 80 per cent of our program problems are related to this matter of race relations—one way or another. Yet, most of us treat it about on the level of deciding what refrigerating unit to buy for an artificial ice rink. [119, p. 36]

Needs and Interests

When the neighborhood centers undertake to study membership needs and interests, they generally reserve their greatest curiosity for the adolescent population. Teenagers are not only their most complex and ambivalent consumers, they have also historically carried the major burden of the agencies' educative and character-building aspirations. Thus studies of adolescents' program preferences, attitudes toward the agency, and other perceptions abound. There is, however, some recent evidence that the work is moving to a higher level of sophistication, focusing less on "market research" and more on a scientific interest in the discovery of psychological and social need.

Levin's (127) scholarly review of research on adolescents and its implications for practice is one such sign; coming from a top administrator of the Chicago Jewish Community Centers, one of the largest neighborhood center complexes in the country, it speaks well for the emergence of an official curiosity about scientific and technical questions related to service. Levin examines the research on adolescent psychology, the subcultural and contracultural perspectives, generational differences in the Jewish family, value similarities and contrasts within the family, the development of sexual activity, problems of Jewish identity within the larger culture, and other factors. In his discussion of findings the emphasis on service is clear—in his call for the recording of practice; for the need to respond to adolescents' "urge to find their own identity, their own goals, their own means" (127, p. 30); and for more research and pooling of information among the centers.

The Jewish centers have in fact produced a number of studies of adolescents over the past five years; Carp (31) compiled a list of such research carried on between 1962 and 1966. An evaluation by Deutschberger (44) of four such studies conducted in Savannah, Georgia (39), Youngstown, Ohio (114), Wilkes-Barre, Pennsylvania (84), and Montreal, Canada (65), raised some basic questions about the applicability of findings and the relationship between local studies and the development of a usable picture of "the present realities of American Jewish teenage life" (44, p. 23). These and similar studies initiated in Pittsburgh (250), New Orleans (220), and New York (30) vary in the range of their interest, from a broad concern with psychosocial problems in the current American scene to a narrower focus on the patterns of Jewish identification and belongingness. In a later section of this chapter a closer look will be taken at some of these studies in the context of group identification.

In the broader field of adolescent study, Bachman and his associates at the Survey Research Center of the Institute for Social Research in Ann Arbor, Michigan, have issued the first volume of their report on a longitudinal study of high school boys, launched under the sponsorship of the United States Office of Education in June 1965 (8). In this first volume they provide an overview of the purpose and design of the research, its relationship to other nationwide youth studies, the conceptual framework, measurement procedures, analytical strategies, and the "major substantive interests to be explored in the study, including the study of schools as organizations" (8, p. iv).

Schwartz and Merten (195), in an "anthropological approach to the youth culture," held that

> contrary to the model of the youth culture as a contra-culture . . . its reality as a subculture does not rest on its power to repudiate or undermine basic adult values. We shall argue that peer-group interaction is guided by expectations which do not govern the behavior of other members of the community. [195, p. 453]

They made their initial contacts through a youth survey agency and established subsequent relationships by tracing friendship networks. Data were obtained from field observation of peer groups in their natural environments and from intensive interviews with selected informants. The researchers found that "adolescent conceptions of the validity of adult goals and values are . . . largely independent of the standards they use to estimate the relative excellence of their peers" (195, p. 459). The adolescents' judgments of personal worth were closely linked to standards of masculinity and femininity. The adolescents described two different life-styles, labeling them "hoody" and "socie" (the researchers perceived a third, residual "conventional" style), and within the two major styles they drew vertical status positions related to how well the individual lives up to the group's standards. The authors concluded:

> We do not hold that the youth subculture is a closed normative system. The normative integrity, coherence and identity of a subculture is not always based upon estrangement from the larger culture nor does it always reside in social organizations which resist integration into larger society. . . . We suggest that the core of the youth culture resides in its distinctive evaluative standards. They endow the adolescent status terminology with qualities and attributes which do not dominate adult status judgments. . . . Finally, our approach emphasizes the element of free cultural play in the genesis of the youth culture. . . . [There are ways in which] the meanings inherent in the adolescent normative order transcend the requirements of simple adjustment to the exigencies of life. [195, p. 468]

Finally, those interested in the literature on the urban adolescent will find a valuable resource in Gottlieb and Reeves's annotated bibliography and discussion of the literature (75). Their work is divided into sections that include the adolescent as consumer, his social institutions, his peers, his preparation for adulthood, "the world in which he lives," and the subject of deviant behavior. They have also included a section on the adolescent subculture, an area of study to which the neighborhood centers may yet make an important contribution from their practice. Taken as a whole, in fact, the research on adolescent needs and behaviors—including the street club studies to be discussed later—is reaching a point at which it will no longer be possible to plead lack of evidence as a reason for operating purely from practice wisdom.

Interest in the preadolescent child produced the next largest volume of research, and several of the national program agencies have been active in this area. Withey and Smith (249) reported a study supported by the National

Council of the Boy Scouts of America as part of an extensive study of children carried out by the Survey Research Center of the Institute for Social Research at the University of Michigan. This long-term series of youth studies has included a national survey of 14–16-year-old boys, two national studies of girls, and a national study of boys aged 11–13 (199, pp. 146–149).

In this study Withey and Smith sought

> to describe as fully as possible the needs, problems, interests, activities and preferences of boys at the age level that Cub Scouting hopes to serve. The picture should be as broadly descriptive as possible, and it should be useful to any group that is interested in this age level. [249, p. 2]

The families chosen were from a national cross-section of those with a boy aged 8–10 in grades two through six of public, private, or parochial schools; it was estimated that this grade and school dimension included 98 percent of boys in this age range. The respondents were selected through a process of multistage probability sampling that developed a total national sample of about 1,000 families—500 in which only the mother was interviewed and 500 in which boys and fathers were also engaged. Focus of the study was on the mother as the major source of information about the children.

Responses to the elaborate questionnaire constituted a detailed account of family characteristics, leisure-time activities, attitudes toward competitive activity, participation in sports and athletics, characteristics favored by parents, their estimates of how they influence their children, their estimates of the age at which children's values are formed, the boys' organizational involvements, and similar data. An attempt was also made to develop categories encompassing the dimensions of rural-urban, urban-suburban, race, religion, and social class.

The chapter accounts follow the thread of the interview, and there is a mass of information too detailed to be summarized here: the report itself makes no effort to develop overall patterns or conclusions. However, the findings themselves are thought provoking, reaching as they do for a wide range of opinions and attitudes and searching for class and racial differences on issues such as parental aspirations, mother-father comparisons, organizational behavior of both parents and boys, and many other significant areas. While many of these questions emerge from the organizational, recruitment-oriented interest of a membership agency, there is evidence here of how such a vested interest can mobilize the resources and technical expertise necessary to generate data of general practice interest.

The Boys' Clubs of America reported on a study (157) of 7–10-year-old members, describing the third and final phase of their National Needs and Interests Study begun in 1958. Here data were derived from the observation of members engaged in activities at four selected Boys' Clubs, chosen to represent a large metropolitan area, a large industrial city, a small industrial city, and a suburban area. One hundred and sixty boys, 40 from each club, were thus observed by student workers especially trained to record activity and interaction among boys and their leaders. The analysis yielded data in five categories—descriptive information, boys' activities in the clubs, boys' likes and dislikes, evaluation of boys' attributes, and boy-leader relationships.

Again the findings are too far ranging to be summarized here, but although the agency pointed out that the sample was not to be considered representative, some of the findings have relevance for those interested in the work of neighborhood centers. It was found, for example, that a large percentage of the boys (86 percent) came from intact families, and that almost half joined before they were 7 years old. With regard to activities, it was shown that the point of entry—first and second choices of activity—was the low-organized games focusing on physical forms of play. The largest number of boys played in groups throughout their four choices of activity, and group play was more likely to be engaged in by the older boys. The highest percentage of boys were judged to be "cooperative," and "very little spontaneity or frustration was observed. Only 3% were said to exhibit any signs of leadership" (157, p. 33). In assessing the quality of "leaders' contact with boy," the highest percentage of contacts (17 percent) was "to reprimand," the next highest (16 percent) was "to instruct," and the next (10 percent) was "regarding behavior to other boys." At the bottom of the scale was "friendly gesture" (4 percent).

A valuable contribution to the study of latency-age boys was made by Hess (90), who, under the auspice of the Boy Scouts of America, contributed a comprehensive review of research and theory on this age group. His review

> recognizes the lack of interest of personality theorists in the 7–10 period, but emphasizes the importance of these years as a time for developing social behavior and orientation toward school and work. It is also a time when a wide range of basic attitudes are laid down. [90, p. 3]

The survey is divided into chapters covering an overview, psychosocial issues in development, "models and masculinity," values and attitudes, interests and leisure, gangs, groups and social interaction, an annotated bibliography, and a general bibliography of 142 items. This is yet another instance of what emerges as the membership agencies turn to scientific methodology in an effort to instruct themselves about the lives and needs of their members.

With regard to the older groups, almost no systematic study of needs and interests could be found since the several researches on young adults reported in the earlier review (199, p. 149). This applied not only to the neighborhood centers and program agencies, but to the published group work literature, which is still mostly descriptive in its accounts of the work in this area.

Special Problems and Populations

The search of the literature turned up considerable evidence that the neighborhood centers are increasingly taking on special populations for service. Much of the work has not yet produced research; the accounts are enthusiastic but unsystematic and the "findings" are generally unsupported by data. Nevertheless some results have begun to accrue: the older work—especially the study of street club youths—is beginning to yield a body of tested knowledge, and there are enough reports of study in the newer areas so that findings can be submitted in a few categories beyond those used in the last review.

Identification and belongingness. The social work research on group identification and ethnic self-awareness has remained largely a monopoly of the Jewish agencies. Despite the burgeoning of group consciousness among blacks, Puerto Ricans, and other minority groups throughout the country, neighborhood center research has not yet focused on them. The situation remains much as it was when the writer noted in the earlier review that

> interest in the problems of minority group members vis-à-vis the larger culture is, of course, not restricted to the Jewish agencies; settlement and other neighborhood workers are continually concerned with these problems. . . . However, no evidence of any systematic study of these issues in these settings could be found. [199, p. 151]

Jewish center research on these questions varies from community to community, but there is a fairly common thread running through the investigations. A central theme has been the development of indexes designed to measure the degree of Jewish group identification. Population samples are then compared (members and nonmembers, participants and nonparticipants, males and females, parents and children, members and professionals), and implications are drawn for agency program and practice. Lazerwitz (123), describing a study conducted at the Jewish Community Centers of Metropolitan Chicago, identified ten indexes of Jewish identification: (1) religious behavior, (2) pietism—involving "those religious items which are at a more intensive level than the standard ones," (3) Jewish education, (4) attitudes toward and involvement with the state of Israel, (5) Jewish organizational activity, (6) degree of acceptance of traditional religious beliefs, (7) concentration of friendship and courtship behavior among Jews, (8) intention to provide one's children with a Jewish education, (9) the "Jewishness" of one's childhood home, and (10) the overall index—"a composite of the nine specific indices" (123, p. 19). Respondents were grouped into four categories—dues-payers (*members,* $N = 102$), nonmembers who attended in the past year (*attending nonmembers,* $N = 134$), previous members who did not attend in the past year (*past members,* $N = 68$), and those who had never joined and did not attend during the past year (*nonattending-never members,* $N = 210$).

Combining the Index of Activity with the Index of Jewish Identification, it was found that members had the largest high-level percentages in nine of the ten measures. Similarly the attending nonmembers provided the largest medium-level percentages in nine of the ten measures. Lowest in identification were those in the past members category, and, interestingly, it was found that the nonattending-never members, while distinctly below the top-identification group, were nevertheless second in the ranking. It was concluded from these figures that "it is most likely that Chicago JCCs attract more identified Jews and then proceed to strengthen their already strong identifications" and further "the often repeated statement that JCC members are like other Jews or are less active in the religious realm is false" (123, p. 38). Amid a considerable amount of other data, the study also produced some interesting comparisons of center members and their workers, on which the author comments as follows:

> On one hand, JCC members are somewhat more religiously oriented and far more traditional in Jewish outlook than past and present Center professionals. On the other hand, the group workers are the more inclined to express their Jewishness through Zionism and their children's Jewish education. Do we find here some insight into possible sources of misunderstanding between Center group workers, members, and the remainder of the Jewish community? Does the membership of JCCs view with alarm their iconoclastic group workers while these professionals regard the members as unthinking, backward-looking Jews? [123, p. 24]

The studies of Jewish adolescents previously mentioned were fairly uniform in their general line of inquiry, their access to large samples of their universe, and the consistent picture they produced of Jewish middle-class adolescents and their connections with the issues of Jewish belongingness and group survival. Hefter (84) described a Jewish center study in Wilkes-Barre, Pennsylvania, in which the adolescents expressed security with non-Jews, a high degree of outgroup dating, and a "liberal approach" to Jewish belief and custom, while at the same time showing belief in God, curiosity about Judaism, a rejection of intermarriage, and a friendship pattern in which their closest relationships were limited to Jews. The conclusion was as follows:

> There were no trends to a wholesale abandonment of their Jewishness . . . [but] a dilution of the specific elements of traditional Judaism . . . which could in time weaken their sense of Jewish identification. [84, p. 68]

In Pittsburgh Yaillen (250) used procedures similar to those of the Wilkes-Barre survey and found that the responses given by the Pittsburgh adolescents were "strikingly similar" to those revealed by the Wilkes-Barre effort. There was an important difference bearing on parental attitudes, and Yaillen felt that this might reflect community size: "The worry parents have in smaller communities about Jewish values produces behavior towards these values which the parents in a larger community take for granted or disregard" (250, p. 7). In addition Yaillen's inquiry into the youngsters' use of the agency yielded

> a virtual tie between a desire for recreation and individual development, when first and second choices are added up. In fact . . . it is rather obvious that these teens are asking for help in growing up as individuals. [250, p. 7]

A study in New Orleans (220) found that the adolescents' own definition of "good Jew" emphasized most strongly their self-identification as Jewish, belief in God, knowledge of the fundamentals of Judaism, and membership in a temple or synagogue, in that order. About half the respondents thought it necessary to marry within the group, although interfaith dating was high, "with the proportion rising to 93% by the 12th grade." The agency was used largely for athletics, "general recreation," and as a gathering-place for ingroup courting and friendship.

In Savannah, Georgia, a study of adolescents, parents, and advisers of local youth groups found strong evidence of a "Jewish teen culture" in which the youngsters identified Jewishness in terms of specific tasks and problems rather than abstract or traditional constructs (39). It was found that the adolescents were generally mistaken when they tried to identify parental attitudes on secular matters, but most often correct when they guessed at parental opinions on issues of Jewishness. The researchers also arrived at some interesting similarities and differences when they compared advisers' and parents' perceptions of various questions affecting the work with adolescent youths.

In Youngstown, Ohio, Kaplan and Walden (114) found that their adolescent respondents viewed the center both as an object of rebellion in their search for independence and as a setting offering a "dependency relationship analogous to the adolescent's position in the family" (114, p. 19). This study probed a number of apparent contradictions and ambivalences with implications for center practice: the youngsters offered "to make friends" as a major reason for joining club groups, but reported that few "meaningful" friendships were formed; parents idealized developmental and growth needs of their children, but were "non-supportive at points of direct confrontation"; parents gave lip-service to individuality, but were fearful of nonconformity. It was concluded that "many of the findings cast doubts as to the Center's effectiveness in working with its adolescent population. The Center is only one institution within the context of the wider community" (114, p. 20). The authors also expressed the familiar concern about the tension between the recreational and the educational-developmental concepts of agency function:

> For the adolescent, the Center is not consciously seen as a place where growth needs and objectives are being met. This is the professional perspective. The adolescent simply seeks a setting in which he can meet friends, have fun and socialize with members of the opposite sex. Considering physiological changes, world uncertainty and pressures at home and school, is it any wonder that teenagers conceive of the Center merely as a place where they relax and perhaps unwind? Desirable or not, these factors seem to color the adolescent's image of the Center. [114, p. 21]

Garfinkle's Montreal study (65) was a sophisticated investigation with a wide range of inquiry and a useful review of the literature. He surveyed 500 adolescents aged 14–17 in residence at eleven summer camps during the 1964 season—a group that comprised 6 percent of the Jewish adolescent community of Montreal. Garfinkle asked questions about their "social values and spheres of social activity," "the relevant sociological or psychological dimensions related to Y membership or participation," and "aspects of Y experience [that] tended to attract or repel membership and participation" (65, p. 1). He found that in his sample peer group acceptance was the dominant social value; "the peer group is clearly telling its members to cultivate social rather than intellectual or athletic skills"; non-"Y" clubs were the dominant social spheres; and, while those from the higher socioeconomic group were more likely to be "Y" members, lower middle-class youngsters were more likely to be participants. Garfinkle explained this by showing data to indicate that "the lower middle class seems more achievement oriented, while the upper middle class [is] more status oriented" (65, p. 107). The study indicated that the "Y" was attracting adolescents who were below average in Jewish identification and that those scored as average were dropping out at a faster rate than they came in. Those who scored above average seemed to have been attracted to other groups and settings. The data amassed in the Montreal study carried many implications for program modification, and the discussion of it by Boeko (16) is a detailed example of the efforts of practitioners to draw practice and program from research findings.

Finally, Carp (30) reported a pilot study in which he used the Taylor Anxiety Scale (derived from the Minnesota Multiphasic Personality Inventory), Hollingshead's Index of Social Class Position, and other measures with a 300-member sample of adolescents in the program of the East Flatbush-Rugby YM-YWHA in New York City. His inquiry was concerned with adolescent anxiety, Jewish identification, and social attitudes and values and he attempted to correlate these variables with those of age, sex, and social class. Some interesting connections were found: girls were more anxious than boys; anxiety increased in the higher social classes; there were no male-female differences on attitudes toward maintaining a "Jewish home"—a responsibility traditionally entrusted to the woman in the family; a "low" sense of values existed on issues such as cheating versus honesty, ends versus means, material things versus happiness, and similar alternatives; and, on the perceptions of the agency and its service, there was little inclination to favor more Jewish programming, regardless of age and class differences.

The studies reported have produced considerable data, much of it thought provoking to those at work in the field. At this stage of development the research is inconclusive and fragmented, but it carries a good deal of interest for its rudimentary attempts at design, its efforts to order the questions, and the nature of its curiosity.

The hard-to-reach. This term itself has already grown strange, expressing as it does the early frustrations of the neighborhood centers in their efforts to serve youngsters who would not respond to the orderly and traditional rules of the agency game. The image of unreachability has by now given way to the realities of considerable practice and research showing that these youths were in fact accessible to any serious effort to reach them. In the past few years some of the most ambitious street club projects and research investigations have been brought to a conclusion and the findings issued. Books are beginning to emerge summarizing and synthesizing the processes and results of street club practice during the past generation.

Short and Strodtbeck's *Group Process and Gang Delinquency* (206), published in 1965, presented the results of a rigorous and comprehensive street club investigation conducted over a five-year period in a collaboration between the Detached Worker Program of the YMCA of Metropolitan Chicago and the Department of Sociology of the University of Chicago. The book discusses the theoretical traditions of street club work and the study of delinquent gangs; the research design and the authors' "departure from conventional notions of research strategy"; the researchers' attempt to bring data to bear on the various theories of gang behavior such as those generated by Cohen (38), Miller (151), and Cloward and Ohlin (37); data designed to "decipher the puzzle of self-conception" in the group context and how the boys' self-concepts affected their group behavior; the early discovery that "delinquent episodes are related to status-maintaining mechanisms within the group"; the group-process emphasis in their findings—the effects of group norms on group responses to status threats, the relationship between social disabilities and delinquent behavior, and other factors; and a summary of the group-process perspective in the context of more recent theoretical formulations (206, pp. vii, viii).

The method and substance of this research are too varied to summarize here, but the "group-process perspective" with which the authors emerge is rich in implications for group work program and practice. The authors' own summary of their position on this theme is as follows:

> We have turned to the face-to-face context of behavior for further guidance and precision. We accept in principle the idea that structural differentiation in the culture of the larger society gives rise to subcultures of social classes characterized by conditions of life which are productive of differential rates of criminal behavior. The focus of this book is on hypotheses relating to mechanisms by which norms and values associated with structural variation become translated into behavior. Between *position in the social order,* including detailed knowledge of the subculture which this implies, and *behavior* there intervene processes of interaction between individuals in groups. For delinquency theory, we feel it is particularly important to link peer-group process and community relations. It is these group-community interactions which impart to delinquent behavior so much of its apparently *ad hoc* character. [206, pp. 269, 270]

The Chicago Youth Development Project, conducted by the Chicago Boys' Clubs with an evaluation team from the Institute for Social Research of the University of Michigan, issued a report in 1964 describing the action program and the research design (147). Reporting as it does work at the halfway mark, much of its interest lies in its account of the relationship between the program and the research, in the "action-research" collaboration that has characterized work with street clubs since its inception.

> Too often the role of the researcher in an action-research project, such as the CYDP, is akin to the role of the archeologist digging through successive levels of an ancient civilization in the hope that he may salvage enough artifacts to reveal the nature of a bygone era. Frequently the meaning of the artifacts, and the relations between them remain problematic because the connecting links required for an accurate interpretation are missing. . . . It is the aim of the CYDP research program to not only evaluate the action program in terms of the changes reflected in the target population, but also to interpret the degree of change effected in relation to the operating causes and effects of the action program. . . . The inquiry of the research program is addressed not only to *what* happened, but also to *how* it happened. [147, p. 50]

This plan is notably achieved in Caplan's (28) ingenious "near-success" concept, to be described later in this chapter in the section on evaluation and outcomes. In its description of research procedures the 1964 report is valuable in presenting its perspectives on the use of record materials, the treatment of arrest data, the interview program, use of the Advisory Committee, the activities analysis, the "crucial determinants" study, and other factors.

Another long-range investigation of work with acting-out youths—although not with street clubs—is in the process of completion at the Seattle Atlantic Street Center, Seattle, Washington. Ikeda (107), the principal investigator, has issued a summary of the final report, and the progress reports of 1967 (46) and 1968 (47) carry collections of documents covering different aspects of the research and action programs. Emphasis is on the effort "to assess the effectiveness of assertive social work among acting-out junior high school boys by comparing performance on school and community indices of experimental group to control group" (107, p. 1). The researchers found that although no differences were produced between the experimental and control groups in the frequency of school disciplinary contacts,

> there is a trend favoring a reduction in the severity of the type of school disciplinary contacts for experimentals, and . . . by the end of the project there was a significant difference in the average severity of disciplinary contacts for the experimental group as a whole in the school environment. [107, p. 3]

The agency was also able to rule out the possibility that the differences were due to "favorable labeling on the part of teachers" (107, p. 3). Berleman and Steinburn's evaluation of the project results (11) will be discussed in a later section of this chapter.

To return to the street club scene, Jansyn (111) reported a study in which he tried to

> illuminate some of the ways in which variations in group activity are related to internal processes of the group and variations in group structure over time. Knowledge of such processes aids in the understanding of the episodic character of gang delinquency. [111, p. 600]

His findings, very much in the group process tradition, pointed to the fact that delinquency in the corner group was often generated as a result of declining solidarity: "The solidarity of the group is important to the boys and its decline beyond a certain level is threatening to them" (111, p. 613). He found too that the boys found it easier to act as a group in a delinquent manner than in a conventional one, and he concluded that the behavior of street corner boys might be understood as activities pursued in reaction to their concern about their own instability as a peer group.

There are, of course, many studies of this nature now going on throughout the country, deriving their interests from many theories and traditions, adding to them, and producing valuable insights for the use of practitioners. It is anticipated that these will be making their contributions to the literature for a long time to come. And as they continue, the tasks of summarizing, synthesizing, and theorizing will become increasingly crucial. Bernstein (12) and Spergel (216) have made contributions to this end.

Bernstein studied a wide range of approaches to work with street groups in different communities, touching the conditions of work, expectations, limitations, theoretical perspectives, relationship to other community services, characteristics of workers, research problems, and other issues. He visited nine cities—Chicago, Cleveland, Los Angeles, San Francisco, Detroit, New York, Philadelphia, Washington, and Boston—interviewing street workers, supervisors, executives, court and police personnel, psychiatrists, school officials, researchers, and groups of youths and their parents. His findings were voluminous, ranging over all of the major issues and providing a kind of encyclopedic view of the historical, theoretical, administrative, programmatic, and practice-oriented perspectives at work over the past two decades. The chapter on research reviews the major findings and calls attention to the fact that little systematic study has been devoted to the problem of method and the skills of street club practice. Bernstein concludes with a discussion of the major sociological problems affecting the ways in which "delinquency is woven into the texture of our society" (12, p. 149).

Spergel's *Street Gang Work: Theory and Practice* is a scholarly and thoroughgoing analysis of practice—"an effort to examine what the street worker does, and what he should do, in his practice with delinquent and potentially delinquent street groups" (216, p. vii). Written from the perspective of an erstwhile street worker and supervisor, the book is divided into two major sections—the development of theory and an analysis of street work practice. The approach is textlike in the best sense of the term, providing a compendium of the major sociological dimensions in gang work and proceeding in Part II to offer a manual of practice on specific tasks like "initiating the relationship," "dealing with the sense of deprivation," decision-making in the group, programming, "terminating the relationship," and others. The book also moves into tasks related to work with individuals, working with other systems (family, neighborhood groups, police, courts, schools, and others), and supervising the street work program. The general approach to street work practice is illustrated in Spergel's concluding remarks:

> Street work may be viewed as a fundamentalist orientation of social organizations to helping people. The basic idea of street work is reaching out to people in need, by the simplest and most direct means possible, to provide service of almost unlimited scope and high personal identity. . . . In the final analysis, the program mobilizes the community's faith in the goodness of and capacity for positive change in its most aggressive, deviant youths. [216, p. 224]

As might be expected, the newest hard-to-reach youths to arouse the interest and concern of the neighborhood centers are members of the "hippie" community. It might also be anticipated that the greatest impetus for studying the problems of this group may emerge from the agencies most closely engaged with middle-class segments of the population.

Solomon (213), working for the Center for Community Research of the Associated YM-YWHAs of Greater New York, conducted a pilot study of hippies in the East Village section of New York City. Motivated partly by the apparent attractiveness of drugs to certain sectors of Jewish middle-class youths and Jewish center constituencies, the researchers moved to test the feasibility of collecting personal data from hippie youths through the use of structured interviews, to develop information on individuals and social structures in the hippie community, and to construct a working definition of the term hippie itself. Five indigenous hippie interviewers were recruited, trained, and deployed to interview 51 of their fellows in the East Village area. Later their data were augmented by returns from a questionnaire on drug abuse published by a hippie newspaper and submitted to the research center for its analysis.

Solomon's findings covered a wide range of questions. Demographically, his respondents were between 18 and 25, with the females averaging almost three years younger than the males; the majority had attended college for a while; most reported fathers as being professionals, executives, or administrators, with annual incomes over $10,000; and over one-third were Jewish, most of whom were males. Drug use was high, with exposure to heroin being low, most admitted to selling as well as using, and the order of drug use seemed to run from marijuana to hashish to LSD to methedrine.

The national sample taken from the newspaper study indicated "a tendency for both groups of data to exhibit more similarities than differences in demographic characteristics and patterns of drug use among respondents" (213, p. 46).

> In terms of the meaning attached to being a "hippie," responses generally can be subsumed under 2 categories of reaction to alienation from the norms and values of the dominant society. These categories are: (1) perceptions of powerlessness and (2) feelings of self-estrangement. [213, p. 12]

There will be more along these lines as agencies continue to make advances toward these youngsters who, very much like the street club youths, need help badly but can only be served on their own turf and in their own style.

The handicapped. The integration of handicapped children into the regular programs of the neighborhood centers has been a focus of agency interest for some years now; the pace of this activity seems to be accelerating and some formal research efforts are beginning to yield results. Further, whereas in the past attention seemed to be given mainly to the physically handicapped, there seems now to be a newer interest in the integration of the mentally retarded. Overall the center of attention is the younger child, with little given to the adolescent or the adult.

The apparent increase in such activity is not yet cause for considerable optimism, according to a study Pappenfort and Kilpatrick (160) made of group work programs for physically handicapped children in Chicago. They interviewed administrators and examined facilities in 95 agencies, of which 19 had programs for the physically handicapped and 42 others had some handicapped children in their regular programs; less than 1 percent of the total agency population was handicapped. Some marked differences were found between agencies with programs and those without, administrators of the latter tending to stereotype the difficulties of programming for the handicapped and to foresee problems unreported by agencies that had such programs. They found too that the larger the agency the more likely it was that it provided services for children with a range of different handicaps.

The New York Service for the Orthopedically Handicapped reported a study of 230 children who participated in a two-year demonstration of the effects on physically handicapped children of organized group activities in community centers and settlements (221). The researchers hypothesized that the children's home and school functioning, as well as their self-images, could be improved by participation in after-school activity with nonhandicapped peers. They further believed that such integration could be achieved without special staff, training, or equipment. Results showed some of the sought-for benefits to the children, but there were many indications that such programs could not be carried on without special staff and facilities. The report lays several action-research problems at the door of the centers, pointing up difficulties agencies experience in disciplining themselves for rigorous program evaluation. Articles by Deschin (42) and Robbins and Schattner (180) have explained some of the processes and problems of this research in greater detail.

The most intensive study of the integration of physically handicapped children into ongoing groups in a neighborhood center was undertaken by the Associated YM-YWHAS of Greater New York at the Mosholu-Montefiore Community Center in New York City, supported by a three-year grant (1962–65) from the U.S. Children's Bureau. Forty-seven physically handicapped children aged 7–14 were placed in existing groups within the center's junior program; the service was augmented with casework and medical consultation to the children, parents, and staff. Directing the research, Holmes (96, 100) used trained observers who accompanied the integrated groups, interaction recording, before-and-after questionnaires designed to elicit parental attitudes, and a number of other measures. He was able to document a "positive and significant impact" on the children, providing data on improvements in adaptive behavior, coping attitudes, social skills, and self-esteem. He further found that the parents developed more realistic and less fantasied appraisals of their children's potentials.

Holmes's interest in group process and in leadership behavior yielded additional findings about the worker skills and group structures through which integration of the handicapped was best achieved. In fact, his developing curiosity about the more general problems of group process resulted in the finding of some important connections between the study of special groups and the study of all groups. His distinction between collections and groups should serve as a useful guide to researchers who need to understand that the mere structural fact of physical integration, without skilled attempts to help the group members come together, may not constitute integration at all or achieve any of the effects hypothesized about it.

The project has been prolific in turning out papers and materials explicating various research problems and procedures and reporting other aspects of the study. Holmes reported on the structured observational schema used in the measurement and evaluation of social interactions in the children's groups (102). Holmes and Smolka (104) described a comparison of attitudes toward child-rearing among mothers of handicapped and nonhandicapped children, finding no support for hypotheses of difference either in the before or after measures, but some evidence of differences in certain subtest scores. In all, the work of Holmes and his associates at the Center for Community Research of the Associated YM-YWHAs of Greater New York is an example of the developing involvement of a segment of the neighborhood center field in the tasks of scientific research.

Added to the work with the physically handicapped, some findings have begun to appear regarding work with mentally retarded children and their parents. Ramsey (171) reviewed a number of studies in which group methods were used to help the parents of these children and found that only three of the fifteen studies utilized objective criteria for measurement. In analyzing the variables of greatest interest to the researchers, Ramsey named the following: modes of recruitment and group formation, size of groups, length of sessions, time span of the group experience, types of group leadership, and the range of group purposes from the structured and formal information-giving to the unstructured counseling and therapy orientation. All studies reported at least partial success, and progress was found in the areas of feeling-ventilation, sharing of practical advice, mutual reassurance, and reality-testing. Ramsey concluded that the studies were generally so poorly designed as to prohibit replication and comparison, and he suggested more taxonomic descriptions of population variables that might affect outcomes; more precise descriptions of group structure, functions, and goals; more information about methods of working; and more objective measures of change.

Schreiber (191), of the Association for the Help of Retarded Children in New York City, reported a program in which 300 retarded children, adolescents, and adults were offered admittance to leisure-time programs in neighborhood agencies. As against the integration orientation, these groups were organized homogeneously, establishing a study population of 25 to 30 groups of mentally retarded clients. Schreiber and Feeley (192), under the same aegis, established and observed a group of siblings of retarded children, working entirely with adolescent siblings between the ages of 13 and 17. The Boy Scouts of America surveyed the number and program disposition of handicapped boys and found 111,100 boys in fifteen categories of handicap, with higher representation of blind, deaf, and mentally retarded children than are found in the general population (222). Fox (56), for the Associated YM-YWHAS of Greater New York in collaboration with the Child Study Association of America, has described a program currently under way to establish and study educational group experiences for parents of retarded children. He reports also that New York State is designing an Institute for Basic Research in Mental Retardation.

The National Institute of Child Health and Human Development (156, pp. 95–96) has been studying the effects of parental counseling on the mentally retarded child. They have reported several emergent trends: parents are more accurate in estimating the child's present abilities than his future adaptability, certain styles of counseling do better in affecting these estimates of future adaptation, parents whose estimates of present ability are poor manage their child less successfully, parents often view the child's difficulties as being separate treatable problems such as poor speech or poor coordination, and counselors often reinforce this view by discussing the child as if his retardation were in fact the sum of separate handicaps (156, p. 95).

The Jewish Community Centers Association of St. Louis conducted an integration study of retarded children similar in scope and discipline to that of the New York Associated YM-YWHAS on the physically handicapped. Flax and Pumphrey (54) and, in a more detailed report, Pumphrey, Goodman, and Flax (170) described a research project financed by the National Institute of Mental Health for a five-year period beginning in 1965. The study was designed "to determine the feasibility of including educable mental retardates (EMRs) in regular Center programs" (54, p. 2), testing the extent to which EMRs could participate with and be tolerated by normal children in the ongoing group activities. Seventy diagnosed EMRs (defined by state law as having IQs between 48 and 78) new to the agency were registered for activities in the period 1965 through 1968. The children were referred by parents, JCC staff, schools, social agencies, and other retardates. The sample consisted of 46 males and 24 females aged 6 through 17, with socioeconomic backgrounds ranging from welfare to upper-class families; 50 of the children were living with both parents; 59 were white and 11 black; 55 were non-Jewish; and the majority had additional handicaps such as poor vision, poor speech, bad coordination, and proneness to seizures. Children and parents were interviewed and placed in activities ranging over day camp, social clubs, resident camp, special interest groups, and athletic groups; 52 of the children chose additional activities at a later point.

A control for each EMR was selected randomly from the group of which he was a member. Measures used were a group participation form, social adjustment rankings, observation schedules, and case histories. The findings were generally favorable to integration, with some interesting complexities. For example, a factor analysis of workers' responses to the group participation scale yielded three independent dimensions of individual performance that explained 87 percent of the common variance among the items—aggressive acting-out, evidence of belongingness and comfort, and behavior directed toward the leader. The EMRs were found not to differ significantly from their controls on the first and third dimensions—aggressiveness and behavior directed toward the leader—but were rated lower, at the .001 level of significance, on the belongingness and comfort factor. The general conclusion was as follows:

> The behavior of two-thirds of the retarded children studied intensively was well within the range of that of the normal children. On the average, their behavior was no more aggressive or focused on adults than that of the other children. Since EMRs were no more inclined to be involved in episodes which caused concern than were other members, but less involved in positive incidents, it seems clear that an optimal expectation for most EMRs would be that they can achieve a level of functioning somewhere among the lower half of a group's total membership. [170, pp. 159, 160]

The researchers also reported a highly favorable reaction from the normal children, their parents, and the staff to the participation of the EMRs.

The aging. The studies at hand are geared mainly to the task of testing the limits of involvement of older people in community activity, as both consumers and providers of service. At Brandeis University's Florence Heller Graduate School for Advanced Studies in Social Welfare, Lambert, Guberman, and Morris (120) set out to test some common assumptions about the role of older citizens in community service. Financed by the Chronic Disease Program of the U.S. Public Health Service, the study sought to determine the extent to which older people were willing and able to participate, and the kind of opportunity structure that existed if they did. The researchers interviewed 297 people in a suburban community of metropolitan Boston, a random sample of all noninstitutionalized residents 65 years of age and over. To assess the opportunity potential, they interviewed the executives of nineteen health and welfare agencies in the community and developed other techniques for involving agencies and old people's organizations in collaborative work on the project itself.

The researchers found that the manpower potential of the aging, considered by itself, was "large enough to make tremendous inroads upon current manpower shortages" (120, p. 44) if transportation, some expenses, and some payment were provided. The old people's task preferences called for interpersonal communication rather than mechanical or physical work, they wanted emotional support and the feeling that the work was needed, not make-work, and they asked for tasks that were specific and feasible. The factors differentiating those who would participate and those who would not were previous volunteer experience, educational level, and self-perception of health; no differences were found with respect to age, sex, and employment status. On the question of availability of opportunity and the extent to which such opportunities were consonant with old people's needs and interests, the researchers found the prospects "rather dismal." They found old people to be underrepresented in full-time paid, part-time paid, and volunteer categories; they were mostly in clerical and maintenance categories. In the case of volunteers, "neither the volunteer nor his function was vital to the goals of his agency" (120, p. 50). No agency had trouble finding aged volunteers, but most found reasons for not being able to use them. "The older volunteer is viewed as an intrusion into the well-organized functioning of an agency. He has three strikes against him; he is a lay person, he is old, and he is a volunteer" (120, p. 50).

Tuckman (228) studied factors related to frequency of attendance at the Adult Health and Recreation Center operated by the Division of Mental Health of the Philadelphia Department of Public Health. He found only two statistically significant factors—health and distance of residence—and failed to find any significance in the factors of age, sex, race, marital status, or education.

Rosenblatt (183), in interviews with 250 older people on New York's Lower East Side, found that "potential volunteers are somewhat younger, healthier, and more neighborly than persons without interest in volunteer activities. They also enjoy life more and make more plans for the future" (183, p. 90). His conclusions also stress the importance of agency commitment to training and job satisfaction for the older volunteer.

In Long Beach, California, Miran and Lemmerman (152), for the Jewish Community Center and Jewish Family Service, surveyed an older adult population for information on home and neighborhood, work and income, leisure-time pursuits, medical care and health, social and emotional adjustment, and need for additional services. They found some excess of leisure time and need for help with transportation, but essentially

> a portrait of an older adult community with comparatively good state of health—physically, socially, emotionally and economically—one that reverberates with intellectual curiosity and a desire for new experiences. [152, p. 34]

The preschool child. When the government accepted—and financed—the proposition that children living in poverty often suffer deprivation in their early childhood learning and need compensatory education before they enter the public schools, the neighborhood centers became a prime setting for the new programs that were implemented. Project Head Start was established by the Office of Economic Opportunity in the summer of 1965 and centers throughout the country have been closely involved with it since that time. Nevertheless, only a small portion of the Head Start research has as yet emanated from that quarter. In New York there was activity by the Center for Community Research of the Associated YM-YWHAS, which examined two such programs conducted for eight weeks in the first summer of Head Start operation.

Holmes's report of this activity pointed out the following:

> These summer programs, and indeed all of the summer Headstart programs, were designed to offset or overcome some of the deficits among children from disadvantaged homes who were scheduled for public school kindergarten or first grade classes starting in the fall of 1965. More specifically, the aim of these programs was to offer the participants a pre-school experience which would help them to learn about the demands of school and teacher, to develop their social skills through participation in an organized group experience with their peers, and to increase the level of their cognitive skills through participation in a wide variety of interesting and stimulating play activities. [97, p. 1]

Holmes thus set out to measure changes in cognitive functioning, patterns of play, and fantasies about peers and adults. Foiled in his effort to do a before-and-after study by the not untypical lateness of the grant award, he studied the ending phase using all of the Head Start children and a matched group of controls. He also followed up at a later point to test for any latent effects that might appear after initial exposure to school.

Thirty-six Head Start children were matched with sixty nonparticipants along the dimensions of age, sex, ethnic background, previous schooling, number of siblings at home, presence or absence of father or mother, and occupation of the major wage earner. Holmes used cognitive measures, projective devices, and a structured observational scheme to observe the children at play. He found significant gains among the Head Start children on cognitive measures and social behavior:

> There was an increase in behavior which was directed toward a fostering of solidarity with others, with a marked decrease in random, nonpurposive, and merely passive "responding" behavior. In other words, at the end of program the goal of the interaction was more likely to be social and affiliative, and less likely to be random or recipient. [97, p. 5]

On the projective device significant differences were found between the participants and the controls on four dimensions—quality of interaction between the characters in the stories, degree of investment of the main characters in the activities, the affect with which the activity was invested, and the degree to which it was constructive or destructive. The Head Start children described the principal characters as being more involved than did the controls, but they also showed more instances of negative interaction, more negative affect, and more destructive fantasies. Holmes's comment on this is as follows:

> Clinically, this finding is striking. It suggests that the initial experience of being in an organized group study has a civilizing effect on behavior, i.e., a decrease in the instances of aggressive behavior is accompanied by an increase in the instances of aggressive fantasies. Thus, hostile impulses are, through this type of experience, less likely to be acted upon and more likely to be represented in fantasy. In other terms, they are more likely to be under the control of the ego. [97, p. 6]

In the follow-up study two months after the children's entrance into school, Holmes found that the differences were eradicated and Head Start children had lost their lead. Surprisingly, however, they had not lost their educational gains; the nonparticipants had simply caught up. Holmes's comment was as follows:

> These findings are not surprising. The first two months of this type of experience are so different from the child's experience in the home, that they have a dramatic effect on fantasy, and on behavior. Both the school and the Head Start program, as it was conducted, are primarily organized nursery school play experiences and, as such, have a great deal in common. It is possible that the first two months of school are so dramatic for children who previously have had no such experience that this was, in fact, the worst time for a recomparison. . . . possibly, if tested at the end of the year, the Head Start children would show more consistent growth than the controls, as a function of the previous summer's experience. [97, p. 7]

In the following year the Associated "Y"s carried forward three new six-month Head Start programs, and Holmes and Holmes (103) studied different classes of participants. Their study groups were defined as follows: (1) the *self-referred,* whose families had sought out the program on their own initiative, (2) the *sought-after,* who responded to active reaching-out by the study staff, (3) the *nonparticipants,* who were contacted by staff but did not enroll in the program, and (4) the *controls,* who were nonparticipating middle-class children with no nursery school experience. The researchers found that the self-referred children were more similar to the middle-class children than to either of the other two categories; that the sought-after and nonparticipant children, although somewhat older, did most poorly; and that the middle-class children, even when younger, did better on the cognitive tests than any of the others. Differences found among the parents reflected closely those found among the children. The researchers' experience also impressed them with the importance of personal contact as a device for recruiting potential users of these kinds of programs. They concluded by calling for comparative studies of "class-integrated" versus "100% disadvantaged" programs and for further research into the reliability of teachers' ratings of children.

The growing concern about the educational preparation of the preschool child has also focused attention on the role of the mother in providing learning experiences in the home. Karnes and his associates studied "the effects of short-term parent training as reflected in the intellectual and linguistic development of the children" and found significant differences between the children and their controls on the Stanford-Binet Individual Intelligence Scale (115, p. 174). They concluded:

> Mothers of low educational and low income level can learn to prepare inexpensive educational materials and to acquire skills for using such materials to foster the intellectual and linguistic development of their children at home. [115, p. 182]

The mothers were paid to attend the sessions, were actively involved in the classroom work, and worked closely with visiting teachers.

Finally, Brittain (18) reviewed several studies of preschool enrichment programs and their effects on the children. He found that although most of the studies reported positive gains, there has been a general inconsistency about whether these gains were maintained over time. Many have concluded that the failure to sustain progress is in large measure a function of the isolation of the family from the enrichment experience of the child.

The school deviant. In the last few years public schools in many communities have turned to the small group as an extra-curricular activity for helping children who are having trouble in the classroom. Leadership for these groups has been drawn from many sources: where there are caseworkers in the system they have been asked to broaden their service, group workers have been attracted into a number of school social work departments, neighborhood clinics have been enlisted to provide consultation and leadership, and neighborhood centers and public schools have increasingly been developing working relationships designed to provide the necessary small group skills and leadership. Again, the programmatic development precedes the research and study by many years and the literature is still largely descriptive.

One of the first systematic efforts to study the work in this area came from a research team at the University of Michigan School of Social Work (187, 240). Financed by the national Office of Juvenile Delinquency and Youth Development, the President's Committee on Juvenile Delinquency and Youth Crime, and the National Institute of Mental Health, the researchers studied five public school systems in which group work practitioners were integrated into school social work services to assist malperforming pupils. They began with the proposition that "malperformance patterns should be viewed as *resultants of the interaction of both pupil characteristics and school conditions*" (240, p. 4) and proceeded to study the role of the social workers in the system, the concept of malperformance itself, and the school conditions reflected in the grading patterns, system of sanctions, and dropout phenomena. Among the findings reported were differential and discriminatory grading patterns in the non-college-preparatory curriculum, "a variety of negative sanction to curb malperformance" (187, p. 23), and a disproportionate number of dropouts among boys, blacks, those from working-class families, those with lower IQs, poor readers, low achievers, and those in the non-college-preparatory curriculum. They concluded:

> The findings from this study and demonstration effort provide substantial support for the proposition that pupil malperformance is most usefully viewed as a consequence of adverse school-pupil interactions. Both with-in-school and between-school variations were noted in teachers' perspectives, in group services, in curriculum placement patterns and outcomes, in grading practices, and in pupil careers. . . . The school itself may maintain or even generate the very malperformance it seeks to eliminate by offering limited opportunity for educational attainment . . . by judging pupils adversely because of attributes which are independent of their actions . . . through unwise use of control practices, and by making it exceedingly difficult for the pupil to "find his way back" once he has been defined as a malperformer. [187, p. 26]

Schafer (188) elaborated the theoretical position of this study, offering an "interactional view" that stressed the social definition of malperformance and the self-fulfilling prophecies that develop from the labeling of deviant acts and the enforcement of norms. Finally, the research team produced a "Pupil Behavior Inventory" designed to draw systematic information about teachers' judgments of malperformers' classroom behavior (241). The PBI was first considered as a response to an earlier need of Detroit's Neighborhood Service Organization to classify pupils referred by the schools for problems defined as misbehavior and underachievement.

The most thorough research effort in this category was undoubtedly the well-known *Girls at Vocational High* (149), a study of the effectiveness of social work services in treating "potential problem cases" referred by a school to a social agency. The inclusion of group counseling in the treatment design was of considerable interest to those working with groups in school systems. Since this was an evaluative study, it will be discussed later in the section on evaluations and outcomes.

The family. The literature and research on the family group is growing rapidly, as is the interest of social workers in the family as a unit of service. Lennard and Bernstein offer an entry into this research from the perspective of the "clinical sociologist" (125, pp. 83–141). Leader (124) reviewed some of the major issues confronting the family therapist. And, closest to the immediate concerns of the neighborhood centers, Kraft and Chilman (118) reviewed a number of programs and studies of parental education in low-income families. Hardy's monograph on *The YMCA and the Changing American Family* (82) is an account of one agency's experience in working with families over the past century.

The most recent connections between the neighborhood agencies and family work have been strengthened by Project ENABLE, of which a review was presented in the December 1967 issue of *Social Casework* (144). An acronym for Education and Neighborhood Action for Better Living Environment, the effort began in September 1965 and was "the first nationwide demonstration designed and implemented by voluntary social agencies to be funded by the Office of Economic Opportunity."

> ENABLE was planned as an effort to forge a new tool for reaching and serving families living in poverty by drawing from the combined expertise and resources of three national organizations: the Child Study Association of America, the Family Service Association of America, and the National Urban League. Expertise in parent education through small group discussion, casework knowledge of individual behavior and family relationships, and skill in community organization were joined in a team approach to help parents discover the strengths within themselves and the resources in their communities to change the situations in which they live and rear their children. [144, p. 609]

Rosenblatt and Wiggins (184) interviewed 4,219 participants in the program, 1,644 nonattenders, and 939 persons who had refused participation. They sought to find the extent to which they were reaching low-income parents in greater proportion than had previous programs, whether they were drawing only the more stable segment of the lower-class families, and whether they could find differences between regular attenders and dropouts. They found that ENABLE had indeed reached a client group that was more deprived than those served previously by FSAA and CSA; there was no evidence that the ENABLE program was reaching only the most advantaged sections of the disadvantaged: "Indeed, there is reason to believe that many of the more enterprising neighborhood residents refused to join ENABLE groups" (184, p. 646). And they found that the project was "slightly less successful in retaining as regular members Negroes and Mexican-Americans and persons with less than twelve years of schooling than whites and those with more education" (184, p. 646). Rosenblatt (182) also reported an evaluative study of attitudinal changes among project participants; this will be reviewed later in this chapter.

Out of a demonstration project on Social Group Work with Parents financed by the U.S. Children's Bureau, Glasser and Navarre (72) developed a description of the one-parent family and the structural variables intervening between their poverty and their single-parenthood. They noted that little study has been made of this subject:

> This seems to be a significant omission in view of the major change of the structure of family life in the United States during this century, and the large number of one-parent families classified as poor. [72, p. 98]

These structures are designated as those of task, communication, power, and affection. In drawing implications for policy and practice, the researchers discussed the need for institutionalizing emotional supports, social outlets, task-oriented groups, provision of male figures, and the subsidization of child care and housekeeping services. They also stressed public services aimed at "diverting family dissolution."

The Group As Client

Although there is still little small group research coming out of group work and the neighborhood centers, the academic study of small groups continues to flourish and the body of knowledge to grow. A by-product of this activity is the increased sophistication of the research compilations and reviews themselves as they become more related to specific research problems and dimensions. McGrath and Altman (140), financed by the Behavioral Sciences Division of the Air Force Office of Scientific Research, published a classification system for organizing and synthesizing information on small group research. Their account contained a case history of their nine-year program of study, some perspectives on the small group field, a discussion of specific research relationships tested in a sample of 250 studies reviewed, annotation of those studies, and a comprehensive bibliography of small group studies up to 1962.

Gerard and Miller (68) reviewed the literature of small group research produced between 1963 and 1966 ("the problem of organizing the research on group dynamics remains insoluble"), beginning with a general overview in which they pointed out that

> none of the new ideas that have appeared in the past three years has catalyzed or focused the activities of researchers to the extent that contributions of Sherif, Lewin, Asch, Heider, and Festinger have mobilized effort in the past. [68, p. 288]

The major interest of small group researchers was indicated as still being in the areas of cooperation-competition and interpersonal attraction, and they went on to review studies concentrating on internal group processes (attraction, problem-solving, conformity and social influence, reinforcement effects, and cooperation-competition) and structural characteristics (communication channels, power structure, leadership and membership characteristics).

Among the other important reviews and bibliographies that appeared were Raven's collection of 3,500 items of small group research (173), Deutsch and Krauss's review of theoretical approaches to problems in social psychology (43), Hoffman's summary of the literature on group problem-solving (94), Allen's description of work on the relationship between situational factors and conformity (4), Glanser and Glaser's review of work on communication networks (71) and the regular evaluations and summaries of studies in game theory appearing in the *Journal of Conflict Resolution.* Other reviews will be mentioned later in the context of specific research categories to be discussed.[1]

In recent years two major areas of study have become especially attractive to group work practitioners: (1) the so-called encounter, sensitivity, and T-group phenomena have increasingly found their way into agency practice and (2) systems theory has undergone elaboration as it has been applied to social work practice. In the sensitivity field, Gifford's "Sensitivity Training and Social Work" (69) was a valuable evaluation of applications of, strengths of, and problems involved in using the work in that field. Schein and Bennis (189) and Bradford, Gibb, and Benne (17) have produced comprehensive expositions of the method and the research on which it is based. Bach (7) wrote an account of the marathon group and its assumptions. In the systems field Buckley (24) edited a source book on the subject and Lathrope (121) tried to bring

> the application of systems logic to some of the problems encountered in day-by-day social work practice. . . . In a search for bridging ideas, it [the paper] attempts some guidelines, raises some cautions, lists some advantages, suggests some habits of mind, and investigates some concepts stemming from systems theory. [121, p. 1]

Moving to the research on some specific problems of group process and structure, the following are a few of the studies recently completed and of specific interest to group workers and their agencies:

The individual in the group. Heslin and Dunphy (89) examined 450 small group studies for dimensions relevant to member satisfaction. They found three major variables—status consensus, perception of progress toward group goals, and perceived freedom to participate. Status consensus involved agreement of members about the statuses of the leader and of each other and was facilitated by having a leader who was high on both group task and group maintenance functions. Perceptions of progress facilitated goal attainment, followed by more member satisfaction. And the members felt more satisfaction when there were more—and more fluid—communication channels within the group. Parker (161), working in a locked ward of a Veterans Administration hospital, found that patients with different psychiatric problems used and benefited from groups in certain specific ways varying in quality of contacts, social integration, and social feeling.

---

[1]Some new journals should also be noted: The old *Journal of Abnormal and Social Psychology* was cleft to produce the *Journal of Abnormal Psychology* and the *Journal of Personality and Social Psychology;* the latter is now a primary source for small group research. The *Journal of Applied Behavioral Sciences* is an outlet for work on T-group and sensitivity training, *Transaction* is of a more popular cast, and the *Journal of Experimental Social Psychology* will also be relevant to group workers.

Ganter and Polansky (63) tried to predict a child's suitability for individual treatment from his participation in a diagnostic group. Defining accessibility as capacity for insight, motivation for change, trust in the worker, and freedom to communicate feelings, they found significant differences on some factors and no differences on others. Important were the ability to talk of painful feelings, identification of the clinic's purpose, sustained activity spans, responsiveness to worker controls, and dependence on the group worker. Not significant were amount of verbalization, direction of responses to other children, flexibility of responses, and attractiveness of the child to the worker. They concluded that the potential of the diagnostic group for predicting accessibility to individual treatment was well demonstrated.

Medow and Zander (148) found in a laboratory experiment that "central" members—those whose actions were needed by fellow members in order to move themselves—did exceed peripheral members in task involvement, self-perception as having more responsibility for outcomes, and desire for the successful performance of the group.

Goodchilds and Smith studied "the wit and his group" and found that "the prediction that a wit will have a relatively positive self-image is supported in the first investigation" (73, p. 28). They found that wits were nonconforming and relatively independent of social norms.

Kazzaz (116) studied the role of the "champion of the cause," describing him, in the Bennis and Shepard framework, as counterdependent during the dependency phase and overpersonal during the intimacy phase of group development.

Levinger (130), in the context of the study of complementarity among married couples, found that structural descriptions of the partners' personalities were less significant than describing these people in interaction with each other. Tharp (224), discussing Levinger's comments on this score, reinforced the need for a situational perspective on complementarity, and Gerard and Miller stated:

> The issues involved here reach far beyond the study of the marriage relationship. The fact that such ferment is occurring in the study of dyadic relations may presage a new stimulus-centered look at the broad field of dynamics. [68, p. 297]

Group composition. Problems of group composition were dealt with by Levine (128) and Shalinsky (203) in doctoral dissertations. Levine sought to determine factors related to "interpersonal balance"—when members could be highly attracted to each other and still be free to disagree with each other—and found that age similarity was the only factor related to a desirable state of high-attraction/low-agreement imbalance, except when those under study were married.

Shalinsky (203, 204), in an experimental field study conducted at a children's summer camp, used Schutz's (193) theory of Fundamental Interpersonal Relations Orientations (FIRO) to seek out factors in the relationship between group composition and "selected aspects of group functioning which have relevance for social group work" (204, p. 42). By grouping campers according to Schutz's three basic needs—inclusion, control, and affection—he created groups deemed compatible and incompatible and then used measures to study four aspects of group functioning—interpersonal attraction, attraction to the group, cooperative behavior, and group productivity. He found support for several of his hypotheses: that (1) more of the compatibles liked each other than did the incompatibles, (2) members of the compatible groups tended to see each other as more attractive, (3) groups of compatibles showed more cooperative behavior, and (4) the compatibles were more productive in competitive tasks. Certain subgroup assumptions were not borne out, raising the question of whether subgrouping is actually a phenomenon related to decline in cohesiveness. Shalinsky concluded that his hypotheses were substantially supported and that FIRO theory is valuable as an approach to group composition in group work practice. The work also included a review and discussion of grouping criteria, as these are elaborated in the literature.

Franseth and Koury's (57) survey of grouping research and its relationship to pupil learning is a summary of nationwide studies on grouping practices in the elementary schools. It deals with ability groupings, normal versus increased range of individual differences, some assumptions underlying grouping by ability, sociometric formations, and some philosophical questions raised by the grouping of children for learning purposes.

Patterns of group interaction. Feldman's doctoral research (50, 52), also located in the summer camp setting, sought to relate certain forms of group integration to variables of power, leadership, and conforming behavior. Defining group integration as the social interaction pattern among members, he examined *normative* integration, in which there is a high consensus about group-relevant behavioral norms; *interpersonal* integration, in which the interaction is based on the members' liking for each other; and *functional* integration, based on specialized activities that meet group requirements. His finding of a high correlation between functional and interpersonal integration was an interesting comment on the popular mode of polarizing the expressive and task-oriented functions.

> For the groups studied, it was found that functional integration and interpersonal integration are highly correlated in a positive direction. That is, groups characterized by effective goal attainment, pattern maintenance, and external relations, and in which responsibility for performance of those functions is distributed among many members, tend to be characterized by high degrees of reciprocal liking. Conversely, groups that are relatively ineffective in the performance of such functions, or in which responsibility for their performance has been monopolized by one or a few members, tend to manifest low levels of interpersonal liking. [50, p. 45]

Bjerstedt (15) studied another aspect of group interaction—the "rotation phenomenon"—in which children tend to rotate the responsibility for tasks, showing what Bjerstedt calls a proper respect for social justice and representing an aspect of the children's "interaction competence." He found that the rotation phenomenon was positively related to other forms of interactional competence and could be used as an indicator of such general competence in group interaction.

Group size. On this factor O'Dell (158) found that in formed leaderless groups the pace and pleasure of group interaction increased as the groupings grew from two to five: "The inhibition that characterizes the dyad is shared also by the triad and, to a decreasing degree, by groups of larger size." Indik (108) investigated the relationship between organizational size and member participation and found that "the results confirm the earlier findings that organizational size is significantly negatively related to member participation in our three sets of organizations" (108, p. 345).

Stages of group development. Tuckman (227) reviewed fifty articles on the developmental sequence in small groups, divided them by setting, and suggested a synthesis descriptive of social and interpersonal group activities.

Group cohesiveness. Lott and Lott (135) surveyed the literature of the past fifteen years, examining work on the determinants and consequences of interpersonal attraction. Goodman (74), at the Jewish Community Center in St. Louis, studied the attractiveness of adult groups to their members and found that in groups led by trained social workers, members tended to respond less favorably to the agency and more to the staff, while the reverse was true of groups that were staffed only to render occasional program and administrative assistance.

Group decision-making. Hall and Williams (79) compared procedures used in established and ad hoc groups and found that the latter tended to resolve differences through compromise while the established groups were more creative and "view conflict as symptomatic of unresolved issues." Handlon and Parloff (80) investigated the specific mechanisms that enhance the production of "good" ideas, finding that a low-critical atmosphere does not necessarily produce the ideas but does increase the probability that they will be reported out when they occur.

Group influences. The earlier work by Festinger, Pepitone, and Newcomb (53) on deindividuation in the group had found that people tended to be much less conservative in revealing themselves in a group than when they were alone, and this had considerable interest for group workers. In this tradition, Wallach, Kogan, and Bem (243) studied the "risky-shift" phenomenon, finding that the group process tends to push decisions in a risky, rather than a conservative, direction; group decision-making reduces the responsibility felt by members, who feel a shared responsibility with others. Thus the group tends to risk more, with more chance of failure, than does an individual acting on his own decision. Taking the problem a step further, Alker and

Kogan (3) found, in three studies conducted with women in college sororities, that discussion alone is not a sufficient condition for the risky-shift phenomenon. When groups converged strongly on standardized ethical norms, the shifts tended to become conservative, whereas those groups that achieved consensus on particularistic unethical alternatives showed shifts toward greater risk-taking.

Finally, group workers will be interested in two studies of nonverbal communication. Exline, Gray, and Schuette (49) found situational variations in people's willingness to engage in mutual glances, and Miller, Banks, and Ogawa (150) sought to identify the relationships between feelings and facial expressions.

The Agency

Following the pattern of the chapter in the first volume of this series (199), agency studies will be presented in three categories: attempts to define agency *function,* studies of internal *structure,* and research on the *program* through which agencies carry out their work. Although the output remained meager, there were a few studies that may lead the way toward more disciplined work in this area.

Function

Research on agency function has often been designed to probe the perceptions, or "image," of the agency held by its users and nonusers in the surrounding community. In this tradition, Alcabes (2) devoted his doctoral research to a study of

> differential perceptions and patterns of use of a complex of Neighborhood Centers by the households of one community—the Lower East Side of New York City. The findings bear upon issues arising from a recurrent dialogue between Neighborhood Centers and their critics as to the centers' effectiveness with the slum community they serve. [2, p. 17]

Alcabes sought to discover (1) the social characteristics of community residents who used and did not use the neighborhood centers, (2) the social characteristics of those who discussed important problems with staff as compared with those who did not, and (3) residents' perceptions of the centers as friendly or alien, positive and negative, and the effect of these perceptions on residents' tendency to discuss important problems with staff.

The study was based on data obtained in a larger survey conducted by Mobilization For Youth in 1961 to develop demographic and attitudinal data on the population of the Lower East Side. The area contains eleven large centers and a number of smaller ones adjunctive to churches and synagogues. Alcabes treated this complex of agencies as one center, "as if they constituted one organization with many branches" (2, p. 45). He conducted interviews in 988 of the 1,252 households selected for the MFY survey, a 79 percent completion rate. Measures were developed for determining residents' awareness and use of the center and their problem-sharing processes.

Alcabes found that 80 percent of the households were aware that a center existed nearby, about half of these had made use of the center, and lower-class families were least likely to be aware that the center existed. He also found that the centers were currently in use by about half of those who had ever used them, lower-class blacks were overrepresented among those who continued to use center resources, and users who had no clear conception of agency staff were more likely to drop out. About a third of the current users shared personal, family, or community problems with staff, and the sharers were overrepresented among households in higher socioeconomic classes, those with no grade school children, and persons who had lived in the community for many years. The households most accessible to the centers were those containing adolescent children. Alcabes concluded that the centers showed a "relatively high recruitment efficiency":

> The critics' charge that the Center selectively recruits middle class households or lower class households with middle class mobility orientation is not substantiated by study findings. The study provides evidence that several factors other than class and mobility orientation are important in determining which households are selected by the recruitment process. However, for some phases of the recruitment process, class does produce an effect in the direction charged by Center critics (the higher the class the higher the recruitment). . . .
>
> When the use phases of the recruitment process are considered, charges that the Center over-recruits middle class Whites or lower class households with middle class mobility orientation become untenable. The effect of class or mobility upon Center use is neither strong nor consistently in the expected direction. Two major factors appear most closely related to Center use: length of residence and composition of household. Location and type of housing, and ethnicity also bear some relation to Center use. [2, pp. 158–159]

Alcabes' findings ran counter to the recent tendency, reported in the earlier review (199, pp. 146–148), to describe the disengagement of the neighborhood centers from the most needy segments of the population. As such it should feed the controversy and hopefully stimulate further careful research of this nature.

Levin (126) analyzed a number of "image" studies conducted by Jewish centers in New York City, Newark, Chicago, and Los Angeles. He concluded that there was a "fairly universal consensus" about the differences in perception of agency function between the professionals and members of the community.

> The data suggest to us that anyone who holds the concept that the membership and the community at large see us as primarily a social group work agency which furthers and fosters individual growth and development and enhances and supports Jewish identification and Jewish values is living, like Alice, in a kind of Wonderland. [126, p. 190]

Levin identifies the points of difference as follows: while the professionals stress Jewish identification and personality development, the community sees the agency as a place for recreation and physical activity; while the professionals hold the image of a family agency, the community perceives the center as primarily a service to children; and while the staff members envisage a broad range of educational, cultural, and social activities designed to develop leadership and participation, the adults invest a substantial portion of their involvement in the health club, cultural arts, interest groups, and social groupings. The professional emphasis on social group work is superseded by a trend toward special interest groups, and the stress on Jewish identification produces a situation wherein "our verbalization far exceeds our practice" (126, p. 207). In short, the professionals tend to speak of the center as a way of life rather than as a variety of specific services. Levy (133) has also explored this range of functional images and its "disparities between idealizations and experience of center personnel."

The need of the neighborhood centers to find a vital function in today's intense struggle for racial democracy produced several studies of problems and strategies. Drake (45) surveyed agency programs and practices on race relations for the National Federation of Settlements and Neighborhood Centers (NFS). Moved by criticism of agency paternalism and rigidity, NFS authorized a study that would stimulate local self-assessment and tap five aspects of agency experience: (1) degree of commitment to integration, (2) integration at the board level, (3) integration at the staff level, (4) modes of social action, and (5) their reactions to the "militant mood" within the civil rights movement. Drake took data from 56 agencies in an interview sample and 86 centers in a general sample that responded to mail questionnaires. The report emerged in a series of case presentations and discussions of community conditions and settlement reactions in Atlanta, Chicago, Philadelphia, Rochester, and other cities. It concluded with a set of guidelines designed to provide agency direction and responsibility during periods of "rapid change in race relations."

For the YMCAs Harlow (83) reported a study of the merger process in which black branches were closed as part of a move toward integration with all-white branches. Here again the emphasis was on racial integration, and here too the study report took the form of case discussion. "It follows the sequence of events from an exploration of early catalytic incidents, the factors behind the incidents, and other contributing causes to the actual closing of the Branch" (83, p. 1).

In another YMCA study Foster and Batchelder (55) examined three different modes of "Y" response to the pressure for racial integration—those agencies that adopted open policies and worked to implement them, those that gradually desegregated without any official policy, and those that, in disagreement with the national council, maintained segregated programs and facilities. They found that the agency image held by "Y" leadership was frequently quite different from that perceived by others in the community, that white and black leadership communicated poorly, and that

> many of the YMCA leaders interviewed in this study felt that the YMCA should not practice racial discrimination, but also made it clear that they felt no responsibility for actually achieving racial integration. [55, p. 30]

These were the people who "make no issue of race," but simply "accept people as they come."

The flow of agency self-studies and surveys designed to relate agency resources to community need seems to have narrowed to a trickle; some of these have already been reported in the various categories presented earlier. The Chicago Jewish Community Centers have been engaged in a comprehensive self-study the final report of which has not yet been received. Holmes (98) surveyed parental interest in nursery school services in three New York communities served by Jewish centers; he found the study rewarding, locating a substantial need that had hitherto been unrevealed and identifying some of the conditions under which it could be met.

Structure

Zald's analysis of "organizations as polities," directed specifically to community organization agencies, had many implications for the neighborhood centers (253). "These concepts and propositions are designed to explain some of the determinants of agency processes and, consequently, the styles and problems of professional practice" (253, p. 56). Four interrelated concepts formed the core of his analysis: that (1) organizations have constitutions, (2) these constitutions serve a constituency that is not the clientele but those groups that control the agency and to whom the executive is most responsible, (3) the community organization agency wishes to affect target populations, other organizations, and centers of decision-making, and (4) the community agencies exist among other agencies and have "foreign relations" that can facilitate or impede their goals.

Zald offered a number of testable propositions, among them the following: (1) To the extent that an agency is heavily dependent on its constituency, it is likely to develop a constitution that gives little room for discretion. (2) The greater the knowledge differential between staff and constituency, the more likely that staff autonomy will be great and the constituency consulted only on "boundary" conditions. (3) Middle- and upper-class constituencies are more apt to work by persuasion and informal negotiation, while lower-class-based organizations will more likely resort to direct action, open propaganda, and agitation. (4) The more an agency has a constituency made up of agencies, the more difficult it is to develop commitment to an action program and the more likely that the agency will serve as a clearinghouse for information and coordination. The analysis is provocative and evokes many of the classic problems and frustrations of the neighborhood group-serving agencies. Zald's "sociological reader" on the social welfare institutions (254) will also be a valuable resource for those interested in the structure of neighborhood agencies and its implications for practice.

In somewhat the same vein Warren (246) identified two constituencies in the "community decision organizations": the input constituency consisted of those parties to which the organization owed responsibility in determining its policies and programs and the output constituency was composed of the appropriate targets of service. Warren found that these two populations were often at variance on specific decisions made by a community organization.

The notion of lay sponsors and boards of directors as constituencies to be served rather than as representative bodies responsible to their clients and members is an effort to align some of the old ideas about agency structure with some persistent realities. The concept may stimulate research designed to explain and document some long-standing inconsistencies between theory and practice in the neighborhood agencies.

On the study of boards of directors and their characteristics, Massarik and Okin (146), for the Jewish Centers Association of Los Angeles, developed a portrait of their board members by age, education, occupation, patterns of religious identification, organizational membership, modes of involvement and influence, satisfactions and dissatisfactions with the board member role, and other factors. They found that their board member was not likely to identify with a specific sect or party in the Jewish community, that his influence tended to be localized to the center itself rather than to Jewish community policy in the larger scene, and that he believed strongly that a small central clique made most of the important decisions. They also found that the "exceptionally satisfied" board member was regarded by others as central and that those perceived as near-central were *less* likely to view their role as exceptionally satisfying than those who were clearly on the fringe. The exceptionally satisfied board members were more likely to report that they had frequent contacts with center executive staff. Only about one in five of the board members believed that he had an almost complete understanding of center philosophy and purpose.

Levy, at the Yeshiva University School of Social Work, sought to uncover elements of knowledge and skill "requisite for effective professional practice with social agency boards" (132, p. 6). He did a content analysis of thirteen process records written by as many center executives to describe their work at a single board meeting. The analysis yielded an inventory of issues with which these agency boards are occupied and he was able to identify—and illustrate with record excerpts—a number of helping roles used by the executives in their direct practice with their boards. Levy emerged with a concept of enabling that he felt was close to the helping role as it is generally understood in other groups and other agencies.

Program

Program studies of depth and general applicability are still hard to come by, and there is little cross-fertilization among the agencies except by way of broadly descriptive accounts published in the various house organs. Mogulof (153) tried to take some more specific measures of a program ingredient much discussed in the Jewish centers:

> The observer of the Jewish Center field "knows" that centers vary in their Jewish practices and that communities, agencies and their leader-

> ship also vary. Could this "knowledge" be made specific in the form of hard data? Could patterns of Jewish achievement and patterns of situational variance be linked to each other statistically so as to suggest that their concurrence was not happenstance? [153, p. 102]

He sent a mail questionnaire including 112 items of Jewish practice and questions dealing with selected variable characteristics to 102 Jewish centers. These were centers that were not linked to synagogues, had autonomous boards of directors, and were not located in Canada or in the metropolitan areas of Los Angeles, Chicago, or New York. The Guttman scale procedure was used to analyze the data, the centers were rated on a continuum from low to high level of Jewish practices, and an effort was made to associate these ratings with characteristics of the general community, the Jewish community, the welfare community, the agency, and the agency leadership.

Mogulof found that in communities marked by a profusion of other cultural patterns centers are more likely to distinguish their practices, achieving a higher level of Jewish content. In communities where Jews had a higher representation on the Community Chest than in the general population, the centers were less likely to distinguish their practices. Other high-level indicators were the center's ability to finance its own operations, a high-density Jewish population, and less extensive welfare community contacts by center leadership. Having hypothesized that "center linkage to the welfare community would be associated with relative failure in the achievement of Jewish goals, and linkage to the Jewish community would be associated with their most successful pursuit," Mogulof concluded that "the findings indicate that one must know a good deal more about the Jewish community before hypothesizing that strong linkage to it is associated with higher levels of distinguishing practices" (153, p. 112). He pointed out that the center field may have considerable difficulty accepting the possibility that two of its major goals may be irreconcilable—the strengthening of Jewish practices and the reinforcement of its connections to the social welfare community.

Brodsky (19) developed data on participation of the Jewish community centers in activities related to the urban crisis. He surveyed 73 centers in 61 cities in the United States and found that "a large majority of Jewish Community Center executives believe that involvement of their Centers in appropriate urban-crisis-related activities is a valid expression of Jewish commitment and values." Centers were involved in three ways: (1) direct services to minorities and disadvantaged groups, including Head Start programs, day care centers, tutorial programs, work training opportunities, camping, and intergroup programming, (2) center participation in Community Action Programs, and (3) public affairs programming involving educative and legislative activity.

For the YMCAs Hardy (81) provided a summary of a national study of work with families in which it was discovered that the goals of the program were unclear, there was little lay involvement, and "there is little coordinated effort in bringing the resources of the Association to bear on family needs" (81, p. 2). He provided program-planning and systematic study guidelines for the development of "Y" work with families. Also for the YMCA, Lucci (136) studied the "Y"s' work with college students, examining the extent and distribution of campus work, the characteristics of leaders and members, the religious orientation of the "Y"s, the relationship between college attributes and "Y" effectiveness, and some implications for policies and practices.

The Boy Scouts of America studied nationwide reactions to their Cub Scout program through the perceptions of scoutmasters (201), Webelos den leaders (247), and the den mothers and Cub Scouts themselves (155). It was found that the tenure of Cub Scout leaders is short, that the emphasis of cubmasters and den mothers is focused heavily on ends and goals, that few of the leaders are trained in the courses supplied by the Scouts, and that while most packs operate uniformly in basic organization and activity, there is considerable variation in the wide range of recommended practices.

The ambiguities surrounding the functions and purposes of the neighborhood centers continue to obstruct efforts to study their structures and processes in depth. The formulation of clear research questions and central theoretical issues is still inhibited by unresolved arguments about whether these agencies are meant to serve as social agencies, social movements, class-homogeneous social clubs, or some definable combination of these.

The Community

The community role of the neighborhood centers has been changing rapidly in the past few years. With the growing national emphasis on local action groups, it may in fact be said that the neighborhood center is no longer at the center of its neighborhood. It has, rather, taken its place within a complex of local community services geared to group activity—ranging from the federally financed CAPs to the "neighborhood service centers" to the community mental health programs to other efforts designed to move hitherto detached and isolated services into the streets and alleys of poor urban neighborhoods (35). At the same time the centers themselves have thrown renewed energy into the work outside their own walls, seeking to become more engaged with militant indigenous groups and to take a part in the activism around them. Further, as other community services have involved themselves in working with groups—in public welfare, child guidance clinics, the schools, ghetto hospitals, and others—the old-time neighborhood center monopoly as the group-serving agency has been broken up.

Thus as we begin with the rubrics of the earlier review—*the community survey, selected social problems,* and *measuring need*—it will soon become apparent that these categories no longer yield the results of bygone years. We will then move on to present some of the more recent—and relevant—work dealing with group services in neighborhoods. The research is still thin, but there is much writing and theorizing, and some of this points with promise to lines of investigation for the future. Trying to stay clear of the territory that belongs to the chapter on community organization, we will describe a few studies on problems of *neighborhood organization* from the perspective of the neighborhood centers, and we will conclude with some work dealing with *related neighborhood services.*

The Community Survey

As noted in the earlier review, the large-scale social survey designed to investigate community needs and bring them to the attention of the people was a major social welfare instrument in the early part of the present century. Its use has dwindled in recent years, but agencies continue to survey their populations and communities in more limited ways and for more specific purposes. Holmes (95) discussed his use of such devices in the agencies comprising the Associated YM-YWHAS of Greater New York. Citing the demographic studies undertaken by his staff, he pointed out that these have a kind of "preresearch" character, leading toward more productive research designs.

> There is no study aim save the collection of data descriptive of the broad memberships of the Associated Y's centers. The variables are not conceptualized except in so far as we have a general notion of what to look for in making any demographic study. There are no hypotheses formulated and there are no sampling requirements save the expectation that all members will be represented on the questionnaire. The variables, as such, are uncontrolled; we want to collect descriptive measures, not to control variables. Similarly, there is no research design as such since this is a preparatory survey. [95, pp. 100–101]

Solomon and Friedman (214) summarized the returns of these Associated "Y" studies over the period 1966–68, providing demographic profiles of each of eight centers reporting to them. They included population information on employment status, age, religious education, religious affiliation, attendance at religious services, participation in Jewish organizations, and patterns of center use. Holmes (99) reported a study of Jewish population mobility in a New York City neighborhood. Using telephone and in-person interviews with Jewish families living in the southeast Bronx, he probed attitudes toward the neighborhood, intentions to move out, and views about the construction of a new agency in the community. He found that those who intended to move were young, had children, and were of a high socioeconomic status.

Selected Social Problems

A reading of the literature suggests that this is a time in which more energy is being put into redefining the problems that the agencies should be studying than in the study of the problems themselves. In such periods historical research is a much-needed commodity, and the field has not been prolific in this area. Gans's reading of settlement history to find a new focus for its work (62) created considerable discussion when it appeared (13). Weissman and Heifetz (248) reviewed the history of the country's oldest settlement—University Settlement on New York's Lower East Side—to illustrate the eras of major concern from the early stress on social reform to the "youth-centered approach" to its current participation in the War on Poverty. They end by calling for an "adult-centered program" emphasizing organized community action and the study of social problems on which it is based: "Settlements cannot do everything, but they can do a great deal more for the urban Negro and Puerto Rican adult than simply take care of his children" (248, p. 49).

Hillman's "People, Places, and Participation" (91), part of a study of local community structure and civic participation financed by the National Commission on Urban Problems, was a sociological examination of the problems attached to citizen participation in the urban scene. The study was conducted by the staff of the National Federation of Settlements and Neighborhood Centers and produced a document that discussed the origins, characteristics, and living patterns of people in slum neighborhoods; the values, conditions, and limitations of civic participation; and the "good community," which encompasses five major factors: (1) the absence of nuisances and freedom from physical fear, (2) adequacy and availability of transportation, (3) sufficiency of public services, (4) provision for the enjoyment of leisure, and (5) wide distribution of political power among skilled and competent groups organized for cooperative action.

One of the more significant studies of a specific and growing social problem was Herman and Sadofsky's examination of nine youth-work programs conducted in major cities throughout the country (88).

> After the termination of the work-training programs for youth undertaken during the Great Depression, more than twenty years elapsed before any comparable programs were created to serve the vocational needs of out-of-school, out-of-work, disadvantaged youth. It was only three years ago that the first of this new group of youth-work programs opened its doors. Similar programs were subsequently established in a large number of cities across the country. Many of these programs received their original impetus from the President's Committee on Juvenile Delinquency and Youth Crime as well as support from the Office of Manpower, Automation and Training (OMAT) for their vocational components. [88, p. v]

Using interviews and workshops the authors undertook a broad survey of the problems of operating youth-work programs, reviewing the tasks of planning, setting objectives, dealing with interagency battles for control, staff training, and others. The chapter on research documents some of the difficulties of conducting effective study programs, pointing out:

> All but one of the executives interviewed in this study believed that research had failed to fulfill its functions in respect to the work program. In fact, at the time they were visited, three of the nine work programs studied had not acquired a research capability of any kind. One program had subcontracted its research to a nearby university, which . . . had pro-

> vided useful observations that had been incorporated in the plans for the program's next year of operations. The five remaining work programs had their own research staffs, but these staffs had produced little of value, in the opinion of our respondents. [88, p. 165]

Measuring Need

In the tradition of the "Youth Project Yardstick" reported from the Welfare Council of Metropolitan Los Angeles by Carter and Frank in the early 1950s, as well as other index-building attempts described in the earlier review (199, pp. 166–168), Staley (217) developed a "recreation needs instrument" as part of a 1966 study of recreational needs and services in south-central Los Angeles. He developed a resources index compounded of the number of professional staff hours per year per 1,000 residents in a given neighborhood, acreage of neighborhood recreation centers per 1,000 residents, and the number of centers per 10,000 persons. His need index consisted of figures on a population of 5–19-year-olds, population density, median family income, and juvenile delinquency rate. With the use of a "C-Scale," he developed scores that related needs to resources and established need priorities for recreational services, neighborhood by neighborhood. His report also included a review of similar attempts to measure recreational and youth needs in American cities over the past twenty years.

In the issue of the journal following that in which Staley's article appeared, Hendon (85) raised some important questions about the value of such studies and the actual relationship between human need and recreational programming. He pointed out that the index was designed to determine neighborhood priority claims within a condition of scarcity. However, he asked, what is meant by *need,* and if recreational resources are increased, what has been said about the human problems they are supposed to meet? He stated:

> We do not know precisely what the relationship is between a given recreational program and human development. We do not know because we have had no extensive explorations of the relationship between particular recreation programs and behavior. [85, p. 189]

Hendon called for an exploration of social and psychological attitudes toward programs such as the Little League, behavioral inputs, parental attitudes, the learning processes involved, the impact of the experience, and other factors. He also criticized the study for its restriction to youths, its use of population density as a criterion, and its assumption that recreation is in some way responsive to problems of delinquency. Stating that current recreational conceptions are class bound and emphasize middle-class forms and structures, Hendon concluded that there is little basis on which to plan recreational facilities "until we approach a point where we can say that expanding recreation resources in a particular way will satisfy a particular set of behavioral criteria for the persons affected" (85, p. 191).

Staley's reply in the same issue (218) further sharpened the dichotomy between structural and process-oriented concerns. He denied having asserted that there is a causal relationship between recreational programs and human behavior and stated that the instrument does not promise to eliminate social problems but simply to indicate that needs exist, that certain social characteristics and resources are related to those needs, and that tensions may be reduced through providing recreation in areas of maximum pressure. He pointed out that there are quantitative and qualitative measurements and his index is in the former category. Staley's emphasis on structural solutions—more facilities—and Hendon's insistence on analyzing the nature and quality of these structures bear upon an important issue, one that is rarely examined by any of the human relations professions.

Neighborhood Organization

Neighborhood center professionals have always been interested in the literature on community power structures, perhaps because their agencies have always found it so difficult to mobilize power as an effective instrument of practice. Walton (244) analyzed 33 studies dealing with 55 communities:

> The purpose of this paper is to review a substantial portion of the existing literature on community power in order to identify what generalizations, if any, can be drawn concerning the methodological and substantive correlates of various types of community power structure. [244, p. 430]

He came to several conclusions about the nature of this work, including the proposition that "the type of power structure identified by studies that rely on a single method may well be an artifact of that method" (244, p. 438).

Neighborhood workers will also be interested in Litwak and Meyer's discussion of the relationship between bureaucratic organizations and community primary groups:

> The general problem we wish to discuss is how bureaucratic organizations and external primary groups (such as the family and neighborhood) coordinate their behavior to maximize social control. It will be argued in this paper that mechanisms exist to coordinate the two forms of organizations, and that these mechanisms of coordination can be systematically interpreted by what we will call a "balance theory of coordination." It will also be argued that this "balance theory" provides a formulation to account for current empirical trends more adequately than traditional sociological theories. [134, p. 246]

Running counter to the prevailing theory that bureaucracies and primary groups, and especially the nuclear family, are inherently antithetical in goals and atmosphere, Litwak and Meyer suggest that "these forms of organization are complementary and that each provides necessary means for achieving a given goal" (134, p. 248). Their balance theory states that maximum social control occurs when coordinating mechanisms develop between organizations and primary groups that balance their relationships in such a way that they are neither too intimate nor isolated from each other. Their search of the literature identified eight mechanisms of coordination currently in operation. Among these are the "detached expert approach," typified by the street club worker who bridges the structures of agency and primary group, and the "settlement house approach," in which facilities, proximity, and professional workers establish a "change-inducing milieu." This effort to develop a theoretical orientation to the task of building bridges between people and their organizations is an important contribution to the advocacy-versus-mediation controversy, more often carried on in rhetorical than in scientific terms.

Hillman and Seever (92), of the National Federation of Settlements Training Center, examined the character of neighborhood organization through interviews, questionnaires, and case material drawn from NFS affiliates in 93 cities. The report raised all of the basic questions, examined agency experiences in detail, and offered guidelines for agency practices in the areas of citizen participation and neighborhood organization.

Related Neighborhood Services

The trend toward the location and integration of services in the heart of a neighborhood is the most recent expression of the reaching-out impulse of the last generation. March (145) summarized the shortcomings of present social service distribution and developed four models designed to offer greater neighborhood participation, more highly articulated services, and an extension of service beyond the individual to the family and the neighborhood. The models include centers for advice and referral, diagnostic centers, centers for "one-stop, multipurpose neighborhood service," and coordinated networks of service systems.

Perlman and Jones (166) reviewed the experience of six neighborhood service centers for a definitive HEW publication. They developed a working definition of this kind of agency, including information and referral; advocacy to protect client interests in their use of other agencies; certain concrete services such as legal aid, day care, employment counseling, and others; and the organization of groups for collective action. They also discussed the role of research in these programs, cited the paucity of resources, and questioned, as had Herman and Sadofsky (88) in the youth-work field, the weakness of research in this area.

The community mental health center is another major neighborhood service phenomenon, and its literature has been growing rapidly in the past few years:

1. Vacher (239) reviewed over 45 journals published from 1957 to 1968 and abstracted articles specific to ten major areas of mental health center operation.

2. Roen and his associates (181) developed and validated an instrument designed to measure "community adaptation" and to serve as a tool for the evaluation of community mental health programs. The community adaptation concept, constructed to operationalize the client's interaction with his environment, was geared to wide application.

3. Richart and Millner studied factors affecting admission to a community mental health center and found that the "regulatory influence" of secure social statuses such as parent, spouse, or employee made such people "less likely to become or remain psychiatric patients than those persons with less tangible positions in life" (179, p. 29).

4. Hinkle, Cole, and Oetting described their efforts at the Southeast Wyoming Mental Health Center to make "research and evaluation, which is quite often a 'spare-time' activity in most mental health centers, an integral part of the ongoing program at Cheyenne" (93, p. 130).

5. Peck and Kaplan (164), in a theoretical discussion of the dynamic exchange between individuals and their groups, pointed out that "the small group has the unique property of enabling us to retain sight of the individual in crisis while we try to gain access to those aspects of his social milieu which are concomitantly involved."

6. The *Community Mental Health Journal,* for seven issues between the spring of 1965 and the winter of 1966, carried a "Program Developments" section that focused on built-in research components. The section seems to have been discontinued after that time.

The interest of the traditional public agencies in the use of groups as a medium of service is illustrated most dramatically by the growing involvement of public welfare programs throughout the country. *Public Welfare* used its October 1968 issue to document this development, publishing summaries of programs across the nation and featuring an account by Schwartz (197) of a four-year process designed to integrate group services in the Bureau of Child Welfare of the New York City Department of Welfare (now the Department of Social Services). Subsequently Feldman (51), also in *Public Welfare,* reported on an exploratory study of group service programs instituted by six public welfare agencies, analyzing factors related to the initiation and development of these programs.

The neighborhood center seems to have gained strength rather than lost it from the breakdown of the old group work agency monopoly. As an established member of a new and growing family of group-oriented services, the center should perhaps have had more to teach. But there are signs, of which the Alcabes study (2) is an example, that the advent of the newer services will involve the center in new investigations that will help to pull together its working experiences over the past seventy-five years and draw generalizations from these.

The Worker

A major development of the past few years was the wide interest in paraprofessionals and their contribution to service in the neighborhoods. The literature on the subject is still largely ideological and hortatory, but there is some recent movement toward systematic role appraisal and analysis. This development has had its counterpart in a growing concern about the differential use of professional manpower and there is some work to report in this area. Beyond that there is evidence that the study of practice itself is at last becoming an object of some scientific interest, mostly in the field of doctoral research.

Continuing to stay close to the format of the earlier review, we will report the studies in three categories: those related to paid, full-time *professionals;* work on *non-professionals,* substituting this rubric for "volunteers" and including material on paraprofessionals; and findings from studies of *method* and the nature of group practice. When the data are thin, some of the subrubrics used in the last review will be abandoned.

Professionals

The neighborhood centers have always been sensitive to the possibility that, while they "are apparently well suited to introduce young people into the social work arena [they] may not promise the kind of professional experience that would attract them into the field of service in which they began" (199, p. 172). Pins's finding that their recruitment role yields only a small return was disconcerting (167).

Following this line of inquiry, Greene, Kasdan, and Segal (76) probed the attitudes toward Jewish center careers of Jewish second-year group work students who had been placed in centers during their first year of training. Thirty-one students in six graduate schools of social work in the New York metropolitan area served as respondents, and the researchers found considerable disaffection: only half of the students felt that the center's goals and purposes were made explicit to staff, three-quarters felt the agencies were unclear in their purpose, more than half felt that social group work principles played little or no part in program-planning, there was a good deal of rejection of and ambivalence about Jewish programming, and they found the social work role in the center confusing and wanted more direct practice by professional staff. The authors concluded that "the Jewish Community Center has to become a more exciting and dynamic setting if it is to attract professional social workers" (76, p. 175).

Related to this area of investigation is the study of occupational mobility, and Scotch (200) built his doctoral research on some problems opened up by Herman (86) in the latter's 1959 study of the mobility of Jewish community center professionals. Scotch pointed out that when Herman did his study the turnover problem in the Jewish center field was an internal one; the field, "in effect, was a closed system of employment" and when a worker left one job he moved to another in the same field. More recently workers are tending to leave the field:

> The annual rate of movement is on the increase, thus shrinking the total number of workers with MSW's. The circulation pattern of workers in the field of social work is virtually one way in terms of movement of workers away from the JCCF [Jewish community center field] with no reciprocal exchange. The future plans of those now working in the JCCF with reference to career commitment would indicate further dwindling of the MSW segment of the JCCF work force to an increasingly smaller percentage. [200, p. 2]

Scotch studied all the graduate social workers employed by the Jewish Community Centers of Chicago for three months or more during the period from 1947 through June of 1967. He was able to enlist all but one of a total population of 141, giving him a response rate of close to 100 percent. Scotch found that the one-way movement of trained social workers out of the Jewish center field "is not so much a product of disenchantment with the JCCF as such but rather, the recent emergence of a number of highly competitive alternative career opportunities" (200, p. 8). Other factors were the newer social work emphasis on institutional change, the emergence of community organization as a more attractive area of work, the shift in emphasis to treatment and problem-solving practice rather than "preventive goals," and the problems of financing professional education.

On the matter of professional manpower utilization, the YMCA's "Preparing for the Seventies" called for a study of their total manpower development program "in view of the crisis in employed leadership" (169, p. 6). Holmes (101), for the Staff Utilization Committee of the Manpower Commission of the National Jewish Welfare Board, interviewed 44 staff members at different levels in eight centers of various sizes in five different states. He found that professional personnel tended to feel that a disproportionate amount of time was required for administrative tasks and not enough for professional activity of appropriate scope and depth, "thus reducing the workers' over-all effectiveness as professionals" (101, p. 36). The committee also produced a number of other studies, all of which are pulled together and summarized by Warach (245).

Nonprofessionals

Books about and anthologies of material on the indigenous nonprofessional have been multiplying, and those by Pearl and Riessman (163), Reiff and Riessman (174), and Grosser, Henry, and Kelley (78) may serve as entries into this field of study. Seidler's paper on the supervision of nonprofessionals (202), prepared as part of an NFS study for the National Commission on Urban Problems, is a good brief introduction to the tasks of incorporating these workers into agency services.

Sobey devoted her doctoral research to a survey of 185 NIMH-financed projects using over 10,000 nonprofessionals; her inquiry was concerned "with the nature, the extent, and the consequences of use of nonprofessionally trained persons in a particular group of projects funded for the purpose of experimenting in new manpower uses" (211, p. 1). The settings ranged "from isolated state mental hospitals to central city community centers, schools and social agencies caring for the young and old, the mentally ill, and those highly vulnerable to emotional disturbance," and the study questions included extent of use, titles, ratio to professional staff, and characteristics of age, sex, race, and educational level, among others. Combining interviews and site visits, she produced a comprehensive array of findings, including the following: the largest single group of projects (39 percent) were in the psychiatric hospitals, paid and volunteer nonprofessionals were represented about equally, the majority of the projects produced a 6:1 ratio favoring nonprofessionals, adults and young adults predominated with limited use made of adolescents and the aged, and the majority of workers were high school graduates, making those with less education an important untapped manpower resource.

Sobey concluded that the boundary lines between the mental health disciplines, as well as the traditional divisions between professional and nonprofessional functions, are blurring. Also less distinct are the lines between the various nonprofessional aide groups; they are all "performing caretaking, therapeutic and community-oriented functions with little evidence of concern that they are moving out of their traditional roles" (211, p. 286). Sobey (212) added another valuable resource with her annotated bibliography on volunteer services in mental health from 1955 to 1969; her introduction gave a historical perspective on voluntarism, some current trends in the field, and the scope of the bibliography. Her book on the "nonprofessional revolution" in mental health is in press at this writing (210).

Some research has begun on role analysis of the indigenous nonprofessional; research on this has, in fact, begun much more quickly than similar investigations in the heyday of the volunteer. Levinson and Schiller (131) conceptualized the agency structure as a three-level pyramid with forms of participation at each level; they identified the key issues as classification of nonprofessionals, simplification and standardization of social work tasks, and the attempt to connect the "discrepant roles" emerging from where the indigenous nonprofessional is heading and the point from which he left.

Gannon (61) examined the nonprofessional role as it was defined by a group of indigenous workers in the Domestic Peace Corps program of the Harlem community in New York City (HDPC). The HDPC was engaged in the recruitment and training of nonprofessionals to work in the social service agencies of central Harlem. From 150 corpsmen and about half of the agencies served, they drew a clear picture of worker aspirations and role implications: the most common reason given for joining was career advancement, the most common response to questions about life satisfaction was related to career and occupation, the most frequent criticisms of HDPC were the low pay and limitation of work hours, and there was dissatisfaction about the quality of the relationship with the professionals. The status of indigenous personnel was poorly defined and seemed to lead to undesirable consequences:

> A source of strain for most workers was the ambivalence within the structure of HDPC regarding the volunteer or employee status of the Corpsmen. This was reflected in difficulties over wages, job benefits and transferring to another job after one's term of service with the Corps is finished. [61, p. 359]

Grosser (77), at MFY, administered a survey questionnaire on perceptions of the neighborhood to community residents, MFY professionals, and indigenous staff workers, with all staff members being asked to predict how the residents would answer the questions. He found that the professionals differed from the residents on many issues related to deprivation, the professionals were most optimistic about the efficacy of social action, the community residents were most optimistic about the chances for success of individual poor persons, indigenous staff perceptions were closer to those of the community residents than were those of the professionals, and the indigenous staff members predicted the responses of community residents more accurately than did the professionals.

Grosser also found, however, that although indigenous staff responses were more like those of the residents than were those of the professionals, on a high proportion of items the indigenous workers were also closer to the professionals than they were to the residents. This suggested that those selected to work in a professional agency were in many ways more like the middle-class professional than the lower-class client. This finding, similar in some important ways to Gannon's data on the Harlem corpsmen, has implications for those who see the "para" as a step toward becoming "professional" rather than as a fixed and permanent role—a "career for the poor."

Specht, Hawkins, and McGee (215), in the Community Development Demonstration Project of Richmond, California, made an important contribution to role and skill analysis when they required all of their "subprofessionals" to keep casebooks of their daily work. The examination of these materials was informal but yielded beginning information on the subprofessionals' tasks, the institutional contacts they were making, and the kinds of skills they were called on to exercise. The researchers found that these workers were required to use skills in interviewing, diagnosis, referral, advocacy, and "brokerage," and often served as a bridge between clients and the institutions. The authors called for more precise means of measuring skills and competence, lest a large number of subprofessional workers be backed into low-paying and unrewarding jobs no matter how great their increasing abilities.

Moving from the indigenous nonprofessional to the more classic frame of reference of the volunteer, several studies explored the roles and characteristics of this category of personnel. Cantor (27), for the Research and Demonstration Center of the Columbia University School of Social Work, followed 111 VISTA Volunteers from the beginning of training through their first four months in jobs located in forty-three different urban projects across the nation. These volunteers, selected randomly by the Washington office from a pool of eligible applicants, were almost all 25 years old and under (90 percent), with two-thirds ranging in age from 20 to 23; girls slightly outnumbered boys; most were white, single, and came from affluent middle-class backgrounds; they were college educated and some had advanced professional training; most had parents who were managers, professionals, and semiprofessionals. On their VISTA jobs the volunteers worked mainly with blacks, children, and young people, and they served in several ways:

> as *bridges* between the ghetto and the world outside; as *catalysts* activating neighbors in social action; as *service agents* giving concrete

> help to individuals and groups; as *innovators* and *gadflies* within the agency trying out new services, criticizing the status quo; and as *symbols* of mobility and concern offering a contact with the outside world. [27, p. 5]

Although somewhat over half indicated that their satisfactions outweighed their frustrations, "almost all had some frustration to tell":

> The major frustrations the volunteers reported . . . related to the nature of their job, agency, relationships with clients and their own personal misgivings. As noted, many Volunteers came to their agencies with the preconception that a VISTA job involved going into the homes and organizing for social action. They were uneasy about their service jobs. Others were concerned with the fact that they did not see immediate results. Some felt that they were not fully utilized or that the agency was too structured and limiting. Volunteers were less bothered by their own agencies than by the fact that other agencies in the community blocked action or did not do their jobs. [27, pp. 44–45]

There were other findings, related to on-the-job training, use of available staff in different ways, supervision, and the impact of neighborhood conditions on the volunteers. "VISTA Volunteers are in no sense indigenous workers" and "culture shock is as real for most VISTA Volunteers as for Peace Corpsmen" (27, p. 47).

Schwartz (194), in a doctoral study, surveyed the volunteer program of the Associated YM-YWHAS of Greater New York, examining the nature of volunteer service, the satisfactions derived from the work, and volunteers' role perceptions together with those of the professional staff. She found:

> The volunteer does not go to the Y primarily to carry out the aims of the agency. He or she goes to satisfy personal purposes related to personal development and education. He is happy to do this while helping the agency, but he is likely to judge the Center on the basis of how well the volunteer program serves him. [194, p. 83]

Schwartz also found that staff members higher up in the hierarchy tended to express more appreciation for the volunteer's contribution, but "these were not the staff members who most frequently worked with volunteers or had the most contact" with them (194, p. 85).

Johnson (112) studied the use of volunteers in community service in North Carolina, developing data on motivation, characteristics, specific contributions, the role of retired and lower income groups, relationships with professional staff persons, and staff willingness to use volunteers in the expansion of social services. Carp (29) investigated the differences among volunteers, older workers, and nonworkers in a population of applicants for public housing for the aged. She found that workers scored as being happier and more self-satisfied than either volunteers or nonworkers on all measures.

> The results suggest that, if volunteer service is to become an effective substitute for work, attention must be paid not only to its time-filling,

time-scheduling activity and sociability components, but also to the purchasing power and the social value inherent in payment. [29, p. 501]

Method

There are signs that the long-awaited interest in the study of practice has begun to appear, both in social work and in related professions. In the field of education Gage (59) edited a superb collection of research pieces on the practice of teaching from which all of the helping professions can learn a great deal. Gage's own chapter on paradigms of research on the teaching process (60) and Broudy's analysis of the historical development of pedagogical concepts (21) are of particular interest to social workers seeking ways of approaching the study of the helping process in groups. Of interest too will be Strupp and Bergin's bibliography of 2,741 items of research in individual psychotherapy, with a major emphasis on studies using a research design and reporting quantitative results (219). They pointed out that "the growth of the field is documented by the fact that the earlier compilation [published by Strupp in 1964] included about 1,000 references whereas the present one, four years later, lists almost three times that number" (219, p. v). The bibliography is indexed by content categories, using rubrics of client, method, and process, among others.

In social work a growing body of doctoral students has begun to produce some fairly substantial contributions to the study of practice with groups. Fresh from their own practice in the neighborhood centers and other settings, many have turned their curiosity loose on problems of method and the output is beginning to mount. Without trying to do a comprehensive review, the writer will describe briefly a few of these studies to give some sense of the kinds of problems they are undertaking.

Garvin (66, 67) investigated the effects of "contractual agreement" between workers and their group members on reciprocal obligations and the role of the worker. Defining contract as "a set of agreements between the worker and the group members regarding the problems to be dealt with in their interaction as well as the means to be utilized in this process" (67, p. 127), he hypothesized that high agreement between workers and members would be associated with a higher quality of performance by both. He found that although all of the variances could not be explained in contractual terms, "the over-all conclusion of this study is that the existence of the 'contract' . . . is an important correlate of worker activity and group movement" (67, p. 145). Brown (22), also working on the contract theme—which promises to become an increasingly popular research subject—found that early attention by the worker to the problem of mutual expectations seemed to produce significant reductions in the amount of time spent on testing, allowing the groups to move to their work more rapidly.

Horowitz (106) and Morgan (154) worked to define the specific techniques of intervention used by social workers in group situations. Horowitz explored the reactions of group workers to hypothetical instances of deviant behavior and tried to trace the effects of selected variables on the workers' projected behavior; he found that his "Study Model" was a useful instrument for differentiating dimensions of worker behavior. Of considerable interest too was the fact that he could derive no meaningful differences between socialization and treatment groups; a high consensus was found on the modes of intervention for the two types. Morgan, analyzing critical incidents reported by professionally trained workers in a New York City neighborhood center, developed a classification system of interventive techniques used with groups and with individuals in groups.

Other method-oriented doctoral investigations were reported by Cleminger (36), who studied group workers' skill in assessing their members' perception of the worker's role (an aspect also related to the contractual theme); Pierce (165), who developed and tested some conceptual models of elements of group practice; Ishikawa (110), who investigated three variables of group workers' verbal acts through time—to whom they were addressed, the nature of the problem situation, and the group resources called on; and Lawrence (122), who, in the classic "leadership style" line of inquiry, tested the effects of group-directed versus worker-directed approaches toward changing the food-buying practices of welfare recipients.

Mention should also be made of a master's degree thesis produced by Agueros and eight associates at the Columbia University School of Social Work (1). Using an analytical instrument previously devised by Schwartz (198), these students isolated and classified over 500 specific helping acts reported by group workers, caseworkers, and community organization practitioners in three statuses—untrained, student, and professional—thus creating nine categories for study and comparison. They stated:

> The attempt is also made to develop some understanding of the complex of factors in which these acts are embedded: to whom they are addressed, the stimuli that set them off, workers' modes of interpreting these stimuli, the hoped-for client responses, and the kinds of assumptions on which these acts are based. The total effort is designed to see as deeply as we can into the detailed events of the helping process, as these events are perceived by the social workers themselves. [1, p. 25]

Comparing the nine worker categories on each of the variables mentioned, the researchers produced a host of subtle and suggestive findings: caseworkers, with high internal consistency among the three degrees of training, were triggered by feeling stimuli significantly more than were group or community workers; group workers tended to be highly susceptible to nonverbal stimuli; the acts of community organization workers tended to be less feeling oriented and more related to advising their clients and providing information intended to be useful; untrained workers were highest on the dimension of directive acts; the three student categories were the most internally consistent in their responses; professionals tended to produce interpretations that related strongly to clients' perceptions of their own situations and to clients' avoidance patterns. In their conclusion the students raised questions about whether the various methods (group work, casework, and community organization) are in some way geared to producing different work-styles, the relationship between work-style and personal styles, and the possibility of effecting comparisons between the workers' and clients' conceptions of what constitutes a helping act. The study also offered a review of the practice research literature and an annotated bibliography of practice studies in social work and related disciplines.

Other studies of group practice were reported from a number of different agency settings. Klein and Snyder (117) studied the work-style phenomenon in the context of gang work, examining the practice of ten detached workers assigned by the Los Angeles Probation Department to the most active gang neighborhoods in the county. They found that interworker variability on practice and the use of time was high, and they concluded that "the agency must build into its structure and program a system for tolerating variability in worker styles." (p. 68.)

Gilbert (70) reported a study of the role of the neighborhood coordinator in the CAP sponsored by the Pittsburgh Mayor's Committee on Human Resources. He probed the question of whether these coordinators were advocates or, as Rein and Riessman (175) had put it, "the cement that binds distributors and consumers," or whether "they operate in a vague shadowland somewhere between these two" (70, p. 136). The study examined these stances carefully and operationally and concluded:

> The coordinators have mastered the essential political and social tools for operating under conflicting pressures in the public spotlight . . . [they] walk the tightrope between advocate and middleman . . . [and] to maintain this balance, they become masters at negotiation, accommodation, and manipulation of citizens and agency staff. [70, p. 144]

From the mental hospital field Yalom and his associates contributed to the research on the contract theme by showing that "anxiety stemming from unclarity of the group task, process, and role expectations in the early meetings of the therapy group may, in fact, be a deterrent to effective therapy" (251, p. 426), and that pretherapy preparatory sessions were able to reduce much of this anxiety. Also from the psychiatric setting, Becker and his associates (10) studied the differences between led and unled therapy groups and found that in the smaller groupings

> the presence of a high-status leader, such as a psychotherapist, leads to less spontaneity, more self-consciousness, and more inhibition. . . . When the size of the group was increased and the role of the participants changed by adding family members to the groups, the inhibiting effect of the therapist's presence was modified, making the activity level of the meetings similar, in some ways, to that of unled group meetings. [10, p. 50]

In a VA hospital in Houston, Rothaus, Johnson, and Lyle (186) assigned 49 psychiatric patients to group discussion roles either similar to their usual behavior (role repetition) or opposite to their usual behavior (role reversal).

They found that passive patients found the role reversal process most difficult, but that role reversal resulted in the greatest feeling of satisfaction for all participants. Further, those assigned to active roles felt more responsible for the group than those assigned to silent ones.

From the camping field Ramsey (172) tested a program designed to produce social and interpersonal activity among mental patients selected from the Texas state mental hospital system. The program was designed to implement the concept that the social structure and processes of the patient community are the essential treatment agents, and Ramsey found a high degree of corroboration for this theory in his examination of worker-patient relations and in his follow-up studies. Levine (129), for the Mental Hygiene Clinic of Henry Street Settlement in New York City, studied the clinic's program of "treatment in the home" and found that efforts to bring mental health skills into the homes of multiproblem families did effect changes in the ways in which parents responded to their children, as well as leading to improved behavior in the children.

On the classic directive-nondirective dimension, Shaw and Blum (205) worked with ninety male undergraduates assigned to eighteen five-member groups. On the same three tasks, nine groups worked under directive leadership and nine under nondirective. The researchers reported:

> This experiment shows clearly that directive leadership is more effective than nondirective when the task is highly structured, that is, when there is only one solution and one way of obtaining this solution. . . . However, on tasks that require varied information and approaches, nondirective leadership is clearly more effective. On such tasks the requirements for leadership are great. Contributions from all members must be encouraged and this requires motivating, advising, rewarding, giving support—in short, nondirective leadership. [205, p. 241]

Thomas (225) and Bruck (23) offered points of departure for the developing study of behavioral approaches to social work practice, both individually and in groups. Thomas related to social work practice the techniques of positive reinforcement, extinction, differential reinforcement, response-shaping, and punishment, and attacked the "mistaken conceptions" that associate such techniques with manipulation and mechanism: "Knowledge is itself ethically neutral and values become engaged only when knowledge is used" (225, p. 25).

Bruck's review of the theory and practice of behavior modification defined the basic tenets "accepted by most behaviorists," evaluated their claims of success, discussed their conception of the individual and the meaning of neurosis, and pointed up some areas of applicability to social work practice. The language of these theorists is strange to most social workers and the frame of reference difficult to handle, but the controversy has grown increasingly lively and may soon produce some valuable practice research in social work as it has in related fields.

The systematic study of practice recording is still in its infancy. Wakeman (242), working out of the Seattle Atlantic Street Center, used high-speed computers to analyze the quality of street worker activity.

> While the keeping of narrative, process, and summary records has served a very useful purpose—and probably always will remain an intrinsic part of the social work education process—the recent and burgeoning development of high-speed computers has introduced a new means for recording social work activity. [242, p. 54]

Garfield and Irizarry (64) described their use of an instrument—the "Record of Service"—that was designed to draw from the worker an account encompassing both the specific focus of his service and the techniques used in carrying it out. From the University of Michigan School of Social Work a Practice Skill Assessment Instrument was offered that gives "quantitative measures of selected aspects of student performance in field instruction" (238). And Shulman's *A Casebook of Social Work with Groups* (207) represented a rare effort to use record materials as a teaching-learning bridge between theory and practice in the helping process. His twenty-seven "interactional techniques" are drawn from theoretical models and illustrated by written accounts of practice.

Concluding with the area of training and supervision, the annotated bibliographies issued by the U.S. Public Health Service on training methodology (234, 235, 236, 237) and on in-service training for key professionals in community mental health (230, 231) have already been mentioned. The neighborhood centers will also be interested in the research reported by the Boys' Clubs of America on their "executive program"—a nationwide effort to establish in-service training for executive and supervisory personnel (176, 177). On a theoretical level, French and his associates (58) systematically applied Homans's formulation on the human group (105) to problems of staff training in group service agencies. Pointing out that

> theory to guide social work practice will develop more rapidly and productively by building on theoretical efforts going forward in the underlying sciences of human behavior, rather than by formulating theory primarily on the basis of observation and analysis of practice [58, p. 379],

they held the Homans frame of reference up against a training program for camp counselors, clerical staff relationships in a group work agency, and the pattern of professional versus volunteer staffing in a community center.

Evaluations and Outcomes

In this final category the picture is that of a few rigorous efforts in a fairly unproductive field. Herman's (87) discussion of the problems of evaluating work training programs for unemployed youths cited the general frustrations of defining criteria of success, using researchers who are unfamiliar with the programs and hence unable to establish the proper categories for data collection, the scientific interest in "basic" research that often obscures the curiosity about specific program data and statistics, and the problems involved in generating reasonable conclusions from specific events.

Brooks (20) described the evaluation process in CAPs, identifying the tasks of determining the extent of goal achievement, fixing the relative importance of the program's key variables, and distinguishing these from variables external to the program and active on it. He also defined levels of evaluation and discussed the various constraints on evaluative research: the long-standing tensions between action and research; the arbitrary boundaries that separate the social sciences from one another; the ethical necessity for the feedback of findings into the program itself, thus changing the very phenomena under study as they are being studied; the brief life expectancies of most projects, creating a pressure for quick results; and the openness of the systems under study, where "the community is *not* a laboratory in which all the variables can be carefully controlled and manipulated at will" (20, p. 39).

It seems fairly clear at this point that the antipoverty programs have failed to live up to the research promises embedded in their grants. However, it may be that the adding-up is still going on and that more productive statements will be forthcoming as many of these projects draw to a close.

Movement Studies

From the Chicago Youth Development Project, Caplan (28) has offered what seems to be a landmark attempt to integrate the study of outcomes and processes so that one may understand the relationship between the two.

> The present study is less concerned with outcome effects as such than it is with the process of behavioral change and with factors that regulate the course of such change through time among subjects involved in a treatment intervention project. Specifically, the major point of interest is the change in behavior of youth who are exposed to a program of counseling and pragmatic help designed to improve their personal and social adjustment; how they change over time; the relationship of behavior changes to program input; and how client and treatment agent behavior are affected by the very interaction system they create. [28, p. 64]

The subjects were 109 inner-city boys being counseled by three experienced street gang workers; each boy was at Stage 5 or above of an eight-stage program adjustment scale developed for an earlier investigation. Going up the scale, Stage 5 was "receptivity to personal counseling," Stage 6 was the ability to demonstrate "meaningful relationship" with the worker, Stage 7 involved "commitment and preparation for change," and Stage 8 called for "transfer and autonomy" (the success stage and the final, rather than instrumental, goal). The variations of treatment input were measured on a "Blood, Sweat, and Tears (BST) Scale," operationalized on six points extending from "minimal worker input" involving only routine recreational and social services to "the supreme effort," calling for a high degree of intimacy and an intensive work level.

The researchers found, as they had in a previous investigation, a striking "near-success pile-up" with 71 percent of the boys in Stages 6 and 7 one year after Stage 5 classification; only 7 percent were in Stage 8 at that time. The study then took some ingenious and creative directions as the researchers turned to explore the "near-success" phenomenon. Was Stage 8 disproportionately small because the study ended too soon for the "additive change model to produce its final summation effects"? The data showed that 89 percent of the subjects had moved to a numerically higher stage through time; however, after Stage 7 the movement was *negative* and there was a backsliding effect followed by a "rebound phase" in which the boys' movement headed back toward Stage 7. Thus it was not a question of time: "in fact, Stage 8 classification after the initial progress through the adjustment stages, became increasingly *less* likely with each successive iteration of the backsliding orders" (28, p. 77).

After further analysis of the complex factors affecting the tendency *nearly* to succeed in taking on the "final change behaviors advocated by the treatment program," Caplan suggested that "instrumental changes proceed independently of or are basically incompatible with the final objectives they are designed to produce." The youngsters can be reached, but "because of the services and favors proffered, there may be considerably more advantage in being 'reached' repeatedly than in being changed" (28, p. 83). And again: "The subjects seemed to have a special affinity for accepting help and a special disaffinity for 'success' in terms of those behaviors which the program ideally wished to produce" (28, p. 85).

Although Caplan noted that "there may be good reason for the [client's] unwillingness to adapt to the external demands required for program success" (28, p. 85), it seemed clear that there was inadequate recognition of the fact that the failure of Stage 8 was a function of the success criteria themselves rather than of the treatment process. If one stopped short of the global and overreaching claims often established for client-worker success, the so-called near-success stage could be accepted as a far more realistic appraisal of what can be achieved by the professional helping process. It seemed clear that in this instance the boys' positive moves were related to stages that reflected the workers' desire to *help;* as soon as the workers began to try to *change* their clients into socially acceptable models (Stage 8), the boys rebelled and forced the workers to persist in their helping behavior. Caplan's interest in the processes of work is stimulating throughout: at one point he draws a fascinating picture of a kind of *folie à deux* between worker and client in which each is "creature and creator of a self-perpetuating drama built upon an interweaving of reciprocal interaction effects" (28, p. 86).

Although not strictly in this category, Maas's (137) inquiry into the connections between preadolescent peer relations and the adult capacity for intimacy would be relevant here. Using the files of a longitudinal study of

248 children born in Berkeley in 1928 and 1929 who were assessed periodically from infancy through adolescence and again at age 30, Maas selected 44 adults who were judged to be at either end of a continuum of capacity-incapacity for intimacy. Evidence of adult capacity for intimacy was the scored distributions on two items of the 100-item California Q-sort deck: Item 35 on warmth, capacity for close relationships, and compassion; and Item 48 on "keeps people at a distance" and "avoids close interpersonal relationships." Independent sorting by two judges, using a third in instances of low agreement, and a search for clearly contrasting cases yielded selection of 22 males (10 "warm" and 12 "aloof") and 22 females (14 warm and 8 aloof). Maas then analyzed the preadolescent peer relations of these men and women. The data were derived from interviews conducted with the subjects during their school years.

Maas found the following:

> There are enduring friendships during preadolescence in both male subsamples—the warm and the aloof. In other aspects of the composition of the peer networks, however, there are notable differences between the warm and the aloof males, and differences in the nature of their interaction with peers. [137, p. 165]

Warm males who had a "chum" had only one, while aloof males tended to have two in sequence, with much evidence of "spoiled friendships" in the aloof male subsample. Warm males tended to have relationships with age-peers and older boys, while aloof males tended to move toward those younger than themselves. Warm males named girls as playmates, while aloof males did not. And aloof males tended to be critical, pejorative, and controlling, explaining somewhat their preference for younger boys. Among the females Maas found fewer differentiating antecedents. The major differences between the warm and aloof females lay in their early attitudes toward boys and in the number of playmates they had at age 12, with a lessening number for the aloof females by that age.

Maas concluded that there were different preadolescent contexts for males and females in developing the capacity for adult intimacy. For the males it seemed to be associated with constancy of enduring friendships, early familiarity with girls, less superordination and rivalry, and being sought after by high-status peers. For the females it was associated with early outgoingness with boys and a large and constant number of playmates. The evidence seemed to support theory on preadolescents' capacity for close and enduring friendships; however, it did not support the proposition that having a preadolescent chum is an essential precondition for the development of the adult capacity for intimacy. Rather, it was the *spoiling* of such friendships that seemed to characterize the aloof adult males. Maas also found that in the larger peer networks reciprocity and collaboration were least characteristic of the aloof males. He concluded with a reminder that he was not trying to establish

> causal connections between these antecedent and subsequent human conditions. Many factors, such as temperament, the age of sexual maturity,

> family relations, and subcultural socialization, not touched on in this paper, probably contribute to the nature of interpersonal relations with peers in both preadolescent and adulthood. [137, p. 172]

Craig and Furst (40) studied the outcomes of boys for whom predictions of future delinquency had been made using the Glueck Social Prediction Table. Those who were judged to have a 50 percent or greater chance of becoming delinquent had been referred for treatment at a child guidance clinic, and these 29 boys and their families had been in therapy over a four-year period. The researchers found few differences between the treatment and the control groups, except that the average age of declared delinquency was two years higher in the treatment group. They concluded:

> This study offers no encouragement for the hope that child guidance therapy offers a means of materially reducing the incidence of serious delinquency in a population of boys selected by the Glueck Social Prediction Table. [40, p. 171]

Macdonald (139) reviewed the New York City Youth Board's test of the table itself, examining both its original and its revised forms in the light of its demonstrated usefulness over the years. She concluded that "high predictive power was not demonstrated by the first table and has not been shown for the new one" (139, p. 182). Further:

> Whether any screening device to identify future delinquents could be used effectively and with proper safeguards remains to be seen. Certainly, effective help for all children when they need help is a more desirable objective. Certainly we now know more about identifying troubled children than about helping them. Clearly the Youth Board's publication of a "Manual" is premature, if not irresponsible, promotion of a screening device that has not yet been proved. [139, p. 182]

From Nashville, McLarnan and Fryer (141) reported on the second year of a research and demonstration project sponsored by the University of Tennessee School of Social Work and the Wesley House Centers and financed by the U.S. Public Health Service. The project was designed

> to help young married couples who are residents in low-rent public housing complexes improve in their performance of family roles. . . . Social group work was selected as the primary method of social work to be used in the demonstration project. Social casework and informal education services were included as additional means of effecting change. [141, p. 1]

The interim report encompassed dimensions of group structure, norms, program, worker function, individualization, and some problems of establishing a clear contract for work.

Program Evaluation

It is beyond the scope of this chapter to render a detailed description of the controversial study by Meyer, Borgatta, and Jones of *Girls at Vocational High* (149). Reviews and discussions abound, ranging from that in the *Washington Post* of March 17, 1966, stating that social workers were "writhing" under the "challenge to their work," to the technical professional reviews of Macdonald (138), Schorr (190), and others. The authors introduced the study rationale and objectives as follows:

> This book describes a study of the consequences of providing social work services to high school girls whose record of earlier performance and behavior at school revealed them to be potentially deviant. Over the course of four years girls with potential problems who entered a vocational high school in New York City were identified from information available to the school. From this pool of students a random sample of cases was referred to an agency where they were offered casework or group counseling services by professional social workers. A control group was also selected at random from the same pool of potential problem cases in order that a comparison could be made between girls who received service and similar girls who did not. Since all these girls were identified as potential problem cases, they may be considered latent or early detected deviants. Services to them consisted in efforts to interrupt deviant careers. [149, p. 15]

The group aspects of the treatment program were somewhat clouded in the authors' description and it is often difficult to understand exactly what happened; apparently the consultants were changed and the groups re-formed, following which there was "almost exclusive use of group approaches after the first phase of the project" (149, p. 149). There are no record excerpts given on which to base any judgments about the quality of individual or group techniques, but the evidence seems clear that both the initial referrals and the "contracts" were vague:

> The specific nature and etiology of their problems were not known at the time of selection and referral. There was no indication of how the girls felt about their problems or whether they were willing or able to attempt to find new and more constructive ways of coping with them. [149, p. 119]

Later, as more concrete tasks were taken on in the groups, the girls' sense of satisfaction seemed to rise:

> The workers continually received comments from the girls regarding their attitudes toward the groups. Aldena Wray, after being in a group for six months, credited her newfound confidence directly to the group experience. Other girls were amazed that they were able to talk about their problems in a group and frequently expressed it. After the group experience, several girls mentioned the meaning it had for them. One girl,

> Edith Casper, had nothing to say while a member of the group, but when she was seen individually much later by a caseworker she gave an unusually good report of many things that had happened in the group and reported on various areas in which she had been helped by the group discussion. . . .
>
> Even some girls whom the workers thought they had failed to reach later returned to the agency asking for help with concrete problems, such as employment. [149, p. 146]

In the end, however, the general conclusions were fairly dismal. Although the researchers indicated that "the findings are not entirely negative," the overall judgment was that "with respect to all of the measures we have used to examine effects of the treatment program, only a minimal effect can be found" (149, p. 204). It is important to recognize that despite the weaknesses of the study and the harshness of the professional reaction, the research effort was a major and a rigorous one, and it created nationwide discussion of a critical subject—the scientific evaluation of social work practice.

Berleman and Steinburn (11) described the pretest phase of an evaluation of a delinquency prevention program begun in 1962 by the Seattle Atlantic Street Center (46, 47) and financed by NIMH for a five-year period. The authors maintained that although the pretest did not represent a real test of the service, it was an opportunity to establish a rigorous technique not generally used in such a program. In the context of another, unnamed, delinquency prevention project, Aronson and Sherwood (6) reviewed the efforts of the research branch to evaluate various aspects of the program. Again the action-research tensions come through explicitly and in detail.

Rosenblatt (182) conducted an extensive study of attendance and attitudes of participants in 301 Project ENABLE groups throughout the country. Processing enormous amounts of attendance and interview data, he found regional differences in attendance, favoring the North, and higher attendance figures emerging from smaller cities and smaller agencies. Measuring attitudinal changes on six items of opinion, he reported on the complex variations, both positive and negative, associated with factors of attendance, group stability, and background characteristics, as these applied to each of the six items. His conclusions were positive, encompassing the rethinking of parental attitudes, the lessening of family isolation, the rise in community action, and other effects.

In the related arena of the Head Start activity, Mann and Elliot (143) studied the 1967 summer Head Start program in seven rural Oklahoma communities and found significant differences between first- and last-week tests. They concluded that although their sample was small, there were indications that the experience had a substantial effect on the cognitive functioning of the children involved.

Endres (48), having offered study-discussion groups as a device for working with disadvantaged parents in Indiana, found that parental self-evaluation yielded evidence of increased confidence and satisfaction. Finally, those interested in both group psychotherapy and the techniques of evaluation will wish to examine Patterson's review of evaluative studies in this area over the past twenty years (162).

Agency Impact

The study of agency effectiveness has never been an area of considerable activity among the neighborhood centers, and now that the classic self-study device has fallen into relative disuse, the output is close to nil. However, Zalba and Stein's report of a study designed to develop a "systematic methodology" for assessing agency effectiveness is an event of some importance to the neighborhood agencies (252). Using two family agencies judged to have high standards of practice, the researchers identified agency input goals on the basis of a content analysis of agency documents and interviews with key staff persons. They then collected data at the "crucial decision points" affecting the screening of clients and judged a sample of 160 cases for treatment success and the development of indexes for the quality of agency output. Normal production data for a given quarter were used to develop indexes of quantity. The conclusions and recommendations are explicit in their instructions relative to use of the model in other settings.

Conclusion

It would be difficult to characterize the complex pattern of the work described in this chapter and to assess its positive and negative aspects in simple terms. Certainly the gaps are still large, the continuity weak, and the commitment spotty. But there can be no doubt that the picture is more developed than it was a half-dozen years ago, and there are several places in which the "official curiosity" called for in the earlier review is growing rapidly. In other settings as well research activity is growing beyond the hobby status to incorporation into the job analysis of the agency itself. In his chapter in the first volume of this series the writer pointed out:

> Ultimately, much will depend on the developing relationship between the neighborhood centers and the social work profession. When the agencies continue to clarify their conceptions of service, they will be increasingly less occupied with questions of faith and doctrine and more with the problems of science. [199, p. 184]

We believe that there was further movement in this direction in the last six years, and indeed such movement seems bound to continue as the agencies are drawn closer to the increasingly desperate problems of war, frustration, and poverty that surround them.

References

1. Agueros, Julie, et al. "A Study of Social Work Practice: An Exploratory Investigation into the Nature of the Helping Process." Unpublished master's thesis, Columbia University School of Social Work, 1965.

2. Alcabes, Abraham. "A Study of a Community's Perception and Use of Neighborhood Centers." Unpublished doctoral dissertation, Columbia University School of Social Work, 1967.
3. Alker, Henry, and Kogan, Nathan. "Effects of Norm-Oriented Group Discussion on Individual Verbal Risk-Taking and Conservation," *Human Relations,* Vol. 21, No. 4 (November 1968), pp. 393–405.
4. Allen, V. L. "Situational Factors in Conformity," in Leonard Berkowitz, ed., *Advances in Experimental Social Psychology.* New York: Academic Press, 1965.
5. Arkava, Morton L. "Social Work Practice and Knowledge: An Examination of Their Relationship," *Journal of Education for Social Work,* Vol. 3, No. 2 (Fall 1967), pp. 5–13.
6. Aronson, Sidney, and Sherwood, Clarence. "Researcher Versus Practitioner: Problems in Social Action Research," *Social Work,* Vol. 12, No. 4 (October 1967), pp. 89–96.
7. Bach, George R. "The Marathon Group. Intensive Practice of Intimate Interaction," *Psychological Reports,* Vol. 18, No. 3 (1966), pp. 995–1002.
8. Bachman, Jerald G., et al. *Youth in Transition. Volume I: Blueprint for a Longitudinal Study of Adolescent Boys.* Ann Arbor: Survey Research Center, Institute for Social Research, University of Michigan, 1967.
9. Batchelder, Richard L., and Buckley, Earle R. (eds.). *YMCA Year Book and Official Roster 1969.* New York: Association Press, 1969.
10. Becker, Robert, et al. "Influence of the Leader on the Activity Level of Therapy Groups," *Journal of Social Psychology,* Vol. 74, No. 1 (February 1968), pp. 39–51.
11. Berleman, William C., and Steinburn, Thomas W. "The Execution and Evaluation of a Delinquency Prevention Program," *Social Problems,* Vol. 14, No. 4 (Spring 1967), pp. 413–423.
12. Bernstein, Saul. *Youth on the Streets: Work with Alienated Youth Groups.* New York: Association Press, 1964.
13. Berry, Margaret E. "Mr. Gans Is Challenged" (Points and Viewpoints), *Social Work,* Vol. 10, No. 1 (January 1965), pp. 104–107.
14. "Bibliography of Research Service Studies." Chicago: Boy Scouts of America, 1969. Mimeographed.
15. Bjerstedt, Ake. "Interaction Competence Among Children: The Rotation Phenomenon in Small Groups," *Journal of Psychology,* Vol. 61, First Half (September 1965), pp. 145–152.
16. Boeko, Jack. "Application of a survey of the Montreal Jewish High School Population," in "Research Papers, National Association of Jewish Center Workers." Papers presented at the National Conference of Jewish Communal Services, Atlantic City, N.J., 1967. New York: National Association of Jewish Center Workers, 1967. Pp. 45–51. Mimeographed.
17. Bradford, L. P., Gibb, J. R., and Benne, Kenneth D. *T-Group Theory and Laboratory Method.* New York: John Wiley & Sons, 1964.

18. Brittain, Clay V. "Preschool Programs for Culturally Deprived Children," *Children,* Vol. 13, No. 4 (July–August 1966), pp. 130–134.
19. Brodsky, Irving. "The Role of the Jewish Community Center in the Urban Crisis," *Associated YM-YWHAs of Greater New York 11th Annual Report, 1968.* New York: Associated YM-YWHAS of Greater New York, 1968.
20. Brooks, Michael P. "The Community Action Program as a Setting for Applied Research," *Journal of Social Issues,* Vol. 21, No. 1 (January 1965), pp. 29–40.
21. Broudy, Harry S. "Historic Exemplars of Teaching Method," in N. L. Gage, ed., *Handbook of Research on Teaching.* Chicago: Rand McNally & Co., 1963. Pp. 1–43.
22. Brown, Leonard N. "Social Workers' Verbal Acts and the Development of Mutual Expectations with Beginning Client Groups." Unpublished doctoral dissertation. Columbia University School of Social Work, 1970.
23. Bruck, Max. "Behavior Modification Theory and Practice: A Critical Review," *Social Work,* Vol. 13, No. 2 (April 1968), pp. 43–55.
24. Buckley, Walter (ed.). *Modern Systems Research for the Behavioral Scientist.* Chicago: Aldine Publishing Co., 1968.
25. Canter, Irving. "Implications of Developments in the Behavioral Sciences for Practice in Jewish Group Service Agencies," *Journal of Jewish Communal Service,* Vol. 41, No. 2 (Winter 1964), pp. 155–167.
26. ——— (ed.). *Research Readings in Jewish Communal Service.* New York: National Association of Jewish Center Workers, 1967.
27. Cantor, Marjorie. "Tomorrow is Today: A Study of VISTA in Urban Poverty, Summary and Implications." New York: Columbia University School of Social Work, Research and Demonstration Center, 1967. Mimeographed.
28. Caplan, Nathan. "Treatment Intervention and Reciprocal Interaction Effects," *Journal of Social Issues,* Vol. 24, No. 1 (January 1968), pp. 63–88.
29. Carp, Frances. "Differences Among Older Workers, Volunteers and Persons Who Are Neither," *Journal of Gerontology,* Vol. 23, No. 4 (October 1968), pp. 497–501.
30. Carp, Joel. "Value Systems of the Jewish Adolescent: A Research Report," in "Conference Papers, Annual Conference of the National Association of Jewish Center Workers," Philadelphia, May-June 1965. New York: National Association of Jewish Center Workers, 1965. Pp. 82–91. Mimeographed.
31. ———. "A List of Selected Reports of Research Projects Conducted in Jewish Community Centers and YM-YWHAS" in "Research Papers, National Association of Jewish Center Workers." Papers presented at the National Conference of Jewish Communal Services, May 1966. New York: National Association of Jewish Center Workers, 1966. Pp. 55–62. Mimeographed.

32. Casper, Max. *The Helping Person in the Group: A KWIC (Key Word in Context) Index of Relevant Journal Articles, 1965–1966.* Vol. 1. Syracuse, N.Y.: Syracuse University School of Social Work, 1967.
33. ———. *The Helping Person in the Group: A KWIC (Key Word in Context) Index of Relevant Journal Articles, 1967–1968.* Vol. 2. Syracuse, N.Y.: Syracuse University School of Social Work, 1969.
34. Center for Community Research. "Newsletter." New York: Associated YM-YWHAs of Greater New York, July 15, 1969. Mimeographed.
35. Chetkow, B. Harold. "Some Factors Influencing the Utilization and Impact of Priority Recommendations in Community Planning," *Social Service Review,* Vol. 41, No. 3 (September 1967), pp. 271–282.
36. Cleminger, Florence. "Congruence Between Members and Workers on Selected Behaviors of the Role of the Social Group Worker." Unpublished doctoral dissertation, University of Southern California School of Social Work, 1965.
37. Cloward, Richard A., and Ohlin, Lloyd E. *Delinquency and Opportunity: A Theory of Delinquent Groups.* Glencoe, Ill.: Free Press, 1960.
38. Cohen, Albert K. *Delinquent Boys: The Culture of the Gang.* Glencoe, Ill.: Free Press, 1955.
39. "Community Self-Study for Jewish Youth." Compilation of documents. Savannah, Ga.: Savannah Jewish Council and National Jewish Welfare Board, 1966. Mimeographed.
40. Craig, Maude and Furst, Philip. "What Happens after Treatment? A Study of Potentially Delinquent Boys," *Social Service Review,* Vol. 39, No. 2 (June 1965), pp. 165–171.
41. *Current Research in Voluntary Social and Health Agencies in New York City: 1969.* New York: Research Department, Community Council of Greater New York, 1969.
42. Deschin, Celia S. "Implications for Schools of a Demonstration Project to Integrate Orthopedically Handicapped Children in Community Centers with their Nonhandicapped Peers." Paper presented at the Research Council of the American School Health Association, Miami Beach, Florida, October 1967.
43. Deutsch, Martin, and Krauss, R. M. *Theories in Social Psychology.* New York: Basic Books, 1965.
44. Deutschberger, Paul. "On the Results of Four Recent Studies of Jewish Teenagers," in "Research Papers, National Association of Jewish Center Workers." Papers presented at the National Conference of Jewish Communal Services, Atlantic City, N.J., May 1967. New York: National Association of Jewish Center Workers, 1967. Pp. 20–24. Mimeographed.
45. Drake, St. Claire. *Race Relations in a Time of Rapid Social Change.* New York: National Federation of Settlements & Neighborhood Centers, 1966.
46. "Effectiveness of Social Work with Acting-Out Youth: Fifth Year Progress Report." Seattle, Wash.: Seattle Atlantic Street Center, 1967. Mimeographed.

47. "Effectiveness of Social Work with Acting-Out Youth: Sixth Year Progress Report." Seattle, Wash.: Seattle Atlantic Street Center, 1968. Mimeographed.
48. Endres, Mary. "The Impact of Parent Education through Study-Discussion Groups in a Poverty Area," *Journal of Marriage and the Family,* Vol. 30, No. 1 (February 1968), pp. 119–122.
49. Exline, Ralph, Gray, David, and Schuette, Dorothy. "Visual Behavior in a Dyad as Affected by Interview Content and Sex of Respondent," *Journal of Personality and Social Psychology,* Vol. 1, No. 1 (January 1965), pp. 201–209.
50. Feldman, Ronald A. "Determinants and Objectives of Social Group Work Intervention," *Social Work Practice, 1967.* New York: Columbia University Press, 1967. Pp. 34–55.
51. ———. "Group Service Programs in Public Welfare: Patterns and Perspectives," *Public Welfare,* Vol. 27, No. 3 (July 1969), pp. 266–271.
52. ———. "Three Types of Group Integration: Their Relationships to Power, Leadership, and Conformity Behavior." Unpublished doctoral dissertation, University of Michigan, 1966.
53. Festinger, Leon, Pepitone, A., and Newcomb, Theodore. "Some Consequences of Deindividuation in a Group," *Journal of Abnormal and Social Psychology,* Vol. 47, No. 2 (April 1952), pp. 382–389.
54. Flax, Norman, and Pumphrey, Muriel. "Serving Educable Mentally Retarded Children and Youth in Regular Center Groups," *Jewish Community Center Program Aids,* Vol. 30, No. 3 (Summer 1969), pp. 2–5.
55. Foster, Barbara R., and Batchelder, Richard L. *Report of the 1965–1966 YMCA Interracial Study.* New York: Research and Development Services, National Board of YMCAs, 1966.
56. Fox, Murray. "Considerations in Developing a Demonstration Program in Parent Education in Child Rearing Practices for Mentally Retarded Children." New York: Associated YM-YWHAS of Greater New York, 1968. Mimeographed.
57. Franseth, Jane, and Koury, Rose. *Survey of Research on Grouping as Related to Pupil Learning.* Washington, D.C.: U.S. Department of Health, Education & Welfare, 1966.
58. French, David G., et al. "Homans' Theory of the Human Group: Applications to Problems of Administration, Policy, and Staff Training in Group Service Agencies," *Journal of Jewish Communal Service,* Vol. 40, No. 4 (Summer 1964), pp. 379–395.
59. Gage, N. L. (ed.). *Handbook of Research on Teaching.* Chicago: Rand McNally & Co., 1963.
60. ———. "Paradigms for Research on Teaching," in Gage, ed., *Handbook of Research on Teaching.* Chicago: Rand McNally & Co., 1963. Pp. 94–141.
61. Gannon, Thomas. "The Role of the Non-professional in the Harlem Domestic Peace Corps," *Sociology and Social Research,* Vol. 52, No. 4 (July 1968), pp. 348–362.

62. Gans, Herbert J. "Redefining the Settlement's Function for the War on Poverty," *Social Work,* Vol. 9, No. 4 (October 1964), pp. 3–12.
63. Ganter, Grace, and Polansky, Norman. "Predicting a Child's Accessibility to Individual Treatment from Diagnostic Groups," *Social Work,* Vol. 9, No. 3 (July 1964), pp. 56–63.
64. Garfield, Goodwin P., and Irizarry, Carol R. "The 'Record of Service': A Way of Describing Social Work Practice," in William Schwartz and Serapio R. Zalba, eds., *The Practice of Group Work.* New York: Columbia University Press, 1970.
65. Garfinkle, Max. "Survey of Montreal Jewish High School Population." May 1965. Mimeographed by the author.
66. Garvin, Charles. "Complementarity of Role Expectations in Groups: Relationship to Worker Performance and Member Problem Solving." Unpublished doctoral dissertation, University of Chicago School of Social Service Administration, 1968.
67. ———. "Complementarity of Role Expectations in Groups: The Member-Worker Contract," *Social Work Practice, 1969.* New York: Columbia University Press, 1969. Pp. 127–145.
68. Gerard, Harold B., and Miller, Norman. "Group Dynamics," in Paul R. Farnsworth, Olga McNemar, and Quinn McNemar, eds., *Annual Review of Psychology.* Vol. 18. Palo Alto: Annual Reviews, 1967. Pp. 287–332.
69. Gifford, C. G. "Sensitivity Training and Social Work," *Social Work,* Vol. 13, No. 2 (April 1968), pp. 78–86.
70. Gilbert, Neil. "Neighborhood Coordinator: Advocate or Middleman?" *Social Service Review,* Vol. 43, No. 2 (June 1969), pp. 136–144.
71. Glanser, Murray, and Glaser, Robert. "Techniques for the Study of Group Structure and Behavior: II. Empirical Studies of the Effects of Structure in Small Groups," *Psychological Bulletin,* Vol. 58, No. 1 (January 1961), pp. 1–27.
72. Glasser, Paul, and Navarre, Elizabeth. "Structural Problems of the One-Parent Family," *Journal of Social Issues,* Vol. 21, No. 1 (January 1965), pp. 98–109.
73. Goodchilds, Jacqueline D., and Smith, Ewart E. "The Wit and his Group," *Human Relations,* Vol. 17, No. 1 (February 1964), pp. 23–31.
74. Goodman, Mortimer. "Preliminary Study of Social Work Intervention with Adults in Social Groups in the Jewish Center," in "Research Papers, National Association of Jewish Center Workers." Papers presented at the National Conference of Jewish Communal Services, Atlantic City, N.J., May 1967. New York: National Association of Jewish Center Workers, 1967. Pp. 25–43. Mimeographed.
75. Gottlieb, David, and Reeves, Jon. *Adolescent Behavior in Urban Areas: A Bibliographic Review and Discussion of the Literature.* New York: Free Press of Glencoe, 1963.
76. Greene, Alan, Kasdan, Barry, and Segal, Brian. "Jewish Social Group Work Students View the Jewish Community Center Field as a Place-

ment and Career," *Journal of Jewish Communal Services,* Vol. 44, No. 2 (Winter 1967), pp. 168–176.

77. Grosser, Charles. "Local Residents as Mediators Between Middle-Class Professional Workers and Lower-Class Clients," *Social Service Review,* Vol. 40, No. 1 (March 1966), pp. 56–63.
78. ———, Henry, William E., and Kelley, James G. (eds.). *Nonprofessionals in the Human Services.* San Francisco: Jossey-Bass, 1969.
79. Hall, Jay, and Williams, Martha S. "A Comparison of Decision-Making Performances in Established and Ad Hoc Groups," *Journal of Personality and Social Psychology,* Vol. 3, No. 2 (February 1966), pp. 214–222.
80. Handlon, Joseph, and Parloff, Morris B. "The Influence of Criticalness on Creative Problem-Solving in Dyads," *Psychiatry,* Vol. 27, No. 1 (February 1964), pp. 17–27.
81. Hardy, James M. *Planning for Impact: A Guide to Planning Effective Family Programs.* New York: Association Press, 1968.
82. ———. *The YMCA and the Changing American Family.* New York: Department of Research and Planning, National Council of YMCAs, 1965.
83. Harlow, Harold C., Jr. *Racial Integration in the Young Men's Christian Associations.* New York: Research and Planning Department, National Council of YMCAs, 1962.
84. Hefter, Sy. "The Wilkes-Barre Survey Results," in "Research Papers, National Association of Jewish Center Workers." Papers presented at the National Conference of Jewish Communal Services, Atlantic City, N.J., May 1967. New York: National Association of Jewish Center Workers, 1967. Pp. 67–73. Mimeographed.
85. Hendon, William S. " 'Determining Neighborhood Recreation Priorities': A Comment," *Journal of Leisure Research,* Vol. 1, No. 2 (Spring 1969), pp. 189–191.
86. Herman, Melvin. *Occupational Mobility in Social Work: The Jewish Community Center Worker.* New York: National Jewish Welfare Board and the Research Institute for Group Work in Jewish Agencies of the National Association of Jewish Center Workers, 1959.
87. ———. "Problems of Evaluation," *American Child,* Vol. 47, No. 2 (March 1965), pp. 5–10.
88. ———, and Sadofsky, Stanley. *Youth-Work Programs: Problems of Planning and Operation.* New York: Center for the Study of Unemployed Youth, Graduate School of Social Work, New York University, 1966.
89. Heslin, Richard, and Dunphy, Dexter. "Three Dimensions of Member Satisfaction in Small Groups," *Human Relations,* Vol. 17, No. 2 (May 1964), pp. 99–112.
90. Hess, Robert D. "The Social and Psychological Development of Six to Ten-Year Old Boys: A Review of Research and Theory." Chicago: Boy Scouts of America, 1963. Mimeographed.

91. Hillman, Arthur. "People, Places and Participation." New York: National Federation of Settlements and Neighborhood Centers, 1969. Mimeographed.
92. ———, and Seever, Frank. *Making Democracy Work: A Study of Neighborhood Organization.* New York: National Federation of Settlements and Neighborhood Centers, 1968.
93. Hinkle, John, Cole, Charles, and Oetting, E. R. "Research in a Community Health Center: A Framework for Action," *Community Mental Health Journal,* Vol. 4, No. 2 (April 1968), pp. 129–133.
94. Hoffman, L. R. "Group Problem Solving," in Louis Berkowitz, ed., *Advances in Experimental Social Psychology.* New York: Academic Press, 1965. Pp. 99–132.
95. Holmes, Douglas. "Bridging the Gap Between Research and Practice in Social Work," *Social Work Practice, 1967.* New York: Columbia University Press, 1967. Pp. 95–108.
96. ———. "Integrating the Handicapped Child: Report of a Research and Demonstration Program," *Journal of Jewish Communal Service,* Vol. 43, No. 2 (Winter 1966), pp. 182–188.
97. ———. "An Objective Evaluation of Certain Aspects of 'Operation Headstart.' " Paper presented at the Eastern Regional Conference, Child Welfare League of America, Atlantic City, N.J., March 1967. Mimeographed.
98. ———. "Potential Use of Associated Y's Nursery Schools." New York: Associated YM-YWHAS of Greater New York, 1969. Mimeographed.
99. ———. "Study of Jewish Population Mobility in the Bronx River Area." New York: Associated YM-YWHAS of Greater New York, 1967. Mimeographed.
100. ———. "A Study of the Problems of Integrating Physically Handicapped Children with Non-Handicapped Children in Recreational Groups." 2 vols. New York: Associated YM-YWHAS of Greater New York, 1966. Mimeographed.
101. ———. "A Study of Staff Utilization: Final Report." New York: National Jewish Welfare Board, 1967. Mimeographed.
102. ———. "The Use of a Structured Observational Schema in Evaluating the Impact of Integrated Social Experiences upon Orthopedically Handicapped Children." Paper presented at a meeting of the American Psychological Association, Chicago, September 1965. Mimeographed.
103. ———, and Holmes, Monica Bychowski. "An Evaluation of Differences Among Different Classes of Head Start Participants." New York: Associated YM-YWHAS of Greater New York, 1966. Mimeographed.
104. ———, and Smolka, Patricia. "A Comparison Between the Attitudes Towards Child Rearing Among Mothers of Orthopedically Handicapped and Non-Handicapped, Pre-Adolescent Children." Paper presented at a meeting of the American Psychological Association, Chicago, September 1965. Mimeographed.

105. Homans, George C. *The Human Group.* New York: Harcourt, Brace & Co., 1950.
106. Horowitz, Gideon. "Worker Interventions in Response to Deviant Behavior in Groups." Unpublished doctoral dissertation, University of Chicago School of Social Service Administration, 1968.
107. Ikeda, Tsuguo. "Final Report Summary: Effectiveness of Social Work with Acting-Out Youth." Seattle, Wash.: Seattle Atlantic Street Center, 1968. Mimeographed.
108. Indik, Bernard. "Organization Size and Member Participation: Some Empirical Tests of Alternative Explanations," *Human Relations,* Vol. 18, No. 4 (November 1965), pp. 339–350.
109. "Is Scouting in Tune with the Times?" Reprint from *Scouting Magazine.* Chicago: Boy Scouts of America, undated.
110. Ishikawa, Wesley. "Verbal Acts of the Social Worker and their Variations Through Time in Release-planning Discussion Group Meetings." Unpublished doctoral dissertation, University of California School of Social Welfare, Los Angeles, 1968.
111. Jansyn, Leon R. "Solidarity and Delinquency in a Street Corner Group," *American Sociological Review,* Vol. 31, No. 5 (October 1966), pp. 600–614.
112. Johnson, Guion Griffis. *Volunteers in Community Service.* Chapel Hill: North Carolina Council of Women's Organizations, 1967.
113. Kaplan, Berton H. "Social Issues and Poverty Research: A Commentary," *Journal of Social Issues,* Vol. 21, No. 1 (January 1965), pp. 1–10.
114. Kaplan, Martin, and Walden, Theodore. "Adolescent Needs and Center Objectives." Paper presented at the Annual Meeting of the National Conference of Jewish Communal Services, Philadelphia, June 1965. Mimeographed.
115. Karnes, Merle, et al. "An Approach for Working with Mothers of Disadvantaged Preschool Children," *Merrill-Palmer Quarterly,* Vol. 14, No. 2 (April 1968), pp. 174–184.
116. Kazzaz, David S. "The Champion of the Cause and the Challenge of Supervising his Anti-Leader Role," *American Journal of Psychiatry,* Vol. 125, No. 6 (December 1968), pp. 737–742.
117. Klein, Malcolm, and Snyder, Neal. "The Detached Worker: Uniformities and Variances in Work Style," *Social Work,* Vol. 10, No. 4 (October 1965), pp. 60–68.
118. Kraft, Ivor, and Chilman, Catherine S. *Helping Low-Income Families Through Parent Education: A Survey of Research.* Washington, D.C.: Children's Bureau, U.S. Department of Health, Education & Welfare, 1966.
119. Kraus, Richard. *Public Recreation and the Negro: A Study of Participation and Administrative Practices.* New York: Center for Urban Education, 1968.

120. Lambert, Camille, Jr., Guberman, Mildred, and Morris, Robert. "Reopening Doors to Community Participation for Older People: How Realistic?" *Social Service Review,* Vol. 38, No. 1 (March 1964), pp. 42–50.

121. Lathrope, Donald E. "Making Use of Systems Thought in Social Work Practice: Some Bridging Ideas." Paper presented at the Conference on Current Trends in Army Social Work, Denver, Colo., September 1969. Mimeographed.

122. Lawrence, Harry. "The Effectiveness of a Group-directed vs. a Worker-directed Style of Leadership in Social Group Work." Unpublished doctoral dissertation, University of California School of Social Welfare, Berkeley, 1967.

123. Lazerwitz, Bernard. "The Jewish Identification of Chicago Jewish Community Center Members and Non-Members," in "Research Papers, National Association of Jewish Center Workers." Papers presented at the National Conference of Jewish Communal Service, Detroit, Michigan, June 1968. New York: National Association of Jewish Center Workers, 1968. Pp. 16–39. Mimeographed.

124. Leader, Arthur L. "Current and Future Issues in Family Therapy," *Social Service Review,* Vol. 43, No. 1 (March 1969), pp. 1–11.

125. Lennard, Henry L., and Bernstein, Arnold. *Patterns in Human Interaction.* San Francisco: Jossey-Bass, 1969.

126. Levin, Morris. "An Analysis of Study Material on the Image of the Jewish Community Center Held by Membership and the Community," in Irving Canter, ed., *Research Readings in Jewish Communal Service.* New York: National Association of Jewish Center Workers, 1967. Pp. 190–207.

127. ———. "A Survey of Research and Program Developments Involving Jewish Adolescents and the Implications for JCC Service." Chicago: Jewish Community Centers of Chicago, 1969. Mimeographed.

128. Levine, Baruch. "Factors Related to Interpersonal Balance in Social Work Treatment Groups." Unpublished doctoral dissertation, University of Chicago School of Social Service Administration, 1968.

129. Levine, Rachel A. "Treatment in the Home," *Social Work,* Vol. 9, No. 1 (January 1964), pp. 19–28.

130. Levinger, George. "Note on Need Complementarity in Marriage," *Psychological Bulletin,* Vol. 61, No. 1 (January 1964), pp. 153–157.

131. Levinson, Perry, and Schiller, Jeffry. "Role Analysis of the Indigenous Nonprofessional," *Social Work,* Vol. 11, No. 3 (July 1966), pp. 95–101.

132. Levy, Charles S. *The Executive and the Jewish Community Center Board.* New York: National Jewish Welfare Board, 1964. Mimeographed.

133. ———. "Professional Practice in the Jewish Community Center: Disparities Between the Idealizations and Experience of Center Personnel,"

in "Research Papers, National Association of Jewish Center Workers." Papers presented at the National Conference of Jewish Communal Services, Atlantic City, N.J., May 1967. New York: National Association of Jewish Center Workers, 1967. Pp. 1–19. Mimeographed.

134. Litwak, Eugene, and Meyer, Henry J. "A Balance Theory of Coordination Between Bureaucratic Organizations and Community Primary Groups," in Edwin J. Thomas, ed., *Behavioral Science for Social Workers.* New York: Free Press, 1967. Pp. 246–264.
135. Lott, Albert J., and Lott, Bernice E. "Group Cohesiveness as Interpersonal Attraction: A Review of Relationships with Antecedent and Consequent Variables," *Psychological Bulletin,* Vol. 64, No. 3 (September 1965), pp. 259–309.
136. Lucci, York. *The Campus YMCA: Highlights from a National Study.* New York: National Board of YMCAs, 1960.
137. Maas, Henry S. "Preadolescent Peer Relations and Adult Intimacy," *Psychiatry: Journal for the Study of Interpersonal Processes,* Vol. 31, No. 2 (May 1968), pp. 161–172.
138. Macdonald, Mary E. "Reunion at Vocational High. An Analysis of *Girls at Vocational High: An Experiment in Social Intervention,*" *Social Service Review,* Vol. 40, No. 2 (June 1966), pp. 175–189.
139. ———. "Verdict Before Trial: A Review of the Test by the New York City Youth Board of the Glueck Social Prediction Table," *Social Service Review,* Vol. 39, No. 2 (June 1965), pp. 172–182.
140. McGrath, Joseph E., and Altman, Irwin. *Small Group Research: A Synthesis and Critique of the Field.* New York: Holt, Rinehart & Winston, 1966.
141. McLarnan, Georgiana, and Fryer, Gideon W. *Improving Decision-Making of Young Low-Income Couples.* Nashville: University of Tennessee School of Social Work and Wesley House Centers, 1967.
142. Maida, Peter R., and McCoy, John L. *The Poor: A Selected Bibliography.* Miscellaneous Publication No. 1145. Washington, D.C.: U.S. Department of Agriculture, Economic Research Service, May 1969.
143. Mann, Edward, and Elliot, Courtney. "Assessment of the Utility of Project Head Start for the Culturally Deprived: An Evaluation of Social and Psychological Functioning," *Training School Bulletin,* Vol. 64, No. 4 (February 1968), pp. 119–125.
144. Manser, Ellen P., Jones, Jeweldean, and Ortof, Selma B. "An Overview of Project ENABLE," *Social Casework,* Vol. 48, No. 10 (December 1967), pp. 609–617.
145. March, Michael. "The Neighborhood Center Concept," *Public Welfare,* Vol. 26, No. 2 (April 1968), pp. 97–111.
146. Massarik, Fred, and Okin, Leo. *Patterns of Board Leadership: A Study of the Jewish Community Center Board Members of Los Angeles, California.* New York: National Jewish Welfare Board, 1964.

147. Mattick, Hans W., and Caplan, Nathan S. *The Chicago Youth Development Project: A Descriptive Account of its Action Program and Research Designs.* Ann Arbor: Institute for Social Research, University of Michigan, 1964.
148. Medow, Herman, and Zander, Alvin. "Aspirations for the Group Chosen by Central and Peripheral Members," *Journal of Personality and Social Psychology,* Vol. 1, No. 3 (1965), pp. 224–228.
149. Meyer, Henry J., Borgatta, Edgar F., and Jones, Wyatt C. *Girls at Vocational High: An Experiment in Social Work Intervention.* New York: Russell Sage Foundation, 1965.
150. Miller, Robert E., Banks, James H., Jr., and Ogawa, Nobuya, "Role of Facial Expression in 'Cooperative-Avoidance Conditioning' in Monkeys," *Journal of Abnormal and Social Psychology,* Vol. 67, No. 1 (July 1963), pp. 24–30.
151. Miller, Walter B. "Lower Class Culture as a Generating Milieu of Gang Delinquency," *Journal of Social Issues,* Vol. 14, No. 3 (1958), pp. 5–19.
152. Miran, Bernard B., and Lemmerman, Mervin N. "Older Adult Population Study and Demonstration Project," in "Research Papers, National Association of Jewish Center Workers." Papers presented at the National Conference of Jewish Communal Services, Washington, D.C., May, 1966. New York: National Association of Jewish Center Workers, 1966. Pp. 21–35. Mimeographed.
153. Mogulof, Melvin. "Toward the Measurement of Jewish Content in Jewish Community Center Practice," *Journal of Jewish Communal Services,* Vol. 41, No. 1 (Fall 1964), pp. 101–113.
154. Morgan, Ruth. "Intervention Techniques in Social Group Work." Unpublished doctoral dissertation, Columbia University School of Social Work, 1966.
155. National Council, Boy Scouts of America. *Cub Scouting: Practices and Attitudes in Packs and Dens.* Princeton, N.J.: Opinion Research Corporation, 1964.
156. National Institutes of Health. *Research Highlights, National Institutes of Health, 1966.* Public Health Service Publication No. 1613. Washington, D.C.: U.S. Department of Health, Education & Welfare, 1966.
157. *Needs and Interests Study of 7-8-9-10 Year-Old Boys' Club Members.* New York: Boys' Clubs of America, 1964.
158. O'Dell, Jerry W. "Group Size and Emotional Interactions," *Journal of Personality and Social Psychology,* Vol. 8, No. 1 (January 1968), pp. 75–78.
159. *Outdoor Recreation Research, A Reference Catalog, 1967.* Washington, D.C.: Bureau of Outdoor Recreation, U.S. Department of the Interior, 1968.
160. Pappenfort, Donnell, and Kilpatrick, Dee Morgan. "Opportunities for Physically Handicapped Children: A Study of Attitudes and Practice in

Settlements and Community Centers," *Social Service Review,* Vol. 41, No. 2 (June 1967), pp. 179–188.

161. Parker, Rolland S. "Patient Variability as a Factor in Group Activities on a Maximum Security Ward," *Psychiatric Quarterly,* Vol. 39, No. 2 (April 1965), pp. 265–278.
162. Patterson, Mansell. "Evaluation Studies of Group Psychotherapy," *International Journal of Psychiatry,* Vol. 4, No. 4 (October 1967), pp. 333–343.
163. Pearl, Arthur, and Riessman, Frank. *New Careers for the Poor.* New York: Free Press, 1965.
164. Peck, Harris, and Kaplan, Seymour. "Crisis Theory and Therapeutic Change in Small Groups: Some Implications for Community Mental Health Programs," *International Journal of Group Psychotherapy,* Vol. 16, No. 2 (April 1966), pp. 135–149.
165. Pierce, Francis. "A Study of the Methodological Components of Social Work with Groups." Unpublished doctoral dissertation, University of Southern California School of Social Work, 1966.
166. Perlman, Robert, and Jones, David. *Neighborhood Service Centers.* Washington, D.C.: Office of Juvenile Delinquency & Youth Development, U.S. Department of Health, Education & Welfare, 1967.
167. Pins, Arnulf M. *Who Chooses Social Work, When and Why?* New York: Council on Social Work Education, 1963.
168. Pope, Hallowell. "Economic Deprivation and Social Participation in a Group of 'Middle Class' Factory Workers," *Social Problems,* Vol. 11, No. 3 (Winter 1964), pp. 290–300.
169. "Preparing for the Seventies." Chicago, Ill.: National Board of YMCAs, 1968. Mimeographed.
170. Pumphrey, Muriel W., Goodman, Mortimer, and Flax, Norman. "Integrating Individuals with Impaired Adaptive Behavior in a Group Work Agency," *Social Work Practice, 1969.* New York: Columbia University Press, 1969. Pp. 146–160.
171. Ramsey, Glenn V. "Review of Group Methods with Parents of the Mentally Retarded," *American Journal of Mental Deficiency,* Vol. 71, No. 5 (March 1967), pp. 857–863.
172. ———. "Sociotherapeutic Camping for the Mentally Ill," *Social Work,* Vol. 9, No. 1 (January 1964), pp. 45–53.
173. Raven, B. H. *Bibliography of Small Group Research.* Technical Report No. 15, 3d ed. Los Angeles: University of California at Los Angeles, 1965.
174. Reiff, Robert, and Riessman, Frank. *The Indigenous Non-Professional.* New York: National Institute of Labor Education, 1964.
175. Rein, Martin, and Riessman, Frank. "A Strategy for Antipoverty Community Action Programs," *Social Work,* Vol. 11, No. 2 (April 1966), pp. 3–12.

176. *A Report on the Executive Program, Part I.* New York: Boys' Clubs of America, undated.
177. *A Report on the Executive Program, Part II.* New York: Boys' Clubs of America, undated.
178. "Research and Demonstration Projects Reported by Members of the National Federation of Settlements, 1962–1965." New York: National Federation of Settlements and Neighborhood Centers, April 1965. Mimeographed.
179. Richart, Robert, and Millner, Lawrence. "Factors Influencing Admission to a Community Mental Health Center," *Community Mental Health Journal,* Vol. 4, No. 1 (February 1968), pp. 27–35.
180. Robbins, Harold, and Schattner, Regina. "Obstacles in the Social Integration of Orthopedically Handicapped Children," *Journal of Jewish Communal Services,* Vol. 45, No. 2 (Winter 1968), pp. 190–199.
181. Roen, Sheldon, et al. "Community Adaptation as an Evaluation Concept in Community Mental Health," *Archives of General Psychiatry,* Vol. 15, No. 1 (July 1966), pp. 36–44.
182. Rosenblatt, Aaron. *Attendance and Attitude Change: A Study of 301 Project* ENABLE *Groups.* New York: Family Service Association of America, 1968.
183. ———. "Interest of Older Persons in Volunteer Activities," *Social Work,* Vol. 11, No. 3 (July 1966), pp. 87–94.
184. ———, and Wiggins, Lee M. "Characteristics of the Parents Served," *Social Casework,* Vol. 48, No. 10 (December 1967), pp. 639–647.
185. Rostov, Barbara W. "Group Work in the Psychiatric Hospital: A Critical Review of the Literature." *Social Work,* Vol. 10, No. 1 (January 1965), pp. 23–31.
186. Rothaus, Paul, Johnson, Dale I., and Lyle, F. A. "Group Participation for Psychiatric Patients," *Journal of Counseling Psychology,* Vol. 11, No. 3 (Fall 1964), pp. 230–240.
187. Sarri, Rosemary C. "Group Approaches to Enhancing Pupil Performance." Paper presented at Wisconsin School Social Workers Association, Madison, April 1968. Mimeographed.
188. Schafer, Walter E. "Deviance in the Public School: An Interactional View," in Edwin J. Thomas, ed., *Behavioral Science for Social Workers.* New York: Free Press, 1967. Pp. 51–58.
189. Schein, Edgar H., and Bennis, Warren G. *Personal and Organizational Change Through Group Methods.* New York: John Wiley & Sons, 1965.
190. Schorr, Alvin L. "Mirror, Mirror on the Wall . . ." (Book Review Essay), *Social Work,* Vol. 10, No. 3 (July 1965), pp. 112–113.
191. Schreiber, Meyer. "Community Recreation Resources for the Mentally Retarded," *Training School Bulletin,* Vol. 62, No. 1 (May 1965), pp. 33–51.

192. ———, and Feeley, Mary. "Siblings of the Retarded—A Guided Group Experience," *Children,* Vol. 12, No. 6 (November-December 1965), pp. 221–225.

193. Schutz, William C. *FIRO, A Three Dimensional Theory of Personal Behavior.* New York: Holt, Rinehart & Winston, 1958.

194. Schwartz, Florence S. "Profit Without Pay: Volunteer Activity in Community Centers," in "Research Papers, National Association of Jewish Center Workers." Papers presented at the National Conference of Jewish Communal Services, Atlantic City, N.J., 1967. New York: National Association of Jewish Center Workers, 1967. Pp. 74–91.

195. Schwartz, Gary, and Merten, Don. "The Language of Adolescence: An Anthropological Approach to thc Youth Culture," *American Journal of Sociology,* Vol. 72, No. 5 (March 1967), pp. 453–468.

196. Schwartz, William. "Group Work and the Social Scene," in Alfred J. Kahn, ed., *Issues in American Social Work.* New York: Columbia University Press, 1959. Pp. 110–137.

197. ———. "Group Work in Public Welfare," *Public Welfare,* Vol. 26, No. 4 (October 1968), pp. 322–370.

198. ———. "Identification of Worker Responses in Group Situations." Memorandum to Gertrude Wilson ct al., Chicago, 1958. Mimeographed.

199. ———. "Neighborhood Centers," in Henry S. Maas, ed., *Five Fields of Social Service: Reviews of Research.* New York: National Association of Social Workers, 1966. Pp. 144–184.

200. Scotch, C. Bernard. "The Impact of Alternative Job Opportunities for MSW's Upon the Manpower Resources of the Jewish Community Center Field," pp. 64–97. Paper presented at the Annual Conference of the National Association of Jewish Center Workers, Detroit, Michigan, June 1968. Mimeographed.

201. "Scoutmasters' Reactions to Cub Scouting." New Brunswick, N.J.: Research Service, Boy Scouts of America, 1964. Mimeographed.

202. Seidler, Morris. "Employment and Supervision of Non-Professionals." Chicago: National Federation of Settlements and Neighborhood Centers, 1968. Mimeographed.

203. Shalinsky, William. "The Effect of Group Composition on Aspects of Group Functioning." Unpublished doctoral dissertation, Western Reserve University School of Applied Social Sciences, 1967.

204. ———. "Group Composition as an Element of Social Group Work Practice," *Social Service Review,* Vol. 43, No. 1 (March 1969), pp. 42–49.

205. Shaw, Marvin E., and Blum, Michael S. "Effects of Leadership Style Upon Group Performance as a Function of Task Structure," *Journal of Personality and Social Psychology,* Vol. 3, No. 2 (February 1966), pp. 238–241.

206. Short, James F., Jr., and Strodtbeck, Fred L. *Group Process and Gang Delinquency.* Chicago: University of Chicago Press, 1965.
207. Shulman, Lawrence. *A Casebook of Social Work with Groups: The Mediating Model.* New York: Council on Social Work Education, 1968.
208. Silverman, Marvin. "Knowledge in Social Group Work: A Review of the Literature," *Social Work,* Vol. 11, No. 3 (July 1966), pp. 56–62.
209. Simon, Edwin. "The AZA Program and Membership—the Problems We Face, the Membership Imbalance." Paper presented at the National Staff Conference of the B'nai B'rith Youth Organization, Washington, D.C., January 1968. Mimeographed.
210. Sobey, Francine S. *The Nonprofessional Revolution in Mental Health.* New York: Columbia University Press, 1970.
211. ———. "Non-Professionals in Mental Health Service: Objectives and Functions in Projects Funded by the National Institute of Mental Health." Unpublished doctoral dissertation, Columbia University School of Social Work, 1968.
212. ———. *Volunteer Services in Mental Health: An Annotated Bibliography, 1955 to 1969.* Publication No. 1002. Washington, D.C.: National Institute of Mental Health, National Clearinghouse for Mental Health Information, 1969.
213. Solomon, Theodore, "A Pilot Study Among East Village 'Hippies.' " Monograph 35. New York: Associated YH-YWHAs of Greater New York, 1968. Mimeographed.
214. ———, and Friedman, Arlene. "The Associated 'Ys' Demographic Study: Summary of Returns, March 1966–January 1968." New York: Associated YM-YWHAs of Greater New York, 1968. Mimeographed.
215. Specht, Harry, Hawkins, Arthur, and McGee, Floyd. "Case Conference on the Neighborhood Sub-Professional Worker: Excerpts from the Casebooks of Sub-Professional Workers," *Children,* Vol. 15, No. 1 (January–February 1968), pp. 7–11.
216. Spergel, Irving. *Street Gang Work: Theory and Practice.* Reading, Mass.: Addison-Wesley Publishing Co., 1966.
217. Staley, Edwin J. "Determining Neighborhood Recreation Priorities: An Instrument," *Journal of Leisure Research,* Vol. 1, No. 1 (Winter 1969), pp. 69–74.
218. ———. " 'Determining Neighborhood Recreation Priorities': A Reply," *Journal of Leisure Research,* Vol. 1, No. 2 (Spring 1969), pp. 193–194.
219. Strupp, Hans H., and Bergin, Allen E. *Research in Individual Psychotherapy: A Bibliography.* Public Health Service Publication No. 1844. Washington, D.C.: U.S. Department of Health, Education & Welfare, 1969.
220. "A Study of Jewish Adolescents of New Orleans." New Orleans: Jewish Welfare Federation of New Orleans, August 1966. Mimeographed.

221. "Summary of a Demonstration Project to Integrate Orthopedically Handicapped Children in Community Centers with their Nonhandicapped Peers." New York: New York Service for the Orthopedically Handicapped, undated. Mimeographed.
222. "A Survey of Boys with Physical or Mental Handicaps Who Are Members of the Boy Scouts of America." New Brunswick, N.J.: Research Service, Boy Scouts of America, 1960. Mimeographed.
223. Taber, Merlin, and Shapiro, Iris. "Social Work and Its Knowledge Base: A Content Analysis of the Periodical Literature," *Social Work,* Vol. 10, No. 4 (October 1965), pp. 100–106.
224. Tharp, Roland G. "Reply to Levinger's Note," *Psychological Bulletin,* Vol. 61, No. 2 (February 1964), pp. 158–160.
225. Thomas, Edwin J. "Selected Sociobehavioral Techniques and Principles: An Approach to Interpersonal Helping," *Social Work,* Vol. 13, No. 1 (January 1968), pp. 12–26.
226. ——— (ed.). *Behavioral Science for Social Workers.* New York: Free Press, 1967.
227. Tuckman, Bruce W. "Developmental Sequence in Small Groups," *Psychological Bulletin,* Vol. 63, No. 6 (June 1965), pp. 384–399.
228. Tuckman, Jacob. "Factors Related to Attendance in a Center for Older People," *Journal of the American Geriatrics Society,* Vol. 15, No. 5 (May 1967), pp. 474–479.
229. U.S. Department of Health, Education, and Welfare, Children's Bureau. *Research Relating to Children.* Bulletin 24. Washington, D.C.: Clearinghouse for Research in Child Life, 1969.
230. U.S. Department of Health, Education, and Welfare, Public Health Service. *Annotated Bibliography on Inservice Training for Allied Professionals and Nonprofessionals in Community Mental Health.* Washington, D.C.: U.S. Government Printing Office, 1969.
231. ———. *Annotated Bibliography on Inservice Training for Key Professionals in Community Mental Health.* Washington, D.C.: U.S. Government Printing Office, 1969.
232. ———. *Community Health Service, Publications Catalog, 1969 Edition.* Public Health Service Publication 1907. Washington, D.C.: U.S. Government Printing Office, March 1969.
233. ———. *Perspectives on Human Deprivation: Biological, Psychological, and Sociological.* Washington, D.C.: National Institute of Child Health and Human Development, 1968.
234. ———. *Training Methodology, Part I: Background Theory and Research: An Annotated Bibliography.* Washington, D.C.: U.S. Government Printing Office, 1969.
235. ———. *Training Methodology, Part II: Planning and Administration: An Annotated Bibliography.* Washington, D.C.: U.S. Government Printing Office, 1969.

236. ———. *Training Methodology, Part III: Instructional Methods and Techniques, An Annotated Bibliography.* Washington, D.C.: U.S. Government Printing Office, 1969.

237. ———. *Training Methodology, Part IV: Audiovisual Theory, Aids, and Equipment, An Annotated Bibliography.* Washington, D.C.: U.S. Government Printing Office, 1969.

238. University of Michigan School of Social Work. *Practice Skill Assessment Instrument.* Ann Arbor, Mich.: Campus Publishers, 1967.

239. Vacher, Carole Doughton. *The Comprehensive Community Mental Health Center: An Annotated Bibliography.* Public Health Service Publication 1980. Chevy Chase, Md.: National Institute of Mental Health, 1969.

240. Vinter, Robert D., and Sarri, Rosemary C. "Malperformance in the Public School: A Group Work Approach," *Social Work,* Vol. 10, No. 1 (January 1965), pp. 3–13.

241. ———, et al. *Pupil Behavior Inventory: A Manual for Administration and Scoring.* Ann Arbor: Campus Publishers, 1966.

242. Wakeman, Roy P. "Using Data Processing to Analyze Worker Activity," *Social Work Practice, 1965.* New York: Columbia University Press, 1965. Pp. 54–64.

243. Wallach, Michael A., Kogan, Nathan, and Bem, Daryl J. "Diffusion of Responsibility and Level of Risk-taking in Groups," *Journal of Abnormal and Social Psychology,* Vol. 68, No. 3 (March 1964), pp. 263–274.

244. Walton, John. "Substance and Artifact: The Current Status of Research on Community Power Structure," *American Journal of Sociology,* Vol. 71, No. 4 (January 1966), pp. 430–438.

245. Warach, Bernard. "Findings on Staff Utilization in Jewish Community Centers and Proposed Recommendations." New York: National Jewish Welfare Board, 1968. Mimeographed.

246. Warren, Roland. "The Interaction of Community Decision Organizations: Some Basic Concepts and Needed Research," *Social Service Review,* Vol. 41, No. 3 (September 1967), pp. 261–270.

247. "Webelos Den Leaders' Reactions to the Webelos Program." New Brunswick, N.J.: Research Service, Boy Scouts of America, 1964. Mimeographed.

248. Weissman, Harold H., and Heifetz, Henry. "Changing Program Emphases of Settlement Houses," *Social Work,* Vol. 13, No. 4 (October 1968), pp. 40–49.

249. Withey, Stephen B., and Smith, Robert L. *A National Study of Boys Eight to Ten Years Old.* Ann Arbor: Survey Research Center, Institute for Social Research, University of Michigan, 1964.

250. Yaillen, Earl. "A Summary of a Survey of Opinions of Jewish Team Members of the Pittsburgh Y-IKC." Pittsburgh: YM-YWHA, Irene Kaufman Centers, November 1967. Mimeographed.

251. Yalom, Irvin, et al. "Preparation of Patients for Group Therapy," *Archives of General Psychiatry,* Vol. 17, No. 4 (October 1967), pp. 416–427.

252. Zalba, Serapio R., and Stein, Herman D. *Assessing Organizational Effectiveness: A Draft Report.* Cleveland, Ohio: School of Applied Social Sciences, Case Western Reserve University, 1969.

253. Zald, Mayer N. "Organizations as Polities: An Analysis of Community Organization Agencies," *Social Work,* Vol. 11, No. 4 (October 1966), pp. 56–65.

254. ——— (ed.). *Social Welfare Institutions: A Sociological Reader.* New York: John Wiley & Sons, 1965.

255. Zimbalist, Sidney E. "Major Trends in Social Work Research: An Analysis of the Nature and Development of Research in Social Work, as Seen in the Periodical Literature, 1900–1950." Unpublished doctoral dissertation, George Warren Brown School of Social Work, Washington University, 1955.

Epilogue

Referring to Bertha Capen Reynolds, Schwartz wrote:

> When a loved one dies everyone feels guilty. We feel we did not do enough to honor her, to show support when she needed it, to let her know we understood what she was doing. We should have talked with her, engaged her, warmed ourselves more before the light went out.
>
> One longs to continue the conversation with her on the issues she raised during her lifetime (1981a, p. 12).

We wish William Schwartz were here to write his own epilogue to his life's work, to lend his vision to our present, to continue our conversations on the issues he raised during his lifetime.

William Schwartz's contributions to the profession of social work were far reaching. He was a thinker and a systematic theory builder, who reached deeply into his practice and his reading of history as the basis for the development of his ideas. His career was distinguished by the generating of a set of still powerful ideas which moved the profession forward in its consideration of professional method and in the practice of its craft. His brilliant teaching inspired thousands of students in the study of professional practice. At the same time his consultation inspired agencies to rethink their premises about practice method and to improve service to clients. Schwartz's scholarship, for example, his attention to detail and familiarity with a wide-ranging relevant literature, is among the very best in our profession. His writing as such was virtually an example of clarity and literateness. He engaged issues of central importance to social work and strengthened the work of countless others who were interested in, and wrote about, method and the mutual aid group. His writing was uncommonly clear, and free of jargon and cant. The active voice and action words were always preferred to preclude the words from becoming obstacles to the ideas themselves. He invested heavily in our professional associations and worked to make visible the connections between the "private troubles" of the practitioners and the "public issues" embedded in our agencies.

No doubt any of these contributions would have been sufficient to earn distinction. But Schwartz's influence was felt not for any one of his valuable achievements, but for the strength of the interrelated effects of these endeavors. His enormous intellectual ability and energy enabled him to work in all areas simultaneously. His abiding interest in contributing to the quality of the profession's practice was seen in his drive to influence the way the profession thought about function and method. Only in this way, he believed, could the profession achieve its social vision. His contribution was important and far reaching, and significant to the advancement of the profession.

Schwartz also defined and identified the work still to be done. He understood that for the most part his ideas were presented in highly conceptual pieces. He hoped that others would take the ideas further, operationalize them further, and show the social worker in action. He also understood that while he had conceptualized the function of social worker as a centripetal force between individuals and systems important to them, more of his attention was focused on the small group system than it was on the relationship between individuals and larger social systems, for example, social service agencies and other bureaucracies. While "Private Troubles and Public Issues: One Social Work Job or Two?" was written to engage some of the debate about his view of the symbiotic tie between individuals and social systems, he believed that no debate as such could or would "settle" the issues. What was needed was further work on the practice details of mediating between individuals and their environment. To show *how* the social worker strengthens the ties, particularly when social institutions and clients seem so alienated from each other, would make his ideas come alive. He believed, as always, that our discussions must be technical, and not about matters of faith.

While sometimes discouraged by the immensity of the professional tasks before us, Schwartz always took pleasure from the small group of colleagues and former students who continued with him in exploring the details of practice. He was encouraged by the work of Lawrence Shulman who, first in 1968 developed a casebook which clearly showed the details of practice and who in 1979 took the interactionist model forward by operationalizing it and showing its details in action. Shulman's most recent effort has been to "develop and test a grounded, holistic theory of social work practice, based on . . . an interactional perspective" (1991, p. 2).[1] The works of Gitterman, Lee, and Berman-Rossi, also continue to

---

[1]The reader may explore these ideas in Shulman's (1968) *A Casebook of Social Work with Groups: The Mediating Model,* New York: Council on Social Work Education; (1979, 1984, 1992) *The Skills of Helping Individuals and Groups;* and (1991) *Interactional Social Work Practice: Toward an Empirical Theory,* all published by Itasca, IL: F. E. Peacock Publishers, Inc.

elaborate and develop Schwartz's ideas.[2] They again show how the efforts of others to go beyond Schwartz's ideas to create their own about professional practice are strengthened and informed by his work.

If Schwartz were here, he would encourage us to form small mutual-aid groups, to band together for the purposes of studying professional practice, to provide support and technical assistance to each other so the study of practice could go forward. I imagine he would still feel as he did in 1962 when he wrote that:

> [d]espite the impatience of those who would like to move as quickly as possible into studies of outcome and effectiveness, our main progress for a time will probably be in studies of process and of limited effects . . . our major tools are still the group record, the life-history, the critical incident, and other techniques for codifying and conceptualizing the experience of practice (1962b, p. 278).

Schwartz hoped that this book of writings would encourage others . . . that energies that lay dormant would be strengthened . . . that social work students would have before them another view of the helping process . . . and that students and colleagues would continue the search for generic elements in the helping process, the expression of skill in social work practice, and how those skills are operationalized with clients and with systems on the clients' behalf.

William Schwartz has provided powerful ideas, and has identified and elaborated a way of working which ties together thinking, feeling, and doing within a social, political, and economic context. He has been an exemplary professional. He never asked of others what he did not ask of himself. He has provided much; the rest is for us to do.

Toby Berman-Rossi

---

[2]See for example Berman-Rossi's (1986) The Fight Against Hopelessness and Despair: Institutionalized Aged, *Mutual Aid Groups and the Life Cycle.* eds. A. Gitterman and L. Shulman, Itasca, IL: F. E. Peacock Publishers, Inc., 1986, pp. 333–58; Lee's (1988) ed. *Social Work with Oppressed Populations,* New York: Haworth Press; Gitterman and Shulman's (1986) *Mutual Aid Groups and the Life Cycle.* eds. A. Gitterman and L. Shulman, Itasca, IL: F. E. Peacock Publishers, Inc., and their (1985–1986) tribute to William Schwartz eds. *The Legacy of William Schwartz: Group Practice as Shared Interaction, Social Work with Groups, 8* (4), and Germain and Gitterman's effort to show how the social worker works between clients and the environment: (1980) *The Life Model of Social Work Practice,* New York: Columbia University Press.

Appendix A: Bibliography

Published and Unpublished Works of William Schwartz

1948 Action research in a group work setting: A record of a cooperative experience. Unpublished master's thesis. New York School of Social Work. Columbia University.

1951 A comparison of background characteristics and performance of paid and volunteer group leaders. *The Jewish Center Worker, XII*(1), 1–12.

1955 Response to Irving Miller Paper. Unpublished. National Conference of Social Work, San Francisco, May 31, 1955.

1959(a) Group work and the social scene. In A. J. Kahn (Ed.), *Issues in American social work* (pp. 110–137). New York: Columbia University Press.

1959(b) Contribution to interdisciplinary symposium. *Nature of the helping process.* Group Work Section. Chicago Chapter. National Association of Social Workers.

1960(a) *Content and process in the educative experience.* Unpublished doctoral dissertation. Teachers College, Columbia University.

1960(b) Camping. *Social work yearbook,* pp. 112–117.

1960(c) Characteristics of the group experience in resident camping. *Social Work, 5*(2), 91–96.

1961 The social worker in the group. *The social welfare forum* (pp. 146–177). New York: Columbia University Press, and *New perspectives on services to groups.* National Association of Social Workers.

1962(a) On certifying each other. *Social Work, 7*(3), 21–26.

1962(b) Toward a strategy of group work practice. *Social Service Review, XXXVI*(3), 268–279.

1962(c) Professional association in social work: Some structural problems. Unpublished paper, presented at a meeting sponsored by the Group Work Section, National Association of Social Workers, at the National Conference on Social Welfare in New York City, May 31, 1962.

1963(a) Small group science and group work practice. *Social Work, 8*(4), 39–46.

1963(b) Some comment on the function of the staff meeting. *Staff Development News,* Official publication of the New York City Department of Welfare. *1*(2).

1964(a) Review of N. Felton and K. T. Wiltes. (Eds.) *Group methods in the public welfare program.* Pacific Books. *Social Casework, XLV*(4), 232.

1964(b) Analysis of working papers. In M. E. Hartford (Ed.), *Working papers toward a frame of reference for social group work* (pp. 53–61). New York: National Association of Social Workers.

1964(c) The classroom teaching of social work with groups: Some central problems. In *A conceptual framework for the teaching of the social group work method in the classroom,* Proceedings, Faculty Conference Day, Council on Social Work Education, January 29, 1964.

1966(a) Discussion of three papers on use of the group method in work with clients, foster families, and adoptive families. *Child Welfare, XLV*(10), 571–575.

1966(b) Neighborhood centers. In H. S. Mass (Ed.) *Five fields of social service: Reviews of research* (pp. 144–184). New York: National Association of Social Workers.

1966(c) Letter to *The Nation. The Nation.* June 27, 1966.

1967 Comments on supervisory practice and social work service in the Neighborhood Center. United Neighborhood Houses Department of Training in New York City, October 20, 1967.

1968 Group work in public welfare. *Public Welfare, XXVI*(4), 322–70.

1968- *Social work with groups: The search for a method.*

1969(a) Private troubles and public issues: One social work job or two? *The social welfare forum* (pp. 22–43). New York: Columbia University Press. The Lindeman Memorial Lecture of the National Conference on Social Welfare, New York City, 1969.

1969(b) The use of groups and school social work function. Unpublished paper. Presented at the New York State School Social Workers Association. May 10, 1969, Saratoga Springs, New York.

1971(a) The practice of child care in residential treatment. In M. F. Mayer and A. Blum (Eds.) *Healing through Living: A symposium on residential treatment* (pp. 38–71). Springfield, Il.: Charles C. Thomas.

1971(b) On the use of groups in social work practice. In W. Schwartz and S. Zalba. (Eds.) *The practice of group work* (pp. 3–21). New York: Columbia University Press. Originally delivered to Annual Workshop for Field Instructors and Faculty, Columbia University School of Social Work, April 21, 1966.

1971(c) *The practice of group work.* (Eds.) W. Schwartz & Zalba, S. New York: Columbia University Press.

1971(d) Neighborhood centers and group work. In H. S. Mass (ed.) *Research in the social services: A five-year review* (pp. 130–191). New York: National Association of Social Workers.

1971(e) The interactionist approach. *Encyclopedia of social work* (pp. 1252–1262). New York: National Association of Social Workers.

1973 Thoughts from abroad: Some recent perspectives on the practice of social work. (1973) Unpublished paper, read at a social work conference in Northern Ireland, at the New University of Ulster, Institute of Continuing Education, Magee University College, Londonderry, on June 25, 1973.

1976 Between client and system: The mediating function. In R. Roberts & Northen, H. (Eds.) *Theories of social work with groups* (pp. 171–197). New York: Columbia University Press.

1977 The interactionist approach. *Encyclopedia of Social Work* (pp. 1328–1338). New York: National Association of Social Workers.

1978 Rosalie. *Social Work With Groups, 1*(3), 265–278.

1979(a) Grace Coyle as educator: A personal note. Presented at the 1979 Symposium of the Committee for the Advancement of Social Work with Groups. Published (1981) Proceedings 1979 Symposium, Committee for the Advancement of Social Work with Groups. (Eds.) Sonia Leib Abels and Paul Abels.

1979(b) Forward to Lawrence Shulman (1979). *The skills of helping individuals and groups.* Itasca, Il.: F. E. Peacock Publishers, Inc.

1979(c) Review of Mano McCaughan (Ed.) *Group work: learning and practice. Contemporary Psychology, 24*(Oct), 858.

1980 Education in the classroom. *Journal of Higher Education, 51*(3), 235–254.

1981(a) Bertha Reynolds as educator. *Catalyst. 3*(11), 5–14.

1981(b) The group work tradition and social work practice. Published in the Rutgers University School of Social Work Symposium of addresses prepared in honor of its 25th birthday. Also published in (1985) *Social Work With Groups, 8*(4), 7–27.

Appendix B: Teaching Tools

Course T6303
William Schwartz

Identification of Worker Responses in Group Situations

The purpose of this exercise is to identify and analyze the acts that group workers perform as they carry out their function within the group situation. For our purposes, we are defining an "act" to include not only the *specific movement of the worker,* but also the *event which precipitated it,* and the *specific intent* of the act itself. This will become clearer as you proceed to provide the data requested below.

This is how you are to proceed:

1. From your recent group recording, choose *two* incidents where you have set down in some detail your efforts to help the members deal with some kind of task or problem that has arisen within the group.
2. In each of the two incidents, underscore the things you did and said. Where a silence or lack of response on your part was deliberate, use the margin to call attention to this *as an act.*
3. Number all of your acts, chronologically, including those noted in the margin. *Do this separately for each incident.*
4. List all of your acts in the left-hand column below. Use the number *and* the words underlined in your record. (e.g., 1. I said, "How about getting started?")
5. Finally, fill out the remaining columns. Here is an explanation of what is asked for in each:

    a. *Response*—Explained above.
    b. *To Whom*—The person, or persons, to whom the speech or movement was particularly addressed.

c. *Stimulus*—Whatever you did or said was precipitated by some remark, or condition or act, by a member or several, or perhaps the group-as-a-whole. *The important thing here is to indicate that stimulus which is most specific and closest in time to what you did.* See examples.

d. *Hypothesis*—How did you "read" this stimulus? What did it mean to you? Again, make your statement as *specific* as possible: *Not* "he wanted acceptance and reassurance," *but* "he seemed worried that if the fellows decided to have a dance, he would have to ask a girl."

e. *Hoped-for immediate response*—The emphasis, here again, is on *immediate,* and *specific.* What did you hope would happen as a result of what you did or said? *Not* "they would learn something about sharing and democracy," *but* "they would see that I was angry," or "they would be ashamed and quiet down."

f. *Interpretation*—What were the *general* assumptions (concepts) about individual or group behavior on which you think your act here was based? Restrict your listing here to a maximum of three per response.

The attached sample sheet should be read over several times before you begin to transcribe your records into the columns.

When you are done, please turn in your underscored records along with the columnar data. Please cross out names and substitute initials before doing so.

Sample Sheet

Record (Excerpt)

I deliberately said nothing here.[4]

R. arrived first, with her small brother in tow, and explained with some disgust that she had to baby-sit. I assured her that she was welcome with or without brothers,[1] and offered a large shirt[2] to protect her clothing. M. came in, announcing with some glee that her grandmother had mumbled repeatedly that "boys paint, not girls." *I smiled.*[3] This had presented no difficulty in her attending, she said; however, her father had wanted to know if any boys would be present.

As they began to paint, A. commented that "things are fun in the club now, we didn't use to do anything," and others nodded a contented sort of agreement. *I offered that they had done a fine job in getting themselves organized and tackling a really tough problem*[5]. . . .

a **Response**	b **To Whom**	c **Stimulus**	d **Hypothesis**	e **Hoped-for immediate response**	f **Interpretation**
1. I assured her, etc.	R.	R's complaint to me about bringing her brother.	She was ashamed to appear with the child tagging along. Also she was ashamed of having a brother so young—she is a teen.	My casual acceptance would make her feel less uncomfortable. Also set the tone of casualness in the group.	*Teenagers hate to show the effects of their domination by adults, before other teens. *Teens are deeply embarrassed by having very young siblings.
2. Offered a large shirt	R.	R's discomfort	The sooner she could get to work the easier it would be for her to stop feeling so different.	She would accept my signal, snap into activity, and think about herself in relation to activity.	*Activity with friends diverts personal anxiety.

3. I smiled	M.	M's comment re: grandmother's reaction to painting as an activity for girls.	Culturally this is a daring defiance of tradition for these girls. M. is excited and pleased by the freedom implied.	She would see that I understood and accepted this and feel even freer to enjoy it.	*Teens need to act out some defiance of familial taboos. *They also need some support while doing it.
4. Said nothing	M. and grp.	M's comment re: father's anxiety.	This is a touchy point with all these fathers. M's meaning: "It's the same old thing."	Didn't want to give them anything to respond to. Rather choose my spot to get into this.	*In some cultures the sexual taboos present even more serious problems for teenagers than in the dominant American pattern.
5. I offered that, etc.	Grp. as a whole	Feeling of contentment and self-satisfaction, verbalized by A.	This was a new feeling for these kids—together, active, independent. They were asking for recognition of their strength.	They would see that I understood and accepted this new feeling and that this freedom was fine with me.	*Recognition given in specific terms is more apt to be perceived as recognition than vague forms of encouragement.

Student: ______________________________

Date: _______________

Record of Service: Group (Peer or Family)

I. Group Description: Begin with a brief (under 200 words) statement about the group-as-a-client, explaining: its purpose, membership, and conditions of formation; psychological and social circumstances leading up to the need for service; its contract with the agency; themes of work thus far; group strengths and weaknesses bearing on the problems of the collective.

II. The Work: Identify one of the problems with which you have tried to help the group thus far. Describe the work you have done, as follows:

Time Period: From ________________ To __________________

Problem: ____

____

Group Task: Formation _______ Structure _____

Relation to Environment _______

Individual Need Satisfaction ______________________________

Now divide your account as follows: (1) When and how the problem came to your attention; (2) A summary of the work, characterizing the techniques you used, and giving dated examples from your record for each characterization (rubric); (3) State where the problem stands now, indications of progress or lack of it, group's use of help, etc.; and (4) Specific next steps that you plan to take, based on your work so far, and where you think matters stand.

III. Conclusions and Comments: Having summarized your work in this way, use this section to give your reactions to several aspects of the exercise: how you identified the problem; how you characterized and classified your techniques; the quality of the work itself; how your knowledge of groups, and of this group in particular, helped or did not help in your approach to this problem; and any other lessons you would care to draw for yourself. Feel free to generalize about implications for social work practice, and to identify any of the group and family literature that seems to bear on the practice problems you have written about.

Student: ______________________________
Date: _______________

Record of Service: Individual

I. Case Description: Begin with a brief (under 200 words) statement about the case as a whole, explaining: how the client got to the agency; some of the psychological and social factors leading up to the need for service; some client strengths and weaknesses bearing on the problems they brought; the services rendered by the agency so far; and the present focus of the contract between client and agency.

II. The Work: Identify one of the problems with which you tried to help in the course of the case thus far. Describe the work you and the client have done on this problem, as follows:

Time Period: From __________ To __________

Problem: ____

____

System: Family _______ Agency _______ Welfare _______

School _______ Peer Group _______ Vocational _______

Housing _______ Other (Name) ____________________________

Now divide your account as follows: (1) When and how the problem came to your attention; (2) A summary of the work, characterizing the techniques you used, and giving dated examples from your record for each characterization (rubric); (3) State where the problem stands now, indications of progress or lack of it, etc.; and (4) Specific next steps you plan to carry out, based on the work that has been done so far.

III. Conclusions and Comments: Having summarized your helping efforts in this way, use this section to give your reactions to several of the elements involved: your identification of the problem; how you characterized your work; the work itself; how your sense of the whole case helped, or didn't help, in approaching this particular problem; and any other lessons you would care to draw for yourself. Feel free to draw any generalizations that occur to you about implications for social work practice, and to identify any of the literature that seems to bear on these questions.